CRIMINAL LAW

This is the third edition of the widely acclaim .R. Sullivan. *Criminal Law: Theory and Doctrine* has estal account of English criminal law, combining a detailed : law with a careful exploration of its theoretical underp dergraduate teaching. It has also established itself as a majc writing, here and abroad, and has been cited in appellate courts throughout the world, including the House of Lords, the High Court of Australia, the Supreme Court of Canada and the Special Tribunal for the former Yugoslavia.

In this edition, besides extensive updating, there is a new chapter on criminalisation as well as detailed new discussions of criminal damage and anti-social behaviour orders (ASBOs).

Criminal Law
Theory and Doctrine

A.P. Simester and G.R. Sullivan

Third Edition

·HART·
PUBLISHING
OXFORD AND PORTLAND, OREGON
2007

Published in North America (US and Canada) by
Hart Publishing
c/o International Specialized Book Services
920 NE 58th Avenue, Suite 300
Portland, OR 97213-3786
USA
Tel: +1 503 287 3093 or toll-free: (1) 800 944 6190
Fax: +1 503 280 8832
E-mail: orders@isbs.com
Website: www.isbs.com

Hart Publishing, 16C Worcester Place, OX1 2JW
Telephone: +44 (0)1865 517530 Fax: +44 (0)1865 510710
E-mail: mail@hartpub.co.uk
Website: http://www.hartpub.co.uk

British Library Cataloguing in Publication Data
Data Available
ISBN-13: 978-1-84113-705-6 (paperback)

Typeset by Forewords, Oxford
Printed and bound in Great Britain by
TJ International Ltd, Padstow, Cornwall

PREFACE TO THE THIRD EDITION

In our preface to the second edition of this work we stated that the new edition was essentially an updated version of the first edition. The distance between this edition and previous editions is greater. One major explanation for this is the passage of time. More than four years of intensive legislative and judicial lawmaking have necessitated much reworking of the existing text. Further, new legislation has required new text, most notably the Fraud Act 2006, which has completely reconceptualised and reshaped the law of fraud and deception. Of our own initiative we have added a new section on criminal damage and a new chapter on criminalisation. This last feature is included not only for the intrinsic interest of its challenging subject matter, but also by way of response to the relentless use of the criminal law as a matter of first recourse to perceived social and moral dangers, rather than as an all-things-considered last resort to those real or imagined phenomena. It is time, we feel, to set out in a scholarly manner how problematic is the decision to make new criminal law and how much deliberation should go into any decision to do so. We are not so naïve as to think that our thoughts on this matter will have any purchase on current legislators and policymakers. But the ideas and considerations we rehearse are of timeless relevance to the appropriate use of the criminal law.

For all these changes found in this third edition, the aspiration remains the same. Our principal motivation is to put before a wide spectrum of readers an accessible yet full account of the theory and doctrine of the criminal law of England and Wales. Help is required even to achieve this in part, and we are lucky to be working at a time of great scholarly interest and achievement in the field of criminal law theory. More directly, we have been assisted on various matters by friends and colleagues, and record particular thanks for suggestions and corrections to Leslie Blake, Antony Duff, and Tony Smith. A special debt of gratitude is owed to Martin Kuzmicki and Lucy Sullivan, for their invaluable research assistance at a time of considerable pressure of work.

A.P. Simester
G.R. Sullivan
Easter 2007

CONTENTS

EXPANDED TABLE OF CONTENTS

ABBREVIATIONS

The following abbreviations for standard textbooks and statutory materials are used in the text and footnotes.

Ashworth, *Principles* Andrew Ashworth, *Principles of Criminal Law* (Oxford: Oxford University Press, 5th ed., 2006)

ECHR European Convention on Human Rights

Hart and Honoré H.L.A. Hart and A.M. Honoré, *Causation in the Law* (Oxford: Oxford University Press, 2nd ed., 1985)

HRA 1998 Human Rights Act 1998

Model Penal Code American Law Institute, *Model Penal Code* (Philadelphia: American Law Institute, Revised ed., 1985).

OAPA 1861 Offences Against the Person Act 1861

Smith and Hogan D. Ormerod, *Smith and Hogan's Criminal Law* (Oxford: Oxford University Press, 11th ed., 2005)

Williams, *TBCL* Glanville Williams, Textbook of Criminal Law (London: Stevens, 2nd ed., 1983)

Williams, *CLGP* Glanville Williams, Criminal Law: The General Part (London: Stevens, 2nd ed., 1961)

TABLE OF CASES

TABLE OF LEGISLATION

United Kingdom

Statutory Instruments

United States of America

1

CRIMINAL LAW: DEFINITION AND AMBIT

The aim of this chapter is to introduce some of the theory that surrounds the criminal law: to explain why the criminal law matters, and to highlight the issues it raises. The chapter begins by considering the defining features of the criminal law, those which distinguish it from other varieties of law. Secondly, the ambit of criminal law is investigated—when is it apt to declare someone a criminal? The discussion in this chapter will lead on, in Chapter 2, to a discussion of the constitutional and Rule of Law principles that constrain the enactment and interpretation of criminal law; and later, in Chapter 16, to consideration of what sorts of actions properly attract criminal prohibitions.

§ 1.1 A search for definition

Like other types of law, the criminal law is a means by which the state participates in the ordering of its citizens' lives. Yet throughout the world, every society with a formal legal system distinguishes between criminal and civil law.[1] This raises a question about the scope of criminal law: what marks a law out as criminal rather than civil? One way of approaching that question is to look for a definition of the criminal law. Broadly speaking, a crime is an event that is prohibited by law, one which can be followed by a prosecution in criminal proceedings and, thereafter, by punishment on conviction:[2]

> "A crime must be defined by reference to the *legal* consequences of the act. We must distinguish, primarily, not between crimes and civil wrongs but between criminal and civil proceedings. A crime then becomes an act that is capable of being followed by criminal proceedings, having one of the types of outcome (punishment etc.) known to follow these proceedings."

Criminal law, in turn, is the variety of law that prohibits such crimes.

But to define criminal law only in these procedural terms fails to shed any light on a more fundamental problem: why does the distinction between criminal and other law matter? It is true that criminal prosecutions follow a different legal procedure from their civil counterparts. But if that is the sole difference, and there is no underlying reason for

---

[1] Robinson, "The Criminal–Civil Distinction and the Utility of Desert" (1996) 76 *Boston ULR* 201, 201–2.
[2] Williams, "The Definition of Crime" (1955) *CLP* 107, 123.

separating the two, drawing the distinction would be pointless.[3] We need to identify the distinguishing features that also justify treating crimes as a separate body of law.

(i) The harmful nature of the prohibited event

One suggestion might be that the harm proscribed by criminal law is greater in degree than that in the civil law, or is somehow public rather than private in nature. For example, across most if not all cultures, the criminal law contains provisions proscribing serious forms of violence and dishonesty. However, while it is true that prevention of harm is central to the criminal law, the distinctiveness of criminal wrongs cannot be captured by reference simply to the moral gravity of the wrongdoing and the importance of the interest being violated. For one thing, most harms are both public and private. The major oil spillage in Sydney harbour that gave rise to the *Wagon Mound* tort cases affected more than one person,[4] while by contrast an ordinary assault typically involves a single victim. Similarly, consider the situation where D plc has placed a large contract for the supply of raw materials with V Ltd. D is aware that without the contract, V would be forced to close with the loss of hundreds of jobs. If, despite this, D breaks the contract in order to obtain supplies from a cheaper overseas source, it commits no offence. Compare this case with the situation where a company fails to send its annual return to the Registrar of Companies within the time limits prescribed by the Companies Act 1985. It seems, therefore, that the events prohibited by criminal laws are not inherently distinguishable from those regulated by other sorts of law. Indeed, the same act can sometimes lead to both criminal and civil liability. If D takes V's car without V's consent, for example, he may be prosecuted for theft. He can also be sued in tort for conversion.

That said, there is intuitive appeal in the idea that criminal wrongs are typically more serious than their civil counterparts; sufficiently serious that, whether or not they also give rise to civil causes of action, the state feels constrained to step in and regulate them directly. This can be seen in the rule that a victim who forgives his attacker may discontinue his civil suit for damages, but cannot stop the prosecution of that attacker. Criminal offences are not merely a private matter. The public as a whole has an interest in their prevention and prosecution. Thus, according to Allen, behaviour is criminalised "because it consists in wrongdoing which directly and in serious degree threatens the security or well-being of society, and because it is not safe to leave it redressable only by compensation of the party injured."[5] Allen's remark is a useful pointer to why assaults are crimes while breaches of contract are not. Assault involves an interference with fundamental rights of the victim, rights which the State is perceived to have a duty to protect. By contrast, individuals are

---

[3] Moreover there would be a problem explaining why the distinction is maintained in those countries which do not observe the procedural safeguards normally found in criminal law. See Robinson, "The Criminal–Civil Distinction and the Utility of Desert" (1996) 76 *Boston ULR* 201, 203.

[4] *Overseas Tankship (UK) Ltd* v. *Morts Dock Engineering* [1961] AC 388; *Overseas Tankship (UK) Ltd* v. *Miller Steamship Co Pty* [1967] AC 617. Cf. public nuisance cases: *Halsey* v. *Esso Petroleum* [1961] 1 WLR 683.

[5] *Legal Duties and Other Essays in Jurisprudence* (1931) 233–4. Compare Coffee: "Characteristically, tort law prices, while criminal law prohibits." On this view, the criminal law should be invoked when the "price" of an action, that the defendant would have to pay in tortious damages, is insufficiently prohibitive. Coffee, "Does 'Unlawful' Mean 'Criminal'?: Reflections on the Disappearing Tort/Crime Distinction in American Law" (1991) 71 *Boston ULR* 193, 194.

normally able to protect themselves against breach of contract, and can satisfactorily undo any damage suffered with the aid of the civil law.

Another possible basis for differentiating civil from criminal law is that criminal acts are those acts which are intrinsically morally wrong. (Such acts are sometimes called *mala in se.*) To some extent this is true of the more serious, stigmatic offences—assault, murder, and so forth.[6] But much of the modern criminal law involves prohibitions which are only wrong because they are illegal (*mala prohibita*). There is little intrinsic moral difference, for instance, between driving at 70 miles per hour on the highway and driving at 75; but the latter is an offence. And conversely, lying may be immoral, but it is not *per se* a criminal act.

More generally, the sheer variety of conduct that has been designated a criminal wrong defies reduction to any "essential" minimum. One finds no unifying thread to the subject matter of the multifarious crimes known to England and Wales.[7] The criminal law has been used—indeed, overused—as a regulatory device, and consequently extends to conduct that can lack any inherent moral turpitude whatsoever, such as failing to notify the licensing authority of a change of address for one's driving licence, or omitting a required statement from a consumer credit contract. In this country, the fact that some particular action is criminal may reflect only a decision on the part of a regulatory body that the public interest requires resort to public means of suppression, and that the matter cannot be left to private redress or bargaining. Amongst the available public means of suppression, the criminal law is the most commonly employed coercive mechanism.

So there are limits to the extent to which we can safely elaborate upon our initial definition by reference to the things that criminal law prohibits. In part, this reflects the fact that criminal law presents political problems as well as legal and analytic ones. In Chapter 16, we shall discuss some of the reasons why the State criminalises certain harms rather than others. But it should always be borne in mind that, in practice, criminal laws are characteristically deployed to control behaviour and events because there is a public, and political, interest in doing so.

(ii) Punishment

A second element of the preliminary definition given in § 1.1 was punishment. Perhaps the main distinction between criminal and civil law is that the criminal law licenses punishment as opposed to compensation? The latter, it might be said, is the province of the civil law.[8]

Punishment is an important facet of the criminal process. Indeed, it is an indispensable feature of criminal prohibitions. Parliament does not say, "Do not assault other people, *please.*" That would not be a law at all. Rather, the law declares, "Do not assault other people, *or else. . . .*" Of course, civil laws also specify sanctions. As Posner points out, however, the nature of the civil sanction differs from that found in criminal law. A defendant who is convicted of a crime will normally be imprisoned or fined. By contrast, someone who loses a civil action faces perhaps an injunction, an order for specific performance, or a requirement to pay damages.

---

[6] Cf. Gross, *A Theory of Criminal Justice* (1979) 13.
[7] See Ashworth, "Is the Criminal Law a Lost Cause?" (2000) 116 *LQR* 225.
[8] Moore, *Law and Psychiatry: Rethinking the Relationship* (1984) 81.

Posner argues that this difference reflects a crucial distinction between the functions of criminal and civil laws. In his opinion, the criminal law exists to impose punishments such as imprisonment in situations where tortious remedies are an insufficient deterrent.[9] But Posner's explanation is doubtful. Both criminal and tortious remedies can operate as deterrents. Each is likely to be regarded as unwelcome by a defendant, and indeed civil damages awards often far exceed criminal fines in magnitude.

On the other hand, it is instructive to consider the reasons *apart from deterrence* which underlie the imposition of sanctions in these cases. In particular, whether or not they have deterrent effects, civil remedies are not normally regarded as punitive. Punishment involves more than simply imposing something unwelcome upon a defendant. A *punitive* sanction imposes hardship *because the recipient deserves it*. Damages in a contract dispute, for instance, are a sanction; but ordinarily they are imposed without censure. It is not necessary to show that a defendant is at fault when he breaches his contractual obligations.

Punishment, by contrast, is imposed with censure as an integral aspect. It responds to the fact that the defendant has done something wrong.[10] Indeed, the level of sentence is one way in which a court signals the wrongfulness of the defendant's actions.[11] Of course, there are also fault-based actions in the law of tort. Nonetheless, damages for tort losses are normally compensatory, not punitive, and are understood as such. That is why one may usually insure against contractual or tortious damages, but not against criminal fines.[12]

Punishment, then, is one function of the criminal law. But punishment is not what is unique about crime. Indeed, punishment is not even a specifically legal phenomenon, let alone specifically the province of criminal law. We do not require a criminal conviction before punishing children or for a footballing foul, and it is sometimes possible to obtain exemplary damages in civil cases. One may be fined or even imprisoned for a civil contempt of court. Conversely, neither is a conviction always accompanied by sanctions. Sometimes offenders are discharged without receiving any sentence for their wrongdoing. This suggests that while punishment is an important facet of the criminal law, it is not its most distinctive feature.

(iii) Convictions

In addition to prohibition and punishment, a third aspect of the criminal process is the conviction itself—the type of verdict that the Court makes. Convictions are the most distinctive aspect of criminal law. In particular, while it also licenses the imposition of sanctions, a criminal conviction (at least for stigmatic offences) is regarded as a penalty *in its own right*, both by legal officials, such as judges, and by the public. This is because it has the effect of labelling the accused as a criminal. A conviction makes a public, condemnatory statement about the defendant: that she is blameworthy for doing the prohibited action. It is, literally, a pronouncement that she is "guilty". By contrast, civil judgments seem merely to

---

[9] Posner, "An Economic Theory of the Criminal Law" (1985) 85 *Col LR* 1193.

[10] For discussion, see von Hirsch, *Censure and Sanctions* (1993).

[11] Cf. *Martineau* (1990) 79 CR (3d) 129, 138 (Lamer CJ): it is a "fundamental principle of a morally based system of law that those causing harm intentionally be punished more severely than those causing harm unintentionally."

[12] *Askey* v. *Golden Wine Co Ltd* [1948] 2 All ER 35; cf. *Clunis* v. *Camden and Islington Health Authority* [1998] QB 978.

pin the salient breach upon a defendant, without necessarily saying anything about her moral culpability. Thus, as we have noted, a claimant can sue for breach of contract without having to show fault by the defendant. The adverse civil verdict is made for the claimant's benefit and entails no formal public censure; the adverse criminal verdict is a pronouncement made on behalf of society and is a form of community condemnation.

This facet is not mentioned in the definition of criminal law that we proposed earlier. Rather, it is something that accompanies the procedural differences. Thus the essential distinction between criminal and civil law lies not so much in the operation as in the social significance of the criminal law—in the way criminal laws and convictions are understood. The criminal law has a communicative function which the civil law does not, and its judgments against the accused have a symbolic significance that civil judgments lack. They are a form of condemnation: a declaration that the accused did wrong. Public recognition of this fact can be seen in the relevance of the criminal law to applications for a visa, or for admission to practise as a lawyer, in which applicants are required to disclose any previous convictions. Or consider the difference between publicly denouncing someone as a "convicted criminal" and calling her a "tortfeasor".[13] The law exists in society, not in the abstract. Correspondingly, the law's labelling of a defendant as "criminal" imports all the resonance and social meaning of that term.

§ 1.2 Ambit

Three salient functions of criminal law emerge from the discussion so far. The first might be called *criminalisation*: the law sets out for citizens those things which must not be done.[14] The second thing the law does is *convict* persons who are proved to have transgressed its prohibitions. Finally, it may *punish* those whom it convicts; and, more generally, the criminal law offers the prospect of punishment to reinforce its function of criminalisation.

The criminal law, then, is a powerful and condemnatory response by the State. It is also a bluntly coercive system, directed at controlling the behaviour of citizens. Criminalisation involves rules backed up by threats. In a sense, criminal law is the means by which the State bullies citizens into complying with its injunctions.

When should the criminal law be invoked? No-one, including the State, should coerce others without good reason. The constriction of people's conduct calls for justification, especially when it is accompanied by censorious and punitive treatment of those who do not comply. Unless there are compelling reasons, the criminal law should not be deployed by Parliament.

Nonetheless, sometimes the use of the criminal law *is* justified. Imagine the following scenario:

One fine September morning, Jim is discovered dead in his home. His skull has been crushed by a blow inflicted with a heavy object. The police are called. Upon further

---

[13] The former is certainly defamatory. Cf. *Carver* v. *Pierce*, an action for slander based on the words, "Thou art a thief, for thou hast stollen my dung" (1648) Sty 66, 82 ER 534.

[14] Or allowed to subsist: below, § 4.1(ii).

investigation, they establish that he was murdered by his daughter, Alice, who killed him in order to receive her inheritance under his will.

Intuitively, most of us would regard this as a classic example of criminal wrongdoing. The reasons are twofold. First, what Alice has done is precisely the sort of activity that the State should prohibit. Murder is both harmful and wrong, and people ought to be protected against it. Secondly, Alice is clearly blameworthy, and deserving of censure for her actions. Thus she is precisely the sort of person who deserves the condemnation of a criminal conviction, as well as the punishment that a conviction exposes her to.

Alice's behaviour is a central case for the application of criminal law. It involves deliberate, culpable infliction of the sort of serious harm that the criminal law is meant to prevent. However, not every case is as clear as this. Suppose the following alternatives:

> Case I: Jim is discovered dead in his home. This time, the police establish that he died instantly after being struck by a vase. The vase was accidentally dislodged from the bookshelf by Barbara.

> Case II: During an argument, Clare insults Jim. Jim is deeply hurt by Clare's words.

It is much less obvious that the criminal law should intervene in these situations. In case I, Barbara has caused Jim's death, but there is no suggestion that she is at fault. Given this, it is inappropriate—indeed, wrong—to apply to her the sanctions of public condemnation and punishment. In case II, Clare has wronged Jim, and deserves censure. But not by the criminal law. Unlike murder, this is not the sort of behaviour that ordinarily should be prohibited by the Draconian technique of criminalisation.

In questioning when application of criminal law is legitimate, guidance may be had from the functions identified earlier. There are two dimensions to the operation of criminal law: *ex ante* and *ex post*. *Ex ante*, the law marks out actions that are prohibited, and warns citizens not to do those actions lest they be punished. *Ex post*, it censures (convicts) and punishes (sentences) persons who transgress its prohibitions. In the following pages, we investigate these two roles separately, and discuss some of the issues affecting when they should be invoked.

(i) Criminalisation ex ante

Why should some behaviour be criminalised, while other behaviour is permitted? The answer to that question is complex and somewhat fragmented. Prima facie, a legislature has the power to proscribe almost any sort of conduct.[15] Earlier, we pointed out that there is no obvious distinction between actions which are criminal and those which generate civil liability (§ 1.1(i)). When the legislature marks some action as criminal, however, it condemns it and rules it out as an acceptable option for citizens. A responsible legislature ought to take such drastic measures only if there are compelling reasons so to do.

---

[15] The Human Rights Act 1998 inhibits the passing of legislation which contravenes ECHR rights. In formal terms, however, the Act leaves Parliamentary sovereignty intact. See further below, § 2.5.

There are a number of reasons to oppose the overuse of criminal law, but the most important of them is concern for individual *autonomy*. The need for tolerance, which underpins any liberal society, is grounded in autonomy. Prohibiting whatever is "wrongful" is likely to intrude much too far upon the liberties of citizens. This is not only to say that, in a liberal society, freedom of choice is to be fostered. It is also to claim that if the law is to respect the right of citizens to control their own lives, it should not deprive them of that control without good reason.

The criminal law stands in the way of free choice. It coerces people by threatening them with criminal liability unless they submit to its commands. Consequently, it circumscribes the individual's capacity to live her own life, in a manner that she herself dictates. By restricting the ways in which a person may shape her life, the law has the potential to prevent her from pursuing the goals and aspirations which matter to her. Indirectly, the criminal law imposes the legislature's view of an acceptable life.

Individual freedom is valuable. Even though it is right, indeed necessary, to have criminal prohibitions, the fact that they restrict autonomy means we should be careful of overextending the reach of the criminal law, and of damaging the right of self-determination. When a person's choices are not voluntary, but instead decided by laws, the life she lives is not entirely her own.[16] Of course, if one considers each crime separately, most criminal prohibitions are unlikely to interfere with someone's freedom in any substantial, pervasive, or long-term sense. Outlawing arson still leaves us with a wide range of alternative activities. But the point about autonomy is more general than that. The effect of criminalisation must be assessed cumulatively, not in isolation. There are already thousands of things the State forbids. Autonomy requires us to have good reason before extending the reach of the criminal law.

None of this is to say that people ought to be allowed to disregard the interests of others, or that there is anything wrong with most of the criminal prohibitions we presently have. But it is a ground for the criminal law to beware of interfering more than the minimum necessary—a prima facie reason against the use of criminal sanctions. Bearing this in mind, once we have discussed various specific offences we will return to this issue in Chapter 16 and ask, what *should* the legislature prohibit through the criminal law? What sorts of considerations should a responsible legislator take into account when deciding whether to create a criminal offence?

(ii) Ex post: *censure*

Our search for definition fastened upon the pronouncement of guilt through conviction as the distinguishing mark of criminal law. This pronouncement connotes fault on the part of the criminal. When the Court finds an accused guilty of committing a crime, and purports to punish her through sentencing, there is a public implication that she is blameworthy. Of course, there are offences of a minor character (e.g. related to parking infringements) where this element of reproof may be relatively trivial—such offences are often characterised as

---

[16] Raz, *The Morality of Freedom* (1986) 382.

not being "truly" criminal in nature. Paradigmatically, though, censure is inherent in criminal convictions.

(a) The need for mens rea

An institution which condemns and punishes people must take care to do so accurately. Being just matters. In particular, if a person is not to blame when something goes wrong, the censure of the criminal law is not appropriate—and if it is inflicted upon her, the public will tend to think that is because she is to blame. When the law labels a defendant as "criminal", it simply cannot avoid this implication. Consequently, it should not convict those for whom that implication is unjustified.

The grounds for wanting to avoid mislabelling defendants are twofold. First, it is unfair and unjust to stigmatise someone as a criminal when they do not deserve condemnation. Secondly, if the criminal law is seen regularly to make mistakes, it will lose its moral credibility. This, Robinson points out, will diminish its effectiveness as a tool of social control:[17]

> "The criminal law can also be more directly effective in increasing compliance with its commands. If it earns a reputation as a reliable statement of what the community perceives as condemnable and not condemnable, people are more likely to defer to its commands as morally authoritative. . . . A distribution of liability that the community perceives as doing justice enhances the criminal law's moral credibility; a distribution of liability that deviates from community perceptions of justice undermines it."

For these reasons, the criminal law ought not to convict people unless they are culpable for doing a prohibited action.[18] Therefore, in so far as possible, criminal offences should be structured so that there can be no conviction without fault. This is achieved by including within every criminal offence some element that reflects culpability.

Suppose the following example:

> Pam has killed Alex. Pam is a doctor, and Alex was one of her patients. Pam gave him a painkiller, to which he had an allergic reaction and died. Causing another's death is generally regarded as a very undesirable thing, and is at the heart of the crimes of murder and manslaughter. The police investigate. They establish that Pam's actions caused Alex's death, and conclude that she has committed a homicide.

On these facts alone, is Pam therefore bad, or blameworthy? Should we convict her of murder? The answer is no. Alex may have been the one patient in a million who was unknowably allergic to the painkiller and died as a consequence. It is important not to kill people, but it does not follow from the fact that killing is undesirable, and normally prohibited, that someone should automatically be convicted or punished for causing another's death. In the criminal law, this principle is expressed by the maxim, *actus non facit reum nisi mens sit rea*:[19] an act does not make a man guilty unless his mind is (also) guilty.

---

[17] "The Criminal–Civil Distinction and the Utility of Desert" (1996) 76 *Boston ULR* 201, 212–13. Robinson's point is made about criminalisation, but applies in this context also.

[18] For an interesting debate which touches on this proposition, see Reiman and van den Haag, "On the Common Saying that it is Better that Ten Guilty Persons Escape than that One Innocent Suffer: Pro and Con" in Paul, Miller and Paul (eds.), *Crime, Culpability, and Remedy* (1990) 226.

[19] Coke, *Third Institute* (1641) 6, 107; an adaptation of the rubric, *reum non facit nisi mens rea*, found in the context of perjury in *Leges Henrici Primi* c. 5, § 28.

There must be *mens rea*—a guilty mind. The action must be done intentionally or recklessly, or wilfully or knowingly, or negligently, or with some other mental state because of which we can say that the defendant is culpable. In Kenny's words, "no external conduct, however serious or even fatal its consequences may have been, is ever punished unless it is produced by some form of *mens rea*."[20]

(b) Theories of culpability

The argument for having a mens rea element in criminal offences assumes that proof of mens rea establishes culpability. However, to what extent this is true is debated by criminal theorists.[21] Academics commonly argue over two accounts of when we may legitimately blame someone for her actions, which can only be sketched here. The first, which is reflected in the law regarding serious crimes, is sometimes called a "subjective" analysis: that culpability depends upon morally defective *choices*. We blame someone for choosing to do a wrong action—for instance, for choosing to set fire to the house. Conversely, fault is not made out unless someone *deliberately* does something bad.

The upshot of this approach is that the *actus non facit reum nisi mens sit rea* maxim transforms into a requirement that we should not convict without advertence. As will be seen in the chapter on mens rea, this would include such mental states as intention and recklessness. If Pam gave Alex the painkiller in order to kill him, we can blame her for causing his death because she intended to do so. Conversely, on the subjective account, it is perfectly reasonable for Pam to dose Alex if she is unaware that the medicine will kill him. Failing to take account of the risk of death is not something for which she can be blamed.

The alternative account is "objective". It grounds fault in *conduct* rather than choices, arguing that an action attracts blame if it inflicts harm when a reasonable person would not have acted that way. Under the objective analysis, awareness of wrongdoing is not essential. If homicide is undesirable, then Pam has a reason not to do it whether or not she foresees the risk. Homicide does not become acceptable just because it is done inadvertently. Since it involves harm, not only does Pam have a moral (and, in this case, legal) duty not to do it, but she also has a duty to *take care* so that she does not do it inadvertently either. On this account, Pam may legitimately be convicted of a crime if she is unreasonably careless.

The objective view works best when explaining why someone may be blamed for negligence, and in giving substance to the idea of the "reasonable man". The "reasonable man" is archetypally a person of decent character. Thus if the defendant has failed to behave like a

---

[20] *Outlines of Criminal Law* (2nd ed., 1904) 39. This proposition is subject to qualification in respect of strict liability (below, § 1.2(ii)(c) and Chapter 6). Note that the present claim is only that mens rea is *necessary* for culpability. Unfortunately, liability for an offence requiring mens rea is sometimes incurred notwithstanding the absence of moral fault: *Yip Chiu-Cheung* v. *R.* [1995] 1 AC 111, following *dicta* in *Kingston* [1995] 2 AC 355, 364–6. These cases are, however, somewhat unusual: where mens rea is present but moral fault is absent, this is usually recognised by the availability of defences. See below, § 1.2(ii)(d); Fletcher, *Rethinking Criminal Law* (1978) 511f, 799f.

[21] See, e.g., Hampton, "Mens Rea" in Paul, Miller and Paul (eds.), *Crime, Culpability, and Remedy* (1990) 1 (also in (1990) 7 *Social Philosophy and Policy* 1); Moore, "Choice, Character, and Excuse" in Paul, Miller and Paul (eds.), *Crime, Culpability and Remedy* (1990) 29; Bayles, "Character, Purpose and Criminal Responsibility" (1982) 1 *Law and Phil* 5; Arenella, "Character, Choice, and Moral Agency" in Paul, Miller and Paul (eds.), *Crime, Culpability and Remedy* (1990) 59; Duff, "Choice, Character and Criminal Liability" (1993) 12 *Law and Phil* 345; Hart, "Negligence, Mens Rea, and Criminal Responsibility" in *Punishment and Responsibility* (1968) 136; Sullivan, "Making Excuses" in Simester and Smith (eds.), *Harm and Culpability* (1996) 131.

reasonable person, we may infer culpability, since her conduct has fallen short of reflecting that decent character.

These subjective and objective approaches are extreme alternatives, and middle ground is available. In the criminal law, inadvertent negligence *is* normally thought to be a standard of fault, but foresight of wrongdoing generally involves *greater* culpability. As we shall see in Chapter 5, adjudicating between the two approaches has not always been easy, particularly in the debate over subjective or objective interpretations of "recklessness", which is the minimum fault requirement for many stigmatic criminal offences. Suppose that David causes a fire in a house and is charged with reckless arson. Traditionally in England, and still in many overseas jurisdictions, recklessness has required some degree of actual foresight. So for David to be guilty he must have actually foreseen the risk of setting fire to the house when he did the act that caused it. Were he merely negligent (or even grossly so), he would have to be acquitted. Where that view is taken, the subjectivist holds sway. On the other hand, for two decades the law in England regarding this offence was objective:[22] David could be convicted of reckless arson even though he did not notice the risk, at least if the risk was an obvious one.

If fault is a prerequisite of criminal liability then it is easy to see why recklessness or other foresight-based mental states are so often required before a defendant can be convicted for his actions. Much more difficult are statutes that define an action to be an offence when it is done negligently. Indeed, subjectivists often argue that people should never be convicted for negligence.[23] We disagree, and it seems to us that one may fairly be blamed for an unreasonable failure to take care; though no doubt the criminalisation of such cases ought to be sparing. But whether one adopts a subjective or objective stance, and whatever one's views regarding the culpability of negligence, one thing is clear. Without at least some form of fault, a defendant should not be convicted of a crime. For the most part, this proposition is reflected in English criminal law where, in the absence of recklessness about the harm (or, in some cases, of negligence), a defendant must generally be acquitted of any serious criminal offence.

(c) Regulatory offences

What, then, of strict liability? There are many crimes for which the prosecution need not prove any element of fault before the defendant may be convicted. In these offences, the defendant's liability is said to be "strict", and the actus non fit reum maxim is said not to apply. For example, under the Water Resources Act 1991 a defendant may be convicted for discharging polluting matter into controlled waters if the prosecution shows merely that he caused the pollutant to be discharged.[24] There is no need to prove that the defendant's involvement was a culpable one.

We deal with strict liability offences more fully in Chapter 6. For now, two observations may be made. The first is that, as we shall see, the courts in some overseas jurisdictions have moved to base "strict" liability on a presumption of fault—where culpability on the part of

---

[22] *Caldwell* [1982] AC 341. The decision in *Caldwell* was eventually reversed by *G* [2003] UKHL 50, [2004] 1 AC 1034, which restored the law to a subjective test. See below, § 5.2.

[23] Below, § 5.5(iv).

[24] Section 85. Cf. *Alphacell Ltd* v. *Woodward* [1972] AC 824.

the defendant is presumed, but may be rebutted. If D can prove that the harm was not at all his fault, he will be acquitted. Thus the essential difference, in other countries, between offences of strict liability and those of negligence is the burden of proof. Arguably, for some minor offences it may be appropriate for that burden to rest upon the defendant rather than the prosecution; and it is to be regretted that English courts have rejected this possibility, which would substantially have ameliorated the harshness of strict liability in this country.

The fact that strict liability offences are often minor raises a second point. Strict liability offences tend not to involve the same level of public censure as serious crimes. A parking offence, for example, comprises an altogether different order of wrongdoing from murder. This is not to deny that traffic offences and their like are part of the criminal law, although perhaps they should not be.[25] But most people distinguish in ordinary life between minor, regulatory-type offences and "true" crimes, and the element of public condemnation is and should be conveyed only by a conviction of the latter type. The difference in social significance is illustrated by the question we mentioned earlier, commonly found in visa and employment applications, about an applicant's criminal record. It is not a request that is intended to elicit disclosure of minor infractions such as parking infringements. To the extent that English law restricts strict liability to minor offences (and it does not do so invariably), its use is therefore somewhat less objectionable.

(d) Allowing defences

The medical homicide example (§ 1.2(ii)(a)), in which Pam kills Alex, illustrates one way in which the defendant may be absolved of fault when a prohibited consequence occurs. Her answer is that, although she killed Alex, it was an accident. She neither intended his death, nor was she negligent in bringing it about: she lacked mens rea. Sometimes, however, a person may not be culpable even though she harms another person deliberately. For example:

> Ian is a policeman in the Armed Offenders squad. He is standing outside a bank when a robbery occurs. John, who is one of the robbers, comes out of the bank and runs toward him, pointing a gun. In order to protect himself, Ian shoots and injures John.

Prima facie, this is a crime. Ian cannot claim that he shot John by accident. Nevertheless, Ian is not to blame. His action, we would say, is *justified*, and he does not deserve to be convicted of any crime.

In order to deal with this sort of case, the law recognises a number of general defences, under which the defendant may acknowledge that he did an otherwise prohibited act and yet escape conviction. Examples of these justificatory defences are self-defence, prevention of crime, and defence of property. In effect such defences allege that, although D's conduct was harmful and normally unlawful, his conduct was nevertheless appropriate in the

---

[25] According to Robinson, "[s]erious deterrent sanctions can and ought to be imposed [for regulatory violations] but they can as easily and effectively be imposed under an administrative system distinct from criminal law that carries a noncriminal label, such as 'violation'": "The Criminal–Civil Distinction and the Utility of Desert" (1996) 76 *Boston ULR* 201, 214. Cf. Mann's proposal for a separate system of justice to deal with such minor crimes, in "Punitive Civil Sanctions: The Middle Ground Between Criminal and Civil Law" (1992) 101 *Yale LJ* 1795.

circumstances.[26] They claim that the defendant's conduct was the right (or an acceptable) thing to do, and so was not deserving of censure. As such, justifications are generalised: they involve judgements about the situation which apply to all the participants; so, e.g., John is not entitled to resist Ian's justified use of force.

There are other predicaments where inflicting harm can be defensible on a more restricted basis. In these cases a person may choose to do something wrong, i.e. unjustified, but we may nevertheless think her insufficiently blameworthy to warrant the censure of the criminal law. For example:

> Susan is arrested after taking part in the bombing of a Government building. She drove the car in which the bombers, a gang of terrorists, had made their escape. After her arrest, it is discovered that she did so only because the terrorists had threatened to kill her otherwise.

In this type of case, Susan's conduct may not be justified, and other people would be entitled to try to stop her. Nevertheless her culpability is lessened by the fact that she was coerced. Thus she has an *excuse*. The rationale for allowing excusatory defences is that advanced by H.L.A. Hart: "unless a man has the capacity and a fair opportunity or chance to alter his behaviour to the law its penalties ought not to be applied to him."[27] Susan's wrongdoing was deliberate, but understandable. By admitting compulsion as a defence,[28] the criminal law acknowledges that Susan did not have a genuine and fair opportunity to choose not to break the law. We may have no reason to praise her. But she does not warrant the penalties of the criminal law, because she is below the threshold of blameworthiness that is appropriate to criminal liability.

(e) Accountability

So far in § 1.2, we have argued that the criminal law should convict only people who are culpable when a prohibited event occurs, and that events should be prohibited only when they are sufficiently harmful to override considerations such as the need to protect the autonomy of citizens. There is, however, a further requirement to be met before the criminal law may convict someone of a crime: accountability. Recall the example with which we began this discussion:

> One fine September morning, Jim is discovered dead in his home. His skull has been crushed by a blow inflicted with a heavy object. The police are called. Upon investigation, they establish that he was murdered by his daughter, Alice, who killed him in order to receive her inheritance under his will.

This, as we said earlier, is a plain case. But it is not just the fact that Alice is culpable which licenses her conviction. Culpability, by itself, is insufficient. Suppose that Jim's brother,

---

[26] Indeed one may say of such cases that no prohibited harm occurred. Thus A.T.H. Smith remarks, "[w]here the defendant's conduct can fairly be described as coming within the terms of the proscribed activity, an offence has, prima facie, been committed: liability will ensue unless he advances some explanation of his conduct which shows that it was justified, in which case there is no actus reus": "On Actus Reus and Mens Rea" in Glazebrook (ed.), *Reshaping the Criminal Law* (1978) 95, 97.

[27] "Punishment and the Elimination of Responsibility" in *Punishment and Responsibility* (1968) 158, 181.

[28] Subject to restrictions: below, Chapter 20.

David, had suspected Alice might try to murder Jim and had done nothing to warn him? David may be blameworthy, but ought we to prosecute him? Certainly not for homicide, at any rate. The difference between David and Alice is that only Alice is legally accountable, or *responsible*, for Jim's death. Only Alice has performed an action that caused Jim's death. Because he is not legally responsible, there is simply no point in prosecuting David, however much we may disapprove of his conduct.[29]

Although a great range of differing conduct can be subjected to criminal sanction, the process of finding guilt and pronouncing a conviction entails certain limits on the boundaries of criminalisation. The finding of guilt on which the conviction is based assumes a degree of accountability for something done or omitted to be done. Unless one subscribes to some extreme version of Calvinism or other doctrine of the damned, guilt is not a state of being, a natural property. Guilt can be generated only in respect of something additional to what the defendant is; something for which he is accountable. Otherwise, the "presumption of innocence" is meaningless. Consider, for example, a nation-state where the government is following a policy of expelling all citizens who are not members of the dominant ethnic group. Acting through civil law process, such a State could pass legislation confiscating the property of minority citizens and impose various forms of disability in terms of profession, marriage, etc., in ways all too familiar. But it would be incoherent for the State to make it a crime simply to be a member of a minority racial grouping; there would be nothing on which the conviction could be based.

The constraint may be ineffective in practice. Where the political environment is so extreme that a State is willing to create an offence simply of being a member of less favoured groups, it is quite likely the judges of that State would be unreceptive to the argument sketched here. But in countries with a judiciary prepared to judge in good faith, the need for accountability—for something additional to one's state of being—should properly limit the scope of criminalisation. This should have been required in the notorious case of *Larsonneur*,[30] a case castigated by Jerome Hall as the "acme of strict injustice!"[31] On what can be ascertained from the available law reports, D, in circumstances wholly beyond her control, was brought from the country then known as Eire into police custody in the United Kingdom. Once here, she was charged with being an alien (she was French) who was in the United Kingdom without permission to land. With an excessively literal interpretation of the legislation in question, the Divisional Court upheld the trial conviction. Lord Hewart ruled that the circumstances of her entry and continuing confinement were "perfectly immaterial". It was enough, said the Court, that she was present in the United Kingdom without permission. In substance then, she was convicted solely for being French. But that, in our submission, is not enough.

Even at the level of principle, the argument from incoherence is narrow. It would be perfectly coherent, however unconscionable, for the nation-state described above to make it a crime for members of a minority group to give birth to children. Neither does the argument rule out what are known as *status*, or *situational*, offences, such as being an illegal immigrant or a parent of a child of compulsory school age who is not regularly attending

---

[29] Or, as Lord Esher MR put it, "[a] man is entitled to be as negligent as he pleases towards the whole world if he owes no duty to them": *Le Lievre v. Gould* [1893] 1 QB 491, 497.

[30] (1933) 149 LT 542. The case is discussed further below, § 4.1(ii)(a).

[31] *General Principles of Criminal Law* (2nd ed., 1960) 329 n. 14.

school. If it can be shown that there were acts or omissions for which D is responsible and by which D could have avoided the proscribed status, then the accountability requirement is satisfied. Translated into criminal law doctrine, this condition is embodied in a requirement of *voluntariness*, which is discussed in § 4.3. Where one's status is involuntary, it cannot legitimately be a criminal offence simply to be what one *is*. The criminal law is concerned with the acts, omissions and, on occasion, acquired status of human beings. It takes human beings as its starting point and then asks what they are accountable *for*.

In addition to the requirement of voluntariness, the need for accountability can raise other difficult issues. Suppose a further variation on the death of Jim:

> Case III: Jim is discovered dead in his home. The police establish that he died after being struck by a vase which fell accidentally from the bookshelf. However, his daughter, Edith, had observed the scene and deliberately failed to summon an ambulance in time to save him.

This is very similar to Alice's case, except for one aspect: our complaint here is not about what Edith did, but about what she *failed* or *omitted* to do. Another way of expressing the difference might be to say that, unlike Alice, Edith did not *cause* Jim's death.[32] Either way, however, because of that distinction, criminal liability does not necessarily follow.

The issues of omission and causation will be discussed in more detail in Chapter 4, but it is important to note that these, too, are crucial matters affecting the range and intrusiveness of the criminal law. Prohibiting an omission is not like prohibiting an action. When the law prevents Ian from (say) punching Bob, it leaves him with plenty of options and rules out only one. Ian is free to choose what to do or not do instead. By contrast, when the law proscribes an omission, it tells him exactly what to do. If Jim is dying, Edith *must* rescue him—she is not free to choose what to do or not do instead. One option is *required*, and all the other options are ruled out. Thus liability for omissions is much more likely to impinge upon individual autonomy and freedom of action.

In a liberal community, the right to autonomy is fundamental.[33] If the law is to acknowledge and respect individuals as independent members of society, then it must judge them according to their own actions, and not those of others. The process of shaping and controlling a person's life should be left to that person, and would be undermined were citizens constantly forced to assume responsibility for events they do not bring about.[34] For this reason, it is a guiding principle of the law that defendants are liable according to what *they* do, not what others do and they might prevent; correspondingly, they should be left free to live their own lives and pursue their own goals without having legal duties to act or intervene constantly thrust upon them, unanticipated, unpredictable, and unwanted, because of the actions of others. This is why there is no general duty to prevent crime.[35] It is also why principles of accountability are so important.[36]

---

[32] Cf. Moore, *Act and Crime* (1993) 267–78. But the law may disagree: see below, § 4.2(iv)(a).

[33] Above, § 1.2(i)(b).

[34] Thus *Hart and Honoré* lxxx–xi: "respect for ourselves and others as distinct persons would be much weakened, if not dissolved, if we could not think of ourselves as the separate authors of the changes we make in the world". For further discussion, see below, § 4.1(i).

[35] Cf. *Coney* (1882) 8 QBD 534, 557–8; *Clarkson* [1971] 3 All ER 344, 347.

[36] There is a pragmatic side to accountability. If a swimmer drowns, the law cannot afford to prosecute every person on the beach. More generally, the State could not possibly contemplate prosecuting everyone who might

Implicit in this reasoning, however, is that omissions are special not because they deny culpability, but because of the implications of their proscription for individual freedom. Thus they are not ruled out *tout court*. In practice, a criminal law duty to intervene is imposed, if at all, only when the defendant has a special connection to the harm—for example, when the defendant is the victim's parent.[37] But even that need not be true. Sometimes an altruistic reason for a stranger to get involved may justify the extension of responsibility. Suppose that Ian, a passer-by, sees a child drowning in a paddling pool. He can rescue the child at no risk to himself. In this situation, for Ian not to intervene would be monstrous. Although English criminal law does not at the moment criminalise such cases, it might justifiably do so, depending upon such factors as the seriousness of the impending harm and the degrees of risk and inconvenience involved in averting it. In many other jurisdictions, it is a crime not to rescue someone in peril when doing so involves no personal danger.[38]

Similarly, the criminal law need not always require D's behaviour to *cause* a specified consequence. For example, the law of secondary liability recognises the responsibility of those who do not themselves perpetrate a crime, but are nevertheless parties to its commission.[39] Suppose, for example, that David plans to kill Tony. Knowing this, Rebecca lends David her gun. Rebecca is a participant in Tony's murder, and his death may be attributed to her as a secondary party. The point here is that Rebecca does not cause Tony's death.[40] (David would have killed him anyway, using someone else's gun.) But she is not like a mere bystander, who can claim that David's action has nothing to do with her; that it is none of her business. Instead, she has involved herself in the murder, and *made* it her business. Thus, although it is David who kills Tony, Rebecca shares in the responsibility for his death.

Like liability for omissions, secondary liability involves an extension of the criminal law beyond the core cases of wrongdoing. As such, it involves a greater intrusion upon people's freedom of action: not only may D not strike V, he may not do anything to help someone else strike V either, a much greater limitation upon what he is left free to do. This raises difficult questions of policy: if Rebecca is a shopkeeper, should she refuse to sell matches to David if she suspects or believes he has an illicit purpose? Secondary liability has the potential to force individuals to police the actions of others, and squarely raises issues of autonomy once more.[41] It is a hard question how far such extensions of responsibility should go, since, like vicarious liability,[42] they can have the effect of imposing liability

---

have prevented it each time a prohibited harm occurs. So the general principle against liability for omissions has a realistic air about it as well as a philosophical justification.

[37] See below, § 4.1(1)(b).

[38] See Ashworth, "The Scope of Criminal Liability for Omissions" (1989) 105 *LQR* 424.

[39] Below, Chapter 7.

[40] See, e.g., *Hart and Honoré* 51ff, 363ff; J.C. Smith, "Aid, Abet, Counsel, or Procure" in Glazebrook (ed.), *Reshaping the Criminal Law* (1978) 120, 131–4.

[41] Particularly in cases of complicit liability for omissions, which may arise when the secondary party has some form of control over the wrongdoer. See for example *Du Cros v. Lambourne* [1907] 1 KB 40, in which the passenger in a car was convicted of being a party to dangerous driving, on the basis that he owned the car and failed to exercise his right of control over the driver's actions. The case is further discussed below, § 7.4(iii).

[42] The doctrine of vicarious liability provides a second route with which a causal requirement may be bypassed. However, vicarious liability is normally to be avoided in criminal law, since it arises out of a more general relationship between the defendant and the actual perpetrator of a wrong, and so is not specific to the wrongful

largely on the basis of the defendant's status rather than his behaviour. Yet, once again, accountability is not ruled out *tout court.*

(iii) Ex post: *sanction*

Although punishment is not a constitutive element of the criminal conviction and lies outside the scope of this text, one cannot overlook its salience in the criminal process. If we were to dismantle punishment and its forbidding infrastructure, much of the *raison d'être* of the criminal law would go with it. Despite its importance, however, the question *why* we punish remains a matter of perennial and irresolvable dispute and has given rise to a vast and challenging literature.[43] In the following paragraphs, we can only sketch the major competing punishment theories, as any attempt to enter the debate would not do it justice.

The common starting point is to require grounds which justify the imposition of punishment on a candidate individual. One should always be sure that the legal verdict which licenses punishment is well founded, a restraint with implications for criminal procedure and evidence. If we can be sure of the facts for the instant case, one group of theorists, commonly known as retributivists, would then ask whether punishment is *deserved.*[44] Desert is a function of the moral quality of the conduct; if it is bad (i.e. wrongful and culpable), a measure of hard treatment may be dispensed, the measure dependent on how bad that conduct is.[45] Once the grounds of desert are present, punishment ceases to be problematic. Indeed, it becomes something that ought to be imposed, something that will restore the moral balance which the malefactor has disturbed. A consistent retributivist will confine punishment to immoral conduct and will typically (though not necessarily) find immorality in the state of mind and disposition of the person to be punished rather than the consequences of her actions.[46] Consistent retributivism would entail a criminal law more scrupulous about finding fault sufficient to allow just punishment.

Retributivism is contrasted with utilitarianism, a species of consequentialism which asserts that any instance of punishment is justified only if the welfare of society is advanced. For a utilitarian, the pain of the person to be punished is a disutility, a diminution in the quantum of general welfare. Accordingly, pain should be inflicted only if it entails net gains in welfare across society: the institution of state punishment must produce overall beneficent effects. The particular effect that utilitarians most commonly seek from punishment is general deterrence, i.e. that without hard treatment of offenders there would be more offending and less welfare overall.[47] As the term "consequentialism" implies, the moral

---

action; consequently the defendant risks being convicted of a crime for which he is not morally responsible. As a rule, "*Qui peccat per alium peccat per se* is not a maxim of criminal law": *Tesco Supermarkets Ltd* v. *Nattrass* [1972] AC 153, 199 (Lord Diplock). See further below, § 8.2.

[43] For excellent introductions to questions of punishment and sentence see Duff and Garland (eds.), *A Reader on Punishment* (1994) and von Hirsch and Ashworth (eds.), *Principles of Sentencing: Readings on Theory and Policy* (2nd ed., 1998).

[44] A classic account is von Hirsch, *Doing Justice* (1976).

[45] On evaluating the gravity of wrongdoing see von Hirsch, *Censure and Sanctions* (1993) chap. 4.

[46] A stimulating example is Ashworth, "Taking the Consequences" in Shute, Gardner and Horder (eds.), *Action and Value in Criminal Law* (1993) 107.

[47] This claim is, of course, an empirical matter. Even if it is true in general terms, there is disagreement whether increasing punishment levels for a particular offences will reduce the incidence of their commission. For a survey of the literature, see von Hirsch et al., *Criminal Deterrence and Sentencing Severity* (1999).

character of a defendant's action is determined primarily by its results. A death remains a death whether it ensues from a brutal killing or a blameless accident. Many attempts have been made to demonstrate that blame and desert matter to utilitarianism,[48] but the relationship is, at best, a contingent one.[49] There is no reason, internal to utilitarianism, why a legal system should differentiate deliberate killings from accidental deaths. If it could be demonstrated that an unvarying penalty of life imprisonment for anyone who causes death in whatever circumstances would radically diminish the number of untimely deaths, then a utilitarian has reason to endorse that practice, and the only permissible objections to such indiscriminate hard treatment must be made in terms of its cost to net social utility. Indeed, consequentialism need not imply a system of criminal law. Other forms of deterrence may be more efficient tools for social control.

Consequentialism and retributivism are incompatible theories. That, of course, does not preclude individuals, even judges, from using consequentialist and retributivist justifications at one and the same time, as when D is sent to prison for a very long time "because you deserve it and because it will deter others of like mind"—an example of belt and braces rather than contradiction. In terms of English sentencing policy, the retributivist approach reached its apogee with the Criminal Justice Act of 1991, whereby proportionality became the primary criterion for deciding penalties. By 1993, concern with the impact of this approach, particularly in the area of fines on motorists, had become politically salient and the then Criminal Justice Act 1993 and Crime (Sentences) Act 1997 departed significantly from the "just deserts" rationale in sentencing.[50] Prior convictions are once again a significant aggravating feature in sentencing decisions, following a shift of emphasis from the moral deserts of the crime at hand toward a law-and-order considerations of the offender's general dangerousness. More recently, the Criminal Justice Act 2003 has further widened the range of sentencing factors by stipulating five explicit principles underlying sentencing: as well as a retributive punishment principle and a consequentialist goal of crime reduction through deterrence, the three new principles are reform and rehabilitation of criminals; public protection (itself a crime-reduction principle); and reparation. Proportionality, thus, is no longer primary. It is no coincidence that rates of incarceration in England and Wales are at an historic high even though general crime rates have fallen.

Some theorists, most notably H.L.A. Hart,[51] have argued for a composite theory of criminal responsibility and punishment, expressed in terms of a distinction between the "general justifying aim" of the criminal law on the one hand and the principles of criminal responsibility and just punishment on the other. For Hart, the general purpose of the criminal law was consequentialist: to deter anti-social conduct. However, this goal is properly inhibited by reference to issues of blame and proportion when adjudicating guilt and passing sentence. The inhibition is necessary to ensure fairness and to maximise autonomy. Although Hart argued for his composite theory with incomparable elegance, the predominating if not the exclusive element within it would appear to be retributivism. To be

---

[48] Hart, *Punishment and Responsibility* (1968) chaps. 1, 7.
[49] See Wootton, *Crime and the Criminal Law* (2nd ed., 1981).
[50] For an account of the background to the 1991 Act and the move away from its principles, see Koffman, "The Rise and Fall of Proportionality: The failure of the Criminal Justice Act 1991" [2006] *Crim LR* 281.
[51] *Punishment and Responsibility* (1968) chaps. 1, 7.

sure, utilitarianism is given the task of determining which conduct will be punished. Yet retributivism would generate many of the same primary norms and it is retributivism which resolves who will be punished and how much punishment will be meted.[52] For the moment, however, the role of retributivism as a limiting principle in a consequetialist matrix is on the wane in England and Wales.

§ 1.3 The structure of a criminal offence

The discussion in this chapter has practical implications for criminal offences. We have characterised the criminal law as a system of prohibition and censure. Correspondingly, the main elements of crimes are twofold, harm and fault. The first of these is primarily an external element:[53] an event or conduct which causes the harm that the law is designed to prevent. For example, the external element in murder is the killing of one human being by another.[54] This external element is known as the *actus reus* of the offence. It sets out the physical thing that must happen before the criminal law can be invoked, and will be discussed in detail in Chapter 4.

Generally, the actus reus is not enough by itself to constitute an offence. In § 1.2(ii)(a) we discussed the example of Pam, a doctor, who killed Alex by injecting him with a painkiller to which he was allergic. Pam has done the actus reus of a murder. But if Alex's allergy was unknowable, then Pam is not to blame, and should not be convicted. Alex's death is simply a tragic accident. The need for fault in an offence gives us the second element, which is known as *mens rea*. This is what might be termed the "mental" element—the guilty mind, such as the intention, knowledge, or recklessness, of the defendant with respect to the actus reus. Mens rea is the subject of Chapter 5.

Like the actus reus, the mens rea varies for each offence. In some crimes, intention or recklessness will be required before D can be convicted, while in others negligence or some other fault element may suffice. An example will help to illustrate. Imagine that Tom has been charged with an offence against section 15(1) of the Forgery and Counterfeiting Act 1981. He recently purchased a toaster from the local shop, paying for it in £10 notes. However, it later turns out that the notes are not genuine, as both Tom and the shopkeeper had thought, but very high quality forgeries. The relevant section provides as follows:

> 15. Offences of passing, etc., counterfeit notes and coins
> (1)   It is an offence for a person—
> (a) to pass or tender as genuine any thing which is, and which he knows or believes to be, a counterfeit of a currency note or of a protected coin. . . .

In this crime, the actus reus is passing or tendering as genuine money which is in fact counterfeit. The mens rea of the crime is knowing or believing that the money is counterfeit.

---

[52] See the critique of Hart's "mixed theory" by Galligan, "The Return to Retribution in Penal Theory" in Tapper (ed.), *Crime, Proof and Punishment* (1981) 144.

[53] Although it may not be entirely external. Sometimes actions acquire a harmful or criminal character only when done with a particular mental state. For illustrative discussion of this point, see Horder, "Crimes of Ulterior Intent" in Simester and Smith (eds.), *Harm and Culpability* (1996) 153; see also below, § 5.3.

[54] Below, Chapter 10.

On the facts given, Tom will not be guilty of passing counterfeit notes since he lacks the mens rea required for an offence against section 15(1).

Sometimes the mens rea can be present without the actus reus. Suppose instead that Tom found the notes on the street and believed that they were counterfeit, but that they were actually genuine. In this case Tom does not commit the offence of passing forged notes, because the actus reus is missing.[55]

(i) Defences: a separate element

The examples above illustrate that both specified parts of the offence, the actus reus and the mens rea, must be proved before there is any question of D's being guilty of a crime. Even if both parts are proved, however, there might still be a defence available, and so we have a third basic element of every crime: the absence of a valid defence.

Suppose, for example, that Tom had indeed known the notes were counterfeit, but had been forced to make the purchase because he had been accosted outside the store by two men who had supplied the notes and "asked" him to buy the toaster, while wielding a shotgun suggestively. Tom has performed the actus reus of section 15(1), with the required mens rea. So we can say that he has committed a *prima facie offence*. Despite this, he will not be convicted since he has a further defence of duress or compulsion.

The word "defence" can sometimes be misleading, because it tends to be used by lawyers to describe any reason why the defendant should be acquitted. Thus if the defendant has an alibi, he will rely on this for his defence. More precisely, however, an alibi is not a defence but rather a denial that there was a prima facie offence at all. If the alibi is accepted, it means that the defendant did not do the actus reus. Similarly, automatism is not so much a defence as a denial of responsibility for the actus reus. Duress and self-defence, by contrast, deny neither actus reus nor mens rea, but rather seek to defend the commission of a prima facie offence by reference to events not contemplated in the actus reus.[56]

Normally, defences reside at large in the common law, and are not expressly set out as part of each offence. Similarly, they are treated in separate chapters of this text. This is because defences are normally of general application to all crimes, unless expressly or impliedly excluded by the statute which creates a particular crime. The fact that defences make up a third element was accepted by Lord Wilberforce in *Lynch*. Duress, he stated:[57]

> "is something which is superimposed on the other ingredients which by themselves would make up an offence, i.e. on the act and the intention. *Coactus volui* sums up the combination: the victim completes the act and knows that he is doing so; but the addition of the element of duress prevents the law from treating what he has done as a crime."

In case it is helpful, we represent this relationship by the following diagram:

---

[55] Cf. *Deller* (1952) 36 Cr App R 184.

[56] Cf. A.T.H. Smith, "On Actus Reus and Mens Rea" in Glazebrook (ed.), *Reshaping the Criminal Law* (1978) 95, 97ff; Simester, "Mistakes in Defence" (1992) 12 *OJLS* 295, 295–6.

[57] [1975] AC 653, 679–80.

The Offence of Passing
Counterfeit Money

s. 15(1)

Actus Reus	Mens Rea	Defences
(T passes a counterfeit currency note as genuine)	(T knows or believes the note is counterfeit)	(e.g. T is not under duress)

2

THE RULE OF LAW AND THE EUROPEAN CONVENTION

It is temptingly easy for a government to misuse the criminal legal system as a convenient means of social ordering. The criminal law, in seeking to secure benefits to society at large, can be a major threat of *in*security for any individual charged with the commission of a crime. Indeed, in some respects the criminal justice system constitutes this country's most potent peace-time threat to the civil rights of those citizens suspected of and prosecuted for crimes. Accordingly society, while endeavouring to control and reduce criminal conduct, must be sensitive to the rights and legitimate expectations of those charged with crime.

Central to the protection of those rights and expectations is the Rule of Law, which demands that those under the State's control should be dealt with by fixed and knowable law, and not according to the discretion of State (including judicial) officials. As such, the Rule of Law embodies a cluster of legal values, including certainty, clarity, and prospectivity; which have at their heart not merely the constitutional premise that government should operate under the law, but also the ideal that citizens should be able successfully to live within the law, by deriving guidance from the law itself.[1] This, in turn, requires that the criminal law must be an organised, ascertainable, system of legal rules—and not *ad hoc* responses to the conduct of individuals.

The Rule of Law exists, first and foremost, at the level of principle. It comprises values to which the law should aspire, and to which legislators and judges should pay heed when enacting and interpreting law.[2] It is not a legally mandatory doctrine in its own right, save in so far as it operates as an informing principle of statutory interpretation.[3] However, with the enactment of the Human Rights Act (HRA) 1998, which provides for the direct applicability of the European Convention on Human Rights and Fundamental Freedoms (ECHR), many of the principles associated with the Rule of Law now have independent constitutional significance. In this chapter, we will explore the significance of those principles for the criminal law; and, more generally, we will consider the impact of the ECHR upon English criminal law.

---

[1] See Raz, *The Authority of Law* (1979) chap. 11; Colvin, "Criminal Law and the Rule of Law" in Fitzgerald (ed.), *Crime, Justice and Codification* (1986) 125.

[2] Cf. Report by the SPTL Committee to the Law Commission, published as Report No. 143, *Codification of the Criminal Law* (1985) para. 1.3: "more accessible, comprehensible, consistent and certain" aspirations for codification.

[3] An illustration of its role in statutory interpretation may be seen in Lord Steyn's assertion in *B (a minor)* v. *DPP* [2000] AC 428, 470 that "in the absence of express words or a truly necessary implication, Parliament must be presumed to legislate on the assumption that the principle of legality will supplement the text."

§ 2.1 No conviction without criminalisation

The first limiting principle is inherent in the definition of criminal law offered at the beginning of Chapter 1: that a crime involves, among other things, an event prohibited by law.[4] This implies that nobody should be convicted of a criminal offence unless what was done is, in law, a crime. *Nullum crimen sine lege*, the maxim goes: no crime without law.[5] Suppose, for example, that Jane is a visitor from another country where adultery is a criinal offence. While in Wales she has an affair with a married man. Even though she believes she is committing a crime, she cannot be convicted of any offence, since adultery is not illegal under English and Welsh criminal law. A case which illustrates this principle is *Deller*.[6] The defendant sold a car, stating as he did so that it was free of encumbrances. In fact, he thought the car was encumbered, because he had earlier mortgaged it to a finance company. Deller was charged with obtaining the proceeds of the car sale under false pretences. As it happened however, the earlier mortgage was apparently invalid, and hence the car *was* un-encumbered. By chance, his pretence was not false. He could not be convicted since he had broken no law.[7]

§ 2.2 Retrospective crimes

A corollary of the *nullum crimen* principle is that there should be no retrospective criminalisation, whereby citizens might be convicted on the basis of conduct which was not, *when they did it*, an offence. In such cases, it is not enough that relevant law is to hand at the time of the trial. It would still be true that at the time of D's conduct he committed no applicable crime. Remedying the legal deficiency by passing a retrospective law, which deemed the offence into existence at the time of its commission, would be to contradict rather than uphold the Rule of Law. Particularly given the dramatic implications of criminal penalties for the lives of individuals, criminal liability is not the sort of nasty surprise that should be sprung on citizens *ex post facto*.

It is important to optimise the transparency and efficacy of the criminal law by stating its rules in advance. Failure to do so undermines the entire operation of the law, as a system of rules designed to guide society's behaviour, when the rules are unknown. When interpreting criminal statutes, the common law contains a presumption against retrospective crimes. Although the presumption may be overridden by the express terms of a legislative enactment,[8] it provides a signal protection against that possibility. Moreover, were Parliament expressly to override that presumption, it would also be in clear contravention of Article 7 of the ECHR, which plainly interdicts retroactive criminal law and retroactive increases in the penalties for existing crimes. As things stand, both at common law and under the terms

---

[4] Above, § 1.1.

[5] Sometimes called the principle of *legality*, especially in the United States. See Hall, *General Principles of Criminal Law* (2nd ed., 1960) 27f.

[6] (1952) 36 Cr App R 184.

[7] At least, at that time. Under modern law, it appears that Deller could now be convicted of an attempt. See below, Chapter 9.

[8] *Waddington v. Miah* [1974] 2 All ER 377; *Deery* [1977] Crim LR 550; *Sutcliffe* [1983] Crim LR 255.

of the HRA 1998, courts are required to accept Parliament's will (subject to the tensions and contradictions described below, in § 2.5). Nonetheless, the incorporation of Article 7 should at least ensure that courts will, in the absence of the clearest language, be loath to interpret a newly created crime, or a statutory increase in penalty, as having retrospective effect. In addition, both the common law presumption and Article 7 may act as a warning sign: any finding that they are overridden involves public acknowledgement that a part of the criminal law transgresses the Rule of Law and contravenes the defendant's basic human rights.

At common law, the courts formerly also had the power to create offences: indeed, this is the foundation of many of the oldest crimes—including murder, which remains undefined by legislation. By the twentieth century, however, the power was exercised less frequently and more controversially, since it inherently involves a retrospective conviction. In *Shaw* v. *DPP*,[9] for example, the defendant was charged with conspiring to corrupt public morals—an offence that had not existed until he was indicted for it. His indictment was upheld by the House of Lords. *Whether or not* the defendant's actions were covered by an existing law, the courts were said to have residual power to criminalise his conduct. The decision led to an outcry, especially among lawyers and academics,[10] and it is now accepted that the courts no longer have the power to create new offences.[11] In the modern legal system, the authority to create new offences lies solely with Parliament:[12]

> "an important democratic principle in this country [is] that it is for those representing the people of the country in Parliament, not the executive and not the judges, to decide what conduct should be treated as lying so far outside the bounds of what is acceptable in our society as to attract criminal penalties."

Neither do the courts have the power to widen existing offences, in order to criminalize conduct that previously was permitted.[13] At the same time, however, this is not to prohibit *any* development of the law. As the European Court of Human Rights (European Court) has observed,[14]

> "However clearly drafted a legal provision may be, in any system of law, including criminal law, there is an inevitable element of judicial interpretation. There will always be a need for elucidation of doubtful points and for adaptation to changing circumstances. Indeed, in the United Kingdom, as in the other Convention States, the progressive development of the criminal law through judicial lawmaking is a well-entrenched and necessary part of legal tradition. Article 7 of the Convention cannot be read as outlawing the gradual clarification of the rules

[9] [1962] AC 220.

[10] *Shaw* is objectionable on a second count: it is also discussed in § 16.000, with respect to criminalising *immoral* activity. See generally Goodhart, "The *Shaw* Case: The Law and Public Morals" (1961) 77 *LQR* 560; Note, (1962) 75 *Harv LR* 1652; Smith, "Judicial Law Making in the Criminal Law" (1984) 100 *LQR* 46.

[11] *Knuller (Publishing, Printing and Promotions) Ltd* v. *DPP* [1973] AC 435; *DPP* v. *Withers* [1975] AC 842.

[12] *Jones et al.* [2006] UKHL 16, para. 29 (Lord Bingham). See also paras. 60–62 (Lord Hoffman); the House rejected the direct incorporation without legislation of new international-law crimes into the domestic law of England and Wales.

[13] *Withers* [1975] AC 842, 863 (Lord Simon); *Rimmington* [2005] UKHL 63, para. 33 (Lord Bingham). None the less, the House of Lords held in *Rimmington* that the common law offence of public nuisance did not breach Article 7, if confined to well-established instances of the offence and not used to evade time limits and sentencing restrictions on more specific statutory offences.

[14] *SW* v. *UK* (1995) 21 EHRR 363, 398 para. 36.

of criminal liability through judicial interpretation from case to case, provided that the resulting development is consistent with the essence of the offence and could reasonably be foreseen."

Yet the evolutionary nature of the common law, and the interpretive role of judges generally, may itself come into conflict with the *nullum crimen* principle. In *R.* v. *R*,[15] for example, the House of Lords abolished an exemption in the common law crime of rape, which had meant that a husband could not be convicted of raping his wife. While that change is to be welcomed as a matter of social and legal policy, the manner in which it was achieved is more controversial, since it led to R's being convicted for conduct that was apparently immune from the charge of rape when done.

Moreover, the decision of the European Court in *SW* v. *UK*[16] shows just how delicate the balance may be between acceptable evolution of common law principles and illegitimate lawmaking. On appeal from *R.* v. *R*, the Court found that there was no breach of Article 7 when the House of Lords ruled against a husband's immunity in rape. There would have been the clearest breach of Article 7[17] if the House of Lords had acknowledged a current, legally valid, immunity but had decided that it was no longer acceptable and would therefore be abolished. That, however, was not the reasoning used by the House of Lords. Instead of abolishing the exemption, their Lordships ruled that the claim for immunity was unfounded in law. That is, they purported to recognise that, by the time of the defendant's actions, the historical immunity for spouses was no longer part of the law. This may seem close to sophistry, but it was a vital distinction. The House of Lords determined that the better view of the law, *at the time of the appellant's conduct,* was that the immunity had gone. Ascertaining the best view of the current state of the law is not a matter of majority prediction, even if the majority is drawn from an expert community of criminal lawyers. The best view consists of the most cogent and intellectually convincing resolution of the issue to be adjudicated.

Their Lordships' dissection of the legal and social grounds of the immunity, together with their demonstration of the incoherence and instability of recent case law which had reluctantly conceded the immunity but, at the same time, had sought to evade its consequences, was the strongest indication that the day of the immunity was done. Indeed, the European Court of Human Rights concluded that the decision by the House of Lords in *R.* v. *R* was predictable. Strictly, however, predictability is not the point. (It is a separate Rule of Law value, considered in § 2.3.) What blocks a claim of retrospective criminalisation here is a demonstration that the defendant's case was decided on the basis of what the law was at the time of the defendant's conduct. The best judgments are not always predictable; a Hercules may surprise but still get it right. Prior to the decision in *R.* v. *R*, most criminal lawyers would have assumed that the husband's immunity in rape was circumscribed but extant. But the convincing reasoning of the House of Lords demonstrates this assumption was incorrect *at the time it was made.* Accordingly, as the European Court found, there was no breach of the *nullum crimen* principle or of Article 7.

---

[15] [1992] 1 AC 599.

[16] (1996) 21 EHRR 363.

[17] Subject to the possibility that the husband's action fell within the exception created by Art. 7(2), noted below in the text.

Unfortunately it is all too easy for a court fixated on the brute merits of a case to shun proper analysis and slip into plain retroactivity. *R.* v. *R* was decided in 1991. Subsequently in *C*,[18] a different defendant was convicted in 2002 of raping his wife *in 1970*. Upholding the conviction, the Court of Appeal expressed itself in the following blunt terms:[19]

> "We need not discuss either the 'declaratory' theory of the effect of judicial decision relating to the development of the common law, nor whether by its decision, the House of Lords was retrospectively creating a new offence where none existed before. The stark fact is that R was convicted. . . . The decision applied to events that had already taken place, as well as those in the future."

This approach effectively abdicates the judicial task. What matters with invocation of precedent is not whether a previous defendant was convicted, but the *reasons* why. In effect, the Court of Appeal's analysis implies that *any* development in the law might be applied retrospectively. While an overly literal reading of the declaratory theory of judical decision-making might support this view, such a reading sits badly with the rule-of-law value of guidance for citizens, recently fortified by the incorporation of Article 7 into English Law. Given the acknowledgement of the spouse's exemption in appellate cases between 1970 and 1991,[20] it is tolerably clear that the Lords' analysis in 1991 was not applicable in 1970. The Court of Appeal asserted, without offering any relevant (and quite a lot of irrelevant) evidence to support its claim, that a solicitor consulted in 1970 would have advised any client that "he might be liable for rape".[21] However implausible that may be, it misses the constitutional point that this is not just a matter of predictability. Lord Bingham sees the distinction in *Rimmington*:[22]

> "There are *two* guiding principles: no one should be punished under a law unless it is sufficiently clear and certain to enable him to know what conduct is forbidden before he does it; and no one should be punished for any act which was not clearly and ascertainably punishable when the act was done."

The first principle concerns fair warning. The second principle expresses the *nullum crimen* rationale: even if retrospective criminalisation is predictable, it is still wrong. It would have been much preferable had the Court of Appeal acknowledged the revisionary nature of its ruling, but defended it as an isolated exception—hence specific to rape—on the grounds of the Article 7(2) exception, which allows for retrospective conviction where a person's act "was criminal according to the general principles of law recognised by civilised nations."

§ 2.3 Fair warning

Apart from its constitutional implications, we have noted that the most important reason for requiring criminal offences to be created prospectively is that failure to do so

---

[18] [2004] EWCA Crim 392, [2004] 1 WLR 2098.
[19] *Ibid.*, para. 22.
[20] E.g. *Steele* (1976) 65 Cr App R 22; *Sharples* [1990] Crim LR 198.
[21] [2004] EWCA Crim 392, [2004] 1 WLR 2098, para. 19.

undermines predictability in the law. In *Shaw* v. *DPP* (above), the enterprising Mr Shaw had been assured by his lawyer that his proposed publication, *The Ladies' Directory*, passed muster in legal terms. Yet the House of Lords found that he, with others, had conspired to corrupt public morality. If even competent legal advice cannot predict the unlawfulness of a defendant's conduct, his attempt to live within the law risks becoming a farce.

However, it is important to notice that, in *Shaw*, predictability was threatened not just because the offence was created retrospectively. Suppose, as some have argued, that the House resurrected rather than invented this species of conspiracy, and that the principle against retroactivity was not breached. Either way, the nebulous terms of the offence leave to speculation what kinds of thing one must not conspire to do. Similarly, even if the view of the European Court that *R.* v. *R* involved no retrospective criminalisation were accepted, the decision remains problematic because of its element of surprise.

This shows that non-retroactive legislation is not the only standard set by the Rule of Law, and that the need for predictability has more general implications. The criminal law is not there solely to tell police and judges what to do after someone offends, but also to tell *citizens* what not to do in advance. As such, it is not enough for there to be a law in place before people can commit a crime. They should also be told about it. That is the reason why non-publication or unavailability of a statutory instrument may be a defence, if a person commits a crime under that instrument while unaware of its existence.[23] There must be an opportunity for defendants to know the law before they are convicted of breaking it:[24]

> "Respect for law, which is the most cogent force in prompting orderly conduct in a civilised community, is weakened, if men are punished for acts which according to the general consensus of opinion they were justified in believing to be morally right *and in accordance with law.*"

The Rule of Law mandates that people should be governed "by rules which are fixed, knowable, and certain."[25] This requires both that the rule be stated in advance, and also that it be stated clearly. Clarity is essential if citizens are to have *fair warning* that by their prospective actions they are in danger of incurring a criminal sanction.[26] If individuals understand the law, they will be able properly to decide what to do in light of the guidance that the law is meant to provide. Only then can the law act as the deterrent it is intended to be. And only then do citizens have a fair opportunity to steer themselves clear of criminal liability.

---

[22] [2005] UKHL 63, para. 33 (emphasis added).

[23] *Grant* v. *Borg* [1982] 1 WLR 638; *Burns* v. *Nowell* (1880) 5 QBD 444; *Lim Chin Aik* v. *R.* [1963] AC 160; *Golden-Brown* v. *Hunt* (1972) 19 Fed LR 438; *Catholique* (1979) 104 DLR (3d) 161.

[24] *State* v. *O'Neil* (1910) 126 NW 454, 456 (emphasis added). See Brett, "Mistake of Law as a Criminal Defence" (1966) 5 *MULR* 179, 204.

[25] Ashworth, *Principles* § 3.5; Raz, *The Authority of Law* (1979) 214–15.

[26] See the discussion in *Misra and Srivastava* [2004] EWCA Crim 2375, paras. 29–34. Compare, in the United States, *Papachristou* v. *City of Jacksonville* 405 US 156, 162 (1972) (vagrancy ordinance void for vagueness). Fair warning is also relevant to inadvertence-based liability, e.g. for negligence. It is one reason why criminal liability for serious crimes should normally be confined to reckless or intentional wrongdoing. This is because if there were widespread exposure to State interference for inadvertent wrongdoing, then it would be much harder for citizens to plan and get on with their lives, without fearing the unforeseen disruption that facing criminal charges entails. See, e.g., Hart, "Punishment and the Elimination of Responsibility" in *Punishment and Responsibility* (1968) 158, 181–2. However, this argument is not insuperable. To the extent that the Rule of Law enjoins unpredictable interference by the State, liability for negligence is reasonably predictable. Moreover, unless negligence liability is no deterrent, the argument prima facie deprives victims of protection from similarly unlooked-for intrusions by other citizens.

Once again, however, fair warning is a Rule of Law aspiration that is not always achieved in practice. Prior to the House of Lords decision in *Ireland*,[27] English criminal lawyers would not generally have predicted that the menace of silent phone calls would be curbed by including them within the definition of assault. Before the decision in *R. v. R* (above), it was widely assumed that a cohabiting husband was immune from the charge of raping his wife. Nonetheless, the House found the immunity to be ungrounded in law. To what extent can we expect greater judicial restraint following the incorporation of the ECHR? In *Kokkinakas v. Greece*, the European Court spoke of the principle that:[28]

> "the criminal law must not be extensively construed to the accused's detriment, for instance by analogy; it follows from this that an offence must be clearly defined in law. This condition is satisfied where the individual can know from the wording of the relevant provision and, if need be, with the assistance of the courts' interpretation of it, what acts and omissions will make him liable."

The passage makes clear that judicial creativity and interpretation—the legitimate principles of which are considered in Chapter 3—can be reviewed under the terms of Article 7. As the European Court has emphasised, even where there are policy grounds favouring an expansive interpretation, they are secondary to the principle that criminal offences must be unambiguously defined:[29]

> "More specifically, . . . the principle that a provision of the criminal law may not be applied extensively to the detriment of the defendant, which is the corollary of the principle of legality in relation to crime and punishment and more generally of the principle of legal certainty, precludes bringing criminal proceedings in respect of conduct not clearly defined as culpable by law. That principle, which is one of the general legal principles underlying the constitutional traditions common to the Member States, has also been enshrined in various international treaties, in particular in Article 7 of the Convention for the Protection of Human Rights and Fundamental Freedoms. . . ."

The importance of this passage has been acknowledged in the House of Lords.[30] But it remains uncertain how far the constraints of Article 7 are being observed, or what factors will be taken into account when reviewing interpretive decisions for compliance.[31] If conduct has been engaged in on the reasonable assumption that it was lawful, that should count as a factor to be considered by a court. But it may be that the *kind* of conduct at issue should properly influence a court. Hence, if the objection is one of fair warning rather than a constitutional one of retrospective criminalisation, the decision in *R. v. R* is defensible, perhaps, on the footing that R's conduct did constitute a crime when done by anyone else, and that the reasons for criminalisation apply just as forcefully to a husband as to anyone else. It should have made no difference had R received an assurance from a lawyer, immediately prior to making his wife submit to intercourse by drawing a knife, that in legal terms he would not be committing rape. That is not, of course, to say that courts may craft new

---

[27] [1998] AC 147. See also Camp, "Section 69 of the Army Act 1955" (1999) 149 *NLJ* 1736. In *Hashman v. United Kingdom* (2000) 30 EHRR 241, the power of a court to bind over persons to "be of good behaviour" was held to be incompatible with the ECHR because the prescribed standard was too imprecise; contrast *Steel v. U.K.* (1999) 28 EHRR 603, where "breach of the peace" was held to be sufficiently certain.

[28] (1993) 17 EHRR 397, 423. Cf. *G v. Federal Republic of Germany* 60 DR 252, 262 (1989).

[29] *Criminal Proceedings against X* Joined cases C-74/95 and C-129/95 [1996] ECR I-6609, 6637 para. 25..

law in order to catch husbands who treat wives in that fashion. It is merely to say that in considering what the current law is, the fact that the defendant thought it was different does not count for much if what the defendant did breached in the most fundamental way his wife's right to bodily integrity. By contrast, if the owner of a factory has done his best to comply with health and safety law and has received professional assurance that he has done enough, this should be recognised when determining whether he has provided a safe system of work "so far as is reasonably practicable."[32]

It is for Parliament to make law and, although judicial interpretation of law may properly be purposive,[33] current legal resources cannot always be stretched to cover the conduct in question. The Rule of Law requires a system of legal ordering, not *ad hoc* responses to the conduct of individuals: as such, it is particularly important in the criminal law to identify where the law and the jurisdiction of judges runs out. We have seen that, in the past, judges have gone beyond that point in order to criminalise conduct they disapproved of even in cases where the policy arguments for criminalisation were not clear cut. That is contrary to adjudication under law. The incorporation of Article 7 enhances the case against such judicial activism.

(i) Use of evaluative concepts

A legal system, then, should seek to provide as much guidance and predictability as it can. However, realism is required when deciding what degree of certainty is attainable in particular laws. Explicitness is necessarily compromised in offences that involve vague and open-ended concepts such as "unreasonable", "rash",[34] and "fraudulent". Similarly, if we drive a car we know, or should know, that we must drive with "due care and attention". The phrase sets a standard for a myriad of driving contexts and inevitably must leave an ultimate assessment to the Court, which will find the phrase of no more than open-ended guidance. What degree of error or inattention will turn us into criminals cannot be stated with exactitude. If the criminal law is to involve itself with standards of safety, which surely it must, it cannot give a rigid specification of the circumstances under which criminal liability will follow.

At the same time, both legislature and judiciary should be cautious about the deployment and interpretation of such expressions. Consider, for example, the imposition of negligence-based criminal liability, through offences which are typically couched in terms of the "unreasonableness" of the defendant's behaviour. The touchstone, be it "unreasonable" or "negligent", is not susceptible of accurate or formal definition. What is "reasonable"? Nowhere does the law say, and to some extent the individual must judge the law's standard for himself, and risk the Court's disagreeing with him. Such gambles ought to be

---

[30] *R (on the application of Junttan Oy)* v. *Bristol Magistrates' Court* [2003] UKHL 55, [2004] 2 All ER 555, para 21 (Lord Nicholls, dissenting).

[31] An instructive example is the common law offence of cheating, cogently criticised by Ormerod, "Cheating the Public Revenue" [1998] *Crim LR* 627, but held to be compatible with the ECHR in *Pattni* [2001] Crim LR 570.

[32] Health and Safety at Work etc. Act 1974, s. 2.

[33] See below, § 3.1.

[34] Cf. s. 362 of the Insolvency Act 1986.

minimised,[35] and where possible these discretionary terms should be replaced by more concrete definitions of what counts as illegal, and what as legitimate.

This reservation should not be overstated, and it cannot be claimed that such terms deprive individuals of advance warning altogether. The defendant's judgement is not purely a guess: words such as "reasonable" are not meaningless.[36] We understand them, and know how to apply the implicit judgements they import. The use of broad evaluative terms such as "negligent" and "fraudulent" may well provide an acceptable level of guidance where there is a high degree of social consensus about appropriate behaviour in the area of activity under regulation. One may assume that degree of necessary consensus, for instance, in matters of road safety; accordingly a requirement to drive with due care and attention may tell us all we really need to know.

Moreover, evaluative standards are useful. Terms like "reasonable" and "dangerous" give the law flexibility to deal with cases that a legislator might not foresee. It is too much to expect a statute to list every single mode of negligent homicide, and meaningful terms like "unreasonable" save us from being straitjacketed by a rigid specification of the circumstances under which criminal liability will or will not follow. Indeed, without such flexibility, the law would be unfair and incomplete. There will always be matters which require regulation, but where a degree of imprecision is inevitable. Over many years, for example, the courts sought a legal definition of when an act was sufficiently close to the commission of a crime to constitute an attempt to commit that crime. Various tests were tried; all were unsatisfactory. Nowadays the jury is simply asked whether an act was "more than merely preparatory".[37]

Nonetheless, evaluative terms *are* imprecise, and for that reason, at least in serious crimes, they should normally be used only sparingly and for clear cases of wrongdoing. This is one justification of the common law's requirement that negligence be "gross" before one may be guilty of manslaughter:[38] it is not merely that D's culpability is greater, but also that we can be more sure D is culpable.[39] Sometimes, the imprecision is such that these terms ought not to be used at all. It is doubtful whether there is a sufficient degree of consensus about the acceptable contents of literature, plays, and film to render the standard "tendency to deprave and corrupt", employed in obscenity law,[40] a sufficient guide to producers and

---

[35] "A statute which either forbids or requires the doing of an act in terms so vague that men of common intelligence must necessarily guess at its meaning and differ as to its application, violates the first essential of due process of law": *Conally* v. *General Construction Company* 269 US 385, 391 (1926). Cf. Rawls, *A Theory of Justice* (1971) 239: "if the precept of no crime without a law is violated, say by statutes being vague and imprecise, what we are at liberty to do is likewise vague and imprecise."

[36] Lucas, "The Philosophy of the Reasonable Man" (1963) 13 *Phil Qtrly* 97.

[37] See below, Chapter 9.

[38] See below, Chapter 10. The use of gross negligence as a culpability standard for manslaughter was held the be compatible with with Article 7 in *Misra* [2005] 1 Cr App R 21.

[39] An interesting discussion is Horder, "Gross Negligence and Criminal Culpability" (1997) 47 *U Toronto LJ* 495.

[40] Obscene Publications Act 1959, s. 1. This statutory test differs from that applicable to "obscene" items sent in the post, which are regulated by the Postal Services Act 2000. The test of "obscenity" in the post is simply that of the word's ordinary meaning, and may include anything that is shocking, lewd, or indecent: *Kirk* [2006] EWCA Crim 725, [2006] Crim LR 850. Yet that standard, too, may be thought rather nebulous; especially since its application is a matter for the jury. Indeed, even in judicial hands the application of evaluative terms may vary. Thus, in *Collins* v. *DPP* [2006] 40, the House of Lords saw fit to overturn a finding by Leicestershire Justices that certain racist telephone messages sent by D were "offensive" but not "grossly offensive". Apparently a reasonable person—but not

publishers operating in those fields. If a government wishes to maintain a regulatory presence there, it is better that it regulates by description, expressly identifying those things which are not to be written, photographed, or filmed: hence the use of a classification system under the Video Recordings Act 1984.

Alas, the ECHR seems unlikely to introduce greater rigour into this area. In *Handyside* v. *UK*,[41] a case resolved by the European Court, the applicant complained that the offence of obscenity in the Obscene Publications Acts 1959–1964 "was so far-reaching and imprecise that it might be applied almost without limit." Under that Act, items which have a tendency "to deprave and corrupt" are obscene unless they are redeemed by some scientific, educational, literary, or artistic merit. In the absence of a societal consensus on what constitutes obscenity, what kinds of sexual or violent material could be published was essentially a matter of guesswork about how the particular jury empanelled for the case would respond to the items with which they were presented. Despite this, the European Court dismissed the applicant's petition, stating that "the requirement of certainty in the law cannot mean that the concrete facts giving rise to criminal liability should be set out in the statute concerned." It was enough that the court was provided with a text, a general definition, which it could amplify and make concrete on a case-by-case basis. This glosses the fact that the formula, "to deprave and corrupt" normally involves a finding of fact. It is not subject to judicial amplification and explication; there are merely the *ad hoc* verdicts of different juries.

§ 2.4 Fair labelling

We have seen that the *ex ante* guidance the law is meant to provide requires it to be clearly stated. However, there is another reason for expecting clarity in criminal offences. When a crime occurs, justice must not only be done, it must be seen to be done. The law needs precision in order to identify exactly what offence the wrongdoer has committed. If he is publicly convicted of "murder", D should *be* a murderer and not a parking offender. At the same time, neither would it be satisfactory for the law simply to label all convicted offenders unspecifically as "criminals", for that would equate the convictions of rapists with those of pickpockets. The criminal law speaks to society as well as wrongdoers when it convicts them, and it should communicate its judgment with precision, by accurately naming the crime of which they are convicted. This requirement is known as the principle of fair labelling.[42]

The need for fair labelling is one reason why we should not merge the separate offences of murder and manslaughter into a single crime of unlawful homicide, as was suggested by Lord Kilbrandon in *Hyam*;[43] nor combine arson and vandalism into a single crime of criminal damage, as was once proposed by the Law Commission.[44] In the eyes of society,

---

the Justices (and indeed not everyone who actually heard the messages)—*would* have found the messages to be grossly offensive. Such variation *ipso facto* suggests the need for more detailed legislative guidance.

[41] 1 EHRR 739 (1976).

[42] Ashworth, "The Elasticity of *Mens Rea*" in Tapper (ed.), *Crime, Proof and Punishment* (1981) 45, 53–6; Williams, "Convictions and Fair Labelling" [1983] *CLJ* 85; Mitchell, "Multiple Wrongdoing and Offence Structure: A Plea for Consistency and Fair Labelling" (2001) 64 *MLR* 395, 398–400.

[43] [1975] AC 55, 98.

[44] Working Paper No. 23, "Malicious Damage" (1969) para. 22.

such offences involve two different types of wrongdoing, and the communicative function of the law would be impaired were the law to blur the difference.[45]

Underlying this objection is the point that different offences may criminalise *actions* which have differing social significance, and not just *outcomes*. So, for example, it would be a mistake to assimilate vandalism with negligent damage to property. Even though the harm to property is the same, vandalism expresses a certain sort of contempt for society and the victim that negligent damage does not. If the criminal law were not to distinguish the two, a conviction would be potentially misleading. (We return to this point in § 16.6(ii).)

The law must make clear what sort of criminal each offender is—what the conviction is *for*. It should communicate this to the defendant, so that he may know exactly what he has done wrong and why he is being punished, in order that his punishment appears meaningful to him, not just an arbitrary harsh treatment. In addition, the law should communicate the crime to the public, so that it too may understand the nature of his transgression. The public record matters. While an employer may have few qualms about hiring a convicted fraudster as an orderly in a children's hospital, it would be an entirely different matter to contemplate employing someone who has been in jail for paedophilia.

§ 2.5 The European Convention on Human Rights

The United Kingdom was one of the original parties to the ECHR.[46] States which contract into the ECHR are obliged to secure the enjoyment of Convention rights for their citizens. Usually, this will require ensuring that State and public officials do not conduct themselves in a manner inimical to Convention rights. Sometimes, however, positive action may be required; including the creation, amendment, or enforcement of criminal offences. If a country is found to be in breach of one or more Articles of the ECHR, it incurs a treaty obligation to bring its law and practices into step with Convention requirements. Alleged breaches of the Convention are adjudicated on by the European Court of Human Rights (European Court) and, since 1966, the United Kingdom has allowed individuals to take cases to the Court. On a variety of occasions the European Court has found against the United Kingdom; a significant number of these adverse judgments concern matters of criminal procedure, criminal law, and sentencing.[47]

Consequently, the Human Rights Act 1998, which requires all public authorities to act compatibly with Convention obligations,[48] is of direct concern to all criminal lawyers.[49] The

---

[45] See Gardner, "Rationality and the Rule of Law in Offences Against the Person" [1994] *CLJ* 502, 504–6, 512–20.

[46] On the law of the Convention generally, consult Harris, Warbrick, Bates and O'Boyle, *Law of the European Convention on Human Rights* (2nd ed., 2007). For consideration of the Convention in the context of criminal law, evidence, and procedure see Emmerson and Ashworth, *Human Rights and Criminal Justice* (2001).

[47] Significant decisions involving findings against the United Kingdom include *McCann and others* v. *UK* (1996) 21 EHRR 97 (permissible force in the prevention of crime); *Tynne, Wilson and Gunnell* v. *UK* (1991) 13 EHRR 666 (discretionary life-sentencing); *Saunders* v. *United Kingdom* (1997) 23 EHRR 313 (compulsory powers of questioning).

[48] For general discussion of the HRA 1998 see Wade, "The United Kingdom's Bill of Rights" in Cambridge Centre for Public Law, *Constitutional Reform in the United Kingdom: Practice and Principles* (1998) 59; Bamforth, "The Application of the Human Rights Act 1998 to Public Authorities and Private Bodies" [1999] *CLJ* 159.

[49] For discussion of the HRA 1998 in the context of criminal law see Cambridge Centre for Public Law, *The Human Rights Act and the Criminal and Regulatory Process* (1999); Smith, "The Human Rights Act and the Criminal

Act enables the defence or the prosecution to raise Convention arguments in any criminal proceedings, whether before the local magistrates or the House of Lords. Should those arguments be found wanting by the English courts, a disappointed individual retains the opportunity to persuade the European Court of the merits of her case by making an application to Strasbourg.[50] From a criminal lawyer's perspective, claims that human rights have been violated are most likely to arise in the contexts of procedure, evidence, and sentencing. Significantly, Article 6 of the ECHR, which guarantees the right to a fair trial, has been construed as having no bearing on the fairness of the substantive law to be applied at the trial.[51] But even the substantive criminal law is not immune: successful challenges to English criminal offences and defences have already been made at Strasbourg.[52]

The following sections offer a brief overview of those Convention Articles most directly affecting the substantive criminal law. More lengthy consideration will be given to particular human rights issues throughout this work where relevant to the subject-matter under discussion. First, however, it is necessary to take a brief overview of the HRA 1998, in order to understand better the manner and extent to which Convention arguments may be put in the context of criminal proceedings.

(i) The Human Rights Act 1998—the framework

At the outset, it should be noted that the HRA 1998 does not elevate the European Convention of Human Rights into a form of higher, fundamental law against which the validity of all other primary legislation may be tested and those laws invalidated if found wanting. Instead, the Act obliges courts to interpret legislation, whenever the legislation was passed, "so far as possible . . . in a way which is compatible with the Convention Rights."[53] If there remains any incompatibility which cannot be erased by interpretation, the validity of offending primary legislation is unimpaired.[54] In such circumstances the High Court and appellate courts may make a *declaration of incompatibility*; but (*per* section 4) that declaration does not affect the validity, continuing operation, or enforcement of any incompatible legislation.

No explicit provision is made in the HRA 1998 for cases of incompatibility between the common law and the Convention. One example of a likely incompatibility is afforded by the common law defence of insanity which, at present, is arguably too broad in treating as

---

Lawyer: The Constitutional Context" [1999] *Crim LR* 251; Arden, "Criminal Law at the Crossroads: The Impact on Human Rights from the Law Commission's Perspective and the Need for a Code" [1999] *Crim LR* 439; Buxton, "The Human Rights Act and the Substantive Criminal Law" [2000] *Crim LR* 331; Ashworth, "The Human Rights Act and the Substantive Criminal Law: A Non-minimalist View" [2000] *Crim LR* 564.

[50] The passing of the HRA 1998 is without prejudice to a right of individual petition to the European Court. However, Art. 34 of the Convention requires that domestic remedies be exhausted before the matter is raised at Strasbourg. Thus Convention rights must first be asserted in the courts of England and Wales.

[51] *Concannon* [2002] Crim LR 213; *Gemmell and Richards* [2002] Crim LR 926; *Z v. UK* (2002) 34 EHRR 3.

[52] Notably in *McCann and others v. UK* (1996) 21 EHRR 97; *A v. UK* (1998) 27 EHRR 611; *Dudgeon v. UK* (1982) 4 EHRR 189.

[53] HRA 1998, s. 3(1). For argument about how English courts should use the interpretive power conferred by s. 3 see Gearty, "Reconciling Parliamentary Democracy and Human Rights" (2002) 118 *LQR* 248 and Phillipson, "(Mis)-Reading Section 3 of the Human Rights Act" 119 (2003) *LQR* 183.

[54] Section 3(2)(b). Subordinate legislation, on the other hand, is likely to be invalid to the extent of any incompatibility with Convention rights: cf. s. 3(2)(c).

insane persons who suffer from conditions such as epilepsy and diabetes, thereby (it has been claimed[55]) contravening Article 5 (right to liberty and security of the person). Suppose a Crown Court judge is persuaded that an insanity verdict in respect of D will contravene Article 5; can he disregard English precedents of the highest authority that require such a verdict in D's case? It has been argued that in this situation he *must* now override previous authority. Section 6 of the HRA 1998 imposes a duty on public authorities to act compatibly with Convention rights. It has been argued that in light of that section, courts—being public bodies—must hand down judgments which are Convention-compatible unless precluded from doing so by the clear terms of a statute or other primary legislation. On that view, the statutory duty under section 6 obliges courts of whatever stature to override any common law authority at odds with the Convention, however high and long-standing that authority may be.[56]

(a) The power to reinterpret

Although, as we have noted, the 1998 Act does not allow a similar power of invalidation in respect of statutes, nonetheless judges should do what they can to render statutes compatible with the Convention. The injunction "so far as it is possible to do so"[57] indicates both the limits placed on the interpretive process and the extent of the judicial effort that must be made to achieve compatibility. Where a statutory provision potentially contravenes Convention rights, interpretation is no longer a matter of divining the intention of Parliament regarding the meaning of that provision but of rendering the Convention provision compatible (if at all possible). The decision of the House of Lords in *Lambert*[58] illustrates the reach of this new power of interpretation. The case concerned a "reverse burden" of proof: to avoid a conviction for possession of a drug with intent to supply, D was required to prove that he neither knew nor suspected or had reason to suspect that he possessed a controlled drug. By a majority of 4:1, the House of Lords decided that the presumption of innocence enshrined in Article 6(2) of the Convention implied that the word "prove" must be interpreted as imposing an evidential rather than a probative burden on D; a remarkable feat of interpretation, notwithstanding the strong terms of section 3(1) of the HRA 1998.

Should Courts go even further and "read in" words into statutory provisions in order to ensure compliance with the Convention? Arden J, considering, extra-judicially, the likely effect of the incorporated Convention on the criminal law, has entertained as a serious possibility the reading in of words to statutory provisions in order to achieve compatibility.[59] She envisaged, for example, that Courts might "write in" due diligence defences for

---

[55] See Sutherland and Gearty, "Insanity and the European Court of Human Rights" [1992] *Crim LR* 418; Baker, "Human Rights, McNaghten and the 1991 Act" [1994] *Crim LR* 84; below, § 18.1(iii). In other respects, the defence is also arguably too narrow, allowing the conviction of some persons in contravention of Art. 3 (torture, inhuman or degrading treatment, or punishment).

[56] For an opinion to this effect see HL Debs., 24 Nov. 1998, col. 783 (Lord Chancellor). For a narrower view of the effect of s. 6, see Kentridge, "The Incorporation of the European Convention on Human Rights" in Cambridge Centre for Public Law, *Constitutional Reform in the United Kingdom: Practice and Principles* (1998) 69. See also Phillipson, "The Human Rights Act, 'Horizontal Effect' and the Common Law: a Bang or a Whimper?" (1999) 62 *MLR* 824.

[57] HRA 1998, s. 3.

[58] [2001] 3 All ER 577.

strict liability offences to avoid convictions which otherwise would violate Article 3 (inhuman or degrading punishment). Save for one Court of Appeal decision reversed by the House of Lords,[60] the courts have refrained from explicit rewriting of statutes but, nonetheless, have made decisions going well beyond the canons of interpretation existing prior to the HRA 1998.[61] In *A*,[62] the House of Lords seemingly went beyond even the broadest conception of interpretation and into the realm of overriding the statutory text under consideration. Concern with the low conviction rate in contested rape trials had led Parliament to place restrictions on the extent to which a rape victim could be cross-examined on her previous sexual history. The House of Lords found these restrictions to be in contravention of the guarantee of fair trial provided by Article 6 of the ECHR. Not even the extended power of interpretation allowed by section 3 of the HRA 1998 could massage the language of the relevant provisions into a form compatible with Article 6. Instead of making a declaration of incompatibility, however, the judgment of the House of Lords requires trial judges to allow cross-examination of V's previous sexual history if necessary to ensure a fair trial, notwithstanding the clear statutory language disallowing the line of questioning.

In *A*, a declaration of incompatibility is taken to be a thing of very last resort, to be avoided if at all possible.[63] By contrast, in the subsequent case of *R (Anderson)* v. *Secretary of State for the Home Department*,[64] the House of Lords straightforwardly made a declaration of incompatibility, after resolving that the statutory provision empowering the Home Secretary to fix the time in prison to be spent by persons serving a mandatory life sentence could not be interpreted in a manner compatible with Article 6. This latter decision seemingly comports better with the scheme of the HRA 1998, in that, although the HRA 1998 provides for new principles of interpretation, they presumably ought to be exercised in a manner compatible with the sovereignty of Parliament. Yet even contrived interpretations have been justified on the basis that, by the HRA, Parliament intended compatible interpretations to be preferred "so far as possible", not "so far as reasonably possible". Thus, according to Lord Bingham in *Attorney-General's Reference (No. 4 of 2002)*:[65]

> "It was argued for the Attorney General that [the contested provision, section 11(2) of the Terrorism Act 2000] could not be read down under section 3 of the [HRA 1998] so as to impose an evidential rather than a legal burden if (contrary to his submissions) the subsection were held to infringe, impermissibly, the presumption of innocence. He submitted that if the presumption of innocence were found to be infringed, a declaration of incompatibility should be

---

[59] "Criminal Law at the Crossroads: the Impact on Human Rights from the Law Commission's Perspective and the Need for a Code" [1999] *Crim LR* 439, 447–50. See also Hooper, "The Impact of the Human Rights Act on Judicial Decision-making" [1998] *EHRLR* 676.

[60] *Re W and B; Re W (Care Plan)* [2001] EWCA Civ 757, [2001] 2 FLR 582; reversed in *Re S (Minors) (Care order: Implementation of care plan); Re W (Minors) (Care order: adequacy of care plan)* [2002] UKHL 10; [2002] 2 AC 291.

[61] Perhaps the most notable example is *Ghaidan* v. *Godin-Mendoza* [2004] 2 AC 557, where the statutory phrase "husband and wife" was interpreted to include same-sex couples.

[62] [2002] 3 All ER 1.

[63] Cf. *Sheldrake* v. *DPP; Attorney-General's Reference (No. 4 of 2002)* [2004] UKHL 43, [2005] 1 AC 264; *Ghaidan* v. *Godin-Mendoza* [2004] UKHL 30.

[64] [2003] 1 AC 837. See too the declaration of incompatibility in *Bellinger* v. *Bellinger* [2003] 2 AC 467.

[65] Cf. *Sheldrake* v. *DPP; Attorney-General's Reference (No. 4 of 2002)* [2004] UKHL 43, [2005] 1 AC 264; *Ghaidan* v. *Godin-Mendoza* [2004] UKHL 30.

made. I cannot accept this submission…. In my opinion, reading down section 11(2) so as to impose an evidential instead of a legal burden falls well within the interpretative principles discussed above. . . . Such was not the intention of Parliament when enacting the 2000 Act, but it was the intention of Parliament when enacting section 3 of the [HRA 1998]."

To summarise Lord Bingham's view: the interpretation inconsistent with Parliament's intention in the 2000 Act is, in fact, mandated by Parliament's intention as expressed in 1998; and so observes the sovereignty of Parliament. The problem with this sleight-of-hand analysis, as all students of Constitutional law will recognise, is that Parliamentary sovereignty requires that, where the intentions of Parliament conflict in domestic legislation, the later expression is to be preferred. It is submitted that the possibility of compatible (re)interpretations contemplated in the HRA 1998 extends only to reasonable interpretations of the legislative will, and not to far-fetched but "possible" readings. The existence of House of Lords cases where declarations of incompatibility have been made[66] shows that there are boundaries to the realm of the possible.

(b) Reviewing legislation "on the face"

As these decisions suggest, the emphasis of the HRA 1998 on interpreting domestic legislation in a manner compatible with the ECHR indicates that the form of review is likely to be "on the face" (a term familiar in US constitutional jurisprudence). That is to say, the reviewing court will look at the impugned statutory provision and evaluate whether the provision, across the range of its likely applications, is compatible with the ECHR. By contrast, there is a form of review known as "as applied": under this approach, the issue to be resolved is whether the provision being challenged contravened the complainant's Convention rights *on a particular occasion*. In its own jurisprudence the European Court takes the "as applied" approach, with its emphasis on whether the rights of the particular applicant have been breached. Yet certain of its decisions are stated in such broad terms as, in effect, to impugn the provision under scrutiny in general terms. For example, in *Saunders v. UK*,[67] the European Court found that the use, at trial, of evidence obtained from the defendant under powers of compulsory questioning was objectionable *per se* and therefore a breach of Article 6(1) (fair trial). This amounts to imposing a general limitation, one not particular to the case. By contrast, in *Salabiaku v. France*,[68] where a reverse burden of proof was under challenge, the European Court—while remarking that reverse burdens were matters for concern and proper issues for judicial scrutiny—found against the appellant on the ground that he had suffered no unfairness in the particular circumstances of the case.

In *Kebilene*,[69] the Divisional Court found certain reverse burdens of proof contained in the Prevention of Terrorism Act 1989 to be in "flagrant" breach of Article 6(2) (presumption of innocence). The finding of the Court was based entirely on the terms of the legislation, i.e. on its face: the Court did not consider whether any unfairness may have been sustained by the particular defendants. Although, on further appeal,[70] the House of

---

[66] E.g. *R (Anderson) v. Secretary of State for the Home Department* [2003] 1 AC 837; *Bellinger v. Bellinger* [2003] 2AC 467.
[67] (1997) 23 EHRR 313.
[68] (1988) 13 EHRR 379.
[69] *R. v. Director of Public Prosecutions, ex p Kebilene* [1999] 3 WLR 175.
[70] [1999] 3 WLR 972.

Lords decided the case on different grounds, Lords Hope and Hobhouse each demurred from the Divisional Court's approach and indicated that the effect upon the defendants of applying the reverse burden would be relevant matters for consideration. Lord Hobhouse spoke of a necessity "to examine each case on its merits" and "to examine whether the relevant provision has in fact resulted in injustice to the complainant."[71] If this approach were to be adopted generally, the impact of the HRA 1998 on the content of domestic legislation would be considerably diminished—and significantly less predictable. It is submitted that the more general perspective adopted by the Divisional Court and contemplated by Lord Steyn's majority judgment better comports with the framework of the Act.[72] Indeed, in subsequent appeals concerning whether reverse burdens within particular offences are in breach of Article 6(2),[73] their Lordships have focused on how such a probative burden will affect trials for the relevant offence *in general*, rather than on the impact of the reverse burden upon the particular appellant's trial. This seems right: it would be odd to conclude that a particular statutory offence imposes a reverse burden on some defendants and not on others. Likewise, in *A*[74] the emphasis is on the fairness of restricting cross-examination in rape trials in general.

The *Kebilene* litigation illustrates how the application of the HRA 1998 can give rise to differences of judicial opinion. The Divisional Court was convinced that the relevant provisions of the Prevention of Terrorism Act 1989 were incompatible with the ECHR[75] and that, as a consequence, any conviction of the defendants would ultimately, assuredly, be quashed on appeal. By contrast, the House of Lords, reversing the Divisional Court, reasoned that even if there were a "flagrant" breach of the ECHR, it does not follow that an appeal would succeed. A more likely outcome, pursuant to section 4 of the HRA 1998, would be a declaration of incompatibility. In any event, their Lordships were not convinced that the provisions under challenge *would* contravene Article 6(2). Lord Steyn, with whom Lords Slynn and Cooke agreed, thought it a distinct possibility that, under the interpretative

---

[71] *Ibid.*, 1009.

[72] It is understandable that the European Court adopts the "as applied" approach. It is not a constitutional court for Europe with power to strike down the laws of States party to the ECHR. In order to have standing the applicant before the European Court must, typically, be a "victim", seeking vindication for wrongs actually endured. Thus the Court will be required to consider whether, *in that particular case*, there was a violation of the applicant's rights under the Convention. By contrast, in domestic law under the HRA 1998, there need be no determination that the defendant's rights are violated. Convention questions can arise as collateral issues in criminal trials, without the same requirement of standing. In that context, the appropriate focus is the condition of English law in terms of its compatibility with the ECHR. This supports the generalist approach of the Divisional Court and of the majority judgment in the House of Lords in *Kebilene*; and is assumed by the framework of the HRA 1998 itself.

[73] *Lambert* [2001] UKHL 37, [2002] 2 AC 545; *Johnstone* [2003] UKHL 28, [2003] 1 WLR 1736, paras. 44–54. In *Sheldrake* v. *DPP*; *Attorney-General's Reference (No. 4 of 2002)* [2004] UKHL 43, [2005] 1 AC 264, para. 21, it was said by Lord Bingham that "The justifiability of any infringement of the presumption of innocence cannot be resolved by any rule of thumb, but on examination of all the facts and circumstances of the particular provision as applied in the particular case." But this assertion needs to be understood in light of the subsequent discussion by his Lordship, which emphasises the generic facts and circumstances of the offence provision, rather than those of the particular defendant (see, especially, paras. 26 and 30).

[74] [2001] 3 All ER 1.

[75] Bingham LCJ reasoned, convincingly, that a reverse burden of proof on a matter central to the wrongdoing alleged against D (i.e. possession of items to be used in connection with terrorism, where the burden of proof was placed on D to show that the items were not used in connection with terrorism once a reasonable suspicion was established by the prosecution), was directly at odds with the presumption of innocence guaranteed by Art. 6(2). See further below, § 2.5(iii).

requirement imposed by section 3 of the HRA 1998, reverse burdens of proof would in future be read as creating merely an evidential burden on a defendant and not, as hitherto, a probative burden. This last possibility has, in fact, sometimes been the outcome in subsequent cases.[76]

The law reform process is also influenced by the ECHR. Under the HRA 1998, a minister in charge of a Bill must inform Parliament whether he is able to make a statement that the provisions of the Bill are compatible with the ECHR.[77] This usefully ensures that ECHR questions must be considered by the civil servants and drafters who prepare legislation. It is notable, for instance, that the Law Commission now pays close attention to ECHR issues when formulating reform proposals.

(ii) The interpretation of Convention rights

In determining the compatibility of statutory provisions and common law with the requirements of the ECHR, some degree of particularity is required concerning the effect and ambit of the various Articles of the ECHR. The terms of the ECHR, an awkward blend of the general and the particular, are not always self-evident. Additionally, when determining a question that arises in connection with an ECHR right, a court must take into account the decisions and judgments of various bodies, in particular the European Court, if the court is of the opinion they are relevant to the proceedings.[78]

These interpretive sources are not binding; they are things to be taken into account. The ECHR has been described by the European Court as "a living instrument",[79] responsive to social and moral change. Accordingly, decisions and opinions of earlier periods may have little or no weight. For instance, early decisions of the European Commission of Human Rights had found that proscriptions of forms of homosexuality were compatible with the ECHR whereas, more recently, the Commission found that stipulating different ages of consent for heterosexual and homosexuals contravened both Article 8 (respect for private life) and Article 14 (principle of non-discrimination).[80]

The ECHR is an international treaty. As such, it is not a constitutional Bill of Rights but an undertaking by party States to observe acceptable standards of human rights in their respective jurisdictions.[81] In the light of this, courts, when exercising the jurisdiction instituted by the HRA 1998, should not derogate from standards clearly set by the European Court. The European Court authoritatively sets the terms for compliance. However, it does not follow that, when construing the ECHR in a domestic context, English courts should go no further to protect rights than does the European Court. In its jurisprudence the European Court has applied a "margin of appreciation",[82] particularly in cases involving Article 10 (freedom of expression) and Article 11 (freedom of assembly and association).

---

[76] For discussion of burdens of proof see below, § 2.5(iii) and § 3.2.

[77] Section 19.

[78] HRA 1998, s. 2. In addition to decisions of the European Court, earlier opinions and decisions of the European Commission on Human Rights and decisions of the Committee of Ministers should also be taken into account.

[79] *Tyrer* v. *UK* (1978) 2 EHRR 1.

[80] *Sutherland and Morris* v. *UK* [1998] EHRLR 117.

[81] See Harris, O'Boyle and Warbrick, *Law of the European Convention on Human Rights* (1995) 9–11.

[82] *Ibid.*, 12–15.

This margin is a recognition that uniform standards cannot be imposed by an international court on States with different histories and sensitivities. Yet no such restraint is required when judges address human rights issues for their own society.[83] If, say, an English judge were to take the view that freedom of speech requires a more robust defence than is found in European Court jurisprudence, she is free to give a fuller effect to the terms of Article 10.[84] That said, a degree of deference is due to the legislative will of a democratically elected Parliament, and where an issue is finely balanced, courts should not be too astute to find that legislation breaches the ECHR. Determining whether or not a legislative provision breaches an Article of the Convention may require consideration of the doctrine of proportionality—is the legislation under consideration a proportionate response in combatting the social mischief or advancing the social policy with which the legislation is concerned? Some degree of diminution in the enjoyment of Convention-protected rights may be an acceptable price for gains in welfare or efficiency and there may well be trade-offs to be made between different Convention-protected rights.[85]

When determining whether a breach of the ECHR has occurred, certain rights are more jealously guarded than others. Articles 2 (the right to life), 3 (the right not to be subjected to torture, inhuman or degrading treatment), and 7 (no retrospective penal law) cannot be derogated from even in times of war or dire emergency. All the other Articles of the ECHR may be derogated from in such circumstances.[86] When the extremities of war and national emergency do not obtain, however, the possibility of derogation does not imply that these other Articles have lesser weight. Article 6 (fair trial and presumption of innocence) in particular has been expansively interpreted.[87]

Apart from drastic circumstances permitting derogation, a Convention right may alternatively be restricted by rulings about its scope. It is fair to say that Article 3 provides an unconditional right: if conduct amounts to torture or inhuman or degrading treatment or punishment, it will violate Article 3 whatever the circumstances. However, in respect of Articles 2 and 7, while non-derogation status underlines the importance of the right at issue, it does not preclude argument about the nature and ambit of these rights. For instance, the uncertain state of the English law of obscenity, and judicial abolition of the husband's immunity in rape, arguably, in each case, involved breaches of Article 7, yet the European Court ruled otherwise.[88] Questions concerned with abortions have been raised

---

[83] In *Kebilene* [1999] 3 WLR 972, 993–4, Lord Hope considered that the margin of appreciation doctrine would not be available to English judges when interpreting the convention. Of course, as Lord Hope recognised, many Convention questions will be matters of broad evaluation affected by matters of national culture and subject-matter even in the absence of that doctrine.

[84] It may be noted that s. 12 of the HRA 1998 makes particular reference to freedom of expression, but only in contexts where the court is considering whether to grant any relief.

[85] The doctrine of proportionality should only come into play if the right is expressed in qualified terms: some Convention rights are absolute, for example the right not to be tortured or subjected to inhuman or degrading treatment (Art. 3). As put by Lord Steyn in *R (Daly)* v. *Secretary of State for Home Department* [2001] 2 WLR 1622, 1634, whether encroachment on a Convention right is a proportionate legislative response requires consideration of "whether: i) the legislative objective is sufficiently important to justify limiting a fundamental right; ii) the measures designed to meet the legislative objective are rationally connected to it; and iii) the means used to impair the right or freedom are no more than is necessary to accomplish the objective."

[86] Article 15.

[87] Harris, O'Boyle and Warbrick, *Law of the European Convention on Human Rights* (1995) chap. 6.

[88] *Handyside* v. *UK* (1976) 1 EHRR 737 (obscenity); *CR and SW* v. *UK* (1996) 21 EHRR 363 (marital rape).

under Article 2 and, in that context, the European Court has applied the margin of appreciation doctrine in light of the considerable differences in the laws of the contracting States.[89] Additionally, even in cases that fall, prima facie, within the general scope of an Article right, exceptions may sometimes be justified. In the case of certain Articles, for instance Articles 8 (the right to private life) and 9 (freedom of thought and religion), the declaration of the right in the ECHR is followed by a statement of the circumstances in which that right may be justifiably interfered with.[90]

(iii) The ECHR and the substantive criminal law

Potentially, the ECHR has considerable implications for the substantive criminal law. Already Strasbourg judgments have had some effect. It may be helpful to list, non-exhaustively, areas of criminal law where the ECHR has the potential to have an impact:[91]

Article 2 (right to life): self-defence; force used in the prevention of crime and to make arrests; abortion; euthanasia.

Article 3 (right not to be subjected to torture or inhuman or degrading treatment): offences against the person arising from staff conduct in prison military and mental health establishments; offences of strict liability, especially 'status' offences; defence of parental chastisement.

Article 5 (right to liberty and security of person): insanity defence; offences against the person in prison, military and mental health establishments.

Article 6 (right to fair hearing and presumption of innocence): offences of strict liability; reverse burdens of proof; entrapment.

Article 7 (right not to be convicted under retroactive law): offences of dishonesty with broad and vague conduct elements; common law assault; the Criminal Justice (Terrorism and Conspiracy) Act 1998, section 5; Crime and Disorder Act 1998, section 5; offences of corrupting public morality and of outraging public decency; Protection from Harassment Act 1997.

Article 8 (right to respect for private life): definition of rape; limits of consent to sexual acts; limits of consent to physical injury; ambit of Protection from Harassment Act 1997; "lifestyle" offences: sections 77–80 of the Criminal Justice and Public Order Act 1994; Proceeds of Crime Act 2002 (onus to prove provenance of funds).

Article 10 (right to freedom of expression): obscenity, and other offensive conduct;[92]

---

[89] "National laws on abortion differ considerably . . . in such a delicate area the contracting states must have a certain discretion": *H* v. *Norway* App. No. 7004/90 (1992).

[90] Arguably, the distinction drawn in Convention jurisprudence between disputes over the scope of an Article right and over exceptions to that right is spurious. On questions of coherence and uncertainty in Convention jurisprudence generally, see McHarg, "Reconciling Rights and the Public Interest: Conceptual Problems and Doctrinal uncertainty in the Jurisprudence of the European Court of Human Rights" (1999) 62 *MLR* 671.

[91] See Ashworth, "The European Convention and Criminal Law" in Cambridge Centre for Public Law, *The Human Rights Act and the Criminal and Regulatory Process* (1999) 37.

[92] Including threatening, abusive, or insulting conduct falling within s. 5(1) of the Public Order Act 1986: *Percy* v. *DPP* [2001] EWHC Admin 1125.

criminal libel; contempt of court; Official Secrets Act 1989; incitement to disaffection.

Article 11 (right to freedom of assembly and association): Criminal Justice & Public Order Act 1994 (control of demonstrations and processions), breach of the peace.

These opportunities for raising Convention issues during criminal trials will not be further developed here. They are mentioned in later chapters as appropriate. However, while it is also addressed in § 3.2 below, it is worth making particular mention here of the burden of proof, which is a pervasive and important issue that straddles the divides between evidential, procedural, and substantive law.[93] Reverse burdens of proof are commonplace in English law[94] and there will, therefore, be many occasions on which to raise this issue. As we noted above, the majority of the House of Lords in *Kebilene*[95] anticipated that reverse burdens may be reinterpreted as imposing merely an evidential burden and not a probative burden on the accused. Yet there may be further possibilities. To what extent does a proscription on reversing burdens of proof carry over to *eliminating* a requirement of proof? To explain, assume there is an offence of, say, knowingly selling food which does not comply with food safety standards. Assume it to be a serious offence with a maximum sentence of, say, ten years' imprisonment. If the onus were placed on D to prove that he did not know that the food which was sold was non-compliant, it may now suffice for D to raise a reasonable possibility that he did not know. What if Parliament were to respond to this finding by dropping any reference to knowledge and making it an offence simply to sell food, even inadvertently, that is non-compliant with safety standards? Is it a sufficient response to say that there are no Article 6 presumption-of-innocence implications because no reverse-burden of proof is employed?[96] Some academics have argued that it is insufficient, an answer that potentially would open up the field of strict liability offences for ECHR scrutiny.[97] However, at least at the present time, the courts have restricted the application of Article 6 to matters of procedural rather than substantive fairness. Thus reversing the burden to prove some offence element may violate Article 6, but eliminating that element altogether from the offence does not.[98]

---

[93] For excellent analysis of the impact of the ECHR on reverse burdens of proof see Dennis, "Reverse Onuses and the Presumption of Innocence: In Search of Principle" [2005] *Crim LR* 901.

[94] Ashworth and Blake, "The Presumption of Innocence in English Criminal Law" [1996] *Crim LR* 306.

[95] [1999] 3 WLR 972; above, § 2.5(i). Burdens of proof are discussed further below, § 3.2.

[96] The offence in English law of selling food that is non-compliant with safety standards (Food Safety Act 1990, s. 8) is an offence of strict liability with a maximum penalty of two years' imprisonment. The strict nature of the offence is mitigated by the provision of a due diligence defence with a reverse onus on D. From the perspective of effective regulation of a problematic industry, one may hope the offence will withstand Convention scrutiny. However, there are some offences of strict liability that carry high terms of imprisonment and are not mitigated by any due diligence defence: e.g. unlawful possession of a firearm as interpreted in *Howells* [1977] QB 614, and rape of a child under 13 as interpreted in *G* [2006] EWCA Crim 821. Such offences are much more difficult to justify.

[97] See, e.g., Tadros and Tierney, "The Presumption of Innocence and the Human Rights Act" (2004) 67 MLR 402; contrast Roberts, "Strict Liability and the Presumption of Innocence" in Simester (ed.), *Appraising Strict Liability* (2005) 151.

[98] *G* [2006] EWCA Crim 821 (rape of a child under 13, contrary to s. 5 of the Sexual Offences Act 2003). The Court of Appeal relied on *Salabiaku v. France* (1991) 13 EHRR 379, where a strict liability offence was held not to contravene Art. 6; below, §§ 3.2(i)(a), (d).

The taking of Convention points is not restricted to the defence. In *A v. UK,*[99] the physical chastisement of children was found to be inhuman and degrading, and thus in breach of Article 3. Clearly, if D is charged with assaulting his son following an act of parental discipline, the prosecution will be entitled to raise Article 3 were D to claim that his conduct was "reasonable chastisement" within the terms of English law. Recourse by the prosecution to the ECHR may well also occur in respect of claims by law enforcement officials to have employed justifiable or excusable force in the course of their duties. Under current English law, even in the case of employing fatal force, D is exempt from any criminal liability if he believed in the existence of circumstances which would have rendered such force reasonable, irrespective of whether D's belief was reasonable.[100] By contrast, under Article 2 of the ECHR (providing for the right to life), the allowance of exceptions only where "absolutely necessary"[101] has been interpreted to require a reasonable belief in the existence of facts which would warrant recourse to fatal force.[102] If English law is brought into line with Article 2 in respect of law enforcement officials, the question may arise whether the same rules should apply to violence employed by private individuals. One should not assume equivalence. In cases of law enforcement we are concerned with the question whether force employed by a public authority is legitimate. In cases confined to private individuals, the immediate ECHR issue is different: whether the United Kingdom, by permitting defences based on unreasonable mistakes in homicide cases, is adequately protecting the lives of its citizens.[103]

At this juncture, the full extent of the ECHR's impact on English substantive criminal law is still a matter of surmise. Yet Convention-based argument has quickly become familiar. A notable feature of ECHR argumentation before English courts is the frequent citation of Commonwealth jurisprudence. Canada, in particular, is a rich source of human rights case law from criminal law contexts. The Canadian courts have employed the term "principles of fundamental justice", which features in section 7 of the Charter of Rights, as a device to open up for discussion fundamental issues in criminal law doctrine such as questions relating to *mens rea,* strict liability, and defences.[104] The ECHR lacks any such sweeping expression; nonetheless, ingenious counsel may well find ways of raising cognate issues, particularly with a judiciary receptive (or at least resigned) to hearing arguments based on rights discourse.

---

[99] [1998] Crim LR 892; and see now *Williams* [2005] UKHL 15.

[100] *Williams (Gladstone)* [1987] 3 All ER 411; *Beckford* [1988] AC 130; below, §§ 18.1(iii), 21.2(viii).

[101] Article 2 (right to life) provides that force may be used in the course of self-defence, lawful arrest, preventing escapes from lawful detention, and quelling riot or insurrection; and that there will be no contravention of the Article notwithstanding the causing of death if the force was "no more than absolutely necessary".

[102] *McCann and others* v. *UK* (1996) 21 EHRR 97.

[103] Criminal lawyers need not engage with the vexed question of "horizontal effect" (the degree to which the Convention regulates the actions of citizens not acting within public authority contexts). In a criminal case, the Convention issue will be whether the offence/defence or procedural/evidential rule at issue is Convention-compliant. However, this is not to deny that courts should take a stricter view of what the Convention requires, particularly under Art. 2, where the conduct of public officials is involved.

[104] Hogg, *Constitutional Law of Canada* (4th ed., 1997) chap. 44; Archibald, "The Constitutionalisation of the General Part of the Criminal Law" (1988) 67 *Can BR* 403; Brudner, "Guilt under the Charter: The Lure of Parliamentary Supremacy" (1998) 40 *Crim LQ* 287.

3

INTERPRETATION AND PROOF

§ 3.1 Statutory interpretation

In Chapter 2 we saw how the Rule of Law embodies values such as fair warning—values which are proper aspirations for the criminal law, now partly cast in justiciable form by the ECHR. However, neither the Rule of Law nor the ECHR supports demands for unattainable measures of predictability and certainty. A degree of imprecision is inherent in the enterprise of legal ordering: statutes are necessarily expressed in general terms, and must be interpreted and applied to particular cases. The agent of this process is the court.[1]

In practice, the judicial task is more substantial than it need be. While legislators cannot be expected to foresee every variant case that might arise when they create an offence, the standard of draftsmanship in this country is such that offences frequently omit to specify quite obvious matters, such as what (if any) mental element an offence requires, on whom a burden of persuasion may lie, and whether omissions as well as acts are within the conduct proscribed. Moreover, some fundamental aspects of the criminal law, such as causation, are untouched by statute. Consequently, the role of judges is pivotal and powerful.

One way of observing the rights and expectations of citizens under the Rule of Law is for judges to show a proper restraint when interpreting the rules of the criminal law. In the civil law—say, a case involving the law of restitution—a judgment may earn praise for the way it reconceptualises the grounds of restitution, thereby vindicating new restitutionary claims. Similar creativity in the criminal law is generally to be avoided, since the scope for condemnation and punishment is thereby enlarged.[2] In Chapter 2 we noted the remark by the European Court of Human Rights (European Court) that "the criminal law must not be extensively construed to the accused's detriment, for instance by analogy."[3] This need for restraint means that interpreting a criminal statute should involve determining its meaning in a non-expansive way. Before examining the interpretation of criminal laws, however, it is useful to sketch a backdrop by commenting first upon the sources of the criminal law.

---

[1] For general discussion, see Ashworth, "Interpreting Criminal Statutes: A Crisis of Legality?" (1991) 107 *LQR* 419; Hall, "Strict or Liberal Construction of Penal Statutes" (1935) 48 *Harv LR* 748; MacCormick and Summers (eds.), *Interpreting Statutes: A Comparative Study* (1991); Jeffries, "Legality, Vagueness, and the Construction of Penal Statutes" (1985) 71 *Va LR* 189; Kremnitzer, "Interpretation in Criminal Law" (1986) 21 *Israel LR* 358.

[2] Cf. Dworkin, "Hard Cases" in *Taking Rights Seriously* (1977) 81, 100: by contrast with "standard civil cases, when the ruling assumption is that one of the parties has a right to win", "[t]he accused in a criminal case has a right to a decision in his favour if he is innocent, but the state has no parallel right to a conviction if he is guilty. The court may therefore find in favour of the accused, in some hard case testing rules of evidence, for example, on an argument of policy that does not suppose that the accused has any right to be acquitted."

[3] *Kokkinakas* v. *Greece* (1994) 17 EHRR 397. See above, § 2.3.

(i) The sources of the criminal law

Until the nineteenth century, English criminal law was essentially common law. The definition of crimes and the rules of criminal responsibility were evolved and developed on a case-by-case basis by judges. Also influential were writers of authority—the institutional writers—most notably Blackstone, Coke, East, Foster, Hale, and Hawkins. Today, English criminal law is no longer predominantly the result of judicial creativity. At the time of writing, there are believed to be something like 8,000 different criminal offences on the statute books, by far the most important source of criminal law. This corpus of statutory law reflects, as Glazebrook puts it, "two centuries of draftsmanship of very uneven quality . . . the product of changing views of morality and of when and how penal measures should be used in the hope of protecting the community against the violent, the lustful, the avaricious, the selfish and the careless."[4]

The predominance of statutory law should not obscure the creative role of the judiciary. Statutes have to be interpreted and, as we have mentioned, the poor draftsmanship to which Glazebrook alludes commonly includes failures to specify the burden of proof or even the *mens rea* requirement in an offence. Perforce, such fundamental issues have to be resolved by interpretation. Even where there is a degree of specificity—e.g. where the offence in question states that intent or recklessness by D is required—in the absence of stipulative definitions for those terms, the judges must resolve their meaning. Moreover, it is still the case that some significant offences, including murder, manslaughter, and assault, remain in large part common law offences. General doctrines affecting criminal liability, such as complicity and causation, remain largely unaffected by statute and new statutory crimes must be received and absorbed into this background.

Even among nations with a common law background, this is unusual. An influential strand in Enlightenment political theory was the conviction that the organs of representative democracy should be more influential than unelected judges in the creation and administration of the criminal law. To that end, criminal codes were promulgated, both here and elsewhere, in the hope that they would stipulate with clarity the content of crimes and the conditions of liability, reducing the role of the judge to that of an agent executing the will of the legislature. These hopes were optimistic, yet by no means wholly unfounded, and the vast majority of developed countries now have criminal codes. Codification passed England and Wales by. From time to time, efforts have been made to remedy the situation. The English Law Commission, for example, has published a Draft Criminal Code Bill. At the present time there is very little prospect of a government setting aside the parliamentary time necessary for the passage of such a bill. The Commission is resigned to modernisation by instalments.

Modernisation is long overdue. Certain statutes, such as the vitally important Offences against the Person Act 1861, are riddled with uncertainty and unhelpful overlaps and duplication. Yet reform and rationalisation should not be at the expense of abolishing offences that constitute a valuable cultural endowment. A Law Commission bill, usefully updating the law of criminal damage, made no provision for an offence of arson.[5] Understandably,

---

[4] Glazebrook, *Blackstone's Statutes on Criminal Law* (9th ed., 1999) xiii.
[5] Working Paper No. 23, *Malicious Damage* (1969) paras. 22, 66f.

Parliament reinstituted the offence—"arson" is an evocative term which should not be lost.[6] The same applies to "robbery", rightly preserved in the Theft Act 1968 as a form of acquisitive violence and not merely retained as an aggravating feature of a general offence of theft. At the same time, the past decade has seen an enormous quantity of legislation relating to the criminal law passed without regard for structure and guiding principles. The role of the judges will be a powerful one for the foreseeable future.

(ii) The interpretation of criminal statutes

It is not possible in a text of this nature to provide more than an overview of the relevant principles. When questions about the meaning of an offence arise, there are three steps for a court to take.

(a) Ordinary meaning

In the first instance, the interpretation of a criminal statute need not differ in technique from the interpretation of a civil statute. Modern statutory interpretation, both civil and criminal, should first take the form of ascertaining the *ordinary meaning in context*.[7] The reference to context is particularly important. It is a feature of language that meaning is not merely lexical, but also depends on the surrounding words and the purpose of the writer. A crucial issue in one famous criminal trial was the meaning of "Let him have it, Chris." Was this an injunction to hand over or to fire a gun? The latter, apparently, and a life as well as an argument was lost. Such uncertainties are not confined to vernacular speech. For example, section 20(2) of the Theft Act 1968 creates an offence *inter alia* of procuring, by deception, another person to indorse a valuable security. On one meaning, to "indorse" something is to express approval of it. But it is quite clear, both from the lexical context (execution of a valuable security) and the purpose of the offence, that the intended meaning is to assign by writing.

When determining the ordinary meaning of a provision, the judge may be addressing a text of considerable age, such as the Offences against the Person Act 1861. Should the judge seek the meaning of any word or expression as of 1861 or in the terms of current usage? It may be that the matter is resolved by previous authority—an appellate case in, say, 1937 may have interpreted the term in a manner clearly applicable to the instant case. But what if there is no such authority? Then it seems the meaning the term bears in present-day English is to be applied, even should it be a meaning clearly not to the mind of the legislature back in 1861. As it was put by the House of Lords in *Burstow*,[8] criminal statutes "are always speaking" and the speech is of the present day.[9] Accordingly the court in construing the expression "actual bodily harm" for the purposes of section 47 of the OAPA 1861 (assault occasioning actual bodily harm) was able to conclude that psychiatric injury was a form of bodily harm.

---

[6] Cf. the discussion of fair labelling, above, § 2.4.
[7] Cf. Bell and Engle, *Cross on Statutory Interpretation* (3rd ed., 1995) 31–3, 48f.
[8] [1998] AC 147.
[9] See too *K* [2002] 1 AC 462; *R (on the application of Smeaton) v. Secretary of State for Health* [2002] NLJR 638.

Even the best-drafted statute can require interpretive decisions by the court. If grammatical context as well as lexical meaning is addressed, one meaning will usually emerge as clearly the best suited to express the purposes of the statute or the relevant part thereof. Where it does so, there can be no objection, even in the case of a criminal statute, to an interpretative choice that goes against the defendant. When one interpretation of a statutory provision is tenable and preferable to any competing interpretation, there is nothing particular about the interpretation of criminal statutes. The "ordinary meaning in context" prevails.

(b) Legislative background

Sometimes the meaning cannot be determined within the four corners of the statute itself. In such cases, the courts have the power to investigate the legislative background of an Act in order to ascertain the intention of Parliament.[10] An illustration of this process is *A-G's Reference (No. 1 of 1988)*,[11] where determining the "ordinary meaning in context" left the Court with a choice between two meanings, each of which was "ordinary". In the course of a consultation with a merchant bank, D had been informed on confidential terms that X plc was to be the subject of a takeover bid. D acquired shares in X in anticipation of the inevitable rise in the share price. This acquisition would have constituted an offence against insider trading legislation, provided D had "obtained" the information. Had D "obtained" inside information? At trial, he argued successfully that he had not, on the basis that the *Oxford English Dictionary* gave "to acquire by endeavour" as the primary meaning of the term. There had been no effort made to obtain this information; he had merely been informed of it while seeking a banker's advice. If this interpretation were to succeed, the offence of insider dealing would be confined to those who seek out inside information in order to deal. However, the legislative history and the overall scheme of the Companies Securities (Insider Dealing) Act 1985 was strongly suggestive that chance recipients of insider information were within the scheme of the Act where the informant was a corporate "insider" (as the merchant bank clearly was). Accordingly, the House of Lords adopted "to get, to come by", the secondary meaning allowed by the *OED*, as the meaning which was to prevail.

Regrettably, whether or not the legislative history is consulted often depends upon the inclination of judges. In the notorious case of *Caldwell*,[12] to which we return in Chapter 5, Lord Diplock conceded that there was an issue of interpretation in respect of the meaning to be given to the culpability term, "reckless". He resolved the issue by recourse to "ordinary" English, which informed him that the term comprehended not only defendants who perceived the likely consequences of their conduct, but also defendants who failed to give thought to the obvious consequences of that conduct. He signally failed to consider a Law Commission report which stated, unequivocally, that only defendants who actually perceived the consequences of their conduct were to be found reckless in cases of criminal

---

[10] *Pepper* v. *Hart* [1993] AC 593. In terms of the Rule of Law, consultation of such sources as Hansard is unobjectionable provided the source is adequately made available to the public, so that potential defendants have fair warning of its import. See Evans, *Statutory Interpretation* (1988) 289.

[11] [1989] AC 971.

[12] [1982] AC 341; reversed ultimately in *G* [2003] UKHL 50, [2004] 1 AC 1034.

damage.[13] Similarly, in *Khan*,[14] resort to a Law Commission report would have informed the Court of Appeal that their decision about the meaning of "intent" for the crime of attempt was contrary to the meaning envisaged by the Commission when proposing the clause subsequently adopted, unamended, by Parliament.[15]

The decisions in *Caldwell* and *Khan* are, unfortunately, only two of many instances of expansive interpretation of statutory offences unsupported by any examination of the policy and legislative history of the offence interpreted. One may even find different approaches in the same case. In *Gomez*,[16] the minority in the House of Lords consulted the report of the Criminal Law Revision Committee which had formulated the provisions under review in that case, namely sections 1 and 15 of the Theft Act 1968. The consultation resolved any doubts: on the facts of the case there could have been a conviction under section 15 for obtaining property by deception but there was no theft within the terms of section 1. Untroubled by an engagement with the legislative history, the majority found that there had been a theft, creating what Sir John Smith has called the "widest imaginable" offence of theft.[17]

(c) Strict construction

Finally if, after examining the statutory context and background, there is still some uncertainty about which interpretation is preferable, then the court should give the benefit of that uncertainty to the accused. This is a presumption of strict construction. It is justified by the requirement to give fair warning, which implies that ambiguity in offences should not be understood to create unpredictable offences; statutes should not require citizens to guess at their meaning, and so should be construed against imposing liability upon a defendant who reasonably thought she was within the terms of the law. The principle of strict interpretation, confined to criminal and taxation statutes, may be expressed as follows:[18]

> "If a penal provision is reasonably capable of two interpretations that interpretation which is most favourable to the accused must be adopted."

This is not to say that *any* measure of doubt over the meaning of a statute should be construed in the defendant's favour. The strict construction principle is a default rule, one to rely on if the meaning of the statute cannot be ascertained by other standard techniques. In the past, the principle of strict construction has sometimes been read as entailing that the benefit of *any* favourable interpretation which passes a minimal threshold of plausibility must always be given to the defendant.[19] Yet, as Lord Reid recognised in *DPP* v. *Ottewell*,[20] this extreme reading is untenable. A lexically possible meaning should not be adopted if the

---

[13] Lord Diplock's approach makes an instructive contrast to the reasoning in *G, ibid.*, where Caldwell was reversed. In the later case, their Lordships paid careful attention to Parliament's intention: see paras. 12–13, 29 (Lord Bingham), 47–50 (Lord Steyn), and 63–4 (Lord Bridge).

[14] [1990] 2 All ER 783. Discussed below, § 9.3(iii)(b).

[15] Law Com. No. 102, *Attempt, and Impossibility in Relation to Attempt, Conspiracy and Incitement* (1980).

[16] *DPP* v. *Gomez* [1993] AC 442. Discussed in detail below, § 13.6(ii).

[17] Commentary at [1993] Crim LR 304, 306.

[18] *Per* Lord Reid in *Sweet* v. *Parsley* [1970] AC 132, 149.

[19] E.g. *Harris* (1836) 7 C & P 446, 173 ER 198.

[20] [1970] AC 642; cf. *Tuck & Sons* v. *Priester* (1887) 19 QBD 629, 638, where Lord Esher MR required that the favourable alternative must be a "reasonable construction".

statutory context makes clear that an alternative interpretation is best suited to the purposes of the statute:[21]

> "The Court of Appeal (Criminal Division) refer to the well-established principle that in doubtful cases a penal provision ought to be given that interpretation which is least unfavourable to the accused. I would never seek to diminish in any way the importance of that principle within its proper sphere. But it only applies where after full inquiry and consideration one is left in real doubt. It is not enough that the provision is ambiguous in the sense that it is capable of having two meanings. The imprecision of the English language (and, so far as I am aware, of any other language) is such that it is extremely difficult to draft any provision which is not ambiguous in that sense. This section is clearly ambiguous in that sense: the Court of Appeal (Criminal Division) attach one meaning to it, and your Lordships are attaching a different meaning to it. But if, after full consideration, your Lordships are satisfied, as I am, that the latter is the meaning which Parliament must have intended the words to convey, then this principle does not prevent us from giving effect to our conclusions."

As a subsidiary principle, then, strict construction is and should be retained in modern criminal law.[22] Nonetheless, it is fair to say that the courts have come to treat the rule as one of "last resort",[23] and sometimes have failed to apply the principle even in a case where it was appropriate. As Glanville Williams observes:[24]

> "The courts cannot manufacture statutes as they manufacture precedents, by they can 'interpret' them. They can cut them down, or expand them. Courts still pay lip-service to the ancient principle that in case of doubt a criminal statute is to be 'strictly construed' in favour of the defendant; but the principle is rarely applied in practice, if there are social reasons for convicting. Indeed, we may make bold to say that the looser the defendant's conduct, the more loosely the judges construe the statute designed to control him."

Just so.[25] Sometimes, the Rule of Law is displaced by the discretionary rule of individual judges. In *Gomez*,[26] for example, D was convicted of theft, contrary to section 1 of the Theft Act 1968, by "appropriating" property that he had deceived V into giving him. The conduct was a plain case of obtaining by deception, contrary to section 15. The House of Lords upheld D's conviction, notwithstanding that the "appropriation" was authorised by V and rested upon a construction that wrenched the crime of theft away from (i) a reasonable alternative meaning more favourable to D,[27] which was also (ii) its intended meaning,[28] and (iii) had been unequivocally embraced in an earlier decision by the House of Lords.[29]

---

[21] *DPP* v. *Ottewell* [1970] AC 642, 649.

[22] Not merely in England and Wales: *US* v. *Kozminski* US 108 SC 2751, 2765 (1988); *Barker* (1983) CLR 338, 350.

[23] *R (on the application of Junttan Oy)* v. *Bristol Magistrates' Court* [2003] UKHL 55, [2004] 2 All ER 555, para 84 (Lord Steyn): "If it has a role to play it is as a rule of last resort: it is only to be applied if all other grounds of determining legislative intent have failed."

[24] *TBCL* 12. Cf. Smith, "Codification of the Criminal Law" [1987] *Denning LJ* 134, 143–4.

[25] Compare, e.g., *Duncalf* [1979] 2 All ER 116; *Delgado* [1984] 1 All ER 449; *R (on the application of Junttan Oy)* v. *Bristol Magistrates' Court* [2003] UKHL 55, [2004] 2 All ER 555, para 84 (*per* Lord Steyn: "In the present context there is at stake a cogent countervailing legal policy: the protection of health and safety at work is of overriding importance").

[26] *DPP* v. *Gomez* [1993] AC 442, discussed in detail below, § 13.6(ii).

[27] Compare *Hinks* [1998] Crim LR 904, where, unlike *Gomez*, D would otherwise have committed no offence at all.

[28] Cf. the dissent by Lord Lowry.

[29] *Morris* [1984] AC 320.

Behind the decision lies the sort of explanation that might be given by an American Legal Realist. D had been charged, incompetently, with theft rather than obtaining by deception. Their Lordships therefore had the alternatives of acquitting altogether a man obviously guilty of the offence under section 15, or of distorting the law of theft. Convicting one dishonest person was, apparently, more important.

Sometimes, then, the courts disregard the principle of strict construction in cases to which it ought to apply. But when they do so, they do bad law. The principle *is* a part of English law, where it operates as a residual doctrine of construction in the way we have described. Moreover, it *ought* not to be ignored. The principle is an important means of upholding the Rule of Law, by making sure that the defendant has fair warning of the scope of the relevant offence, and that (in a case like *Gomez*, where D was plainly guilty of something else[30]) his wrongdoing is fairly labelled. If, after considering the context and legislative history, a criminal prohibition is reasonably capable of being interpreted in two different ways, it is wrong not to give the defendant the benefit of the doubt. Indeed, in our view the principle is mandated by Article 7 of the ECHR.[31] A strict approach to construction helps to prevent criminal liability from coming as a surprise to defendants. It ensures that the scope of an offence extends only to those cases where its application, *ex ante*, was clear and predictable.

(d) Summary

The correct approach to statutory interpretation, it is submitted, is first to seek the ordinary meaning in context. Where, like the example of "indorse" in section 20(2) of the Theft Act 1968, the meaning of a phrase emerges clearly from the context and purpose of the statute, that meaning should be adopted even though it goes against the defendant. Otherwise, if the meaning is not apparent from the Act or the relevant part of the Act, a thorough review of the legislative history should be undertaken. If, after that exercise, the interpretation of the provision remains a matter of reasonable dispute, the benefit of the doubt should be given to the defendant. In practice, as we noted above, the approach argued for here is sometimes vulnerable to judges minded to override interpretive uncertainty in the interests of crime-control. Such vulnerability is unfortunate. Compromising the Rule of Law for the sake of short-term policy objectives is improper adjudication.

(e) The obvious drafting error?

The above is the correct general approach. Apparently, however, there is one special case—although, in our view, it involves a regrettable compromise of the Rule of Law. The case involves the correction of an "obvious drafting error", as in *R (on the application of the CPS) v. Bow Street Magistrates Court and others*.[32] In that case, the defendants were charged with possessing a false passport on 4 April 2006, formerly an offence under section 5 of the Forgery and Counterfeiting Act 1981. Unfortunately, section 44(2) of the Identity Cards Act 2006, which came into force on 30 March 2006, repealed the relevant offence under the 1981 Act. It was intended that they be replaced by corresponding provisions in sections 25

---

[30] See Shute and Horder, "Thieving and Deceiving: What is the Difference" (1993) 56 *MLR* 548.
[31] See above, §§ 2.2-3.
[32] [2006] EWHC 1763 (Admin).

and 26 of the new 2006 Act; but those new provisions had not themselves yet come into force. Section 44(3) suspended the coming into force of most of the 1981 Act, although not of section 44 itself:

> This Act (apart from this section and sections 36 and 38) shall come into force on such day as the Secretary of State may by order appoint; and different days may be appointed for different purposes.

No doubt there is a slip-up here. By section 44(3), section 44(2) came into force on 30 March 2006 to repeal the offence charged under the 1981 Act; but the new sections did not come into force. The Divisional Court ruled that the statute could be corrected. Words are to be read into section 44(3), so that it is to be interpreted as follows:[33]

> This Act (apart from this section, *other than subsection (2) hereof,* and sections 36 and 38) shall come into force on such day as the Secretary of State may by order appoint; and different days may be appointed for different purposes.

It seems that there are three criteria which must be met before such an intervention can be made. The criteria are laid down by the House of Lords in *Inco Europe Ltd and others* v. *First Choice Distribution (a Firm) and Others*:[34]

> "This power is confined to plain cases of drafting mistakes. The courts are ever mindful that their constitutional role in this field is interpretative. They must abstain from any course which might have the appearance of judicial legislation. A statute is expressed in language approved and enacted by the legislature. So the courts exercise considerable caution before adding or omitting or substituting words. Before interpreting a statute in this way the court must be abundantly sure of three matters: (1) the intended purpose of the statute or provision in question; (2) that by inadvertence the draftsman and Parliament failed to give effect to that purpose in the provision in question; and (3) the substance of the provision Parliament would have made, although not necessarily the precise words Parliament would have used, had the error in the Bill been noticed."

No doubt those criteria were met in the present case. But *Inco Europe* was a civil case, not criminal, and the House of Lords emphasised the point:[35]

> "Sometimes, even when these conditions are met, the court may find itself inhibited from interpreting the statutory provision in accordance with what it is satisfied was the underlying intention of Parliament. The alteration in language may be too far-reaching. . . . Or the subject matter may call for a strict interpretation of the statutory language, as in penal legislation. None of these considerations apply in the present case. Here, the court is able to give effect to a construction of the statute which accords with the intention of the legislature."

It is submitted that the Divisional Court wrongly discounted this qualification.[36] Civil law contains no direct equivalent of the *nullum crimen* rule, discussed earlier in §§ 2.1–2. In the criminal law, it is not appropriate to read words into a statute to create an offence that,

---

[33] See *ibid.*, para. 44.
[34] [2000] 1 WLR 586, 592.
[35] *Ibid.*, 592–3.
[36] The Court dealt with the point by opining that the novel construction of s. 44(3) of the 2006 Act did not inflict any detriment or greater detriment upon any of the defendants or any other person, because it merely continued the existing law until its replacement by the new provisions and that no increase in penalty was involved at any stage

on the clear meaning of the statute when applying the correct approach outlined on the pages above, does not exist. The "obvious error" rule in *Inco Europe* should be confined to the civil law.

(iii) Interpretation and development of common law offences

Contrasts are frequently made between statutory interpretation, on the one hand, and the creation and development of the common law. Despite the importance of statutory law for vast tracts of English law, statutes, it is claimed, do not become part of a general body of law, organically linked to the other statutory and common law norms that already occupy the relevant legal domain. Each statute remains a thing apart, to be interpreted within its own four corners and legislative history and not to be used as a means of extrapolation and analogy for the treatment of issues that do not arise under the statute itself. By contrast, the common law is said to be an entity which subsumes its constituent parts, thereby allowing ideas developed in one branch of common law to be deployed freely in other branches should cognate issues arise. The self-confident and conscious development of common law rules and doctrines finds no counterpart in statutory interpretation.[37]

Although that account risks parody, it contains a core of truth: for the civil law. The criminal law is different. The criminal branch of the common law is essentially a realm apart.[38] It has not been integrated with contract and property; nor even, to any significant extent, with the law of tort. In the criminal law, a comparison between statutory interpretation and the development and interpretation of common law crimes reveals parallel tendencies toward expansive interpretation, usually done in the interests of crime control. One point of difference is that the common law has contained rules of such breadth and imprecision that expansive interpretation frequently was not required. In effect, the common law was there ready and waiting to rubber-stamp a prosecutor's decision to proceed.

Perhaps the best illustration of the flexibility of common law crimes is the common-law version of conspiracy—an agreement between two or more persons to effect some unlawful purpose.[39] Left to judicial devices, "unlawful" was allowed free rein and led to the criminalisation of many actions which, if done by individuals acting alone, would not have been criminal. This freedom, was exercised to large and controversial effect,[40] and at the price of the Rule of Law, until finally limited by the Criminal Law Act of 1977. Even so, the "elasticity" was not completely forsworn. Conspiracies to defraud, to corrupt public

---

([2006] EWHC 1763 (Admin), paras. 47-8). But of course it does: the interposition of words created an offence where there was otherwise none.

[37] See the classic article by Pound, "Common Law and Legislation" (1907) 21 *Harv LR* 383. The contrast still retains substance but statutes are no longer treated so circumspectly as formerly they were. As Atiyah has demonstrated ("Common Law and Statute Law" (1985) 48 *MLR* 1), statutes may be used by judges as sources of analogy and policy for legal development generally, though this tends to occur on a haphazard, *ad hoc*, basis.

[38] "The miserable history of crime in England can be shortly told. There is no achievement to trace. Nothing worthwhile was created." With these words, Milsom introduces a chapter in which he demonstrates, by contrast with the rest of the common law, the impoverished development and lack of resources of the law of crime: *Historical Foundations of the Common Law* (1969) 353.

[39] Wright, *Law of Criminal Conspiracies and Agreements* (1873) 63–5.

[40] *Kamara v. DPP* [1974] AC 104, 109.

morality, and to outrage public decency were retained by the 1977 Act pending their replacement by narrower, statutory offences. These forms of conspiracy are still in rude health. Conspiracy to defraud, in particular, is defined in the widest of terms:[41] it includes any agreement to cause loss to another by dishonest means, or by dishonest means to induce persons to act contrary to a duty.

The requirement for an "agreement" in conspiracy offences provides at least an element of restraint on their interpretation. Should conspiracy to defraud ever become an offence capable of commission by individuals, large parts of the criminal law could be made redundant. Indeed, at one time the common law was held to contain just such a catch-all offence, applicable to single individuals. In *Manley*,[42] a prosecution was launched against D for deliberately wasting police time. In the absence of anything more suitable to hand, the Court of Criminal Appeal approved the trial judge's resurrection of the offence of "public mischief", a public mischief being anything injurious to the public interest. It is perhaps needless to emphasise the extent to which such an offence undermines any aspiration to fair warning[43] in the criminal law. Happily, the offence was infrequently resorted to and eventually consigned to legal history by the House of Lords in *DPP v. Withers*.[44]

Whatever criticisms may be made of modern parliaments, it is doubtful whether offences based on phrases so nebulous, extensible, and threatening[45] as "public mischief" or "corrupting public morality" would survive the modern legislative process.[46] Yet even modern parliaments seem disinclined to abolish established, widely phrased offences.[47] In a modern democracy, judges should not be allowed to help themselves to such untrammelled power. Yet we have seen that modern statutes are not always a sufficient constraint on judicial activism, and it seems the internal resources of the criminal law are an insufficient bulwark.

The need is pressing. Judicial activism shows no sign of abating, as evidenced by the decision of the House of Lords in *Ireland*.[48] The case decided that silent telephone calls which occasion psychological distress may constitute assaults. For hundreds of years, an assault required the threat of imminent violence; that is, the threat of some immediate, unwanted bodily contact. Remarkably, the House found that this condition could be satisfied despite the caller's being miles away from his victim. As we will see in Chapter 11, the reasoning of the House does not convince. Also remarkably, this decision was reached despite the fact that in future such conduct would have been caught by sections 1 and 2 of the Protection from Harassment Act 1997. Yet the House reached its interpretation not merely to avoid an acquittal in the instant case. It also considered that the penalties provided by the new Act were insufficient and that recourse to the greater penalties

---

[41] Below, Chapter 15. Remarkably the Fraud Act 2006, which creates a general fraud offence, does not abolish common law conspiracy to defraud. We can assume that this protean and widely prosecuted offence will be with us for the indefinite future.

[42] [1933] 1 KB 529.

[43] And fair labelling: above, § 2.4.

[44] [1975] AC 842.

[45] Potentially, such phrases permit criminalisation on the basis of immorality rather than harm or offence: below, § 16.3.

[46] The latter term was retained by the Criminal Law Act 1977, but only pending replacement.

[47] As can be seen in the omission by the Fraud Act 2006 to abolish common law conspiracy to defraud, when reforming the law of fraud. See below, Chapter 15.

[48] [1998] AC 147. See above, § 2.3; below, § 11.2(i)(c).

provided by the sanctions for aggravated assaults was required. Accordingly, their Lordships decided to customise centuries of common law in order to circumnavigate the new Act.

§ 3.2 The burden of proving actus reus and mens rea

In Chapter 1, we argued that convicting an innocent person would be seriously to defame him. Punishing him, of course, compounds the wrong. Because criminal liability is so serious, every citizen has the right not to have the State inflict such liability on him unless he is, in fact, guilty. That right is fundamental: it is profoundly wrong for the State to mistreat an innocent person, and to do so breaches one of the keystones of an individual's relationship with the State.

So when the State brands someone a criminal, it needs to be sure that it is right—or at least, in the absence of omniscience, as sure as it can be.[49] For that reason, there is a basic presumption in English law that the defendant in a trial is innocent until proved guilty. The presumption is also codified in Article 6(2) of the ECHR, which provides that a person "charged with a criminal offence shall be presumed innocent until proved guilty according to the law." In the words of the European Court of Human Rights:[50]

> "Paragraph 2 embodies the principle of the presumption of innocence. It requires, *inter alia*, that when carrying out their duties, the members of a court should not start with the preconceived idea that the accused has committed the offence charged; the burden of proof is on the prosecution, and any doubt should benefit the accused. It also follows that it is for the prosecution to inform the accused of the case that will be made against him, so that he may prepare and present his defence accordingly, and to adduce evidence sufficient to convict him."

None of this is novel. The presumption of innocence predates the ECHR, and has been a part of the common law at least since *Woolmington* v. *DPP*.[51] In *Woolmington*, a murder case, the trial judge had relied on earlier authorities to direct the jury that, once the prosecution has proved the actus reus, mens rea can be presumed and it was up to the defendant to "satisfy" the jury either that mens rea was absent and the killing had been accidental, or that it had been justified. On this view, the prosecution had to prove only the actus reus, and the burden then lay on the defendant to prove either the lack of mens rea or any defence. Not so, said the House of Lords:[52]

> "Throughout the web of the English Criminal Law one golden thread is always to be seen, that it is the duty of the prosecution to prove the prisoner's guilt. . . . If, at the end of and on the whole of the case, there is a reasonable doubt, created by the evidence given by either the prosecution or the prisoner, as to whether the prisoner killed the deceased with a malicious intention, the prosecution has not made out the case and the prisoner is entitled to an acquittal. No matter what the charge or where the trial, the principle that the prosecution must prove the guilt of the prisoner is part of the common law of England and no attempt to whittle it down can be entertained."

---

[49] Cf. the judgment of Brennan J in *Re Winship* 397 US 358 (1970) (SC).
[50] *Barberà, Messegué and Jabardo* v. *Spain* (1989) 11 EHRR 360.
[51] [1935] AC 462.
[52] [1935] AC 462, 481–2 (Viscount Sankey LC). See also *Mancini* v. *DPP* [1942] AC 1, 11 (Viscount Simon LC).

It was not for the defendant to demonstrate that the actus reus was an accident; the prosecution must establish mens rea beyond reasonable doubt. The effect of *Woolmington* may be summarised in the following steps:

(i)　　The prosecution has the burden to bring evidence which prima facie proves all actus reus and mens rea elements of the offence *beyond reasonable doubt.*

(ii)　　Once the prosecution has done so, it is then open to the defendant either to raise a reasonable doubt about the evidence the prosecution has brought, or to point to some further evidence which raises a doubt whether the prosecution's evidence is in fact sufficient to prove both actus reus[53] and mens rea beyond reasonable doubt.

(iii)　　Alternatively, if the prosecution proves both actus reus and mens rea, the defendant has an *evidentiary burden* to raise any evidence which suggests the possible availability of a defence (e.g. that the actus reus was done in self-defence).[54] If he does so, or if the evidence introduced by the prosecution does so,[55] then the prosecution assumes the burden of proving beyond reasonable doubt that the relevant defence is not available in this case.[56] This rule applies to common law defences with the exception of insanity; there is also an exception for statutory defences. We will consider these exceptions below.

The defendant does *not* have to prove that he is innocent. The jury may think that he is untrustworthy, and be unconvinced by his story. But if it thinks there is a reasonable possibility that he is not guilty of the crime charged, then he must be acquitted. As the Privy Council put it, in *Jayasena v. R.*, "the only burden laid upon the accused in this respect is to collect from the evidence enough material to make it possible for a reasonable jury to acquit."[57] in practical terms, the effect of the *Woolmington* approach is that a defendant need not collaborate in his own conviction; however strong the grounds of suspicion against him he need not give any account of himself or in any other way assist the prosecution make its case. As such, the presumption of innocence is an essential counterpart to the defendant's right of non-self-incrimination.

The crux of the presumption is the standard "beyond reasonable doubt".[58] It means that the jury must acquit if there is a realistic or genuine doubt about the defendant's guilt, although not if the doubt is only vague or fanciful.[59] Such a high standard is needed for the

---

[53] This includes claims of involuntariness or automatism: *Bratty v. A-G for Northern Ireland* [1963] AC 386, 406–7, 413–14. See below, § 4.3(iv).

[54] *Lobell* [1957] 1 QB 547, 551 (self-defence); *Gill* [1963] 2 All ER 688, 691 (duress). The evidentiary burden to introduce defences differs from the option to refute evidence of actus reus or mens rea in step (ii). The latter is sometimes called a *tactical burden* on the defendant. The difference is that, where there is an evidential burden on D to suggest (e.g.) a defence, its absence will be *presumed* by the court unless D discharges that burden. By contrast, a tactical burden involves no presumption. Thus, D may choose not to respond to the prosecution's evidence of actus reus and mens rea, and simply hope that the jury is not convinced by it.

[55] Thus the defence must be considered even if the defendant has not raised it himself: *Palmer v. R.* [1971] 1 AC 814, 823; *Wheeler* (1967) 52 Cr App R 28, 30–1; *Hammond* (1985) 82 Cr App R 65.

[56] *Lobell* [1957] 1 QB 547; *Gill* [1963] 2 All ER 688; *Chan Kau v. R* [1955] AC 206, 211; *Mancini v. DPP* [1942] AC 1.

[57] [1970] AC 618, 623.

[58] This may be a more stringent standard than that required by Art. 6(2) of the ECHR, which demands evidence "sufficiently strong in the eyes of the law to establish his guilt": *Austria v. Italy* 6 YB 740, 784 (1963) Com Rep; CM Res DH (63) 3.

[59] *Miller v. Minister of Pensions* [1947] 2 All ER 372, 373–4 (Denning J).

State to be sufficiently sure that it is imposing criminal liability accurately. It is not enough that the defendant "very likely", or even "probably", did the crime; otherwise there would be too many cases of error and consequent miscarriages of justice. The possibility of error is all the greater when it is also remembered that the State typically has far greater resources with which to conduct a prosecution than the defendant has with which to defend himself. In addition, the high standard of proof acts as a constraint upon the decision to prosecute. Without the presumption of innocence, those who make that decision would have an immense and potentially oppressive power to disrupt the lives of citizens.[60]

(i) Exceptions

(a) Parliament

It is not uncommon for a statute to modify the normal burden of proof, especially in respect of particular elements within the offence. An example of this is the offence of child abduction contrary to section 2 of the Child Abduction Act 1984. Subsection (3) provides a defence, *inter alia*, if the defendant proves "that, at the time of the alleged offence, he believed that the child had attained the age of sixteen." In this case, once the prosecution has proved the other elements of an offence against section 2, the defendant has a legal (and not merely evidential) burden to prove that the conditions of the defence exist. In all such cases, the defendant must prove to the civil standard, of balance of probabilities.[61]

This is not a textbook on evidence. However, it is submitted that for the reasons given in the last section, statutory exceptions of this sort are generally to be deplored.[62] Effectively, they reverse the presumption of innocence, and replace it with a presumption of criminality, whereby the defendant is to be convicted of a crime unless she exculpates herself. As such, they expose the defendant to conviction for a crime without the prosecution being required, at any stage, to lead evidence which proves her guilt beyond reasonable doubt. There *may* be occasions when it is apt to require the defendant, in respect of matters that lie peculiarly within her knowledge, to suggest reasons why she should not be convicted.[63] But rather like the tort doctrine of *res ipsa loquitur*, this is a principle to be sparingly used and only if the prosecution has established a prima facie case. Moreover, even then the desired result can usually be achieved by imposing an *evidential* burden to introduce defences upon the defendant, without requiring her to discharge the full legal burden of persuading the court that she is innocent. The defendant should not, on any occasion, be required to prove her innocence.

Be that as it may, statutory reversal of the burden of proof occurs quite frequently, and may be done either expressly or impliedly.[64] Moreover, in *Lingens* v. *Austria*[65] the European

---

[60] As Ashworth points out: *Principles* 83.

[61] *Carr-Briant* [1943] KB 607.

[62] See, e.g., Roberts, "Taking the Burden of Proof Seriously" [1995] *Crim LR* 783; Jeffries and Stephan, "Defences, Presumptions and Burden of Proof in Criminal Law" (1979) 88 *Yale LJ* 1325.

[63] Cf. *Jayasena* v. *R.* [1970] AC 618, 626–7 (PC). See also the discussion of (and reservations about) strict liability, below, Chapter 6.

[64] *Hunt* [1987] AC 352, 374 (Lord Griffiths), 379–80 (Lord Ackner). See the survey by Ashworth and Blake, "The Presumption of Innocence in English Criminal Law" [1996] *Crim LR* 306.

[65] (1982) 4 EHRR 373.

Court has ruled that the practice does not necessarily contravene Article 6(2) of the ECHR. Similarly, statutory presumptions of fact, where the onus of rebuttal falls on the accused, have been held consistent with Article 6(2), provided the presumption operates "within reasonable limits which take into account the importance of what is at stake and maintain the rights of the defence."[66] The proviso does, at least, offer hope that in extreme cases the imposition of a persuasive burden on the defendant will be disallowed by Article 6(2). But it seems the case would have to be extreme. In *Salabiaku* v. *France*,[67] D had been found in possession of drugs in the "green" channel at Paris airport. He was charged with the serious, imprisonable, offence of drugs smuggling. Under French law, smuggling was presumed from the fact of possession in such circumstances unless D could establish to the satisfaction of the court that he was unaware of the nature of the items possessed. The Court found that this presumption did not contravene Article 6(2). Similar findings have been made in respect of a presumption that D, a company director, was guilty of an offence if the offence has been proved against his company[68] and in respect of a presumption that D was living off immoral earnings if it is proved that D was cohabiting with a prostitute.[69]

Fortunately, a series of House of Lords decisions has established a somewhat less permissive attitude to reverse burdens of proof, at least in this country.[70] While there is no general bar to reverse burdens and each offence must be considered on its merits,[71] on some occasions at least a reverse burden has been ruled incompatible with Article 6(2). An example is *Lambert*,[72] where, in order to avoid conviction for an offence of drug trafficking under section 5 of the Misuse of Drugs Act 1971, D was required to prove that he neither knew nor suspected nor had reason to know or suspect that the substance in his possession was a controlled drug. By a majority of 4:1, the House of Lords decided that, notwithstanding the public interest in prohibiting the trade in illegal drugs, to impose a legal burden on a defendant was a disproportionate legislative response and, consequently, a breach of Article 6(2). It was held that, within the interpretive possibilities allowed for by section 3 of the HRA 1998, the requirement to "prove" lack of knowledge, suspicion, etc., could be reinterpreted to require D merely to raise the possibility that he neither knew nor suspected—merely an evidential burden and not a probative burden. A notable feature of the decision was a refusal to rely upon any formal distinction between definitional elements of an offence and matters of defence when determining the acceptability of a reverse burden. What mattered was whether D would be found guilty of an offence unless he could prove the particular matter in dispute.

---

[66] *Salabiaku* v. *France* (1988) 13 EHRR 379; cf. *X* v. *UK* No 5124/71, 42 CD 135 (1972). In *Duhs* v. *Sweden* No 12995/87, 67 DR 204 (1990), the Court held that imposition of a parking fine on the basis of car ownership was within such reasonable limits, and hence was permissible. See also *A-G of Hong Kong* v. *Lee Kwong-Kut* [1993] AC 951 (in the context of the Hong Kong Bill of Rights); *Vasquez* v. *R* [1994] 3 All ER 674 (constitution of Belize).

[67] (1988) 13 EHRR 379.

[68] *G* v. *Malta* No 16641/90 (1991).

[69] *X* v. *UK* No 5124/71, 42 CD 135 (1972).

[70] *R.* v. *DPP, ex p. Kebilene* [2000] AC 326, *Lambert* [2001] UKHL 37, [2002] 2 AC 545; *Johnstone* [2003] UKHL 28, [2003] 1 WLR 1736; *Sheldrake* v. *DPP; Attorney-General's Reference (No. 4 of 2002)* [2004] UKHL 43, [2005] 1 AC 264.

[71] *Lambert* [2001] UKHL 37, [2002] 2 AC 545, paras. 34, 152; *Sheldrake* v. *DPP; Attorney-General's Reference (No. 4 of 2002)* [2004] UKHL 43, [2005] 1 AC 264, para. 21.

[72] [2001] 3 All ER 577.

In so far as the various decisions by their Lordships can be distilled,[73] it seems that the proper approach is as follows. Where, on ordinary techniques of statutory interpretation (above, § 3.1), a particular piece of legislation imposes a probative, and not merely evidential, burden on the defendant, the court must then enquire whether doing so is an unjustifiable infringement of the presumption of innocence in Article 6(2). Qualification of the presumption may sometimes be justifiable and proportionate, depending on the context and reasons why the reverse burden is imposed. However, where the presumption of innocence is held to be unjustifiably infringed, the court must, if possible, reinterpret the legislative provision so as to impose an evidential burden;[74] or, if that interpretation is precluded by the terms of the legislation, a declaration of incompatibility with the ECHR should be made.[75]

The key question, of course, is whether the imposition of a reverse burden is justifiable and proportionate. In deciding that question, one should balance, on the one hand, society's interest in the effective suppression of the social mischief with which the offence is concerned and, on the other hand, D's right to a fair trial. When weighing up these two competing interests, the courts have emphasised the importance of the seriousness of the offence at issue (usually marked by the severity of the maximum sentence), the relative ease of proof for one party or the other in relation to the element at issue, and the likely risk that the reverse burden creates of convicting innocent defendants.

However, the extent to which these considerations are capable of supplying adequate general guidance for future cases has rightly been doubted.[76] The assessments of proportionality in cases to date have been rather *ad hoc*, and it is worth observing that, in the main, reverse burdens have been upheld. It would be very much in the interests of justice and consistency if the House of Lords were to resort to more general principles when adjudicating upon reverse burdens. Indeed, it is submitted that the primary general principle should be that, for stigmatic crimes involving proof of culpability and a potential sentence of imprisonment, reverse probative burdens should *always* be reduced to evidential burdens.[77] Support for a more assertive approach to the presumption of innocence can be found in the important sentencing case of *Newton*[78] and its associated jurisprudence. At the sentencing stage, any disputed fact unfavourable to D must be proved beyond reasonable doubt. This fundamental principle of criminal justice is even more in point when the grounds of liability are contested at trial.

It would also be helpful if the European Court adopted this principle, a stance that would complement the strong line it has taken on matters of self-incrimination. In *Funke* v. *France*,[79] the Court ruled that answers obtained from D in relation to his tax affairs under statutory powers of compulsion could not be put before the judge at his subsequent

---

[73] See, in particular, the valuable discussion by Dennis, "Reverse Onuses and the Presumption of Innocence: In Search of Principle" [2005] *Crim LR* 901.

[74] As required by s. 3 of the HRA 1998; see above, § 2.5(i).

[75] HRA 1998, s. 4.

[76] By Ashworth, in the commentary on *Sheldrake* v. *DPP* [2005] Crim LR 218.

[77] Indeed, the distinct hostility to reverse burden provisions evinced in *Lambert* [2001] UKHL 37, [2002] 2 AC 545 supports such a general principle.

[78] (1982) 77 Cr App R 13.

[79] [1993] 1 CMLR 897.

criminal trial for tax evasion; a decision to the same effect was reached in *Saunders* v. *UK*,[80] in respect of answers obtained under compulsory powers of questioning allowed under companies legislation. These decisions sit uneasily beside the relaxed attitude exhibited by the Court to the reversal of burdens of proof. The protection against self-incrimination is rendered largely meaningless if there is a presumption of guilt, whereby the prosecution need not prove guilt at all and it falls to the defendant to demonstrate his innocence.

Another statutory incursion upon the principle that the defendant is not required to prove innocence is the enactment of sections 34–37 of the Criminal Justice and Public Order Act 1994, which permit the fact that a defendant was silent in the face of police questioning, or fails to testify at trial, to be used as evidence for the purpose of drawing adverse inferences of guilt. As Ashworth has remarked, "if there is to be a presumption that a person is innocent until proved guilty by the prosecution, there appears to be some inconsistency in holding that the defendant can through his or her silence supply an element in that case."[81] The practical effect of modifying a defendant's right to silence is partially to reallocate the burden of proof. For this and other reasons,[82] the provisions of the Criminal Justice and Public Order Act 1994 remain profoundly controversial.

(b) Statutory defences

The previous section contemplates statutory shifts in the burden of proof within *particular* offences. One situation where the burden of proof is *generally* reversed is in respect of any exonerating circumstances provided for by the statute creating the offence. Where the offence is a summary trial before a Magistrates' Court, section 101 of the Magistrates' Courts Act 1908 provides that the burden of proving any "exception, exemption, proviso, excuse or qualification" shall fall upon the defendant (as always in such cases, to the balance of probabilities[83]). It has now been held by the House of Lords in *Hunt*[84] that the same rule exists at common law, applicable to indictable offences as well as to summary proceedings.

The upshot of *Hunt* is that statutory defences must normally be proved by the defendant. By contrast, in common law defences (such as self-defence and duress) the defendant bears only an evidential burden, and the existence of the defence must then be negated beyond reasonable doubt by the prosecution.

The merits of this rule may be doubted. First, the concerns expressed in the last section, over imposing persuasive burdens on defendants, apply here also. Moreover, there is a further problem. One implication of the decision in *Hunt* is that it makes crucial the question whether the particular exonerating factor is an element of the statutory *offence*— which the prosecution must negate beyond reasonable doubt, in the normal way—or a supplementary *defence*, in which case the defendant bears the onus of proof. This distinction,

---

[80] (1997) 23 EHRR 313.

[81] *The Criminal Process: An Evaluative Study* (1994) 112. Cf. *Funcke, Cremieux and Miailhe* v. *France* [1993] 1 CMLR 897. See, e.g., Jackson, "Curtailing the Right to Silence: Lessons from Northern Ireland" [1991] *Crim LR* 404; Galligan, "The Right to Silence Reconsidered" [1988] *CLP* 69; Dennis, "The Criminal Justice and Public Order Act 1994: The Evidence Provisions" [1995] *Crim LR* 4, 9ff. In *Murray* v. *UK* (1996) 22 EHRR 29, however, the Court ruled that inferences drawn from the accused's refusal to give evidence were not in breach of Art. 6.

[82] E.g. the suspect's right to privacy and her privilege against self-incrimination.

[83] *Hunt* [1987] AC 352, 385.

[84] *Ibid.* See Smith, "The Presumption of Innocence" (1987) 38 *NILQ* 223.

between ingredients of offences and defences, is not always easy to draw. Suppose an (imaginary) statute were to be enacted prohibiting assaults, where "assault" were defined as "the application of force without consent or some other lawful excuse." Is the victim's absence of consent an ingredient of the offence definition, or is his consent a matter of defence? There is no easy answer, and the guidance available from the cases is limited[85]—so limited, indeed, that an Australian judge once remarked that "judges are inclined eventually to assert that a case falls on one side of the line or the other without really being able to assign reasons for their view."[86] Given the implications of the categorisation being made, this is a thoroughly unsatisfactory state of affairs.

(c) Insanity

A third exception is the defence of insanity. The common law makes a default presumption of sanity.[87] Once again, the defendant must prove this defence on the balance of probabilities—an incongruous anomaly, given that the defendant bears only an evidential burden in respect of other general defences; and that the consequence of proving insanity may be incarceration.[88] A similar rule applies to the statutory defence of diminished responsibility. Note, however, that the need for a defendant to show insanity or diminished responsibility arises only if the prosecution can prove the actus reus (and, in diminished responsibility, the mens rea) beyond reasonable doubt in the normal way.[89] Insanity is discussed in detail in § 19.1; diminished responsibility is considered in § 19.2.

(d) Strict liability

A most important exception is the subject of Chapter 6. In offences of strict liability, the prosecution has only to prove the actus reus, and there is no mens rea element to be proved. (Sometimes the defendant has the possibility of proving some alternative, statutory defence, to the balance of probabilities.) The European Court has decided,[90] and the Court of Appeal has agreed,[91] that strict liability offences, of which there are a multitude in the criminal law, are not prohibited by Article 6(2). Typically, the use of strict liability is regarded as a matter of substantive rather than procedural criminal law, even though (as we shall see) a standard rationale for imposing strict liability is convenience of proof for prosecutors. It is a false dichotomy. Strict liability has the capacity almost entirely to circumvent the values protected by the presumption of innocence.[92]

---

[85] See *Hunt* [1987] AC 352, 374 (Lord Griffiths); *Nimmo* v. *Alexander Cowan & Sons Ltd* [1968] AC 107, 135 (Lord Pearson). A useful discussion of this aspect of *Hunt* is Orchard, "The Golden Thread—Somewhat Frayed" (1988) 6 *Otago LR* 615, 624ff.

[86] *Francis* v. *Flood* [1978] 1 NSWLR 113, 119 (Sheppard J).

[87] Cf. the *M'Naghten* rules, 10 Cl & F 200, 210, 8 ER 718, 722; *Woolmington* v. *DPP* [1935] AC 462, 475.

[88] For excellent discussion, see Jones, "Insanity, Automatism, and the Burden of Proof on the Accused" (1995) 111 *LQR* 475.

[89] *A-G's Reference (No. 3 of 1998)* [1999] 3 All ER 40.

[90] *Salabiaku* v. *France* (1988) 13 EHRR 379.

[91] *G* [2006] EWCA Crim 821.

[92] For discussion of whether the presumption of innocence does have necessary implications for the imposition of strict liability see Sullivan, "Strict Liability for Criminal Offences in England and Wales following Incorporation into English Law of the European Convention on Human Rights" in Simester, (ed.), *Appraising Strict Liability* (2005) 195; Tadros and Tierney, "The Presumption of Innocence and the Human Rights Act" (2004) 67 *MLR* 404; Ashworth,

(ii) The "golden thread": somewhat frayed?[93]

At the time, the decision in *Woolmington* was delivered with great conviction and rhetorical effect. According to Viscount Sankey, the proposition that the burden of proof always falls upon the prosecution is "the one golden thread always to be seen throughout the web of the English criminal law."[94] It might be thought, therefore, that the presumption in Article 6(2) of the ECHR merely reflects a state of affairs that exists already in England and Wales.

The rhetoric is misleading. On many occasions, the presumption of innocence has been ruled compatible with imposing a burden of proof (to the balance of probabilities) on the defendant. We have seen, for example, that it is for a defendant to establish that he is insane or suffering from diminished responsibility. There are many examples of statutory provisions where burdens are placed on the defendant. And in *Hunt*,[95] the House of Lords confirmed that such a burden may be imposed, not only by express provision, but also by necessary implication. In an illuminating study, Ashworth and Blake have found that, in 40 per cent of offences triable before the Crown Court, a burden of proof on one or more issues was imposed on the defendant.[96] The authors discovered little that was systematic about the allocation of proof burdens; it tends to be happenstance, with similar proof issues allocated differently under different statutes.

Worse still, in the jurisprudence of the European Court, the presumption of innocence under Article 6(2) has been treated as compatible with the imposition of reverse burdens of proof, entailing only a degree of restraint in their deployment. To date, no ECHR challenge to a reverse burden has succeeded. As matters stand, therefore, it cannot be said that English practice with respect to the burden of proof, unsatisfactory though it is, contravenes ECHR standards.

Still, the situation is not hopeless. The clear iteration of a presumption of innocence in Article 6(2), combined with decisions such as *Lambert* and with the restrictive approach displayed by the ECHR to self-incrimination,[97] may yet prompt a better shielding of the presumption of innocence. It cannot be satisfactory, particularly for serious crimes, that D must prove facts crucial to the maintenance of her innocence. This objection is exacerbated by the unsystematic treatment, noted by Ashworth and Blake, of very similar exculpatory factors in different offences. Moreover, the random variation they describe is not just a matter of statutory stipulation. It is not uncommon, for example, for a defendant charged with murder to plead in the alternative the defences of provocation and diminished responsibility. As we shall see,[98] as the law stands it may be very difficult to determine whether particular evidence will give rise to one or other of these defences; it may be too that the evidence will satisfy the differing criteria for each of these defences. But as provocation, the evidence need only be suggestive of the defence: if it is, the prosecution (*à la Woolmington*)

"Four Threats to the Presumption of Innocence" (2006) 123 *SALJ* 62; and, *contra*, Roberts, "Strict Liability and the Presumption of Innocence: An Exposé of Functionalist Assumptions" in Simester, (ed.), *Appraising Strict Liability* (2005) 195.

[93] Orchard, "The Golden Thread—Somewhat Frayed" (1988) 6 *Otago LR* 615.

[94] See the quotation above, in the text at n. 43.

[95] Above, § 3.2(i)(b).

[96] "The Presumption of Innocence in English Criminal Law" [1996] *Crim LR* 306.

[97] Above, § 3.2(i)(a).

[98] Below, §§ 10.5, 19.2.

must negate the defence. Yet under the head of diminished responsibility, the defendant has the onus of establishing the defence. Not only is this confusing for juries dealing with the same evidence under different heads of defence: it is unsustainable as a matter of principle.

4

THE ACTUS REUS

In Chapter 1 we discussed some of the reasons why a person cannot and should not be guilty of a crime unless both (a) he has caused or is otherwise responsible for the external event prohibited by law—the actus reus—and (b) he had a specified mental state (falling within the requirements of the particular crime) with respect to that external event—the mens rea. If D kills V, she may have brought about the actus reus of murder, but it does not follow that she has committed any offence. When the doctor gives a painkiller to her patient, who turns out to be unknowably allergic to it, she may kill that patient: but it is an accident, and no criminal liability will follow. The mens rea is missing. Conversely, if she administers the drug intending it to kill him, and he dies of an unrelated heart attack, she does not murder him.[1] The actus reus is missing. In the next two chapters, we investigate the orthodox general principles of criminal law regarding these two elements. It is convenient to begin here with the actus reus.

For the purposes of identifying the constituent elements of an offence, it is conventional to identify the actus reus of a crime with that part of the definition which does not refer to the defendant's mental state.[2] The actus reus can usefully be divided into three types of ingredient: behaviour, consequences, and circumstances. Often the circumstances or consequences surrounding something the defendant does are relevant to her wrongdoing, and so the offence does not just turn on D's behaviour. It is an essential part of our concept of murder, for instance, that someone dies. Thus the victim's death—a consequence—is a constitutive part of the actus reus of murder. Such offences are sometimes called "result crimes",[3] because they cannot be committed unless the defendant's actions cause the specified result or consequence actually to occur.

An example of a crime requiring *circumstances* is bigamy, which involves D's going through a marriage ceremony (the behaviour) while being married to someone else (the circumstance). It is important to realise that, since specification of the actus reus of each offence differs, there is no requirement that all three types of ingredient be present in the actus reus of each offence. Hence the actus reus of murder—i.e. the killing of one person by another—requires that there be (i) some (unspecified) behaviour on the part of the defendant with (ii) the consequence that another person dies. By contrast, the actus reus of

---

[1] *White* [1910] 2 KB 124.

[2] This division of crimes into actus reus and mens rea elements is a helpful expository device but not an analytical necessity. Sometimes, moreover, it is not easy to divide a crime in this way. For instance, as we will see in § 5.6(ii), whether D is in "possession" of something may depend both on her physical conduct and on her understandings about that conduct.

[3] The term is from Gordon, *Criminal Law of Scotland* (2nd ed., 1978) 61.

rape is made out if there is (i) behaviour (sexual intercourse) by the defendant with the victim, in (ii) circumstances where the victim does not consent to it. No consequence is necessary.

§ 4.1 The behaviour element

Normally, the actus reus doctrine requires an action of some sort: something *done* by the defendant. This is not always obvious. It might sometimes appear as though result crimes such as murder could be specified solely by reference to the consequence, and without the actus reus containing any behavioural element. Thus it is the outcome which is emphasised in Kenny's definition of actus reus: "such result of human conduct as the law seeks to prevent."[4] And consider, for instance, the crime of murder. Surely it is the result, death, which is central to that crime? V's death is the harmful result that, as Kenny puts it, the law seeks to prevent. Without that death, murder is not and cannot be committed. The relevant harm has not occurred.

But the view that it is only the consequence or result that matters is not quite right. The law is not concerned with deaths *per se*, but rather with deaths that other people bring about. "A dead man with a knife in his back is not the *actus reus* of a murder. It is putting the knife in the back thereby causing the death which is the *actus reus*."[5] The result *is* important: it helps to mark out what type of wrongdoing the law is concerned with. Indeed, it is the nature of the result, rather than of the behaviour which causes it, that gives homicide its special moral and social significance. Murder is murder whether done by knife or poison, and this is why the behaviour element of the actus reus is unspecific. But it exists all the same.

On the other hand, it is possible for an actus reus to consist *only* of behaviour. This is especially true of inchoate crimes, such as incitement, where there is no requirement that the incitement be effective.[6] Crimes of this type are sometimes termed "conduct crimes", since the actus reus requires proof only of specified conduct by the defendant and does not specify any particular circumstances or consequences.

(i) Behaviour and omissions

Where behaviour is an element of the actus reus, standard legal doctrine stipulates that the behaviour requirement is a requirement of positive action by the defendant. Except occasionally, an omission will not do. Thus it is a crime for D deliberately to drown V, but no crime for D gleefully to stand on the beach and watch while his enemy, V, is caught in the tide and drowns nearby.[7]

---

[4] Turner, *Kenny's Outlines of Criminal Law* (19th ed., 1965) 17.
[5] *Smith and Hogan* 37.
[6] Below, Chapter 9.
[7] Cf. Stephen, *Digest of the Criminal Law* (4th ed., 1887) Art. 212. Other writing includes Hughes, "Criminal Omissions" (1958) 67 *Yale LJ* 590; Glazebrook, "Criminal Omissions: The Duty Requirement in Offences Against the Person" (1960) 76 *LQR* 386; Ashworth, "The Scope of Criminal Liability for Omissions" (1989) 105 *LQR* 424; Alexander, "Criminal Liability for Omissions: An Inventory of Issues" in Simester and Shute (eds.), *Criminal Law Theory: Doctrines of the General Part* (2000) 121.

This standard doctrine in fact comprises two rules. First, behaviour specified in an actus reus can prima facie be satisfied only by a positive act on the part of the defendant, and not by the defendant's omission. Secondly, there are certain exceptions to the first, prima facie rule. These exceptions usually arise when the defendant has a *duty* to intervene and prevent the prohibited harm from occurring, whereupon his failure to do so counts as an omission satisfying the behavioural element of that actus reus. The first rule is general in nature: the exceptions, and the duties on which they are based, are specific and confined.

In the above approach the criminal law resembles the civil law, which is generally averse to imposing liability for omissions,[8] and is willing to do so only in special cases where the reasons in favour are strong enough to override that aversion. The distinction between misfeasance and non-feasance is, as Fleming has said, "deeply rooted in the common law."[9] Civil law duties to intervene are dependent upon, for example, the defendant's having created the risk[10] or in some other way having assumed responsibility for it.[11] Similarly, an omission to reject a contractual offer cannot constitute its acceptance.[12] Silence is no representation in the tort of deceit;[13] neither is it *per se* a misrepresentation when negotiating a contract.[14]

(a) Why omissions are special

One might, of course, accept that the law often does distinguish between acts and omissions, but still ask why that distinction *should* make any practical difference to criminal liability. There are various reasons. One is based upon considerations of autonomy. We value living in a society where citizens are respected as individuals—where they are free to live their own lives and pursue their own priorities without having their choices determined by legal duties to act or intervene. The prohibition of omissions is far more intrusive upon individuals' autonomy and freedom than is the prohibition of acts, which is why the systematic imposition of (criminal or civil) liability for failures to act is to be resisted.[15]

---

[8] Per Lord Keith in *Yuen Kun-Yeu* v. *A-G of Hong Kong* [1988] AC 175, 192, there is no liability in negligence "on the part of one who sees another about to walk over a cliff with his head in the air, and forbears to shout a warning." Cf. *Ancell* v. *McDermott* [1993] 4 All ER 355; *Alexandrou* v. *Oxford* [1993] 4 All ER 328; *Hill* v. *Chief Constable of West Yorkshire* [1989] AC 53; *Curran* v. *Northern Ireland Housing Association Ltd* [1987] AC 718; *East Suffolk Catchment Board* v. *Kent* [1941] AC 74; *Gautret* v. *Egerton* (1867) LR 2 CP 371, 375. According to Salmond and Heuston, *The Law of Torts* (20th ed., 1992) 224, "in the absence of some existing duty the general principle is that there is no liability for a mere omission to act."

[9] *The Law of Torts* (8th ed., 1992) 146.

[10] *Johnson* v. *Rea* [1961] 1 WLR 1400.

[11] E.g. *Dorset Yacht Co* v. *Home Office* [1970] AC 1004; *Barnett* v. *Chelsea and Kensington Hospital Management Committee* [1969] 1 QB 428.

[12] *Felthouse* v. *Bindley* (1862) 11 CB (NS) 869, 142 ER 1037; cf. *The Leonidas* [1985] 2 All ER 796; *The Santa Clara* [1995] 3 All ER 971.

[13] *Peek* v. *Gurney* (1873) LR 6 HL 377, 392, 403; *Arkwright* v. *Newbold* (1881) 17 Ch D 301, 318; *Banque Keyser Ullman* v. *Skandia* [1990] 1 QB 665.

[14] *Fox* v. *Mackreth* (1788) 2 Cox Eq Cas 320, 321; *Keates* v. *Lord Cadogan* (1851) 10 CB 591, 138 ER 234; *Bell* v. *Lever Bros Ltd* [1932] AC 161, 227.

[15] See, very generally, Simester, "Why Omissions Are Special" (1995) 1 *Legal Theory* 311; also the earlier discussion in §§ 1.2(i)(b), 1.2(ii)(e). There is philosophical controversy whether the act–omission distinction, of and by itself, is morally significant. Nonetheless, it is worth observing that acts usually manifest a greater level of hostility than do omissions, and we tend to feel very differently about killers than about non-savers. Omissions are often incidental to the defendant's practical deliberations—they disclose a different and lesser fault, of limited imagination or empathy, rather than malice.

This is not to suggest that there should never be liability for omissions. Those writers who advocate a criminal law duty of easy rescue, for example, have at least an arguable case.[16] Rather, the present argument is that liability for omissions should be exceptional, and not as widespread as liability for actions. At any moment in time, the number of positive actions we are doing is very small. But the number of things we are failing to do is enormous. This is because there are very few ways in which one can do an action, whereas the number of ways in which one can fail to do something is much greater. For example, while D is not saving the drowning swimmer she may be walking, reading a book, swimming herself, playing cricket, etc. But she cannot do any of these things while she *is* saving the swimmer. The burden the law imposes when it prohibits a person from doing something is therefore lighter and less intrusive than when it orders that person to act. Enforced forbearance involves the sacrifice of fewer options, and is more likely to leave the defendant with a chance of conforming to law without significant derangement. "Compare being banished to Liechtenstein with being banished from Liechtenstein."[17] Or, in a more apposite example, compare being prohibited from drowning the other swimmers when sunbathing at a beach to being required to save (or, indeed, drown) them. Wholesale liability for omissions would force us constantly to interrupt our own actions and plans in order to prevent outcomes that are brought about by others: to become, in effect, our brothers' keepers. It would be incompatible with a country's ambition to be a liberal State.

A second consideration is that if prohibited omissions involve the sacrifice of more options, then they are also likely to require a greater sacrifice of our own interests. If D buys a piece of furniture for his home, why is he not held responsible for the lives that money would save in, say, Ethiopia? One factor is our widespread acceptance that people are to some extent entitled to prefer their own interests, and the interests of those near to them, above the interests of others. A mother who gives her own child pocket-money warrants no reproof when she does not do the same for the child next door. Of course, such a view may be no more than a moral mistake. But if so, it is an inescapable feature of our society, and the law must bow to its almost universal acceptance. Moreover, given that individuals exist in different and specific situations, they are typically better placed to assess and contribute to their own lives, and to the lives of those they know, than to the lives of strangers. These points help to explain examples where someone does not save starving children in foreign countries: they limit the extent to which the needs of strangers take precedence over and mandate the sacrifice of our own plans and interests. We cannot do everything, and it would be absurd to expect us to try. When we make decisions, we are entitled to acknowledge that our own lives, and the lives of people we are close to, are important to us. So, even apart from questions of autonomy, the law's presumption against penalising omissions can be justified as a simple and workable means by which the law can recognise the priority individuals are entitled to accord the content of their own lives.

---

[16] See, e.g., Ashworth, "The Scope of Criminal Liability for Omissions" (1989) 105 *LQR* 424; Hughes, "Criminal Omissions" (1958) 67 *Yale LJ* 590.

[17] Bennett, "Morality and Consequences" in McMurrin (ed.), *The Tanner Lectures in Human Values* (1981) 47, 78; cf. Bennett, *The Act Itself* (1995) 92. A similar principle applies in the context of false imprisonment: *Bird* v. *Jones* (1845) 7 QB 742.

(b) The exceptions

Case 1: Specific statutory and common law offences.
Many statutes now contain offences which expressly impose liability for an omission. Often these are offences which can *only* be committed by omission, such as failing to provide a breath specimen,[18] or failing to file an annual return as required by the Companies Act 1985. Similarly, section 1(2)(a) of the Children and Young Persons Act 1933 requires persons to supply legally dependent children with adequate food, clothing, medical aid, and lodging; an offence is committed when D fails to discharge that duty. The common law also knows some, though very few, offences specifically of omission. Perhaps the most significant of these is the refusal to assist a police officer when called upon to aid in restoring the peace.[19]

The above offences involve specific reference to a behavioural element on the part of the defendant. A second variety of statutory crime which can be done, indirectly, by omission is that where the actus reus names no behavioural element at all, and requires only proof of certain events or circumstances. (This type of offence is discussed below, in § 4.1(b).) Characteristically, offences of the latter sort are an indirect imposition of liability for D's omission to prevent the specified event or outcome occurring. Of course, in these cases liability will also lie for bringing the outcome about by a positive act. But no such act is *required*.

Case 2: Duties imposed on persons in a special relationship to the victim.
Sometimes, even without a specific offence, the law holds that considerations such as autonomy and self-interest are outweighed. This occurs when the defendant is found to be under a more general legal duty, such as the duty of parents to their children. A stranger can stand by and watch a child starve or drown. But that child's parent cannot.

The law does not normally require us to be guardians of the interests of others. But parents already *are* the guardians of their children, and are responsible for their welfare. The law does no more than reflect that by imposing a legal duty upon parents to intervene on behalf of their children. To some extent these duties now have parallels in statute: we noted in the last section that the Children and Young Persons Act 1933 requires legally dependent children to be supplied with adequate food and other necessaries. However, that Act merely creates a particular and confined offence. The common law duties of parents are wider ranging than this, and prima facie apply to any offence (unless excluded: below, § 4.1(i)(c)). Thus a parent's failure to effect an easy rescue of her child would count as the actus reus of murder even though it is scarcely a failure to supply necessaries.[20] And more generally, it is submitted that a parent who willingly permits another to assault his child (when he can prevent this happening) is himself guilty of an assault.[21]

---

[18] Contrary to s. 6 of the Road Traffic Act 1988. Cf. *Raymond Parry* v. *Department for Work and Pensions* [2005] EWHC 1486 (Admin) (failing to disclose employment when in receipt of an incapacity benefit).

[19] *Brown* (1841) Car & M 314, 174 ER 522; Nicholson, "The Citizen's Duty to Assist the Police" [1992] *Crim LR* 611. It is also a common law offence of misconduct in a public office for a police constable to refuse to perform his duty to preserve the Queen's peace: *Dytham* [1979] QB 722.

[20] *Handley* (1874) 13 Cox CC 79; *White* (1871) 12 Cox CC 83, 86 (Blackburn J).

[21] Cf. *Emery* (1993) 14 Cr App R (S) 394 (cruelty); *Russell* [1933] VLR 59 (manslaughter); *Commonwealth* v. *Howard* 402 A 2d 674 (1979) (manslaughter). See also the discussion below, § 4.1(i)(c).

So a parent has a duty to rescue his child from harm. But is this so if the child is 30? Where the child is no longer dependent upon her parents, a special relationship still exists between them, but it no longer involves the same commitment to responsibility for the child's welfare.[22] The latter is surely the more important feature. In the old cases governing the relationship of master to apprentice, the duty of care is said to arise from the master's assumption of responsibility and the apprentice's dependence, so that it was necessary to allege the apprentice was of tender years: "[t]here is a clear distinction between treatment of this sort to a child and to an adult."[23] Similarly, it is submitted, parents do not ordinarily owe legal duties to rescue their adult children.[24] Neither do children owe such duties to their parents. This is not to deny that people have moral obligations to their relatives. But it is quite a different matter to hold them criminally liable for failing to discharge those obligations.

The view that, rather than the closeness of their emotional or other relationship, it is D's responsibility for V's welfare that is the decisive feature is consistent with the case law regarding legal duties owed toward someone who is in the defendant's care. In *Stone and Dobinson*,[25] S and his mistress D (both somewhat backward) were held to have assumed responsibility for the care of S's sister, who died from a combination of anorexia nervosa and their incompetent neglect. *Both* were convicted of manslaughter, irrespective of the fact that only S was related to V.[26]

Also consistent is *Smith*,[27] in which the Court of Appeal assumed that the institution of marriage does not itself generate a duty of care between spouses, although an assumption of responsibility for the welfare of one's spouse or partner will readily be inferred.[28] If this is right,[29] the Australian decision of *Russell* would not be followed here: R's wife had drowned herself and their sons while R was present, whereupon R was convicted of the manslaughter not only of the sons but also of the wife.[30] By implication, a mutual obligation to protect would not extend to the partners in a merely casual sexual relationship.[31]

---

[22] Compare s. 1 of the Children and Young Persons Act 1933, the application of which terminates when the child reaches the age of 16 years.

[23] *Ridley* (1811) 2 Camp 650, 652, 170 ER 1282, 1283; *Friend* (1802) Russ & Ry 20, 168 ER 662. See also *Charlotte Smith* (1865) 10 Cox CC 82 (servant).

[24] *Smith* (1826) 2 C & P 449, 172 ER 203; *Shepherd* (1862) 9 Cox CC 123; *contra Chattaway* (1922) 17 Cr App R 7.

[25] [1977] QB 354. Arguably, the Court's finding of an assumed responsibility was doubtful on the facts; see Ashworth, "The Scope of Criminal Liability for Omissions" (1989) 105 *LQR* 424, 443. The case is also unsatisfactory on questions of causation (did the neglect make any difference?) and of gross negligence (given the couple's intellectual limitations—compare the discussion of *Elliott* v. *C* [1983] 2 All ER 1005, below, § 5.5(ii)).

[26] Cf. *R.* v. *West London Coroner, ex p. Gray* [1987] 2 All ER 129; *Condé* (1867) 10 Cox 547; *Instan* [1893] 1 QB 450; *Marriott* (1838) 8 C & P 425, 173 ER 559; *Nicholls* (1874) 13 Cox CC 75; *Bubb* (1841) 4 Cox CC 455. See Williams, "Criminal Omissions—The Conventional View" (1991) 107 *LQR* 86, 90. A valuable and wide-ranging discussion may be found in the Australian case of *Taktak* (1988) 14 NSWLR 226.

[27] [1979] Crim LR 251. This decision throws doubt on the assertion made by Horder and McGowan, "Manslaughter by Causing Another's Suicide" [2006] *Crim LR* 1035, 1044, that "[t]here is no doubt that a duty of care exists between spouses." The authors cite the case of *Hood* [2003] EWCA Crim 2772, which in our view illustrates that an assumption of a duty of care between spouses will be readily inferred but not that a duty of care arises from marital status *per se*.

[28] E.g. where D is the sole carer for his disabled wife, as in *Hood* [2003] EWCA Crim 2772, [2004] 1 Cr App R (S) 73.

[29] *Contra Plummer* (1844) 1 C & K 600, 174 ER 954 (estranged spouse).

[30] [1933] VLR 59 (McArthur J dissenting).

[31] Cf. *People* v. *Beardsley* 113 NW 1128 (1907); discussed by Hughes, "Criminal Omissions" (1958) 67 *Yale LJ* 590, 624. See also *Lewis* v. *CPS* [2002] EWHC Crim 1049, where the Court upheld a refusal to prosecute after D left his intoxicated friend asleep in an unlocked car during a very hot day, with the result that the friend died.

Case 3: Duties imposed on persons assuming a particular responsibility.
The cases discussed so far have been concerned with duties arising from a wide-ranging and unspecific responsibility for another's welfare. Such duties tend to be general in nature, with the result that the criminal law treats omissions like actions for most purposes. A more complex relationship is that between a doctor and her patient.[32] This duty is a confined one—a doctor on her way home may drive past the scene of an accident without attracting criminal liability for doing so. The duty applies only to the patients in her care. In such cases, injury resulting from the doctor's failure to provide proper care is regarded by the criminal law just as if it were brought about by an act of improper treatment.

Even to her patients, however, the doctor's duty is not all-encompassing. She may not kill by positive act, but it appears that she may withdraw care, with judicial approval, from a patient in a persistent vegetative state.[33] The duty is not to keep the patient alive, but to make reasonable efforts to do so, consonant with proper medical practice,[34] and only in so far as doing so is in the patient's best interests.[35]

Another source of specific criminal law duties is civil law obligations. The classic case is *Pittwood*.[36] D had been employed by a railway company to keep the gate at a level crossing. He went to lunch forgetting to close the gate. A haycart subsequently entered the crossing and was struck by a train. D was convicted of manslaughter. It is not clear whether D's duty depended upon his having been hired to discharge a duty to the public that was owed by his employers,[37] or was grounded on the fact that he was hired to protect other people and that they were likely to be injured by his dereliction. The latter seems to have been the rationale adopted by Wright J,[38] but there is reason to support the former view. Consider a hypothetical case in which D, a nurse, has signed a contract that contains a term requiring her to intervene and save people at large—that is, even when off duty and away from the hospital. In such a case, D's failure to rescue someone when at the beach may be a breach of contract, but surely would not be a criminal offence.

Case 4: The continuing act doctrine.
Sometimes a defendant brings about an actus reus without mens rea but then, while the harmful consequences continue, intentionally omits to remedy or discontinue them. In such

---

[32] For another example of role-based responsibility, see *Curtis* (1885) 15 Cox CC 746 (duty of a local authority officer to provide medical assistance to a destitute person).

[33] *Airedale NHS Trust* v. *Bland* [1993] AC 789. See also the note by Finnis, "*Bland*: Crossing the Rubicon?" (1993) 109 *LQR* 329.

[34] Cf. *TBCL* 236.

[35] *Airedale NHS Trust* v. *Bland* [1993] AC 789, 868–9 (Lord Goff); *R (Burke)* v. *GMC* [2004] EWHC 1879 (Admin). See also the difficult cases involving the degree of care owed by doctors to handicapped neonates: *Arthur* (1981) 12 B Med LR 1; *Re B* (1981) [1990] 3 All ER 927; *Re F* [1990] 2 AC 1.

[36] (1902) 19 TLR 37. See also *Hughes* (1857) Dears & B 248, 169 ER 996; approved in *Roberts* [1942] 1 All ER 187, 192; *Kelly* v. *The King* [1923] VLR 704, 708 (reversed on a different ground in 32 CLR 509).

[37] Compare *Smith* (1869) 11 Cox CC 210, where a watchman who deserted his post was held not liable for manslaughter because his employer has no duty to provide a watchman; also *Singh (Gurphal)* [1999] Crim LR 582 where D, who was in charge of a lodging house while the landlord was away, was held to owe a duty of care to the tenant such that both D and the landlord were guilty of manslaughter when a faulty gas fire caused the tenant's death by carbon monoxide poisoning. The decision in *Smith* is criticised by J.W.C. Turner in Kenny's *Outlines of Criminal Law* (17th ed., 1958) 169.

[38] "The man was paid to keep the gate shut and protect the public. . . . A man might incur criminal liability from a duty arising out of contract": (1902) 19 TLR 37, 38.

cases the "continuing act" doctrine may be applied, and liability imposed without the need to find a legal duty owed by the defendant.[39] In *Fagan* v. *Metropolitan Police Commissioner*,[40] F accidentally drove onto a policeman's foot. When apprised of his action, he refused to move the car. He was convicted of assault on the basis that his refusal to remove the vehicle amounted to a continuation of the original (positive) act of battery,[41] and was not a mere omission. Hence it could satisfy the actus reus requirement.

A similar case is *Kaitamaki*.[42] D had sexual intercourse with V without her consent. D's evidence was that he became aware V was not consenting only after penetration had occurred. However, he did not then withdraw from intercourse. The trial judge directed the jury that "if, having realised she is not willing, he continues with the act of intercourse, it then becomes rape." On appeal, the correctness of the direction was affirmed by the Privy Council.

Case 5: Duties imposed on persons with a special relationship to the harm.
In *Miller*,[43] a vagrant set fire to his mattress with a cigarette while sleeping. He awoke to find the mattress smouldering. Without taking any steps to extinguish the fire, he simply moved to the next room and went to sleep. The house itself caught fire, and he was charged with arson. Although the Court of Appeal upheld his conviction on the basis of a continuing act, the House of Lords took a different approach. It acknowledged that the arson had been committed by M's knowing omission to deal with the fire, and held that this omission could satisfy the actus reus requirement because M's unintentional starting of the fire *created* a legal duty. The duty is "to take measures that lie within one's power to counteract a danger that one has oneself created."[44] The relevant sorts of "danger" are those which threaten an interest protected by the criminal law—thus the duty arises where, unless D intervenes, his earlier (positive) act will bring about the prohibited harm.

Note that a defendant's subsequent failure to prevent the risk will not by itself constitute an offence—it must be accompanied by such other elements of the offence as are required, e.g. mens rea.

It is important to distinguish the basis of liability in *Miller* from the continuing act doctrine (above). The approach taken in *Miller* is generally to be preferred, and indeed *Fagan* can itself be explained as a case where D created the harm and therefore had a duty to counteract that harm.[45] Nonetheless, it is sometimes necessary to rely on the continuing act doctrine. Because *Miller* imposes liability for an omission, it is inapplicable to those offences that cannot be committed by omission, i.e. where the terms of the offence exclude liability for omissions. Offences of this type are the subject of the next section.

---

[39] Compare, in contract, the law governing a representation which later becomes false but where the change of circumstances is not disclosed: *With* v. *O'Flanagan* [1936] Ch 575 ("continuing representation").

[40] [1969] 1 QB 438.

[41] Which had not itself been an assault because F lacked mens rea at that time.

[42] [1985] AC 147. See also *Cooper and Schaub* [1994] Crim LR 531.

[43] [1983] 2 AC 161; see J.C. Smith [1982] *Crim LR* 526; Williams [1982] *Crim LR* 773. Compare also *Santana Bermudez* [2004] Crim LR 471. For an extension of this type of case see *Speck* [1977] 2 All ER 859, in which D was convicted of gross indecency because he passively allowed an 8-year-old girl to touch him indecently.

[44] [1983] 2 AC 161, 176.

[45] Where necessary, however, the two cases can be distinguished, since (unlike *Miller*) in *Fagan* the actus reus had already occurred by the time D acquired *mens rea*.

(c) Statutory restrictions: offences that cannot be committed by omission

Some offences exclude liability for omissions by specifying the particular type of behaviour that is required. For example, section 32 of the OAPA 1861 makes it an offence (*inter alia*) to "put or throw" objects onto a railway. It would seem that this manner of behaving can only be done by a positive act. Similarly, the actus reus of rape requires active sexual intercourse with, including penetration of, the victim; an omission cannot suffice.[46]

In these offences, liability for omissions is restricted because the behavioural element of the actus reus has been specified quite precisely by statute. Conversely, omission-based liability should normally be possible where an offence has an unspecific behaviour element, and its actus reus is defined mainly by reference to consequences or circumstances. An example of this is murder, for which, in essence, the actus reus requires the causing of one person's death by another.[47]

Homicide is a clear case. It is settled law that culpable homicide can be committed by omission.[48] But what about other offences? An assault by battery, for example, requires *inter alia* the unlawful application of force to another person.[49] Can this be done by omission? Consider the following example proposed by Smith and Hogan:[50]

"It is generally said that D must have done some act and that it is not enough that he stood still and obstructed V's passage like an inanimate object. But suppose D is sitting at the corner of a corridor with his legs stretched across it. He hears V running down the corridor and deliberately remains still with the intention that V, on turning the corner, shall fall over his legs. Why should this not be a battery? It would be if D had put out his legs with the intention of tripping up V."

Glanville Williams, however, was doubtful. In his view, the example put by Smith and Hogan:[51]

"is a case of special type. The man presumably committed an act when he put his foot there in the first place, though initially it was without wrongful intent. When he later failed to remove his foot, with the requisite mental element, he became guilty of an assault under the rule [in *Miller*[52]]."

According to Williams, assault cannot be committed by a pure omission:[53]

"if a person merely stands stock still, being 'entirely passive like a door or a wall' as it was put in one case, it is not an assault, however inconvenient his presence at that particular spot may have been. . . ."

With respect to Williams, the example cannot be analysed as a *Miller*-type situation, unless P was already running down the corridor when D (without mens rea) stretched out his legs.

---

[46] Sections 1, 44 Sexual Offences Act 1956. See also the offence of throwing missiles, contrary to the Football (Offences) Act 1991, s. 2.

[47] Cf. *Dyson* [1908] 2 KB 454, 457; below, Chapter 10.

[48] Cf. *Gibbins and Proctor* (1918) 13 Cr App R 134.

[49] Below, Chapter 11.

[50] *Smith and Hogan* 522.

[51] "What Should the Code Do about Omissions?" (1987) 7 *LS* 92, 116.

[52] See above, § 4.1(i)(b) (Case 5).

[53] *TBCL*, 179; citing *Innes v. Wylie* (1844) 1 C & K 257, 263, 174 ER 800, 803 (Lord Denman CJ).

The case proposed by Smith and Hogan should not normally be a battery. However, this is not, *contra* Williams, because assault cannot be committed by omission. Rather, it is for the reasons given earlier, in § 4.1(i): that a stranger generally does not owe duties to act. By contrast, consider a case where the duty *is* owed. It seems implausible to say that a parent who intentionally trips his child in the way Smith and Hogan describe cannot be convicted of assault. He certainly ought to be. It is submitted that where an offence is unspecific as to the manner of behaviour required, it should be possible to commit that offence by omission. The fact that an offence is defined in terms of "action", as such, should not be determinative.[54] This is especially since positive action is the default requirement of offences with a behavioural element anyway—the entire sphere of omissions liability is predicated on an exception from that requirement.

Sometimes, as we have seen, the action requirement *is* excluded by linguistic considerations. It would be unfair to convict a defendant for conduct the statutory language clearly excludes.[55] But such instances are and should be rare. There is no judicial compunction about saying that a parent can kill a child by failing to feed it, however odd that may sound,[56] and it is submitted that linguistic conventions unreflective of valid moral principles or distinctions should normally not pre-empt the possibility of liability for omissions.

If such harms as "killing", "obstructing",[57] "harassing",[58] cheating,[59] and "falsely imprisoning"[60] can be done by omission, and if the difference between various offences over whether one can be convicted for an omission is not to be arbitrary and piecemeal, then a coherent general approach should be taken. Unless the legislature has demonstrated a contrary intention by specifying the particular manner of behaviour in which the offence must be committed, a criminal offence should be capable of being committed by omission. This is the only approach capable of producing predictable and consistent rather than random law. Any concern over the width of that approach should be tempered by the knowledge that the defendant would have to be under a legal duty to act, and that mens rea would still have to be proved.[61]

As was noted in the previous section, even if omission-based liability is excluded by the terms of the offence, a conviction may still be obtained under the continuing act doctrine (above). Suppose that D and V are having consensual sexual intercourse, and that sexual connection has already occurred. During intercourse, V withdraws her consent. D, however, remains in a state of sexual connection with V. His failure to withdraw is a continuation of

---

[54] As it was in *Ahmad* (1986) 84 Cr App R 64; contrast *Speck* [1977] 2 All ER 859.

[55] See the fair warning discussion in § 2.3. For this reason, Williams argues in a letter to the editor of the *Criminal Law Review* that "the courts should not create liability for omissions without statutory authority. Verbs used in defining offences and prima facie implying active conduct should not be stretched by interpretation to include omissions": [1982] *Crim LR* 773. See also his "Criminal Omissions—The Conventional View" (1991) 107 *LQR* 86, 87–9; "What should the Code do about Omissions?" (1987) 7 *LS* 92, 94–5.

[56] And for other examples, see *Shama* [1990] 2 All ER 602; *Firth* (1990) 91 Cr App R 217.

[57] *Stunt* v. *Bolton* [1972] RTR 435; *Gully* v. *Smith* (1883) 12 QBD 121.

[58] *Yuthiwattana* (1984) 80 Cr App R 55.

[59] *Mavji* [1987] 2 All ER 758; *Tonner* [1985] 1 All ER 807.

[60] *TBCL* 179; *Smith and Hogan* 571.

[61] The requirement for mens rea, in particular, seems to meet Williams's concern that "it would be unfair to describe a slack and ineffective tenant who lets the premises burn as an arsonist": *TBCL* 152.

the original act of having sexual intercourse with V. Since it is no longer consensual, he commits the actus reus of rape.[62]

(d) Omissions and consequences: causation

One problem that arises for omissions is whether or not they can be said to "cause" things. Characteristically, what is significant about omissions is that they fail to prevent *other* factors from bringing about the harm. If D watches from the beach while V drowns, a post mortem will conclude that V's death was caused by his sojourn underwater. D merely failed to intervene: can she truly be said to have caused V's death? We shall consider this question more fully in § 4.2(iv), when we discuss causation. But it is clear that in the law omissions can be causes—or perhaps one should say, causal factors. If D could have saved V, then her failure to do so was *a* reason why V drowned. And if D had a legal duty to save her, then that failure will be a cause of death in law.

(e) Distinguishing acts from omissions

Given that, as we have seen, there is normally no liability for omissions, it is important to be able to distinguish acts from omissions in order to decide whether a defendant's behaviour counts as one or the other. Unfortunately, the line between them is not easily drawn:[63]

> "If a doctor is keeping a patient alive by cranking the handle of a machine and he stops, this looks like a clear case of omission. So too if the machine is electrically operated but switches itself off every 24 hours and the doctor deliberately does not re-start it. Switching off a functioning machine looks like an act; but is it any different in substance from the first two cases? On the other hand, is it any different from cutting the high-wire on which a tight-rope walker is balancing?—which is an act, if ever there was one. Is the ending of a programme of dialysis an omission, while switching off a ventilator is an act? Is the discontinuance of a drip feed, which is keeping a patient alive, by withdrawing the tube from his body an act and failure to replace an emptied bag an omission? It seems offensive if liability for homicide depends on distinctions of this kind; but it appears to be so."

Why is switching off a ventilator an act, and failing to (re)start it an omission? The difference seems to be that the former *requires* certain bodily movements, whereas the latter does not. Switching the ventilator off can be done in only one way,[64] but failing to switch the ventilator on (or off) can be done while doing any number of things—one might be talking to the nurse, reading a journal, taking a walk, booking dinner at a restaurant, etc. Similarly, cranking the handle of a machine and cutting the high-wire are actions because they require very specific behaviour by D: "not cranking the handle" and "not replacing the emptied bag" are not specific about D's behaviour at all.

As we saw earlier, this difference is an important facet of the rationale for separating omissions from acts when it comes to criminalisation. Prohibiting omissions rules out many more options than does prohibiting acts. If D is enjoined by law not to strike V, that leaves

---

[62] *Kaitamaki* [1985] AC 147; *Cooper and Schaub* [1994] Crim LR 531. These decisions are now entrenched in legislation by s. 79(2) of the Sexual Offences Act 2003.

[63] *Smith and Hogan* 86–7. See, in respect of the examples, Williams, *TBCL* 236–7; Kennedy, "Switching Off Life Support Machines: The Legal Implications" [1977] *Crim LR* 443; Beynon, "Doctors as Murderers" [1982] *Crim LR* 17.

[64] Or, at most, in only a few ways.

him with plenty of freedom for legal movement of his arm, not to mention the rest of his body. But if D is *required* to strike V (i.e. prohibited from omitting to do so) then his freedom of movement is severely curtailed. His options are down to one.

The difference is legally irrelevant, however, where the defendant is held responsible for the actus reus through the existence of a legal duty. With this in mind, we should reconsider Smith and Hogan's remark that "it seems offensive if liability for homicide depends on distinctions of this kind; but it appears to be so." The obvious response is that liability does not *just* depend on the act/omission distinction, but also on the issue in each case whether D is under a duty to intervene. What the examples do suggest, though, is that one might be doubtful of the judicial reasoning in life-and-death medical cases. In *Airedale NHS Trust* v. *Bland*,[65] B had been in a persistent vegetative state for 3 1/2 years without medical hope of improvement. Having obtained parental consent, the hospital applied for a declaration that it would be lawful to discontinue artificial feeding and hydration, with the intention that B should be allowed to die. The House of Lords upheld the declaration. Their Lordships affirmed that for the doctors to bring about B's death by lethal injection or suchlike would be murder, but reasoned that (i) what was proposed was an omission rather than an act, and (ii) the legal duty of the doctors did not extend to prolonging treatment of a patient when it was no longer in his best interests to do so.[66]

The difficulty with this reasoning is that ceasing treatment normally involves switching off a ventilator or other life-support machine. Notwithstanding that the House of Lords explicitly countenanced this step,[67] it is an act, not an omission. An intruder who does such a thing commits murder, even though she has no legal duty to save the patient's life. The true explanation of these cases must surely be that there is a limited justification available to doctors, in certain circumstances, to take some quite specific measures toward ending life. Those measures can include particular acts as well as omissions; although the permissible scope of such measures remains, of course, a matter of intense and shifting ethical debate.[68]

(ii) Crimes with no (explicit) behaviour element

Some academic writers have suggested that there can be no criminal liability without a "voluntary act" on the part of the defendant; meaning by this that there must be (i) a behavioural element specified in every actus reus, which (ii) must be done "voluntarily" by the defendant.[69] For the most part, the second aspect of this suggestion seems right (see below, § 4.3). The first claim, however, is less plausible.

---

[65] [1993] AC 789. See Keown, "Restoring Moral and Intellectual Shape to the Law after *Bland*" (1997) 113 *LQR* 481.

[66] [1993] AC 789, 868–9 (Lord Goff). Compare *Re A (Children)* [2001] Fam 147, where surgical intervention was ruled to be a positive act.

[67] [1993] AC 789, 866 (Lord Goff), 881–2 (Lord Browne-Wilkinson).

[68] Contrast the decisions in *R (on the application of Pretty)* [2001] UKHL 61, [2002] 1 AC 800 and *Re B* [2002] EWHC 429, [2002] 2 All ER 449.

[69] E.g. Stephen, *A History of the Criminal Law of England* (1883) vol. II, 97; Cross and Jones, *An Introduction to Criminal Law* (3rd ed., 1953) 32; Turner, *Kenny's Outlines of Criminal Law* (17th ed., 1958) 26 7; O'Connor and Fairall, *Criminal Defences* (2nd ed., 1988) 2, 6–7; Moore, *Act and Crime* (1993) chap. 2. The claim made is normally, in fact, even stronger: that there must be a positive (and voluntary) act by the defendant specified in every actus reus. The phrasing in the text is designed to allow for omissions.

It is certainly true that crimes such as murder, rape, and assault—with which ordinary citizens are most familiar, and which have the greatest moral resonance—are crimes which require wrong*doing*, and necessarily involve some behaviour (whether act or omission) by the defendant. But many other crimes stipulate no behavioural element on the part of the defendant. These are offences which penalise a defendant on the basis of the situation in which she finds herself. It is the circumstances themselves which make up the harm that the criminal law is designed to address, and so it is possible to specify the actus reus of these crimes solely by reference to those circumstances.

For convenience, we can divide offences of this sort into two main types: crimes where the actus reus specifies only the occurrence of some state of affairs; and crimes of possession.

(a) Crimes involving states of affairs

Sometimes known as crimes of "situational liability",[70] these are crimes where the actus reus is simply an event or circumstance that is in some way connected to the defendant. An example is provided by section 3(1) of the Prevention of Oil Pollution Act 1971:

> If any oil to which section 1 of this Act applies, or any mixture containing such oil, is discharged into any part of the sea (a) from a pipe-line . . . then, subject to the following provisions of this Act, the owner of the pipe-line . . . shall be guilty of an offence. . . .

Here the actus reus of the offence is apparently complete without the need to prove any act or omission on the part of the defendant.[71]

Of course, it is not enough for a defendant to be criminally liable for an offence just because something bad happens—e.g. because a pipe-line leaks oil into the sea. The defendant must in some way be connected to, and responsible for, the actus reus. Normally this connection is through his having a particular status, or relationship, with respect to that actus reus. If a pipe-line discharges oil, it is the pipe-line's *owner* who is picked out for attention by the criminal law, and not, for instance, every person living or sailing nearby. Situational offences are in this respect similar to offences of omission, in that they raise the problem of attribution to defendants, discussed earlier (§ 1.2(ii)(e)). The potential for over-broad criminalisation means that there is a need on the part of the legislator to contain liability by specifying only defendants who are responsible for, and in a position to control, the prohibited situation.

The requirement for a particular status or relationship is typically found in another type of situational liability, being the vicarious criminal liability sometimes imposed on employers for the acts of their employees. Vicarious liability is dealt with further in Chapter 8.[72] A third form of connection may be seen in the notorious case of *Larsonneur*.[73] In that case, L was convicted of being found in the United Kingdom when permission for her to

---

[70] Glazebrook, "Situational Liability" in Glazebrook (ed.), *Reshaping the Criminal Law* (1978) 108; Cohen, "The 'Actus Reus' and Offences of 'Situation'" (1972) 7 *Israel LR* 186. Crimes of this sort are sometimes ruled unconstitutional in the United States: *Robinson* v. *California* 370 US 660 (1962) (being addicted to narcotics); *Papachristou* v. *City of Jacksonville* 405 US 156 (1972) (being a vagrant).

[71] Limited defences are, however, provided by ss. 3(1) and 6 of the same Act.

[72] See also above, § 1.2(ii)(e).

[73] (1933) 149 LT 542.

enter the country had previously been refused. It was, however, undisputed that the only reason for her being back on UK soil was that she had been brought there against her will by the police. In convicting her of a situational liability offence, the law has picked out Larsonneur because it was she to whom the actus reus happened, and not because of anything she did.[74]

Larsonneur has been widely criticised, and rightly so.[75] But the proper reason for criticising it is less clear. One problem with the case is that the language used in many situational offences appears not to require any mens rea or fault element on the part of the defendant, and thereby imposes what is known as *strict liability*. This is an important criticism, and we shall return to it in § 6.3. But that has not been the only ground of opposition. Ashworth, for instance, once disapproved of "defining an offence in a way that seems to require no act by the defendant as a basis for liability."[76] The objection was that, quite apart from there being no mens rea element, there is no behavioural requirement in the actus reus. However, this is not a valid objection. There is nothing inherently defective or unjust about an offence that contains no behaviour element.

To see this, *Larsonneur* may be contrasted with the New Zealand case of *Finau* v. *Department of Labour*,[77] where F was prosecuted under the Immigration Act 1964 for remaining in New Zealand after the expiry of her visitor's permit. The Court of Appeal upheld F's appeal against conviction on the basis that it had been impossible for her to leave the country, owing to her pregnancy and the consequent refusal of any airline to carry her.

The result in the New Zealand case demonstrates that there need be no injustice, and there is nothing intrinsically wrong, in criminalising states of affairs, so long as the class of potential defendants is clearly identified. However, what *Finau* does is to make clear a further requirement under New Zealand law: that the defendant could have done something about it. The actus reus, although it specifies no act or omission, must still have been *voluntary* . It is the failure of English law to observe *this* requirement which seems to us the main problem with *Larsonneur,* and the reason why the decision in that case is so objectionable.[78]

At the level of theory, two points emerge from this comparison between the jurisdictions. First, where, by contrast with the facts of *Larsonneur*, the defendant *could* have prevented the actus reus from occurring, then situational liability operates, in effect, just like liability for voluntary omissions. Indirectly, it involves the defendant being prosecuted for her failure or omission to prevent the actus reus from happening.[79]

---

[74] Though see Lanham, "Larsonneur Revisited" [1976] *Crim LR* 276, who suggests the possibility of prior fault.

[75] E.g. Hall, *GPCL* 329, n. 14; Williams, *CLGP* 11; Howard, *Strict Responsibility* (1963) 47.

[76] *Principles of Criminal Law* (2nd ed., 1995) 105. Ashworth's discussion of *Larsonneur* has since been modified, withdrawing the phrasing quoted here: *Principles*, § 4.3(a).

[77] [1984] 2 NZLR 396; also with *Martin* v. *State of Alabama* (1944) 17 So 2d 427. Contrast the approach of the House of Lords in *Porter* v. *Honey* [1988] 3 All ER 1045, which sought to exculpate a blameless defendant through techniques of statutory interpretation, rather than by reference to impossibility: see below, § 4.3(ii)(b).

[78] For an argument that to convict D on facts such as *Larsonneur* contravenes D's right to a fair trial guaranteed by Art 6(1) of the European Convention for Human Rights, see Sullivan, "Strict Liability and the ECHR" in Simester (ed.), *Appraising Strict Liability* (2005) 195, 207–10. An argument that a conviction in such circumstances breaches the presumption of innocence guaranteed by Art 6(2) of the Convention failed, however, in *Barnfather* v. *London Borough of Islington Education Authority* [2003] EWHC Admin 418.

[79] An illustrative New Zealand case of this sort is *Tifaga* v. *Department of Labour* [1980] 2 NZLR 235. There D *was* convicted of overstaying, following the termination of his temporary entry permit, because his inability to leave the country was due to his own failure to retain sufficient funds to do so.

Conversely, it is submitted that, unless there is a requirement of voluntariness, situational offences are at odds with the deepest presuppositions of the criminal law. The very notion of a trial, of a plea, assumes putative answerability for something. One is not answerable for a state of affairs (e.g. having red hair), and it should not be the actus reus of an offence, unless one is able to avoid that state of affairs (e.g. by shaving one's head or dyeing the hair another colour).

Turning to matters of doctrine, it is clear that English law admits the existence of situational offences, where there is no formal necessity to prove an act or omission by the defendant. However, in light of cases such as *Larsonneur*,[80] it appears that situational offences do not incorporate a defence of involuntariness. We consider this point in detail below (§§ 4.3(ii), 6.2(i)).

(b) Crimes of possession

Possessory offences are a creation of statute. They are not found in the common law.[81] There are a number of such offences especially relating to controlled drugs, and to weapons or tools of crime.[82] According to section 5(2) of the Misuse of Drugs Act 1971, for example, "it is an offence for a person to have a controlled drug in his possession." The offence makes no reference to the defendant's conduct.

Characteristically, possession is criminalised as a convenient substitute for the harm that is really objected to, being the *use* of the thing possessed.[83] Criminalisation at the earlier stage both simplifies evidential issues and makes an offence out of behaviour which might otherwise not even count as an *attempt* to do the ultimate crime contemplated. Thus, if offences of this sort did not exist, the police would not be able to intervene at an early stage to prevent many crimes without the prospective offender's escaping the clutches of the criminal law. It is undesirable as well as wasteful of resources that they should have to wait until the contraband is actually used before making an arrest.[84]

In crimes of possession, there is no formal requirement for an act or omission by the defendant.[85] No doubt D put the crowbar in his car before heading out to commit a burglary, but the offence of going equipped for stealing requires only that he *has* it.[86] So far

---

[80] A later case to similar effect is *Winzar* v. *Chief Constable of Kent*, *The Times*, 28 March 1983. D, who had been brought to hospital but found merely to be drunk, was subsequently removed by the police to their car parked on the road outside; whereupon he was charged with being found drunk on the highway. His conviction was upheld by the Divisional Court. Contrast *Winzar* with decisions in other jurisdictions: *O'Sullivan* v. *Fisher* [1954] SASR 33; *Palmer-Brown* v. *Police* [1985] 1 NZLR 365.

[81] Compare, e.g., *Heath* (1810) Russ & Ry 184, 168 ER 750; *Dugdale* v. *R.* (1853) 1 E & B 435, 118 ER 499.

[82] E.g. s. 25 of the Theft Act 1968 (going equipped for stealing); s. 1 of the Firearms Act 1968.

[83] Alternatively, the wrong is sometimes in the *making* of the thing, as in the possession of indecent photographs of children contrary to s. 160(1) of the Criminal Justice Act 1988 (the making of such photographs itself being a criminal offence under s. 17(1) of the Protection of Children Act 1978).

[84] For criticism of this rationale, see Fletcher, *Rethinking Criminal Law* (1978) 197–205.

[85] It is otherwise in the United States; § 2.01(4) of the Model Penal Code states that possession is established "if the possessor knowingly procured or received the thing possessed or was aware of his control thereof for a sufficient period to have been able to terminate his possession."

[86] Theft Act 1968, s. 25. The physical nature of the possession requirement varies for different offences. Under s. 25, it is necessary to show that D "has with him" the instrument of theft, burglary, etc.; which requires personal possession, either upon one's person or in one's car nearby: cf. *Doukas* [1978] 1 All ER 1061; *McCalla* (1988) 87 Cr App R 372, 378. By contrast, it will ordinarily be enough for possession that the prohibited item is held by a third party on behalf of D: *Kelt* [1977] 1 WLR 1365; *Sullivan* v. *Earl of Caithness* [1976] QB 966. In the case of drugs, the

as proving the actus reus is concerned, it does not matter how that situation came about.[87] Nonetheless, like offences of situational liability, possessory offences can normally be thought of as having an implicit behavioural element, albeit one that the prosecution need not prove. In effect, criminalisation of D's possession of the crowbar may be treated as imposing an indirect liability, either for the act of obtaining the crowbar (i.e. acquiring possession) or for the omission by D to dispose of it.[88]

So possession and situational offences contain no formal requirement for proof of a behavioural element on the part of the defendant. Despite this, criminal convictions in these cases can usually be explained in terms of an implicit act or omission by the defendant. Recognition of this implicit element helps to explain some of the more difficult cases where D did not obtain the prohibited item by dint of his own efforts. Suppose that D is stopped while in his car, and is found to have with him a package containing cannabis. He claims, however, that he had nothing to do with the presence of the package in his car, and that it had been placed there by a friend. While that claim would suggest that D is not responsible—and therefore should not be criminally liable[89]—for the fact that the cannabis is in his possession, the law may still be justified in imposing criminal liability because of his voluntary failure to dispose of the item. The difficult cases for this analysis occur when D's possession (whether by acquisition or non-disposal) is *involuntary*. We shall return to this issue in § 4.3(ii).

§ 4.2 Consequences: the need for causation

Not all consequences involve persons. For example, the sudden arrival of a very large meteor is thought to have caused the extinction of dinosaurs; and the collapse of many of San Francisco's buildings in 1906 occurred because of an earthquake rather than by human hand. But for the purposes of the criminal law, consequences are those circumstances, events, or states of affairs which are the result of (i.e. *caused* by) the defendant's behaviour. Thus, whenever a consequence, such as death, is specified as part of the actus reus of an offence, the prosecution must prove both that the consequence occurred and that the defendant's behaviour caused that consequence.

This does not mean that D must in any immediate physical sense cause the consequence. A post-disaster inquiry may find that D was in flagrant breach of his duty in failing to pass on a flood warning to the emergency services of the devastated city. The flooding is the most direct physical cause of the deaths by drowning; but, in law, D's behaviour will also be regarded as *one* of the causes of the deaths of those who would have been saved had he done his duty. It is enough that there is *a* causal link from D's behaviour to the consequence.

---

physical element of possession will be established if the substance is present at a place which is subject to D's dominion or control: *Lewis* (1988) 87 Cr App R 270.

[87] However, the mode of acquisition may be relevant to mens rea. In particular, the possibility of inadvertent possession is usually excluded by the mens rea requirement of knowledge that the courts have held is implicit in the word "possess". Cf. *Cugullere* [1961] 1 2 ALL ER 343; *Warner v. Metropolitan Police Comr* [1969] 2 AC 256; below, §§ 4.3(ii)(c), 5.6(ii).

[88] Cf. Williams, *CLGP* 8; Husak, *Philosophy of the Criminal Law* (1987) 12; Moore, *Act and Crime* (1993) 21; *Porter* [2006] EWCA Crim 560, [2006] 1 WLR 2633 (rendering electronic images irretrievable, at least to D).

[89] Cf. § 1.2(ii)ff; also below, § 4.3.

The requirement of causation is fundamental to our understanding of the actus reus in criminal law. Suppose, for example, that V dies. The result, death, is an element of the actus reus of murder. But normally it would be wrong to hold someone guilty of murder who does not cause V's death. Imagine B is a bystander who happens to be standing beside V when, suddenly, D rushes up to V and stabs him fatally. Here our criminal law takes a very individualistic approach, emphasising the distinctive responsibility of citizens for their own actions. Thus the law does not prosecute D's parents, who brought D up in such a way that he was not adequately instilled with the values that would have stopped him from killing V. Neither would it hold B guilty of murder even if B had, in fact, been planning to kill V himself, and had delightedly stood aside upon perceiving D's murderous intentions.[90] In short, there is no doctrine of collective social responsibility in our criminal law. This reflects the nature of our society. Even in team games, such as a football match, the newspaper statistics record the names of those who scored goals. Of course, other approaches are possible.[91] At one time, it was the practice in Greece to hold the entire city punishable for the crimes of its leaders. Similarly, the Chinese doctrine of *lian-tsua* would result in a whole family or village being punished for the wrongdoing of one of its members. But these are not the ways of most modern societies.. Moreover, to impose criminal liability upon someone for the actions of others would not only be out of step with public perceptions, but would also substantially restrict individual liberty.[92] It is inappropriate in a liberal culture to force us to be the guardian of others on pain of criminal conviction.

(i) The rule of thumb

The starting, and frequently finishing, point of any causation problem is the "but for" or *sine qua non* test: would the consequence specified in the actus reus have occurred *but for* the defendant's behaviour? If it would not have occurred except for the defendant's acting as he did, then prima facie his behaviour caused that consequence. Conversely, if it would have occurred anyway, that is a reason to deny the existence of causation (and consequently to refrain from holding the defendant criminally liable for the occurrence of the actus reus).

Suppose, for example, that a doctor injects his patient with a painkiller, and the patient subsequently dies. Whether or not the doctor is guilty of manslaughter or murder depends upon a number of factors, but he definitely commits neither unless injecting the painkiller caused that patient's death. If the patient would have died when she did whether or not the doctor had injected her (e.g. of an unrelated heart attack), then the *but for* test is not satisfied and we have grounds for saying that the doctor's actions did not cause her death.[93] Conversely, if it can be proved that (subject to a *de minimis* exception[94]) she would not have died when she did without the doctor's intervention, then prima facie he killed her.

---

[90] B may, however, become guilty of murder if he manifests his delight in a manner which is intended to encourage D. Not all liability for outcomes is predicated on *the defendant's* having caused the outcome; he may be held responsible for the consequence of someone else's actions as a secondary party. See below, Chapter 7.

[91] See, e.g., Fauconnet, *La Responsabilité: Étude de Sociologie* (1920).

[92] Cf. the argument against liability for omissions, above, § 4.1(i)(a); also the discussion in Chapter 1.

[93] Cf. *Dalloway* (1847) 2 Cox CC 273; *White* [1910] 2 KB 124.

[94] Below, § 4.2(ii)(a).

Most of the time, the *sine qua non* test will be an entirely adequate yardstick of causation, and in the absence of any unusual circumstances the prima facie answer it gives will be a conclusive one. But it is important to realise that *but for* causation is no more than indicative of true legal causation. Suppose, for instance, that D invites V to meet her for lunch. Unfortunately, while driving to their rendezvous, V's car is hit by a truck, the brakes of which have failed. But for D's inviting V to lunch, the accident would not have occurred. Yet D did not cause the accident. Another useful illustration is *Hensler*.[95] D sent V a begging letter in which he misrepresented his plight. V was not deceived, but nevertheless sent D some money. On these facts, although V would not have sent the money but for D's letter, D could not be convicted of obtaining by false pretences, because the false pretence had not caused D to send the money.[96]

So the presence of *but for* causation does not mean that there is true legal causation. Conversely, the absence of *but for* causation does not imply an absence of true legal causation either. Suppose this time that D sets fire to V's house, razing it. It turns out, however, that there was a faulty electrical circuit in the house that was about to overheat and cause a similar fire. We cannot say that, but for D's conduct, V's house would not have burned down. Yet despite this, it *is* D who causes the damage.

The difficulty arises because so-called *but for* "causation" *is actually not a species of causation at all*. Rather, it is a formula which merely expresses a certain sort of relationship between two things: that, in the circumstances, it was impossible for the second event (the "consequence") to happen without the first action (the "cause") having occurred. As such, the *sine qua non* relationship simply expresses a proposition of logic, and not of causation. What really matters in the law is not whether there is a logical *but for* relationship between the defendant's behaviour and the prohibited consequence, but whether there is a true causal relationship *at law*.

(ii) Causation in law

Some causal relationships are very mechanical, and present no problems for the law. This sort of causation occurs when the action leads to the relevant consequence through the ordinary workings of physics, biology, and the like. Thus the connection between D's knocking over the tumbler and its watery contents pouring out is a simple mechanical one; the consequence follows straightforwardly given the existence of gravity and the fluidity of the liquid inside, without the intervention of subsequent events. The connection between D's shooting V and V's consequential death is normally just as straightforward, something that a pathologist might be able to discuss in technical rather than, say, legal or moral terms.

The real difficulties arise when there are other actions, or events of nature, which *also* play a role in bringing about the relevant consequence. Consider, for example, the facts in *Pittwood*,[97] where D failed to close the gate at a railway crossing, with the result that a cart entered the crossing and was hit by a train. One can say, of this case, that the arrival of the

---

[95] (1870) 11 Cox CC 570.

[96] D was, however, convicted of an attempt to obtain by false pretences. Compare *Mills* (1857) 1 Dears & Bell 205, 169 ER 978.

[97] (1902) 19 TLR 37.

train was itself a causal factor in the accident. Yet we can still agree that D's negligence caused the crash. Why?

It is not possible to give a definitive analysis of the principles of causation here.[98] But over the next few pages a number of guiding principles will be suggested. Perhaps the most important point to remember during the discussion which follows is that, while causation frequently depends upon physical, mechanical, relationships between actions and outcomes (such as the relationship that D's firing a gun may bear to V's death a moment later), causation is also and very often a function of moral and policy evaluations. When we state that Pittwood's dereliction "caused" an accident, we are articulating a view that his behaviour was responsible for that accident. In other words, the ascription of causation in *Pittwood* is not so much a *prerequisite* of his being held responsible as it is an expression of the moral *conclusion* that, through his behaviour, he is responsible, and legally answerable, for the accident that resulted. The moral considerations underlying that conclusion find legal expression in the guiding principles outlined below.

(a) Significant cause

Whatever other causes play a role in bringing the actus reus about, the first requirement is that D's behaviour must contribute in some significant way to its occurrence. In *White*,[99] W gave his mother poison. Before it could take effect, however, she died of an unrelated heart attack. W was guilty of an attempted murder. But he did not commit murder because the poison played no role in his mother's death.

The contribution that D makes must be more than insignificant or *de minimis*.[100] If a doctor takes a blood sample from a patient who is dying from gunshot wounds, the additional loss of blood for the sample may further weaken the patient and hasten death by a few moments. But the doctor's role in the patient's death is, in this context, causally insignificant, and the law will impute the death solely to the gunshot wounds.[101]

However, the defendant's contribution need not be a substantial one. In *Hennigan*,[102] for example, it was ruled wrong to direct a jury that D was not liable if less than one-fifth to blame for the actus reus. Certainly, D's behaviour need not be the main cause of death. It is enough that her conduct plays a part which is not "insubstantial", or not "insignificant".[103]

(b) Causal salience

As well as making a "not insignificant" contribution, D's causal role must also be *salient*. Suppose that D is driving to work at a speed in excess of the speed limit. He slows to the correct speed in advance of an intersection, but is involved in an accident on the intersection with another car. If he had not been speeding he would not have arrived at the

---

[98] The classic work is *Hart and Honoré*. See also Kadish, *Blame and Punishment* (1987) chap. 8; Williams, *TBCL* chap. 14. For more philosophical discussion, see Honoré, "Necessary and Sufficient Conditions in Tort Law" in Owen (ed.), *Philosophical Foundations of Tort Law* (1995) 363; Mackie, "Causes and Conditions" in Sosa (ed.), *Causation and Conditionals* (1975) 15.

[99] [1910] 2 KB 124.

[100] See *Cato* [1976] 1 All ER 260, 265–6.

[101] Cf. *Adams* [1957] Crim LR 365. The direction to the jury by Devlin J is reproduced in Arlidge, "The Trial of Dr David Moor" [2000] Crim LR 31, 34–5.

[102] [1971] 3 All ER 133. Cf. *Garforth* [1954] Crim LR 936.

[103] *Cato* [1976] 1 All ER 260, 265–6; *Cheshire* [1991] 3 All ER 670, 677.

intersection when he did, and the accident would not have occurred. But his speeding is not a cause of the accident. Its only role was to ensure that D was present in a particular place at a particular time, and this in no way affected the likelihood of an accident occurring. The risk would have been just as great had he arrived later;[104] indeed, neither would the accident have happened if his speed had been even *more* excessive. A slightly different example is put by Hart and Honoré:[105]

> "If it is negligent of the defendant to hand a child a loaded gun, and the child drops the gun on his foot and injures it, the injury to the foot is not within the risk (shooting) that made it negligent to hand the child the loaded gun. It is also true that the aspect of the defendant's conduct which made it negligent, the fact that the gun was loaded, was not causally relevant to the injury, since that fact did not significantly increase the gun's weight."

Here D, by giving the gun to the child at all (whether loaded or not), played a causal role in V's subsequent injury. But the reasons why D is at fault—which concern the risk that the child will discharge the gun—are in no way salient to the injury that V sustains.

Salience is frequently in point in cases of manslaughter, whether by gross negligence or by an unlawful and dangerous act. In each case, it must be the conduct constituting the gross negligence or the unlawful and dangerous act that caused death. Conversely, it is impermissible for the Crown to prove gross negligence by reference to conduct, even grossly culpable conduct, that is not causatively salient to the fatality. In the New Zealand case of *Fenton*,[106] for example, D had caused the death of a passenger in the utility vehicle he was driving when he failed to exercise reasonable care to avoid danger to human life, in conduct that established ordinary negligence. It was held that further failings which were merely part of the background to the accident (in this case, the vehicle's lack of a warrant of fitness and registration, the appellant's failure to wear a seatbelt, and the fact he had converted the vehicle without the owner's permission), were inadmissible to prove gross negligence causing death. Similarly, in *Carey*,[107] the defendants were convicted of affray and of manslaughter by unlawful and dangerous act, after a confrontation in which one of them punched V. Subsequently V, a seemingly healthy 15-year-old girl, died from unexpected ventricular fibrillation triggered, apparently, by her flight. The Court of Appeal quashed the manslaughter convictions. The punch, which was certainly an unlawful and dangerous act, was not the cause of death; while the affray, in the view of the Court, was not itself dangerous.

(c) Multiple causes

A further principle is that there may be multiple causes. In *Pittwood*,[108] both the arrival of the train and the defendant's failure to close the gate were causes of the accident. This may be true even when more than one person is at fault.[109] Suppose that D shoots V who is taken to hospital. While in hospital, V is attended to by E, an inexperienced doctor who

---

[104] Cf. *Berry* v. *Borough of Sugar Notch* 43 Atl 240 (Pa) (1899); *Hart and Honoré* 168–70; Williams, *TBCL* § 16.7.
[105] *Hart and Honoré* lxiii. Cf. *Wrigley* (1829) 1 Lew CC 171, 168 ER 1001; *Gorris* v. *Scott* (1874) LR 9 Ex 125; Fleming, *The Law of Torts* (7th ed., 1987) 174.
[106] [2003] 3 NZLR 439, especially para. 14.
[107] [2006] EWCA Crim 17.
[108] (1902) 19 TLR 37; above, § 4.1(i)(b) (Case 2).
[109] Cf. *Benge* (1865) 4 F & F 504, 176 ER 665.

negligently fails to recognise the true extent of her injuries. V dies because those injuries are improperly left untreated. In this case, the actions of both D and E cause V's death, and (depending on mens rea considerations) both D and E may be guilty of homicide-related offences. Similarly, if both A and B simultaneously shoot C fatally through the heart, and C dies instantly, then both A and B kill him; even though we cannot say "but for" each shot, C would not have died.[110] It is enough that the actus reus or consequence can be attributed to the defendant's conduct as *a*, not *the*, cause. The general test when there are multiple causes is whether the defendant's contribution was, by the time the consequence came about, still a "significant and operating cause".[111] If so, then it is irrelevant whether that same consequence can also be attributed to other defendants.[112]

Moreover, when multiple causes are concurrently at work, there is no requirement that a defendant's conduct must have been sufficient to cause the prohibited outcome by itself. As we shall see on the following pages, there are many cases where the actus reus occurs only because of the contribution of a third party or of the victim himself.[113] An example of this is the case of *National Rivers Authority* v. *Yorkshire Water Services*,[114] where the defendant company was charged with causing noxious matter to enter a river. The company regularly and legitimately discharged treated sewage into the river. One night, however, somebody covertly introduced a prohibited substance into the sewer, with the result that when the sewage was discharged, the prohibited material also entered the river. On appeal, the Divisional Court reversed the Crown Court and held that the defendant *had* caused the noxious substance to enter the river: the fact that a stranger also caused the pollution was "neither here nor there."[115] This seems correct. Although the defendant did not cause the sewage to become polluted, it did cause the contents of the sewer to enter the river. It was, of course, blameless in doing so; but that is another matter.[116] Where, as here, the pollution occurs only because of the cumulative actions of defendant and vandal, *both* may be said to have caused the harm. Once again, the general test is the same: whether the particular defendant's own conduct was a significant contributor in bringing about the actus reus.

(iii) Intervening causes

In such cases as *Pittwood* and *National Rivers Authority* v. *Yorkshire Water Services*, the other causal factors operated in tandem with D's conduct to bring about the prohibited harm. Sometimes, however, D's contribution is followed by an action by someone else, or a

---

[110] *Jones* v. *Commonwealth* (1955) 281 SW 2d 920, 922–3. From a moral and legal perspective, no other conclusion is possible, even though this type of case presents difficulty for philosophical accounts of causation.

[111] Usually "substantial and operating"—cf. *Smith* [1959] 2 QB 35, 42–3; but see above, § 4.2(ii)(a).

[112] Cf. *Haines* (1847) 2 Car & K 368, 175 ER 152; *Malcherek* [1981] 2 All ER 422; *Blaue* [1975] 3 All ER 446.

[113] E.g. *Pagett* (1983) 76 Cr App R 279 (third party), below, § 4.2(iii)(b); *Roberts* (1971) 56 Cr App R 95 (victim), below, § 4.2(iii)(c).

[114] [1994] 4 All ER 274; reversed on another ground by the House of Lords, [1995] 1 All ER 225.

[115] [1994] 4 All ER 274, 279–80.

[116] The case should be distinguished from *National Rivers Authority* v. *Wright Engineering Ltd* [1994] 4 All ER 281. In that case D used a tank to store oil near a brook. Vandals opened a tap on the tank, with the result that the oil flowed into the brook. D was acquitted of causing a noxious substance to enter the brook—again, correctly. This is a clear case of *novus actus interveniens*, discussed below, § 4.2(iii)ff. By contrast, in *Yorkshire Water Services*, the vandal's intervention occurred prior to the company's processing and discharging the effluent. The distinction is not, of course, one that tracks culpability.

coincidental event, that is the more immediate (or "proximate") cause of death and which displaces D's causal responsibility for the actus reus. A good example of this is the case of *White*, mentioned earlier.[117] Suppose that in the normal course of events the poison D gave his mother would have caused her death.[118] Nonetheless, it was a subsequent, unrelated, heart attack that killed her. The occurrence of the heart attack overtook the effects of D's conduct and usurped his causal responsibility for her death.

Where the later event displaces D's responsibility in this way, it is often called a *novus actus interveniens*. A *novus actus* is an action or event which "intervenes" to "break the causal chain" leading from D to the eventual harm. Where the prohibited consequence is attributable to a *novus actus*, D is not criminally liable for bringing about that consequence. His behaviour is no longer a significant and operating cause.

We look now at the main types of intervening causes in more detail.

(a) Natural events

Where the other causal factors involve natural events rather than persons, the basic rule is that causation is attributed to the defendant *unless* the intervening natural event was not reasonably foreseeable. Another way of putting this test, in the language preferred by Lord Hoffmann, is to say that an intervening natural event is a *novus actus interveniens* only if its occurrence is "something extraordinary" rather than an ordinary occurrence or ordinary fact of life.[119] A number of overseas cases have usefully illustrated this point. In *Hart*,[120] D assaulted V, leaving her lying unconscious on a beach below the high-water mark. V was subsequently drowned by the incoming tide. The Court of Appeal held that D had caused the death of the victim. It is thought that D would not have killed her had V been left lying above the high-water mark and had only drowned because of a freak tidal wave.[121]

The idea here is that the further cause is not merely a coincidence. Rather, it is the sort of risk that is created or increased by D's initial actions; and the prospect of the prohibited consequence coming about by that further means is one of the reasons we might sensibly give when stating why D should not act as he does.[122] Thus in cases such as *Gowans*,[123] where D inflicted serious injuries upon V, sending him into coma and thereby making V susceptible to serious infection which V later contracted and from which he died, it was held that D's conduct, in rendering V especially vulnerable to the further, immediate cause of death, was a sufficient cause for the death to be attributable to D. A contrasting case with different result is *Bush v. Commonwealth*.[124] In that case D shot V, who subsequently died of scarlet fever, transmitted to him in hospital by the surgeon who operated on the bullet

---

[117] Above, § 4.2(ii)(a).

[118] In fact, although D probably thought otherwise, it appears that the quantity given was insufficient to cause death, save perhaps as part of a cumulative dose.

[119] *Environment Agency v. Empress Car Co. (Abertillery) Ltd.* [1999] 2 AC 22, 34–6. Provided it is borne in mind that what must be foreseeable is events of the same *type*, rather than the *particular* intervening event, these alternative ways of phrasing the causation test involve little practical difference.

[120] [1986] 2 NZLR 408. See also *Hallett* [1969] SASR 141; *Phillips* [1971] ALR 740; *Hill* [1953] NZLR 688, 694–5.

[121] Perkins, "The Law of Homicide" (1946) 36 *J Crim L & Crim* 391, 393–4.

[122] Cf. the requirement for salience, above, § 4.2(ii)(b).

[123] [2003] EWCA Crim 3935. Cf. *Forrest* (1886) 20 SASR 78; *D* [2003] EWCA Crim 2772, [2004] 1 Cr App R (S) 73, para. 6.

[124] (1880) 78 Ky 268.

wound. D was acquitted of unlawful homicide. His attack on V did not substantially increase the risk of V's contracting scarlet fever; neither was that risk a significant reason why we would think D's initial actions wrong. A different view might have been taken if D had succumbed to an infection characteristically associated with his injuries.

The outcome in *Bush* v. *Commonwealth* would also have been different if the fever had caused death only *in conjunction with* the fact that V was weakened by the wound D had inflicted. The latter would be a case of multiple concurrent causes, rather than of *novus actus*, since the original injury would still be making an ongoing (operating) contribution to V's death.

There is another important exception to the rule that unforeseeable or extraordinary events are capable of breaking the causal chain linking defendant to eventual outcome. A coincidental or fortuitous route involving natural events will not normally be a *novus actus* when the ultimate result was *intended* by the defendant.[125] For example:

> D shoots at V on a mountainside, meaning to kill him. She misses, but the noise of her shot triggers an avalanche in which V is swept away and killed. D is guilty of murder. She has brought about the intended result, and cannot escape responsibility by pointing to the unexpected causal detour of the means that she herself initiated.

This exception is sometimes described as a rule that "intended consequences are never too remote." It is preferable not to characterise the exception in that way, and indeed to do so would be inaccurate. For example, D's intended contribution to an outcome may be superceded by the *novus actus* of a third party.[126] It is to that possibility that we now turn.

(b) Other persons

In some respects, there are similarities between the causal status of natural events and the intervening actions of third parties. If D stabs V, and V later dies, D is nevertheless not causally responsible if it turns out that V dies because the ambulance within which he was being carried to hospital was crushed by a runaway lorry. Neither does D kill V if, after being fatally wounded and left for dead, V is chanced upon by his old enemy T, who shoots V, killing him instantly.[127] In these situations, the unforeseeable intervention of another breaks the causal chain between D's contribution and the eventual outcome. However, there are also significant differences between the attribution of causation where there are intervening natural events and that where there are intervening actions by other persons. In the former case, as we have seen, the main test is one of "ordinariness" or reasonable foreseeability. In the latter, this is only one aspect of a more complex enquiry.

At a very generalised level, there are two main principles guiding causation when a third person intervenes. First is the proposition that T's intervention which causes the actus reus will normally be a *novus actus*, and absolve D of responsibility, when that intervention is "free, deliberate and informed."[128] This occurs when T *knowingly* intervenes to bring about

---

[125] E.g. *Anon* ("The Harlot's Case"), Crompton's *Justice* 24, discussed in *TBCL* 389; *Michael* (1840) 9 C & P 356, 173 ER 867 (where the intervention was by another person); *Demirian* [1989] VR 97, 113–4.

[126] The rule would also be subject to a salience requirement regarding unexpected interventions: § 4.2(ii)(b).

[127] Cf. *State* v. *Wood* (1881) 53 Vt 558; *Evans and Gardner* [1976] VR 523, 527–8. See below, § 4.2(iii)(b) (Case 2).

[128] *Pagett* (1983) 76 Cr App R 279, 288–9; *Latif* [1996] 1 WLR 104, 115 (HL). In *Kennedy* v. *R* [2005] EWCA Crim

the prohibited outcome, without her choice to do so being induced, fettered, or constrained by the situation D has created. In that situation T assumes full responsibility for the outcome, displacing or pre-empting its attribution to D. The rationale for this is ably expressed by Glanville Williams:[129]

> "Underlying this rule there is, undoubtedly, a philosophical attitude. Moralists and lawyers regard the individual's will as the autonomous prime cause of his behaviour. What a person does (if he has reached adult years, is of sound mind and is not acting under mistake, intimidation or similar pressure) is his own responsibility, and is not regarded as having been caused by other people. An intervening act of this kind, therefore, breaks the causal connection that would otherwise have been perceived between previous acts and the forbidden consequence."

Very often T's knowing intercession will not meet those criteria. The doctor's intervention in treating V is not free or unconstrained, but rather is a justified response to the need for treatment that D has engendered. This point can be stated more generally: T's participation in begetting the actus reus is insufficiently free, and *cannot* be a *novus actus*, when it is justified or excused by the demands of the situation that D's conduct has placed her in. While T's conduct may itself be a cause of the harm, it is not an independent cause; rather, in law, it has the status of being itself a consequence of D's wrongdoing. Thus, instead of T's becoming fully (and exclusively) responsible for the eventual outcome, D remains at least partly responsible for that intervention by T, and for its effects.

Neither will T's input be "free, deliberate and informed" when T is ignorant of the relevant facts. In this sort of case, T's contribution to the harm is an inadvertent one. Her role may be innocent or accidental, but need not be, and may instead be negligent. Either way, there is no deliberate choice by T to bring the harm about, and so she cannot be said to assume full responsibility for that harm to the exclusion of D.

The second main principle applies where, because of her ignorance or mistake, T's intervention does not meet the "free, deliberate and informed" criteria. In that case the third-party intervention is, in effect, no different from a natural event. Thus it is subject to the further tests that govern intervention by a natural event. In particular, it can only count as a *novus actus* if its occurrence was independent of D's wrongdoing and was not reasonably foreseeable.[130] One new factor in examining this issue will be T's culpability for her conduct: if the harm occurred only following T's gross negligence, it is less likely to be reasonably foreseeable and the sort of risk which provides a reason why D should not have acted as he did in the first place.[131]

As with any intervening cause, whether natural or human, a third principle also applies: that even if the intervention was independent of D and unforeseeable, it will be no more than a concurrent cause if D's contribution is still playing a direct, contributory role at the

---

685, the Court of Appeal has suggested a qualification to this principle: to count as a novus actus, the free, deliberate, and informed intervention must also not be done "in concert" with D. This qualification is critiqued below, at § 4.2(iii)(d) (Case 2).

[129] *TBCL* 391.

[130] Or, in Lord Hoffmann's phrasing, if its occurrence was "extraordinary": above, n. 117.

[131] Above, § 4.2(iii)(a). Less likely, but not impossible: cf. *Benge* (1865) 1 F & F 504, 176 ER 665, where a railway accident occurred only because the risk created by D's negligence was not counteracted when others also failed to observe proper procedures. See further below, § 4.2(iii)(b) (Case 3).

time the harm eventually occurs. This is a straightforward application of the proposition that there can be multiple causes of an outcome.[132]

In the following subsections, we will consider these rather abstract principles in the more practical context of the leading cases, and in light of judicial dicta.

Case 1: Foreseeable and innocent interventions.
Cases where another's intervention does not break the causal chain occur in a variety of ways. In some of the most dramatic examples, D will still be ascribed with causal responsibility if the contribution of the other party is both predictable (i.e. reasonably foreseeable) and itself innocent.

A famous case of this variety is *Michael*.[133] D wished to murder her illegitimate child, who was in the care of a foster-mother. She gave a bottle of poison to the foster-mother, telling her it was medicine and instructing her to administer it to the baby. The foster-mother decided not to give the medicine and put it on the mantelpiece. Some days later the foster-mother's own five-year-old child removed the bottle and administered a fatal dose to the child. D was convicted of murder.[134]

The events in *Michael* involved the input of a young child, undoubtedly an innocent for the purposes of legal responsibility. But they would be treated no differently by the law if T were an adult whose foreseeable intervention was inadvertent and blameless. Suppose, for example, that an altercation occurs between D and V on the pavement of a busy city street. D pushes V, who stumbles onto the road and is run over and killed by a passing car.[135] In such a case, the intervention of the car (unintended by its driver) could not be regarded as a *novus actus*, and D would properly be treated as having caused V's death.

By contrast, the innocent intervention will be regarded as a *novus actus* where it is unforeseeable. In *Martin*,[136] D was held not to have caused death after he offered his child a sip of an alcoholic drink, whereupon the child seized and consumed the entire drink. Similarly, the example in the last paragraph may be compared with a situation in which D assaults V, leaving her unconscious in a quiet and well-lit street. Prima facie, he should not be held responsible for V's death if, subsequently, she is run over by a driver who had ample opportunity to avoid her.[137]

Where T's actions are not inadvertent but instead justified or excused because of the situation D has created, T will effectively be counted as an innocent intervener. The most important case of this type is *Pagett*,[138] in which the defendant holed up in a building, then emerged firing at police and using his hostage as a human shield. The police returned fire in the dark, killing the hostage. The consequence, that the police would—quite understandably—return fire, and so kill the girl, was an entirely foreseeable upshot of what the

---

[132] See above, § 4.2(ii)(c). Cf. *Hennigan* [1971] 3 All ER 133.

[133] (1840) 9 C & P 356, 173 ER 867; see also *Tessymond* (1828) 1 Lew CC 169, 168 ER 1000.

[134] It is thought that T's intervention was reasonably foreseeable. (See *TBCL* 394.) However, even if it were unforeseeable and extraordinary, D's conviction can be justified on the basis that, T's intervention being innocent, it should be treated like a natural event and the rule about intended consequences applied. See above, § 4.2(iii)(a).

[135] *Fleeting* [1977] 1 NZLR 343.

[136] (1827) 3 C & P 211, 172 ER 390.

[137] *Knutsen* [1963] Qd R 157.

[138] (1983) 76 Cr App R 279.

defendant did, and so could not break the chain of causation which led from his behaviour to the hostage's death.

It was said in *Pagett* that the policeman's reaction in returning fire was instinctive and "involuntary". But it need not be involuntary. It was enough that the reaction was a reasonable response, justifiable in terms either of self-defence or the execution of a legal duty. Either way, it is not sufficiently "free" to usurp the defendant's causal responsibility for the eventual consequences.

An extension of the decision in *Pagett* may be seen in the tort case of *Scott v. Shepherd*.[139] D threw a lighted squib into the market house, where it landed beside T. T, in order to protect himself, threw the squib across the warehouse. It landed beside R, who in turn also threw the squib away, such that it struck P and exploded, blinding P in one eye. D was held to have caused P's injury, on principles that were said in the case to be analogous to those applying in the criminal law.[140] From the point of view of the criminal law, this seems to be right. The case is slightly different from *Pagett*, in that T's (and R's) reaction involved necessity rather than self-defence, and was excusable rather than justifiable. But it was reasonably foreseeable, and moreover one for which T could not be blamed—a response induced by the circumstances that D himself had generated. Thus T's reaction is allowed to be a mistake,[141] and unjustified, provided it is a reasonable or understandable response made in the heat or emergency of the moment.

One other case worth mention is *Martin*.[142] Intending to cause confusion and terror, D put out the gaslights on a staircase to the exit of a theatre, and placed an iron bar across the exit doorway. In the subsequent panic, a number of persons were seriously injured. D's conviction for inflicting grievous bodily harm was affirmed on appeal. Again, rightly so. The immediate cause of injury was no doubt the stampeding of the audience. Yet the behaviour of the audience was hardly "free, deliberate, and informed." Rather, it was a foreseeable and understandable consequence of the panic induced by D.

Case 2: Foreseeable and intentional interventions.
The cases above illustrate the general rule that, where the intervention is both innocent and foreseeable, it will not normally suffice to break the causal chain linking the defendant to the actus reus. But what if the third party's free intervention is foreseeable, yet not innocent or blameless? Here things get a little more complicated. The reason for this is the importance of individual autonomy and responsibility in the law. A person's actions are not usually regarded as caused by others, and the law stipulates that a defendant is responsible for her own actions but is normally not responsible for the wrongdoing of a third party even if it was foreseeable, and would not have occurred but for the defendant's contribution. So if D inflicts serious injuries upon V during a mugging, and another assailant later chances upon and shoots V (killing him instantly), then D does not cause death even if it was foreseeable[143] that another person might subsequently kill V. Similarly, the result in

---

[139] (1773) 2 Bl W 892, 96 ER 525. Cf. *Tomars* [1978] 2 NZLR 505; *Madison v. State* 234 Ind 517, 130 NE 2d 35 (1955).
[140] (1773) 2 Bl W 892, 899, 96 ER 525, 528 (De Grey CJ).
[141] Cf. *McKechnie* (1992) 94 Cr App R 51, 58.
[142] (1881) 8 QBD 54. See also the cases involving interventions by the victim: below, § 4.2(iii)(e).
[143] Or even made "likely" by D's actions: *Dalby* [1982] 1 ALL ER 916. As Glanville Williams states, "[t]he fact that

Michael [144] would have been different if T had been a mature adult who knew the details of D's plans when she administered the poison to D's baby. [145]

Where the third party's wrongful intervention is itself intentional, something other than causation is required before the outcome can *also* be ascribed to the original actor-defendant. Characteristically, the extra ingredient is supplied when the third party's intervention is in some way induced or underwritten by the defendant. In these cases, D's liability is predicated on a derivative, or secondary party basis, rather than upon causation. [146] Thus when D deliberately incites or assists T to commit a crime, D too will be criminally liable alongside T for its commission. Secondary liability is dealt with separately in Chapter 7.

Sometimes an intervention to bring about the actus reus may be intentional without necessarily being culpable. As we saw in the preceding section, where this occurs because of a justification or excuse arising from D's conduct, T is treated as if his were an innocent intervention. However, where T's intervention is intentional, free, and unconstrained by justificatory or excusatory circumstances, it will usually break the causal link between defendant and outcome. In *Latif*, [147] D was charged, *inter alia*, with importing a controlled drug. The drug was in fact brought into the country by a customs officer with full knowledge of the contents of the packages he carried. The House of Lords held that the officer's voluntary and knowing intervention relieved D of causal responsibility for importation of the drugs, and that the most he could be convicted of was an attempt to commit the offence. [148]

Case 3: Foreseeable and culpable interventions.
Normally, when there is no *intentional* wrongdoing by the intervener, it is less likely—but not impossible—that the culpable intervention will break the causal link between D and the eventual outcome. [149] This is because, as was stated at the beginning of § 4.2(iii)(b), T cannot be said to have assumed a full responsibility for the effects of her intervention. Nonetheless, it is still possible for T's conduct to disrupt the causal path joining D with the actus reus. [150] For example, where V is injured by D, but killed in an accident en route to hospital, the fact that the accident was unintended by T is no bar to an application of the *novus actus* doctrine and denial of D's responsibility. The most instructive legal examples of this variety arise in a medical context, where D inflicts injuries upon V the extent of which are at least exacerbated by the medical treatment V subsequently receives.

[D's] own conduct, rightful or wrongful, provided the background for a subsequent voluntary act by another does not make him responsible for it. What he does may be a but-for cause of the injurious act, but he did not do it": "*Finis* for *Novus Actus?*" (1989) 48 *CLJ* 391.

[144] Above, § 4.2(iii)(b) (Case 1).

[145] Compare *Hilton* (1838) 2 Lew CC 214, 168 ER 1132, where a stranger's intervention was a *novus actus*, with *Lowe* (1850) 3 Car & Kir 123, 175 ER 489, where the intermediary was an "ignorant boy" and D was not absolved of responsibility. Cf. *People* v. *Elder* 100 Mich 515, 59 NW 237 (1894); *Commonwealth* v. *Root* 403 Pa 571, 170 A 2d 310 (1961).

[146] Cf. G. Fletcher, *Rethinking Criminal Law* (1978) 582.

[147] [1996] 1 WLR 104. To similar effect is *Tse Hung-Lit* [1986] AC 876. For another, extraordinary, example, see *People* v. *Campbell* 124 Mich App 333, 335 NW 2d 27 (1983).

[148] It is possible that the officer's intervention could be regarded as culpable since the House of Lords treated him as having committed an offence himself. But this was not required in *Horsey* (1862) 3 F & F 287, 176 ER 129.

[149] Cf. *Benge* (1865) 4 F & F 504, 176 ER 665.

[150] E.g. *Ledger* (1862) 2 F & F 857, 175 ER 1319.

A case where "palpably" bad medical treatment was held to cause death to the exclusion of D's original actions is *Jordan*.[151] In that case the defendant had stabbed V, who was admitted to hospital and died eight days later. On appeal, evidence was admitted to show that when he died, the original injury had substantially healed. V's death was in fact caused by his allergic reaction to the antibiotic he was given in hospital and by the intravenous administration of too much liquid. Moreover, the antibiotic was introduced to prevent infection only after he had shown he was intolerant of it. The Court of Criminal Appeal, in quashing Jordan's conviction, held that the grossly negligent[152] medical treatment broke the causal link between the stabbing and V's death.

While we submit that *Jordan* was rightly decided, it must be regarded as a very unusual case, distinguished by its rather extreme facts. Acknowledging this, the Court was "disposed to accept it as law that death resulting from any normal treatment employed to deal with a felonious injury may be regarded as caused by the felonious injury."[153] Thus where death results from normal treatment applied to the injury, then both the treatment and the injury are causes of death and the treatment does not break the chain of causation from the original injury to death.

Even if the intervening treatment is abnormal, however, it will not necessarily count as a *novus actus*. In *Smith*,[154] V was stabbed by P with a bayonet. His lung was pierced, but this injury went unrecognised by those who attended to him. He was dropped twice on the way to the medical reception station. There the medical officer failed to diagnose the seriousness of the situation and gave the wrong treatment, which very likely increased the risk of death.[155] On appeal, it was held that where the original injury is still an operating and significant[156] cause of death, then—regardless of other contributing causes—the death can still be attributed to the defendant. It is only if the original wound is merely a *historical setting* for the second injury (here, the treatment), which is then the major operating cause of death, that there can be a break in the causal chain. By contrast with the facts in *Jordan*, in *Smith* the stab wound and consequent haemorrhage were still immediate medical factors explaining V's death.

There appear, therefore, to be two conditions which must be satisfied before the intervening behaviour can supersede the defendant's causal role. Loosely stated:

(I)   The original harm inflicted by D must no longer be contributing to the occurrence of the eventual result (i.e. as a concurrent cause).

This condition applies even if T's wrongdoing is intentional. For example, if D inflicts a non-fatal stab wound upon V, then D (as well as T) causes V's death if T later also stabs V and the loss of blood from both wounds is a contributing factor bringing about V's death.[157] Contrast this example with the example mentioned earlier, where D stabs V and T

---

[151] (1956) 40 Cr App R 152.
[152] See Williams, "Causation in Homicide" [1957] *Crim LR* 429.
[153] (1956) 40 Cr App R 152, 157.
[154] [1959] 2 QB 35.
[155] Indeed, it was said in evidence at the trial that V's chances of recovery were 75 per cent given proper treatment.
[156] "Substantial" in the speech of Lord Parker CJ [1959] 2 QB 35, 42–3. But see above, § 4.2(ii)(a).
[157] This may be the best explanation of *Dear* [1996] *Crim LR* 595.

later chances upon V and shoots her, killing her instantly. In that case T and not D causes V's death.

The second condition is as follows:

(II)   The relevant intervention by T must be independent (i.e. not itself a consequence) of the original wrongdoing by D.

This condition is conveniently illustrated by the New Zealand case of *Kirikiri*.[158] In that case, V was the victim of a serious assault by D, which caused structural damage to her face. At the hospital where she was first treated, a temporary tracheostomy was performed in order to assist her breathing. She was then transferred to another hospital for reconstructive surgery, which was to take place four days later and was not essential to save her life. Before surgery, however, the inserted tracheal tube slipped. Attempts to replace it failed and V died. The High Court held, on a pre-trial motion, that there was "ample evidence" on these facts for a jury to hold that D caused V's death. This seems right. The immediate cause of death was the failure of the tracheostomy and of the surgeons' attempts to repair it. But the tracheostomy itself was a medically appropriate response, made necessary by the injuries D had inflicted upon V. D might therefore be regarded as causally responsible for the (necessitous, appropriate) intervention that, in turn, led to V's death.

It may be helpful to illustrate the different legal character of the causal sequences in these cases with diagrams. In *Jordan*, the conduct of the doctor amounted to a *novus actus* independent of D's actions:

Jordan: D ⟶ stabs V ⊣   T ⟶ injects antibiotics ⟶ V dies

By contrast, in *Kirikiri* the doctor's intervention was a direct response to the injuries D had inflicted, and thus could be treated as a consequence of D's actions:

Kirikiri: D ⟶ attacks V ⟶ T performs tracheostomy ⟶ V dies

In *Smith*, the doctor's conduct made an independent contribution to V's death. But the stab wound inflicted by D remained a concurrent, operating cause of death:

Smith: D ⟶ stabs V
                                        ⟶ V dies
             T ⟶ exacerbates wounds

One important factor in determining whether the medical intervention counts as a consequence for the purposes of condition II will be the extent to which that treatment is negligent. "Palpably" wrong—i.e. grossly negligent—treatment is obviously not a consequential intervention falling within condition II. (As *Smith* illustrates, the question whether it is a *novus actus interveniens* will then depend upon condition I.) On the other hand, reasonable, even if ultimately incorrect and harmful, treatment *is* a consequence.[159]

---

[158] [1982] 2 NZLR 648. Condition II is also crucial to the explanation of *Cheshire* [1991] 3 All ER 670, the most important recent case on medical interventions. However, because of the complexity of that case its analysis is deferred to the end of our discussion of causation, in § 4.2(iv)(c). For present purposes, *Kirikiri* provides the better illustration.

[159] *McKechnie* (1992) 94 Cr App R 51, 58; *Kirikiri* [1982] 2 NZLR 648.

However, the status of treatment which is negligent, but not grossly negligent, is not clear. Authority on this question is both *obiter* and inconsistent.[160] It is submitted that, by analogy with the principles stated in § 4.2(iii)(b) above (Case 1) and § 4.2(iii)(e) below, medically erroneous treatment that is neither reasonable nor reasonably foreseeable should count as independent action within condition II.

(c) Distinction from the innocent agent doctrine

Sometimes persons bring about outcomes deliberately through the agency of another person. If D gives V's daughter a lethal draught of poison, telling her it is for V's cold, and the daughter administers the poison to V, D is guilty of murder as if he had administered the poison himself.[161] Similarly, D may be convicted of importing prohibited drugs even though the means of conveyance was an airline.[162] The doctrine of innocent agency renders the intervening participant the mere instrument of D, enabling courts to find that D has committed the offence as a principal offender.

Discussion of this doctrine belongs in Chapter 7, on secondary parties. It is mentioned here in order to distinguish it from the causation question that arises upon an innocent third party's intervention. Innocent agency requires that D knowingly uses T as his agent to bring about the prohibited result. Thus *Michael*, where a child later and independently administered the poison that D had instructed V's nurse to give to V, is not a suitable case for application of the doctrine.

Innocent agency and causal principles nonetheless share some common ground. Like causation, innocent agency requires that T should be ignorant of the true nature of her actions. Where this is not so, and T is aware that her conduct constitutes an actus reus, responsibility for her actions and their result cannot then be imputed back to D.

(d) Two special cases of intentional interventions: pollution and co-operation in a drug overdose

There are two problematic cases governing deliberate third-party interventions, which we discuss here as special cases.

Case 1: Pollution and the problem of Empress.
The first is the decision by the House of Lords in *Environmental Agency* v. *Empress Car Co. (Abertillery) Ltd.*[163] In that case, D had attached a tap to a diesel tank in its yard. The tap overrode existing barriers designed to contain spillage from the tank, meaning that it was possible for overflows from the tap to drain into the nearby river. On 20 March 1995 the tap was opened by an unknown person, with the result that the entire contents of the tank were drained and flowed into the river. D was convicted of "causing polluting matter to enter controlled waters,"[164] a conviction that was affirmed by the House of Lords.

The leading judgment, given by Lord Hoffmann, contains a number of useful statements of principle.[165] But it is, in one respect, profoundly unsatisfactory. Apparently, the intervention

---

[160] For a survey of the case law, see *Hart and Honoré* 352ff. The more recent case of *McKechnie* (1992) 94 Cr App R 51 suggests a standard of simple negligence.
[161] *Anon* (1634) Kel 53, 84 ER 1079.
[162] *White* v. *Ridley* (1978) 140 CLR 342.
[163] [1999] 2 AC 22.
[164] Contrary to s. 85(1) of the Water Resources Act 1991.
[165] E.g. [1999] 2 AC 22, 29F, 30e–31b.

of the third party was free, deliberate, informed, and indeed malicious. Prima facie, therefore, it was a *novus actus*. But Lord Hoffmann accorded no special status to such interventions and failed to distinguish informed acts by third persons from acts which are either uninformed or unfree, or indeed from interventions of nature. "By parity of reasoning",[166] the same test was said to apply to all:

> "The true common sense distinction is, in my view, between acts and events which, although not necessarily foreseeable in the particular case,[167] are in the generality a normal and familiar fact of life, and acts or events which are abnormal and extraordinary."

The main effect of this conclusion is to assimilate interventions by third parties with interventions by natural events, thereby extending the appropriate test of the latter (discussed in § 4.2(iii)(a)) also to the former. Hence a normal or foreseeable intervention, even if fully informed and deliberate, would not break the chain of causation linking D to the ultimate outcome.

This holding is contrary to both principle and law. At the level of principle, it is unexplained how D's lawful storage of oil on its land had any causal effect. V may lawfully park his car in a street. D may come along and vandalise the vehicle. V inadvertently gives D the opportunity to cause criminal damage but his parking of his car was not a cause of its being damaged. If the physical location of the car is regarded as a cause of the damage, all other features of the environment which made it possible for D to damage it should be regarded too as causes of the damage. The same reasoning applies to D's storage of the oil in *Empress*. The winnowing out of such factors is, in part, accomplished by the long-standing precept of causation rules in the criminal law that a person is responsible for his own autonomous actions and not for those of others. As Williams puts it, "[w]hat a person does . . . is his own responsibility, and is not regarded as having been caused by other people."[168] Otherwise, D's criminal liability for causing an actus reus would not be under his own control, but would instead be subject to the autonomous choice of someone else. Giving other citizens the power to render D guilty of a crime not only disempowers D and undermines his autonomy, but is also contrary to the importance attached in modern English law to an individual's separate identity and responsibility.[169]

The dealer who sells T a gun does not shoot V. T does. It may sometimes be appropriate to criminalise the dealer's actions, but not on the basis of causation. Similarly, in the present case, D did not pollute the river. T did. It was possible for the legislature to make D responsible for that outcome by stipulating vicarious or situational liability; but the legislation did

---

[166] [1999] 2 AC 22, 33d, 35d.

[167] Thus his Lordship eschews the language of "foreseeability" in favour of "ordinariness", although the distinction is unlikely to be of great practical significance. See above, n. 117.

[168] *TBCL* 391; the passage is quoted more fully above, § 4.2(iii)(b). Cf. *Hart and Honoré* 364–5. Certain jurisdictions take the view that conduct, while remaining free, deliberate, and informed, can be causally influenced by the interventions of other human agents as when, say, P resolves to kill V as a result of being offered £10,000 by D to do so. In Germany, for instance, D would be regarded as "the principal behind the principal" in the murder of V: Fletcher, *Rethinking Criminal Law* (1978) 657ff. Whatever the merits of this less restricted approach, it cannot suddenly be adopted *ad hoc* for England and Wales at the cost of a major disruption in settled doctrine and resulting uncertainty, particularly in the area of parties to crimes. In English and Wales, such a case is properly handled within the law of complicity.

[169] Cf. the principle of personal responsibility argued for in Simester, "The Mental Element in Complicity" [2006] 122 *LQR* 578, 580–1.

not do that. The statute requires causation by the *defendant*, in the normal way. The House of Lords trampled upon a fundamental precept of criminal law.

Bad principle, then. Bad law, too. The decision is inconsistent with the reasoning in such decisions as *Latif*,[170] *Hilton*,[171] and *Dalby*,[172] mentioned earlier.[173] Glanville Williams's conclusion on *Dalby* holds just as aptly for *Empress*:[174]

> "The fact that [D's] own conduct, rightful or wrongful, provided the background for a subsequent voluntary act by another does not make him responsible for it. What he does may be a but-for cause of the injurious act, but he did not do it."

In *Empress*, D's storage of oil provided no more than the opportunity for T's vandalous act. Were it otherwise, the law of complicity would be largely redundant. One who assists another to commit a crime could be held to have caused the prohibited harm, and so be convicted of the crime as a principal. Lord Hoffmann's analysis virtually demolishes the need for liability of secondary parties. Yet the decision in *Empress* purports to follow law. Unfortunately, in the face of extensive criminal law precedent to the contrary, the only unequivocal authority Lord Hoffmann cited for his conclusion was a tort case.[175] Moreover, his Lordship placed great weight on the statement attributed to Lord Wilberforce in *Alphacell* v. *Woodward* that "the *deliberate* act of a third party does not necessarily negative causal connection."[176] But Lord Wilberforce did not use the word "deliberate". During his speech in *Alphacell* v. *Woodward*, Lord Wilberforce had, *obiter*, merely rejected the proposition that "in every case the act of a third party necessarily interrupts the chain of causation"; a warranted rejection that provides no support whatsoever for the reasoning in *Empress*. So: bad principle, bad law, and bad reasoning.

It is to be hoped that the decision will not prevail, or (at worst) that it will be confined to the sphere of regulatory offences such as those governing pollution. The Court of Appeal has itself sought to limit the effect of the case, treating it as a matter of specific statutory interpretation.[177] That is, in our view, a suitable analysis.

Case 2: Drug overdoses and acting in concert.
The other problematic decision concerning deliberate third-party interventions is *Kennedy* v. *R*,[178] the leading decision in a line of drug overdose cases. D had prepared a heroin mixture for V in a syringe which he then gave to V. V injected himself with the heroin and sub-

---

[170] [1996] 1 ALL ER 353; also *Tse Hung-Lit* [1986] AC 876.

[171] (1838) 2 Lew CC 214, 168 ER 1132.

[172] [1982] 1 ALL ER 916.

[173] Above, § 4.2(iii)(b). See also *People* v. *Elder* 100 Mich 515, 59 NW 237 (1894); *Commonwealth* v. *Root* 403 Pa 571, 170 A 2d 310 (1961); *People* v. *Campbell* 124 Mich App 333, 335 NW 2d 27 (1983); *Horsey* (1862) 3 F & F 287, 176 ER 129. *Empress* is also inconsistent with *Impress (Worcester) Ltd* v. *Rees* [1971] 2 All ER 357, which Lord Hoffmann asserted was wrongly decided, notwithstanding that the result in that case had been endorsed by the House of Lords in *Alphacell* v. *Woodward* [1972] AC 824, 835 (Lord Wilberforce) 847 (Lord Salmon).

[174] "*Finis* for *Novus Actus?*" (1989) 48 *CLJ* 391; above, n. 141.

[175] *Stansbie* v. *Troman* [1948] 2 KB 48.

[176] *Empress* [1999] 2 AC 22, 33C. See *Alphacell* v. *Woodward* [1972] AC 824, 835.

[177] *Kennedy* v. *R* [2005] EWCA Crim 685, paras 36–9; discussed immediately below as Case 2. The Court rejected the wider reading of *Empress* adopted previously in *Finlay* [2003] EWCA Crim 3868 (CA).

[178] [2005] EWCA Crim 685. For discussion, see Ormerod and Fortson, "Drug Suppliers as Manslaughterers (Again)" [2005] *Crim LR* 819; Jones, "Causation, Homicide and the Supply of Drugs" (2006) 26 *LS* 139.

sequently died. D was convicted of manslaughter. On appeal,[179] the issue was whether D had caused V's death by an unlawful act. The main difficulty was that, even though D's contribution was unlawful (being the supply of a controlled substance), and had played a part in the events leading to V's death, prima facie there was an intervening act by another, V himself, who had self-administered the injection. The intervention by V was free, deliberate, and informed; as such, it seemed to be a novus actus, absolving D of causal responsibility for the homicide.

The Court circumnavigated this issue by ruling that the relevant act causing death was the administration of a noxious substance, contrary to section 23 of the OAPA 1861; and that D could be held responsible for that act because D and V had *acted in concert* in administering the heroin:[180]

> "If a defendant is acting in concert with the deceased, what the deceased does in concert with the defendant will not break the chain of causation, even though the general principles as to causation have to be applied. . . . If Kennedy either caused the deceased to administer the drug or was acting jointly with the deceased in administering the drug, Kennedy would be acting in concert with the deceased and there would be no breach in the chain of causation."

This appears to create a new principle of causation: even where an intervening agent is free, deliberate and informed,[181] the intervention will not break the chain of causation if it is done "in concert" with the defendant.

The idea seems to be that where D's and V's actions are intimately bound together, it is artificial to divide up what in reality is a joint operation, a single "combined" transaction for which both are responsible.[182] In *Kennedy*, the key features that rendered their actions "in concert", thereby invoking this new general principle, were (i) that D was present throughout the events; (ii) that D's own contribution was immediately and intimately connected to V's conduct; and (iii) that D's contribution was pursuant to a shared understanding that encompassed V's subsequent conduct.

The problem with this decision is that, notwithstanding the collaborative nature of the project, it was V, not D, who administered the drug. Properly, cases such as these are the domain of secondary liability: D was a party to the self-administration of the heroin (an action that is not itself an offence). To see this, suppose that instead of there being two parties, there had been three. D, let us say, prepared a syringe for P, who injected V—or, indeed, handed over a knife with which P stabbed V. In such cases, D does not cause V's death even though he is criminally responsible for it. Rather, P is straightforwardly guilty of manslaughter as a principal and D as a secondary party.[183] This is the best explanation of

---

[179] In fact, this was D's second appeal. The first saw his conviction upheld: see [1999] Crim LR 65. However, following uncertainty in the subsequent case law, the case was referred back to the Court of Appeal for reconsideration by the UK Criminal Cases Review Commission. Appellate decisions in the more-or-less similar cases of *Dalby* [1982] 1 All ER 916, *Dias* [2002] 2 Cr App R 41, and *Richards* [2002] EWCA Crim 3175 had resulted in the defendant's conviction being quashed; whereas in *Rogers* [2003] 1 WLR 1374 and *Finlay* [2003] EWCA Crim 3868 the convictions had been upheld.

[180] [2005] EWCA Crim 685, paras. 42–3.

[181] Above, § 4.2(iii)(b); *Pagett* (1983) 76 Cr App R 279, 288, 289.

[182] [2005] EWCA Crim 685, para. 53.

[183] Secondary liability is discussed in detail below, Chapter 7.

the proviso in *Latif*, on which *Kennedy* placed great weight.[184] According to Lord Steyn in *Latif*:[185]

> "the free, deliberate and informed intervention of a second person, who intends to exploit the situation created by the first, *but is not acting in concert with him*, is held to relieve the first actor of criminal responsibility."

It is certainly true that, if they are acting in concert, the first is not relieved of criminal responsibility—but this is because he is complicit, not because he causes the outcome personally.

Like *Empress*, it is to be hoped that the decision in *Kennedy* will find no general place in the criminal law; that, at most, it will be confined to cases of intervention by the victim. This new doctrine of causation through another's "acting-in-concert" is no more than a device to evade the problem that arises when D helps P to inflict *self*-harm rather than harm to a third person. Because self-harm is not generally a crime, secondary liability usually does not apply and D cannot be convicted of complicity in P's offence. But general principles of causation should not be invented on an *ad hoc* basis to deal with specific problems such as this.[186]

(e) The victim

What about cases where the intervention is by V himself, rather than by a third party, and D and V are not acting in concert? The general rule is that the consequences of V's intervention are attributable to D provided that:

1. V's conduct is in reaction to D's wrongdoing; and
2. V's reaction was a reasonably foreseeable possibility.

In *Roberts*[187] the defendant made sexual advances to V while driving a car. V leapt out of the moving vehicle and suffered resulting injuries. D's conviction for assault occasioning actual bodily harm was upheld by the Court of Appeal, which asked whether the injury was "the natural result of what the alleged assailant said and did, in the sense that it was something that could reasonably have been foreseen as the consequence of what he was saying or doing?"[188] The same principle is capable of explaining the American case of *People v. Lewis*,[189] in which V, who was dying painfully from a gunshot wound, committed suicide by

---

[184] [2005] EWCA Crim 685, para. 42.

[185] [1996] 1 WLR 104, 115 (HL) (emphasis added).

[186] Jones has urged that English law should adopt the straightforward Scottish approach that the supply of a drug by D to V which V takes with fatal consequences should of itself and by itself be regarded as a cause of V's death: "Causation, Homicide and the Supply of Drugs" (2006) 26 *LS* 139. But this is an *ad hoc* approach, resting on an unsustainably wide conception of causation that attributes causal properties to what are mere enabling conditions for subsequent actions. (Why merely controlled-drug sellers? Why not also sellers, particularly large scale sellers, of alcohol and tobacco?) It is submitted that any major reallocation of the boundary between self-responsibility and victimhood should not proceed by way of *ad hoc* judicial decision-making.

[187] (1971) 56 Cr App R 95. Other cases include *Marjoram* [2000] Crim LR 372; *DPP v. Daley* [1980] AC 237; *Williams* [1992] 2 All ER 183; *Pitts* (1842) Car & M 284, 174 ER 509; *Halliday* [1886–90] ALL ER 1028; *Lewis* [1970] Crim LR 647. See Elliott, "Frightening a Person into Injuring Himself" [1974] *Crim LR* 15.

[188] (1971) 56 Cr App R 95, 102.

[189] 124 Cal 551, 57 P 470 (1898).

cutting his throat. D was held to have caused V's death.[190] It would be otherwise, however, if V had killed himself not in reaction to the suffering that D had inflicted, but rather in order to shield D or, indeed, in an attempt to make D liable for a homicide offence.

The second requirement, of reasonable foreseeability, may not be met where the victim's reaction is disproportionate. Although it is sometimes said that "the victim must be taken as he is found,"[191] in *People* v. *Lewis* D would not have been guilty of murder if the wound had merely been painful rather than dangerous and, knowing this, V had taken his life only in order to escape pain.[192] In general, V's reaction will not be a *novus actus* where it is "in the foreseeable range",[193] and is not "daft".[194] This remains so even if that reaction is negligent or unlawful.[195]

As is the case with third-party interventions, the possibility of a victim's contribution being a *novus actus interveniens* remains subject to the proviso that the original harm inflicted by D must no longer be contributing to the occurrence of the eventual result. In *Wall*,[196] the defendant (a colonial governor) sentenced V to an illegal flogging of some 800 lashes. V died from the punishment. It appeared that V had drunk alcohol after the flogging, which may well have accelerated his death. If so, however, it did so in combination with the effects of the flogging, and so would have been no more than an accompanying rather than overriding causal factor. The defendant therefore remained causally responsible for V's death.

(f) Summary of approach to intervening causes

It is impossible to be precise and comprehensive about the principles governing the attribution of causation. The rich detail of the cases defies reduction to a list of simple rules: sometimes when confronting new situations, the best technique may be simply to argue by analogy to one or more decided cases. Nonetheless, at the risk of oversimplification we offer the following general guidelines to causation problems where there are intervening causes.

Begin by considering whether D's original act is still making an ongoing contribution, in its own right, to the prohibited result at the time that result occurs (e.g. where V dies after losing blood from D's wound as well as T's). If so, then regardless of the other interventions, D's act is a concurrent cause of the result (§ 4.2(ii)(c)) and the causal chain is not broken by any *novus actus interveniens*. The analysis is concluded.

If the conclusion is not determined by that first step, it then becomes necessary to

---

[190] Although the *ratio* of the decision was multiple causes (that V died from loss of blood from the combined wounds), the court would have been prepared to decide the case on this ground if the facts had been clear regarding D's motive for cutting his own throat. See also *State* v. *Angelina* 73 WVa 146, 80 SE 141 (1913); *Jones* v. *State* 220 Ind 384, 43 NE 2d 1017 (1942); *Stephenson* v. *State* 205 Ind 141, 179 NE 633 (1932) (torture).

[191] E.g. *Blaue* [1975] 3 All ER 446, 450; below, § 4.2(iv)(b).

[192] *Pace* the *obiter dicta* in *D* [2006] EWCA Crim 1139, [2006] Crim LR 923, where it is suggested that a minor assault on a person with a fragile and vulnerable personality, who then committed suicide, might be capable of constituting manslaughter. At least in most such cases, deliberate suicide would not be "in the foreseeable range."

[193] *Corbett* [1996] Crim LR 594 (CA); *pace Dear* [1996] Crim LR 595 (CA). It is submitted that the former case is to be preferred on this point, being consistent with existing case law (see, e.g., the cases cited in n. 137 above).

[194] *Roberts* (1971) 56 Cr App R 95, 102.

[195] Cf. *Walker* (1824) 1 C & P 320, 171 ER 1213; *Swindall and Osborne* (1846) 2 Car & Kir 230, 2 Cox CC 141, 175 ER 95.

[196] (1802) 28 St Tr 51, 145. See also *Flynn* (1867) 16 WR 319 (Ir); *Mubila* [1956] SA 31.

enquire whether D's original act is a cause of the prohibited result *through the medium of* T's intervention. This question is approached as follows.

First, assuming T is a human agent, consider whether T's intervention is free, deliberate, and informed (§ 4.2(iii)(b)). If it meets these criteria in full, then, regardless of its predictability, T's intervention is a *novus actus interveniens* that breaks the causal chain between D's original act and the prohibited result. *Pace Empress* (§ 4.2(iii)(d) Case 1), D is absolved of causal responsibility and the analysis is concluded. (There may be an exception to this where T is the victim and T's action is one of self-harm done in concert with D—see § 4.2(iii)(d) Case 2. But that exception remains controversial.)

Alternatively, if T is not a human agent (§ 4.2(iii)(a)) or the intervention was not free, deliberate, and informed, consider whether that intervention was reasonably foreseeable, as opposed to unforeseeable and extraordinary. If the former, then it may be expected not to sever the causal chain linking D's original act to the prohibited result; if the latter, then the intervention is a *novus actus interveniens*.

(iv) Omissions

(a) As causes

It is sometimes suggested that omissions cannot be causes.[197] This idea is founded on the notion that non-events, like failures to intercede and rescue a drowning victim, cannot bring things about: they are merely failures to prevent. To some extent this is true. If D watches without intervening while in a position to save V, her causal contribution to D's death is not of the same order as that when D herself holds V's head under water. One thing that is distinctive about omissions is that they do not initiate causal processes. Instead, they permit other causal processes to bring about the harm.

Nonetheless, neither ordinary language nor the law has much compunction about attributing causal responsibility to omissions. Both within and outside the courtroom, it is acceptable to say that the railway gatekeeper's failure in *Pittwood*[198] to close the gate before the train came through caused the resulting accident. By contrast, it would be misleading just to state that the train's arrival caused the accident, although that was also a causal factor. We tend to reserve the language of causation for those factors which are most relevant to our explanations.

All this reflects the point made earlier in § 4.2(ii), that causation in law is rarely a simple mechanical issue. Rather, it is intimately connected with the process of ascribing *responsibility* for the actus reus. Active intervention, while an obvious means of "causing" harm in the mechanical sense, is not the only way of being involved in bringing that harm about. In law, responsibility for the consequences of omissions involves a twofold test. D is normally held legally responsible for the consequences of an omission when (i) he has a duty to

---

[197] E.g. Moore, *Act and Crime* (1993) 267–78. For discussion, see Hughes, "Criminal Omissions" (1958) 67 *Yale LJ* 590, 627–31; Husak, *Philosophy of Criminal Law* (1987) chap. 6; Leavens, "A Causative Approach to Omissions" (1988) 76 *Cal LR* 547; Beynon, "Causation, Omissions and Complicity" [1987] *Crim LR* 539. Fletcher, "On the Moral Irrelevance of Bodily Movements" (1994) 142 *U Pa L Rev* 1443; *Hart and Honoré* 38; Fletcher, *Rethinking Criminal Law* (1978) 589ff.

[198] (1902) 19 TLR 37. Cf. the discussion in *Hart and Honoré* 32ff; also Feinberg, *Harm to Others* (1984) 172ff.

prevent those consequences from occurring (considered earlier in § 4.1(i)(b)), and (ii) his omission to intervene made a difference: that is, *if he had intervened, his intervention would have made a difference*. Part (ii) is the causal test.[199] For omissions, it is usually satisfied by proof of "but for" causation. In other words, D's omission causes an outcome if, but for that omission by D, the outcome would not have occurred.[200] If it would have resulted anyway, then D's omission made no difference and D cannot be held causally responsible for that outcome. As an example:

> Suppose that D, a doctor, does not notice that V has stopped breathing and fails to give him artificial respiration. She cannot be held causally responsible for his death unless it can be shown that V would have survived if D had discharged her duty to intervene and artificially respirate him.

A similar example is *Dalloway*,[201] in which D was driving a cart without retaining a proper grip on the reins. A young child ran out in front of the cart and was struck and killed. It was ruled that D might be convicted of manslaughter only if it were proved that, had D been using the reins correctly, the child would have been saved.

Note that the prosecution must show, beyond reasonable doubt, that D's intervention *would*—not *might*—have made a difference. This rule is made clear in *Morby*, the facts of which were as follows:[202]

> D's child, aged 8, died of smallpox. Owing to D's religious beliefs, he obtained no medical aid for his son. At trial, it was established that proper medical treatment might have saved or prolonged the child's life, and would certainly have increased his chances of survival; but it could not definitely be said that treatment would have made any difference. It might have been of no avail.

On these facts, the Court for Crown Cases Reserved held unanimously that D's conviction could not be sustained. In this respect the stringency of the causal test for omissions matches that for acts: it must positively be proved that D's conduct *did* cause death, not that it may have done.

It is worth emphasising that even where it can be shown that D's omission is a "but for" cause of the harm, the omission will not be a legal cause if a *novus actus* intervenes. It is also subject to the requirement of salience.[203] Suppose, for example, that Alice makes a luncheon appointment with James. Later she discovers that she will not be free on the day they have arranged. Unfortunately, she discourteously fails to telephone James and cancel the appointment. While en route to the restaurant, James is killed in an automobile accident. If Alice had remembered to cancel, James would have eaten lunch at his office. Thus, but for Alice's omission, James would not have died. In this situation, however, Alice's omission is not a cause of death.

---

[199] *Quaere* whether this requirement was overlooked in *Stone and Dobinson* [1977] QB 354.
[200] *Morby* (1882) 8 QBD 571; *Barnett* v. *Chelsea and Kensington Hospital Mgmt Cttee* [1969] 1 QB 428.
[201] (1847) 2 Cox CC 273.
[202] (1882) 8 QBD 571. See Williams, "What Should the Code Do About Omissions?" (1987) 7 *LS* 92, 106.
[203] Above, § 4.2(ii)(b).

(b) As interventions

The general rule is that, while an omission by a third party can be a causal factor, it cannot be a *novus actus interveniens*. Where D omits to prevent harm, his omission may be a legal cause of that harm, but it is normally a *concurrent* cause; that is, alongside those causal processes that the omission has failed to prevent. To illustrate:

> Suppose that D stabs V, who is admitted to hospital with substantial loss of blood and in urgent need of a blood transfusion to save her life. Apart from the loss of blood, V's injuries are not life-threatening. T, the doctor who attends V, recognises that she needs a blood transfusion and prepares to give her one. While waiting for the blood to arrive, he goes to check on another patient. Unfortunately, he is distracted by a conversation with the patient and forgets to return and administer the transfusion to V. V dies from the loss of blood. Had the transfusion been performed, she would have survived.

In this case, *both* D and T cause V's death. Diagrammatically, their actions are multiple concurrent causes:

T's omission is not a *novus actus* that intervenes to break the causal chain from D's conduct to V's death. The whole reason why T's omission is causally significant is that it *fails to break* the causal sequence from D's action's to V's death. Indeed, we fault T and hold him (as well as D) liable for V's death precisely because he should have intervened and broken that chain before it reached its fatal culmination.

The proposition that an omission normally does not break a pre-existing causal chain is the proper explanation of *Blaue*.[204] In that case V was stabbed, and was admitted to hospital having lost a large quantity of blood. She was a Jehovah's Witness, and refused the blood transfusion that was necessary to save her life. Consequently, the following day she died. D was convicted of her manslaughter. He appealed, contending that V's refusal to have a blood transfusion had broken the causal chain between the stabbing and V's death.

While it was accepted by the Crown that V's refusal to have a transfusion was *a* cause of her death, the Court of Appeal quite rightly ruled, using an analogy with *Smith*,[205] that the original wound inflicted by D was still an operating cause of death. However, faced with the submission by D's counsel that V's decision was an unreasonable one, the Court responded that:[206]

> "It has long been the policy of the law that those who use violence on other people must take their victims as they find them. This in our judgment means the whole man, not just the physical man. It does not lie in the mouth of the assailant to say that his victim's religious beliefs which inhibited him from accepting certain kinds of treatment were unreasonable."

---

[204] [1975] 3 All ER 446; also of *Holland* (1841) 2 Mood & R 351, 174 ER 313.
[205] See above, § 4.2(iii)(b) (Case 3).
[206] [1975] 3 All ER 446, 450.

As a general proposition, this is not valid law. Cases such as *Roberts*, discussed in §
4.2(iii)(e), establish that an intervening reaction by V *does* break the chain of causation
where it is not a reasonably foreseeable possibility—or, as was said in that case, where the
reaction is "so daft" that it is really V's own voluntary act.[207] This means that D does not
have to take his victim however he finds her, but only in so far as her reaction is a
reasonably foreseeable or understandable one.

Suppose, then, that V's refusal of a transfusion *was* "daft", and not a sensible or
foreseeable possibility (this was not decided by the Court). Prima facie, on the authority of
Roberts and similar cases, this would then be a *novus actus* for which D was not responsible.
In *Blaue*, however, the difference from those other cases was that V's intervening conduct
involved not an act but an omission.[208] Thus, while it played a causal role in bringing about
her death, and was a factor (unlike *Roberts*) for which D was not responsible, it did not
break the causal chain from the stabbing to V's death. D's appeal, in effect, was that by her
refusing to break the causal sequence D had set in motion, V broke the chain of causation.
But an omission cannot, by itself, do that.[209]

The difference between the two cases can be illustrated, once again, with causal diagrams:

Roberts: D ⟶ frightens V ⟶ V jumps from car ⟶ V is injured

Blaue: D ⟶ stabs V ⟶ V loses blood ┐
                                              ├⟶ V dies
                V ⟶ refuses transfusion of blood ┘

(c) Two case studies

By way of conclusion, it may be helpful to consider two more complex examples. One case
that combines both omissions and the issue of medical interventions is *McKechnie*.[210] The
facts of the case were as follows:

> D attacked V, inflicting serious head injuries. V was taken, deeply unconscious, to hospital,
> where he was discovered to be suffering from a duodenal ulcer which required surgery. How-
> ever, the attending doctors decided not to operate on the ulcer. This decision was taken
> because, in the doctors' view, administration of the necessary anaesthesia to someone with
> such extensive head injuries could be fatal. A month later, the ulcer burst, and V died without
> having regained consciousness.

On these facts, D's conviction for manslaughter was upheld by the Court of Appeal. How
should the question of causation be analysed? One cause of V's death is, of course, the ulcer.
But another, concurrent, causal factor is the doctors' omission to operate: if it had been safe
to operate, there was no doubt but that the ulcer would have been removed.[211] What is
therefore crucial to D's liability is whether the omission to operate, which *was* a cause of
death, can be said in turn to be a consequence of D's actions in inflicting the head injuries

---

[207] (1971) 56 Cr App R 95, 102.

[208] More precisely, an action (refusal) whose causal role depends upon an omission (non-transfusion).

[209] *Contra Hart and Honoré* 361. Occasionally, an omission may be a *novus actus* when *combined* with a positive
intervention: e.g. when the railway gatekeeper fails to close the gate, causing the ambulance taking V to hospital to
be hit by a train. The gatekeeper causes V's death, not V's original assailant.

[210] (1992) 94 Cr App R 51.

[211] *Ibid.*, 57.

upon V. And it seems clear enough that it was. The doctors' decision not to operate was made precisely because of the injuries D inflicted. Moreover, although expert testimony at trial conflicted over whether it was *possible* to proceed with the operation without endangering V's life, there was no dispute that the decision was a reasonable one to take. Hence it was not a *novus actus interveniens*. We may represent the causal analysis as follows:

McKechnie:

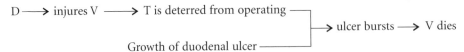

We are also in a position now to consider the difficult case of *Cheshire*.[212] The relevant facts of the case were as follows:

> In early December 1987, D shot V in the leg and stomach. V was taken to hospital where his injuries were operated on and he was then transferred to the intensive care unit. He developed respiratory problems and in mid-December a tracheotomy tube was inserted into his windpipe, where it remained for some four weeks. In early February his condition began to improve, and it appears that by this time the injuries inflicted by D's bullets had ceased to threaten his life. Unfortunately, he then began to develop breathing difficulties. These arose because his windpipe had narrowed near the site of the tracheotomy—a rare but known side-effect of tracheotomies. The medical staff negligently failed to diagnose the cause of the breathing difficulties, and V died in mid-February.

The Court of Appeal upheld D's conviction for murder, and properly so. Both D and V's doctors caused V's death. The key point is that the tracheotomy and subsequent complication occurred without negligence by the doctors. Thus there is no disruption of the causal chain between D's act of shooting V and the narrowing of V's windpipe. This being so, the question then becomes whether the doctors' subsequent negligence is a *novus actus interveniens* that breaks the causal chain between the narrowing of the windpipe and V's death. And the answer to that question is no—because it constitutes an omission. The complaint against the doctors is that they *failed* to prevent the (natural, albeit rare) complication from causing death. Diagrammatically:

Cheshire:

D —→ injures V —→ T performs tracheotomy —→ windpipe narrows ⌐
                                                                ├→ V dies
                         T(2) —→ fails to rectify windpipe ⌐

§ 4.3 The requirement of voluntariness

It is a fundamental requirement of the criminal law that D cannot be held liable for the occurrence of an actus reus unless he was *responsible* for it: unless its occurrence can in some way be attributed to D.

---

212 [1991] 3 All ER 670.

We noted in Chapter 1 that when an actus reus occurs (e.g. Jim is murdered), the criminal law begins with every member of society as a potential defendant.[213] The legal criteria that define responsibility for an actus reus also help to tell us which members of society are suitable defendants. Suppose that while investigating Jim's death, the police learn that his daughter Alice had secretly wished him dead because she stood to gain from his will. Despite her desires, the need for responsibility means that Alice is not guilty of murder unless she actually played some role in bringing about his death.

In respect of consequences, responsibility is established by showing causation. The police may conclude that although Alice wanted Jim's death, she did not cause it. Hence she did not murder Jim. More generally, causation is necessary to establish a link between D's behaviour and the prohibited consequences. If an actus reus includes specification of such consequences (e.g. a person's death), the prosecution must prove causation in order to show that D's behaviour was responsible for that consequence, as part of showing that the actus reus as a whole can be attributed to D.

However, before she can be criminally liable the defendant must also be responsible for the *behaviour* element of the actus reus. This requirement is met when her behaviour is voluntary. Suppose that Alice did in fact cause Jim's death, but that she did so while suffering an epileptic seizure, during which her movements caused a heavy object to fall and crush Jim. Alice's behaviour, which causes Jim's death, is not voluntary. She is not responsible for his death, and cannot be convicted of murder.

Very often, acquittal in these circumstances need not be based upon involuntariness. Crimes such as murder require proof of some mental element on the part of the defendant, i.e. proof of some form of mens rea.[214] In most cases, murder itself cannot be committed unless D intends to kill or cause serious injury.[215] Thus, even though Alice's behaviour may have caused death, she lacks the mental element required to be guilty of murder. She lacks mens rea.

But it is important to emphasise that involuntariness is *not* merely a denial of intention, or of other forms of mens rea, or even a denial of fault in general.[216] Alice does not claim that she killed Jim by *accident*. Her denial is much more profound. It is a claim that the movements of her body which caused Jim's death do not belong to Alice as a reasoning person.

This deserves elaboration. As part of our conception of what it is to be a human being, we draw a distinction between a deliberative person and her body. Not all movements of one's body can be identified with the person whose body it is that moves. When the doctor tests Simon's reflexes by tapping him on the knee, the swinging of his leg cannot be attributed to Simon. It is merely an event in the history of his body, rather like the lurching of passengers standing in a crowded bus. These are not actions that a person is answerable for doing. They are things that happen to him, over which he has no control, and for which he is not responsible. So it is with Alice in the example above. Her behaviour is part of her

---

[213] See §§ 1.2(ii)(e), 7.1.

[214] Below, Chapter 5.

[215] Below, Chapter 10.

[216] For useful discussion of this point, see Patient, "Some Remarks about the Element of Voluntariness in Offences of Absolute Liability" [1968] *Crim LR* 23.

body's history, but is not attributable to her as a reasoning person. It is not produced by any exercise of the capacities that identify Alice as a moral agent. In the words of H.L.A. Hart:[217]

> "What is missing in these cases appears to most people as a vital link between mind and body; and both the ordinary man and the lawyer might well insist on this by saying that in these cases there is not 'really' a human action at all and certainly nothing for which anyone should be made criminally responsible however 'strict' legal responsibility might be."

(i) Involuntary behaviour

In general, D's deliberative control over her behaviour can be lost or impaired in two ways. First, D's normal capacity to reason about her behaviour may be suppressed because of an impaired consciousness. Alternatively, even if D is able to reason normally about her actions, she may have lost physical control over the movements of her body. In either case, her actions are not responsive to reason. They are "movements of the body which occurred though the agent had no reason for moving his body in that way."[218]

(a) Loss of physical control

Imagine the following assault:

> Deborah is standing between Vicky and Tanya. Suddenly, Tanya grasps Deborah's arm and forces it into Vicky's midriff. Tanya is more powerful than Deborah, and Deborah has no chance to resist her. Vicky is winded.

In this situation, Deborah does not commit an assault on Vicky, because her behaviour is involuntary.[219] The movement of Deborah's arm does not occur under her control, and she cannot prevent its occurrence. Thus she is not responsible for the actus reus which eventuates. (Indeed, it is Tanya who assaults Vicky, using Deborah's arm.) Comparable instances are where D's arm strikes V as the result of a reflex movement or a muscular convulsion or spasm.[220]

(b) Impaired consciousness

It has also been held that if D, while driving, were to be stunned by a blow and rendered incapable of controlling his car, his consequent failure to give way to a pedestrian at a pedestrian crossing would be involuntary and not subject to criminal liability.[221] An analogous situation is sleepwalking. In Hughes, a woman had got out of bed during the night and had gone to the kitchen "to peel potatoes", whence she had taken a knife and returned to the bedroom to stab her husband. She was acquitted of wounding with intent.[222]

---

[217] Hart, "Acts of Will and Responsibility" in Punishment and Responsibility (1968) 90, 107.

[218] The definition of involuntariness proposed by Hart, Punishment and Responsibility (1968) 255–6.

[219] Farduto (1912) 10 DLR 669, 673; compare O'Sullivan v. Fisher [1954] SASR 33, 39–40.

[220] Bratty v. A-G for Northern Ireland [1963] AC 386, 409.

[221] Hill v. Baxter [1958] 1 QB 277, 282–3, 286; Burns v. Bidder [1967] 2 QB 227, 36; Kay v. Butterworth (1945) 61 TLR 452, 453; Spurge [1961] 2 QB 205; Bell [1984] 3 All ER 842, 846.

[222] Reported in The Times, 3 May 1978, p. 5. Cf. Bratty v. A-G for Northern Ireland [1963] AC 386, 403, 409; Carpenter, The Times, 14 October 1976; Carter [1959] VR 105; Fain v. Commonwealth (1879) 39 Am Rep 213. Seemingly, the case should have been regarded as one of insane automatism: below, §18.1(ii)(c).

Sleepwalking is an instructive case, because D's behaviour in this state may well be purposive,[223] and exhibit many outward signs of intentionality. Glanville Williams makes this point vividly:[224]

> "The sleep-walker does not always proceed as the cartoonists imagine him, with eyes tightly closed and arms outstretched. His eyes may be open and he may appear to be in perfect control. He will open a door and turn a corner, walk downstairs, open a drawer, take out a carving-knife, and return to the bedroom where his wife is asleep. But after waking up he will not remember his deed (except sometimes as a dream). Although his acts have a certain purpose (indeed, he may have an understandable reason for killing his wife), it is the purpose of a dream-state. He is not acting with his normal conscious mind."

When Lady Macbeth is observed "washing" her hands at night,[225] her movements are hardly random or uncontrolled. They exude purpose. Her actions are, in some sense, a subintentional product of her unconscious or subconscious mind. Certainly they are not mere reflex movements. But the control that Lady Macbeth has over them is in no way a conscious control—indeed, she is incapable of acting intentionally at all. Her "acts" are, in law, involuntary.

In the criminal law, these forms of involuntary behaviour are known as automatism. Like Lady Macbeth, the defendant may be unconscious or semi-conscious when she does the actus reus. Where this is so, and her actions are the product of that impaired consciousness, those actions are described as automatic. However, as the assault example involving Deborah, Tanya, and Vicky shows, automatism predicated upon unconsciousness or impaired consciousness is not *required* for the defendant to be absolved of responsibility for her behaviour. Whether she was conscious or unconscious, what is essential to the denial of responsibility for a defendant's involuntary behaviour is that *she was unable deliberatively to control that behaviour and to prevent it from occurring.*

In most cases, there will be a connection between consciousness and control: the greater the degree of consciousness a defendant has, the greater the degree of conscious or deliberative control she will have over her actions. This raises the further question: where D's claim of involuntariness is based upon automatism and an impaired consciousness, must D have lost *all* conscious control over her limbs?

The law is unclear. The leading recent case is *A-G's Reference (No. 2 of 1992)*, and it sets a very high standard indeed. In that case, D was charged with causing death by reckless driving. He had steered his truck onto the hard shoulder of the motorway and then into a stationary vehicle. At the time, D had been driving for six of the past 12 hours. The defence adduced evidence that D had entered a condition known as "driving without awareness", in which a driver's ability to avoid a collision was negated because repetitive stimuli experienced during long motorway journeys induced a trance-like state in which the focal point for forward vision gradually came nearer and nearer until the driver was focusing just ahead of his windscreen. The Court of Appeal held that such evidence could not support a defence of automatism. In the Court's words, "the defence of automatism requires a total destruction

---

[223] Compare also *Charlson* [1955] 1 All ER 859.
[224] *TBCL* 665.
[225] *Macbeth*, Act V, scene i.

of voluntary control on the defendant's part. Impaired, reduced, or partial control is not enough."[226] By contrast, someone driving without awareness "retains some control. He would be able to steer the vehicle and usually to react and return to full awareness when confronted by significant stimuli."[227] The Court observed that although "very little" may intrude upon the driver's consciousness, he is not entirely (just "largely") unaware of steering or of the road ahead.[228]

This standard accords with that in the earlier case of *Watmore* v. *Jenkins*, where automatism was said to connote no "wider or looser concept than involuntary movement of the body or limbs."[229] Similarly, in *Broome* v. *Perkins*, the contrast between normal and automatic driving was described as follows:[230]

> "When driving a motor vehicle, the driver's conscious mind receives signals from his eyes and ears, decides on the appropriate course of action as a result of those signals, and gives directions to the limbs to control the vehicle. When a person's actions are involuntary and automatic his mind is not controlling or directing his limbs."

On this footing, the defendant Perkins was convicted of driving without due care and attention, even though in a hypoglycaemic state. Since his erratic driving manifested reaction to stimuli (e.g. veering away from another vehicle, braking behind traffic), his mind must, at least from time to time, have been in control of his limbs. During those periods he was driving, and therefore, in the view of the Divisional Court, the offence was made out. On a similar rationale, the defendant in *Watmore* v. *Jenkins* was convicted of dangerous driving when in a hypoglycaemic state.[231]

These decisions are somewhat rigid in their approach, and are difficult to reconcile with a second body of cases not involving driving offences. In *Charlson*,[232] D was charged with causing grievous bodily harm to his 10-year-old son, after he had suddenly struck the child on the head with a mallet and then defenestrated him. D may well have been suffering from a cerebral tumour, which would render him liable to an outburst of impulsive violence over which he had no control. On these facts, D was permitted to raise a defence of automatism (and found not guilty) even though he could recall hitting V on the head. Similarly, in *Quick*, on a charge of assault D was allowed to raise automatism consequent upon hypoglycaemia, notwithstanding that his condition was one of semi-consciousness.[233] It is hard to see how the same condition, hypoglycaemia, may ground a claim of automatism in *Quick* but not in *Watmore* v. *Jenkins* or *Broome* v. *Perkins*.

The latter cases are to be preferred. It is noteworthy that the cases in which the most stringent demands are made all concern driving offences, and it may be that they should be

---

[226] [1994] QB 91, 105.

[227] [1994] QB 91, 105.

[228] [1994] QB 91, 102.

[229] [1962] 2 QB 572, 586.

[230] (1987) 85 Cr App R 321, 332.

[231] *Isitt* (1978) 67 Cr App R 44 may be thought of as a similar authority, in that D's claim of hysterical fugue did not forestall his conviction for dangerous driving. However, on the facts his conduct appears to have involved action for a purpose—merely without moral inhibition (see at 48–9).

[232] [1955] 1 All ER 859. Strictly speaking, since D was suffering from an "internal" disorder, the case should be regarded as one of *insane* automatism: below, §§ 4.3(i)(d), 18.1(ii)(c).

[233] [1973] QB 910, 916b.

restricted to that context. In offences that involve more complex activities, such as robbery and assault, there is certainly no requirement that D be altogether unconscious.[234] What is striking about the driving cases is the simplistic approach of the courts. No middle ground is acknowledged: in which D may not be fully unconscious, yet may have no conscious control over his actions. His limbs may respond to subconscious commands, but not to reason.

In this context it is helpful to consider *Bratty v. Attorney-General for Northern Ireland*, in which Lord Denning stated:[235]

> "No act is punishable if it is done involuntarily: and an involuntary act in this context—some people nowadays prefer to speak of it as 'automatism'—means an act which is done by the muscles without any control of the mind, such as a spasm, a reflex action or a convulsion; or an act done by a person who is not conscious of what he is doing, such as an act done whilst suffering from concussion or whilst sleep-walking."

At first blush, this passage may seem to contemplate only situations where there is a complete loss of consciousness. However, Lord Denning's definition is asserted in order to draw a contrast, later in the same judgment, with an act that the accused merely cannot remember, or which "is unintentional or its consequences merely foreseen." Understood in this context, there is no suggestion that his Lordship intended to equate involuntariness with unconsciousness; indeed concussion, expressly included in the definition, is a clear case where behaviour is not consciously but at some lower level *willed*. Moreover, the judgment goes on to discuss, without reservation on this point, the direction given in *Charlson*;[236] in which (as we saw) D's actions were not only conscious but remembered.

If Lord Denning meant that the accused person must be absolutely unconscious, it would be meaningless to speak of "an act which is done by the muscles without any control by the mind," since muscles cannot be moved without stimulus of some sort from the mind. The conclusion is inescapable that his Lordship envisaged the conscious, reasoning control of the mind as what must be lacking in automatism.[237] Moreover, at the level of principle, this analysis seems correct. What counts is the inability *deliberatively* to control one's conduct—that one's movements are not responsive to a capacity to reason and deliberate about one's conduct. Obviously, where the defendant is altogether unconscious her reasoning capacities will be inactive. But a defendant need *not* be unconscious before those capacities may be suppressed or inoperative. A hypnotised patient who carries out the instructions of the hypnotist must be able to comprehend and implement those instructions at some level of consciousness. Yet he has no capacity to deliberate about what actions to

---

[234] The possibility of semi-conscious automatism appears to have been accepted also in *Stripp* (1978) 69 Cr App R 318, 320–1; cf. *Toner* (1991) 93 Cr App R 382; *Carter* [1959] VR 105, 108–9.

[235] [1963] AC 386, 409. See also the judgment of Viscount Kilmuir LC, at 401, 527.

[236] [1955] 1 All ER 859; see *Bratty* [1963] AC 386, 411. (Lord Denning thought, however, that case should have been regarded as insane rather than sane automatism. See above, n. 229.)

[237] A conclusion reached by the New Zealand Court of Appeal in *Burr* [1969] NZLR 736, 744–5 (North P), when considering the same passage. In *Broome v. Perkins* (1987) 85 Cr App R 321, the prosecution's submission (at 325) that "automatism meant an act which was done by the muscles without any control by the mind such as a spasm, a reflex action or a convulsion" seems to reveal a fundamental confusion between automatism and loss of physical control over one's limbs (§ 4.3(i)(a)).

take or his reasons for taking them. He is an automaton, and is not responsible for his behaviour.[238]

Apart from sleepwalking and hypnotism, standard cases of semi-conscious conduct which are capable of qualifying as automatic and involuntary behaviour include acts done while in a state of concussion,[239] dissociation,[240] and advanced stages of hypoglycaemia.[241] In each of these instances, a loss of the capacity deliberatively to control D's behaviour will mean that he cannot be held criminally responsible for his actions and their consequences.

(c) Imperfect deliberative capacity?

Although the above cases show that semi-conscious action can be automatic, they all involve a *complete* loss of deliberative control. It must be emphasised, on the other hand, that where D does in fact form an intention to commit a crime, then however clouded and confused D's awareness may have been, automatism is excluded. Responsibility for behaviour is not denied merely because D's deliberative faculties are not functioning perfectly, or "not working in top gear."[242] "Not thinking clearly" implies that D is still thinking about his actions, even if not very well. He is still exercising some deliberative control over his conduct, and cannot claim that his conduct was involuntary—it is a far cry from this state to one in which D is not reasoning at all. Rather than automatism, the appropriate defence (if applicable) is one of absence of mens rea. An instructive case is *Kingston*, the facts of which were as follows:[243]

> D was invited to a flat for ostensibly innocent purposes. While there, he was given coffee laced with disinhibiting drugs. He was then taken into a bedroom where a 15-year-old boy lay, also drugged, on a bed. D performed sexual acts with the boy, and was subsequently charged with an indecent assault. His conviction was upheld by the House of Lords.

It is quite likely that D would not have acted as he did had he not (unknown to him) ingested the drugs, which may well have affected his judgement by freeing him of his usual self-restraint. But a disinhibited intent is still an intent, and the explanation cannot amount to a denial of responsibility for D. He acts for reasons—albeit perhaps not reasons that would normally motivate him—and thus is not automatic.[244] More generally, it is no defence that D acted upon an *irresistible impulse*, if he knew what he was doing and acted

---

[238] For interesting discussion, see Williams, "The Actus Reus of Dr Caligari" (1994) 142 *U Pa L Rev* 1661, 1667f.

[239] Cf. *Bratty v. A-G for Northern Ireland* [1963] AC 386, 403; *Quick* [1973] QB 910, 918, 920–2.

[240] Cf. *Toner* (1991) 93 Cr App R 382; *T* [1990] Crim LR 256; *Rabey* (1980) 15 CR (3d) 225.

[241] *Quick* [1973] QB 910.

[242] *Isitt* (1977) 67 Cr App R 44, 48.

[243] [1995] 2 AC 355.

[244] Cf. *Isitt* (1977) 67 Cr App R 44, 49; *A-G for South Australia v. Brown* [1960] AC 432; *Bratty v. A-G or Northern Ireland* [1963] AC 386, 409; *HM Advocate v. Kidd* [1960] SLT 82. A similar analysis would apply to provocation; D's provoked intention is still an intention. Thus the defence functions as an excuse rather than as a denial of voluntariness. See below, § 10.5. For an argument that *Kingston* might deserve an excusatory defence, see Sullivan, "Making Excuses" in Simester and Smith (eds.), *Harm and Culpability* (1996) 131.

[245] *Bratty v. A-G for Northern Ireland* [1963] AC 386, 409; *A-G for South Australia v. Brown* [1960] AC 432; cf. *Dodd* (1974) 7 SASR 151, 157; *Burr* [1969] NZLR 736, 750.

intentionally.[245] An impulsive action is conscious and intentional—it is action for a reason, not action uncontrolled by reason.

(d) Insane automatism

Whenever a defendant's involuntariness is found to be due to automatism, the court must then determine whether it is to be classified as *sane* or *insane* automatism. This classification depends upon the cause of the automatism. Where the defendant loses consciousness as a result of a blow on the head, for example, his behaviour will be regarded as occurring in a state of sane automatism. By contrast, behaviour occurring during an epileptic fit will be exculpated on the footing of insane automatism.

The test for differentiating these types of automatism will be discussed in Chapter 19, when we consider the defence of insanity. The importance of the distinction is that sane automatism operates as a straightforward denial of voluntariness and thus leads to an outright acquittal. By contrast, insane automatism is treated in law as a species of insanity, for which there is a special verdict and a different burden of proof upon the defendant.

(ii) Omissions, states of affairs, and possession

So far we have considered involuntariness in the context of positive actions by a defendant. However, we saw earlier in this chapter (§ 4.1) that not every actus reus requires a positive action. For example, if D stands by while her child drowns in the bath, her omission to save him is prima facie the actus reus of culpable homicide.[246]

Obviously, the involuntariness of omissions cannot be explained in the same way as actions. It would be odd indeed to talk of a reflex or convulsive omission. Nonetheless, even for omissions the criminal law in general requires that D must be responsible for her behaviour before she commits the actus reus of a crime. D's omission is involuntary, and her responsibility for the actus reus is negated, when she fails to discharge a duty to intervene because it was *impossible* for her to do so. There is extensive authority for this proposition.[247] As Sir William Scott put the point, in *The Generous*:[248]

> "But the law itself, and the administration of it, must yield to that to which everything must bend—to necessity. The law, in its most positive and peremptory injunctions, is understood to disclaim, as it does in its general aphorisms, all intention of compelling them to impossibilities; and the administration of law must adopt that general exception in the consideration of all particular cases."

That general exception was adopted in *Bamber*,[249] where a landowner charged with non-repair of a highway across his land was absolved of liability on the ground that repair of the highway was impossible:[250]

---

[246] Above, § 4.1(i)(a) (Case 2).
[247] *Stockdale* v. *Coulson* [1974] 3 All ER 154; *Brown* (1841) Car & M 314, 318, 174 ER 521, 524 ("without any physical impossibility" a proviso); *Mary Hogan* (1851) 2 Den 277, 169 ER 504; *Burns* v. *Bidder* [1967] 2 QB 227; *Vann* (1851) Cox CC 379. A valuable discussion is Smart, "Criminal Responsibility for Failing to Do the Impossible" (1987) 103 *LQR* 532. See also Williams, *CLGP* 746–8.
[248] (1812) 2 Dods 322, 323, 165 ER 1501.
[249] (1843) 5 QB 279, 114 ER 1254.
[250] *Ibid.*, 287, 1257.

"Both the road which the defendant is charged with liability to repair, and the land over which it passes, are washed away by the sea. To restore the road, as he is required to do, he must create a part of the earth anew. . . . But here all the materials of which a road could be made have been swept away by the act of God. Under those circumstances can the defendant be liable for not repairing the road? We want an authority for such a proposition; and none has been found."

In the context of an offence more familiar to students, suppose the following example:

After an earthquake, D observes that his daughter is suffocating under a pile of rubble. D fails to rescue her because he is pinned beneath some collapsed masonry from which he cannot escape. D is not responsible for failing to rescue his daughter, and cannot be attributed with the actus reus of a homicide.

This is true even if, for some reason, D had wanted his daughter dead, and would not have rescued her had it been possible to do so.[251]

In such cases, where a defendant would not have complied with the law even if possible, it is sometimes important to distinguish between involuntary *behaviour* and unavoidable *consequences*. In the earthquake example, D has no control over his behaviour. But imagine the following case:

E is sunbathing on the beach when he observes his young daughter entering the sea and starting to swim in shallow water. Unfortunately, she encounters difficulties and is caught in an outgoing tide. E does not lift a finger to help, despite her cries to him, and watches as she is swept out to sea and drowned.

E may be able to deny responsibility for his daughter's death on the basis of *causation*. In a prosecution for murder or manslaughter, the prosecution must prove that E's omission to intervene caused his daughter's death. If in fact there was a riptide, and E would have been unable to save her anyway, then he is not responsible for the fatal consequence and cannot be convicted of a homicide offence.

The difference between this case and the earthquake example is that E denies responsibility for a *consequence* of his omission, on the basis of causation, while D denies responsibility for his *behaviour*, on the basis of involuntariness. Either way, a vital element of the actus reus of homicide is missing. But unlike D, E may still be criminally liable for any relevant offence where consequences are not part of the actus reus,[252] including an *attempt*. Because E's behaviour was not involuntary, it is capable in principle of constituting the actus reus of an attempted murder.[253] (Whether he would be convicted then depends upon questions of mens rea and proximity.) By contrast, it is impossible for D even to attempt a rescue. Therefore he cannot be held responsible for failing to do so.

---

[251] Cf. *Starri* v. *SA Police* (1995) 80 A Crim R 197.

[252] Compare *Brown* (1841) Car & M 314, 318, 174 ER 522, 524.

[253] Subject to the language of the Criminal Attempts Act 1981, which prima facie requires an "act": below, § 9.3(ii)(c)

(a) Omission cases that derogate from principle

In *Stockdale* v. *Coulson* it was said that "nobody ought to be prosecuted for that which it is impossible to do."[254] Similarly, in *Burns* v. *Nowell*:[255]

> "before a continuous act or proceeding, not originally unlawful, can be treated as unlawful by reason of the passing of an Act of Parliament, . . . a reasonable time must be allowed for its discontinuance. . . ."

At the level of principle, these sentiments endorse a defence of impossibility in ringing terms. Yet there are cases where such a defence has not been allowed. In *Davey* v. *Towle*,[256] for example, the driver of a car was not excused for failing to produce a test certificate, even though it was impossible for him to do so because the car owner was unable or unwilling to produce the certificate. Such cases should be regarded as exceptional. Derogation from the principle *lex non cogit ad impossibilia* is not to be encouraged: it is both morally undesirable and inconsistent with a significant body of case law.[257]

It may be that the exceptional cases such as *Davey* v. *Towle* can be explained, and therefore confined. They all involve strict liability offences—especially driving offences— where the defendant chose to engage in a specialist, risk-creating activity, and thereby brought himself within the scope of the relevant criminal law duty. Moreover, the defendant had an opportunity, before doing so (e.g. commencing to drive), to ensure that he had the ability to comply with the law.[258] In such circumstances, it may be reasonable to expect the onus to lie on the defendant to make sure in advance that he has the wherewithal to comply with the law. Failure to do so would then count as a species of antecedent fault: discussed below, § 4.3(iii).

An additional consideration is that, in *Davey* v. *Towle*, to permit D to shelter behind the recalcitrance of the car owner would undermine the effectiveness and purpose of the offence itself. Provided there is the possibility of ensuring compliance in advance, this would seem a legitimate reason for excluding a defence of impossibility at the time of the infraction. Where, however, the features identified here do not apply, it is submitted that the general rule is that impossibility is a defence to crimes of omission.

(b) States of affairs

In principle, the test of responsibility for crimes which specify no behavioural element, and which criminalise states of affairs, ought to be similar to the impossibility test for crimes of omission. This follows from the point made earlier (in § 4.1(ii)(a)) that such offences, while formally needing no proof of particular behaviour by the defendant, can be seen as indirectly imposing liability for a defendant's omission to prevent the actus reus from occurring.

Unfortunately, English courts have not acknowledged this point. Instead, they have

---

[254] [1974] 3 All ER 154, 157.
[255] (1880) 5 QBD 444, 454.
[256] [1973] RTR 328. Cf. *Strowger* v. *John* [1974] RTR 124; *Pilgram* v. *Dean* [1974] 2 All ER 751.
[257] See the cases cited above, n. 244.
[258] Compare *Strowger* v. *John* [1974] RTR 124, 130, where, on a charge of failing to display a vehicle excise licence (which had fallen off the windscreen), Lord Widgery CJ observed that it might be different if a stranger had broken into the car and removed the licence without the defendant's knowledge.

treated the issue essentially as a question of statutory interpretation: does the statute creating the offence refer to the defendant's behaviour? In the case of liability for omissions, where the behaviour element of the actus reus is explicit, it has therefore been possible to deny responsibility for the actus reus by claiming that D's behaviour was involuntary. By contrast, where the offence specifies no explicit behavioural element at all, the courts have tended to regard such claims as legally irrelevant.

It need not be thus. In *Dr Bonham's Case*, Coke CJ used words of great power:[259]

> "when an Act of Parliament is against common right and reason, or repugnant, *or impossible to be performed*, the common law will controul it. . . ."

The defence of impossibility, it may be observed, has venerable spiritual heritage: a law that demands the impossible surely is against common right and reason, warranting an exception. Consistently with this, Lord Uthwatt commented in 1948 that a driver who failed to accord precedence at a pedestrian crossing "has, subject only to the application of the principle *Lex non cogit ad impossibilia*, broken the regulation."[260] Yet in 1988 such grand sentiments were nowhere to be found in the Court of Appeal. In *Porter* v. *Honey*[261] D, an estate agent, was prosecuted for displaying a "for sale" board on a property at a time when a second board was also displayed. D had erected the board at a time when no other board was displayed, and prima facie committed an offence only when (unknown to D) a competing estate agent erected a second "for sale" board on the same property. Faced with this situation, the House of Lords succeeded in exculpating D only by a convoluted (and far-fetched) exercise in statutory reinterpretation. The moral poverty of this technique was captured, without irony, by Lord Griffiths' first words:

> "the question for your Lordships is whether on the true construction of the relevant legislation an estate agent who lawfully places a 'for sale' board on a property should be held to have committed a criminal offence because another estate agent unlawfully and without the knowledge or consent of the first estate agent places a second 'for sale' board on the same property. I suggest that any layman would not hesitate to answer, 'No, Parliament cannot have intended such an unjust and absurd result'. Unfortunately, the legislation poses a more difficult problem of construction for the lawyer. . . ."

The "modern" approach has had greatest impact upon situational crimes. In English law, by contrast with other jurisdictions,[262] it appears that impossibility is no defence to crimes that impose liability purely for a state of affairs. Authority for this proposition includes *Larsonneur*,[263] discussed earlier, and a number of other cases.[264] In *Larsonneur*, it will be recalled, D was brought into the United Kingdom against her will by the police, and consequently convicted of "being found" in the country when permission for her to enter had

---

[259] 8 Co Rep 113b, 118a, 77 ER 646, 652. Coke CJ's words must now be read in light of the doctrine of Parliamentary Sovereignty. But there is nothing in that doctrine that prevents recognition of a common law defence of necessity.

[260] *London Passenger Transport Board* v. *Upson* [1949] AC 155.

[261] [1988] 3 All ER 1045. Compare *Leicester* v. *Pearson* [1952] 2 QB 668.

[262] See, e.g., *O'Sullivan* v. *Fisher* [1954] SASR 33; *Finau* v. *Dept of Labour* [1984] 2 NZLR 396.

[263] (1933) 149 LT 542; above, § 4.1(ii)(a).

[264] Cf. *Hawkins* v. *Holmes* [1974] RTR 436; *Duck* v. *Peacock* [1949] 1 All ER 318; *Crump* v. *Gilmore* [1970] Crim LR 28; *Smedleys Ltd* v. *Breed* [1974] AC 839; also the cases mentioned above, n. 244.

previously been refused. A similar case is *Winzar* v. *Chief Constable of Kent*.[265] D, who had been brought to hospital but found merely to be drunk, was later removed by the police to their car parked on the road outside. He was then charged with being found drunk on a highway, and his conviction was upheld by the Divisional Court. "Being found", it was held, refers only to the perceptions or actions of the finder and not to any conduct by the defendant. Given the language used in the statute, the fact that the defendant's involvement was involuntary was said therefore to be immaterial.

Since the defendants were said to be guilty of offences in these cases, presumably the policemen involved should have been charged with procuring. So far as responsibility for the offence is concerned, its commission in each case was brought about by the police and had nothing to do with the defendant.[266] Yet it was the defendant who was convicted. Cases such as *Larsonneur* and *Winzar* show a lack of regard for fundamental principles of humanity and justice.[267]

(c) Involuntary possession

Like situational offences, criminal possession (e.g. of an instrument of burglary[268] or of a controlled drug[269]) can be established without proving any behaviour by D (above, § 4.1(ii)(b)). The physical element of "being in possession" is a state of affairs in which D has control, with or without custody,[270] of the prohibited item. It is usually sufficient for the actus reus to show that the item is at a location where it is subject to D's power of control.[271]

As it happens, most offences of possession are unlikely to raise issues of involuntariness, since they generally require proof of a mental element in addition to proof of the actus reus. Thus, according to Lord Morris in *Warner* v. *Metropolitan Police Commissioner*, possession involves "being *knowingly* in control of a thing in circumstances which have involved an opportunity (whether availed of or not) to learn or discover, at least in a general way, what the thing is."[272] We will consider mens rea issues surrounding possession below, in § 5.6(ii). For present purposes, suppose that D is asleep when another person places controlled drugs in her hand. There is no need to address the question of voluntariness, since D lacks the knowledge required to constitute possession of the drugs.[273]

---

[265] *The Times*, 28 March 1983.

[266] Subject to the argument by Lanham, "Larsonneur Revisited" [1976] *Crim LR*, that *Larsonneur* involved prior fault; a rationale not, however, relied upon in the Court's decision.

[267] For a consideration of the potential impact of the European Convention of Human Rights on such cases, see Sullivan, "Strict Liability for Criminal Offences in England and Wales following Incorporation into English Law of the European Convention on Human Rights" in Simester, (ed.), *Appraising Strict Liability* (2005) 195.

[268] Theft Act 1968, s. 25.

[269] Misuse of Drugs Act 1971, s. 5.

[270] Cf. *Kelt* [1977] 1 WLR 1365; *Sullivan* v. *Earl of Caithness* [1976] QB 966 (item held on behalf of D by third party). In some offences control without the availability of imminent custody may not suffice: *Lester* (1955) 39 Cr App R 157.

[271] At least in respect of drugs: *Lewis* (1987) 87 Cr App R 270.

[272] [1969] 2 AC 256, 289.

[273] See, e.g., the hypothetical case posed by Parker LCJ in *Lockyer* v. *Gibb* [1967] 2 QB 243, 248; discussed by the House of Lords in *Warner* v. *Metropolitan Police Comr* [1969] 2 AC 256, 282, 286, 300, 303, 311; below, § 5.6(ii). In addition, even if it were held that D "possessed" the drugs, she would have a defence of justified ignorance under s. 28 of the Misuse of Drugs Act 1971.

As we shall see in Chapter 5, the view that "possession" has an embedded mental element has been criticised. If that criticism were to be accepted by the courts, the question of involuntary possession would become more important. However, it is possible to construct situations in which, even if Lord Morris is right, one may involuntarily be in possession:

> Imagine that D acquires possession of controlled drugs but not by means of his own voluntary actions—for example, if a visitor to his house leaves the drugs behind when she departs. D may not be responsible for acquiring possession, but normally he is still responsible for *being* in possession because he fails to divest himself of the drugs. Suppose further, however, that D knows that he has been left the drugs yet happens to be bed-ridden through illness and is thus unable to dispose of them.

It is submitted that, by analogy with offences involving omissions, D should not be held responsible for the actus reus and his involuntary possession should not be attributed to him for the purposes of criminal liability. Indirect authority for this proposition may be inferred from the reasoning of the House of Lords in *Warner*. Presumably the reason Lord Morris required an opportunity to discover possession is in order that the defendant should have the chance to divest himself of contraband unknowingly acquired. It would seem both harsh and unlikely that, the instant some stranger thrusts a package into D's arms while D is out walking, he should be held criminally responsible for possession before he has had even the chance to drop it.[274]

(d) Distinction between impossibility and ignorance of duty

Impossibility amounting to involuntariness should be distinguished from situations where D is reasonably unaware of the existence of facts that trigger a duty to act in a certain manner. For example, one does not, apparently, commit an offence of remaining in Singapore when one's presence there becomes unlawful pursuant to an unpublished law.[275] Exculpation in such cases does not depend upon any claim of involuntariness, but rather upon the source and reasonableness of D's ignorance of law or fact. It is thus a matter for particular defences.

(iii) Involuntariness: responsibility by antecedent fault

Sometimes, even though the actus reus occurs involuntarily, D may still be held criminally responsible. One way in which this may occur is through vicarious liability, which is discussed below in Chapter 8. Leaving that possibility aside, however, D may also be liable for an offence if his involuntariness, and in turn the actus reus, was the consequence of earlier conduct by D in respect of which D was at fault. There are three main situations in which this can occur.

---

[274] Compare *Wright* (1975) 62 Cr App R 169.
[275] *Lim Chin Aik* v. *R.* [1963] AC 160. Cf. *Harding* v. *Price* [1948] 1 KB 695 (failing to report an accident when D did not know it had occurred); *Hampson* v. *Powell* [1970] 1 All ER 929, 931; *Hardcastle* v. *Bielby* [1892] 1 QB 709; *Simons* v. *Rhodes and Son Ltd* [1956] 1 WLR 642; *Belling* v. *O'Sullivan* [1950] SASR 43. See below, § 18.2(iii).

(a) Intoxication

The first is voluntary intoxication. Suppose that D drinks himself into a stupor, and then commits an assault. Even if the court accepts his claim that the assault occurred while D was an automaton, it will not negate his criminal responsibility for the actus reus. In such circumstances, the presence of intoxication has two roles. First, it precludes the claim of involuntariness. Secondly, it is constitutive of certain mens rea states, including recklessness (the mens rea element in assault). A helpful illustration is provided by *Lipman*, the facts of which were as follows:[276]

> L and his female friend, V, took a quantity of LSD while in V's flat. During the hallu-cination which followed, L suffocated V by cramming bed sheet into her mouth. He believed when he did so that he was fighting snakes while descending to the centre of the earth.

L's behaviour while hallucinating is analogous to sleepwalking. It did not occur under his conscious or deliberative control. However, the automatism was self-induced, and moreover induced by D's own fault in becoming intoxicated. His claim to be exculpated on the basis of automatism was therefore refused, and L was convicted of manslaughter.[277]

The legal ramifications of intoxication will be explored further below, in Chapter 18. It is worth mentioning here, however, that English law on this point is out of line with that prevailing in other common law jurisdictions; where, unless one of the two further excep-tions (below, § 4.3(iii)(b)–(c)) applied, automatism would be available and L would not be convicted.[278] The reasoning in other jurisdictions is as follows. Even though L is responsible for his automatism, becoming automatic is not a criminal offence. It does *not* follow that he is responsible for the further consequences of his automatism. Before that can be the case, L must have the required mens rea not merely in respect of becoming automatic, but also in respect of those further consequences which make up the actus reus. Thus if an offence requires proof that the defendant foresaw the actus reus, the claim of automatism or invol-untariness denies responsibility unless she actually foresaw the possibility of her incapacity *and* the resulting offence.[279]

Ignoring such reasoning, English courts have focused on public policy concerns surrounding the inherent dangerousness of the defendant's conduct, and generally impose strict liability for the consequences of voluntary intoxication.

(b) Recklessness

The doctrine by which voluntary intoxication overrides a defence of automatism operates

---

[276] [1970] 1 QB 152.

[277] Approved in *DPP* v. *Majewski* [1977] AC 443. See MacKay, "Intoxication as a Factor in Automatism" [1982] *Crim LR* 146; Horder, "Pleading Involuntary Lack of Capacity" [1993] *CLJ* 298, 304ff.

[278] *O'Connor* (1980) 146 CLR 64; *Martin* (1984) 51 ALR 540; *Kamipeli* [1975] 2 NZLR 610; *Cottle* [1958] NZLR 999, 1002, 1007 (Gresson P); *Daviault* (1994) 118 DLR (4th) 469; Orchard, "Surviving without Majewski—A View from Down Under" [1993] *Crim LR* 426.

[279] *O'Connor* (1980) 146 CLR 64, 73 (Barwick CJ), 103 (Stephen J); cf. *Egan* (1897) 23 VLR 159; *Sione* v. *Labour Dept* [1972] NZLR 278; *Ryan* (1967) 121 CLR 205. In these other jurisdictions, Lipman might have been convicted of manslaughter if the risk of killing someone while under the influence of LSD were such as to make his taking the drug "grossly negligent". (For discussion of the mens rea element in manslaughter see below, § 10.6.)

only if the intoxication is self-induced through D's taking alcohol or non-soporific drugs (such as LSD). Thus it does not apply in a case such as *Bailey* [280] where D, a diabetic, failed to take sufficient food after a normal dose of insulin and lapsed into automatism. Similarly, the doctrine does not apply if D's automatism arises from taking valium, a sedative. [281]

The distinction appears to be that, in the latter cases, the substance that induces automatism is not one with generally recognised tendencies to produce aggressive, dangerous behaviour. Consequently, the public policy considerations that underlie decisions such as *Lipman* are less pressing, and there is no need to regard the defendant as being "on notice" of the dangerous consequences of his becoming intoxicated.

Where the defendant's automatism is not self-induced by alcohol or non-soporific drugs, the test is different. The defendant may rely upon his involuntariness as a defence *unless* he actually foresaw the risk of his behaviour becoming "aggressive, unpredictable and uncontrolled with the result that he may cause some injury to others." [282] The standard of prior fault required is known as subjective *recklessness*, which is discussed further in the chapter on mens rea (below, § 5.2).

(c) Antecedent actus reus

In each of the above situations, the actus reus occurs while the defendant is automatic, and the defendant is simply precluded in law from claiming that automatism to exculpate herself. A third alternative for prosecutors is to show that the behavioural element of the actus reus occurred *before* the defendant became automatic. One such case arises where D falls asleep while driving and then has an accident. Although D's driving was involuntary at the time of the collision, he will be guilty of careless driving at the earlier time when he continued to drive despite feeling sleepy. [283] Indeed, D will have committed the offence even if no accident should occur.

Another example may be the phenomenon sometimes called "Dutch courage": where D, intending to murder V, drinks himself into a stupor *in order* to perpetrate the killing. [284] The ordinary rule governing intoxication (above, § 4.3(iii)(a)) will make D guilty of manslaughter, but is not sufficient to make him guilty of murder, since the mental element required for murder is intention rather than recklessness. Nonetheless, it is arguable that his conduct in becoming drunk is itself a cause of death, and therefore constitutes the actus reus of murder. Hence, rather than focusing upon D's actions while automatic, his responsibility will be based upon his earlier conduct, which caused the prohibited harm, and which was itself accompanied by the fault element required for the crime.

---

[280] [1983] 2 All ER 503.

[281] *Hardie* [1984] 3 All ER 848.

[282] *Bailey* [1983] 2 All ER 503, 507, overruling the earlier decision in *Quick* [1973] QB 910, 922, where it was said that automatism would not be available where its onset "could have been reasonably foreseen as a result of either doing, or omitting to do something, as, for example, taking alcohol against medical advice after using certain prescribed drugs, or failing to have regular meals while taking insulin." See generally Ashworth, "Reason, Logic and Criminal Liability" (1975) 91 *LQR* 102, 106–9; Robinson, "Causing the Conditions of One's Own Defence: A Study in the Limits of Theory in Criminal Law Doctrine" (1985) 71 *Va LR* 1.

[283] *Kay v. Butterworth* (1945) 173 LT 191; *Spurge* [1961] 2 QB 205; below, § 5.8(i)(c)–(d).

[284] *A-G for Northern Ireland v. Gallagher* [1963] AC 349, 382 (Lord Denning).

To illustrate this type of analysis, consider the following facts:[285]

> D attempts to rob a jeweller's shop. He threatens those in the shop by pointing a loaded and cocked gun at them with his finger on the trigger. V, the shopkeeper, then springs at him. D is jolted back against the door, causing his finger to depress the trigger involuntarily. V is killed when the gun goes off, and D is charged with murder.

In such a case, D commits homicide. Even if the immediate cause of death is an involuntary act by D, that is not a *novus actus interveniens*; his actions leading up to that point, in threatening V and other people in the shop by pointing a gun at them with his finger on the trigger, are (also) a cause of death.[286] Thus D's earlier conduct, rather than the firing of the gun itself, is the actus reus of murder.

(d) Strict liability offences?

For the sake of clarity, special mention should be made of offences that do not require proof of mens rea. Such offences, involving what is known as strict or absolute liability, are considered in Chapter 6. Unless one of the foregoing exceptions applies, it is submitted that because voluntariness is fundamental to D's responsibility for the actus reus, and not merely relevant to mens rea, in principle its absence will still result in there being no criminal liability for D's conduct:[287]

> "When a man is charged with dangerous driving, it is no defence for him to say, however truly, 'I did not mean to drive dangerously.' There is said to be an absolute prohibition against that offence, whether he had a guilty mind or not, see *Hill* v. *Baxter* [288] by Lord Goddard CJ. But even though it is absolutely prohibited, nevertheless he has a defence if he can show that it was an involuntary act in the sense that he was unconscious at the time and did not know what he was doing, see *H.M. Advocate* v. *Ritchie*,[289] *Reg.* v. *Minor* [290] and *Cooper* v. *McKenna, Ex parte Cooper*.[291]"

The exception, as we saw earlier, is in respect of pure situational offences, which the courts in cases such as *Larsonneur* [292] have construed as imposing criminal liability notwithstanding that it may be impossible to prevent the actus reus from occurring.

It is also worth noting that some offences impose strict liability only for a part of the actus reus, and require mens rea for other parts of the offence. The first case to recognise strict liability, *Woodrow*,[293] is a convenient example. D was convicted of possessing adulterated

---

[285] Taken from *Wickliffe* [1987] 1 NZLR 55, 60, where the approach suggested here was accepted as a possible analysis by the New Zealand Court of Appeal; also by the Australian High Court in *Ryan* v. *R.* (1967) 121 CLR 205, 218–19, 231, 233, 239; cf. Elliott, "Responsibility for Involuntary Acts: Ryan v The Queen" (1968) 41 *ALJ* 497. See also the commentary on *Burke* [1987] Crim LR 480, 484.

[286] See also the discussion of causation earlier in this chapter, § 4.2(iii)ff.

[287] *Bratty* v. *A-G for Northern Ireland* [1963] AC 386, 409–10. Cf. *Hill* v. *Baxter* [1958] 1 QB 277; *O'Connor* (1980) 146 CLR 64; Williams, "Absolute Liability in Traffic Offences" [1967] *Crim LR* 142 and 194, 199ff.

[288] [1958] 1 QB 277, 282.

[289] [1926] SC(J) 45.

[290] (1955) 15 WWR (NS) 433.

[291] [1960] QLR 406.

[292] Above, § 4.3(ii)(d).

[293] (1846) 15 M & W 404.

tobacco, even though he did not know it was adulterated. The offence was held to impose strict liability in respect of the fact that the tobacco was adulterated. But there was no suggestion that liability in respect of the *possession* was also strict. Had someone put the tobacco in his hand while D was sleeping, then involuntariness would have precluded liability in the normal way.[294]

(e) Evidential issues

A claim of involuntariness or automatism is often described by lawyers as a "defence". In terms of substantive legal doctrine, it is not. It is a denial of the actus reus, rather than a plea that the defendant's actions were justified or excused. As such, it is for the prosecution to prove voluntariness on the part of the defendant alongside the rest of the actus reus. So far as the burden of proof is concerned, however, automatism is like a defence. In practice, there is a presumption of deliberative capacity to control one's actions, and voluntariness will become an issue only if there is evidence which genuinely raises the issue.[295] Thus, if the defendant wishes to deny responsibility on this basis, she must point to credible evidence that supports her claim. It is said that "blackout is one of the first refuges of a guilty conscience."[296] In general, since it is so easily feigned, the defendant's testimony of automatism will not be accepted unless it is buttressed by relevant evidence of surrounding circumstances or medical conditions.[297]

---

[294] See above, § 4.3(ii)(e).

[295] *Bratty* v. *A-G for Northern Ireland* [1963] AC 386, 406–7, 413, 416–17. Similarly for impossibility: cf. *Bailey* [1983] 1 WLR 760, 765–6. For further discussion of the burden of proof, see above, § 3.2.

[296] *Cooper* v. *McKenna* [1960] Qd R 406, 419 (Stable J); *Bratty* v. *A-G for Northern Ireland* [1963] AC 386, 413–14 (Lord Denning).

[297] *Cook* v. *Atchison* [1968] Crim LR 266; cf. *Hill* v. *Baxter* [1958] 1 QB 277; *Stripp* (1978) 69 Cr App R 318; contrast *Budd* [1962] Crim LR 49.

5

MENS REA

The mens rea of a crime is, generally speaking, that part of the offence which refers to the defendant's mental state. Consider, for example, section 15(1) of the Forgery and Counterfeiting Act 1981:

> It is an offence for a person—
> (a) to pass or tender as genuine any thing which is, and which he knows or believes to be, a counterfeit of a currency note or of a protected coin. . . .

When Tom is charged with an offence of passing a counterfeit note under section 15(1)(a), the offence may be established only if Tom *knew or believed that the "note" was counterfeit*. The italicised part of the last sentence is the mens rea requirement.

In the case of section 15(1)(a), the mental element is fairly straightforward. But it is possible for an offence to contain a variety of actus reus elements for which the corresponding mens rea requirements differ. One such offence is section 3 of the Criminal Damage Act 1971, which provides, in part, that:

> A person who has anything in his custody or under his control intending without lawful excuse to use it . . .
> (b) to destroy or damage his own . . . property in a way which he knows is likely to endanger the life of some other person;
> shall be guilty of an offence.

There are two parts to the mens rea for this offence. A defendant must (i) have *intended* to use the item in question to damage his own property, and (ii) have *known* that doing so was likely to endanger another person's life.

Although mens rea is often regarded as the requirement that the defendant have a "guilty mind", and is taken to contain the fault elements of each offence, it is in practice a rather technical area of law. For a prosecutor, mens rea requires her to establish only that the defendant had the specified mental state toward the actus reus which is required for that crime. In particular, proof that the defendant has the requisite mens rea of an offence does not mean that she must know her conduct is illegal,[1] or wrong. Similarly, a laudable motive which prompts the defendant to commit an offence is no defence. In *Smith*,[2] for instance, the defendant offered a bribe to the town mayor. He did so in order to expose the mayor as corrupt. Despite his good motive, he was convicted of offering a bribe to a public servant

---

[1] See below, § 18.2 (ignorance of law).
[2] [1960] 2 QB 423.

since he had intentionally (the mens rea) offered the bribe (the actus reus). At that stage the offence was complete, and his motive could not help him.[3]

There are three steps to be taken in establishing whether a defendant has mens rea. The first step is to determine what mens rea standard is required in respect of each separate element of the actus reus. The second is to interpret the criteria of those mens rea element(s). Third is the factual question: did the defendant in fact act with the mens rea element(s) required?

The present chapter is concerned with the second of those steps; its purpose is to explain the main types of mens rea which the law might require. There are in fact a great variety of possible mens rea states, including purpose, intention, recklessness, wilfulness, knowledge, belief, suspicion, reasonable cause to believe, maliciousness, fraudulence, dishonesty, corruptness, and negligence. However, in this chapter we will confine our discussion to the most common, and most important, types of fault element.

§ 5.1 Intention

The central, and usually the most grave, case of wrongdoing occurs when the defendant's crime is intentional.[4] Both in law and in society at large, praise and blame are most obviously incurred for conduct that a person intends: D attracts greater censure if she deliberately breaks V's vase than if she carelessly drops it. For the majority of offences, it is not necessary to prove that the actus reus was intended, since recklessness will normally suffice for a conviction. (Intention will therefore often be most relevant at the sentencing stage.) But this is not always so—murder, for example, requires an intention to kill or inflict grievous bodily harm; recklessness will not suffice. Other offences requiring proof of an intent include theft, burglary, and wounding with intent. There are other important reasons for distinguishing intention from recklessness, and we shall return to these later.

There is normally no need for an elaborate definition of intention in order to decide whether an actus reus was intended. A few exceptional situations may present difficulty, but usually the analysis will be intuitively obvious: "[t]he general legal opinion is that 'intention' cannot be satisfactorily defined and does not need a definition, since everybody knows what it means."[5] Nonetheless, the fact that some cases are difficult means that we do sometimes

---

[3] The decision does not sit well with *Clarke* (1984) 80 Cr App R 344, which holds that a citizen has a defence if acting honestly and solely to reveal crime and recover its proceeds. However, the view that mens rea means no more than the mental element for the offence is endorsed in *Hinklin* (1868) LR 3 QB 360, 370–2; *Yip Chiu-Cheung* [1995] 1 AC 111; also *Kingston* [1995] 2 AC 355. This approach, which disconnects a finding of mens rea from the presence of fault, is appropriate only if a suitable range of defences is available. See above, § 1.2(ii); also Brett, *Inquiry into Criminal Guilt* (1960).

[4] See, e.g., Smith, "Intention in Criminal Law" (1974) 27 *CLP* 93; White, "Intention, Purpose, Foresight and Desire" (1976) 92 *LQR* 569; Buzzard, "'Intent'" [1978] *Crim LR* 5; Smith, "'Intent': A Reply" [1978] *Crim LR* 14; Duff, "The Obscure Intentions of the House of Lords" [1986] *Crim LR* 771; Williams, "Oblique Intention" (1987) 46 *CLJ* 417; Buxton, "Some Simple Thoughts on Intention" [1988] *Crim LR* 484; Duff, "Intentions Legal and Philosophical" (1989) 9 *OJLS* 76; Smith, "A Note on 'Intention'" [1990] *Crim LR* 85; Simester and Chan, "Intention Thus Far" [1997] *Crim LR* 704; Norrie, "After *Woollin*" [1999] *Crim LR* 532; Kaveny, "Inferring Intention from Foresight" (2004) 120 *LQR* 81.

[5] Williams, *TBCL* 74. *Per* Lord Bridge, in *Moloney* [1985] AC 905, 926, "[t]he golden rule should be that . . . the judge should avoid any elaboration or paraphrase of what is meant by intent, and leave it to the jury's good sense to decide whether the accused acted with the necessary intent." Cf. *Belfon* [1976] 3 All ER 46 (CA); *Nedrick* [1986] 1 WLR 1025, 1027 (CA).

need guidelines about what intention means. The legal territory of intention comprises two alternative categories. D may be found to have intended the actus reus if:

(I)   D *intended* the actus reus in the ordinary, core sense of "intention"; or

(II)   D recognised that the actus reus was a *virtually certain* consequence of his actions.

The first case, (I), is the standard or core variety and largely reflects the ordinary language meaning of "intention". In this paradigm case, D tries (seeks, attempts) to bring about the relevant outcome. For whatever reason, he wants or needs to bring about that outcome, and that is why he acts as he does. By contrast, in the virtual certainty case, (II), D does not act in order to bring about the intended outcome. He acts for other reasons. However, he knows that the actus reus is a virtually certain consequence of his actions. Though that is not what he is trying to bring about, it is a practically inevitable concomitant.

In the following sections, we will elaborate upon these definitions. In §§ 5.1(i)–(iii), the paradigm category of intention (I) will be discussed. The virtual certainty case (II) is considered in § 5.1(iv).

(i) Ways of speaking about intention (in its core sense)

As a starting point, it may be helpful to consider how "intention" has been paraphrased by judges and academic writers. In *Cunliffe* v. *Goodman*, Lord Asquith stated that intention "connotes a state of affairs which the party 'intending' . . . does more than merely contemplate: it connotes a state of affairs which, on the contrary, he decides, so far as in him lies, to bring about."[6] In other words, D generally intends an outcome if it is something that he decides, or seeks, to bring about.[7] Additionally, it seems clear that D intends a result if he acts with the *purpose*,[8] or object, of bringing it about. In Smith and Hogan's useful example:[9]

> "If D has resolved to kill P and he fires a loaded gun at him with the object of doing so, he intends to kill. It is immaterial that he is aware that he is a poor shot, the P is nearly out of range, and that his chances of success are small. It is sufficient that killing is his object or purpose, . . . that he acts in order to kill."

At the heart of this approach is a recognition that D intends to kill P if he means to bring about P's death by his actions—if he acts with the aim, object, or purpose of killing P.[10]

Antony Duff has built on this idea. Suppose that D fires a gun knowing that P is nearby, and we are trying to decide whether he intended to kill P. Duff argues that if D aims to cause P's death by his actions, then we can say that D *attempts* to kill P.[11] Furthermore, an attempt can be either a success or a failure. Therefore, Duff shows, one feature of intention

---

[6] [1950] 2 KB 237, 253.

[7] Cf. *Mohan* [1976] 1 QB 1, 11 (CA); *Pearman* (1984) 80 Cr App R 259 (CA).

[8] *Burke* [1991] 1 AC 135, 147 (HL).

[9] *Smith and Hogan* 93.

[10] Cf. *Gollins* v. *Gollins* [1964] AC 644, 663 (Lord Reid); *DPP* v. *Smith* [1961] AC 290, 327 (Viscount Kilmuir LC); *Hyam* v. *DPP* [1975] AC 55, 79 (Lord Hailsham).

[11] This point was made by the Court of Appeal in *Moloney, The Times*, 22 December 1983 (May LJ); see *Moloney* [1985] AC 905, 919 (Lord Bridge). Compare also *Walker* (1989) 90 Cr App R 226, 230: "'[t]rying to kill' is synonymous with purpose. It has never been suggested that a man does not intend what he is trying to achieve."

is that a defendant who intends (aims, tries, attempts) to kill P would regard himself as having "failed" in some sense if P does not die.[12] By contrast, if he does not intend P's death, then he would not think he had failed if P survives. So this is another way of testing whether D intended P's death.

An illustration of Duff's argument is provided by the case of *Hyam*.[13] D had poured petrol through the letterbox of V's house and set fire to the petrol, intending only to frighten V but realising her actions risked causing death. Duff remarks:[14]

> "Mrs Hyam intended to set fire to Mrs Booth's house; her action would have failed had the house not caught fire. . . . She intended thereby to frighten Mrs Booth: had the fire not frightened Mrs Booth, her action (though successful as one of 'setting fire to the house') would have failed as one of 'frightening Mrs Booth'. But she did not intend to cause death or injury: though she foresaw death or injury as a likely effect of her action, her action would not have been a failure had no one been killed or injured; death or injury were foreseen side-effects, not intended effects, of her action."

By frightening Mrs Booth, the defendant would have succeeded in her purpose; her actions would not have been a failure if no-one had died, since it was no part of her purpose to kill. Neither, we would say, was she trying to kill anyone. Thus the deaths were not intended (at least not in the core sense).

(ii) A formal definition of intention in its core sense

The differences noted above between intended and unintended actions can also be set out in terms of means, ends, and side-effects. Things done as means or ends are intended; side-effects are not.[15] In *Hyam*, D set fire to the house as a means of frightening Mrs Booth. Hence, both setting fire to the house and frightening Mrs Booth were intended. But the ensuing fatalities were neither a means nor an end. They were side-effects of her actions, and as such unintended.

Ideas of means, ends, and purpose point to a more formal way of thinking about intention. The purposes or ends for which one acts are the reasons *why* one acts. They motivate and explain one's action. Intention embraces both these and the intermediate steps (the means) that one undertakes in order to achieve those ends. Formally, we can capture the central cases of intention as follows. D intends to do an action (or to bring about some consequence) if:

(a)   He *wants* to do that action (or to bring about that consequence), or

(b)   He *believes* it is possible for him to achieve something he wants by doing that action (or by bringing about that consequence);

and

(c)   He behaves as he does *because*[16] of his desire in (a) or his belief in (b).

---

[12] Duff, *Intention, Agency and Criminal Liability* (1990) 61–3. See now his *Criminal Attempts* (1996) chap. 1.

[13] [1975] AC 55.

[14] Duff, *Intention, Agency and Criminal Liability* (1990) 61.

[15] Finnis, "Intention and Side-effects" in Frey and Morris (eds.), *Liability and Responsibility* (1991) 32. See also Williams, "Oblique Intention" (1987) 46 *CLJ* 417, 421.

Notice that nothing in this definition requires that D should believe the action or consequence is probable, highly likely, or anything more than merely possible. This is shown by Smith and Hogan's example cited earlier, where D attempts to kill P despite the chances of doing so being small. The combination of (a) with (c) covers actions which are done as ends:

(a)   He *wants* to do that action (or to bring about that consequence); and
(c)   He behaves as he does *because* of that desire.

Mrs Hyam wanted to frighten Mrs Booth, and she set fire to the house because she wanted to frighten her. Therefore she intended to frighten Mrs Booth. Her desire to frighten, which is the desire contemplated in (a) above, is often termed the defendant's *motive*. But it is important to recognise that a desire, or motive, is not enough by itself to establish intention. Often people want things which they never set out to achieve. If D stands to inherit from his mother's will, he may have a reason for wanting her death. But the mere wish that another person were deceased is not an intention to kill that person: "intention is something quite different from motive or desire."[17] Distinguishing between desire and intention here is (c), the requirement that the defendant act because of that motive. A motive is irrelevant to intention unless it is also *why* D did the actus reus.

On the other hand, desire is not an essential component of intention.[18] Often, we bring things about not because we want them, but because they are a *means* to something else (that we do want).[19] The parent who punishes a child for misbehaving may do so regretfully, believing it to be her only option and wishing very much that there were something else she could do; yet she intends to punish him all the same.[20] What she wants (say) is to deter her child from behaving that way again, and she punishes him in order to achieve that aim. But she does not desire his punishment, at least not for its own sake. This sort of case, where the actus reus is done as a means to an end, is captured by the combination of (b) with (c):

(b)   He *believes* it is possible for him to achieve something he wants by doing that action (or by bringing about that consequence); and
(c)   He behaves as he does *because* of that belief.

In *Smith*,[21] D believed that by bribing the mayor he would be able to expose him. This was why he acted as he did. Therefore he intended to bribe[22] the official, even though his ultimate aim was to expose him. It may be helpful to show D's reasoning with a diagram:

---

[16] Or, at least *in part because*. We consider the possibility of multiple intentions below, in § 5.1(vi).

[17] *Per* Lord Bridge in *Moloney* [1985] AC 905, 926.

[18] Cf. *Mohan* [1976] QB 1, 11 (James LJ): intention is "a decision to bring about, in so far as it lies within the accused's power, the commission of the offence . . . no matter whether the accused desired that consequence of his act or not."

[19] See *Hyam* [1974] 2 All ER 41, 74 (Lord Hailsham): intention includes "the means as well as the end"; also Williams, *CLGP* §16.

[20] Compare *Lang* v. *Lang* [1955] AC 402, 428–9.

[21] [1960] 2 QB 423. See above, § 5.

[22] Or, more accurately, to "corrupt" the official. In fact s. 1(2) of the Public Bodies Corrupt Practices Act 1889 requires that the defendant act "corruptly". The Court interpreted this to mean only that he must intend to induce a corrupt bargain. See above, n. 3; Shyllon, "The Corruption of 'Corruptly'" [1969] *Crim LR* 250.

Smith: S ——————→ bribe mayor$_{\text{Means}}$ ——————→ expose corruption$_{\text{End}}$

Similarly, Mrs Hyam believed that by setting fire to the house she would be able to frighten Mrs Booth. That was why she acted as she did. Therefore she intended to set fire to the house:

Hyam: H ——————→ set fire to house$_{\text{Means}}$ ——————→ frighten V$_{\text{End}}$

                                                        kill V$_{\text{Side-effect}}$

But as this diagram shows, it was no part of her intentions to kill V or do grievous bodily harm to her.

In practice, of course, looking at the defendant's desires and beliefs is an indispensible aid in helping us to ascertain her intentions. Even in (b), the case of doing something as a means to an end, there must be a motive in the background. And although it does not matter in principle what that background motive is, often it will be important for evidential purposes. "To prove the intention, you may show the motive, and this is a link in the chain of evidence."[23]

(iii) Foresight of consequences is not enough

The key ingredient of any account of intention is (c), that the defendant acts because of her desire or belief. Without it, there cannot be intention. If D foresees an outcome, and indeed welcomes it, but that outcome nonetheless plays no part in her decision to act, then she does not intend it.[24] The outcome is, for D, incidental. Mrs Hyam foresaw the possibility of killing Mrs Booth, but she did not set fire to the house because of her belief that doing so might bring about Mrs Booth's death. Hence, although she was reckless,[25] she did not intend to kill. Similarly, a judge who awards compensatory damages against a defendant may realise that, in so doing, he might cause the bankruptcy of the defendant, but that has nothing to do with why he awards the damages. The bankruptcy is no more than a foreseen but unintended side-effect.

The law has not always been clear on this point. In *Hardy* v. *Motor Insurers' Bureau*, for instance, it was said of the accused that "he must have foreseen, when he did the act, that it would in all probability injure the other person. Therefore he had the intent to injure the other person."[26] And in *Jakac*, the Supreme Court of Victoria was of similar mind: if the defendant "knew what the consequences were likely to be, and with that knowledge he deliberately did the act and if the consequences in fact did follow, he must be taken to intend them."[27] Indeed, in 1960 the House of Lords in *DPP* v. *Smith* simply presumed (*inter alia*)

---

[23] *Heeson* (1878) 14 Cox CC 40, 44 (Lush J).

[24] A point made by Kenny, "Intention and Purpose in Law" in Summers (ed.), *Essays in Legal Philosophy* (1968) 146, 155.

[25] Below, § 5.2.

[26] [1964] 2 QB 745, 764 (Pearson LJ); see also at 758 (Lord Denning MR). Cf. Lord Diplock's definition of "purpose" in *Chandler* v. *DPP* [1964] AC 763, 805 to "designate those objects which he knows will probably be achieved by the act, whether he wants them or not."

[27] [1961] VR 367, 371. Cf. Saunders, *Mozley & Whitley's Law Dictionary* (9th ed., 1977) 175: "a person who contemplates any result, as not unlikely to follow from a deliberate act of his own, may be said to intend that result, whether he desire it or not. . . ."

that Jim Smith intended whatever he foresaw.[28] The House of Lords later divided on this question in *Hyam*. Although Lord Hailsham declared it "clear that 'intention' is clearly to be distinguished alike from 'desire' and from foresight of the probable consequences,"[29] his Lordship's view does not reflect a consensus. Viscount Dilhorne, for instance, remarked that if someone does an act "knowing when he does it that it is highly probable that grievous bodily harm will result, I think that most people would say and be justified in saying that whatever other intentions he may have had as well, he at least intended grievous bodily harm."[30] Indeed, Lord Diplock felt able, following *Hyam*, to hold that the law was now "well-settled":[31]

> "Where intention to produce a particular result was a necessary element of an offence, no distinction was to be drawn in law between the state of mind of one who did an act because he desired it to produce that particular result and the state of mind of one who, when he did the act, was aware that it was likely to produce that result but was prepared to take the risk that it might do so. . . ."

More recently, however, the distinction between intention and mere foresight has been accepted by the House of Lords. The key cases are *Moloney*[32] and *Hancock and Shankland*.[33] In *Moloney*, the defendant was charged with murder after shooting his stepfather during a drunken game. It was not clear that, when he pulled the trigger, he realised the gun was pointing at the victim. His conviction was quashed because the trial judge was ruled to have misdirected the jury in stating:[34]

> "a man intends the consequence of his voluntary act (a) when he desires it to happen, whether or not he foresees that it probably will happen, and (b) when he foresees that it will happen, whether he desires it or not."

Contrast that direction (which was based upon *Hyam*) with the view of Lord Bridge, who was "firmly of opinion that foresight of consequences, as an element bearing on the issue of intention in murder, or indeed any other crime of specific intent, belongs, not to the substantive law, but to the law of evidence."[35]

Strictly speaking, Lord Bridge's remarks were *obiter dicta*,[36] since the decisive factor in the decision was that D apparently did not think about the risk of death at all,[37] and the case was therefore not one of foresight.[38] Fortunately, the point was not *obiter* in *Hancock and*

---

[28] [1961] AC 290. Cf. Viscount Kilmuir LC, at 326: "the test of what a reasonable man would contemplate as the probable result of his acts, and, therefore, would intend. . . ." See also *Ward* [1956] 1 QB 351; Kenny, "Intention and Purpose in Law" in Summers (ed.), *Essays in Legal Philosophy* (1968) 146.

[29] [1975] AC 55, 74.

[30] *Ibid.*, 82.

[31] *Lemon* [1979] AC 617, 638. See also a similar dictum in *Hyam* [1975] AC 55, 86.

[32] [1985] AC 905.

[33] [1986] AC 455.

[34] [1985] AC 905, 917.

[35] *Ibid.*, 928.

[36] Cf. *ibid.*, 920; *Hancock* [1986] AC 455, 460 (CA), [1986] AC 455, 468 (HL).

[37] See *Moloney* [1985] AC 905, 920B–D. Their Lordships must have overlooked the jury's finding that D foresaw death or grievous bodily harm.

[38] Thus, strictly, the decision rules only that inadvertence forecloses intention—contra *DPP v. Smith* [1961] AC 290. Apart from being undone by s. 8 of the Criminal Justice Act 1967, *DPP v. Smith* itself was effectively overruled by the Privy Council in *Frankland and Moore* v. *R.* [1987] AC 576.

Shankland. In that case the defendants, miners who were on strike, pushed concrete blocks off a bridge onto the motorway below. The blocks struck a taxi ferrying another miner to work. The taxi driver was killed. The defendants, it appears, recognised the dangerousness of their actions but claimed they intended only to frighten the miner and prevent him from going to work, but not to harm anyone. Their convictions for murder were quashed. As Lord Scarman put it, "foresight does not necessarily imply the existence of intention."[39] This rule has since been reiterated by the Court of Appeal in *Nedrick* [40] and *Mathews*,[41] and by the House of Lords in *Woollin*.[42] It may safely be regarded as now prevailing.[43]

(iv) Virtually certain consequences: the second category of intention

Mere foresight of a consequence, then, does not establish an intention. But one question is still unresolved: what if the consequence is foreseen not merely as possible, but as *certain* to occur—does "intention" include such a case? Consider the following example used by a number of philosophers. V, a fat man, is trapped in the mouth of a cave. The waters in the cave are rapidly rising, and the cave will soon be flooded. The trapped man is immovable, and is preventing the escape and survival of his fellow speleologists. The only way of unblocking the exit is by blowing him up with a stick of dynamite. Can they do so without intending his death?[44] The case can be represented as follows:

$$\textit{Speleologist}: \quad S \longrightarrow \text{blow up V} \longrightarrow \text{escape and survive}$$
$$\| \ \|$$
$$\text{kill V}$$

As this example illustrates, some consequences which are not themselves sought (as either means or end) are nevertheless much too close to the intended effects to be separated off as mere side-effects. V's colleagues would be delighted if they could blow him up, and free themselves, without killing V. But they cannot. It is a certainty that V will die. In this respect, it is worth noting the definition of intention contemplated by the Law Commission in its Report on homicide:[45]

(1) A person should be taken to intend a result if he or she acts in order to bring it about.

(2) An intention to bring about a result may be found if it is shown that the defendant thought that the result was a virtually certain consequence of his or her action.

---

[39] [1986] 1 AC 455, 472.

[40] [1986] 1 WLR 1025.

[41] [2003] EWCA Crim 192.

[42] [1999] 1 AC 82.

[43] In the *Law Quarterly Review*, Lord Goff concludes that "after the journey through *Smith, Hyam, Moloney* and *Hancock*, the law is really back where it was. . . . Foresight of consequences is not the same as intent, but is material from which the jury may, having regard to the circumstances of the case, infer that the defendant really had the relevant intent": "The Mental Element in the Crime of Murder" (1988) 104 *LQR* 30, 41.

[44] For philosophical discussion of the case see Geddes, "On the Intrinsic Wrongness of Killing Innocent People" (1973) 33 *Analysis* 93; Duff, "Intentionally Killing the Innocent" (1973) 34 *Analysis* 16; Finnis, "The Rights and Wrongs of Abortion: a Reply to Judith Jarvis Thomson" (1973) 2 *Philosophy and Public Affairs* 117; Hanink, "Some Light on Double Effect" (1975) 35 *Analysis* 147.

[45] Law Com. No. 304, *Murder, Manslaughter and Infanticide* (2006) 3.27. For earlier proposals, see *A New Homicide Act for England and Wales?* LCCP No. 177 (2006) 4.3; and see the discussion in Part 4 generally. See too Law Com. No. 218 7.1–7.14 and Law Com. No. 122 (1992) 5.4–5.11.

Limb (2) captures the case of the speleologists. The language of virtual certainty reflects the need for something more than just foresight that the result is likely or possible; the latter would be a case of recklessness.

In the past, the courts have been equivocal about this type of case. Although Lord Hailsham did not think that "foresight as such of a high degree of probability is at all the same thing as intention,"[46] he nevertheless stated explicitly that intention includes not only those things done as ends or means but also "the inseparable consequences of the end as well as the means." The extension is supported by reference to an example developed by Glanville Williams:[47]

> "suppose that a villain of the deepest dye blows up an aircraft in flight with a time-bomb, merely for the purpose of collecting on insurance. It is not his aim to cause the people on board to perish, but he knows that success in his scheme will inevitably involve their deaths as a side-effect."

According to Lord Hailsham, "if any passengers are killed he is guilty of murder, as their death will be a moral certainty if he carries out his intention."[48] In *Moloney*, Lord Bridge, too, accepted that there may be cases where things which are seemingly not sought as ends or means should be analysed as cases of intention:[49]

> "A man who, at London Airport, boards a plane which he knows to be bound for Manchester, clearly intends to travel to Manchester, even though Manchester is the last place he wants to be and his motive for boarding the plane is simply to escape pursuit. . . . By boarding the Manchester plane, the man conclusively demonstrates his intention to go there, because it is a moral certainty that that is where he will arrive."

In such a case the law would say that the "morally certain" consequence is intended. But the basis on which it does so is unclear.[50] There are two main alternatives: either there is, *by definition*, a second category of (indirect) intention involving morally certain consequences,[51] or there is not and moral certainty is simply evidence of an intention in its core sense. In the latter case, there is no second category of intention: foresight of a moral certainty is no more than a ground for inferring that the consequence was (directly) intended,[52] and the inference may be rebutted by other evidence.

There is something to be said for thinking the link is merely evidential, and that there is no second category. Even consequences that are certain to occur may appear not to be intended. If D drinks a bottle of scotch one evening, he may be sure that he will get a

---

[46] *Hyam* [1975] AC 55, 77.

[47] "Oblique Intention" (1987) 46 *CLJ* 417, 423; cf. his earlier *The Mental Element in Crime* (1965) 34–5. For discussion of these types of cases and the surrounding literature, see Pedain, "Intention and the Terrorist Example" [2004] *Crim LR* 284. More generally, see also Kugler, *Direct and Oblique Intention in the Criminal Law* (2002).

[48] *Hyam* [1975] AC 55, 74.

[49] *Moloney* [1985] AC 905, 926.

[50] Duff, *Intention, Agency and Criminal Liability* (1990) 21–2; also Duff, "The Obscure Intentions of the House of Lords" [1986] *Crim LR* 771.

[51] Cf. Lord Bridge in *Moloney* [1985] AC 905, 925: an overwhelming probability "will *suffice to establish* the necessary intent" (emphasis added). Compare also the use of "conclusively" in the quotation above at n. 49.

[52] Cf. *Nedrick* [1986] 1 WLR 1025, 1029: where D realises that a consequence is inevitable, "the inference *may* be irresistible that he intended that result" (emphasis added).

hangover in the morning, but he does not drink the scotch with the intention of having a hangover.[53] Support for this position is found in decisions subsequent to *Moloney*, where the courts frequently tended to read Lord Bridge's remarks as pertaining to evidential matters. In *Nedrick*, Lord Lane CJ held that "if the jury are satisfied that at the material time the defendant recognised that death or serious harm would be virtually certain (barring some unforeseen intervention) to result from his voluntary act, then that is a fact from which they may find it easy to infer that he intended to kill or do serious bodily harm."[54] Writing extra-judicially in 1987, Lord Goff condemned the extension of intention to embrace moral certainty as "illegitimate".[55]

If Lord Lane and Lord Goff are right, then the explanation of cases like the flight to Manchester has nothing to do with moral certainty. Rather, it is that the fugitive intentionally travels to Manchester as a *means* of leaving London. This is consistent with the account of intention stated earlier, in § 5.1(ii):

Traveller :   T ————→ go to Manchester ————→ leave London

But this answer does not help to deal with the insurance-bombing case proposed by Glanville Williams, where the deaths of the airline passengers are clearly not a means to anything. Despite this, it does seem that the passengers' deaths are so intimately bound up with the villain's intended actions as to be inseparable, and it would be wrong to call them mere side-effects. It appears, therefore, that there is a special category of intention, which falls outside the standard definition given in § 5.1(ii). This second category arises where the defendant recognises that the additional effect is inseparable from those which he intends. A useful definition of this type of case is the rule proposed by H.L.A. Hart: a foreseen outcome is to be regarded as intended when it "is so immediately and invariably connected with the action done that the suggestion that the action might not have that outcome would by ordinary standards be regarded as absurd, or such as only a mentally abnormal person would seriously entertain."[56] These outcomes are intended even though D is not trying or aiming to bring them about. They represent a supplement to the core definition of intention stated in § 5.1(ii).

Fortunately, there is now a House of Lords decision that supports this analysis. In *Woollin*,[57] D had lost his temper and thrown his three-month-old son against a hard surface. The child's skull fractured and death ensued. In D's trial for murder, the prosecution expressly disavowed that D had intended (in the core sense) his son's death or serious injury. His conviction implies, therefore, that foreseeing a result as a virtual certainty is an alternative category of intention, and not just evidence from which to infer the core definition of

---

[53] Duff, *Intention, Agency and Criminal Liability* (1990) 89–90.

[54] [1986] 1 WLR 1025. See also the judgment by Lord Scarman in *Hancock*, above at n. 39.

[55] "The Mental Element in the Crime of Murder" (1988) 104 *LQR* 30, 59.

[56] "Intention and Punishment" in *Punishment and Responsibility* (1968) 113, 120. Hart continues, "the connexion between action and outcome seems therefore to be not merely contingent but rather to be conceptual." See further Simester, "Moral Certainty, and the Boundaries of Intention" (1996) 16 *OJLS* 445. This is a tighter connection (as with respect it ought to be) than that required by the Canadian Supreme Court in *Chartrand* (1994) 116 DLR (4th) 207, 225–30.

[57] [1999] 1 AC 82.

intention. On appeal,[58] Lord Steyn accepted this and explicitly rejected the language of inference. Distilled from his judgment, his Lordship asserts that:[59]

> "in the rare cases where the [standard] direction that it is for the jury simply to decide whether the defendant intended to kill or to do serious bodily harm is not enough, the jury should be directed that they are not entitled to *find* the necessary intention, unless they feel sure that death or serious bodily harm was a virtual certainty (barring some unforeseen intervention) as a result of the defendant's actions and that the defendant appreciated that such was the case."

There are, therefore, two types of intention. First, the normal, core variety is that defined in § 5.1(ii): where an outcome is sought directly by D (because he wants it for its own sake or as a means to something else). Secondly, there are outcomes which, in D's eyes, are so closely bound to normally intended outcomes that they are virtually certain to occur alongside. They may also be regarded as (indirectly) intended.

Cases requiring a *Woollin* direction are rare. Normally, as Lord Steyn said, the jury should consider only the core sense of intention.[60] The *Woollin* decision gives the prosecution an alternative way of proving that an outcome was intended; it is supplementary to, and not a substitute for, intention in the core sense.[61]

However, while clarifying the independent status of this second category of intention, *Woollin* does leave its precise definition unresolved. Lord Steyn's model direction is expressed in negative terms: "the jury should be directed that they are not entitled to find the necessary intention, unless they feel sure that death or serious bodily harm was a virtual certainty." This suggests that, although foresight of virtual certainty is *necessary* before the alternative category of intention is satisfied, it may not always be *sufficient*.[62] It seems that, where there is virtual certainty, the jury is permitted to conclude that the defendant intended the outcome and, absent any special considerations, the jury should normally so conclude;[63] but they are entitled not to find intention should there be such considerations. For example, a doctor may know that by injecting a terminally ill patient with the morphine necessary to dull pain, incidentally it is virtually certain that she will shorten the patient's life. The doctor does not aim to shorten the patient's life, and does not intend his death in

---

[58] Ultimately, D's conviction was quashed and a conviction for manslaughter substituted, because the trial judge had misdirected the jury on the alternative limb by requiring only that D foresaw a "substantial risk" (rather than virtual certainty) of serious injury or death.

[59] [1999] 1 AC 82, 96.

[60] Cf. *Phillips* [2004] EWCA Crim 112, para. 10; *Allen* [2005] EWCA Crim 1344.

[61] *D* [2004] EWCA Crim 1391, [2004] All ER (D) 11, para. 29: "*Woollin* is designed to help the prosecution to fill a gap in the rare circumstances in which a defendant does an act which caused the death without the purpose of killing or causing serious injury, but in circumstances where death or serious bodily harm had been a virtual certainty (barring some unforeseen intervention) as a result of the defendant's actions and the defendant had appreciated that such was the case."

[62] Hence the Court of Appeal was right to judge, in *Matthews* [2003] EWCA Crim 192; [2003] 2 Cr App R 461, para. 43, that "the law has not yet reached a definition of intent in murder in terms of appreciation of a virtual certainty." Foresight of virtual certainty is not the same thing as (indirect) intention, but rather a basis on which it may be found.

[63] Compare, e.g., the analysis of the events in *Matthews, ibid.*, para. 46: "If the jury were sure that the appellants appreciated the virtual certainty of Jonathan's death when they threw him from the bridge and also that they then had no intention of saving him from such death, it is impossible to see how the jury could not have found that the appellants intended Jonathan to die."

the core sense. In such a case, notwithstanding that it is a virtually certain side-effect, the jury may well conclude that she does not intend his death, even indirectly.[64]

(a) Objective and subjective virtual certainty?

There is another oddity about the *Woollin* direction. Lord Steyn requires not only that the defendant *think* the outcome is virtually certain; it must also in fact *be* virtually certain. Arguably, however, it is only the former that counts. Intention is a measure of the agent's perceptions and mental state, and should be unaffected by facts of which the agent is unaware. Suppose that D is a fugitive who accelerates her car toward a policeman who is blocking her escape. The fugitive, let us say, wishes only to escape but thinks it is virtually certain that, by knocking over the policeman, she will cause grievous bodily harm. In fact, there is a 20 per cent chance in such collisions that the victim will not be seriously injured; but D does not know this and, as it happens, the policeman is severely hurt. In our view, D should be held to have intended the injury.[65]

(b) Definitions and evidence

What, then, is the role of evidential inference? Where the prosecution seeks to prove that D (directly) intended the actus reus under the standard definition, foresight of a probability is evidence from which that intention may be *inferred*. Notice, however, that reference to probability forms no part of that standard definition (given in § 5.1(ii)). In terms of the paradigm type of intention, there is no reason to require virtual certainty before inferring (direct) intent. If D aims a pistol at V and pulls the trigger, it may not be virtually certain, or even very likely, that V will die—perhaps it is a difficult shot—yet we would normally infer that D's intention was to kill; that he was trying to kill.[66] The connection between (standard, direct) intention and foresight of probability is purely evidential.

On the other hand, the connection between foresight of probability and the virtually certain category of intention is not even evidential. It is non-existent. Without foresight of an outcome that D perceives to be virtually certain, the second category of (indirect) intention is simply not in play.

(v) Intention and circumstances

The account of intention we have given so far needs qualification when applied to any circumstances which form a part of the actus reus. This is best seen by means of an example. Rape can only be committed by D's having sexual intercourse with V without her consent. The circumstance, that V does not consent, is part of the actus reus of the offence.

---

[64] For a discussion of cases that contain *dicta* to this effect, see Ashworth, "Criminal Liability in a Medical Context: The Treatment of Good Intentions" in Simester and Smith (eds.), *Harm and Culpability* (1996) 173. Cf. *Re A (Children)* [2001] Fam 147, 251-2 (Robert Walker LJ).

[65] Cf. Simester, "Moral certainty, and the boundaries of intention" (1996) 16 *OJLS* 445, 465-466.

[66] Cf. *D* [2004] EWCA Crim 1391, [2004] All ER (D) 11, para. 29: "*Woollin* is not designed to make the prosecution's task more difficult. Many murderers whose purpose was to kill or cause serious injury would escape conviction for murder if the jury was given only a *Woollin* direction. The man who kills another with a gun would be able to escape liability for murder if he could show that he was such a bad shot that death or serious bodily harm was not a virtual certainty or that the defendant had thought that death or serious bodily harm was not a virtual certainty."

There are two ways in which D's mental state regarding V's non-consent can satisfy the demands of intention. The plain case occurs where D rapes V by intentionally having sexual intercourse with her, *hoping or desiring* that she does not consent. In this case D intends "sexual intercourse without consent" in its full sense, because it is part of his purpose not merely to have sexual intercourse with V, but to have it without her consent. Duff's test of failure shows this clearly:[67] D would regard himself as having "failed" if V did in fact consent to having sexual intercourse with him.

Although the clearest sort of case, this is the less common variety of intention where circumstances are at issue, and probably occurs only rarely. More often, rape is intentional when D is aware that V does not consent, yet neither intends nor hopes (and does not care) that V is not consenting. In this situation, D intends to have "sexual intercourse without consent", because he intends to have sexual intercourse *believing* that V does not consent.

So there are two ways of showing that an actus reus is intended when it involves circumstances. The first is by showing that the behaviour and consequences are intended, and that D hopes the circumstances are present. The second is by showing that the behaviour and consequences are intended, and that D believes the circumstances are present. What does "believing" mean in this context? In our view "believing" has the same meaning as "knowing", with one exception. We consider the meaning of knowledge below,[68] but in essence what is required is that the defendant hold a positive belief, amounting to an acceptance, that the circumstance exists.

The one difference, in law, between knowledge and belief is that a belief need not be correct. The defendant may believe something wrongly, but she cannot "know" something that is false. Usually the difference will not matter very much. For example, if D wrongly believes that V does *not* consent to sexual intercourse, when in fact she does consent, then regardless of his mens rea he cannot commit rape, because the actus reus is missing. But sometimes it will still be important to establish whether D has mens rea, since even without the actus reus he might nonetheless be guilty of an attempt. In this example, his false belief that V does not consent will be sufficient to help constitute an intention for the purposes of attempted rape.[69]

(vi) Multiple intentions

Very often, a person has more than one reason for acting as he does. By cooking dinner, John might intend not only to assuage his hunger, but also to use up the contents of the fridge, as well as surprise and please his flatmates. All three results are intended. The mere fact that a defendant can point to some other result that he was also trying to achieve does not mean that he cannot have intended the actus reus. It is no answer for a newspaper that deliberately publishes *sub judice* material to say that it was really trying to increase its circu-

---

[67] Above, § 5.1(i).

[68] See § 5.4.

[69] The claim here is merely that knowledge or belief satisfies the demands of intention. It is a further question (taken up in Chapter 9) whether, with respect to circumstances, intention is *required* to establish the mens rea of attempt offences. The cases of *Khan* [1990] 2 All ER 783 (CA) and *A-G's Reference (No. 3 of 1992)* [1994] 1 WLR 409 (CA) suggest otherwise. Fortunately, the reasoning in those cases remains specific to attempts, and has not been carried over to substantive offences.

lation. Ignoring extraneous intentions, the criminal law focuses only on the actus reus; and asks, whatever else he intended, did D intend that *actus*?

(vii) "With intent" or "ulterior intent" crimes

Sometimes the intentional doing of an actus reus is not itself an offence, and becomes criminal only when done for some further purpose. For example, if D carries a crowbar in his bag he does nothing wrong; but if he carries the crowbar with intent to use it in a burglary, he is guilty of an offence.[70] Crimes of this sort require what is often called an "ulterior intent".[71] The main feature of such crimes is that they specify, as part of the mens rea, an intent to do something that is not part of the actus reus. In the example above, the actus reus is simple possession of the crowbar—it does not matter whether the crowbar is actually used in a burglary.[72] This is why such crimes are said to involve "ulterior" intent: because the eventual intention is ulterior to the actus reus.

In other respects, however, these crimes are no different from crimes of ordinary intent. In particular, where a crime specifies an ulterior intent as part of the mens rea, it seems clear that mere foresight of the further consequence will not do. The crime can be committed only if the defendant intends that consequence.[73] This is the explanation of the controversial case of *Steane*.[74] Steane had been compelled, through concern for the safety of his family, to make broadcasts on behalf of the Germans during the Second World War. He was prosecuted under English wartime regulations for doing an act likely to assist the enemy (the actus reus), "with intent to assist the enemy". The Court of Criminal Appeal quashed his conviction for lack of mens rea, and rightly so. Although in making the broadcasts Steane had done an act likely to assist the enemy, the prosecution had failed to prove that he intended thereby to assist the enemy (i.e. that assisting the enemy was a part of his purposes in broadcasting). It is important to emphasise that the mens rea required is ulterior to the actus reus. The actus reus is "*any act likely* to assist the enemy", and does not involve proof that the defendant in fact did assist the enemy. The mens rea is an intent "to assist the enemy"; which goes beyond the actus reus. Steane intended to make the broadcasts, but his ulterior intent in so doing had been to protect his family. It would be otherwise if the foreseen further consequence were "morally certain" to accompany his intended actions; in which case they too would be intended.[75]

(viii) Conditional intent

Sometimes a person is willing to commit a crime but her actions will not necessarily result in one. For example, if a thief makes off with a handbag, meaning to keep the contents, she steals those contents only if there are any. In this situation, her intention to take the contents

---

[70] Theft Act 1968, s. 25. Cf. *Ellames* [1974] 3 All ER 130; *Hargreaves* [1985] Crim LR 243.

[71] See generally Horder, "Crimes of Ulterior Intent" in Simester and Smith (eds.), *Harm and Culpability* (1996) 153.

[72] Cf. *Rodley* (1913) 9 Cr App R 69, 76.

[73] *Belfon* [1976] 3 All ER 46, 49.

[74] [1947] KB 997. See, e.g., Williams, "Oblique Intention" (1987) 46 *CLJ* 417, 428.

[75] See above, § 5.1(iv); also *Chartrand* (1994) 116 DLR (4th) 207, 225–30.

is conditional upon there being anything to steal. Such cases are not uncommon in the criminal law, especially in the context of offences involving an ulterior intent. The general rule is that an intention to do or bring about something only if particular conditions hold is in law, an intention. Thus a burglar who enters a flat with intent to steal a television set provided there be a set to steal, intends to steal.[76]

(ix) No presumption of intention

Proving mens rea is often difficult. It is impossible to look directly into the minds of defendants in order to know whether they had mens rea at the time of the offence. Usually, if the defendant does not himself confess to having it, the prosecution will be put to proving the relevant state of mind through supporting evidence, e.g. of the defendant's actions before, during, and after the actus reus occurred. Suppose that D is found to have shot V. If there is evidence that D planned the shooting in advance, this may be admissible to support the allegation that D's actions were intentional. The same is true if it is shown that D took careful aim at V's heart before pulling the trigger. In this case, proof by the prosecution that the prohibited harm (i.e. V's death) was a natural consequence of D's actions will support the inference that D intended it. Similarly, proof that the defendant foresaw the outcome (e.g. because D knew the gun was loaded) may also help to support such a conclusion. Inferences of this variety depend upon a recognition that there is no reasonable interpretation of the evidence other than that the defendant had mens rea.

But such inferences are a matter of evidence only. They are neither irrebuttable, nor are they substantive rules of criminal law. Intention is a subjective concept, and any inference made from the evidence is *not* a presumption. Where the prosecution is obliged to prove mens rea, it must do so beyond reasonable doubt. Supporting evidence, e.g. of foresight, is simply a part of what the prosecution may show in order to convince the court that, in light of all the evidence,[77] it may safely conclude, beyond reasonable doubt, that D had the required mens rea.

It was not always so. In *DPP v. Smith*,[78] the House of Lords held there was an irrebuttable presumption in law that a person intends the reasonably foreseeable consequences of his acts. Fortunately, this highly controversial decision has been reversed by section 8 of the Criminal Justice Act 1967. In any offence requiring the prosecution to prove mens rea on the part of the defendant, section 8 provides that the court:

(a) shall not be bound in law to infer that he intended or foresaw a result of his actions by reason only of its being a natural and probable consequence of those actions; but
(b) shall decide whether he did intend or foresee that result by reference to all the evidence, drawing such inferences from the evidence as appear proper in the circumstances.

The section does not, alas, offer a definition of "intention"—hence the difficulties seen earlier in this chapter. Its only role is to govern, and restrict, evidential rules of inference.

---

[76] *A-G's References (Nos. 1 and 2 of 1979)* [1980] QB 180 (noted [1979] Crim LR 585), distinguishing and confining *Husseyn* (1977) 67 Cr App R 131n; *Walkington* [1979] 2 All ER 716, noted [1979] Crim LR 526; *Buckingham* (1976) 63 Cr App R 159. See Campbell, "Conditional Intention" (1982) 2 *LS* 77.

[77] Cf. *Hales* [2005] EWCA Crim 1118, [2005] All ER (D) 371, para. 17: "The jury has to put all the circumstances together, leaving out nothing of potential relevance."

§ 5.2 Recklessness

Often people cause injury without intending to—that is, without acting in order to do so. The doctor who injects her patient with a painkiller may unintentionally kill him, if the patient proves to be allergic to the drug that she injects. But the fact that an injury is unintended does not mean that the person who causes it is blameless; the doctor may have been aware of the risk of injury, a risk that she nevertheless chose to run. In such cases, we would say, she foresaw (but did not intend) the harm.

Not every case of foresight amounts to recklessness. In order for a defendant to be reckless, the risk that she chooses to run must also be an unreasonable one.[79] Although in practice this issue does not often arise, the qualification is important. It means that anaesthetists, who knowingly undertake a slight risk that the patient will have a fatal allergic reaction when anaesthetised before an operation, are not necessarily guilty of reckless homicide when the patient dies. The question of what is reasonable is an objective question, and it is not an issue of whether the defendant thought the risk was reasonable; rather, it is a question whether an ordinary and prudent person would have been prepared to take that risk. To this extent defendants cannot be permitted to judge what is right for themselves.

There are a number of factors for the law to consider when deciding whether a particular risk was reasonable. These include the probability of the risk occurring, and the nature and gravity of the harm being risked. Driving at 30 mph on a busy road may be reasonable; driving at 50 may not be, because of the increased risk of accidents and the more serious injuries that are likely to ensue should there be a crash. Against these considerations should be balanced the value and likelihood of achieving what the defendant was trying to do while running that risk. A high-risk surgical operation may be justifiable when it is done as a last resort or in an emergency to save the patient's life. But the risks involved may not be acceptable if less dangerous alternatives are available, or if the purpose of the operation is trivial, or if reasonable steps are not taken to reduce those risks.

One point that should be made here is that the incorporation of a standard of reasonableness means that there is no need for a separate "threshold" criterion of probability or likelihood. Obviously, if a risk is thought to be minimal or only an "outside chance", running that risk is likely to be unobjectionable. But even a very slight risk will be enough for recklessness if the harm being risked is serious enough and the act concerned has no social value. A game of "Russian roulette" would be reckless even if the chances of being killed were thought to be only one in 200.[80] In such cases, it may be necessary to abandon an activity altogether if the defendant cannot eliminate the risk entirely. One example of this is provided by *Chief Constable of Avon and Somerset Constabulary v. Shimmen*.[81] D, a martial arts expert, was demonstrating his skill to friends by kicking close to a window without intending to break it. This experiment in controlled risk-taking failed: he smashed the window. Even though he thought he had "eliminated as much risk as possible," he was

---

[78] [1961] AC 290. The decision was treated as wrongly decided by the Privy Council in *Frankland* v. *R.* [1987] AC 576.

[79] Cf. *Renouf* [1986] 2 All ER 449.

[80] Cf. *Vehicle Inspectorate* v. *Nuttall* [1999] 1 WLR 629, 636. Indeed, whether an outcome is sufficiently probable to be, in law, "likely" also depends on the gravity of the outcome at risk: *Whitehouse* [2000] Crim LR 172.

[81] (1987) 84 Cr App R 7.

nevertheless guilty of reckless criminal damage since he had chosen to run the slight and unjustifiable risk which remained. Conversely, there may be a very substantial risk of injury or death in certain "last resort" surgical operations, but those operations are not necessarily unreasonable when undertaken.

There are two definitions of recklessness known to English law: "subjective" or *Cunningham* recklessness, and "objective" or *Caldwell* recklessness. Of the two, subjective recklessness can be regarded as the standard variety. Formally, under the subjective definition, D acts recklessly if:

(a)   He believes his conduct will give rise to a risk of harm; and

(b)   It is unreasonable for D to run the risk that he foresees.

The main difference between intention and recklessness is that while in both cases the defendant must foresee the possibility of realising the actus reus, in recklessness he need not seek or be motivated to bring it about. In recent times, however, there have been rulings to the effect that element (a), actual foresight of the risk, should not always be required. We consider this issue in the next section.

(i) *The need for foresight*

The leading modern case to require that there be actual foresight before a defendant can be considered reckless is *Cunningham*.[82] In that case, D interfered with the coin-operated gas meter in an unoccupied house in order to steal money from it. The gas escaped, seeped into an adjoining house, and endangered the life of a person living there. Upon his appeal against conviction for maliciously administering a noxious thing so as to endanger life,[83] the Court of Criminal Appeal held that "malice" required either intention or recklessness. Recklessness would be present if "the accused has foreseen that the particular kind of harm might be done, and yet has gone on to take the risk of it."[84]

On this view, failing to think about a risk is not a ground of criminal culpability. An illustration of this principle is found in *Stephenson*,[85] where D lit a fire in order to warm himself while sheltering in a haystack, and was charged with reckless arson after the haystack itself caught fire and was destroyed. Stephenson's conviction was quashed on appeal because (as he suffered from schizophrenia) he might not have been aware of the risk to the haystack.[86]

On the other hand, the law as stated in *Cunningham* does not entitle a defendant deliberately to close her mind to an obvious risk when she is aware of the risk but does not think about it because she does not care. In *Parker* [87] D slammed down a public telephone receiver with such force that he broke it. The Court rejected his defence that he had been too

---

[82] [1957] 2 QB 396. Cf. *Briggs* [1977] 1 All ER 475, 477; *Stephenson* [1979] QB 695, 1203; *Mullins* [1980] Crim LR 37; *Flack* v. *Hunt* [1980] Crim LR 44.

[83] Contrary to the OAPA 1861, s. 23.

[84] [1957] 2 QB 396, 399. Quoting with approval from Turner, *Kenny's Outlines of Criminal Law* (16th ed., 1952) 186.

[85] [1979] QB 695.

[86] Note that on these facts, D might properly have been obliged to plead insanity. See below, Chapter 19.

[87] [1977] 2 All ER 37.

enraged to think about the risk. The inherent association of his violent action with its consequence meant that he could be taken to have appreciated the risk without the awareness of that risk being at the forefront of his mind, and without the need for sober or careful deliberation in advance.

The inference made in *Parker* must arise clearly from the facts if it is to be properly drawn.[88] In *Briggs*,[89] D took hold of the door handle to V's car and tried to open the door, apparently with a normal arm movement. The handle broke. On appeal, the Court of Appeal quashed D's conviction for misdirection. The trial judge had failed to instruct the jury that, in order to be held reckless, D must have given thought to the risk of damaging the door handle; it was possible that D had not done so.

Unlike in *Parker*, the risk created by the defendant in *Briggs* was not so inherent in his actions that it was inevitable that D had appreciated it. *Briggs* reinforces the point that there must be awareness of the risk at some level of the defendant's consciousness before he can be found reckless.

(a) An alternative, objective version of recklessness

The above states the established position after *Cunningham*. In 1981 the House of Lords invented a second version of recklessness in *Metropolitan Police Commissioner* v. *Caldwell*[90] and the companion case of *Lawrence*.[91] In *Caldwell*, the defendant set fire to a hotel while intoxicated. He was charged, *inter alia*, with an offence against section 1(1) of the Criminal Damage Act 1971, which makes it an offence to damage another's property "being reckless as to whether any such property would be destroyed or damaged." The House of Lords held that a defendant is reckless in law if:[92]

> "(1) he does an act which in fact creates an obvious [and serious][93] risk that property would be destroyed or damaged and (2) when he does the act he either has not given any thought to the possibility of there being any such risk or has recognised that there was some risk involved and has nonetheless gone on to do it."

The essence of the decision was to create a second category of recklessness in criminal law. In addition to the cases of actual foresight covered by *Cunningham*, the defendant would also be treated as reckless if he failed to think of a risk when that risk was a glaring one. In effect, the *Caldwell* definition of recklessness embraces both advertent wrongdoing and gross negligence.[94]

---

[88] Indeed, it is arguable that the inference was inappropriate in *Parker* itself. As such the decision by the Court of Appeal may be a precursor of *Caldwell*, discussed below in the next subsection. If so, however, the approach in *Parker* is narrower than that taken by the House of Lords in *Caldwell*; it would justify inferring recklessness only where D "deliberately closes his mind" to obvious consequences because he is "in a self-induced state of temper", or for a similarly discreditable reason. See [1977] 2 All ER 37, 40.

[89] [1977] 1 All ER 475.

[90] [1982] AC 341.

[91] [1982] AC 510. Cf. also *Miller* [1983] 2 AC 161.

[92] [1982] AC 341, 354.

[93] Interpolated in *Lawrence* [1982] AC 510, 527. The requirement of obviousness does not apply where the risk is in fact foreseen: *Reid* [1992] 3 All ER 673, 691.

[94] See below, § 5.5(iv). Cf. *Adomako* [1995] 1 AC 171, 187, 189 (Lord Mackay).

(b) Rejection of the objective version, and the future of recklessness

The extension of recklessness proposed in *Caldwell* was always controversial.[95] Although the decision exercised a considerable influence over English criminal law during the 1980s,[96] its importance quickly diminished, to the point that its application came to be restricted to the offence in *Caldwell* itself (criminal damage and its variants), and to a few other statutory offences.[97] Eventually, in *G*,[98] the House of Lords overruled the application of objective recklessness even to criminal damage, reversing the very decision in *Caldwell*. Advertent recklessness is, once more, the dominant—perhaps even the only—form.

In *G*, two children aged 11 and 12 had stolen away camping without their parents' permission. During the night they entered the back yard of a Co-op shop, where they found some bundles of newspapers. After opening the newspapers, they set fire to some of them and threw them under a wheelie-bin in the yard. The defendant children then left the yard without putting out the fire. Subsequently, the fire spread to the bin and to the adjacent shop, causing approximately £1 million worth of damage. The defendants apparently expected the newspapers to burn themselves out on the concrete floor of the yard, and did not foresee the risk of the fire spreading to the building. At trial, following a *Caldwell* direction, they were convicted of reckless arson, a conviction upheld by the Court of Appeal. The House of Lords, however, quashed the convictions. *Caldwell* was overruled: it was held to have misinterpreted Parliament's intention when enacting the Criminal Damage Act 1971. More generally, the objective test of recklessness established in *Caldwell* was labeled "unjust".

Technically, the current law is that, whenever a court comes to interpret the meaning of an offence requiring "recklessness", it always has two options: to follow *Cunningham* and read it as requiring actual foresight, or to require the objective, *Caldwell* version. It therefore remains possible that, in some future context, the courts will interpret a specific statutory requirement of recklessness as entailing *Caldwell* and not *Cunningham* recklessness. Indeed, this possibility was left open by Lords Bingham and Rodger in *G*.[99]

But the likelihood that courts will ever adopt *Caldwell* recklessness in a statutory interpretation exercise is surely now remote, notwithstanding that there are some ordinary-language senses of "recklessness" which are not subjective (below, § 5.2(ii)). In general, unless the statute expressly precludes it, the fault element for criminal offences should usually be subjective. As the House of Lords itself acknowledged in *G*, convictions of serious crimes should not normally be visited on the inadvertent. In the absence of compelling reasons, such as a clear legislative indication, we should not normally make criminals of

---

[95] See, e.g., Smith [1981] *Crim LR* 393, 410; Williams, "Recklessness Redefined" [1981] *CLJ* 252; Griew, "Reckless Damage and Reckless Driving: Living with *Caldwell* and *Lawrence*" [1981] *Crim LR* 743; McEwan and Robilliard, "Recklessness: The House of Lords and the Criminal Law" (1981) 1 *LS* 267; Syrota, "A Radical Change in the Law of Recklessness?" [1982] *Crim LR* 97; Duff, "Professor Williams and Conditional Subjectivism" [1982] *CLJ* 273; Duff, *Intention, Agency and Criminal Liability* (1990) chap. 7; Williams, "The Unresolved Problem of Recklessness" (1988) 8 *LS* 74.

[96] Contrast other jurisdictions, where *Caldwell* generally failed to take hold: *Smith* (1982) 7 A Crim R 437; *Sansregret* v. *R.* (1985) 17 DLR (4th) 577; *Harney* [1987] 2 NZLR 576.

[97] E.g. *Large* v. *Mainprize* [1989] Crim LR 213.

[98] [2003] UKHL 50; [2004] 1 AC 1034.

[99] *Ibid.*, paras. 28 (Lord Bingham) and 69 (Lord Rodger).

those who act without any intent or awareness of wrongdoing, since they may not be suffi-ciently blameworthy to warrant conviction or punishment:[100]

> "But it is not clearly blameworthy to do something involving a risk of injury to another if . . . one genuinely does not perceive the risk. Such a person may fairly be accused of stupidity or lack of imagination, but neither of those failings should expose him to conviction of serious crime or the risk of punishment."

Indeed, especially where the defendant suffers from limitations of age, intellect, or the like, to apply the *Caldwell* standard would be manifestly unfair, since it could lead to the conviction of persons, including children, who lacked even the *capacity* to appreciate risks that would be obvious to ordinary adults:[101]

> "It is neither moral nor just to convict a defendant (least of all a child) on the strength of what someone else would have apprehended if the defendant himself had no such apprehen-sion. Nor, the defendant having been convicted, is the problem cured by imposition of a nominal penalty."

We concur. The justification of *Caldwell*, according to Lord Diplock, was that inadver-tence to an obvious risk frequently is just as blameworthy as choosing to run a risk which is foreseen, and so should be treated the same way. There is some force in this: it is an unattractive option to acquit a defendant who did not consider the risks because he was too drunk, too temperamental, or too uncaring a person to bother thinking about them.[102] But, as we shall see in § 5.2(iv), there are already special rules in place which deal with intoxi-cation. Moreover, a question might be asked whether the moral equation constructed by Lord Diplock will always (or almost always) hold—which ought to be the case before a court makes such a comprehensive extension. In particular, it seems harsh to treat as reckless those whose inadvertence was due to preoccupation or distraction,[103] and who may be utterly horrified when they recognise the consequences of their actions. It is even more harsh to equate with advertent recklessness the actions of those who were *incapable* of perceiving the risk.[104]

(ii) Recklessness as an actus reus term

The plausibility of an objective approach in cases involving reckless driving, such as *Lawrence*, rests upon a distinction that we drew in Chapter 4.[105] In *Lawrence*, the actus reus of the offence was concerned only with D's *behaviour* (i.e. with his reckless driving). By contrast, in many other offences D's behaviour alone is not sufficient to establish the actus reus. There

[100] *Ibid.*, para. 32 (Lord Bingham); see also para. 55 (Lord Steyn).

[101] *Ibid.*, para. 33 (Lord Bingham); cf. paras. 52-4 (Lord Steyn). The House rejected a modified test, of whether the risk would have been obvious to one with *the defendant's* capacities: *ibid.*, paras. 37-8 (Lord Bingham). See further below, § 5.5(ii).

[102] Cf. Lord Goff in *Reid* [1992] 3 All ER 673, 687ff. This seems to have been the thinking underlying *Parker* (above, § 5.2(i)).

[103] Cf. Griew, "Reckless Damage and Reckless Driving: Living with *Caldwell* and *Lawrence*" [1981] *Crim LR* 743, 747; in tort, *West Ky. Tel. Co.* v. *Pharis* 25 Ky LR 1838 (1904).

[104] As, following *Caldwell*, was done in *Elliott* v. *C (a minor)* [1983] 1 WLR 939; discussed further below, § 5.5(ii).

[105] See §§ 4, 4.1.

must be an additional element, e.g. that the victim is not consenting, or that she dies. Where an offence involves *circumstances* and *consequences*, it is natural for a lawyer to think of recklessness as a mens rea term, requiring advertence to the specific circumstance or consequence named in that offence. For example, to commit a reckless homicide one has to foresee the possibility of death ensuing. But matters are different when the actus reus is concerned only with the behaviour of the defendant. In an offence of reckless driving the court did not ask, "Was the defendant aware of the possibility that she might be driving a car?" Rather, what counted was whether the *manner* of her behaviour was sufficiently dangerous—not what she thought about that behaviour. "Reckless", in this context, qualifies the nature of the behaviour that is needed for the offence. Hence, it is an actus reus term. One might, for example, drive in a reckless manner (the *actus*) deliberately (the *mens*).[106]

(iii) Recklessness and circumstances

Just as with consequences, recklessness as to circumstances requires that the defendant acts believing that there is a possibility, or risk, that the circumstance might exist. This is sometimes called "reckless knowledge", but the term is a misleading one, since "knowledge" as such is not needed, and it will be enough if the defendant merely recognises that the circumstance *may* exist.

The definition just stated is derived from general principles. Recklessness requires that the defendant be aware of the possibility that the actus reus, as a whole, may occur. Hence it requires the defendant to be aware that each element of that actus reus may be present, including circumstances. A useful illustration of this is the offence of indecent assault. One element of that offence is the victim's lack of consent. The mens rea for this element is recklessness.[107] Thus the defendant cannot be guilty if he believes that his victim consents, and may only be convicted if he goes ahead recognising that she may not be consenting. As Lord Bingham put it in *G*, a person is reckless with respect to a circumstance "when he is aware of a risk that it exists or will exist."[108]

The difference between recklessness and intention can be shown by the following example. If D has sexual intercourse with V recognising (but not caring) that she may not be consenting, then if V does not consent D commits a reckless rape. On the other hand, if D has sexual intercourse *believing* positively that V does not consent, he rapes her intentionally. (In either case D commits the offence of rape.[109])

The above states the law in principle. Sometimes, however, this definition leads to difficulties where the defendant acts without giving thought to attendant circumstances. This may occur, for example, where D indecently touches another person but claims it did not occur to him that she might not consent. What if D did not think about the possibility because he did not care, and would have gone ahead anyway? Should he be acquitted? In

---

[106] Winslade, "Brady on Recklessness" (1972) 33 *Analysis* 31.

[107] *C* [1992] Crim LR 642.

[108] [2003] UKHL 50; [2004] 1 AC 1034, para. 41, quoting from the proposed clause 18(c) in *A Draft Code for England and Wales* Law. Com. No. 177 (1989).

[109] Whether D's recklessness would be sufficient for him to be convicted of an attempt (if V in fact does consent) is discussed below, in Chapter 9.

order to deal with such situations, recent cases have suggested two alternative ways of finding recklessness by the defendant.

The first suggested extension is that a defendant may be held reckless about a circumstance, such as non-consent, if he was indifferent to, or could not care less about, whether the victim was consenting. The validity of this extension is doubtful. Its genesis seems to be the references to indifference found in *Lawrence*. It is endorsed in a number of decisions, for example *Kimber*, where in the Court of Appeal's words, D's "attitude to [V] was one of indifference to her feelings and wishes. This state of mind is aptly described in the colloquial expression, 'couldn't care less'. In law this is recklessness."[110] But if that proposition was ever correct, it is not now. *Caldwell*, as we have noted, is no longer good law. Mens rea is not normally concerned with the *attitudes* of defendants; it is concerned with what they intended, knew, and did not know. This is why a worthy attitude, or a good motive, is no defence under the criminal law.[111] It is also why, under the *Cunningham* approach to recklessness, defendants are not to be convicted merely on the basis of an unworthy attitude or bad motive, e.g. for indifference. Correspondingly, the law should not be concerned to enquire *why* D failed to foresee a risk, and whether it was because he did not care or exhibited some other indifferent attitude.[112] Such fine nuances have no practical place in the law.

The second extension to traditional recklessness is more plausible, and is now almost certainly part of the law. On this test, D will be held reckless about a circumstantial element in an offence *unless* he has a positive belief that the circumstance is lacking. Thus, if D deliberately and indecently touches V, it is an indecent assault unless he believes that V consents. More generally, where recklessness about non-consent is required to establish mens rea, it suffices *either* if D recognised V might not be consenting, *or* if D did *not* believe that she was consenting. This test was accepted by the House of Lords in *B (a minor)* v. *DPP*.[113] In effect, the prosecution need prove only that D lacked a genuine belief that V consented, without having to prove, in addition, that he believed there was a risk that she did not consent. This formulation of recklessness will not convict defendants who wrongly assume that V consents, but will catch those who proceed to harm V without believing they have V's agreement. The advantage of this test is that (like *Cunningham*) its focus is restricted to D's cognitive beliefs, whereas the test suggested in *Kimber* requires consideration of D's attitude. Moreover, *Kimber* itself also falls within this second category.

---

[110] [1983] 1 WLR 1118, 1123. Cf. *Pigg* [1982] 2 All ER 591 (reversed on different ground [1983] 1 All ER 56); *Millard* [1987] Crim LR 393; *Khan* [1990] 2 All ER 783 (CA); *Paine* [1998] 1 Cr App R 36. Compare, in Australia, *Tolmie* (1995) 37 NSWLR 660; *Kitchener* (1993) 29 NSWLR 696; *Vehicle Inspectorate* v. *Nuttall* [1999] 1 WLR 629, 636. The approach in *Tolmie* was endorsed by Callinan J in *Banditt* v. *R.* [2005] HCA 80, para. 86, but not by the majority, which favoured a subjective test: see paras. 20, 25, 33–6.

[111] Cf. *Smith* [1960] 2 QB 423; above, §§ 5, 5.1(ii). For the rule that a positive attitude, of hoping the actus reus would not happen, supplies no defence, see *Crabbe* (1985) 156 CLR 464, 470.

[112] Moreover, as Norrie points out, there are different kinds of indifferent attitude: "Between Orthodox Subjectivism and Moral Contextualism: Intention and the Consultation Paper" [2006] *Crim LR* 486, 492-3. Thus the objection is compounded by ambiguity about *which* standard to apply.

[113] [2000] 2 AC 428, 459 (Lord Mackay), 466 (Lord Nicholls). Cf. *K* [2002] 1 AC 462, 471 (Lord Bingham), 479 (Lord Hobhouse); also *Satnam and Kewal Singh* (1983) 78 Cr App R 149. Contrast, however, the quotation from Lord Bingham in *G* [2003] UKHL 50, [2004] 1 AC 1034, para. 41, in the text above at n. 108.

(iv) Intoxication and the presumption of recklessness

In general, there is no presumption of recklessness, and the prosecution is obliged to prove recklessness without the assistance of irrebuttable inferences.[114] As always, the prosecution may rely on evidential inferences in the normal way: for example, the fact that D took precautions, say by wearing fire-resistant clothing when dealing with flammable materials, may be relied on to suggest that he recognised his conduct was dangerous. However, there is no rule of substantive law by which the defendant is deemed to have foreseen a consequence merely because it was likely or obvious.[115]

This generalisation is subject to one exception. If the defendant fails to foresee a risk because he was voluntarily intoxicated, he may be treated, in law, as having foreseen that risk.[116] Voluntary intoxication can lead, as a matter of law, to a finding of recklessness—including *Cunningham* recklessness. The legal significance of intoxication will be discussed in more detail below, in Chapter 18.

§ 5.3 Why distinguish intention from recklessness?

In practice, recklessness satisfies the mens rea requirement in most crimes. This raises an obvious question: why bother discussing a separate category of intention at all? There are three reasons for doing so. First, some actions can only be done intentionally. For example, a person attempts to harm another only if he intends to do so. It would be a misuse of language to describe a knowing risk-taker as "attempting" to inflict harm.

Often this linguistic difference reflects a moral distinction,[117] because the presence of intention can alter the very nature of what is done. As Glanville Williams once pointed out, "[t]he act constituting a crime may in some circumstances be objectively innocent, and take its criminal colouring entirely from the intent with which it is done."[118] It was the defendant's intention which changed the action from simple assault to indecent assault in *Court*,[119] a case where D spanked a young girl on the seat of her shorts. He was convicted of indecent assault because he had not done so in order to administer discipline, but rather for sexual gratification—his intention made the behaviour "indecent".[120] Similarly, the difference between negligent appropriation of property and theft lies not merely in the degree of culpability but also in the nature of the action itself (even though the physical harm may be the same). Theft cannot fully be defined in terms of its consequence because the action itself expresses a certain sort of contempt for property rights, and for the victim, which the mere appropriation of property does not.

---

[114] See s. 8 of the Criminal Justice Act 1967; above, § 5.1(ix).

[115] *Caldwell* [1982] AC 341, discussed earlier in § 5.2(i), is not such a decision; rather, it holds that for the objective variety of recklessness actual foresight by the defendant is not a required element.

[116] *Bennett* [1995] Crim LR 877.

[117] See, e.g., Duff, "Attempted Homicide" (1995) 1 *Legal Theory* 149; Horder, "Crimes of Ulterior Intent" in Simester and Smith (eds.), *Harm and Culpability* (1996) 153.

[118] *CLGP* 22. See also Lynch, "The Mental Element in the Actus Reus" (1982) 98 *LQR* 109.

[119] [1989] AC 28; discussed in Sullivan, "The Need for a Crime of Sexual Assault" [1989] *Crim LR* 331.

[120] *Per* Lord Ackner (at 230), "[t]o decide whether or not right-minded persons might think that the assault was indecent, the following factors were clearly relevant: the relationship of the defendant to this victim . . ., how had the defendant come to embark on this conduct and *why* was he behaving in this way?"

The second rationale for distinguishing intention from recklessness is that, as we have seen, recklessness is established only if the defendant risked doing the actus reus *unreasonably*. By contrast, there is no condition of unreasonableness attaching to intention. Neither is there a general defence known to the criminal law of reasonable action.[121]

The third ground also involves defences, which is a topic we have not yet discussed. As the law presently stands, in order to claim a defence such as self-defence, the defendant must *intend* to defend himself when he does the actus reus. This point is illustrated by the well-known case of *Dadson*,[122] in which a policeman shot and wounded a thief who was stealing wood. It was then, as now, an offence intentionally to shoot another, and both the actus reus and mens rea were made out in Dadson's case. However, the thief was in fact a felon, and a defence existed at that time to the effect that the policeman would be justified in shooting to prevent the escape of a felon. The difficulty was that the policeman had not realised that the person he was shooting was a felon. Hence, although he intended to shoot V, he did not intend the justification: i.e. to prevent the escape of a felon. Therefore, the Court ruled, he was not entitled to claim the defence, and he was convicted.[123]

§ 5.4 Knowledge

Where an offence is formulated so as to require that the defendant act "knowing" that some circumstance exists, this demands a positive (and correct[124]) belief on the part of the defendant that the relevant circumstance does indeed exist.[125] If Tom purchases goods suspecting they may well be stolen, he commits no offence of handling stolen goods because he does not "know" that they are stolen—he merely suspects they are.[126] Belief or knowledge that a circumstance *may* obtain, which would be sufficient for recklessness, is not knowledge that it does obtain. Hence it is inadequate to satisfy the mens rea of any offence which requires knowledge or intention that some circumstance exists.[127] In this respect "knowledge" of circumstances is the cognitive cousin of intention, rather than recklessness.

What is not necessary, however, is that the defendant should think that the relevant circumstance exists with provable certainty. In law, it is sufficient that the defendant accepts, or assumes, and has no serious doubt, at the time he acts, that the circumstance is present.[128] Hence if Tom refrains from investigating further whether or not the goods are indeed stolen,

---

[121] Cf. *Yip Chiu-cheung* v. R. [1995] 1 AC 111. For a discussion of this point in the context of medical necessity, see Ashworth, "Criminal Liability in a Medical Context: the Treatment of Good Intentions" in Simester and Smith (eds.), *Harm and Culpability* (1996) 173.

[122] (1850) 4 Cox CC 358.

[123] See also *Thain* [1985] NI 457; Sullivan, "Bad Thoughts and Bad Acts" [1990] *Crim LR* 559; Hogan, "The *Dadson* Principle" [1989] *Crim LR* 679.

[124] *US* v. *Dynar* (1977) 147 DLR 4th 399, 424.

[125] See generally Shute, "Knowledge and Belief in the Criminal Law" and Sullivan, "Knowledge, Belief and Culpability" in Shute and Simester (eds.), *Criminal Law Theory: Doctrines of the General Part* (2002) 184 and 207 respectively.

[126] *Grainge* [1974] 1 All ER 928 (CA).

[127] *Hall* (1985) 81 Cr App R 260 (CA); *Ismael* [1977] *Crim LR* 557.

[128] Cf. Smith, noting *Charles* [1977] *Crim LR* 615, 620: "doubts are inconsistent with belief"—at least if those doubts are serious ones. See the interesting discussion by Griew, "Consistency, Communication and Codification—Reflections on Two Mens Rea Words" in Glazebrook (ed.), *Reshaping the Criminal Law* (1978) 57, 69ff.

and goes ahead with the purchase believing that they may well be, he is not guilty of handling. It is not enough for him to believe there is a possibility or likelihood that they are stolen.[129] But if, despite the fact that he has not actually seen proof of another's ownership, he accepts the vendor's disclosure to him that the goods are purloined, then he handles them when he goes ahead with the purchase.

(i) Wilful blindness

The situation where Tom realises there is a chance the goods are stolen, yet deliberately refrains from checking his suspicion, raises the issue of "wilful blindness". Cases of wilful blindness often appear to fall between the mens rea alternatives (i) recklessness as to the circumstance ("reckless knowledge"), and (ii) (actual) knowledge, which satisfies intention. One alternative is straightforward. *Every* case where a defendant realises or suspects the circumstance might exist and refrains from investigating further is a case of reckless knowledge (i). Even without further investigation, the defendant knows already that there is a risk that the circumstance is present. So if the mens rea of an offence requires only recklessness, then the defendant may be convicted.[130]

Finding actual knowledge is more difficult. In some cases of deliberate non-inquiry by a defendant, the court will invoke what is known as the "doctrine" of wilful blindness. This doctrine applies where the defendant intentionally chooses not to inquire whether something is true because he has no real doubt what the answer is going to be. Its effect is to attribute knowledge of the circumstance to the defendant. In other words, where the wilful blindness doctrine applies, the law will treat the defendant as having actual knowledge (ii), and not merely the reckless knowledge that he otherwise would have.

The conditions under which the doctrine applies are not capable of being stated precisely.[131] Broadly speaking, if there is an obvious way of finding something out and the defendant deliberately shuts his eyes to a risk by failing to find out, he will not be permitted to exculpate himself by claiming that he did not know the truth. Wilful blindness covers the case where D "deliberately refrained from making inquiries the results of which he might not care to have."[132] Or, as the House of Lords stated in *Westminster CC v. Croyalgrange Ltd*:[133]

> "it is always open to the tribunal of fact, when knowledge on the part of a defendant is required to be proved, to base a finding of knowledge on evidence that the defendant had deliberately shut his eyes to the obvious or refrained from enquiry because he suspected the truth but did not want to have his suspicion confirmed."

---

[129] *Griffiths* (1974) 60 Cr App R 14 (CA); *Woods* [1969] 1 QB 447 (CCA).

[130] Above, § 5.2(iii).

[131] See Wasik and Thompson, "Turning a Blind Eye as Constituting Mens Rea" (1981) 32 *NILQ* 328; *CLGP* § 57; Lanham, "Wilful Blindness and the Criminal Law" (1985) 9 *Crim LJ* 261; Ryan, "Reckless Transmission of HIV: Knowledge and Culpability" [2006] *Crim LR* 981, 984–9.

[132] *Roper v. Taylor's Central Garages Ltd* [1951] 2 TLR 284, 288, quoting from *Evans v. Dell* [1937] 1 All ER 349, 353.

[133] *Westminster CC v. Croyalgrange Ltd* [1986] 2 All ER 353, 359.

On the other hand, wilful blindness cannot be invoked just because D *should* have inquired into the facts, or even if he suspected the truth;[134] otherwise knowledge would effectively be indistinguishable from recklessness. However, the line between recklessness and wilful blindness is a fine one. It appears that the defendant is wilfully blind in two situations. The first is if he shuts his eyes and fails to enquire because he is virtually certain what the answer will be.[135] This approach squares with the test once proposed by the Law Commission:[136]

> "The standard test of knowledge is—Did the person whose conduct is in issue either know of the relevant circumstances or have no substantial doubt of their existence?"

Alternatively, the wilful blindness doctrine will also apply if the means of knowledge are easily to hand, and D realises the likely truth of a matter but refrains from enquiry *in order* not to know. In such circumstances, although D in fact lacks knowledge there are clear normative grounds for inculpation. This type of case is helpfully elucidated by the judgment of Lord Sumner in *The Zamora*:[137]

> "There are two senses in which a man is said not to know something because he does not want to know it. A thing may be troublesome to learn, and the knowledge of it, when acquired, may be uninteresting or distasteful. To refuse to know any more about the subject or anything at all is then a wilful but a real ignorance. On the other hand, a man is said not to know because he does not want to know, where the substance of the thing is borne in upon his mind with a conviction that full details or precise proofs may be dangerous, because they may embarrass his denials or compromise his protests. In such a case he flatters himself that where ignorance is safe, 'tis folly to be wise, but there he is wrong, for he has been put upon notice and his further ignorance . . . is a mere affectation and disguise."

It should be emphasised that wilful blindness is a doctrine of substantive rather than evidential law. It imputes knowledge to the defendant for legal purposes where there is not, in fact, such knowledge. Even if the doctrine does not apply, however, there remains the further possibility that a jury may *infer* actual knowledge on the part of the defendant (i.e. that in fact he accepted the truth and had no serious doubt), from evidence that D recognised the likely circumstances and made no further enquiry.[138] Nonetheless, proof of the latter does not constitute proof of the former.

§ 5.5 Negligence

Unlike such mens rea varieties as recklessness, intention, and knowledge, negligence does not presuppose any particular state of mind on the part of the defendant. It is, however, a

---

[134] *Griffiths* (1974) 60 Cr App R 14; *Court* [1954] Crim LR 622; *Havard* (1914) 11 Cr App R 2. Cf. *Saik* [2007] 1 AC 18, at para. 32 (Lord Nicholls), para. 78 (Lord Hope), and para. 120 (Lord Brown).

[135] E.g. *Ross* v. *Moss* [1965] 2 QB 396.

[136] Draft Criminal Liability (Mental Element) Bill, Law Com. No. 89 (1978) cl. 3(1). This is a more demanding test than that finally endorsed by the Law Commission: Law Com. No. 177, *A Criminal Code for England and Wales* (1989) cl. 18(a).

[137] [1921] 1 AC 801, 812. See *Borthwick-Norton* v. *Romney Warwick Estates Ltd* [1950] 1 All ER 362, 365–6; *Redgate* v. *Haynes* (1876) LR 1 QB 89; *Somerset* v. *Wade* [1894] 1 QB 574. Cf. *Sansregret* v. *R.* [1985] 1 SCR 570, 584–6; *Barbeau* (1996) 110 CCC (3d) 69, 92–5 (Que CA).

[138] *Smith (Albert)* (1976) 64 Cr App R 217.

standard that reflects fault on the part of the defendant, and so it is appropriately discussed alongside the other mens rea categories. The main feature distinguishing negligence from the categories we have mentioned so far is that, in negligence, there is no requirement that the defendant foresee the risk that the actus reus might occur. Sometimes we blame people precisely because they have *failed* to think about something—because they were careless or thoughtless. It is this sort of case that is captured by negligence.

(i) The test for negligence

Even though negligence permits the finding of fault for inadvertent wrongdoing, it does not actually matter whether the defendant attends to or contemplates the risks. As Glanville Williams asserts, "the essential question, at any rate for legal purposes, is whether it was reasonable for you to go ahead with your conduct in the circumstances."[139] Of course, normally one who foresees and runs an unreasonable risk will be reckless as well as negligent. Negligence does not, however, *require* inadvertence. This is for two reasons. The first is that in the criminal law, the lesser fault standard incorporates the greater. A defendant should not be able to exculpate herself by pleading that her actions were reckless or intentional rather than negligent. It follows that where negligence is enough for criminal liability, then, *a fortiori*, there is liability for intention or recklessness.

The second reason is that, as we mentioned earlier, a defendant can foresee the actus reus without being reckless, yet may still be negligent. For example, an anaesthetist who recognises there is a slight risk of killing his patient is not normally reckless. But if he has unknowingly miscalculated the dose, then he is negligent even though not reckless. Recklessness involves an objective assessment of the subjectively perceived risk. Negligence involves an objective assessment of an objectively recognisable risk.[140]

So the emphasis is on the unreasonableness of the defendant's behaviour. Formally, the defendant is negligent if a reasonable person in the same circumstances (a) would have been aware of the risks of doing the actus reus and (b) would not have run those risks. It does not matter if the defendant herself was unaware of the risks. What counts is that her behaviour falls short of the standard of conduct that we would expect of a reasonable person—that she failed to take reasonable precautions against the harm specified in the actus reus.

(a) Ordinary or gross negligence?

The criminal law knows two types of negligence: ordinary negligence and gross negligence. One example of an offence requiring ordinary negligence is that of driving without due care and attention, contrary to section 3 of the Road Traffic Act 1988.[141] D commits an offence by making an error while driving that a reasonably prudent and skilful driver would not make;[142] in other words, by driving in a manner which involves a risk of harm that the

---

[139] Williams in Fitzpatrick and Williams, "Carelessness, Indifference and Recklessness: Two Replies" (1962) 25 *MLR* 49, 57.
[140] Although this proposition will be qualified below, in § 5.5(ii).
[141] Cf. Gas Act 1995, sched. 2 para. 10.
[142] *Simpson v. Peat* [1952] 2 QB 24, 27.

reasonable man would regard as unjustifiable. A standard of ordinary negligence may also be imported by the requirement that D exhibit "due diligence", for example in section 21 of the Food Safety Act 1990. Alternatively, there may be a direct reference to the reasonableness of D's mental state: in rape, for instance, it is sufficient that D "does not reasonably believe" that his victim consents.[143] In these cases, it is enough that D has failed to exercise a reasonable level of care in exercising the required diligence or considering whether V has consented.

Sometimes, however, the mens rea of an offence cannot be satisfied by anything less than gross negligence. For example, the Road Traffic Act 1988 also contains the offence of dangerous driving, which is committed by a defendant if:[144]

(a) the way he drives falls far below what would be expected of a competent and careful driver, and
(b) it would be obvious to a competent and careful driver that driving in that way would be dangerous.

The standard is that of gross rather than ordinary negligence. While the difference between the two is a matter of degree and judgement in each case, broadly speaking, negligence will be gross if the defendant's conduct not merely fails to meet the standard set by the reasonable man test, but falls short of that standard by a considerable margin—i.e. if the defendant's conduct is not merely unreasonable, but *very* unreasonable:[145]

"in order to establish criminal liability the facts must be such that, in the opinion of the jury, the negligence of the accused went beyond a mere matter of compensation between subjects and showed such disregard for the life and safety of others as to amount to a crime against the State and conduct deserving punishment."

It may be negligent to drive around a particular bend at 50 mph; if so, it is grossly negligent to do so at 80 mph. Hart puts the test another way: "[n]egligence is gross if the precautions to be taken against harm are very simple, such as persons who are but poorly endowed with physical and mental capacities can easily take."[146]

At common law, a conviction for manslaughter may be predicated on gross negligence. A recent example is provided by *Adomako*.[147] D, an anaesthetist, was attending an operation when the tube supplying oxygen to the patient became dislodged. D failed to notice the signs of disconnection, in consequence of which the patient, some nine minutes later, suffered cardiac arrest and subsequently died. D was convicted of manslaughter, on the footing that his failure to notice and remedy the problem was a gross dereliction of the standard of care that may reasonably be expected from a competent anaesthetist.

(b) Emergency

One of the features of *Adomako* was that the situation was urgent: the defendant, in his own testimony, stated that "after things went wrong I think I did panic a bit."[148] The test of

---

[143] Sexual Offences Act 2003, s. 1; below, ch. 12.
[144] Section 2A.
[145] *Bateman* (1925) 19 Cr App R 8, 11.
[146] "Negligence, *Mens Rea*, and Criminal Responsibility" in *Punishment and Responsibility* (1968) 136, 149.
[147] [1995] 1 AC 171.
[148] [1995] 1 AC 171, 182.

negligence has sometimes been criticised for being insensitive to circumstances, and for assessing emergency judgements in the cold light of the courtroom. Jeremy Horder has argued that in such situations we should not demand clinical accuracy, and that legitimate emotions such as fear and compassion, which sometimes lead us to make mistakes, are not properly allowed for by the orthodox test of negligence.[149] But this underestimates the legal test. We usually excuse a prima facie "negligent" mistake because it was not unreasonable *in the circumstances*. Although the evaluation of a defendant's conduct is done in a courtroom, in each case it must be done in the light of the defendant's particular circumstances and of normal social and personal values—including those of compassion and self-preservation. This is why it is sometimes reasonable to react precipitously.[150] The law does make allowance for emergencies: as Holmes J once noted, "detached reflection cannot be demanded in the presence of an uplifted knife."[151] A nice illustration of this principle is given in *Simpson* v. *Peat*:[152]

> "Suppose a driver is confronted with a sudden emergency through no fault of his own; in an endeavour to avert a collision he swerves to his right—it is shown that had he swerved to the left the accident would not have happened : that is being wise after the event and, if the driver was in fact exercising the degree of care and attention which a reasonably prudent driver would exercise, he ought not to be convicted, even though another and perhaps more highly skilled driver would have acted differently."

Horder claims that negligence in such cases "is not culpable". But if it is not culpable, this will be because it is not negligence at all.

(ii) Abnormal defendants—does the reasonable man share any of their characteristics?

The tests of negligence that we have identified seem at first blush to be objective. We complain of the defendant's *conduct*, and decide that she was negligent simply by determining that her conduct does not match a standard of behaviour that would have been acceptable in the circumstances. However, if negligence is truly a measure of culpability, there would seem to be a problem with this approach. In other categories of mens rea, the defendant is blameworthy because she *knowingly* does the wrong thing—not merely because her behaviour is wrong. But that ground of fault cannot apply here. In negligence, the law says that the defendant *should* have done whatever the reasonable man would have done: but why? Why should the defendant be regarded as blameworthy, and attract the odium of criminal culpability, just because her behaviour causes some harm that she did not foresee?[153]

---

[149] "Cognition, Emotion and Criminal Culpability" (1990) 106 *LQR* 469, 482. Compare Glanville Williams, "Offences and Defences" (1982) 2 *LS* 233, 242. See also Merry and McCall-Smith, *Errors, Medicine and the Law* (2001) 58-64.

[150] As Bernard Williams notes: *Ethics and the Limits of Philosophy* (1985) 185. See Horder, "Cognition, Emotion and Criminal Culpability" (1990) 106 *LQR* 469, 481.

[151] *Brown* v. *US* 256 US 335, 343 (1921). More prosaically, see *Wood* v. *Richards* (1977) 65 Cr App R 300; also Williams, *TBCL* 90.

[152] [1952] 2 QB 24, 28.

[153] Simester, "Can Negligence be Culpable?" in Horder (ed.), *Oxford Essays in Jurisprudence* (Fourth Series, 2000) 85.

The law's response is to assume that the reasonable man test incorporates the require-ments of blame. If the defendant's conduct is objectively unreasonable, then it manifests a failing on the part of the defendant for which she may properly be blamed. Putting things the other way around, had she not been deserving of blame, her behaviour would not have failed the reasonable man test.

Most of the time this is a satisfactory answer. For example, if D had been a properly attentive and caring parent, she would not have left her child unattended by the swimming pool—we may hold her negligent, and blame her, for doing so where a reasonable parent would not. And the fact that D was not a naturally caring parent is no excuse. But not every case is so straightforward. What if D is in some way abnormal? Suppose, for example, that D fails to observe a child climbing into the pool. A normal person would have seen the child. Is D negligent? Perhaps not, if it turns out that D is blind. The example suggests that, although the reasonable man test is mostly independent of the particular defendant, it is not entirely so. We do not expect D to behave as if she were sighted, but rather as a reasonable blind person would.

Generally speaking, the law states that behaviour is negligent if it involves a failure to exercise that "care and caution which a reasonable and prudent person ordinarily would exercise under like conditions or circumstances."[154] But what exactly is meant by the "reasonable and prudent person"? The illustration above suggests that we do not replace the defendant altogether with objective characteristics, otherwise the youngest child would receive no allowance for immaturity[155] and the blind would be expected to see.[156] *Smith and Hogan*, however, characterises the reasonable man standard rather more robustly: "if D has less knowledge or capacity for foresight than the reasonable person this, it seems, will not generally help him."[157] Similarly, asked "what if the defendant is substandard in abilities?", Williams responds, "the reasonable man is not imagined to be substandard in intelligence or foresight."[158]

It will be clear that we disagree. The test is mostly objective, but it can, if properly and sensitively applied, be in part, subjective. In particular, the reasonable man should be endowed with any peculiar physical characteristic of the defendant—including sight, hearing,[159] and age.[160] If his colleague's electrocution could have been avoided simply by throwing the mains switch, D is not negligent if he fails to do so because he is a paraplegic. (This partially subjective approach is also, increasingly, favoured in the context of defences such as provocation and duress, which we consider later in this book.)

---

[154] *Cordas* v. *Peerless Transportation Co* 27 NYS 2d 198, 4 Am LR 2d 147 (1941).

[155] Gray, "The Standard of Care for Children Revisited" (1980) 45 *Mo LR* 597; Shulman, "The Standard of Care Required of Children" (1928) 37 *Yale LJ* 618. See e.g. *Charbonneau* v. *MacRury* 153 A 457 (1931); *McHale* v. *Watson* (1966) 115 CLR 199; *Yorkton Agricultural Assoc* v. *Morley* (1967) 66 DLR (2d) 37. Compare *DPP* v. *Camplin* [1978] AC 705, 718 (provocation).

[156] Compare, in tort law, *Bernard* v. *Russell* 164 A 2d 577 (1960); *Keith* v. *Worcester St R.R.* 82 NE 680 (1907); *Balcom* v. *City of Independence* 160 NW 305 (1921). See Weisiger, "Negligence of the Physically Infirm" (1946) 24 *NCLR* 187; Lowry, "The Blind and the Law of Tort" (1972) 20 *Chittys LJ* 253.

[157] *Smith and Hogan* 130 (emphasis omitted).

[158] *TBCL* 94.

[159] Cf. *S.A. Ambulance* v. *Waldheim* (1948) 77 CLR 215.

[160] Note 149 above.

Sometimes this can work against the defendant. If she has additional knowledge, over and above that which a reasonable man would possess, then she will be held to the standard of that extra knowledge.[161] Thus a driver with exceptionally good vision would be expected to avoid the cyclist she notices ahead of her even if drivers with normal vision would not see that cyclist in time. And a professional, acting in a professional capacity,[162] will be judged by the standard of a reasonably skilful and competent practitioner;[163] not by the standard of a layman.

In what other ways is the reasonable man test to be influenced by facts about the particular defendant? In order to answer that question, consider why we would expect the apparently "objective" standard in negligence to be affected by a defendant's physical limitations. The reason is that to convict a blind person for failing to see would be wrong and unfair. The blind do not deserve blame for failing to see. This, it is submitted, is the right way to approach the question of objectivity in negligence. The reasonable man test should be subjective to the extent that the defendant's shortcomings do not disclose fault. In particular, apart from physical limitations there is one other failing for which an abnormal defendant should not be blamed: intelligence. Consider the facts of *Elliott* v. *C (a minor)*.[164] C, a 14-year-old girl of low intelligence, had wandered away from home and spent the night outdoors without sleep before ending up in a garden shed. There she found some white spirit, which she poured onto the floor and ignited by dropping lighted matches on it. The shed was destroyed in the ensuing fire. Although someone of normal intelligence would no doubt have appreciated the risk of burning down the shed, it was found as a fact that the risk would not have been obvious to one of her limited capacities.[165] Under the objective test of recklessness prevailing at the time, C was convicted of criminal damage.[166] But this seems to us highly problematic. It is submitted that to regard her even as having destroyed the shed *negligently* would be wrong.

That having been said, however, it is not clear whether the criminal law currently makes any allowance for low intelligence when assessing negligence. Academic argument favours taking account of personal incapacities. H.L.A. Hart proposed a general precondition for criminal liability of the form, "*could* the accused, given his mental and physical capacities have taken [the required] precautions?"[167] Although the Canadian Supreme Court has approved a similar requirement,[168] there is *obiter dicta* from the High Court of Australia endorsing an objective test, one that disregards individual capacities.[169] In England there is little relevant legal authority. The suggestion of a test like Hart's may be found in *Hudson*,[170]

---

[161] Cf. *Lamb* [1967] 2 QB 981; *Gossett* (1993) 105 DLR (4th) 681, 694–6; Road Traffic Act 1988, s. 3.

[162] This qualification may not apply in tort: *McComiskey* v. *McDermott* [1974] IR 75.

[163] *Bateman* (1925) 19 Cr App R 8, 12–13; *Adomako* [1995] 1 AC 171, 188.

[164] [1983] 1 WLR 939.

[165] *Ibid.*, 945 ("in the circumstances this risk [that the shed would be destroyed] would not have been obvious to her or appreciated by her if she had given thought to the matter").

[166] By application of the *Caldwell* definition of recklessness, now reversed by the House of Lords in *G*: above, § 5.2(i)(a)–(b).

[167] "Negligence, Mens Rea and Criminal Responsibility" in *Punishment and Responsibility* (1968) 136, 154. See also Simester, "Can Negligence be Culpable?" in Horder (ed.), *Oxford Essays in Jurisprudence*, Fourth Series (2000) 85; Ashworth, *Principles* § 5.3(f).

[168] *Creighton* (1993) 105 DLR (4th) 632.

[169] *Lavender* [2005] HCA 37, para. 128 (Kirby J).

[170] [1966] 1 QB 448. See also *Hardie* [1985] 1 WLR 64.

where the defendant was charged with having sexual intercourse with a defective woman.[171] It is a defence to this charge that the defendant "does not know and has no reason to suspect her to be a defective." In adjudicating the defence, the court was prepared to consider the limitations of the particular defendant:[172]

> "There may be cases, of which this is not one, where there is evidence before the jury that the accused himself is a person of limited intelligence, or possibly suffering from some handicap which would prevent him from appreciating the state of affairs which an ordinary man might realise."

Contra, subjective allowances are impliedly excluded by *Elliott* v. *C*[173] (above), where C was held to have acted recklessly on the *Caldwell* standard because the risk was obvious to a normal adult. The Court of Appeal also excluded the defendant's schizophrenia in *C (Sean Peter)*,[174] when determining whether, under section 1(2) of the Protection from Harassment Act 1997, a reasonable person would think that threatening letters sent by the defendant to his local MP amounted to harassment.

The question awaits definitive resolution by the House of Lords. Nonetheless, there are signs of a more compassionate approach in House of Lords decisions. Lord McKay suggests in *Adomako* that gross negligence involves conduct so bad that it may be characterised as reckless "in the ordinary connotation of that word";[175] in *Elliott* v. *C*, C was certainly not "reckless" in ordinary language. There are also dicta in *Reid* to the effect that fault should be assessed by reference to the capacities of the particular defendant: Lord Keith makes it clear that a defendant should not be liable where his inadvertence is owing to "some condition not involving fault on his part",[176] while Lord Goff refers to "illness of shock",[177] and Lord Browne-Wilkinson to "sudden disability".[178] More recently, in *G*, the House of Lords was plainly hostile to the unfairness of convicting of arson "a defendant (least of all a child) on the strength of what someone else would have apprehended."[179] In Lord Steyn's view:[180]

> "it is contrary to art 40(1) [of the United Nations Convention on the Rights of the Child] to ignore in a crime punishable by life imprisonment, or detention during Her Majesty's pleasure, the age of a child in judging whether the mental element has been satisfied. . . . If it is wrong to ignore the special characteristics of children in the context of recklessness under s 1 of the 1971 [Criminal Damage] Act, an adult who suffers from a lack of mental capacity or a

---

171 Contrary to the Sexual Offences Act 1956, s. 7.

172 [1966] 1 QB 448, 455.

173 [1983] 1 WLR 939, above , § 5.2(i); also *R (Stephen)* (1984) 79 Cr App R 334; *Stone and Dobinson* [1977] QB 354; *Ward* [1956] 1 QB 351.

174 [2001] EWCA Crim 1251; [2001] Crim LR 845. See also below, § 11.8. The decision is perhaps explicable on policy grounds specific to the statute (at paras. 18–19): "The conduct at which the Act is aimed, and from which it seeks to provide protection, is particularly likely to be conduct pursued by those of obsessive or otherwise unusual psychological make-up and very frequently by those suffering from an identifiable mental illness. . . . We are satisfied that to give the Act the construction for which [counsel] contends would be to remove from its protection a very large number of victims and indeed to run the risk of significantly thwarting the purpose of the Act."

175 [1995] 1 AC 171, 187. See the note by Gardner (1995) 111 *LQR* 22, 23–4.

176 [1992] 3 All ER 673, 675c. But D's paranoid schizophrenia was disregarded by the Court of Appeal in *Colohan* [2001] Crim LR 845, when determining whether D ought to have known that his conduct amounted to harassment contrary to s. 1 of the Protection from Harassment Act 1997.

177 *Ibid.*, 690J.

178 *Ibid.*, 696F.

179 [2003] UKHL 50, [2004] 1 AC 1034, para. 33 (Lord Bingham).

relevant personality disorder may be entitled to the same standard of justice. Recognising the special characteristics of children and mentally disabled people goes some way towards reducing the scope of s 1 of the 1971 Act for producing unjust results which are inherent in the objective mould into which the *Caldwell* analysis forced recklessness."

There is room, therefore, for optimism that ultimately the approach of the Court of Criminal Appeal in *Hudson* will prevail.

(iii) Negligence with respect to behaviour rather than consequences or circumstances

As with recklessness, negligence sometimes operates like an actus reus term. It does so when it qualifies the *behavioural* element in the actus reus, as opposed to elements of consequence or circumstance. So, for example, in an offence of careless driving the carelessness—i.e. negligence—of the driving is not a mens rea term meaning that a reasonable person would (and the defendant should) have realised that he was driving. Rather, it is effectively an actus reus term: meaning that the defendant was driving in a *manner* that fell short of the standard a reasonable person would set. Thus careless driving is a different type of negligence offence from negligent rape, where the law's concern is not so much with the manner of the defendant's action as with the fact that it was done at all.

Most of the time the difference will not be important, since even as a mens rea term negligence is assessed by reference to the defendant's conduct. However, it seems that the subjective elements of the reasonable man test may not apply when negligence is operating as an actus reus standard. Hence in *McCrone* v. *Riding* it was said that the standard of care in driving:[181]

"is an objective standard, impersonal and universal, fixed in relation to the safety of other users of the highway. It is in no way related to the degree of proficiency or degree of experience to be attained by the individual driver."

The justification for this is the need for a co-operative standard that other drivers can rely upon, together with the fact that driving is a voluntary activity, and those who engage in it may be thought to hold themselves out as being reasonably competent to do so.

(iv) The place of negligence

A number of writers have argued that people should never be subject to criminal liability on the basis of negligence,[182] and that its place lies properly in the arena of torts and compensation rather than of crimes and punishment. There is force in this argument, since it would

---

[180] *Ibid.*, paras. 53–4.

[181] [1938] 1 All ER 157, 158. See too *Gosney* [1971] 2 QB 674, 680; *Preston Justices, ex p Lyons* [1982] RTR 173; Wasik, "A Learner's Careless Driving" [1982] *Crim LR* 411.

[182] Hall, "Negligent Behaviour Should be Excluded from Penal Liability" (1963) 63 *Columbia LR* 632; Turner, "The Mental Element in Crimes at Common Law" in Radzinowicz and Turner (eds.), *The Modern Approach to Criminal Law* (1948) 195, 207–11; Hall, *General Principles of Criminal Law* (2nd ed., 1960) 138. Hart's refutation of Turner's argument is convincing: "Negligence, *Mens Rea*, and Criminal Responsibility" in *Punishment and Responsibility* (1968) 136. See also Moore, "Choice, Character, and Excuse" in Paul, Miller and Paul (eds.), *Crime, Culpability and Remedy* (1990) 29, 58; Keedy, "Ignorance and Mistake in the Criminal Law" (1908) 22 *Harv LR* 75, 83–5.

normally be harsh to equate those who do wrong inadvertently with others who break the law intentionally or recklessly. The person who inadvertently does harm might well have refrained from doing so, had she only realised the risk. But the fact that negligence is often not as bad as recklessness or intention does not mean that it is never serious enough to warrant criminalisation. Baker's example is instructive:[183]

> "Carelessly handling loaded firearms in a crowded area, or speeding through a school zone at lunch hour oblivious to the dangers to others because one is absorbed in an interesting conversation, is more culpable . . . than deliberately taking a $0.50 store item without payment or than many other knowing offences against property."

Sometimes, one who knowingly takes the risk of a minor crime is not so deserving of a criminal sanction as another who carelessly risks serious harm. It would be wrong for the criminal law only ever to convict in the former case.

Such instances are properly exceptional, and normally the law is reluctant to inflict serious criminal (rather than civil) sanctions upon people who have merely been negligent. Nonetheless, it would be a mistake to discount the significance of negligence. Quite apart from setting the mens rea standard for manslaughter and various statutory offences, it remains very important in the context of defences, both common law and statutory. For example, duress is available only if the defendant's reaction is reasonable, while in many sexual offences the defendant's ignorance (e.g. of V's age or mental impairment) must also be reasonable if it is to found a defence.

§ 5.6 Other mens rea states

We have mentioned that there is a variety of other mens rea terms used in the criminal law. Some of these, such as "dishonestly", occur primarily in the context of property crimes such as theft, and will be explored in some detail when we come to look at the specific offences.[184]

(i) "With a view to"

The phrase, "with a view to", introduces a form of ulterior intention. A person does X with a view to Y when Y supplies one of the reasons why she does X.[185] Foresight that Y is likely to occur is insufficient. On the other hand, it is not necessary that Y be the ultimate motive, or even the dominant objective, behind the doing of X.[186] It is enough that it be *one* of the objectives or intentions with which X is done.

---

[183] Baker, "Mens Rea, Negligence and Criminal Law Reform" (1987) 6 *Law and Phil* 53, 81. In *Principles* 193, Ashworth posits the following example: "D, a shot-gun champion, fires at a target, knowing that there is a slight risk that the bullet will ricochet and injure a spectator, which it does; E, who rarely handles guns, is invited to participate in a shooting party and fires wildly into bushes, failing to consider the possibility of others being there, and one is injured. Is D manifestly more culpable than E?"

[184] Below, Chapter 13.

[185] *Dooley* [2005] EWCA Crim 3093, [2006] Crim LR 544, para. 14.

[186] Cf. *J. Lyons and Sons* v. *Wilkins* [1899] 1 Ch 255, 269; Bevans (1988) 87 Cr App R 64.

As such, the phrase is cognate to intention rather than recklessness, and overlaps considerably with "with an intention to". It goes beyond intention, however, in that there is no requirement for any crystallized intention to be formed by D. It is enough if, for example, X is done *in case* Y will later be sought. Thus the phrase is apt to capture preparatory conduct such as taking certain preliminary steps (X) in readiness for the possibility of later pursuing an unlawful objective (Y).

(ii) Wilfulness

Historically, the case law regarding this term is inconsistent.[187] Fortunately, a lead has now been taken by the House of Lords in *Sheppard*.[188] The defendants in that case were charged with wilfully neglecting their young child. They had failed to ensure adequate medical care for the child, but apparently had not realised how ill he was. At trial, the judge directed the jury that wilful neglect was established if a reasonable parent would have appreciated the danger to the child in the same circumstances. On appeal, the House of Lords quashed the defendants' conviction. Wilfulness, it was held, requires either a deliberate decision to neglect the child, by refraining from calling a doctor when it is known that a doctor is needed; or a failure to call the doctor because the defendant does not care whether the child may need a medical examination. In essence, this means that wilfulness is an alternative term for objective (i.e. *Caldwell*) recklessness, and is satisfied if the defendant either consciously disregards the child's needs or ignores those needs because he is indifferent to the child's welfare.

The link between wilfulness and objective recklessness is perhaps not surprising in a decision handed down only a few months before *Caldwell* itself. It remains to be seen whether, like recklessness, wilfulness will in future be restricted to situations where the defendant actually foresees the prohibited outcome. In addition to earlier case law,[189] some support for this possibility may be found in *Sheppard*, where, according to Lord Keith:[190]

> "The primary meaning of 'wilful' is 'deliberate'. So a parent who knows that his child needs medical care and deliberately, that is by conscious decision, refrains from calling a doctor, is guilty under the subsection. As a matter of general principle, recklessness is to be equiparated with deliberation."

The analogy with deliberateness does, however, raise a question. Recklessness, we saw earlier, requires that the actus reus be an unreasonable risk. Is it possible that "wilfully", like "deliberately", imports no such requirement? If so, a surgeon who carries out a risky yet medically justified operation might be said to injure her patient willfully, even though she is not reckless. It is submitted, however, that in the context of the criminal law "wilfully" should bear the more restricted meaning, i.e. of recklessness. The defendant who, without intending

---

[187] Andrews, "Wilfulness: A Lesson in Ambiguity" (1981) 1 *LS* 303, 315ff.

[188] *Sheppard* [1981] AC 394.

[189] E.g. *Holroyd* (1841) 2 M & Rob 339, 174 ER 308; *Eaton* v. *Cobb* [1950] 1 All ER 1016; *Bullock* v. *Turnbull* [1952] 2 Lloyd's Rep 303; *Wilmott* v. *Attack* [1977] QB 498; *Ostler* v. *Elliott* [1980] Crim LR 584. Contrast *Cotterill* v. *Penn* [1936] 1 KB 53, rightly criticised by Andrews, "Wilfulness: A Lesson in Ambiguity" (1981) 1 *LS* 303, 316–17; *McPherson* [1980] Crim LR 654, criticised by Williams, [1981] *Crim LR* 796.

[190] [1981] AC 394, 418.

the actus reus, takes a reasonable risk of bringing that actus about should not be regarded as having brought it about wilfully.

(iii) Malice

Many older statutes use the term "maliciously" when specifying crimes. Section 48 of the Malicious Damage Act 1861, for instance, provides that "whosoever shall unlawfully and maliciously cut away, cast adrift, remove, alter, deface, sink, or destroy . . . any boat, buoy, buoy rope, perch, or mark used or intended for the guidance of seamen" commits an offence imprisonable for up to seven years. It is settled law that "maliciously" comprises intention or *Cunningham* recklessness.[191] Inadvertence, even *Caldwell* recklessness, will not do. On the other hand, there is no requirement that D's actions must be accompanied by "malice" in the ordinary sense of that term (i.e. by animosity or spite).[192] Foresight or intention is sufficient.

One special case is section 20 of the OAPA 1861, which provides that "whosoever shall unlawfully and maliciously wound or inflict any grievous bodily harm upon any other person" commits an offence. Although it is clear that "maliciously" in section 20 requires subjective foresight, the courts have held that D need only foresee the prospect of *some* bodily harm, and need not foresee a wounding or grievous bodily harm.[193] The rule makes a crucial part of the offence—the occurrence of an injury more serious than mere bodily harm—effectively a matter of strict liability. Quite apart from distorting the meaning of "maliciously", such a departure from principle[194] is particularly undesirable in the context of a serious crime like that in section 20. Fortunately, the definition of maliciousness has not suffered from similar judicial creativity when appearing in other offences.

(iv) Possession

Although primarily an actus reus term,[195] "possession" typically imports into the offence a concomitant mental ingredient. The leading decision, at least in the context of drug offences, is *Warner*.[196] D was convicted of unauthorised possession of a controlled drug, contrary to section 1 of the then Misuse of Drugs Act 1964, after being found with a box containing 20,000 amphetamine tablets. He claimed that he had thought the box contained scent. The House of Lords upheld his conviction. Although a *ratio decidendi* is difficult to distil from the judgments, it appears a majority of their Lordships were prepared to accept that the mens rea of possession requires only that D should know he is in possession of *something*, provided the something he thinks he possesses is not completely different from

---

[191] *Cunningham* [1957] 2 QB 396, 399; *Savage; Parmenter* [1991] 4 All ER 698, 721; *CLGP* § 30; Turner, *Kenny's Outlines of Criminal Law* (16th ed., 1952) 186.

[192] *Solanke* [1969] 3 All ER 1383.

[193] *Mowatt* [1968] 1 QB 421; *Savage; Parmenter* [1991] 4 All ER 698; *Rushworth* (1992) 95 Cr App R 252. The offence is discussed in detail below, § 11.5.

[194] Cf. "the ordinary principle that, where it is required that an offence should have been knowingly committed, the requisite knowledge must embrace all the elements of the offence": *Westminster City Council v. Croyalgrange Ltd* [1985] 1 All ER 740, 744 (DC); affd [1986] 2 All ER 353 (HL).

[195] Above, § 4.1(ii)(b).

[196] [1969] 2 AC 256; cf. *McNamara* (1988) 87 Cr App R 246. Amongst earlier cases, see *Southern* (1821) R & R 444, 168 ER 889; *Woodrow* (1846) 15 M & W 404, 153 ER 907; *Pearson* (1908) 1 Cr App R 79.

the thing he actually has. D need not know the precise nature of the material he possesses. Thus, if D had thought the box was empty, he would not have been in possession of its contents—yet since, on the facts, he thought it contained scent, he had sufficient mens rea to be in possession of the drugs (because scent, apparently, is not sufficiently different from drugs). Lord Pearce summarised the law as follows:[197]

> "I think that the term 'possession' is satisfied by a knowledge only of the existence of the thing itself and not its qualities, and that ignorance or mistake as to its qualities is not an excuse. This would comply with the general understanding of the word 'possess'. Though I reasonably believe the tablet which I possess to be aspirin, yet if they turn out to be heroin I am in possession of heroin tablets. This would be so I think even if I believed them to be sweets."

Where the contraband is not in a container, the rule is the same. Suppose that a stranger plants a cannabis cigarette in D's handbag or car, without D's knowledge. According to *Warner*, D would lack the mental element required to be in possession of the cannabis: "if someone surreptitiously puts something into my pocket, I am not in possession of it until I know it is there."[198]

The rule stated here is subject to certain qualifications. First, even though D does not realise he is in physical possession of something, he will nevertheless be in legal possession if he invited receipt of the thing. In *Peastol*,[199] D ordered a delivery of amphetamines, which arrived in the post. He was held to be in possession of the drugs as soon as the envelope was delivered through the letter box, even though he was not yet aware it had arrived.

Secondly, certain passages in *Warner* suggest that as well as knowing one is in possession of something, one must also have had a right or opportunity to discover the nature of that thing, e.g. (in *Warner* itself) by opening the box. Lord Morris characterised possession as "being knowingly in control of a thing in circumstances which have involved an opportunity (whether availed of or not) to learn or to discover, at least in a general way, what the thing is."[200] This additional requirement became redundant when the Misuse of Drugs Act 1971, section 28, enacted a defence that the defendant neither believed, suspected, nor had reason to suspect that the thing in his possession was a controlled drug; it was abandoned by the Court of Appeal in *McNamara*.[201] However, in *Lewis* [202] the requirement was resurrected, not as a necessary (i.e. exculpatory) condition of possession, but as a sufficient (i.e. *inculpatory*) one. The Court of Appeal held in that case that the sole tenant of a house may be in possession of drugs found there even though he visited the house infrequently and did not know they were on the premises, provided he had an opportunity to find out they were present. The decision is unfortunate and should not be followed. It seriously misconstrues Lord Morris's words by turning a dual requirement, for knowledge of the thing's being within his physical custody (whatever it might be) *and* opportunity to discover its nature, into *alternative* tests, of knowledge *or* opportunity to discover the drug.

---

[197] [1969] 2 AC 256, 305. Lord Pearce's subsequent qualification, that "it would be otherwise if I believed them to be something of a wholly different nature", is hard to justify and has not been observed in subsequent cases: *Marriott* [1971] 1 All ER 595; *McNamara* (1988) 87 Cr App R 246, noted [1988] *Crim LR* 440, (1988) 34 *MLR* 582.

[198] [1969] 2 AC 256, 299 (Lord Guest). Cf. *ibid.*, 305 (Lord Pearce); *Ashton-Rickardt* [1978] 1 All ER 173; *Irving* [1970] Crim LR 642; *Cugullere* [1961] 2 All ER 343 ("having with him an offensive weapon").

[199] (1978) 69 Cr App R 203.

[200] [1969] 2 AC 256, 289.

[201] (1988) 87 Cr App R 246.

[202] (1988) 87 Cr App R 270, criticised [1988] *Crim LR* 517.

By now, it may be apparent that *Warner* is a deeply problematic decision. Unfortunately, the section under which D was charged contained no explicit mens rea requirement. With the exception of Lord Reid, who was prepared to imply a requirement for mens rea into the offence as a whole, their Lordships therefore saw themselves as constrained to choose between the options of making drug possession a no-fault, strict liability, offence or implying a mental ingredient into the term "possession" itself. The House resorted to a fictional, artificial, construction rather than face squarely the true root of the difficulty, i.e. the absence of an express mens rea element in the statute. Smith's comment encapsulates the problem nicely:[203]

> "The difficulty arises because possession has become the criterion of guilt, yet possession is a neutral concept, not involving blame or fault. We shrink from saying that the lady with the shopping basket is in possession of the packet slipped in without her knowledge because it contains controlled drugs. If it were a box of chocolates dropped in by a friend as a birthday present, would any of the judges in *Warner* have hesitated to hold that she was in possession of it? If it were removed by a thief would they have had any doubt that it was stolen from her . . . ? Of course not. So far as the question of possession is concerned, there should be no distinction between the drugs and the chocolates. If the House in *Warner* had followed the lead of Lord Reid, these difficulties would have been largely if not entirely avoided. . . ."

§ 5.7 Transferred mens rea

It is a general rule that, if the defendant does an actus reus with the required mens rea (and without being able to plead any relevant defence), she is guilty of an offence even though the occurrence of the actus reus may be unexpected in a way which is immaterial to the definition.[204] To illustrate:

> Suppose that Duncan takes aim at Tom with intent to kill him, and pulls the trigger. Just as Duncan shoots, however, Tom bends down to pick a flower. Duncan's shot misses Tom and hits Bill, who was standing behind Tom. Bill is killed instantly. In this situation Duncan is guilty of murdering Bill, notwithstanding that he did not foresee that possible outcome. The actus reus of murder is to kill a *person*.[205] Thus, although Duncan intended to kill Tom rather than Bill, he had the mens rea for murder since he intended to kill a *person*; the identity of that person is immaterial to the definition of the offence.

The doctrine of "transferred malice", as it is popularly known, is not confined to murder.[206] Neither is it a doctrine merely of transferred *intention*. Imagine, this time, that Jane bears a

---

[203] [1988] *Crim LR* 519.

[204] For critical discussion, see Ashworth, "Transferred Malice and Punishment for Unforeseen Consequences" in Glazebrook (ed.), *Reshaping the Criminal Law* (1978) 77; Ashworth, "The Elasticity of Mens Rea" in Tapper (ed.), *Crime, Proof and Punishment* (1981) 45; Williams, "Convictions and Fair Labelling" [1983] *CLJ* 85; Horder, "Transferred Malice and the Remoteness of Unexpected Outcomes from Intentions" [2006] *Crim LR* 383. More abstract treatments include Husak, "Transferred Intent" (1996) 10 *Notre Dame Journal of Legal Ethics and Public Policy* 65; also Dillof, "Transferred Intent: an Enquiry into the Nature of Criminal Culpability" [1998] *Buffalo Crim LR* 501.

[205] *Gore* (1611) 9 Co Rep 81, 77 ER 853; *A-G's Reference (No. 3 of 1994)* [1996] 2 All ER 10; *Hopwood* (1913) 8 Cr App R 143.

[206] E.g. *Mitchell* [1983] QB 741 (unlawful act manslaughter); *Gross* (1913) 77 JP 352 (voluntary manslaughter); *Latimer* (1886) 17 QBD 359 (wounding); *McCullum* (1973) 57 Cr App R 645 (handling stolen goods).

grudge against Daniel. She throws a stone at the brickwork of his house, No. 6 King Street. She recognises that the stone may break one of Daniel's windows, although she does not intend it to do so. As it happens, the stone misses the windows of No. 6 but ricochets off the brickwork and breaks Pat's window at No. 8. Jane's recklessness is sufficient mens rea for the crime of damaging property,[207] and is transferrable to the (otherwise unanticipated) result: damage to *Pat's* property.

However, transferred malice does not operate when the divergence between actus reus and mens rea *is* relevant to the definition of the offence. In particular, it is not possible to convict someone on the basis of an actus reus for one offence accompanied by the mens rea for a different offence. If Jane were to throw a stone at Daniel and miss but inadvertently break his window, she is not guilty of criminal damage (unless she foresaw a risk to the window when throwing the stone at Daniel).[208] Her intent to injure Daniel does not satisfy the mens rea requirement for damage to property.

When malice is transferred, so also are defences. Imagine one last variant: Duncan attempts to shoot Tom only because Tom is attacking him and Duncan is in immediate peril of his life. He misses and unexpectedly kills Bill. Duncan's intention may be transferred, but so too is his claim of self-defence. He is not guilty of murder.[209]

Although the transferred malice doctrine has been criticised,[210] in its modern incarnation (i.e. as stated here) the doctrine is unobjectionable. Indeed, it is not really a doctrine at all—merely a particular type of immaterial variation. The causal miscarriage of D's actions in transferred malice cases has exactly the same legal status as, for example, cases of immaterial mistake. If Ian steals a cheap painting because he thinks it is a valuable Constable, he has the mens rea (and commits the actus reus) of theft since the specific identity of the property stolen forms no necessary part of the offence definition. It is enough that he takes "property belonging to another", whether or not that property is of great value.[211] Transferred malice cases are governed by the same principle: D's actions cause an outcome that is in some way unexpected,[212] but not in a way relevant to the offence definition.[213]

---

[207] Criminal Damage Act 1971, s. 1(1).

[208] Compare *Pembliton* (1874) LR 2 CCC 119; *Taaffe* [1984] AC 539. (Jane could, of course, have been convicted straightforwardly if she had foreseen the risk of breaking the window.) Compare however *Ellis and Street* (1986) 84 Cr App R 235, which pays lip service to the principle that the actus reus and mens rea must correspond, but at the same time subverts that fundamental requirement for the sake of enforcement convenience.

[209] Cf. *Gross* (1913) 77 JP 352 (provocation). Note that the transfer of a defence will not necessarily preclude liability for an independent offence. It may, for example, have been grossly negligent to shoot at Tom because of the risk of hitting Bill.

[210] See, e.g., *A-G's Reference (No. 3 of 1994)* [1998] AC 245, 259–62 (Lord Mustill); below, § 10.2(i)(a).

[211] Cf. *Wrigley* [1957] Crim LR 57.

[212] A proviso: transferred malice is unproblematic only if causal principles are properly observed. This explains the otherwise troubling case of *Heigho* 18 Idaho 566 (1910), discussed in Williams, *TBCL* 181 n. 1. In that case, D assaulted W, and an onlooker died of fright. D was convicted of the manslaughter of W. It is submitted the conviction was wrong; D was not causally responsible for the onlooker's death. Horder disagrees with this view ("Transferred Malice and the Remoteness of Unexpected Outcomes from Intentions" [2006] *Crim LR* 383, 389–90), but one of the criteria of causal responsibility here is that the intervening event be reasonably foreseeable: above, § 4.2(iii)(a)–(b).

[213] Cf. *Wrigley* [1957] Crim LR 57.

(i) "Incompatible" or "remote" transfers where the offence elements are satisfied?

Lord Mustill has observed of transferring mens rea that "to make any sense of this process there must, as it seems to me, be some compatibility between the original intention and the actual occurrence, and this is, indeed, what one finds in the cases."[214] We have suggested above that the need for compatibility is satisfied when the variation is immaterial to the definition of the offence. However, Jeremy Horder has suggested an additional limitation, which would sometimes prevent the transfer of mens rea even though the mens rea and actus reus elements are present. In his view, an outcome is too "remote" for mens rea to be transferred if (i) the victim was not the intended victim and (ii) the victim was killed in an unexpected way, in a manner unforeseen by the defendant.[215] Thus consider the following example:

> D shoots at V1, intending to kill him. The bullet misses, but enters a factory behind V1. There, it strikes an electrical transformer, causing the transformer to explode. The explosion kills a factory worker, V2.

There is general agreement that the intention to kill V1 cannot be transferred to any charge of criminal damage involving the unanticipated explosion. At the same time, on the transferred mens rea analysis we have set out, D is straightforwardly guilty of murder, since by her act she intended to, and did, kill a human being. However, if we were to accept Horder's limiting principle of "remoteness" or "incompatibility", it seems that D would not be convicted of murder but, rather, of the attempted murder of V1 and of the manslaughter of V2.[216]

In our view, such a limiting principle should be rejected. First, it promotes uncertainty. When is the manner in which an outcome is caused sufficiently different and unexpected to count as incompatible? One might think that causation doctrines already have this in hand, but Horder's principle is meant to apply *after* causal responsibility for V2's death is established. It is undesirable to compound the complexity of the enquiry into D's guilt, since the criteria of any additional limitation do not seem susceptible of clear enunciation. Moreover, the moral case for a limitation seems unmeritorious. Suppose that the unexpected explosion had, in fact, killed V1. Convicting D of murder is then straightforward. Why should it make al the difference that it was V2 instead who died? Both are human beings. All the elements of the offence are present. As was observed in *Mitchell*, "the criminality of the doer of the act is precisely the same whether it is A or B who dies."[217] To convict D of unlawful-act manslaughter, on the basis of an attempted murder causing death, is an unnecessary sophistication.

---

[214] *A-G's Reference (No. 3 of 1994)* [1998] AC 245, 262.

[215] "Transferred Malice and the Remoteness of Unexpected Outcomes from Intentions" [2006] *Crim LR* 383, 388-9.

[216] In this he aligns himself with Ashworth: "Transferred Malice and Punishment for Unforeseen Consequences" in Glazebrook (ed.), *Reshaping the Criminal Law* (1978) 77.

[217] [1983] QB 741, 748.

§ 5.8 Concurrence

As a general rule, the actus reus and mens rea of a crime must coincide in time. That is, the behavioural and circumstantial elements of the actus reus must occur at the same time as the mens rea requirements are satisfied. Unless there is a moment in time, a *scintilla temporis*, at which these elements are all present, the crime is not committed.[218] Consider the following illustration:

> D is an assassin who has been hired to kill V. One evening she drives over to V's house in order to shoot him when he comes home. On the way, however, she is involved in an accident when she collides with a cyclist who has suddenly cut in front of her car. Upon getting out of the car, D recognises that the cyclist is V. Thinking V is unconscious but alive, she shoots him through the heart. V, however, was already dead as a result of the accident.

D has not murdered V. Although she may have caused his death (the actus reus) by driving into him, when she did so she did not have a present intention to kill. Later, when she shot V, she had the mens rea for murder but her behaviour did not cause his death, so could not constitute the actus reus. Thus there is no moment in time at which both the actus reus and mens rea of murder are present.

Neither can an antecedent mens rea be added to a subsequent actus reus in order to support a conviction. For example:

> D takes a new umbrella to the law library one morning. When she departs, she cannot remember exactly what her umbrella looked like. Seeing an attractive umbrella in the stand, she decides to take and keep that one instead—not realising that it is in fact her own umbrella. Later, she begins to feel guilty. She returns to the law library, and replaces the attractive umbrella. In its place, she takes with her a different umbrella which she mistakenly thinks is the one she originally came with.

When D first leaves the library, she attempts to steal an umbrella but fails to do so because the one she takes is her own. She has the mens rea for theft but does not commit the actus reus.[219] Later, when she departs for a second time, she commits the actus reus of theft by taking another person's umbrella, but does so innocently—without an "intention of permanently depriving the other."[220] There is no moment in time at which all elements of the definition of theft are co-existent.

Where the actus reus includes consequences, the requirement for concurrence applies to the behavioural element rather than its consequence. If D deliberately poisons V, and V takes some hours to die, the fact that D repents in the meantime will not absolve her of murder.[221] Conversely, if D is driving and accidentally hits a cyclist, the fact that she realises the cyclist is V, her enemy, and rejoices while he is dying of his injuries will not make her guilty of a homicide offence. For the purposes of concurrence, the actus reus has already occurred.

---

[218] *Fowler v. Padget* (1798) 7 Term Rep 509, 101 ER 1103.
[219] The umbrella is not property belonging to another: Theft Act 1968, s. 1(1).
[220] Theft Act 1968, s. 1(1).
[221] Cf. *Jakeman* (1982) 76 Cr App R 223.

Although concurrence is a standard requirement for offences involving mens rea, there are some situations where the need for concurrence does not operate or can be circumnavigated.[222] We consider these below.

(i) Circumventing the concurrence requirement

(a) Fresh acts, continuing acts, and subsequent omissions

Where an actus reus by D precedes his having mens rea, one technique available to the prosecutor is to show another, later, occurrence of the actus reus which coincides with D's mens rea—i.e. to look for a different moment in time at which the offence can be proved to have occurred.

A standard, if unusual, case of this would be where D does a second positive act which also brings about the actus reus. Suppose, in the days when tort actions died with the plaintiff,[223] that while driving D accidentally runs over V. V, fatally injured, lies dying. D is uninsured and, panicking, she backs up hoping thereby to avoid tortious liability. If the further injuries D inflicts by reversing over V play any causal role by accelerating V's death then D becomes guilty of murder, on the basis of the second and not the first incident.

Absent a fresh causative act by the defendant, the prosecution may try instead to show a *continuing* act: that the actus reus, although initiated by D without mens rea, is still occurring or being perpetrated by D at a later moment when D now has the required mens rea. This type of case is discussed in § 4.1(i)(b).[224] It is exemplified by *Fagan* v. *Metropolitan Police Commissioner*,[225] in which D accidentally stopped his car on a policeman's foot. That itself was no assault, since D did not yet have mens rea. However, when he deliberately refrained from moving his car, an assault was established. There was an ongoing application of force to the policeman by D (the actus reus), which was now accompanied by mens rea.[226]

Alternatively, the prosecution can try to bring its case within the ambit of *Miller*.[227] In this situation, a subsequent omission to prevent harm may constitute the actus reus if it amounts to a failure to prevent a danger that D has himself created by his earlier actions. *Miller* is discussed further in § 4.1(i)(b).[228]

(b) The complex single transaction

The law is different when the actus reus of an offence occurs *after* D has mens rea. Here it will sometimes be possible to convict D on the basis that the particular act that caused harm was part of a larger, complex series of actions which should be viewed as a whole, where D has mens rea at some earlier point during that "transaction".

---

[222] Marston, "Contemporaneity of Act and Intention in Crimes" (1970) 86 *LQR* 208. See also White, "The Identity and Time of the Actus Reus" [1977] *Crim LR* 148.

[223] Winfield, "Death as Affecting Liability in Tort" (1929) 29 *Col L Rev* 239.

[224] See Case 4.

[225] [1969] 1 QB 439.

[226] See also *Kaitamaki* v. *R.* [1985] AC 147; *Cooper and Schaub* [1994] Crim LR 531.

[227] [1983] 2 AC 161.

[228] See Case 5.

The classic case is *Thabo Meli* v. *R*.[229] In that case, four defendants conspired to kill V and dispose of his body. In accordance with their plan, they struck V on the head (with intent thereby to kill him). Thinking him dead, they rolled him over a cliff. In fact, V was not killed by the blow and died from exposure suffered after falling down the cliff. Prima facie, the act of disposal, which caused V's death, was unaccompanied by the mens rea for murder since the defendants believed he was already dead. Nonetheless, the Privy Council upheld their convictions for murder. Rather than slicing up the events of the killing into component moments of time and then looking for a single moment at which actus reus and mens rea coincide:[230]

> "It appears to their Lordships impossible to divide up what was really one series of acts in this way. There is no doubt that the accused set out to do all these acts in order to achieve their plan, and as parts of their plan; and it is much too refined a ground of judgment to say that, because they were under a misapprehension at one stage and thought that their guilty purpose was achieved before, in fact, it was achieved, therefore they are to escape the penalties of the law."

It is hard to disagree with this decision, which represents a genuine exception to the concurrence requirement.[231] The defendants did exactly what they planned to do, and brought about exactly the result they had intended. The fact that the manner in which their success occurred was unexpected seems no ground for exculpation.

As the quotation above emphasises, the actions of the defendants were deliberate and pursuant to a preconceived plan. However, these elements of preplanning and intent have not been required in subsequent cases. In *Church*[232] the defendant knocked the victim unconscious during a fight and, mistakenly believing he had killed her, threw her into a river where she drowned. His conviction for manslaughter was upheld. Similarly, in *Le Brun*[233] D, in an argument with his wife, knocked her unconscious and, while attempting to drag her body away, dropped and killed her. On appeal, the trial judge was held correctly to have directed the jury that they could convict D of murder or manslaughter (depending on the intention with which he first struck his wife) if D had accidentally dropped her while either attempting to move her to her home against her known wishes, and/or attempting to dispose of the body or cover up the assault. In such circumstances, English law[234] holds that the the sequence of wrongful acts by the defendant may be regarded as elements of a single episode of unlawful conduct, where the transaction as a whole incorporates both mens rea and actus reus elements of a crime.

---

[229] [1954] 1 All ER 373.

[230] [1954] 1 All ER 373, 374.

[231] It is worth noting, however, that the case could have been decided on a more straightforward causation basis, to be discussed in § 5.8(i)(c). The same could be said of *Church*, considered below in the next paragraph. Arguably, *Le Brun* (also considered below) is the only case where the one transaction analysis was actually needed.

[232] [1966] 1 QB 59.

[233] [1991] 4 All ER 673. See also *Moore and Dorn* [1975] Crim LR 229; *Le Brun* [1991] 4 All ER 673; *A-G's Reference (No. 4 of 1980)* [1981] 2 All ER 617. For discussion, see Sullivan, "Cause and the Contemporaneity of Actus Reus and Mens Rea" [1993] CLJ 487, 495–9.

[234] Contrast some other jurisdictions: *Ramsay* [1967] NZLR 1005; *Chiswibo* 1960 (2) SA 714; *Shorty* [1950] SR 280; *Khandu* (1890) ILR 15 Bom 194.

Le Brun does suggest one limitation to the *Thabo Meli* principle. The Court of Appeal appeared to acquiesce in the trial judge's direction that:[235]

> "if the fatal injury had happened in the course of . . . well-intentioned efforts to help her, he would be guilty neither of murder nor manslaughter . . . the distinction I am drawing [is] between as it were an extension or a furtherance or a continuation of the unlawful conduct and a different tack where whatever he has done to her before he is trying his best to help or comfort her even if in a misguided way. . . ."

According to Lord Lane CJ, "the judge was drawing a sharp distinction between actions by the appellant which were designed to help his wife and actions which were not so designed." This suggests the *Thabo Meli* doctrine will apply only where the ongoing actions are still tainted by D's unlawful purpose. Had D dropped his wife while carrying her to hospital, his doing so would have been a separate incident, divisible from the earlier, unlawful transaction.

(c) A causation approach

Where the defendant's mens rea precedes the action that most obviously constitutes the actus reus, another way of circumventing concurrence difficulties is to show that some earlier action by the defendant, done at the time when he had mens rea, was *also* a cause of the prohibited harm. The clearest illustrations of this approach are to be found in overseas cases. In *McKinnon*,[236] D assaulted V and knocked him unconscious. D then manhandled V, apparently causing an accidental nose-bleed, before leaving V lying on the ground and running off. While V was lying unconscious, the blood from his nose entered his lungs and he suffocated. The New Zealand Court of Appeal upheld D's conviction for murder. Although D may not have had the required mens rea when he caused the injury to V's nose, he did have mens rea when he struck V and knocked him unconscious. Moreover, the Court ruled, D's striking V was a contributory cause of his death, in combination with the nose-bleed, since it rendered V unable to deal with the bleeding. Thus there was no need to invoke a series-of-acts analysis, of the sort found in *Thabo Meli*, since there was already a *scintilla temporis* at which both an actus reus and the mens rea of murder were present.

Indeed, it is arguable that *Thabo Meli* could itself have been decided on a causation basis.[237] On this approach, the *Thabo Meli* doctrine would still be necessary in some cases, but only where the second event was overwhelmingly the cause of death, and amounted to a *novus actus interveniens* (e.g. where V is killed instantly by the impact after he is thrown over a cliff).[238] Conversely, the causation analysis will be necessary in situations where *Thabo Meli* cannot apply, for example because D's second intervention was innocent and well-meaning, or where the intervention is by a stranger rather than by D.

---

[235] [1991] 1 QB 61.

[236] [1980] 2 NZLR 31. Compare *S* v. *Masilela* 1968 (2) SA 558. For discussion of multiple causes see above, § 4.2(ii)(c).

[237] Adams, "Homicide and the Supposed Corpse" (1968) 1 *Otago LR* 278, 287; Marston, "Contemporaneity of Act and Intention in Crimes" (1970) 86 *LQR* 208, 218–19; *McKinnon* [1980] 2 NZLR 31, 36–7.

[238] Compare *Le Brun* [1991] 1 QB 61.

(d) Involuntariness and antecedent fault

If D perpetrates an actus reus while in an automatic state, normally the concurrence requirement will not be satisfied. Exceptionally, however, it may be possible to convict D, on the basis that his automatism is a consequence of his own earlier actions which occurred at a time when he had the mens rea for the offence. This type of case is discussed more fully in § 4.3(iii). Suppose, for example, that David is a diabetic. One day he deliberately takes insulin without eating any food. He does this in the hope of reducing himself into a semi-conscious state, where he knows that he is likely to become violent and assault his flatmate whom he does not like. Should his plan be successful, David will be guilty of an intentional assault, notwithstanding his automatism at the time the assault occurs.

Sometimes the offence may be proved without reference to the defendant's subsequent, involuntary conduct. In *Kay v. Butterworth*,[239] D fell asleep while driving and collided with soldiers marching on the road. He was convicted of careless driving, but not because he drove into the soldiers. (At that time he was asleep and his behaviour was involuntary.) Rather, the offence was complete when he continued to drive while drowsy—that, in itself, was careless driving. Indeed, D would have committed the offence even if he had not run into the soldiers.[240] Glanville Williams illustrates this point in a lucid example:[241]

> "When, for example, a driver proceeds along Church Lane in a sleepy condition, and falls asleep at the wheel just before entering High Street, where he is involved in an accident, he cannot be convicted of careless driving in High Street, because in contemplation of law he did not 'drive' in High Street, and it makes no difference that his involuntary accident in High Street was the result of his own previous fault. He can, indeed, be convicted of careless driving, but this must be laid as having taken place in Church Lane, when the driver was undoubtedly 'driving'."

The offence occurs in Church Lane.

---

[239] (1945) 61 TLR 452. Cf. *Moses* v. *Winder* [1980] Crim LR 232. For a rather more dramatic example, see *People* v. *Decina* 2 NY 2d 133 (1956).

[240] *Spurge* [1961] 2 QB 205, 210.

[241] *TBCL* 682. Obviously, this analysis works only if the time-frame for commission of the actus reus is sufficiently elastic, and not tied to a particular incident. Contrast *Burns* v. *Bidder* [1967] 2 QB 227 (failing to accord precedence at a pedestrian crossing).

6

STRICT AND CONSTRUCTIVE LIABILITY

Not every offence against the criminal law involves the sort of public condemnation that is implicit in a conviction for homicide. We argued in Chapter 1 that serious criminal offences, where considerable public stigma attaches to a conviction, should always stipulate some form of mens rea element that must be proved before the defendant may be convicted, in order to avoid inflicting "the disgrace of criminality"[1] upon defendants who are not at fault when harm occurs. By contrast, a parking offence, for instance, involves little or no stigma, so the need for a mens rea element is not as pressing.[2]

In recognition of this, there are many offences of a regulatory nature which lack a true mens rea ingredient.[3] These offences impose *strict* (sometimes called *absolute*[4]) *liability*: the prosecution is required to prove the actus reus, but in relation to one or more elements of the actus reus, there is no mens rea element to prove. The defendant will be convicted even if he was entirely without fault. Thus, in *Pharmaceutical Society of Great Britain* v. *Storkwain Ltd*,[5] the defendant chemists were convicted of selling controlled medicines without prescription even though they neither knew nor had reason to suspect that the "prescriptions" they filled were forgeries. Offences of this sort have been in existence for over 150 years: in 1846 a dealer was convicted in *Woodrow*[6] of possessing adulterated tobacco even though he had no ground for suspecting the tobacco was adulterated, and could only have discovered it to be so by a chemical analysis that it would be unreasonable to expect of dealers. Similarly, in *Lundy* v. *Le Cocq*,[7] D was convicted of selling intoxicating liquor to a drunken person, contrary to section 13 of the Licensing Act 1872, which provided that "if any licensed person . . . sells any intoxicating liquor to any drunken person, he shall be liable to a penalty." Although D neither knew nor had reason to suspect the buyer was drunk, the Divisional Court held the offence was absolute, and ignorance of the buyer's condition was irrelevant.

According to Lord Edmund-Davies, an offence may properly be regarded as being of strict liability even though mens rea is required regarding other elements of the actus reus.[8]

---

[1] *Warner* v. *Metropolitan Police Comr* [1969] 2 AC 256, 272 (Lord Reid).

[2] Cf. "acts not criminal in any real sense" *per* Wright J in *Sherras* v. *De Rutzen* [1895] 1 QB 918, 922.

[3] See, Simester (ed.), *Appraising Strict Liability* (2005); Sayre, "Public Welfare Offences" (1933) 33 *Col LR* 55; Howard, *Strict Responsibility* (1963); Kadish, "Some Observations on the Use of Criminal Sanctions in Enforcing Economic Regulations" (1963) 30 *U Chicago LR* 423; Leigh, *Strict and Vicarious Liability* (1982); Richardson, "Strict Liability for Regulatory Crime: The Empirical Research" [1987] *Crim LR* 295; Horder, "Strict Liability, Statutory Construction, and the Spirit of Liberty" (2002) 118 *LQR* 458.

[4] Although a distinction between these terms is drawn elsewhere in the Commonwealth: below, § 6.2.

[5] [1986] 2 All ER 635. See too *Harrow London BC* v. *Shah* [1999] 3 All ER 302.

[6] (1846) 15 M & W 404, 153 ER 907. The case is generally thought to be the first to impose strict liability.

[7] (1884) 13 QBD 207.

This is an important point, since most offences containing a strict liability element will also involve some actus reus elements in respect of which mens rea is required. In *Storkwain* (above), D's belief that the forged prescriptions were valid was irrelevant—the prohibition was absolute. Yet it is clear that the offence involves mens rea regarding other elements of the actus reus. It must be shown that D intended to sell controlled medicines. In principle, if a chemist were to pick up the wrong packet, and hand over controlled medicines thinking they were headache tablets, he could not be convicted.

Sometimes, however, the classification of an offence as one of strict liability may be misleading, if strict liability applies only to a foreseeable consequence of D's conduct and proof of culpability is required for the other actus reus elements. In truth, such offences impose *constructive* rather than strict liability. Causing death by dangerous driving, contrary to section 1 of the Road Traffic Act 1988, is an offence of this type; the fact that no culpability is required about the death does not make the overall offence in substance one of strict liability. Indeed, fatalities are precisely the sort of reason why dangerous driving is blameworthy. The objections to imposing strict liability in *Storkwain* (which we consider in § 6.3) therefore do not apply with the same force to causing death by dangerous driving. The nature and limits of legitimate constructive liability are considered below, in § 6.5.

With isolated exceptions, strict liability offences are a creation of statute rather than the common law.[9] The opportunity to impose them arises from the fact that criminal legislation is very often silent regarding the mens rea element, leaving it to the courts either to imply a mens rea requirement or to interpret the offence literally as one of strict liability. Originally, the courts recognised a principle that in such cases mens rea was to be implied: "Acts of Parliament are to be so construed, as no man that is innocent, or free from injury or wrong, be by a literal construction punished or endamaged."[10] Although operation of the principle could be overridden by Parliament itself, the legislation would have to be clear on the point:[11]

> "it is contrary to the whole established law of England (unless the legislation on the subject has clearly enacted it), to say that a person can be guilty of a crime in England without a wrongful intent—without an attempt to do that which the law has forbidden."

Extensive authority can be found in support of this proposition, which applied even to summary offences.[12] Indeed, as we shall see in § 6.1, it remains the point of departure for courts when determining whether a particular statute creates an offence of strict liability or one requiring mens rea. But the principle is not always decisive, and the courts are often willing to read statutes literally, i.e. without implying a mens rea requirement. The seeds of

---

[8] *Lemon* [1979] AC 617, 656.

[9] The common law exceptions include an employer's liability for public nuisance and criminal libel. Common law contempt of court, previously thought to be a matter of strict liability, has now been said, *obiter*, to require mens rea: *Yousaf* [2006] EWCA Crim 469, para. 19.

[10] *Margate Pier Co* v. *Hannam* (1819) 3 B & Ald 266, 270, 106 ER 661, 663, quoting Lord Coke; cf. *Tolson* (1889) 23 QBD 168, 187 (Stephen J).

[11] *A-G* v. *Bradlaugh* (1885) 14 QBD 667, 689 (Brett MR); cf. *Chisholm* v. *Doulton* (1889) 22 QBD 736, 741 (Cave J).

[12] E.g. *Fowler* v. *Padget* (1798) 7 Term Rep 509, 101 ER 1103; *Batting* v. *Bristol and Exeter Ry Co* (1860) 3 LT 665; *Hearne* v. *Garton* (1859) 2 El & El 66, 121 ER 26; *Sleep* (1861) L & C 44, 169 ER 1296; *Cope* v. *James* (1871) LR 7 QB 135; *Paul* v. *Hargreaves* [1908] 2 KB 289; *Sherras* v. *de Rutzen* [1895] 1 QB 918.

this willingness were sown during the later part of the nineteenth century, when strict liability offences began to emerge as a convenient means of dealing with rapidly changing social and industrial practices.[13] Most often they owe their existence to a perception that the need to protect the public might on occasion justify convicting people of offences even where they were not necessarily at fault;[14] especially, though not invariably, where the harm involved resulted from a specialised activity, one which might naturally lend itself to control by regulatory rather than "truly criminal" prohibitions. Even the enforcement of such offences tends to be distinctive. They are frequently the responsibility not of the police, but by specialist agencies created to monitor and control the effects of particular types of activity such as pollution and industrial safety. Habits of prosecution differ also. In practice, it appears that while prosecution is a typical response of the police to breaches of the law, regulatory agencies by contrast tend to prosecute only for recurring or very serious breaches of the law; characteristically, in the hands of regulatory agencies, the fact that an offence imposes strict liability operates as an important background consideration in compliance negotiations.[15]

§ 6.1 Recognition of strict liability in a statutory offence

In this and the previous chapter, the discussion of mens rea and strict liability has so far concentrated on defining the leading terms. But a further question arises every time we consider a particular offence. *Which* mens rea state is required to satisfy *that* offence? The answer varies from offence to offence: for assault, recklessness will suffice; for murder, an intention is required; driving while disqualified, by contrast, is an offence of strict liability. Often the answer will be found straightforwardly in the explicit words of the statute that creates the offence. For example, section 2 of the Explosive Substances Act 1883 makes it an offence "maliciously" to cause an explosion likely to endanger life or property: the offence cannot be committed inadvertently. But, frequently, a statute will specify only the actus reus elements, and be silent regarding whether a form of mens rea is required. In such instances the courts must decide.

The first point to consider is whether the mens rea standard has been settled by judicial precedent. The offence of driving while disqualified, for example, has been held to impose strict liability in *Bowshe*[16] and *Miller*.[17] In light of this, and unless the offence becomes

---

[13] See, e.g., Carson, "Symbolic and Instrumental Dimensions of Early Factory Legislation" in Hood (ed.), *Crime, Criminology and Public Policy* (1974); Carson, "The Conventionalisation of Early Factory Crime" (1979) 7 *Int J Soc Law* 37.

[14] Cf. *Hobbs* v. *Winchester Corporation* [1910] 2 KB 471, 483 (Kennedy LJ): "the natural inference from the statute and its object is that the peril to the butcher from innocently selling unsound meat is deemed by the legislature to be much less than the peril to the public which would follow from the necessity of proving in each case a *mens rea*."

[15] See, e.g., Hawkins, *Law as Last Resort* (2003); Reiss, "Selecting Strategies of Social Control over Organizational Life" in Hawkins and Thomas (eds.), *Enforcing Regulation* (1984) 25; Hutter, *The Reasonable Arm of the Law* (1988); Hawkins, *Environment and Enforcement* (1984). But the discretionary nature of prosecutions in such instances is not without rule of law problems: Simester, "Is Strict Liability Always Wrong?" in Simester (ed.), *Appraising Strict Liability* (2005) 21, 32–3.

[16] [1973] RTR 202.

[17] [1975] 2 All ER 974.

altered by legislation,[18] there would seem to be no reason for another court to reconsider the question in future.

If the mens rea standard for the offence is not settled by statute or case law, the court will have to make a fresh decision. The guiding principles affecting that decision are stated in the subsections following this paragraph. By way of introduction, however, it may be helpful to quote from the Privy Council's summary of those principles in *Gammon Ltd* v. *A-G of Hong Kong*:[19]

> "In their Lordships' opinion, the law relevant to this appeal may be stated in the following propositions . . . : (1) there is a presumption of law that mens rea is required before a person can be held guilty of a criminal offence; (2) the presumption is particularly strong where the offence is 'truly criminal' in character; (3) the presumption applies to statutory offences, and can be displaced only if this is clearly or by necessary implication the effect of the statute; (4) the only situation in which the presumption can be displaced is where the statute is concerned with an issue of social concern, and public safety is such an issue; (5) mens rea stands unless it an also be shown that the creation of strict liability will be effective to promote the objects of the statute by encouraging greater vigilance to prevent the commission of the prohibited act."

(i) The initial presumption

The basic presumption from which one starts is that mens rea is required for every offence. Traditional authority for this is found in *Sherras* v. *De Rutzen*:[20]

> "There is a presumption that mens rea . . . is an essential ingredient in every offence; but that presumption is liable to be displaced either by the words of the statute creating the offence or by the subject matter with which it deals, and both must be considered."

During the first part of the twentieth century the status of this proposition was called into question on a number of occasions,[21] and reaffirmed on others.[22] However, its place has been secured by the House of Lords in the two leading modern decisions on strict liability, *Sweet* v. *Parsley*[23] and *B* v. *DPP*.[24]

In *Sweet* v. *Parsley*, a schoolteacher was prosecuted for "being concerned in the management of premises used for the purpose of smoking cannabis."[25] She had sublet her farmhouse to a group of students who, without her knowledge, smoked cannabis there. Even

---

[18] The offence, formerly contained in s. 99 of the Road Traffic Act 1972, was re-enacted by s. 103 of the Road Traffic Act 1988 without substantive change.

[19] [1985] 1 AC 1, 14.

[20] [1895] 1 QB 918, 921. D was charged with supplying liquor to a constable on duty, contrary to s. 16(2) of the Licensing Act 1872. At the time, the constable was not wearing his duty band, which he was expected to wear when on duty. D consequently assumed the constable was off duty. See also *Williamson* v. *Norris* [1899] 1 QB 7, 14; *Duncan* v. *State* 7 Humph. 148, 150 (1846) (Tenn.).

[21] E.g., "in construing a modern statute this presumption as to *mens rea* does not exist": *Hobbs* v. *Winchester Corporation* [1910] 2 KB 471, 483; *St Margaret's Trust Ltd* [1958] 2 All ER 289.

[22] E.g. *Brent* v. *Wood* (1946) 175 LT 306, 307; *Harding* v. *Price* [1948] 1 KB 695, 700; *Reynolds* v. *G.H. Austin and Sons* [1951] 2 KB 135, 143, 145, 147–9.

[23] [1970] AC 132.

[24] [2000] 2 AC 428.

[25] Contrary to s. 5(b) of the (then) Dangerous Drugs Act 1965.

[26] [1970] AC 132, 148 (Lord Reid).

though the terms of the statute prima facie were satisfied—she was concerned in the management of the premises, and cannabis was smoked there—the House of Lords quashed her conviction. Mens rea, albeit unstated, was an element of the offence:[26]

> "there has for centuries been a presumption that Parliament did not intend to make criminals of persons who were in no way blameworthy in what they did. This means that, whenever a section is silent as to mens rea there is a presumption that, in order to give effect to the will of Parliament, we must read in words appropriate to require mens rea."

The justification for this starting-point, which is made explicit by Lord Reid in the quotation above, rests in the issues discussed in Chapter 1 and in § 3.2. According to Lord Diplock:[27]

> "the mere fact that Parliament has made the conduct a criminal offence gives rise to *some* implication about the mental element of the conduct proscribed. . . . This implication stems from the principle that it is contrary to a rational and civilised criminal code, such as Parliament must be presumed to have intended, to penalise one who has performed his duty as a citizen to ascertain what acts are prohibited by law (ignorantia juris non excusat) and has taken all proper care to inform himself of any facts which would make his conduct lawful."

Parliament normally does not, and indeed should not, intend to make criminals of those who are not blameworthy and do not warrant that label.

In practice, the presumption in *Sherras v. De Rutzen* very often has operated merely as a point of departure, a prelude to assessment of further considerations (to be noted below). As we shall see, even imprisonable offences have on occasion been held to be of strict liability.[28] But the presumption does have weight. *Sweet v. Parsley* stipulates that mens rea is the default position for an offence unless its implication is *clearly* outweighed by other factors. This implication is buttressed by Lord Reid's judgment in *Sweet v. Parsley:*[29]

> "it is a universal principle that if a penal provision is reasonably capable of two interpreta-
> · tions, that interpretation which is most favourable to the accused must be adopted."

Thus, following *Sweet,* the presumption for mens rea is abrogated, in favour of strict liability, only when it would be positively unreasonable (in light of the factors stated below) to interpret the offence as requiring mens rea.

B v. DPP [30] strengthens the presumption even further. During a bus journey B, a boy aged 15, persistently requested a 13-year-old girl to perform oral sex. He was charged with inciting a girl under 14 to commit an act of gross indecency contrary to section 1(1) of the Indecency with Children Act 1960. B claimed that he had honestly believed that the girl was over 14. However, the Youth Court justices ruled, following the leading early case of *Prince,*[31] that the offence was one of strict liability in respect of the victim's age, and that

---

[27] [1970] AC 132, 162–3. See also at 153 (Lord Morris).

[28] E.g. *Gammon Ltd* v. *A-G of Hong Kong* [1985] 1 AC 1; *Howells* [1977] QB 614.

[29] [1970] AC 132, 149.

[30] [2000] 2 AC 428.

[31] (1875) LR 2 CCR 154. In *Prince*, D was convicted of an offence against s. 55 OAPA 1861, which enacted that "whosoever shall unlawfully take . . . any unmarried girl, being under the age of sixteen years, out of the possession and against the will of her father or mother . . . shall be guilty of a misdemeanour." D did exactly that, but reasonably believed the girl's age was 18. The Court for Crown Cases Reserved held that the age of the girl was a

therefore his state of mind concerning her age was irrelevant. B appealed ultimately to the House of Lords, arguing that since the Act did not specify a mens rea requirement, the common law presumption that mens rea was necessary should apply: and that, since he had thought the girl was over 14, he lacked the intent or recklessness presumptively required.

The House of Lords allowed B's appeal. It ruled that the common-law presumption of mens rea applied to section 1(1) of the 1960 Act:[32]

> "In these circumstances the starting point for a court is the established common law presumption that a mental element, traditionally labelled mens rea, is an essential ingredient unless Parliament has indicated a contrary intention either expressly or by necessary implication. The common law presumes that, unless Parliament indicated otherwise, the appropriate mental element is an unexpressed ingredient of every statutory offence."

Thus the presumption is only to be overridden, according to their Lordships, if there is a *necessary* implication that Parliament intended the offence to be strict:[33]

> "[T]he test is not whether it is a reasonable implication that the statute rules out mens rea as a constituent part of the crime–the test is whether it is a *necessary* implication."

This constraint is not always applied to the letter. Frequently in the past, the courts have ruled that the only reasonable construction of regulatory offences is that they are intended to be of strict liability, and they remain willing to do so notwithstanding B v. DPP.[34] But, at least for serious crimes, B v. DPP sets down an important marker in the law of strict liability (although not, ironically, in the new law of sexual offences).[35] In K,[36] decided shortly afterwards, the defendant, aged 26, indecently assaulted V contrary to section 14 of the Sexual Offences Act 1956. V was aged 14, and by section 14(2) of the 1956 Act a girl under the age of 16 cannot in law consent to an indecent assault. However, K believed that V was aged 16. (She had told him so.) The Court of Appeal upheld K's conviction, refusing to overrule previous decisions that liability is strict as to age in the offence of indecent assault. This need not have been inconsistent with B v. DPP. In K, the Court of Appeal rightly started with a presumption that the offence in section 14 required mens rea as to all elements, but was led by various factors (in particular, the statutory history) to conclude that the presumption was overridden in respect of age where the victim was under 16, and that Parliament had intended that particular element of the offence to be one of strict liability.

---

matter of strict liability, so that D's belief was irrelevant. Notwithstanding that *Prince* was a leading decision for 125 years, in the light of B v. DPP it must now be regarded as unsound. See, however, Horder, "How Culpability Can, and Cannot, be Denied in Under-age Sex Crimes" [2001] *Crim LR* 15.

[32] [2000] 2 AC 428, 460 (Lord Nicholls), citing the passage from Lord Reid's judgment (above in the text) in *Sweet v. Parsley* [1970] AC 132, 148–9.

[33] [2000] 2 AC 428, 481 (Lord Hutton: emphasis in original). This requirement was said to be fulfilled only if such a reading is "compellingly clear" (according to Lord Nicholls, with whom Lord Irvine agreed), "sufficiently clear" (per Lord Steyn), or "necessary" (Lord Hutton, whose speech Lord Steyn also endorsed; also Lord Mackay).

[34] See, e.g., *Muhamad* [2003] EWCA Crim 1856, [2003] QB 1031 (materially contributing to insolvency by gambling); *Hart* v. *Anglian Water Services Ltd* (causing a discharge of effluent); *Mutadi* [2004] EWCA Crim 697 (importing contrabanded animal products); *G* [2006] EWCA Crim 821 (rape of a child under 13; below, § 12.7).

[35] As we see below, the Sexual Offences Act 2003 subsequently introduced a regime of designedly strict liability offences with respect to sexual offences involving children aged under 13 years.

[36] [2002] 1 AC 462.

Despite this, the House of Lords overruled the Court of Appeal. Notwithstanding the history, it is not a *necessary* implication of the legislation that, in respect of V's age, the offence is one of strict liability. Given the strength of the arguments in favour of the view that section 14 imposes strict liability (indeed, as Lord Millett noted, that was clearly Parliament's intention), their Lordships' decision in *K* signals clearly that, in serious criminal offences, the courts will strive to uphold the presumption in favour of mens rea.[37]

It should be emphasised that the presumption of mens rea generally means intention or recklessness (or, as appropriate, knowledge or belief). Negligence is thought to be not blameworthy enough to warrant criminal sanctions for "truly criminal" offences, and apparently cannot be implied by the courts as a middle-ground alternative to strict liability for less serious offences. Authority for this proposition includes *Sweet* v. *Parsley* itself, where the House noted the possibility of alternative approaches in other jurisdictions,[38] but ultimately regarded itself as able to choose only between strict liability and full mens rea.[39]

(ii) Overriding the presumption: subject matter of the offence

In deciding whether to override the presumption in favour of mens rea, the courts have had regard to a number of considerations.

Put most broadly, the most important concern is whether the offence is "serious" or "truly criminal", as opposed to a "quasi-criminal",[40] "public welfare", or "regulatory" offence. At the heart of this issue is the nature of the mischief the offence is designed to suppress. Very obviously, an offence will be of the truly criminal variety, and require mens rea, when it prohibits an activity that is, in itself, overtly wrongful (e.g. murder, assault, and the like). In these cases the activity may occasion moral condemnation even without being criminalised, and a conviction is therefore likely to attract a substantial level of moral stigma. By contrast, where conviction for the offence is likely to occasion little or no public stigma (as in the case of a parking infringement), the courts will be more willing to find strict liability. Such instances are said to fall within the "class of acts . . . which are not criminal in any real sense, but are acts which in the public interest are prohibited under a penalty."[41]

More difficult are cases where the defendant's activity is not necessarily or inherently wrongful, but becomes the actus reus of an offence when done in a particular manner.

---

[37] Compare *Kumar* [2004] EWCA Crim 3207, where the Court of Appeal cited both *B* and *K* in ruling that, in the former offence of buggery contrary to s. 12 of the Sexual Offences Act 1956, a mens rea requirement with respect to the victim's age had been neither expressly nor necessarily excluded by the legislation. The case may be contrasted with *G* [2006] EWCA Crim 821, where a presumption of mens rea in the offence of rape of a child, contrary to s. 5 of the Sexual Offences Act 2003, was (rightly, if regrettably) excluded altogether by the intention of Parliament as manifested in the scheme of the statute. See below, § 12.7. Unfortunately, the Court in *G* went on to rule further that this interpretation was consistent with Art. 6(2) of the ECHR: above, § 2.5(iii).

[38] See below, § 6.4.

[39] See Devlin's discussion of this point in *Samples of Lawmaking* (1962) 67–82. For a suggestion that due diligence defences may be "read in" to comply with Art. 3 of the ECHR see Arden, "Criminal Law at the Crossroads: The Impact on Human Rights from the Law Commission's Perspective and the Need for a Code" [1999] *Crim LR* 439, 450. Contrast, however, *Salabiaku* v. *France* (1988) 13 EHRR 379.

[40] *Pearks, Gunston & Tee Ltd* v. *Ward* [1902] 2 KB 1, 11. Cf. *London Borough of Harrow* v. *Shah* [1999] 3 All ER 302 ("not truly criminal in character" *per* Mitchell J).

[41] *Sherras* v. *De Rutzen* [1895] 1 QB 918, 922.

Driving a vehicle may be a legitimate activity, but driving a vehicle without insurance is a strict liability offence.[42] Factors relevant to the assessment of such offences include whether the offence is directed at regulating trades, activities, and the like, especially those which involve specialist skills and those for which one must be licensed. Where this is the case, it is more likely to be treated as a public welfare offence, i.e. as one that regulates and controls excesses in an otherwise acceptable practice. The fact that the activity is a specialist one increases the probability that its regulation will involve strict liability. One reason for this is that the use of strict liability simplifies prosecutions, a factor that is especially salient when the defendant may be expected to know far better than the prosecutor what went wrong and how to prevent it. In such circumstances, it may be unreasonable to suppose that the prosecutor will be able to acquire sufficiently accurate knowledge of the workings of the defendant's business organisation to prove mens rea. As Lord Salmon commented in *Alphacell Ltd* v. *Woodward*, on a charge brought under the Rivers (Prevention of Pollution) Act 1951:[43]

> "If . . . no conviction could be obtained under the 1951 Act unless the prosecution could discharge the often impossible onus of proving that the pollution was caused intentionally or negligently, a great deal of pollution would go unpunished and undeterred to the relief of many riparian factory owners."

This reasoning is reinforced (at least in the eyes of the courts) by the fact that regulation of a voluntary specialist activity does not lead to the conviction of citizens for doing ordinary things without being on notice that their conduct was in danger of breaching the criminal law. Concerns about fair warning[44] are thus less pressing where the defendant may be said to some extent to have assumed the risks of liability by voluntarily bringing herself within the particular sphere of operation of a regulatory law. In *Hobbs* v. *Winchester Corporation*, a butcher suing for compensation in respect of unsound meat that had been destroyed was held to have been in default, and so barred from recovering, even though he had no reasonable means of discovering the condition of the meat:[45]

> "the policy of the Act is this: that if a man chooses for profit to engage in a business which involves offering for sale of that which may be deadly or injurious to health he must take that risk, and that it is not a sufficient defence for anyone who chooses to embark on such a business to say 'I could not have discovered the disease unless I had an analyst on the premises'. "

A similar point was made in *Sweet* v. *Parsley* by Lord Diplock:[46]

> "Where penal provisions are of general application to the conduct of ordinary citizens in the course of their every day life, the presumption is that the standard of care required of them in informing themselves of facts which would make their conduct unlawful, is that of the familiar common law duty of care. But where the subject-matter of a statute is the regulation of a particular activity involving potential danger to public health, safety or morals, in which citi-

---

[42] Contrary to s. 143 of the Road Traffic Act 1988; *Tapsell* v. *Maslen* [1967] Crim LR 53.
[43] [1972] AC 824. Cf. *Woodrow* (1846) 15 M & W 404, 417, 153 ER 907, 913.
[44] See above, § 2.3.
[45] [1910] 2 KB 471, 483.
[46] [1970] AC 132, 163. One interesting philosophical discussion which makes a point of this type is Honoré, "Responsibility and Luck: The Moral Basis of Strict Liability" (1988) 104 *LQR* 530.

zens have a choice whether they participate or not, the court may feel driven to infer an intention of Parliament to impose, by penal sanctions, a higher duty of care on those who choose to participate."

Whether this is a *good* argument for imposing strict liability will be considered below, in § 6.3. For the moment it is sufficient to note that some judges think it is, and we may anticipate a greater willingness to find strict liability where the statute governs a specialist activity.

As Lord Diplock contemplates, the likelihood of a law's being declared strict is also increased if the activities it regulates have a tendency to endanger sections of the public[47] (or, in recent times, the environment[48]). Obvious places for such laws are regulations governing the quality of food products,[49] the distribution of drugs,[50] and safety on the road[51] or in the workplace. An important instance of the last type is *Gammon (Hong Kong) Ltd v. A-G for Hong Kong.*[52] Following the collapse of construction work on a building site, the defendants responsible for the site were charged with deviating in a material way from the approved plan, contrary to the local construction regulations. The offence carried a substantial fine and possible imprisonment for up to three years. Noting that the presumption of mens rea is "particularly strong" in such circumstances, since the offence did appear to be "truly criminal" in character, the Privy Council nonetheless advised that the offence was one of strict liability. Lord Scarman highlighted the importance of the danger that the offence sought to guard against: "the only situation in which the presumption can be displaced is where the statute is concerned with an issue of social concern, and public safety is such an issue."[53]

Lord Scarman goes on to describe an additional condition that should be met: efficacy. Overriding the presumption of mens rea should not be done simply as a matter of convenience—something more substantial must be gained by doing so:[54]

"Even where a statute is concerned with such an issue [of social concern], the presumption of mens rea stands unless it can also be shown that the creation of strict liability will be effective to promote the objects of the statute by encouraging greater vigilance to prevent the commission of the prohibited act."

Another factor is that, if one element of the actus reus involves the arbitrary drawing of a line over such matters as time, quantity, or size, mens rea may be less likely to be required in respect of that particular aspect. The most obvious case is a speeding offence, where the

---

[47] Or, it seems, the economy: *St Margaret's Trust Ltd* [1958] 2 All ER 289, 293: "[t]he present generation has witnessed the collapse of the currency in other countries and the consequent chaos, misery and widespread ruin".

[48] Cf. *Alphacell Ltd* v. *Woodward* [1972] AC 824, 848 ("many rivers which are now filthy would become filthier still and many rivers which are now clean would lose their cleanliness"); *Kirkland* v. *Robinson* [1987] Crim LR 643. This notwithstanding that environmental offences now appear to involve significant social stigma.

[49] Especially prior to the introduction of a statutory "due diligence" defence in s. 21 of the Food Safety Act 1990. Cf. *Lim Chin Aik* [1963] AC 160, 174; *CLGP* § 77.

[50] *Pharmaceutical Society of Great Britain* v. *Storkwain Ltd* [1986] 2 All ER 635; *Warner* v. *Metropolitan Police Commr* [1969] 2 AC 256.

[51] *Bowsher* [1973] RTR 202; *Reynolds* v. *Austin & Sons* [1951] 2 KB 135.

[52] [1985] AC 1.

[53] Ibid., 14.

[54] Ibid. Cf. *Lim Chin Aik* [1963] AC 160, 175; *Sweet* v. *Parsley* [1970] AC 132, 163; *Reynolds* v. *Austin & Sons* [1951] 2 KB 135, 150 (Devlin J).

difference between 30 and 31 m.p.h. may have a significance that is purely the result of law.[55] It would be indulgent to require knowledge of one's speed in such cases, and in the absence of a default negligence standard, strict liability becomes the leading alternative.

At the other end of the spectrum, if an element of the actus reus involves the legal assessment of certain facts, then the defendant need possess only whatever mens rea is required regarding the facts themselves. She need not be aware of the legal assessment itself, which is a legal conclusion in the nature of a value judgement that the defendant is not permitted to second-guess.[56] For example, it is irrelevant whether, in the circumstances as she perceives them, a defendant believes she is using "*reasonable* force" in self-defence: it is for the court to decide whether the force she then uses is reasonable.[57] (Indeed, sometimes a failure to recognise the status of one's actions—e.g. that the force one uses is excessive—may itself disclose culpability.[58]) The presence of a legal assessment within the actus reus raises conflicting concerns between the need to prevent individuals from undermining the law's values, and the need to give them fair warning of the criminal implications of their conduct. We will return to this issue in the discussion of ignorance of law (§ 18.2).

(iii) Severity of punishment

The range and severity of punishments prescribed upon conviction should also be taken into account. In *Gammon*, for example, the fact that the maximum penalty for the offence was a substantial fine and imprisonment for three years was said by the Privy Council to be a "formidable point"[59] militating against strict liability. The potential for imprisonment is a clear indication that an offence is "truly criminal" rather than merely "regulatory" in character, and in such cases the presumption of mens rea normally should not be displaced.

It seems, however, that the courts do not regard the mere prospect of imprisonment as enough to make a crime "serious". In *Muhamad*,[60] the offence of materially contributing to one's insolvency by gambling, contrary to section 362(1)(a) of the Insolvency Act 1986, was held to involve strict liability notwithstanding the maximum sentence of two years' imprisonment. In the view of Dyson LJ, doing so:[61]

---

[55] This principle does not apply to age, at least in the context of sexual offences—where V's age has independent moral significance: *B* v. *DPP* [2000] 2 AC 428 (HL).

[56] As in *Doring* [2002] EWCA Crim 1695 (being concerned in the management of a company while being an undisclosed bankrupt). D had been involved in the publicity, promotion, and design activities of the company but had neither hired nor fired staff and made no financial decisions or contracts for the company. Apparently, D believed that in doing so she was not directly or indirectly managing the company. The Court of Appeal upheld her conviction, ruling that it was a matter of strict liability whether her acts, objectively understood, amounted to being concerned in the management of the company. Cf. *Lemon and Gay News Ltd* [1979] AC 617 (whether a statement is "calculated to outrage the feelings of Christians"); also the discussion of evaluative terms, above, § 2.3(i). But compare the dissent on this point by Barwick CJ in *Iannella* v. *French* (1968) 119 CLR 84, 97.

[57] *Armstrong-Williams (Gladstone)* [1987] 3 All ER 411; *Clegg* [1995] 1 All ER 334; *Owino* [1996] 2 Cr App R 128; *DPP* v. *Braun* [1999] Crim LR 416. To the extent that *Scarlett* [1993] 4 All ER 629 might seem to suggest the contrary, it should be regarded as wrong: below, § 17.1(v).

[58] For brief discussion of this point, see Simester, "Is Strict Liability Always Wrong?" in Simester (ed.), *Appraising Strict Liability* (2005) 21, 42–4.

[59] [1985] AC 1, 17.

[60] [2003] EWCA Crim 1856, [2003] QB 1031, para. 16.

[61] *Ibid.* Cf. *Lim Chin Aik* [1963] AC 160, 175; *Sweet* v. *Parsley* [1970] AC 132, 163; *Reynolds* v. *Austin & Sons* [1951] 2 KB 135, 150 (Devlin J).

"The starting point, therefore, is to determine how serious an offence is created by section 362(1)(a), and accordingly how much weight, if any, should be attached to the presumption. Some weight must undoubtedly be given to the presumption, but in our judgment it can be readily displaced. As we have said, the maximum sentence indicates that Parliament considered this to be an offence of some significance, but not one of the utmost seriousness. This is not surprising. We do not believe that great stigma attaches to a conviction of this offence."

It is not clear why an offence must be of "the utmost seriousness" if the presumption of mens rea is not to be readily displaced. There is much to be said for the approach adopted in the Model Penal Code, which asserts that the possibility of imprisonment for any term should be a conclusive reason against imposing strict liability.[62] Nonetheless, in UK courts some quite substantial maximum sentences have been ruled to impose strict liability, after taking into account such considerations as the interest (e.g. public safety) being protected.[63] These include the offence in *Gammon* itself, where the Privy Council, immediately after acknowledging the severity of the maximum penalties, continued with a "but": "there is nothing inconsistent with the purpose of the Ordinance in imposing severe penalties for offences of strict liability."[64]

One may ask whether the Privy Council has missed the point. Perhaps one may have reason to impose strict liability if it is inconsistent with the purpose of a statute *not* to do so. But surely not the other way round? The mere fact that strict liability is "not inconsistent" with the purpose of the statute is hardly a reason to impose it, and in no way meets the objection that in *Gammon* the maximum penalties were severe and clearly criminal in character. Neither does the logic in *Gammon* conform to the requirement—now laid down in *B* v. *DPP* [65]—that the imposition of strict liability must be a *necessary implication* of the statute, and not merely consistent with it. At least for serious offences, it is to be hoped that *B* v. *DPP* will make decisions such as *Gammon* rarer in the future.

That having been said, the potential for heavy penalties in an offence gives rise to a tension. Severe sanctions generally give the offence a criminal character, yet they may also reflect the fact that the subject matter of the offence—the social danger or harm involved—is itself substantial, a factor (as we have seen) weighing in favour of strict liability. The type of offence most suitable for strict liability would involve substantial ultimate public harm or inconvenience (whether directly or cumulatively), and relatively little stigma for an individual offence. This may occur, for example, in certain road traffic offences. Similarly, the offence in *Alphacell Ltd* v. *Woodward*[66] of causing polluted material to enter a stream, which carried a low maximum penalty, was also relatively well-suited to strict liability; especially in 1972 when pollution offences tended to be regarded as "acts not criminal in any real sense."[67] It is clear from the case law that in practice the courts have extended their recognition of strict liability well beyond these paradigms.[68] Moreover, paradigms shift.

---

[62] § 6.02(4).

[63] E.g. *Pharmaceutical Society of Great Britain* v. *Storkwain Ltd* [1986] 2 All ER 635; *Howells* [1977] QB 614; *R.* v. *Wells Street Magistrates' Court and Martin, ex p Westminster City Council* [1986] *Crim LR* 695.

[64] [1985] AC 1, 17.

[65] [2000] 2 AC 428; above, § 6.1(i).

[66] [1972] AC 824.

[67] *Sherras* v. *De Rutzen* [1895] 1 QB 918, 922.

[68] See the cases noted above, n. 63.

Destruction and despoliation of the natural environment is now a very salient concern and acts degrading and threatening an environment would now readily be regarded as "truly criminal". On the face of it, that would give greater weight to the the presumption in favour of mens rea for environmental offences, a move not likely to be favoured by anyone committed to optimum enforcement of environmental law.

(iv) Implying mens rea from statutory language

Sometimes, rather than being presumed or explicit, or established by the judicial history, the Legislature's intent to include or exclude a mens rea requirement can be *implied* directly from the words or scheme of the statute. This may occur in a number of ways.[69]

First, a verb specifying part of the actus reus may import a mental element. An example of this is "possession", the meaning of which was discussed in § 5.6(i). According to the House of Lords,[70] D is not in possession of an article unless she is *aware* that she possesses something.[71] Similarly, it has been held that "permitting" another to use a vehicle when equipped with defective brakes can only be done knowingly. As a matter of ordinary language, the Divisional Court said, permitting "in our opinion, at once imports a state of mind."[72] Thus it is impossible, at least in that offence, to "permit" inadvertently.[73]

Secondly, the court may look to the scheme of the statute. Some of the earliest strict liability cases turned on this point. In *Betts* v. *Armstead*[74] the defendant was charged with selling adulterated bread, contrary to section 6 of the Sale of Food and Drugs Act 1875. He was apparently unaware the loaf was adulterated; nonetheless, he was convicted, since under section 5 an absence of knowledge had expressly been made a defence to offences enacted by sections 2–4, but not to section 6. The validity of this type of inference was, however, subsequently doubted by Lord Goddard CJ,[75] since verbal distinctions of this sort may arise from the vagaries of parliamentary amendment or even of imperfect draftsmanship. Present law appears to be that linguistic difference between sections is a factor that may be taken into account, but is not itself decisive:[76]

> "It is also firmly established that the fact that other sections of the Act expressly require *mens rea*, for example because they contain the word 'knowingly', is not itself sufficient to justify a decision that a section which is silent as to *mens rea* creates an absolute offence."

The difference is more likely to be decisive, however, where the relevant statute was drawn up as a coherent regime, especially where the legislature has created parallel pairs of offences

[69] Cf. Manchester, "Knowledge, Due Diligence and Strict Liability in Regulatory Offences" [2006] *Crim LR* 213, 216–9, 223–6.

[70] *Warner* v. *Metropolitan Police Comr* [1969] 2 AC 256.

[71] Although she need not be aware of the item's character; to that extent, therefore, a possession offence which specifies no further mens rea element can be regarded, in substance, as an offence of strict liability.

[72] *James & Son Ltd* v. *Smee* [1955] 1 QB 78, 91.

[73] Although the same may not hold for other offences: *DPP* v. *Fisher* [1991] *Crim LR* 787 (permitting a vehicle to be used without insurance a strict liability offence).

[74] (1888) 20 QBD 771. Cf. *Parker* v. *Alder* [1899] 1 QB 20; *Fitzpatrick* v. *Kelly* (1873) LR 8 QB 337.

[75] *Lines* v. *Hersom* [1951] 2 KB 682, 686–7.

[76] *Sweet* v. *Parsley* [1970] AC 132, 149 (Lord Reid). This factor will be particularly weak if the statute is a consolidation of previous statutes passed at different times: cf. *K* [2002] 1 AC 462, 467 (Lord Bingham).

only one of which specifies a mens rea requirement. The leading example of this is the Sexual Offences Act,[77] which enacts a regime of four offences of non-consensual sexual activity (in sections 1–4) followed by four offences of the same activity committed with a child under 13. The former require proof of negligence; the latter do not, and the conclusion is unavoidable that they are intended to impose strict liability.[78]

A more straightforward indication that an offence is of strict liability occurs when the statute itself creates a specific defence, e.g. of non-negligence. Such a defence would be otiose if the offence were to require proof of full mens rea. Section 21 of the Food Safety Act 1990, for example, provides, in respect of offences created by sections 1–20 of the Act, that "it shall . . . be a defence for the person charged to prove that he took all reasonable precautions and exercised all due diligence to avoid the commission of the offence." By implication, the offences enacted in those preceding sections are otherwise of strict liability. This type of statutory "due diligence" defence is now a common feature of regulatory offences.[79]

(v) The ability of others to affect D's liability?

In overseas jurisdictions, it has sometimes been said that if strict liability is to be imposed at all, it should be done only in offences that are set out in the clearest terms, so that it is possible for a defendant to know in advance what are the boundaries of the offence: "When there is absolute liability there ought to be absolute certainty as to the ingredients of the offence so that the offender cannot say that he was unable beforehand to conduct himself so as to avoid the offence."[80] As part of this general approach, the New Zealand courts have been reluctant to ascribe absolute liability in cases where the defendant's activity is affected by what others are doing. Thus, in *Jackson* v. *Attorney-General*,[81] the High Court held that one reason for not imposing absolute liability for the (former) offence of possessing cannabis in a prison cell, contrary to section 32 of the Penal Institutions Act 1954 (NZ), was that imposition of absolute liability would tend to encourage inmates to take retribution against another inmate by placing cannabis or other drugs in the other's cell.[82] The potential for third parties to bring D within the scope of an offence should not normally be accompanied by strict liability on the part of the defendant.[83] It is submitted that these considerations, which involve principles applicable to the common law generally, deserve also to be given weight by UK courts when determining whether a particular offence imposes strict liability.

---

[77] Discussed in detail below, Chapter 12.

[78] *G* [2006] EWCA Crim 821.

[79] See, e.g., Simester and Roberts, "Strict Liability in UK Regulation" in Macrory, *Regulatory Justice: Sanctioning in a post-Hampton World* (2006) annex E.

[80] *Re Wairarapa Election Petition* [1988] 2 NZLR 74, 117 (HC).

[81] [2006] 2 NZLR 534, 542 (HC).

[82] Compare, too, *Police* v. *Creedon* [1976] 1 NZLR 571, 573, a prosecution for failing to yield the right of way at an intersection, where the Court of Appeal emphasised the importance of the fact that "the regulation requires a driver of a motor vehicle to take a specific course of action if, and only if, something else is being done by someone else." By contrast with (say) failing to stop at an intersection governed by a stop sign, the offence in Creedon does "not impose an omnipresent and unvarying obligation" (*ibid.*, 574). Its uncertain boundaries were said therefore to militate against strict liability.

[83] Cf. *Re Wairarapa Election Petition* [1988] 2 NZLR 74, 117 ll. 36–38 (HC). For related discussion of this point, see Simester, "The Mental Element in Complicity" (2006) 122 *LQR* 578, 580–1.

§ 6.2 The availability of common law defences

We have seen that D may plead neither absence of mens rea nor absence of fault when charged with a strict liability offence. However, apart from any statutory defences that may expressly be made available, it appears that D may still plead common law defences. There appears to be nothing, even in the older case law on strict liability, that forecloses such defences as duress. Moreover, there is modern appellate authority expressly recognising that duress, whether by threats or circumstances, is available as a defence to the strict liability offence of driving while disqualified.[84] Defences such as duress, necessity, and self-defence therefore seem to be available. We saw in Chapter 4 that the same is true for automatism and involuntariness.[85]

The position is less clear regarding insanity. In principle, this defence should also be available to strict liability offences. But in *DPP* v. *H*, McCowan LJ stated that:[86]

> "The [insanity] defence is based on the absence of mens rea, but none is required for the offence of driving with an excess of alcohol. Hence the defence of insanity has no relevance to such a charge as it is an offence of strict liability."

This is wrong. Insanity, in law, is not based on the absence of mens rea. As we shall see in the chapter on insanity (Chapter 19), the defence comes in two main forms: either as (effectively) insane automatism or as incapacity to recognise the wrongness of one's act. Regarding the first variety: automatism—whether sane or insane—is not merely a denial of mens rea, as a matter either of law or of principle. It is clearly established that automatism is a general defence to strict liability as well as other offences, and there is Court of Appeal authority that this includes insane automatism[87]—which, at the level of principle, is surely right. There is no reason to distinguish sane from insane automatism for the purposes of strict liability. Regarding the second variety: there is no denial of mens rea at all. The defendant *has* mens rea, and is simply incapable of recognising that his actions (of which he is aware) are wrong. McCowan LJ's analysis contains a fundamental error.

The nature of the insanity defence will be further discussed in Chapter 19. So far as strict liability offences are concerned, it suffices to say there is dubious Divisional Court authority that insanity is not available as a defence—and to hope that the decision, which is contrary to principle, will be overruled by a more senior court.

(i) Exception for situational offences

In Chapter 4, during the discussion of involuntariness, a distinction was drawn between state-of-affairs offences and other types of offences, e.g. those involving an act or omission

---

[84] *Martin* [1989] 1 All ER 652 (CA); but see *Cichon* v. *DPP*, noted and criticised [1994] Crim LR 918 (DC). Canadian authority supports the availability of such defences as a general proposition: *R.* v. *Cancoil Thermal Corp and Parkinson* (1986) 27 CCC (3d) 295, 301–2; *Walker* (1979) 48 CCC (2d) 126, 134–5; *Kennedy* (1972) 7 CCC (2d) 42; *Breau* (1959) 125 CCC 84. There is a brief discussion of these questions in Sayre, "Public Welfare Offences" (1933) 33 *Col LR* 55, 75–8.

[85] Above, § 4.3(iii)(d).

[86] [1997] 1 WLR 1406. Cf. *R.* v. *Horseferry Road Magistrates' Court, ex parte K* [1996] 3 All ER 769, and see the criticism of *DPP* v. *H* by Ward, "Magistrates, Insanity and the Common Law" [1997] *Crim LR* 796, 800–2.

[87] *Hennessey* [1989] 2 All ER 9 (CA); *Isitt* [197867 Cr App R 44 (CA); cf. *Hill* v. *Baxter* [1958] 1 QB 277, 283, 285–6.

by the defendant. As we saw in § 4.3(ii)(b), it appears that automatism and impossibility are not available to offences that comprise purely a state of affairs, and which make no reference to the defendant's behaviour. It may be that the same is true for other common law defences such as duress. If so, then although duress seems generally to be available for strict liability offences, it would not be available when the particular strict liability offence criminalises a pure state of affairs. The point appears to be undecided.[88]

A second distinction reinforces this possibility. In those strict liability cases where a common law defence has been recognised, the offence has always been a mixed one, containing a strict liability element together with one or more actus reus elements for which mens rea is required.[89] However, where the offence is mixed, defences such as duress will be available anyway, since they can attach in respect of the components that require mens rea. By contrast, strict liability offences which criminalise states of affairs *simpliciter* are likely to contain no mens rea element whatsoever. There is no case of this type in which a common law defence has been allowed.

§ 6.3 The justification of strict liability

Like it or not, strict liability appears to be well entrenched in our legal system. Indeed, studies have suggested that approximately half of all offences involve at least one strict liability element.[90] But is it ever *morally* right to impose strict liability for a criminal offence? Without a mens rea requirement, strict liability inevitably licenses the conviction of the blameless. Can doing so ever be justified?

One problem with approaching this question in England is that, in the absence of statutory guidance, the courts have treated strict liability as the only alternative to a full mens rea requirement, i.e. of intention or recklessness. Consequently, the arguments for and against requiring full mens rea tend to be interpreted as arguments (respectively) against and for strict liability. This is fallacious. Mens rea and strict liability are not complementary. As we shall see, there is middle ground; in particular, negligence liability. It follows that arguments against requiring mens rea are not necessarily arguments for imposing strict liability, and that arguments against strict liability are not necessarily arguments in favour of mens rea. In order to show this more clearly, we will consider the moral argument for imposing a strict liability standard as two separate issues. The first is the question whether, for certain offences, requiring something less than full mens rea (intention or recklessness) may be appropriate. The second issue is whether, if mens rea should be dispensed with, strict liability is an appropriate alternative.

(i) The argument for sometimes dispensing with mens rea

The reason most often given for abandoning a full mens rea requirement is that protection

---

[88] In this respect, *Larsonneur* (1933) 149 LT 542 is authority only that *lawful* compulsion by another would be no defence.

[89] See above, § 6.2.

[90] Ashworth and Blake, "The Presumption of Innocence in English Criminal Law" [1996] *Crim LR* 306; JUSTICE, *Breaking the Rules* (1980).

of the public sometimes requires a high standard of care on the part of those who undertake risk-creating activities.[91] Proper care needs to be taken by such persons, and without
liability for inadvertence the careless will be able to transfer the considerable costs of their
foolishness to the rest of society, without having any serious incentive to reduce or eliminate
those risks. The threat of criminal liability supplies a motive for persons in risk-generating
activities to adopt precautions, which might not otherwise be taken, in order to ensure that
unforeseen mishaps and errors are eliminated.[92] Lady Wootton's writing is a useful example
of this type of argument:[93]

> "If the object of the criminal law is to prevent the occurrence of socially damaging actions, it
> would be absurd to turn a blind eye to those which were due to carelessness, negligence, or
> even accident. . . . [I]n the modern world as much and more damage is done by negligence, or
> by indifference to the welfare or safety of others, as by deliberate wickedness. . . . If the law
> says that certain things are not to be done, it is illogical to confine this prohibition to occa-
> sions on which they are done from malice aforethought; for at least the material consequences
> of an action, and the reasons for prohibiting it are the same whether it is the result of sinister
> malicious plotting, of negligence, or of sheer accident."

In practice, such deterrence-based reasoning seems to be reflected in the law, since, as we
have observed already, regulatory offences are often found where there is a need to protect
the public from risks created by industrial and other specialist activities. Particularly where
the harmful impact of the actus reus is severe and widespread, the law has reason to provide
incentives through criminalisation for persons not only to refrain from advertent wrongdoing, but also to take care against inadvertent harms.

Of course, the public protection/deterrence argument cannot, by itself, be a decisive justification. The public needs also to be protected from assaults, damage to property, and the
like, yet these are not strict liability offences; they require proof of mens rea in the ordinary
way.[94] The difference, it is said, is that assault is a "true" crime, conviction for which entails
serious social stigma—hence the need for a higher standard of fault, which partially
overrides the deterrence argument—whereas regulatory offences control "quasi-" (i.e. not
truly) criminal actions.[95]

The force of the deterrence factor is reinforced by a further consideration. Very often, the
activities controlled by regulatory offences involve the commercial behaviour of corporations rather than the private conduct of individuals. Strict liability seems particularly useful
where the offence is directed toward controlling the activity of corporations. There are three
reasons for this. First, corporate convictions do not normally involve the same level of
stigma as do those attaching to individuals, nor the same practical implications. Secondly,

---

[91] For an elaboration of the assumption of risk argument, see Honoré, "Responsibility and Luck: The Moral Basis
of Strict Liability" (1988) 104 *LQR* 530.

[92] *R. v. City of Sault Ste. Marie* (1978) 85 DLR (3d) 161, 171. Cf. the criterion of efficacy, above, § 6.1(ii).

[93] *Crime and the Criminal Law* (2nd ed., 1981) 47, 50, 51. The claim of illogicality is, incidentally, false. Sometimes
the presence of mens rea is crucial to the wrongfulness of what is done: cf. above, § 5.3. Wootton's argument
therefore applies only to those harms whose nature is independent of the mens rea with which they are caused, and
which (as such) are sufficiently severe to warrant criminalisation.

[94] Cf. Mannheim, "Mens Rea in German and English Criminal Law" (1936) 18 *J Comp Leg* 78, 90: "the number of
larcenies committed, e.g., is also very great; nevertheless, nobody would suggest that acts of larceny should be
punished when committed without *mens rea*."

[95] See above, § 6.1(ii).

corporate activity is characteristically on a larger scale than that by individuals, and correspondingly creates greater levels of social threat. Finally, and most importantly, the proof of mens rea presents special difficulty in the context of corporate bodies, since there may be no one person who can be identified as the agent when a corporation acts. Strict liability, by contrast, is much more easily applied to companies and the like, since it can be administered without reference to the defendant's mental state.

(ii) The argument for always requiring mens rea

Prima facie, the foregoing are good reasons to dispense with mens rea in some offences. But there are also arguments going the other way. First, the reasons given above do not establish why *criminal* rather than civil sanctions should be used to regulate the activities involved. Even if private individuals cannot pursue a claim for damages, it may be open to the State, by legislative reform, to pursue miscreants through an administrative system of regulations that applies a standard of strict liability without the accompanying connotations of a criminal conviction—a welcome move that has been contemplated by the Cabinet Office.[96] Arguably, as things stand now, the moral authority of the criminal law is being undermined by the extension of liability to what are, in essence, mere regulatory violations.[97]

(Against this argument it may be noted that the description, "mere regulatory violations", somewhat underplays the vital public protection role that construction standards, work-safety standards, pollution standards, etc., discharge. Setting up a new system to try these matters as civil infractions rather than crimes would be a major task, and might be seen as downgrading the importance of effective regulation. There is little evidence that the proliferation of regulatory crimes has blunted the distinction between doing wrong and getting something wrong.)

Secondly, the arguments against mens rea trade upon the fact that conviction for a strict liability offence does not carry the same moral opprobrium and social stigma as does conviction for an offence that is "truly" criminal in nature. Indeed, in the context of strict liability both the House of Lords and the Privy Council have recognised a distinction between "truly criminal" and "regulatory" offences.[98] Therefore a cautionary note is appropriate. In *Woolmington*, Viscount Sankey LC had stated that, apart from insanity and statutory exceptions, the prosecution must prove guilt "no matter what the charge or where the trial."[99] Danger lies in the fact that, if a defendant's interests are to be subordinated to those of the general public in "regulatory" offences, the line—denied in *Woolmington*—between such offences and "true" crimes is not always easy to draw. We have seen already (§ 6.1) that categorising offences is a difficult exercise, involving conflicting factors whose force

---

[96] Macrory, *Regulatory Justice: Sanctioning in a Post-Hampton World* (2006). The Macrory Review recommends introducing a complementary regime of Monetary Administrative Penalties, using strict liability to enforce regulatory breaches outside the criminal law.

[97] Compare Robinson, "The Criminal–Civil Distinction and the Utility of Desert" (1996) 76 *Boston ULR* 201, 212–14.

[98] *Sweet* v. *Parsley* [1970] AC 132, 149 (Lord Reid), 163 (Lord Diplock); *Alphacell Ltd* v. *Woodward* [1972] AC 824, 839 (Viscount Dilhorne), 848 (Lord Salmon); *Gammon (Hong Kong) Ltd* v. *A-G for Hong Kong* [1985] AC 1, 12–14.

[99] [1935] AC 462, 481; compare *Mancini* v. *DPP* [1942] AC 1, 11 (Viscount Simon LC); Orchard, "The Judicial Categorisation of Offences" (1983) 2 *Cantérbury LR* 81, 94.

is not readily quantified. Indeed, the courts have sometimes imposed strict liability for offences that are punishable by imprisonment;[100] surely an *indicium* of serious rather than minor transgression?[101] If a clear distinction between "regulatory" and "truly criminal" offences cannot be drawn, or if that distinction fails to capture the public imagination, then the arguments[102] for retaining the presumption of innocence—and for always requiring proof of mens rea—are much harder to surmount.

(iii) The argument for strict liability

Even assuming that, on balance, there is sometimes good reason to dispense with the requirement of full mens rea, the second question is whether strict liability is a suitable alternative. The best argument for abandoning all fault requirements is convenience. Administration of justice would be more expensive and greatly slowed if the prosecution were put to proving mens rea—even negligence—in respect of every minor offence before the courts. This is especially true in areas regulated by public welfare offences, where the defendant may be far better placed to understand the nature of her own specialist activity, and thus to prevent the occurrence of harm, than is the prosecutor to learn the nature of the defendant's activity in order to prove fault; all the more so in the case of activities (and transgressions) by large and complex corporations, where it may be very difficult for an external prosecutor to prove that particular individuals were at fault within such organisations.

Regulatory enforcement needs to be done efficiently—a government cannot afford to spend large amounts of money on prosecutions, especially where the offences involved are common and individually involve no serious harm. (Where substantial harm does ensue for individual transgressions, the prosecution should in any event be for a more serious crime involving mens rea and greater penalties.) Moreover, individual offences that involve no serious stigma can protect against a cumulative harm that may be very substantial indeed. These costs of controlling economic activity are, in truth, part of the costs of carrying on that activity, and it therefore makes some economic sense that the burden of criminal penalties should be borne as a form of production expense by those who voluntarily initiate risk-creating activities.[103]

(iv) The argument against strict liability

Let us assume, though it is not obviously true, that a clear distinction can be drawn between "truly" criminal and those offences which are merely regulatory, or "quasi-criminal", and that the public understands the nature and significance of that distinction. Even if this is

---

[102] Above, § 6.1(iii).

[101] It is worth noting that the US Model Penal Code eschews such a possibility, asserting that the possibility of imprisonment should be a conclusive reason against imposing strict liability: § 6.02(4), though a contrary statute would not be unconstitutional: *US* v. *Freed* 401 US 601 (1971).

[102] See above, §§ 3.2, 3.2(i)(a).

[103] "In the case of a minor pollution . . . a comparatively nominal fine will no doubt be imposed. This may be regarded as a not unfair hazard of carrying on a business which may cause pollution on the banks of a river": *Alphacell Ltd* v. *Woodward* [1972] AC 824, 848 (Lord Salmon).

conceded, however, all the arguments above, either in favour of abandoning mens rea or in favour of imposing strict liability, can be met.

The first point is that both the arguments given for abandoning mens rea are, in fact, arguments in favour of imposing *negligence* as the fault standard, not strict liability. It is true that regulatory offences seek to deter those entering into specialist activities from inflicting harm upon others, and by criminalising negligence such offences may help to deter the careless and indifferent and not merely the malicious or wicked. But strict liability goes beyond that, by criminalising accidents and reasonable conduct. This goes further than is necessary or desirable.

The legal implications of risk without fault lie within the realms of insurance and tort liability, not in criminal law. It is foolish for the law to demand that defendants do more than what is reasonable,[104] and there is no evidence that strict liability is a more effective deterrent than mens rea or negligence offences.[105] The effect of demanding the unreasonable, through strict liability, is to force a defendant either to desist from the risk-creating activity altogether, or to persist and accept that he must run all risks, however esoteric and unlikely, of the prohibited harm occurring; and incur the ensuing conviction. The first option cannot be taken seriously. It is surely not the intention of the law to discourage people from entering into productive activity altogether. The nation's economy would not last very long if that were the outcome. Rather, the aim of regulatory laws must be to discourage people from entering into an activity (or from executing it in a manner) which creates *unreasonable* risks of the unwanted harm occurring. But *that* aim can be achieved by negligence liability. Strict liability forces the blameless defendant to become a gratuitous risk-taker, subject to a criminal legal lottery over which he has no reasonable control. If he is unlucky, he will be convicted. A lottery is no basis on which to conduct the nation's criminal law. Such a Draconian system, moreover, is likely to promote cynicism and disrespect for the law among innocent people who are labelled criminal "offenders" by their conviction.

The other reason given in § 6.3(i) for abandoning mens rea requirements was that they are ill-suited to corporate liability.[106] Again, however, negligence would seem to fit the bill. Proof of negligence can be established without reference to the company's mental state (i.e. without proving the state of mind of a controlling officer), since negligence is measured in terms of conduct. It is, of course, true that negligence obliges the prosecution to establish behaviour by the employee that can be attributed to the company—but the same constraint applies to strict liability.

The argument for strict liability, in § 6.3(iii), is more sophisticated. It applies even if the required fault standard is negligence, since proof even of negligence may present difficulties

---

[104] *Pace* Lord Salmon: strict liability "encourages riparian factory owners not only to take reasonable steps to prevent pollution but to do everything possible to ensure that they do not cause it": *Alphacell Ltd* v. *Woodward* [1972] AC 824, 848–9. See also Donovan J, in *St Margaret's Trust Ltd* [1958] 2 All ER 289, 293: "[t]here would be little point in enacting that no one should breach the defences against a flood, and at the same time excusing any one who did it innocently."

[105] See Jackson, "*Storkwain*: A Case Study in Strict liability and Self-Regulation" [1991] *Crim LR* 892; Richardson, "Strict Liability for Regulatory Crime: The Empirical Research" [1987] *Crim LR* 295; Baldwin, "Why Rules Don't Work" (1990) 53 *MLR* 321; Hall, *General Principles of Criminal Law* (2nd ed., 1960) 344–6. In terms of economic incentives, it is possible that strict liability may lead to reduced rather than increased deterrence: Simester, "Is Strict Liability Always Wrong?" in Simester (ed.), *Appraising Strict Liability* (2005) 21, 30–1.

[106] Below, § 8.2.

where the defendant's activity is a specialist one, not readily understood by a prosecutor or court. But there is a profound moral problem with the argument: it presents an issue of *procedural* convenience as a reason to change *substantive* law. The better answer, surely, is to change the procedure: by reversing the onus of proof.[107] This approach has been taken elsewhere in the Commonwealth, where "strict liability" offences require the prosecution to prove the actus reus beyond reasonable doubt, whereupon the defendant may exculpate himself by proving absence of fault (i.e. a "no-negligence" defence) on the balance of probabilities. Moreover, the question whether the defendant is at fault in a strict liability offence will still be relevant to any common-law defence and, in particular, to sentencing. Indeed, fault is likely to be relevant even to the decision to prosecute.[108] In light of this, it seems that the evidence may as well be heard straightforwardly before conviction. The judge certainly cannot pass sentence without deciding whether the offence was committed knowingly, negligently, or blamelessly,[109] and will, if the facts are disputed, in any case have to hold a further hearing to determine them.[110] Given the advantage the defendant may have, of familiarity with the nature of his specialist activity, it is arguable that, as well as being more efficient, the shift in evidential burdens may also result in better justice.

It is, in short, doubtful whether there are any significant advantages to be gained from the device of strict liability. But even more important is the intrinsic moral objection. It is wrong to convict the innocent. To do so is a misuse of criminal law, the most condemnatory institution available to society. If someone does not deserve to be convicted, then they should not be. To convict innocent people violates this most basic tenet of criminal liability.[111] It also breaches the requirement for fair warning, since citizens have no way of knowing or predicting when they may be about to incur criminal liability.[112] No doubt the public need to be protected from the harms that regulatory offences are designed to prevent. But the public need to be protected, too, from random liability.

To the claim that strict liability tends to be imposed only for offences which involve little or no public stigma, it may be responded that transgressors still suffer the rigours of the criminal process, with associated costs and loss of time, not to mention the fact of a conviction and a criminal record. And if the conviction is a trivial consideration, why make the wrongdoing a criminal rather than civil or administrative matter? "When it becomes respectable to be convicted, the vitality of the criminal law has been sapped."[113]

---

[107] See, however, *Lambert* [2001] 3 ALL ER 577, where, in the context of the application of the HRA 1998 to s. 28 of the Misuse of Drugs Act 1971, the House of Lords interpreted a reverse burden of proof as imposing only an evidential and not a probative burden. For discussion of this and other impacts of the HRA 1998 upon strict liability, see above, §§ 2.5(i), 2.5(iii), 3.2(i)(a).

[108] Richardson, Ogus, and Burrows, *Policing Prosecution* (1982); Hutter, *The Reasonable Arm of the Law* (1988); *Smedleys Ltd* v. *Breed* [1974] AC 839, 856 (Viscount Dilhorne); *James & Son* v. *Smee* [1955] 1 QB 78, 93 (Parker J). Compare *Hart* v. *Bex* [1957] Crim LR 622, where the Court convicted but thought that a prosecution should not have been brought.

[109] See, e.g., *Smedleys Ltd* v. *Breed* [1974] AC 839, 857 (Viscount Dilhorne); *Lester* (1975) 63 Cr App R 144.

[110] *Newton* (1983) 77 Cr App R 13.

[111] See above, § 1.2(ii)(a).

[112] Cf. above, § 2.3.

[113] Sayre, "The Present Significance of *Mens Rea* in the Criminal Law" in Pound (ed.), *Harvard Legal Essays* (1934) 399, 409.

§ 6.4 Middle ground: strict liability in the Commonwealth

In parts of the Commonwealth, a distinction is drawn between the terms "strict liability" and "absolute liability". In "strict liability" offences, the prosecution is required to prove the actus reus but, in relation to one or more elements of the actus reus, there is no mens rea element to prove. Nonetheless, the defendant can prove absence of fault in order to escape liability. In essence, the offences are negligence-based, but with a reversed burden of proof. "Absolute liability", by contrast, refers to what in England is known as "strict liability". The offence is complete upon proof of the actus reus, without any requirement to prove mens rea; neither can the defendant claim an absence of fault in his own defence.

The leading Commonwealth case on strict liability is *R. v. City of Sault Ste Marie*,[114] in which the Supreme Court of Canada decided that although mens rea need not be an essential ingredient of an offence, an alternative to absolute liability was nonetheless possible: there might be a defence available of "total absence of fault", the onus of proof for which would lie on the defendant. This third category, which the Court named strict liability, was characterised as follows:[115]

> "the doing of the prohibited act *prima facie* imports the offence, leaving it open to the accused to avoid liability by proving that he took all reasonable care. This involves consideration of what a reasonable man would have done in the circumstances. The defence will be available if the accused reasonably believed in a mistaken set of facts which, if true, would render the act or omission innocent, or if he took all reasonable steps to avoid the particular event."

The Supreme Court thus claimed a middle ground that the House of Lords denied itself in *Sweet v. Parsley*.[116] Indeed, it went further and held that regulatory offences, if they were not found to require proof of full mens rea, should presumptively involve "strict" rather than "absolute" liability.[117] Absolute liability is now a rare phenomenon: as a matter of principle, it should be applied only if imposed by the legislation "in clear terms or by necessary implication."[118]

Why did the House of Lords tread a different path, and reject the possibility of a negligence-based middle ground? The answer is that, although a "halfway house" between mens rea and "absolute" liability was looked upon favourably by many of their Lordships in *Sweet v. Parsley*,[119] the House regarded the imposition of a persuasive burden of proof upon the defendant as inconsistent with *Woolmington*. In *Woolmington*, Viscount Sankey LC had said that, saving insanity and express statutory exceptions, the prosecution was required to prove guilt "no matter what the charge or where the trial."[120] The objection raised by the House is

---

[114] (1978) 85 DLR (3d) 161 (water pollution). See, for analysis, Hutchinson, "Sault Ste. Marie, Mens Rea and the Halfway House: Public Welfare Offences Get a Home of Their Own" (1979) 17 *Osgoode Hall LJ* 415.

[115] (1978) 85 DLR (3d) 161, 181–2. Compare, in Australia, *Proudman v. Dayman* (1941) 67 CLR 536, 540 (Dixon J); Howard, "Strict Responsibility in the High Court of Australia" (1960) 76 *LQR* 547. See also Brett, "Strict Responsibility: Possible Solutions" (1974) 37 *MLR* 417; Orchard, "The Defence of Absence of Fault in Australasia and Canada" in Smith (ed.), *Criminal Law: Essays in Honour of J.C. Smith* (1987) 114.

[116] [1970] AC 132; above, § 6.1(i)

[117] (1978) 85 DLR (3d) 161, 182. The policy reasons for preferring strict liability are stated at 171–2.

[118] *Millar v. MOT* [1986] 1 NZLR 660 (CA).

[119] [1970] AC 132, 150 (Lord Reid), 158 (Lord Pearce), 164 (Lord Diplock).

[120] [1935] AC 462, 481; cf. *Mancini v. DPP* [1942] AC 1, 11: the rule is "of general application in all charges under the criminal law."

not merely of technical precedent: the Commonwealth version of strict liability contravenes the fundamental principle espoused in *Woolmington* that the prosecution must prove the whole of its case, and it is not for the defendant to prove his innocence.

The irony of this is surely obvious, even if lost upon their Lordships.[121] *Woolmington* is, and was meant to be, a bastion for the defendant, a fortress against conviction of the innocent. How extraordinary that, in *Sweet* v. *Parsley*, it led to an "absolute" liability doctrine whereby the innocent defendant is denied even the *opportunity* to exculpate himself.

It is, moreover, not clear that the English view of strict liability was genuinely entailed by the precedent set by *Woolmington*. First, the point made by the Supreme Court in *Sault Ste Marie*, that *Woolmington* was concerned with "criminal offences in the true sense" and not with regulatory offences,[122] has much force. There is no reason to suppose that Viscount Sankey intended or even envisaged the implication later drawn from his words. Secondly, if it comes to judicial creativity, the House of Lords has more recently shown little compunction about trampling upon *Woolmington* in *Hunt*, when (as we saw earlier) it ruled that the defendant bears the onus of proving any statutory exceptions to an offence, even where the statute does not expressly impose that burden.[123] Finally, if *Woolmington* really does foreclose the Commonwealth version of strict liability, alternatives were available. In particular, a defence of absence of fault where the *evidential* (rather than persuasive) burden lies on the defendant is certainly consistent with *Woolmington*, and was favoured by Lord Diplock in *Sweet* v. *Parsley*.[124] But the House was having none of this. Rather than adopt a morally defensible course, and impose some form of negligence-based liability, the Lords bequeathed English law with the harshness of strict liability.

§ 6.5 The correspondence principle, constructive liability, and moral luck

In § 5.8, we discussed a requirement of *concurrence*: that the actus reus and mens rea of an offence must coincide in time. The concurrence requirement reflects a more general principle, of *correspondence*, in criminal law. Loosely stated, the standard version of the correspondence principle maintains that for every offence there should be both an actus reus element and a mens rea element which relates to that actus reus, and that both of these elements must simultaneously be satisfied before the offence is committed. One way of expressing the objection to strict liability offences, therefore, is that they breach this correspondence principle.

The correspondence principle has an ancient pedigree. As long ago as 1798 Lord Kenyon described it as "a principle of natural justice, and of our law, that *actus non facit reum nisi mens sit rea*. The intent and the act must both concur to constitute the crime." Before that,

---

[121] Not, however, upon others: *R.* v. *City of Sault Ste Marie* (1978) 85 DLR (3d) 161, 175; *Millar* v. *MOT* [1986] 1 NZLR 660, 666; Cooke, "One Golden Thread?" in *Turning Points of the Common Law* (1997) 28, 47.

[122] (1978) 85 DLR (3d) 161, 174–5; cf. *Civil Aviation Dept* v. *MacKenzie* [1983] NZLR 78, 84.

[123] Above, § 3.2(i)(b).

[124] [1970] AC 132, 164. More accurately, the defence was said to be one of "honest and reasonable belief in a state of affairs which, had it existed, would have made his act innocent" (in effect, an absence of fault). Lord Diplock's preference was subsequently adopted by the New Zealand Court of Appeal in *Strawbridge* [1970] NZLR 909, but that decision is now superceded: *Millar* v. *MOT* [1986] 1 NZLR 660, 668.

references to the principle may be found in Bracton and Coke. According to Bracton, for example:[125]

> "For take away the will and every act will be indifferent, because it is your intent which gives meaning to your act, and a crime is not committed unless an intent to injure exists; neither is a theft committed without the intention to steal."

Certainly in the centuries after Coke,[126] these early sentiments had become so entrenched in the common law that mens rea could properly be described as "one of the fundamental requisites of criminality."[127] "The general rule of English law is, that no crime can be committed unless there is mens rea."[128] Criminal conviction, therefore, required something more than the mere occurrence of harm. Subject to limited exceptions whose genesis, we have observed, lay in the nineteenth century,[129] strict liability would not do.

Understood in this way, the principle of correspondence is a limited ethical principal, one which recognises that criminal liability should depend not only upon a person's acts but also upon her moral guilt with respect to those acts. However, some writers have claimed a larger role for the correspondence principle. They defend what may be termed a "rigid version" of the principle. According to the rigid version, for *every* actus reus element there should be a corresponding mens rea element, every one of which should simultaneously be satisfied before the offence is committed. Thus, according to Ashworth:[130]

> "If the conduct element of a crime is 'causing serious injury', the principle of correspondence demands that the fault element should be intention or recklessness as to causing serious injury, and not intention or recklessness as to some lesser consequence such as a mere assault. Another example, as we shall see, is the law of murder: in English law a person may be convicted of murder if he either intended to kill or intended to cause grievous bodily harm. However, the latter species of fault breaches the principle of correspondence: the fault element does not correspond with the conduct element (which is, causing death), and so a person is liable to conviction for a higher crime than contemplated."

Another offence that violates the rigid version of the correspondence principle is section 1 of the Road Traffic Act 1988, causing death by dangerous driving. Once the preliminary offence of dangerous driving is committed,[131] liability for the greater offence in section 1 becomes a matter of strict liability, because the only difference in the definitions of these two offences is whether D causes someone's death; and that is an actus reus element for which no additional mens rea element is required.

---

[125] *De Legibus et Consuetudinibus Angliae*, 101b. Cf. Coke, *Third Institute* (1641) 6, 107.

[126] For discussion see Sayre, "*Mens Rea*" (1932) 45 *Harv LR* 974.

[127] Sayre, "The Present Significance of *Mens Rea* in the Criminal Law" in Pound (ed.), *Harvard Legal Essays* (1934) 399, 399.

[128] *Williamson v. Norris* [1899] 1 QB 7, 14 (Lord Russell).

[129] "It is true that there are cases where the Legislature in its wisdom has declared that, in the particular class of cases dealt with, a man is to be treated as guilty of the offence in question, although he has not acted with negligence, and had no guilty mind. There are several such cases, but they form an exception to the general rule of law": *ibid.*

[130] *Principles* 85. See Horder, "A Critique of the Correspondence Principle in Criminal Law" [1995] *Crim LR* 759; Mitchell, "In Defence of a Principle of Correspondence" [1999] *Crim LR* 195; Horder, "Questioning the Correspondence Principle—A Reply" [1999] *Crim LR* 206.

[131] Road Traffic Act 1988, s. 2.

Offences of this sort are said to impose *constructive liability*. Perhaps the best-known constructive liability offence is manslaughter by an unlawful act. If D commits a crime which creates a reasonably foreseeable risk of *some* harm to V, D becomes guilty of manslaughter should his preliminary crime in fact cause V's death.[132] This form of manslaughter contains no mens rea ingredient referring to the crucial actus reus element, death.

Constructive liability breaches the correspondence principle, at least in the rigid form. But is constructive liability necessarily a bad thing, or is the correspondence principle over-rated? The answer, surely, is a bit of both. The rigid version of the correspondence principle is not and never has been a part of the criminal law.[133] On the other hand, the case for the standard version of the correspondence principle is much stronger. The maxim *actus non facit reum nisi mens sit rea* is rightly a venerable one because we want convictions for causing harm to be a matter of culpability and not of luck. We have seen that strict liability is objectionable because it exposes defendants to convictions purely on the basis of luck rather than fault. Constructive liability has the potential, if misused, to do the same.

To see this, let us set out two examples, illustrating situations where the use of constructive liability would and would not be legitimate.

> Example 1: Jane bears a grudge against Daniel. When Daniel's back is turned she throws a stone at him, intending to injure him. She misses. The stone damages Daniel's binoculars, which were lying concealed in the long grass.

A similar case was discussed in § 5.7, in the context of transferred malice. As we saw then, Jane is not guilty of criminal damage. The mens rea and actus reus do not coincide, and the most she can be convicted of is an attempted assault. Rightly so. The correspondence principle is applicable to this sort of case. The fact that Jane has a "guilty mind" and intends a criminal act gives us no basis for convicting her of intentionally damaging Daniel's property, since vandalism is a very different type of offence from assault. To impose constructive liability here would be wrong because there is no connection between Jane's culpability and the harm she has done. Morally speaking, to convict Jane would be equivalent to imposing *strict* rather than constructive liability; with all the objections (in § 6.3) that strict liability imports.

Contrast Jane's case, however, with a second example:

> Example 2: Deborah is driving through a village at a speed 20 miles per hour in excess of the speed limit. Unexpectedly she loses control of her car, mounts the pavement, and kills Allan, who had been walking quietly toward the corner shop in order to buy a newspaper.

Driving through the village at such excessive speed is, we may conclude, dangerous driving. As such, Jane commits the offence of causing death by dangerous driving notwithstanding that she does not foresee Allan's death. Under section 1 of the Road Traffic Act 1988, the offence requires no mens rea element to be proved in respect of the death. It is a constructive liability offence. But there is nothing wrong with that. Certainly it is, in one sense, a matter of luck that Allan was killed. But the luck is not random or unrelated in the

---

[132] Below, § 10.6(ii). See especially the critique in § 10.6(ii)(f).
[133] Gardner, "Rationality and the Rule of Law in Offences Against the Person" [1994] *CLJ* 502, 509.

way it was for Jane. Here, the possibility of this type of outcome forms part of the very reason why dangerous driving is wrongful and, indeed, itself criminalised (by section 2 of the same Act).

(i) Moral luck

Even if it can be distinguished from strict liability, however, constructive liability may still be thought problematic, because—like strict liability—it has the effect of making liability depend on D's bad luck. Of course, in this sense luck is integral to the criminal law. If D shoots at V and misses, for example, the most she can be guilty of is attempted murder. If V dies, D becomes liable for murder; a different conviction with different penal consequences. Yet, once D has pulled the trigger, the outcome is a matter of luck. "We never do more than move our bodies: the rest is up to nature."[134]

The problem is as follows. Luck, it may be thought, is involuntary—the antithesis of control. And culpability, surely, should be dependent upon control rather than luck. As Nagel puts it:[135]

> "Prior to reflection it is intuitively plausible that people cannot be morally assessed for what is not their fault, or for what is due to factors beyond their control. [Moral] judgment is different from the evaluation of something as a good or bad thing, or state of affairs. The latter may be present in addition to moral judgment, but when we blame someone for his actions we are not merely saying it is bad that they happened, or bad that he exists: we are judging *him*, saying he is bad. . . . Without being able to explain exactly why, we feel that the appropriateness of moral assessment is easily undermined by the discovery that the act or attribute, no matter how good or bad, is not under the person's control."

If that is so, there is an obvious difficulty because outcomes—harms—unavoidably involve luck. Nagel continues:[136]

> "Whether we succeed or fail in what we try to do nearly always depends to some extent on factors beyond our control. This is true of murder, altruism, revolution, the sacrifice of certain interests for the sake of others—almost any morally important act. What has been done, and what is morally judged, is partly determined by other factors. However jewel-like[137] the good will may be in its own right, there is a morally significant difference between rescuing someone from a burning building and dropping him from a twelfth-storey window while trying to rescue him. Similarly, there is a morally significant difference between reckless driving and manslaughter. But whether a reckless driver hits a pedestrian depends on the presence of the pedestrian at the point where he recklessly passes a red light."

And that, we have noted, is a matter of luck.

Ashworth, amongst others, has used this type of point to oppose segregating attempt

---

[134] Davidson, "Agency" in *Essays on Actions and Events* (1980) 43, 59. Cf. Ashworth, "Taking the Consequences" in Shute, Gardner and Horder, *Action and Value in Criminal Law* (1993) 107.

[135] "Moral Luck" in *Mortal Questions* (1979) 24, 25. See, *inter alia*, André, "Nagel, Williams and Moral Luck" (1983) 43 *Analysis* 202; Honoré, "Responsibility and Luck: The Moral Basis of Strict Liability" (1989) 104 *LQR* 530; Mandil, "Chance, Freedom and Criminal Liability" (1987) 87 *Cal LR* 125; Schulhofer, "Harm and Punishment: A Critique of Emphasis on the Results of Conduct in the Criminal Law" (1974) 122 *U Pa LR* 1497; Smith, "The Element of Chance in Criminal Liability" [1971] *Crim LR* 63; Williams, "Moral Luck" in *Moral Luck* (1981).

[136] "Moral Luck" in *Mortal Questions* (1979) 24, 25.

liability: where the difference is merely down to luck, a failed attempt to kill ought to be punished just as severely as if it had succeeded, and vice versa.[138] On Ashworth's view, any substantive offence, such as murder, is analogous to a constructive liability offence: the preliminary crime committed by D is attempted murder, and what elevates D's crime to murder is (like dangerous driving causing death) merely the actus reus element of causing death—for which no additional mens rea element is required.

It is not possible, in a book of this nature, to answer these objections in full; here, we can only sketch a defence of moral luck in the criminal law. The key point is that in dangerous driving, like murder, death is not *merely* a matter of luck. To see this, consider the following example proposed by Smith:[139]

> "the daughter of a business executive has been assigned a science project of investigating the distribution of blood-types within the population. To assist her, the executive asks his secretary to survey the office staff and prepare a report on their blood-types by noon. Instead of carrying out this request, the secretary reads a spy novel. At 11:45 a co-worker suffers massive bleeding as a result of an office accident. Paramedics arrive, and could start a transfusion immediately if the workers' blood-type were known. Unfortunately he is unconscious, cannot provide this information, and so dies before the transfusion can be started. Had the secretary followed her boss's orders, she would have known the worker's blood-type and his life would have been saved. Her failure to obtain this information is both objectively wrong *and* culpable, and it led to her inability to save her co-worker's life. But [there is] no inclination to say that the secretary is to blame for the co-worker's death."

A comparison between this example and that of Deborah's driving shows that there are two types of luck: intrinsic and extrinsic.[140] The secretary is not blameworthy for the co-worker's death, and Jane is not guilty of wilful damage to Daniel's property, because these risks were *extrinsic* to each actor's culpability. Such risks affect the outcome, and perhaps affect our retrospective judgements about what D *did*, but they are not factors to take into account when deciding, *in advance*, what D should do. By contrast, in the dangerous driving case and in the attempted murder case, the risk of death was *intrinsic* to D's culpability: it formed part of the reason why, even *ex ante*, D's behaviour was wrong.

Ashworth and Nagel are right to observe that many factors affecting an outcome are beyond our control. But this does not imply that the outcome itself is beyond our control. It is only *given* D's behaviour that the outcome is—thereafter—beyond her control. D does have control over the outcome; she exercises that control *through* her behaviour. It is D's dangerous driving, or her pulling the trigger, that brings the uncontrolled factors into play, and makes the luck relevant. Where that luck is intrinsic, there seems no difficulty about holding D responsible and culpable for the outcome.

---

[137] A reference to Kant, *Foundations of the Metaphysics of Morals* (1785) §1.

[138] "Criminal Attempts and the Role of Resulting Harm" (1988) 19 *Rutgers LJ* 725; "Belief, Intent, and Criminal Liability" in Eekelaar and Bell (eds.), *Oxford Essays in Jurisprudence* (3rd Series, 1987) 1. The argument is restricted to "complete" rather than "incomplete" attempts: cf. *Principles* 443–5. For an interesting discussion of these issues see Lewis, "The Punishment that Leaves Something to Chance" (1989) 18 *Phil & Pub Aff* 53. See also below, § 9.3(vi).

[139] "Culpable Ignorance" (1983) 92 *The Philosophical Review* 543, 550.

[140] Williams, "Moral Luck" in *Moral Luck* (1981) 20, 25–6. This distinction supports a better analysis of Horder's gun-cleaning example than the author himself offers: "A Critique of the Correspondence Principle in Criminal Law" [1995] *Crim LR* 759, 764. Suppose I clean my gun outside *in order* to upset V. Although my deliberate wrong changes my normative position, it does not does not do so with respect to extrinsic risks such as an accidental discharge that causes V's death by shock.

Moreover, constructive liability is consistent with the rule of law. Where such offences are predicated on intrinsic luck, they do not defeat the desire to give fair warning in criminal law.[141] Indeed, D may be regarded as already warned, since she has committed the preliminary crime (e.g. dangerous driving) with mens rea;[142] and the intrinsic luck forms part of the rationale for blaming D and regarding that preliminary crime as wrong.[143]

At the same time, constructive liability advances the goal of representative labelling in the law.[144] If D shoots and kills V, we do not reprove the attack and, separately, regret V's death. No: we reprove the murder. It does not sufficiently describe D's act to say that she attempted to murder V. She murdered him. Similarly, it would be incomplete and therefore inaccurate to describe Deborah's conduct as dangerous driving. Even where the mens rea for two offences is the same, representative labelling in the criminal law is constrained by harm. Why are reckless endangerment by dangerous driving, attempts to kill, and the like wrongful? The answer is not because they involve any direct (e.g. physical) harm to the victim, but because D wrongfully manipulates, subordinates, or attacks V's interests and autonomy. But when an attempt succeeds, when dangerous driving kills, the harm is rather different. V is dead. Only by acknowledging that fact can the criminal law communicate what D has done.

---

[141] Discussed above, § 2.3.

[142] See Gardner, "Rationality and the Rule of Law in Offences Against the Person" [1994] *CLJ* 502, 521–3.

[143] This further point presupposes that the goal of giving potential offenders fair warning of their crimes does not always require advertence by defendants to the actus reus. It is submitted that crimes of negligence are capable of giving fair warning.

[144] Above, § 2.4.

7

SECONDARY PARTICIPATION

§ 7.1 The possibility of derivative liability

In Chapter 1, we considered the following example:[1]

> One fine September morning, Jim is discovered dead in his home. His skull has been crushed by a blow inflicted with a heavy object. The police are called. Upon investigation, they establish that he was murdered by his daughter, Alice, who killed him in order to receive her inheritance under his will.

This, as we said earlier, is a paradigm case of criminal wrongdoing by Alice, involving deliberate, culpable infliction of the sort of serious harm that the criminal law seeks to prevent. Alice is precisely the sort of person who deserves the condemnation of a criminal conviction. But she may not be the only person culpable in respect of Jim's death. Imagine the following additional details:

> During the course of their investigation, the police unearth a number of related facts. Frank, Jim's cousin, had learned by accident of Alice's plan to murder Jim, but had done nothing because he, too, stood to inherit under the will. Alice had planned the murder with the help of Gertrude, whom she had consulted about possible methods of carrying out the killing. The baseball bat that Alice eventually used belongs to Harry, who lent it to Alice for the purpose.

When an offence is committed it is not only the immediate perpetrator of the actus reus who may incur criminal liability. Others may also be held accountable by the criminal law. Usually, this will occur when those others have participated in the commission of the crime, albeit without themselves satisfying the actus reus.[2] Such persons, when they are held to be criminally accountable, are said to be *parties* to the offence.

The difficult questions, for both theory and doctrine in criminal law, are *when* and *why* persons other than the perpetrator of a crime should be held liable. When Jim dies every legally competent person within the jurisdiction is a potential defendant, yet it is inappropriate to regard every member of society as involved in the crime that Alice commits. But how do we narrow the field in a principled way? In short, when a crime occurs, who are the suitable defendants?

---

[1] Above, § 1.2 and, especially, § 1.2(ii)(e).
[2] Note, however, *Empress Car Co* v. *NRA* [1998] 1 All ER 481, the logic of which threatens to undermine this proposition—and in turn, much of the rationale for secondary liability. The case is discussed above, § 4.2(iii)(d) and below, § 7.7(i).

In Chapter 4 we considered the criminal law's doctrines of omissions and causation, which play a vital role in identifying those persons who may be ascribed with legal responsibility for committing a crime. Because of the law regarding omissions, for example, Frank will not be held responsible for Jim's death. On the other hand, these are not the only doctrines of responsibility in criminal law. Gertrude and Harry did not cause Jim's death: Alice's action was free and unconstrained.[3] Nonetheless they, as well as Alice, will be held guilty of Jim's murder.

In this and the following chapter, we consider the doctrines by which a defendant may be held responsible for a crime she does not herself commit.[4] There are two main ways in which this may occur. The first gives rise to *secondary liability*. Although they did not perpetrate the crime, Gertrude and Harry have participated in Jim's murder by rendering aid and encouragement to Alice. Hence, they are known as secondary parties to the murder and are guilty of the offence alongside Alice. The second doctrine of responsibility occurs when a person is held responsible, at large, for the various acts of another person. This is known as *vicarious liability* and is much more common in civil than in criminal law. For example, an employer may sometimes be sued in tort for the damage its employee causes to P's property, but cannot itself be prosecuted for vandalism.

Both forms of liability are *derivative*. The defendant is indirectly held responsible for a crime committed by another and, as such, her liability is dependent upon the criminal actions of that other person. If no crime is committed, there is generally nothing of a criminal character that can be secondarily or vicariously attributed to the defendant.[5] As was noted in § 1.2(ii)(e), and will be seen below, the fact that liability is derived from the crime of another raises difficult questions of principle and policy. The level of involvement required to make D guilty when P commits a crime must balance the consideration that D is often just as culpable as P (and indeed sometimes more culpable), even though it was not D who pulled the trigger, against the difficulty that derivative liability casts the net of criminalisation well beyond the direct infliction of criminal harms, to catch ostensibly innocent conduct such as lending (or selling[6]) Alice a baseball bat or even sitting as a passenger in a car.[7] It is for this reason that the mens rea requirements of secondary liability, in particular, are generally more complex than those for the underlying offence.

For similar reasons, vicarious liability is normally to be avoided altogether in criminal law, since it arises simply out of a pre-existing relationship between the defendant and the actual perpetrator of a crime, and so is not specific to the crime or to any conduct by D relevant to that crime. It follows that D risks being convicted of a crime to which he has not contributed and for which he is in no way at fault. As Chapter 1 argued, that would be an undesirable outcome, especially in the context of stigmatic crimes. Consequently, it will be

---

[3] See above, § 4.2ff. Their assistance need not even be a *sine qua non* of the crime—Alice, we may suppose, would have received the same advice and aid from others had Gertrude and Harry been unavailable or unwilling.

[4] A classic discussion is Sayre, "Criminal Responsibility for the Acts of Another" (1930) 43 *Harv LR* 678. Other American writings include Perkins, "Parties to Crime" (1941) 89 *U Pa LR* 581; Dressler, "Reassessing the Theoretical Underpinnings of Accomplice Liability: New Solutions to an Old Problem" (1985) 37 *Hastings LJ* 91.

[5] Kadish, *Blame and Punishment* (1987) 146ff. This proposition is subject to certain exceptions, e.g. where S has procured P to do the actus reus of an offence without mens rea, or under duress: see below, § 7.6(ii).

[6] Cf. *NCB v. Gamble* [1959] 1 QB 1. See, e.g., Duff, "'Can I Help You?' Accessorial Liability and the Intention to Assist" (1990) 10 *LS* 165; Williams, "Complicity, Purpose and the Draft Code" [1990] *Crim LR* 4.

[7] E.g. *Du Cros v. Lambourne* [1907] 1 KB 40; below, § 7.4(iii).

seen in Chapter 8 that vicarious liability is not a general doctrine of the criminal law, being normally restricted to regulatory offences and imposed only when it is found that Parliament must have intended it.

In the second part of Chapter 8, we will turn our attention to the liability of corporations. Although corporations are sometimes credited with a legal capacity to act, or omit, and to commit crimes directly, as will be seen, corporate liability often is to be explained as a specialised variety of vicarious liability.

§ 7.2 Modes of participation

The law recognises two main varieties of participation in a crime. For convenience, we begin with a summary. Participation in an offence may occur in the following ways:

(i)   As principal (the person who carries out the offence); or
(ii) As secondary party: either
  (a) through assistance or encouragement—by aiding, abetting, counselling, or procuring the commission of that offence; or
  (b) through membership of a joint enterprise that led to the offence.

Suppose that D commits an assault by hitting V during an argument. In this case, D acts as the *principal*—the person who actually commits the crime. In general, D will be a principal offender if he personally fulfils the actus reus and mens rea requirements of the crime.

Alternatively, the crime itself may be done by P, but S may be involved as a *secondary party*. Secondary parties are those persons whose role in giving assistance or encouragement to P is sufficient to make them also participants in and guilty of the crime committed by the principal, notwithstanding that they do not themselves satisfy the actus reus and mens rea elements of the crime. *Per* section 8 of the Accessories and Abettors Act 1861, as amended by the Criminal Law Act 1977:

> Whosoever shall aid, abet, counsel or procure the commission of any indictable offence,[8] whether the same be an offence at common law or by virtue of any Act passed or to be passed, shall be liable to be tried, indicted, and punished as a principal offender.

A secondary party should be distinguished from a person who assists someone else (who may be either a principal or secondary party) who has committed an offence, *after* the crime has been completed. Such a person does not participate in the crime itself, and his liability is not for the original crime committed, but instead arises independently as an offence under section 4 of the Criminal Law Act 1967.[9] By contrast, participation by a party to the offence must occur before that offence is completed.[10]

---

[8] Similar rules apply to summary trials: Magistrates' Courts Act 1980, s. 44.

[9] This rule differs from the common law, which was repealed by the Criminal Law Act 1967. At common law, whenever D subsequently gave assistance to any person committing or party to a felony, which assistance tended to and had the object of enabling that person to avoid arrest, trial, or conviction, D also became a party to the original felony and did not commit an independent offence.

[10] *King* (1817) Russ & Ry 332, 168 ER 830; *Stally* [1959] 3 All ER 814. In the case of a continuing offence, such

The distinction between principals and secondary offenders is now of little practical significance in criminal law since each is deemed to be guilty of the full offence. Thus it will not affect his resulting conviction for, say, murder, whether D himself killed another person or was simply a secondary party. Indeed, it can be very difficult on the facts of some cases to differentiate between principals and secondary parties,[11] and the form of charge need not specify the nature of D's participation, but may simply allege guilt.[12]

Nonetheless, the terminology is still to be found in the case law. One reason for this is that the distinction is still crucial to the operation of section 8 itself. If D was not a principal, the enquiry whether D was a secondary party will depend in part upon the existence of a principal who did perpetrate the offence, and will take a different form—with a different actus reus and different mens rea—from the enquiry into the principal's liability. The elements of the principal's liability are specific to each offence: in murder, for example, the prosecution must prove an intent to kill or inflict grievous bodily injury (Chapter 10), while strict liability offences require no proof of mens rea on the part of a principal (Chapter 6). By contrast, for both types of offence the elements of secondary liability are the same; they are as set out in this chapter *whatever* the main offence.

The difference between principals and secondary parties matters for at least two other reasons. First, some offences are defined so that certain participants are excluded from liability, either because only a named class of persons may commit the offence as a principal or (more rarely) because the possibility of secondary participation is excluded.[13] Secondly, there is no vicarious liability for the acts of secondary parties.[14]

§ 7.3 The principal

Before considering the varieties of secondary participation falling within section 8, it is necessary to make some observations regarding the participation of principal offenders. First, there may be more than one principal offender. If P and Q assault V by jointly raining blows on him, they are each principals. If V dies from the combination of blows, they will each be guilty of manslaughter or murder.[15] There are two ways in which multiple defendants may be held to be principals. First, each may separately satisfy all the required ingredients of the relevant offence. In the above example, P and Q are each independently guilty of an assault. Alternatively, each may separately satisfy *some* part of the actus reus for the offence where their actions, in combination, fulfil the complete actus reus requirement and each has the requisite mens rea. The latter is a true case of joint principals, in that it is sufficient for liability that each party does a part of the actus reus.[16]

---

as rape (cf. Sexual Offences Act 2003, s. 79(2); *Kaitamaki* [1985] AC 147), the participation may occur after commencement of the offence but must happen before its completion (i.e. prior to withdrawal by the rapist): *Mok Wei Tak* v. *R.* [1990] 2 AC 333 (PC); *Mayberry* [1973] Qd R 211.

[11] See, e.g., *Swindall and Osborne* (1846) 2 C & K 230, 175 ER 95; *Du Cros* v. *Lambourne* [1907] 1 KB 40.

[12] However, it is desirable wherever possible for the prosecution to specify the form of participation when laying the charge: *Maxwell* v. *DPP for Northern Ireland* [1978] 3 All ER 1140, 1142.

[13] See below, § 7.6(iv).

[14] *Ferguson* v. *Weaving* [1951] 11 KB 814.

[15] Cf. *Langman* v. *Valentine* [1952] 2 All ER 803 (joint drivers).

[16] E.g. *Bingley* (1821) Russ & Ry 446 (each forged part of a banknote); *Cornwall* (1730) 2 Str 881, 93 ER 914 (breaking and entering). See Lanham, "Complicity, Concert and Conspiracy" (1980) 4 *Crim LJ* 276.

Note, however, that there must be *some* contribution to the occurrence of the actus reus before one can be held to have committed the offence as a principal. Thus if S and P attack C in concert, yet it is a particular blow by P that causes death independent of the effect of the earlier blows by S, then S cannot be convicted of murder as a principal and must be convicted as a secondary party. While the outcome may be the same (both are convicted of murder), the importance of this is that the actus reus and mens rea elements required to be proved in order to convict S as a secondary party are formally different from those required to convict P.

(i) Innocent agents

Sometimes the actus reus is not perpetrated personally by the defendant, but instead P arranges for it to be brought about by T, who is unaware of the significance of his actions.. Where the defendant deliberately[17] *uses* an "innocent agent" to bring about the actus reus, the participation of the intervening actor is disregarded and the law treats the defendant as the principal.[18] Conceptually, it is as if P "stands in the shoes" of the innocent agent. An example is when the host at a party gives a waiter a glass of wine to take out to the victim, when only the host knows that the wine contains poison. Although the waiter gives the victim poison, he is merely an innocent agent and it is the host who is the perpetrator of the crime.[19]

The doctrine of innocent agency does not apply if the intervening agent is herself guilty of the offence; consequently, it is normally inapplicable to strict liability offences.[20] Further, it may only be invoked, and the agent can only be categorised as an *innocent* agent, either if she does not know that she is doing the actus reus or if she lacks criminal capacity, in particular through being insane[21] or an infant.[22]

There are also some crimes for which the doctrine is excluded altogether because, by the very nature of those crimes, direct perpetration of the crime is required of the principal offender. This will depend upon the interpretation of each particular offence, but in general such cases are of two types.

First, innocent agency is more likely to be excluded where the essence of the crime is specified *behaviour* by the criminal, rather than the bringing about of some *consequence*.[23] In bigamy, for example, it seems impossible to say that P has gone through a ceremony of

---

[17] Exceptionally, an actus reus brought about by an innocent agent may also be attributed to D if it resulted from D's negligence, when negligence is sufficient to establish mens rea: *Tessymond* (1828) 1 Lewin 169.

[18] For discussion, see Alldridge, "The Doctrine of Innocent Agency" (1990) 2 *Crim L Forum* 45; Williams, "Innocent Agency and Causation" (1992) 3 *Crim L Forum* 289; Alldridge, "Common Sense, Innocent Agency, and Causation" (1992) 3 *Crim L Forum* 299. By contrast, secondary liability is thought to depend upon the existence of a principal offender: a striking illustration is *Demirian* [1989] VR 97. This requirement is considered below, § 7.6(i).

[19] Cf. *Anon* (1634) Kel 53, 84 ER 1079; *Johnson* (1805) 7 East 65, 103 ER 26; *Butcher* (1858) Bell 6, 169 ER 1145; *Butt* (1884) 15 Cox CC 56; *White v. Ridley* (1978) 140 CLR 342.

[20] Where, despite her innocence, the intervening agent is guilty of an offence, D should be convicted as a secondary party: *A-G's Reference (No 1 of 1975)* [1975] QB 773; below, § 7.4(i)(d).

[21] *Tyler* (1838) 8 C & P 616, 173 ER 643—notwithstanding that the insane "innocent agent" in that case was the ringleader!

[22] *Manley* (1844) 1 Cox CC 104; *Mazeau* (1840) 9 C & P 676, 173 ER 1006.

[23] See the distinction made between behavioural, circumstantial, and consequential elements of the actus reus, above, § 4.

marriage with V (the actus reus) when he has procured T to do so. The same is true for rape (notwithstanding the contrary decision in *Cogan and Leak*[24]), and for crimes such as careless driving[25] and driving with excess alcohol.[26] The doctrine of innocent agency operates only where it is possible for P to fulfil the elements of the actus reus by the instrument of some other person. That is straightforwardly done where the actus reus does not specify particular behaviour by the defendant. For example, in murder, which requires the causing of another's death, it is apt to view P as having killed V herself, even though she in fact procures the waiter to deliver the poison.[27] It is rather less easy to treat P as having done the actus reus personally when the gist of the wrong is T's actual conduct, rather than its consequence.

However, while the distinction may seem clear enough in principle, the question whether the conduct element of a particular offence requires P's direct, personal involvement can involve fine—indeed, seemingly arbitrary—distinctions. For instance, it is apparently possible to "enter" premises as a burglar through the agency of another;[28] but one cannot "buy" liquor on licensed premises unless personally present on those premises.[29] Thus the range of offences to which the innocent agent doctrine applies is somewhat uncertain.

Secondly, innocent agency is also excluded if P is not a member of the class of persons eligible to commit the offence as a principal. A typical example is an offence that can only be committed by a licensee. A useful illustration of this sort of offence, though not one involving innocent agency, is *Morris v. Tolman*:[30]

> D obtained a licence to use his vehicle on the highway. S, his employee, then used the vehicle for a purpose not covered by the licence. It was a statutory offence for the licensee to use the vehicle outside the terms of the licence.

On these facts, no offence was committed by either P or S. P had not used the vehicle himself (hence no actus reus by P). S had used the vehicle, but could not be guilty of the offence since he was not the licensee (hence no actus reus by S).

Suppose, instead, that by a trick S procures P, the innocent licensee, to use the vehicle outside the terms of the licence. Because he is not the licensee, S is incapable of committing the offence personally; therefore the innocent agency doctrine cannot apply and he cannot be convicted as principal. A crime will be committed in such cases only if the main offence

---

[24] [1976] QB 217; see the commentary in [1975] *Crim LR* 584. *Cogan and Leak* was followed by the Victorian Court of Appeal in *Hewitt* (1996) 84 A Crim R 440, but should now be explained on the basis of procurement: below, § 7.6(ii)(b).

[25] *Thornton* v. *Mitchell* [1940] 1 All ER 339, considered in *CLGP* § 129 n. 11. Cf. *Millward* [1994] Crim LR 527. Both cases are discussed in the text below, §§ 7.6(i), 7.6(ii)(b).

[26] Cf. *A-G's Reference (No. 1 of 1975)* [1975] QB 773, in which D secretly laced P's drink. (Note that the offence in that case was held to be one of strict liability, and that P was therefore guilty of committing the offence as a principal, notwithstanding his "innocence". D, in turn, was a secondary party.)

[27] Cf. *Butt* (1884) 15 Cox CC 56 (D guilty as principal of falsifying his employer's accounts by making a false statement to the employer's innocent bookkeeper).

[28] Hale 1 PC 555 (1736). Cf. *Brisac* (1803) 4 East 164, 102 ER 792 (conspiracy to cheat). By contrast, in *Pratt* v. *Martin* [1911] 2 KB 90, D was held not to have effected "entry" within the meaning of the Game Act 1831, s. 30, when he sent a dog onto land.

[29] Hence, in *Woby* v. *B and O* [1986] Crim LR 183, the two defendant minors, who had sent an adult into an off-licence to buy lager on their behalf, were ruled not to be guilty of "buying intoxicating liquor on licensed premises, being aged under 18 years" since they were not on the premises when they did so.

[30] [1923] 1 KB 166.

is one of strict liability; in which case P is himself guilty as principal and S, in turn, is guilty as a secondary party who procures the offence.

§ 7.4 Secondary parties who assist or encourage crime

Section 8 applies to persons who involve themselves in a crime by giving assistance or encouragement to its commission. The section mentions four varieties of conduct counting as secondary participation: aiding, abetting, counselling, and procuring. These are also the categories of participation recognised at common law, which section 8 essentially enacts.[31] Because, as we shall see, the categories overlap, it appears that they include the actus reus of virtually any form of assistance, encouragement, or contribution toward a crime by the principal.

(i) The conduct element

Although section 8 identifies four types of conduct constituting participation, it is not necessary in the charge to specify which type of conduct is relied on, and all four verbs may also be used together.[32] Indeed, to some extent the overlap in meanings between the words makes this a sensible practice,[33] and it is slightly artificial to analyse the terms as independent, alternative, actus reus elements. Nonetheless, each word has a different meaning,[34] and makes a particular contribution to the scope of participation covered by section 8. They will therefore be examined separately.

(a) Aiding

S aids P by assisting, helping, or giving support to P in the commission of a crime.[35] There must be actual assistance: merely trying to help is not enough.[36] If S, knowing that P is going to rob a bank, plans to lend P her gun, she does not aid the offence if her car breaks down on the way over to P's house and P leaves to commit the robbery before S arrives. On the other hand, the assistance need not be substantial. If T acts as lookout for P during the bank robbery, he is a party to the robbery even should there be no need to give a warning.[37]

---

[31] *Benford* v. *Sims* [1898] 2 QB 641.

[32] *Ferguson* v. *Weaving* [1951] KB 814.

[33] Albeit not a desirable one in cases where the evidence allows the particular form of participation to be specified: *Maxwell* [1978] 3 All ER 1140; *Gaughan* [1990] Crim LR 880.

[34] As was pointed out by Lord Widgery CJ in *A-G's Reference (No. 1 of 1975)* [1975] 1 QB 773, 779. The Chief Justice's view is a departure from traditional learning (cf. criticism by Smith, "Aid, Abet, Counsel, or Procure" in Glazebrook (ed.), *Reshaping the Criminal Law* (1978) 120, 125). It is submitted that the modern view is now to be preferred, given that traditional distinctions between aiders and abetters (present at the time of the offence) and counsellors and procurers (accessories before the fact) is no longer of legal effect. See below, § 7.4(i)(a).

[35] E.g. *Bainbridge* [1960] 1 QB 129 (supplying oxygen cutting equipment for use in a burglary); *Stansfeld & Co* v. *Andrews* (1909) 22 Cox 84 (supplying beer for illegal sale).

[36] See Smith, "Secondary Participation and Inchoate Offences" in Tapper (ed.), *Crime, Proof and Punishment* (1981) 21, 36–9. Cf. *A-G* v. *Able* [1984] 1 QB 795, 812 (Woolf J): no offence unless the reader "was assisted or encouraged by so reading the booklet to take or attempt to take his own life, otherwise the alleged offender cannot be guilty of more than an attempt." Note that there is no general offence of attempting to aid another to commit a crime: Criminal Law Act 1977, s. 1(4)(b).

[37] "The assistance given, however, need not contribute to the criminal result in the sense that but for it the result

It is no longer necessary that the assistance should take place at the scene of the offence.[38] Traditionally, the common law divided secondary parties into two groups. Aiders and abettors were said to be "principals in the second degree", and distinguished from counsellors and procurers—"accessories before the fact"—by their actual or constructive presence *at the time* the offence is committed.[39] The division is now only of historical interest, and it seems that the requirement of presence for aiders and abettors, and conversely the requirement of absence for counsellors and procurers, has also disappeared.[40] This seems to follow from the Court of Appeal's instruction in *A-G's Reference (No. 1 of 1975)*[41] that the four terms are, in so far as possible, to be interpreted according to their ordinary meanings.

Although there is no English case establishing the point, neither is it required that the principal should be aware of the assistance, provided she is in fact assisted.[42] Suppose that P plans a robbery, intending to use her gun. The day before the robbery takes place, S notices that P's gun is missing from its drawer. Without telling P, he places his own gun, a similar model, in the drawer for P to use instead. P carries out the robbery using S's gun. In this case S has aided P and is a party to the robbery even though P is ignorant of S's contribution. A well-known illustration is the American case of *State v. Tally*.[43] Judge Tally, whose brothers-in-law were pursuing and planning to kill V, prevented a third party from warning V of the danger, thereby making it easier for the pursuers to kill V. Tally was guilty of aiding murder, notwithstanding that his brothers-in-law were unaware of the assistance.[44]

(b) Abetting

In terms of its dictionary definition, "to abet" means to incite by aid, to instigate, or to encourage. In practice, because of its overlap with the other forms of participation in section 8, abetment is typically associated with encouragement.[45] Even so, there is extensive overlap with other forms of participation in crime. For example, in cases where S is alleged

would not have ensued. It is quite sufficient if it facilitated a result that would have transpired without it": *State v. Tally* 102 Ala 25, 15 So 722 (1894). Cf. *Gogerly* (1818) R & R 343, 168 ER 836.

[38] *Blakely* v. *DPP* [1991] RTR 405, 411; *Thambiah* v. *R.* [1966] AC 37 (PC).

[39] *Ferguson* v. *Weaving* [1951] 1 KB 814, 819; *Bowker* v. *Premier Drug Co* [1928] 1 KB 217. "Constructive" presence tended to be interpreted broadly. It included any assistance rendered while the offence was being carried out, even if such assistance was from afar—compare *State* v. *Tally* 102 Ala 25, 15 So 722 (1894); as well as being near enough to render assistance if called upon, cf. *Betts* (1930) 22 Cr App R 148. For discussion, see Smith, "Aid, Abet, Counsel, or Procure" in Glazebrook (ed.), *Reshaping the Criminal Law* (1978) 120, 125f; *CLGP* § 120.

[40] Compare *A-G* v. *Able* [1984] 1 QB 795, where advice given in advance was regarded as within the scope of aiding and abetting, with *Bainbridge* [1960] 1 QB 129, where it was treated as counselling or procuring.

[41] [1975] QB 773, 779 (Lord Widgery CJ).

[42] Cf. *Kupferberg* (1918) 13 Cr App R 166, 168: "in many cases aiding and abetting is done by the mutual consent of the criminals but it is not essential that it should be." Per Turner, *Russell on Crime* (12th ed., 1964) 147, "it is quite possible for a complete stranger to be guilty of aiding and abetting a crime committed by a principal offender who does not even know that he is being aided." This passage was approved by Martin JA in *Hobart* v. *R.* (1982) 25 CR (3d) 214, 236 (Ont CA).

[43] 102 Ala 25, 15 So 722 (1894).

[44] See also *Larkins* v. *Police* [1987] 2 NZLR 282, where S spontaneously decided to act as lookout during a robbery. Per Eichelbaum J (at 290), "the appellant's action in providing the principal offenders with, as counsel put it, an extra pair of eyes was at least evidence of actual assistance regardless whether those offenders were aware of its availability."

[45] Cf. *Clarkson* [1971] 3 All ER 344.

to "assist" P by offering support (e.g. as a lookout) on which P relies, the reliance itself may be sufficient encouragement for P to be abetted, whether or not any assistance is in fact provided. Similarly, encouragement of P to commit an offence is likely also to constitute counselling.[46]

The encouragement may be by words[47] or conduct—nodding one's head in endorsement of a crime may be just as effective as a verbal indication of agreement. Indeed, mere presence may constitute abetment where that presence supplies an incentive to the principal to go ahead. For example, in *Coney*[48] it was said that attendance at an illegal prize-fight might be evidence of abetting battery by the fighters, since, as Mathew J observed:[49]

> "The chief incentive to the wretched combatants to fight on until (as happens too often) dreadful injuries have been inflicted and life endangered or sacrificed, is the presence of spectators watching with keen interest every incident of the fight."

Simply by watching, S may encourage the fighters (although, as we shall see below, the mens rea requirement means that S must also *intend* this result).

However, such cases are exceptional, because it is necessary to show that S did *in fact* encourage P in the commission of a crime.[50] A good illustration of this principle is *Clarkson*.[51] Two soldiers, hearing noises emanating from a room at their barracks, entered the room where they found other soldiers raping a young woman. The two remained in the room to watch. Apparently, they neither did nor said anything, either to encourage or discourage continuance of the rape. The Court of Appeal quashed their convictions for aiding and abetting, because the Judge-advocate had not clearly stated that it must be proved the appellants intended to and did encourage commission of the crime. While the Court acknowledged it was possible that the rapists *might* in fact have received encouragement from the appellants' presence,[52] that encouragement had to be proved. Mere presence *which does not by itself encourage* is insufficient: "[t]here must be an intention to encourage; and there must also be encouragement in fact."[53] Edmund Davies J, giving the judgment of the Court of Criminal Appeal in *Allan*, stated the point as follows:[54]

> "In our judgment, before a jury can properly convict an accused person of being a principal in the second degree to an affray, they must be convinced by the evidence that, at the very least, he by some means or other encouraged the participants. To hold otherwise would be, in effect, as counsel for the appellants rightly expressed it, to convict a man on his thoughts, unaccompanied by any physical act other than the fact of his mere presence."

---

[46] In fact, at common law the main difference between abetting and counselling was merely the timing of the encouragement. If it occurred prior to the crime, S would be an "accessory before the fact" (counsellor or procurer) rather than a "principal in the second degree" (abettor or aider). See, e.g., the discussion in *A-G v. Able* [1984] QB 795, 809.

[47] *Royce* (1767) 4 Burr 2073, 2082, 98 ER 81, 86.

[48] (1882) 8 QBD 534.

[49] *Ibid.*, 544 (dissenting).

[50] *Coney* (1882) 8 QBD 534; *Young* (1838) 8 C & P 644, 173 ER 655; *Atkinson* (1869) 11 Cox CC 330; below, §§ 7.4(ii), (iii).

[51] [1971] 3 All ER 344.

[52] *Ibid.*, 347A.

[53] *Ibid.*, 348.

[54] [1965] 1 QB 130, 138.

In practice, therefore, the inference of encouragement will usually require something further, such as proof of some additional action by S (e.g. words or gestures) or of a particular circumstance that implies support,[55] for example that P and S are members of the same gang or that S's presence is pursuant to some prior arrangement.[56] Alternatively, it may be sufficient that S is part of a group offering encouragement, and that P is aware of the group's behaviour, albeit unaware of S's individual conduct.[57]

By contrast with aid, which can be rendered to P without P's knowledge (above, § 7.4(i)(a)), it is essential that the encouragement be communicated successfully to P. There cannot be "encouragement in fact" by S unless P knows of it. Suppose, for example, that S knows P intends to commit a robbery. S posts a letter to P in which she encourages P to commit the robbery, but the letter is never delivered. On these facts alone, S cannot be a party to the robbery because her encouragement, although offered, is not received by P.

This point, which applies also to incitement and counselling, is considered further below (§ 7.4(ii)). But it is important to emphasise that the requirement, that S's encouragement be communicated to P, is not a requirement that the encouragement had any effect upon P, by inducing him to commit the offence. It is unnecessary to show that P would not have offended but for the encouragement, or even that P was in any way influenced by it. P must be aware of his being encouraged (the encouragement must be communicated), but it need not make a difference.[58]

(c) Counselling

"Counselling" has two varieties of meaning. First, it includes the provision of advice or information,[59] though such conduct may also amount to aiding or abetting.[60] Alternatively, counselling may contemplate "urging" someone to commit an offence[61]—in which sense the overlap is with abetting and, to a lesser extent, procuring. In this second context, counselling may also constitute the inchoate offence of incitement (below, § 9.1).

(d) Procuring

By contrast with the other varieties of secondary participation, procurement of an offence requires that the secondary party deliberately *induces* or *influences* the principal to commit the offence. Therefore the requisite connection between S and commission of the offence must be rather stronger than for aiding, abetting, or counselling. By contrast with those other terms, which require only that S play some part in the crime:[62]

---

[55] See also *Wilcox* v. *Jeffery* [1951] 1 All ER 464, where S attended a concert by Coleman Hawkins in his capacity as a jazz critic and, further, paid a fee to attend. The concert was unlawful since Hawkins was an American who did not have a work permit. S was held to have abetted P's contravention of the Aliens Order 1920: "his presence and his payment to go there was an encouragement" (at 466 *per* Lord Goddard CJ).

[56] E.g. *Smith* v. *Reynolds* [1986] Crim LR 559 (presence pursuant to a prior agreement).

[57] Cf. *Coney* (1882) 8 QBD 534.

[58] Cf. *Wilcox* v. *Jeffery* [1951] 1 All ER 464.

[59] A classic example is *Baker* (1909) 28 NZLR 536, where S wrote to P with advice how to break into a safe using explosives. The case is criticised by Williams, *CLGP* §125, but only on the issue of mens rea.

[60] Cf. *A-G* v. *Able* [1985] QB 795, 809, where it was noted that "[i]gnorance how to commit suicide must by itself be a deterrent. . . . The contents of the booklet provide information as to methods which are less likely to result in an unsuccessful attempt. This assistance must encourage some readers to commit or attempt to commit suicide."

[61] *Calhaem* [1985] QB 808; cf. *Stuart* v. *R.* (1976) 134 CLR 426.

[62] *A-G's Reference (No. 1 of 1975)* [1975] QB 773. See also *Millward* [1994] Crim LR 527; *Beck* [1985] 1 WLR 22; *Reed* [1982] Crim LR 819; *Broadfoot* [1976] 3 All ER 753; *Bryce* [2004] EWCA Crim 1231.

"To procure means to produce by endeavour. You procure a thing by setting out to see that it happens and taking the appropriate steps to produce that happening."

Thus the perpetration of the principal crime must in some sense be a consequence of the procurement by S.[63] However, S's contribution need not be a decisive, or *sine qua non* ingredient of the decision by P to commit the offence: it is enough that the procurement was influential. Even if there were other reasons why, without S's contribution, P might have chosen to commit the offence anyway, that does not matter. Provided that S's conduct in fact played some part in influencing P, S will be guilty of procurement.[64]

Normally, procurement by S will take the form of persuasion, inducement, or threats. Sometimes, however, the causation element of a procurement may operate without influencing P's reasons; indeed, P may be entirely ignorant of S's role. In cases where an offence can be committed without mens rea, and the innocent agent doctrine does not apply,[65] S may become a secondary party to an offence by causing P to commit it. In *A-G's Reference (No. 1 of 1975)*[66] S secretly laced the drinks of P, who was subsequently convicted of driving with excess alcohol (a strict liability offence). S was guilty of procuring the offence.

(ii) The need for a connection

Secondary liability is derived from S's *involvement* in the principal offence, and not merely her attempt to become involved. It follows that S's conduct must somehow be connected to the commission of the offence by P. As we have seen, in the case of aiding this requirement is manifested by the need to demonstrate that assistance of some sort *was in fact* provided to P; similarly, in the case of procuring, it is reflected in the need to show a link of influence or inducement between S's conduct and perpetration of the offence. The same is true for abetting and counselling. Although causation need not be shown, it must be established by the prosecution that the principal *received* encouragement, urging, or advice, before S's conduct may count as participation falling within section 8.[67]

This point is fundamental to the nature of secondary participation. Derivative liability is *not* a form of inchoate liability. Liability is not based on S's act of encouragement (for example) *per se*, as it is in inchoate offences such as incitement. Rather, it is derived from S's *participation in* the offence perpetrated by P. If P is not aware of the encouragement, urging, or advice, S necessarily fails to participate in the commission of the offence. In such a case, S cannot be a party to its commission.

---

[63] See the summary by Smith, "Aid, Abet, Counsel, or Procure" in Glazebrook (ed.), *Reshaping the Criminal Law* (1978) 120, 134.

[64] For a civil law illustration see *Barton* v. *Armstrong* [1976] AC 104, 121 (execution of deed voidable for duress, even though P had other reasons to execute the deed apart from D's threat): "the illegitimate means used was a reason (not the reason, nor the predominant reason nor the clinching reason) why the complainant acted as he did. We are also prepared to accept that a decisive answer is not obtainable by asking the question whether the contract would have been made even if there had been no threats because, even if the answer to this question is affirmative, that does not prove that the contract was not made because of the threats."

[65] Above, § 7.3(i).

[66] [1975] QB 773. The decision has considerable untapped potential for the liability of hosts and publicans: see below, § 7.4(iv)(a).

[67] *Clarkson* [1971] 3 All ER 344 (abetting); *Calhaem* [1985] QB 808 (counselling). Cf. Smith, "Aid, Abet, Counsel, or Procure" in Glazebrook (ed.), *Reshaping the Criminal Law* (1978) 120, 131–4.

The result is the same if the encouragement was so long ago that P has forgotten about it by the time she resolves to commit the offence, in which case S will not be a party to the offence.[68] This type of "forgotten advice" case is covered by a further *connection-based* requirement, suggested in the extraordinary case of *Calhaem*:[69] P must not only be aware of S's encouragement (for example), but he must also act in accordance with, or within the scope of, the endorsement provided by S's encouragement. The Court of Appeal provided the following illustration:[70]

> "For example, if the principal offender happened to be involved in a football riot in the course of which he laid about him with a weapon of some sort and killed someone who, unknown to him, was the person whom he had been counselled to kill, he would not, in our view, have been acting within the scope of his authority; he would have been acting outside it, albeit what he had done was what he had been counselled to do."

This is not to require that the encouragement, counselling, etc., actually "made a difference" in influencing P to commit the offence. As Woolf J stated in *A-G v. Able*, "it does not make any difference that the person [counselled] would have tried to commit suicide anyway."[71] P must have received and been aware of, say, encouragement by S, but the encouragement need not have played any further role.

(iii) Omissions

S may aid or abet an offence by omission. Most obviously, this may occur where S's failure to discharge a legal duty assists P to commit an offence: for example, when the security guard at a warehouse deliberately fails to lock a door, intending that P may readily gain entry into the building and steal some of the goods stored inside.

Rather more problematic are cases where a person is held liable as a party for omitting to interfere and prevent an offence when she has a duty to do so and/or a power of control over the principal or the victim. Standard examples of this variety of abetment are said to occur if a parent permits another to commit an offence against her child, or if the owner of a car, while sitting in the passenger seat, permits the driver to break the law. However, these are not the same type of case.

Consider, first, the case where S, a parent, permits another to inflict fatal injuries upon his child when he is in a position to prevent the assault from taking place. It is sometimes suggested that such a person would be party to a culpable homicide if, by not intervening, S encouraged (and—the mens rea element—intended to encourage) the principal offender.[72] As far as secondary liability is concerned, this seems to understate the position. It is

---

[68] Cf. *A-G v. Able* [1984] 1 QB 795.

[69] [1985] QB 808. S had hired P to murder her rival V. It was said that P, after having second thoughts, had decided not to kill V but went to V's house in order to act out a pretence so that both S and V would think an attempt had been made to kill V. However, after V screamed, P apparently went "berserk" and killed V by hitting her several times with a hammer. On these facts, the Court of Appeal upheld S's conviction for counselling murder.

[70] *Ibid.*, 813.

[71] *A-G v. Able* [1984] 1 QB 795, 812.

[72] E.g. *Foreman and Ford* [1988] Crim LR 677 (police officer); *Witika* (1991) 7 CRNZ 621(CA); *Nixon* (1990) 57 CCC (3d) 97, 109–110; cf. *Witika* [1993] 2 NZLR 424 (CA). For discussion, see Finn, "Culpable Non-Intervention: Reconsidering the Basis for Party Liability by Omission" (1994) 18 *Crim LJ* 90.

submitted that where S has a legal duty and the present ability to prevent V's death, his failure to do so, *in itself*, constitutes *aiding*, and not merely evidence of encouragement.[73] The case is analogous to that of the warehouse security guard (above); in both examples, the conduct would be aiding whether or not P knew of the decision by S to refrain from performing his duty.[74]

Indeed, arguably S is not merely a secondary party; he may be independently guilty as a principal. Provided his intervention would have been causally efficacious in preventing the actus reus from occurring, it seems open to conclude that death results from his culpable failure to discharge his duty as a parent to intervene,[75] in which case this is a plain case of direct liability for murder or manslaughter resulting from his omission to perform a legal duty.[76]

At the other end of the scale is the case where S, a stranger, chances upon the commission of a crime and remains to watch. As we have noted already, such facts by themselves are insufficient to make S a party to the crime. This point is illustrated by *Clarkson*,[77] which was discussed in § 7.4(i)(b). Two soldiers entered a room where a rape was taking place. They stayed to observe the events, purportedly without either encouraging or discouraging commission of the offence. The Court of Appeal quashed their convictions for aiding and abetting. In the absence of actual and intended encouragement, their failure to intervene attracted no criminal liability, since they were under no duty to intervene.

The difficult case arises when S is not under a duty but has a specific legal power to control P's activity. Consider the facts of *Du Cros* v. *Lambourne*.[78] S was the owner of a car that had been driven dangerously, but it was not clear whether S or his companion, P, was driving at the time. Nonetheless, S was convicted of being a party to dangerous driving, it being irrelevant whether he was principal or abettor. If P was driving, S had the legal power as owner to direct the manner in which P drove; his acquiescence in the manner of P's driving was therefore held to constitute abetment of the offence of dangerous driving.

Du Cros v. *Lambourne* is generally taken as authority that failure by S to exercise a legal *power* (not duty) of control over P's activity may be, without more, constitutive of secondary participation in crime.[79] In other words, there is no need to show that S's non-intervention actually assisted or encouraged P. However, the judgments in that case are in fact equivocal on the point.[80] Moreover, in *Cassady* v. *Reg. Morris Transport Ltd* it was held

---

[73] This appears to be the analysis in *Russell* [1933] VLR 59, 66 (Cussen ACJ), 76 (Mann J) (Vic SC); *Popen* (1981) 60 CCC (2d) 232 (Ont CA). Cf. *Rubie* v. *Faulkner* [1940] 1 KB 571; *Russell and Russell* (1987) 85 Cr App R 388.

[74] Although in *Russell* [1933] VLR 59, 67, Cussen ACJ suggests the spouse must have known of S's acquiescence. R's wife drowned herself and their sons in R's presence, wherefore R was convicted of manslaughter. See above, § 4.1(i)(b) (Case 2).

[75] This would require analysis of the case as involving concurrent causes (i.e. P's action and S's omission), rather than a novus actus by P. Yet such an approach seems plausible, provided that S is able to prevent P's conduct.

[76] See the judgment of McArthur J in *Russell* [1933] VLR 59. The existence of such a duty is discussed above, § 4.1(i)(b) (Case 2).

[77] [1971] 3 All ER 344.

[78] [1907] 1 KB 40. See generally on this topic Smith, *A Modern Treatise on the Law of Criminal Complicity* (1991) 39ff.

[79] See, e.g., *Webster* [2006] EWCA Crim 415, para. [28].

[80] Darling J appears to have regarded non-intervention as abetment *per se* ([1907] 1 KB 40, 46–7); Lord Alverstone CJ, with whom Ridley J agreed, refused to "attempt to lay down any general rule or principle, but having regard to these findings of fact, it is, in my opinion, impossible to say that there was in this case no evidence of aiding and abetting" (at 46).

that an employer's failure to forbid an offence by its employee was merely *evidence* (and not constitutive) of encouragement.[81] Thus it remains open for a defendant to argue that where D has a mere power, not only must there be a failure to intervene, but the non-intervention must in fact encourage (and be intended to encourage) P in her commission of the offence.

In any event, the gulf between specific power and duty is easily bridged. Where S has a supervisory role, e.g. as the instructor of a learner-driver, it seems clear that a mere omission to intervene is sufficient to establish liability as a secondary party, and that the instructor is under a *duty* (and does not merely have a right) to intervene and prevent a dangerous manoeuvre by the learner-driver.[82] And in *Tuck* v. *Robson*,[83] a public house licensee was held to have assisted others in drinking after hours through "passive assistance", which the Court defined as "presence with no steps being taken to enforce his right either to eject the customers or at any rate to revoke their licence to be on the premises."[84] The decision is problematic: although the Court relied upon the publican's "right" (i.e. power) and did not use the language of duties, the decision effectively imposes a duty on the publican to revoke his customers' licence. Seemingly, that duty rests on nothing other than the existence of a corresponding power.

In light of these cases, it appears that the current law regarding omissions is as follows:

(i)   If S has a *legal duty* to prevent an offence (e.g. in the case of a parent to protect his child), then a failure by S to take reasonable steps to intervene *in itself* constitutes the actus reus of aiding and abetting. (Indeed, if causation can be established, S may be guilty as a principal.)

(ii) If S has neither a duty nor a particular power, then he must intend by his non-intervention to encourage P, and, in fact, his inaction must also encourage P.

(iii) If S has a power of control over P, but no particular legal duty, it seems that the position is the same as in (i): a failure by S to take reasonable steps to intervene *in itself* constitutes the actus reus of aiding and abetting.

Alternatively, if *Cassady* v. *Reg. Morris Transport Ltd* is right, the position of those such as the owner-passenger in (iii) is identical to that in (ii), i.e. he is in the same legal position as the onlookers to the rape in *Clarkson*, or the casual spectators at the prize-fight in *Coney*.[85]

There are arguments in favour of *Cassady*. To impose liability in such cases is, effectively, to extend criminal liability for omissions. As we saw in § 4.1, the law is reluctant to impose liability for omissions, and for good reason. Forcing persons to intervene and regulate the actions of others (e.g. requiring property-owners to police the actions of users) substantially widens the umbrella of criminal responsibility for wrongdoing and, in turn, risks intruding severely upon the autonomy of citizens.[86] This point is particularly significant when one

---

[81] [1975] RTR 470. Cf. *Duxley* v. *Gilmore* (1959) 123 JP 331, but contrast *Ferguson* v. *Weaving* [1951] 1 KB 814, 819; *Thomas* v. *Lindop* [1950] 1 All ER 966, 968.

[82] *Rubie* v. *Faulkner* [1940] 1 KB 571, 575: "[f]or him to refrain from doing anything when he could see that an unlawful act was about to be done, and his duty was to prevent an unlawful act if he could, was for him to aid and abet." See also *Harris* [1964] Crim LR 54; Wasik, "A Learner's Careless Driving" [1982] *Crim LR* 411; Lanham, "Drivers, Control, and Accomplices" [1982] *Crim LR* 419.

[83] [1970] 1 All ER 1171.

[84] *Ibid.*, 1175.

[85] (1882) 8 QBD 534; above, § 7.4(i)(b).

[86] For elaboration of this argument, see above, §§ 4.1(i)(a), 1.2(i)(b), 1.2(ii)(e). See also Bronitt, "Defending *Giorgianni*—Part Two: New Solutions for Old Problems in Complicity" (1993) 17 *Crim LJ* 305, 310–11.

takes into account the fact that *everyone* has a power to control the criminal activities of others, by virtue of section 3(1) of the Criminal Law Act 1967.[87] If a mere power were sufficient to make S an accomplice, then anyone, stranger or friend, who is in position to intervene to prevent a crime would become an accessory to that crime. *That, surely, cannot be allowed*, since it would entirely subvert the policy of the law against generally criminalising omissions.

On the other hand, in the difficult case, S is not a mere stranger, a passer-by who stumbles upon a crime that she is under no duty to prevent. An important distinction can be drawn between the background general power to prevent crimes, under section 3(1) of the Criminal Law Act 1967, and the more specific powers of control at issue in cases such as *Du Cros v. Lambourne*: it is only in the latter cases that S is entitled to control P's activity *whether or not* an offence is being committed. Although there is no general obligation to prevent crime,[88] it seems reasonable to conclude that those with specific legal powers to prevent a crime *do* contribute to—hence, participate in—the wrongdoing by refraining from exercising their authority and, thus, deliberately permitting that crime to occur.

As with active forms of secondary participation, the omission to intervene must occur at a time when S also has the requisite mens rea—i.e., as we see below, knowledge of the essential matters of P's crime. In the specific context of omissions, however, it is worth noting that the courts have emphasised that S's knowledge must arise at a point when she has an opportunity to intervene. Mere knowledge of P's misconduct is not enough if it is too late for S to prevent it.[89]

(iv) Mens rea for participation by assistance or encouragement

The mens rea for secondary participation (by aiding, abetting, counseling, or procuring[90]) is intention: S must intend to participate in the crime committed by P.[91] Stated in this way, the fault element appears straightforward. However, it is in fact quite complex, because the mens rea element must relate to two different matters: S's own conduct, in assisting or encouraging P, and the fact that P's actions are criminal in nature. We may summarise the mens rea requirement as follows:

(i) S must intend his own contribution (i.e. to aid, abet, counsel, or procure P); and

(ii) S must appreciate the nature of P's actions. That is, S must know or foresee the "essential matters" relating to P's actions which make those actions an offence.

(a) S's own contribution: the intention to aid, abet, counsel or procure

Although section 8 itself is silent on the question of mens rea, it is clear that the essence of aiding and abetting is intentional help or encouragement. This means that not only must S

---

[87] "A person may use such force as is reasonable in the circumstances in the prevention of crime, or in effecting or assisting in the lawful arrest of offenders or suspected offenders or of persons unlawfully at large."

[88] Cf. *Allan* [1965] 1 QB 130.

[89] *Dennis v. Pite* [1968] 11 FLR 458; cf. *Webster* [2006] EWCA Crim 415, para. 28.

[90] For the mens rea requirements of participation by joint enterprise see below, § 7.5(iii).

[91] See generally Dennis, "The Mental Element for Accessories" in P. Smith (ed.), *Criminal Law: Essays in Honour of J.C. Smith* (1987) 40; K. J. M. Smith, *A Modern Treatise on Criminal Complicity* (1991) part II; Sullivan, "Intent, Purpose and Complicity" [1988] *Crim LR* 641; Dennis, "Intention and Complicity: A Reply" [1988] *Crim LR* 649.

intend her actions, but she must also act with the intent thereby to aid, abet, counsel, or procure P's conduct.

The criteria of intention are considered above, in § 5.1. In the context of secondary parties, there is no requirement for S to desire that P commit the offence she aids (abets, etc.). It is the *assistance* or the *encouragement*, not the ultimate crime, that must be intended by S.[92] Consider, for example, the following facts, which are based on *Cafferata* v. *Wilson*:[93]

> Stephen is a firearms wholesaler. He sells a firearm to Pamela, a general shopkeeper. Stephen knows that Pamela will re-sell the firearm in her shop, and that Pamela does not have a license to deal in firearms. Stephen does not sell the firearm to Pamela because he wants her to resell it, but rather because he wants the money that Pamela is prepared to pay for it.

The claim that Stephen does not want or intend Pamela to resell the firearm is irrelevant. It may be characterised as a claim about Stephen's motive, or ultimate purpose, which is of course to make money. But what matters is whether he intended to assist Pamela. The answer to that question is, yes: Stephen intended to provide Pamela with an ingredient essential to the selling of a firearm. It is this facilitation, not the ultimate offence, that must be intended; whether that aid is itself rendered for the further purpose of bringing about the offence is simply beside the point. Indeed, any requirement that the *offence* must be intended would deprive secondary liability of much of its current scope.

On the other hand, the help must be *intended*. Recklessness is insufficient.[94] Thus it would not be enough for secondary liability that S merely thinks it is likely P may be assisted. Suppose, for example, the following variation:

> Susan is an auctioneer of various goods. She sells an unlabelled box of goods to Peter, a wholesaler. Because the goods are in bond, she is unsure (i.e. reckless) whether the goods are toy pistols or real guns. Susan knows that Peter does not have a license to deal in firearms.

On these facts, Susan lacks the mens rea for secondary participation because she is merely reckless whether Peter is assisted or encouraged.

S's own contribution: the intention to procure.
In respect of S's intending her own contribution, procurement is a special case. By contrast with assistance and encouragement, the connection is necessarily tighter. S must still be proved to have intended her act of procurement. However, because procurement requires a causal contribution that influences or induces P to commit the crime, it follows that S must

---

[92] See *Bryce* [2004] EWCA Crim 1231 at [61], citing this proposition from the first edition. Cf. *National Coal Board* v. *Gamble* [1959] 1 QB 11, 23; *Lynch* v. *DPP for Northern Ireland* [1975] AC 653, 678; *A-G* v. *Able* [1984] 1 QB 795; *Clarke* (1984) 80 Cr App R 344. Note that the connection is necessarily tighter in cases of participation by procurement. S must similarly be proved to have intended his act of procurement; however, because procurement requires a causal contribution that influences or induces P to commit the crime, it follows that S must intend to help bring it about that P will commit the crime itself. For this reason, it was said in *A-G's Reference (No. 1 of 1975)* [1975] QB 773, 779 that, by contrast with aiding, abetting, or counseling, procuring an offence requires an "endeavour" or "setting out" to cause the commission of the offence.

[93] [1936] 3 All ER 149.

[94] *Scott* (1978) 68 Cr App R 164 (suspicion not enough).

intend to help bring it about that P will commit the crime itself. For this reason, it was said by the Court of Appeal in *A-G's Reference (No. 1 of 1975)*[95] that, unlike aiding, abetting, inciting, or counselling, procuring an offence requires an "endeavour" or "setting out" to cause the commission of the offence.

An exception for duress or necessity?

Suppose that S aids P out of some further reason such as fear. This may, of course, give rise to a supervening defence of duress or necessity. Sometimes, however, the courts have treated such circumstances as vitiating S's intent to aid. In *Gillick*,[96] the House of Lords appeared to hold that a doctor who gives contraceptive advice or treatment to a girl aged under 16 years, for clinical reasons, while recognising that this would facilitate acts of unlawful sexual intercourse, would lack the intent to aid and abet unlawful sexual intercourse. Similarly, in *Fretwell*[97] S reluctantly supplied an abortifacient to a woman who had threatened to kill herself should S not do so. Although S hoped P would not take the drug, she did so and died. S was held not liable for murder as an accessory (to the crime of *felo de se*, or "self-murder") because he was "unwilling that the woman should take the poison."[98]

The analysis in these decisions is understandable—Fretwell, in particular, faced the death penalty—but problematic. Notwithstanding the language of the judgments, in both cases the aid *is* intended by S. Like the example of Susan and Peter above, in both *Fretwell* and *Gillick* S may hope that P will not ultimately engage in the criminal conduct. Nonetheless, S's own help is intended: it is reluctant, justified, and deliberate. Moreover, as we have seen, the benevolent further purpose of S is irrelevant to the question whether S has mens rea. Contrast the analysis in *Lynch* v. *DPP for Northern Ireland* where, under duress, S drove P to a garage where P planned to murder a policeman. According to Lord Morris:[99]

> "If in the present case the jury were satisfied that the car was driven towards the garage in pursuance of a murderous plan and that the appellant knew that was the plan and intentionally drove the car in execution of that plan he could be held to have aided and abetted even though he regretted the plan or indeed was horrified by it."

The better approach in cases such as *Fretwell* and *Lynch* is to accept that S has the mens rea to aid and abet, but to allow S a defence based on duress or necessity. This is precisely the view taken by Lord Morris in *Lynch*. His Lordship continued:[100]

---

[95] [1975] QB 773, 779 (CA).

[96] *Gillick* v. *West Norfolk and Wisbech Area Health Authority* [1986] AC 112 (HL), adopting Woolf J's views on the criminal law aspects of the case (which was brought as a civil action for a declaration) at [1984] QB 581, 589 (QBD). Cf. *Janaway* v. *Salford Health Authority* [1989] AC 537, 550–1 (Slade LJ), 558 (Stocker LJ), CA; contrast at 572 (Lord Keith), 572–3 (Lord Lowry), HL. For general discussion, see Ashworth, "Criminal Liability in a Medical Context: The Treatment of Good Intentions" in Simester and Smith (eds.), *Harm and Culpability* (1996) 173; J.C. Smith, *Justification and Excuse in the Criminal Law* (1989) 64–70; Spencer, "Trying to Help Another Person Commit a Crime" in P. Smith (ed.), *Criminal Law: Essays in Honour of J.C. Smith* (1987) 148.

[97] (1862) Le & Ca 161, 169 ER 1345. *Per* Woolf J, in *A-G* v. *Able* [1984] 1 QB 795, *Fretwell* should be regarded as "confined to its own facts."

[98] (1862) Le & Ca 161, 164, 169 ER 1345, 1346.

[99] [1975] AC 653, 678.

[100] *Ibid.* Cf. *Hibbert* (1995) 99 CCC (3d) 193. Note that duress is no longer available as a defence to participation in murder: below, § 20.1(i)(d).

"But if that intention and all that he did only came about because of the compulsion of duress of the nature that I have described he would, in my view, have a defence."

The decisions in *Fretwell* and *Gillick* were constrained from taking such an enlightened approach by the fact that, at the time, it was thought that the defences of duress and necessity did not cover those cases.[101] It is to be hoped that the fiction of denying an intent by S will not be required in future and that, in particular, the scope of the necessity defence will ultimately be accepted as embracing such instances of *bona fide* medical treatment.

An exception for performance of a duty?

Consider the following facts, which occurred in *National Coal Board* v. *Gamble*:[102]

> S (the National Coal Board) sold P's employer a large quantity of coal. P, a lorry driver, was despatched to collect some of the coal. Once loaded, the lorry was weighed before leaving the colliery. S's employee, the weighbridge clerk, realised the load exceeded that permitted to be carried on the highway. He drew P's attention to the illegality. P said that he was prepared to take the risk of being caught, whereupon the clerk issued P with a weighbridge ticket. The weighbridge clerk's function in issuing the ticket to P was to record how much coal had been taken, in order that S could then charge the buyer for that amount of coal, and also to pass title in the coal to the buyer.

On these facts, it was held by a majority of the Divisional Court[103] that S, through its servant, was an accessory to the offence committed by P. In handing over the ticket and passing title to the coal, S aided P by enabling the lorry to depart from the colliery with the coal (and thereby to commit an offence). The fact that the clerk was motivated only by considerations of accounting was irrelevant to the question whether he intended that aid.

In the majority judgments, a great deal was made of the fact that ownership of the coal had not passed before the clerk handed over the weighbridge ticket. Implicit in this is the proposition that if P already owns some item possessed by S, then by handing the item over S merely performs her legal duty to deliver up possession to P; she does not aid or abet P to commit an offence with that item. Regard the facts of *Lomas*:[104]

> S has possession of a jemmy, which she borrowed from P. S knows that P is a professional burglar. P asks for return of the jemmy and S gives it to him. P then uses the jemmy to commit a burglary.

S was held not to be a party to P's crime. Properly so, observed Devlin J in *NCB* v. *Gamble*:[105]

> "In a sense a man who gives up to a criminal a weapon which the latter has a right to demand from him aids in the commission of the crime as much as if he sold or lent the article, but this has never been held to be aiding in law. . . . In the transfer of property there must be either a physical delivery or a positive act of assent to a taking. But a man who hands over to

---

[101] For discussion of the current scope of these defences, see below, §§ 20.1, 21.3.

[102] [1959] 1 QB 11. See Duff, "'Can I Help You?' Accessorial Liability and the Intention to Assist" (1990) 10 *LS* 165; Williams, "Complicity, Purpose and the Draft Code" [1990] *Crim LR* 4.

[103] Lord Goddard CJ and Devlin J, Slade J dissenting.

[104] (1913) 9 Cr App R 220; discussed in *Bullock* [1955] 1 All ER 15.

[105] [1959] 1 QB 11, 20.

another his own property on demand, although he may physically be performing a positive act, in law is only refraining from detinue. Thus in law the former act is one of assistance voluntarily given and the latter is only a failure to prevent the commission of a crime by means of forcible detention."

By contrast, the act of a shopkeeper who knows P's criminal purpose before selling P the jemmy would be an act "of assistance voluntarily given":[106]

"If one man deliberately sells to another a gun to be used for murdering a third, he may be indifferent about whether the third man lives or dies and interested only in the cash profit to be made out of the sale, but he can still be an aider and abettor. To hold otherwise would be to negative the rule that mens rea is a matter of intent only and does not depend on desire or motive."

Prima facie, then, the law after *NCB* v. *Gamble* is as follows. S intentionally aids P to commit a crime when he intentionally provides material assistance (e.g. by handing over an instrument of burglary), *except* when P has a legal right to receive that assistance from S and S renders the assistance only because he owes a legal duty to do so.

Unfortunately, this summary of the law involves a false distinction. The underlying rationale identified by Devlin J is spurious. Whether or not P owns the jemmy, he is aided when S gives it to him, because he now has possession when before he did not. In both cases (i.e. owned and unowned), the aid itself is intended. The fact that the jemmy belongs to P is relevant, once again, only to motive.

Neither does P's ownership establish a legal duty on S to hand over the jemmy. While there is normally a civil law duty on bailees-at-will to return borrowed property upon demand, it is defeated by the duty not to commit a crime. Just as it is "incumbent on a court of equity to act by such rule as tends most to discountenance the crime,"[107] so it is that the rules of the civil law must always be subject to exception whenever they would tend to undermine the criminal law. This point was recognised by Parker LCJ in *Garrett* v. *Arthur Churchill (Glass) Ltd*:[108]

"albeit there was a legal duty in ordinary circumstances to hand over the goblet to the owners once the agency was determined, I do not think that an action would lie for breach of that duty if the handing over would constitute the offence of being knowingly concerned in its exportation."

The inevitable conclusion must be that, in terms of legal principle, ownership makes no difference. Assuming in each case that S knows the essential matters of P's offence, there is no distinction to be drawn between the situation in *Lomas* and that in *NCB* v. *Gamble*. Both cases, moreover, are inseparable from the case of a shopkeeper who sells a jemmy to P knowing his purpose. Notwithstanding the distinction laid down in *NCB* v. *Gamble*, in principle all three situations ought to result in the same outcome: the conviction of S.

---

[106] [1959] 1 QB 11, 23.

[107] *Bridgman* v. *Green* (1855) 2 Ves Sen 627, 628, 28 ER 399. Cf. *Amicable Society* v. *Bolland* (1830) 4 Bligh (NS) 194, 211, 5 ER 70; *Re Estate of Crippen, decd.* [1911] P 108, 112; Smith, "Civil Law Concepts in the Criminal Law" [1972B] *CLJ* 197, 208–11.

[108] [1970] 1 QB 92, 99.

Civil liberties and the interests of victims.

Accordingly, liability for complicity is a real possibility for persons who are merely performing the routines of their jobs or trades. Given this possibility, it is important to consider whether, morally speaking, an exception *ought* to be allowed in such cases as those of the weighbridge clerk, the bailee, and/or the shopkeeper? Williams argues that, at least in the case of the shopkeeper, there should be an exception:[109]

> "From the point of view of policy the question is one of some complexity. On the one side are the policy of repressing crime, and the difficulty of distinguishing between the merchant who knowingly assists a crime and the ordinary accessory before the fact. On the other side stand the undesirability of giving too great an extension to the criminal law, and the inconvenience to legitimate trade of requiring a merchant to concern himself with the affairs of his custom- ers. . . . It is submitted that . . . the seller of an ordinary marketable commodity is not his buyer's keeper in criminal law unless he is specifically made so by statute. Any other rule would be too wide an extension of criminal responsibility."

Williams suggests that the exception should be confined to sellers of "an ordinary marketable commodity." Some American states have a general exception for shopkeepers, provided it is not the *purpose* of the seller to assist the buyer's offence.[110] In respect of bailment cases like *Lomas*, a further possibility would be to create an exception covering those who return property to its owner, provided that it is not S's purpose thereby to assist the owner to commit a crime, and that the contemplated crime is not a serious one (say, a crime triable only on indictment).[111]

In our view, the criminal law should take priority over the civil law in this matter. Sometimes, where criminal and civil law overlap, the criminal law must perforce follow the civil law, e.g. where it is the civil law that defines the relevant harm. An example is the law of theft; where property rights, the interests being safeguarded by the criminal law, are a creature of civil law.[112] But complicity is not like theft. When S hands P a weapon, P is aided, and the victim's rights are put at risk, equally *whoever* of them owns it.

The argument against our view is a strong one. Williams highlights the inconvenience to shopkeepers if they are required to concern themselves with the affairs of their customers. A similar point may be made regarding ordinary citizens who return the belongings of others. It is important that persons engaging in ordinary activities should be able to perform those activities—i.e. to live their lives—without being harassed by the criminal law; especially if the harassment requires them to modify their own activities because of the plans and conduct of others, and not because of anything they have done themselves. It is significant that the duty not to help P arises out of P's intentions, and not from S's conduct or plans. Thus, as Williams objects (in the context of the weighbridge operator's case):[113]

> "It seems a strong thing to hold that a man who is simply pursuing his ordinary and lawful vocation, and takes no special steps to assist illegalities, becomes involved as a third party to a

---

[109] *CLGP* § 124.

[110] Cf. Model Penal Code, § 2.06(3).

[111] Williams, "Obedience to Law as a Crime" (1990) 53 *MLR* 445; Sullivan, "The Law Commission Consultation Paper on Complicity: Fault Elements and Joint Enterprise" [1994] *Crim LR* 252.

[112] For discussion of this proposition, and of derogations from it by the courts, see below, Chapter 13.

[113] *TBCL* 342.

crime committed by the customer merely because he realises that his customer will be enabled by what he himself does to commit a crime."

Consider also the case of *A-G's Reference (No. 1 of 1975)*,[114] mentioned earlier, in which S was convicted of procuring P to drive with excess alcohol after secretly lacing P's drinks. Although P was ignorant of S's actions in that case, one possible implication of the decision is that publicans—and indeed, generous hosts at a dinner party—could be regarded as aiding and abetting whenever their customers or guests then drive home drunk.[115] Williams's objection may be extended to these cases too, and one should hesitate before allowing the criminal law to reach so far into the ordinary commercial and private activities of citizens.

Nonetheless, while Williams's reasoning is powerful, it is not in our view conclusive. These are not cases where S stands by passively and omits to prevent P's crime. S *actively and intentionally helps* P to commit that crime. Indeed, S's aid may even be an indispensable feature of P's wrongdoing.[116] The rights of victims not to be burgled, assaulted, etc., mean that it is sometimes necessary to curtail the liberty of citizens to intervene and assist criminals, as well as the liberty of shopkeepers to sell goods to anyone at will. Those rights should prevail here. Moreover, the intrusive implications of this position for the lives of citizens are not as great as they may seem. S's duty is not to refuse aid to those suspected of having a criminal purpose; as will be seen below, the duty arises only if S *knows or foresees* that a crime will be committed.[117] Thus S is not required to police the actions of P. She does not have to enquire into P's purpose; neither must she take active steps, either to stop P or to inform the police. She is simply not free to assist P deliberately when she realises that P plans to commit a crime.

There is room for compromise, one which balances individual liberty against the need to prevent crime. The potential intrusiveness of criminal liability for ordinary activities—including the activities of bailees otherwise mandated by the civil law—would be reduced by excluding party liability for persons who assist or encourage summary offences.[118] A similar step has already been taken in respect of attempts liability,[119] and there seems little reason not to carry the logic over to complicity. Apart from fostering individual autonomy, such a move would give due recognition to the seriousness of the underlying offence and the interests being protected by that offence, while avoiding the uncertainties of a "relative seriousness" or "balance of evils" defence[120] in these difficult cases.

---

[114] [1975] QB 773; above, § 7.4(i)(d).

[115] Williams, *TBCL* 338–41. Widgery LCJ refers to the question of hosts in the case itself, and argues that they are unaffected by the decision, since where the provision of alcohol is overt rather than by lacing, guests make up their own minds whether or not to take drink—hence, no procurement by the host. Unfortunately, this reasoning is unconvincing since it applies only to the case of secondary participation by procurement; and not to aiding, abetting, or counselling, which lack a requirement of causation: above, § 7.4(i)(d).

[116] Cf. *NCB v. Gamble* [1959] 1 QB 11.

[117] For discussion of the trade-off between a stringent mens rea requirement and the reach of criminalisation, see Simester, "The Mental Element in Complicity" (2006) 122 *LQR* 578, 591–2.

[118] Cf. *TBCL* 343; Spencer, "Trying to Help Another Person Commit a Crime" in P. Smith (ed.), *Criminal Law: Essays in Honour of J.C. Smith* (1987) 148, 162.

[119] Below, § 9.3(ii)(a).

[120] Advocated by Ashworth, *Principles* 420. Cf. *NCB v. Gamble* [1959] 1 QB 11, 20 ("except in the case of a felony" *per* Devlin J).

(b) P's criminal conduct: S must have knowledge or foresight of essential matters

The classic statement of this requirement is to be found in *Johnson* v. *Youdan*, where it was said that:[121]

> "Before a person can be convicted of aiding and abetting the commission of an offence he must at least know the essential matters which constitute that offence."

Two issues arise: (i) what degree of "knowledge" must S have, and (ii) what "essential matters" of an offence must S know about?

The meaning of "knowledge" is considered earlier, in § 5.4: S must accept, or assume, and have no substantial doubt that the relevant facts are true. There must be actual knowledge: it is not enough that S *ought* to have known the facts.[122] Neither is it sufficient if S suspects that they may well be true, even if accompanied by a negligent[123] or reckless failure to enquire into the facts;[124] although in the more extreme case of wilful blindness, S will be treated as having knowledge.[125]

This analysis would exclude from liability a person who renders assistance to P believing that P may be about to commit a crime but not knowing that he will. Mere belief in the possible existence of a set of facts amounts to recklessness, not intention.[126] Consider the following variant of an example used in section § 7.4(iv)(a):

> S is a firearms wholesaler. He sells a firearm to P, a general shopkeeper. S knows that P does not have a license to deal in firearms. S does not sell the firearm to P because he wants her to resell it, but rather because he wants the money that P is prepared to pay for it. However, (this time) S is unsure whether P intends to resell the firearm in her shop or to keep the firearm for her own use. In fact, P does resell the firearm.

On these facts, S is merely reckless about the essential facts of the crime ultimately committed by P. Assuming S does not satisfy the criteria of wilful blindness,[127] he does not *know* those facts. As such, according to the criteria laid down in *Johnson* v. *Youden* (above), S is innocent of secondary participation in P's crime.

The requirement of knowledge has been adopted expressly in numerous cases,[128] and has in the past received the endorsement of the House of Lords.[129] However, it appears that the law has moved on. In its 1993 Consultation Paper on *Assisting and Encouraging Crime*, the Law Commission suggested that notwithstanding the dicta in *Johnson* v. *Youden*, whenever a case has turned on the point, recklessness has been sufficient to convict the accessory:[130]

---

[121] [1950] 1 KB 544, 546.

[122] *Webster* [2006] EWCA Crim 415, at para. 25.

[123] Cf. *Callow* v. *Tillstone* (1900) 64 JP 823.

[124] *Bainbridge* [1960] 1 QB 129, 134; *DPP for Northern Ireland* v. *Maxwell* [1978] 3 All ER 1140, 1146–8.

[125] *Antonelli* (1905) 70 JP 4. The doctrine of wilful blindness is examined above, § 5.4(i).

[126] See above, §§ 5.2(iii), 5.4.

[127] Above, § 5.4(i).

[128] E.g. *Ackroyds Air Travel Ltd* v. *DPP* [1950] 1 All ER 933; *Thomas* v. *Lindop* [1950] 1 All ER 966; *Ferguson* v. *Weaving* [1951] 1 KB 814; *Smith* v. *Jenner* [1968] Crim LR 99; *Patel* [1970] Crim LR 274. More recently, compare *Webster* [2006] EWCA Crim 415, at para. 21.

[129] *Churchill* [1967] 2 AC 224, 236–7; *Maxwell* v. *DPP for Northern Ireland* [1978] 3 All ER 1140. Cf. the decision by the High Court of Australia in *Giorgianni* v. *R.* (1984) 156 CLR 473.

[130] Consultation Paper No. 131 (1993) para. 2.58. The Law Commission's final Report prefers a requirement that S intend (directly or obliquely) that P will commit the offence: *Participating in Crime* Law Com. No. 305 (2007).

"there is no case which rejects the awareness of a mere possibility of the commission of the principal offence as a ground of accessorial liability, and at least some authority that seems to support that analysis."

One such authority appears to be *Carter* v. *Richardson*,[131] where S was supervising P, a learner driver, who was driving with excess alcohol. Even though it was impossible for S to know precisely P's blood-alcohol level, S was convicted of aiding and abetting the offence committed by P. On a case stated, the Divisional Court held that "it was sufficient if the defendant was aware that the principal offender had consumed excessive alcohol even though the precise amount had not been determined";[132] a test satisfied, Lord Widgery CJ continued, if S "*knew* that [P] had been drinking to such an extent that it was *probable* that his blood alcohol content was over the limit."[133] The first statement is unobjectionable. However, it seems that the second quotation pitches the standard lower than "knowledge" in that, prima facie, it does not require S to have a settled belief, or no substantial doubt, that P's blood alcohol content was over the limit. To the extent that this is so, the test shades into (subjective[134]) recklessness.

It is not clear that, on the facts of *Carter* v. *Richardson*, the Court needed to go so far as this. The case seems better analysed as a situation where (given, e.g., S's awareness of P's behaviour and of the amount of alcohol consumed by P) the court could readily infer from the facts of the case that S had no substantial doubt that, whatever the precise blood-alcohol measurement, it was in excess of the permitted level.[135] Nonetheless, foresight of the probable existence of the essential matters of P's crime apparently now satisfies the mens rea requirement of aiding and abetting. A similar standard is endorsed by the Court of Appeal in *Rook*,[136] where contemplation or foresight of the crime "as a real or serious risk" was said to suffice; in *Reardon*,[137] where foresight by S of the "strong possibility" of P's crime was sufficient; and in *Bryce*,[138] where (following *Rook*) a "real or substantial risk" would do. Although the (*obiter*) reasoning in those cases is open to criticism,[139] especially regarding the analogy they draw to joint enterprise liability,[140] for the moment foresight of probability seems to be enough.[141]

It is arguable, moreover, that the broadening of the law on this point is to be welcomed at the level of principle. An argument favouring this approach might be summarised as follows:

[131] [1974] RTR 314. Contrast *Tinsley* [1963] Crim LR 520.

[132] [1974] RTR 314, 318 (Lord Widgery CJ).

[133] *Ibid.* (emphasis added).

[134] Objective or *Caldwell*-recklessness is insufficient: *Blakely and Sutton* v. *DPP* [1991] RTR 405.

[135] Indeed, S had originally pretended he himself was the driver, presumably for this very reason. Cf. *Crampton* v. *Fish* [1970] Crim LR 235, where "the evidence was apparently so overwhelming that no reasonable magistrate could fail to be satisfied of the accused's knowledge."

[136] [1993] 2 All ER 955, 960.

[137] [1999] Crim LR 392 (CA).

[138] [2004] EWCA Crim 1231 at para. 71.

[139] See Simester, "The Mental Element in Complicity" (2006) 122 *LQR* 578, 583–8.

[140] Below, § 7.5.

[141] In *Webster* [2006] EWCA Crim 415, the Court of Appeal appeared not to notice the difference, concluding, in para. 26, that in order to establish S's aiding and abetting of P's dangerous driving, the prosecution must prove that S "foresaw that [P] was likely to drive in a dangerous manner"; and, in para. 29, that it must prove that S "knew that [P] was, by virtue of the speed the vehicle was travelling, driving dangerously."

Why should full knowledge be necessary for there to be an intention to help or encourage P? No doubt S should be required to know of any relevant circumstance where knowledge is required of P. But it does *not* follow that recklessness should be insufficient for S's liability when it suffices for P's. Otherwise, S would escape liability in many cases where she willingly assists P to commit a crime, and has the same mens rea (i.e. recklessness) toward that crime as has P; and there is no merit in that. Surely S has crossed the threshold justifying conviction, both in terms of her culpability and her conduct?

Despite the attractiveness of this argument, in our view the relaxation, in recent years, of the requirement for "knowledge" into one of foresight is to be regretted.[142] The basis of secondary liability is different from that of a principal. There is no suggestion that the secondary party actually commits the offence himself or that he satisfies the actus reus requirements of the relevant crime. The actus reus element of secondary participation is entirely independent of the actus reus of the principal offence. This being so, there seems no reason why the mens rea requirement for participation should be determined by that principal offence. Moreover, derivative liability of any variety involves widening the net of the criminal law beyond those who actually perpetrate offences: not only may S not strike V, she may not do anything to help anyone else strike V either.[143] Because of this widening, the grounds of derivative liability ought correspondingly to be constricted, in order to prevent excessive criminalisation of conduct that does not itself cause a criminal harm. Otherwise, over-criminalisation may lead, in turn, to a disproportionate intrusion upon the freedoms of citizens who do not themselves commit crimes, forcing them constantly to modify their own actions because of the potential conduct of others.

Strict liability offences.
One implication of the analysis above is that an intention to assist or encourage, and foresight of essential matters, is still required notwithstanding that the principal offence may be one of negligence or even strict liability. The classic authority for this proposition is *Callow v. Tillstone*.[144] In that case, P, a butcher, was convicted of the strict liability offence of exposing unsound meat for sale. P had offered the meat for sale only after asking S, a veterinary surgeon, to examine the meat and certify whether it was sound. S had performed the examination negligently, and wrongly certified the meat as sound. Despite his negligence, S's conviction for abetting the offence by P was quashed. S did not know the meat was unsound.

The result in *Callow v. Tillstone* seems odd. P, who lacked fault, was convicted while S, whose fault induced the offence, was acquitted. Once again, however, it is important to note that, unlike P, S did not commit the actus reus of any offence. (The doctrine of innocent agency was ruled out by the fact that S fell outside the class of persons who could commit that offence.) The anomalous-looking outcome in the case should be attributed not to the law governing secondary parties, but rather to the morally indefensible phenomenon of strict liability for principals.

---

[142] See Simester, "The Mental Element in Complicity" (2006) 122 *LQR* 578, 588–92.
[143] Above, § 1.2(ii)(e).
[144] (1900) 64 JP 823.

(c) P's criminal conduct: what "essential matters" must S know about?

It is also a difficult question what aspects of P's crime count as "essential matters", such that they must be foreseen by S. The following propositions may be asserted.

First, S must appreciate that P intends or contemplates doing actions which constitute the actus reus of an offence, although S need not recognise that those actions in fact constitute an offence.[145] Secondly, S need not know all the details of the proposed offence, such as the time or place of its commission.[146] However, mere knowledge that "something illegal" is intended by P is not enough. S must at least foresee either:

(i)   the *type* of offence intended (and eventually committed) by P; or

(ii) that P would commit any one of a number of offences, the "list" of which includes the type of offence that eventually was committed.

The leading cases are *Bainbridge*[147] and *Maxwell*.[148] In *Bainbridge*, S supplied oxygen-cutting equipment to P who later used it to break into the Midland Bank at Stoke Newington. S claimed that he had suspected P wanted the equipment for some illegal purpose (e.g. to break up stolen goods), but had not known it would be used to break into a bank, let alone the Midland Bank at Stoke Newington. While his claim failed on the evidence, the Court of Criminal Appeal ruled that, on those facts, S would have lacked mens rea. His knowledge that he was aiding "some illegal venture" would be insufficient:[149] he had to know what *type* of crime would be committed by P. On the other hand, S need only appreciate the type and not the details. It was sufficient that S knew P intended to break and enter, and steal. S did not have to know the particulars of the plan, e.g. that the target was a particular bank in Stoke Newington.

An example may be helpful. Suppose that S is charged with aiding and abetting a burglary.[150] S had encouraged P to steal V's wallet, but had not anticipated that P would steal the wallet from V's house. In such a case, it would be a misdirection for the trial judge to state that S need not know that P proposed to steal from the house. Trespassory entry into a building is an essential element of the offence of burglary; indeed, it is the distinguishing feature of that offence. It follows that burglary cannot be regarded as being the same *type* of offence as simple theft. S can only be convicted as a party to burglary if, as well as foreseeing that P contemplated a theft, he also realised that P contemplated doing so within a building.

Bainbridge, decided in 1959, establishes alternative (i) above. In 1978, the House of Lords in *DPP for Northern Ireland* v. *Maxwell*[151] extended the reasoning in *Bainbridge* to cover alternative (ii). S was a member of the UVF, a terrorist organisation. One night he was called upon to drive a car guiding other UVF members to a public house. He did so

---

[145] *Johnson* v. *Youden* [1950] 1 KB 544, 546: "[h]e need not actually know that an offence has been committed, because he may not know that the facts constitute an offence and ignorance of the law is not a defence."

[146] *Bainbridge* [1960] 1 QB 129; *Bullock* [1955] 1 All ER 15; cf. *Lomas* [1913] 9 Cr App R 220.

[147] [1960] 1 QB 129.

[148] [1978] 3 All ER 1140.

[149] [1960] 1 QB 129, 133; *Scott* (1978) 68 Cr App R 164; *Patel* [1970] Crim LR 274.

[150] Contrary to s. 9 of the Theft Act 1968; below, § 14.3. Cf. *Barnard* (1980) 70 Cr App R 28 (D's agreement to a theft did not establish his liability for conspiracy to rob); below, § 9.2(ii)(b) (Case 1).

[151] [1978] 3 All ER 1140.

knowing that a terrorist attack was planned, though uncertain whether the attack was to be perpetrated by bomb, gun, or other means. In fact, the attack was carried out using a bomb. S was guilty of aiding two offences against the Explosive Substances Act 1883, since these offences were within the range of types of crime that S contemplated P would commit. According to Lord Scarman, the accessory:[152]

> "may have in contemplation only one [type of[153]] offence, or several; and the several which he contemplates he may see as alternatives. An accessory who leaves it to his principal to choose is liable, provided always the choice is made from the range of offences from which the accessory contemplates the choice will be made. Although the court's formulation of the principle goes further than [Bainbridge], it is a sound development of the law and in no way inconsistent."

Thus S would instead have been guilty of murder if, alternatively, P had killed the publican by shooting him. Conversely, and odd as it might seem, S would not have been liable had the principals entered the pub and stolen a bottle of whiskey—notwithstanding that the latter offence is so much lesser than those actually contemplated by S.[154]

Other variations within a type.
Suppose that P plans to set fire to V's house. Knowing the details of the plan, S helps P by giving him V's address. P goes to the house, then changes his mind and instead sets fire to V's car.[155] Is S guilty of arson? Yes. As cases like *Bainbridge* establish, incidental variations of detail such as time and place are immaterial since they do not alter the type of crime committed by P (and assisted by S). Therefore, because P commits the same offence (arson) either way, S's liability is normally unaffected by this variation.

The exception is if S's assistance or encouragement is directed specifically to the aspect of P's offence that was varied. In such cases, even though that aspect be immaterial to P's guilt, it becomes essential to S's complicity. For example:

> S counsels P to murder a particular person, V. P, having set out to kill V, then changes his mind and decides instead to kill W. S is not a party to the murder of W.[156]

It is otherwise if the identity of the victim to be killed—or the identity of the property to be fired, in our earlier example—were of no particular relevance to S's intervention. Thus, for instance, if P were to receive S's help with obtaining a weapon in order to kill someone ("as it happens, X"), S would still be liable when Y is shot instead.

---

[152] [1978] 3 All ER 1151 (Lord Scarman).

[153] The insertion is an implication of *Bainbridge*.

[154] It is an interesting question why the correspondence principle (above, § 6.5) is observed even when, as here, D is prepared to do an actus reus more heinous (albeit of a different type) than he in fact does. The point perhaps deserves closer attention than it has yet received in the literature.

[155] The facts of *Dunning and Graham* (unreported, Preston Crown Court, Dec. 1985), discussed in *Smith and Hogan* 145.

[156] *Saunders and Archer* (1573) 2 Plowd 473, 75 ER 706; *Leahy* [1985] Crim LR 99; *S v. Robinson* 1968 (1) SA 666; Hawkins, 2 PC ch. 29, §§ 20, 21; Foster, *Crown Law* 369; Stephen, *Digest* art. 43. For criticism of this rule, see Smith, *A Modern Treatise on the Law of Criminal Complicity* (1991) 200ff; Clarkson, "Complicity, *Powell* and Manslaughter" [1998] *Crim LR* 556, 559.

At first glance, although this states the law, the law looks somewhat odd. Since the difference between shooting V and shooting W is immaterial to the definition of murder, the variation would seem to be covered by the doctrine of transferred malice.[157] It is murder of any human being, and participation therein, that the law criminalises; not murder of a particular person. In principle, since the identity of the victim does not matter to P's liability for murder, prima facie neither should it make a difference to the liability of S.

Notwithstanding its apparent oddity, however, the exception is defensible on the basis of the *Calhaem* principle, that P must act within the scope of the encouragement.[158] As such, it is submitted that the rule applies to encouragement rather than assistance; a distinction that is consistent with the case law. Assistance should always be covered by the transferred malice doctrine, but encouragement (say) to murder V can be expressed in such confined terms that it does not encourage murder generally, i.e. of anyone else; in which case the *Calhaem* principle may appropriately displace S's liability.[159]

The oddity is anyway avoided, and S remains liable, if the variation is unintentional. Suppose that P does not change his mind, and carries out his attempt to shoot V. Unfortunately, he mistakes W for V and kills W. Here, the transferred malice doctrine applies to S as well as P, and both S and P are guilty of murdering W.[160]

Mens rea of the principal.
P's mens rea is also an essential matter. S must foresee that P will do the actus reus with the level of mens rea required for it to amount to an offence. S cannot abet murder, for example, if S recognises that P is about to kill V negligently,[161] since negligence is insufficient mens rea for P to be guilty of murder. Similarly, if P's offence requires proof of an ulterior intention, S must be aware of that intent by P.[162] To illustrate: on a charge of abetting possession of a controlled drug with intent to supply,[163] S would have to foresee not only P's possession, but also her intent to supply the drug to another.[164]

Strict or constructive liability for consequences of P's conduct.
Many offences contain a mixture of actus reus elements where, for some of those elements, the prosecution must prove mens rea on the part of the principal and, for other actus reus elements, no mens rea is required. In the context of secondary liability, where no mens rea as to consequences need be proved against P, neither need any mens rea in repect of those consequences be proved against S. Effectively, those consequences are not part of the essential matters of P's conduct. For example, S need not foresee the consequence (death) in order to abet the offence of "dangerous driving causing death". Provided S foresees the essential elements of P's dangerous driving, he will be liable for the further consequences to

---

[157] Above, § 5.7.
[158] Above, § 7.4(ii).
[159] This distinction would support S's conviction in *Reardon* [1999] Crim LR 392.
[160] Hawkins, 2 PC ch. 29, § 22; Foster, *Crown Law* 370; Stephen, *Digest* art. 41.
[161] *Cruse* (1838) 8 C & P 541, 173 ER 610; *Quick* [1973] QB 910, 923; Dennis, "The Mental Element for Accessories" in P. Smith (ed.), *Criminal Law: Essays in Honour of J.C. Smith* (1987) 40, 46–7, 55.
[162] *DPP for Northern Ireland* v. *Maxwell* [1978] 3 All ER 1140.
[163] Contrary to s. 5(3) of the Misuse of Drugs Act 1971.
[164] Cf. *Samuels* [1985] 1 NZLR 350.
[165] *Robert Millar (Contractors) Ltd* [1970] 2 QB 54; *Harris* [1964] Crim LR 54.

the same extent as is P.[165] Similarly, if S aids or abets P to inflict a common assault upon V, and V dies, both S and P are guilty of manslaughter even though neither may have foreseen the prospect of V's death. P is guilty because causing death by an unlawful act satisfies the required elements of manslaughter as a principal;[166] upon proof of the criminal assault, death is a strict liability element. Correspondingly, death is not an "essential matter" and S need not foresee V's death for the purposes of secondary liability.[167] Thus V's death need be foreseen by neither P nor S.

§ 7.5 Secondary parties pursuant to joint unlawful enterprise

In § 7.4, we considered the standard forms of secondary participation; those which are mentioned expressly by section 8 of the Accessories and Abettors Act 1861.[168] In these standard cases, liability is established on the basis that S assists or encourages the principal by aiding, abetting, counselling, or procuring the relevant offence. As an accessory, S knows the essential facts of the offence charged and intends to assist or encourage P in committing that offence.

In principle, the standard forms of complicity involve a single offence: i.e. the offence that is deliberately aided or encouraged by S and which ultimately is committed by P. By contrast, joint enterprise liability characteristically involves *two* offences: i.e. an offence (A) that is jointly undertaken by S and P,[169] and the further offence (B) then committed by P alone. The secondary party need not specifically assist or encourage offence B to become liable for its commission. He becomes a party to the offence if he foresaw that its commission was a possible consequence of proceeding with the original plan to commit some different crime (A); even though he may not have intended or even been directly involved in the commission of that further, or "collateral", offence that was perpetrated by P. For example:

> P and S agree to commit a burglary. Together they break into V's home. In the course of the burglary, P is challenged by V whom he attacks and injures. S does not participate physically in the assault. However, S knew that P has a propensity toward violence, and realised that P might well assault the occupier of the house were they to be confronted. S is guilty, with P, of assault occasioning actual bodily harm.

It matters not that S did not intend that an assault should be committed; nor that S was uncertain whether the assault would occur; nor that S did not intend to help or encourage its commission. Liability arises because S has participated in a criminal enterprise with P, pursuant to which P has committed a further, "collateral", offence which S knew might occur. In simple terms, we may say that the parties set out to commit one crime and

---

[166] See below, Chapter 10.

[167] *Creamer* [1966] 1 QB 72; *Buck* (1960) 44 Cr App R 213; *Baldessare* (1930) 22 Cr App R 70; *Reid* (1976) 62 Cr App R 109; *Swindall and Osborne* (1846) 2 C & K 230, 175 ER 95.

[168] Set out in the text above, § 7.2.

[169] Note there is no requirement in joint enterprise liability that offence A must successfully be perpetrated. If it is perpetrated by P, however, joint enterprise liability would also apply; but S will normally be liable anyway for the offence on standard principles of abetment.

become liable for a different one. The difference between the two varieties of secondary participation, in so far as the conduct element is concerned, is that there is no need to show specifically that S assisted or encouraged the second offence.

As the example illustrates, the idea of secondary participation by joint enterprise has an affinity with the inchoate offence of conspiracy:[170] S and P must form a common purpose to commit a crime. The elements of this form of participation are as follows:

(i) S and P jointly embark on the commission of crime A.
(ii) S foresees that, in the course of the joint enterprise to commit crime A, P might commit crime B (with the requisite mens rea for that crime).
(iii) P commits crime B.
(iv) The commission of crime B must occur as an incident of the joint enterprise, and not in a manner that is fundamentally different from the possibility foreseen by S.

If these requirements are met, then in addition to any liability S may have for conspiracy to commit a crime, and as a (principal or secondary) party to crime A, S will be liable as a party to crime B. Indeed, where S and P form a common purpose to commit a crime, S is liable for every offence committed by P in carrying out that purpose which S knew to be a possible consequence of carrying out the common purpose.

In the following sections, we consider the requirements of joint enterprise liability in more detail.

(i) Joint embarkation on crime A

There must be a joint enterprise: an agreement, or reciprocal understanding, between S and P to pursue crime A; so that S and P act in concert.[171] This requirement is usefully illustrated by *Petters and Parfitt*:[172]

> V died after being assaulted in a car park. Both S and P had participated in the assault, but had arrived on the scene independently. At trial, they were convicted of manslaughter after the judge directed the jury that there was a joint enterprise, even though there was no pre-arranged plan, provided both were attacking V at the same time and there was a common intention that V should suffer harm (and the fatal blow was within the scope of that common intention).

The Court of Appeal allowed the appeals. It was not enough that S and P each intended the same thing, i.e. to assault V. That purpose had to be shared.

The agreement that makes a purpose common (and the enterprise *joint*) need not be explicit or formal, or even prearranged. The agreement may be tacit, and a shared

---

[170] See below, § 7.5(v).

[171] Cf. *Moland* (1843) 2 Mood CC 276, 169 ER 110 ("concert"); *Chan Wing-siu* v. R. [1985] AC 168, 175 ("concert"); *Matusevich* v. R. (1977) 137 CLR 633, 636–7 ("agreement, arrangement, or understanding"); *Baldessare* (1930) 22 Cr App R 70, 72 ("community of purpose"). See also *Smith (Wesley)* [1963] 3 All ER 597, 601, noted below, § 7.5(v).

[172] [1995] Crim LR 501. Cf. *Savard* [1946] 3 DLR 468. In any event, strictly speaking *Petters and Parfitt* could not have been a case of joint enterprise, since there was only one crime at issue. The case was, properly, one of joint principals or of ordinary aiding and abetting.

understanding may emerge from their actions in the course of committing offence A. Sir John Smith put the point thus:[173]

> "S and P see a policeman approaching, they exchange glances, and S goes for the officer while P stands by, ready to intervene if S seems to need his assistance. There is now evidence on which a jury could find an agreement to collaborate in the commission of the offence, a joint enterprise. If P knocks down the second approaching policeman, S will be liable for that assault. The agreement has to be deduced from their conduct, but that is usual in joint enterprise cases."

Contrast this analysis with liability for assisting or encouraging. Suppose, in Smith's example, there had been no mutual understanding reached between P and S, but that P had merely decided, spontaneously, to assist S by knocking down the second policeman and preventing him from stopping S's assault. In that case, there would be no joint enterprise. P would be liable for the S's assault under ordinary principles of aiding and abetting; S, however, would not be liable for the assault committed by P.

(ii) Foresight of crime B

S must actually foresee the prospect that P might go on to commit the essential matters of the collateral offence (crime B). In *Davies* v. *DPP*,[174] S and a number of youths attacked a second group, using only their fists. During the attack P pulled out a knife and stabbed one of their opponents to death. The House of Lords ruled that S was not an accomplice. The enterprise into which S joined was one of common assault, and S was unaware that P or anyone else had brought a weapon with him; as such, S did not foresee the possibility of a stabbing.[175]

On the other hand, foresight of possibility[176] is sufficient. In *Powell*,[177] S1 and S2 went with P to buy drugs from V, a drug dealer. Before the transaction could take place, the dealer was shot dead using a gun carried by P. S1 and S2 knew that P was armed, and had realised P might use the gun to kill or inflict grievous bodily injury on V. On these facts the House upheld their convictions for murder. Notwithstanding that the mens rea for murder as principal is *intention* to kill or inflict grievous bodily injury, it is sufficient if secondary parties to a joint unlawful enterprise *foresee* that murder by P as possible. In so holding, their Lordships followed the lead taken in a number of decisions by the Court of Appeal and Privy Council[178] and overruled *Barr*[179] and *Smith*,[180] two earlier cases which had

---

[173] *Petters and Parfitt* [1995] Crim LR 501, 502. (The characters' names are substituted.) The same is true for liability under the inchoate offence of conspiracy: below, § 9.2(iv).

[174] [1954] AC 378. Cf. *Mahmood* [1994] Crim LR 368.

[175] Cf. *A-G's Reference (No. 3 of 2004)* [2005] EWCA Crim 1882, in which S recruited P1 and P2 to terrorise V, knowing that they might deliberately discharge a firearm near V but not (on the agreed facts) foreseeing the possibility that they might cause V any physical injury. In the event, the principals deliberately shot V in the head at point-blank range, killing him. S was ruled not to be guilty of manslaughter.

[176] Not probability: cf. *Powell; English* [1997] 4 All ER 545, 551B (Lord Steyn), 566G (Lord Hutton).

[177] *Powell; English* [1997] 4 All ER 545.

[178] *Smith (Wesley)* [1963] 3 All ER 597 (CCA); *Anderson and Morris* [1966] 2 QB 110 (CCA); *Chan Wing-siu* v. *R.* [1985] AC 168 (PC); *Hui Chi-ming* v. *R.* [1992] 1 AC 34 (PC). See Smith, "Criminal Liability of Accessories: Law and Law Reform" (1997) 113 *LQR* 453.

[179] (1986) 88 Cr App R 362.

[180] [1988] Crim LR 616.

suggested that, in order to be guilty of an offence, secondary parties must have no less a degree of mens rea than is required of the principal—i.e. on a charge of murder, that S must have intended P should kill or inflict grievous bodily harm upon the victim.

At first sight, it may appear odd that a person who merely foresees a possibility of death (or serious injury) should be guilty of murder. That would certainly not be true if S were charged as principal. It is submitted, however, that the result in *Powell* can be justified, and is consistent with the rationale underlying participation by joint enterprise. It is S's commitment to a common unlawful purpose that adds the crucial extra normative ingredient, justifying the law's requiring only that S must foresee the possibility of P's crime.[181] We shall return to this issue below, in § 7.5(v).

(iii) An incident of the joint enterprise and not fundamentally different

Prior to *Powell*, there was authority suggesting that, in addition to being foreseen, P's commission of crime B must have been *authorised* by S as being within the scope of the joint enterprise. Thus, in *Anderson and Morris*, Lord Parker CJ asserted:[182]

> "if one of the adventurers goes beyond what has been tacitly agreed as part of the common enterprise, his co-adventurer is not liable for the consequences of that unauthorised act. . . . [i]t is for the jury to decide whether what was done was part of the joint enterprise, or went beyond it and was in fact an act unauthorised by that joint enterprise."

Similarly, in *Chan Wing-Siu* v. *R.*, the Privy Council stated:[183]

> "The case must depend on the wider principle whereby a secondary party is criminally liable for acts by the primary offender of a type which the former foresees but does not necessarily intend. That there is such a principle is not in doubt. It turns on contemplation or, putting the same idea in other words, authorisation, which may be express but is more usually implied. It meets the case of a crime foreseen as a possible incident of the common unlawful enterprise. The criminal culpability lies in participating in the venture with that foresight."

There is a difference between contemplation of possibility and (tacit or express) authorisation. Suppose S participates in a burglary knowing P has both a knife and a propensity for violence. S, however, makes it clear to P that she is opposed to his using the knife. If P, confronted during the burglary, stabs his victim, the stabbing is foreseen but unauthorised.

If there were previously any uncertainty regarding this point, after *Powell* there is none. In such cases S is a party to the stabbing.[184] Foresight, or contemplation, is the key ingredient.

---

[181] Notice is that there is no logical incongruity here. The basis of P's liability is different: he is liable because he satisfies the actus reus and mens rea requirements of murder. S is liable because she satisfies the actus reus and mens rea requirements of secondary participation (and note that this means she must foresee the prospect of P's acts being intentional; it is not enough merely to foresee the possibility of V's death). Since the actus reus requirements are different, logic does not compel the mens rea requirements to be the same.

[182] [1966] 2 QB 110, 118–19 (adopting the submission of Geoffrey Lane QC: "at any rate for the last 130 or 140 years that has been the true position").

[183] [1985] AC 168, 175.

[184] *Powell*; *English* [1997] 4 All ER 545, 556–8; *Hui Chi-Ming* v. *R.* [1992] 1 AC 34, 53; *Hyde* [1991] 1 QB 134, 139. Cf. *Day* [2001] Crim LR 984, where S's conviction was upheld because he foresaw that P might kick V in the head, notwithstanding that apparently he did not approve of it.

Nevertheless, the criterion that P's further crime must be "an incident of the joint enterprise" does introduce an extra constraint, or at least a refinement of the requirement for foresight by S. As the Privy Council put it, in *Hui Chi-ming* v. *R.*:[185]

> "mere foresight is not enough: the accessory, in order to be guilty, must have foreseen the relevant offence which the principal may commit as a possible *incident* of the common unlawful enterprise."

P's actions must be of the same *type*[186] that S foresees, and must not be "fundamentally different" from those recognised by S to be possible incidents of the enterprise. This requirement was regarded as crucial in *English*,[187] a separate appeal decided together with *Powell*. The facts of *English* were as follows:

> S and P jointly attacked a police office with wooden posts, causing injury. During the attack, P produced a knife and stabbed the police officer. The officer died of the stab wound. Apparently S had not known that P was carrying a knife, and did not foresee the stabbing.

The House of Lords ruled that the stabbing fell outside the scope or possible incidents of the joint enterprise, as contemplated by S. According to Lord Hutton, "the secondary party must foresee an act of the type which the principal party committed, and in the present case the use of a knife was fundamentally different to the use of a wooden post."[188] This is so even though an assault with wooden posts may itself cause death—but (at least in the circumstances envisaged) it was very much less likely to do so. Their Lordships did not much elaborate on the test when P's actions will be "fundamentally different" from any contemplated by S, but dangerousness was regarded as an important factor:[189]

> "if the weapon used by the primary party is different to, but as dangerous as, the weapon which the secondary party contemplated he might use, the secondary party should not escape liability for murder because of the difference in the weapon, for example, if he foresaw that the primary party might use a gun to kill and the latter used a knife to kill, or vice versa."

One instructive case in this respect is *Gamble*,[190] a decision approved in *Powell*.[191] The relevant facts of *Gamble* were as follows:

> S1 and S2 agreed with P1 and P2 upon a joint enterprise to attack V. S1 and S2 expected that V would be given a severe beating and might be "kneecapped" (i.e. a bullet might be fired into V's kneecap). However, during the attack V was deliberately murdered by the principals, who cut his throat. (V was also shot four times, not in the kneecap; two of the bullets would have been fatal but for the fact that V first bled to death from the cut to his throat.) Neither S1 nor S2 foresaw that V might be killed with a knife or that he might be shot other than in the knee.

S1 and S2 had a common purpose, with P1 and P2, to inflict grievous bodily harm, and if the beating or kneecapping had caused V's death each would have been guilty of murder.

---

[185] [1992] 1 AC 34, 53 (emphasis added).
[186] *Chan Wing-siu* v. *R.* [1985] AC 168, 175.
[187] *Powell; English* [1997] 4 All ER 545.
[188] *Ibid.*, 564. Cf. *Crooks* [1999] NI 226, 234 (Lord Carswell CJ).
[189] [1997] 4 All ER 545, 566 (Lord Hutton). See the commentary by Smith [1998] *Crim LR* 48, 50–2; *CLGP* § 133.
[190] [1989] NI 268. See also *Uddin* [1998] 2 All ER 744 and *Greatrex* [1999] 1 Cr App R 126.
[191] *Powell; English* [1997] 4 All ER 545, 564–5.

But the principals departed fundamentally from the scope of the enterprise contemplated by S1 and S2. Their actions were, from a moral perspective, significantly different from those to which S1 and S2 had agreed—both because they involved an intention to kill and because they were much more likely to cause death. There is no reason to suppose S1 or S2 would have agreed to participate in an enterprise on such terms. Hence, they could not be attributed with responsibility for the acts that caused V's death.

Whether P's act counts as "fundamentally different" is a matter of fact for the jury to determine[192] and, in directing the jury, the meaning of that expression is not normally to be elaborated upon by the judge.[193] The question turns on the nature of P's *conduct* rather than on the intention with which the conduct is performed, and it is not sufficient to make a fundamental difference that P unexpectedly has an intention to kill rather than the foreseen intention to do grievous bodily harm.[194] What matters is what P *does*, and in this respect it seems clear that dangerousness is the most important factor, something emphasised by the Court of Appeal in *Uddin*:[195]

> In deciding whether the actions are of such a different type the use by that party of a weapon is a significant factor. If the character of the weapon, e.g. its propensity to cause death, is different from any weapon used or contemplated by the others and if it is used with a specific intent to kill, the others are not responsible for the death unless it is proved that they knew or foresaw the likelihood of the use of such a weapon. . . . If some or all of the others are using weapons which could be regarded as equally likely to inflict fatal injury, the mere fact that a different weapon was used is immaterial.

However, some constraints must be emphasised. First, the "fundamental difference" exception does not apply if, despite S's lack of advance foresight of P's use of a weapon, S continues to participate in the joint enterprise after the weapon is produced and she realises that it may be used by P:[196]

> If in the course of the concerted attack a weapon is produced by one of the participants and the others knowing that he has it in circumstances where he may use it in the course of the attack participate or continue to participate in the attack, they will be guilty of murder if the weapon is used to inflict a fatal wound.

Secondly, in respect of murder, the exception does not apply if S realised it was possible that, in the course of the joint enterprise, P might kill V *with intent to kill V*. That is, the fundamental difference rule is available where S foresaw only that P might act with intent to inflict grievous bodily harm (rather than death).[197] Finally, it should not be forgotten that

---

[192] *O'Flaherty* [2004] EWCA Crim 526, at para. 56.

[193] *Rahman* [2007] EWCA Crim 342, at para. 70.

[194] *Ibid.*, at paras. 29–46, especially para. 43.

[195] [1999] QB 431, 441 (CA). The relative dangerousness of P's actions is emphasised also in *Greatrex* [1999] 1 Cr App R 126, 135ff (CA).

[196] *Uddin* [1999] QB 431, 441 (CA). See the discussion of withdrawal below, § 7.6(vi)(a).

[197] This constraint is established explicitly by the Court of Appeal in *Rahman* [2007] EWCA Crim 342, at paras. 20, 22; notwithstanding that the same case suggests, as is noted in the text above, that fundamental difference is a function of conduct rather than mens rea. The semantic answer appears to be that foresight of an intent to kill *disapplies* the common purpose rule rather than modifies its scope (in the sense of what qualifies as a fundamental departure). Either way, however, a limitation of S's liability has been done away with.

even where S is exempted from liability for murder by the rule, she may nonetheless be guilty of lesser offences, including offences against the person and conspiracy.[198]

The assessment of dangerousness must be made in context and across all the evidence, and not just by focusing on the abstract nature of the particular weapons deployed. In *Rahman*,[199] the defendants took part in a group attack upon V using, as well as their fists and feet, various blunt weapons including chair legs, pieces of fencing, baseball bats, metal tubing, and a length of scaffolding pole. Ultimately, one of the attackers produced a knife and fatally stabbed V; something the defendants denied having foreseen. In dismissing their appeals against conviction for murder, the Court of Appeal ruled that there was evidence from which the jury could reasonably infer they had foreseen the possible use of a knife.[200] However, it also held that, in light of the evidence as a whole, including the sheer ferocity of the attack, the stabbing was not *inherently* or *necessarily* fundamentally different (and therefore falling outside the scope of the common purpose), so that the judge was justified in leaving "to the jury the issue of whether or not the stabbing was so fundamentally different an action as to take it outside the common purpose. For the avoidance of doubt, we find the judge's decision to be justified whether or not the appellant foresaw the use of a knife."[201]

More generally, the Court went on to summarise the correct approach to fundamental difference problems in a murder case, as follows:[202]

In order to convict S of murder the jury must first be sure that P unlawfully caused the death of V intending to kill him or cause him really serious bodily harm and secondly be sure that S played some part in the attack on V. The route to verdict could then be:

1. Are you sure that S intended that one of the attackers would kill V intending to kill him or that S realised that one of the attackers might kill V with intent to kill him? If yes, guilty of murder. If no, go to 2.

2. Are you sure that either:
a) S realised that one of the attackers might kill V with intent to cause him really serious bodily harm; or
b) S intended that serious really bodily harm would be caused to V; or
c) S realised that one of the attackers might cause serious bodily harm to V intending to cause him such harm?
If no, not guilty of murder. If yes, go to question 3.

3. What was P's act which caused the death of V? (e.g. stabbing, shooting, kicking, beating). Go to question 4.

4. Did S realise that one of the attackers might do this act? If yes, guilty of murder. If no, go to the question 5.

---

[198] Alternative offences can be charged: cf. *Greatrex* [1999] 1 Cr App R 126 (CA).
[199] [2007] EWCA Crim 342.
[200] *Ibid.*, para. 99.
[201] *Ibid.*, para. 81; and see paras. 77–80.
[202] *Ibid.*, [69]. The Court regarded "realise" and "foresee" as synonymous: para. 54. In the quotation, we have substituted "S" for the Court's use of "D" to designate the secondary party.

5. What act or acts are you sure S realised that one of the attackers might do to cause V really serious harm? Go to question 6.

6. Are you sure that this act or these acts (which S realised one of the attackers might do) is/are not of a fundamentally different nature to P's act which caused the death of V? If yes, guilty of murder. If no, not guilty of murder.

Steps 1 and 2 are concerned with establishing whether the fundamental difference exception is available at all to the defendant; if it is, the jury should proceed to steps 3–6 in deciding whether what was done by P was indeed fundamentally different from that foreseen by S.

(iv) Conviction for a different offence?

Where P departs from the scope of the joint enterprise and commits a crime different from that foreseen by S, the denial of responsibility for P's actions generally means that S is entitled to a complete acquittal in respect of that further crime. However, in principle it seems possible in some circumstances for S to be guilty of manslaughter in circumstances where P is guilty of murder. Suppose the following example, which is set out by the Court of Appeal in *Day*:[203]

> "Suppose that the participants in a joint enterprise all propose or foresee the same kind of violence being inflicted on their victim, let it be punching with the possibility of kicking to follow. On that they are at one. But two [of] them harbour a subjective intention to inflict serious injury by means of such violence. The third harbours only, or foresees or intends only, that some harm might be done. One of those actuated by an intent to do grievous bodily harm punches or kicks the victim just as all three foresaw. The victim falls and suffers a subdural haemorrhage and dies."

While the first two participants are guilty of murder, the third is not since he did not foresee that P would act with the mens rea for murder. Nonetheless, and unlike the facts of *English*, P's behaviour and its consequence seem to be within the scope of the common purpose. As such, it appears that the third participant is guilty of manslaughter.[204]

Put more generally, in cases where P is guilty of murder and the fundamental difference rule does not apply, then where S failed to foresee the essential elements of murder —e.g. by failing to foresee the likelihood that P would act with sufficient mens rea for murder —S may nonetheless be convicted of manslaughter if she foresaw the probability that P may act with the culpability required for a manslaughter conviction: for example, by committing an unlawful act, such as an assault, that involved some risk of physical harm to another person.[205] Because death is a strict liability element in manslaughter (and hence not an essential matter), S need not foresee that death was a likely consequence of carrying out the

---

[203] [2001] Crim LR 984.

[204] *Gilmour* [2000] 2 Cr App R 407; *Day* [2001] Crim LR 984; below, § 7.6(iii). Cf. *Stewart and Schofield* [1995] 1 Cr App R 441, discussed by Clarkson, "Complicity, *Powell* and Manslaughter" [1998] *Crim LR* 556, 560. *Contra* Clarkson (and by contrast with the example in the text), P's physical behaviour in *Stewart and Schofield* went beyond that agreed to by S. Although S had contemplated a mere battery, that mere battery did not cause death (it was, rather, the unexpectedly severe battering that did so). Query whether this was true also on the facts in *Gilmour*, as the commentary suggests at [2000] Crim LR 763, 764–5 (see also letters to the editor at [2001] Crim LR 333–5).

[205] Below, § 10.6.

joint enterprise. In principle, an analogous approach will apply also to the overlapping hierarchy of aggravated assault crimes found in the Offences Against the Person Act 1861.[206]

(v) The rationale of joint enterprise liability

"Intellectually", said Lord Mustill, "there are problems with the concept of a joint venture, but they do not detract from its general practical worth."[207] One may hesitate to distinguish so readily between matters of intellectual coherence and those of practicality, but it is true that the rationale for joint enterprise liability is somewhat unclear. Smith and Hogan claim that joint enterprise is simply an aspect of aiding, abetting, counselling, or procuring, which therefore falls to be "governed by the ordinary principles of secondary participation."[208] We think, however, that joint enterprise is a special case of secondary participation and not merely a sub-species of assistance and encouragement.

The gist of a joint enterprise is concerted action, or agreement acted out.[209] It is this element of an implemented agreement to commit crime A that triggers the doctrines of joint enterprise liability. That this is so is recognised in *Smith (Wesley)*, where Slade J notes that "the terms 'agreement', 'confederacy', 'acting in concert', and 'conspiracy', all pre-suppose an agreement express or by implication to achieve a common purpose."[210] By contrast, none of aiding, abetting, counselling, or procuring presupposes an agreement or common purpose.[211] S may, for example, render aid without P's knowledge, or she may offer advice to P without endorsing or allying herself with P's conduct ("if you must do it, and I want no part of it and wish you wouldn't, then do at least take these precautions"[212]). Similarly, it is enough for abetment if S's encouragement is merely received by P: there is no need for that endorsement to influence P or even be acknowledged.[213]

It is submitted that to analyse joint enterprise as a special case of aiding and abetting is misleading, in terms of both criminal law doctrine and its underlying justification.[214] This is because the actus reus requirements of joint enterprise liability *differ* from those applying to participation by assistance or encouragement. There is no need to show a common purpose in standard cases of aiding and abetting. But it is S's commitment to that common unlawful purpose (to commit crime A) that arguably justifies the law's requiring only that S must foresee the possibility of crime B, rather than demanding that S must *help or encourage* crime B—which, as we saw, is required in the standard cases.

---

[206] Below, Chapter 11.

[207] *Powell; English* [1997] 4 All ER 545, 548.

[208] *Smith and Hogan* 190–1. See also Smith, "Secondary Participation in Crime—Can We Do Without It?" (1994) 144 *NLJ* 679.

[209] Above, § 7.5(i).

[210] [1963] 3 All ER 597, 601. The passage is cited by Lord Hutton in *Powell; English* [1997] 4 All ER 545, 555. Cf. *CLGP* § 133.

[211] *Kupferberg* (1918) 13 Cr App R 166, 168. See above, § 7.4(i)(a).

[212] Compare *Gillick* v. *West Norfolk and Wisbech Area Health Authority* [1986] AC 112; noted above, § 7.4(iv)(a).

[213] Above, § 7.4(ii).

[214] Simester, "The Mental Element in Complicity" (2006) 122 LQR 578, 592–600; an argument accepted by the High Court of Australia: *Clayton* v. *R* [2006] HCA 58, at para. 20. The Law Commission also favours retaining separate doctrines: *Murder, Manslaughter and Infanticide* Law Com. No. 304 (2006) part 4.

Aiding/abetting and joint enterprise are structurally unalike. In cases of aiding and abetting only one crime is at issue: crime A.[215] S directly participates in crime A by her intended act of aiding or abetting that very crime. The wrong which makes S responsible for crime A is that deliberate assistance or encouragement: it is her act of directly associating herself with P's crime. In joint enterprise cases, the wrong is the agreement or confederacy.[216] That agreement (to commit crime A) opens a wider door to liability; it exposes S to conviction for any foreseen crimes B, C, and D, committed by P in the course of executing the agreement. As such, S's connection to crime B is *indirect*. It operates only through the agreement.

It is important to recognise that aiding, abetting, counselling, and procuring are not doctrines that operate as ends in themselves. They exist as formally recognised channels via which the law transcends the normal limitations of autonomy, individual responsibility, and causation doctrines in order to associate one person with responsibility for a crime committed by another. There is no in-principle reason, therefore, why the law should not recognise complementary doctrines where a similar rationale for extending responsibility applies.[217] Joint enterprise presents just that situation.

Even so, an important policy question remains. Why should the agreement or confederacy make such a difference? Clearly, the law regards the joint unlawful enterprise as upping the ante, such that S becomes liable to be convicted of crimes to which she has in no way contributed.

By entering into an agreement or joint enterprise, S changes her normative position. She becomes, through her own deliberate choice, a participant in a group action to commit a crime.[218] Moreover, her new status has moral significance: she associates herself with the conduct of the other members of the group in a way that the mere aider or abettor, who remains an independent character throughout the episode, does not. The law has a particular hostility to criminal groups. As with the inchoate crime of conspiracy, the rationale is partly one of dangerousness: "experience has shown that joint criminal enterprises only too readily escalate into the commission of greater offences."[219] Criminal associations are

---

[215] Although, of course, crime A may be committed on more than one occasion; as when P uses the jemmy supplied by S to commit several burglaries.

[216] Compare the American rule that one who enters into a conspiracy thereby becomes liable for every reasonably foreseeable crime committed by his co-conspirators in furtherance of the conspiracy: *Pinkerton v. United States* 328 US 640 (1946); Johnson, "The Unnecessary Crime of Conspiracy" (1973) 61 *Calif LR* 1137, 1146ff. The (overbroad) rule is not found in the Model Penal Code (see § 2.06).

[217] Admittedly, a pragmatic consideration is whether to do so would over-complicate the law and associated jury directions: cf. *Clayton* [2006] HCA 58, at [113–17] (Kirby J, dissenting). On the other hand, joint enterprise doctrine offers real practical gains in overcoming the evidential difficulties, where there is concerted action, of distinguishing between the contributions made by individual actors and of establishing precisely what part was taken by each member of the combination.

[218] In *Clayton, ibid.*, at para. 107, Kirby J (dissenting) rejects this argument: "The law may indeed dislike anti-social activities, particularly where they result in death. But a rational and just legal system will dislike such activities equally, whether the conduct charged is prosecuted as an offence of acting in concert or of aiding and abetting others in carrying out the group activity." (See also Sullivan, "Complicity for First Degree Murder and Complicity in an Unlawful Killing" [2006] *Crim LR* 502, 509–10.) Yet the point being made here in the text is that S's activity is not merely anti-social but independently criminal. By contrast, aiding and abetting need involve no otherwise criminal conduct; it is S's intention to aid, abet, etc. that turns her otherwise lawful conduct into the stuff of criminality. Hence a rational legal system may distinguish between the two, especially with respect to the mens rea requirement.

[219] *Powell; English* [1997] 4 All ER 545, 551; cf. *Rahman* [2007] EWCA Crim 342, at para. 61; Marshall, Webb and Tilley, *Rationalisation of Current Research on Guns, Gangs and other Weapons: Phase 1* (2005), § 3.4.

dangerous. They present a threat to public safety that ordinary criminal prohibitions, addressed to individual actors, do not entirely address. Moreover, the danger is not just of an immediately physical nature. A group is a form of society, and a group constituted by a joint unlawful enterprise is a form of society that has set itself against the law and order of society at large. Individuals offending alone do not do this. Thus concerted wrongdoing imports additional and special reasons for the the law to intervene.[220]

§ 7.6 General principles applying to all secondary parties

Whether it arises on the basis of assistance or encouragement, or on the basis of joint enterprise, secondary liability is subject to certain general doctrines governing the nature of the link required between the participant's actions and the commission of the offence to which she is party. These doctrines are discussed below.

(i) Liability is normally dependent on commission of the offence

As we have observed already, and unlike inchoate crimes of incitement and conspiracy, secondary participation is derivative, and not itself an offence. Rather, it involves S in being ascribed with legal responsibility for the offence that P commits. It follows that, subject to certain exceptions, S may only be attributed with that offence *if it actually is committed.* For example:

> S urges P to shoot V, a common enemy. P purchases a gun, but before he has the opportunity to purchase any ammunition the gun dealer becomes suspicious and alerts the police, who cancel P's gun licence and confiscate the weapon.

S is guilty of the inchoate offence of incitement to commit a crime, but since P does not actually commit the crime, S cannot be a party to murder.[221] In these standard examples, there can be no secondary liability because there is no actus reus by the principal. Consider the facts of *Thornton* v. *Mitchell*:[222]

> S, a bus conductor, negligently directed the bus driver to reverse. Two pedestrians were in consequence hit by the bus. However, the driver was acquitted of careless driving, since he had quite properly relied upon the instructions of the conductor.

In these circumstances, S was acquitted of aiding and abetting the offence of careless driving. There was no actus reus by the bus driver—he had not been driving carelessly[223]—and thus nothing at all of a criminal character from which S's liability might derive.

---

[220] In some situations, an alternative form of intervention might be to make S guilty of an aggravated version of the offence she herself commits. For instance, where crime A is a burglary, foresight by S that P might be violent during the burglary could be made a ground for a holding S guilty of aggravated burglary (rather than murder). The practicability of this alternative would depend upon there being a suitable battery of aggravated versions of typical "crime A" offences.

[221] Cf. *Demirian* [1989] VR 97; Lanham, "Primary and Derivative Criminal Liability: An Australian Perspective" [2000] *Crim LR* 707.

[222] [1940] 1 All ER 339. See also *Loukes* [1996] Crim LR 341; Taylor, "Complicity and Excuses" [1983] *Crim LR* 656. In *Pickford* [1995] QB 203, 213 the Court of Appeal noted, *obiter*, that S could not be convicted of aiding an abetting an offence by P if P was not a member of the class of persons who, in law, could commit the offence.

[223] For explanation, see above, § 5.5(iii).

(ii) Exceptions: secondary liability without the primary offence

The case is straightforward where P does not commit an actus reus at all. However, there are certain circumstances where something less than the full offence by P is required. The first occurs when P commits the actus reus of the offence, but is not criminally responsible for doing so because of infancy or insanity. To illustrate, consider the following facts from the Australian case of *Schultz v. Pettitt*:[224]

> D allowed P, his five-year-old daughter, to operate a power boat. P pushed the throttle too far and the boat ploughed into another boat. D was charged with carelessly operating the boat.

Prima facie, P has operated the boat carelessly. However, as we shall see in Chapter 19, P could not be convicted because of her infancy. Therefore, no offence was committed by P. Despite this, Cox J would have been willing to uphold D's conviction as a secondary party. This analysis seems right in principle.[225]

English law recognises at least two further exceptions to the requirement that P be guilty of an offence, although the scope of these exceptions is not fully settled. We consider them in the following subsections.

(a) When S is responsible for P's excuse

The first exception is for other possible defences, apart from infancy and insanity, that P may claim but which do not negate S's liability as a party. There is at least one such general defence:[226] that of duress, when S is the source of the duress. In *Bourne*,[227] S forced his wife to have sexual connection with an animal. S was convicted of abetting her to commit buggery notwithstanding that it was assumed his wife, had she been charged with the same offence, would have been acquitted owing to the availability of a defence of duress.[228] It appears that this defence operates only as a personal excuse. Similar reasoning would not, therefore, carry over to situations where (for example) P acted in justifying self-defence.[229]

(b) When S procures P to act without mens rea

The second exception arises when P does the actus reus of an offence but lacks mens rea.[230]

---

[224] (1980) 25 SASR 427. Note that the innocent agency doctrine was held not to apply: see §§ 7.3(i), 7.6(ii)(b).

[225] As it happened, this ground for upholding the conviction failed on the facts, because the father apparently lacked the mens rea required for secondary participation.

[226] And see also below, § 7.6(iii).

[227] (1952) 36 Cr App R 125. See Edwards, "Duress and Aiding and Abetting" (1953) 69 *LQR* 227; Cross, "Duress and Aiding and Abetting (A Reply)" (1953) 69 *LQR* 354.

[228] Compare *Howe* [1987] AC 417, 458, where Lord Mackay highlighted the fact that duress involved a "reason special to [P] himself." Note that this was not the reasoning used by the Court in *Bourne* itself: see below, n. 205, and accompanying discussion in § 7.6(ii)(b) of the limitations of such reasoning. The best explanation of *Bourne* is that highlighted by Lord Mackay and adopted here. For discussion of the distinction between justification and excuse see below, § 17.2.

[229] Strictly, the appropriate defence would have been coercion, a special, extended, variety of the duress defence, available to wives who commit crimes in the presence of their husbands. See below, § 20.2.

[230] Cf. *DPP v. K and B* [1997] 1 Cr App R 36, in which two girls, B and K, used threats of violence to order V to have sexual intercourse with P, an unknown boy apparently under 14 years of age. Note, however, that the analysis in that case is flawed. The Divisional Court treated P as lacking mens rea on the basis of the *doli incapax* presumption (*ibid.*, 42). This was wrong: the *doli incapax* presumption is not against mens rea but against P's having the capacity to distinguish right from wrong (below, § 19.4(ii)). It is therefore a denial of criminal responsibility, like insanity

In limited circumstances, S may be liable as a secondary party when she procures P to commit the actus reus of an offence for which P lacks mens rea. In *Cogan and Leak*,[231] P had sexual intercourse with S's wife, apparently believing (on the basis of what S told him) that the wife was consenting. On appeal, P's conviction for rape was quashed, but S's conviction was upheld. The main ground for upholding his conviction was said to be that P was an innocent agent through whom S had acted as a principal in committing the offence. However, as *Smith and Hogan* points out, "the agency theory is misconceived. If it were right, a woman could be convicted of rape as the principal and it is plain that she cannot commit that offence."[232] Rape is one of a number of offences that cannot be committed through an innocent agent.[233]

Alternatively, the Court of Appeal reasoned that S was guilty of procuring rape, since even though P could not be convicted, S's wife had "clearly" been raped: "Cogan had sexual intercourse with her without her consent. The fact that Cogan was innocent of rape because he believed that she was consenting does not affect the position that she was raped."[234]

This, with respect, is also poor reasoning. Rape is not an absolute liability crime, constituted simply by its actus reus. The fact that P lacked mens rea means that, for the purposes of the criminal law (and by contrast with ordinary language), no rape occurred.[235] Nonetheless, S's conviction seems a just result. If so, the better analysis seems to be that, where S *procures* P to commit the actus reus of an offence without mens rea, S may be convicted of procuring that offence. The Court of Appeal subsequently accepted this account in *Millward*,[236] the facts of which were as follows:

> S instructed P, his employee, to drive S's tractor on the highway. The tractor was in a defective condition, and by driving it on the highway P (the Court assumed[237]) committed the actus reus of reckless driving. S knew, and P did not know, that the vehicle was unroadworthy. While on the highway, the tractor's condition caused an accident, killing the passenger of another car.

On these facts, P was acquitted of causing death by reckless driving but S was convicted as a party to the offence. The Court of Appeal upheld S's conviction explicitly on the basis that he had procured commission of the actus reus by P.

and the irrebuttable presumption of *doli incapax* for infants below 10 years of age. For criticism, see the commentary at [1997] Crim LR 121.

[231] [1976] QB 217.

[232] *Smith and Hogan* 173.

[233] See above, § 7.3(i).

[234] *Cogan and Leak* [1976] QB 217, 223.

[235] A similar example of this reasoning appears in *Bourne* (1952) 36 Cr App R 125, discussed in the previous section (see especially n. 198). Lord Goddard asserted (at 128) that the fact that P would have been acquitted of buggery presented no impediment to S's conviction for complicity because "that [P] could have set up duress . . . means that she admits that she has committed the crime but prays to be excused from punishment." Yet an acquittal would mean that she committed no crime.

[236] [1994] Crim LR 527; see also *Wheelhouse* [1994] Crim LR 756.

[237] Erroneously. In fact, the case was like *Thornton* v. *Mitchell*, discussed above in § 7.6(i), where no actus reus occurred. Cf. the acceptance of this criticism of *Millward* by Smith, in his discussion of *Loukes* [1996] *Crim LR* 341, 343.

The propriety of this new exception to the rule that P must be guilty of the offence has been doubted,[238] but its place in English law now seems secure.[239] In any event, such cases will be rare, since whenever the actus reus involves consequences, S may normally be convicted as a principal offender (either on the basis of having caused the actus reus personally or by means of the innocent agent doctrine).

(iii) Conviction for different offences with the same actus reus

A variant situation arises when there are two offences constituted by the same actus reus, and differentiated only by degree of culpability. The leading example of this is murder and manslaughter. Suppose, for instance, the following situation:

> S lends P a cosh, which he knows P plans to use to in order to assault V. S knows that the blow may cause V's death, but believes P intends only to knock V out and does not mean to kill him. In this, however, S is mistaken. P intends to kill V. Unfortunately, although P hits V no harder than agreed, she succeeds in her aim of killing him.

It appears that, in cases of this sort, S and P need not be convicted of the same offence, and that where P is guilty of murder, it is possible to convict S only of manslaughter. This possibility has already been noted in the context of joint enterprises.[240] In respect of secondary participation by assistance or encouragement (i.e. aiding, abetting, counselling, or procuring), the rationale for S's lesser conviction would be similar: that S's participation was with the intention of assisting or encouraging P whose proposed conduct was such that, were V to die, P would be guilty of manslaughter; in circumstances where, ultimately, P performed the envisaged conduct with sufficient mens rea for murder.[241]

The fact that these two offences share the same actus reus means that any incursion upon the principle that S's liability is derivative upon P's is minimal. Indeed, manslaughter may be regarded as a lesser included offence within murder. Moreover, arguably the jury has a constitutional power on a charge of murder (improperly) to return a verdict of manslaughter, even though the jury is satisfied that every element necessary to constitute the crime of murder has been established.[242]

---

[238] See, e.g., Kadish, "Complicity, Cause and Blame" in *Essays in the Criminal Law* (1987) 135, 180; Law Commission Consultation Paper No. 131, *Assisting and Encouraging Crime* (1993) para. 4.207.

[239] It is worth noting that the Law Commission's Draft Criminal Code makes special provision for these cases in clause 26(3)(a), which treats S as a perpetrator. Arguably, this is preferable to using standard complicity doctrines as a way of capturing the nature and significance of S's actions.

[240] Above, § 7.5(iv).

[241] Cf. *Gilmour* [2000] 2 Cr App R 407; *Murtagh and Kennedy* [1955] Crim LR 315.

[242] See, e.g., *Gammage v. R.* (1969) 122 CLR 444, 450–1, 453, 460, 463, 465 (HCA). English courts have not determined the point authoritatively, but in *Shipley* (1784) 4 Doug KB 73, 178, 99 ER 774, 828, Ashurst J drew a distinction similar to that accepted by the Australian High Court in *Gammage*: "I admit the jury have the power of finding a verdict against the law, and so they have of finding a verdict against the evidence, but I deny that they have a right to do so." In *Meany* (1862) L & C 213, 216, 169 ER 1368, 1370, Pollock CB noted that the judge "is not bound to receive their verdict unless they insist upon his doing so." A manslaughter verdict contrary to direction has been accepted, reluctantly, by the judge in at least one case, noted (1942) 86 *Sol LJ* 251; see also *Soanes* [1948] 1 All ER 289, 290 (infanticide); *Clement v. Blunt* (1623) 2 Rolle 460, 81 ER 916. In *Smith, The Times*, 14 January 1804 (discussed by Williams, "Homicide and the Supernatural" (1949) 65 *LQR* 491, 500–3), however, the Court refused to

However, the reverse is not true, and it does not follow from the above that S may be convicted of murder if the principal party is guilty only of manslaughter. This possibility requires separate consideration. Imagine the following example:

> S encourages P to punch V. S knows, and P does not, that V has an "egg-shell skull", and she hopes that the blow will cause V's death. P strikes V, killing him.

P is guilty of manslaughter. But is S guilty of murder, or only of manslaughter? In *Richards*,[243] the Court of Appeal first suggested that S can only be guilty of manslaughter. The facts of that case were as follows:

> S hired P1 and P2 to beat up V, her husband, badly enough to hospitalise him for a month. P1 and P2 then attacked V and inflicted a minor but no serious wound. The principals were acquitted of wounding with intent to cause grievous bodily harm and convicted instead of unlawful wounding, a lesser offence. S was convicted of wounding with intent to cause grievous bodily harm.

The Court of Appeal quashed S's conviction, and substituted a conviction for unlawful wounding. However, the decision has been powerfully criticised,[244] and was disapproved by both the Court of Appeal and the House of Lords in *Howe*.[245] It appears, therefore, that under current law S may be found guilty of the greater offence (e.g. murder) even though, because of lack of mens rea, P is guilty of only of the lesser offence (e.g. manslaughter).

It may be the law, but does the position after *Howe* accord with principle? According to Ashworth:[246]

> "this new rule involves a patent departure from the derivative theory of accomplice liability: the (intended) higher offence was never committed, and so the accomplice's liability cannot derive from any such offence. The theory underlying the *Howe* ruling is that the culpability of the accomplice should be viewed as a separate issue from that of the principal, and based upon what the accomplice intended to happen or believed would happen."

It is true that P has acted without the mens rea for murder. Prior to *Howe* the only permitted exception in such cases (i.e. where S may be convicted despite P's lacking mens rea) was restricted to situations in which S has actively procured the actus reus through P;[247] and that is a special case, justified by analogy with the doctrine of innocent agency. The exception approved in *Howe* can claim no such analogy.

Nonetheless, there are reasons why S should be convicted of murder. It is misleading to present murder and manslaughter as independent offences. Although the wrong in each is

---

receive the jury's first verdict of manslaughter, and sent the jury back out with a direction to convict of murder or acquit; see also Snelling, "The Alternative Verdict of Manslaughter" (1958) 32 *ALJ* 137.

[243] [1974] QB 776.

[244] E.g. [1974] Crim LR 96; Smith, "Aid, Abet, Counsel, or Procure" in Glazebrook (ed.), *Reshaping the Criminal Law* (1978) 120, 128–30; *TBCL* § 15.18. Contrast Kadish, "Complicity, Cause and Blame" in *Blame and Punishment* (1987) 135, 184–6.

[245] [1987] AC 417 (HL), *sub nom. Burke* [1986] QB 626, 641–2 (CA).

[246] *Principles* 432.

[247] Above, § 7.6(ii)(c). Where S's participation is by procurement, it may even be possible in such cases to convict her as principal on ordinary principles of causation. See Alldridge, "The Doctrine of Innocent Agency" (1990) 2 *Crim L Forum* 45, 61ff.

not *precisely* the same (there are some reasons against killing someone deliberately which do not apply to killing someone inadvertently, and vice versa), the core of the wrong is identical. The dominant rationale for each offence is the protection of life. Indeed, it is generally appropriate to think of manslaughter as an alternative rather than separate charge, available when the mens rea of murder cannot be proved or when the defendant has some limited defence such as provocation. Arguably therefore, Ashworth is wrong to characterise the theory underlying the *dicta* in *Howe* as a matter of culpability triumphing over the principles of derivative liability; in the context of derivation, these offences should not be regarded as separate.

It is important to bear in mind that the principles of derivative liability do not have a life of their own. They exist only for a further purpose: to supplement ordinary actus reus doctrines (governing omissions, causation, etc.) by identifying other persons who are answerable when a criminal wrong is done. Once we consider this underlying rationale, it becomes apparent that S *can* be attributed with responsibility for the actus reus of murder in these cases. At least arguably, the underlying function of derivative liability doctrines is properly served by the ruling in *Howe*.

In any event, there is one further, uncontroversial, exception. Consistent with the case of duress above (§ 7.6(ii)(a)), it arises when there is a personal excusatory defence available to P. Culpable homicide admits of palliative defences: especially, for provocation, diminished responsibility,[248] suicide pacts,[249] and infanticide.[250] Where such a defence is open to the principal, the secondary party's liability for murder (or manslaughter, in the case of infanticide) will not be correspondingly reduced.

(iv) Limitations on secondary liability

(a) The Tyrrell principle

The common law contains a limited exemption from secondary liability for victims of crime. The exemption arises in respect of offences that exist for the *protection* of a certain class of person, i.e. persons who are regarded by the statute as victims rather than co-offenders. Such persons are treated as incapable of participating in crimes against themselves. The leading case is *Tyrrell*, where it was held that D, a girl under the age of 16 years, could not be convicted of abetting unlawful sexual intercourse with herself, because the Act that created the offence "was passed for the purpose of protecting women and girls against themselves."[251] However, the common law principle espoused in *Tyrrell* is of uncertain scope,[252] and its application may be doubtful in areas other than offences against

---

[248] Cf. Homicide Act 1957, s. 2(4).

[249] Homicide Act 1957, s. 4(1).

[250] Infanticide Act 1938, s. 1(1).

[251] [1894] 1 QB 710, 712 (Lord Coleridge CJ). See also *Whitehouse* [1977] QB 868; *Pickford* [1995] 1 Cr App R 420, 428; *Congdon* [1990] NLJR 1221. However, while these three cases were decided on the basis of the *Tyrrell* principle, they are better analysed as falling within the next type of exceptions (§ 7.6(iv)(b)), where liability is excluded as a matter of statutory interpretation. See Williams, "Victims and Other Exempt Parties in Crime" (1990) 10 *LS* 245, 249–50.

[252] Williams, "Victims and Other Exempt Parties in Crime" (1990) 10 *LS* 245; Hogan, "Victims as Parties to Crime" [1962] *Crim LR* 683; Williams, "Victims as Parties to Crimes—A Further Comment" [1964] *Crim LR* 686; Heydon, "The Corroboration of Accomplices" [1973] *Crim LR* 264, 274.

young persons and persons suffering from a disability. Indeed, its place even in sexual offences involving the young is now uncertain, following enactment of the Sexual Offences Act 2003. That Act, while not explicitly excluding the *Tyrell* principle,[253] frequently fails to identify with consistency or clarity whether its various offences are designed to protect particular classes of persons, and allows that young persons can commit many of the Act's offences even as principals.[254] Consequently, we must await future rulings about which, if any, of its offences remain subject to the common law exception.[255]

The possibility of applying the *Tyrell* principle depends on the purpose of the relevant legislation, and arises only if the statute is directed toward protecting an identified class of persons. There is certainly no *general* exception for victims of crime. Thus if, for example, in the course of a sadomasochistic episode S asks P to inflict injury on him, it appears that both P and S commit an offence of assault occasioning actual bodily harm contrary to section 47 of the Offences Against the Person Act 1861, since that offence protects the public at large.[256]

(b) Specific legislation

Quite apart from situations where the policy of a statute invokes the *Tyrrell* principle, the relevant primary offence may also be defined by legislation in such a way that it delimits the class of persons who may commit that offence. In such instances, secondary participation is excluded except in so far as such participants qualify within the class stipulated by the primary offence. One example is the offence of living on the earnings of prostitution which, according to section 30(1) of the Sexual Offences Act 1956, can be committed only by a man. Evidently Parliament intended thereby to make pimps punishable for the offence, but not prostitutes; it follows that neither should prostitutes be guilty of abetting those who live off their earnings.[257]

Another instance of statutory restriction on the range of secondary participants was suggested, *obiter*, by Lord Parker CJ in *Carmichael & Sons Ltd v. Cottle*.[258] The Chief Justice observed that, in the context of regulations prohibiting the use or causing or permitting of

---

[253] See s. 73(3), which preserves existing exceptions to complicity liability.

[254] Below, Chapter 12.

[255] Bohlander, "The Sexual Offences Act 2003 and the *Tyrell* Principle—Criminalising the Victims" [2005] *Crim LR* 701.

[256] Cf. *Brown* [1994] 1 AC 212. Interestingly, since the rhetoric of the majority judgments in that case emphasises the paternalistic aspect of not allowing the masochist legally to consent to violence perpetrated by the sadist, arguably it follows that the masochist ought to be treated as a victim falling within the protected class to which the *Tyrrell* principle applies. It is legal moralism, not paternalism, that indicts the masochist.

[257] Cf. *Murphy* (1981) 21 CR (3d) 39, 52–5; Heydon, "The Corroboration of Accomplices" [1973] *Crim LR* 264, 270, 276; Williams, *TBCL* § 15.15. In *Congdon* [1990] NLJR 1221, it was said that prostitutes were exempted from complicity in the offence on the basis of the *Tyrrell* principle, but, as Williams points out, the offence is not designed primarily to protect prostitutes as victims: "Victims and Other Exempt Parties in Crime" (1990) 10 *LS* 245, 249. In 11 BGHSt. 268 (1958), the German Supreme Court decided that S could be guilty as accessory of attempting to murder himself, notwithstanding that (like English law) the German definition of murder excludes suicide, and requires that the killing must be "of another".

[258] [1971] RTR 11, 14. Cf. *Crawford* v. *Haughton* [1972] 1 ALL ER 535; *Farr* [1982] Crim LR 745. Arguably, *Sockett* (1908) 72 JP 428 should have been treated as such a case: see *TBCL* § 15.15 n. 11. S, who was not pregnant, was convicted of aiding and abetting P to use an instrument on S with intent to procure a miscarriage; even though the statute made it no offence for someone not pregnant to use such an instrument on herself, so that S fell outside the class of persons who could commit the offence as principal.

use of a defective vehicle on the road, since "normally, 'using' is applicable to the actual driver" it may follow that:

> "when the words used are 'using or causing or permitting [to be used]', there is no room for the application of the principle in regard to aiders and abettors. The statute in other words itself provides the alternatives, and, if a person is to be charged as an aider and abettor or an accessory, he should be so charged, and under these provisions should be specifically charged with causing or permitting the user."

However, such cases are rare. More commonly, the statute may define a class of persons who may commit the offence *as a principal*, without restricting the class of persons who may be guilty of the offence as a secondary party.[259] A good example is the offence of rape, which can only be committed by a male against a female.[260] This criterion means that a female cannot commit rape as a principal. But she may nonetheless aid and abet a rape committed by someone else.[261]

(c) Law enforcement

Law enforcement is a problematic and partial exception to secondary liability. Suppose that S is a police officer (or indeed a private individual), and assists P to commit a crime in order to gather evidence against P. Is S too guilty of the crime? The answer appears to depend on the nature of S's participation. Consider first the case where S instigates the crime herself. According to the House of Lords in *Sang*, in that case S has no defence:[262]

> "I would now refer to what is, I believe and hope, the unusual case in which a dishonest policeman, anxious to improve his detection record, tries very hard with the help of an *agent provocateur* to induce a young man with no criminal tendencies to commit a serious crime, and ultimately the young man succumbs to the inducement. . . . The policeman and the informer who acted together in inciting him to commit the crime should . . . both be prosecuted and suitably punished."

(So too, added their Lordships, should the young man.[263]) By contrast, where P has instigated the offence and S then participates solely in order to trap P, or to prevent the offence from coming to fruition, S appears to be exempted from liability as a secondary party even though he may satisfy the actus reus and mens rea elements required for liability. According to the Court of Appeal in *Birtles*:[264]

> "It is one thing for the police to make use of information concerning an offence that is already laid on. In such a case the police are clearly entitled, and indeed it is their duty, to mitigate the consequences of the proposed offence, for example, to protect the proposed victim, and to that end it may be perfectly proper for them to encourage the informer to take part in the offence or for the police officer himself to do so. But it is quite another thing, and something of which

---

[259] Cf. the actual decision in *Sockett, ibid.*; also *Mok Wei Tak v. R.* [1990] 2 AC 333; Heydon, "The Corroboration of Accomplices" [1973] *Crim LR* 264, 271.

[260] Sexual Offences Act 1956, s. 1, as substituted by s. 142 of the Criminal Justice and Public Order Act 1994.

[261] See *Ram* (1893) 17 Cox CC 609.

[262] [1980] AC 402 (Lord Salmon).

[263] See further the discussion of entrapment: below, § 20.4.

[264] [1969] 2 All ER 1131n, 1132 (Lord Parker CJ). Cf. *Bainbridge* [1991] *Crim LR* 535; *Clarke* (1984) 80 Cr App R 344; *McEvilly* (1973) 60 Cr App R 150; *McCann* (1971) 56 Cr App R 359.

this court thoroughly disapproves, to use an informer to encourage another to commit an offence or indeed an offence of a more serious character, which he would not otherwise commit."

There is difficult middle ground.[265] In *Williams* v. *DPP*,[266] police officers exposed cartons of cigarettes, apparently unguarded, in the back of a van parked in the street; then prosecuted P after he helped himself to some of them. The Divisional Court stated that the police had not aided or abetted P's crime; yet it is arguable that they did so. Provision of the "bait" constituted an essential ingredient of the crime, not to mention encouragement. Perhaps there is a subtle distinction to be drawn between "instigation" and mere "temptation"; a distinction favourably construed where S's motive is law enforcement. It is impossible, in a text of this nature, to resolve the many difficulties raised by these cases. Suffice it to note, however, that the judgment in *Birtles* is very difficult to reconcile with decisions such as *Yip Chiu-cheung* v. *R.*,[267] where an undercover police officer (who was not charged) was said by the House of Lords to be a co-conspirator with D to export heroin, even though the officer had entered into the conspiracy solely in order to expose the operation. A look behind the judgments is revealing. By ruling the officer a conspirator in *Yip*, their Lordships secured D's conviction for conspiracy. By ruling the officer a non-participant in *Birtles*, the Court of Appeal freed him from the rules constraining evidence given by accomplices, so that his evidence against D did not need corroboration. Making law for ulterior purposes like these, it must be said, is a recipe for bad law.

(v) Secondary liability and inchoate offences

We have observed that secondary participation is not *per se* a crime. Its doctrines do not create offences. They operate as a conduit to S's responsibility for some other form of criminal wrongdoing. Therefore, since aiding and abetting is not an offence, it follows that S cannot commit the inchoate crime of attempting to aid and abet.[268] If there were ever any doubt about this at common law, it has been resolved by section 1(4)(b) of the Criminal Attempts Act 1981, which expressly excludes aiding, abetting, counselling, and procuring from the ambit of the crime of attempting to commit an offence.[269]

The corresponding propositions that one may not commit an offence of inciting, or conspiring, to aid and abet have not been established authoritatively. While the Court of Appeal has held that the offence of conspiracy under section 1 of the Criminal Law Act 1977 excludes any offence of conspiring to aid and abet,[270] the point was left open by the House of Lords.[271]

[265] See Ashworth, "Testing Fidelity to Legal Values: Official Involvement and Criminal Justice" in Shute and Simester (eds.), *Criminal Law: Doctrines of the General Part* (2002) 299.

[266] (1993) 98 Cr App R 209.

[267] [1995] 1 AC 111; below, § 9.2(iv). Cf. *Latif* [1996] 1 ALL ER 353; above, § 4.2(iii)(b) (Case 2).

[268] Smith, "Secondary Participation and Inchoate Offences" in Tapper (ed.), *Crime, Proof and Punishment* (1981) 21. See also Spencer, "Trying to Help Another Person Commit a Crime" in P. Smith (ed.), *Criminal Law: Essays in Honour of J.C. Smith* (1987) 148; below, § 7.7. Contrast the Model Penal Code, § 2.06(3)(a)(ii).

[269] Cf. *Dunnington* [1984] QB 472.

[270] *Hollinshead* [1985] 1 All ER 850, 857–8 (CA).

[271] *Hollinshead* [1985] AC 975 (HL).

Conceptually, the view that there can be no inchoate offence of attempted participation in crime seems right. If S has failed to participate in a crime, she has no connection with it and should not be convicted. Her conduct is, one might say, too remote from manifest criminality to warrant the attention of the criminal law; attention that would be tantamount to punishing for little more than wrongful thoughts.[272] Conversely, however, the inchoate offences *are* offences in themselves, independent of the further crime that is attempted, incited, or conspired toward. Therefore, S may be a party to (aid, abet, etc.) an attempt,[273] incitement, or conspiracy[274] by P to commit an offence.

An exception to the general rule that there is no inchoate liability for participation arises if assistance or encouragement is itself made a substantive offence by legislation. In *McShane*,[275] D visited her mother in hospital where they discussed the possibility of the mother's suicide. D was convicted of attempting to counsel or procure her mother's suicide. She appealed on the ground that no such offence was known to law. However, the Court of Appeal dismissed the appeal. Section 2(1) of the Suicide Act 1961 creates a substantive offence in the following terms:

> A person who aids, abets, counsels or procures the suicide of another, or an attempt by another to commit suicide, shall be liable on conviction to imprisonment for a term not exceeding 14 years.

Under this section, the counselling or procuring is not a secondary form of participation in some further offence; it constitutes an offence in its own right. Consequently, there can be an inchoate offence of attempting to commit an offence against section 2(1), and D was rightly convicted of attempting to counsel or procure another's suicide.

The Law Commission has recently proposed to generalise this last technique, by making assisting or encouraging crime an inchoate offence *in its own right*, independently of the perpetration of the principal's crime.[276] If its proposals become law,[277] one who (say) encourages P to commit a murder becomes, herself, immediately guilty of the inchoate offence of *encouraging crime* and, subsequently, guilty of *murder* if P then carries out the crime as encouraged. These proposals are discussed further in § 7.7 and in Chapter 9.

(vi) Withdrawal

When perpetrating the principal offence, P cannot undo his crime. Once the elements of the offence are concurrently satisfied the offence is committed and cannot be "uncommitted". By contrast, secondary participation *can* be undone. S may withdraw her participation,[278]

---

[272] *Per* Fletcher, *Rethinking Criminal Law* (1978) 680–1: "there is no social wrong in acting to aid the crime of another, unless the aid actually furthers the criminal objective."

[273] *Hapgood v. Wyatt* (1870) LR 1 CCR 221, 11 Cox CC 471; *Clayton* (1843) 1 C & K 128, 174 ER 743. Cf. *Mackie* [1957] NZLR 669 (CA).

[274] *Anderson* (1984) 80 Cr App R 64; cf. *McNamara (No 1)* (1981) 56 CCC (2d) 193.

[275] (1977) 66 Cr App R 97.

[276] *Inchoate Liability for Assisting and Encouraging Crime* Law Com. No. 300 (2006).

[277] Serious Crime Bill, part 2.

[278] "A person who unequivocally withdraws from the joint enterprise before the moment of the actual commission of the crime by the principal, here murder, should not be liable for that crime, although his acts before withdrawing may render him liable for other offences." *O'Flaherty* [2004] 2 Cr App R 20, para. 58.

although she must do so before the crime is committed or attempted. Withdrawal, however, is not easy. Repentance is insufficient.[279] The participation must not merely be discontinued. It must be countermanded.

(a) Withdrawal from participation in a joint enterprise

Where S has participated simply by joining in a common purpose to commit a crime, the common purpose may be abandoned by S's communicating his withdrawal in an unequivocal and timely way. This may become particularly important if, having agreed to participate in a joint crime A, S realises *subsequently* that P may go beyond what was agreed and perpetrate some further crime B: for example, if, in the course of burgling a house, S suddenly realises that her companion is armed with a knife and may use it on anyone found in the house. In this or any other joint enterprise case,[280] S can avoid liability for crime B by then withdrawing from the joint enterprise before crime B is committed.

The leading statement of the criteria for withdrawing from a joint enterprise is found in the Canadian case of *Whitehouse*:[281]

> "where practical and reasonable there must be timely communication of the intention to abandon the common purpose from those who wish to dissociate themselves from the contemplated crime to those who decide to continue in it."

The notice of withdrawal, whether made by words or actions,[282] must be "unequivocal";[283] a perfunctory disclaimer is likely to be insufficient,[284] as is merely leaving the scene,[285] or simply not turning up.[286] It must also be timely, occurring before the crime is committed, and perhaps before its commission is even commenced.[287]

There is no general requirement that S must, in addition to withdrawing unequivocally, also take reasonable steps to prevent P from committing the offence.[288] However, where the situation is such that communication of withdrawal to the other parties is impossible or impractical, withdrawal may alternatively be effected by taking steps to prevent the commission of the offence, e.g. by warning the victim or the police.[289] There may come a point when events are so far advanced that efficacious withdrawal by S is impossible.[290]

---

[279] *Croft* [1944] 1 KB 295; *Becerra and Cooper* (1976) 62 Cr App R 212; Hale, 1 PC 618.

[280] Cf. *Downing* [2005] EWCA Crim 1981.

[281] [1941] 1 DLR 683, 685; see also *Henderson* v. R. [1949] 2 DLR 121. The statement is approved by English authorities: *Becerra and Cooper* (1976) 62 Cr App R 212; *Whitefield* (1983) 79 Cr App R 36; *Rook* [1993] 2 All ER 955. For discussion of the common law and recommendations for reform see K.J.M. Smith, "Withdrawal in Complicity: A Restatement of Principles" [2001] *Crim LR* 769.

[282] E.g., by S's action of quitting the company he has joined: *Hyde* (1672) 1 Hale PC 537; Foster, *Crown Law* 354; *Edmeades* (1828) 3 C & P 390, 392, 172 ER 469, 470.

[283] *Rook* [1993] 2 All ER 955, 962; *Baker* [1994] Crim LR 444.

[284] Cf. *Fletcher* [1962] Crim LR 551.

[285] *Becerra and Cooper* (1976) 62 Cr App R 212.

[286] *Goodspeed* (1911) 6 Cr App R 133; *Rook* [1993] 2 All ER 955.

[287] A possibility raised in *Perman* [1996] 1 Cr App R 24, 34.

[288] *O'Flaherty* [2004] 2 Cr App R 20, paras. 60–61.

[289] *Becerra and Cooper* (1976) 62 Cr App R 212. Cf. Lanham, "Accomplices and Withdrawal" (1981) 97 *LQR* 575, 580ff; *Eldredge* v. *United States* (1932) 62 F 2d 449; *Commonwealth* v. *Huber* (1958) 15 D & C 2d 726.

[290] As appears to have occurred in *White* v. *Ridley* (1978) 140 CLR 342.

(b) Withdrawal from assistance or encouragement

When S has provided supplementary assistance or encouragement toward the commission of a crime, countermanding that participation is more onerous. Mere cessation of further participatory activity will be insufficient.[291] Withdrawal may only be effected by taking steps to counteract the effect of his previous actions. What steps are sufficient will, it seems, depend upon the circumstances and upon the extent of S's prior participation: the greater the involvement, the more S must do to withdraw.[292] Encouragement can normally be undone by an express statement to the opposite effect.[293] However, if material assistance has been rendered, there may have to be some form of physical intervention to impede the crime. For example, S may have to try to recover the knife loaned to P or attempt to protect the victim, perhaps even by restraining P physically.[294] Advice or counsel, on the other hand, cannot as such be undone, but may be countermanded by attempts to dissuade P from proceeding with the crime. In *Grundy*,[295] S had provided P1 and P2 with information about premises they were planning to burgle. Two weeks before the burglary was to be committed, however, S apparently had a change of heart and thereafter had been trying to stop the principals from carrying out their plan. The Court of Appeal ruled that the trial judge had erred by refusing to leave S's defence of withdrawal to the jury.

§ 7.7 Do we need complicity?

Should the day ever arrive when England and Wales join with the rest of the civilised world in codifying their criminal law, Peter Glazebrook has suggested that we might dispense with doctrines of complicity.[296] Glazebrook would simply specify the various modes of involvement in crimes—i.e. modes by which one may become guilty of committing a crime—without drawing a formal distinction between principals and accessories.

It is certainly possible to express a person's involvement in wrongs that are perpetrated by others without resorting to a formal notion of complicity, as the law on joint tortfeasors demonstrates. Removing the labels, however, may not dissolve the reasons that begat them. Even on Glazebrook's draft provisions,[297] helping and encouraging crime are only modes of committing an offence *if* some other person (let us call her the "principal") actually commits that offence. So the liability of the helper or encourager is dependent. Moreover, the actus reus of offending by helping will necessarily differ from the actus reus of offending by

---

[291] *Johnson and Jones* (1841) Car & M 218, 174 ER 479.

[292] Australian case law requires that S take "all reasonable steps" to undo the impact of his participation: *Menniti* [1985] 1 Qd R 520, noted at (1986) 10 *Crim LJ* 236; *Wilton* (1993) 64 A Crim R 359. The proposition that S must seek to "neutralise" the effect of previous assistance was left undecided by the Court of Appeal in *Rook* [1993] 2 All ER 955, 962–3, but seems implicit in *Becerra and Cooper* (1976) 62 Cr App R 212, 219; where S handed over the knife to P, "something vastly different and vastly more effective" than an announced departure was required to constitute withdrawal.

[293] *Saunders and Archer* (1573) 2 Plowd 473, 75 ER 706. Cf. *Croft* [1944] KB 295; *Rook* [1993] 2 All ER 955.

[294] *Becerra and Cooper* (1976) 62 Cr App R 212; *Baker* [1994] Crim LR 444.

[295] [1977] Crim LR 534; cf. *Whitefield* (1984) 79 Cr App R 36.

[296] "Structuring the Criminal Code: Functional Approaches to Complicity, Incomplete Offences and General Offences" in Simester and Smith (eds.), *Harm and Culpability* (1996) 195.

[297] *Ibid.*, 211–12.

committing (i.e. as principal). It looks as if distinct principles will still be needed, in order separately to identify those who independently commit the offence and those who commit it only by helping or encouraging another.

An alternative, more radical proposal, made by the Law Commission and currently before Parliament,[298] is to supplement the law of complicity with two inchoate offences of assisting and encouraging crime.[299] If enacted, S's liability for the new offences will become constituted by her own actions and intentions, and will arise independently of whether the relevant substantive offence is, ultimately, committed by P. The attraction of such a proposal is that, like any inchoate offence, it would reduce the element of luck in S's conviction. The point is made by Spencer:[300]

> "If you commit the crime I knew you intended with my help to commit, I am likely to be an accessory, but if you do not, I may well commit no offence at all. . . . This is very strange. In either case, I have done all that I have to do to incur criminal liability. It is no fault of mine—or to be accurate, it is not due to any lack of fault on my part—that the crime was never committed. If my behaviour was bad enough to punish where you actually made use of the help I gave you, it was surely bad enough to punish where I fully expected you to use it but you got caught before you had the chance."

Reasonable disagreement is possible on this issue. It is worth pausing, however, to note that there are some considerations militating against the creation of inchoate offences of aiding or abetting (depending, especially, on the level of mens rea that they require). It may be that Spencer's argument understates the importance both of the harm principle and of the derivative rationale that underlies accomplice liability. Consider the following case:

> P, wishing to commit a burglary, asks S to lend him a jemmy, and S does so in full knowledge of P's purpose. That night, however, P changes his mind and decides not to proceed with the burglary.

Spencer puts the same case with a different ending:[301]

> "P, wishing to commit a burglary, asks S to lend him a jemmy, and S does so in full knowledge of P's purpose. That night, the police arrest P as he is about to leave his house on burglary bent."

In principle, however, his analysis applies to both cases. On either set of facts, P has committed no offence at all. Not even an attempt: it is mere preparation. Yet, if an inchoate offence of assisting crime were to exist, S would already be guilty. How so? The justification, Spencer argues, is that the basis for exculpating P provides no reason to exculpate S:[302]

> "The reason [the law does not wish to penalise P], surely, is that he is still a long way from his objective, and has a number of psychological barriers to cross before he reaches it, at any one

---

[298] Serious Crime Bill, part 2; *Inchoate Liability for Assisting and Encouraging Crime* Law Com. No. 300 (2006). See Sullivan, "Inchoate Liability for Assisting and Encouraging Crime—The Law Commission Report" [2006] *Crim LR* 1047.

[299] Cf. Spencer, "Trying to Help Another Person Commit a Crime" in P. Smith (ed.), *Criminal Law: Essays in Honour of J.C. Smith* (1987) 148; Buxton, "Complicity in the Criminal Code" (1969) 85 *LQR* 252.

[300] Trying to Help Another Person Commit a Crime" in P. Smith (ed.), *Criminal Law: Essays in Honour of J.C. Smith* (1987) 148, 148.

[301] *Ibid.*, 159.

[302] *Ibid.* (emphasis added). "P" and "S" are substituted for Spencer's use of "A" and "B".

of which he may change his mind and abandon his wicked plan. *It seems unduly harsh to punish someone who may yet decide to behave himself,* and it is practically unwise as well, because if a man stands to be punished as soon as he has begin to carry out his plan, having begun he may think he has nothing to lose by going on. But this reasoning does not apply to S who has knowingly supplied him with help such as advice or equipment. S has done the last act that he is able to do. He has passed his final psychological barrier. There is no question of his changing his mind and simply not doing it: as far as S is concerned *the deed is done.* So it is neither unjust nor foolish to punish S for helping P when we do not punish P."

One objection to this answer is that "it seems unduly harsh" is not the only reason we refrain from punishing P. As our variant example illustrates, the main difficulty about punishing P is not that his psychological culpability is still conditional, as Spencer seems to suggest, but the remoteness of P's conduct from any criminal harm. Earlier, in § 1.2(i), we noted that the requirement for harm is a fundamental restraint on the use of criminal sanctions; a discussion to which we return in Chapter 16. Without harm, or at least proximity to harm (e.g. in crimes of attempt), the State has no justification to intervene. If that is right, to punish P is not merely "unduly harsh": it is potentially to violate the harm principle. Thus the example need not be viewed, as Spencer seems to contemplate, as one where State punishment is prima facie justified, and merely defrayed by the fact that P "may yet decide to behave himself". Rather, it can be seen as a scenario where the grounds for punishing are insufficient.

Derivatively, S may make the same answer. S's deed is done, Spencer notes. This is true, and as such S's conduct can be distinguished clearly from P's. But to punish S threatens still to violate the harm principle. P's deed is *not* done, or even started. And in cases of assistance or encouragement, whether criminalised in secondary or inchoate form, the harm caused or risked by P should be an indispensable part of the justification for punishing S: it is not S's conduct that triggers the harm principle and justifies state intervention, but P's. In turn, on the facts of Spencer's example, P's actions are not yet criminal because they are only preparatory, and too remote from the harm that warrants the criminalisation of burglary. In terms of criminalisation, no event of a sufficiently criminal character has yet occurred. If this goes for P, then it goes for S's involvement too.

Admittedly, the harm-based considerations advanced here have implications for inchoate liability more generally, especially for offences of incitement. But in inchoate offences one would expect a much stronger mens rea element, requiring that one *intend* the crime to be committed; which constrains and offsets the remoteness of the harm to be committed by P. More generally, it must be said that the increasing use of incitement offences to regulate conduct (such as incitement to racial hatred, terrorism, and the like), is a worrying trend in modern society. Criminalisation on the basis of risk prevention is potentially far more invasive, and restrictive of human freedom, than the prohibition of crystallised or attempted harms.

One upshot of the argument set out above in this section—to which the Law Commission makes no reply—is the phenomenon to which Spencer and presumably subjectivists such as Ashworth[303] would object: that S's liability becomes a matter of moral

---

[303] Cf. Ashworth, "Taking the Consequences" in Shute, Gardner, and Horder (eds.), *Action and Value in Criminal Law* (1993) 107.

luck. So far as S is concerned, it is no more than luck that determines whether he is guilty of burglary as a secondary party or escapes scot-free. S has made a complete attempt to aid P's offence. Therefore, the subjectivists would say, he *deserves* to be convicted.

The issue of moral luck was considered earlier, in § 6.5(i). Suffice it to say here that moral luck of this variety is an indispensable aspect both of ordinary life and of the criminal law. It establishes what action D *does*, and therefore what D is guilty *for doing*. Correspondingly, convicting S for complicity in a particular crime captures the moral quality of the events in which S was involved better than would her conviction for an inchoate offence.[304] The difference between being convicted, say, for attempted murder and for murder may be a matter of luck (e.g. whether D's shot misses; whether the bomb fails to explode). But it matters nonetheless. So too in secondary participation. Moreover, the luck is not random. The defendant *makes* his guilt a matter of luck, by attempting to kill or by attempting to aid another's crime. If other areas of the criminal law are properly subject to moral luck, so too is secondary liability.

(i) A causation analysis?

An even more radical suggestion would be to extend the "causal" analysis of complicity, identified by K.J.M. Smith.[305] Smith suggests that complicity liability is best understood as resting on a causal basis, i.e. that S is liable because of her causal contribution to the crime that P commits. Of course, to adopt that analysis would require a much wider notion of causation than is usually employed by the criminal law. Yet it would still be implausible.[306] Even the most generous and broad version of causation is absent in some cases of secondary liability—at least, absent in any sense that leaves causation a meaningful concept. S abets P to offend, for instance, by communicating encouragement to P, whether or not the encouragement makes any difference to P.[307] A person may be sufficiently involved in the crime of another to merit condemnation and punishment without that involvement creating any causal ripples.

Nonetheless, it is worth noting that one or two recent cases have suggested just such a widening of causation, of the sort that Smith's analysis would require. In *Empress*,[308] D was charged with causing a pollutant to enter the nearby river.[309] D had removed a protective device which would otherwise have contained overflows from the drum in which the pollutant was contained. Subsequently, an unknown person (T) opened the tap on the drum, whereupon the contents poured out and overflowed into the river. D's conviction was upheld by the House of Lords. T also caused the pollution, but his act was not a *novus actus* because, according to Lord Hoffmann, it was not "extraordinary":[310]

---

[304] For a valuable general discussion of these questions, see Kadish, "Complicity, Cause and Blame" in *Blame and Punishment* (1987) 135.

[305] *A Modern Treatise on the Law of Criminal Complicity* (1991).

[306] A causal analysis is rejected, for instance, by Smith, "Aid, Abet, Counsel, or Procure"in Glazebrook (ed.), *Reshaping the Criminal Law* (1978) 120; also *Hart and Honoré* 377–88.

[307] See, e.g., *Wilcox* v. *Jeffery* [1951] 1 All ER 464; above, §§ 7.4(i)(b), 7.4(ii).

[308] *Empress Car Co (Abertillery) Ltd* v. *National Rivers Authority* [1988] 1 All ER 481.

[309] Contrary to s. 85(1) of the Water Resources Act 1991.

[310] [1988] 1 All ER 481, 492–3.

"If the defendant did something which produced a situation in which the polluting matter could escape but a necessary condition of the actual escape which happened was also the act of a third party or a natural event, the justices should consider whether that act or event should be regarded as a normal fact of life or something extraordinary. If it was in the general run of things a matter of ordinary occurrence, it will not negative the causal effect of the defendant's acts, even if it was not foreseeable that it would happen to that particular defendant or take that particular form. If it can be regarded as something extraordinary, it will be open to the justices to hold that the defendant did not cause the pollution."

With respect to his Lordship, if this were a correct statement of the criminal law on causation, it would undermine almost entirely the need for complicity liability.[311] The action of P will virtually never count as extraordinary where it is aided or abetted by S, and so will not count as a *novus actus*. Therefore it would almost always be possible to convict S as a principal for the crime that P commits.

Fortunately, as we saw when discussing *Empress* in § 4.2(iii)(d), the passage quoted is not a correct statement of the law. Notwithstanding Lord Hoffmann's purported denial, T's action was a *novus actus*. It was free, deliberate, and informed,[312] and meets all the criteria of a fresh intervening act outlined in § 4.2(iii)(b). The reasoning in *Empress* is inconsistent with the case law discussed in that section;[313] it is, quite simply, wrong.

The core of Lord Hoffmann's error is his likening of deliberate intervening acts *by persons* to the interventions of nature. They are not the same, and are not governed by the same rules. Lord Hoffmann has correctly stated the relevant test for whether a natural event[314] (or a third party's action which is not free, deliberate, and informed[315]) counts as a *novus actus*. But when T's intervention is free, deliberate, and informed, it breaks existing chains of causation *whether or not* it is predictable, foreseeable, or ordinary.

The rationale for distinguishing human from natural intervention was discussed in § 4.2(iii)(b). In the context of secondary liability, recall the example with which we began this chapter:

One fine September morning, Jim is discovered dead in his home. His skull has been crushed by a blow inflicted with a heavy object. The police are called. Upon investigation, they establish that he was murdered by his daughter, Alice, who killed him in order to receive her inheritance under his will. The baseball bat that Alice used to murder Jim belongs to Harry, who lent it to Alice for the purpose.

It matters who killed Jim. Alice did, not Harry. Neither was it a joint murder. Without special causal rules of some form for intervening human agents, we would be forced to say that both Harry and Alice caused Jim's death. But to do so would disregard the claim Harry and Alice each has to be treated as a separate, human, moral agent.

Why is secondary liability special? The answer is that, normally, liability ought to depend on a person's own intentions and actions. Rightly, the law is profoundly reluctant to put one person's criminal liability at the mercy of another person's deliberate choice. This is true as a

---

[311] Cf. *Kennedy* [1999] Crim LR 65, cogently criticised at 67–8 by Smith.
[312] *Pagett* (1983) 76 Cr App R 279, 288–9.
[313] E.g. *Latif* [1996] 1 ALL ER 353, noted in §§ 4.2(iii)(b) (Case 2).
[314] Above, § 4.2(iii)(a).
[315] Above, § 4.2(iii)(b); especially at n. 123.

general proposition. Consider, for example, the question posed once by Smith and Hogan in the context of liability for omissions:[316]

> "If D is sitting in a corridor and, hearing P running towards him, he stretches out his leg with the intention that P shall fall over it, and he does, that is plainly an assault. Is it not an assault if D's leg is stretched out already and he deliberately omits to move it, with the same intention and effect?"

But if D has a duty to remove his leg, then P is granted a power to put D under that duty, simply by running toward him. The law that facilitates this has become a tool by which P may subject D's will to his own. More generally, under a legal system of this sort, D's choices and liability would be governed not merely by his own goals and values but equally by the whims of others.

So, too, principles of causation and secondary liability. Free, deliberate, and informed interventions by third parties have a distinctive causal status because we do not want T to have the power to choose that D shall become guilty of a crime. Complicity liability is a special case. The aider or abettor, deliberately by her actions, places her liability in the hands of P, and cannot complain when responsibility for P's crime is attributed also to her. But S does not commit the offence as a principal, in the way that causation-based approaches to her liability may suggest. It *is* a special case, properly constituted by actus reus and mens rea elements that are quite distinct from those applying to the principal.

---

[316] *Criminal Law* (5th ed., 1983) 45.

8

VICARIOUS AND CORPORATE LIABILITY

§ 8.1 Vicarious Liability

The term "vicarious liability"[1] must be treated with circumspection. The criminal law contains nothing like the general doctrine of vicarious liability that we know from tort. Tort law imposes extensive liability upon employers for torts committed by employees in the course of their employment.[2] This is not surprising. The predominant rationale of the law of negligence is to provide compensation for injury: as between the employer and a third party injured by an employee, it may well be unjust for a judgment debt against the employee to go unsatisfied because of lack of means. There is no equivalent pressure to forge such a doctrine in the criminal law. The traditional concern of the criminal law is with individuals who commit or participate in crimes.[3] Vicarious liability involves the *attribution* to D of conduct and states of mind possessed by another. A judicial disinclination to create a doctrine of vicarious liability is clearly to be seen in the well-known case of *Huggins*,[4] where D, the governor of a prison, was charged with aiding and abetting E, a warder, to murder V, a prisoner who had died on account of E's mistreatment. D was open to considerable criticism in the manner in which he discharged his office. Yet he had not encouraged nor did he know of E's mistreatment of V. Accordingly, no question of criminal liability on the part of D arose:[5]

> "It is not a point to be disputed but that in criminal cases the principal is not answerable for the act of the deputy, as he is in civil cases; they must each answer for their own acts and stand or fall by their own behaviour."

It would not be strictly accurate to state that there is no doctrine at all of criminal vicarious liability at common law. In the crime of public nuisance, an employer may be liable for the act of an employee despite the lack of any instruction or knowledge in respect of the employee's act.[6] Public nuisance is, however, an anomalous crime and in some respects has

---

[1] Glazebrook, "Situational Liability" in Glazebrook (ed.), *Reshaping the Criminal Law* (1978) 108; Leigh, *Strict and Vicarious Liability* (1982); *CLGP* chap. 7.

[2] Atiyah, *Vicarious Liability* (1969).

[3] For critiques of the criminal law's preoccupation with individuals and its presuppositions of liability see Norrie, *Crime, Reason and History* (1993) chaps. 2, 3; Norrie, "'Simulacra of Morality?' Beyond the Ideal/Actual Antinomies of Criminal Justice" in Duff (ed.), *Philosophy and the Criminal Law* (1998) 101; Wells, *Corporations and Criminal Responsibility* (2nd ed., 2001) chap. 3.

[4] (1730) 2 Str 883, 93 ER 915.

[5] *Ibid.*, 885 (Str), 917 (ER).

[6] *Stephens* (1866) LR 1 QB 702; *Medley* (1834) 6 C & P 292, [1824–34] All ER Rep 123.

more affinity with the law of tort than the law of crime.[7] At one time, too, the offence of criminal libel imposed vicarious liability on owners of newspapers for libels published by employees without requiring proof of any knowledge or instruction on the part of the proprietor;[8] but the position has been modified by statutory intervention.[9] In substance, there is no doctrine of vicarious liability in the common law of crime.

In respect of statutory offences, it seems that there are now four ways in which vicarious or quasi-vicarious liability may arise:

(i)   By express legislation.

(ii)   By the delegation doctrine. This arises where a licence is awarded to a named individual to manage a property or activity within the terms of that licence. Should the individual to whom the licence is awarded delegate the performance of the terms of the licence to another person then, in matters relevant to the licence, the conduct *and state of mind* of the other person is attributed to the delegator.[10]

(iii) Where the employee/agent's actions are, in civil law, the actions of the employer/principal (e.g. selling or possessing something in the course of employment). Properly, this is not an instance of vicarious liability, since it requires no attribution of another person's actus reus to the defendant; although it may be loosely described as generating vicarious liability, in the sense that the liability of D is triggered by the conduct of another. These cases generally involve offences of strict liability.

(iv)   Finally, there is a fourth, anomalous, category of cases where vicarious liability for acts of employees has been imposed without delegation.

In the following sections, we consider each of these categories in turn.

(i) Express legislation

Constitutionally, there is nothing to prevent Parliament from explicitly imposing vicarious liability, and sometimes this is done. For example, where a licence is awarded to D to keep or manage a public house he may breach the terms of that licence if he should "by himself of by his servant or agent sell or supply to any person in licensed premises . . . any intoxicating liquor outside permitted hours."[11] Parliament has even gone so far as to deem D the perpetrator of certain minor traffic offences by conclusively presuming him to be the driver of a vehicle at the material time if he is the owner of that vehicle, a form of vicarious liability which even extends to companies.[12] Typically, however, vicarious liability is inferred by the judges as an exercise in interpretation rather than expressly imposed by the terms of legislation.

---

[7] In *Stephens* (1866) LR 1 QB 702, the proceedings were said to be civil in substance.
[8] *Walter* (1799) 3 Esp 21, 170 ER 524; *Gutch, Fisher and Alexander* (1829) Mood & M 433, 173 ER 1214.
[9] Libel Act 1843, s. 7.
[10] *Allen* v. *Whitehead* [1930] 1 KB 211; *Mullins* v. *Collins* (1874) LR QB 292
[11] Licensing Act 1964, s. 59.
[12] Road Traffic Offenders Act 1988, s. 64(5).

(ii) Delegation

Vicarious liability based on the principle of delegation[13] is a judicial creation made in response to a perceived legislative deficiency. Suppose that, pursuant to legislation, a licence is granted to a named person of presumed good character. Typically, the legislation will be silent about the legal position if the licence holder devolves compliance with the terms of that licence to someone else. Of course, if the legislation allows criminal liability for breaches of the licence terms to be imposed on the delegate, enforcing such offences is possible notwithstanding the fact of delegation. Frequently, however, the only person who may commit the offence is the licensee. For instance, section 44 of the Metropolitan Police Act 1839 states that it is an offence for:

> every person who shall have or keep any house, shop, room or place of public resort within the metropolitan police district wherein . . .refreshments of any kind shall be sold . . .and who shall knowingly permit or suffer prostitutes or persons of notoriously bad character to meet together and remain therein.

It will be noted that the persons who may commit offences under this provision are the owner, tenant, or keeper of a house, shop, room, or place of public resort. Prima facie, it must be a person within that class who *knowingly* permits, suffers prostitutes etc. Accordingly, in the leading case of *Allen* v. *Whitehead*,[14] when D, the occupier and licensee of a café, was charged with an offence under section 44, he defended himself on the basis that, as an occasional visitor to his own café, he was unaware that his manager E was allowing prostitutes to remain on the premises. Indeed, he had instructed E not to allow this to happen and had arranged notices in the café warning prostitutes off. Confirming D's conviction, Lord Hewart CJ held that, if D had delegated to E the conduct of the café, "knowledge in the manager was knowledge in the keeper of the house." Were it otherwise, the Chief Justice reasoned, "this statute would be rendered nugatory."[15]

In so ruling, Lord Hewart CJ confirmed a line of authority to the same effect which, though varying in expression and emphasis, can best be explained as imposing vicarious liability based on a delegation principle. This line of authority was reviewed by the House of Lords in *Vane* v. *Yiannopoullos*[16] where E, a waitress employed by D, knowingly sold drinks to customers who were not ordering a meal, in contravention of the terms of D's licence. The doctrine of vicarious liability based on delegation was not accepted with any great enthusiasm by their Lordships: Lords Morris and Donovan thought that the delegation/vicarious liability doctrine was a judicial gloss on statutory provisions; Lord Hodson expressed no opinion on its legitimacy; while Lord Reid found it dubious but too entrenched for judicial uprooting. Only Lord Evershed thought it a "fair and sensible" doctrine. As it happens, all these opinions were *obiter* since it was found on the facts that no delegation had occurred: D, the licensee, remained on the premises, albeit on the upper floor of his restaurant, while E served the drinks two floors below. Their Lordships took the view that a delegation required the non-involvement of the licence holder in the

---

[13] Pace, "Delegation: A Doctrine in Search of a Definition" [1982] *Crim LR* 627.
[14] [1930] 1 KB 211.
[15] *Ibid.*, 214.

management of the licensed premises. This was not the case here. D was involved in the running of his business, even if he could not be everywhere at once. Accordingly, he had not contravened the terms of his licence because he was unaware of the illicit sales by E. Only if he had delegated management to E would E's knowledge have been attributed to him.

This view of delegation has been attacked.[17] It has been regarded as paradoxical that, if D is miles away, she should be fixed with knowledge on the basis of delegation but can evade the attribution of her employee's knowledge when she is much closer to the action. But there is no paradox. Let us accept, if only for the moment, the legitimacy of vicarious liability based on delegation. It follows that where D, the licence holder, remains involved in the management of the licensed premises, it is entirely appropriate that his criminal liability be determined by reference to D's own culpability: if liability requires knowledge, he must be proved to have knowledge. By contrast, if he accepts the obligations of a licence by becoming a licence holder but leaves it to another to ensure compliance with its terms, there need be no inconsistency in fixing the licence holder with the delegate's knowledge. D has assumed the risk. That said, such reasoning will not always resolve liabilities fairly. D may take great care in appointing his delegate but be fixed with any knowledge the delegate acquires. Contrast E, who remains on the premises but manages them very slackly. He will not be imputed with the knowledge of his employees. It cannot be said, therefore, that the delegation principle ensures an even-handed pattern of enforcement for licenses.

Given the potential harshness of the doctrine of vicarious liability by delegation, it is unsurprising that it has come under attack in the courtroom as well as in the literature. In *Winson*,[18] defence counsel argued that, given the division of opinion amongst their Lordships in *Vane* concerning the propriety of the doctrine, the Court of Appeal was free to reject this body of law. However, the Court of Appeal demurred, ruling that vicarious liability based on delegation was too firmly established to have been unsettled by the doubts expressed *obiter* in *Vane*. Further, said the Court, the doctrine was justified by the need to prevent a licensee from evading her responsibilities by delegating them to another.

At the same time, the Court of Appeal in *Winson* emphasised that only a *complete* delegation of the principal's legal duties would trigger the doctrine. Similar sentiments were expressed by their Lordships in *Vane*.[19] Given this, the decision of the Divisional Court in *Howker v. Robinson*[20] is difficult to accommodate. In that case, the Divisional Court upheld D's conviction for knowingly selling alcohol to a person under the age of 18. The sale was made by E, an employee who served in the lounge bar. At the time of the sale D was in the public bar. The magistrates had made a finding of fact that there had been a delegation of authority to E in respect of the lounge bar, which the Divisional Court refused to disturb on the ground that the finding was not plainly unreasonable. Yet it clearly emerges from *Vane* and *Winson* that, as a matter of law, the delegation principle will come into play only if D has devolved to another his obligation to ensure that the terms of the licence are complied with. There seems to have been no evidence of that in *Howker*. D was serving in the public

---

[16] [1965] AC 486.
[17] Pace, "Delegation: A Doctrine in Search of a Definition" [1982] *Crim LR* 627, 629, 636.
[18] [1969] 1 QB 371.
[19] [1965] AC 486, 497 (Lord Reid), 504–5 (Lord Evershed), 510–11 (Lord Hodson).
[20] [1973] QB 178.

bar while E was in the lounge bar, but there was nothing in the facts to suggest that the lounge bar was in any sense E's "domain" where he enjoyed a managerial authority. E was just a barman. Besides, the offence in question was an offence not exclusive to licensees; it could also be committed by employees, undermining the "rendered nugatory" rationale of vicarious liability in this instance. It is submitted that *Howker* is wrong and should not be followed. It was not followed in a non-licensee case, *Bradshaw* v. *Ewart-James*,[21] where it was held that a ship's master had not delegated his responsibilities as master when he took himself off to bed leaving the first mate with temporary responsibility for the vessel. Such temporary delegations are not enough for vicarious liability to arise. Only a complete delegation of authority will suffice.[22]

(iii) When the act of an employee/agent is that of the employer/principal

There is another group of cases which are sometimes said to involve vicarious liability but which, on ultimate analysis, are cases of *strict* liability. Unfortunately, as we discussed in Chapter 6, English law quite often allows conviction without the need to establish mens rea on the part of D. To illustrate: consider the offence of being the parent of a child of compulsory school-age who fails to attend regularly at school.[23] In *Crump* v. *Gilmore*,[24] the Divisional Court confirmed the conviction of D, the parent of E, where E was making too few appearances at school. The court took the offence to be one of strict liability, and therefore it was irrelevant that D neither knew nor had cause to know of E's sporadic school attendances. Accordingly, D's liability was attributable to E's conduct but it was not truly vicarious; she was directly responsible on the basis of her involuntary acquisition of a particular status.[25] It is not unnatural to perceive such liability as vicarious, because D's liability arises out of the conduct of a third party. Legally, however, D's liability is directly imposed.

A similar analysis applies where D Ltd, a company, sells food not complying with food safety standards and thereby contravenes section 8 of the Food Safety Act 1990. Since the offence is strict, liability ensues if it can be proved the seller sold non-compliant food; there is no need to demonstrate any form of knowledge, recklessness, or negligence by anyone.[26] D Ltd sells food each time one of its shop assistants makes a sale to a customer and, if the food is non-compliant, D commits the offence. This situation is often described as an instance of vicarious liability, with liability imposed on the company in respect of the act of its assistant. But, structurally, the facts may be analysed in the same manner as the facts of *Crump* v. *Gilmore*. Each time a sale is made by an assistant to a customer, the company, as

---

[21] [1983] QB 671.

[22] For further discussion of *Bradshaw*, see Sullivan and Warbrick, "Ship Routeing Schemes and the Criminal Liability of the Master" [1983] *LMCLQ* 23.

[23] Formerly Education Act 1944, s. 39(1); now Education Act 1993, s. 199. For critical discussion of the line of authority imposing this exreme form of strict liability, see Horder, "Whose Values Should Determine When Liability Is Strict?" in Simester, (ed.), *Appraising Strict Liability* (2005) 105, and Sullivan "Strict Liability for Criminal Offences in England and Wales Following Incorporation into English Law of the ECHR" in *ibid.*, 195, 207–10.

[24] [1970] Crim LR 28.

[25] See the discussion in Glazebrook, "Situational Liability" in Glazebrook (ed.), *Reshaping the Criminal Law* (1978) 108, 108–14.

[26] Although s. 21 of the Act provides for a defence of due diligence with a reverse burden of proof.

legal owner of the item sold, is selling to the customer. Thus the company commits the offence *directly*. An illustration is *Coppen* v. *Moore (No. 2)*,[27] where a shop assistant sold food under a false description to a customer. The sale, in the legal sense of the term, was made by D, the employer and owner of the goods sold. Consequently, since the offence of selling goods under a false trade description did not require any form of knowledge, recklessness, or negligence to be proved against D, liability was established against him on proof that the assistant sold the item under a false description.

That this is not a case of true vicarious liability can be clearly demonstrated by a contrasting example of a selling offence requiring proof of mens rea. Consider, for instance, the offence of knowingly selling intoxicating liquor to an under-age person. Here D, the owner of the liquor (and the licensee) makes a sale each time liquor is sold by one of his employees; but D will only be liable for the offence if *he* knows that the customer is under-age (direct personal liability), or if he has delegated the running of the licensed premises to the employee who then knowingly sells to an under-age customer (a case of true vicarious liability).

In this category of cases, then, no doctrine, vicarious or other, is involved; there is merely a determination whether an actus reus has been proved personally against D. In particular, it is also necessary still to prove any mens rea element of the offence personally against D. Mens rea may only be attributed vicariously to D if the delegation principle applies (above, § 8.1(ii)).

Consequently, these types of case will normally involve offences of strict liability: typically, offences of sale or possession. There are many offences which penalise the bare possession of particular items. Possession, in legal terms, need not require any physical custody or control of the items alleged to be possessed.[28] A company, for instance, will be in possession of all those items stored in its warehouses and stores for the purposes of its business. Any contraband items delivered, carried, or used by its servants or agents on the company's behalf in the course of employment will be in the possession of the company.

If the varieties of vicarious and quasi-vicarious liability ended here there would be (relatively) little controversy about the topic. Unfortunately, there are some anomalous cases where, unlike sale or possession offences, the actus reus of an offence seemingly requires a degree of *personal* involvement on the part of D but where liability has been imposed on D notwithstanding the lack of D's personal involvement in committing the offence. These are cases of genuine vicarious liability because the actus reus is not proved directly against D but *attributed* to him. This form of vicarious liability is not expressly recognised as such in the case law, precluding the statement of any general principle justifying its imposition. We turn now to consider this further variety of vicarious liability.

(iv) Anomalous cases of liability for an employee's act

In straightforward cases such as selling or possession there can be no objection to attributing an actus reus to D. Activities like "selling" and "possessing" are, in law, technical terms. They are legally constructed activities whose application is determined by the civil law. Thus

---

[27] [1898] 2 QB 306.
[28] *Lewis* (1988) 87 Cr App R 270.

it comes as no surprise that, legally, one can sell or possess through the instrumentality of others. The injustice, if any, does not arise from the way in which the actus reus is established but from the fact that liability may be imposed on proof of actus reus alone.

The picture changes where the actus reus is not a technical legal act but seemingly requires personal conduct on the part of D. That necessary element of liability is missing if the conduct proved was the conduct of someone else. If D is charged as a principal offender with a driving offence, she can quite properly complain if the driving in question was the driving of E and not her own. Driving is not a civil law term but an ordinary physical activity. The courts have therefore required the driving to be by D if she is to be convicted as a principal offender of a driving offence.[29]

Not, unfortunately, without exception. In *James & Son Ltd* v. *Smee*,[30] D, a company, claimed that "using" a vehicle required the same degree of personal involvement as driving a vehicle. A company employee had used a vehicle with defective brakes in the course of his employment. The condition of the brakes was not known to the defendant company. The company was charged under the Motor Vehicles (Construction and Use) Regulations 1951 with "using or causing or permitting to be used . . . a motor vehicle which did not comply with [these] regulations."

The company conceded that it may have "caused" or "permitted" the vehicle to be used, but liability could not be imposed under those heads because, under the statute, proof of causing or permitting a vehicle to be used in a defective condition required proof that D was aware of the condition of the vehicle. Nonetheless, the Divisional Court imposed liability for "using" the vehicle.[31] That term, as the court interpreted it, simply required the vehicle to be used by an employee in the course of employment and did not require any knowledge of the state of the vehicle. In its statutory context, this would appear a strained interpretation. The juxtaposition of the term "using" as an alternative to "causing or permitting to be used" is strongly suggestive that a personal physical act (D itself using) is being contrasted with a permitting or causing of the same physical act (of using by another person). Be that as it may, the Divisional Court considered that a use of the vehicle by an employee in the course of employment was also a use by the employer.

The decision appears to be confined to the employer–employee relationship. It has been held that the owner of a vehicle does not use it when he lends it to a friend,[32] nor when it is taken by a stranger.[33] This suggests that *James & Son Ltd* v. *Smee* is a case, *sub silentio*, of true vicarious liability (outside the sphere of managerial delegation); of an attributed actus reus, not an example of an actus reus requirement that can be fulfilled by the conduct of someone other than the defendant.

An even starker example of this phenomenon is *Slatcher* v. *George Mence Smith Ltd*[34]

---

[29] *Richmond London Borough Council* v. *Pinn & Wheeler Ltd* [1989] RTR 354 (DC).
[30] [1955] 1 QB 78; *Green* v. *Burnett* [1955] 1 QB 78.
[31] *Evans* v. *Dell* [1937] 1 All ER 349.
[32] *Crawford* v. *Haughton* [1972] 1 All ER 535.
[33] *Strutt* v. *Cliff* [1911] 1 KB 1.
[34] [1951] 2 KB 631. In a prosecution under s. 2 of the Merchandise Marks Act 1887, D was entitled to a defence (*per* s. 2(2)(c)) if he could establish "that otherwise he had acted innocently." The Divisional Court disallowed the defence because, although D personally had acted innocently, its employee had not. See also *Sopp* v. *Long* [1970] 1 QB 518 ("caused").

where the "act" of an employee was taken, in law, to be the "act" of the employer. One could not imagine a word more redolent of personal involvement than "act". In the pungent words of Glanville Williams, "a mere statement of this decision is sufficient to show that something must have gone wrong with the reasoning."[35]

(a) A scope-of-employment limitation

This occasional overriding of the requirement for personal conduct is not confined to the regulatory sphere. We have already encountered decisions such as *Cogan and Leak*,[36] where the Court of Appeal—it is generally thought, wrongly[37]—held that the offence of rape can be committed by a principal through the innocent agency of another notwithstanding the plain requirement for the offence of rape to prove that a principal offender had sexual intercourse with the victim. Such decisions are not necessarily insupportable. It may well be appropriate, on occasion, to rule that D is, in substance, the principal offender despite the fact that his conduct does not satisfy, in literal terms, the actus reus specified for the offence.[38] Yet the debate required to justify this form of liability is suppressed by judicial assertions that D has directly committed the actus reus of the offence when the facts of the case clearly indicate the contrary.

In the regulatory sphere, it seems clear that the type of vicarious liability found in *James & Son Ltd v. Smee*, of an employer for acts of an employee, will be subject to at least one limitation: the employee's act must be in the course of employment. Where the employee acts outside the scope of his employment or of the authority conferred, the defendant will not be liable. For example, in *Adams v. Camfoni*[39] it was held that a master was not liable when a servant boy, who had no authority to do so, supplied his master's liquor to a customer out of hours. Similarly, if a cleaner, lacking any authority to do so, opens a hotel bar outside the legal hours and sells liquor to customers, the licensee will not be liable.[40] The cleaner's acts are clearly outside the scope of his employment and are not the acts of the licensee who employs him.

On the other hand, it seems that an employee will not necessarily exceed the scope of his authority simply because he acts in a way contrary to instructions given. One illustration of this is *Coppen v. Moore (No. 2)*,[41] discussed in § 8.1(iii). Where an assistant sold hams as "Scotch ham", despite the employer's express instructions that they were only to be sold as "breakfast hams", the sale nonetheless was made by the employer and constituted an offence by the latter.

(v) Summary

To summarise, the occurrence of true vicarious liability is confined to statutes which expressly impose such liability and to situations where a duty of compliance with the terms

---

[35] *CLGP* 223.

[36] [1976] QB 217.

[37] See above, §§ 7.3(i), 7(6)(ii)(b).

[38] For instance, § 2.06(2) of the Model Penal Code provides that "a person is legally accountable for the conduct of another person when: (a) acting with the kind of culpability that is sufficient for the commission of the offence, he causes an innocent or irresponsible person to engage in such conduct. . . ."

[39] [1929] 1 KB 95.

of a licence has been delegated. There are some cases of strict liability which may be described as cases of vicarious liability but which merely demonstrate that certain activities, such as selling or possessing, can be done through the agency of others. By contrast, other verbs imply personal involvement. A company, for instance, can sell a car through a sales-person but does not itself "use" or "drive" a car when a company car is used or driven by a company employee. In these cases, liability can only be vicarious.

In these other cases, however, D has sometimes been held vicariously liable without there being any finding of delegation. Decisions such as *James & Son Ltd* v. *Smee* (above) have credited D with the actus reus of an offence which requires personal involvement even though D was not personally involved. Such cases involve a form of vicarious liability because an activity such as, say, driving can only be *attributed* to a person who was not in fact driving. This last form of vicarious liability is *ad hoc* and unacknowledged even when imposed. But, alas, it exists.

It is also worth noting here that it can be said that, as a result of the decision of the House of Lords in *Environmental Agency* v. *Empress Car Co. (Abertillery) Ltd*,[42] in substance the scope of unacknowledged vicarious liability has been extended. Recall that the defendant company was found to have "caused" pollution to a river when the immediate cause of the pollution was the act of an unknown intruder who had turned the tap of the oil tank sited on the company's land. We will not rehearse again here our criticism of the finding that the mere presence of oil on the company's land was a cause of the pollution: it suffices to say if those criticisms are well founded then in substance the company was made vicariously liable for the intruder's act.

(vi) Reform

In its Draft Criminal Code, the Law Commission provides no statutory version of the delegation principle. Under the Code, if vicarious liability is to be imposed, it must be done so expressly.[43] This is welcome. The judicial creation of the delegation principle is an undis-criminating way of enforcing the duties of licensees. As we have acknowledged, there is some reason to discriminate between cases where D retains a responsibility for complying with the terms of the licence and cases where he wholly delegates discharge of his duties to another. Yet it is an unsatisfactory distinction. D1 may remain on his premises, manage his business inattentively, and take no care in the discharge of his legal duties. Conversely, D2 may take particular care in appointing a delegate and have good reason to think that the appointed person will be scrupulous in her observance of the delegated duties. Yet the former case is treated more indulgently than the latter.

Where vicarious liability results in liability being imposed on blameless persons, an issue may arise under the terms of Article 3 of the European Convention on Human Rights which proscribes, *inter alia*, inhumane or degrading punishment.[44] But even if a defendant's

---

[40] See *Jull v Treanor* (1896) 14 NZLR 513.
[41] [1898] 2 QB 306.
[42] [1999] AC 22; discussed above, § 4.2(iii)(d).
[43] Law Com. No. 177, *A Criminal Code for England and Wales* (1989) cl. 29.
[44] In *Reynolds* v. *G H Austin & Sons Ltd* [1951] 2 KB 149, Devlin J remarked, apropos the imposition of vicarious liability, that "if a man is punished because of an act done by another, whom he cannot reasonably be expected to

invocation of Article 3 were successful, that would be something of a patchwork fix. Article 3 is likely to have purchase only in cases where the blameless defendant is an individual subjected to imprisonment, rather than a company. What is long overdue is a complete rethink about defining and enforcing regulatory law, a matter which runs to strict liability as well as to vicarious liability. The fundamental issue is ensuring that any offence which carries the stigma of a formal conviction must be premised on some degree of culpability on the part of the person convicted; a culpability that, in certain circumstances, could be simple as opposed to gross negligence.

§ 8.2 Corporate liability [45]

(i) The justification of corporate liability

Since the mid-nineteenth century, it has been established that companies may commit crimes of strict liability.[46] Where no culpability is required in the definition of the offence, the fact that a company is, at law, a separate person distinct from its directors, employees, and shareholders presents no barrier to the imposition of criminal liability. For example, evirontmental legislation may require that the carbon levels of smoke emissions must not exceed a given level, a matter of strict liability.[47] If the smoke emissions of a factory owned by D plc should exceed permitted levels, then D, as owner of the factory, will be liable straightforwardly for the offence. Historically, there was a view that companies by virtue of their artificial nature were incapable of being guilty of any crime because guilt was perceived to be exclusively a human property.[48] That view did not survive long into the era of industrialisation and the advent of the joint-stock company. The application of regulatory law to limited companies is now almost completely uncontroversial. There may be argument whether such regulation should ever take the form of strict liability, but hardly anyone objects specifically to the fact that companies are held liable for such offences. Indeed, given the overwhelming predominance of the limited company in industrial, transport, and commercial activity,[49] corporate liability is essential for the efficacy of any legislation concerned with pollution, health, safety, and trading standards.

---

influence or control, the law is engaged, not in punishing thoughtlessness or inefficiency, and thereby promoting the welfare of the community, but in pouncing upon the most convenient victim. Without the authority of express words, I am not willing to conclude that Parliament can intend what would seem to the ordinary man to be the useless and unjust infliction of a penalty."

[45] Wells, *Corporations and Criminal Responsibility* (2nd ed., 2001); Fisse and Braithwaite, *Corporations, Crime and Accountability* (1993); Clarkson, "Kicking Corporate Bodies and Damning Their Souls" (1996) 59 *MLR* 557; Gobert, "Corporate Criminality: New Crimes for the Times" [1994] *Crim LR* 722; Gobert and Punch, *Rethinking Corporate Crime* (2003); Sullivan, "Expressing Corporate Guilt" (1995) 15 *OJLS* 551; Sullivan, "The Attribution of Culpability to Limited Companies" [1996] *CLJ* 515.

[46] *Birmingham and Gloucester Railway Co.* (1842) 3 QB 223, 114 ER 492.

[47] Clean Air Act 1993, s. 2.

[48] In the famous words of Edward, First Baron Thurlow, a company has "no soul to be damned and no body to be kicked": Mencken, *A New Dictionary of Quotations* (1942) 223.

[49] There are over a million registered companies: *Companies* (HMSO, 1998).

Nonetheless, some writers have queried the need for any form of corporate criminal liability, even with respect to regulatory law.[50] It has been objected that the fines paid by the company ultimately will be borne by the shareholders who are not, in any sense, responsible for the offence. However, this stance overlooks the nature of an investment as a shareholder in a limited company. An investment on the terms of limited liability is a legally created privilege, and the terms on which sums of capital can be aggregated and deployed have, from the controversial inception of limited companies, been a matter of continuing legislative scrutiny and revision. The funds of limited companies are subject to a host of different financial imposts imposed in what is taken to be the public interest. Investments must be made on the assumption that companies will not seek illegitimate competitive advantages by non-compliance with regulatory law. From that perspective, there is no difference in principle between fines and other forms of financial exaction (e.g. by a regulator for underperformance on agreed targets). The impact of fines on investors, arising from non-compliance with law, is merely one of a large number of investment risks. In our view, it is not enough to punish the individuals responsible for breaching regulations. In fairness to companies which commit resources to meet their legal obligations, companies found in breach should be fined at least to the extent necessary to correct any competitive advantage gained thereby.

(ii) Crimes of strict liability

For crimes of strict liability, the artificial personality of a limited company poses few conceptual difficulties in imposing corporate liability. In a limited sense all corporate liability can be spoken of as vicarious liability because corporate conduct is ultimately referable to some form of human conduct.[51] When the corporately owned factory chimney belches pollution, it does so as a product of a set of acts and omissions by human agents. In legal terms, however, companies will commit offences of strict liability directly: the company, of itself, will fulfil the offence specifications of regulatory crimes (in terms of selling, leasing, possessing, using, etc.) if done in the course of business of the company. This type of case is discussed in more detail above, in § 8.1(iii).

(iii) Crimes of mens rea

(a) The policy issue: how is corporate culpability possible?

For crimes where forms of mens rea are required—defrauding the revenue, acting dishonestly when appropriating property belonging to another with an intent permanently to deprive, killing V by an act of gross negligence, etc.—some legal means of attributing the requisite mens rea to the company is required. Whether such legal means should be deployed at all and, if so, what kind of legal means, is a controversial area of law and policy. The view might be taken that "culpability", in the non-legal sense of the term, is an entirely

---

[50] See, e.g., the view of the former authors of Smith and Hogan, *Criminal Law* (10th ed., 2002) 207: "the necessity for corporate criminal liability awaits demonstration."
[51] Although this claim may be disputed, a matter to be discussed below, § 8.2(v).

human property, something which a corporation with its inherently artificial form cannot possess.[52] Acceptance of that view allows two responses. First, any question of companies becoming responsible for what may be termed culpability-crimes is categorically dismissed and the imposition of corporate liability for such crimes is regarded as a mistake. An alternative response is to allow liability for such crimes while recognising that the attribution of culpability to companies is a matter of form rather than substance (for companies cannot *really* be culpable), a matter of form engaged in for whatever consequentialist returns may be had. On this second approach (the approach by and large taken by English law), the conduct and state of mind of an individual is attributed to the company and becomes corporate conduct and a corporate state of mind (while remaining also, for legal purposes, the conduct and state of mind of the given individual). So, to take manslaughter by gross negligence as an example, if E, an employee of D plc, exhibits the culpability for manslaughter when causing the death of V in the course of his employment with D, it may be possible to attribute E's conduct and culpability to D, allowing both D and E to be convicted of manslaughter. That possibility would not arise, however, if the death of V were to occur as a consequence of the activities of D where no individual associated with D could be shown to have the culpability required for manslaughter.[53]

A radically different approach is in order if the view is taken, as increasingly it is, that companies are culpability-bearing agents in their own right, manifesting an inherently *corporate* agency and culpability not reducible to a matter of human agency. If corporations *as corporations* can possess intentionality, concoct schemes to injure or defraud, etc., then rules and doctrines must be crafted to capture (in a forensically manageable way) this form of culpability.

In the next section, we will consider how liability for crimes of mens rea is imposed on companies in English law. This will involve an examination of what is known as the doctrine of identification, which is currently the predominant legal basis for attributing states of mind to companies. However, the territory at one time exclusively occupied by the identification doctrine may sometimes be encroached upon by judicial recourse to vicarious liability, which will be discussed in § 8.2(iii)(c)–(d). Finally, we will consider options for future reform, including possible alternatives to the identification doctrine and to vicarious liability.

(b) Attributing culpability to limited companies: the doctrine of identification

The idea that forms the basis of this doctrine is a simple one, even simplistic. The identification doctrine, sometimes known as the *alter ego* principle, takes the conduct and state of mind of certain high-ranking corporate officials to be the conduct and state of mind of the company itself. If, for example, a company director of sufficient stature to be regarded as a corporate *alter ego* were to form a dishonest intent in the course of transacting company business, so too his company would possess the same dishonest intent.

---

[52] Wolf, "The Legal and Moral Responsibility of Organisations" in Pennock and Chapman (eds.), *Criminal Justice* (1985) 267.

[53] *R. v. H M Coroner for East Kent, ex p Spooner* (1989) 88 Cr App Rep 10; *P & O Ferries (Dover) Ltd* (1990) 93 Cr App R 72; *Great Western Trains Co* (unreported: Central Criminal Court, Scott Baker J, 30 June 1999).

This anthropomorphic doctrine first surfaced in the civil case of *Lennards Carrying Co Ltd v. Asiatic Petroleum Ltd,*[54] where the defendants were being sued by plaintiff cargo-owners for the loss of cargo caused by the unseaworthiness of the vessel managed by the defendants. Under applicable legislation, the defendant's liability in damages would be capped unless it could be proved that the loss was attributable to the defendant's "fault". As interpreted by Lord Haldane for the Privy Council, "fault" required personal fault on the part of *Lennards,* the company that managed the ship on behalf of the owners. This was supplied by Mr Lennard, the managing director of Lennards, who was aware of the condition of the vessel yet permitted it to be taken to sea. According to Lord Haldane:[55]

> "Mr Lennard was the directing mind of the company . . . his action was the action of the company itself . . . [his] fault is not merely that of a servant or agent for whom the company is liable upon the footing *respondent superior* but somebody for whom the company is liable because his action is the very action of the company itself."

This identification of high-ranking officials with the company itself was adopted into the criminal law in the cases of *DPP v. Kent and Sussex Contractors*[56] and *ICR Haulage Ltd,*[57] where companies were held liable (for intending to deceive the Revenue and for conspiracy to defraud, respectively) after the court in each case identified the culpable states of mind of corporate officials with their companies.

Over time, the doctrine became well embedded into both civil and criminal law and, with familiarity, an increasingly liberal approach was taken to the question of which corporate officials could be identified with the company.[58] This liberality was checked by the House of Lords decision in *Tesco Supermarkets Ltd v. Nattrass,*[59] where it was ruled that only individuals at the apex of the corporate hierarchy could be identified with the company. Lord Diplock took a rigid and formal approach to this question: only officials granted plenary authority in the articles of association over a company's affairs could be so identified. For him, that would include the board of directors making decisions on behalf of the company, together with the chief executive and, possibly, any other executive possessing a plenary authority for the activity at issue in a particular case.[60] Lord Reid, too, required a plenary authority as opposed to a delegated responsibility but was prepared to look at substance as well as form; he did not make a grant of authority in the articles of association a precondition for identification.[61]

The narrowness of the doctrine is exemplified by the decision in *Redfern,*[62] where Dunlop (Europe) Ltd was charged with knowingly exporting combat equipment to Iran in contravention of agreed sanctions. The facts of the matter were known to the European sales manager but he was considered insufficiently important in Dunlop's scheme of things to be identified with his company. Similarly, in *P&O Ferries (Dover) Ltd,*[63] where P&O Ltd

---

[54] [1915] AC 705.
[55] *Ibid.,* 713, 714.
[56] [1944] KB 146.
[57] [1944] KB 551.
[58] E.g. *The Lady Gwendolen* [1965] 2 All ER 283.
[59] [1972] AC 153.
[60] *Ibid.,* 199.
[61] *Ibid.,* 171.
[62] [1993] Crim LR 43.
[63] (1990) 93 Cr App R 72.

were charged with manslaughter following the Zeebrugge sinking, the ship's master was ruled not to be a person who could be identified with the company.

The one thing to be said in favour of the doctrine of identification is that, provided it is confined to the very top echelon of corporate officials, the operation of the doctrine allows a fair measure of predictability. Lord Diplock, in *Tesco*,[64] reasoned that this exclusive focus on top management was integral to the very nature of the doctrine. He insisted that it involved a form of *direct* corporate responsibility in contradistinction to vicarious liability. As the doctrine identifies the very state of mind of the company itself, that entity is to be located solely at the top—the very "brains" of the company in Lord Denning's quaint idiom.[65] Yet a scrutiny of the way that the doctrine works reveals it, in substance, to be very close to vicarious liability. The company's culpability is a derivative of human culpability. Within the doctrine's own terms, a finding that the company possessed the mens rea for an offence may only be made if some decision-making organ or individual of sufficient seniority possessed the mens rea for the offence. This narrowness is the doctrine's major limitation in terms of obtaining corporate convictions. If we confine our attention to charges of corporate manslaughter, by 2005 there had been only 34 prosecutions for manslaughter brought against companies, with no convictions against companies of any size or complexity.[66] Successful prosecutions have been confined to small companies where the top management ran the company in a "hands on" manner. In any larger company, it is exceedingly unlikely that an official of sufficient stature to count as an *alter ego* of the company would be found grossly negligent in respect of particular safety matters; as the failed *P&O* ("a company infected with the disease of sloppiness"[67]) prosecution demonstrates. Notwithstanding the increasing public concern with corporate safety standards, the Court of Appeal has confirmed in *A-G's Reference (No. 2 of 1999)*[68] that liability for gross negligence manslaughter can only be imposed on a company under the principle of identification.

(c) Vicarious corporate liability

Until comparatively recently, it would have been accurate to say that vicarious liability in its full sense was not imposed on companies in the sphere of criminal law. To be sure, any employee selling, using, possessing, etc., in the course of employment might incriminate the company for a strict liability offence. But for a mens rea offence, identification was required.

In *Tesco Supermarkets plc* v. *Brent LBC*,[69] an issue arose concerning whether Tesco "knew or had reasonable cause to believe" that a hirer of a restricted video was under the age of 18; a matter of culpability which, according to Professor Sir John Smith, had to be resolved under the terms of the identification doctrine.[70] However, the Divisional Court confirmed the company's conviction, ruling that the state of mind of the checkout assistant could be identified with Tesco. Staughton LJ blithely distinguished the earlier *Tesco* decision on the

---

[64] [1972] AC 153, 199f.
[65] *Bolton (Engineering) Co Ltd* v. *Graham & Sons* [1957] 1 QB 159, 172.
[66] Home Office, *Corporate Manslaughter: The Government's Draft Bill for Reform* Cm. 6497 (2005).
[67] *Report of Court No. 8074* (HMSO, 1987) para. 14.1 ("Sheen Report").
[68] [2000] 1 QB 796.
[69] [1993] 2 All ER 718.
[70] [1993] Crim LR 624, 626.

basis that it concerned a provision in a different statute. The House of Lords took a similar line in *Director General of Fair-Trading* v. *Pioneer Concrete plc*,[71] finding that the knowledge and conduct of a company's sales force sufficed to place the company in contempt of court. These, and other decisions, may give the impression that identification is in the process of being supplanted by vicarious liability. Yet prospects of an orderly demise are confounded by the House of Lords decision in *Seaboard Offshore Ltd* v. *Secretary of State for Transport*,[72] where a company was charged with failing to take reasonable steps to secure maritime safety. The human fault lay with a company engineer, who allowed the ship to sail despite an inadequate inspection of the engines. One might expect that, in a regulatory offence concerned with safety standards, vicarious liability might be imposed. Instead, identification was the principle applied, entailing an acquittal of the company on the ground that the engineer was insufficiently senior to generate criminal liability for the company. Consequently, there is now considerable confusion over the appropriate rule of attribution to employ when resolving corporate liability for a regulatory offence that requires proof of some form of culpability.

(d) A via media?

This uncertainty in the law was directly addressed by Lord Hoffmann in the Privy Council case of *Meridian Global Funds* v. *Management Asia Ltd*.[73] Conducting a broad review of previous authority, Lord Hoffmann concluded that there is no general theory of attribution in the matter of assigning states of culpability to companies. Instead, there are specific rules of attribution tailored for the terms and policies of the statutory or common law offence at issue in particular cases. What were previously thought to be leading cases on the theory of attribution—*Tesco Supermarkets Ltd* and *Asiatic Petroleum Ltd*—are downgraded by Lord Hoffmann to authorities dealing with specific statutory provisions.[74] For him, the way to proceed in determining a question of corporate criminal liability is, first, to resolve whether the offence in question is an offence that may be committed by a company. If it is, one then moves on to consider the level in the corporate hierarchy where culpability should be located in order best to give expression to the terms and policy of the offence under consideration.[75]

According to the *Meridian* analysis, the identification doctrine on the one hand and vicarious liability on the other are the two polar extremes of a range of different rules of attribution. One must allow this as a theoretical possibility. Yet the fact is that, of the rules of attribution on offer, the choices made have been confined to either identification or vicarious liability. The case law does not disclose a spectrum of choices but only two. It is not difficult to understand why choices made to date divide into these two possibilities. If uppermost in a court's mind is the need for an effective law that maximises deterrence of companies, the broad-based inculpation offered by vicarious liability becomes attractive. Thus, in *Meridian* itself, the issue was whether the company "knew" that it had acquired a

---

[71] [1995] 1 AC 456.
[72] [1994] 1 WLR 541.
[73] [1995] 2 AC 500.
[74] Trade Descriptions Act 1968 (*Tesco*); Merchant Shipping Act 1894 (*Asiatic Petroleum*).
[75] [1995] 2 AC 500, 507.

shareholding in another company.[76] The knowledge of a fund manager of insufficient status to be identified with the company was, nonetheless, found to be knowledge attributable to the company. The Privy Council advised that the statutory policy informing the offence—the need for prompt disclosure of acquisitions to provide transparency in securities markets—required the imposition of vicarious liability.[77]

Militating against a wholesale adoption of vicarious liability is the concern to be fair to companies and to their constituencies. The more serious the offence, the greater the potential for damage to corporate reputation, the more compelling the value of fairness. Restraint in the imposition of corporate liability for serious offences has been expressed, until now, by insisting on the applicability of the identification doctrine. *Post Meridian*, we must now allow the possibility of some *via media* between vicarious liability and identification. To date there has been no experiment along those lines. The decision in *A-G's Reference (No. 2 of 1999)*,[78] which rigidly confirms that the doctrine of identification is the rule of attribution for corporate manslaughter, is not a good augury for a more flexible approach—at least, not in the area of serious, stigmatic criminal offences.

(iv) Summary: the current law

Any summary of the current law of corporate criminal liability must, inevitably, be tentative:

    (i)   If an offence is of a regulatory nature, makes no reference to mens rea, and concerns activities which can straightforwardly be attributed to companies ("selling", "possession", "polluting", etc.), corporate guilt will be a simple exercise in the imposition of strict liability.

    (ii)   Recalling the earlier general discussion of vicarious liability, vicarious liability will be imposed for mens rea offences concerned with compliance with the terms of a licence should it be found that the company has delegated to another the task of compliance with its duties. This follows on ordinary vicarious liability principles, applicable to corporate and individual defendants alike.

    (iii)   Even in the absence of delegation, mens rea may be attributed to a company on the basis of vicarious corporate liability if the offence concerns retail regulation (*Tesco Supermarkets* v. *Brent*[79]) or market regulation (*Meridian*[80]).

    (iv)   In the light of *Seaboard Offshore*,[81] it cannot be assumed that vicarious liability will always be the rule of attribution for corporate defendants even where the offence is of a regulatory nature. As the *Seaboard* decision shows, if a regulatory offence requires mens rea the identification doctrine can be chosen as the rule of attribution. However, it is fair to say that vicarious liability is typically more likely to be adopted in the regulatory sphere, even where the offence involves proof of mens rea.

---

[76] Securities Amendment Act 1988 (New Zealand), s. 20(3)(4).
[77] [1995] 2 AC 500, 511.
[78] [2000] 1 QB 796.
[79] [1993] 2 All ER 718.
[80] [1995] 2 AC 500.
[81] [1994] 1 WLR 541.

That leaves the question when, if ever, the doctrine of identification will be put aside where serious, stigmatic criminal offences are involved. Recall that, in *Pioneer Concrete*,[82] the House of Lords found companies to be in contempt of court on the basis of vicarious liability. Contempt is a matter of grave reputational consequence and may give rise to unlimited fines. But its nature is too anomalous to warrant any general conclusions. In recent cases where serious crimes have been charged, including manslaughter, identification has remained the basis of attribution.[83] In *Meridian*, Lord Hoffmann particularly warned against assuming that anything in his judgment had any implications for corporate manslaughter;[84] a warning corroborated by the decision in *A-G's Reference (No. 2 of 1999)*,[85] which confirmed identification as the rule of attribution for corporate manslaughter in the context of a prosecution following a large-scale rail crash. It may well be the case that identification will remain the principal, even the sole, basis of attribution of culpability for serious, stigmatic crimes.

(v) Reform: new conceptions of corporate action and responsibility

There is a growing strand of opinion that the unsatisfactory state of the law regarding corporate criminal liability is in large part explained by a failure to ask the right questions. To date in English law, the approach has been to ask questions first about the culpability of *individuals* associated with companies, and then to ask further questions concerning how the culpability of these individuals has implications for the culpability of their companies. To proceed in this way, it may be argued, overlooks the crucial fact that there is such a thing as genuine corporate agency and, in turn, corporate culpability—a free-standing culpability that need not be derived from the faults of individuals associated with the company.[86] Indeed, it has been asserted that corporate culpability may be present even if no one associated individual has been in any degree at fault.[87] Two attempts to capture this form of culpability will now be examined. This is of more than academic interest because, as will be seen, there have been legislative proposals for England and Wales which attempt to formulate a "corporate" corporate criminal liability.

(a) Reactive fault

"Reactive fault" is a proposal of Professors Fisse and Braithwaite for a new basis of corporate liability.[88] They are committed to the view that companies, in moral terms, amount to

---

[82] [1995] 1 AC 456.

[83] See, e.g., *H M Coroner for East Kent* (1989) 88 Cr App R 10; *P & O Ferries (Dover) Ltd* (1990) 93 Cr App R 72; *Great Western Trains Co* (unreported: Central Criminal Court, Scott Baker J, 30 June 1999).

[84] [1995] 2 AC 500, 512.

[85] [2000] 1 QB 796.

[86] French, *Collective and Corporate Responsibility* (1984) esp. 30–65. French appears to claim that the structure and practice of decision-making in companies may constitute a distinctive form of corporate intentionality which is not reducible to the mental states, past and present, of human agents associated with companies. For a view that French is offering merely a semantic account of the agency of companies see Oryang and Shiner, "Organisations and Agency" (1995) 1 *Legal Theory* 283.

[87] Dan-Cohen, *Rights, Persons and Organisations: A Legal Theory for Bureaucratic Society* (1986) chap. 3.

[88] See Fisse and Braithwaite, *Corporations, Crime and Accountability* (1993); Fisse and Braithwaite, "The Allocation of Responsibility for Corporate Crime: Individualism, Collectivism and Accountability" (1988) 11 *Sydney LR* 468. Cf. French, "Fishing the Red Herrings out of a Sea of Moral Responsibility" in LePore and McLaughlin (eds.), *Actions and Events: Perspectives on the Philosophy of Donald Davidson* (1985) 73.

something more than the sum of the individuals associated with them, that something important is lost if corporate conduct is represented exclusively as a function of human conduct.[89] This perspective forms the backdrop of their proposal; they do not, however, try to devise a new regime which gives direct expression to an intrinsically corporate form of culpability. Their proposal dispenses entirely with the need to establish culpability at the time of the actus reus. The fault of the company is to be found in terms of its reaction, or lack of reaction, to the commission of the actus reus. In their words:[90]

> "Reactive fault [is] . . . an unreasonable corporate failure to devise and undertake satisfactory preventative or corrective measures in response to the commission of the actus reus of the offence."

Finding culpability from acts, omissions, and states of mind which arise *after* the commission of the actus reus is a radical departure from the norm. Yet we would not have left behind the appraisal of the conduct of human beings. Let us assume that the actus reus is the death of a worker caused, say, during the course of building activities undertaken by D Ltd. There would, of course, have to be an initial investigation of the death-causing incident. There would follow an examination of what could and should have been done to make the working practices of D Ltd safer for the future. It is hard to see how the conduct of individuals associated with D Ltd would not form a key element at the trial. There are other, allied, problems. What charge would be brought against D Ltd? Would it, could it, depend on the degree of reactive fault found to be present? How would it be determined whether the degree of reactive fault proved against D Ltd merited a conviction for manslaughter? If the jury brought in a verdict of manslaughter against D Ltd, what would be the position of individuals associated with D Ltd whose conduct was found to be wanting? Would there be a possibility of complicity charges and, if so, on what conceptual basis? If such charges are not to be brought, would and should any civil law consequences follow for individuals closely associated with the guilty verdict against the company?

The adoption of reactive fault would signal an enormous change in corporate liability. Deaths or injuries occurring in the context of manufacturing, construction, mining, air, rail and sea transport activities, road accidents involving corporately owned vehicles, etc., potentially involve serious criminal liability on the part of companies. The issues arising at trial would not turn on the culpability at the time of a particular incident but instead would require a review of corporate safety and other procedures within an open-ended time frame.[91] The prosecutorial and forensic burden would be enormous. Reactive fault is an untenable basis for corporate liability.

(b) The theory of aggregation

Under this theory,[92] the faults of any two or more persons associated with the company may be aggregated and attributed *in toto* to the company. A judgment then has to be made

---

[89] Fisse and Braithwaite, *Corporations, Crime and Accountability* (1993) chap. 2.

[90] *Ibid.*, 48.

[91] The efficacy and acceptability of trial by jury comes under increasing pressure the more protracted and complex the issue to be resolved, as is evidenced by the difficulties experienced in effectively prosecuting serious fraud. See Sullivan, "The Particularity of Serious Fraud" in Birks (ed.), *Pressing Problems in the Law* vol. 1 (1995) 99, 102–3.

[92] Discussed by Wells, *Corporations and Criminal Responsibility* (1993) 132–3.

whether the totality of this consolidated fault constitutes, for the company, the culpability required for the offence. If one or more of the associated individuals is possessed in full of the culpability the offence requires, the aggregation theory will not, in that particular application, extend beyond vicarious liability. The theory comes into its own when it cannot be said of any associated individual that she possesses the culpability the offence requires. If, for example, a company is charged with manslaughter by gross negligence, it may be that none of its directors or employees can be shown individually to have been grossly negligent but, nonetheless, two or more individuals are open collectively to criticism in relation to the incident which caused the death of V. The question then is whether the sum of these criticisms constitutes gross negligence on the part of the company. This theory can attain some degree of metaphysical coherence only if one assumes that the company has the moral and agency properties of a real person, absorbing, over time and space, the faults of those associated with it. In that sense, the theory of aggregation is a theory genuinely concerned with *corporate* corporate guilt.

Yet, again, one may have reservations about the implications of this approach. It is closely associated with criticisms made against individuals. Persons connected with the company who have been subjected to criticism at public trials will be closely linked to any guilty verdict sustained by the company, with possible adverse legal consequences, at least at civil law. They will be tainted, in our manslaughter example, with the stigma of that offence without it being proved against them, or the elements of it.[93]

In its proposal for an offence of "corporate killing" the Law Commission seemingly adopts the principle of aggregation (despite its statement to the contrary).[94] The terms of this offence provide:

> "A corporation is guilty of corporate killing if—
> (a) a management failure by the corporation is the cause or one of the causes of a person's death; and
> (b) that failure constitutes conduct falling far below what can reasonably be expected of the corporation in the circumstances.
> (c) . . . there is a management failure by the corporation if the way in which its activities are managed or organised fails to ensure the health and safety of persons employed in or affected by those activities. . . ."

Under the Commission's proposal, a management failure will occur for the purposes of this offence whenever a death would not have occurred had the company been better managed or if it had better organised its health and safety policies and practices. The crucial issue will be whether the company's conduct fell far below what could reasonably have been expected in the circumstances. The Commission intends to capture in this formulation its commitment to the view that there should be brought into legal discourse the concept of an organisational liability which is not merely derivative of the faults of individuals associated with the organisation. It intends that the offence of corporate killing should impose liability on companies even in circumstances where it cannot be said of any connected individual

---

[93] Aggregation was rejected as a suitable basis of liability for corporate manslaughter in such cases as *H M Coroner for East Kent* (1989) 88 Cr App R 10; *P & O Ferries (Dover) Ltd* (1990) 93 Cr App R 72; *Great Western Trains Co* (unreported: Central Criminal Court, Scott Baker J, 30 June 1999).

[94] Law Com. No. 237, *Legislating the Criminal Code: Involuntary Manslaughter* (1996) paras. 8.1–8–77.

that her conduct fell far below what could reasonably have been expected of her. Still, the finding against the company cannot come from thin air; it must, perforce, arise from an appraisal of the conduct of those individuals who make up the totality of the company's safety performance.[95]

(c) The future of corporate liability

The enactment of the Law Commission's proposal for corporate killing could have implications for corporate liability in general. Currently before Parliament is a Corporate Manslaughter and Corporate Homicide Bill which reflects the Commission's proposals, albeit with significant differences.[96] Should the Bill be enacted, there will be, for the first time, statutory recognition of a principle that companies *qua* companies can bear guilt and warrant punishment. Under the Bill, a company[97] will be guilty of corporate manslaughter[98] if a "gross" breach of a duty of care on the part of the organisation causes the death of V. The gross organisational failure on which proof of the offence depends will be established if "the conduct alleged to amount to a breach of that duty falls far below of what can reasonably be expected of the organisation in the circumstances."[99]

Although expression is given to the idea of a purely corporate liability—indeed, individuals cannot be liable for this offence, neither as principals nor in a secondary capacity[100]—the terms of expression are narrower than the Law Commission proposals. In particular, a finding of a gross breach of duty may only be made if the way in which its activities are managed or organised by its *senior* management is a substantial element in the company's gross breach of duty.[101] To be a senior manager, a person associated with the organisation must play a significant role in the making of decisions about how the whole or a substantial part of its activities are to be managed or organised, or actually manage or organise the whole or a substantial part of its activities.[102] One need not be a highly paid corporate lawyer to appreciate the considerable scope for litigation about who counts as a senior manager. The only certainty is that the smaller the organisation, the more likely it will be that senior management will have direct responsibility for safety matters. Indeed, there is evidence that, in anticipation of legislation along these lines, companies are

---

[95] At para. 8.4, the Commission envisages juries finding whether a risk "was or should have been obvious to any individual or group of individuals within the company who were or should have been responsible for taking safety measures, in deciding whether the company's conduct fell below the required standard."

[96] Home Office, *Reforming the Law on Involuntary Manslaughter: The Government Proposals* (2000). For comment, see Sullivan "Corporate Killing—Some Government Proposals" [2001] *Crim LR* 31. These proposals were examined and modified by the House of Commons Home Affairs and Work and Pensions Committees, *Draft Corporate Manslaughter Bill, First Joint Report of Session 2005–06*, Vols. 1–111(2005); responded to by the Government at 2005–06 HC 540. For comment see Clarkson, "Corporate Manslaughter: Yet More Government Proposals" [2005] *Crim LR* 677. From this process emerged the Bill currently before Parliament.

[97] Which is deemed to include various non-corporate bodies, including emergency services and the Prison Service. At the time of writing, parliamentary diputes about the appropriate reach of this proposed legislation, particularly its applicability to deaths in police and prison custody, have created uncertainty about whether the measure will become law.

[98] On, in Scotland, corporate homicide.

[99] Corporate Manslaughter and Homicide Bill, cl. 1(4).

[100] *Ibid.*, cl. 16.

[101] *Ibid.*, cl. 1(3).

[102] *Ibid.*, cl 1(4)(c).

delegating health and safety resposibilities to more junior employees.[103] These uncertainties and manoeuvres give force to the argument that enhancing corporate safety standards will be better served by legislating for aggravated versions of familiar regulatory health and safety offences.[104]

Be that as it may, if we do have a corporate manslaughter offence along these lines, we will have an offence where the grounds of corporate liability are expressed in organisational terms, so that guilt is not dependent on establishing that any individual associated with the company possessed the culpability for the crime. Can this idea be carried forward for other crimes? That may prove difficult. Corporate manslaughter has a close affinity with manslaughter by gross negligence and, whatever the reservations expressed above, the negligence standard—which is assessed primarily by reference to a defendant's conduct—is well adapted to a holistic appraisal of the company's performance in safety matters. Many other serious offences have states of mind such as intent, dishonesty, or recklessness as definitional elements. These states of mind would not be captured by posing questions relating to general corporate performance. Attributing intentionality and other states of mind to a company directly, without any mediation through the intentions and states of mind of persons connected with it, would require full adoption of the view that companies are, sufficient unto themselves, moral agents or "intelligent machines".

This seems an unlikely prospect. In line with English traditions of empiricism is the assertion of Lord Hoffman that "there is no such thing as the company itself, no *ding an sich*. . . ."[105] The traditional view of English company law is that companies are inherently and exclusively *legal* regimes with no transcendent reality beyond the merely legal.[106] That view of companies fits well with a rejection of the claim that human agency may be submerged and transmuted by social and bureaucratic structures. Instead, one may assert that companies, in terms of their activities and planning, depend on human agency and are not, in terms of conduct and states of mind, some form of non-human sentient creature.[107] This perspective does not need to deny the force of corporate culture on behavioural patterns. It merely insists that those cultures emanate from the interactions, past and present, of human beings.[108]

On this view, the gateway to corporate guilt lies through the conduct and states of mind of persons connected with the company. If it is thought right to convict companies for serious offences on a broader front than is currently the case, the most straightforward way of doing this would be to convict companies on the basis of vicarious liability. It may be

---

[103] Home Affairs and Work and Pensions Committees, *Draft Corporate Manslaughter Bill, First Joint Report of Session 2005–06*, para. 135.

[104] See Glazebrook, "A Better Way of Convicting Businesses of Avoidable Deaths and Injuries" (2002) 61 *Cambridge LJ* 405. For an example of such an offence, see the Occupational Health and Safety Act 2000, s. 36A (NSW), which creates an offence of reckless conduct causing death at a workplace by a person with health and safety duties.

[105] *Meridian Global Funds Management Asia Ltd* v. *Securities Commission* [1995] 2 AC 500, 507.

[106] Hart, "Definition and Theory in Jurisprudence" (1954) 70 *LQR* 37.

[107] A perspective identified as "methodological individualism": Popper, *The Poverty of Historicism* (1957); Watkins, "Historical Explanation in the Social Sciences" (1957–58) 8 *British Journal for the Philosophy of Science* 104.

[108] For an account which accepts methodological individualism but which emphasises the formative influence of group and social structures in creating forms of "collective intentionality" see Searle, *The Construction of Social Reality* (1995).

objected that this would be too undiscriminating: why, it might be asked, should, say, a reputable insurance company be found guilty of obtaining property by deception because one of its salesforce on a particular occasion made false and dishonest statements when selling a policy to a customer. The objection has considerable force. Vicarious liability would be far more acceptable if companies were allowed a due diligence defence. In the insurance company example, the company should be exonerated if it could demonstrate that its recruiting, training, and monitoring practices emphasised and supported honesty in sales and penalised dishonesty.

If companies are regularly to be convicted for serious offences, it is necessary to consider what forms of sanction are appropriate. It should be uncontroversial that companies, by way of fines, should be stripped of any illicit gains and of any quantifiable competitive advantage attributable to the crimes and breaches of regulation occurring in the course of their activities. But what level of sanction beyond that? There is an intractable tension between imposing monetary penalties aimed at deterrence and avoiding adverse consequences for employees, creditors, and shareholders unimplicated in the wrongdoing. If the company is forced into liquidation, a valuable source of employment and goods and services may be lost. Adaptation of monetary penalties such as the "equity" fine and non-monetary alternatives such as corporate probation have been suggested but are fraught with difficulty in both theory and practice.[109] These problems have yet to be resolved. Corporate punishment, like corporate liability, remains a rich source of philosophical and economic challenges.[110]

---

[109] For discussion of the forms of sanction that may be deployed against companies see Wells, *Corporations and Criminal Responsibility* (1993) 31–8, 146–9; Coffee, "No Soul to Damn: No Body to Kick: An Unscandalized Inquiry into the Problem of Corporate Punishment" (1981) 79 *Michigan LR* 386.

[110] See Lederman, "Models for Imposing Corporate Criminal Liability: from adaptation and imitation towards aggregation and the search for self-identity" [2001] *Buffalo Criminal LR* 642, for a thoughtful account of recent theorising in the area.

9

THE INCHOATE OFFENCES

The offences of incitement, conspiracy, and attempt are known as the inchoate offences[1] because liability for these crimes may arise before, or indeed without, the commission of any principal offence.[2] The essentials of these offences are readily grasped. D will be liable for inciting theft as soon as he urges P to steal property from V. D and P will be liable for a conspiracy to commit theft the moment P agrees with D that she should steal from V. P will be guilty of attempted theft from V if and when, intending to steal from V, he does anything that comes sufficiently close to appropriating property from V.

The obvious virtue of inchoate offences is that they permit the lawful restraint and arrest of aspirant criminals prior to the realisation of any concrete harm.[3] If D, lacking any justification or excuse, were to shoot at V, it is a matter for great relief should the bullet miss its target and harmlessly fall to ground. Yet it would be a remarkably indulgent system of criminal law that allowed the absence of concrete harm to preclude any criminal offence by D. From a consequentialist perspective, her liability for attempted murder is justified by society's need to restrain and deter dangerous persons. Provided there was a clear and present danger of the violation of a protected interest of any innocent person, the use of restraining and punitive measures against D is justified. Indeed, it may be argued that to subject an innocent person to an unwarranted risk of death is, *in itself*, the harmful violation of a protected interest.

From a retributivist position, moreover, many "desert" theorists would maintain that a person who tries to do harm but fails to achieve her objective is, in terms of culpability, not materially different from the person who tries and succeeds.[4] Further, even theorists who insist that the occurrence of harm does have moral significance (i.e. that it matters to D's culpability whether she succeeds or fails) would not question the restraint and punishment of a person who has unequivocally tried to harm another; they merely dispute whether failure should be penalised as heavily as success.[5]

The consequentialist and retributivist justifications for inchoate offences are most

---

[1] Robinson, *Criminal Law* (1997) 611–21.

[2] The terms "principal offence", "full offence", and "substantive offence" will be used in this chapter to denote the crime that is the objective of the incitor, conspirator, or attemptor.

[3] Despite the evident utility of these offences they have been criticised for their potential to punish conduct too remote from the realisation of any concrete harm. Some of these criticisms will be addressed below in this chapter. For a general critical survey, see Husak, "The Nature and Justifiability of Nonconsummate Offences" (1995) 37 *Arizona LR* 151.

[4] Ashworth, "Criminal Attempts and the Role of Resulting Harm under the Code and in the Common Law" (1988) 19 *Rutgers LJ* 725.

[5] Duff, *Criminal Attempts* (1996) chap. 4. For further discussion and references, see below, § 9.3(vi).

graphically demonstrated when, as in our shooting example, D has done everything that she intends to do in her attempt to harm V. In that case, D's attempt is complete. The appropriateness of penalising conduct which is of a more preliminary nature is controversial. For instance, there has been considerable debate whether agreeing with another to commit a crime at some future date warrants criminalisation.[6] In the United States, certain jurisdictions and federal law require, before liability for conspiracy may arise, that at least one overt act in pursuance of the criminal objective be carried out by a party to the agreement.[7] In England and Wales, however, incitement and conspiracy are well entrenched and permit restraint and coercion well before the commission of the substantive offence. Indeed, a policy of early intervention is not confined to inchoate crimes. Many substantive offences, particularly those offences which proscribe possession of such things as guns, explosives, and drugs, are designed indirectly to prevent future harms.[8]

§ 9.1 Incitement

(i) The actus reus

Since the decision in *Higgins*,[9] it has been a crime at common law for D to urge or persuade others to perpetrate crimes. In *Goldman*,[10] the Court of Appeal approved the following passage from the South African case of *Mykosiana*:[11]

> "An inciter . . . is one who reaches and seeks to influence the mind of another to the commission of a crime. The machinations of criminal ingenuity being legion, the approach to the other's mind may take many forms, such as a suggestion, proposal, request, exhortation, gesture, argument, persuasion, inducement or arousal of cupidity."

Despite the many modes of incitement identified in this "gamut of words",[12] it omits what an earlier Court of Appeal took to be the essence of the matter: "'Encourage' represents as well as any modern word can the concept involved."[13] Following this lead, we will take encouragement as the best synonym for the term incitement.[14]

---

[6] Johnson, "The Unnecessary Crime of Conspiracy" (1973) 61 *Cal LR* 1137; Marcus, "Criminal Conspiracy Law: Time to Turn Back from an Ever Expanding, Ever More Troubling Area" (1992) 1 *Wm and Mary Bill Rts J* 1.

[7] Perkins and Boyce, *Criminal Law* (3rd ed., 1982) 685–7.

[8] To this category, one might add crimes involving the proscription of conduct associated with drug-taking, forms of sexuality, and obscenity; which are frequently justified by reference to the ultimate impact that such conduct may have on the social order. The link between the proscribed activities and such generalised further or underlying harm may be very tenuous. For an interesting discussion of the role of remote harms in the creation of criminal offences, see von Hirsch, "Extending the Harm Principle: 'Remote' Harms and Fair Imputation" in Simester and Smith (eds.), *Harm and Culpability* (1996) 259.

[9] (1801) 2 East 5, 102 ER 269.

[10] [1997] Crim LR 894.

[11] (1966) 4 SA 655 at 658 (Holmes JA).

[12] The description of the Court of Appeal in *Marlow* [1997] Crim LR 897.

[13] *Ibid.*

[14] If the Serious Crime Bill currently before Parliament (at April 2007) enters into law there will be a statutory offence of encouraging crime.

With that in mind, we can see that the typical case of incitement will involve some conduct by D with the potential to encourage P to commit a crime. Although incitement has a conduct element, an actus reus, D's attitude or motivation may also be relevant in detemining whether his conduct constituted the actus reus of incitement. For instance, P may ask D whether V, P's wife is still seeing F. D answers truthfully that she is although aware that this information may lead to P killing V. But if D simply felt constrained to tell P the truth, no incitement to murder arises. Contrast if D seeks P out to impart this information, or if he seeks P out in order to deceive P into thinking that V is seeing F. For cases such as these, we will also need to discuss (as we do below) whether the idea of incitement includes circumstances where D manipulates P into a state of mind conducive to the commission of a crime.

If some communication or gesture on the part of D is received by P that may influence P to commit a crime, the actus reus of incitement is made out. It is not necessary for D's incitement to have any effect on the intentions or conduct of others. Accordingly it is immaterial if, as in *DPP* v. *Armstrong*,[15] the incitee is an undercover police officer uninfluenced by D's solicitation. The target of the incitement may be either a particular individual or people generally—as when D addresses a meeting or writes a newspaper article.[16] The fact that unavailing attempts to get others to commit crimes suffices in itself for criminal liability has not escaped criticism on the grounds of the remoteness of D's conduct from the commission of any substantive offence,[17] but incitement is too well established to be removed by anything other than legislation and there seems no prospect of that.[18]

Whether the necessary potential of D's conduct to encourage criminal activety on the part of P is present may require some close judgements. Encouragement was found to be present in *Invicta Plastics* v. *Claire*[19] where D, a company, advertised in a motoring magazine a device, "Radatec", which indicated the presence of a police radar device monitoring traffic. It is illegal for private persons to install such devices.[20] Pictorial detail in the advertisement illustrated the utility of "Radatec" in avoiding detection for speeding. The Divisional Court confirmed D's conviction for inciting the commission of offences. The company was endeavouring to persuade motorists to acquire the device to assist them in contravening the laws against speeding. *Invicta Plastics* may be contrasted with *James*,[21] where the Court of Appeal held that the mere intention to manufacture and sell "black boxes"—devices which have no utility other than for the illegal abstraction of electricity—did not amount to

---

[15] [2000] Crim LR 379.

[16] *Most* (1881) 7 QBD 244.

[17] For a critique of the offence of incitement see Robbins, "Double Inchoate Crimes" (1989) 26 *Harv J Legis* 1. Robbins argues that incitement essentially penalises attempts to conspire and, consequently, targets conduct too remote from the principal offence. There is some force in his critique, but it should be remembered that there must always be some element of active persuasion or pressure in order to make out a case of incitement. Additionally, incitement may occur in circumstances where no conspiracy is envisaged, e.g. when D addresses his incitement to a large number of people, as in *Most* (1881) 7 QBD 244.

[18] Incitement will be put into statutory form by way of an inchoate offence of "encouraging crime" should the Serious Crime Bill be enacted in its current form. The setting up of the Serious Organised Crime Agency in 2005 with its remit of increasing the effectiveness of the criminal law in dealing with the background figures who organise the criminal activities of others is likely to encourage recourse to inchoate crimes such as incitement and conspiracy.

[19] [1976] RTR 251.

[20] Wireless Telegraphy Act 1949, s. 1(1).

[21] (1985) 82 Cr App R 226.

inciting offences against section 13 of the Theft Act 1968. In *Marlow*,[22] D was convicted of incitement on the basis of publishing instructions on the growing of cannabis, something which clearly might encourage others to follow suit.[23]

A rather more dubious decision is *Goldman*,[24] where D was held to have incited E by responding positively to an advertisement placed by E which offered the sale of indecent photographs of children. That E's advertisment constituted incitement is not in doubt. D's role, however, seems to have been confined to that of a willing recipient of E's criminal services. D's incitement allegedly took the form of "arousing [E's] cupidity", yet D did nothing more than show himself to be a purchaser of E's child pornography. It would be odd to think that we, say, incite the sale of a sweater by Marks & Spencer when we present the item at the counter. On the facts, the crucial element of inducement or persuasion appears to be missing. It is difficult to overlook the fact that the Court of Appeal's rather strained analysis enabled D to be found criminally liable for conduct in England in respect of seeking to access child pornography supplied from overseas. An understandable zeal to curb this vile trade seems to have distorted the natural meaning of incitement. The same impetus may explain *O'Shea* v. *Coventry Magistrates' Court*,[25] where D had accessesd internet sites featuring child pornography. He was charged with inciting P, who ran the site, to distribute indecent photographs of children. D's defence was that he had incited no-one, merely downloaded images from his computer. The Divisional Court confirmed D's conviction on the basis that by accessing the site D would encourage P to maintain the site. It seemed that no evidence was required that P was aware that D had visited the site. This stretches any reasonable conception of incitement to its limits and beyond.

It is true that confining the law to the natural meaning of incitement, as argued for here and *contra* the decisions in *Goldman* and *O'Shea*, will exempt from liability conduct that may *facilitate* but not strictly encourage crime. Without buyers, the child pornographer cannot sell his illegal wares. Peter Glazebrook considers that to punish acts of encouragement or persuasion to commit crimes, yet to withhold punishments for acts that materially assist crimes, is absurd: it is to treat words more seriously than deeds.[26]

If D encourages P to kill V, she will be guilty of incitement to murder. If she sells a gun to P, aware of P's murderous intention but without giving him any verbal or other encouragement, she will avoid liability for incitement. This may seem difficult to justify in terms of culpability and social defence; indeed, in either case, should P actually kill V, D will be an accomplice in V's murder.[27] Linguistically, however, the distinction is sound. If D, without

---

[22] [1997] Crim LR 897 (CA).

[23] A challenge against the decision in *Marlow* on the ground that it contravened D's right to freedom of expression guaranteed by Article 10 ECHR was held by the European Court to be inadmissible on the ground that the derogation from that freedom was in pursuit of the legitimate aim of suppressing the foresseable commission of crimes: [2001] EHRLR 444.

[24] [2001] Crim LR 822.

[25] CO/6342/2003.

[26] Glazebrook, "Structuring the Criminal Code: Functional Approaches to Complicity, Incomplete Offences and General Defences" in Simester and Smith (eds.), *Harm and Culpability* (1996) 195, 201.

[27] The Serious Crime Bill currently before Parliament will, if enacted, create inchoate offences of encouraging crime and assisting crime, thereby penalising the gun supplier in the text above at the point of supply: it would be immaterial for her liability for the assisting offence if the gun she supplied were not used by P. For discussion of the Law Commission Proposals for these inchoate offences see Sullivan, "Inchoate Liability for Assisting and Encouraging Crime: the Law Commission Proposals" [2006] *Crim LR* 1047.

doing anything more, sells a gun to P, aware of P's intention to kill V but interested only in the cash profit to be made from the sale, it is apposite to describe D's conduct as assistance but not as incitement.

Lord Denning, when determining the scope of the statutory offence of incitement to racial hatred in *Race Relations Board* v. *Applin*,[28] considered that threats as well as encouragement and persuasion fell within the legal conception of incitement.[29] His view was approved, *obiter*, by the Divisional Court in *Invicta Plastics* in the context of the general law of incitement.[30] There is much to be said for this view notwithstanding that as a matter of ordinary language we would not describe coercing or threatening a reluctant P to do some crime as "inciting" P. But in the case of threats, to go with the grain of ordinary language would be perverse. Take a case where D seeks to persuade her employee P to commit an offence within the course of employment. If she offers a rise in salary by way of inducement, she unequivocally commits incitement. The same must surely follow if she uses the stick of redundancy rather than carrot of financial reward. Threats are a mode of influence along with encouragement and persuasion, and it is conduct which seeks to arouse and influence the commission of crimes that constitutes the legal conception of incitement. Returning to an example given earlier, where D falsely tells P that his wife V is seeing F, knowing that receiving this misinformation may induce P to kill V, D is seeking to arouse D to kill V and his conduct may properly be thought to be within the bounds of incitement.

Accordingly, D commits incitement when she seeks to influence P by encouragement, persuasion, arousal or coercion to commit a crime. A preparedness to assist P to commit an offence is insufficient unless an inference of persuasion, encouragement, arousal, or coercion can be drawn from the totality of the circumstances.

(a) The conduct incited

Indictable offences, summary offences, and complicity.
D will be guilty of incitement if the conduct he encourages would constitute an indictable or summary offence on the part of P were she to act as D proposes. In *Bodin*,[31] the trial judge ruled that the conduct D incites must involve an offence by P in the capacity of a principal offender. It was held that D did not commit incitement when the conduct he proposed to P would amount to complicity in a crime but would not involve a crime directly perpetrated by P. Accordingly, on this view of the law, D will commit incitement to murder if he suggests to P that, say, she kill V by injecting him with anthrax, but he will not be guilty of that offence if his suggestion is that P should distribute anthrax to as many potential killers as she is able to locate.

The reason given for this limitation on the scope of incitement is that D must incite conduct on the part of P which is "criminal *per se*". This "reason" merely states the limitation and neither explains nor justifies it. Perhaps what lies behind the ruling in *Bodin* is the idea that acts of complicity are too remote from the commission of the principal offence to fall within the mischief of incitement. If this is the reason, it does not sit well with

---

[28] [1973] QB 815.
[29] *Ibid.*, 827.
[30] [1976] RTR 251
[31] [1979] Crim LR 176.

the fact that it is quite irrelevant to liability for incitement whether or not the principal offence is committed. The reason cannot be that complicitous conduct is systemically less serious than acts of perpetration; in *Howe*,[32] the House of Lords decisively rejected the view that acts of complicity were generally less heinous than acts of perpetration. Although the ruling in *Bodin* was referred to uncritically by the Court of Appeal in *Sirat*[33] and receives sub silentio support from section 30(4) of the Criminal Law Act 1977,[34] strictly it is merely a Crown Court ruling of no formal authority. It is submitted that the ruling should not be followed by other courts. Complicitous conduct should fall within the ambit of conduct that it is criminal to incite.

Inchoate offences.

An inchoate offence is something criminal in its own right. Logically, there is nothing to preclude bringing a charge of incitement in respect of inciting the commission of an inchoate offence (e.g. inciting T to incite P to commit an offence). Reservations may be had, however, about criminalising conduct which may be considered too remote from the commission of a substantive offence. Parliament has given effect to this reservation, but only partially. Section 5(7) of the Criminal Law Act 1977 disallows any charge of incitement to conspire. Nothing is said about incitement to incite or incitement to attempt. In *Sirat*,[35] the Court of Appeal was of the view that incitement to incite remains an offence. However, such a charge cannot be brought, according to *Sirat*, if the form of incitement which D incites P to undertake will involve P entering conspiracies with third parties, because then such a charge would flout the statutory restriction on charges of incitement to conspire. The ruling is intelligible and justifiable as a matter of statutory interpretation. Yet it allows absurd distinctions. For instance, suppose that D urges P to attend a clandestine meeting of terrorists and advocate the immediate resumption of a bombing strategy. For reasons of security, D instructs P to leave immediately after he has addressed the meeting and on no account to enter into any conversation. Alternatively, D may require P to make calls on individual terrorists and obtain their respective agreements to resume bombing activities. All other things being equal, D will be guilty of incitement in the first scenario but not in the second—an inexplicable distinction in terms of policy and respective culpability. In its proposed Criminal Code, the Law Commission recommends re-establishing the offence of incitement to conspire.[36] Alternatively, if it is considered that bringing together two inchoate offences in one charge risks criminalising conduct too remote from the occurrence of a concrete harm, the appropriate course would be to abolish incitement to incite.

Almost invariably, the problem will not arise for incitement to attempt because, in most imaginable circumstances, D would anyway be urging P to commit the full offence. Very occasionally however, D may incite P to commit an offence which it is, in fact, impossible to commit. The defence of impossibility has been abolished for the statutory offence of

---

[32] [1987] AC 417.

[33] (1985) 83 Cr App R 41.

[34] Which deals with penalties applicable to those who incite others "to commit a summary offence", with no reference to other modes of participation. However, it is submitted that a provision dealing with penalties should not be read as determining the scope and ambit of offences.

[35] (1985) 83 Cr App R 41.

[36] Law Com. No. 177, *A Criminal Code for England and Wales* (1989) cl. 47.

attempt.[37] Suppose D orders P to enter V's bedroom at night and shoot V in his bed. D knows that V is already dead; she wants the unwitting P to shoot a bullet into V's corpse to obfuscate the true cause of death. P would be guilty of attempted murder. D, with her knowledge of the true facts, should be guilty of inciting attempted murder but not of inciting murder. She was aware that murder was impossible and therefore she was not seeking, through the agency of P, to bring about that crime. Nonetheless, she was inciting conduct which constituted attempted murder on P's part and a conviction for inciting P's attempt appropriately reflects her culpability.[38]

Inciting an actus reus.

In our discussion of the liability of accomplices, we saw that the perpetration of a mere actus reus by P may sometimes ground a charge of complicity against D.[39] Recall that if, say, D persuades P to have intercourse with V by alleging that V's genuine protestations will be feigned, D may yet be an accomplice to rape even if P is acquitted of the principal offence because of lack of proof of mens rea. D's conviction as an accomplice to rape is appropriate because D has procured the occurrence of the harm associated with commission of the substantive offence. In principle, this reasoning should carry over to incitement. On the facts above, D should be guilty of incitement to rape as soon as he urges or persuades P to have intercourse with V, whether or not P goes on to rape V, because the harm of rape, i.e. sexual violation, is still being sought through D's actions.

However, there is authority which, implicitly, is to the contrary. In *Curr*,[40] D's conviction for inciting P to obtain payments by deception was quashed because it had not been established whether P had acted with intent to deceive. Since P had made untrue statements, the actus reus of the substantive offence had occurred. Accordingly, the decision in *Curr* is strongly suggestive that liability for incitement requires a proposal entailing perpetration of the full offence, and not just of the actus reus. However, *Curr* pre-dates the adoption of the "actus reus suffices" principle in cases of complicity by procurement. Further, as will be discussed below, the idea that the incitor and the incitee must have the same mens rea has been rejected in subsequent appellate cases.[41] In light of this, the position for incitement may yet be reviewed, particularly in a case, such as the rape example above, where the terrible harms associated with the full offence can occur even where P lacks mens rea.

Even if *Curr* is wrong, there must, at least, be encouragement of what in law constitutes an actus reus. In *C*,[42] D incited P, a boy of 12, to sodomise him. At the time of the event there was a conclusive presumption of law that a boy under the age of 13 was incapable of

---

[37] Criminal Attempts Act 1981, s. 1(3).

[38] The decision in *Hapgood* (1870) LR 1 CCR 221 indicates that D would also be liable as a secondary party to P's attempt. See further Smith, "Secondary Participation and Inchoate Offences" in Tapper (ed.), *Crime, Proof and Punishment* (1981) 21, 26–7. Paradoxically, if, in the shooting example given in the text, D was unaware that V was dead and took herself to be encouraging P to kill V, she would not be guilty of incitement to murder, as it remains a defence to *incitement* (unlike attempt) to demonstrate that it was impossible to commit the offence incited: see further below, § 9.4. By contrast, where she is aware of the true facts, she incites an offence—attempted murder— that it is possible, on the facts, to commit.

[39] Above, § 7.6(i)(b).

[40] [1968] 2 QB 944; see also *Whitehouse* [1977] QB 868.

[41] *DPP* v. *Armstrong* [2000] Crim LR 379 (DC); *C* [2005] EWCA Crim 2827 (CA); see also below, § 9.1(ii).

[42] *Ibid.*

sexual intercourse.[43] It followed from the presumption that any act of sodomy by P would not constitute an offence on his part and the Court of Appeal reluctantly held that this entailed the failure of the charge of incitement to sodomy made against D. Of course, in a physical sense, an act of anal intercourse did occur when P penetrated D. But in the realm of law, P was incapable of doing that which he actually did, so in this very artificial sense there was not even an actus reus.

Future crimes

It is immaterial that the crime D incites P to commit will become possible only at some time in the future. For example, D will be liable for incitement if he urges the killing, at birth, of a baby unborn[44] or the receiving of goods yet to be stolen.[45] On the other hand, the defence of impossibility will be available to D if, in these examples, a live birth is no longer possible *at the time D incites* the future murder, or the goods she has in mind will never materialise.

Within its own terms, this distinction is tenable. Inciting a crime that, all other things equal, it will be possible to commit at some future date constitutes a greater social threat than inciting a crime that is already impossible by the time of the incitement. While tenable, however, it is arguably inappropriate for the law to continue making this distinction. The impossibility defence has been abolished for the statutory offences of conspiracy[46] and attempt.[47] It is highly anomalous that the impossibility of committing the substantive offence does not provide a defence for conspiracy, which requires the making of an agreement to carry out the substantive offence, nor for attempt, where there must be conduct which is sufficiently proximate to the offence, but provides a defence for incitement which does not require that there be any step whatsoever to carry out the substantive offence. Under the proposed Criminal Code, the defence of impossibility will be abolished for incitement.[48] It is an overdue reform.

(b) The sufficiency of communication

The offence of incitement is complete as soon as D communicates persuasion or pressure to P to commit an offence. Indeed, D commits the offence of attempting to incite if she does something sufficiently close to an act of communication. In *Banks*,[49] D's letter to P advising P to kill V was intercepted in the post. D was convicted of attempting to incite.

As *Banks* indicates, there must be communication for the full offence but, thereafter, as we have noted, it is of no consequence that D's incitement was without effect or influence on P's future conduct.[50] As D's offence is complete at the point of communication, it follows in principle that any countermanding or withdrawal of her initial incitement by D should count, at most, as mitigation but cannot undo the crime she has already committed. In the

---

[43] Now repealed by Crimnal Justice Act 1993.
[44] *Banks* (1873) 12 Cox CC 393.
[45] *McDonough* (1962) 47 Cr App R 37.
[46] Criminal Law Act 1977, s. 1(1).
[47] Criminal Attempts Act 1981, s. 1(3).
[48] Law Com. No.177, *A Criminal Code for England and Wales* (1989) cl. 50.
[49] (1873) 12 Cox CC 393.
[50] *Krause* (1902) 18 TLR 238.

cognate sphere of complicity, if D counsels P to commit an offence but then, prior to the commission of the offence, revokes her earlier counselling or contacts an appropriate person in authority, she will no longer be a party to the offence if P goes on to commit it.[51] Should a defence of revocation be available for incitement? Incitement and counselling are not precisely parallel. D will not be an accomplice until the principal offence is carried out, whereas, as we know, incitement is complete on communication. And yet the counsellor and the incitor are very much alike. In either case, all the elements of liability personal to D are present as soon as advice or encouragement is given. The public policy considerations that allow a withdrawal defence where the charge is one of complicity also seem germane to a charge of incitement. Furthermore, it would undermine the policy behind the withdrawal defence in complicity if the prosecution could obviate it by charging incitement on the same facts. Consequently, it is submitted that there is a good case for reforming the current law, to allow the incitor a defence if, prior to the commission of the offence incited, she counter-mands encouragement of the crime to persons she has incited or informs an appropriate authority (such as the police) of the details of her conduct.

(ii) Mens rea

Incitement, being a common law offence, requires proof of a mental element on the part of D. By its very nature, incitement involves an intention on the part of D that P should carry out the crime that D is persuading, pressurising, or arousing him to perform. This may, for convenience, be broken down as follows:

(i)   an intention by D that P carry out the course of conduct (including bringing about any consequences specified in the actus reus of the crime) that D has incited; and

(ii)   knowledge or belief by D that, at the time of P's conduct, any circumstances required for the actus reus of the incited crime will be present.[52]

A misleading case on the mental element required for incitement is *Curr*,[53] in which D was charged with inciting P and others to obtain social security payments by deception. D's conviction was quashed by the Court of Appeal on the basis that it was not established that P intended to deceive; there was a possibility, unresolved at the trial, that P may have acted without intending to deceive and therefore would not have committed the principal offence. The appellate court misdirected itself. The issue was not whether P did, in fact, have mens rea but whether D *believed* that P would have mens rea. If he had a belief to that effect then, on the facts as D understood them, he would have been inciting P to commit a crime, irrespective of P's actual state of mind. Recall that incitement is complete as soon as D communicates with P, and it is immaterial that D's persuasion or pressure has no effect on P. It is out of keeping with the essential nature of incitement, which focuses on the culpability of D and not that of P, to insist that P must have mens rea when perpetrating the actus reus

---

[51] See the discussion above, § 7.6(iv).

[52] This assumes that D's liability for incitement does not require incitement of the full offence, merely the actus reus of that offence. For discussion, see above, § 9.1(i)(a) (inciting an actus reus).

[53] [1968] 2 QB 944.

of the crime incited. Thus, in *DPP* v. *Armstrong*,[54] the fact that P was an undercover police-man with no intention of committing the principal offence did not preclude a conviction of D for inciting P. Although *Armstrong* can be distinguished from *Curr*—in the former case P did not commit the actus reus of the principal offence at all—the distinction is irrelevant to the nature and purpose of incitement. In *C*,[55] the Court of Appeal gave careful consideration to *Curr* and although ultimately the matter did not call for a decision it was considered to be an erroneous decision.

As with any other offence of mens rea, a distinction must be made, when relevant, between mens rea on the one hand and motive on the other. Such a distinction was not drawn by the Court of Appeal in *Shaw*.[56] D incited P and others, fellow employees, to commit thefts against their employer. D's motivation, apparently, was to bring deficiencies in the security system to the notice of the employer. It was held that D's motivation was incompatible with liability for incitement to steal. Yet what P was persuaded by D to do was clearly theft[57] and D was aware of all the material circumstances which rendered P's conduct theft. Recall the decision of the Privy Council in *Yip Chiu-cheung*,[58] where it was assumed that D would commit a serious drugs offence even though his sole motivation in importing drugs was to expose the activities of drug traffickers. The approach of English law, though not beyond criticism,[59] is that mens rea may be present even though D's conduct may lack moral culpability; indeed, it may be present even if his conduct merits praise. The decision in *Shaw* cannot be reconciled with this stance; there are no particular features of incitement which argue for a different approach. Accordingly, *Shaw* should be regarded as wrongly decided. At the very least it has been regarded as authoratative only in terms of the wording of the charge: in *DPP* v. *Armstrong*,[60] the decision in *Shaw* was given guarded approval because D was charged with *dishonestly* inciting P to commit theft. The reference to dishonesty in the charge was otiose, since dishonesty is not a constituent element of incitement.

(iii) Victims as incitors

Like the rule in complicity, a person regarded as a victim of an offence committed by P cannot be regarded as an incitor of P, notwithstanding any persuasion or pressure she has brought to bear directed towards the commission of the offence by P.[61] "Victim" is not a term of general application in this context; to be a victim in the restricted sense applicable, one must be a member of a defined, vulnerable class, most typically a person under the age of consent.[62]

---

[54] [2000] Crim LR 379.
[55] [2005] EWCA Crim 2827.
[56] [1994] Crim LR 365.
[57] Note that P, unlike D, was dishonest since he was unaware of D's reason for encouraging the thefts.
[58] [1995] 1 AC 111.
[59] See above, § 1.2(ii).
[60] [2000] Crim LR 379 (QBD).
[61] *Tyrrell* [1894] 1 QB 710. In *Tyrrell*, D was acquitted of incitement as well as on a charge of complicity.
[62] For further discussion of this principle in the context of complicity see above, § 7.6(iv)(a).

§ 9.2 Conspiracy

Conspiracy is predominantly a statutory offence, defined by section 1 of the Criminal Law Act 1977. The essence of statutory conspiracy is an agreement between two or more persons which, if carried out in accordance with the intentions of the parties, will result in the commission of a statutory or common law crime by at least one of the parties to the agreement.

Apart from statutory conspiracy, there are also some forms of conspiracy surviving at common law. Prior to the passing of the Criminal Law Act 1977, the Law Commission examined the common law of conspiracy and prepared a bill which, with some significant alterations by Parliament, became the substance of the 1977 Act.[63] The aspiration of the Law Commission, echoed in ministerial statements, was ultimately to replace entirely common law conspiracy by a statutory offence. However, at the time the Act was passed, abolition in its entirety of common law conspiracy was not regarded as a feasible option.[64] Three heads of common law conspiracy were felt to be indispensable until new offences, as yet unresolved, were created to replace them. The common law conspiracies retained were (i) to outrage public decency; (ii) to corrupt public morality; and (iii) to defraud. Accordingly, common law conspiracy, to this diminished extent, still exists.[65]

These three heads of common law conspiracy were retained, as it was unclear to what extent these respective heads of conspiracy criminalise agreements to carry out conduct that would not be criminal if done by an individual acting alone. Statutory conspiracy is confined to agreements to commit crimes that individuals can commit when acting alone. Rightly or otherwise, it was the opinion of Parliament at the time that a continuing regulatory presence was required in these three areas, even if that required penalising conduct which would not be criminal but for the presence of a conspiracy. However, since the passing of the 1977 Act, *Gibson*[66] has resolved that conduct outraging public decency constitutes a substantive offence in its own right. Accordingly, an agreement to outrage public decency will fall within the ambit of statutory conspiracy as outlined above.[67] The position in respect of corrupting public morality is less clear cut, but is probably the same as for outraging public decency.[68] Consequently these offences are now covered by statutory conspiracy and will not be further considered here.

By contrast, in the case of conspiracy to defraud, it is incontrovertibly the case that forms of dishonest conduct which would not otherwise be criminal are rendered criminal only by virtue of the common law conspiracy.[69] This form of conspiracy, which is of enormous

---

[63] Law Com. No. 76, *Conspiracy and Criminal Law Reform* (1976).

[64] HL Vol. 379, col. 206 (Lord Harris of Greenwich).

[65] Criminal Law Act 1977, s. 5.

[66] [1990] 2 QB 619 (CA).

[67] Under the terms of s. 5(3) of the Criminal Law Act 1977, if there is a substantive offence of outraging public decency, as now appears to be the case, an agreement to commit that offence must be charged as a statutory conspiracy, falling within s. 1 of the Act, and may not be charged as a common law conspiracy.

[68] In *Shaw* v. *DPP* [1962] AC 220, the Court of Criminal Appeal held that there was a substantive offence of corrupting public morality. However, the House of Lords confirmed the appellant's conviction for conspiracy to corrupt public morality and did not go on to confirm whether or not there was a substantive offence.

[69] Conduct which clearly falls within the ambit of a substantive offence involving dishonesty, such as theft, will almost invariably fall within the ambit of conspiracy to defraud if two or more persons are involved. Section 12 of the Criminal Justice Act 1987, resolving an interpretative conflict that had arisen over the effect of s. 5(2) of the Criminal Law Act 1977, provides that in such circumstances the conduct may be charged as either a statutory

breadth, is frequently resorted to, particularly in the sphere of large-scale commercial fraud. Moreover, it seems that this last vestige of common law conspiracy is to be retained on a permanent basis. It was widely anticipated that the Fraud Act 2006 would abolish the offence but the Government has not done so; fearful, it seems, of leaving gaps in the coverage of dishonest conduct.[70] The offence will be considered in detail below, in the context of property offences.[71] In this chapter, we will examine the elements of statutory conspiracy. Unfortunately, as we shall see, the Criminal Law Act 1977 does not provide clear answers to many of the points of interpretation that arise.[72] Consequently, resort to pre-Act common law authority may still be required to assist the resolution of interpretative difficulties.

(i) Statutory conspiracy—definition and ambit

(a) Indictable and summary offences

Section 1 of the Criminal Law Act 1977 provides that:

> if a person agrees with any other person or persons that a course of conduct will be pursued which, if the agreement is carried out in accordance with their intentions, either—
> (a) will necessarily amount to or involve the commission of any offence or offences by one or more parties to the agreement, or
> (b) would do so but for the existence of facts which render the commission of the offence or any offences impossible, he is guilty of conspiracy to commit the offence or offences in question.

At the core of statutory conspiracy is an agreement between two or more persons which will necessarily involve the commission of an offence by one or more of the parties should the agreement be carried out in accordance with their intentions. The offence may be common law or statutory, indictable or summary.

Formerly, any conspiracy charged under the Criminal Law Act 1977 had to involve an agreement to commit an offence triable within England and Wales.[73] An agreement made in Birmingham to rob a bank in Brussels has never been indictable under the terms of section 1. However, such an agreement will now constitute a conspiracy triable in England and Wales under the recently interpolated section 1A.[74] In remarkably broad terms, section 1A of the Criminal Law Act 1977 turns agreements to contravene the laws of foreign states into conspiracies under English law. The new section is a reaction to the international dimensions of some forms of modern criminal activity. It will be discussed in more detail below (§ 9.5), when we address the issue of jurisdiction over inchoate offences.

---

conspiracy or a common law conspiracy. Contrast s. 5(3) of the Criminal Law Act 1977, which clearly provides that if corrupting public morality, or outraging public decency, constitute substantive offences, only a charge of statutory conspiracy may be brought in respect of any agreement to commit such offences.

[70] Ormerod, "The Fraud Act 2006: Criminalising Lying?" [2007] *Crim LR* 193, 194.

[71] § 15.6.

[72] See Smith, "Conspiracy under the Criminal Law Act 1977" [1977] *Crim LR* 598 and 638 for a remarkably prescient discussion of the interpretative difficulties that have arisen.

[73] Criminal Law Act 1977, s. 1(4); *Board of Trade v. Owen* [1957] AC 602.

[74] Criminal Justice (Terrorism and Conspiracy) Act 1998, s. 5.

(b) Inchoate offences

The phrase "commission of any offence" employed in section 1 of the Criminal Law Act 1977 is perfectly apt to cover inchoate offences. Accordingly, a conspiracy to incite would be a possible charge on (for instance) facts similar to *Invicta Plastics* v. *Clare*.[75] Managers of that company would be guilty of conspiracy to incite when they agreed the specifics of the "Radatec" advertisement that, when published, constituted an incitement to motorists to commit offences under the Wireless Telegraphy Act 1949. One implication of this is that the reach of the criminal law may extend far back from the point of commission of the principal offence. Serious doubts may be entertained on the propriety of such charges for conduct so remote from the substantive crime,[76] yet there appears to be no legal impediment to such a prosecution.

Similarly, in principle there are no legal difficulties precluding charges of conspiracy to conspire or conspiracy to attempt. However, such charges will rarely be apt. It is hard to envisage a conspiracy to conspire which is not, more straightforwardly, a conspiracy to commit a substantive offence. Likewise, a conspiracy to attempt will be a conspiracy to commit the substantive offence, save for some very rare cases of impossibility in relation to the substantive offence.[77]

(c) Secondary liability

"Commission" is a term appropriate to acts of perpetration but unsuited to convey complicity in the offence of another. It is unlikely that an agreement between and *confined* to D and E to assist the commission of an offence by P will constitute a statutory conspiracy on the part of D and E. The fact that section 1 of the Criminal Law Act 1977 contemplates that only "*one* or more parties to the agreement" may commit the agreed crime strengthens this view. If "commission" were a term that covered complicitous conduct, conspirators would become secondary parties or principals to the substantive offence upon the commission of the offence agreed upon. Accordingly it would always be the case that implementation of the agreement would involve commission of the offence by at least two persons.[78]

(ii) The agreement

(a) Conspiracy as collaboration

Agreement[79] is the essence of conspiracy; in the terms of section 1 of the Criminal Law Act 1977, it is required that D "agrees with any other person or persons that a course of conduct shall be pursued." Yet the term must be regarded with some caution, particularly by lawyers familiar with the concept of agreement as used in other areas of law such as contract. It is

---

[75] [1976] RTR 251.

[76] For critical discussion, see Johnson, "The Unnecessary Crime of Conspiracy" (1973) 61 *California LR* 1137; Marcus, "Criminal Conspiracy Law: Time to Turn Back from an Ever Expanding, Ever More Troubling Area" (1992) 1 *William and Mary Bill of Rights J* 1.

[77] See the discussion above, § 9.1(i)(a) (inchoate offences); the example given there could be adapted to conspiracy.

[78] *Hollinshead* [1985] 1 All ER 850, 858 (CA).

[79] Orchard, "Agreement in Criminal Conspiracy" [1974] *Crim LR* 297, 335; Marcus, "The Criminal Agreement in Theory and in Practice" (1977) 65 *Geo LJ* 925.

not enough that D and E agree a course of conduct that necessarily involves the commission of an offence. The commission of that offence must constitute a project that they have in common; their agreement must be indicative of a collaboration to achieve that end. The *collaborative* nature of the agreement necessary for a criminal conspiracy was usefully highlighted by the Court of Appeal in *Ardarlan*:[80]

> "Is it true to say that the acts of the accused were done in pursuance of a criminal purpose held in common between them?"

The Criminal Law Act 1977 provides no definition of agreement. Accordingly, we may assume that the Act intends no change from the common law regarding the nature of the agreement required for conspiracy. The Canadian case of *Sokoloski* [81] provides a useful illustration of an agreement directed at criminal activity which falls short of a criminal conspiracy. D and E arranged a rendezvous at which D could hand over drugs for cash to E. The selling of drugs by D constituted the crime of drug-trafficking on his part. E was charged with conspiracy with D to traffic in drugs. On appeal, it was ruled that there was no drug-trafficking conspiracy between D and E. Selling drugs for cash was D's project, and his alone. The fact that E agreed arrangements with D which enabled D to sell drugs did not alter the fact that E's role in these arrangements was that of a buyer of drugs, an activity which did not constitute drug trafficking. But for this limitation on the kind of agreement required for conspiracy, all manner of consumption of illegal services could be brought within the net of conspiracy.[82]

Commonality of purpose was signally lacking in the much-criticised case of *Meyrick*.[83] D and E separately owned nightclubs occupying adjacent premises. Each acting on his own initiative, D and E paid bribes to the same police officer in return for non-enforcement of the licensing laws in respect of their own premises. Notwithstanding the lack of any personal communication between D and E regarding the bribes, a verdict of conspiracy to corrupt was reached on the basis that "each well knew what the other was doing."[84] *Griffiths* [85] provides a useful contrast with *Meyrick*. In *Griffiths*, the defendants were all farmers who employed the same accountant. The accountant had instructed the defendants in various ways of dishonestly obtaining subsidies from the Ministry of Agriculture. The Court of Appeal found that while individual defendants may have been aware that fellow defendants were employing the same accountant to similar fraudulent effect, this did not, of itself, make them conspirators: each was engaging in fraudulent conduct in the course of his own affairs. *Meyrick* was "explained" in *Griffiths* on the basis of the proximity of the respective premises. Why should that matter? If D and E, both shoplifters, should notice what the other is doing, that would not make for a conspiracy to steal, however close together they stood. *Meyrick* should be regarded as wrong, both in light of the decision in *Griffiths* and by reference to the statement of general principle in *Ardarlan* (quoted above).

---

[80] [1972] All ER 257, 261.
[81] [1977] 2 SCR 523.
[82] But see the criticism of just such a development in the law of incitement above, § 9.1(i).
[83] (1929) 21 Cr App R 94.
[84] *Ibid.*, 102.
[85] (1965) 49 Cr App R 279.

The existence of a common purpose may be questioned when D's role is merely to supply some weapon or other object to be used in the commission of the offence. If D agrees with E that V should be killed and volunteers to provide a weapon, clearly he is E's partner in the project of killing V. By contrast, that appears not to be the case where D supplies a weapon to E for cash, aware that E intends to use the weapon to kill V but without agreeing with E that V should be killed. In *Gemmell*,[86] the Court of Appeal of New Zealand held that where D knows that other persons have agreed to commit a crime but where he is not a party to their agreement, if he does certain acts intended to assist the commission of the crime, he does not become a party to the conspiracy. *Gemmell* lays down the correct approach. No doubt D is a secondary party to the substantive offence, if and when it is committed, but he is uninvolved in the conspiracy.

(b) Differences between the parties over what has been agreed

To what extent can it be said that D and E have reached agreement on a course of conduct when the evidence reveals differences between them as to the content of their agreement? Two situations must be distinguished: (i) where D and E have different offences in mind; and (ii) where the differences between D and E do not preclude an agreement to commit the same offence.

Case 1: Different offences in mind.
In *Barnard*,[87] E and F (and others) agreed to commit robbery. D agreed to assist them, but he thought the scheme was to commit a less serious offence of theft. The Court of Appeal ruled that D was not guilty of conspiracy to rob; an intention to agree to the lesser offence of theft was not equivalent to an intention to agree to commit robbery. In *Patel*,[88] Woolf LJ (as he then was) considered, *obiter*, the converse situation; he instanced circumstances where D took himself to be agreeing to the importation of heroin, whereas his fellow conspirators planned to import cannabis, a lesser offence. Given that the offences were of the same type, Woolf LJ took the view that the greater implied the lesser and D could not disassociate himself from the conspiracy merely because the crime to be committed was less serious than the offence he had contemplated. Woolf LJ's view receives support from *dicta* of the Court of Appeal in *Taylor (Robert John)*,[89] where the Court ruled that an agreement to import Class B drugs would not encompass the importation of Class A drugs. However, the converse did not apply: if D agreed to import Class A drugs he would be liable for a conspiracy to import Class B drugs if that was what his co-conspirators had agreed to.

In terms of policy, the conclusion is entirely reasonable if the matter is assessed from the perspective of D's culpability; he has demonstrated his preparedness to do something that was cognate with, yet even more serious than, the crime his fellow conspirators had in mind. The problem with this culpability-driven approach, however, is that in purely conceptual terms it blurs the lines between actus reus (the agreement) and mens rea (the intention to commit a particular crime). In strict terms, the presence of agreement should first be

---

[86] [1985] 2 NZLR 740.
[87] (1980) 70 Cr App R 28.
[88] Unreported, 7 August 1991 (CA). Transcript 89/4351/51.
[89] [2002] Crim LR 205.

established and one should *then* move on to determine whether the mens rea of each party is consonant with the objectively established agreement.

In *Barnard*, the conduct of the parties, assessed objectively, amounted to formation of a conspiracy to rob, a conspiracy to which D was a party. The actus reus of conspiracy—agreement—was present. The reason D was not guilty of the offence was that he lacked mens rea; a readiness to thieve was not equivalent to a willingness to rob. Likewise, in the situation discussed by Woolf LJ in *Patel*, there was a conspiracy to import cannabis which D had, by his actions, joined; unlike Barnard, D would be guilty of conspiracy to import cannabis as an intent to import heroin was sufficient mens rea for the smuggling offence with which he was charged.[90] In some cases, however, differences between the parties may preclude the formation of an agreement if an objective approach is taken. Suppose that D and E agree to import drugs; D assumes the agreement concerns a consignment of heroin, a Class A drug, whereas E has in mind a consignment of cannabis, a Class B drug. It may be that, objectively, one view of their agreement is more reasonable than the other; on the evidence, a court may find that this was a conspiracy to import heroin or it was a conspiracy to import cannabis, as the case may be. In that case, there will be an objective act of agreement ascribable to both parties and their ultimate liability will hinge on their respective states of mind and whether it suffices for liability for the crime each, respectively, had in mind to commit. Alternatively, their actions may be genuinely ambiguous, so that both views of the agreement are plausible. If the presence of agreement is to be judged objectively, then there is none to be found.

Understandably, a criminal court court may be reluctant to reach such a conclusion as it would involve the acquittal of persons who had demonstrated a commitment to perpetrate crimes. There would be a natural temptation to reason that each defendant is to be judged from his own, subjective, perspective; even if, in the light of their differing perspectives, there is no agreement in the strict contractual sense. A less strict approach would, in our example, enable a court to find D guilty of conspiracy to import heroin and E guilty of conspiracy to import cannabis. Both parties have the mens rea for importation contrary to section 170 of the Customs and Excise Management Act 1979, and no great injustice is done if they are convicted of conspiracy to commit the offence, provided the punishment that each party receives is appropriate to his mens rea.

Case 2: Same offence in mind.
In *Broad*,[91] D and E agreed to manufacture drugs. D believed their agreement was to produce heroin whereas E thought they had arranged to produce cocaine. The Court of Appeal held the difference to be immaterial: on either view of the agreement, the objective would constitute the same offence, i.e. production of a Class A drug. *Broad* should be read as settling a general principle to the effect that differences over the content of their agreement between the parties do not vitiate any agreement between them if the respective

---

[90] Importation of a controlled drug contravenes s. 170 of the Customs and Excise Management Act 1979. As interpreted, the mens rea for the offence is awareness that some form of contraband is being imported even though penalties vary markedly (potentially life imprisonment for importing a Class A drug) according to the objects actually imported: *Taafe* [1984] AC 539.
[91] [1997] Crim LR 666.

course of conduct that each party contemplates will result in the commission of the same offence.

Professor Sir John Smith, however, queries the generality of *Broad*.[92] He contrasts the facts of that case with a hypothetical situation where D takes himself to be agreeing with E to murder V and is subsequently horrified to learn that the victim E intends is W. Smith suggests that differences regarding the kind of Class A drug are immaterial but the identity of the victim is a matter of substance. On that view, D would not be liable for conspiracy to murder. This conclusion may be doubted. The mens rea for murder takes no account of the identity of the victim. In the terms of section 1 of the Criminal Law Act 1977, D had agreed a course of conduct which, "will necessarily amount to or involve the commission of [an] offence."

Nonetheless, Professor Smith's view gains some support from the House of Lords decision on joint enterprise in complicity in *Powell and English*.[93] The House ruled that if the manner in which the principal commits the offence takes a form fundamentally different from that contemplated by the accomplice, the conduct of the principal will fall outside the scope of their joint enterprise. In *Powell*, D would have been liable for murder had P killed V with a wooden stave, the weapon that D contemplated that P would use, but he was not implicated when P chose to kill V with a knife. Prima facie, a change of victim is in some respects even more fundamental than a change of weapon. However, it is submitted that the influence of *Powell* should not be extended to statutory conspiracy. *Powell* involved a choice between two conflicting lines of common law authority in complicity, a matter which has no bearing on the correct interpretation of statutory conspiracy. Accordingly, differences between the parties as to the particulars of their agreement should not preclude liability for conspiracy if, notwithstanding those differences, the parties have agreed to commit the same offence. (If, on account of such differences, there are variations in the moral standing of the respective defendants, normally they can be taken into account at the sentencing stage.)

(c) Conditional agreements

The parties must conclude an agreement before liability for conspiracy can arise. This means that if D makes the resolution of certain matters a precondition to final agreement,[94] there is no conspiracy; as in *Walker*,[95] where D agreed in principle to robbery but then withdrew because of unresolved differences between himself and the other parties on how the robbery was to be carried out. The Court of Appeal quashed D's conviction for conspiracy, reasoning that he had not concluded a final agreement with the other parties because his conditions for joining their criminal project had not been met.

If, however, the parties have unequivocally agreed a criminal project, liability arises at that point. Such liability is unaffected by its being contingent on future events. In *O'Hadhmaill*,[96] the defendants, members of the IRA, resolved to carry out a bombing

---

[92] *Ibid.*, 668.
[93] [1997] 4 All ER 545.
[94] Broderick, "Conditional Objectives of Conspiracies" (1985) 94 *Yale LJ* 895.
[95] [1962] Crim LR 458.
[96] [1966] Crim LR 509.

campaign. They agreed not to give effect to this project unless and until the IRA abandoned a ceasefire policy. In confirming the defendants' convictions for conspiracy to cause explosions, the Court of Appeal held that this condition did not preclude the formation of an agreement on a course of conduct which, in the words of section 1 of the Criminal Law Act 1977, "if carried out in accordance with their intentions . . . will necessarily amount to or involve the commission of any offence." The agreement was in no sense equivocal. It was the intention of the parties to carry it out should a particular state of affairs arise. *O'Hadhmaill* is salutary. Practically all future projects will be subject to implicit conditions. For instance, suppose D and E agree to rob a bank. They are asked by some third party what they will do should they find the bank surrounded by armed police at the time they propose to rob it. A reply that they would then abandon their scheme in no way alters the fact that they have unequivocally agreed to rob a bank.

The reasoning in *O'Hadhmaill* clearly applies where the project of D and E is intrinsically criminal, e.g. to cause explosions or to rob banks. According to dicta in *Reed*,[97] such reasoning does not extend to situations where D and E conceive an objective which may be realised lawfully but agree to act in a criminal manner should that prove necessary in order to attain their goal. The following example was given in *Reed*:[98]

> "A and B agree to drive from London to Edinburgh in a time which can be achieved without exceeding the speed limits, but only if the traffic which they encounter is exceptionally light. Their agreement will not necessarily involve the commission of any offence, even if it is carried out in accordance with their intentions, and they do arrive from London to Edinburgh in the stated time."

Apparently, conditional agreements of that description fall outside the ambit of statutory conspiracy. This conclusion rests on a questionable interpretation of the phrase, "course of conduct" which appears in section 1 of the Criminal Law Act 1977; the matter will be dealt with more fully below, in § 9.2(iii), when we examine the meaning of that phrase.

(d) The sufficiency of agreement

Liability for conspiracy arises as soon as a course of conduct is agreed which is sufficiently specific to identify the crime(s) that would be committed should the agreement be carried out. Consequently, conduct which is very remote from the commission of a substantive offence may constitute a conspiracy. Suppose D and E agree to hire themselves out as "contract killers". From that point, they are parties to a conspiracy to murder notwithstanding that vital matters such as clients, victims, and rates of payment have yet to be resolved. In certain jurisdictions, there is a further requirement for an overt act done in pursuit of the agreed criminal objective before liability in conspiracy can arise.[99] This has much to commend it. The overt act is evidence that the agreement is a serious one and constitutes a real social threat. Moreover, such a requirement has the potential to lessen reliance on confessions as a mode of proof. However, the overt act requirement has not been received into English law to date and its introduction has not been proposed by any law reform agency.

---

[97] [1982] Crim LR 819 (CA).
[98] *Ibid.*, 820.
[99] See above, § 9.

In principle, once liability for conspiracy has arisen, it cannot be undone through any voluntary revocation of the agreement by all the parties to it or, in terms of the liability of specific individuals, through any voluntary withdrawal by a party to the agreement. In *Walker*,[100] D's conviction for conspiracy was quashed on the basis that he withdrew from negotiations with other parties *prior* to reaching an agreement with them; the Court of Appeal indicated, *obiter*, that had the point of agreement already been reached, a subsequent voluntary withdrawal would have provided at most mitigation and not a defence. As we have seen, a voluntary withdrawal defence is allowed for accomplices.[101] Although the conceptual bases of conspiracy and complicity differ—conspiracy is a form of direct liability which arises at the point of agreement; complicity is a form of derivative liability which arises on the commission of a substantive offence by another person—providing an incentive to withdraw from a criminal project prior to the commission of the substantive offence is equally in point for conspiracy. Moreover, many accomplices will be parties to a conspiracy made with the principal offender. In terms of policy, it seems be inconsistent to allow D a defence of voluntary withdrawal in respect of a complicity charge yet to impose liability upon D as a conspirator. Currently, providing a defence of voluntary revocation and withdrawal for alleged conspirators would be within the competence of a trial judge, there being no binding appellate authority disallowing such a defence.

(iii) The "course of conduct"

Under the terms of section 1(1) of the Criminal Law Act 1977, the parties must agree that:

> a course of conduct shall be pursued which, if the agreement is carried out in accordance with their intentions, . . . will necessarily amount to or involve the commission of any offence or offences.

On the face of it, this statutory requirement is straightforward: it demands proof of what it was the parties had agreed to do and proof that doing what had been agreed would *necessarily* have involved the commission of one or more crimes by at least one party of the agreement. Unfortunately, the position is not as straightforward as it should be. Interpretative difficulties have arisen over the phrase, "course of conduct". Two areas of ambiguity will be discussed: (i) how broadly or narrowly should the phrase be construed? and (ii) how many "course[s] of conduct" may a particular episode of conduct contain?

(a) A broad or narrow construction?

At its broadest, "course of conduct" may be construed as including any acts or omissions the parties propose to do and any consequences that will arise from the perpetration of those acts or omissions. At its narrowest, the reference to conduct could be read as signifying simply the acts or omissions the parties propose without reference to ensuing consequences. The broad interpretation best comports with the language of the Act and the rationale of conspiracy. The Act speaks of a "course of conduct . . . carried out *in accordance with their intentions*," which seems to imply that the consequences the parties intend to bring about

---

[100] [1962] Crim LR 458.
[101] Above, § 7.6(vi).

are to be included within the expression, "course of conduct". Suppose that D and E agree to tamper with the brakes of V's car with the intention that it should crash and V be killed. That agreement is, surely, a conspiracy to murder, a judgment confirmed if "course of conduct" includes the results that D and E intend their conduct to achieve. If that is the correct interpretation of the phrase, then the course of conduct they have agreed, "will *necessarily* amount to or involve the commission of [an] offence." However, if the narrow interpretation prevails and the course of conduct that D and E have agreed is confined to the physical interference with the brakes of the car, then it cannot be said that their conduct will necessarily cause the death of V. V might survive any ensuing crash, the tampering might prove ineffective, and so on. The narrow interpretation attains a measure of plausibility from the fact that it is common practice to break down the elements of "result" crimes into a tripartite division of conduct elements, circumstance elements, and consequence elements; where the "conduct" element encompasses only the physical movements of D.[102] But that is merely done for the purposes of exposition and in no sense determines the correct interpretation of section 1(1). In ordinary English speech, it is perfectly permissible to describe the same incident in a manner whereby D's conduct includes consequential results (as in "D killed V by shooting him") or in a manner which separates D's conduct from its consequence (as in "D fired a gun at V causing V to die").[103] Therefore, in terms of the wording of the Act and an effective law of conspiracy, the conduct of the parties should be taken to include the intended consequences of their agreed acts and omissions. There is no theory of language nor legal principle which precludes this interpretation.

Unfortunately, the approach argued for here is contrary to the approach of the House of Lords in *Nock*.[104] The case itself involved common law conspiracy, on which the Act has no bearing. Lord Scarman, however, adverted to the defining elements of statutory conspiracy and regarded them as an effective summary of the common law position for conspiracies where the objective of the conspiracy was the commission of a crime. D and E had attempted to produce cocaine from a set of materials which, unknown to them, did not contain any coca-base, rendering their project impossible. Lord Scarman construed the phrase "course of conduct" as a reference to what D and E physically proposed to do, i.e. to apply certain chemical procedures to the material they had. The consequence they intended to bring about from applying these procedures was not, itself, to be taken as part of their course of conduct; it was the objective of their agreed course of conduct but was not part of it.[105] Accordingly, D and E were not parties to a conspiracy to produce cocaine because the implementation of what they had agreed would not "necessarily" involve the commission of a crime.

The actual decision in *Nock* was reversed by an amendment of the Criminal Law Act 1977. It now it suffices that an offence would have been committed, "but for the existence of facts which render the commission of the offence . . . *impossible*."[106] Lord Scarman's reasoning has therefore been displaced for cases of impossibility. Seemingly, however, it

---

[102] See above, § 7.4.

[103] Feinberg describes this as the "accordion effect": "Action and Responsibility" in Black (ed.), *Philosophy in America* (1965) 134.

[104] [1978] AC 979.

[105] *Ibid.*, 995–6, 998.

[106] Section 1(1)(b) of the Criminal Law Act 1977, as amended by the Criminal Attempts Act 1981.

remains in place for cases where attainable objectives are pursued by ineffectual means. On this view, D and E would now be conspirators on the original facts of *Nock* but not in circumstances, say, where it was *possible* to manufacture cocaine from the materials D and E possessed but not by the method they agreed to use.

This conclusion is so perverse that one is tempted peremptorily to reject it. However, if the interpretation we have argued for—that the course of conduct includes the consequences the parties intend to achieve—is correct, the amendment to the Act for the case of impossibility was unnecessary. Under our preferred interpretation, a course of conduct includes intended consequences and is thus irrelevant whether those consequences are possible or impossible of attainment.

Lord Scarman's analysis in *Nock* may be contrasted with the decision of the Court of Appeal in *Bolton*.[107] The latter case concerned a dishonest scheme agreed between D and E to obtain a mortgage advance from a building society. They anticipated that they would receive the advance by way of a cheque, a valuable security, but, because of changes in the society's payments system, they received the advance by way of electronic transfer, a method that did not involve creation of a valuable security. It was held that they had conspired to procure the execution of a valuable security as their expectation of receiving a cheque was to be regarded as part of the "course of conduct" they had agreed. Unfortunately, Lord Scarman's contrary analysis of this phrase was not considered by the Court of Appeal. Recall that, although Lord Scarman construed the terms of the Act, he was taking the Act as a guide to the common law. His Lordship's reading of section 1(1) is of only persuasive authority. It is submitted that the analysis in *Bolton* is to be preferred. Further, the amendment of the Criminal Law Act 1977 relating to the cases of impossibility should be treated as being intended to remove the long-standing common law defence of impossibility to the crime of statutory conspiracy. It should not be regarded as confirming Lord Scarman's analysis by way of creating a special exemption to it.

(b) How many courses of conduct?

Suppose that D and E agree, say, to commit a burglary and contingently agree also to commit some further offence, such as murder, should they encounter opposition in the course of the burglary. It may be asked how many conspiracies arise in these cases. Clearly, in our example, there is a conspiracy to commit burglary. Is there an additional conspiracy to commit murder? If we characterise their agreement as an agreement involving but one agreed course of conduct—to commit burglary—then there is no conspiracy to murder. They may successfully conclude the burglary without necessarily committing murder. However, it is possible to separate the strands of their overall agreement; an agreement to burgle and an agreement to murder on a particular eventuality. Linguistically, it is perfectly apt to regard them as two separate agreements to pursue two different courses of conduct. It is true that their project is burglary rather than murder: the murder, if it should occur, would be but a means to an end. But that has no bearing on the wrongfulness of agreeing to murder someone. *O'Hadhmaill*[108] decides that it is no answer to a charge of conspiracy that the implementation of an agreement was subject to a condition which may not be fulfilled,

---

[107] (1991) 94 Cr App R 74.
[108] [1966] Crim LR 509.

provided the parties have unequivocally agreed to pursue a criminal course of conduct should the terms of the condition be fulfilled. It is submitted that the better view is that in such circumstances there are as many separate courses of conduct as there are crimes the parties have unequivocally agreed to commit. This conclusion is supported by *A-G's Reference (No. 4 of 2003)*,[109] where the Court of Appeal was sympathetic to the view that if D and others agree to steal a particular item and resolve that should it be necessary they will commit burglary or robbery to get it, there are conspiracies for theft, burglary, and robbery.

Recall, however, our discussion of the "driving to Edinburgh" example put by Lord Lane in *Reed*.[110] Lord Lane took the view that if the objective of D and E—arriving in Edinburgh in time, say, for lunch—could be achieved by driving within speed limits, their agreement to exceed those limits, should need arise, did not constitute a conspiracy to exceed statutory limits. Their course of conduct could reach a successful conclusion without necessarily involving the commission of a crime. His view appears to be that courses of conduct are identified by reference to the ultimate objective of the parties and to any means employed to attain that objective which are intrinsically necessary and not merely contingently necessary. On that view, the Edinburgh agreement takes in lunching and driving to lunch, two separate courses of conduct, but not speeding to lunch.

Employing a distinction between intrinsically necessary means and contingently necessary means to delimit the ambit of conspiracy entails some fine distinctions. Suppose that D and E agree to obtain money from V. They agree to try first to obtain the money by a hard-luck story; should that not succeed they agree to kill V and then take his money. Here the distinction between intrinsically necessary means and contingently necessary means does not apply. They contemplate the possibility of having to try two means to the same end, plan A and plan B. Surely there is a conspiracy to defraud *and* a conspiracy to murder? Distinguishing between situations such as the lunch in Edinburgh scenario and the money plot is too refined for the practical concerns of the criminal law. It is submitted that, in the spirit of the decision in *O'Hadhmaill*, if the parties have unequivocally agreed to commit an offence should a particular eventuality arise, they have agreed "a course of conduct shall be pursued which . . . will necessarily . . . involve the commission of an offence." The dictum to the contrary of Lord Lane in *Reed* should not be followed.

(iv) *The mens rea of conspiracy*

There is an element of contrivance in subdividing the constituents of conspiracy into sections dealing with actus reus—the agreement—on the one hand, and mens rea on the other. After all, agreement, the meeting of minds, involves a mental operation. That said, the presence of a consensus does not exhaust what is required by way of a mental element for this offence. Agreements operate on the surface of things and the fact of agreement may coexist with secret reservations or betrayals that one or more of the parties may have in mind. For example, suppose D and E agree to meet later that night in order to carry out a burglary at the house of V. D has no intention of showing up. He agrees with E because he is disinclined to admit that the lacks the courage to commit burglary. E, on the other hand,

---

[109] [2004] EWCA Crim 1944.
[110] [1982] Crim LR 819 (CA).

is an undercover policeman who plans to arrest D. If neither D nor E is guilty of conspiracy, as is likely the case, it will be because each lacks mens rea.

(a) Intention to carry out the course of conduct agreed

Section 1 of the Criminal Law Act 1977 refers to an agreement, "carried out in accordance with the intentions of [the parties]." This indicates that liability in conspiracy is predicated on the intention of the parties to carry out their agreement. The requirement for this form of intention is a matter of implication rather than express stipulation. The Law Commission recommended that there be express stipulation on the matter. It drafted the following provision:[111]

> "both he and the other person or persons with whom he agrees must intend to bring about any consequence which is an element of that offence, even where the offence in question may be committed without that consequence actually being intended by the person committing it."

In the debates on the Bill that became the Criminal Law Act 1977, this provision was rejected on the ground of excessive complexity. Nonetheless, the Lord Chancellor, when agreeing to the deletion of the clause, stated that what is now section 1 of the Criminal Law Act 1977 required "full intention and knowledge before conspiracy can be established."[112]

This legislative history needs to be borne in mind[113] when considering the implications of the House of Lords decision in *Anderson*.[114] Seemingly, a unanimous House decided that an intention to carry out the agreed *course of conduct* was not a defining element of conspiracy. It sufficed that D had agreed a criminal project with others and intended to play *his assigned part* in it. Further than that, nothing else was required. In particular, the prosecution need not establish that D intended that the agreement be carried through to completion.

The ruling in *Anderson* was novel. Previously, it had never been suggested, let alone decided, that an intention to realise the objective of the conspiracy was not essential to liability as a conspirator.[115] The elements of liability will, of course, be the same for each conspirator. Consequently, *Anderson* raises the possibility of liability for conspiracy in circumstances where none of the parties to a particular agreement intends that it be carried out. So radical is this interpretation and so out of accord with the legislative history of statutory conspiracy and the history of conspiracy generally, it is necessary to examine the facts of *Anderson* to see if any limitations or special considerations can be brought to bear on the ambit of the decision:

> The appellant D had been a prisoner, along with E and F. E and F conceived a plan to effect the escape from prison of G. D agreed with E and F to help effect G's escape and undertook that when he, D, was released from prison he would procure some diamond cutting equipment and arrange for it to be smuggled into the prison. D sought to defend himself from liability for conspiracy on the basis that his sole interest in this venture was to make some

---

[111] Law Com. No. 76, *Conspiracy and Criminal Law Reform* (1976); Law Com. No. 177, *A Criminal Code for England and Wales* (1989) cl. 1(3).

[112] HL Debs, vol. 379, col. 55.

[113] Including reference to Ministerial statements to Parliament, pursuant to *Pepper* v. *Hart* [1993] AC 593.

[114] [1986] AC 27.

[115] In *Thompson* (1965) Cr App R 1, for example, the Court of Criminal Appeal had ruled that to be guilty of conspiracy a person must not only agree a criminal project but also intend that the project be carried out.

money from selling the equipment to E and F. He claimed that he envisaged no prospect that E and F would succeed in their plan.

There was no necessity for the House to revamp the mental element of conspiracy in order to sustain D's conviction for the offence. D had entered into an agreement with E and F, the object of which was to bring about the escape of G. D's role was not as a mere supplier of materials; he was part of the plot to spring G. The plot was a real one in the sense that D knew that E and F would try to put it into effect. Not infrequently, a party will join a conspiracy in circumstances where it is not envisaged that he himself will take any part in the commission of the substantive offence. For such a party, his "intent" that the substantive offence be carried out is constituted by the knowledge that his co-conspirators intend to do so. In *Anderson*, D knew that E and F intended to carry out the substantive offence and he assisted that project. He did not intend to frustrate their scheme by, say, reporting them to the relevant authorities. That he thought nothing or little of E and F's prospects of success would seem neither here nor there. His conviction was perfectly in accord with the orthodox understanding of the mental element in conspiracy. Any reference to his ultimate motive (i.e. to make money) was irrelevant: the House of Lords simply confused D's motive with his intent.

An appreciation that the innovative approach of the House of Lords was unnecessary for the decision in *Anderson* increases one's confidence in the validity and authority of several appellate decisions and dicta which subsequently have sought to minimise the effects of that decision.

One such case is *McPhillips*,[116] where Lowry LCJ, giving judgment for the Court of Appeal of Northern Ireland, ruled that section 1(1) of the Criminal Law Act 1977 required an intention on the part of a conspirator that the object of the conspiracy be carried out. Accordingly, D was not liable for conspiracy to murder in *McPhillips* because he intended to alert the relevant authorities prior to the explosion of the bomb he and his partners had set. Lord Lowry distinguished the decision in *Anderson* on the basis that on the facts of that case D had had no intention of frustrating the plans of his fellow conspirators to effect the escape of a prisoner. The facts of the respective cases do differ in the manner indicated by his Lordship. Yet if one were to remain faithful to the decision in *Anderson*, it is unclear why this factual difference should be of any consequence. By becoming a party to an agreement to murder and intending to play a part (indeed playing a part) in carrying out the agreement, the appellant in *McPhillips* fulfilled the requirements for liability in conspiracy as set down by Lord Bridge in *Anderson*.

In other cases, too, Lord Bridge's requirements have not been taken as either a necessary or a sufficient basis for liability in conspiracy. In *Edwards*,[117] the Court of Appeal ruled that D could incur liability for conspiracy to supply amphetamine only if he intended that amphetamine be supplied. No reference to *Anderson* was made in the judgment. In *Yip Chiu-Cheung*, again without reference to *Anderson*, Lord Griffiths stated that "the crime of conspiracy requires an agreement between two or more persons to commit an unlawful act with the intention of carrying it out. *It is the intention to carry out the crime* that constitutes the mens rea of the offence."[118]

---

[116] [1989] NI 360.
[117] [1991] Crim LR 45.
[118] [1995] 1 AC 111, 118 (emphasis added). And see too *Harvey* [1999] Crim LR 70.

Of course, this post-*Anderson* case law, comprising, as it does, a decision of the Court of Appeal of Northern Ireland, a *per incuriam* decision of the Court of Appeal, and dicta of the Privy Council, cannot overturn an unequivocal ruling of the House of Lords. Yet, in estimating the future influence of the *Anderson* ruling, it is pertinent to recall our previous discussion of the legislative history of statutory conspiracy. That history clearly indicates that it was not the intention of Parliament, when enacting section 1(1) of the Criminal Law Act 1977, to dispense with the venerable requirement of an intention to carry out the agreement; section 1(1) was understood to require such an intention. Furthermore, as will be seen below, section 1(2) requires proof of intent or knowledge with respect to any circumstances necessary for the commission of the substantive offence. It would have been quite bizarre for Parliament to insist on full mens rea as to circumstance elements of the substantive offence yet, at same time, dispense with mens rea as to any consequence element required to establish the substantive offence. Finally, as we have already argued, if the nature of the intention required for the crime of conspiracy had been properly analysed by the House of Lords in *Anderson*, the appellant's conviction could have been sustained without recourse to the legal innovations to which the House resorted. Accordingly it is submitted, with some confidence, that to be a guilty party to a conspiracy, D must intend that the course of conduct that the parties have agreed should be carried out in circumstances which would necessarily amount to the commission of an offence by at least one of the parties to the agreement.

(b) Intention and foresight of certainty

Where the substantive offence is the very object of the conspiracy, mens rea is straight-forward. Assuredly, there will be a conspiracy to murder where D and E agree to firebomb V's house with the objective of killing V. Suppose, however, that D and E conceive of a plan to set fire to a house, occupied by V, in order to make a fraudulent insurance claim for destruction of the building. They appreciate the life-threatening potential of their projected conduct, yet the prospect of death or injury to V is not a motivating factor in the making of their agreement. From the perspective of potential conspiracy charges, there are obvious charges in relation to their fraudulent objective and there is also a conspiracy to commit arson, since arson is an intended means to their fraudulent end. Assume that it can be proved that D and E contemplate the death of V as a virtual certainty if the course of conduct they have agreed is carried out according to their intentions. Can we say that their agreement is, also, a conspiracy to murder?

English criminal law consistently, though not invariably, permits inferences of intent to be drawn with respect to side-effects which are the virtually certain outcome of D's conduct, if D foresaw the outcome as virtually certain.[119] At common law, the conflation of knowledge with intent has been carried over to conspiracy. For example, in *Cooke*,[120] D and others, railway employees, were found guilty of conspiracy to defraud British Rail on the basis that in scheming to sell their own food and drink to British Rail customers, they intended to cause loss to their employer. Of course, it was no part of D's purpose to cause loss; that was merely the inevitable concomitant of making such gains. It may well be that

---

[119] See above, § 5.1(iv).
[120] [1986] AC 909.

the same analysis will be made in the context of statutory conspiracy.[121] Should that prove to be the case, then in our house-burning example D and E would be liable for conspiracy to murder.

Intention, as always, must be distinguished from motive. In *Yip Chiu-Cheung*,[122] it was the view of the Privy Council that D would incur liability for conspiracy to import drugs from Hong Kong to Sydney if he intended that the agreement be carried out notwithstanding his secret role as an undercover police officer, to bring his fellow conspirators to justice. If he had planned to secure the arrest of the others prior to the implementation of the agreement he would then not have been guilty of conspiracy, since he would have lacked an intention to carry out the agreement. In either of those scenarios, the timing of any arrests may depend on contingencies which would have no bearing on the moral quality of D's conduct. Despite this, English courts regard mens rea as a technical legal description of D's state of mind which need not necessarily involve any culpability on the part of D.[123] Accordingly, the analysis in *Yip* represents current English law.[124]

(c) Intention to take some part in carrying out the agreement

As we have discussed, the decision in *Anderson* sought to dispense with the requirement of an intent that the agreement be carried out. According to Lord Bridge, the relevant intent to be established is simply an intent by D to take some part in carrying out the agreement:[125]

> "But, beyond the mere fact of agreement, the necessary mens rea of the crime is, in my opinion, established if, and only if, it is shown that the accused, when he entered into the agreement, intended to play some part in the agreed course of conduct in furtherance of the criminal purpose which the agreed course of conduct was intended to achieve. Nothing less will suffice; nothing more is required."

Prior to *Anderson*, a requirement that D must intend to *play some part* in carrying out the agreement was unknown to English law. From the origin of the offence until the present time, liability for conspiracy has been founded on the fact of *agreement*.[126] Suppose, for the moment, we take *Anderson* at face value and accept that the requirement of an intention to play some part in implementing the agreement is a part of English law. It appears that D, for instance, would no longer be liable for conspiracy to murder if he induced E and F to agree to kill V by offering a financial incentive. D's conduct would have brought about an agreement to kill to which she was a party but, assuming the validity of *Anderson*, she cannot incur liability for conspiracy unless she intended to play some part in implementing this agreement.

---

[121] Cf. *Walker* (1989) 90 Cr App R 226, where a similar analysis was adopted in respect of statutory attempt.

[122] [1995] 1 AC 111.

[123] See also the discussion earlier, § 5.

[124] In *Somchai Liangsiriprasert v. US Government* (1991) 92 Cr App R 77, 82 the Privy Council had left open the question whether law enforcement officials should be given dispensation to enter conpiracies in order to frustrate criminal objectives, but *Yip Chiu-cheung* suggests no such dispensation will be given. For valuable discussion of the issues of principle and policy in condoning illegal actions in the interests of law enforcement see Ashworth, "Testing Fidelity to Legal Values: Official Involvment and Criminal Justice" in Shute and Simester (eds.), *Criminal Law Theory: Doctrines of the General Part* (2002) 299.

[125] [1986] AC 27, 39.

[126] *Poulterer's Case* (1611) 9 Co Rep 55b, 77 ER 813; *Starling* (1664) 1 Sid 174, 82 ER 1039.

What does "taking some part" require by way of conduct? In our agreement-to-murder example from the last paragraph, it would be enough, by analogy with the facts of *Anderson*, for D to provide some practical assistance to E and F, such as providing them with a weapon. Presumably, it would suffice if D, say, informed E and F of V's whereabouts. But if D had no active role to play in implementing the agreement, he would not be liable for conspiracy. Yet surely one can be party to an agreement—and thus a member of a conspiracy—without being allocated an active role in its implementation? The test in *Anderson* apportions liability on the basis of differences that are irrelevant to the gist of conspiracy. The gist of conspiracy is the entry into the agreement.

With that in mind, the approach of the Court of Appeal in *Siracusa* is to be welcomed. D had recruited and agreed with E and others that offences be committed in contravention of section 170(2)(b) of the Customs and Excise Management Act 1979. It could not be proved against him that he intended to play an active part in implementing this agreement. O'Connor LJ confirmed his conviction for conspiracy on the basis that his "intention to participate in the furtherance of the criminal purpose is . . . established by his failure to stop the unlawful activity. Lord Bridge's dictum does not require anything more."[127] On O'Connor LJ's approach, D, in our agreement-to-kill example, would intend to play some part in carrying out the agreement should she fail to report their agreement to the police or take some similar steps.

O'Connor LJ's analysis is artificial: not preventing an offence is hardly "playing a part" in its commission. But the artificiality is forced by the need to pay lip-service to *Anderson*. It would labour the obvious to say anything more than that O'Connor LJ is departing from the view of the law held by Lord Bridge under the guise of complying with it. As Lord Bridge's conception of the mental element in conspiracy is so novel, so strange, and so destructive of the rationale of conspiracy, there must, surely, be a good prospect that O'Connor LJ's "interpretation" of Lord Bridge will prevail.

(d) Intention and knowledge as to facts or circumstances necessary for the commission of the offence

Section 1(2) of the Criminal Law Act 1977 provides:

> Where liability for any offence may be incurred without knowledge on the part of the person committing it of any particular fact or circumstance necessary for the commission of the offence, a person shall nevertheless not be guilty of conspiracy to commit that offence by virtue of subsection (1) above unless he and at least one other party of the agreement intend or know that that fact or circumstance shall or will exist at the time when the conduct constituting the offence is to take place.

Section 1(2) is the only provision of the Act which deals explicitly with the mens rea requirements for conspiracy. Ostensibly, its terms are of limited effect. It deals with the situation where liability for the *substantive* offence may be incurred without knowledge on the part of D of any particular fact or circumstance necessary for the commission of the offence; for example, where the substantive offence is one of strict liability. If a conspiracy charge relating to an agreement to commit an offence of strict liability is brought, section

---

[127] (1989) 90 Cr App Rep 340.

1(2) makes clear that intention or knowledge as to the facts or circumstances of the substantive offence is required even if such proof would not be required for the substantive offence itself.

Does the provision have any wider effect? No reference is made to any conduct or consequence elements of the substantive offence. No indication is given about the mens rea required for conspiracy when the substantive offence does require proof of knowledge of any particular fact or circumstance necessary for the commission of the offence. A basic principle of statutory interpretation is that if express provision is made for a particular matter or issue and no provision is made for cognate matters or issues falling outside the situation expressly provided for, the inference to be drawn is that the same provision does not extend to those cognate matters or issues.[128] Prima facie, applying that rule of construction, we reach what has been aptly described as a "scandalous paradox":[129] on a conspiracy charge, knowledge or intent must be proved for any particular fact or circumstance necessary for the commission of the offence if such knowledge or intent would *not* be required in a trial for the substantive offence but proof of such knowledge or intent may be dispensed with where such knowledge or intent *is* required for the substantive offence. Furthermore, on a conspiracy charge, no mens rea need be proved with respect to conduct and consequence elements of the substantive offence regardless of whether such mens rea is required for the substantive offence.

This prima facie conclusion defies logic and cannot be defended in terms of policy. It is relevant to refer again to the legislative history of the Act. Recall that the original Bill put before Parliament contained a clause that provided for proof of intention as to any consequence elements necessary for commission of the substantive offence on a charge of conspiracy. Although the clause was deleted on the ground that it was excessively complex, the Lord Chancellor assured Parliament that what is now section 1(1) of the Criminal Law Act 1977 required proof of "*full* intention and knowledge before conspiracy can be established."[130] If these words are taken as an authoritative guide to the interpretation of section 1(1), intention or knowledge should be required as to all elements that make up the substantive offence. That is the position at common law;[131] one would have anticipated express provision in the Act were the well-established and long-standing common law position to be departed from. If we accept that section 1(1) requires intention or knowledge for all elements of the substantive offence, then section 1(2) may be regarded as a provision inserted to avoid any doubt that the same level of intention or knowledge is required on a conspiracy charge even when it is not required by the substantive offence. The word "nevertheless" adds force to this interpretation; it may be taken to stress that even in cases where there is an element of strict liability within the substantive offence, mens rea as to those elements is required for conspiracy; *a fortiori* such intention or knowledge is required when proof of such intention or knowledge is required for the substantive offence. This reading,

---

[128] *Expressio unius est exclusio alterius*—"the mention of one thing is the exclusion of another": Bell and Engle, *Cross on Statutory Interpretation* (3rd ed., 1995) 140–1.

[129] Elliot, "Mens Rea in Statutory Conspiracy" [1978] *Crim LR* 202, 204.

[130] See above, § 9.2(iv)(a).

[131] See below, § 15.6(iv), regarding the mens rea for conspiracy to defraud.

originally proposed by Sir John Smith,[132] was recently endorsed by the House of Lords in *Saik*[133] and can be taken as established.

Accordingly, it seems clear that D will not be liable for conspiracy unless she intends or knows of any particular fact or circumstance necessary for the commission of the substantive offence. Recklessness, even of the *Cunningham*[134] variety, will not suffice for conspiracy. Suppose D and E agree to cut down a tree that they think may belong either to E or to V. Should it be the case that the ownership of the tree is V's, destruction of the tree by D and E would constitute criminal damage on their part, recklessness being sufficient culpability for the offence.[135] However, there would not be a conspiracy to commit criminal damage: they would neither know[136] nor intend that the tree belongs to V.

(e) Future facts

Under the terms of section 1(2), D must *intend* or *know* that "facts or circumstances necessary for the commission of [the substantive offence] *shall* or *will* exist at the time when the conduct constituting the offence is to take place." Clearly, it is possible to intend a future fact or circumstance. If D invites V for dinner on 1 November, he intends to have dinner with V on that day. Suppose that D and E agree to invite V to dinner on the 1st and to kill him when he comes on that day. D and E are, of course, guilty of conspiracy to murder as they *intend* a fact necessary for the commission of the crime—the presence of V for dinner—to occur.

Ordinarily, however, one would not say that D *knows* V will come to dinner on 1 November, at least until V responds affirmatively to the invitation. It is therefore possible to conceive of situations where D and E plan to kill V and it cannot be said that they intend or know of V's necessary presence. For example, suppose that D and E are aware that always V drives home by either route A or route B. They agree that, should V take route B on 1 November, they will intercept him and kill him. Strictly, they cannot *intend* the presence of V unless they have (or think they have) some means of influencing V to take route B. Moreover, they do not *know* which route V will take. Accordingly, on a literal interpretation of section 1(2), there is no conspiracy.

Such a literal interpretation would seriously undermine the law of conspiracy. As we saw earlier, when discussing conditional agreements (§ 9.2(ii)(c)), the successful implementation of agreements will often require the presence of facts or circumstances which can be neither known nor intended when the agreement is struck. Since it is generally not possible to "know" the future outcome of unresolved contingencies,[137] the interpretation of *intend* becomes crucial. It is submitted that, for the purpose of section 1(2), D's "intention" must embrace the preconditions of that intention, such that D should be taken to intend the

---

[132] "Mens Rea in Statutory Conspiracy: (3) Some Answers" [1978] *Crim LR* 210.

[133] [2007] 1 AC 18, at paras. 16–21 (Lord Nichols).

[134] [1957] 2 QB 396.

[135] Criminal Damage Act 1971, s. 1(1).

[136] For general discussion of knowledge as a culpability term in criminal law, see Shute "Knowledge and Belief in the Criminal Law" and Sullivan "Knowledge, Belief and Culpability", in Shute and Simester (eds.), *Criminal Law Theory: Doctrines of the General Part* (2002) 184 and 207 respectively.

[137] Above, § 5.4. Cf. *Sunair Holidays Ltd* [1973] 2 All ER 1233, where the Court of Appeal held that D could not be taken to "know" the existence of a future, contingent fact (the date of completion of a swimming-pool).

existence of those facts or circumstances which he contemplates as necessary for the commission of the intended substantive offence.[138]

Subject to that qualification, whatever the mens rea requirements for the substantive offence, or the lack thereof, to be convicted of conspiracy D must know of or intend the presence of any material circumstances necessary for proof of the principal offence. The decision in *Sakavicas*[139] is in flat contradiction of this statement of the law. The money-laundering offences at issue in that case required proof of knowledge or suspicion of the illegal provenance of the funds: the Court of Appeal held that D and E were guilty of conspiracy to commit these offences on the basis of their suspicion that the funds they agreed to process were the proceeds of drug trafficking or other illegal activity. Happily, we need not consider the tortuous reasoning behind the decision.[140] In *Saik*[141] the House of Lords ruled that even where liability for an offence could be incurred without knowledge on the part of the person committing it of any particular fact or circumstance necessary for the commission of the offence, section 1(2) of the 1977 Act required proof that any conspirator knew or intended that the fact or circumstance "shall or will" exist when the conspiracy was put into effect. Baroness Hale, dissenting, considered that D would intend in a conditional sense the fact of the illegal provenance of the funds if he agreed to accept them for changing into another currency despite his suspicions.[142] But the concept of conditional intent is best reserved where D resolves a course of action subject to a contingency as in "I will steal that necklace if those are real diamonds." To adapt the concept in the manner of Baroness Hale is to render it a synonym for suspicion.

Special mention should be made of cases involving conspiracies to import a deal in controlled drugs. It seems that, if D takes himself to be agreeing to the importation of a Class A, he will be liable for conspiracy to import a Class B or C drug if that is what his co-conspirators take themselves to have agreed.[143] Even though importation of a Class A is a different offence from importation of a Class B or Class C drug, the mens rea for each different importation offence is the same. It suffices that there was awareness that the item in possession was some form of contraband.[144] Yet, strictly speaking, D neither knew nor intended the existence of the facts necessary for the commission of this lesser offence. The finding of conspiracy to commit the lesser offence can be defended if we are prepared to say in this context that the greater offence can comprehend the lesser offence, so that an intention to import a Class A drug can be taken to be an intent to import a Class B or Class C drug.

---

[138] Such an interpretation must underlie decisions such as *O'Hadmaill* [1996] Crim LR 509 (CA), discussed above in § 9.2(ii)(c). In that case, D and others agreed to resume a bombing campaign if and when a cease fire was revoked. Strictly, they could neither have known nor intended that hostilities would restart (the matter was not for them to decide). Their conviction for conspiracy indicates that it was enough for them to *contemplate* circumstances whereupon their agreement would take effect.

[139] [2004] EWCA Crim 2686 and see too *Ali* [2005] EWCA Crim 87.

[140] Expertly and critically dissected by Ormerod, " Making Sense of Mens Rea in Statutory Conspiracies" [2006] *Current Legal Problems* 185, an analysis endorsed by Lord Nicholls in *Saik* [2007] 1 AC 18, para. 37.

[141] *Ibid.*

[142] *Ibid.*, paras. 97–100.

[143] *Patel*, unreported, 7 August 1991 (CA), transcript 89/4351/51; *Taylor* [2002] Crim LR 205.

[144] *Taafe* [1984] AC 539.

(f) Mens rea for statutory conspiracy—a summary

It may be helpful to summarise our conclusions on the mental element required for conspiracy:

(i)   D must intend that the agreement to which she is a party should be carried out.

(ii)   D must know of or intend the existence of any fact or circumstance necessary for the commission of the agreed offence.

(iii) Where a fact or circumstance necessary for the commission of the agreed offence is not in existence at the time of the agreement, D must intend, know, or contemplate that any such fact or circumstance will exist at the time the offence takes place.

(iv)   If D is to be guilty of conspiracy, at least one other party to the agreement must satisfy conditions (i) through (iii) above.

(v)   It is not necessary for D to intend to play any active part in carrying out the agreement.

(v) D's co-conspirators: some limitations

Once it has been proved that D is a party to an agreement to commit a crime and is possessed of the necessary mens rea, and that at least one other party to the agreement has mens rea, liability for conspiracy will normally ensue against D and the other party with mens rea. However, liability will not arise if that other party is the only other party to the agreement and is either (a) D's spouse; (b) a person under the age of criminal responsibility; (c) a victim of the intended substantive offence; or (d) a limited company. We must also consider the position (e) when the only other party to the agreement is acquitted.

(a) Spouses

It was probably a rule at common law that an agreement between a husband and wife alone to commit a crime did not constitute a conspiracy. The common law was based upon the legal fiction that husband and wife constituted a single legal person.[145] In R,[146] the House of Lords decided that the same fiction no longer had any role to play in providing the husband with a defence to a charge of raping his wife. The view expressed in R, that this fiction was fundamentally at odds with the status of women in modern English life, is of general application and in principle would enable common law conspiracy charges to be brought on the basis of agreements confined to a husband and wife.[147] However, section 2(2) of the Criminal Law Act 1977 expressly provides that an agreement confined to a husband and wife will not constitute a statutory conspiracy.

This provision was endorsed by the Law Commission as safeguarding "the stability of marriage."[148] One might think there are more serious threats to a marriage than conspiracy charges and, in any event, wives may be charged as secondary parties to their husband's crimes should the conspiracy be carried out. Be that as it may, section 2(2) is unequivocal.

---

[145] *CLGP* 799–803.

[146] [1992] 1 AC 599.

[147] There is no English decision which rules that husband and wife cannot conspire at common law, although there is a statement to that effect in Hawkins 1 PC, ch. 27, § 8 and dicta in *Mawji* v. *R.* [1957] AC 126 (PC). At civil law, a husband and wife can conspire: *Midland Bank Trust Co Ltd* v. *Green (No 3)* [1979] Ch 496.

[148] Law Com. No. 76, *Conspiracy and Criminal Law Reform* (1976) paras. 1.46–1.49.

Its terms are confined to agreements where the parties are the husband and wife alone. Should they be joined by any other party, such as a child of the marriage, all parties will be liable for conspiracy. It may be noted, too, that apart from being an accomplice of her partner, a spouse may also incur liability under section 4 of the Criminal Law Act 1967 if anything is done with intent to impede the apprehension or prosecution of the principal offender. The immunity in respect of conspiracy is anomalous and anachronistic but is undeniably part of the modern law of statutory conspiracy.

(b) Persons under the age of criminal responsibility

Section 2(2) further provides that D will not be guilty of conspiracy if the only other person with whom he agrees is a person under the age of criminal responsibility. If E is the only other party to agreement and is under the age of 10, E has a complete defence to a charge of statutory conspiracy.[149] Section 2(2) makes it clear that, in such cases, D too is exempt from liability in conspiracy. It is not obvious why E's lack of criminal capacity should also provide immunity for D if E was capable of entering into an agreement with an intention that the agreement be carried out. However, arguably persons under 10 are generally incapable in any meaningful sense of making criminal agreements; if so, then one way of viewing (and of justifying) the subsection is to see it as a form of conclusive presumption against the existence of the actus reus. On that view, there would be no agreement to which D can be a party in any case where E, the only other party, is under 10.

(c) Where the only other party is a victim

At common law, where E would otherwise be party to a conspiracy with D, E will not be liable if she is to be regarded as the victim of the agreed crime. So, in *Tyrrell*,[150] E, a girl under the age of 14, was not a conspirator with D in the crime of unlawful sexual intercourse despite her readiness to participate. Section 2(2) confirms this immunity for statutory conspiracy. It also provides that D, too, is not liable for statutory conspiracy if the only other party to the agreement is an "intended victim" of the agreed offence.

It is difficult to appreciate why, in principle, this should be so. If E, notwithstanding her victim status, possesses the capacity to enter agreements with intent that they be carried out, there is a sufficient actus reus for D's liability to be assessed by reference to his own culpability. The rule in *Tyrrell* is protective of victims and, it is submitted, should confer no immunity on non-victim participants in the criminal activity. The effect of section 2(2) is to pass on the protection accorded to victims to persons who are fully accountable for the agreements they enter.

The range of persons who fall within the category of victim is not defined by the Act. At common law, in the context of immunity from charges of complicity and conspiracy, a "victim" has always been a member of a defined, vulnerable class, such as a young person below the age of consent or a statutorily protected tenant.[151] The absence of such limiting characteristics specified in section 2(2)—there is simply an unqualified reference to "intended victim"—invites consideration whether the term is to be taken in a broader sense.

---

[149] The defence of infancy is discussed below, § 19.4.
[150] [1894] 1 QB 710. See above, § 7.6(iv)(a).
[151] *Grace Rymer Investment* v. *Waite* [1958] Ch 831.

Certainly, the principle underlying cases such as *Tyrrell* could be applied more expansively. Whether a narrow or broad interpretation will be taken is a matter of conjecture. It cannot be said that section 2(2) merely preserves the established common law position, as the common law is solely concerned with the immunity of the victim, whereas this section additionally provides immunity for a party who enters into an agreement where the only other party is a victim. As the policy of the provision is anyway questionable, it is submitted that a narrow interpretation of "victim" should be adopted.[152]

The express provision in section 2(2) for the cases of infants (above, § 9.2(v)(b)) and for victims indicates that D will otherwise be liable for conspiracy in any situation where the only other party to the agreement is exempt from prosecution on some other ground (provided the ground of exemption is compatible with the capacity to enter an agreement with the intention that it be carried out). An illustration from the common law is provided by *Duguid*[153] where D agreed with E, the mother of a child, to remove her child from the possession of the lawful guardian. Had the agreement been carried out D would have been liable for an offence under section 56 of the Offences against the Person Act 1861 but not E, as it was provided that a mother could not be prosecuted for taking her own child. It was held that E's immunity from prosecution for the substantive offence did not preclude D from being convicted for conspiracy to commit the offence. The same should follow for statutory conspiracy.

(d) Limited companies

The position of limited companies as parties to conspiracies is not dealt with by the Act. It may be assumed that the common law rules will continue to apply in statutory conspiracy.

Companies, as legal persons with an identity, separate from that of shareholders and directors,[154] may commit crimes in their own right. It has been held that companies may become parties to conspiracies provided an agreement on behalf of the company is made by a person sufficiently senior to be identified with the company.[155] In *McDonnell*,[156] Nield J ruled there was no conspiracy where D, the managing director and sole shareholder in E Ltd, arranged the tax affairs of E so as to evade fraudulently the payment of corporation tax. For Nield J, conspiracy required the involvement of at least two human agents; he rejected the view that E could be regarded as possessing a mind separate from D's as "too artificial".

It may be noted that if, in *McDonnell*, D had enlisted the help of, say, F, an accountant, to create the fraudulent scheme of corporate tax evasion, a conviction of D, F, *and* E Ltd for conspiracy to evade corporation tax would have been possible. Yet a conviction of E Ltd for conspiracy in those circumstances would involve the same degree of artificiality which the learned judge found unacceptable on the facts of *McDonnell*. The conviction of E Ltd would

---

[152] This would comport with the view that the passive masochists who featured in *Brown* [1994] AC 212 (below, § 21.1) are to be regarded as fully responsible participants in criminal acts perpetrated on them by their partners, and therefore liable in a derivative capacity for any offences arising from this consensual activity. The point was not tested in *Brown* but such a conclusion goes with the grain of the legal moralism so evident in the majority judgments of that case.

[153] (1906) 70 JP 294.

[154] *Salomon v. Salomon* [1897] AC 22 (HL).

[155] *Kent and Sussex Contractors Ltd* [1944] KB 146.

[156] [1966] 1 QB 233.

be on the basis that D's agreement with F entailed the agreement of E Ltd. Whenever a company is convicted for conspiracy an artificial duality is involved to the effect that the state of mind of D (a person of requisite seniority) is not merely her own state of mind but, additionally, a state of mind attributable to the company. The same logic can be carried over to one-person companies; as the Privy Council decision in *Lee* v. *Lee's Air Farming*,[157] a civil case, demonstrates. Nonetheless, *McDonnell* indicates that in criminal law, common sense will triumph over logic where the company is alleged to have conspired with only one human agent, who is the very person identified with that company.

(e) Acquittal of the only other party

Suppose that D and E are jointly tried for conspiracy and no other persons are alleged to have conspired with them. At one time the common law rule was that the acquittal of one of the alleged conspirators entailed the acquittal of the other. The reasoning behind this rule was that the acquittal of one conspirator and the conviction of the other in circumstances where only two persons had been charged with conspiracy would be incompatible with the requirement that two or more parties are necessary to constitute a conspiracy. The rule was criticised for confusing the requirements of formal legal proof with actual facts in the world. It may be the case that a confession or hearsay evidence is admissible against D but not against E,[158] resulting in proof beyond reasonable doubt against D but not against E. This criticism of the common law proved decisive for the House of Lords in *DPP* v. *Shannon*.[159] Thereafter, the acquittal of one party to the conspiracy was no bar to the conviction of the other even for cases where only two parties were alleged to have formed a conspiracy. The Criminal Law Act 1977, in section 5(8) and (9), confirms the rule in *Shannon* for both statutory and common law conspiracies.

(vi) Conspiracies involving the commission of more than one offence

Section 1(1) of the Criminal Law Act 1977 refers to a course of conduct involving "the commission of any offence or *offences*," indicating that a course of conduct charged as a single conspiracy may have as its objective the commission of two or more offences. It is even permissible for a number of offences of differing degrees of seriousness to be charged in a single conspiracy; provided it can be proved against each conspirator that she agreed to the commission of the most serious offences referred to in the indictment. The effect of the proviso can be seen in *Roberts*,[160] where there was evidence that some of the defendants had agreed to acts of aggravated criminal damage whereas other defendants had agreed only to acts of simple criminal damage. The Court of Appeal ruled that the defendants in the latter group were not parties to the conspiracy as charged. Presumably, they would have been parties if the indictment had charged only a conspiracy to commit acts of simple criminal damage.

---

[157] [1961] AC 12 (PC). It was held that Mr Lee could be identified with his company in his capacity as managing director and could be regarded as an employee, under the direction of the company, in his capacity as the company's one and only pilot. According to Lord Morris, "such is the logic of *Salomon*."

[158] *CLGP* 678–9.

[159] [1975] AC 717.

[160] [1998] 1 Cr App R 441.

When an agreement to commit two or more crimes is charged as a single conspiracy, particular care must be taken not to bring into association parties who are not truly partners in the same objectives. D and E may agree to rob V and W banks but decide that they will need the assistance of F with a further robbery of X bank. Accordingly, they enlist F for the X bank project. In a trial where only D and E are the defendants, the most appropriate course may be to charge D and E with a single conspiracy to rob V, W, and X banks. Such a course may be more economical of court-time and provide a jury with a better overall perspective of their wrongdoing. If F is joined too as a defendant, he may only properly be charged with conspiring to rob the X bank, thus precluding the use against him of evidence that relates only to the robbery of the V and W banks.

Although multi-offence conspiracies may be charged as a single conspiracy, there is nothing to preclude several, distinct conspiracy charges. In *Lavercombe*,[161] D and E agreed to buy cannabis in Thailand for importing into the United Kingdom. Although already convicted in Thailand for conspiracy to possess cannabis, the Court of Appeal confirmed their liability for conspiracy to import cannabis into the United Kingdom. Since there were two distinct offences there could be two distinct conspiracies and it was immaterial that both conspiracies were constituted by the one agreement on a course of conduct.

(vii) Conspiracy—an unnecessary offence?

If statutory conspiracy were to be abolished,[162] persons who agreed to commit a crime would be beyond the reach of the criminal law only until they incited others to commit crimes, committed some offence of a preliminary or possessory kind by way of preparation for the offence agreed, or engaged in conduct sufficiently proximate to the full offence to constitute an attempt. The ground covered by conspiracy and conspiracy alone is narrow. Moreover, in practical terms, conspiracies which have manifested themselves in nothing more than the fact of agreement are rarely prosecuted. Such bare agreements will seldom come to light, since criminals do not plan their crimes on the public record. Typically, evidence of a conspiracy is inferred from concerted criminal activity.[163] Moreover, when a crime has been committed, anyone who has agreed to its commission will, almost invariably, be an accomplice of the principal offenders. It may be doubted whether it is worth retaining such a complex body of law merely to proscribe non-consummated agreements.

Against that view, retentionists would argue that multi-party agreements to commit crimes are more dangerous and subversive than commitments to crime on the part of individuals.[164] There is a degree of plausibility in that claim, yet, as we have noted, prosecutions are seldom brought in respect of conspiracies which do not result in the commission of substantive offences.[165] A joint trial of principals and accomplices in respect of the

---

[161] [1988] Crim LR 435.

[162] Johnson, "The Unnecessary Crime of Conspiracy" (1973) 61 *Cal LR* 1137; Dennis, "The Rationale of Criminal Conspiracy" (1977) 93 *LQR* 39.

[163] *Mulcahy* (1868) LR 3 HL 306, 317; *Hammersley* (1958) 42 Cr App R 207. For discussion, see *TBCL* 422–23.

[164] *Griffiths* [1966] 1 QB 589.

[165] Non-consummated conspiracies are occasionally prosecuted as, for example, in the case of terrorist conspiracies to cause explosions which are intercepted by police at a preparatory stage.

substantive offences actually committed or attempted will enable the prosecution to lay appropriate stress on the dangers that may be posed by well organised criminal activity.

At common law, conspiracy was employed for what has been described as its "useful elasticity". When conspiracy was entirely a common law crime, prosecutors were allowed to use conspiracy charges to evade time limits, sentencing restrictions, and procedural requirements imposed in respect of particular statutory offences. Happily such elasticity is no longer permitted; the Criminal Law Act 1977 ensures that the penalty for conspiracy cannot exceed that imposed for the substantive offence[166] and that any time or procedural requirements associated with the substantive offence equally apply to conspiracies to commit that offence.[167] As we noted at the outset of our discussion of conspiracy, one form of elasticity remains. It is still the case that some forms of conduct which would not be criminal if perpetrated by an individual may become criminal if done in pursuance of an agreement by two or more persons, most notably in conspiracy to defraud.[168] It is very much a matter for regret that the Fraud Act 2006 did not abolish conspiracy to defraud depite the Law Commission's intention that it would.[169]

Supporters of conspiracy charges emphasise their procedural and evidential advantages. Following an allegation of conspiracy, each alleged conspirator may be treated as the agent of his co-defendants. Accordingly, evidence pertaining to one particular defendant becomes admissible against all other defendants for the purposes of the conspiracy charge that yokes them together.[170] Conspiracy counts, it is claimed, give proper emphasis to the group character of multi-party offending and allow the jury a clearer, more rounded, picture of what the defendants have done.[171] This is particularly useful, it is said, where the role played by one or more of the parties in the perpetration of the substantive offences is unclear. Yet, as Professor Glanville Williams pointed out many years ago, these benefits are equally accessible if defendants are charged with being each other's accomplices.[172] It is habit of mind and long-standing practice that favours recourse to conspiracy rather than any unique advantage that the charge brings.

The Law Commission has recently proposed two inchoate offences relating, respectively, to encouraging crimes and assisting crimes.[173] Neither proposed offence requires the commission of a substantive offence. On enactment of these proposals, the ground covered exclusively by conspiracy would be limited to non-consummated agreements where D's agreement with E that E should commit a crime does not constitute any form of encouragement or assistance in relation to the projected offence. Even if such forms of agreements are theoretically possible, it would hardly seem worthwhile retaining conspiracy to deal merely with them.

---

[166] Section 3.

[167] Section 4.

[168] Below, § 15.3.

[169] Law Com. Consultation Paper No. 155, *Fraud and Deception* (1999).

[170] Cf. *Griffiths* [1966] 1 QB 589.

[171] *Cox and Mead, The Times,* 6 December 1984, discussed in Law Com. No. 104, *Conspiracy to Defraud* (1987) para 6.6; *Simmonds* [1969] 1 QB 685, 690.

[172] *The Proof of Guilt* (2nd ed., 1958) chap. 9.

[173] Law Com. No. 300, *Inchoate Liability for Assisting and Encouraging Crime* (2006). These proposals are now reflected in clauses of the Serious Crime Bill currently before Parliament.

§ 9.3 Attempt

The inchoate offence of attempt[174] penalises conduct which is sufficiently proximate to the commission of an indictable offence, when done with intent to commit that offence. At common law, attempt was a complex, vacillating body of law.[175] Considerable, albeit imperfect, simplification has been achieved by the Criminal Attempts Act 1981, which abolishes the common law offence and replaces it with the following statutory offence contained in section 1:[176]

> If, with intent to commit an offence to which this section applies, a person does an act which is more than merely preparatory to the commission of the offence, he is guilty of an attempt to commit the offence.

The most obvious justification for having a general law of attempts is to allow the timely prevention of a future criminal harm. A concern with harms yet to be realised can be seen even in the early development of the common law. For instance, burglary, from its emergence in the twelfth century, penalised individuals who entered walled cities or inhabited premises at night with felonious intent. The threat to security from such entry called for intervention; it was not necessary to demonstrate that the felony D had in mind ultimately was committed.[177] Likewise, the offence of assault was devised to proscribe *threats* of immediate violence, supplementing the earlier offence of battery which penalised the actual use of force.[178] The crime of attempt itself, dealing in general terms with threatened harms, did not emerge until much later. We owe to the Star Chamber the notion that, if a crime exists, it is also an offence to attempt to commit that crime.[179] This idea was received into the common law and by the early nineteenth century it was possible to speak in terms of a general common law crime of attempt,[180] now replaced by the present statutory offence.

Inherent in the very idea of an attempt is something done that is proximate to commission of a full criminal offence. This necessary proximity was found to be lacking in *Geddes*[181] where D, a trespasser, was apprehended in a school lavatory while in possession of a kitchen knife, rope, and binding tape. There was compelling reason to believe that D intended to abduct a pupil of the school. The Court of Appeal ruled that D's conduct did not constitute attempted false imprisonment because, at the time of his arrest, he had not tried to restrict anyone's movements. Not unreasonably, the decision in *Geddes* could be castigated as a failure to afford adequate social protection. Had D trespassed in the school with intent to steal, or rape, or inflict grievous bodily harm, or cause damage to property, he could have been convicted of burglary.[182] Prior to the Criminal Attempts Act 1981, he could have been convicted of procuring an instrument to commit a crime,[183] were it the case that

---

[174] Duff, *Criminal Attempts* (1996).

[175] See the definitive account in *CLGP* chap. 14.

[176] The Act broadly gives effect to the recommendations in Law Com. No.102, *Attempt and Impossibility in Relation to Attempt, Conspiracy and Incitement* (1980).

[177] Kenny, *Outlines of the Criminal Law* (1902) 170–1.

[178] Hawkins, *Pleas of the Crown*, chap. 62, § 1.

[179] Stephen, *History of the Criminal Law of England* (1883) vol. 2, 221–3.

[180] *Higgins* [1801] 2 East 5, 102 ER 269.

[181] [1996] Crim LR 894 (CA).

[182] Theft Act 1968, s. 9.

[183] As in *Gurmit Singh* [1986] 2 QB 53; but see now s. 6 of the Criminal Attempts Act 1981.

he obtained the knife, rope, or tape as aids to abduction. Under the current law, there is no suitable crime covering the situation which confronted the courts in *Geddes*.[184]

The appropriate response to this gap in social protection is not to reintroduce a general offence of procuring materials to commit a crime nor to relax the interpretation of the proximity requirement in attempt. If we were to take the former path, any convicted pædophile would obtain items like a rope or a kitchen knife at his peril. Likewise, if we were to extend the actus reus of attempted false imprisonment to encompass any step, however preliminary, towards the commission of the offence, his freedom from arrest would be threatened whenever he was in the vicinity of children. Such steps, if taken to fill the gap exposed by *Geddes*, carry an undue risk of oppressive policing and unsafe convictions based on dubious confessions. This said, intervention at a stage earlier than currently allowed by the law of attempt *is* warranted in respect of situations notoriously associated with particular kinds of harm. We are aware that we acquire such things as guns, or explosives, at our peril should we lack a licence or justification to do so. If we drive a car, we should know that we will be in trouble if we drive dangerously, or allow our vehicle to become unsafe, even if no accident results. Convictions for offences of this kind do not violate legitimate expectations of fair warning nor require undue reliance on confession evidence. Consequently, there could be no complaint if Parliament were to respond to the acquittal in *Geddes* by adding false imprisonment and kidnapping to the list of burglarious offences.

(i) Actus reus: the requirement of proximity

Resolving when conduct is sufficiently close to the commission of an offence to constitute an attempt has been a matter of intractable difficulty for English law.[185] It would be unfair to characterise this failure to devise a simple and clear test of proximity as a matter of judicial ineptitude. Ordinary language supplies little help in distinguishing conduct that is merely *preparatory* from conduct that is close enough to constitute an *attempt*.[186] We would not say of D, a high jumper, that she was attempting to clear the bar until she had commenced her run-up to the jump. We can assume a general agreement that earlier conduct (warm-up, removal of track suit, etc.) is conduct preliminary to an attempt to clear the bar. Thereafter, dispute may arise. Some may argue that an attempt to clear the bar does not begin until D launches herself upwards, whereas others may insist that we are within the ambit of an attempt once the run-up commences. In terms of the rules of athletic competitions, the latter group would win the argument if the rule for competitions is that a run-up to the bar, however faltering and incomplete, constitutes an attempt at a jump. It will be readily appreciated that this rule would be a matter of stipulation and does not rest on any "correct" view of what, in any natural or philosophical sense, constitutes an attempt at jumping obstacles.

---

[184] Even possession of the knife in a public place would not necessarily have entailed commission of a crime because liability for the offence of possessing an offensive weapon (Prevention of Crime Act 1953, s. 1) requires proof that D intended to use the weapon *to injure* in cases where (as in *Geddes*) the weapon is not offensive *per se*.

[185] Duff, *Criminal Attempts* (1996) chap. 2; Smith, "Proximity in Attempt: Lord Lane's Midway Course" [1991] *Crim LR* 576; Stuart, "The Actus Reus in Attempts" [1970] *Crim LR* 505.

[186] For instructive discussion see Duff, *Criminal Attempts* (1996) 33–5.

(a) The proximity requirement at common law

Unsurprisingly, the common law has failed to agree a general test. Consensus on a test for proximity has been undermined by an unresolved tension between the claims of social protection, on the one hand, and an insistence that criminal liability should be confined to those who have perpetrated some wrongful deed, on the other. The latter approach was given its best expression in what was known as the "last act" test.[187] Under that test, D would not be liable for the attempted murder of V until, say, she had aimed the gun and squeezed the trigger (i.e. D had done the last act required of her to commit the crime). The test has its attractions. It allows certainty of application and confines liability to those who have perpetrated a wrong.[188] From the perspective of V, however, the test has grave limitations. Provided we can be sure that D has resolved to kill V, there is much to be said for intervening and stopping D well before V's life is imperilled by D's actually firing at him.

Such concerns were reflected in alternative formulations to the last act test such as the "substantial step"[189] test and the "unequivocal act" test.[190] Under the substantial step test, D could be convicted of attempted arson on the basis of, say, walking towards a haystack with matches in his pocket (should it be proved that he intended to set fire to the stack). Objections to D's conviction can be raised on the basis that until he strikes a match in order to ignite the stack, he has done nothing *wrong*; there is nothing reprehensible about walking in a field with matches in one's pocket.[191] An additional objection is that convictions in such circumstances may be unduly dependent on confession evidence. The "unequivocal act" test addressed these concerns. Under its terms, in our arson example, D would not commit attempted arson until his extrinsic conduct indicated in the clearest terms that his immediate project was arson. In application, however, this test was not consistently or strictly applied, and resort to D's state of mind was permitted to resolve the ambiguities of his conduct.[192]

(b) The proximity requirement under statute

No particular test achieved primacy at common law, although it is fair to say that the predominant trend in the thirty years or so prior to the Criminal Attempts Act 1981 was toward a restrictive rather than expansive approach to the test of sufficient proximity.[193] Following the recommendations of the Law Commission, the Criminal Attempts Act 1981 dispenses with any formal legal test of proximity. Instead, it addresses the proximity issue in terms of a question of fact to be placed before the jury: did D do an act with intent to commit an offence which was "more than merely preparatory to the commission of the offence"?[194]

The Act provides explicitly that whether an act by D is more than merely preparatory "is

---

[187] *Eagleton* (1855) 6 Cox CC 559.

[188] Assuming, as we do, that D can do wrong though she causes no material harm (even in the sense of alarm and apprehension). D does wrong if she fires at V, even if V remains unaware of D's actions.

[189] *Roberts* (1855) Dears 539, 169 ER 836.

[190] *Davey* v. *Lee* [1968] 1 QB 366.

[191] On this view, punishing D might well be regarded as a form of preventative detention and a violation of D's rights.

[192] In *Davey* v. *Lee* [1968] 1 QB 366, the Court of Criminal Appeal adopted the unequivocal act test and, at the same time, permitted resort to confession evidence in order to clarify D's otherwise ambiguous conduct.

[193] E.g. *Kyprianou* v. *Reynolds* [1969] Crim LR 656; *Comer* v. *Bloomfield* (1971) 55 Cr App R 305.

[194] Criminal Attempts Act 1981, s. 1(1).

a question of fact"[195] to be answered by the jury, provided that there is evidence sufficient in law to support such a finding. Accordingly, a judge must satisfy herself that the prosecution has adduced enough evidence to support a finding that D's act was more than merely preparatory to the commission of an offence. If the judge is satisfied, the question of sufficient proximity is put to the jury who must then make their own decision on the issue. However compellingly obvious it may seem that particular conduct is more than merely preparatory, it is a misdirection for a judge to instruct a jury that they *must* find the actus reus is proved.[196]

(c) The approach in recent cases

The long title to the Criminal Attempts Act 1981 indicates that the Act is to reform the previous law.[197] Accordingly, it would be reasonable to suppose that the common law on the issue of sufficient proximity was superseded. Despite this, in the early cases decided under the Act, reference was made to pre-Act case law when addressing the question of sufficient proximity.[198] By contrast, subsequent cases, most notably *Jones*,[199] have stressed that the words "more than merely preparatory" must be allowed their natural meaning and not be expansively or restrictively glossed by reference to cases decided before the Act. This seems now to be the law. It follows that an appellate court, when reviewing a conviction for attempt, must satisfy itself merely that there was sufficient evidence to sustain the finding that D's conduct was more than merely preparatory. On the face of it, that is a question of evaluating the facts of each particular case. In *Geddes*, however, Lord Bingham LJ introduced a degree of rigour into the question by insisting that the necessary proximity would not occur until D reached the stage of *trying* to commit the offence:[200]

> "It is, we think, an accurate paraphrase of the statutory test and not an illegitimate gloss upon
> it to ask whether the available evidence, if accepted, could show that a defendant has done an
> act which shows that he has actually tried to commit the offence in question, or whether he
> has only got ready or put himself in a position or equipped himself to do so."

Recall that, in *Geddes*, D had not tried before his arrest to detain any victim:[201] accordingly, applying Lord Bingham's test, he was not guilty of attempted false imprisonment.

In light of *Geddes*, it seems that a person does not reach the stage of trying to commit the offence until he broaches commission of the actus reus of the substantive offence; as occurred in *Jones*,[202] where D was convicted of attempted murder upon unlocking the safety-catch and pointing a loaded firearm at V. In *A-G's Reference (No. 1 of 1992)*,[203] a

---

[195] Criminal Attempts Act 1981, s. 4(3).

[196] See *Stonehouse* [1978] AC 55 (HL), which resolved the position under the common law. The reasoning in *Stonehouse* is *a fortiori* applicable to the position under the Criminal Attempts Act 1981 which provides explicitly that the question of proximity is one of fact. Questions of fact, even of "evaluative" fact such as whether conduct is "more than merely preparatory", fall within the exclusive province of the jury.

[197] "An Act to amend the Law of England and Wales as to attempt to commit offences. . . ."

[198] *Widdowsen* (1985) 82 Cr App R 314; *Boyle* (1987) 84 Cr App R 270.

[199] [1990] 3 All ER 886.

[200] [1966] Crim LR 894, 895.

[201] Above, § 9.3.

[202] (1990) 91 Cr App R 351 (CA). Contrast at common law, *Stevens* v. *R.* [1985] LRC (Crim) 17, noted (1986) 50 *J Crim L* 247.

[203] [1993] 2 All ER 190 (CA).

conviction for attempted rape was upheld where D had thrown V to the ground and exposed his person. Contrast the facts of *Campbell*,[204] where D, in possession of a imitation firearm, was arrested just before entering a post office that he intended to rob. The quashing of his conviction for attempted robbery follows from the fact that, however close he came to committing robbery, he had yet to commence those acts which would constitute theft by force—which is the actus reus of robbery. Less easily explained in terms of Lord Bingham's test is *Tosti*.[205] D was observed concealing oxyacetylene equipment behind a hedge, approaching a barn door, and bending down to examine a padlock. His conviction for attempted burglary was sustained by the Court of Appeal. The line dividing *Campbell* from *Tosti* may be considered so faint as to be invisible. It could, perhaps, be asserted that, by examining the padlock in *Tosti*, D was getting physically to grips with committing the crime itself, something that had yet to occur in *Campbell*. That at least was the view of Beldam LJ, who described the defendant in *Tosti* as taking "the first steps in the commission of the offence."[206]

Broadly, the approach to the question of sufficient proximity taken by Lord Bingham in *Geddes* is to be welcomed. In insisting that D must have commenced that series of acts which will constitute, if and when completed, the actus reus of the substantive offence, liability for attempt is confined to those who have demonstrated by their overt conduct that they are prepared to commit crimes. Moreover, a law of attempt cast in these restrictive terms is less dependent on confession evidence for convictions than would be the case under a more expansive test. To be sure, as in many areas of law, there will be decisions not easy to reconcile, as the contrasting decisions in *Campbell* and *Tosti* demonstrate. Yet, in general terms, the current law governing sufficient proximity in attempt is far more straightforward than it was under the common law, where incompatible legal tests competed for supremacy.

All that said, it does appear that the modern law of attempt may, on occasion, offer scant protection to potential victims of serious crimes; as is vividly illustrated by the acquittals in *Geddes* and *Campbell*. The way forward, argued for already, is not to create a more broadly formulated law of attempt but to craft specific offences for particular situations which presage the occurrence of serious harm. As suggested, to repair the gap exposed in *Geddes* it could be made an offence to trespass with intent to imprison falsely or to kidnap. In *Campbell*, D was convicted for possession of an imitation firearm.[207] It is better to proceed in this piecemeal way than to resort to a broad and vague law of attempt susceptible to uncertainties of interpretation and oppressive modes of enforcement.

(ii) The scope of the actus reus of attempt

(a) Summary offences

To be guilty of an attempt D must intend to commit an offence to which section 1 of the Criminal Attempts Act 1981 applies.[208] Section 1(4) of the Act provides that the offence

---

[204] [1990] 93 Cr App R 350 (CA).
[205] [1997] Crim LR 746 (CA).
[206] *Ibid.*, 747.
[207] Firearms Act 1968, s. 16A.
[208] Section 1(1).

must be an offence that would be triable in England and Wales as an indictable offence. In general terms, therefore, there is no offence of attempting to commit a summary offence. This must reflect the legislative view that attempts are systemically less serious than the perpetration of substantive offences and do not merit criminalisation where the substantive crime is of a minor nature. There are, however, a number of specific statutory offences of attempting to commit particular summary offences.[209]

(b) Inchoate offences and complicity

Additionally, section 1(4) provides that the offence of attempt does not apply to common law or statutory conspiracy nor aiding, abetting, counselling, procuring, or suborning the commission of an offence. The reasoning lying behind these exceptions appears, in the case of conspiracy, to be its remoteness from any substantive offence and, in the case of secondary participation, the view that complicity is somehow less heinous than perpetration. Whatever the merits of these exemptions, they are subject to exceptions. Section 1(4) makes no reference to incitement and it must be assumed that the common law position still holds that incitement is an offence that may be attempted.[210] Furthermore, complicitous conduct may be made the gravamen of a specific offence, as in the (substantive) statutory crimes of aiding and abetting suicide and of procuring an act of gross indecency. These statutory offences can, in turn, be attempted.[211]

(c) Omissions

Section 1 of the Act makes reference to "a person who *does an act* which is more than merely preparatory" (emphasis added). There is authority that statutory phrases which make reference to the "doing of acts" import a legislative intent to preclude liability for omission.[212] In the context of attempts, the practical effect of this limitation is likely to be limited. On occasion, however, it may leave unpunished conduct which should be censured. Suppose that D, a carer who is wholly responsible for the welfare of the bedridden V, intentionally omits to provide food or drink. All other things equal, it would be appropriate to find D liable for the attempted murder if and when V's health becomes seriously impaired by a lack of sustenance.[213] Under the terms of the Act, however, it seems that D will not be liable for attempted murder, notwithstanding how parlous V's condition may become.

(d) Offences of negligence and strict liability

As will be discussed below in § 9.3(iii), liability for attempt requires proof of an intent to commit the substantive offence. It has been argued that this requirement places limits on the kind of offences that can be attempted:[214]

---

[209] Section 3 of the Criminal Attempts Act 1981 provides that, if any special statutory provision permits a charge of attempt in respect of a summary offence, liability for such an attempt will be governed by the same principles that apply to charges of attempt brought under the 1981 Act.

[210] *Banks* (1873) 12 Cox CC 393.

[211] *McShane* (1977) 66 Cr App R 97 (CA).

[212] *Ahmad* (1986) 84 Cr App R 64 (CA).

[213] The possibility of liability for attempts by omission may give rise to difficult questions of proximity. Suppose that V falls down a hole and D is under a duty to rescue V. D, however, walks away hoping that V will not be found and will perish of starvation. Does D's conduct amount to an attempt as soon as she walks away, or must V first come close to death?

[214] Card, Cross, and Jones, *Criminal Law* (14th ed., 1998) 557.

"the requirement of an intent to commit the offence whose attempt is charged means that there cannot be a conviction for an attempt to commit involuntary manslaughter because the essence of that offence is that the killing was unintentional, and the same is true of an offence whose essence is recklessness or negligence."

Not so. Admittedly, it would be odd to charge, say, attempted manslaughter by gross negligence. Negligence is a failure to attain reasonable standards and a person intentionally flouting such standards is acting culpably but not in a manner we would ordinarily call "negligent". To say that one is attempting to be negligent seems a contradiction in terms.

The oddity arises, however, not because manslaughter is an offence of negligence but because, if the actus reus of manslaughter is intended, the appropriate offence is normally murder (since manslaughter and murder share the same actus reus and are differentiated by gradations of mens rea).[215] Even so, there is nothing that prevents an intentional killing from being charged as manslaughter—the greater includes the lesser.[216] The lesser forms of culpability provided for manslaughter are sufficient but not necessary conditions of liability. Accordingly, a charge of attempted manslaughter[217] is not a contradiction in terms but must be proved by evidence which establishes an intent to kill. The fact that such evidence would satisfy the requirements of attempted murder does not preclude the lesser charge from being brought.

The point at issue here is simple but important. Most substantive offences do not require proof of an intent to commit them—many offences require no proof of culpability at all.[218] If they can be tried on indictment, these crimes can be attempted (provided D intended to commit the crime). For example, if D takes a vehicle which is in a dangerous condition onto the highway, she will commit the offence of dangerous driving if the state of the vehicle should have been obvious to a careful and competent driver.[219] For the substantive offence, it is irrelevant that D herself was unaware of the danger her vehicle posed. Suppose she were to be stopped immediately prior to driving onto the highway and her vehicle examined. In principle, she would be guilty of attempted dangerous driving should she be aware of the dangerous condition of her vehicle but not otherwise.[220]

(iii) The mens rea of attempt

The mens rea requirement is simply stated: according to the Criminal Attempts Act 1981, D must act "with intent to commit [the substantive] offence".[221] Alas, judicial interpretation has rendered the explication of this requirement less straightforward than, ideally, it should be. It will assist our discussion if we look at the question of intent sequentially in respect of

---

[215] See below, Chapter 10.

[216] Not infrequently, prosecutors lay manslaughter charges where the evidence would support a charge of murder. They may do so for a variety of reasons, including evasion of time-consuming trial issues and avoidance of the mandatory sentence associated with murder. For discussion, see Farrier, "The Distinction between Murder and Manslaughter in its Procedure Context" (1976) 39 MLR 415, esp. at 430–1.

[217] Particularly of the constructive variety: below, § 10.6(ii).

[218] See above, Chapter 6.

[219] Road Traffic Act 1988, s. 2, as substituted by s. 1 of the Road Traffic Act 1991.

[220] This assumes that the "missing element" analysis, proposed in A-G's Reference (No. 3 of 1992) [1994] 2 All ER 121, does not prevail. See below, § 9.3(iii)(c).

[221] Section 1(1).

the separate elements that may make up the actus reus of a substantive offence. Almost invariably an offence will require some form of *conduct* on the part of D,[222] usually conduct perpetrated in particular *circumstances*. For some offences, an additional *consequence* element is required; it must be proved that D's conduct caused a particular result, such as a wound or a death. The concept of intent is not univocal across these three elements. Hence, we need to discuss the intent required for attempt liability by reference separately to these elements.

(a) Conduct

By "conduct", we mean those movements on the part of D which are required of her as part of the actus reus of the substantive offence. In a case of murder by shooting, for example, the conduct element would include D's aiming of the gun and her squeezing of the trigger. Typically, such conduct will speak for itself in terms of its intentionality.[223] Were we to observe D picking up the gun and aiming it at V, we would thereby directly observe her intentionality. Generally, we would only be unsure whether or not her conduct was intentional were we to be told that despite her appearance of consciousness she was, say, sleepwalking or in a hypnotic trance. Outside such very special cases as these and the more common cases of altered states of consciousness induced by drink or drugs, the intentionality of conduct will be straightforwardly established.

(b) Circumstances

Conduct is the most basic element of an offence and will rarely constitute the actus reus by itself. Attendant circumstances will need to be present. Frequently, the presence or absence of such circumstances will be matters beyond the control of D and, consequently, matters beyond the scope of his intentionality. Consider the case of D who finds a book on a seat in an airport lounge. Make two alternative assumptions: (i) the book was deliberately abandoned by its owner V, thereby divesting V of ownership; or (ii) V left the book inadvertently and would recover it if he could, entailing that ownership remains with V. Suppose that D is about to deface the book but is prevented from doing so by the intervention of X. The substantive offence of criminal damage would have been possible only if the book were property belonging to another, e.g. on the facts of assumption (ii).[224] Whether or not the book belongs to V is a circumstance that, strictly, D cannot have intentions about—the facts are whatever they are. If the facts are those of assumption (ii) and D is aware of those facts, then clearly he intends to damage property belonging to another and is guilty of an attempt. His *knowledge* of the circumstances makes for an intention to damage someone else's property.[225] That intentionality would also subsist if D has a true *belief* that the facts were

---

[222] For possible exceptions see above, § 4.1(ii).

[223] See Duff, *Intention, Agency and Criminal Liability* (1990) 116–20, where it is argued convincingly that intentions may take a form which can be directly observed and are inappropriately characterised as inner mental states severable from the conduct of the agent.

[224] On assumption (i), ownership in the book would not vest in the owners or tenants of the airport lounge but in the first person taking possession of the book intending to keep it: *Parker* v. *British Airways Board* [1982] QB 1004; below, § 13.4(5).

[225] Unless he made a mistake of civil law and believed that he was entitled to assume ownership of the book in such circumstances: cf. *Smith* [1974] QB 354.

those of assumption (ii). His belief, though falling short of knowledge, still entails an intent to damage property belonging to another. The same applies if D has a *false* belief that the facts are as in (ii), where the truth is that V has indeed abandoned the book. Under the Criminal Attempts Act 1981, even in this last case D is guilty of an attempt—notwithstanding that the full offence is impossible to commit.[226] His false belief makes for an *intention* to damage property belonging to another.

But what if D lacks knowledge or any true or false belief? He observes V leaving for his flight and is unsure whether V has abandoned or inadvertently left the book. If he defaces the book, lacking any knowledge or belief about its ownership, it could not be said that he intends to damage property belonging to another—that would not be his purpose, neither would damage to another's property be something that he foresees as virtually certain. Here we should say that he is merely reckless about damaging *another's* property. He apparently lacks the intent that the Act requires. This conclusion is supported by section 1(3) of the Criminal Attempts Act 1981, which provides that if the commission of the offence is impossible, he shall be regarded as having an intent to commit the offence, "if the facts of the case had been as he *believed* them to be" (emphasis added). These words demonstrate that, even where V has in fact abandoned the book, D may still be convicted of attempted criminal damage if, *and only if*, he has a *belief* that the property is owned by another. Unfortunately, there is no express provision covering the position where the facts *are* as D believes them to be; but as a matter of general principle it may be said that only a belief (here a true belief) that the property is owned property should allow a conviction for attempted criminal damage. Recklessness should not suffice. That was the position taken, at the time, by the Law Commission.[227]

However, in the light of the Court of Appeal decision in *Khan*,[228] we are obliged to differentiate between situations where commission of the full offence is impossible and situations where D attempts a crime which it *is* possible to commit. In *Khan*, D attempted to have intercourse with V, aware that she might not consent to the act. On the Law Commission's view of the effect of the Act, outlined above, D would intend to commit rape and hence be liable for attempted rape if, and only if, he knew that V did not consent to intercourse or if he believed she did not consent. His actual state of mind fell short of knowledge or belief: D was found to be reckless about V's consent, i.e. aware that she *might* not consent but neither aware nor believing that she *did* not consent. In confirming D's conviction for attempted rape, the Court of Appeal ruled that, provided D possessed an intention with respect to the conduct element of the full offence (and D clearly intended to have sex), proof of recklessness as to any circumstance element would permit a finding that D intended to commit rape within the meaning of section 1 of the Criminal Attempts Act 1981.

Conceptually, the court's reasoning is unconvincing.[229] Where D lacks knowledge or

---

[226] Criminal Attempts Act 1981, s. 1(2).

[227] Law Com. No. 102, *Attempt and Impossibility in Relation to Attempt, Conspiracy and Incitement* (1980) paras. 214–218. Note that the Law Commission later changed its mind in the underlying policy questions: Law. Com. No. 177, *A Criminal Code for England and Wales* (1989) cl. 49(2).

[228] [1990] 2 All ER 783.

[229] See Sullivan, "Intent, Subjective Recklessness and Culpability" (1992) 12 *OJLS* 380, where the reasoning but not the outcome in *Khan* is criticised. For a defence and rigorous explication of the reasoning in *Khan*, see Duff, "The Circumstances of an Attempt" [1991] *CLJ* 100.

belief regarding the absence of V's consent, D intends to rape only if it is his purpose "to have sexual intercourse without consent"—i.e. if it was *part* of his design that V should not consent.[230] Alternatively, if D's purpose was simply "to have sex", it being incidental to him whether V consents, then he would certainly intend "to have sexual intercourse" but would intend "to have sexual intercourse without consent" only if he knew or believed that V would not consent (i.e. a case of virtual certainty[231]). It was found in *Khan* that D was in the former category and, lacking knowledge or belief as to V's lack of consent, it cannot be said that he acted in order to rape or that he foresaw the rape of V as a virtual certainty.

In confirming the conviction in *Khan*, the Court was heavily influenced by the fact that, had D succeeded in having intercourse, he would have been liable for the full offence of rape, an offence which can be committed intentionally or recklessly. In the interests of public protection, the Court of Appeal considered that the mens rea for attempt should be aligned as closely as possible with the mens rea for the full offence. This is a powerful consideration. Undeniably, the conduct involved in *Khan* was gravely wrong and a considerable gap in social protection would have been allowed had his conviction been quashed. Nonetheless, the Court of Appeal seems to have departed from the statutory requirement of an intent to commit the full offence. As explained above, an intent will still be required for the rare cases where the full offence is impossible to commit but, for other cases, following *Khan*, if there is intent as to the conduct element of the offence, knowledge, belief, or recklessness will suffice for circumstance elements. This considerably diminishes the culpability required for attempts. Yet it is safe to assume that *Khan* represents the current state of the law. As we shall see below, the reasoning in that case has even been carried over to consequence elements, thereby entrenching its status.[232]

(c) Consequences

Prior to the Criminal Attempts Act 1981, in order to be liable for attempt D had to intend to cause any consequence specified in the actus reus of the full offence. A leading pre-Act case is *Whybrow*,[233] where D was charged with the attempted murder of his wife. Asserting that, in the case of attempt, "intent becomes the principal ingredient of the crime", Goddard LCJ ruled that for D to be guilty of attempted murder he must have intended to cause the death of V. He explicitly rejected the argument that, because an intent to cause grievous bodily harm would suffice for the full offence, it would also suffice for the attempt to commit it. The centrality of intent to attempt liability was confirmed in another pre-Act case, *Mohan*, where James LJ spoke of:[234]

> "a decision to bring about, in so far as it lies within the accused's power, the commission of the offence which it is alleged the accused attempted to commit, no matter whether the accused desired that consequence of his act or not."

---

[230] Above, § 5.1(v).

[231] Above, § 5.1(iv).

[232] Furthermore, the Law Commission, reversing the position it took at the time the Criminal Attempts Act 1981 was framed (Law Com. No. 102, *Attempt and Impossibility in Relation to Attempt, Conspiracy and Incitement* (1980)), adopts the reasoning in *Khan* in its proposed Criminal Code: Law Com. No. 177, *A Criminal Code for England and Wales* (1989) cl. 49(2).

[233] (1951) 35 Cr App R 141 (CCA).

[234] [1976] QB 1, 3 (CA).

In *Pearman*,[235] the Court of Appeal stated that this passage remained an authoritative guide to the interpretation of intent under the Criminal Attempt Act 1981. The words employed by James LJ in *Mohan* comprehend not only the primary meaning of the term intent (what is sometimes called *direct* intent), but also foresight that a consequence was a virtual certainty. This was confirmed in *Pearman*, where it was stated that:[236]

> "a man who is cornered by the police when he is in a car may have the primary purpose of simply escaping from that situation. If he drives straight at police officers at high speed, a jury is likely to conclude that he intended to injure a police officer and maybe cause him serious grievous bodily harm."

In the light of the House of Lords decision in *Woollin*,[237] where the consequence is not directly intended by D, a jury should be invited to make a finding of intent only where that consequence was a virtually certain upshot of D's conduct and where D was aware of this virtual certainty. Only then, in the words of James LJ, can we speak convincingly of a "decision to bring about, in so far as it lies within the accused's power, the commission of the offence which it is alleged the accused attempted to commit."

It has been argued that this constitutes too broad a view of what is required for a finding of intent as to consequences in the law of attempt. The argument runs that the term "attempt" is synonymous with "trying" and it can only be said that D is attempting to achieve a consequence if he is acting in order to bring that consequence about.[238] But ordinary English usage is not always clear cut in these matters, and need not foreclose discussion of issues of principle or policy in criminal law.[239] Suppose, to use Glanville Williams's example,[240] that D places a bomb in the hold of a departing passenger plane. When asked why, he may truthfully reply that he was looking to make an insurance claim based on the loss of the plane and deny that his purpose was to take life. Yet he knows that success in his objective is inseparable from the sacrifice of people's lives. Arguably, it is not open to D to deny, even on ordinary language, that he was trying to kill—only to deny that this was his ultimate motive. Moreover, the grave wrongdoing involved and the requirements of social protection supply compelling reason to treat such a case as one of attempted murder. The conclusion is supported by *Mohan*, by *Pearman*, and by the Court of Appeal decision in *Walker and Hayles*.[241]

Thus far, the mens rea required for consequence elements seems straightforward—direct intent or foresight of a virtual certainty. Unfortunately, our interim conclusion must now be tested against the decision of the Court of Appeal in *A-G's Reference (No. 3 of 1992)*.[242] D and others had thrown lighted petrol bombs at a car where V and others were passengers. The bombs missed the car and smashed against a wall. D was charged with attempted arson being reckless whether life be endangered, contrary to section 1(2) of the Criminal Damage

---

[235] (1985) 80 Cr App R 259.
[236] *Ibid.*, 263.
[237] [1999] 1 AC 82.
[238] Fletcher, *Rethinking Criminal Law* (1978) 161.
[239] Ashworth, *Principles* 445–6.
[240] Above, § 5.1(iv).
[241] (1989) 90 Cr App R 226 (CA).
[242] [1994] 2 All ER 121.

Act 1971. The trial judge directed that D would not be guilty of this aggravated form of attempted criminal damage unless it were proved that he *intended* that V's life be endangered. The Court of Appeal, much influenced by its earlier decision in *Khan*, disagreed. It adopted what has been called the "missing element"[243] analysis of the intent requirement in attempt:[244]

> "a defendant, in order to be guilty of an attempt, must be in one of the states of mind required for the commission of the offence, and did [sic] his best, so far as he could, to supply what was missing from the completion of the offence. It is the policy of the law that such people should be punished notwithstanding that in fact the intentions of such a defendant have not been fulfilled."

The Court effectively divided the actus reus of an attempt into those elements of the substantive offence that D *had* satisfied, and those elements that were still "missing". For the former, whatever mens rea was required by the substantive offence would suffice also for the attempt. For the latter, intent would be required.

Applying this analysis to the facts of *A-G's Reference* itself, the only element missing from commission of the full offence was damage to property, an element which, in the quaint language of the court, D was doing his best to supply. This was the only element D was required to intend. So far as the remaining elements were required, for the full offence it sufficed that D be *Caldwell*-reckless as to whether life would be endangered by his conduct. The Court ruled that *Caldwell* recklessness would equally suffice for the attempt.

On the face of it, *A-G's Reference (No. 3 of 1992)* decides that, on a charge of attempt, recklessness may suffice for any "present" consequence element of the full offence provided that D intends to bring about any "missing" consequence or other element. It is a requirement of aggravated criminal damage that D's damage to or destruction of property brings about a situation that would be perceived as dangerous to life by an ordinary prudent person. That requirement seems best characterised as a consequence of D's conduct, since it is a state of affairs that arises because of D's conduct. The cases decided prior to *A-G's Reference* are reconcilable on the basis that, in the earlier decisions, the relevant consequence had always been a "missing element", i.e. something that had not materialised. An intention to bring about a non-realised consequence is still required, if this reading of *A-G's Reference* is accepted.

Even if reconciliation with earlier cases is theoretically possible, however, the truth of the matter is that the approach to the mens rea of attempt in *A-G's Reference (No. 3 of 1992)* is a radical departure from them. If intention is required only for those elements of the full offence which D has not brought about the scope of attempt is considerably enlarged. A noteworthy feature of *A-G's Reference* was that *Caldwell* recklessness (which was at that time sufficient mens rea for the substantive offence of arson) was found to constitute adequate culpability in the context of attempts liability. It is hardly any step further to allow negligence to suffice.[245] Suppose D is stopped immediately before joining the highway driving a

---

[243] Stannard, "Making up for the Missing Element: A Sideways Look at Attempts" (1987) 7 *LS* 194.

[244] [1994] 2 All ER 121, 128.

[245] See above, § 5.2(i). The abolition of *Caldwell* recklessness in *G* [2004] 1 AC 1034 and the House of Lords endorsement of a subjective approach to mens rea in serious offences may make such a prospect less likely; but in *Misra* [2005] 1 Cr App R 21 it was held that the decision in *G* had no implications for gross negligence manslaughter.

dangerous vehicle. It is established that he intended to drive onto the highway, but the evidence falls short of proof that he was aware of the condition of his car. If, however, a careful competent driver would have been aware, then D intended to bring about the missing element and possessed the culpability for other elements required for the full offence.[246] On the authority of *A-G's Reference*, D would be guilty of a negligent attempt to drive dangerously. This is a bizarre result. Doubtless there is something to be said for this approach in terms of public safety, but it goes beyond anything Parliament intended when passing the Criminal Attempts Act 1981. To avoid undue extensions of liability, it is submitted that *A-G's Reference* should be confined to its very particular facts. First, and obviously, it has no application to consequences yet to be realised, i.e. to "missing elements". Secondly, the consequence element involved was of an unusual kind. The consequence at issue was a state of affairs—danger to life or a situation that would be perceived as dangerous by an ordinary prudent person—and not, as is far more typically the case, a realised harm such as a death, wounding or damage to property. It would be possible to confine the *ratio* of the case to state-of-affairs consequences that do not comprise realised harms.[247] Such a fact-specific ground of distinction is unattractive. But sometimes it is the lesser evil.

(d) Conditional intent

Does a "conditional intent" satisfy the intent requirement for attempt? In *Husseyn*,[248] D was charged with attempting to steal sub-aqua equipment. He had been on the point of opening a holdall which contained the equipment. His conviction for attempted theft was quashed on the basis that he was searching for something that, for him, would be worth taking. A "present" intent to steal would not arise until D determined to take some particular item of property. By contrast, an intent to steal if and when some precondition should be satisfied was not sufficient: it was not a "present" intent to steal.

The ramifications of *Husseyn* were considerable.[249] Many persons enter property with intent to steal but propose only to steal things which are valuable, concealable, and portable, such as money or jewellery. Prima facie, on the reasoning in *Husseyn*, such persons would not be burglars until they encountered some property that they resolved to steal since, until then, there is no "present" intent. However, a subsequent Court of Appeal decision, *A-G's Reference (Nos. 1 and 2 of 1979)*,[250] holds that a conditional intent to steal is a "present" intent for the purposes of burglary.

How are the decisions in *Husseyn* and *A-G's Reference (Nos. 1 and 2 of 1979)* to be reconciled? In the latter case, the Court of Appeal put forward an explanation of *Husseyn* in procedural terms. In *Husseyn*, D had been charged with attempting to steal sub-aqua

---

[246] Under s. 2 of the Road Traffic Act 1988, as substituted by s. 1 of the Road Traffic Act 1991, it suffices that the dangerous condition of the vehicle "would be obvious to a competent and careful driver."

[247] Indeed, it may be argued that mere changes in probabilities (such as underlie the judgment of dangerousness) are not perspicuously characterised as consequences. On that understanding, *A-G's Reference (No. 3 of 1992)* is truly *sui generis*. Contrast, however, Bennett, *The Act Itself* (1995) 55–6, where changes in probabilities are regarded as "non-causal consequences".

[248] (1977) 67 Cr App R 131n. See also below, § 13.7(i)(g).

[249] See Williams, "Three Rogues' Charters" [1980] *Crim LR* 263.

[250] [1980] QB 180. And see too *Toothill* [1998] *Crim LR* 876.

equipment. Such a charge could not succeed as D never formed an intent to steal sub-aqua equipment as such. Had he been charged with attempting to steal "some or all of the contents of the holdall", a conviction for attempted theft would have been sustainable. Yet, as observed in *Smith and Hogan*, unless it could be proved that D would have taken something from the receptacle, the issue found to be decisive in *Husseyn* is left intact.[251] In the circumstances that arose in that case, they suggest that D be charged with "attempting to steal from a holdall."

Yet even if that procedural solution is accepted, a further difficulty may remain. Liability for attempt still requires an act of sufficient proximity which, in the case of attempted theft, implies an act that is proximate to the appropriation of someone else's property.[252] If D has demonstrated that he does not want *that* property—he opens the door to a room and then closes it without taking its contents—how close has D come to appropriating *those* contents? Proving a sufficiently proximate act in these circumstances requires a fictional supposition that D did intend to acquire the items which, in reality, he went on to reject.[253]

(e) Mens rea for attempt—a summary

Regarding the mens rea for attempt, the Criminal Attempts Act 1981 merely refers to "an intent to commit the offence." We can now appreciate that this beguilingly simple statement requires considerable explication in the light of interpretative case law. It will be helpful to summarise the conclusions reached here:

(i)   D must intend to perpetrate any conduct element specified for the full offence.

(ii)   For any circumstance elements of the full offence, it is sufficient if D intends, knows, or believes that, or is reckless whether, those circumstances are or may be present at the time of her conduct.

(iii)   If it is impossible for the relevant circumstance element to be present, D must intend or believe that the element is present at the time of her conduct. Recklessness will not suffice.

(iv)   For consequence elements, in respect of any consequence that D's conduct has *not* realised, it must be proved that D intended to realise that consequence.

(v)   For any consequence that D's conduct *has* realised, in addition to intent, it seems that the required mens rea is the same as it is for the full offence: *A-G's Reference (No. 3 of 1992)*. This proposition remains controversial, however, and may yet be confined to state-of-affairs consequences.

(vi)   Finally, a conditional intent may be sufficient mens rea provided that D has resolved to commit the crime at issue should the condition be satisfied.[254]

---

[251] *Smith and Hogan* 407.

[252] The problem does not arise in burglary, the offence at issue in *A-G's Reference (No. 3 of 1992)*; there the intent to steal can be established in general terms; there is no need to prove that D came close to stealing something in particular.

[253] Fictional, or counterfactual, assumptions of this sort may properly to used to resolve the issue of proximity in cases where it is *impossible* to commit the substantive crime: Criminal Attempts Act 1981, s. 1(3), and see further § 9.4 below. This provision does not, however, apply to cases of unwanted property, since it is clearly possible to steal such property.

[254] Although, as noted above in § 9.3(iii)(d), there may be difficulties with the actus reus requirement of proximity in such cases.

(iv) Voluntary withdrawal

In the case of substantive offences, full repentance and restoration after commission of the offence will be merely matters of mitigation. If D, say, surreptitiously picks up an item in a department store, dishonestly intending to avoid paying for it, he commits theft notwithstanding a subsequent pang of conscience which leads him to put it back. What if that change of heart should strike D as he reaches for the artefact but before he makes contact with it?[255] The answer is the same. Analytically, if the actus reus and mens rea of attempted theft are present, he has reached the point of no return. In conceptual terms, liability for attempt should ensue if actus reus and mens rea are present unless D can lay claim to any justification or excuse for his conduct.

In the case of attempts, however, there is something inapt about such an unyielding analysis. Although attempt is a crime in its own right, its principal rationales are to allow timely interventions by law enforcement personnel prior to realisation of any harm and to allow lawful restraint of the socially dangerous. A genuine change of heart by D prior to bringing about harm indicates that intervention and restraint were not required for that occasion. Further, some voluntary withdrawals can considerably reduce D's culpability. As we shall argue in a following section, should D take aim at V and shoot with intent to kill, D's innate culpability remains the same whether or not she succeeds in killing V. Yet if D should take aim and then voluntarily desist, the survival of V is to her credit. Besides, from a purely instrumental perspective, there is something to be said for the law's giving D an incentive for voluntary withdrawal in such cases.

At the present time, such English case law as touches on voluntary withdrawal in attempt is inconclusive on whether, currently, a "change of heart" defence is allowed.[256] Ideally a defence should be created by legislation. The main problem about providing such a defence concerns the difficulty of differentiating between voluntary and involuntary desistance. In *Page*,[257] for instance, D was observed climbing a ladder and inserting the point of a crowbar under a window frame. He then withdrew the implement and climbed down the ladder. He claimed that thoughts of his mother had brought him back to his good self. An alternative explanation was that he had become aware of police observation. To obviate these difficulties of establishing true motive, there is something to be said for placing the onus of proof, on a balance of probabilities, on the defendant. As a matter of general principle, the burden of proving constituent elements of the crime and of disproving any excuse or justification arising from the facts should lie with the prosecution.[258] Yet the defence proposed is highly exceptional. The defence would be raised where the formal elements of guilt were present and where there was nothing to suggest that the defendant lacked the capacity to choose to conform her conduct to law. Accordingly, a reverse burden of proof would not work undue hardship and may encourage acceptance of such a defence.

---

[255] See Wasik, "Abandoning Criminal Intent" [1980] *Crim LR* 785.

[256] For discussion of English and Commonwealth authority, see Stuart, "The *Actus Reus* in Attempts" [1970] *Crim LR* 505, 519–21.

[257] [1933] Argus LR 374 (Victoria). Cf. *Taylor* (1859) 1 F & F 511, 175 ER 831; *Lankford* [1959] Crim LR 209.

[258] See Roberts, "Taking the Burden of Proof Seriously" [1995] *Crim LR* 783.

(v) Liability for attempt and commission of the full offence

Failure is implicit in the ordinary notion of an attempt. When we watch a high jump competitor sail effortlessly over the bar, we do not describe her effort as a "commendable attempt" to clear the bar. For the purposes of legal analysis, it has been argued that the offence of attempt is subsumed and eclipsed by commission of the full offence.[259] If this idea of merger is taken literally then were D, say, to be charged with attempted murder, she would be able to answer the charge by demonstrating that she had, in fact, committed murder. Attempt liability would no longer subsist as it would have been eclipsed by the commission of the full offence.

This argument has found favour in some jurisdictions[260] but is manifestly unsatisfactory. As a matter of ordinary English usage, the term "attempt" may imply a failure to complete but there is no need here slavishly to follow the contours of ordinary language when addressing issues of principle and policy. For the purposes of the criminal law, "attempt" need not be construed as a description of D's conduct as a whole but should be regarded as a description of the kind of liability his conduct will attract at a particular stage in his sequence of acts. That liability, once established, remains free-standing and is not subsumed within any subsequent liability for the full offence. This analysis is supported by section 6(4) of the Criminal Law Act 1967, which provides that D may be convicted for an attempt "notwithstanding that he is shown to be guilty of the completed offence." Indeed, attempt charges have been permitted in circumstances where the evidence supporting the charge was unequivocally evidence of the full offence. Such was the case in Cox,[261] a case of "mercy killing". The evidence of poisoning which secured a conviction for attempted murder, the only charge preferred, was overwhelming evidence that V had met her death by poisoning.[262] A charge of attempted murder may have been preferred in order to avoid confronting the jury with a duty to send a doctor, acting on the request of and from compassion for his patient, to prison for life. Whatever the merits of this prosecutorial decision, the conviction of Dr Cox suggests that liability for the attempt survives the commission of the full offence.

(vi) Attempt, luck, and punishment

Consider the following scenarios:

> D leaves a house heavily intoxicated. He makes for his car in the driveway but is so drunk that he stumbles before he reaches the driveway and falls asleep. Alternatively, he may succeed in getting to his car but be so befuddled by drink that he cannot fit his key into the ignition. Or, he may manage to drive his car onto the road and, despite his intoxicated condition, reach his destination without mishap. On the other

---

[259] Hall, General Principles of Criminal Law (2nd ed., 1960) 577; Fletcher, Rethinking Criminal Law (1978) 131.
[260] E.g. Commonwealth v. Crow (1931) 303 Pa 91.
[261] (1992) 12 BMLR 38.
[262] On the facts of Cox, V was unquestionably alive when the poison was administered, and the dosage was sufficient to kill anyone instantly, whatever their state of health. See too Burke [2000] Crim LR 409, where there was a conviction for attempt despite evidence of commission of the full offence.

hand, he may be involved in a collision with another vehicle and deaths or injuries may, or may not, ensue. Why was D drunk? He may be an alcoholic and that condition may have arisen because of a genetic disposition, the vagaries of life, weakness of will, or any combination thereof. Or he may be an overseas visitor, unfamiliar with alcohol, who is taken completely unawares by the effect it has on him.

The possible narratives sketched above reflect the all-pervasive influence of chance factors on the prospect of criminal liability, the kind of offence committed, and what punishment, if any, will be received. Certain forms of contingency are so intrinsic to the very substance of life that a system of criminal law must merely take them as read, and can seek no form of accommodation with them.[263] Social circumstances, the particularities of character, and the patterns of opportunity for criminal acts constitute the most powerful crimogenic factors in play—but only exceptionally will they generate matters to be taken into account when determining whether D has committed a crime. Critical theorists such as Kelman[264] and Norrie[265] rebuke the failure of the criminal law to take account of these background factors, particularly the question of social disadvantage. Mainstream theorists, such as Ashworth,[266] accept that the criminal law as currently theorised and practised must, save for exceptional circumstances, assume that persons subjected to the criminal law are capable of autonomy and choice. Nonetheless, indeed because of that assumption, Ashworth insists that a rational criminal law should seek to eradicate, so far as practicable, the influence of luck on a person's criminal liability and punishment. In our drunken driver scenario, what would matter for Ashworth is that D attempted to drive while in a condition that posed a serious threat to others: provided he committed an act sufficiently proximate to driving the car, his culpability would hold constant; irrespective of whether he succeeded in driving, whether he was involved in an accident, and whether fatalities or injuries ensued from the accident. In Ashworth's view, D should be punished in a manner commensurate with his culpability and his just punishment should not be affected by the vagaries of chance.

The impact of luck is particularly marked in the sphere of liability for attempt. A Chicago-based study revealed that over 45 per cent of gunshot victims struck in the head by a high-calibre bullet survive their ordeal.[267] If D shoots V in the head with intent to kill him and succeeds, in many US jurisdictions he will face the prospect of the death penalty and in England he will receive a mandatory life sentence. Should V survive, D will not be a murderer and, in general, he will receive a lesser sentence.[268] Here Ashworth's "culpability

---

[263] See above, § 6.5(i). On the appropriate treatment of chance and contingency in the making of moral judgments see, especially, Williams, "Moral Luck" in *Moral Luck* (1981) 20; Nagel, "Moral Luck" in *Mortal Questions* (1979) 24.

[264] Kelman, "Interpretative Construction in the Substantive Criminal Law" (1981) 33 *Stanford LR* 591.

[265] *Crime, Reason and History* (1993) chap. 3; also his "'Simulacra of Morality'? Beyond the Ideal/Actual Antinomies of Criminal Justice" in Duff (ed.), *Philosophy of Criminal Law* (1998) 101.

[266] "Criminal Attempts and the Role of Resulting Harm under the Code and in the Common Law" (1988) 19 *Rutgers LJ* 19; "Taking the Consequences" in Shute, Gardner, and Horder (eds.), *Action and Value in Criminal Law* (1993) 107.

[267] Zimring, "The Medium is the Message: Firearm Caliber as a Determinant of Death from Assault" (1972) 1 *J Legal Studies* 97, 104.

[268] Attempts are consistently punished less severely than the equivalent full offence. For a defence of this practice, see Robinson and Darley, "Objectivist Versus Subjectivist View of Criminality: A Study in the Role of Social Science in Criminal Law Theory" (1998) 18 *OJLS* 409.

holds constant" argument has particular force: it is not obvious how contingencies such as the availability of timely and skilled surgery put D in different moral case even if the deftness of a surgeon allows him to evade the status of murderer. Still, on one scenario D will have killed and brought into the world such harms as the loss of a life, feelings of loss and grief for those persons close to V, the elimination of a productive member of society, etc.; whereas if death does not ensue, the harm actually brought about by D will be less. Anthony Duff, in his exhaustive and richly layered treatise on criminal attempts, argues forcefully from a deontological perspective that results do matter morally; that the greater the harm we bring about, the deeper our culpability.[269] On this perspective, differential punishment for attempts and completed crimes is justified.

To minimise the influence of luck upon the imposition of blame and punishment is attractive, even if contrary to popular sentiment. Famously, Kant argued for the primacy of *trying*, in contradistinction to *succeeding*, in making moral judgements. Assuming the presence of autonomy and the capacity for choice, an agent is in control of her decisions but is not in control of outcomes. If moral judgement is to be based on the quality of our autonomous choices, outcomes matter for such judgements only in so far as they cast light on our choices and indicate our resolve. That said, outcomes matter enormously in terms of human welfare and our relations with others. We may invite a friend for dinner and laugh with relief when he catches reflexively a bottle he has carelessly elbowed from the table. Laughter may be absent for a while should a mop and bucket be needed. Clearly, if a bad outcome does not arise, the emotional drive to impose full severity of sanction loses force. That is no cause for concern—in fact the opposite. Merely because D has put himself in a position where he may be justly punished does not, *pace* Kant, entail that he must be punished to the full measure of his culpability.[270] If all just punishment were fully exacted, the world would be even worse than it already is.[271] Indeed, a much greater cause for concern is excessive punishment. Frequently, outcome-specific sanctions, such as mandatory life sentences, inflict a punishment which exceeds D's innate culpability.[272] That is of more concern than any undue leniency offered to those guilty of attempts.

§ 9.4 Impossibility and inchoate offences

(i) The principle of an impossibility defence

In principle, if the substantive offence is impossible to commit, this need not preclude liability for incitement, conspiracy, or attempt. V may already be dead, but that does not rule out the possibility that D and E, unaware of his recent death, could make an agreement to kill V. The question then arises whether this agreement constitutes a criminal conspiracy.

---

[269] *Criminal Attempts* (1996) chap. 12.

[270] Kant, *Philosophy of Law* (1796; transl. Clarke, 1887). Kant believed that mercy had no place in criminal justice and should be confined to dealings between individuals. In his view, the State is under a duty not to pardon or forgive crimes.

[271] For attempts to justify acts of mercy under specified circumstances in criminal justice settings, see Smart, "Mercy" (1968) 43 *Philosophy* 345; Card, "Mercy" (1972) 81 *Philosophical Review* 182.

[272] See the discussion below, § 10.3(ii).

Prior to 1981, the common law position was that if the full offence was impossible to commit, there could be no liability for any incitement, conspiracy, or attempt to commit it. Since 1981, the position has now changed for attempts[273] and statutory conspiracy,[274] but impossibility remains a defence to incitement and common law conspiracy. Accordingly, we still have to consider how the defence operates, and why impossibility should preclude liability when otherwise liability would ensue.

In the case law and voluminous literature that the impossibility issue has generated, no predominant rationale for the defence of impossibility emerges. It has been argued that impossibility necessarily provides a defence to a charge of attempt on grounds of lack of proximity, yet this explanation does not carry over to incitement and conspiracy. Besides, the proximity objection is circular. It implicitly assumes the conclusion that impossibility should provide a defence: if we allow liability to be proved on the basis of facts that D assumes, then his act may have been sufficiently proximate on the facts mistakenly assumed. More persuasive is the view that, since no harm was in fact threatened, the matter is insufficiently serious to warrant criminal liability; a conclusion attractive for those theorists who assert that criminal liability should be for conduct which causes harm or threatens harm and should not be imposed just because of one's character, however bad that may be.[275] On this view, when D and E agree to kill V, a person already dead, the agreement does not give rise to any social danger. Yet impossibility defences have been allowed even when danger beckoned. Picking an empty pocket has been regarded as a case of impossibility,[276] yet such conduct is menacing. Moreover, conduct may deserve censure irrespective of its propensity for harm: trying to kill someone without justification or excuse, for instance, is a very bad thing to do and merits punishment for its badness alone whatever danger, if any, was threatened. The lack of a consistent rationale has given rise to unstable and shifting case law in jurisdictions which recognise an impossibility defence.[277]

This lack of focus entails difficulties in the legal application of impossibility defences. Insufficiency of means to attain an achievable end will generally not constitute an impossibility defence, yet radical insufficiency of means may do so. Further distinctions have been drawn concerning the relevance of the success or failure of D's project. Where D's project was to obtain a video recorder as cheaply as possible, it has been ruled by the House of Lords that D did not attempt to handle stolen goods when she acquired a second-hand recorder which, erroneously, she thought was stolen.[278] On the other hand, D was held to be guilty of attempting to traffic in heroin when he acquired a substance which he took to be heroin but which in fact was snuff, thereby frustrating his scheme to acquire the drug.[279] One way to defend these different outcomes is to maintain that a project brought to fruition without committing a crime cannot be regarded as an attempt to commit a crime, render-

---

[273] Criminal Attempts Act 1981, s. 1(2).

[274] Criminal Law Act 1977, s. 1(1)(b) as amended by the Criminal Attempts Act 1981.

[275] For a robust statement of this view see Hogan, "The Criminal Attempts Act and Attempting the Impossible" [1984] *Crim LR* 584.

[276] *Collins* (1864) Le & Ca 471, 169 ER 1477; but contrast *Ring* (1892) 61 LJMC 116.

[277] For a discussion of cases from a variety of US jurisdictions see Perkins and Boyle, *Criminal Law* (3rd ed., 1982) 627–35.

[278] *Anderton* v. *Ryan* [1985] 1 AC 560; below, § 9.4(iii).

[279] *Shivpuri* [1987] AC 1; below, § 9.4(iii).

ing irrelevant the question of impossibility as a defence.[280] Alternatively, some theorists acknowledge that in both situations an issue of impossibility arises but that only in the case of the failure to obtain drugs can there be said to be an intent to commit an offence.[281] These matters will require more discussion below. Enough has been said for now to indicate the vagaries and complexity of the topic of impossibility; a topic which, thankfully, has diminished in importance since the 1981 reforms.

The impossibility at issue here concerns matters of fact and not questions of law. There is a broad consensus that an impossibility of law should not lead to criminal liability. It is impossible to commit, say, the crime of adultery, because adultery is not a crime. The consensus is not, perhaps, uniform: it has been claimed that it is inconsistent to deny a defence of factual impossibility and yet acquit someone who commits adultery in the belief that he is committing a crime.[282] Yet the principle of legality requires that attempt liability take its bounds from the norms of the substantive criminal law.[283] Non-existent crimes are in entirely different case from a crime which, in particular circumstances, it may be impossible to commit.

Less straightforward is the situation where D takes his conduct to fall within the boundaries of an extant offence because he is mistaken about the ambit of the offence. Suppose that D "borrows" V's lawnmower for the weekend when V is away, aware that V would not have given D permission to use it. On the basis of a conversation with E (a confused law student), D believes that dishonestly borrowing the mower constitutes theft despite his lack of intention to deprive V permanently of the mower. D has demonstrated that he is prepared to do something which he assumes is theft, a crime that assuredly exists. Yet, legally, he is in the same case as our adulterer. He believes that dishonestly borrowing a lawnmower is a crime: it is not. Even more complex is the case where the mistake as to the ambit of a crime is the product of a mistake of civil law. For exculpatory purposes, a mistake of civil law is put on the same footing as a mistake of fact[284] and, arguably, this should cut both ways. Suppose that D cuts down a particular tree that he mistakenly thinks belongs to V. The fence separating D's land from V's had been moved by V without D noticing this change for six years, and D assumes that ownership in the tree is vested in V because he believes that ownership to land is acquired by adverse possession after six years; whereas the legally effective period is twelve years. If D's belief were true he would be intentionally destroying property belonging to another, a clear case of criminal damage. There seems little difference here from the situation where D makes a valid contract for the acquisition of a video recorder in the mistaken belief that the item was stolen. Both cases should come out the same way on the question whether an inchoate offence has been committed. But which way remains a matter of controversy, as we shall see.

---

[280] Hogan, "The Criminal Attempts Act and Attempting the Impossible" [1984] *Crim LR* 584; *Anderton v. Ryan* [1985] 1 AC 560.

[281] Duff, *Criminal Attempts* (1996) 112–13.

[282] Gross, *A Theory of Criminal Justice* (1979) 209.

[283] See *CLGP* 633–5.

[284] *Smith* [1974] QB 354.

(ii) Impossibility at common law

The House of Lords decisions in *Haughton* v. *Smith*[285] and *DPP* v. *Nock*[286] established a defence of impossibility for inchoate offences at common law. As we have noted, these decisions still govern for the common law offence of incitement and for common law conspiracy.[287] Three distinctive situations were identified in *Haughton* and confirmed in *Nock*. They will be discussed in turn.

(a) Inefficient and insufficient means

Seeking an attainable end in a manner which will not attain success is not to be regarded as a case of impossibility. That D and E dishonestly agree to relieve V of money through a scheme never likely to fool V will not preclude a conviction for conspiracy to defraud. By and large, this category is straightforward and uncontroversial.

However, in those rare cases where D commits himself to a criminal endeavour by means which are radically deficient and which threaten no-one's interests, there may be a temptation to classify deficiency of means as intrinsic impossibility. If D were to incite E to kill V by sticking pins into an effigy of V, one may be inclined not to take the matter seriously—however convinced D may be of E's diabolical powers. It appears natural to dismiss any charge of incitement on the ground of impossibility. On the other hand, since the particular result *is* achievable, by some means or other, and is genuinely, if ineffectually, striven for, the situation does seem to be one of ineffective means. Duff suggests that this sort of case should be dealt with by providing for an acquittal if the conduct alleged "failed to engage with the world as an attempt to commit [the] offence."[288] As matters stand, one would have to rely on prosecutorial discretion. Given the absence of reported cases, the employment of radically deficient means does not appear to attract prosecution, perhaps because it does not normally come to light or is not taken seriously when it does.[289]

(b) Physical impossibility

Perhaps the voodoo doll case would be treated by the courts as one of physical impossibility. In *Nock*,[290] D and others were in possession of an admixture of substances from which they attempted to obtain cocaine. The mixture was incapable of yielding cocaine whatever processes it was subjected to. The House ruled that should a particular objective be physically impossible, whatever the means employed, the defence of impossibility applied. Suppose that V falsely informs D and E that he has a large credit balance at X bank. In fact V has no funds at all at the bank. If D and E contrive a dishonest scheme in an attempt to access V's supposed account, they have a defence of impossibility to conspiracy to defraud.

This head of impossibility has given rise to great dissatisfaction. In the example above, V

---

[285] [1975] AC 476.

[286] [1978] AC 979.

[287] For attempt and statutory conspiracy, the defence is now abolished by the Criminal Attempts Act 1981: below, § 9.4(iii).

[288] *Criminal Attempts* (1996) 398.

[289] In a study conducted by Finkel *et al.*, subjects almost unanimously considered that a case involving radically deficient means (pins in a wax effigy) did not merit prosecution: "Lay Perspectives on Legal Conundrums: Impossible and Mistaken Act Cases" (1995) 19 *Law and Human Behaviour* 593.

may have suspected the dishonest designs of D and E and led them a false trail in order to entrap. Should this be regarded as a case of physical impossibility if V had the large balance he claimed, but at the Y bank? In the past, it has been ruled to be a case of impossibility when D shot at a tree stump thinking the stump was a human being;[291] but not a case of impossibility when D shoots into an empty room while V is located elsewhere in the house.[292] The "empty pocket" cases, too, have divided courts,[293] with exceptional variables (such as property situated elsewhere on the victim or the proximity of other victims) generating convictions for attempted theft against the general trend of acquittals. There are few academic defenders of acquittals in cases of physical impossibility (subject to Duff's "engagement with the world" reservation referred to earlier) and the matter is less important than it was. Nonetheless, the continuing presence of this defence for incitement and common law conspiracies underscores the desirability of statutory intervention in respect of these offences.

(c) Completion of intended conduct without the commission of a substantive offence

This category is exemplified by *Haughton*,[294] where D arranged to take possession of corned beef that he assumed would be stolen. When he did take possession, the beef was no longer stolen as it had been taken into police custody[295] and then released under police supervision in order to entrap D. The House of Lords ruled that D was not guilty of attempting to handle stolen goods. His (physical) conduct was "objectively innocent" and his belief that the goods were stolen did not alter that fact.

This notion of "objective innocence" has proved tenacious. Indeed, for some time it even withstood the statutory abolition of an impossibility defence in attempt and statutory conspiracy (discussed in the following section). Two arguments support acquittals in these cases. First, it is claimed that situations which consist of D achieving everything he set out to do are ineptly described as attempts, which imply some form of miscarriage or failure. Secondly, where the conduct is "objectively innocent", convictions in these cases may arguably be castigated as involving punishment for thought alone. It is submitted that neither claim is defensible. As we noted earlier (§ 9.3(v)), "attempt" as a legal term of art need not imply any form of failure. Moreover, "impossible" attempts are no more thought crimes than are other attempts. D must do something which is more than merely preparatory on the facts that he assumed.

(iii) Impossibility in attempt and statutory conspiracy

Decisions such as *Haughton* and *Nock* were subjected to considerable criticism, principally on the ground that persons unequivocally embarked on criminal projects, such as receiving stolen goods on a large scale or producing cocaine for trafficking purposes, were evading

---

[290] [1978] AC 979.
[291] *McPherson* (1857) 7 Cox CC 281, 169 ER 975 (CCR).
[292] *State* v. *Mitchell* (1902) 170 Mo 633.
[293] Contrast *Collins* (1864) Le & Ca 471, 169 ER 1477 with *Ring* (1892) 61 LJMC 116.
[294] [1975] AC 476.
[295] Theft Act 1968, s. 24(3).

justified censure and restraint because of flukes which, although precluding concrete harm on particular occasions, allowed dangerous actors to remain at large.[296] This sentiment ultimately proved decisive and the Criminal Attempts Act 1981 abolished the impossibility defence for statutory conspiracy and attempt. For both offences it is provided that D may conspire or attempt to commit an offence, "even though the facts are such that the commission of the offence is impossible."[297] Those words seem apt to eradicate the defence of impossibility in all its forms. D and E will conspire to traffick in a Class A drug even if the suitcase they agree to collect contains snuff and not, as they believe, heroin. D will attempt to handle stolen corned beef, notwithstanding that the beef has lost its stolen character, if D thinks the beef is stolen. In the case of attempt, for the avoidance of any conceivable doubt, it is provided that D's intention is to be judged as if "the facts of the case had been as he believed them to be."[298] This renders completely untenable the always fallacious argument which took the form, on facts such as *Haughton*, that "D intended to handle that particular consignment of beef: that particular consignment of beef was not stolen beef; accordingly, D did not intend to handle stolen beef."

Yet even the most clearly drafted legislation, emerging from a transparent and easily verifiable legislative history,[299] may not be proof against firmly entrenched judicial views, particularly where the facts of the instant case put these views in the best light. In *Anderton v. Ryan*,[300] D was questioned by police about her acquisition of a video recorder at a low price. She admitted that she believed the item was stolen, although it was never proved that it had been. She was charged with attempted handling. Clearly what D did was not *intrinsically* a criminal project. The project was the acquisition of a video recorder and D was not so perverse as to prefer a recorder that was actually stolen. Moreover, there was no evidence that she was anything in the nature of a trader in stolen goods, rendering her prosecution heavy-handed, if not oppressive. Yet her conviction would seem assured. If the facts had been as she believed them to be, she would have acquired a stolen item. Judging her intent against the facts she supposed, she intended to handle stolen goods.

A unanimous House of Lords quashed D's conviction. The language of the 1981 Act was not so much interpreted as swept aside by the idea of "objective innocence". She had done everything she had wanted to do, it was said, and she had not been proved to have committed a crime. How could everyday, lawful acts such as acquiring goods for payment be turned into crimes by mere beliefs which could not be shown to correspond with the facts? The conduct was not of the sort intended to be regulated by the Criminal Attempts Act 1981 and, accordingly, application of the impossibility provisions to D's conduct simply, seemingly, did not arise.

Within a matter of months, in *Shivpuri*,[301] the House of Lords was confronted with facts

---

[296] See the discussion at Law Com. No. 102, *Attempt and Impossibility in Relation to Attempt, Conspiracy and Incitement* (1980) paras. 2.85–2.100.

[297] Criminal Attempts Act 1981, s. 1(2); Criminal Law Act 1977, s. 1(1)(b).

[298] Criminal Attempts Act 1981, s. 1(3)(b).

[299] In the discussion at Law Com. No. 102, *Attempt and Impossibility in Relation to Attempt, Conspiracy and Incitement* (1980) paras. 2.85–2.100, no distinction is drawn between cases such as *Anderton* and cases such as *Shivpuri*. The provisions in the Commission's draft Bill, reflecting this analysis, were adopted unchanged by Parliament.

[300] [1985] 1 AC 560.

[301] [1987] AC 1.

from a very different milieu from *Anderton*. D was a suspected drug trafficker. In the context of an undercover police operation, he was induced to take possession of a suitcase full of snuff which he had been assured contained heroin, and was subsequently charged with attempting to commit the offence of being knowingly concerned with dealing in controlled drugs. Here D's project was intrinsically criminal. The absence of heroin entailed the failure of his project. Moreover, it is clearly in the public interest that "sting" operations should be carried out, where possible, with the aid of such props as powder masquerading as a drug, fake firearms, or explosives, etc., without risking circulation of the real things. It is not surprising then, that D's conviction for attempted drug trafficking was upheld by a unanimous House. More surprising, perhaps, was that *Anderton* v. *Ryan* was overturned. A majority of the House considered that differing outcomes in these cases could not be reconciled. Interestingly, two law Lords considered that the two cases could be reconciled[302] but they were not prepared to take this opinion to the point of dissent. Accordingly, *Anderton* v. *Ryan* is unequivocally overruled.

That there are differences between *Shivpuri* and *Anderton* is undeniable. But, as the majority in *Shivpuri* recognised, these differences can gain no purchase on the language of the 1981 Act.[303] If we judge Mrs Ryan on the facts that she supposed, she would have obtained a stolen item and would have intended to obtain a stolen item. The fact that this criminal act (on the supposed facts) was not done for its own sake but to gain some ulterior advantage is true of a great many acts which are indubitably criminal. That Mrs Ryan did not in fact obtain a stolen item (or could not be proved to have done so) prompts reactions of indulgence for her case. Yet it has not proved feasible to draft legislation on impossibility which leaves out a Ryan but includes a Shivpuri.

Duff, in his exhaustive treatise on attempts, maintains that the two cases can and should have different outcomes and, moreover, that different outcomes are compatible with the language of the Criminal Attempts Act 1981.[304] His position is that while Shivpuri intended to traffick in drugs, Ryan did not intend to handle stolen goods. According to Duff, Ryan lacks the requisite intent as obtaining a stolen recorder played no motivational part in her conduct. She wanted a cheap recorder, nothing else, and therefore the stolen quality which she mistakenly attributed to the item she acquired was not part, as Duff terms it, of the "content" of her intent. He does acknowledge, however, that had her belief been congruent with the facts, she would have intended to obtain a stolen item.

Duff's explication of this perceived difference is complex and subtle. Suffice it here to say that he would draw distinctions which, however fine-grained, do not necessarily carry moral weight. He says of D who intends to kill V, a person he takes to be the prime minister but whose identity is immaterial to D (a contract killer, say), that D intends to kill the prime minister if V *is* the prime minister but not if D mistakenly takes V to be the prime minister. Either way, of course, D is guilty of murder. But surely, in either case, he intends to kill a

---

[302] Lords Hailsham and Mackay took the view that in *Shivpuri* D intended to deal in drugs whereas in *Anderton* D merely believed the recorder was stolen and did not intend to acquire a stolen recorder. It is submitted that, although there certainly is a distinction between the cases, the difference is one of motive or purpose rather than a lack of intention.

[303] Lord Bridge, in giving judgment for the House, acknowledged his indebtedness to an article by Glanville Williams, "The Lords and Impossible Attempts" [1986] *CLJ* 33.

[304] Duff, *Criminal Attempts* (1996) 378–84.

prime minister? Duff ties "intent" too tightly to "motive". Intention is a cognitive as well as a motivational state: the "content" of one's intent includes circumstances that are known about or believed even when not desired. Moreover, the claim that the content of one's intentions depends upon what actually happens is profoundly implausible. Intention is a mental state, a subjective phenomenon. We intend those acts and results which provide *us* with a reason for which *we* act—it is hard to see how those reasons could be constituted by unknown truths.

§ 9.5 Jurisdiction and inchoate offences

At common law, the dependence of jurisdiction upon territory ensured that "all crime is local."[305] For statutory crimes, there is a very strong presumption that criminal statutes are concerned only with the regulation of acts or omissions perpetrated in the United Kingdom.[306] There are, however, some long-standing statutory exceptions to the territoriality principle[307] and, in recent times, significant further exceptions have been enacted in response to the transnational character of some forms of criminality.[308]

In principle, inchoate offences need not be constrained by the territoriality principle, provided the inchoate offence in question relates to an offence to be perpetrated in England or Wales. As Lord Salmon observed, what difference does it make if a plan to rob a bank in London is hatched in Birmingham or Brussels?[309] In that spirit, the Privy Council in *Somchai Liangsiriprasent* v. *United States*[310] considered that parties to agreements made abroad to perpetrate offences in England are subject to English criminal jurisdiction, notwithstanding the absence of any steps taken in England to put the agreements into effect. The Court of Appeal has made similar rulings in *Sansom*[311] and *Naina*.[312] The position established for conspiracy may well apply also to attempt. In *DPP* v. *Stonehouse*,[313] D faked his death by drowning in Miami so that his wife, who was uninvolved in the fraud, could claim on life assurance policies. The House of Lords asserted jurisdiction over this attempted criminal deception. The majority of the House justified the assumption of jurisdiction on the basis that "effects" (reports in the press) of D's conduct in Miami were felt in England.[314] Lord Diplock, however, asserted jurisdiction on a different basis: that D's conduct abroad was sufficiently proximate to the commission of an offence of criminal deception in England. His Lordship's more straightforward approach gains strength from the subsequent adoption, in cases such as *Sansom* (above), of the same approach to cases of conspiracy. If attempts or conspiracies are focused on substantive crimes which are

---

[305] Williams, "Venue and Ambit of the Criminal Law" (1965) 81 *LQR* 276, 395, 518.

[306] *Cox* v. *Army Council* [1963] AC 48; *Air India* v. *Wiggins* [1980] 1 WLR 815.

[307] Notably murder, manslaughter, and bigamy: OAPA 1861, ss. 9, 57.

[308] E.g. Criminal Justice Act 1975, s. 1; Criminal Justice Act 1993, part 1; Suppression of Terrorism Act 1978, s. 4; Taking of Hostages Act 1982, s.1(1).

[309] *DPP* v. *Doot* [1973] AC 602.

[310] [1991] AC 225.

[311] [1991] 2 QB 130.

[312] 22 April 1999 (CA No. 9900442X3).

[313] [1978] AC 55.

[314] For criticism of that approach see Sullivan, "Crossing the Rubicon in Miami" (1978) 41 *MLR* 215.

themselves triable in England or Wales, there is no reason in principle why the attempt or conspiracy should take place in England or Wales.[315]

For most offences of fraud and dishonesty, it is now clearly the case, following the implementation of Part I of the Criminal Justice Act 1993,[316] that conspiracies and attempts directed at those offences need not take place in England and Wales provided that English courts would have jurisdiction over the substantive offence.[317] As we have seen, that position has been established judicially for conspiracy in general and probably extends generally for attempts too.

We now turn to the converse case of incitements, conspiracies, and attempts in England and Wales to commit crimes within foreign jurisdictions. Classically, inchoate activity directed at breaching foreign laws did not constitute an offence under English law.[318] For conspiracy the position is now radically changed by section 1A of the Criminal Law Act 1977,[319] which provides jurisdiction over conspiracies notwithstanding that implementation of the agreement will involve an act or event by one or more of the parties taking place outside the United Kingdom. The act or event must constitute an offence in the country where it is to take place and must also constitute an offence under English law were the act or event to take place in England or Wales. Jurisdiction is triggered if "anything" relating to the conspiracy—e.g. the posting of a letter—is done in England by a party to the conspiracy or by the "agent" of a party. The breadth of coverage is enormous. For instance, D and E, Australian tourists passing through London, could be tried for conspiracy were they to agree in a London pub to cheat on the Paris Metro. The Attorney-General must give consent to any prosecution under section 1A. It will be interesting to see how he approaches that task in practice.[320]

---

[315] The same, in principle, should apply to incitement. However, there is no authority on the point.

[316] SI 1999 No. 1189 (32); SI 1999 No. 1499 (42). For discussion of Part 1 of the Criminal Justice Act 1993 in relation to substantive offences of fraud and dishonesty, see below, § 13.9.

[317] Criminal Justice Act 1993, ss. 3, 4. No provision is made for incitement.

[318] *Board of Trade* v. *Owen* [1957] AC 602.

[319] Interpolated by s. 5 of the Criminal Justice (Terrorism and Conspiracy) Act 1998. No provision is made for attempt or incitement. Note, however, s. 5 of the Criminal Justice Act 1993, which extends conspiracy to defraud and incitement to commit specified offences of fraud and dishonesty to situations where the fraudulent or dishonest conduct will take place outside England and Wales.

[320] The Criminal Justice (Terrorism and Conspiracy) Act 1998 was hurriedly passed during an emergency session of Parliament. There is no reference in the debates to the provision extending jurisdiction for conspiracy. Political groups active in London suspected of organising violent acts to take place overseas are generally considered to be the target group.

10

HOMICIDE

§ 10.1 Death and liability

Homicide is the death of a human being in circumstances where the death can be attributed to the conduct of one or more other human beings. A homicide may be lawful or unlawful. An example of lawful homicide is where D kills V in justifiable self-defence.[1] If the homicide is unlawful it may be one of a variety of offences (including diverse forms of vehicular homicide): in this chapter we will consider murder, manslaughter, and infanticide.

If D is found to be causally responsible for V's death, important penal consequences may follow that are unparalleled elsewhere in the criminal law. For instance, in *Mallet*,[2] D quarrelled with his neighbour V and, regrettably, punched V in the face. Ordinarily, this would have been a case of simple assault as the punch itself inflicted no injury upon V. Unfortunately, V fell awkwardly and died as a result of striking his head on a paving stone. The affair was therefore, as will be explained later, a case of manslaughter[3] and the Court of Appeal confirmed D's custodial sentence[4] even though it found that D was not at fault with regard to causing V's death. If a motorist, by his dangerous driving, were to cause dreadful but non-fatal injuries, he would receive, at most, a two-year prison sentence.[5] If his driving were to cause death, the maximum sentence would extend to fourteen years.[6] A person may cause another individual serious injury by grossly negligent conduct. Outside special contexts, such conduct will not result in criminal liability. Should death ensue, however, liability may be incurred for manslaughter.[7] Formerly, all persons found guilty of murder would receive a mandatory death sentence.[8] Nowadays, the mandatory sentence is life imprisonment,[9] a unique case of penal inflexibility for a crime which, like many other crimes, can encompass substantial variations of culpability in its range of applications.

Of course, the criminal law must take killings seriously. By its very finality, death is an

---

[1] At one time the common law formally distinguished between justifiable homicides and merely excusable homicides. While an acquittal followed upon verdicts either of justifiable or excusable homicide, in the case of the latter D's goods were forfeited. In 1828 forfeiture was abolished and, so far as D is concerned, there is no difference between the various defences to homicide (or to any other crime).

[2] [1972] Crim LR 260.

[3] Below, § 10.6ff.

[4] Imprisonment for one year.

[5] Criminal Justice Act 2003, s. 285.

[6] *Ibid.*, s. 1.

[7] *Adomako* [1995] 1 AC 171.

[8] That is, until s. 5 of the Homicide Act 1957 (now repealed) created a distinction between capital and non-capital murder. Non-capital murder attracted a mandatory life sentence.

[9] Murder (Abolition of Death Penalty) Act 1965.

irremediable harm and even if V is killed instantly and painlessly in circumstances which did not cause her any prior anxiety, she will normally have been done a very great wrong. Yet it is a mistake to hold that death as a harm will invariably transcend all other harms. True, death is the negation of life and life is a precondition for all other forms of value and disvalue. Yet it does not follow that death is always the worst alternative. There may be circumstances where death is the preferred outcome for a particular person for reasons that strike us as rational, whereas only in the most bizarre circumstances would a person welcome the infliction upon herself of significant disablement or other forms of serious harm. Death is special in terms of the impact it has on those with strong emotional[10] and material bonds with the person deceased. The anger and resentment of these "secondary" victims,[11] amplified in the press, is perhaps the most potent factor inhibiting a more equable penal response to causing death. As the following pages will show, causing death may involve morally debatable forms of liability and risk exposure to excessive punishment.

§ 10.2 Homicide defined

A homicide must contain the following elements:

(a)   The victim must be a human being.
(b)   Death must be caused through the act or omission of one or more human beings.
(c)   Death must occur within the Queen's peace.

We will now examine these elements.

(i) Human beings

Homicide is defined in terms of the taking of human life. In certain rare situations, dispute may arise about the human status of a victim of an alleged homicide. First, a foetus, even to the point of delivery at birth, is not accorded full human status, and until birth the interests of the foetus are protected by laws falling outwith the law of homicide.[12] Secondly, at one time, the advent of death—identified in terms of the absence of pulse and respiration—was a clearly defined terminus of homicide law. Advances in medical techniques have undermined the certainty with which we can apply or disapply the concept of death to persons with profound and permanent disabilities whose existence is sustained by artificial means.[13] Accordingly, homicide law requires criteria by which to establish the presence of independent human life at the time of birth and to determine the life/death status of persons who may exhibit one or more of the traditional indicia of life, but only by virtue of technological intervention.

---

[10] For a searching study of impact on family and significant others see Rock, *After Homicide: Practical and Political Responses to Bereavement* (1998).

[11] It may be noted that close relatives of persons deceased have been treated as "victims" for the purposes of bringing actions before the European Court of Human Rights (*McCann and Others* v. *UK* (1996) 21 EHRR 97) in order to contest the legality of State action resulting in fatalities.

[12] Infant Life (Preservation) Act 1929; OAPA 1861, s. 58.

[13] See Skegg, *Law, Ethics and Medicine* (1984) chap. 9.

(a) Life at birth

In *A-G's Reference (No. 3 of 1994)*,[14] the House of Lords confirmed, *obiter*, previous understanding that to destroy a viable foetus, however late in term, would not constitute any form of homicide. This is so whether the act of destruction terminates the life of the foetus in the womb or causes the foetus to be stillborn. For a live foetus to attain full personhood, the whole body of the child must emerge into the world and must sustain an existence independently of the mother for however brief a period of time. There is no modern case law on what constitutes an existence independently of the mother.[15] The preponderance of nineteenth-century authority on the topic favours a test of independent respiration,[16] which provides a serviceable criterion for the existence of life.[17]

The failure to accord full human status to a late-term viable foetus has been rationalised on the basis that until the foetus is expelled from the mother, it is to be regarded as belonging to the mother and not constituting any kind of entity in its own right.[18] This rationalisation was forcefully rejected by Lord Mustill in *A-G's Reference (No. 3 of 1994)*[19] on the ground that it contradicted incontrovertible biological fact. From an early stage in pregnancy, a foetus becomes an entity unto itself, whose habitat is in the womb. Indeed, after eight months of pregnancy, no further metamorphic development of the foetus occurs, and from then on the difference between a foetus and a neonate is purely a matter of location.[20] The legal conferment of personhood reflects societal perceptions which are not underpinned by biological data. This results in some uncomfortable anomalies. If a late-term viable foetus is destroyed in the womb without justification or excuse, the applicable offences are child destruction or unlawfully procuring a miscarriage.[21] If, however, the pre-term attempt to destroy the foetus (when "*en ventre sa mere*") is unsuccessful and a birth ensues, yet the neonate dies as a consequence of injuries sustained in the earlier attempt to destroy it, a verdict of murder or manslaughter may ensue.[22] Similarly, a lawful abortion may be performed outside the normally permitted period of 24 weeks if it seems likely that a child, if born, would be seriously handicapped.[23] By contrast, there seems little doubt that if a pre-term child is sustained alive outside the womb, the destruction of the child would be regarded as the destruction of a person, however handicapped the child.[24]

---

[14] [1997] 3 All ER 936.

[15] For general discussion see Temkin, "Pre-Natal Injury, Homicide and the Draft Criminal Code" [1986] *CLJ* 414.

[16] *Poulton* (1832) 5 C & P 329, 172 ER 997; *Brain* (1834) 6 C & P 349, 172 ER 1272; *West* (1848) 2 Cox CC 500; *Crutchley* (1857) 7 C & P 814, 173 ER 355.

[17] The Criminal Law Revision Committee, in its Fourteenth Report, *Offences Against the Person* Cmnd. 7844 (1980), did not recommend any statutory change in the law.

[18] A view adopted by the Court of Appeal in *A-G's Reference (No. 3 of 1994)* [1996] 2 All ER 10, 18.

[19] [1997] 3 All ER 936, 943.

[20] Although, of course, the location of a foetus has implications when the interests of the foetus are irreconcilable with respect for the autonomous choices of the pregnant woman: *St George's Health Care NHS Trust v. S* [1998] 3 All ER 673.

[21] Infant Life (Preservation) Act 1929; OAPA 1861, s. 58.

[22] Confirmed by the House of Lords in *A-G's Reference (No. 3 of 1994)* [1997] 3 All ER 936.

[23] Abortion Act 1967, s. 1(1)(d).

[24] There are civil cases, such as *Re C* [1989] 3 WLR 240; *Re J* [1990] 3 All ER 930; and the criminal trial case of *Arthur* (1981) 12 B Med LR 1, which indicate that lesser degrees of medical care may be owed to profoundly disabled neonates, but the deliberate killing of any person is murder regardless of the state of disability: *Airedale National Health Trust v. Bland* [1993] AC 789, *passim*. In the very special circumstances of *ReA (Children) (Conjoined Twins: Surgical Seperation)* [2001] 1 Fam 147, the separation of conjoined twins was held to be a lawful

Debate about the appropriate legal status of the late-term foetus has arisen in other juris-dictions, most notably in the United States.[25] South Carolina has legislated that a late-term foetus is legally to be regarded as a full human subject.[26] A considerable number of states have enacted "feticide" statutes, which fall short of attributing personhood to foetuses but which stipulate that the non-therapeutic destruction of a foetus is to be regarded as equiv-alent to the taking of human life.[27] In England, however, there is high authority that a late-term foetus is *not* to be regarded as a person. The House of Lords in *A-G's Reference (No. 3 of 1994)*[28] regarded the matter as beyond argument and refused to convict D of murder on the assumption that V had died from the effects of an injury sustained when V was a foetus in the womb of E. D had stabbed E when she was pregnant with the intent only to injure E. The House of Lords considered that it would be extending the concept of trans-ferred malice too far to transfer from the mother to the foetus and then to the child V that the foetus subsequently became. Although the ruling was expressed in terms of discounte-nancing a "double" transfer of malice, that objection could not have been sustained had there not been a perceived discontinuity and a lesser status as between the foetus and the child. Furthermore, in a civil case, it has been ruled unlawful to make a woman submit to surgery in order to save the life of the foetus (and her own life) at the time of confinement.[29] Such an assertion of autonomy would be difficult to sustain in legal terms had the claimant been regarded as the mother of a child.

Moreover, the passing of the Infant Life Preservation Act 1929 can be said to reinforce the non-person status of a late-term foetus. The Act was passed on the assumption that to destroy a foetus in the process of birth would not constitute an offence unless it could be proved that the child had taken breath after complete expulsion from the mother. Therefore, it may be asserted with some confidence that the recognition of a late-term foetus as a full person would require legislative intervention.[30] Any such initiative should proceed cautiously. As we have discussed, the present law gives rise to some anomalous distinctions when tested against the biological facts. Yet the reception of a child into the world after the point of birth is an event of enormous cultural significance, laden with symbolism. These social facts may weigh more heavily than biological facts when resolving the parameters of the law of homicide.[31]

---

procedure even though it was known that it would entail the death of the weaker twin. The difficulty and signifi-cance of the case arise from the fact that the weaker, profoundly handicapped twin was, properly, accorded full human status: see further § 21(ii)(e). In the case of late-term abortions, a foetus may be delivered capable of survival outside the womb but, particularly in a case of handicap, be allowed to die. For a view that such an omission may result in culpable homicide unless the law allows selective non-treatment of defective neonates, see Mason and McCall Smith, *Law and Medical Ethics* (5th ed., 1999) at 132–3.

[25] There are decisions to the effect that the common law recognises the personhood of a late-term viable foetus: *Commonwealth* v. *Lawrence* (1998) 404 Mass 378 (Mass SC).

[26] Code of Laws of South Carolina, Offences Against the Person, s. 16–3–90.

[27] Schott, "Fetal Protection—An Overview of Recent State Legislative Responses" (1991) 22 *Memphis State University LR* 119; Kaufman, "Legal Recognition of Independent Fetal Rights" (1997) 17 *Children's Legal Rights J* 20.

[28] [1997] 3 All ER 936.

[29] *St George's Healthcare NHS Trust* v. *S* [1998] 3 All ER 673.

[30] Currently, the jurisprudence on Art. 2 of the ECHR seems unlikely to require any judge made change: *Vo* v. *France* (2005) 40 EHRR 259.

[31] Becker, "Human Being: The Boundaries of the Concept" (1974) 4 *Phil & Public Aff* 334; Engelhardt, "The Ontology of Abortion" (1973) 84 *Ethics* 217.

Post-natal deaths from pre-natal injuries.

Once a child has an existence independently of the mother, the death of the child by the agency of another will constitute homicide. This applies where a pre-birth injury causes a post-birth death. The early case of *Senior* [32] indicates the potential scope of the liability that may arise in such circumstances. D, a midwife, ineptly supervised a birth. As a consequence, the child died shortly after the birth and D was successfully prosecuted for manslaughter by gross negligence. A wide range of pre-birth conduct on the part of pregnant women may be associated with the deaths of infants, including substance abuse and sexual risk-taking. In English case law, at the present time, there is no reported case of a prosecution arising from such circumstances. There may be a very understandable ambivalence on the part of prosecuting authorities in seeking penal sanctions against persons who are in thrall to addictions of various kinds or burdened by other forms of social dysfunction, but in principle such prosecutions are possible. [33]

A-G's Reference (No. 3 of 1994) confirms that post-natal deaths resulting from pre-natal injury fall within the domain of homicide. In actus reus terms this is quite straightforward: a neonate is a person even when born in a condition inimical to ultimate survival. Yet the fact that the fatal injury was inflicted prior to birth may well have a bearing upon questions of mens rea. If D intends to destroy a foetus in the womb, he will lack an intent to kill *a person* and therefore will lack the mens rea for murder. Consequently, should the foetus survive D's destructive efforts but die some time after the birth as a consequence of them, a murder charge would seem to be ruled out. [34] D will be liable for murder only if he inflicts a pre-birth injury intending to cause the child to die after the birth [35] or to be born with a serious injury. [36]

Recall that on the facts of *A-G's Reference (No. 3 of 1994)*, D did not direct his violence at the foetus. His target was the pregnant woman, whom he stabbed in the small of the back. The mother gave birth but the child died some days thereafter as a consequence of premature birth induced by the attack. The House of Lords considered D guilty of manslaughter of the kind known as constructive manslaughter, which merely requires a dangerous criminal act causally associated with the death. It is not necessary that the dangerous act be targeted at the deceased. [37]

In ruling that D would be guilty of manslaughter, the House of Lords differed from the Court of Appeal. Below, [38] a murder verdict had been thought possible on the basis of the transferred intent principle. [39] D had intended to cause grievous bodily harm to his pregnant

---

[32] (183?) 1 Mood CC 346, 168 ER 1298.

[33] Prosecutions and civil law injunctions have been sought against substance-abusing pregnant women in the United States: Jos, Marshall and Perlmutter, "The Charleston Policy on Cocaine use during Pregnancy: A Cautionary Tale" (1995) 23 *J Law, Med and Ethics* 120; Glaze, "Combatting Prenatal Substance Abuse: Court Ordered Protective Custody of the Fetus" (1997) 80 *Marquette LR* 793.

[34] D would, however, be guilty of constructive manslaughter, on the basis that he has caused death by an unlawful and dangerous act. See further below, § 10.6ff.

[35] According to Lord Mustill, in these circumstances D's mens rea may be regarded as not directed to the foetus but to the human being if and when it comes into existence: [1997] 3 All ER 936, 949.

[36] This should follow from the rule that an intent to cause grievous bodily harm is sufficient mens rea for murder.

[37] *Mitchell* [1983] QB 741, confirmed in *A-G's Reference (No. 3 of 1994)* [1997] 3 All ER 936, 957.

[38] [1996] 2 All ER 10.

[39] Above, § 5.7.

girlfriend, and with that intention he had done an act causing the subsequent death of the child. Lord Mustill, in rejecting this view, expressed his dislike both of the rule that intent to cause grievous bodily harm sufficed as mens rea for murder and of the transferred intent principle generally. He accepted that these grounds of inculpation were too well entrenched to remove. Yet he declined, as we noted above, he put it, to "extend" the transferred intent principle to "double" transfers (first from the mother to the foetus, then from the foetus to the child it became).[40]

Clearly, *A-G's Reference (No. 3 of 1994)* decides that if D intends to cause serious harm to a pregnant V (which is sufficient mens rea for murder should V herself die) but does not intend to harm the foetus, he will be guilty of manslaughter but not murder should the foetus become a child who dies as a consequence of D's attack on the mother. The basis of this decision is elusive, giving rise to speculation about its ambit. Lord Mustill disliked the principle of transferred intent because he regarded it as based on a fiction. The fictional character of the transferred intent principle may, however, be queried. The principle may, instead, be taken to prescribe that the mere occurrence of unforeseen consequences does not preclude liability if the presence of those consequences is compatible with proof of the elements of the offence, in this case intending serious bodily harm and causing death thereby. Moreover, the House of Lords clearly accepted the substance of the transferred intent principle when it ruled that, in the case of manslaughter, it sufficed that D's conduct was dangerous and that the dangerousness of the act need not be identified in terms of any threat to the actual victim. Furthermore, recall that Lord Mustill refused to confirm the murder conviction on the basis of a compound dislike of the transferred intent principle and the rule that intent to cause serious harm sufficed as culpability for murder. Accordingly, we cannot be sure what the outcome would have been had D acted with intent to kill his girlfriend. Would Lord Mustill have countenanced a "double" transfer of intent then?

(b) Death[41]

At one time an entirely satisfactory legal account of death could be given in terms of the irreversible cessation of respiration and heartbeat. In most circumstances, such an account will still suffice. Take a person recovered unconscious from the sea. No heartbeat or respiration may be detectable, yet we would not pronounce that person dead if those faculties could be restored by manual or technological means. If the point of no return has been reached, ruling out recourse to such means, then the person is assuredly dead. But suppose it is possible to re-establish respiration and heartbeat by artificial means. Can we assume that life has been restored?

The answer to that question will depend on the condition of the patient. It may be that because of the length of time that the patient's brain was deprived of oxygen, the condition known as "brain-death" has arisen. This is an irreversible condition involving the complete non-functioning of the brain stem.[42] Identification of this condition is straightforward—a confirmed flat printout from an electroencephalography (EEG) machine.[43] There is an

---

[40] [1997] 3 All ER 936, 949.

[41] Dickens, "Death" in Kennedy and Grubb (eds.), *Principles of Medical Law* (1998) chap. 17.

[42] The brain stem controls reflexive functions of the body including breathing and heartbeat.

[43] "Criteria for the Diagnosis of Brain Stem Death" (1995) 29 *J Royal College of Physicians* 381–2.

[44] For references to international legislation, see Giesen, *International Medical Malpractice Law* (1988) 612, n. 73.

international medical consensus that brain-death is death *ipso facto* and many jurisdictions have passed legislation stipulating brain-death as a criterion of death.[44] There has been no legislative response for England and Wales. However, in *Bland*,[45] three law lords assumed that destruction of the brain stem entailed death.[46] In *Re A (a minor)*,[47] a civil case, there was a first instance ruling that brain stem death was, for legal purposes, death. It would be surprising if a contrary view were to be taken.

Nonetheless, it is not universally agreed that brain-dead persons sustained mechanically are to be regarded as dead. Peter Singer, for instance, maintains that the locution "pink, supple and dead" is contradictory.[48] Certainly the body of a continuously respirated brain-dead person is a living organism. Should terminating the vitality of such an organism be regarded as causing the death of a human being? Current medical practice assumes that such organisms are no longer persons.[49] Considerable expense would be incurred and beneficent transplant and grafting surgery precluded were an appellate court to rule that brain-dead persons are live persons. It is not easy to see what value such a judgment would advance and, accordingly, we will assume here that brain-death is death *tout court.*

Any condition affecting the brain which is less radical than brain-death is unlikely to be legally designated a form of death. The House of Lords in *Bland*[50] decided that a person in a persistent vegetative state (PVS) was alive and made the same assumption for persons in profound and permanent coma. One may ponder whether persons permanently lacking any form of sentient life, wholly cut off from any form of interaction with other people, are in morally different case from persons who are brain dead. Yet there are strong pragmatic reasons for drawing a distinction between brain-death and other forms of non-sentience. There are reliable and easily applied criteria for determining the presence of brain-death.[51] The condition is completely irreversible and there is no prospect of any effective medical intervention. By contrast, diagnosis of the profundity and duration of states which fall short of brain-death is a far less certain procedure. Questions about the appropriate treatment of PVS and comatose patients can and should be debated in terms of the quality and meaning of life, a debate which should not be foreclosed by any stipulative definition of death.[52] Accordingly, it is submitted that any mental condition which does not amount to brain-death should be regarded as compatible with the presence of life.

(ii) Causation in homicide

We have already discussed principles of causation in criminal law.[53] As there are no principles of causation distinctive to homicide, we need not discuss causation in any detail here. Nonetheless, some reference to causation is in order as homicide cases provide some striking

---

[44] [1993] 1 AC 789 (HL).
[45] *Ibid.*, 856 (Lord Keith), 863 (Lord Goff), 878 (Lord Browne-Wilkinson).
[47] [1992] 3 Med L Rev 303 (Fam D).
[48] *Rethinking Life and Death* (1994) 24.
[49] Dickens, "Death" in Kennedy and Grubb (eds.), *Principles of Medical Law* (1998) 870–3.
[50] [1993] 1 AC 789.
[51] "Criteria for the Diagnosis of Brain Stem Death" (1995) 29 *J Royal College of Physicians* 381–2.
[52] Dworkin, *Life's Dominion* (1993) chap. 7.
[53] Above, § 4.2.

examples of cases where causal principles are taken to their limits—and even beyond. When a person who is at fault is somehow connected to a result so grave as death, there is a disposition to attribute causal responsibility to the blameworthy agent. This sometimes results in strained causal attributions, particularly in cases where some other person, not morally at fault, seems more directly responsible for causing the death.

Pagett[54] is a case in point. D took V hostage before emerging from a house, which was circled by armed police, with V clasped to him as a human shield. D fired at the police, who returned his fire. V died after being struck by a police bullet. The police response was found to be lawful conduct by way of self-defence. D was found guilty of manslaughter on the basis that his conduct was a cause of V's death.

Before we scrutinise the reasoning in the case, it should be stated at the outset that there would have been a failure of justice had not D been found guilty of the manslaughter of V as a principal offender. The police reaction was a reasonable one to an emergency not of their making. Goff LJ, however, eased the way for a finding of causal agency against D by describing the police reaction as "involuntary". Under that description, the police involved need not be regarded as voluntary informed actors and were allowed to drop out of the causal picture.

Yet it is possible to envisage circumstances where it would be inapt to describe interventions such as the police action in *Pagett* as involuntary conduct but where the moral pressure to attribute causal agency to someone not obviously the causal agent of the death would be as strong. Suppose that T, an armed duty policeman, is observing D, a terrorist. He sees that E is about to activate a control device which will detonate a bomb planted further down the crowded street. There are only seconds left, with no way to stop D except by shooting her. T takes the decision to shoot, aware of the risk that the bullet may strike someone else. The bullet kills V, an innocent person. There is a powerful case for holding D responsible for V's death. But it would be implausible to describe T's conduct as involuntary.

This example reveals that, in the context of intervening agents, something deeper than mechanical causal principles is at work when we designate a blameworthy person a causal agent. The sentiment laying behind the causal findings in such cases depends in part on a recognition of who bears primary moral responsibility for the untoward outcome. Such a finding may be made against a person who, under mechanical accounts of cause and effect, is not a causal agent. Risking a generalisation, we may say that if D, by her wrongful act or omission, places V in a situation where he is killed by the justified conduct of T, responsibility for the fact of V's death will be attributed to D as a principal offender.[55] Moreover, the same conclusion will follow even if T's conduct is merely excused, provided T's conduct is a reasonably foreseeable response to the situation D has created. In these situations, T's conduct may even be fully informed and voluntary. As we saw in Chapter 4, what counts is not whether her conduct is "involuntary" but whether—to borrow a different phrase from *Pagett*—whether T's conduct is "free, deliberate and informed."[56] Because of D's conduct, T does not intervene freely. D remains causally responsible for V's death.

---

[54] (1983) 76 Cr App R 279 (CA).

[55] For discussion of the nature of justification and of excuse see further below, § 17.2.

[56] (1983) 76 Cr App R 279, 288–9. See above, § 4.2(iii)(b), in particular Case 1, and § 4.2(iii)(e).

Moral questions of justification and excuse, as well as questions of foreseeability, can therefore affect the attribution of an actus reus to D. In practice, however, the dependence of causation on moral accountability is sometimes pushed too far by the courts, especially in cases of homicide. In *Kennedy*,[57] for example, D handed V a syringe containing heroin which V used to inject herself. V died from the effect of the drug. D was held responsible, qua principal, for the death. But, as we saw in § 4.2(iii)(d), the decision seems wrong: V died by her own hand. On standard doctrine, V's conduct was free, deliberate, and informed and therefore a *novus actus interveniens*, notwithstanding D's associated culpability. Less straightforward is a situation, as in *Daliwal*,[58] where V committed suicide after enduring considerable physical abuse over an extended period of time. The Court of Appeal was open to the argument that a suicide that was influenced by D's abuse could be considered an event caused by D.[59] That would seem a reasonable conclusion if V's suicide was an act of desperation induced by the abusive (and criminal) conduct of D.

The entanglement of moral issues with causal questions is evident in Devlin J's widely discussed judgment in *Adams*,[60] where he considered the position of a doctor dispensing analgesic drugs to a terminal patient. On the assumption that the drugs were administered to relieve pain, the underlying pathology responsible for the patient's terminal condition should, according to the learned judge, be regarded as the sole cause of death even if the drugs had brought forward the time of death by "minutes, hours or even, perhaps, days." This analysis should be doubted. It confuses motive with cause. If the same acceleration of death were brought about with a malevolent motive—say, to enjoy an inheritance sooner— then death would surely have been attributable to the drugs.[61] Similarly, subject to the *de minimis* proviso,[62] medical treatment that hastens death *is* a cause of death. (It is mens rea that is missing, not the actus reus.) Particularly in a homicide context, we must be alert to the drawing of causal distinctions, like Devlin J's, which are unwarranted by causal doctrine.[63]

---

[57] [1999] 1 Cr App R 54; upheld on an alternative ground of principal responsibility in *Kennedy (No. 2)* [2005] EWCA Crim 685: whereas, in *Kennedy (No. 1)*, D was held straightforwardly to have caused death, on appeal it was said that V's conduct was not a *novus actus* because D and V had "acted in concert"—so that they were, in effect, treated as joint principals. On the facts of the case, the substitute explanation is no more satisfactory. See further above, § 4.2(iii)(d) (Case 2).

[58] [2006] EWCA Crim 1139.

[59] In the event, the conviction for manslaughter was quashed as the prosecution based its case on the allegation that the last assault made by D on V was the cause of V's decision to commit suicide, declining to argue that D's abusive conduct overall was the cause of her suicide. The Court of Appeal considered that D's last assault in isolation was an insufficient cause of V's suicide but considered that the manslaughter charge might have succeeded had the prosecution's case proceeded on a wider basis: see further Horder and McGowan, "Manslaughter by Causing Another's Suicide" [2006] *Crim LR* 1035.

[60] [1957] Crim LR 365.

[61] See too *Le Brun* [1992] 1 QB 61 where, in the context of a manslaughter charge, different motivations made for different conclusions concerning the causal status of an act. D knocked V unconscious with a non-life-threatening blow and subsequently caused her death by picking her up and accidentally dropping her. The Court of Appeal held that the assault was to be regarded as a cause of death because D picked up V for a bad reason (to take her to a place where she did not want to go). If, however, he had picked her up with a good motive (seeking medical help) the assault would not have been, legally, a cause of death. The result reached in the case seems the right one but it is unnecessary to resolve the issue in these confused causal terms: see further Sullivan, "Contemporaneity of Actus Reus and Mens Rea" [1993] *CLJ* 487, 495–500. The case is properly dealt with on the *Thabo Meli* principle: above, § 5.8(i)(b).

[62] Above, § 4.2(ii)(a). This seems to be the best explanation of *Adams* itself.

[63] For an effective critique of causal doctrine featuring some well-known homicide decisions, see Norrie, "A Critique of Criminal Causation" (1991) 54 *MLR* 685.

(iii) Acts, omissions, and homicide

Well-known definitions of murder and manslaughter given by institutional authors such as Coke employ the terms "kill" and "killing" in their formulations of the conduct to be proved against D.[64] Accordingly, at one time, there was scope for an argument that "merely" allowing V to die could not constitute the actus reus of either murder or manslaughter, even if it could be established that D owed V a duty of care. This argument was put forward in *Gibbins and Proctor*,[65] where D was charged with murder on the basis of a deliberate failure to feed her infant stepdaughter. Unsurprisingly, on the facts of the case, the argument failed. A deliberate strategy to starve someone to death can legitimately be described as a killing— "I killed him by starving him to death" is a perfectly sensible locution. By contrast, failures to provide essential sustenance by mismanagement and incompetence, as in *Instan*,[66] or failures of supervision, such as the negligent failure of the railway crossing keeper in *Pittwood*[67] to close the gates before the arrival of the train, are less obviously designated "killings". The conviction for manslaughter in each of these cases indicates that the expressions "kill" and "killing" are not to be taken too literally. They should be regarded as synonymous with "cause death" and "causing death".[68] The notion of cause will accommodate failures by D to prevent the avoidable death of V where it can be maintained that it was D's duty to prevent V's death and that she possessed the capacity to do so.[69]

Accordingly, the distinction between acts and omissions presents no difficulties that are peculiar to homicide. That said, *ad hoc* use of the act/omissions distinction has sometimes been judicially employed in order to contain the scope of certain forms of homicide. The form of manslaughter known as constructive manslaughter is, as we shall see below, of very wide ambit. It would be broader still had not unlawful omissions been excluded from its scope by the definitional fiat of the Court of Appeal in *Lowe*.[70] In the same vein, it appears that D does not commit suicide should he refuse food or essential medical treatment while aware that refusal entails his certain death;[71] a matter of great moment for those caring for D, who might otherwise find themselves accomplices in his suicide.[72] Likewise, V does not commit suicide should she ask to be removed from a life-support system;[73] but V will be asking for help in an act of suicide should she request assistance to take an active substance

---

[64] "Murder is when a man of sound memory, and of the age of discretion, unlawfully killeth within any county of the realm any reasonable creature in *rerum natura* under the king's peace, with malice aforethought, either expressed by the party or implied by law": Coke, 3 Inst 47.

[65] (1918) 13 Cr App R 134.

[66] [1893] 1 QB 450.

[67] (1902) 19 TLR 37.

[68] Stephen, *Digest of Criminal Law* (4th ed., 1887) 138, cited with approval in *A-G's Reference (No. 3 of 1994)* [1998] AC 245 (HL).

[69] Moore, amongst others, has argued against the view that omissions can be causes of events: *Act and Crime* (1993) 30–1. His position seems well founded in terms of mechanical causation. As is argued above, § 4.2(iv)(a), causative effect may only be attributed to omissions on the basis of a counterfactual narrative—the daughter would have lived had she been fed; the driver of the cart would not have been killed had the gate been shut etc. Bearing in mind the burden of proof, one should have great confidence that death would have been averted if D performed the relevant duty. Unfortunately, this requirement is sometimes overlooked: see *Stone* [1977] QB 354.

[70] [1973] QB 702 (CA).

[71] *Secretary of State v. Robb* [1995] 1 All ER 677 (CA).

[72] Suicide Act 1961, s. 2.

[73] *Re B (adult: refusal of Medical Treatment)* [2002] 2 All ER 449.

that will end her life.[74] In both cases, the exercise of V's autonomy requires the assistance of others. However, the former situation is characterised as the refusal of treatment: her physical removed from life support is, legally, an omission to provide further treatment where active assistance in the taking of a fatal substence remains an illegal act.[75] Liability for omissions will arise only if D can be said to be under a duty to prevent V's death. In medical contexts, in particular, D may find herself under a duty to sustain V's life in the first instance but then be relieved from that duty should it be determined that V's best interests do not require the sustaining of his life.[76] The cessation of the duty to keep V alive is, of course, without prejudice to the overarching duty imposed on us all not to cause the death of others by a positive act.[77] That latter duty sits awkwardly with the well-established practice of closing down systems of life support in the light of a patient's wishes or a decision that the patient's best interests no longer require the sustaining of his life. On the face of it, the step-by-step procedure involved in shutting down a life-support system seems, indubitably, an act of commission comparable, say, to the simpler task of switching off a television. Be that as it may, Lord Goff in *Bland* considered that the removal of life support was to be regarded as an omission: in such cases the cause of death is attributed to the underlying pathology which necessitated life support and the removal of life support, is merely a failure to suppress this underlying cause.[78] Lord Goff's argument proves too much. It would equally apply to, say, a situation where D conceals V's insulin intending that V should die from his unpalliated diabetic symptoms. Nonetheless, Lord Goff's position, though analytically unconvincing, has the instrumental value of protecting medical personnel from liability for murder or manslaughter when carrying out what are now routine procedures of terminating life support.

(iv) Abolition of the year and a day rule

At common law, in order for D to be held responsible for V's death, the death had to occur within one year and a day of the act or omission by D that caused it.[79] The rule was of great antiquity and obscure in origin and rationale.[80] By early modern times, the rule was justified in terms of the difficulty of proving that D's conduct was a cause of V's death after the lapse of such a period of time. The current wide availability of life-support technology for the seriously injured renders such a rationalisation untenable, and the rule is now abolished by the Law Reform (Year and a Day Rule) Act 1996[81] in respect of offences concerned with the causing of death and of suicide.

The Act brings homicide cases into line with other indictable offences. However, there are

---

[74] *R (on the application of Pretty)* [2002] 1 All ER 1.

[75] For critical discussion see Tur, "Legislative Technique and Human Rights: The Sad Case of Assisted Suicide [2003] *Crim LR* 3.

[76] *Airedale NHS Trust v. Bland* [1993] AC 789.

[77] All the judgments in *Bland* emphasise that although it may be in a patient's best interests not to be kept alive, no patient, whatever her condition and whatever her wishes, may be killed. See too *Cox* (1992) 12 BMLR 38.

[78] [1993] AC 789, 866.

[79] In the classic definition of murder given by Coke, V must die "of the wound or hurt, etc., within a year or a day of the same": 3 Inst, 47.

[80] Yale, "A Year and a Day in Homicide" [1989] *CLJ* 202.

[81] Section 1.

potentially oppressive situations for an accused person which may arise in homicide contexts. There may be a considerable lapse of time occurring between the injury caused by D and the ultimate death of V. During that time D will face the prospect of prosecution for some form of homicide in circumstances where he may already have been tried and convicted for an offence arising from the initial injury. Accordingly, the Act provides that proceedings in respect of a "fatal offence" may be instituted only if the Attorney-General gives consent whenever the injury that causes death is sustained more than three years before death occurs or if the accused has previously been convicted of an offence in circumstances alleged to be connected with the death.[82]

(v) The Queen's Peace

Any human being can be the victim of homicide with the exception of persons who are not "under the Queen's Peace". Accordingly, causing the deaths of alien enemies in the course of war lays no ground for a homicide prosecution.[83] The same probably applies to rebels who, at the time they were killed, were engaged in hostile operations against the Crown.[84]

As a matter of history, operations of war involving subjects of the Crown have been predominantly carried out overseas. On normal rules of criminal jurisdiction, which apply a territoriality principle, killings perpetrated overseas would in any event not be justiciable here. However, section 9 of the OAPA 1861 provides that any murder or manslaughter committed by any subject of the Crown on land out of the United Kingdom may be tried and punished in England. The specific exception for those not under the Queen's Peace is therefore essential.

§ 10.3 Murder

(i) The mental element in murder[85]

The traditional definition of murder is that it is a homicide committed with "malice aforethought". This definition is no longer useful; neither malice[86] nor forethought[87] is necessary, or sufficient, for a finding of murder. For many years past, malice aforethought has been a purely technical expression meaning nothing more than those mental states recognised by the common law as sufficiently culpable to make a homicide murder. Before the Homicide Act 1957, there were three kinds of malice aforethought—"express", "implied", and

---

[82] Section 2.

[83] It is homicide if an enemy alien is killed other than in the course of war: *Maria v. Hall* (1807) 1 Taunt 33, 36, 127 ER 741.

[84] 1 Hale PC 433.

[85] Goff, "The Mental Element in the Crime of Murder" (1988) 104 *LQR* 30; Williams, "The Mens Rea for Murder: Leave it Alone" (1989) 105 *LQR* 387; Wilson, "A Plea for Rationality in the Law of Murder" (1990) 10 *LS* 307; House of Lords, *Report of the Select Committee on Murder and Life Imprisonment* (Session 1988–89) HL Paper 78, paras. 30–38.

[86] It is murder, for example, if D's intentional killing of V is done from motives of compassion, say because V has a painful, terminal illness.

[87] A spontaneous intentional killing is murder in the absence of any justification, excuse, or extenuation.

"constructive". Express malice required an intent to cause death. Implied malice was established by proof of an intention to cause grievous bodily harm. Constructive malice aforethought was present if D caused death while committing or attempting to commit a felony or when resisting lawful arrest. If a causal connection between the causing of death and commission of the felony or resistance to the arrest was established, it was immaterial that D intended neither to kill nor to cause grievous bodily harm.[88]

Constructive malice was taken to be too indiscriminate in its operation[89] and was abolished by section 1 of the Homicide Act 1957. The Act makes clear that implied as well as express malice survives the abolition of constructive malice.[90] We will not further employ these anachronistic terms; it is better simply to refer to *an intent to cause death* and *an intent to cause grievous bodily harm* as the two forms of mental element currently sufficient under English law to constitute the mens rea of murder.

(a) Intent to cause grievous bodily harm

As indicated, an intent to cause grievous bodily harm remains sufficient mens rea for murder. It has survived several attempts to unseat it. In *Vickers*,[91] D had been convicted of murder on the basis that he intended to cause grievous bodily harm. The argument was put on behalf of D that, since causing grievous bodily harm with intent was, at that time, a felony in its own right, to convict someone of murder on the ground of proof of such an intent was effectively to resurrect the principle of constructive malice. The Court of Criminal Appeal rejected this argument. To kill by causing grievous bodily harm was not to cause death by an offence separate from the killing. The infliction of bodily harm was the direct cause of death.

In the subsequent case of *Hyam*,[92] where the House of Lords sought to resolve the definition of the mens rea for murder, Lord Diplock, with the assent of Lord Kilbrandon, rejected as a sufficient mental element the mere intent to cause grievous bodily harm. He considered that, historically, the erstwhile constructive malice doctrine had unduly inhibited the development and refinement of the mental element for the crime. Without that restraint, he divined judges would have confined murder to circumstances where D either intended to kill or intentionally caused grievous bodily harm *knowing* that his conduct threatened the life of the victim.[93] With constructive malice abolished, Lord Diplock concluded that the House was free to express the mens rea for murder in the form it would have attained without the constraint of the felony/murder rule.

Of the three remaining law lords in *Hyam*, Lords Hailsham and Dilhorne refused to go

---

[88] In *Beard* [1920] AC 479, evidence of intoxication was admissible on the question whether D had formed an intent to kill or cause grievous bodily harm to V. However, the evidence clearly established that D had attempted to rape V and in the course of his attempt had killed V. Under the felony murder doctrine, that in itself made the killing murder. As stated in the text above, the doctrine is now abolished.

[89] *Royal Commission on Capital Punishment* Cmnd. 8932 (1953) 24–8.

[90] Homicide Act 1957, s. 1: "where a person kills another in the course or furtherance of some other offence, the killing shall not amount to murder unless done with the same malice aforethought (*express or implied*) as is required for a killing or to amount to murder when not done in the course or furtherance of some other offence" (emphasis added).

[91] [1957] 2 QB 664.

[92] [1975] AC 55.

[93] *Ibid.*, 89–93.

along with Lord Diplock's striking version of counterfactual history. Remarkably, the fifth judge, Lord Cross, refused to make a decision on the matter, acknowledging force in both positions. Instead, he confirmed the verdict of murder on the "assumption" that an intent to cause grievous bodily harm constituted sufficient mens rea.[94] This lack of resolution entailed a subsequent appeal on the matter in *Cunningham*.[95] Here, a differently constituted House of Lords ruled by a majority that an intent to cause grievous bodily harm was sufficient mens rea for murder. Criticism continues at the highest judicial level of a law of murder which allows convictions for this grave offence without proof of any culpability element that refers to the element of death—a "fiction" according to Lord Mustill.[96] The criticism has particular force in circumstances where the harm in question, although "really serious", is not harm which constitutes, of itself, a threat to life. As Lord Edmund-Davies observed in his dissenting speech in *Cunningham*, a broken arm is "really serious"[97] but an intent to inflict such an injury should be regarded as insufficient for the most serious of crimes.[98] Yet despite the continuing vein of judicial criticism,[99] the law is settled by *Cunningham* and any future change will require legislation.

(b) Intent is subjective

The intent to be proved in a case of murder is the intent possessed by D *herself* at the time of the acts or omissions alleged to be the cause of death. This may appear so obvious a requirement as not to be worth stating. Such a statement of the obvious needs to be made, however, because of the notorious decision of the House of Lords in *DPP* v. *Smith*.[100] The House of Lords startled professional and academic opinion by ruling that D could be presumed to have intended to cause death or grievous bodily harm to V if a reasonable person, placed in the same situation as D and with D's knowledge of the surrounding circumstances, would have foreseen the causing of death or grievous bodily harm to V as a natural and probable consequence of her conduct. What precisely this formulation conveyed was a matter of intense debate.[101] An entirely tenable view of the decision was that it allowed a conviction for murder on the basis of negligence, on the foresight of the reasonable person rather than the accused. The controversy the decision aroused led to the preparation of a two-clause Bill by the Law Commission which, had it been enacted as it stood, would clearly have overturned *Smith*.[102] However, only one clause was enacted, being the clause that subsequently became section 8 of the Criminal Justice Act 1967. The clause that focused directly on the decision in *Smith* was dropped.

---

[94] *Ibid.*, 97–8.

[95] [1982] AC 566.

[96] *A-G's Reference (No. 3 of 1994)* [1998] AC 245, 262.

[97] The interpretation of grievous bodily harm given in *DPP* v. *Smith* [1961] AC 290, 334. And see now *Bollom* [2003] EWCA Crim 2846 where the court of Appeal confirmed that harm which raised no risk to the life of V could constitute serious bodily harm.

[98] [1982] AC 566, 582–3. In terms of the discussion of moral luck above, § 6.5(i), this would be an injury where consequent death was a matter of extrinsic rather than intrinsic luck.

[99] *Powell, Daniels and English* [1999] 1 AC 1, 11 (Lord Mustill), 14–15 (Lord Steyn); *Woollin* [1999] AC 82, 90 (Lord Steyn).

[100] [1961] AC 290.

[101] Contrast Denning, *Responsibility Before the Law* (1961) with Williams, *The Mental Element in Crime* (1965) chap. 1.

[102] Law Com. No. 10, *Imported Criminal Intent (Director of Public Prosecutions v. Smith)* (1967) 17.

It will be recalled that section 8 deals with *proof* of intent and foresight;[103] it has nothing to say on the definition of these terms, or about when intent or foresight need be proved. On one reading of this legislative history, the decision in *Smith* remained intact, Parliament having explicitly rejected a provision that would have reversed it. If *Smith* still stood, it followed that murder was defined in a manner that did not require proof of intent or foresight on the part of D. Accordingly, section 8 would be irrelevant to the issue of the culpability required for murder; the section applies only when the definition of an offence requires proof of intent or foresight on the part of D.

Whatever the force of this reasoning, from the moment section 8 came into force, appellate courts regarded *Smith* as overturned[104] and this has been uncritically reiterated many times, most recently by the House of Lords in *Woollin*.[105] Furthermore, the Privy Council in *Frankland*[106] advised that *Smith* had been based on a misunderstanding of the common law and should no longer be followed in a common law jurisdiction which did not possess the equivalent of section 8. *Smith*, it seems, has been remaindered safely to legal history: the intent required for murder is an intent that the accused herself must be proved to have possessed.

(c) The meaning of intent in murder

In our discussion in Chapter 5 of intent, a "core" meaning of the term was identified as well as an alternative, non-core meaning. D intends to cause V's death (or grievous bodily harm), in the core or primary sense, if he acts in order to cause death (or grievous bodily harm) to V or if he causes death (or grievous bodily harm) as a necessary means to some other end. When D acts in one of these states of mind, his conduct will normally take the form of a direct attack on V. In such cases Lord Bridge's "Golden Rule" applies:[107]

> "When directing a jury on the mental element necessary in a crime of specific intent, the judge should avoid any elaboration or paraphrase of what is meant by intent and leave it to the jury's good sense to decide whether the accused acted with the necessary intent."

This approach is commendably straightforward. Where V has died following an attack by D with a gun, knife, or heavy implement, a very strong inference arises that D attacked in order to kill or seriously hurt V. The jury may be safely left to draw that inference in the absence of any reason why they should not do so.

Such an uncomplicated approach is impossible where there is no compelling evidence that D intended to kill or cause grievous bodily harm in this core sense. Take a case where D sets fire to a house in order to make a fraudulent insurance claim in respect of the damage he will cause. He is aware that the house is occupied by V and that it is virtually certain that V will perish in the fire. Here there may be no evidence that D intends the death of V in the core sense of that term. He may be wholly indifferent whether V lives or dies. The existence or non-existence of V may have no bearing whatever on the success of his fraudulent claim. Consequently, were D to be charged with the murder of V, this would be one of those "rare

---

[103] See above, § 5.1(ix), where s. 8 is quoted in the text.
[104] *Wallett* [1968] 2 QB 367.
[105] [1999] AC 82.
[106] [1987] AC 576.
[107] *Moloney* [1985] AC 905, 926.

cases" where a direction on intention of the kind laid down by the House of Lords in *Woollin* would be required:[108]

> "the jury should be directed that they are not entitled to find the necessary intention, unless they feel sure that death or serious injury was a virtual certainty (barring some unforeseen intervention) as a result of the defendant's actions and that the defendant appreciated that such was the case."

As we saw above in § 5.1(iv), *Woollin* establishes that foresight of virtual certainty is the basis of finding intention in the secondary, non-core sense. Ideally, *Woollin* should be read as establishing that proof of foresight on the part of D that it is virtually certain he will cause death (or grievous bodily harm) to V *constitutes* an intent, in the secondary non-core sense, to cause death (or grievous bodily harm).[109] But, as previously discussed, because of the way the *Woollin* direction is expressed and because of pre-*Woollin* case law, there is space for an interpretation to the effect that proof of the state of mind the direction identifies is merely evidence from which intent may be inferred and does not constitute intent *per se*.[110] Such a reading was endorsed by the Court of Appeal in *Matthews and Alleyne*.[111] To read the decision in this manner is unfortunate. It is when we lack evidence of intent in the core sense that a *Woollin* direction is required. It would be puzzling to insist that foresight that an outcome is virtually certain is mere evidence on which a finding of intent (in the secondary sense) to cause that outcome may be based. Far better to hold that appreciation on the part of D that his conduct is virtually certain to cause a particular result *constitutes* an intent (in a secondary, non-core sense) to cause that result, otherwise we are in the dark as to what constitutes this alternative form of intent. This is exemplified by *Mathews and Alleyne* itself. D and others threw V into the River Trent when it was in mid-winter flood and despite their awareness that V could not swim. The trial judge directed the jury that they should convict D of murder if D appreciated that V's death by drowning was a virtual certainty. That was held to be a misdirection. The jury should have been told that they were entitled to find D guilty of murder should they choose to do so. Yet the conviction for murder was confirmed on the basis that any reasonable jury properly directed would have convicted on such evidence. Why such certainty? Because the jury could have had no doubt that D knew V was virtually certain to drown. So it seems that for non-core intent there is in reality nothing beyond the perception of practical certainty; it is unfortunate that obfuscation was not put to one side.

To conclude, we can say that D will have the mens rea for murder if:

(i)   he acts in order to kill or cause grievous bodily harm; or

(ii)   he kills or causes grievous bodily harm as a means to some other end he is seeking to achieve.

Additionally, a jury can be told that they are entitled to make a finding of intent against D if:

---

108 [1999] AC 82, 90.
109 Simester, "Murder, Mens Rea and the House of Lords—Again" (1999) 115 *LQR* 17.
110 Above, § 5.1(iv). See also Norrie, "After *Woollin*" [1999] *Crim LR* 532.
111 [2003] 2 Cr App R 30.

(iii)   his conduct is virtually certain to cause death or grievous bodily harm and he appreciates that his conduct is virtually certain to cause death or grievous bodily harm.

There may be one sphere, however, where the state of mind identified in (iii) may not suffice. In *Bland*, Lord Goff considered that a doctor administering pain-relieving drugs to a terminal patient would not be guilty of murder, or any other offence, if the patient's death were accelerated as a known side-effect of this palliative care.[112] *Dicta* from other appellate cases[113] indicate that a doctor will not be criminally responsible for any consequences brought about as a side-effect of treatment given in what a responsible body of medical opinion would consider the best interests of the patient. Indeed, in *Gillick* Lord Scarman went so far as to state that "the bona fide exercise by a doctor of his clinical judgment must be a complete negation of the guilty mind."[114] Whatever scope is given to that statement, in the context of murder it is clear that any exemption for medical personnel from the scope of the offence is confined to the side-effects of treatment and does not embrace fatal means to a desired objective. If, as in *Cox*,[115] the acceleration of death is used as a means of terminating pain, liability will be incurred irrespective of the gravity of the pain, the lack of any other means of palliation, and the considered wishes of the patient. Whether a distinction between means and side-effects should be accorded such decisive effect in these distressing cases is, of course, a matter of intense ethical debate.

In a recent report,[116] the English Law Commission has in substance recommended codifying the law relating to intent in murder. Under their proposals, D will be taken to intend a result if she acts in order to bring it about and, additionally, a jury "*may*" make a finding of intent if it is shown that D "thought the result was a virtually certain consequence of his or her action." A welcome advance on the current position is that D need only think a result to have been virtually certain: the prosecution would not have to prove that the result was in fact virtually certain, ensuring an exclusive focus on the culpability of D. But, as under the current law, the jury in this case of non-core intent may choose whether or not to make the ultimate finding of intent. The basis of such a finding is left a deliberate blank by the Commission, who favour unstructured moral evaluations as a basis for findings of intent.

(ii)   The ambit of murder—an evaluation

Any evaluation of the defining elements of murder cannot leave out of account the mandatory sentence of life imprisonment that the offence attracts.[117] Many offences are defined in very general terms and encompass conduct that varies enormously in terms of its content and its culpability. Theft, for instance, ranges from taking the apple from the orchard to sophisticated frauds involving the electronic manipulation of huge sums of

---

[112] [1993] AC 789.

[113] *Re J* [1990] 3 All ER 930, 938.

[114] [1986] 1 AC 112, 190.

[115] (1992) 12 BMLR 38.

[116] *Murder, Manslaughter and Infanticide*, Law Com. No. 304 (2006). For discussion, see Norrie, "Between Orthodox and Moral Contextualism" [2006] *Crim LR* 486.

[117] Murder (Abolition of the Death Penalty) Act 1965.

money. Of course, the apple thief and the large-scale fraudster will receive very different treatment at the hands of the court, a latitude facilitated by the discretionary sentencing scheme provided in the event of a conviction for theft.[118] By contrast, because each murder receives the same draconian penalty, in principle there ought to be a large degree of similarity in the culpability evinced by each particular murder. A moment's reflection, however, reveals that murder, like other offences, spans a range of differing culpabilities:[119]

> "Murder, as every practitioner of the law knows, though often described as one of the utmost heinousness, is not in fact necessarily so, but consists in a whole bundle of offences of vastly differing degrees of culpability, ranging from brutal, cynical and repeated offences like the so-called Moors murders (*R v. Brady and Hindley* (6 May 1966, unreported)) to the almost venial, if objectively immoral, 'mercy killing' of a beloved partner."

Why, then, the unyielding fixed penalty? The origin of the mandatory life sentence is to be found in the political process that lead to the passing of the Murder (Abolition of Death Penalty) Act 1965. There would not have been a parliamentary majority for the abolition of the death penalty in murder had not the supporters of abolition undertaken that each and every conviction for murder should attract a mandatory life sentence.[120] There was then, and remains now, a strong public sentiment that murder is a special offence which should be marked on each occasion by a special penalty. Those who argue for retention of the mandatory life sentence (or for reintroduction of the death penalty) assert that the intentional taking of any life merits a life sentence and/or that an unyielding and draconian response is an effective deterrent for those who would otherwise kill. *Contra*, two authoritative committees which have investigated the issue found neither argument persuasive and recommended a discretionary sentencing regime for the offence.[121] Nonetheless, the Government has indicated its intention to retain the mandatory sentence.[122]

The continuation of the mandatory life sentence for the indefinite future makes it all the more important that the definition of murder should be focused on the most culpable forms of killing. Beyond argument, the current definition of murder includes many persons convicted of the offence who do not merit a life term. Even though legal forms of extenuation, such as the defences of provocation and diminished responsibility, take outside the ambit of murder some defendants who would otherwise be convicted for the offence, murder remains too inclusive an offence. It may be argued that the situation is not as draconian as it may seem because, as is well known, a prisoner serving a mandatory life term will rarely spend the rest of her life in prison. Nonetheless, the position of a person serving a mandatory life sentence is unenviable. A life sentence contains a literal truth in that any release is a release on licence that may be revoked by administrative rather than judicial decision. The release decision for a mandatory lifer is now entrusted to the Parole Board rather than the Home Secretary, following reform of the mandatory life-sentencing

---

[118] From an absolute discharge to 7 years' imprisonment: Criminal Justice Act 1991, s. 26.

[119] *Howe* [1987] 1 All ER 771, 781.

[120] The Bill that became the Murder (Abolition of Death Penalty) Act 1965 was a private member's Bill passed on a free vote.

[121] Report of the Advisory Council on the Penal System: *Sentences of Imprisonment* (1978) paras. 235–244; House of Lords, Select Committee on Murder and Life Imprisonment (Session 1988–89) HL Paper 78, paras. 108–118.

[122] *Hansard*, HL, 11 June 1997, WA 83.

process instituted by the Criminal Justice Act 2003.[123] Under the scheme of the Act, the trial judge must determine what term of years the prisoner should serve by way of retribution for his offence. Although what period of time should be served on this retributive basis is ultimately a matter for the judge,[124] there is a strong statutory presumption that the term should be at least 15 years or, according to the circumstances of the offence, 30 years or whole life. When the retributive part of the sentence is served, the Parole Board may delay release on licence if the prisoner's release is considered a risk for particular persons or the public generally. This regime is severe. Unlike prisoners serving a fixed term of years who are normally released after serving one-half of the term, persons subject to a mandatory life sentence must serve the retributive period of the sentence in full. It is imperative, therefore, that the scope of the offence of murder ensures as far as is possible that only those who warrant such treatment are convicted of the offence.

Criticism of the current scope of murder predominantly fixes on the fact that, in addition to an intention to kill, an intention to cause grievous bodily harm will suffice as mens rea. Those who support the current position argue that an intention to cause "really serious harm" is sufficiently heinous to warrant full responsibility for the fact of death, should that occur. Yet even if this is sometimes true, as a general proposition it is too broad; it may, for example, be murder if V dies as an untoward consequence of D's act of deliberately breaking V's arm. In the light of judicial criticism of this form of culpability,[125] it is surprising that grievous bodily harm has not been reinterpreted in the context of murder to require the causing of harm that is intrinsically dangerous to life. Yet even if that were done, there remains force in the argument that an offence designed to pick out the worst kinds of killings should require some advertence to the chance of causing death.

The Law Commission has recently proposed an offence of first-degree murder along these lines.[126] As recommended, it would be first-degree murder to kill with intent to kill, or to kill with intent to cause serious injury when aware of a serious risk of causing death.[127] Only first-degree murder with this welcome narrowing of culpability would attract a mandatory life sentence.[128]

Suppose the mens rea for the form of murder attracting a mandatory sentence were to be reformulated along these lines. The range of culpability falling within the compass of the offence, though significantly narrower than the current offence, nonetheless would remain extensive, as the range of circumstances where the mens rea for the offence may arise would still be considerable. At one time, English law looked to features beyond mens rea in an attempt to identify what forms of murder should attract a capital sentence. The same technique might be employed to determine which kinds of murder should attract a mandatory

---

[123] Section 269 and schedule 21.

[124] *Sullivan* [2004] EWCA Crim 1762, [2005] 1 Cr App R 3.

[125] *Cunningham* [1982] AC 566, 582–3 (Lord Edmund-Davies); *Powell and Daniels and English* [1999] 1 AC 1, 11 (Lord Mustill), 14–15 (Lord Steyn); *Woollin* [1999] AC 82, 90 (Lord Steyn).

[126] *Murder, Manslaughter and Infanticide*, Law Com. No. 304. (2006).

[127] For discussion, see Wilson, "The Structure of Criminal Homicide" [2006] *Crim LR* 471.

[128] The Commission proposes an offence of second-degree murder defined in terms of killings done with intent to cause serious injury or intended to cause injury or fear or risk of injury if D was aware of a serious risk of causing death. Additionally, it would be second-degree murder if D successfully raised diminished responsibility or provocation to a charge of first-degree murder. This second form of murder would not attract the mandatory penalty but could be punished with a life term if appropriate.

life sentence. Under now-repealed provisions of the Homicide Act 1957, factors such as killing a policeman or use of a firearm would make the offence a capital one.[129] Other jurisdictions make reference to such matters as the use of torture,[130] the use of poison,[131] a sexual motive, or the age of the victim.[132] However, in England, such an approach proved unsatisfactory. The grounds of aggravation were controversial and it was generally agreed that these subdivisions of the offence entailed fine distinctions which did not reliably track gradations of culpability.[133] Because, for political reasons, the mandatory penalty seems set to remain for the indefinite future,[134] there is much to be said for a definition of first-degree murder confined to killings done with intent to kill and it is to be regretted that the Law Commission did not remain faithful to their original proposal to this effect.[135] The partial defences to murder of provocation and diminished responsibility will remain important palliatives for an offence punished in such a rigid fashion.

§ 10.4 Manslaughter

(i) Introduction

At one time, under the common law, any killing which was unlawful but insufficiently grave to amount to murder would be designated manslaughter.[136] Nowadays, the element of unlawfulness attendant on the killing of V by D no longer suffices *per se*. The unlawfulness must take particular forms if a verdict of manslaughter is to follow. Yet even in its modern form, manslaughter is a crime of enormous scope. It is an offence that can be committed with several differing forms of culpability. Between these various ways of committing what is but a single offence, there is a major divide: the division between voluntary and involuntary manslaughter. Voluntary manslaughter refers to those killings perpetrated with an intent to kill or to cause grievous bodily harm, in circumstances which do not disclose any justification or excuse but where there is some form of legally recognised extenuation, established at the trial stage, which reduces what would otherwise be murder to manslaughter. Involuntary manslaughter does not require proof of an intent to kill or cause grievous bodily harm. In the sphere of involuntary manslaughter recklessness, or gross negligence, or

---

[129] Section 5(1) provided that murders done in furtherance of theft, by shooting or explosion, when avoiding arrest or escaping from custody, or of police officers and prison officers (and those assisting them) would constitute capital murder.

[130] Selaho Code, s. 18–4003(a).

[131] California Penal Code, s. 189.

[132] Ariz. Rev. Stat. Ann; s. 13–604.01(A).

[133] The class of capital murder in England and Wales was designed to capture not so much the worst killings in terms of innate culpability but those killings which most threatened order and stability, thereby warranting maximum deterrence. But this approach became discredited precisely because the line between capital and non-capital murder did not reliably track differing degrees of heinousness.

[134] The terms of reference given to the English Law Commission by the Home Office for a review of the law of murder instructed t.hat the mandatory penalty was to remain.

[135] LCCP No. 177.

[136] Up to the 19th century manslaughter was regarded as the residual category of homicide, into which fell all killings that were not justified, excusable, or murder: see Turner, *Kenny's Outlines of Criminal Law* (16th ed., 1952) 139–40.

the commission of certain "dangerous" criminal acts each provides a sufficient culpability for a manslaughter conviction.

(ii) Voluntary manslaughter

There are three forms of voluntary manslaughter: committing a prima facie murder in response to some incident or event which constitutes legally adequate provocation; committing a prima facie murder when afflicted by one or more of the conditions specified in section 2 of the Homicide Act 1957 (diminished responsibility); and committing prima facie murder in pursuance of a suicide pact. In each case, these grounds of mitigation will be relevant as legal extenuation only if it can be proved that D acted with intent to cause death or to cause grievous bodily harm; in the absence of proof of the culpability for murder, D may, in any event, be guilty of involuntary manslaughter or one of the statutory forms of homicide. Evidence of provocation or of mental conditions falling within section 2 may also be used to throw reasonable doubt on whether D did intend to kill or cause grievous bodily harm.[137] If, by reason of such evidence or by reference to other evidence, proof of the mens rea for murder is not established, evidence of provocation or mental disorder may still be relevant, but only at the sentencing stage following a verdict of manslaughter. But that is not our present concern, which is with *legal* extenuation; that is, situations where all the elements of murder are made out and provocation, diminished responsibility, or membership of a suicide pact is adduced to reduce the conviction to manslaughter.

At this juncture, only provocation will be discussed. The defence of diminished responsibility was introduced to remedy some of the deficiencies of the defence of insanity; diminished responsibility and insanity will be considered when we discuss the mental condition defences.[138] Membership of suicide pacts will be discussed when we consider the legal response to suicide and to those who assist it.[139]

§ 10.5 Provocation[140]

(i) Common law and statute

For many centuries, English law has partially condoned killings when done in a state of anger aroused by some form of provocation. The origins of this form of extenuation have been traced back to verdicts of medieval juries whereby certain spontaneous angry killings were treated, indulgently, as killing *se defendendo*, thereby avoiding a verdict of murder and

---

[137] As was pointed out in the context of provocation in *Richens* [1993] 4 All ER 877, the loss of self-control induced by the provocation must be compatible with proof of an intent to kill or to cause grievous bodily harm.

[138] Below, Chapter 19.

[139] Below, § 10.8.

[140] Ashworth, "The Doctrine of Provocation" [1976] *CLJ* 292; Dressler, "Rethinking Heat of Passion: A Defence in Search of a Rationale" (1982) 73 *J Crim L and Crim* 421; Horder, *Provocation and Responsibility* (1992); Sullivan, "Anger and Excuse: Reassessing Provocation" (1992) 12 *OJLS* 380; Nourse, "Passion's Progress; Modern Law Reform and the Provocation Defence" (1997) 106 *Yale LJ* 1331.

all its consequences.[141] From these beginnings, provocation ultimately emerged as a distinct partial defence to murder and generated its own body of principles and rules. The Royal Commission on Capital Punishment, which reported in 1953, concluded that the defence was, in some respects, too rigid and exclusionary.[142] Its recommendations led to the enactment of section 3 of the Homicide Act 1957:

> Where on a charge of murder there is evidence on which a jury can find that the person charged was provoked (whether by things done or by things said or by both together) to lose his self-control, the question whether the provocation was enough to make a reasonable man do as he did shall be left to be determined by the jury; and in determining that question the jury shall take into account everything both done and said according to the effect which, in their opinion, it would have on a reasonable man.

Section 3 does not replace the previous law. Its purpose is to amend and supplement the common law. The section itself has nothing to say about the effect of a successful plea of provocation which is still governed by the common law. The Act confirms that provocation is a matter of *legal* extenuation to be resolved at the trial stage and is confined to trials for murder.[143] Nothing is said about the burden of proof: at common law the burden of disproof is placed on the prosecution should there be any evidential foundation for a plea of provocation.[144]

The impact of section 3 on the common law has been the subject of many appeals. Before we turn to what was and may yet remain a disputatious and unstable body of law, it will be useful to summarise briefly those changes which statute has clearly brought about. The most fundamental of those changes is that, if there is evidence that D has lost self-control as a consequence of provocation, the issue of provocation *must* be put before a jury.[145] Prior to the enactment of section 3, there were two ways in which a trial judge could remove the issue from the jury despite evidence that D had killed in a state of anger induced by provocation. First, what might constitute adequate provocation fit to go to the jury was constrained by judicial discretion. In general terms, only violence or an *act* of adultery witnessed by D were allowed to count. Other forms of conduct and, in particular, "mere words" were ruled to be inadequate.[146] Secondly, even if D had responded to conduct which was a recognised form of provocation, his plea could nonetheless be dismissed by the judge's ruling that D's response to the provocation was disproportionate: "the mode of resentment must bear a reasonable relationship to the provocation if the offence is to be reduced to manslaughter."[147]

These two restrictions on the availability of the defence are expressly removed by the terms of section 3. Provocation may now take the form of "anything said or done", thereby

---

[141] Horder, *Provocation and Responsibility* (1992) chap. 1.

[142] Cmnd. 8932, para. 141.

[143] In *Cunningham* [1958] 3 All ER 711, where a charge of wounding with intent to cause grievous bodily harm was brought, and in *Bruzas* [1972] Crim LR 367, which concerned a charge of attempted murder, it was confirmed that provocation could not be argued at trial in order to avoid conviction for the offence charged: outwith murder, provocation arises only at the sentencing stage as a possible ground of mitigation.

[144] The principle in *Woolmington* [1935] AC 462 applies. See above, § 3.2.

[145] *Doughty* (1986) 83 Cr App R 319; *Johnson* [1989] 1 WLR 740.

[146] *Holmes* [1946] AC 588, 600.

[147] *Mancini* [1942] AC 1, 9.

opening up in the broadest terms the kinds of conduct, physical or verbal, which are admissible provocation. Once there is credible evidence of provocation, it is for the jury and not the judge to resolve the issue of proportionality: it is for them to decide "whether the provocation was enough to make a reasonable man do as he did." Indeed, the latter change has been widely construed. Ordinarily, on general principles, a judge is entitled to withdraw a question of fact from the consideration of the jury if he considers that the factual issue to be resolved does not arise on the evidence before him. On that approach, were a judge to take the view that D's response was grossly disproportionate to the provocation he endured, he would be entitled to withdraw the issue on the basis that no reasonable jury would find that a reasonable man would have done as D did. As interpreted, however, section 3 requires that the jury must resolve this issue, although they may receive guidance on the issue from the judge.[148]

Further interpretations of section 3 remove other restrictions. At common law, provocation as typically formulated is something done by the deceased to the accused.[149] D could not raise a plea of provocation if he killed V in response to something done by W.[150] It was less clear what the position was if he killed V on account of something V did to W rather than to D.[151] However, in *Davies*,[152] the Court of Appeal ruled that the phrase "everything both done and said" in section 3 implies that all sources of provocation, whether or not they emanated from the deceased, must now be considered. Likewise, there are no restrictions on a jury's assessment of the question whether the reasonable man would have done as the accused had done; the jury has to consider D's conduct, whatever it was, and then evaluate it in the terms of section 3.

Whenever a provocation plea is raised, relevant issues fall within two spheres, commonly referred to as the subjective element and the objective element. The subjective element of the defence concerns whether D actually lost self-control because of something that counts as provocation. If that condition is satisfied, the jury must go on to consider the objective element, the issue of how a reasonable person would have responded to the provocation. Two questions arise from this ground of the defence: would the reasonable person have lost control on account of provocation of the same kind that was endured by D? And if a reasonable person would have lost her self-control, would she have acted as did D?

(ii) The subjective element

The subjective requirements of provocation are as follows:[153]

(i)   there must be something done or said;
(ii)   in consequence of which D lost self-control.

We consider these elements in turn.

---

[148] *Phillips* (1968) 58 Cr App R 133 (PC); *Brown* [1972] 3 WLR 506 (CA).
[149] See the "classic" direction of Devlin J in *Duffy* [1949] 1 All ER 932n (CCA).
[150] *Simpson* (1915) 84 LJKB 1893 (CCA).
[151] There was authority that provocation could be raised in those circumstances: *Harrington* (1866) 10 Cox CC 370.
[152] [1975] QB 691 (CA).
[153] See generally Horder, "Re-Shaping the Subjective Element in the Provocation Defence" (2005) 25 *Oxford Journal of Legal Studies* 123.

(a) Provoked by things done or said

The requirement that something be done or said reaffirms that the provocation is something that arises from human agency. D, a farmer, may look out upon his flood-devastated land and feel a great surge of anger towards V, his prosperous neighbour, who farms higher ground. Should D's resentment lead him to kill V, the subsequent trial of D for murder would be uncomplicated by any issue of provocation if V said and did nothing which enraged D. Contrast a situation where D, a securities dealer, is infuriated because V, a professional rival, has more shrewdly anticipated the future and divested himself of investments prior to a falling market. Were D, in his fury, to kill V, any plea of provocation could not necessarily be so easily dismissed. V's conduct was part of the explanation of why D was angry with V.[154]

At root, these two examples have an affinity transcending any differences. One would be inclined to say that there is nothing *provocative* about owning an unflooded farm or being a successful share-dealer. It should not be enough that something was said or done by V which angered D. In addition it should be "something *unwarranted* which is likely to make a reasonable person angry or indignant."[155] For that reason, the Privy Council in *Edwards* [156] was of the view, *obiter*, that an attack by V upon D, which was prompted by D's own black-mailing behaviour, could not, in law, constitute provocation of D if V's response was a predictable reaction to the blackmail by D. Unfortunately, the *dicta* in *Edwards* were not followed in *Johnson*,[157] where D was allowed to raise provocation on the fact of V's reaction to D's own objectionable and aggressive behaviour notwithstanding that V's response was a predictable response to D's behaviour. In the same vein, the Court of Appeal ruled in *Doughty* [158] that a baby's persistent crying could constitute a *provocative* incident. Here, the line between aggravation arising from natural events and events attributable to human agency may be considered so thin as to be invisible. Babies presage tears just as clouds imply rain. However, the Court of Appeal considered that the terms of section 3 allowed a trial judge no choice: if there was evidence that D may have lost self-control as a result of something said or done the issue of provocation must go to the jury. It is submitted that this approach is mistaken. The Court of Appeal has conflated *provocation* with any conduct by V which causes anger to D. By this interpretation, the old common law is not merely liberalised but remaindered. However, despite these reservations, this undiscriminating approach must be taken to represent current law.[159]

There must at least be evidence of *something* said or done. In *Acott*,[160] D had killed his mother, V, with whom he lived. V died as a result of D's frenzied attack and it was not in the least improbable that, prior to the attack, V had done or said something to D which

---

[154] No doubt, however, there would be grave difficulty in establishing the other elements of provocation in such a case.

[155] *Browne* [1973] NI 96, 108 (Lowry LCJ).

[156] [1973] 1 All ER 152 (PC).

[157] [1989] 1 WLR 740 (CA).

[158] (1986) 83 Cr App R 319.

[159] For further discussion of what kinds of conduct may be regarded as provocative see Dressler, "Provocation: Partial Justification or Partial Excuse" (1988) 51 *MLR* 467; McAuley, "Anticipating the Past: The Defence of Provocation in Irish Law" (1987) 50 *MLR* 133.

[160] [1996] 4 All ER 443 (HL).

precipitated the attack. D, himself, professed no recollection of the incident. Understandably, the House of Lords confirmed that a plea of provocation could not be raised. V may well have said or done something but there was no *evidence* that she had.

(b) Loss of self-control

Even if there is evidence of the gravest provocation endured by D, it will not avail him unless there is also evidence that D lost self-control. So, in *Cocker*,[161] where D killed his depressive wife in response to her incessant requests for him to do so, no issue of provocation arose. The circumstances of the killing indicated calm and deliberation. Exactly what psychological state represents a loss of self-control cannot precisely be pinned down. The "classic" direction on the matter given by Devlin J in *Duffy*[162] speaks of a:

> "sudden and temporary loss of self-control, rendering the accused so subject to passion as to make him or her not master of his [*sic*] mind."

Obviously, then, D must be in some extremity of anger. The anger need not be so overwhelming as to render D incapable of knowing what he was doing. In principle, if S's anger was as radically unstabilising as that, he could claim that he lacked the mens rea for murder. In *Richens*,[163] it was stressed that awareness of the nature and quality of one's actions and of the consequences that will ensue from them was quite compatible with a successful plea of provocation. All that is required is that D must be so angry that he is unable to restrain himself.

The need for a "sudden and temporary loss of self-control" indicates that there must be something in the nature of a spontaneous response to the provocation if it is to be claimed that D lost self-control. Any indication of a plan or design to kill V would sit uncomfortably with a plea that the killing was something beyond D's control. Similarly, any lapse of time between the last provocative incident and D's reaction will undermine D's claim to have lost control. Both of these indicia were problematic in *Ibrams*.[164] The last provocative act perpetrated by V occurred on 7 October. On 10 October, D planned with others the killing of V. The attack was successfully carried out on 12 October. On such facts, it is hardly surprising that the trial judge ruled that there was no evidence of any loss of self-control. It is submitted that the important feature in *Ibrams* was the planning and deliberation, with the lapse of time underscoring the organised nature of the killing. Unfortunately, the Court of Appeal, when upholding the trial verdict, unduly stressed the lapse of time between the last bout of provocative behaviour and the killing. On a questionable interpretation of a passage from the leading case of *Camplin*,[165] it was ruled that for a plea of provocation to succeed, there must be an *immediate* response to the provocation. This is to turn what should be an issue of fact into a dubious ruling of law.[166] Lapse of time will never assist a

---

[161] [1989] Crim LR 740 (CA).
[162] [1949] 1 All ER 932n (CCA).
[163] [1993] 4 All ER 877 (CA).
[164] (1982) 74 Cr App R 154 (CA).
[165] [1978] AC 705.
[166] In *Ibrams* (1982) 74 Cr App R 154, 159, Lawton LJ based his ruling on Lord Diplock's insistence in *Camplin* [1978] AC 705, 716 upon a loss of self-control "at the time of the act which caused the death." Although, clearly, there must be a loss of self-control, there is nothing in Lord Diplock's words which require that the loss of self-control should occur *immediately* after the last provocative incident.

plea of provocation but it should not, of itself, defeat the plea. What is important is that D should have lost control at the time she killed V. There is no psychological learning indicating that such loss cannot occur once a given period of time has elapsed since the last provocative incident.[167]

The ruling in *Ibrams* has not formally been overturned but, since then, there has been a series of cases where trial judges have allowed the issue of provocation to go to the jury despite significant passages of time between the killing and the last provocative incident. In none of these cases did the Court of Appeal deprecate this more accommodating approach. These authorities, which include prominent "battered women" cases such as *Thornton*[168] and *Ahluwalia*,[169] are to be welcomed[170] in as much as they reduce the importance of lapse of time from a formal legal barrier into an item of evidence relevant to the subjective issue of whether D did, in fact, lose self-control.[171] *Ibrams* would appear no longer authoritative on the question of the legal effect of delayed response.

This more permissive approach is less satisfactory when, in addition to a lapse of time, there is evidence of premeditation and planning. In *Thornton*, for instance, D declared her intention of killing V, her brutal husband, went into another room to obtain and sharpen a knife, before returning and stabbing V. In *Ahluwalia*, D waited until her abusive husband V was asleep, fetched a can of petrol, doused his bed with fuel, and then set a fire. Most strikingly, in *Pearson*,[172] D and E had armed themselves with weapons and killed V in the course of a planned joint enterprise. In each of these cases, the jury were asked to consider whether D had acted in a state of loss of control. This insistence upon a finding of loss of self-control has been criticised, criticism founded on a very understandable concern with the provocation endured by the defendants in these cases.[173] But section 3 is quite explicit on the point: there must be in fact a loss of self-control.

In cases of this type, juries may be placed in a considerable quandary. Their sympathies may well be engaged by the ordeal suffered by the defendant at the hands of the deceased. At the same time, they will face evidence of planning and deliberation which impedes the expression of their sentiment by way of a verdict in favour of the defendant. Such contradiction encourages a "sympathy lottery" rather than equal treatment of defendants, and underscores the need to resolve such cases in a manner more suitable than the current law allows.[174]

On the subjective limb of the defence, the exclusive focus is on whether D killed in circumstances indicative of a loss of self-control. If D recovers his composure immediately

---

[167] Brett, "The Physiology of Provocation" [1970] *Crim LR* 640.

[168] [1992] 1 All ER 306 (CA).

[169] [1992] 4 All ER 889 (CA).

[170] See also *Baille* [1995] Crim LR 739 (CA); *Pearson* [1992] Crim LR 193 (CA).

[171] In *Logan* [1996] AC 871, 887, Lord Steyn regarded the relevance of "cooling-time" as a common-sense matter for the jury.

[172] [1992] Crim LR 193 (CA).

[173] O'Donovan, "Defences for Battered Women Who Kill" (1991) 18 *J Law and Soc* 219; Nicholson, "Telling Tales: Gender Discrimination Gender Construction and Battered Women Who Kill" (1995) 3 *Feminist Leg Stud* 185; McColgan, "In Defence of Battered Women Who Kill" (1993) 130 *J Law and Soc* 508; Wells, "Battered Women Syndrome and Defences to Homicide: Where Now?" (1994) 14 *LS* 266; Dressler, "Battered Women Who Kill Their Sleeping Tormenters: Reflections on Maintaining Respect for Human Life while Killing Moral Monsters" in Shute and Simester (eds.), *Criminal Law Theory: Doctrines of the General Part* (2002) 259.

[174] See further below, § 10.5(vii).

after the killing, the only relevance this immediate restoration of self-control should have is on the credibility of whether there was an initial loss of self-control. In *Clarke*,[175] D strangled V and then placed live wires into her mouth. Had V been alive, she would have been electrocuted, but the prosecution was unable to prove that V was still alive when D inserted the wires into her mouth. There was evidence that D had lost control when he strangled V but had regained control immediately afterward and then sought to disguise the cause of death. The Court of Appeal upheld the trial judge's ruling that the whole course of conduct should be considered by the jury: "everything done and said", in the terms of section 3. But if the possibility that V was already dead when the wires were placed in her mouth could not be discounted, then the only relevance of the later incident was the light, if any, that it threw on D's claim to have lost control when he strangled V.

(iii) The objective element

(a) Provocation and context

When dealing with the objective limb of the provocation defence, the jury must consider the impact that the provocation would have had on a reasonable person. Essentially, they must ask whether a reasonable person might have lost control and, if she had done so, might she have acted as D did. In resolving these questions the jury can take into account "*everything both done and said*" which has a bearing on the loss of control claimed by D. Note, however, that the jury may consider only those factors that affected D. If, in the course of the trial, evidence of provocative conduct emerges in addition to the provocative acts which D claims caused her to lose self-control, the jury cannot consider that additional evidence in terms of the likely effect on the reasonable person if it was irrelevant to D's loss of self-control. That special case aside, the widest range of events may be considered. In the pre-Act case of *McArthy*,[176] D lost control after receiving an unwelcome sexual request from V. The jury were entitled to consider the fact that, some 20 minutes earlier, V had indecently assaulted D. This broad approach is reinforced by the wide terms of section 3. Consequently, it is surprising that the Court of Appeal in *Davies*[177] considered that the trial judge had been too generous in directing that the jury could take into account "the whole course of conduct of [V] right through that turbulent year of 1972." A different and more appropriate stance was taken in both *Thornton*[178] and *Ahluwalia*,[179] where the whole course of marital discord endured by the respective defendants was admitted as evidence relevant to the weight of the provocation and the impact it would have had.

(b) The reasonable person standard

In *Welsh*,[180] we find a clear reference to the reasonable man as a standard of evaluation in provocation. If the yardstick of the reasonable person is taken literally as a normative test,

---

[175] [1991] Crim LR 383.
[176] [1954] 2 QB 105 (CCA).
[177] [1975] QB 691 (CA).
[178] [1992] 1 All ER 306 (CA).
[179] [1992] 4 All ER 889.
[180] (1869) 2 Cox CC 336.

two things should follow. First, this ground of extenuation should rarely succeed: for how often, surely, would the *reasonable* person intentionally kill, in peacetime, except in self-defence or to protect the lives of others? Secondly, if it really were true that a reasonable person in D's situation would also have killed V, the appropriate verdict should be an acquittal. Reasonable conduct should not be punished. If a reasonableness standard were truly applied in provocation cases, we should anticipate absolute discharges as the typical sentencing outcome of a successful plea. Yet considerable terms of imprisonment are imposed on persons found guilty of manslaughter on this ground. Such sentences can only be justified if D's behaviour, albeit provoked, remains blameworthy.

In truth, the reasonable person has never operated in this sphere of law in the manner of the reasonable person familiar from the law of negligence. At common law, the reasonable person standard in provocation was not only a standard for estimating fault but also a judicial controlling device to prevent what were seen as undeserving pleas from being placed before a jury. For instance, a claim to have been provoked by a confession of adultery could be withheld from the jury by ruling that a reasonable person would not lose self-control in like circumstances.[181] At the present time, because of section 3, a claim of provocation must go to the jury if there is evidence that D has lost control because of something done or said by anyone else. It is now for the jury to resolve whether or not a reasonable person would have done as D did. Somewhat paradoxically, this has enhanced the normative bite of the reasonable person standard: no longer a mechanism for keeping from the jury what were judicially perceived as unmeritorious claims but now the principal means by which the jury resolves the issue of mitigation. In some cases, guidance to the juries on this issue has been made in strongly normative terms.

Happily, this form of guidance has been undermined by the judgment of the House of Lords in the important case of *Morhall*.[182] D was addicted to solvents and on that account he was taunted by V. It was argued for D that, in resolving how a reasonable person would have reacted in these circumstances, the test should be how a reasonable person afflicted with such an addiction would have reacted. At first instance, the trial judge, upheld by the Court of Appeal, considered that an addiction was reprehensible and thus incompatible with the status of a reasonable person.[183] Accordingly the jury were instructed to disregard any question of addiction when evaluating how a reasonable person would have reacted to taunts directed at a state of addiction. Lord Goff, giving judgment for the House of Lords, castigated that reasoning as resting on a fundamental misunderstanding of the role and nature of the reasonable person in the law of provocation. He explained that in this sphere of law, a reasonable person is in no sense an exemplary person. The expression merely indicates that the point of reference in provocation is the *ordinary* person from whom a normal capacity to exercise self-control should be expected.[184] A "reasonable person", so understood, can readily be attributed with a condition such as substance addiction. An ordinary person, so afflicted, would therefore remain within the class of persons from whom normal standards of restraint can be expected.

---

[181] *Holmes* [1946] AC 588, 600 (HL).
[182] [1996] AC 90.
[183] [1993] 4 All ER 888.
[184] [1996] AC 90, 97–8.

Lord Goff's judgment is very valuable in clarifying the nature of the extenuation at work in provocation (although whether it makes for a convincing ground of extenuation is another matter, yet to be discussed). The reasonable person standard accommodates the notion of an ordinary person committing an act which is, prima facie, murder. The question for the jury then becomes whether the loss of self-control by D was *understandable* in terms of the responses of ordinary people (themselves) and, if it was, whether that goes some way to extenuating D's culpability while leaving in place what may still be a considerable residuum of blame for the killing.

(c) The "characteristics" of the reasonable person

We have seen that the jury must evaluate the response of the defendant applying the standard of the ordinary person. However, there may well be particular facets of the defendant herself which go to explain the loss of self-control and its fatal consequences. D may be unusually pugnacious, abnormally sensitive, mocked about a particular form of affliction, and so on. The question thus arises what particularities associated with the defendant— what "characteristics", to use the expression employed in the cases[185]—can be attributed to the reasonable person when assessing whether the reasonable person would have acted as D did.

Much of the case law in the years following the passing of the Homicide Act 1957 has approached this question with an underlying division in play. Some characteristics of the defendant may be relevant to the *sting* of the particular provocative words or actions. Taunting D about her height may be more provocative to D if D is extremely short-statured. By contrast, other characteristics of the defendant may affect her capacity for self-control in general. An adolescent may have less capacity for self-control than a mature adult. As we shall see, this distinction is not at all clear-cut. Neither has it been accepted in all the cases. However, it is a convenient division with which to approach the analysis of which of D's subjective characteristics are allowed for when assessing whether the reasonable person would have acted as did D.

(d) Characteristics which aggravate the sting of the provocation

Prior to the Homicide Act 1957, the nature and attributes of the reasonable person were judicially controlled. A reasonable person was taken to possess normal capacities for self-control,[186] the effect of alcohol or drugs taken by D were to be disregarded.[187] Most controversially, any physical characteristics of D which made for a particular susceptibility to the kind of provocation at issue were also to be ignored. That last restriction could work serious injustice. In the leading pre-1957 case, *Bedder*,[188] the House of Lords ruled that the trial judge was correct to instruct the jury to disregard the fact of D's impotence when applying the reasonable man test, even though V's provocative conduct was expressly focused on D's impotence.

---

[185] The term was introduced into the New Zealand law of provocation in *McGregor* [1962] NZLR 1069 and adopted into English law in *Camplin* [1978] AC 705; see Orchard, "Provocation—Recharacterisation of 'Characteristics'" (1996) 6 *Canterbury LR* 202.
[186] *Lesbini* [1914] 3 KB 1116 (CCA).
[187] *McCarthy* [1954] 2 KB 105.
[188] [1954] 2 All ER 80.

It was not obvious what effect section 3 had on this body of law.[189] One view was that, effectively, nothing had changed. The reasonable man test had been retained and the judge could direct the jury on the make-up of the reasonable person when instructing the jury. The judge would be bound by previous authority in doing so. That was the stance taken by the trial judge in *Camplin*,[190] where D, a 15-year-old boy, struck and killed V after V had sodomised and subsequently mocked him. His counsel had argued the jury should be allowed to take into account D's age when determining the degree of self-control to be expected, arguing that an adolescent would typically be more sensitive and volatile, when mocked, than would a person of mature years. The argument was dismissed at trial on the basis that *Bedder* required a direction instructing the jury to ignore D's age while deliberating upon the likely reaction of a reasonable person to the humiliation that D had endured. The Court of Appeal reversed the trial judge on the cogent ground that to instruct a jury to assess the reaction of a reasonable 15-year-old boy was perfectly compatible with *Bedder*. There was nothing exceptional about being 15. Condescending to the defendant's age was not to derogate from a standard of self-control to be expected of everyone; that is, everyone according to age.[191] The House of Lords confirmed this reasoning, adding that gender too could be taken into account by the jury when determining whether a reasonable person would have acted as D did.[192]

Unlike in *Bedder*, there is nothing in the actual decision in *Camplin* which relates to *exceptional* vulnerabilities or afflictions that may make D sensitive to particular forms of affront. Yet the importance of *Camplin* goes well beyond the actual decision. Lord Diplock, giving the main judgment, took the opportunity to revise and reform the law on a broader front. He took the view that the approach taken in *Bedder* was incompatible with section 3. That section explicitly provides that a jury may take into account words as well as deeds on a plea of provocation. How then, Lord Diplock pertinently asked, could a jury be instructed to take into account the provocative weight of specific words and, at one and the same time, ignore particular characteristics of D which rendered those words offensive. Accordingly, he concluded that *Bedder* should no longer be regarded as binding.[193] Instead, juries should be directed to consider how a reasonable person of the age and gender of D would have responded to the provocation in question, bearing in mind, if relevant, any characteristics of D rendering D particularly susceptible to the kind of provocative conduct in issue.

Camplin is a humane and liberalising decision, of great importance for the modern law. What it did not do, however, is give much guidance about which specific facets of a person's make-up would count as admissible "characteristics". Some indications were offered by the Court of Appeal in the post-*Camplin* case of *Newell*,[194] where D had killed V after V had made a derogatory remark concerning D's ex-girlfriend and had made what was, for D, an offensive offer of sex. At the time, D's life was a turbulent one. He was an alcoholic recently deserted by his girlfriend. The desertion had prompted D's state of depression, a failed but serious suicide attempt, and voluminous consumption of drink and drugs, culminating, at

---

[189] English, "What Did Section Three Do to the Law of Provocation?" [1970] *Crim LR* 249.
[190] [1978] AC 705.
[191] [1978] 1 All ER 1236.
[192] [1978] AC 705, 718.
[193] *Ibid.*
[194] (1980) 71 Cr App R 331 (CA).

the time of the killing, in a state of toxic exhaustion. The Court of Appeal considered that, save possibly for his alcoholism, none of these features could constitute "characteristics". Influenced by New Zealand case law which had devised and explicated the notion of a "characteristic",[195] the Court ruled that a relevant characteristic must be something with a degree of permanence and gravity, something "which makes [D] a different person from the ordinary run of mankind."[196] Everything in D's personal situation, with the possible exception of the alcoholism, was "transitory in nature" and did not constitute relevant characteristics.[197] Thus provocative conduct directed at these afflictions would not advance D's case. The court declined to make any judgment on the status of D's alcoholism since V's provocation did not advert to that trait.

In the light of the subsequent decision of the House of Lords in *Morhall*,[198] we now know that a state of addiction does count as a relevant characteristic for the purposes of assessing the sting of the provocation. Furthermore, Lord Goff, when giving judgment for the House, queried whether, in order to qualify as a characteristic, D's particular condition need be a permanent or a long-term state of affairs. He instanced eczema as a condition which may be temporary but which should constitute a characteristic for as long as the condition, and D's sensitivity about it, endures.[199] His judgment, with its emphasis on provocation as a defence based on the reactions of *ordinary* people, makes a welcome contrast to the "different person from the run of mankind" approach to characteristics employed in *Newell*. A person's particular ethnicity or sexual orientation does not, one would hope, mark her out from the rest of mankind, yet such matters must surely be taken into account if the provocation in issue is directed towards such aspects of their person-hood.[200] Further, we may assume, post-*Morhall*, that such conditions as depression, or sensitivity concerning a recent suicide attempt should be attributed to the reasonable person if such conditions apply to D and the sting of the provocation is related to them.

On the basis of the authorities discussed so far, the defence of provocation is reasonably coherent in conceptual terms. In terms of the *Camplin* analysis, it is a defence for *ordinary people*, in that it is a defence premised on the reactions of persons capable of an ordinary level of self-restraint. (On that matter, an objective standard of expectation applies, mediated only by the age or gender of the particular defendant[201]—but more on this below.) However, when considering the weight or sting of the provocation, particular facets of the defendant may be attributed to the reasonable person if germane to the provocation at issue in the case.[202] There is a strong line drawn in *Camplin* between the ordinary powers of self-control to be expected of D or anyone else (an objective test) and an assessment of how provocative for D was the particular provocation.

Unfortunately, in practice, this conceptual framework may give rise to an unwelcome

---

[195] Discussed in Orchard, "Provocation—Re-characterisation of 'Characteristics'" (1996) 6 *Canterbury LR* 202.
[196] (1980) 71 Cr App R 331, 339.
[197] *Ibid.*, 340.
[198] [1996] AC 90. See Norrie, "From Criminal Law to Legal Theory: The Mysterious Case of the Reasonable Glue Sniffer"(2002) 65 *MLR* 538
[199] *Ibid.*, 99.
[200] Yeo, "Sex, Ethnicity, Power of Self-Control and Provocation Revisited" (1996) 18 *Sydney LR* 304.
[201] *Camplin* [1978] AC 705.
[202] *Ibid.*; *Morhall* [1996] AC 90.

degree of artificiality. Take facts similar to those arising in *Newell*.[203] In the light of *Morhall*, we have argued that if V were to make a derogatory reference to D's recent suicide attempt and fragile mental condition, the jury should be permitted to consider the likely reaction of an ordinary person afflicted with such a history. A person with such a history is likely (i) to be sensitive to any reference to it and (ii) to find self-control difficult because of the instability induced by her current mental condition. Yet only the matter covered in (i) can be taken into account. On the issue of self-control, normal stability must be assumed subject to the variations in the capacity for self-control that are presumed to accompany the age and gender of D. This rigid distinction is not a natural means to employ when assessing whether a particular killing should be adjudged murder or manslaughter.

(e) Characteristics which affect self-control

Controversy has followed. The intelligible, yet problematic, division in *Camplin* between those characteristics which go to the sting of provocation and those of sex and age which, alone, can be taken into account when setting the expected standard of self-control has been variously undermined and reasserted by the Court of Appeal, House of Lords, and Privy Council, in a series of appellate cases involving defendants suffering from forms of personality disorder or mental impairment. It is necessary to set out the recent history in some detail.

Undermining objective self-control: the Court of Appeal versus the Privy Council.
The revisionary initiative came from a series of decisions by the Court of Appeal, in which the principal cases were *Ahluwalia*[204] and *Thornton (No. 2)*,[205] which featured battered woman's syndrome; *Humphreys*,[206] which concerned immaturity and attention seeking by wrist slashing; and *Dryden*,[207] involving "obsessive and eccentric" personality. Common to all these cases was the presence of expert testimony indicating that these conditions were beyond the normal range of personality variation and constituted discrete syndromes. On that basis, these respective conditions were accepted, in legal terms, as characteristics in the sense laid down in *Newell*.[208] But, going beyond anything decided in *Newell*, these "syndrome" characteristics straddle the divide between characteristics going to weight of provocation and matters that may be taken into account on the issue of self-control. They were deemed relevant should the provocation be directed towards the personality trait and, *whether or not the provocation was so directed*, they were ruled to be relevant when estimating whether a reasonable person (with that syndrome) would have acted in a manner similar to D.

The approach taken in these cases was intended to apply only if the defendant is afflicted with a specific personality syndrome identified by expert evidence. In the absence of such evidence, normal standards of self-control will be expected. For instance, in *Roberts*,[209]

---

[203] (1980) 71 Cr App R 331.
[204] [1992] 4 All ER 889.
[205] [1996] 2 All ER 1023.
[206] [1995] 4 All ER 1008.
[207] [1995] 4 All ER 987.
[208] (1980) 71 Cr App R 331.
[209] [1990] Crim LR 122 (CA).

expert witnesses were prepared to testify that pre-lingual deaf-mutes typically experienced raised anger levels because of the frustrations inherent in coping with their disability. If such a person were, like D, taunted about this condition he would find it harder to exercise self-control than would, *mutatis mutandis,* a person with normal hearing provoked on some matter germane to himself. The Court of Appeal ruled that this evidence was rightly excluded. Deaf-mutes, as a class, are not afflicted with any form of personality syndrome. Accordingly, the degree of self-control to be required of a deaf-mute was the same degree of self-control to be expected of any normal person of D's age and gender.

However, the Court of Appeal's willingness to admit syndrome evidence on the issue of the standard of self-control attributable to the reasonable person was subsequently criticised by Lord Goff in *Luc Thiet-Thuan* v. *R.,*[210] where, in the majority opinion of the Privy Council, he advised that D's brain damage (which induced impulsive behaviour in D) should not be taken into account when applying the reasonable person standard. Lord Goff cogently argued that the admission of such evidence was incompatible with the long-established nature of provocation as defence available for ordinary persons. He considered that the Court of Appeal of Hong Kong, in admitting syndrome evidence, had paid insufficient attention to the analysis of the nature of provocation as a defence made by the House of Lords in *Camplin* and *Morhall* and had been unduly influenced by New Zealand case law,[211] which had stretched the defence beyond its natural limits in order to ameliorate the absence of a defence of diminished responsibility in that jurisdiction.[212]

Lord Goff's remarks have considerable force. If provocation is to be a defence confined to ordinary people, then admissible syndrome evidence on the question of self-control should, at most, include those syndromes which would be contracted by a significant number of persons of normal psychological disposition were they to share the same history as the defendant. In that sense "life experience" syndromes, such as "battered woman's" syndrome, can be accommodated within the terms of reference set by an ordinary, reasonable person standard. Contrast conditions such as organic brain damage, obsessive reclusive personality, and immaturity; which the Court of Appeal had also ruled admissible on the question of self-control.[213] To the extent that these conditions are physiologically derived, they would have afflicted the respective defendants in these cases irrespective of their life experience. Of course, such conditions are relevant to D's level of culpability but, as Lord Goff observed, in the context of murder their appropriate place is within the statutory defence of diminished responsibility.[214]

Although Lord Goff's views carried the majority of the Privy Council, there was a powerful dissent from Lord Steyn.[215] He approved the admission of syndrome evidence on the issue of self-control, taking the view that nothing said in *Camplin* or *Morhall* precluded this approach. With respect, that view is tenable only in the sense that the particular matter of syndrome evidence is not discussed in either of those cases. Yet on any fair reading of those authorities, the only matters relevant to the issue of self-control were taken to be age

---

[210] [1997] AC 131.
[211] *McGregor* [1962] NZLR 1069.
[212] [1997] AC 131.
[213] *Humphreys* [1995] 4 All ER 1008; *Dryden* [1995] 4 All ER 987.
[214] Homicide Act 1957, s. 2.
[215] [1997] AC 131.

and gender. More importantly, Lord Steyn was also concerned with the artificiality of allowing evidence to be called in order to explain the sting of the provocation—in *Humphreys*, for instance, D was mocked by V on account of her immaturity and wrist-slashing tendencies—and, at one and the same time, instructing juries to disregard the evidence on the question of self-control. In *Humphreys*, if a court were to follow Lord Goff, the immaturity and tendency to hysteria of D would have to be set aside when considering how the ordinary reasonable person would have responded to such taunts.

In terms of substantive justice, this criticism is so powerful as to override matters of conceptual clarity. Lord Steyn's dissent emboldened the Court of Appeal, post-*Luc Thiet-Thuan*, to continue the line of authority criticised by Lord Goff. In three cases, *Parker*,[216] *Campbell (No. 2)*,[217] and *Smith*,[218] the Court of Appeal approved the admission of evidence of personality disorders and organic mental impairment as relevant to the issue of self-control.

Reasserting objective self-control: the Privy Council versus the House of Lords.
Ongoing disagreement was in due course seemingly resolved in favour of a subjective approach by the House of Lords, when it confirmed the decision of the Court of Appeal in the last of those cases, *Smith*.[219] The majority decision of the House is expansive, particularly the judgments of Lords Hoffman and Clyde. D was suffering from depression, but the quarrel leading to V's death at the hands of D did not involve any pejorative reference by V to D's depressed condition. Nonetheless, the majority ruled that D's state of depression should have been taken into account by the jury when considering whether a reasonable person would have done as D did when reacting to V's taunts. Of the majority judgments, Lord Slynn's is the least wide-ranging. In essence, he considered that it would be forensically unworkable to draw any strict division between, on the one hand, characteristics admissible on the matter of the weight of the provocation and, on the other hand, characteristics allowable on the question of capacity for self-control. Accordingly, his Lordship considered that when applying the reasonable man standard to the facts of the instant case, the jury should have been directed to consider how a reasonable man afflicted with D's state of depression would have reacted to the provocation.

Lords Hoffman and Clyde went further in reshaping the concepts and language used in this area of law. Neither judge considered it obligatory for trial judges to make any reference to the reasonable person when directing juries.[220] Both were of the view that the nature of the extenuation at issue in provocation was best explained without reference to any such concept. Juries should be told that an acceptable standard of self-control was to be expected from everyone. No license was to be given to persons with defective characters, such as the pugnacious, the unduly excitable, the short-tempered, or the morbidly jealous. On the other hand, the jury must consider any characteristic possessed by D that has a just bearing on his

---

[216] [1997] Crim LR 760.
[217] [1997] Crim LR 227.
[218] [1999] 1 QB 1079 (CA).
[219] [2001] 1 AC 146 (HL). For critical commentary on *Smith* see Gardner and Macklem, "Compassion without Respect? Nine Fallacies in *R. v. Smith*" [2001] *Crim LR* 623; Macklem and Gardner, "Provocation and Pluralism" (2001) 64 *MLR* 815.
[220] But to do so is, quite rightly, still permissible: *Jenkins* [2002] EWCA 749.

capacity to exercise self-control. It was accepted that this would not make for clear and coherent doctrine; yet a loss of clarity was thought to be an acceptable price of doing justice for defendants.

What is the difference between non-admissible defect of character and allowable characteristics? As Lord Slynn acknowledged, there are difficult borderline questions here. Of particular interest is Lord Hoffman's discussion of the Australian case of *Stingel* v. *The Queen*,[221] where D had killed V, the boyfriend of his former partner, on witnessing (as he had supposed) their act of sexual intercourse. Lord Hoffman agreed with the High Court of Australia that D's obsession with his former partner was not to be attributed to the reasonable person: "Male possessiveness and jealousy should not today be an acceptable reason for loss of self-control leading to homicide. . . ." Indeed, but how do we distinguish conceptually between *Stingel* and a case such as *Dryden*,[222] where D's obsessive personality (in matters relating to his land and his rights thereon) was deemed attributable to the reasonable person? All that may be safely gleaned from the judgments of Lords Hoffman and Clyde is that, under the approach in *Smith*, an admissible characteristic may be temporary or permanent, may fall short of any recognised medical disorder, but would not include the destabilising effects of drugs or alcohol and shortcomings of character. The very unclarity of what limits were to be placed on attributable characteristics made further litigation inevitable.

Moreover, while the majority of the House therefore preferred the approach of the Court of Appeal to that of the Privy Council, however, the decision was far from unanimous— indeed, a bare three to two majority. The dissenting judgments forcefully rejected the majority position in terms of legal analysis and even more forcefully in terms of policy. In their view, unless characteristics relating to the capacity for self-control are confined to age and gender, the distinctiveness of the separate defences of provocation and diminished responsibility is undermined. Undoubtedly, persons with any form of mental instability who have lost self-control because of something done or said will find section 3 of the Homicide Act 1957 more receptive to their needs than section 2. Of particular note is the opinion of both dissentients to the effect that the majority judgments in *Smith* are incompatible with the earlier decision of the House of Lords in *Morhall*.[223] If there is incompatibility then, of course, the majority view need not be followed in subsequent litigation.

So it is, perhaps, not entirely surprising that the majority decision in *Smith* has itself been rejected by a six to three majority of the Privy Council in *A-G for Jersey* v. *Holley*.[224] This appeal from Jersey concerned the relevance of D's alcoholism to the reasonable person test in provocation from a jurisdiction that followed the same principles as English law in matters relating to provocation as a partial defence to murder. The majority of the Privy Council considered that *Smith* was incompatible with the earlier of the House of Lords in *Camplin* and *Morhall* and that those decisions should be followed in the event of any conflict with the decision in *Smith*. For the majority in *Holley*, D's alcoholism might have been a relevant consideration in evaluating the provocative sting of V's conduct had his

[221] [1990] 171 CLR 312.
[222] [1995] 4 All ER 987.
[223] [1996] AC 90.
[224] [2005] UKPC 23, [2005] 2 AC 580.

quarrel with V related to his state of addiction. His addiction had no relevance to the level of self-control to be expected of him. On that matter the only variables that the jury should take into account were age and gender.

The current position: a constitutional problem.
The Privy Council's advice in *Holley* purports to reassert the legal analysis of provocation that was laid down in *Camplin* and *Morhall*. So are we back to the pre-*Smith* law in England and Wales? That was certainly the view of the majority in *Holley*, which considered that trial judges and the Court of Appeal should follow the majority's judgment. But this raises a constitutional difficulty: how could an appeal from Jersey settle the law for England and Wales, particularly as the Judicial Committee's view of the relevant law departed from *Smith*, the latest decision of the House of Lords? We need hardly remind ourselves that House of Lords decisions are binding on all other courts in our jurisdiction, whereas Privy Council decisions, however respected, are merely persuasive for English courts of whatever status. For the majority, the binding quality of their decision for England and Wales rested essentially on a headcount: a majority of current judicial members of the House of Lords had taken the *Camplin/Morhall* line in recent appeals before the House, rather than the *Smith* approach. In the light of that, the Privy Council advised that any appeal to the House of Lords arguing a view of the law based on *Smith* was "doomed" to fail; and that, accordingly, its opinion should be treated as binding. The reasoning is problematic.[225] Nonetheless, it has been accepted by the Court of Appeal[226] and, at least in the lower courts, this vexatious matter must be regarded as for the moment resolved—so that the decision in *Smith* is somehow effectively overruled. Whether it leaves the law in a satisfactory condition will be considered below. Either way, however, another visit to the House of Lords is in order.

(iv) The relationship between provocation and diminished responsibility[227]

Having discussed the role of characteristics such as personality disorders and mental impairment in provocation pleas, it may be helpful to consider the close practical relationship that can arise between the defences of provocation and diminished responsibility[228] when evidence germane to both defences arises during a trial for murder. The overlap in practice became more extensive under the line of authority ultimately endorsed in *Smith*, allowing evidence of mental disorder on the issue of capacity to exercise self-control. Indeed, during that time, the number of successful diminished responsibility pleas fell to about 20 cases a year compared with about 80 cases in the early 1990s.[229] The

---

[225] The matter is of constitutional significance, and cannot be gone into in detail here. However, some obvious reservations should be expressed. The time span before any further appeal to the House of Lords is uncertain and it is impossible to know who the personnel then sitting on the appeal will be; and it is not clear that identifying the individual judges is a relevant feature of the decision of a *court*. Each appeal is, by its very nature, a fresh start that must be heard before open judicial minds; and what counts is not the individual views, but the decision of the panel. It is therefore quite wrong to suggest that some future appeal is, notwithstanding precedent, "doomed" before it starts. See, further, the note at (2006) 122 *LQR* 329.

[226] *Mohammed* [2005] EWCA Crim 1880; *James* [2006] EWCA Crim 14, [2006] QB 588.

[227] Mackay, *Mental Condition Defences in the Criminal Law* (1995) 198–202; Mackay, "Pleading Provocation and Diminished Responsibility Together" [1988] *Crim LR* 411.

[228] Diminished responsibility is discussed in detail below, § 19.2.

[229] Law Com. No. 304, para. 5.84.

decision in *Holley*, confining such evidence to the *weight* of the provocation, brings with it a greater practical separation of the two defences and it may be that the number of diminished responsibility pleas will rise again in the context of a narrower reading of provocation.

Clearly, any diagnosable personality disorder or mental impairment presumptively falls within section 2 of the Homicide Act 1957[230] and may well lead a jury to conclude that D's responsibility for his acts was substantially impaired within the terms of that section. Equally, as we have seen, such evidence may well be relevant to a plea of provocation;[231] at least to the extent that, post-*Holley*, the evidence is relevant.[232] In an appropriate case, therefore, D may raise both defences of her own motion. Even if she were to plead diminished responsibility only, a judge is obliged to give a direction of provocation if he thinks the evidence raises that possibility. This points up a major anomaly. For diminished responsibility, the burden of proof, on a balance of probabilities, lies with the defendant.[233] For provocation, where the burden of proof is a matter of common law, the burden of disproof is on the prosecution once an evidential issue of provocation has been raised. This burden is discharged by proof beyond any reasonable doubt. It cannot be easy, even for the most conscientious and capable jury, to deal with the same evidence under different heads, applying differential burdens and quantums of proof.

(v) The manner of response

In provocation, the essential evaluative question for the jury is whether the reasonable person would have responded to the provocation in the same manner as the defendant: "whether the provocation was enough to make a reasonable man do as he did." With the enactment of section 3, it is a matter for the jury whose decision on the issue can no longer be pre-empted by the judge as a matter of law.[234] However, as with any other question of fact, a judge may provide guidance for the jury—even, in an appropriate case, strong guidance—provided such guidance falls short of any mandatory direction.[235]

In *Phillips*,[236] this judicial function was challenged. V had spat at E, D's mother. In swift, enraged response, D decapitated V with a machete. The trial judge had directed the jury to

---

[230] Section 2 provides that "where a person kills or is a party to the killing of another, he shall not be convicted of murder if he was suffering from such abnormality of mind (whether arising from a condition of arrested or retarded development of mind or any inherent causes or induced by disease or injury) as substantially impaired his mental responsibility for his acts and omissions in doing or being a party to the killing."

[231] In *Ahluwalia* [1992] 4 All ER 889 and *Thornton (No. 2)* [1996] 2 All ER 1023, evidence of battered woman's syndrome was taken to be relevant to provocation and diminished responsibility. Both grounds of extenuation may be raised in the same trial.

[232] As explained earlier, syndrome evidence post-*Holley* is only relevant to the provocation plea if the provocative conduct of V was in some manner focused on D's syndrome, so that the syndrome evidence is relevant to show the weight or sting of the provocation, rather than attesting to D's personal capacity for self-control.

[233] Homicide Act 1957 s. 2(2).

[234] The effect of decisions such as *Doughty* (1986) 83 Cr App R 319 and *Johnson* [1989] 1 WLR 740 is that D must not be deprived of his chance of a perverse jury verdict even in circumstances where the trial judge is convinced that no reasonable jury could find that a reasonable person would have acted as did D. However, if a judge were, wrongly, not to allow provocation to go to the jury, D's conviction may yet be confirmed if the appellate court is sure that at least 10 of the jurors would have rejected the defence: *Dhillon* [1997] 2 Cr App R 104, 114–15.

[235] A mandatory direction must not be given on a question of fact even in the plainest of cases: *Stonehouse* [1978] AC 55.

[236] (1968) 53 Cr App R 133.

consider whether the degree of disproportion between the insulting behaviour of V and D's response was so gross as to exclude provocation. It was argued on behalf of D that since any successful plea of provocation must be based on a finding of loss of self-control by D, it was illogical to give a direction in terms of proportionality because D, *ex hypothesi*, was out of control. This argument was found wanting by the Privy Council, and with good reason. The argument on behalf of D was a purely semantic one. In ordinary usage, we readily use a locution as "she was out of control" to describe persons well short of homicidal rage. We may ascribe loss of self-control, for instance, to a person losing an argument who is raising her voice and resorting to verbal abuse. As the Privy Council observed, there are degrees of loss of self-control (gestural, verbal, physical).[237] In the context of mitigating D's responsibility for a killing, the degree of loss of control must no doubt be extreme, yet, in all the circumstances, it must still bear some comparison with the likely reaction of an ordinary person. *Phillips* has been followed in England;[238] appropriate judicial guidance on this matter is perfectly compatible with the terms of section 3 and with standard judicial practice in offering guidance on matters of fact.

(vi) Provocation and mistake

Even at common law, where provocation was confined to something done by the deceased to the defendant, it was accepted that if D mistakenly assumed V had done something to him amounting to provocation, he was entitled to be tried on the basis that his mistaken assumptions were true.[239] The inclusionary terms of section 3 underscore this concession. Furthermore, at common law, this concession was available even if the mistake were induced by drink,[240] making an exception to the principle prevailing for much of this century that a mistake, to count in terms of defence, had to be based on reasonable grounds.[241] Perhaps this dispensation can be explained on the basis that a successful plea of provocation merely extenuates and does not completely excuse. Be that as it may, the inclusionary language of section 3 fortifies this position, as does the reversal, in general terms, of the old rule that mistakes going to defence had to be based on reasonable grounds. However, doubt has been thrown on the effect of intoxicated mistakes in cases of specific intent crimes by the cases of *O'Grady*,[242] *O'Connor*,[243] and now *Hatton*.[244] Cases concerned with drunken mistakes in the context of provocation were not discussed in any of these cases.[245] For reasons to be discussed later, it is submitted that these are unsound authorities[246] and that evidence of mistakes induced by intoxication should continue to be admissible in provocation cases.

---

[237] *Ibid.*, 135.
[238] *Brown* [1972] 3 WLR 506: *Van Dongen* [2005] Crim LR 971.
[239] *Brown* (1776) 1 Leach 148, 168 ER 177.
[240] *Letenock* (1917) 12 Cr App R 221 (CCA); *Wardrope* [1960] Crim LR 770.
[241] Cf. 11 *Halsbury's Laws* (4th ed.) para. 21; below, § 18.1.
[242] [1987] QB 995 (CA).
[243] [1991] Crim LR 135 (CA).
[244] [2005]
[245] These cases were concerned with drink-induced beliefs in the need to employ defensive force. The view was expressed that such beliefs would be disregarded even in the context of a murder charge, notwithstanding that it is established law that evidence of voluntary intoxication may be admitted on the issue of whether D formed the mens rea for murder.
[246] Below, § 18.3(iii)(b).

(vii) The future of provocation

One important monograph on the defence of provocation concludes by recommending the abolition of the defence.[247] It is a proposal that merits serious consideration, as the force and rationale of this ground of extenuation are not easy to state.[248] A condition of angry loss of self-control is at the core of provocation. Yet anger is a criminogenic emotion and one of the key deterrent tasks of the criminal law is to provide incentives for citizens to curb violent responses induced by their angry states. A person disposed to respond to frustrations and setbacks with an angry loss of control culminating in serious violence would thereby demonstrate a dangerous and deficient character and should not be accorded any form of condonation. Moreover, the partial condonation of angry violence through a provocation defence comes with an inbuilt gender bias because it clearly privileges persons with an effective capacity and disposition spontaneously to kill others. Such killings occur frequently in domestic contexts against physically vulnerable members of the household.[249] The historical origins of provocation lay in a perception, long discarded as part of our law, that killings emerging from sudden falling-outs (chance-medleys) were less heinous than killings which were the product of premeditation. From the early modern period the continuation of the defence was reinforced by an acceptance that male honour can (even should) be vindicated by acts of retaliatory violence.[250] These paradigms are unsuited to a modern liberal democracy. They merely strengthen the view that the survival of the defence is an historical anomaly that is acceptable, if at all, only because of the mandatory penalty for murder.

Attempts have been made to offer a modern rationale for the defence. Finbar McAuley[251] defends the extenuating force of provocation on the basis of what he terms "partial justification". For him, there must be some element of the victim's "asking for it" so that blame for the killing is in some sense shared between defendant and victim. As Macauley observes himself, such a rationale cannot underpin the English version of the provocation defence because, since the passage of section 3, provocation will run where the victim is someone other than the provocateur and, more importantly, the issue is raised if D is provoked by *anything*, such as the crying of a baby or a predictable reaction to his own unlawful or offensive behaviour. These are not cases where the victim "asks for it". In any event, the notion of partial justification is incoherent. Conduct is either justified, all things considered, or it is not (although in the latter case it may be condonable). Even in the case of the gravest provocation—say D has just witnessed the murder of his wife by V—D's killing V cannot be justified. Understandable, yes. Excusable, perhaps. But not justified. Viewed from the perspective of a general rule of conduct, his action is clearly wrong and impermissible.

Joshua Dressler, in a thoughtful article,[252] locates the rationale of the provocation defence

---

[247] Horder, *Provocation and Responsibility* (1992) chap. 9.

[248] For an interesting argument that provocation remains salvageable, see Freedman, "Restoring Order to the Reasonable Person Test in the Reference of Provocation" [1998] *King's College LJ* 26.

[249] In 1996, of 217 female homicide victims, 44% were killed by partners and 20% by members of their families. Of the 410 male homicide victims, 6% were killed by partners and 16% by members of their families: *Criminal Statistics, England and Wales 1996* Cmnd. 3764, (1997); Clarkson and Keating, *Criminal Law: Cases and Materials* (4th ed., 1998) 627–8.

[250] Horder, *Provocation and Responsibility* (1992) chaps. 1–3.

[251] "Anticipating the Past: The Defence of Provocation in Irish Law" (1987) 50 *MLR* 133.

[252] "Rethinking Heat of Passion: A Defence in Search of a Rationale" (1982) 73 *J Crim L and Crim* 421.

in the realm of excuse, the excuse consisting of D's reduced capacity to conform his conduct to law when induced to lose self-control in angry reaction to provocation. But, as he recognises, our judgmental reaction to loss of control greatly depends on the nature of the conduct which caused the reaction. In the example where V kills D's wife, we readily condone, at least in part, D's response. By contrast, where the precipitating incident is trivial, we may, quite reasonably, see E's loss of self-control as a ground of censure. Yet the emotions gripping E may be just as strong, just as choice-constraining, as the emotions aroused in a person who has endured grave provocation. The loss of self-control does not in itself explain why we feel blame is extenuated in some cases. Indeed, in some cases where murder verdicts have been sustained because of insufficient evidence of loss of self-control (*Ibrams, Ahluwalia,* and *Thornton*), there may be a strong case for extenuation, even in a case of considered, deliberate killing.

The rigidity of the mandatory sentence in murder calls for flexible, fact-sensitive grounds of extenuation. Some members of the judiciary have, with the best of intentions, sought to make provocation more flexible and fact-sensitive, particularly through reception of syndrome evidence on the subjective and objective grounds. In so doing, they created an awkward overlap with the grounds of extenuation afforded by diminished responsibility, undermining the coherence of provocation as a defence for ordinary people. That tendency has been halted by the decision in *Holley*; but there are grounds for thinking that this is but to swap one set of concerns for another. Take, for instance, the post-*Holley* decision in *Mohammed*.[253] D had killed his daughter V, enraged that she was continuing a relationship with a man after he had ordered her to end the connection. Not merely was this defiance but, according to the version of the Muslim faith to which D subscribed, it was in breach of V's religious obligation to obey her father, placing her beyond the bounds of her community. In an accurate rendering of the post-*Holley* law, the trial judge, in a direction approved by the Court of Appeal, instructed the jury that they should consider D's religion and culture in determining how a reasonable person so situated would have regarded V's defiance of her father. When it came to evaluating how a reasonable person would have reacted to the defiance (on discovering the couple in his house), the test to be employed was the likely reaction of a person of ordinary stability and temperament. This awkward amalgam of cultural relativism and mainstream expectations concerning self-control cannot be easy material for a jury to work justice with. Such a case raises, yet again, the question whether a soundly based defence of provocation can be worked out or whether the defence should be abolished.

The English Law Commission has recently published its final proposals for a reformed law of provocation.[254] The recommendations come in two parts: situations where (i) D acts in response to a fear of serious violence; and (ii) D acts in response to words or conduct that constitute "gross provocation". In cases of fear of serious violence, D will be convicted of second-degree murder (which is punished at the discretion of the judge) rather than

---

[253] [2005] EWCA Crim 1880.

[254] Law Com. No. 304, part 5. The proposals are in substance the same as recommended in LCCP No. 177, part 6; on which see Mackay and Mitchell, "But Is this Provocation? Some Thoughts on the Law Commission's Report on Partial Defences to Murder" [2005] *Crim LR* 44; Quick and Wells "Getting Tough with Defences" [2006] *Crim LR* 514.

first-degree murder (mandatory life sentence), provided "a person of [D]'s age and of ordinary temperament, i.e., ordinary tolerance and self restraint, in the circumstances of [D] might have reacted in the same or similar way." This can be welcomed without reservation. It seems entirely suitable to cover without strain domestic violence cases such as *Thorton*[255] and *Ahluwalia*.[256] Furthermore, it repairs the failure of English law to provide some extenuation for cases where there is a right to use some force in self-defence but where the right was abused by D's recourse to excessive force.[257]

The proposal relating to gross provocation is problematic. To be grossly provocative, V's words or conduct must cause D to have a "justifiable sense of being seriously wronged". In one aspect this is to be welcomed, since vexations such as crying babies or predictable reactions to one's own aggressive behaviour would no longer raise the partial defence. But cultural variables may give rise to considerable difficulty in resolving what constitutes gross provocation. Returning to the troubling case of *Mohammed*,[258] could D claim to have been grossly provoked by his daughter's continuance of the relationship he had forbidden? Yes, if we attend to the norms of his religion and culture: by those norms he would have a "justifiable sense of being seriously wronged". Might a person of "ordinary tolerance and self restraint, *in the circumstances of the defendant*" have reacted in the same or similar way? Again, and disturbingly, the answer may be affirmative if there was significant support from his religious and cultural group for his drastic response.[259]

The rationale of this limb of the proposed defence is hard to grasp. There need be no loss of self-control on the part of D. He need not fear violence, present or future, on the part of V or anyone else. Perhaps the most fundamental purpose of the criminal law is to make force and physical coercion the monopoly of the State, save for circumstances where D alone can act to save himself or those for whom he is responsible. The current law of provocation makes some partial accommodation for D where he could not control himself even though he was not in any physical danger. But if there is no loss of self-control and no present and future danger, on what ground do we even partially condone an intentional killing perpetrated by a person of ordinary temperament? Unless this question is answered in a manner acceptable to members of all cultures in the multicultural jurisdiction of England and Wales, the case for this part of the Law Commission's reform of provocation is not made out.[260]

---

[255] [1992] 1 All ER 306.

[256] [1992] 4 All ER 889.

[257] [1995] 1 AC 482.

[258] [2005] EWCA Crim 1880.

[259] For further and valuable discussion of the problem of formulating a defence of provocation fairly applicable to members of radically different cultures, see Power, "Provocation and Culture" [2006] *Crim LR* 871.

[260] It is noteworthy that the Law Commission proposes that, under the reformed law of provocation, the judge should be given a power to withdraw the defence from the jury unless there is evidence on which a reasonable jury, properly directed, could conclude that the defence applies. This is not the standard power to withdraw a defence on grounds of insufficiency of evidence. This is a power of withdrawal even in the face of evidence that raises the defence in terms of the applicable grounds. That such an unusual gatekeeping role is deemed necessary should lead to a rethink of the applicable grounds.

§ 10.6 Involuntary manslaughter

(i) Introduction

The term "involuntary manslaughter" refers to those killings made criminal at common law notwithstanding a lack of intention to kill or cause grievous bodily harm.[261] The ambit of involuntary manslaughter is wide, ranging from killings which have a strong affinity with murder to situations where D would lack the culpability for any serious criminal offence had he not caused death. Nowhere is the role of chance factors more prevalent. Beyond the sphere of regulatory offences, negligence does not attract criminal liability unless the negligence is gross and results in death.[262] Assault is now a summary offence;[263] should a death be causally linked to an assault a manslaughter verdict will likely ensue, however unexpected and unforeseeable that eventuality may have been.[264] Certain forms of eccentric sexuality, not in themselves criminal, may attract a manslaughter verdict should death inadvertently arise.[265] The various ways in which liability for involuntary manslaughter may arise are not explicable by reference to any conceptual scheme or overarching principle. They merely reflect the assessments of judges down the years of which killings merit a punitive response. To an extent, the wide scope of involuntary manslaughter is a function of the complete sentencing discretion that judges are permitted at common law; D may receive anything from an absolute discharge to life imprisonment. If judges had accepted as a restraining principle that the minimum culpability requirement for manslaughter should, at least normally, be such as to merit a substantial custodial sentence, we would have narrower and more defensible law of manslaughter.

It is impossible to state the ambit of involuntary manslaughter with precision. Three broad areas of liability can be identified and will now be discussed.

(ii) Constructive manslaughter

What is now known as constructive manslaughter, or "unlawful act" manslaughter,[266] used to be the manslaughter counterpart of the felony/murder rule. If the unlawful act responsible for the death was not a felony but involved any other form of illegality, criminal or civil, then automatically the perpetrator of the unlawful act was guilty of manslaughter.[267] The extraordinary breadth of this form of liability needs no emphasis. Unfortunately, unlike the felony/murder rule itself, constructive manslaughter has not been abolished. The kinds of unlawful act on which a manslaughter verdict may be based have been significantly narrowed since the eighteenth century, yet it remains a broad and frequently unpredictable ground of liability. Constructive manslaughter requires:

---

[261] 1 Russ 611–33 (views about the scope of manslaughter from Coke, Hale, Hawkins, Forster, Black, and East).
[262] *Adomako* [1995] 1 AC 171 (HL).
[263] Criminal Justice Act 1988, s. 39.
[264] See the facts of *Mallett* [1972] Crim LR 260 (CA).
[265] *Pike* [1961] Crim LR 547.
[266] Kenny, *Outlines of Criminal Law* (1902) 119–20.
[267] Buxton, "By Any Unlawful Act" (1966) 82 *LQR* 174.

(i)   a criminal act which causes death;

(ii)   an act which is criminal *per se*; and

(iii)   an act which is dangerous.

(iii) The unlawful act

(a) A criminal act

In *Franklin*,[268] D was strolling along Brighton Pier on a bank holiday Monday and, we know not why, threw an empty wooden beer crate into the sea. The crate struck and killed V, who had been swimming in the sea below. The prosecution argued that liability for constructive manslaughter followed from the trespass to goods perpetrated by D on taking and disposing of the stallholder's crate. Field J rejected this argument by insisting that the unlawful act that causes V's death must be a crime. While merely a trial direction, it has been widely cited as authoritative, and despite the breadth of *dicta* employed by the House of Lords in *Newbury*[269] (where there was, *obiter*, undiscriminating reference to an "unlawful act" *tout court*[270]), since *Franklin* there has been no imposition of liability for constructive man-slaughter on the basis of mere civil-law wrongdoing.[271] That this absence reflects doctrinal limitations rather than mere prosecutorial practice is implied by the Court of Appeal decision in *Scarlett*.[272] D had been convicted of constructive manslaughter on the basis that he had assaulted V. His conviction was quashed on appeal because the trial court, improperly according to the Court of Appeal, had not permitted D to defend himself on the basis that he had thought that the force he had employed to eject a trespasser was reasonable even though, in objective terms, it was found by the jury to have been excessive.[273] There is little doubt that, under civil law, by employing excessive force D had committed the tort of battery, and it is notable that no attempt was made to argue that this civil liability was a sufficient underpinning to sustain the conviction for manslaughter.

(b) An act of commission

Since the Court of Appeal decision in *Lowe*,[274] it appears that the criminal act must take the

---

[268] (1883) 15 Cox CC 163.

[269] [1977] AC 500.

[270] In *Newbury*, D threw a piece of paving stone from a bridge as a train approached: it smashed through the cab window, killing V. We cannot assume the commission of any underlying offence against the person because, as will be discussed below, the House of Lords rejected, as a requirement for constructive manslaughter, any need for D to foresee that his act would cause physical harm to someone. Nonetheless, D seems to have committed the offences of criminal damage contrary to the Criminal Damage Act 1971 and of endangering passengers contrary to s. 32 of the OAPA 1861. Accordingly, there is no need to resort to the tort of trespass to sustain D's conviction for constructive manslaughter.

[271] In *Lamb* [1967] 2 QB 981, a case of horseplay involving a gun but not involving any assault, Sachs LJ held that it was a misdirection to speak in general terms of "an unlawful and dangerous act" and "not in point to consider whether an act is unlawful merely from the angle of civil liabilities." What was required was an act "unlawful in the criminal sense of the word."

[272] [1993] 4 All ER 629.

[273] But see now *Owino* [1996] 2 Cr App R 128 and *Armstrong-Braun* [1999] Crim LR 416.

[274] [1973] QB 702; disapproving *Senior* [1899] 1 QB 283. Although *Lowe* has been superseded in other respects by *Sheppard* [1981] AC 394, it remains authoritative on the present point.

form of an act rather than an omission. D was found to have wilfully neglected her child contrary to section 1 of the Children and Young Persons Act 1933 by her failure to arrange for medical treatment despite the obvious need of her child for medical attention. Phillimore LJ drew a sharp distinction between a child's dying as the result of a parent's blow and death resulting from parental neglect of the child. The former incident but not the latter will attract liability for constructive manslaughter. His Lordship did not offer any defence of this distinction and it is not obvious why indifference and neglect of one's parental duties to catastrophic effect is systemically less culpable than parental violence. Yet it is well to remember that we are dealing here with *constructive* liability, in the sense that there need be no mens rea regarding death or serious injury: if the ruling had been the other way, *all* child deaths associated with wilful neglect would constitute manslaughter without any necessity to demonstrate parental culpability in respect of the risk of death. Cases of egregious parental neglect resulting in the death of children can be charged as manslaughter on the basis of the gross negligence of the parents. For that form of manslaughter, the better view is that the negligence must relate to the risk of death.[275] With this in mind, the decision in *Lowe* may be welcomed. It is regrettable enough that the causing of inadvertent death by a positive criminal act may frequently sustain a charge of manslaughter; there is no virtue in imposing this harsh doctrine on omissions, even on the assumption that, other things being equal, acts and omissions are morally equivalent.[276]

(c) An act criminal *per se*

The sheer number of criminal offences, particularly regulatory offences, leaves enormous scope for constructive manslaughter. A random example is the selling of food non-compliant with food safety standards, an offence of strict liability.[277] Each year, deaths ensue from food-poisoning. The lack of manslaughter verdicts associated with such deaths is, in part, attributable to the decision of the House of Lords in *Andrews*.[278] D had committed the offence of dangerous driving, and in so doing had caused the death of V. According to Lord Atkin, a verdict of manslaughter did not necessarily flow from such facts. For constructive manslaughter there had to be an underlying crime which was intrinsically criminal and not merely "a lawful act [done] with a degree of carelessness which the legislature makes criminal."[279] The distinction is not an easy one but in practical terms the effect of *Andrews* has been to take driving offences and regulatory offences concerned with public and work-place safety outside the ambit of constructive manslaughter.[280] Serious transgressions in those areas which result in death may, instead, constitute manslaughter by gross negligence.

Although the practical effect of *Andrews* is easily grasped, its conceptual underpinning is problematic. Lord Atkin's informing idea is straightforward: driving is not of itself illegal; it

---

[275] See below, § 10.6(iv).

[276] On the question of equivalence, see the penetrating discussion in Bennett, *The Act Itself* (1995) 139–42.

[277] Food Safety Act 1990, s. 8. A defence of due diligence, with an onus of proof on D, is provided by s. 21.

[278] [1937] AC 576.

[279] *Ibid.*, 585.

[280] According to the *Mortality Statistics—Injury and Poisoning* (cited by Clarkson and Keating, *Criminal Law: Text and Materials* (4th ed., 1998) 669) report for 1992 (1994), there were 16,781 deaths by violence or accident in that year. Many of these deaths in workplace and road-traffic situations will involve criminal offences, yet the number of prosecutions for manslaughter form a tiny percentage of prosecutions compared with the prosecutions for health and safety offences and road traffic offences that may be brought following death from unnatural causes.

becomes illegal if done carelessly or dangerously. Therefore, dangerous or careless driving does not, of itself, provide a basis for manslaughter. But this distinction soon runs into difficulties. What if D takes his car on to the public roads with a blood alcohol level above the permitted limit or drives a vehicle which contravenes the Use and Safety of Vehicles Regulations? And why is it the case that driving in a manner which is dangerous or, indeed, which exceeds the speed limit is not something intrinsically illegal? There is a host of things which are otherwise legal but which become illegal if done the wrong way or with the wrong motivation, and it is odd to base any classificatory scheme on this otherwise unremarkable fact. Here, we may discern judicial policy masquerading as a conceptually driven distinction. As we will see, constructive manslaughter is allowed free rein over such conduct as fighting, vandalism, drug-taking, and exotic sexual practices. It does not spill over to the quotidian criminalities of the majority population. This, it must be stressed, is not an argument for employing constructive manslaughter to its full extent.[281] It is an argument for abolition of this form of liability.[282]

Some writers have interpreted *Andrews* as authority for a much simpler proposition: that the unlawful act must be not merely a crime, but a crime of more than negligence or strict liability.[283] Strictly speaking, this is a misreading of the distinction drawn by Lord Atkin. But it is perhaps defensible to reread the decision in this way, since doing so provides a better underpinning to the practical distinction Lord Atkin sought to make.

(d) A dangerous criminal act

The House of Lords in *Newbury*[284] confirmed earlier authority to the effect that the criminal act in question must also be "dangerous". Because dangerousness may be so readily inferred from the fact that death has arisen, it should be stressed that the requirement for a dangerous act is a principle of limitation. The House adopted an earlier statement of the law made by the Court of Appeal in *Church*:[285]

> "the unlawful act must be such that all sober and reasonable people would inevitably recognise it as an act which must subject the other person to at least the risk of some harm resulting therefrom albeit not serious harm."

Two points may be made about this passage. First, the property of dangerousness need not be perceived by D; it is a matter of objective appraisal from the perspective of an ordinary, prudent person. Secondly, the danger in question need not relate to a risk of death or even serious bodily harm; the risk of minor physical harm is quite sufficient. Thus the constructive nature of unlawful act manslaughter is mitigated only to a slight degree. Nonetheless, the requirement for a dangerous act is not without limiting effect. In *Dawson*,[286] D pointed an imitation firearm at V in the course of a robbery. V, a middle-aged

---

[281] But see Wells, *Corporations and Criminal Responsibility* (2nd ed., 2001) 75–8, who argues for more frequent resort to this category of manslaughter in the interests of industrial and transportation safety.

[282] As recommended by the Law Commission in *Involuntary Manslaughter*: Law Com. No. 237 (1996) 127. Unfortunately, as will be discussed below, the Commission then substantially reversed its earlier position in Law Com. No. 304.

[283] See, e.g., *Smith and Hogan* 382; Ashworth, *Principles* 301.

[284] [1977] AC 500.

[285] [1966] 1 QB 59, 70.

[286] (1985) 81 Cr App R 150 (CA).

man with coronary illness, suffered a fatal heart attack induced by the fright engendered by his confrontation with D. This was held not to be a case of constructive manslaughter. The ordinary person would have foreseen that V would be frightened, even extremely frightened, but fright *per se* (falling short of psychiatric injury) was not a form of harm within the *Church* formulation. According to the Court of Appeal, it was clear that some form of bodily harm is required. A coronary was to be regarded as a form of bodily harm but the ordinary person would not inevitably have recognised the risk of that eventuality arising from these circumstances. The ordinary person was to be invested with the knowledge available to D at the time of his act, no less, no more.[287] Middle-aged men did not comprise a class of individuals susceptible to heart attacks induced by fright. By contrast, in *Watson*,[288] *Dawson* was distinguished on facts where an 87-year-old man died as a result of a coronary induced by the stress of D's burglarious entry into his home. Elderly men did comprise a class of individuals susceptible to stress-induced heart attacks. D knew his victim to be an elderly man so it followed that the ordinary person test should be applied with that in mind.

Dawson was also distinguished, questionably, in *Ball*.[289] D was quarrelling with V and reached into his pocket to take a cartridge which he placed in his shotgun. He fired the gun, killing V. The pocket contained live and blank cartridges. D claimed that he had intended to load his gun with a blank cartridge. His counsel argued that the reasoning in *Dawson* obliged the judge to direct the jury that, in applying the ordinary person test, the ordinary person must be taken to assume the presence of a blank cartridge in the gun because that was the assumption made by D. The Court of Appeal dismissed this argument on the ground that *Dawson* was a case concerned with the vulnerability of the victim, whereas the facts of *Ball* involved a question about the inherent danger of D's act. In the latter kind of case the jury was entitled to appraise the dangerousness of the act in the light of all the circumstances actually present at the time of D's act, not merely those circumstances known to D himself. Yet this distinction would lead to absurd consequences. Suppose that, on facts otherwise similar to *Ball*, D had bought a carton of blank cartridges which, due to a packaging mishap of which he was unaware, contained some live cartridges. In those circumstances, surely, the ordinary person should be invested with the same assumption as D; the assumption that the gun was loaded with a blank cartridge. Moreover, distinguishing *Dawson* was unnecessary. On the actual facts of *Ball*, D was aware that his pocket contained live cartridges as well as blanks. His manslaughter conviction is entirely in keeping with the reasoning of *Dawson*: D's act was dangerous given the facts that D knew. The argument of defence counsel in *Ball*, as sketched here, was a fallacious reading of *Dawson*. It should have been dismissed on that ground.

(e) No "aimed at" requirement

In the now discredited case of *DPP* v. *Smith*,[290] the House of Lords spoke in terms of an act "aimed at the victim" as a defining element of the crime of murder. That requirement, if

---

[287] *Ibid.*, 157.
[288] (1989) 89 Cr App R 211 (CA).
[289] [1989] Crim LR 730.
[290] [1961] AC 290. In *Frankland* [1987] AC 576, the Privy Council ruled that *Smith* had been based on a misunderstanding of the law of murder.

such it ever was, did not survive the later decision of the House in *Hyam*.[291] Yet in *Dalby*,[292] Waller LJ, giving the judgment of the Court of Appeal, incorporated this limitation into the definition of constructive manslaughter. D unlawfully supplied V with drugs contrary to section 4 of the Misuse of Drugs Act 1971. V injected the drugs intravenously and subsequently died from their effects. The illegal supply of drugs was not a sufficient predicate for a verdict of manslaughter because, according to Waller LJ, it lacked the quality of being "directed at the victim."[293] The validity of this requirement was soon tested against the facts of *Mitchell*,[294] where D began a fight with E in a crowded post office. In the ensuing fracas, V, a frail old lady, was crushed to death. D's manslaughter conviction was confirmed by the Court of Appeal notwithstanding that D's violence was directed at E and not V. All that was required was a criminal and dangerous act which was a legal cause of V's death, an approach followed by the Court of Appeal in *Goodfellow*[295] and vindicated by the House of Lords in *A-G's Reference (No. 3 of 1994)*.[296]

How, then, can *Dalby* be explained in the absence of an "aimed at" requirement? A better reason for ruling out manslaughter in *Dalby*, it is submitted, is the absence of any causal nexus between D's act of supply and V's subsequent death. V was aware that he was injecting drugs into his bloodstream; it was his fully informed decision. V's intervention amounted to a *novus actus*, breaking the casual chain. This justification of the decision in *Dalby* was suggested in *Mitchell*.[297] The decision of the Court of Appeal in *Kennedy*[298] confirms that there is no "aimed at" requirement in constructive manslaughter. (Disconcertingly, however, *Kennedy* itself confirmed a conviction for manslaughter based on D's supply of a drug to V. But V took the drug voluntarily. Accordingly, D's conviction should have been quashed on the basis of V's *novus actus*.[299])

(f) Constructive manslaughter—a critique

In the late Victorian case of *Franklin*,[300] Field J expressed a "horror" of constructive crime. Such a reaction is by no means universal. In *Cato*,[301] two drug addicts, D and V, obtained heroin of a high degree of purity. As was their practice, they consensually injected heroin for each other. Each of them became comatose. Because of contingencies with no bearing on the respective culpability of each actor, D received medical treatment and survived, whereas V died. D was successfully prosecuted for manslaughter, receiving five years' imprisonment. At trial, the unlawful act was found to be the malicious administration of a noxious substance.[302] On appeal, Lord Widgery CJ suppressed his doubts about the propriety of that

---

[291] [1975] AC 55.
[292] [1982] 1 All ER 916 (CA).
[293] *Ibid.*, 919.
[294] [1983] QB 741.
[295] (1986) 83 Cr App R 23.
[296] [1998] AC 245.
[297] [1982] 1 All ER 916,
[298] (1999) 1 Cr App R 54.
[299] Unfortunately in *Kennedy (No. 2)* [2005] EWCA Crim 685, the conviction was affirmed on the problematic ground that D had "acted in concert" with the deceased. See above, § 4.2(iii)(d) (Case 2).
[300] (1883) 15 Cox CC 163.
[301] [1976] 1 All ER 260 (CA). See the valuable note by Wells (1976) 39 *MLR* 474.
[302] OAPA 1861, s. 23.

finding[303] by ruling that, alternatively, the unlawful act was "injecting [V] with a mixture of heroin and water which at the time of the injection and for the purposes of the injection [D] had unlawfully taken into his possession."[304] The difficulty about the latter "offence", a difficulty which should have daunted even a judge so robust as Lord Widgery CJ, is that no such crime is known to English law.[305]

What drives Lord Widgery CJ's judgment is an abhorrence of drug-taking and a determination to impose penal consequences on those involved in it. It is hard to discern any moral or social difference between drugs taken by an individual and those taken with the assistance of a mutual addict. Yet it was only the latter feature that allowed elbow-room for constructive manslaughter in *Cato*[306] (and even then the decision is hard to justify in legal terms). A striking feature is the fortuity surrounding the verdict. Both V and D may easily have died; equally likely was joint survival or the sole death of D.

In our discussion of the law of attempt, we conceded both the impossibility of eradicating "outcome luck" from the criminal law, and that outcome luck could have legitimate implications for the grading of offences and the quantum of punishment.[307] But luck is too potent a factor in the imposition of liability for constructive manslaughter. It can turn a "trivial" assault between quarrelling neighbours into a serious crime involving a custodial sentence where, as in *Mallett*,[308] V falls awkwardly and fatally bumps his head on concrete. Such a verdict can be defended only on the basis that if D engages in criminal conduct, he must take responsibility for the consequences of his criminality, whatever those consequences may be. No doubt such reasoning may have its place where D's conduct gives rise to a clear and vivid danger that serious consequences may occur. Yet in constructive manslaughter, the connection between the unlawfulness of D's act and its dangerousness may be extremely tenuous. In *Arobieke*,[309] D terrified V by following him closely to the railway station and then searching for him on the train V had boarded. V had good reason to fear serious violence at the hands of D and, in his fear, sought to escape across the live tracks, thereby electrocuting himself. A conviction of constructive manslaughter against D was properly ruled out because, *inter alia*, the facts disclosed no unlawful act on his part. Contrast *Mallett*, where there was no threat of serious violence but D was nonetheless convicted of manslaughter.

Unfortunately, there is no likelihood that the legislature will abolish constructive manslaughter. Rather, the Government does not hesitate to impose heavy penalties based substantially on the fact of causing death, as witness the recent increase in the maximum penalty for dangerous driving causing death from five years' to ten years' imprisonment and thence to 14 years'.[310] The (in many ways admirable) heightened concern with the wrongs

---

[303] The effect of V's consent to the injection was insufficiently considered at trial in relation to a conviction under s. 23. Difficult questions would require resolution particularly, at the present time, concerning the impact of the House of Lords decision in *Brown* [1994] 1 AC 212.

[304] [1976] 1 All ER 260, 267.

[305] While *possession* and *supply* of controlled drugs are criminalised, it is not an offence to *administer* a controlled drug.

[306] But see *Kennedy* (1999) 1 Cr App R 54, criticised above in § 4.2(iii)(d).

[307] Above, § 9.3(vi). See also above, § 6.5.

[308] [1972] Crim LR 260.

[309] [1988] Crim LR 314 (CA).

[310] Criminal Justice Act 1993, s. 67; Criminal Justice Act 2003, s. 285. Contrast the maximum penalty for dangerous driving *simpliciter* (contrary to s. 2 of the Road Traffic Act 1988), which remains pegged at two years' imprisonment.

suffered by the victims of crime and the relatives of those victims appears for now to militate against rational appraisals of culpability in the face of death. The most recent Law Commission proposals[311] recommend the creation of an offence of criminal act manslaughter, to cover cases where D kills V intending to cause injury or foreseeing a serious risk of causing injury. Although the trigger for liability is a subjective state of mind, a conviction for an offence which carries a possible penalty of life imprisonment is possible without proof of any culpability relating to death or even substantial harm.

(iv) Manslaughter by gross negligence

Carelessness may be thought to be a problematic form of culpability for a serious criminal offence. The breadth of constructive manslaughter has been criticised. Nonetheless, liability for that form of manslaughter will be triggered by some form of chosen, criminal conduct. By contrast, gross negligence manslaughter requires no advertent wrongdoing and may penalise "the ethically well-disposed agent",[312] a person who lacks any violent or predatory designs on the persons or property of others. To be convicted of manslaughter by gross negligence, it is enough for D to cause the death of V by doing something or omitting to do something in circumstances which reveal a clear failure to exhibit minimum standards of competence or concern. Such standards are largely objective.[313] It was no answer for D to claim, in *Stone*,[314] that his intelligence and skills were so deficient as to preclude performance of the most basic of social tasks. Yet if we do not pay heed to such deficiencies, what is the basis of our censure?[315] If a person is capable of attaining basic skills and competence, then it is conventional and acceptable to criticise her for failure to exercise that competence. If the consequences of such failure are minor, criticism should normally be restrained. She would rightly be aggrieved to receive the same degree of censure for carelessly losing another person's £10 as for dishonestly taking that £10. Yet what if D, a childminder, allows V, an infant in her care, to wander with fatal consequences onto a busy road because she was preoccupied by a conversation with E? The urge to punish would arise. Would it be in point that D was distraught at what she had allowed to happen? If the child had survived, however badly injured, no criminal offence would have been committed by D. Does the impact of death override the lack of recklessness or intent, levels of culpability that otherwise are required for a stigmatic offence? Or should gross negligence receive criminal censure on a broader and more consistent basis than it now does?[316] The answer to such questions depends ultimately on value judgements which are psychologically grounded, lying beyond proof and refutation.[317]

---

[311] Law Com. No. 304, para. 9.9

[312] An expression attributable to Bernard Williams.

[313] There is, however, uncertainty whether the standards are *entirely* objective: above, § 5.5(ii).

[314] [1977] QB 354 (CA).

[315] See too the facts of *Elliot* v. *C* [1983] 2 All ER 1005.

[316] As is argued in Schulhofer, "Harm and Punishment: A Critique of the Emphasis on the Results of Conduct in the Criminal Law" (1974) 122 *U Pa L Rev* 1497, 1605.

[317] Acceptance of the salience of psychological reactions as precipitates for moral judgments entails the rejection of moral realism but not an acceptance of moral relativism. On psychological reactions and moral judgments see Bennett, *The Act Itself* (1995) 12–16.

(a) The meaning of gross negligence

To cause or allow the death of another negligently will not, of itself, incur liability in manslaughter. The failure of care or concern must be rather more egregious than is required for civil liability. According to Lord Hewart CJ in *Bateman*, it must be the case that:[318]

> "in the opinion of the jury, the negligence of the accused went beyond a mere matter of compensation between subjects and showed such disregard for the life and safety of others, as to amount to a crime against the state and conduct deserving of punishment."

The dictum has been criticised for vacuity, yet it usefully stresses that juries should be cautious when attributing criminality to a defendant who has neither intended nor foreseen that she would cause or allow harm to another. The dictum was approved by the House of Lords in *Andrews*[319] and reflects a consistent pattern of jury directions. Exemplifying this approach is the decision in *Finney*[320] where D, an asylum attendant, was not found guilty of manslaughter even though he made no visual check to see if his patient, V, had left the bath following D's direction to do so. V had remained in the bath and had been killed when, for cleaning purposes, D released scalding water into the bath. The evidence fell short of establishing the abject failure of care necessary to justify a finding of gross negligence.

Sometimes, the courts equate gross negligence with a form of recklessness. For instance, Lord Atkin opined in *Andrews* that a useful synonym for gross negligence was the term recklessness. It is clear from the context (the approval of the decision in *Bateman*) that Lord Atkin was not in any sense seeking to dilute the degree of egregiousness required for a finding of gross negligence.[321] However, the House of Lords went further in *Seymour*.[322] Lord Roskill, in giving judgment for the House, took recklessness to be the most suitable term to express the kind of culpability required for this head of manslaughter. Moreover, he ruled that the recklessness required should be of the kind expounded in *Caldwell*[323] and *Lawrence*.[324] Furthermore, whereas the better view had been that gross negligence should relate to the risk of death or, at least, grievous bodily harm, for Lord Roskill recklessness as to the risk of any degree of harm would suffice.[325] The upshot was an enormously wide form of manslaughter. Liability would ensue if D's conduct had given rise to an obvious and serious risk of physical harm, a risk which D had either foreseen or failed to give any thought to. The breadth of this new approach is readily appreciated if we return to the facts of *Finney*; a manslaughter verdict would seem assured were a jury to be directed along the lines indicated by Lord Roskill.

In *Adomako*,[326] the House of Lords reviewed the fundamentals of this form of manslaughter. *Seymour* was not overruled but seen as no longer relevant. Lord Mackay noted

---

[318] (1925) 19 Cr App R 8, 11.

[319] [1937] AC 576, 582–3.

[320] (1874) 12 Cox CC 625.

[321] [1937] AC 576, 583.

[322] [1983] 2 AC 493.

[323] [1982] AC 341.

[324] [1982] AC 510.

[325] [1982] 2 AC 493, 505 where the elements of reckless manslaughter are assimilated to the elements of reckless driving.

[326] [1995] 1 AC 171. For valuable notes discussing the decision see Smith [1994] *Crim LR* 758; Virgo [1995] *CLJ* 14; and Gardner (1995) 111 *LQR* 22.

that the House in *Seymour* was concerned with liability for the offence of causing death by reckless driving alongside liability for manslaughter. Indeed it was, and one of the most telling criticisms of *Seymour* was that Lord Roskill took the constituents of each offence exactly to correspond. According to Lord Mackay, the statutory abolition of causing death by reckless driving therefore remaindered *Seymour* to legal history. Unfortunately, he did not explain the mystery of how the abolition of the offence of reckless driving had also undone what *Seymour* had decided about manslaughter. It would have been far better to have overruled by using the 1966 Practice Direction. Judicial comity restrains judicial candour.

Be that as it may, *Caldwell* recklessness has been removed from the ambit of manslaughter. *Adomako* asserts the continuing relevance of the approach taken in *Andrews* and *Bateman* and reinstates gross negligence as the required form of culpability. To incur liability for this form of manslaughter, D must have been in breach of a duty of care under the ordinary principles of negligence and her negligence must have caused the death of V. It seems the reference to the civil law of negligence must not be taken too literally. It is more a reference to a basic principle of human association to take care not to cause avoidable and non-excusable deaths to those affected by one's conduct, rather than any strict application of the rules allowing recovery in negligence.[327] So if D and V are engaged on a joint criminal enterprise—illegal immigration;[328] arson of a building[329]—D may be liable for the manslaughter of V on the basis of his gross negligence irrespective of the fact that public policy would preclude a successful action in negligence against V.

While there is a general duty imposed on us all not to cause death by a positive act, the duty requirement does require closer attention where the allegation of gross negligence takes the form of a failure to discharge a legal obligation, such as D's omission to close the railway crossing gate in *Pittwood*.[330] D's liability for manslaughter rested on a finding that his responsibility for closing the gate was more than a contractual duty owed to his employer, but also constituted a general duty of care owed to users of the crossing.

Once the duty of care (in the qualified sense identified above) and causation are satisfied, the jury must next ask themselves (for Lord Mackay, it is "supremely a jury question"):[331]

"having regard to the risk of death involved, [was] the conduct of the defendant . . . so bad in all the circumstances as to amount to a criminal act or omission?"

The harshness introduced by *Seymour* is, for the moment at least, a thing of the past; witness the quashing of several of the convictions in the consolidated appeals heard by the House in *Adomako*, convictions which were entirely well-founded under a *Caldwell* recklessness standard. The phrase of Lord Mackay's, "having regard to the risk of death involved," suggests that the gross negligence of D must be as to death and not as to any lesser harm. As Glanville Williams observed, if gross negligence as to any physical harm were to suffice, constructive manslaughter would effectively be made redundant[332]—an

---

[327] For a view that there is more to it than that see Herring, "The Duty of Care in Gross Negligence Manslaughter" [2007] *Crim LR* 24.
[328] *Wacker* [2003] 1 Cr App R 22.
[329] *Willoughby* [2004] EWCA Crim 3365.
[330] (1902) 19 TLR 37; above, § 4.1(i)(b) (Case 3).
[331] [1995] 1 AC 171, 187.
[332] *CLGP*, 111.

assessment now confirmed by authority.[333] Note, too, that "badness" in this context is not a matter of evil disposition or even indifference to the victim's welfare. It is a matter of D's conduct. In one of the cases disposed of in *Adomako* where a conviction for gross negligence manslaughter was confirmed, an anaesthetist had failed for 11 minutes or so to identify the cause of the patient's respiratory difficulty as a dislodged endotracheal tube. Other means of restoring the supply of oxygen were frantically tried but the simple and obvious procedure of reattaching the tube was not performed, something that, according to expert evidence, would have been done by a competent anaesthetist within 30 seconds of observing the patient's difficulties. As a qualified professional person, he was required to demonstrate competence. His incompetence was so bad as to allow his conviction for manslaughter to be confirmed.

(b) A critique of gross negligence manslaughter

Whether negligence, however gross, is a sufficient form of culpability for a serious offence is a matter that has divided theorists.[334] In the light of the House of Lords decision in *G*,[335] which rejected objective recklessness as a suitable form of culpability for serious offences, the optimistic argument was put in *Misra*[336] that abolition of objective recklessness implied the abolition of gross negligence as a form of culpability for an offence as serious as manslaughter. The argument predictably failed,[337] since gross negligence manslaughter has been well established for many years and was recently endorsed and refurbished by the House of Lords in *Adomako*. Moreover, there is clearly ground for serious criticism of D if she has failed to conduct herself to the standard that she is reasonably capable of; equally so were she to attempt a task that she knows she is incapable of. It has been argued that penal consequences in respect of negligence are pointless because the thoughtless and the careless cannot be deterred, whereas reckless or intentional criminality can be influenced by the prospect of hard treatment. The point has been put as a matter of logic but it is a question of fact. We all have prudential reasons to drive carefully because, if we do, our chances of being killed or injured on the road are diminished. Another reason for driving carefully is to avoid liability for the crime of driving without due care and attention.[338] Whether that offence and other motoring offences improve driving standards on a significant scale is something to be investigated and not dismissed out of hand.[339] The argument from deterrence has gained force recently, particularly by way of reaction to several large transportation disasters. The Law Commission is now of the view, reversing an earlier stance, that there is a valid role for the offence of gross-negligence manslaughter in English law.[340] Further, gross negligence—"conduct falling far below what can reasonably be expected"—is the informing idea behind the offence of corporate manslaughter which is currently before

---

[333] *Singh* [1999] Crim LR 582.

[334] See above, § 5.5(iv).

[335] [2004] 1 AC 1034; above, § 5.2(i)(b).

[336] [2005] 1 Cr App R 21.

[337] As was also the case in *Mark* [2004] EWCA Crim 2490.

[338] Road Traffic Act 1988, s. 3, as substituted by s. 2 of the Road Traffic Act 1991.

[339] Although the difficulties of measuring the deterrent effects of criminal laws are very considerable: see Walker and Padfield, *Sentencing: Theory, Practice and Law* (2nd ed., 1996) 79–95.

[340] Law Com. No. 304, para 9.9.

Parliament.[341] Yet legitimate concern with effective deterrence should not override an insistence that convictions for serious, stigmatic, offences should be based on a sufficient degree of culpability. Should an anaesthetist, doing his hapless and inadequate best, receive a custodial sentence for the disastrous consequences of his ineptitude? Yes, it might be answered, if he was capable of doing better or had reason to know that he was not up to the demands of his job. A negative response would be made by those who would restrict imprisonment to persons who *choose* to harm the interests of others. We can introduce but not resolve this issue here. As was said earlier, disagreement arises from different psychological responses to the occurrence of harm and cannot be resolved by any resort to principle. Even if we allow findings of negligence to be a basis of criminal liability, liability for manslaughter is based not on mere negligence but *gross* negligence which is "so bad . . . as to amount to a criminal act or omission." This judgment is to be made by the jury and allows considerable scope for different verdicts on similar facts. Such is the latitude for the fact finder, the argument was put in *Misra* that this variant of manslaughter failed to give the fair notice required by Article 7 of the ECHR. The argument failed. As we have seen, the fair notice requirements of Article 7 have not been rigorously applied.[342] Furthermore the criminalisation of negligence entails fact-specific judgments made on the basis of general criteria. It is simply impossible to lay down specific rules about the standard of care for the myriad of circumstances where a claim can be made that D has acted negligently.

(v) Reckless manslaughter

In *Hyam*,[343] the House of Lords ruled by a majority that a high degree of *Cunningham* recklessness—foresight of the probability of death or grievous bodily harm—sufficed for malice aforethought in murder. *Hyam* was, in substance, reversed by *Moloney*[344] where the House decided that nothing less than an intent to kill or cause grievous bodily harm would suffice as the culpability required for murder. The dissenting judges in *Hyam* assumed that the high form of recklessness that the majority found sufficient for murder would suffice to support a verdict of manslaughter. This must surely be the case, at least where D foresees he may kill or seriously injure V; yet there is a dearth of authority on subjective recklessness as a form of culpability for manslaughter.[345] In the vast majority of cases when there is foresight on the part of D that his conduct may unjustifiably or inexcusably kill or seriously injure V, his conduct will involve the commission of some offence, irrespective of the causing of any injury or death to V. In *Hyam* itself, D had perpetrated arson. Consequently, a conviction for constructive manslaughter would straightforwardly be obtained on facts such as those without regard to the question whether D foresaw death or serious injury to another.

There may, nonetheless, occasionally be circumstances where D is subjectively reckless as to the causing of death or serious injury but where his conduct would not involve any offence. For instance, D, an archer, might continue with his target practice even though V is

---

[341] As at April 2007: Corporate Manslaughter and Homicide Bill, discussed above, § 8.2(iii)(b)-(c).
[342] See above, § 2.2.
[343] [1975] AC 55.
[344] [1985] AC 905.
[345] The existence of this form of manslaughter was confirmed in *Lidar* [2000] 4 Archbold News 3.

present within the vicinity. When aiming at the target, D would not necessarily commit any offence against V.[346] Accordingly, if V were killed by D's overshooting arrow, it might not be a case of constructive manslaughter but it would be reckless manslaughter if D foresaw a risk of causing death or serious bodily harm.

Does foresight of harm of a lesser magnitude than death or serious harm suffice? In *Adomako*, Lord Mackay gave his approval to earlier *dicta* which suggest that the mens rea for manslaughter will be present in circumstances where D foresees that his acts or omissions may cause physical harm to V or where D is indifferent to the effects of his conduct upon V's health or welfare.[347] It is unfortunate that Lord Mackay approved these *dicta*, which are vaguely expressed and of uncertain ambit. In any event, they are no more than *obiter dicta*: the cases wherein they occur involved questions of gross negligence regarding V's death.[348] There is nothing to preclude the adoption of a rule that the mens rea for reckless manslaughter is foresight of an unwarranted risk of death or grievous bodily harm. In *Lidar*,[349] the Court of Appeal assumed that foresight of death or serious harm was required.

This form of manslaughter is rarely prosecuted, because any qualifying cases are likely also to fall within the ambit of either constructive manslaughter, as noted above, or gross negligence manslaughter. In *A-G's Reference (No. 2 of 1999)*,[350] Rose LJ considered that recklessness in the form of advertence to risk or indifference to risk, might lead to a finding of gross negligence in the criminal law; confirming the view that there is very little scope for a species of manslaughter based exclusively on recklessness. It is true that a finding of gross negligence must rest on a finding that D's conduct was "so bad in all the circumstances as to amount to a criminal act or omission", but that quality is surely present where D takes or is indifferent to an unwarranted risk of causing death or serious bodily harm. It seems negligent as well as reckless to take a known risk—and frequently grossly negligent. The only discrete ground covered by this variant of manslaughter would be situations where D knowingly takes an unwarranted risk of causing serious bodily harm but is not grossly negligent as to causing V's death, essentially a theoretical rather than practical possibility. It is noteworthy that in the Law Commission's final report on the reform of homicide, no provision is made for a statutory version of reckless manslaughter.

§ 10.7 Reform of the law of homicide

In the past few years the English Law Commission has conducted a major review of the English law of homicide, with consultation papers and a final report on the partial defences to murder,[351] and a consultation paper and final report on the structure and content of homicide.[352] Looking in the round at this body of work,[353] and without repeating our

---

[346] There might be an assault if V were made apprehensive by D's continuing to shoot his arrows and D was aware that this was the case but not otherwise.

[347] [1995] 1 AC 171, 187.

[348] *Stone* [1977] QB 354; *West London Coroner, Ex parte Gray* [1988] QB 467.

[349] [2004] 4 Archbold News.

[350] [2000] 3 All ER 182.

[351] LCCP No. 173 (2003); Law Com. No. 290 (2004).

[352] LCCP No. 177; Law Com. No. 304 (2006).

[353] For reviews, see Wilson, "The Structure of Criminal Homicide" [2006] *Crim LR* 471; Ashworth, "Principles, Pragmatism and the Law Commission's Recommendations on Homicide Law Reform" [2007] *Crim LR* 345.

earlier remarks on specific aspects of the proposals, the principal impression is how much the future envisaged by the Commission is so similar to the present. There will be a crime of murder—first-degree murder—with a mandatory penalty of life imprisonment. There will be, as now, partial defences of provocation and diminished responsibility reducing first-degree murder to second-degree murder, displacing the mandatory penalty. Gross negligence manslaughter will be retained and the proposal for an offence of criminal act manslaughter has a large affinity with the current constructive manslaughter. To be sure, there are some significant changes. First-degree murder will require some degree of culpability as to causing death and duress will be a defence to first-degree and second-degree murder, albeit with a reverse burden of proof. There are some important differences between the current versions of provocation and diminished responsibility and the reformulations of these partial defences. But it is a refurbishment rather than a new blueprint.

The crucial decision was the retention of one form of murder attracting a mandatory penalty. Much of the design and content of the new dispensation follows from that. A radical, simplifying reform, suggested by Lord Kilbrandon in *Hyam*,[354] would be to reduce all the categories of homicide to one: a general, all-embracing offence of unlawful homicide.This proposal has been defended and elaborated by Blom-Cooper and Morris.[355] Certainly, many of the post-*Hyam* appeals on the demarcation of the murder/manslaughter boundary, the limits of the provocation defence, and the applicability of duress to murder would have been unnecessary had this bold proposal been taken up by the legislature. The principal casualty of such a change would be a distinct crime of murder. The pay-off would be radical simplification of a complex body of law and a sentencing discretion for every case of homicide.

These are powerful attractions, yet it may cogently be objected that to scrap all the current gradations of homicide would bring under one label an enormous range of differing conduct with very different forms of culpability. Besides, there is a strong sentiment to retain the evocative term murder; a feeling that an important cultural value would be lost if the worst killings did not attract that label. That sentiment proved decisive for the Law Commission.[356] It remains to be seen what price must be paid in terms of appeals and complexity should these reforms be implemented.

§ 10.8 Suicide, complicity in suicide, and suicide pacts

(i) Suicide

For centuries, death by suicide entailed for the deceased a form of post-mortem disgrace. Burial rites were prohibited and real and personal property were forfeit to the Crown.[357] That stigma was reflected in law. Until the passing of the Suicide Act 1961, it was an offence at common law to attempt suicide. Because of the Act, however, a survivor of a suicide

---

[354] [1975] AC 55, 98.
[355] *With Malice Aforethought* (2004).
[356] Law Com. No. 304, part 2.
[357] Kenny, *Outlines of Criminal Law* (1902) 112–14.

attempt will no longer attract criminal liability for her self-directed conduct.[358] However, as will be seen, it remains criminal to assist in the suicide of others, whether by helping others to kill themselves[359] or by killing at the request of a person wishing to die.[360]

The residual criminality still associated with suicide attempts requires some attempt at determining what acts are to be regarded as suicides.[361] In *Bland*,[362] Lord Goff took the view that a person was legitimately entitled to insist on the cessation of forms of life support such as mechanical respiration. Such an exercise of autonomy was not to be regarded as a form of suicide, merely a refusal of medical treatment. Lord Goff does not explain why, in particular circumstances, to decline further treatment is not to opt for suicide. It is not obvious why a request to be taken off life support is not a form of suicide in circumstances where the removal of support entails a rapid and certain death. Prima facie, it seems to be a case of opting for non-existence by rejecting an unacceptable form of life. Be that as it may, Lord Goff's denial that such a choice was equivalent to suicide both ensures patient autonomy and shields doctors and other medical personnel from the possibility of criminal liability in respect of assisting suicide. It remains the case that the taking of any drug or poison to end life will be suicide whatever the degree of pain and disability the patient must otherwise endure. That position has not changed following the incorporation of the ECHR into English law.[363]

In *Bland*, Hoffmann LJ (as he then was) took the decriminalistion of suicide to be a recognition of the principle of self-determination.[364] If this is indicative of a right in the strict sense, it should follow that if a person of sufficient maturity and competent decision-making capacity has resolved to take her life, any physical intervention to prevent her from doing so will constitute an assault. This analysis throws into question the legality of such interventions as non-consensual medical treatment to prevent loss of life following a suicide attempt. It may be doubted, however, whether there is a right to commit suicide, at least in the full sense. If there were such a right, the rightholder should be entitled to call upon others to help her in the vindication of the right. But it is quite clear that if others were to help her they would become liable for complicity in suicide, contrary to section 2 of the Suicide Act 1961. The existence of section 2 rather suggests that the abolition of the offence of attempted suicide does not make the choice to commit suicide a legally protected sphere of autonomy, merely that such a choice will not incur a criminal sanction. On the other hand, the mere fact that life-preserving intervention *may* be lawful does not mean that it *should* be employed in every possible case.

---

[358] Suicide Act 1961, s. 1.

[359] *Ibid.*, s. 2.

[360] Homicide Act 1957, s. 4.

[361] See also Wheat, "The Law's Treatment of the Suicidal" [2000] *Med LR* 182.

[362] [1993] AC 789, 864.

[363] In *Re B (Adult: refusal of medical treatment)* [2002] 2 All ER 449, the Court of Appeal ruled that the continuation of life support should cease on notification by a competent patient that such treatment was no longer wanted. However, assisting a person wishing to die by providing a substance that will terminate life is unlawfully to assist that person's suicide: *R (on the application of Pretty)* [2002] 1 All ER 1. For critical discussion, *see* Tur, "Legislative Technique and Human Rights: The Sad Case of Assisted Suicide" [2003] *Crim LR* 3.

[364] [1993] AC 789, 827.

(ii) Complicity in suicide

As mentioned already, complicity in the suicide of another remains a criminal offence.[365] There is no statutory definition of suicide, something that does not assist precision in identifying what life-terminating assistance is permitted. It seems tolerably clear that any help rendered to assist a person to take her life by an act of commission will constitute complicity in that person's suicide. Furthermore, although in medical contexts life-sustaining treatment can be withdrawn or refused without embroiling medical or caring personnel in complicity-in-suicide charges, it is not safe to assume that, outside these contexts, self-determination by way of omission is a similarly protected zone. So, if V determines to die by way of starvation, D may incur liability under section 2 were he to encourage and strengthen her resolve not to take food during the critical period. However, if V were to go on a hunger strike to make a political point, it is by no means obvious that persons strengthening her resolve up to the point of death will incur liability under section 2. It may well be that the doctrine of double effect will operate in this context,[366] so that D's liability will depend on whether he intended V to die or merely foresaw death as a side-effect.

Section 2 uses the formula, "aid, abet, counsel or procure", the standard complicity formula. However, the section creates a free-standing crime, not a way of participating in the crime of another. Accordingly, a person will be liable for *attempted* complicity in another's suicide should she be unsuccessful in persuading that person to take his own life; notwithstanding that, under the general law, there is no offence of attempted complicity in the crime of another.[367]

Because it is a free-standing offence attracting a further layer of inchoate liability, this may be seen as indicative of a legislative intent that conduct falling within section 2 is to be penalised within its own terms and is not to be regarded as a direct cause of D's death. Recall, however, the analyses of causation and action-in-concert adopted across the two *Kennedy*[368] cases. If the approaches in those cases were to be taken seriously, should D supply a syringe of poison to V in the knowledge that V would use it to commit suicide, D would then become exposed to direct liability, *as a principal*, for a homicide offence. On the view favoured here and in chapter four, the proper charge is under section 2: complicity in V's death.

(iii) Suicide pacts

If D kills V with the "settled intention" of dying too in pursuance of a suicide pact between herself and V, D will be guilty of manslaughter rather than murder by virtue of section 4 of the Homicide Act 1957. To be a member of such a pact, one must intend to die in pursuance of the pact. If that is not the case D will be guilty of murder. It is not a defining element of a suicide pact that each member of it must intend to die on the same occasion.

---

[365] Suicide Act 1961, s. 2.
[366] *Secretary of State for the Home Department v. Robb* [1995] 1 All ER 677.
[367] *McShane* [1977] 66 Cr App R 97.
[368] [1999] 1 Cr App R 54; [2005] EWCA Crim 685; above, § 4.2(iii)(d) (Case 2).

Accordingly, D should be entitled to a verdict of manslaughter even if a time comes when she no longer intends to fulfil the pact, provided she intended to observe the pact at the time she killed V. One aspect of the extenuation that underlines section 4 is that D's mental state must be so desperate as to induce a decision to commit suicide *at the time of the killing.* It is irrelevant that the condition may pass.

For obvious reasons, it may be difficult to resolve what part the survivor of a suicide pact played in enacting the pact. The Suicide Act 1961 provides that on a charge of murder or manslaughter in pursuance of the pact, a verdict of complicity in suicide may be given.[369]

---

[369] Suicide Act 1961, s. 2(2).

11

NON-FATAL OFFENCES AGAINST THE PERSON

Offences of violence cover an enormous spectrum of human conduct. D commits battery if he takes hold of V's arm, should V have made it clear that she objects to such contact by D.[1] Or D may shoot and seriously injure V and thereby commit serious offences such as attempted murder or wounding with intent. What links the arm-holding with the shooting is the right of all persons not to be subjected to any unwarranted intrusion upon the body.[2] This most basic of rights is jealously guarded by the criminal law and, because of this, the concept of violence employed in the foundation offences of assault and battery extends to the mere touching of the clothes of the victim and even to the threat thereof.[3] This is not overreaction: the right not to be physically touched, outside the sphere of consensual touchings and the exigencies of normal life, is fundamental to ordered liberty. Even where no harm occurs, the raw battery or assault *in itself* violates D's right to be left alone and not be interfered with by others. This shows that there is a further dimension to the offences against the person, additional to the concern for personal integrity and our right not to be hurt. The further dimension is a matter of privacy. The very act of interfering with another's person is a wrong; not because of any harmful consequences, but because it violates one of the core interests implicated in the right to privacy, guaranteed by Article 8 of the ECHR.

There are a considerable number of offences which deal with the infliction or the threat of violence. Many of them are to be found in the Offences against the Person Act 1861, an enactment which remains of central importance today. The Act is in no sense a codification of non-fatal violent offences; it merely brings together a disparate collection of existing statutory offences. There is much overlap and inconsistent terminology. Even at the time of its enactment it was castigated as "singularly fragmentary and unsystematic".[4] Yet it remains, today, at the centre of the law's response to violence against the person[5] and continues to generate a stream of appellate, interpretative case law.

---

[1] *Collins* v. *Willcock* [1984] 3 All ER 37 (CA).

[2] The right inheres in all persons capable of autonomous choices, however irrational the choice made by the particular agent: *St George's Healthcare NHS Trust* v. *S* [1998] 3 All ER 673. By contrast, if a person is considered unable to choose, quite drastic physical interventions may become lawful, such as the sterilisation of a learning-disabled woman: *F* v. *West Berkshire Health Authority* [1990] 2 AC 1 (HL).

[3] *Day* (1845) 1 Cox CC 207; *Thomas* (1985) 81 Cr App R 331 (CA).

[4] Greaves, *The Criminal Law Consolidation and Amendment Acts* (2nd ed., 1862) 3–4.

[5] It is assumed that "person" is a reference to a human being and that pre-natal injury does not fall within provisions relating to the inflicting, occasioning, or causing of injury. There is no authority or dictum to the contrary and no reason of principle why the law relating to non-fatal offences against the person should differ on this point from the law of homicide (see above, § 10.2(i)(a)). If V should be born in an injured condition because of something

In this chapter, no attempt will be made at a comprehensive coverage of offences of violence. We will look first at the two basic offences, assault and battery, which police the frontier between lawful conduct and violent acts. Then we will turn to offences involving some form of bodily (which now includes psychiatric) harm, namely assault occasioning actual bodily harm, the malicious infliction of wounds or grievous bodily harm, and the intentional causing of wounds or grievous bodily harm with intent to do grievous bodily harm. As we shall see, these offences have been extended to include the intentional and reckless transmission of diseases and infection. Following that, we will briefly consider offences concerned with poisons and noxious substances and then go on to discuss harassment offences—what might be termed psychic violence. Finally, we will examine versions of these offences aggravated by racial or religious hostility.

§ 11.1 Assault and battery

Assault and battery are two distinct offences. V is assaulted if she *apprehends* the possibility of imminent unlawful violence.[6] A battery is inflicted upon V if unlawful violence is *inflicted* upon her. The distinction may seem odd. Ordinary people, and lawyers too, would naturally describe D's punching V as an assault. It would seem pedantry of the most tiresome kind to insist that, if V saw the punch coming, she was first assaulted as she apprehended its impact and subsequently battered when the punch landed. The pedant might add for good measure that if V was struck without warning from behind by D, D would be guilty of battery but not of assault. It would be far better to do away with such nit-picking and use the term "assault" to cover situations where V *either* apprehends *or* suffers violence (in the latter case, whether she apprehended it or not). The term battery could be allowed to wither away as an archaism. Indeed it looked as if that was the way that things were going. In 1980, the Criminal Law Revision Committee took the view that the term "assault" could be safely used in legal discourse to cover assaults in the narrow sense (i.e. causing an apprehension of violence) and in the sense of inflicting violence, rendering the term battery otiose.[7] The same position is taken in the current Home Office proposals for reforming this area of law.[8]

Pedantry returned with a vengeance in *DPP* v. *Little*.[9] The information laid against D charged that he "did unlawfully assault and batter [V] contrary to [section 39 of the Criminal Justice Act 1988]." The Divisional Court ruled that the information was bad for duplicity because it charged two separate offences instead of the permissible single offence. Assault, said the Court, was to cause an apprehension of violence and battery was to inflict violence. If assault and battery were to be charged, they would have to be laid by separate informations. It is not, as might have formerly been thought, mere verbiage to charge D's

---

done by D prior to V's birth, applying the reasoning in *A-G's Reference* (*No. 3 of 1994*) [1998] AC 245, in principle a charge against D under a suitable provision of the OAPA 1861 should be possible.

[6] See *Logdon* [1976] Crim LR 121 (DC) for an example of a "pure" assault, i.e. a situation where D intended V to apprehend violence by showing him a gun in a desk drawer but lacked any present intention to inflict violence.

[7] Criminal Law Revision Committee, Fourteenth Report, *Offences Against the Person* Cmnd. 7844 (1980).

[8] Home Office, *Violence: Reforming the Offences Against the Person Act 1861* (1998), discussed below, § 11.10.

[9] [1992] QB 645 (DC).

physical attack on V as an assault and battery: it is to charge D with two separate offences with different definitions.

In historical terms, the decision in *Little* is correct. Battery emerged as a crime from the tort of trespass to the person.[10] The etymology of assault—*adsaltare*, to jump at—indicates the focus on frightening rather than hitting people.[11] Yet it is remarkably inconvenient to revert to the medieval origins of these offences. For example, section 47 of the OAPA 1861 penalises "any *assault* occasioning actual bodily harm." There is no reference whatever to battery. By far and away the most common incident giving rise to a charge under section 47 is a direct attack by D on V. The standard form of indictment for such an occurrence is "D assaulted V, thereby occasioning him actual bodily harm." If V apprehended the attack the reference to assault is sustainable in terms of the presence of the elements of the offence. Yet it is the battery rather than the assault that occasions the actual bodily harm. What if D succeeds in striking V without first causing him apprehension? (Suppose V is looking the other way or is asleep.) As *Smith and Hogan* observes, it would be "incredible" if such circumstances did not involve a section 47 offence.[12]

In *Little*, the Divisional Court accepted that the legislature, in section 47 and in other provisions, used the term "assault" to embrace both assault in the pure sense of the term and the offence of battery. That points up the fact that the standard form of indictment referred to above, used in respect of section 47, is duplicitous, in that the term "assault" when used in that section is a reference to the two distinct offences of assault or battery. It follows that, as Smith and Hogan reflect, "thousands of people have been convicted on defective indictments ever since 1861." Understandably, the authors now advise prosecutors to "draft particulars of an indictment or information so as to make clear that it charges either an assault or a battery, but not both."[13]

Until the long-overdue reform of offences against the person is in place,[14] we must take seriously the separateness of assault and battery.

§ 11.2 Assault

(i) The actus reus

According to the decision in *Little*,[15] assault is a statutory offence. Therefore, one should consult the statutory definition prior to any account of the actus reus of the offence. But there is no statutory definition. *Little* states that assault became a statutory offence upon the passing into law of section 47 of the OAPA 1861. This is a puzzling conclusion, since section 47 merely states that the maximum penalty for the offence is five years' imprisonment and that it may be tried on indictment. *Little* goes on to rule that the relevant constitutive

[10] Milsom, *Historical Foundations of the Common Law* (2nd ed., 1981) chap. 11.
[11] Williams, *TBCL* 172.
[12] *Smith and Hogan* 519.
[13] *Ibid.*
[14] See below, § 11.10.
[15] [1992] QB 645 (DC).

statutory provision is now section 39 of the Criminal Justice Act 1988, which provides that common assault (and battery) are summary offences punishable by a fine not exceeding level 5 or a term of imprisonment not exceeding six months. Again, no definition of assault is to be found there. We must still turn to the common law in order to delineate the nature and ambit of the offence, notwithstanding that the practice after *Little* is for informations to refer to assault as an offence charged under section 39.[16]

The actus reus of assault is any act by D that causes V to apprehend immediate and unlawful personal violence. There is high authority endorsing this depiction of the actus reus in assault and a degree of stability of definition has been achieved.[17] However, as we shall see, key elements of this judicially derived formula have been expansively interpreted. Before turning to those elements, some general remarks concerning the actus reus may be made.

(a) Unlawfulness and consent

V must apprehend *unlawful* violence. Sometimes, the application of force may be quite lawful, as in the application of defensive or preventive force.[18] Consent, too, may legitimate what would otherwise count as unlawful violence. Although consent is further discussed below,[19] given the crucial role that it may play in constituting an assault, some additional discussion of that element is appropriate here.

There is some uncertainty whether lack of consent is an element of the actus reus of assault or a defence to assault.[20] The former is the better view. The threshold of violence in assault is, properly, set at a very low level. V suffers the actus reus of an assault if she apprehends an imminent touching by D to which she has not consented and which is not an inevitable concomitant of ordinary life (like being jostled on a crowded tube-train). Because an assault may include the threat of things that (should they happen) will not even hurt, we can see that lack of consent, and D's corresponding disrespect for V's autonomy and privacy, are at the heart of the wrong that constitutes an assault.[21] Certain forceful interventions may

---

[16] It is completely obscure why providing statutory penalties for a common law offence changes the offence into a statutory offence. If it does, murder, for instance, becomes a statutory offence because the penalty for murder is prescribed by the Murder (Abolition of Death Penalty) Act 1965. That conclusion has never been suggested. Subsequently, the Court of Appeal has left open the question whether assault and battery should be regarded as separate statutory offences: *Lynsey* [1995] 3 All ER 654. Further, in *Haystead* v. *Chief Constable of Derbyshire* [2000] 3 All ER 890, Laws LJ observed that assault and battery were "in truth" common law offences. However, unless and until *Little* is overruled, charges of assault and battery should be brought under s. 39 of the Criminal Justice Act 1988.

[17] *Ireland* [1998] AC 147.

[18] Below, § 21.2.

[19] § 21.1.

[20] In *Brown* [1994] 1 AC 212 (HL), Lords Jauncey, Lowry, and Templeman considered consent to be a defence to assault, whereas Lords Mustill and Slynn considered the absence of consent to be part of the harm that constituted the offence. However, the views expressed on this point were *obiter* in respect of simple assault, since the case involved the causing of actual bodily harm—which in the circumstances was taken by the majority to negative the relevance of consent altogether (below, § 21.1(iv)). In *Kimber* [1983] 3 All ER 316, the Court of Appeal considered non-consent to be an integral element of the actus reus in assault.

[21] Consequently, in principle there should be no finding of *assault*, even where D has caused significant physical harm to V, if D acts with V's consent. (There may well be liability for other offences which do not require an assault upon V, such as ss. 18 and 20 of the OAPA 1861.) However, this may not be the position under English law at present; on the majority view in *Brown* (see previous note), the most minor of apprehended contacts will constitute the actus reus of assault and consent is simply a qualified defence.

be well intentioned and, from a paternalist standpoint, be in the interests of V. But it is for V to decide what is in her interest. In *St George's Trust*,[22] a tort case, D performed an operation to save V's life and the late-term foetus she was carrying. However, he did so despite V's lack of consent. This was held to be trespass to the person and, undoubtedly, was also an assault.

Consequently, it is not necessary for V in any sense to be *frightened* by what D intends to do. It is enough that she does not want D to do it. If D threatens any form of immediate touching which V has not consented to, or which need not be tolerated as an incident of everyday life, D commits assault.

(b) The conduct element in assault

In *Fagan* v. *MPC*,[23] the Divisional Court reiterated the traditional view that assault requires a positive act and that a mere omission will not suffice. In *Fagan*, D's conviction for assault[24] was confirmed on the basis of intentional failure to remove the wheel of a car which he had inadvertently parked on V's foot. The decision demonstrates that the act requirement will be fulfilled if D persists with a threatening posture that he may have adopted without any intent to cause fright. So, if D is sitting alone in, say, a railway carriage and puts on a "horror" mask to amuse himself, the actus reus of assault will occur when, on being joined by V, a fellow passenger, D does not remove the mask despite the fact that it has caused V to fear an imminent attack from him.

The act requirement will not be satisfied, however, if D's lawful presence, without more, is perceived as a threat by V. Suppose that D enters an enclosed railway carriage on a train. The only other occupant is V, a lone woman. D notes that V seems agitated: moments later she says, "Please do not touch me." It would be appropriate socially for D to remove himself from the carriage at the first safe opportunity, but his failure to do so should not constitute the actus reus of assault. Arguably, that conclusion would not hold if D had knowingly entered a "women-only" carriage, i.e. if D were a trespasser. In *Smith* v. *Superintendent of Woking Police Station*,[25] D had trespassed onto enclosed grounds and looked through the window of a ground-floor bedroom. V, undressing for sleep, was terrified when she saw him standing there; conduct which constituted an act of assault.

To speak is clearly an act. However, there are dicta to the effect that "mere words" would not constitute an assault.[26] Applying such *dicta*, the Court of Appeal of British Columbia ruled in *Byrne*[27] that to say, threatingly, "I've got a gun, give me all your money or I will shoot" did not constitute an assault. The court insisted on some form of physical act. This remarkable indulgence is no longer on offer in England and Wales. The decision in *Smith*, above, holds that mere presence in unlawful threatening circumstances may constitute an assault. Those features were present in *Byrne* and, in addition, there were threatening words, making *Byrne* an *a fortiori* case from the standpoint of *Smith*. Any remaining doubt on the

---

[22] [1998] 3 All ER 673 (CA).

[23] [1969] 1 QB 439 (DC); above, § 4.1(i)(b) (Case 4).

[24] Strictly, the case involved battery rather than assault, as it was concerned with the application of force and not the threat of force. The Divisional Court spoke in terms of assault and there is no reason to suppose that its reasoning does not extend to assault in the pure sense of that term.

[25] (1983) 76 Cr App R 234 (DC).

[26] *Meade and Belt* (1823) 1 Lew CC 184.

[27] [1968] 3 CCC 179.

matter is resolved by the decision of the House of Lords in *Ireland*.[28] One of the matters requiring resolution in this important case was whether silent telephone calls could, *in principle*, constitute an assault. (The ruling was in principle because D had pleaded guilty to a charge of assault causing actual bodily harm in the sense of psychiatric harm by silent telephone calls; accordingly the facts of the case were not under review.) The court ruled unanimously that a silent telephone call would constitute an assault if, *inter alia*, it caused V to apprehend the possibility of immediate violence. Although it would be possible to draw a distinction between telephone calls *per se* and "mere words", the two full judgments given in *Ireland* take their decision to have abolished the rule that mere words cannot constitute an assault if it ever truly existed in English law.[29] Similarly, in *Constanza*[30] (discussed below), the Court of Appeal held that written threats could found an assault.

(c) A threat of immediate violence

Assault in its pure form is a *threat* offence, whereas battery is a *contact* offence. Although they have differing histories, the two offences are closely linked. The actus reus of assault is the threat of an immediate battery. But it would be a mistake to describe assault as an attempted battery. To be guilty of assault, D need not possess any intention to inflict violence on V; it is enough that he intentionally or recklessly causes V *to apprehend* immediate violence.[31] On the other hand a threat to inflict violence later is not enough. So, if D were to say, "I will come round next Monday and cut your right leg off" he would not have assaulted V, notwithstanding V's state of terror.

    An understandable judicial concern with the life-wrecking consequences of the abusive conduct familiarly called "harassment" has led to a significant attenuation of the immediacy requirement in assault, making for considerable doubt about the current scope of the offence. In *Constanza*, the Court of Appeal reviewed D's conviction for assault occasioning actual bodily harm arising from circumstances where D, among other things, sent threatening letters to V. Confirming D's conviction, the Court noted that D lived in the same neighbourhood as V and that it was enough to prove "fear of violence at some time not excluding the immediate future."[32] These words are not conspicuously clear but, in the context of the case, they appear to mean that it sufficed that among the fears that V entertained was the fear of a possible imminent attack. That this is enough is confirmed by the House of Lords in *Ireland* where Lord Steyn, speaking for the judicial committee, concluded that the immediacy requirement was made out if D's conduct caused V to apprehend the "possibility" of an immediate attack.[33]

    In *Ireland*, D's conduct took the form of silent telephone calls, calls made miles from the homes of his victims. As mentioned already, their Lordships did not decide whether the actual calls placed by D constituted assaults; in the light of D's guilty plea it merely had to be decided whether silent calls could in principle constitute assaults. Of course, on

---

[28] [1998] AC 147 (HL).

[29] *Ibid.*, 161–2 (Lord Steyn), 166 (Lord Hope).

[30] [1997] 2 Cr App R 492 (CA).

[31] *Logdon* [1976[Crim LR 121 (DC). For a discussion of assaults not culminating in bodily contact see Horder, "Reconsidering Psychic Assault" [1998] *Crim LR* 392.

[32] [1997] 2 Cr App R 492, 494.

[33] [1998] AC 147, 162.

particular facts, a silent call might cause a fear of an immediate attack (e.g. where V believes the caller is in the flat below). Yet, even though V may know that the caller is many miles away, she may still be reduced to a state of great fear. It seems from *Ireland* that in such cases the issue of assault may now be put to the jury. As Lord Steyn acknowledges, whether V is put in fear of the possibility of an immediate attack is a question of fact. Nonetheless, he recommended that trial judges might advise juries that, if they found that V was put in fear, they should consider "what, if not the possibility of imminent personal violence, was the victim terrified about?"[34]

This, with respect, relaxes the imminence requirement in assault beyond any point previously contemplated. It is simply not the case that a state of fear is, necessarily, a fear of the possibility of imminent attack. It is perfectly possible to experience fear and, at one and the same time, be aware that one is perfectly safe, as anyone who has watched a well-crafted horror film well knows. Many recipients of such hateful things as threatening letters or calls may be traumatised by the experience, particularly if it is an extended one, yet at no time fear an *immediate* attack. Certainly, there should be legal protection from such conduct.[35] But the law of assault is the wrong medium (as Lord Steyn seemingly concedes at one point in his judgment[36]). In cases involving threatening calls or letters, it is submitted that judges should refrain from leaving assault-based offences to juries unless there is some evidence from the facts of the instant case that V was actually put in fear of the possibility of an immediate attack. *Pace* Lord Steyn, evidence of fear of something inchoate or non-immediate should not be placed before juries with an invitation to find that the only plausible basis for the fear was the threat of immediate attack.

(d) Conditional threats

There is some authority that a "conditional" threat cannot constitute an assault. In *Blake* v. *Barnard*,[37] there was held to be no assault where D pointed a pistol at V's head with the words, "Shut up or I will blow your brains out." The reasoning behind this remarkable decision was that there was no threat of immediate violence because V could negate the threat by doing what he was told.

Several criticisms may be made. In *Blake*, the famous civil case of *Tuberville* v. *Savage*[38] was perceived to be in point. This was an error. As is well known, in *Tuberville*, D touched his sword and informed V that "If it were not assize time, I would not take such language." We can see that D was informing V that, despite V's impertinence, D was not going to use his sword for fear of being tried and hanged:[39] a case of a non-threat rather than a conditional threat. Moreover, as already discussed, assault is as much about the protection of autonomy as protection from hurt. In *Blake*, D had no right to put such a coercive condition to V. Accordingly, V was under no duty to comply with the threat and was being

---

[34] *Ibid.*, 162. See also *DPP* v. *Ramos* [2000] Crim LR 768.

[35] Protection from Harassment Act 1997; Communications Act 2003. On the latter see *Collins* [2005] Crim LR 794.

[36] [1998] AC 147, 162

[37] (1840) 9 C & P 626, 173 ER 985.

[38] (1669) 1 Mod Rep 3, 86 ER 684.

[39] Assuming, as the Court seemingly did, that D's words were a reliable indication that V was in no immediate danger. It is easy to imagine circumstances where reaching for a weapon is construed as a threat of immediate violence despite placatory words.

confronted with a risk of violence should he assert his right to speak. In principle, such threats should normally constitute assaults. Indeed, there are *dicta* in the later case of *Read* v. *Coker*[40] to that effect.

(ii) The mens rea for assault

The mental element for the crime of assault can be stated briefly and with some assurance. D must intend that V should fear the possibility of immediate violence, or recklessly cause V to fear the possibility of immediate violence.[41] There is no authority or any reason of principle why intent should bear any special or restricted meaning in this context. The recklessness in question is *Cunningham* recklessness:[42] accordingly, D must intend or foresee that V will fear the possibility of immediate violence.

Because assault is a crime which may be committed recklessly, it is, in the confusing terminology employed by the courts, a crime of "basic" intent and therefore a crime where the liability of voluntarily intoxicated persons is resolved under the principles of *Majewski*.[43]

§ 11.3 Battery

(i) Actus reus

The actus reus of battery is the infliction of violence on V by D. It has emerged from our discussion of assault that violence is used in a very extended sense, reflecting the values of autonomy and privacy as well as protection from physical harm. Accordingly, D commits battery if he makes contact with V in any fashion to which she has not consented or which is not a contact in keeping with the normal expectations of the relevant time and place.[44] To kiss someone without consent has been considered a battery,[45] as has the act of spitting upon someone,[46] and the unauthorised cutting of hair.[47] If D makes contact with clothes that V is wearing, that will also suffice for battery.[48]

If one wishes to have the benefits of moving about in a modern urban society, one must accept the inevitable bodily contacts arising therefrom. Suppose that V has a horror of bodily contact with strangers but must take an underground train in order to get to work.

---

[40] (1853) 13 CB 850, 138 ER 1437.

[41] *Savage* [1992] 1 AC 699.

[42] In *K* [1990] 1 All ER 331, the Divisional Court ruled that *Caldwell* recklessness applied to a case of battery and, in so far as no distinction is drawn in the case law between the two offences in terms of mens rea, to assault also. *K* was overruled by the Court of Appeal in *Spratt* [1991] 2 All ER 210 and *Spratt* was confirmed on this point by the same Court in *Parmenter* [1991] 2 All ER 225. *Dicta* in the House of Lords in *Savage* (which overruled *Spratt* and *Parmenter* on other grounds) assume that advertence is required for assault: [1992] 1 AC 699, 736 (Lord Ackner).

[43] [1977] AC 443 (HL); discussed below, § 18.3(ii).

[44] "An assault [*sc.* meaning "battery"] is an "intentional touching of another person without the consent of that person and without lawful excuse": *Faulkner* v. *Talbot* [1981] 3 All ER 468, 471; applied in *Thomas* (1985) 81 Cr App R 331 (CA).

[45] *Dungey* (1864) 4 F & F 99, 102, 176 ER 487.

[46] *Smith* (1866) F & F 1066, 176 ER 910.

[47] *Smith* [2006] EWHC 94.

[48] *Day* (1845) 1 Cox CC 207.

She cannot complain of battery when she is crushed together with others in the rush hour. However, she is entitled to resist what would otherwise be normal lawful contact provided she has made it clear to D that she does not want such contact with him and it is practicable for him to desist from such contact.[49]

There is dispute about how direct the contact with V must be to constitute battery. Person-to-person contact is obviously sufficient but not necessary. Using any form of weapon will suffice. Just as a knife wielded in the hand is within the offence, so too a knife that is thrown. As *Scott v. Shepherd*[50] illustrates, it does not matter if a dangerous weapon, such as a grenade, passes through several panic-stricken hands after being thrown by D prior to the impact on V. Such a response would not constitute a *novus actus interveniens*. Extending the offence further, there are *dicta* to the effect that to set a booby trap[51] or to cause crushing by inducing panic[52] may constitute battery. There seems a clear public interest in including such events within the scope of the offence; it should not matter in principle whether D causes violence to the person of V by direct or indirect means, provided the causing of violence is attributable to some act by D.

As with assault, battery requires an act. However, it seems that the normal rules about omissions apply.[53] Thus a qualifying "act" was found to be present in *Santana-Bermudez*,[54] where V's finger was pierced by a syringe-needle lying in D's pocket. Prior to searching D, V (a police officer) asked if he had any needles on his person and D replied, "No". The danger that D had created was found to come within the decision in *Miller*[55] and on the Divisional Court's reading of that decision his failure to inform V was tantamount to an act of battery.

Accordingly, acts indirectly causing violence seem to fall within the crime of battery. However, in *Ireland*, Lord Steyn strongly discountenanced any assumption that a battery had occurred on the facts of that case. The silent telephone calls had caused psychiatric injury to V, injury which was taken to constitute bodily harm. The prosecution had argued that causing such bodily harm through the medium of the telephone was a form of battery. This was decisively rejected, on the ground that the concept of battery could not accommodate the causing of psychiatric injury by telephone.[56] Moreover, in *Wilson*,[57] the House of Lords had earlier ruled that the statutory offence of maliciously inflicting a wound or grievous bodily harm would encompass percussive and impact injuries whether directly or indirectly caused. In so ruling, their Lordships had considered that, so construed, the offence of malicious wounding[58] would take in a broader swathe of conduct than battery. The cases which take a broader view of battery are not, of course, binding on the House of Lords.[59] In

---

[49] *Collins* v. *Wilcock* [1984] 3 All ER 374 (CA).

[50] (1773) 3 Wils 403, 96 ER 525; above, § 4.2(iii)(b) (Case 1). *Scott* v. *Shepherd* is a civil case but there is no reason why a narrower conception should be adopted in the criminal law.

[51] *Clarence* (1888) 22 QBD 23, 36 (Wills J), 45 (Stephen J) (CCR).

[52] *Martin* (1881) 8 QBD 54 (CCR); see also *Lewis* [1970] Crim LR 647 (CA).

[53] Above, § 4.1(i).

[54] [2004] Crim LR 471.

[55] [1983] 2 AC 161. See above, § 4.1(i)(b) (Case 5).

[56] [1998] AC 147, 161. The conduct was held to constitute an assault.

[57] [1984] AC 242; followed in *Mandair* [1995] 1 AC 208 (HL).

[58] OAPA 1861, s. 20.

[59] *Martin* (1881) 8 QBD 54 and *Lewis* [1970] Crim LR 647 did involve assumptions that a battery had occurred, as the view was taken in those cases that a conviction under s. 20 of the OAPA 1861 required proof of a battery; an assumption no longer tenable in the light of *Wilson* [1984] AC 242 and *Mandair* [1995] 1 AC 208.

the one decision directly in point (and uncomplicated by any creative use of the *Miller* principle), *DPP* v. *K*,[60] the Divisional Court held that a battery had occurred where D had secreted acid in a hand-dryer, causing V to be burnt with acid upon using the machine. It is submitted that the Divisional Court was correct. Particularly in cases where such means are intentionally employed to cause harm, it would be absurd to draw any distinction between indirect methods and more standard forms of weapon. The idea that battery requires a very direct form of violence gains force from the term "inflict", which features in standard formulations of the offence.[61] Yet the same verb also features in the statutory offence of malicious wounding and, in that context, is no longer taken to require a directly caused injury.[62] Indeed in *Burstow*, an appeal heard jointly with *Ireland*, the House of Lords approved (in the context of maliciously inflicting grievous bodily harm) a reading of inflict as a near synonym for cause when the harm consisted of psychiatric injury.[63] The restrictive view of battery taken in *Ireland* was *obiter*.[64] It is submitted that in cases of physical contact, the more relaxed reading of inflict in *Wilson*[65] should be extended to battery. The indirect infliction of violence should suffice.[66]

(ii) Hostility

In *Brown*,[67] the House of Lords confirmed that the contact required for battery was a "hostile" contact. This requirement is not straightforwardly classified as an element of either actus reus or mens rea. The presence of hostility is a function of the motivation and attitude of D (seemingly a matter of mens rea) but which serves to fix and identify the nature of the conduct itself (prima facie, a matter of actus reus). A hand placed on V's shoulder in friendship is different in kind from a hand that will pull V into the violent clutches of D, notwithstanding that the force applied in the initial placing of the hand may be the same.

The requirement for hostility has come under strong judicial and academic attack. Lord Goff, in particular, has criticised the requirement as too vague and restrictive. For him, the boundaries of "physical contact which is generally acceptable in the ordinary conduct of daily life" should inform decisions concerning the ambit of the offence.[68] But does this provide a clearer cutting edge? Suppose V is embraced by D, an exuberant stranger, in a crowded bar one minute after midnight on New Year's Day. He does not like it. Is this a

---

[60] [1990] 1 All ER 331.

[61] Battery "consists in the infliction of unlawful violence by D upon P": *Smith and Hogan* 416.

[62] See *Wilson* [1984] AC 242 and *Mandair* [1995] 1 AC 208.

[63] [1998] AC 147, 160 (Lord Steyn), 164 (Lord Hope).

[64] The convictions were sustained on a finding of assault.

[65] [1984] AC 242.

[66] For a view that this conclusion, while desirable in terms of policy, is untenable on the state of the authorities, see Hirst, "Assault, Battery and Indirect Violence" [1999] *Crim LR* 557. But see also *Haystead* v. *Chief Constable of Derbyshire* [2000] 3 All ER 890, where D caused V, a baby, to fall to the floor by hitting V's mother who was carrying V. Laws LJ took the view that battery did not require a directly inflicted injury. Although this opinion was strictly *obiter* (on the facts there was, on analysis, a directly inflicted injury), Laws LJ made it clear that he would have confirmed D's conviction even had he found V's injuries to be indirectly inflicted.

[67] [1994] 1 AC 212. A requirement for hostility was also endorsed by the Court of Appeal in the civil case of *Wilson* v. *Pringle* [1987] QB 237.

[68] *Collins* v. *Wilcock* [1984] 3 All ER 374, 378 (CA); see too *F* v. *West Berkshire Health Authority* [1990] 2 AC 1 (HL).

battery or, in the context of the time and place, an "acceptable standard of conduct"? If one takes the view that a *faux pas* should not necessarily entail criminal liability, there may be something to be said for a requirement of hostility.

While the majority in *Brown* endorsed the need for hostility in battery, it has been remarked that, in the context of that case, the endorsement was vacuous.[69] In Brown, all the defendants had fully consented to participation in sadomasochistic activities. Nonetheless, the hostility requirement was found to be satisfied. The contacts between the defendants in *Brown* caused actual bodily harm or wounds and were intended to do so. They were more than mere batteries. From *Brown*, we may infer that conduct intentionally causing that degree of harm for a purpose not judicially recognised as acceptable will *ipso facto* be found to be hostile.[70] In such cases the requirement is meaningless. That still leaves a role for the hostility requirement in cases where the contact does not cause bodily harm or where bodily harm was unintended and unforeseen.

(iii) Mens rea

The mens rea for battery mirrors the mens rea for assault. D must intend to inflict unlawful violence or do so recklessly. The recklessness is *Cunningham* recklessness.[71] D must actually have foreseen the risk of inflicting violence upon V. This requirement is subject to the standard *Majewski* exception for voluntary intoxication.[72]

§ 11.4 Assault occasioning actual bodily harm

Section 47 of the OAPA 1861 provides:

> whosoever shall be convicted upon an indictment of any assault occasioning actual bodily harm shall be liable to be imprisoned for any term not exceeding five years.

(i) Actus reus

The term assault is used here as an umbrella term to cover the discrete offence of assault, in the pure sense of that term, and the offence of battery.[73] By far and away the most common form of this offence will be a battery which causes the requisite degree of bodily harm. However, it is possible for a pure assault to occasion bodily harm; in *Lewis*,[74] a frightened V was injured when escaping the threatened violence of D. In "fright" cases such as *Lewis*,

---

[69] *Smith and Hogan* 412.

[70] But see *Wilson* [1997] QB 47 (CA); discussed below, § 21.1(v).

[71] *Savage* [1992] 1 AC 699; *Fagan* v. *Metropolitan Police Commissioner* [1969] 1 QB 439. The cases do not discriminate between the separate offences of assault and battery when discussing mens rea issues; it is safe to assume equivalence.

[72] Below, § 18.3(ii).

[73] In *Savage* [1992] 1 AC 699, 736, 740, Lord Ackner described the mens rea for s. 47 in terms of the mens rea for assault and in terms of the mens rea for battery: we can safely assume that in this context, the term "assault" covers "pure" assault and battery.

[74] [1970] Crim LR 647 (CA); see also *Cartledge* v. *Allen* [1973] Crim LR 530.

where harm arises in the course of a reaction to a threat of violence, a causal link between D's threatening conduct and V's injury exists even though V's frightened reaction may be considered ill-advised. It is unrealistic to expect frightened people to take measured responses and it is quite foreseeable that they will not do so. In the leading case of *Roberts*,[75] where V jumped from a moving car in order to escape the sexual gropings of D, causal responsibility for V's injuries was attributed to D on the footing that V's reaction was not so "daft" as to be unforeseeable.[76] There seems, in this context, to be no difference between "occasioning" bodily harm and "causing" bodily harm.[77]

What constitutes actual bodily harm is set at a very low threshold: "any hurt or injury calculated to interfere with the health or comfort of [D]", provided it is more than "transient and trifling."[78] Bruisings, abrasions, blooded noses, etc., will be enough, as will even momentary unconsciousness.[79] Practically any sustained attack or fighting will involve occasioning actual bodily harm. Enormous scope is thus afforded to prosecutorial discretion.[80] The vast majority of the common assaults that are tried summarily by virtue of section 39 of the Criminal Justice Act 1988 were also triable on indictment under section 47 of the OAPA 1861, with the maximum term of imprisonment inflated from six months to five years. The gravity of the injury is but one of the many variables determining whether a violent incident is tried summarily or indictably, or, indeed, tried at all.[81]

The expression *actual* bodily harm might be taken to signify that only physical harm will fall within the section. However, as interpreted in *Miller*, the expression includes "a hysterical and nervous condition."[82] In *Chan-Fook*,[83] the Court of Appeal asserted that non-physical harm falls within section 47 provided that it constitutes some form of psychiatric injury attested to by expert evidence. This ruling was confirmed by the House of Lords in *Burstow*.[84] Accordingly, mere fright will not constitute bodily harm, even where a nervous or hysterical condition is induced, unless there is uncontroverted expert testimony that V's state constitutes a form of psychiatric injury.[85]

---

[75] (1972) 56 Cr App R 95 (CA).

[76] *Ibid.*, 102. *Williams* [1992] 2 All ER 183 (CA) adopts the same approach to causation in homicide. For discussion of interventions by victims see above, § 4.2(iii)(e).

[77] John Gardner has claimed that "occasion" is a broader term than "cause" and includes liability for outcomes which would not be attributed on the basis of a causal analysis: "Rationality and the Rule of Law in Offences against the Person" [1994] *CLJ* 502, 509–10. Gardner cites no authority for his claim, merely stating that the distinction between "occasion" and "cause" was "neglected" in *Roberts*.

[78] *Donovan* [1934] 2 KB 498 (CCA).

[79] *T v. DPP* [2003] EWHC 255 (Admin).

[80] The charging standards agreed by the police and the Crown Prosecution Service state that s. 47 should be charged when there is the loss or breakage of teeth, temporary loss of sensory function, extensive or multiple bruising, broken nose, minor factures, minor cuts requiring stitches, or psychiatric injury which is more than fear, distress, or panic: *Offences Against the Person Charging Standards* (2nd ed., 1996).

[81] For an illuminating study, in the context of assaults, of which factors determine a decision to prosecute and for what offence, see Clarkson, Cretney, Davis, and Shepherd, "Assaults: The Relationship between Seriousness, Criminalisation and Punishment" [1994] *Crim LR* 4.

[82] *Miller* [1954] 2 QB 282, 292.

[83] [1994] 2 All ER 552.

[84] [1998] AC 147.

[85] In *Morris* [1998] 1 Cr App R 386, evidence from a general practitioner that V suffered anxiety, fear, and sleeplessness was held to be insufficient to establish actual bodily harm. Ashworth argues that the insistence on psychiatric injury is unduly limiting in the light of research which demonstrates that fright and lasting fear are produced by many attacks: *Principles*, 312. A more expansive approach to the question of harm, however, would entail considerable difficulties of definition and proof in cases of non-corporeal bodily harm.

The inclusion of psychiatric injury as a harm within the sphere of offences concerned with violence has considerable ramifications, discussed in more detail below.[86] In the context of section 47, the range of conduct penalised which caused psychiatric injury is limited by the need for an assault or battery: D must threaten or inflict unlawful violence on V. Only if psychiatric injury ensues from those circumstances is a charge under section 47 in order.

(ii) Mens rea

The mens rea for section 47 is the mens rea for assault or battery, discussed previously. There is no need to prove any mental element with respect to occasioning bodily harm.[87] Accordingly, this is an offence of constructive liability.[88] The element of the offence constituting the aggravating feature is an element of strict liability. In the context of aggravated offences of violence, constructive liability seems wrong in principle. This is disputed by John Gardner, who argues that persons who threaten or use violence cross a moral threshold when they do so and occupy a position of responsibility for any consequences that ensue from such conduct.[89] Gardner's view finds great support in popular sentiments and from some judges. By contrast, in the context of offences against the person the correspondence principle mandates that sufficient culpability is most reliably evidenced by proof that D intended or at least foresaw those consequences of her conduct which are elements of the offence with which she is charged.[90] There is room in the criminal law for liability based on negligence (even, perhaps, strict liability for minor regulatory offences[91]) but not when the crimes are concerned with violence (as opposed to its consequences). It is true that many cases of assault occasioning actual bodily harm will arise spontaneously in street and re-creational settings, frequently where D has consumed significant quantities of drink or drugs.[92] Difficulties of proving mens rea in such circumstances are considerably eased by the special regime for the voluntarily intoxicated.[93] For the least serious of the aggravated offences, assault occasioning absolute bodily harm, it may be that on proof of mens rea for the *assault* element, negligence as to the consequence—the infliction of actual bodily harm—would be an acceptable form of culpability. But there should be some form of culpability for the aggravating element of the offence.

---

[86] § 11.5(i).
[87] *Savage* [1992] 1 AC 699 (HL), affirming *Roberts* (1971) 56 Cr App R 95 (CA), overruling *Spratt* [1991] 2 All ER 210 (CA) and *Parmenter* [1991] 2 All ER 225 (CA).
[88] Above, § 6.5.
[89] "Rationality and the Rule of Law in Offences Against the Person" [1994] *CLJ* 502. For different views on the merits of the correspondence principle, see Horder, "A Critique of the Correspondence Principle" [1995] *Crim LR* 759 and Mitchell, "In Defence of the Correspondence Principle" [1999] *Crim LR* 195.
[90] Above, § 6.5.
[91] Though see above, § 6.3, for a full discussion of this issue.
[92] Nicholas *et al.*, *Crime in England and Wales 2004–05* (2005) 85.
[93] See below, § 18.3

§ 11.5 Maliciously inflicting wounds or grievous bodily harm

Section 20 of the OAPA 1861 provides:

> whosoever shall unlawfully and maliciously wound or inflict any grievous bodily harm upon any other person, either with or without any weapon or instrument, shall be guilty of an offence, and being convicted thereof shall be liable . . . to imprisonment for a term not exceeding five years.

It is noteworthy that the maximum penalty, five years, is the same penalty provided under section 47. In practice, section 20 is regarded as the more serious offence, and the charging policy of the Crown Prosecution Service reflects this.[94] Further, in terms of punishment, the sentences handed down in respect of section 20 convictions are typically in a higher range than are the sentences imposed in respect of section 47.[95]

(i) Actus reus

(a) Wounds or inflicts grievous bodily harm

The harm element of the offence is present if D inflicts a wound or grievous bodily harm on V. A wound, as defined, requires all the layers of the skin to be pierced.[96] There must be an external aspect to an injury for it to be regarded as a wound. Internal ruptures, even if they cause significant internal bleeding, are not wounds.[97] Even so, the range of what counts as a wound is considerable. If sufficiently serious, a wound may also constitute grievous bodily harm while, at the other end of the spectrum, even a very minor injury may satisfy the definitional requirement of a wound.

In *Metheram*,[98] the phrase "really serious harm" was thought best to express the meaning of grievous bodily harm. As explained in *Grundy*,[99] the totality of the injuries suffered by V should be taken into account; it may be that no one particular injury is really serious yet, taken as a whole, V's injuries may amount to grievous bodily harm. This approach was confirmed in *Bollom*[100] where it was applied with the sensible observation that far less by way of bodily harm would constitute serious harm if V were a young child.

In *Burstow*,[101] the House of Lords confirmed that psychiatric injury, attested to by expert evidence, could constitute *bodily* harm. Further, if the adverse psychiatric condition inflicted on V by D were sufficiently serious, it would constitute grievous bodily harm falling within section 20 (and section 18) of the OAPA 1861. In the context of psychiatric injury, it was ruled in *Burstow* that D would "inflict" psychiatric such harm if his conduct was a cause of V's psychiatric condition, a matter to be determined on normal causal principles.[102]

---

[94] Crown Prosecution Service, *Offences Against the Person Charging Standards* (2nd ed., 1996).
[95] Moxon, *Sentencing Practice in the Crown Court* (1988).
[96] Both the dermis and the epidermis must be broken: *Moriarty* v. *Brooks* (1834) 6 C & P 684, 172 ER 1419; a break in the outer skin is insufficient: *M'Loughlin* (1838) 8 C & P 635, 173 ER 651.
[97] *JCC (a minor)* v. *Eisenhower* (1984) 78 Cr App R 48 (DC).
[98] [1961] 3 All ER 200 (CCA).
[99] [1977] Crim LR 543 (CA).
[100] [2004] 2 Cr App R 50.
[101] [1998] AC 147.
[102] *Ibid.*, 160, 164.

The effect of *Burstow* is to enlarge significantly the kinds of setback to personal wellbeing that fall within the section and, consequentially, the kinds of conduct coming within the scope of the offence. On the facts of *Burstow*, there was no physical contact that impacted upon V, directly or indirectly. V had endured a long process of harassment by D, which included such abuses as threatening letters and telephone calls, following, photographing, etc. A reading of the case leaves no doubt about the extent of V's suffering and the wrongfulness of D's conduct. There can be no qualms about the actual decision in the case. However, the limits of the decision are difficult to identify.[103]

In *Burstow*, psychiatric injury was held to be a form of *bodily* injury. How literally are we to take this? If no distinction is to be taken between psychiatric and physical injury *in general* , the effects of the decision could be profound. For example, suppose that D, an employer, wishes to terminate the contract of V, her employee. D has good reason to consider V's job performance unacceptable. Of course, in no circumstances whatsoever may D inflict physical harm on V to force his resignation. Instead of that, however, she calls V to her office, gives him three months' salary in lieu of notice and explains how he has fallen down on his job. She is aware of V's previous psychiatric history and foresees that his mental health will once again break down if sacked. That proves to be the case. On these facts, D has caused psychiatric injury and foresaw that she would do so. A section 20 offence? One's initial response is to stress that section 20 requires *unlawful* conduct on the part of D. How can a legitimate termination of employment be unlawful? The answer, if one takes literally the finding in *Burstow*, is that any course of conduct whereby D foresees that she will cause V grievous *bodily* harm cannot be legitimate conduct unless she is acting in self-defence or under duress.

It is unlikely that the limits of *Burstow* will be tested in this way. The Crown Prosecution Service will probably not prosecute in those cases where such commonplaces as adultery, verbal cruelty, termination of employment, promises made for the purposes of seduction, and the like cause serious mental distress amounting to psychiatric injury. These things will be tolerated as part of "normal" life, as they should be. Any attempt rigorously to police such matters would make for an intolerable society. There would need to be something extreme and visible—the kind of conduct that occurred in *Burstow* or, perhaps, sustained classroom or workplace bullying, to trigger a police investigation and a file of evidence for the Crown Prosecution Service. Psychiatric injury may have devastating consequences but it is *different* from physical injury. Policing the causing of psychiatric injury by way of nineteenth-century laws focused on matters physical is not the way forward. New legislation is required which should pay particular attention to the kind of conduct which is to be penalised.[104]

(b) Inflict

The verb "inflict", which features in section 20, was for a very long time thought to include a narrower range of conduct than would be captured by employing the term "cause". In the context of psychiatric injury, *Burstow* has decided that inflict is now to be interpreted as a

---

[103] For an incisive discussion see Gardner, "Stalking" (1998) 114 *LQR* 33.

[104] To some extent, the Protection from Harassment Act 1997 provides appropriate protection from conduct of this kind but there are deficiencies of coverage: see below, § 11.8.

synonym for cause.[105] We will consider first the meaning of inflict derived in cases of physical injury, and then consider whether the extensive interpretation adopted in *Burstow* has implications for cases which involve physical injury.

For many years *Clarence*[106] was regarded as the leading case on the meaning of "inflict". D had been charged with the malicious infliction of grievous bodily harm upon V, on account of his infecting V with gonorrhoea. Despite V's ignorance of D's infected state, her consent to intercourse was taken to be valid; accordingly, the bodily contact involved in intercourse did not constitute a battery by D. For the majority, this ruled out a conviction under section 20 because of the need for a:[107]

> "direct causing of some grievous injury to the body itself with a weapon, as by a cut with a knife, or without a weapon, as by a blow with the fist, or by pushing a person down. Indeed, ['inflict' implies] an assault and battery of which a wound or grievous bodily harm is the manifest immediate and obvious result."

The restrictive definition in *Clarence* was relaxed to a degree in cases such as *Martin*[108] and *Halliday*.[109] These and other cases were considered by the House of Lords in *Wilson*, where the House of Lords ruled, contra *Clarence*, that section 20 did not require the commission of an assault or battery:[110]

> "grievous bodily harm may be inflicted where the accused has directly or violently inflicted it by assaulting the victim or where the accused has 'inflicted' it by doing something intentionally which though it is not in itself a direct application of force to the body of the victim does directly result in some force being applied violently to the body of the victim so that he suffers grievous bodily harm."

This passage was subsequently endorsed by the House of Lords in *Mandair*.[111] An injury caused by way of an "infliction" is an injury caused by an impact or percussion set in motion by D. The injury must arise directly from the impact but the impact itself need not be something that D has directly caused; any direct or indirectly caused impact or percussive connection will suffice. Returning to the facts of *Clarence*, we can now appreciate that if an assault or battery is no longer required, the fact of consensual intercourse will not, of itself, be a barrier to a conviction. Yet to convict on the facts of *Clarence*, we must still find that "force [was] applied violently" and that, because of the violent application of force, injury (infection) was sustained. Even if we regard consensual intercourse as involving the violent application of force (which is doubtful), the injury is not caused by the application of force but by the process of infection.

To allow diseases and infections within the scope of section 20, "inflict" must be interpreted as a near synonym for cause. That, as we know, was the course taken in the context of

---

[105] [1998] AC 147.

[106] (1888) 22 QBD 23 (CCR).

[107] *Ibid.*, 41 (Stephen J).

[108] (1881) 8 QBD 54 (CCR) (D held to have inflicted grievous bodily harm by causing victims to rush to locked exits).

[109] [1886–90] All ER 1028 (CCR) (D held to have inflicted grievous bodily harm when V was injured in the course of escaping the threatened violence of D).

[110] [1984] AC 242.

[111] [1995] 1 AC 208.

psychiatric injury in *Burstow*, where there had been no physical contact between D and V. Lord Hope considered that inflict bore the same meaning as cause, save that for the former term there was an implication that the consequences of the act were likely to be unpleasant or harmful.[112] In the context of crimes, his approach effectively assimilates "inflict" to "cause", and would ensure a conviction on facts such as *Clarence*. Lord Steyn, whose judgment was that of the majority, was more circumspect. He did not consider the two terms to be synonymous but took it to be natural to speak of inflicting psychiatric injury without implying, in that context, any direct or indirect violent contact.[113] In the important decisions of *Dica*[114] and *Konzani*,[115] the Court of Appeal took the analysis of Lord Hope to be of general application. Departing from the ruling in *Clarence*, it was held in both cases that for D to pass on a sexually transmitted disease to his sexual partner V, where V was unaware and had not consented to the risk of infection, was conduct falling within section 20. These cases have considerable ramifications for questions relating to what constitutes a valid consent to harm, for the scope of some key sexual offences, and for the appropriatness of using laws designed to curb violence to penalise sexual risk-taking. The first two issues will be treated in later chapters,[116] and the third matter later in this chapter (§ 11.7). But for now we need merely note that unless and until they are overruled by the House of Lords, *Dica* and *Konzani* resolve that "inflict" is a synonym for "cause" for the purposes of section 20.

(ii) Mens rea

The key term is malice: in modern English criminal law this is interpreted as intention or recklessness. The recklessness is *Cunningham* recklessness.[117] However, the foresight required for this offence is not foresight on the part of D *that he will inflict a wound or grievous bodily harm* on V. It is enough, according to a line of authority originating in *Mowatt* and endorsed by the House of Lords in *Savage and Parmenter*,[118] that D foresees that he *may*[119] inflict *some*, even *minor*, bodily harm on V. This is unfortunate. More than that: this violation of the correspondence principle is reprehensible in the context of a serious offence.

Most section 20 cases will involve physical attacks. The Court of Appeal sensibly ruled in *Beeson*[120] that, if a wound or grievous bodily harm is caused by a direct attack inherently likely to cause physical harm, no guidance to the jury on the meaning of malice is necessary. Guidance should be given only if D raises an argument that his conduct was in some sense mistaken or accidental or that, for some other reason, he failed to recognise that he might cause harm.

---

[112] [1998] AC 147.

[113] *Ibid.*, 160–1.

[114] [2004] QB 1257

[115] [2005] EWCA Crim 706.

[116] See chaps. 21 and 12 respectively.

[117] *Savage* [1992] 1 AC 699.

[118] *Ibid.*, affirming *Mowatt* [1968] 1 QB 421 (CA).

[119] *Rushworth* (1992) 95 Cr App R 252, 255 (CA), dismissing an argument that D must foresee that some harm to V will result from his conduct.

[120] [1994] Crim LR 190 (CA).

§ 11.6 Wounding with intent

Section 18 of the OAPA 1861 provides:

> Whosoever shall unlawfully and maliciously by any means whatsoever wound or cause griev-
> ous bodily harm to any person . . . with intent . . . to do some . . . grievous bodily harm to
> any person, or with intent to resist or prevent the lawful apprehension or detainer of any per-
> son, shall be guilty of an offence, and being convicted thereof shall be liable . . . to
> imprisonment for life.

Section 18 creates one offence with several modes of commission. It may be helpful to set
out these various modes of commission:

(a)   unlawfully and maliciously wounding, with intent to do grievous bodily harm;
(b)   unlawfully and maliciously wounding, with intent to resist or prevent the lawful
      apprehension or detainer of any person;
(c)   unlawfully and maliciously causing grievous bodily harm, with intent to do grievous
      bodily harm;
(d)   unlawfully and maliciously causing grievous bodily harm, with intent to resist or
      prevent the lawful apprehension or detainer of any person.

(i) Actus reus

We are already familiar with the meanings of "wounding" and "causing grievous bodily
harm."[121] What constitutes "lawful apprehension or detention" will, of course, depend on
the validity of the arrest and detention, a matter dependent on the particular facts of each
case. As we have discussed, the term "grievous bodily harm" includes serious psychiatric
injury and now will include serious infection or disease. In the context of section 18, where
the culpability requirement is intention, there may be less concern about the extension of
liability into these areas. The requirement of intention will narrow and focus the potential
range of conduct that may be penalised and ensure a culpability that warrants a criminal
sanction.

With the omission of the verb "inflict", the former uncertainties associated with that term
in section 20[122] are avoided. It is necessary only that D causes the wound or serious injury.
Normal principles of causation apply.[123]

(ii) Mens rea

The core of the offence is intention. In variants (a), (b), and (d) (set out above), this is an
ulterior intent,[124] while in variant (c) the required intent coincides with the actus reus. The
most common variants of the offence are (a) where D wounds V with intent to cause grievous

---

[121] Above, § 11.5(i)(a).
[122] For the moment resolved: above, § 11.5(i)(b).
[123] See above, § 4.2.
[124] Above, § 5.1(vii).

bodily harm or (c) where D causes V grievous bodily harm with intent to cause grievous bodily harm.

In variant (c), where mens rea coincides with actus reus, if the grievous bodily harm is caused by way of a direct attack the jury should simply be invited to consider whether D intended that result: there is no need for any direction on the meaning of intent.[125] By contrast, where D has caused V grievous bodily harm by some dangerous act not in the nature of direct attack and asserts that she did not act in order to cause such harm, it will be sufficient for the matter to go to the jury if she foresaw that harm is virtually certain to occur.[126] In both of the cases under discussion—direct attack causing grievous bodily harm; dangerous act causing grievous bodily harm—the term "maliciously", which appears in section 18, is redundant. The mens rea issue is whether D intended grievous bodily harm: if she did, *a fortiori* it was done maliciously in the sense that term carries in modern English criminal law.

Under variant (b), where the section 18 offence takes the form of a wound falling short of grievous bodily harm, an ulterior intent to cause grievous bodily must be proved. In practice, there is no room in this kind of case for intent proved on the basis of foresight that the grievous bodily harm was a virtual certainty: if grievous bodily harm did not arise, then it could not have been a virtually certain result of D's actual conduct. Accordingly it must be proved that D acted with intent in the core sense[127] to cause V grievous bodily harm. Again, the term maliciously is redundant; if D acted in order to cause serious harm, *a fortiori* he acted maliciously with respect to that consequence.

The requirement of malice may have a role to play in variants (b) and (d), where D's intent is to prevent or resist the lawful apprehension or detention of any person. In principle, the requirement of malice in section 18 entails that D must at least foresee the possibility that she might cause a wound or grievous bodily harm in cases where her intent is to resist arrest or detention.[128]

In variants (b) and (d), it is clear from the terms of section 18 that D must *intend* to resist an apprehension or detention. Recklessness does not suffice. However, section 18 further requires that D must intend to resist a *lawful* apprehension or detention. What mens rea is required for the element of lawfulness? In principle, what is needed is that, in the circumstances that D believes to exist, the arrest is lawful. Thus if D wrongly believes in facts which, if true, would have made the arrest unlawful, he lacks mens rea. On the other hand, if D has made no mistake about the circumstances, it suffices that the apprehension or detention is, in fact, lawful. It would not go to liability, merely mitigation, that D believed the apprehension or detention was illegal.[129]

---

[125] *Moloney* [1985] AC 905, 926 (HL).

[126] *Woollin* [1999] AC 282 (HL); above, § 5.1(iv).

[127] Above, § 5.1.

[128] *Morrison* (1989) 89 Cr App R 17. The case confirms that the test is actual foresight of injury on the part of D but did not rehearse the question whether the foresight must be of a wound or grievous bodily harm. In principle it should; but see *Mowatt* [1968] 1 QB 421.

[129] Cf. *Bentley* (1850) 4 Cox CC 406. Such a mistake should be characterised as a mistake of law, discussed below, § 18.2.

§ 11.7 Transmitting diseases and infection

Concern about the spread of Acquired Immune Deficiency Syndrome (AIDS) has led to consideration whether current offences against the person may apply to conduct associated with transmission of that condition.[130] More generally, as we will see, there are justified concerns over the appropriateness of the existing range of offences that protect the person in the context of harms inflicted by the transmission of diseases and infection. Our discussion will focus on AIDS; there are, of course, implications for other forms of transmission of disease and infection whether sexually transmitted or otherwise.

(i) Cases where harm was intended

The most straightforward situation will be where V dies as a consequence of AIDS and it can be proved that D infected V with Human Immunodeficiency Virus (HIV) in order that she should die. With the abolition of the year-and-a-day rule,[131] there is no impediment to a charge of murder. Such cases are likely to be very rare (although they are not unknown).

What offences, if any, are committed if D intentionally causes V to become HIV-positive? From the decisions in *Dica*[132] and *Konzani*,[133] we know that to be made HIV-positive is to be seriously harmed in a bodily sense. If the infection is intentionally transmitted there seems no impediment to a conviction under section 18 of the OAPA 1861, a conclusion made by Stephen J in *Clarence*.[134] Nonetheless, the condition of being HIV-positive is compatible with years of normal healthy existence, given access to suitable drugs. Yet the condition is a significant setback to the interests of the person so afflicted and the setback is, in a broad sense, to bodily integrity. Whatever reservations there may be concerning the extension of bodily harm to psychiatric injury,[135] it would, in the light of that extension, have been perverse to hold that the condition of being HIV-positive did not amount to grievous bodily harm. That said, the expression is not a natural one to employ in this context, pointing up the need for specific legislation.[136]

(ii) Cases where the harm was knowingly risked

Far more common than intentionally transmitting infection will be taking risks relating to infection, notably through forms of unprotected sexual activity engaged in by persons who are aware that they have a condition that can be passed on by sexual contact. By reading "inflict" as synonymous with cause, the Court of Appeal in *Dica* and *Konzani* has laid the ground for straightforward convictions of maliciously inflicting grievous bodily harm,

---

[130] Bronitt, "Spreading Disease and the Criminal Law" [1994] *Crim LR* 21.
[131] Law Reform (Year and a Day Rule) Act 1996; discussed above, § 10.2(iv).
[132] [2004] QB 1257.
[133] [2005] EWCA Crim 706.
[134] (1888) 22 QBD 23.
[135] *Burstow* [1998] AC 147 (HL); *Chan-Fook* [1994] 2 All ER 552 (CA).
[136] The Home Office Draft Bill for Offences Against the Person (*Violence: Reforming the Offences Against the Person Act 1861* (1998)) proposes that injury should not include anything caused by disease save for the proposed offence of intentionally causing serious injury.

within the terms of section 20, in cases where D infects his sexual partner having foreseen the risk of doing so, and where V has not consented to that risk.

In *Dica*, on the facts assumed for the purposes of the appeal and on the facts themselves in *Konzani*, V had not consented to the risk of infection. Prima facie, however, whether V actually consented should have been irrelevant, in light of the House of Lords decision in *Brown*,[137] which (save for special circumstances[138]) restricts the scope of valid consent to the infliction of harms falling short of actual bodily harm. According to the law set out in *Brown*, consent to the risk of infection on the part of V might mitigate D's offence, but would not preclude liability.

Nonetheless, there is a distinct possibility that in some circumstances V's consent might be effectual. In *Dica*, reference was made to a couple trying to start a family and to another couple organising their sex life according to the strictures of the Roman Catholic church. The assumption was made that in those circumstances it would be legitimate to take the risk of becoming HIV-positive.

Nothing could better exemplify the unsuitability of using the current law of violence to regulate risky sexual conduct than these opaque speculations in *Dica* concerning the limits of consent. The line is uncertain and the penalties for crossing it are high. At the point of transmission there is liability for a serious offence against the person. If V should subsequently die, D could face charges of manslaughter of the constructive or gross negligence variety.[139]

If V has not given a valid consent to the risk of HIV, will each incident of risky sexual intercourse constitute rape of the penetrated V? Is V's consent to the sex act vitiated? According to *Clarence*,[140] the answer is no: V, even in her state of ignorance, understood the essential nature of the act to which she was consenting. The matter is controversial, yet on balance it is submitted that *Clarence* is correct on this point and is supported by dicta in *Dica* and *Konzani*. In such circumstances, D shows disregard for V's health and welfare rather than for her sexual autonomy; and the gravamen of that kind of wrong is not properly captured by charges of rape.[141] We return to this matter in the next chapter.

(iii) Administering noxious things

Finally, brief mention should be made of section 23 of the OAPA 1861, which concerns the malicious administration (or causing to be administered or taken) of noxious things which endanger life or inflict grievous bodily harm. It has been argued that bodily fluids containing HIV are "noxious" things and that sexual transmission of fluids can be regarded as an "administration" or a "taking" within the meaning of this section.[142] These are by no means untenable claims and, if this interpretation is accepted, a defendant could be

---

[137] [1994] 1 AC 212.

[138] Such as organised sport; one may safely assume that sexual activity would not in itself qualify as a special circumstance. See below, § 21.1(iv).

[139] See the discussion of these ways of committing manslaughter in chapter 10.

[140] (1888) 22 QBD 23; confirmed in EB [2006] EWCA 2945. See below § 21.1(ii)(d).

[141] Gardner and Shute, "The Wrongness of Rape" in Horder (ed.), *Oxford Essays in Jurisprudence* (4th Series, 2000) 193.

[142] Bronnitt, "Spreading Disease and the Criminal Law" [1994] *Crim LR* 21.

convicted on the basis of having unprotected sex knowing himself to be HIV-positive since that fact, of itself, would be life-endangering to an HIV-negative person. Under the section, the element of malice (recklessness) merely relates to the noxious substance; seemingly it need not be proved that D foresaw life endangerment or the infliction of grievous bodily harm.[143]

Save for cases involving the intentional transmission of disease, it is submitted that the vigorous application of the laws regulating physical and sexual violence to cases involving transmission of diseases would be a far from ideal response to a difficult area of social and health policy, where confident and confidential reporting of an HIV status is at least as important as deterring sexual irresposibility.[144]

§ 11.8 Harassment

The Protection from Harassment Act 1997[145] provides, *inter alia*:[146]

1(1) A person must not pursue a course of conduct—
    (a) which amounts to the harassment of another, and
    (b) which he knows or ought to know amounts to harassment of the other.

1(A) A person must not pursue a course of conduct—
    (a) which involves harassment of two or more persons, and
    (b) which he knows or ought to know involves harassment of those persons, and
    (c) by which he intends to persuade any person (whether or not one of those persons mentioned above)—
        (i) not to do something that he is entitled or required to do, or
        (ii) to do something that he is not under any obligation to do.

(2) For the purposes of this section, the person whose course of conduct is in question ought to know that it amounts to or involves harassment of another if a reasonable person in possession of the same information would think the course of conduct amounted to or involved harassment of the other.

. . .

4(1) A person whose course of conduct causes another to fear, on at least two occasions, that violence will be used against him is guilty of an offence if he knows or ought to know that his course of conduct will cause the other so to fear on each of these occasions.

---

[143] *Cato* [1976] 1 All ER 260. For a well-founded criticism of this position, see *TBCL* 213–16.

[144] This is the position adopted in the Home Office's Draft Bill for Offences Against the Person: *Violence: Reforming the Offences Against the Person Act 1861* (1998). See the critiques in Weait, "Taking the Blame: Criminal Law, Social Responsibility and the Sexual Transmission of HIV" (2001) 23 *Journal of Social Welfare and Family Law* 441 and Weait, "Knowledge, Autonomy and Consent: *R v Konzani*" [2005] *Crim LR* 763.

[145] Wells, "Stalking: the Criminal Law Response" [1997] *Crim LR* 463; Finch, *The Criminalisation of Stalking* (2001); Finch "The Perfect Stalking Law: An Evaluation of the Efficacy of the Protection from Harrasment Act 1997" [2002] *Crim LR* 702.

[146] Section 1A was inserted by s. 125 of the Serious and Organised Crime and Police Act 2005.

[147] [1998] AC 147 (HL).

(2) For the purposes of this section, the person whose course of conduct is in question ought to know that it will cause another to fear that violence will be used against him on any occasion if a reasonable person in possession of the same information would think the course of conduct would cause the other so to fear on the occasion.

The expression "violence" evokes some kind of physical attack. As we have seen in this chapter, in *Ireland and Burstow*[147] the House of Lords brought non-contact acts that cause psychiatric injury into the mainstream of the criminal law in terms of offences and punishment. While the reasoning and ultimate implications of these decisions have been questioned, no-one would deny that courses of conduct aimed at destabilising and diminishing the quality of the victim's life are properly, without metaphor, regarded as species of violence, notwithstanding the lack of any blow or physical attack. The activities known as stalking and harassment are now widely regarded as serious wrongs in our culture and cause considerable suffering.[148]

The Protection from Harassment Act 1997 is a legislative attempt directly to confront these wrongs, although it will impinge on other conduct too, such as protests, demonstrations, and intrusive press activity. In its criminal law part, the Act creates the three offences set out above: two harassment offences in section 1 and a fear of violence offence in section 4. We consider these offences in turn.

(i) Harassment of another

Turning to the first, and primary, harassment offence set out in section 1 of the Act, the most striking feature is the absence of any definition of "harassment", the very activity to be proscribed. Subsection (2), in effect, provides that if a reasonable person would interpret D's course of conduct as amounting to harassment, then that course of conduct is harassment. Since the offence may be tried only summarily, the "reasonable person" in effect will be the stipendiary magistrate or the lay justices trying the case.

The scope of the primary offence is quite enormous. An admissions tutor may understandably consider herself harassed after the fifth telephone call from an importunate applicant. But, even in her blackest mood, the tutor is unlikely to regard herself as the victim of an offence. The scope of the offence is curbed to a degree by section 1(3), which provides a defence, with the burden of proof on D, of preventing or detecting crime, complying with a statutory enactment, or acting reasonably.

There must, at least, be a "course of conduct". This has been interpreted as requiring the harassment of V on at least two occasions and some degree of connection between the two occasions.[149] The Act provides that if if D aids, abets, counsels, or procures E's conduct on one occasion and should E's conduct on a subsequent occasion taken with the first occasion make for a course of conduct by E, there is also a course of conduct on D's part whether or not D was present on the second occasion.[150] However, two self-contained incidents

---

[148] The National Anti-stalking and Harassment campaign reported contact from over 7,000 victims of stalking between January 1994 and November 1995; 95% of victims are women: Home Office, *Stalking the Solutions: A Consultation Paper* (1996) para. 1.8.

[149] *Lau* v. *DPP* [2000] Crim LR 580; *Hills* [2001] Crim LR 318.

[150] As inserted by the the Criminal Justice and Police Act 2001.

involving interactions between the same persons will not suffice, as where D is unpleasant to V after some disagreement, is then reconciled to V, but on some future occasion is unpleasant again. But provided there is the necessary degree of connection between the two episodes of harassment, it will not matter if there is a considerable time elapsing between the two incidents—annual demonstrations outside, say, a synagogue, on a particular anniversary might well constitute an offence of harassment.

Although the offence requires the harassment of another by way of at least two episodes of conduct (to make for a course of conduct), it is not necessary that V be present to experience the harassment. In *Dunn*,[151] the Court of Appeal ruled that V had been harassed by D's conduct at V's home. D had intended to frighten all members of the household (including V) and it was immaterial that she was not present at the time.

To be guilty of the primary harassment offence, contrary to secton 1(1), D must know or ought to know that his conduct is harassment. One might think that a negligence requirement is rather low for a serious offence, but in fact the requirement here falls short even of true negligence, especially in the context of group activity. If D aids, abets, counsels, or procures E's conduct on one occasion, D will be taken to know any matter that E knew or ought to have known on a subsequent occasion—whether or not D was present on that subsequent occasion.[152] Moreover, in determining what D ought to have known (even when acting alone), no account is to be taken of a cognitive disability such as schizophrenia.[153] The alternative requirement for proof of actual or constructive knowledge does not really assist clarity in cases at the margins of the offence: given that "harassment" is undefined, the matter is essentially at the disposal of the magistrates. In *Thomas* v. *News Group Newspapers*,[154] in a preliminary ruling in civil proceedings,[155] the Court of Appeal held that there was no reason in principle why articles in a newspaper showing V in an unfavorable light should not constitute harassment of V. The decision in *Thomas* confirms that the parameters of this offence are very broad indeed, and it may well be that prosecutions on particular facts will be open to objections under Articles 7 (non-retroactivity), 10 (freedom of expression), and 11 (freedom of peaceful assembly and association) of the ECHR.

(ii) "Persuasive" harassment of others

The second, subsidiary harassment offence has many features in common with the primary offence but also points of difference. First, at least two persons must be subjected to conduct which *involved* harassment. For the primary offence one or more persons must be subjected to conduct which *amounted* to harassment. The difference between amounting and involving is far from obvious: if conduct does not amount to harassment it can hardly involve harassment. Perhaps different terms are used because for the primary offence it is enough that D's conduct amounts to harassment, he need not have any particular objective. By contrast, for the second offence, D must intend to persuade at least two persons not to

---

[151] *Dunn* [2001] Crim LR 130.
[152] *Ibid.*
[153] *Colohan* [2001] EWCA Crim 1251.
[154] [2001] All ER (D) 246.
[155] The 1997 Act also provides civil remedies for harassment.

engage in some form of lawful conduct. The different phraseology is perhaps to emphasise that conduct which is part of a bigger scheme than harassment for harassment's sake is within the offence. (And yet the same is true of the primary offence!) Be that as it may, this form of the harassment offence seems designed to cover a situation where, say, D, an animal rights activist, seeks to persuade employees not to continue working for a company that tests its products on animals. If her persuasive efforts constitute harassment by the lights of a reasonable person and if a judgment is made that she should have known this, she will be guilty of the offence.

(iii) Causing fear of violence

The offence created by section 4, of putting another in fear of violence, is not open to the same measure of objection as the harassment offences because what constitutes violence, though again undefined, has a greater core of certainty. It should be noted that, unlike assault, the fear of violence need not be fear of immediate violence. But a blatant threat, say, to kneecap V next Wednesday will not of itself fall within section 4. V's fear of violence must be caused by D on at least two occasions. Moreover V must fear that violence *will* be used against her.[156] A well-founded apprehension even of the probability of violence will not suffice.[157] In the light of these factors, Lord Steyn in *Ireland and Burstow* considered that the Act offered deficient protection to recipients of telephone calls or messages redolent with threatened violence but short on the specifics of intended action.[158] Lord Steyn was right.

The offence under section 4 does not require any intent or recklessness on the part of D in causing V to fear violence. It is enough that a reasonable person would have foreseen that result. It might be thought that an offence which can be committed negligently should not have a maximum sentence of imprisonment for five years. Lord Steyn, on the other hand, considered five years too low a sentence for the worst kind of offending within section 4. That may well be true for cases where D has intentionally subjected V to a reign of terror with devastating effect. It would have been far better had there been gradations of offence in terms of a hierarchy of intention, recklessness and, if need be, negligence, with differential penalties attached.

The Protection of Harassment Act 1997 is an unimpressive measure; a hasty product driven by political exigencies with legislative revisions and extensions made in the same vein. It uses undefined terms and takes objective liability to the extent of deeming D to know of matters which were the thoughts and motivations of others at ocassions where he was not present. A better solution to the genuine problem of threats and harassment is required.

---

[156] Fear that D will be violent to someone other than V does not suffice: *Caurti* v. *DPP* [2002] Crim LR 131.

[157] In *Henley* [2002] Crim LR 582, it was held to be an error to rule that it sufficed that V was "seriously frightened as to what *might* happen."

[158] [1998] AC 147, 153.

§ 11.9 Racial and religious aggravation

There is considerable evidence that a significant number of violent attacks which take place in public are racially motivated and that the number of such attacks is on the increase.[159] Part II of the Crime and Disorder Act 1998 seeks to strengthen the law's response to such attacks by providing that a racist motivation for violent and some cognate offences will constitute a racially aggravated form of the offence (a separate offence) subject to higher penalties.[160] Pursuant to section 39 of the Anti-Terrorism Crime and Security Act 2001 religious aggravation is folded into this legislation on the same terms. Of the offences we have examined in this chapter, the maximum term of imprisonment for a racially or religiously aggravated assault is two years' imprisonment; for racially or religiously aggravated assault occasioning actual bodily harm, seven years; for racially or religiously aggravated malicious wounding or grievous bodily harm, seven years; for racially or religiously aggravated harassment, two years; and for racially or religiously aggravated putting people in fear of violence, seven years.[161] As the aggravated version of these offences are separate offences in their own right, the element of D's hostility to V based on V's race or religion is something that has to be proved at trial or conceded by the defence. There is no provision for a racially or religiously aggravated version of wounding with intent. As the maximum penalty for that offence is life imprisonment there is, of course, no scope for further aggravation. However, section 82 of the Crime and Disorder Act 1998 provides that racial or religious motivation is an aggravating factor in sentencing for all offences and if either form of hostility is proved there must be an announcement to that effect in open court.

Racial or religious aggravation is defined in section 28 of the Crime and Disorder 1998. The section provides:

(1) An offence is racially or religiously aggravated . . . if—
    (a) at the time of committing the offence, or immediately before or after doing so, the offender demonstrates towards the victim of the offence hostility based on the victim's membership (or presumed membership) of a racial or religious group; or
    (b) the offence is racially motivated (wholly or partly) by hostility towards members of a racial or religious group based on their membership of that group.
(2) In subsection (1) (a) above—
    "membership" in relation to a racial or religious group includes association with members of that group;
    "presumed" means presumed by the offender.
(3) It is immaterial for the purposes of paragraph (a) or (b) of subsection (1) above whether or not the offender's hostility is also based to any extent, on a factor not mentioned in that paragraph.
(4) In this section "racial group" means a group of persons defined by reference to race, colour, nationality (including citizenship) or ethnic or national origins.
(5) In this section "religious group" means a group of persons defined by reference to religious belief or lack of religious belief.

---

[159] In 1988 there were 4,383 racial incidents reported to the police, rising to 12,222 reports in 1995–6: Home Office, *Racial Violence and Harassment: A Consultation Document* (1997).
[160] Crime and Disorder Act 1998, s. 28.
[161] See ss. 29 and 32 of the Crime and Disorder Act 1998.

If D assaults V, a member of a different racial or religious group, the fact that his victim belongs to a different group will not of itself establish the element of racial aggravation. The possibility of proving racial aggravation will arise only if D is aware that V is a member of a particular racial group or presumes, rightly or wrongly, that V is a member of the group.

Ultimate proof of racial or religous aggravation may take two forms. First, under section 28(1)(a) of the Crime and Disorder Act 1998 the prosecution may be able to prove that at the time of the offence, or immediately before it, or immediately after it, D "demonstrated" racial or religious hostility towards V based on V's membership or presumed membership of a racial or religious group. Here, the racial hostility is something extraneous to the offence itself. It is something that accompanies offences, not something to be inferred from an offence *per se*, even if D is aware of V's membership of a particular racial or religious group. So, something like a racial or religious insult aimed at V immediately before, during, or after the attack is required.[162] It is not necessary to show that racial or religious hostility is at least part of the explanation for the attack: it suffices that hostility is manifested in some way.

By contrast, under section 28(1)(b) it must be proved that in the absence of any demonstration of racial or religious hostility, D's offence was motivated by hostility towards V, a hostility explained by V's membership or presumed membership of a racial or religious group.

What constitutes membership of a racial group has been widely construed. In *White*,[163] D referred to V as an "African". This was held sufficiently specific to indicate hostility to V because of her membership of a racial group. Similarly in *M (A minor)*,[164] "bloody foreigner" sufficed as did "immigrant doctor" in *A-G's Reference (No. 4 of 2004)*.[165] These are undeniably broad interpretations of what constitutes membership of a racial group; but any other approach would lead to some unedifying distinctions and benefit those who express their racial hostility in a coarse-grained way. A similar approach to "religious group" is more problematic. Understandably, there is no legislative list of approved religions. So a cult where V claims some special relationship with the supernatural, and persuades D and other followers that the best guarantee of the afterlife is to follow his precepts, may well constitute a religious group. Should D lose his faith in V and physically attack him on the ground that he is a false prophet, his attack may be considered aggravated by religious hostility. That hardly seems in the public interest.

Sensibly, what makes for hostility is undefined. Where abusive language is used immediately before, during, or immediately after the offence, making pejorative references to race or religion hostility of the relevant kind will typically be present. But not invariably. In *DPP* v. *Pal*,[166] D referred to V as a "brown Englishman" and a "white man's arse-licker". Racial aggravation was held not to be present: D had taken exception to V's conduct, not to his race. D's hostility to V was based on his conception of how members of their racial group should interact with members of another racial group. The decision is understandable as an

---

[162] In *Parry* [2004] EWHC 3112, an admission to the police 20 minutes after D's attack that his attack on V was racially motivated was held to be a demonstration of racial hostility immediately after the attack.

[163] [2001] 1 WLR 1352.

[164] [2004] EWHC 1453; similarly *Rogers* [2005] EWCA Crim 2863.

[165] [2005] EWCA Crim 889.

[166] [2000] Crim LR 756.

interpretation of the provisions but is uncomfortable in terms of social policy.[167] Suppose that V marries outside her religious group, an act of apostasy according to the groups' religious norms, for which the sanction is a severe beating. The beating would not be religiously aggravated on the logic of *Pal*.[168] Perhaps the most disturbing feature of *Pal* is that it comports with the grain of the provisions. But protection can also be needed from the strictures of religion and claims of dominion or containment based on ethnic loyalties.[169]

Proof of an attack by D on a member of a different racial or religious group will not, of itself, establish racial or religious hostility. That fact will not even be prima facie proof of hostility if there is evidence of some non-racial or religious explanation for the attack. On the other hand, as a matter of evidence, if the prosecution can prove that D knew or presumed that V was a member of a different racial or religious group and there is no overt explanation for D's aggression (such as a non-religious or non-racial quarrel), D may legitimately be expected to raise some credible evidence of non-racial or non-religious motivation. If he does not do so, the prosecution's allegation of racial or religious hostility is likely to be sustained. In the absence of a credible explanation, actions may be allowed to speak loudly and clearly.[170]

§ 11.10 Reforming the law of violence

Judges and commentators have expressed a great deal of dissatisfaction with the law relating to non-fatal offences.[171] The main focus of discontent has been with sections 47, 20, and 18 of the OAPA 1861, by far the most important sections of that Act in terms of the number of prosecutions. On one view, these offences may be viewed as an escalating ladder of gravity, in terms of the harm caused to the victim. From that perspective, the coverage provided is quirky and not easily rationalised. Section 47 requires an assault or battery which must occasion actual bodily harm. No mental element is required in respect of the bodily harm. What degree of directness is required for a battery is unclear. The maximum penalty for section 47 is five years' imprisonment, the same as for malicious wounding or grievous bodily harm under section 20, which does not reflect the fact that section 20 is regarded as a more serious offence.

In turn, section 20 concerns two different forms of harm—wounds and grievous bodily harm—which may well involve very different orders of magnitude. Whereas grievous bodily harm is by definition serious, a wound may be a very minor affair. There seems no obvious reason to bracket wounds and serious bodily harm within the actus reus of one offence. The wound or grievous bodily harm must be "inflicted"; a term that, as the case law stands, may

---

[167] In *Mcfarlane* [2002] EWHC Admin 485, *Pal* was said to be heavily dependent on its facts and that normally that where a racialist epithet was used during an attack racial hostility would be made out.

[168] In *Pal*, the court claimed that its reasoning would not extend, in the Court's own example, to a white man attacking another white man because of the latter's association with a black woman; but is hard to see the difference in principle between this example and the facts of the case.

[169] Section 28(5) of the Crime and Disorder Act 1998 makes some movement in this direction by aggravating attacks on atheists where hostility to atheism is demonstrated, or is at least in part a motivation for the attack.

[170] Inferences against D may be drawn from a failure to give evidence: Criminal Justice and Public Order Act 1994, s. 35.

[171] For cogent criticism and further references see Ashworth, *Principles of Criminal Law* (3rd ed., 1999) 344–5.

well mean different things according to the kind of injury that has occurred. For physical injuries, the need to prove an infliction probably requires some form of causation involving a violent or percussive impact (though not necessarily in so direct a form as is required for battery). For psychiatric injuries, any causal connection suffices. For diseases and infections, the position is obscure. Further, under section 20 a minimum mens rea of recklessness is required, but not as to a wound or grievous bodily harm; foresight of some, minor, bodily harm suffices.

Section 18 has given less ground for criticism. Although wounds and grievous bodily harm are again bracketed together, there must always be proof of an intent to cause grievous bodily harm or to resist lawful arrest or detention. This ensures that some measure of serious wrongdoing is involved for this very serious offence with its maximum term of life imprisonment. The requirement of a causal connection and nothing more avoids the morally dubious distinction between "cause" and "inflict" and allows a greater degree of certainty. Nonetheless, it remains an offence that draws together things not obviously connected. Questions relating to arrest and detention are best dealt with in the family of offences relating to assaults on policemen and other criminal justice officials. The term grievous bodily harm covers a wide range of injury, from, say, a broken arm to horrendous life-threatening injuries. Moreover the offence takes two very different forms: as either an offence where a serious harm was intentionally caused or an offence where a serious harm was intended but not brought about.

The Home Office has proposed replacement offences which would constitute a simpler and more coherent pattern of offences.[172] The three offences under discussion would be replaced by the following provisions:

(i)   A person is guilty of an offence if he intentionally causes serious injury to another.
(ii) A person is guilty of an offence if he recklessly causes serious injury to another.
(iii) A person is guilty of an offence if he intentionally or recklessly causes injury to another.
(iv) A person act intentionally with respect to a result of—
      (a) it is his purpose to cause it, or
      (b) although it is not his purpose to cause it, he knows that it would occur in the ordinary course of events if he were to succeed in his purpose of causing some other result.
(v)   A person acts recklessly with respect to a result if he is aware of a risk that it will occur and it is unreasonable to take that risk having regard to the circumstances as he knows or believes them to be.
(vi) "Injury" means—
      physical injury, or
      mental injury.
(vii) [Save for the offence of intentionally causing serious injury] physical injury does not include anything caused by disease but (subject to that) it includes pain, unconsciousness and any other impairment of a person's physical condition.

For many criminal lawyers, the enactment of these proposals in place of sections 47, 20, and 18 would constitute a significant advance. The most obvious feature of the proposed

---

[172] Home Office, *Violence: Reforming the Offences Against the Person Act 1861* (1998). The Home Office proposals largely reflect the earlier recommendations of the Law Commission: Law Com. No. 218, *Legislating the Criminal Code: Offences Against the Person and General Principles* (1993).

offences is the absence of clutter; the expression is simple and direct, with actus reus linked to mens rea through nothing more than a causal connection. Mens rea corresponds to the actus reus and the mens rea and actus reus terms are defined. It is difficult to imagine that this scheme of offences would give rise to the same number of appeals, confusions, and complexities as does the current order.

If simplicity and economy of means are taken to be virtues (and this has been contested), there are nonetheless some criticisms that may be offered. The exclusion of disease, save for the offence of causing serious injury intentionally, may be characterised as a licence for reprehensible sexual risk-taking. Yet there is much to be said for caution in this area. A public health perspective favours a policy which encourages the sexually irresponsible to report their own condition and provide information about their sexual contacts. A law and a prosecution policy favouring rigorous policing of persons who have unprotected sex when suffering from sexually transmissible infections would be at odds with public health concerns (and require oppressive police investigations).

A similar caution may be urged with respect to mental injury. If mental injury is intentionally caused in the core sense of intention, the conduct concerned will, in the main, be conduct which should be proscribed. Yet there are many situations in ordinary life where a person may cause another mental injury as a likely *side-effect* of conduct that she should remain free to engage in. Under the terms of the proposed reforms, such conduct might well be covered by the offences of recklessly causing serious injury or recklessly causing injury.

More generally, the proposals draw a distinction between injuries and serious injuries, yet provide no guidance on seriousness. As under the current law, what constitutes a serious injury will be a question of fact. Potentially, this brings an unduly large swathe of injury into the most grave offence—intentionally causing serious injury—which, like the present section 18, carries a maximum term of life imprisonment. There is something to be said in favour of a greater particularity here, with a tripartite division of physical harm offences into cases of (i) injury, (ii) serious injury, and (iii) grievous injury. These terms should have some degree of definition, with grievous injury confined to physical or mental harm that causes extreme pain and suffering, significant disfigurement, or significant disability. In the sphere of serious injury, the proposals sharply demarcate causing serious injury with intent (maximum penalty life imprisonment) from recklessly causing serious injury (five years maximum). For cases of causing injury, however, there is but one offence which can be committed either intentionally or recklessly. It is difficult to appreciate why the distinction between intent and recklessness loses its moral significance for cases involving lesser injury.[173]

The mens rea terms are unexceptional from the perspective of subjectivism and the correspondence principle. A stipulative definition of intent is offered which includes injuries brought about as a side-effect of some other purpose. The definition would be further improved by providing that, to count as intended result, a side-effect should be something

---

[173] If, as we believe, the distinction between intention and recklessness retains moral purchase at this lower level of offending, the provision of separate offences of intentionally causing injury and recklessly causing injury would provide the further advantage that the former offence, being a crime where the culpability is confined to intent, would not come within the *Majewski* principle: see further below, § 18.3.

that is virtually certain to occur.[174] The definition of recklessness is in straightforward *Cunningham* terms.

The conditional welcome given here for these proposals is by no means universally shared. Jeremy Horder complains that the proposed reforms strip the law of too much moral substance.[175] He emphasises the importance of "representative" or "fair" labelling,[176] which is achieved only if the definition of an offence conveys an accurate moral picture of what the defendant has done. To that end, he favours the use of such graphic terms as "castrates, disables, disfigures, or dismembers . . . or removes an internal body part" in the definition of offences.[177] One may question, however, whether the awful details of the worst forms of violence need to feature in the *definition* of offences. Such cases receive close attention from the media and the factual details are widely disseminated in the press. The moral resonance of an offence need not require details of the *modus operandi*. For example, the term "murder" has great evocative power. Murder may extend over a vast range of particulars from, say, a painless lethal injection to agonising and protracted forms of death; but there is no need to identify gruesome ways of killing in order to convey the gravity of murder. Besides, if charges were to contain the amount of particularity recommended by Horder, there arises the risk of unmeritorious arguments on the applicability of the charge brought. Arguments concerning whether D's act was a disablement or disfigurement would be thoroughly unattractive. That said, we have commented already on the fact that the term "serious injury" is too broad and that a greater degree of subdivision and definition is required. To this extent Horder is clearly right.

Another critical voice is that of John Gardner.[178] For him sections 47, 20, and 18 of the OAPA 1861 each has a distinctive value and ambit, which would be swept away by the Government's proposals. Gardner argues that the central point about section 47 is that liability is triggered by an assault or battery: "By committing an assault one changes one's own normative position, so that certain adverse consequences and circumstances which would not have counted against one but for one's original assault now count against one automatically, and add to one's crime."[179] On this view, it is no surprise that section 47 has the same maximum penalty as section 20, that no mental element is required for the occasioning of actual bodily harm, and that (according to Gardner) "occasion" is a broader term than cause.

In Gardner's scheme, section 20 concerns the *infliction* of violence, which can take in a broader field of conduct than assault but keeps the offence away from such things as transmitting diseases. Here some degree of foresight should be required about the possible infliction of physical harm. Section 18, in dealing with *intended* consequences, appropriately moves to a broader *causal* standard when determining the presence of actus reus. We cannot discuss here whether this schema is persuasive in normative terms. What can be said is that Gardner's schema has never been firmly established as part of English law. In actus reus

---

[174] For further discussion of virtually certain consequences see above, § 5.1(iv), where the Law Commission's formulation (adopted by the Home Office) is noted: see, especially, n. 45.
[175] "Rethinking Non-fatal Offences Against the Person" (1994) 14 *OJLS* 335.
[176] See above, § 2.4.
[177] Horder, "Rethinking Non-fatal Offences Against the Person" (1994) 14 *OJLS* 335, 345.
[178] "Rationality and the Rule of Law in Offences Against the Person" [1994] *CLJ* 502.
[179] *Ibid.*, 509.

terms, there was for many years a close association between sections 47 and 20, as it was considered that "inflict" required proof of an assault or battery. Although that connection was relaxed in *Wilson*,[180] there remains considerable doubt about the extent to which battery itself can accommodate forms of indirectly caused injury, rendering problematic the degree of disassociation between sections 47 and 20 when physical injury is in issue. Moreover, there is no authority that "occasion" in section 47 is a broader term than cause, although there is authority that it is synonymous with cause.[181] Indeed when psychiatric injury is an issue, "inflict" itself has been interpreted as "cause",[182] making for points of contact between sections 20 and 18 as well as section 47. Gardner seems to be seeking a preservation order on a house never built. The degrees of difference and similarity between the three offences follow no overarching pattern, a fact which by itself makes a case for reform.

Something should finally be said about the reform proposals for the offences of assault and battery. There is to be a single offence, which may take two forms:

(viii)   A person is guilty of an offence if—
    (a)   he intentionally or recklessly applies force to or causes an impact on the body of another, or
    (b)   he intentionally or recklessly causes the other to believe that any such force or impact is imminent.

It will be noted that the offence is a single offence which can be committed in two ways, avoiding the tiresome question of duplicity. Battery is, at long last, jettisoned as a term and with it the question of what degree of directness that offence requires. The offence requires the application of force or *causing* an impact on the body, clearly bringing a case like K[183] within its terms. No offence is committed if the force or impact is neither intended nor likely and D's conduct is "such as is generally acceptable in the ordinary conduct of daily life" and is not known or believed to be unacceptable to V.[184] The hostility requirement is dropped and replaced by Lord Goff's "daily life" criterion.[185] In the case of contacts inherently unlikely to cause physical injury, the line between acceptable and unacceptable conduct will remain hazy, but this is inevitable, once the requirement of hostility is omitted, given the imprecision of that boundary in social life. As under the present law, the mens rea is intention or recklessness. The proposal builds sensibly on the current law with useful simplification and clarification.

---

[180] [1984] AC 242 (HL).
[181] *Roberts* (1971) 56 Cr App R 95 (CA).
[182] *Burstow* [1998] AC 147 (HL).
[183] (1990) 91 Cr App R 23 (CA). See above, § 11.3(i).
[184] Home Office, *Violence: Reforming the Offences Against the Person Act 1861* (1998) cl. 4(2).
[185] *Collins* v. *Wilcock* [1984] 3 All ER 374, 378 (CA). See above, § 11.3(ii).

12

NON-CONSENSUAL SEXUAL OFFENCES

The Sexual Offences Act 2003 contains four major offences that penalise D in respect of non-consensual sexual acts. These offences are, respectively, rape; assault by penetration; sexual assault; and causing a person to engage in sexual activity without consent. They replace the former version of rape and the offence of indecent assault, offences which covered conduct that broadly may be termed "sexual violence".[1] Almost without exception, the new offences cover such conduct and, arguably, other forms of conduct too. Certainly, some conduct that fell within the former offence of indecent assault will now be treated more seriously within the new offences.[2]

The genesis of these new offences can be traced through a major Home Office report,[3] followed by intensive parliamentary debates and committee revision,[4] prior to royal assent. Although some of the details of these new offences were significantly changed from the original Home Office proposals, certain themes remained constant: the need for modernisation of the law, and particularly for greater clarity; gender neutrality in the law whenever possible; effective protection for victims, thereby encouraging victims to come forward; and fairness to defendants.[5] Of course, a reasonable period of time must elapse before any assessment can be made about whether these aims have been achieved. What can be said at present is that, in certain particulars, there seem to be improvements over the old law. Yet, without indulging in pessimism, there are also a number of difficulties and obscurities that seem sure to engender appellate litigation.

Below, the specifics of the new offences will be discussed. They share certain common features. First, each of these offences involves "sexual" conduct. In rape, as we shall argue, the sexuality involved is self-evident, whereas the other offences may include conduct that is not patently sexual. The Act makes provision for determining when conduct is sexual,[6] and we consider this provision in § 12.5. Further, common to these new offences is that they all

---

[1] Formerly found in the Sexual Offences Act 1956, ss. 1 (rape), 14–15 (indecent assault).

[2] For instance, manual penetration of a vagina or anus will come within the new offence of assault by penetration—an offence, like rape, punishable with life imprisonment. Formerly such conduct fell merely within the offence of indecent assault.

[3] *Setting the Boundaries: Reforming the Law on Sex Offences* (Home Office, 2000); Lacey, "Beset by Boundaries: The Home Office Review of Sex Offences" [2001] *Crim LR* 3; Rumney, "The Review of Sex Offences and Rape Law" (2001) 64 *MLR* 890.

[4] Home Affairs Committee, *Sexual Offences Bill* (Fifth Report of Session 2002–03, HC 639, 2003); *The Government Reply to the Fifth Report from the Home Affairs Committee Session 2002–2003* HC 639; *Sexual Offences Bill* (CM 5986, 2003).

[5] For exposition and critique of the four offences under discussion, see Temkin and Ashworth, "The Sexual Offences Act 2003, Rape, Sexual Assaults and the Problems of Consent" [2004] *Crim LR* 328.

[6] Sexual Offences Act 2003, s. 78.

dispense with proof of knowledge or recklessness as to lack of consent, something required by the former offences of indecent assault and rape.[7] The position now is that, after proof that D intentionally committed the conduct elements of one of these offences with relevant accompanying circumstances, liability will ensue unless D *reasonably believed* that V consented. Moreover, the Act makes provision whereby, in certain circumstances, an evidential[8] or a conclusive[9] presumption is to be made about V's non-consent and about the lack of D's reasonable belief in consent. We return to those matters in § 12.6, after we have examined the distinctive features of each new offence. Finally, as things stand, it seems that unusual rules apply to sections 1–4 concerning the role of intoxication. We consider these in § 12.8.

§12.1 Rape

Section 1 of the Sexual Offences Act 2003 provides:

> (1) A person (A) commits an offence if—
>   (a) he intentionally penetrates the vagina, anus or mouth of another person (B) with his penis,
>   (b) B does not consent to the penetration, and
>   (c) A does not reasonably believe that B consents.

Of the four new offences, rape is the only one that requires a male perpetrator, someone who intentionally penetrates the vagina, anus, or mouth of another non-consenting person with *his* penis. There was some controversial authority that the former offence of rape could be committed through the instrumentality of an innocent agent;[10] however, such a verdict now seems precluded by the new wording of the offence.[11] Penetration is required on the part of D and continues from entry to withdrawal.[12] Accordingly, D may rape V if he continues to penetrate V when an initial consent is revoked prior to withdrawal.[13] Vaginal penetration occurs as soon as there is entry of the vulva.[14] It is immaterial if the vagina penetrated is surgically constructed, for example through gender reassignment surgery.[15] Anal and oral penetration also constitutes rape, entailing male as well as female victims.

The penetration must be intentional. In practice, if an act of penetration is proved almost invariably the inference will be that it was intentional. What if D was very intoxicated at the time of intercourse? Even then, the action may be expected to speak for itself. The activity is not like, say, falling against someone or other forms of mistaken or accidental

---

[7] Of course, the previous law will be the governing law in respect of conduct prior to May 2004. For an account of the previous law of rape and indecent assault, see Chapter 12 of the first edition of this work.

[8] Sexual Offence Act 2003, s. 75.

[9] *Ibid.*, s. 76.

[10] *Cogan and Leak* [1976] 2 QB 217; above, § 7.3(i).

[11] Secondary liability remains possible. If D1 assists or encourages D2 to penetrate V's vagina, mouth, or anus with his penis, D1 will be an accomplice to any rape that D2 perpetrates. Further, should D1 procure D2 so to act while D2 reasonably believes that V consents, D2 would nonetheless have committed the actus reus of rape, a sufficient basis with which to find complicity by D1: *DPP* v. *K and B* [1997] 1 Cr App Rep 36; above, § 7.6(ii)(b).

[12] Sexual Offences Act 2003, s. 79(2).

[13] As was the position under the previous law: *Kaitamaki* [1985] AC 147; *Cooper* [1994] Crim LR 541.

[14] Sexual Offences Act 2003, s. 79(9).

[15] *Ibid.*, s. 79(3).

contact. Its very nature argues against any finding that penetration occurred by accident or mistake, even in states of extreme intoxication.[16] We return to this point, in the context of intoxication, below in § 12.8.

Requirements (b) and (c) in section 1(1), concerning V's non-consent and the absence of a reasonable belief in V's consent, are considered below in § 12.6.

§ 12.2 Assault by penetration

Section 2 of the Sexual Offences Act 2003 provides:

> (1) A person (A) commits an offence if—
>   (a) he intentionally penetrates the vagina or anus of another person (B) with a part of his body or anything else,
>   (b) the penetration is sexual,
>   (c) B does not consent to the penetration, and
>   (d) A does not reasonably believe that B consents.

A striking feature of this offence is its potential breadth, particularly considering the maximum penalty of life imprisonment. Although the intentional, non-consensual, penetration must be of the anus or vagina, it may be done with any part of the body or with anything else. Many routine medical procedures—involving thermometers, swabs, and the like—lie on the cusp of this offence. Of course, consent to such procedures will normally be present. But what if D, a doctor, takes a vaginal swab from his patient, ostensibly for the sake of a treatment required by V but, covertly, to collect data for a study unconnected with V's medical needs? In such circumstances, much will hang on the meaning to be given to "sexual", a matter we examine in § 12.5.

It will be noted that there is an overlap with the offence of rape whenever the vagina or anus of V is penetrated by D's penis. This was deliberate, to allow for cases where it can be proved that D was responsible for an act of penetration by some bodily part or anything else but it cannot be proved that D used his penis (although he may have done). The retention of a crime of rape indicates that the legislature thinks that there is a particular form of heinousness associated with penile penetration. Such penetration may be thought to be the ultimate kind of forced intimacy, as well as being the form most redolent of risk of disease and unwanted pregnancy.[17] Given that there is now an offence with the same

---

[16] Under its previous definition, rape was construed as a crime of basic intent, entailing that proof of recklessness was presumed if D was voluntarily intoxicated when he penetrated V: *Woods* (1982) 74 Cr App Rep 312; *Fotheringham* (1988) 88 Cr App Rep 206.

[17] It has been argued that the core of the wrong of rape is disrespect for V's autonomy, the use of her body in a purely instrumental manner which disregards her personhood. As such, rape in its "pure" form would take place where D, using a condom, penetrates an insensate V who never becomes aware of what D has done and suffers no adverse physical or psychological effects: Gardner and Shute, "The Wrongness of Rape" in Horder (ed.), *Oxford Essays in Jurisprudence* (4th series, 2000) 193. On this view, the "core" wrong would have occurred whenever D uses the body of an insensate V for sexual gratification and whatever form his conduct takes, implying no difference in the basic wrong of the offences of rape, assault by penetration, and sexual assault. But, of course, a typical instance of rape will be fully experienced by the victim and will inflict serious psychological trauma, as well as risking physical injury, infection, and—in the case of vaginal penetration—unwanted pregnancy. Although such effects are not within the formal definition of rape, they are very much part of our conception of rape and explain why rape is appropriately characterised as a form of violence against V as well as a wrong of disregard for V's autonomy.

maximum penalty of life imprisonment but which covers a much broader swathe of conduct, the distinctive wrongness of rape is now reflected only by the labelling.

Requirements (c) and (d) in section 2(1), concerning V's non-consent and the absence of a reasonable belief in V's consent, are considered below in § 12.6. The role of voluntary intoxication in attributing a finding of intentional penetration will be discussed in § 12.8.

§ 12.3 Sexual assault

Section 3 of the Sexual Offences Act 2003 provides:

> (1) A person (A) commits an offence if—
>   (a) he intentionally touches another person (B),
>   (b) the touching is sexual,
>   (c) B does not consent to the touching, and
>   (d) A does not reasonably believe that B consents.

The offence covers non-consensual, non-penetrative, sexual acts, requiring proof that D touched V. V's person includes reference to a body part surgically constructed, in particular through gender reassignment surgery.[18]

A "touching" includes a touching amounting to penetration.[19] The term covers much else besides, including touching made with any part of the body, or using anything else, and *through* anything.[20] It was confirmed in *H*[21] that V's body includes her clothes and it seems that no pressure on her body need be felt by V. For example, should D intentionally brush V's fully clothed breast without her consent, he may well commit sexual assault.

One point of restriction, however, is that the offence is *confined* to touching; which, in the pedantic terms of English law, is strictly speaking a battery. Accordingly, to continue our example, if D attempts but fails to touch V's breast, yet puts her in fear of an imminent touching, he may well perpetrate a simple assault but not a sexual assault. Alternatively, there may well be an attempted sexual assault on such facts.

The touching must also be intentional, a requirement that has considerable practical importance; it is easy to envisage circumstances where the touching of a fully clothed person may be completely inadvertent, as when travelling on a crowded bus or railway carriage. There is, however, some controversy about whether a touching will be regarded as intentional if it results from D's state of intoxication. As always, deliberate contact will suffice even if D would not have chosen to touch V had he been sober, on the standard premise that a drunken intention is none the less an intention. Yet it seems that accidental contact pursuant to a drunken stumble will not be treated as intentional. The issue is discussed further below, in § 12.8.

Requirement (b) in section 3(1), concerning the sexual nature of the touching, is dealt with below, in § 12.5. Requirements (c) and (d), concerning V's non-consent and the absence of a reasonable belief in V's consent, are considered in § 12.6.

---

[18] Section 79(3).
[19] Sexual Offences Act 2003, s. 79(8).
[20] *Ibid.*
[21] [2005] EWCA Crim 732, continuing the pre-2003 Act approach.

§ 12.4 Causing a person to engage in sexual activity without consent

Section 4 of the Sexual Offences Act 2003 provides:

(1) A person (A) commits an offence if—
    (a) he intentionally causes another person (B) to engage in an activity,
    (b) the activity is sexual,
    (c) B does not consent to engaging in the activity, and
    (d) A does not reasonably believe that B consents.

A perusal of this offence immediately informs that where the interchange is between D and V, and no-one else, much of the conduct covered in the preceding offences will fall also within this offence. With the exception of sexual violations of overwhelmed or passive victims (who could not be said to be "engaged in an activity"), the overlap of section 4 with the other three offences is considerable.

What, then, is the distinctive coverage of this offence? For the moment, confining ourselves to interactions between D and V, situations where D causes V to touch him sexually, or causes V to touch herself sexually, seem to be included. The same would apply if we reverse the genders, including situations where D compels V to have intercourse with her. Moving beyond two party interactions, D commits this offence if he causes V to engage in non-consensual sexual activity with T: T may be innocent of D's machinations, an accomplice of D, or even a co-victim with V.

D must *cause* V to engage in an activity to which she does not consent. If V acts as she does because of something violent or coercive that D does, or threatens to do, it is inevitable that D will be found to have caused her to do it. As we shall see in § 12.6, the very same facts will also establish V's lack of consent. But the two elements may not coincide. On a very loose view of causation, for example, D might be said to have "caused" V to have sex with him by overcoming her reluctance with a very large sum of money.[22] It does not necessarily follow that the ensuing sexual act was non-consensual, even in cases where D has exploited the economic circumstances of V.

It is worth dwelling briefly on the last point. A real difficulty in this area is that dire economic necessities may be highly coercive. Suppose that V is an asylum seeker deprived of any benefits, following adjudication that she did not declare her intention to seek asylum at the point of entry; and D, a brothel keeper who is aware of her circumstances, offers her work. If, from desperation, she becomes a sex worker it is no stretch of language to say that she has been caused to engage in sexual activity. (Moreover, as will be noted in § 12.6, it may be but a short step to go further and conclude that she does not consent to any of the sex acts she performs or endures in the course of her work.) Such a conclusion would have significant implications not merely for the scope of section 4 but also for the other

---

[22] A broad view of causation, one that would plot a causal pathway connecting the conduct of D and the voluntary actions of V, has occasionally been taken in cases such as *Kennedy* [1999] Crim LR 65 and *Kennedy (No. 2)* [2005] EWCA Crim 685, and is supported by the reasoning of the House of Lords in *Environmental Agency* v. *Empress Car Co* [1999] 2 AC 22. But see the critical analysis at § 4.2(d). It may be noted that the variant of this offence created in s. 8 of the Sexual Offence Act 2003, for the protection of children under the age of 13 years, proscribes "causing or *inciting*" a child under 13 to engage in sexual activity. The absence of any reference to inciting in the core offence lends support to the view that, in line with the standard approach to causation, the deliberate, free, and informed decision of V is to be regarded as a *novus actus*.

non-consensual offences in the Act. No doubt those responsible for formulating and implementing a Draconian asylum policy are effectively beyond the purview of this offence and, if they are exempt, so should be D. Yet it is remarkable that legislation so recently formulated can give rise to such conjectures on the scope of these very serious offences.

§ 12.5 Sexual conduct or activity

The offences of assault by penetration, sexual assault, and causing a person to engage in sexual activity explicitly require proof of sexual conduct or activity. The same requirement is not included in the definition of rape. The reason for this, presumably, is that the sexuality of penile penetration is self-evident and requires no further explication. If this is correct, then every case of penile penetration is, inherently, a case of sexual conduct. Alternatively, if this view were not accepted, the way would be open to argue that the definition of rape may include "non-sexual" penile penetrations, as where D penetrates V not for sexual gratification but to cause distress and humiliation. We think, however, that any argument that penetrations so motivated are not sexual should be summarily dismissed. The humiliation and distress arises from enforced *sexual* connection, regardless of whether D seeks sexual gratification from his conduct.[23]

In respect of the other three offences, it will only be in a small minority of cases that the question is problematic whether D's conduct was sexual. Should the answer not be obvious, and serious consideration be required, section 78 of the Sexual Offences Act 2003 provides that activity is sexual if:

(a) whatever its circumstances or any person's purpose in relation to it, it is because of its nature sexual, or
(b) because of its nature it may be sexual and because of its circumstances or the purpose of any person in relation to it (or both) it is sexual.

(i) Activity "by its nature" sexual

Paragraph (a) mirrors the position adopted above: that certain conduct is inherently sexual whatever D's purpose. Unequivocally within this category would be penetration of orifices by a penis and oral connection by D with any of V's intimate parts.

Beyond that, one should proceed cautiously. Arguably, touching V's intimate parts manually or with an implement may, or may not, be sexual conduct; in which case it falls under paragraph (b). However, such an analysis was rejected under the former offence of indecent assault. In *Court*,[24] the opinion was expressed that the touching of a vagina was *inherently* indecent even if done for a non-sexual reason. Lord Ackner proposed a case where D, a doctor, takes a vaginal sample from V under the guise of diagnosis but, in reality, takes the sample for the purposes of some general research he is undertaking. No valid

---

[23] It is noteworthy that Lord Ackner, in giving judgment for the House of Lords in *Court* [1989] AC 28, considered that intimate touching not motivated by sexual gratification would fall within the (former) offence of indecent assault.

[24] [1989] AC 28, 44.

consent would be given in such circumstances and, since D's act is (according to Lord Ackner) inherently indecent, the offence of indecent assault would be committed. A similar view was applied in *Tabassum*,[25] again to convict D of the former offence of indecent assault, where D examined V's breasts for a non-sexual reason.

Arguably, this takes findings of sexual violation beyond their appropriate scope.[26] The hypothetical doctor in *Court* would now be guilty of assault by penetration, an offence as serious as rape. If fully informed consent is not given to a non-sexual examination of an intimate body part, criminal liability should ensue—but for simple assault rather than sexual assault. One implication of *Court* and *Tabassum* seems to be that even a fully consensual medical examination, carried out properly and for a legitimate purpose, would be sexual if it concerned any intimate part of the body. The mere fact of consent—a "circumstance" and so excluded from the ambit of section 78(a)—cannot be decisive of that point. This suggests that, while there must be a large presumption that any intimate touching is by its nature sexual, it is not a foregone conclusion. Indeed, to characterise the many thousands of medically essential intimate examinations that occur in clinical settings each day as sexual episodes kept lawful by consent is absurd.

(ii) Activity ambiguous by nature

Where conduct is not inherently sexual, paragraph (b) requires us to consider its surrounding circumstances and D's purposes. The facts of *Court* provide a good example: D put V, a twelve-year-old girl, over his knee and smacked her fully clothed bottom. If it was an act of unauthorised discipline for misbehaviour by V it was a case of simple assault. In fact, D was smacking V's bottom for sexual gratification and accordingly was guilty of indecent assault. D would nowadays be guilty of sexual assault.

The phase "because of its nature it may be sexual" could potentially be taken to imply that certain acts, because of their nature, *cannot* be regarded as sexual even if done for sexual gratification. That was certainly the position under the old law of indecent assault. For example, it was held in *George*[27] that when, for fetishist reasons, D touched the shoes that V was wearing, D's sexual motive could not make an inherently decent act into an indecent act. This approach is reinforced under the new Act by *H*, where it was considered doubtful whether a sexual assault would occur on facts such as *George*, although the Court acknowledged that the ultimate decision might be for the jury within the terms of section 78(b).[28] In our view, however, a jury *should* be asked to consider whether a sexual assault occurred on facts such as *George*.

H distinguished between two questions in the context of section 78(b): first, whether the

---

[25] [2000] 2 Cr App R 328. D carried out what may have been genuine research into breast-cancer, aware that women whom he examined mistakenly assumed he was a medical doctor. The Court of Appeal held that their mistake vitiated the women's consent (as to which see below, § 12.6) and that, even if the research was genuine, the examinations were inherently indecent and therefore indecent assaults rather than mere assaults.

[26] Cf. Sullivan, "The Need for a Crime of Sexual Assault" [1989] *Crim LR* 331, where it was argued that the term "indecent assault", now superseded by "sexual assault", was both over-inclusive (in that the touching of intimate bodily parts was taken to be inherently indecent whatever D's reasons for touching V's body) and under-inclusive (in that certain acts, even if done in pursuit of sexual arousal, would remain inherently decent).

[27] [1956] Crim LR 52.

[28] *H* [2005] EWCA Crim 732, [2005] 2 All ER 859, para. 11.

touching because of its nature *could* be sexual; and secondly, whether the touching because of its circumstances or its purpose *was* sexual. But it is submitted that the first question is not significant, in that the answer is *always* yes. *Contra* the doubts expressed in *H*, the nature of any act can be changed into a sexual act if done in pursuit of sexual release. If D touches V in any manner to attain a state of arousal, a sexual assault has occurred (assuming the touching is non-consensual). Such a touching is qualitatively different to, not to mention more threatening than, a touching where D, say, takes hold of V's shod foot in order to ascertain V's shoe size.[29]

§12.6 Consent

For each of these offences, it must be proved that V did not consent. Prior to the 2003 Act, a somewhat uninformative distinction was drawn between consent, however reluctant, and mere "submission" falling short of consent.[30] Section 74 of the Sexual Offence Act 2003 now provides that a person consents, "if he agrees by choice, and has the freedom and capacity to make that choice." Capacity to choose focuses attention on V's mental capacities at the time of the sexual act, the ability to understand the meaning and implications of his decisions. Those questions, at least, involve consideration of matters of objective fact, albeit of a psychological rather than palpable kind. However, the question whether D had the "freedom" to choose is a much more metaphysical matter when we go beyond questions of force, the threat of force, and insensibility. For instance, what if D offers V work in his brothel, fully aware that V, an asylum seeker who has not applied for asylum at the port of entry, is without means of support. If working as a sex-worker is something she detests, has she been "caused to engage in sexual activity without consent" or has she taken, however reluctantly, an opportunity to earn money provided by D?[31] What if D had forcibly taken what money she had before offering her work in the brothel?

We will consider the general difficulties about consent further in § 21.1(iii)(c). To some extent, the answer to such questions is made easier by the Act's providing in section 76 for two circumstances which, if proved, lead to *conclusive* presumptions that V did not consent. Additionally, the Act lists a set of circumstances in section 75 where an *evidential* presumption arises against D that V did not consent. (None of these includes situations such as the brothel example.)

As we shall see, however, any difficulty in proving non-consent may only be postponed by the evidential presumptions. If D is able to overcome the evidential presumption by pointing to evidence suggestive that, notwithstanding the countervailing circumstances, V did possess the freedom and capacity to choose, the burden of proof reverts in the normal way to the prosecution, who must then establish the lack of freedom or incapacity of V within the terms of section 74.

---

[29] Sullivan, "The Need for a Crime of Sexual Assault" [1989] *Crim LR* 331.

[30] *Olugboja* [1989] QB 320 (CA). The decision has its defenders: Gardner, "Appreciating *Olugboja*" (1996) 16 *Legal Studies* 275.

[31] Note, too, the question whether her conduct is "caused": above, § 12.4.

The presumptions relating to consent must now be considered before returning, in § 12.6(iii), to the default test of consent laid down in section 74.

(i) Evidential presumptions about consent

In respect of each of the four offences we have examined, section 75 of the Sexual Offences Act 2003 provides for evidential presumptions (i) about consent and (ii) about a reasonable belief in consent. For such presumptions to arise, the prosecution must prove (a) that D committed the conduct element of the actus reus of the offence with which he is charged; (b) that any of the circumstances specified in section 75 existed; and (c) that D knew those circumstances existed. If these conditions are satisfied, V is to be presumed not to have consented to the relevant act unless sufficient evidence is adduced to raise an issue as to whether V consented. Likewise, if D claims to have reasonably believed that V consented when aware that any of the specified circumstances existed, he is presumed not to have reasonably believed that V consented, unless sufficient evidence is adduced to raise an issue as to whether he reasonably believed that V consented. In other words, an evidential onus is imposed on D.

The specified circumstances will be listed below. First, we will take one of these specified circumstances, the use or threat of immediate violence by D against V,[32] to illustrate the working of an evidential presumption. Let us say that D threatened violence against V immediately before he had sexual intercourse with V. This much is proved by the prosecution. If nothing further is heard from D, the jury will be entitled to find, without any further consideration, that V did not consent to intercourse with D. Suppose D claims that the threat of violence was part of a sex game he was playing with V, and produces a letter to him from V agreeing to the kind of encounter that D claimed occurred. If the presiding judge considered D might be telling the truth, D will have raised an issue as to whether V consented. It will be then for the prosecution to prove to the jury that V was not consenting. The same evidence may well raise an issue as to a reasonable belief in consent and, if so, the prosecution must then prove that D did not reasonably believe that V consented.

(a) On what basis does the prosecution prove non-consent by V if D has succeeded in raising an evidential issue?

Most straightforwardly, the prosecution may refute D's claim that the threat of violence was part of a game, showing that D was simply being violent. In such a case the evidential presumption locks in again and V's lack of consent is presumed. But if the prosecution cannot refute that the violence was on the face of it consensual, the presumption falls away. From then on the prosecution must prove lack of consent in terms of section 74. The prosecution must prove that, on this occasion, V either did not agree to sexual intercourse, or that she lacked the freedom and capacity to make that choice. Such might be the case, for example, where D and V had agreed to some role playing involving violence but during the interchange V made it clear that she did not wish to have sex with him.

---

[32] Sexual Offences Act, s. 75(2)(a)–(b).

(b) On what basis does the prosecution prove that D did not reasonably believe that V consented if D has succeeded in raising an evidential issue?

To continue our example, suppose the prosecution has not refuted the game claim by D but has established that V nonetheless did not consent. D claims a reasonable belief in V's consent. How does the prosecution defeat this claim? Is it enough to establish that a reasonable person, in the same circumstances as D, would not have believed that V was consenting?

At one time, it was proposed that the reasonableness of D's belief should be resolved by applying an objective reasonable person standard. That proposal was rejected by Parliament, on the basis that a person with learning disabilities would be judged by standards he could not attain.[33] The test to be applied, for all four offences under discussion, is as follows:[34]

> whether a belief is reasonable is to be determined having regard to all the circumstances, including any steps A has taken to ascertain whether B consents.

Accordingly, the test is whether D's belief in the circumstances of his case that V consented was reasonable with a particular emphasis on what efforts he made to ascertain the true state of V's consent.[35]

What if, in our example, D had been drinking to such an extent that his judgment was impaired? Could regard be had to that circumstance? Evidently not: if D would not have formed the belief but for drink, that demonstrates the unreasonableness of the belief. For this reason, it is uncertain whether Parliament's intention to mitigate an objective standard, in favour of learning-disabled persons and others in like case, has succeeded. The question is "whether a *belief* is reasonable". Reference to all the circumstances may well explain *why* D came to have an unreasonable belief—D1 was drunk, say, whereas D2 was learning disabled. And, of course, the two cases are not comparable—D1 is to be blamed for losing his usual bearings through drink, whereas it was understandable (and condonable) for D2 to have formed an unreasonable belief. Yet it does not follow that to understand and condone *why* a particular belief was formed makes the belief itself *reasonable*.

We may judge that D's failure, say, to jump a fence was a reasonable effort given his weight, age, lack of training, and the like. But the same conclusion cannot be made of an erroneous belief that D has formed but which would not be shared by a person with normal reasoning competence. If D, a learning-disabled person, misconstrues V's affectionate pat on the shoulder as a sexual invitation, the belief is unreasonable even if held in good faith by D. The fact that we are able to take into account D's reduced mental capacity makes his mistake a condonable one but does not elevate it into a reasonable belief. To exempt

---

[33] Home Affairs Committee, *Sexual Offences Bill* Fifth Report of Session 2002–03, HC639, para. 23.

[34] Sexual Offences Act 2003, ss. 1(2), 2(2), 3(2), 4(2).

[35] In our example, no doubt D will wish to bring in evidence the history of his sexual relationship with V, which raises difficult and controversial issues concerning the parameters of admissible evidence; issues that lie beyond the compass of this book. (Those issues would have arisen even if the reasonable person standard had been retained by Parliament.) The Youth Justice and Criminal Evidence Act 1999, s. 41, places limits on the extent to which V can be questioned about her previous sexual history even when it concerns the nature of her relationship with D. Nonetheless, in *A* [2001] 3 All ER 1, the House of Lords decided that, in light of the fair trial guarantee provided by Article 6 of the European Convention of Human Rights, the restrictions on cross-examination imposed by s. 41 had to be interpreted in a manner compatible with Article 6.

learned-disabled persons and others in like case, courts will have to construe the requirement for a reasonable belief in consent to be satisfied where it was understandable and condonable for D to believe that V consented, irrespective of the objective justification for such a belief.

(c) Circumstances where evidential presumptions about consent arise

Section 75(2) lists the circumstances that give rise to evidential presumptions. They arise where:

(a) any person, at the time of the relevant act or immediately before it began, used violence against V or caused V to fear that immediate violence would be used against her;

(b) any person, at the time of the relevant act or immediately before it began, caused V to fear that violence was being used, or that immediate violence would be used, against another person;

(c) V was, and D was not, unlawfully detained at the time of the relevant act;

(d) V was asleep or otherwise unconscious at the time of the relevant act;

(e) because of V's physical disability, V was not able at the time of the relevant act to communicate to D whether she consented;

(f) any person had administered to or caused to be taken by V, without her consent, a substance which, having regard to when it was administered or taken, was capable of causing or enabling V to be stupefied or overpowered at the time of the relevant act.

One may wonder why conditions (a)–(c) required specific provisions. Under the general test set down in section 74, one would have thought that, in such circumstances, a lack of freedom and capacity to consent would readily be inferred. D would have to produce some exceptional evidence to rebut an inference of non-consent. And that is, effectively, the position under section 75(2)(a)–(c); the use or threat of immediate violence or unlawful detention must surely, ordinarily, be incompatible with the free consent of V and, indeed, with any reasonable belief on D's part that V consented.

Condition (d) is very puzzling; under the previous law, the fact that V was asleep or otherwise unconscious would normally be constitutive of an incapacity to consent.[36] Perhaps the effect of the condition is to allow for a possibility that, between persons with an intimate relationship, one of them may sometimes, legitimately, sexually fondle his sleeping partner. In such a case, while V's non-consent (and D's lack of reasonable belief in consent) is to be presumed, D still has an opportunity to raise a reasonable doubt about these matters, making them a live issue. Similarly, issues relating to condition (e) might arise in the context of existing sexual relationships: in normal circumstances where a person performs a sexual act on a person who cannot at the time communicate consent because of disability, a very serious wrong is perpetrated.

Condition (f) requires some examination. We must assume circumstances where someone has slipped V a substance capable of causing, or enabling, V to be overpowered or stupefied at the time of the relevant act. Where, in fact, D is overpowered or stupefied, the finding of non-consent within the terms of section 74 would normally be straightforward, even without the benefit of condition (f).[37] In circumstances where the substance has no or

---

[36] *Mayers* (1872) 12 Cox CC 311; *Larter* [1995] Crim LR 75 (CA).

[37] To raise an issue, D would presumably have to adduce evidence that V agreed in advance that D could make covert attempts to stupify or overpower her and could be allowed intercourse (or whatever sexual touching is at

little effect, D may no doubt raise an evidential issue, notwithstanding his nefarious intention (although issues of attempt liability may arise).

More problematic is the case where V is neither overpowered nor stupefied but influenced to the extent of becoming disinhibited and participating in sexual acts which, if unaffected, she would have declined.[38] In the context of involuntary intoxication raised as a defence to a sexual offence, it has been asserted by appellate courts that "a drunken intent is nevertheless an intent."[39] Does it follow that a consent given in a state of involuntary intoxication is still a consent? We think not. Judgments about consent, or the lack of consent, can be a function of disapproval of D's conduct quite as much as estimates of V's state of mind.[40] Thus, where D has administered or caused V to take a substance without her consent, it may be said her consent was not valid where she does things that she would not have done but for the disinhibiting effects of the substance. It is otherwise of course if V voluntarily takes drink or drugs and becomes disinhibited. The effects of drink and drugs are well known and, as the Court of Appeal emphasised in *Bree*,[41] persons who take these intoxicants must take responsibility for their actions and not be patronised into victimhood. Accordingly, in *Bree*, a case of voluntary but advanced intoxication, the court ruled that consent should not be categorically ruled out: it was for the jury to decide in conformity with section 74 whether V retained the capacity for consent.

(ii) Conclusive presumptions about consent and reasonable belief in consent

Section 76 of the Sexual Offences Act 2003 provides for two sets of circumstances where it is to be conclusively presumed that V did not consent to the relevant [sexual] act and that D did not reasonably believe that V consented. The circumstances are that:

(a) D intentionally deceived V as to the nature or purpose of the relevant act;
(b) D intentionally induced V to consent to the relevant act by impersonating a person known personally to V

Condition (a) contains two elements: nature and purpose. In stipulating that deceptions as to the nature of the act vitiate V's consent, the condition preserves the pre-Act position. If D passes off a sexual act to V as something other than a sexual act, it will be conclusively presumed that V did not consent to the act; as in the old case of *Flattery*,[42] where D passed off his act of intercourse as a medically approved method of improving V's singing voice.

---

issue) if she were reduced to that condition. In *R (on the application of T)* v. *DPP* [2003] EWHC 226 (AC), it was held that even a momentary loss of consciousness constituted actual bodily harm for purposes of s. 47 of the OAPA 1861. In the light of the decision in *Brown* [1994] 1 AC 212 (HL), which precludes the validity of any consent to the infliction of actual bodily harm save in limited circumstances (below, § 21.1, 21.1(iv)), D may well commit an offence against ss. 47 or 23 of the OAPA 1861.

[38] For an account of the difficult issues that arise in estimating the effect on consent of drink, drugs, and mind-altering substances, see Finch and Munro, "Intoxicated Consent and the Boundaries of Drug Assisted Rape" [2003] *Crim LR* 773.

[39] *Kingston* [1995] 2 AC 355, 369 (Lord Mustill), quoting from *Sheehan* [1975] 1 WLR 739, 744 (CA).

[40] For proposals to define rape more in terms of the conduct of D rather than the state of mind of V, see Dripps, "For a Negative, Normative Model of Consent, with a Comment on Preference-Skepticism" (1996) 2 *Legal Theory* 113 and West, "A Comment on Consent, Sex and Rape"(1996) 2 *Legal Theory* 233. Contrast Bogart, "Commodification and Phenomenology: Evading Consent in Theory Regarding Rape" (1996) 2 *Legal Theory* 253.

[41] [2007] EWCA Crim 256.

[42] (1877) 2 QBD 410 (CCR); see too *Williams* [1923] 1 KB 340 (CCA).

Implicit in the concept of the *nature* of an act is a distinction between the essence of the act and its non-essential attributes. Provided V understands the essence of the act she will consent to it, even if mistaken or ignorant as to one or more non-essential attributes. It has been held in *B* that, if D does not disclose that he may pass on a sexually transmitted disease to V, this does not vitiate V's consent to the *sexual* act.[43] (At the same time, because V does not consent to the risk of infection, D may commit a non-sexual offence against the person.[44])

However, under condition (a), a deception as to the *purpose* of the act will also give rise to a conclusive presumption. Frequently, deception about the purpose of the act will be indistinguishable from a deception about its nature; but it is possible for cases to fall exclusively into this latter category. An example of this would be the hypothetical scenario discussed by Lord Ackner in *Court*:[45] where D, a doctor, takes a vaginal sample from V under the guise of diagnosis but, in reality, takes the sample for the purposes of some general research he is undertaking. In this scenario, V may have a sufficient understanding of the physical *nature* of D's conduct but be deceived as to its *purpose*. No valid consent is given in such circumstances.

There will also be clear cases where V is deceived, but neither as to the nature nor the purpose of D's act; as when V has been led to expect by D to be paid for providing sex.[46] In this situation, V understands both that it is a sex act and that D's purpose is to have sex with her. Her position is the same as anyone who has offered a service as a consequence of a deception about payment. The gravamen of D's wrongdoing is dishonesty rather than sexual violation. This conclusion has been criticised by Jonathan Herring, on the ground that V lacks any true understanding of the nature of D's conduct if, but for some ignorance of fact or false belief on her part she would not have consented.[47] It is submitted, however, that Herring adopts an untenably narrow view of consent in the context of very serious offences.[48] Suppose, for instance, that V, a sex worker, were to ask D if he is a supporter of Celtic Football Club. She informs him, truthfully, that she would not have sex with him if he were in that category because of her strong allegiance to Rangers. D untruthfully replies that he does not support Celtic and pays her for sexual intercourse. It would be absurd to claim

---

[43] [2006] EWCA Crim 2945; confirming *dicta* in *Dica* [2004] EWCA Crim 1103 and *Konzani* [2005] 2 Cr App R 13.

[44] In *Dica*, the Court of Appeal considered *Clarence* to be overruled by *Wilson* [1984] AC 242, *Ireland and Burstow* [1998] AC 147, and *Chan-Fook* (1994) 99 Cr App R 147, in so far as *Clarence* was authority to the effect that s. 20 of the OAPA 1861 required proof of assault or battery. It was held in *Dica* that to cause V to become HIV positive was to cause her grievous bodily harm, and that a s. 20 offence would be committed if D was aware of the risk of infecting V and had not informed her of that risk, an analysis upheld in *Konzani*. Interestingly, in *Dica* the Court considered that, notwithstanding the decision in *Brown* [1994] 1AC 212, V could consent to certain risks in the context of sexual activity if informed of the risk. An example was given of a Roman Catholic married couple who could not practice protection despite the infection of one of the partners. As it had not been ascertained at trial in *Dica* whether the victim had known of the risk, the appeal resulted in an order for a retrial.

[45] [1989] AC 28 (HL). Note that in § 12.5 above, we argue that this scenario should be regarded as an assault rather than a *sexual* assault.

[46] *Linekar* [1995] QB 250.

[47] Herring, "Mistaken Sex" [2005] *Crim LR* 519.

[48] See further Gross, "Rape, Moralism and Human Rights" [2007] *Crim LR* 220; Herring, "Human Rights and Rape: A reply to Hyman Gross" [2007] *Crim LR* 228.

that V has been raped. None of the unpleasantness surrounding this episode engages with the wrongs of rape.[49]

Finally, a conclusive presumption will arise under section 76 if D impersonates someone known to V and V is induced by the impersonation to consent to the sexual act. The requirement for *personal* acquaintance will exculpate someone who exploits a strong resemblance to, say, David Beckham. (This notwithstanding that Herring's argument would extend to such cases also.) The impersonation must *induce* consent: if there is evidence that D's impersonation—of, say, a second cousin who V has not seen in 15 years—did not play any part in V's decision to engage in sexual activity with D, the prosecution will have to refute that evidence before a conclusive presumption that V did not consent applies.

(iii) Consent and reasonable belief apart from evidential and conclusive presumptions

The particular factual circumstances to which sections 75 and 76 apply are not exhaustive. If a prosecution is brought on facts not covered by any evidential or conclusive presumption (or, indeed, if an evidential presumption is overcome by D), the normal rules of proof will apply: the prosecution must establish that V did not consent and/or that D lacked any reasonable belief that V consented. If we return to the example of D's exploiting the economic plight of the asylum seeker, V, in order to induce her to work in his brothel, in any charge against D of causing V to engage in sexual activity without consent, the issue of V's consent would be addressed under the terms of section 74: did she have "the freedom and capacity to make that choice"? Particularly in the variant of the example where D does no more than offer her work in his brothel, D may seek to argue that it was her choice. He may firmly believe this, but that of itself will not ground a claim of a reasonable belief in V's consent. If a finding of non-consent is made by the jury on these facts, then they are unlikely to hold that it was reasonable for D to believe that V consented, since D was aware of the salient facts which induced the jury to find non-consent. The question, whether on the facts (as D reasonably believes them to be) V's consent is vitiated, is not a question for D to decide; it is, rather, a question for the jury.[50]

If is far from easy to determine whether the brothel keeper D would be found guilty of the offence of causing V to engage in sexual activity offence.[51] Many other examples giving rise to the uncertainty could be given, particularly outside the circumstances covered by presumptions. For instance, as we saw in § 12.6(i), an evidential presumption that V did not consent arises if D makes a threat of *immediate* violence to V or another.[52] What if D threatens to disfigure V in a few days time if she does not have sex with him now? As such a

---

[49] This might be disputed by Gardner and Shute, who place the use of V as a mere sex object by D at the core of the wrong of rape: "The Wrongness of Rape" in Horder (ed.), *Oxford Essays in Jurisprudence* (4th series, 2000) 193. It is all too likely in our example that D's interest in V is purely confined to sex. But the commodification of sex is neither a necessary or sufficient condition of rape, the essence of which is penetration without consent.

[50] An analogy may be drawn with a situation where D uses what he himself *believes* to be reasonable force in self-defence but where a jury finds that the force used was excessive. Notwithstanding the decision in *Scarlett* [1993] 4 All ER 629 (CA), D cannot rely on a mistake of fact based on his own normative standards: *Owino* (1996) 2 Cr App R 128 (CA); *Martin (David)* [2000] 2 Cr App R 42 (CA); § 18.1(v). *A fortiori*, this will be the case where a *reasonable* belief is required.

[51] For general discussion of the circumstances that vitiate consent at common law, see below, § 21.1(iii).

[52] Sexual Offences Act 2003, s. 75(2)(a)–(b).

threat does not give rise to an evidential presumption, are we to infer that such threats are of a lesser order of magnitude? Such as inference should be resisted: the issue is, simply, whether V had the freedom and capacity to choose. Given the nature of this particular threat, the jury may readily find a lack of consent. But make the threat less horrific and expand the timeline, and uncertainties may arise.

§12.7 The irrelevance of consent by children under 13

Although English law has for a long time penalised sexual activity with children, there were no conclusive presumptions concerning young children and their capacity to consent to sexual acts.[53] Of course, young children who did not consent to sexual activities could be victims of crimes such as rape; yet, however young the child, the issue of whether or not there was consent to the act had to be addressed. If they did consent, the proper charge was not rape or indecent assault but an age-based sexual offence.[54] That has now changed. Regarding the four non-consensual sexual offences just examined—rape, assault by penetration, sexual assault, and causing a person to engage in sexual activity—there is a version of each created specifically for victims under the age of 13 years: rape of a child under 13,[55] assault of a child under 13 by penetration,[56] sexual assault of a child under 13,[57] and causing or inciting a child under 13 to engage in sexual activity.[58]

With one exception, considered below, the core of the proscribed activity remains exactly the same. For instance, in the case of the offence of rape of a child under 13, the prosecution must prove that D intentionally penetrated the vagina, anus, or mouth of V with his penis. *Mutatis mutandis*, the same applies for assault by penetration and sexual assault. However, the offence of causing a person to engage in sexual activity is extended in section 8 to cover, additionally, *inciting* a person under 13 to engage in sexual activity. This makes clear that persuading a young child to participate in sexual activity, perhaps by offering various forms of treats or other inducements, is as much within the offence as threats and other forms of coercion. However, unexpectedly, section 8 is also turned by this extension into an inchoate offence. Where D incites V, there is no requirement that the sexual activity actually occurs. For the other three offences, and also for liability by *causing* sexual activity under section 8, perpetration of the relevant conduct is the actus reus of the appropriate offence.

Most importantly, these offences entirely omit the element of non-consent from the actus reus, and replace it with the element that V is aged under 13. Hence there is no question of

---

[53] In *Howard* [1965] 3 All ER 684 (CCA), it was held to be a misdirection for a trial judge to rule that, as a matter of law, a child of six was incapable of consent.

[54] See, e.g., s. 5 of the (former) Sexual Offences Act 1956, which made it an offence to have sexual intercourse with a girl under 13 years of age.

[55] *Per* s. 6(1), D commits an offence if "(a) he intentionally penetrates the vagina, anus or mouth of another person with his penis, and (b) the other person is under 13."

[56] *Per* s. 6(1), D commits an offence if "(a) he intentionally penetrates the vagina or anus of another person with a part of his body or anything else, (b) the penetration is sexual, and (c) the other person is under 13."

[57] *Per* s. 7(1), D commits an offence if "(a) he intentionally touches another person, (b) the touching is sexual, and (c) the other person is under 13."

[58] *Per* s. 8(1), D commits an offence if "(a) he intentionally causes or incites another person (B) to engage in an activity, (b) the activity is sexual, and (c) B is under 13." The Sexual Offences Act 2003 also enacts a complementary range of age-based, child sex offences: see, e.g., s. 9 (criminalizing sexual activity with a child).

a presumption of non-consent, or of there being strict liability as to consent. The consent, or otherwise, of V is simply not an issue.

In many respects, the creation of these offences is very welcome. If we take D, a 50-year-old man, who befriends and then has sexual intercourse with V, a 12-year-old girl, there is no injustice to D in treating his conduct as a form of rape and dispensing with the unseemly process of cross-examining V to ascertain her understanding of and consent to the sexual act.[59] But what if D is 13? Or 12—perhaps even younger than V?[60] It is a fact of contemporary life that sexual activity, including intercourse, is by no means uncommon in the early teens.[61] There are very good reasons why children of this age should not engage in sexual intercourse with each other; but should the 13-year-old boy be designated and punished as a rapist? The current answer in English law is yes. In G,[62] a boy of 15 had intercourse with V, a girl of 12, whom he believed to be 15. He was convicted of rape. The imposition of such serious criminal liability on one so young—and on a strict basis—did not, according to the Court of Appeal, contravene the presumption of innocence guaranteed by Article 6(2) of the ECHR. Neither did the custodial sentence or the requirement to register as a sex offender after release infringe D's right to privacy and private life guaranteed by Article 8 of the ECHR. Forms of sexual activity falling well short of sexual intercourse will fall within the offence of assault by penetration and almost any form of sexual activity—kissing, say—will fall within the purview of sexual assault. Even what may, otherwise, be quite innocuous behaviour by children may fall within the purview of these offences.[63]

On the face of it, these offences are offences of strict liability with respect to V's age, despite their stigmatic quality and the potentially very high terms of imprisonment.[64] No mens rea element is specified regarding the requirement that V is under 13. Moreover, if we look to the child sex offences that the Sexual Offences Act 2003 creates in respect of victims aged from 13 to 15, defendants are not guilty of the offence if they reasonably believed V to be 16 years of age or older.[65] The most natural inference by way of contrasting those provisions is that the offences dealing with victims under the age of 13 are offences of strict liability (irrespective of the age of the defendant).

Under the previous regime of sexual offences, the House of Lords held that mens rea, in the form of a lack of honest belief that the child was older than the age specified in the offence, was to be implied in the former offences of inciting a child under the age of 14 to commit an act of gross indecency[66] and indecent assault on a girl under the age of 16.[67]

---

[59] There was even authority to the effect that arousing "animal instinct" might found a valid consent: *Fletcher* (1866) LR 1 CCR 39; *Barratt* (1873) LR 2 CCR 81.

[60] Frequently, in this case, V too may commit an offence against s. 8. For possible defences of infancy, see below, § 19.4.

[61] Erens, McManus, Prescott, Field, *et al.*, *National Survey of Sexual Attitudes and Lifestyles II* (National Centre for Social Research, 2003) 5; cited in Spencer, "The Sexual Offences Act 2003: Child and Family Offences" [2004] *Crim LR* 347.

[62] [2006] EWCA Crim 821.

[63] For a forceful critique, see Spencer, *ibid.*, 348–54.

[64] The maximum penalties are life imprisonment for rape and assault by penetration, and 14 years' imprisonment for sexual assault and causing or inciting sexual activity.

[65] Sexual Offences Act 2003, ss. 9(1)(c)(i), 10(1)(c)(i). No mens rea is required as to age if the child is under 13: ss. 9(1)(c)(ii), 10(1)(c)(ii).

[66] *B (a minor)* v. *DPP* [2000] 2 AC 428. See above, § 6.1(i).

[67] *K* [2002] 1 AC 462.

Those offences, too, were on the face of it strict as to the element of age, and a contrast between those offences and other sexual offences—which provided for a "young persons" defence on the basis of reasonable belief that V was older than the relevant age—was noted, but their Lordships nonetheless rejected the inference of strict liability where no such defence was provided. In both cases, the House of Lords strongly endorsed a subjective approach to mens rea and a strong presumption in favour of mens rea for serious offences, an approach further fortified by decision in G.[68] In B (a minor) v. DPP, Lord Hutton said:[69]

> "the test is not whether it is a reasonable implication that the statute rules out mens rea as constituent part of the crime—the test is whether it is a *necessary* implication."

Be that as it may, the contrast drawn now is between offences created within a single coherent Act, postdating these decisions and no mere consolidating statute. If Parliament had wished to sustain their Lordships' approach to the mens rea requirements concerning age in sexual offences, it could have straightforwardly specified a mens rea element. That it did not is strong evidence that, for child victims under the age of 13, no mental element as to the age of the victim need be proved. Accordingly, it was no surprise that the Court of Appeal held in G[70] that the element of age for an under-13 offence required no mental element on the part of D. The surprise was, rather, that the Court thought this compatible with the ECHR.

§12.8 Intoxication

Each of the four offences considered in this chapter imposes a requirement of intention concerning the conduct element: an intentional penetration with the penis in section 1 (rape); an intentional penetration in section 2 (assault by penetration); an intentional touching of another person in section 3 (sexual assault); and intentionally causing another person to engage in an activity (which is sexual) in section 4. What if D does the actus reus unintentionally, where the lack of intention arises from voluntary intoxication?

The criminal law doctrines governing voluntary intoxication are set out below, in § 18.3. In general, where D lacks the requisite mens rea in respect of one or more elements of the actus reus, the doctrines allow a fictional inference to be made that he actually has mens rea (in effect, deeming him to have mens rea), for any "basic intent" offence—but not where the offence requires proof of a "specific intent". In turn, this raises the question whether the offences in sections 1–4 are crimes of basic or specific intent.

The question was considered in Heard.[71] D, who was waiting to be seen at a hospital, became angry and punched one of the police officers accompanying him. He then undid his

---

[68] [2003] UKHL 50. The House of Lords reverted to a test of "*Cunningham*" rather than "*Caldwell*" recklessness for the offence of criminal damage. Four of the judgments favour a culpability element expressed in terms of subjective mens rea for serious offences. Only Lord Rodger, while concurring in the decision, thought that *Caldwell* recklessness might be an appropriate basis of liability in certain circumstances.

[69] [2000] 2 AC 428, 481.

[70] [2006] EWCA Crim 821.

[71] [2007] EWCA Crim 125.

trousers, took his penis in his hand, and rubbed it up and down the thigh of the officer. He was arrested and charged with sexual assault. D was at the time extremely drunk.

The Court of Appeal ruled that the intention at issue in section 3 was a basic intent, on the ground that no purposive element was involved in the section: a deliberate touching that was in fact sexual sufficed, and it was not necessary to show that the touching was done for any purpose. Accordingly, had it been necessary, the Court of Appeal would have ruled that D's state of extreme intoxication was inadmissible to deflect a finding that D's act of rubbing his penis against V's trousered leg was deliberate. Presumably, a similar analysis will apply to a charge of rape where D achieves penetration despite his intoxication (should it be necessary), and to the other offences considered in this chapter.

As it happens, the ruling was *obiter*, since the special rules related to voluntary intoxication[72] were not actually applied in *Heard*. It was, on the facts, "perfectly clear that this was a case of drunken intentional touching."[73] But it must be said that the decision is problematic. Prior to *Heard*, the range of offences that have been ruled to require specific intention comprise the offences where an intention must be proved and recklessless does not suffice. The relevant intention may (as in theft) but need not (as in handling and murder) be purposive; what matters is that intention must specifically be proved. On this point, *Heard* is out of line with existing authorities.

Admittedly, the remaining elements of each offence in sections 1–4 are generally of basic intent; but the voluntary intoxication rules ought to apply element by element, rather than in a coarse fashion across the whole of an offence. If D believes, drunkenly that his touching V is not sexual or that V has consented, D's intoxication cannot exculpate. But this should not foreclose separate consideration of the element of touching, to determine the case where D's act of touching V is unintentional because of intoxication. (The same applies in cases where the determination whether D's otherwise ambiguous conduct is sexual requires reference to D's purpose: above, § 12.5(ii).)

The Court's decision also depends upon a further, somewhat refined distinction. According to *Heard*, the voluntary intoxication rules apply if D's touching of V is a seemingly "deliberate" act: because the offence is now one of basic intent, evidence of intoxication will not be admissible to refute the inference of intention. But where D bumps into V while in a drugged or drunken state, the crucial requirement of intentional touching (or penetration, as the case may be) is not supplied by the standard intoxication doctrines. As recognised in *Heard* itself, even in a case of basic intent, a finding of such intent will not be made if "the mind did not go with the physical act."[74] It seems that "a drunken accident is still an accident":[75] where, viewed objectively, the physical conduct that caused the actus reus was patently non-intentional, the law of voluntary intoxication will not convert accidents into acts of deliberation.

---

[72] Discussed below, § 19.3.
[73] [2007] EWCA Crim 125, para. 17.
[74] *Ibid.*, paras. 19–23. See also the decision in *Brady* [2006] EWCA Crim 2413; and discussion below, § 19.3(iii).
[75] [2007] EWCA Crim 125, para. 23.

13

THEFT

§ 13.1 Property, rights, and justice

> "A man's property is something related to him: This relation is not natural, but moral and founded upon justice. 'Tis very preposterous, therefore, to imagine, that we can have any idea of property, without fully comprehending the nature of justice. . . . The origin of justice explains that of property."[1]

The recognition and protection of property rights in our society raise deep questions of political philosophy. In part, this is because the concept of "property" is itself amorphous. There is a tendency to associate property with "things"—to think of property in terms of objects endowed with spatial dimensions, that can be touched and seen. The association is often appropriate, but can be misleading. Property, understood in the context of a legal system, is a legal phenomenon—and rights of property are not physical things but legal constructs. Indeed, in an important sense proprietary rights are a species of personal right. They are rights between persons, which are held by one person against another person or persons.[2] That I own something means, in law, that I have certain rights to deal with that thing which others do not have and that others owe me certain duties not to deal with it.

These rights and duties are not absolute. D is not free to torture her cat. Ownership of land does not mean the police have no right, under any circumstances, to enter; neither does it make one free to build upon the land without permission. Property may be subject to taxation and even expropriation by the State.

Moreover, the rights associated with ownership of property vary across different types of property. As we shall see, the human body is not susceptible of ownership in the same way as is a kettle. Similarly, the legal nature of property has varied across different periods of social and legal development. In the early common law, ownership was conceived of in terms of the right to possession,[3] which explains the emphasis on possession in the Larceny Act 1916, the statutory predecessor to our modern law of theft; and also why the tort of conversion could only be committed against a plaintiff in possession or with an immediate proprietary right to possession.[4]

---

[1] Hume, *A Treatise of Human Nature* (Selby-Bigge and Nidditch, eds., 2nd ed., 1978) 491.

[2] Cf. Hohfeld, *Fundamental Legal Conceptions as Applied in Judicial Reasoning* (1919) 71ff; Harris, *Property and Justice* (1996) 120ff. According to Grey, "The Disintegration of Property" in *NOMOS xxii: Property* (1980) 69, 81, "the substitution of a bundle-of-rights for a thing-ownership conception of property has the ultimate consequence that property ceases to be an important category in legal and political theory."

[3] Pollock and Maitland, *The History of English Law* (2nd ed., 1911) vol. I, 57, vol. II, 153ff; Tigar, "The Right of Property and the Law of Theft" (1984) 62 *Texas LR* 1443.

[4] Who may be the bailee rather than the owner: *Gordon* v. *Harper* (1796) 7 TR 9; *Wertheim* v. *Cheel* (1885) 11 VLR

The extent to which property is a pre-legal concept (rather than a creation of law) is a matter of controversy. Property rights are distinguished from other interpersonal rights by the fact that they exist in respect of some *thing*, yet that thing may be tangible or intangible and, independent of the law, property seems to lack any clear-cut definition.[5] Despite this, much of our law and society takes property to be a foundational concept. In both civil and criminal law, sanctions for wrongs such as conversion, theft, and the like, normally require proof of a harm. Implicitly, these sanctions take it for granted that there is some right of property that can be harmed, such that corrective justice is called for; or even, in Locke's work, so that the government of a society is warranted.[6] This sort of proposition—that property may be prior to tort and criminal law, and even prior to law—informs much political theory, especially by libertarian philosophers.[7] Property rights are defended by liberal political philosophers, too, on the ground that autonomy is augmented when individuals are able to choose for themselves how they deal with their property, spend their money, etc.[8] If my well-being is increased by breaking crockery from time to time, without risking harm to others, that should be my affair—provided the crockery is mine.

At the same time, the reasons for law to recognise property are not only individualistic. Donne's admonition that no man is an island also has communitarian implications for the law of property. In a social context, property rights help to co-ordinate the activities of society members, by limiting the freedom of citizens to conduct themselves without trespassing unduly upon the private lives of others. Property rights can enhance liberty, yet their free use by one may restrict the capacity for well-being of another. Even in societies which endorse free-market economic activity, the law typically contains a panoply of constraints on monopolistic, exploitative, or otherwise unfair action. Similarly, taxation derogates from absolute notions of dominion over property, but may be justified by redistributive arguments—including the need to foster minimum standards of living in others. In economic terms, a selective recognition of property rights offers chances both to foster economic prosperity and to provide for values that markets may not deliver, including values related to basic needs and human rights.

Legal institutions of property, therefore, must accommodate both the principles and privileges of ownership, with its implications for corrective justice, and the need to allocate social wealth, driven by concerns of distributive justice. However, by contrast with corrective justice, which presupposes a notion of property, distributive justice may operate prior to the law's conception of property.[9] An absolutist legal conception of property would generate a system in which autonomy, consent, and individual fault are determinative. These concepts

---

107; *Nyberg* v. *Handelaar* [1892] 2 QB 202; Warren, "Qualifying as Plaintiff in an Action for Conversion" (1936) 49 *Harv LR* 1084. Indeed, even the owner is capable of converting her own goods, if someone else has an indefeasible possessory right to them: *Roberts* v. *Wyatt* (1810) 2 Taunt 268, 127 ER 1080; *City Motors* v. *S. Aerial Service* (1961) 106 CLR 477.

   [5] Gray, "Property in Thin Air" [1991] *CLJ* 252.

   [6] Locke, *Two Treatises of Government*, Book II § 123. Cf. *Entick* v. *Carrington* (1765) 19 St Tr 1029, 1060: "The great end for which men entered into society was to secure their property."

   [7] See, e.g., Nozick, *Anarchy, State and Utopia* (1974).

   [8] See Waldron, *The Right to Private Property* (1988); Simmonds, "The Possibility of Private Law" in Tasioulas (ed.), *Law, Values and Social Practices* (1997) 129.

   [9] Cf. Simester and Sullivan, "On the Nature and Rationale of Property Offences" in Duff and Green (eds.), *Defining Crimes: Essays on the Criminal Law's Special Part* (2005) 168, §§ 1–2.

are certainly important to the common law. But they are not the only considerations. For example, in many jurisdictions constructive trusts are now imposed for reasons of fairness, say upon the break-up of a domestic relationship where no formal arrangements existed regarding distribution of property. Land owners may now owe involuntary duties to trespassers.[10] The recognition of property in commercial contexts may be determined by the need to allocate risk in unforeseen circumstances, or by considerations of priority in insolvency. Indeed, the Canadian Supreme Court has even suggested that proprietary remedies can be created, or even refused, on a discretionary basis according to whether "there is reason to grant to the plaintiff the additional rights that flow from a recognition of a right of property."[11]

By and large, these distributive factors are not the concern of the criminal law, since it is not for the criminal law to decide when property rights exist. Rather, property offences exist primarily to reinforce and protect those rights once recognised by the civil law. Indirectly, therefore, property offences are not merely a means to protect individuals' autonomous rights over property, but also a tool for reinforcing political decisions about the distribution of scarce resources in society. Prima facie rules of property arise in the civil law for a variety of underlying reasons. Yet the criminal law does not look behind the prima facie rules. It takes ownership, and its facets, as an axiom.

Inevitably so. Both civil and criminal law share a conception of ownership. Notwithstanding what has been said here about *when* ownership should be recognised, its recognition necessarily involves certain legal consequences, at least in a liberal society.[12] Ownership of property confers upon the owner a set of powers, in particular to use and to alienate (transfer) the property, and to exclude others from doing the same. Without these powers there is no ownership. In the context of property offences, the function of the criminal law is to protect those rights of ownership. This means that the criminal law must take its lead from the civil law: the creature it protects is a creation of the civil law.

In the criminal law, that protection is achieved by a variety of offences which impose obligations on non-owners not to usurp the powers of an owner. First among them, and the subject of this chapter, is the prohibition of theft.

§ 13.2 The definition of theft

Theft is defined in section 1(1) of the Theft Act 1968, which provides:

> A person is guilty of theft if he dishonestly appropriates property belonging to another with the intention of permanently depriving the other of it; and "thief" and "steal" shall be construed accordingly.

The offence contains five elements, each of which must be proved by the prosecution. The first three elements comprise the actus reus:

(i)   there must be *property* (i.e. something capable of being stolen);

---

[10] Occupiers' Liability Act 1984.
[11] *Lac Minerals v. Corona Ltd* (1989) 61 DLR 14, 51.
[12] Cf. Honoré, "Ownership" in Guest (ed.), *Oxford Essays in Jurisprudence* (1961) 107.

(ii)   that property must *belong* to another; and

(iii) D must *appropriate* the property.

The final two elements constitute the mens rea:

(iv)   D must intend permanently to deprive another person of the property; and

(v)   D must act dishonestly.

Each of these elements will be considered below.

§ 13.3 Property

Most things can be stolen. At common law and under the Larceny Act 1916, land and intangible property were excluded from the ambit of a larceny. This limitation is undone by section 4(1) of the 1968 Act, which enacts a general rule that:

> "Property" includes any money and all other property, real or personal, including things in action and other intangible property.

The current position is therefore that, subject to certain exceptions in section 4(2)–(4), any type of property can be stolen. But it remains necessary to show (a) that the thing stolen is, in law, an item of property; and (b) that none of the exceptions apply.

(i) What counts as property?

To fall within section 4(1), the thing stolen must first be some type of property (real or personal, tangible or intangible). Most instances of theft are straightforward: D absconds with a television set or some other chattel—a piece of tangible personal property. Other cases, however, may be less obvious. Suppose D usurps V's right of way, or takes a train ride without first buying a ticket. Are these cases of theft? In order to answer that question, we need first to know whether the thing taken is, in law, "property". That term is not defined by the Theft Act, and its definition is a matter for the civil law. Although most things are capable of being owned, even in the civil law it is sometimes unclear whether particular rights constitute a form of legal or equitable property (i.e. rights *in rem*) or merely give rise to entitlements to sue others in contract, tort, or equity (rights *in personam*). In what follows we will survey the main areas of difficulty.

(a) Things in action and other intangible property

A thing in action, also called a chose in action, is something in which the law acknowledges property rights but which has no physical existence. The rights cannot be asserted physically and can be vindicated only by legal action (hence a thing "in action"). Examples of choses in action are a debt, shares in a company,[13] and a trade mark or copyright. Under section 4(1), all these things are capable of being stolen.

---

[13] Cf. *Grubb* [1915] 2 KB 683.

However, mere information, even a trade secret, does not qualify for protection as intangible property.[14] In *Oxford* v. *Moss*,[15] a university student took an examination paper before the examination and copied it before returning the paper to its original location. He was held not to have committed theft. Even though the information on the examination paper was no longer confidential, in the eyes of the law the university had not been deprived of any property. It would have been different if the student had not returned the examination paper itself, since he could then have been convicted of stealing the paper on which the examination was typed.

Even where the right being interfered with is property for the purposes of the Act, the interference may not always count as theft. Breach of copyright, for instance, violates a chose in action. But photocopying a textbook does not deprive the copyright owner of the book. Neither does it deprive her of copyright in that book.[16]

There are hard questions of policy at issue here. Industrial espionage is a serious matter. Information can be worth an enormous amount of money. It may be the subject of contract, and its acquisition often involves the expenditure of considerable human and financial resources. We take it for granted that the recipe for Coca Cola is secret, both from us and from the manufacturer's competitors. Certainly it receives protection under the civil law, albeit not from the law of property.[17] Why not from the law of theft? In modern times, a nation's economic activity depends upon owners being able to protect the intangible rewards of their labours just as much as the tangible chattels they produce. The knowledge generated by research and development activities is vital to economic growth, and the case for criminalising theft of that knowledge is at least arguable.[18]

On the other hand, this is not to say that the decision in *Oxford* v. *Moss* was wrong. Extending the law of theft to include the appropriation of information raises difficult questions concerning the proper scope of protection. Should all confidential information be protected, or just trade secrets? When is information sufficiently confidential? What if the information is a matter of public interest?[19] The area, while ripe for reform, calls for legislative rather than judicial innovation.

(b) Services

A service is not by itself property.[20] So, for example, a ride on a train cannot be stolen,[21]

---

[14] Cf. *The Federal Commissioner of Taxation* v. *United Aircraft Corp* (1943) 68 CLR 525, 534–5 (Latham CJ); *Boardman* v. *Phipps* [1967] 2 AC 46, 102–3 (Lord Cohen), 127–8 (Lord Upjohn), though for more equivocal views see at 89–91 (Viscount Dilhorne), 107 (Lord Hodson), 115 (Lord Guest).

[15] (1978) 68 Cr App R 183. See [1979] Crim LR 119.

[16] Cf. *Lloyd* [1985] QB 829; *Rank Film Distributors Ltd* v. *Video Information Centre* [1982] AC 380, 445; *Storrow and Poole* [1983] Crim LR 332.

[17] *Fraser* v. *Thames Television* [1984] QB 44; *A-G* v. *Observer Ltd* [1990] 1 AC 107, Stuckey, "The Equitable Action for Breach of Confidence: Is Information Ever Property?" (1981) 9 *Sydney LR* 402.

[18] See Cross, "Protecting Confidential Information under the Criminal Law of Theft and Fraud" (1991) 11 *OJLS* 264; Davies, "Protection of Intellectual Property—A Myth?" [2004] *J Crim Law* 398. Compare the Model Penal Code, § 223.0(6): "'Property' means anything of value."

[19] Cf. Cripps, "The Public Interest Defence to the Action for Breach of Confidence and the Law Commission's Proposals on Disclosure in the Public Interest" (1984) 4 *OJLS* 361.

[20] *Bagley* (1923) 17 Cr App R 162.

[21] Cf. *Boulton* (1849) 1 Den 508, 169 ER 349; *Beecham* (1851) 5 Cox 181.

though D's activity may comprise some other offence such as obtaining services dishonestly;[22] and one may steal the piece of paper on which the ticket is printed.

(c) Bank accounts

The relationship between banker and customer is one of debtor and creditor[23] or, if the account is in overdraft, vice versa. Since debts are a type of chose in action, it follows that the customer's right to draw on a credit balance is property within the scope of section 4(1), and can be stolen. Additionally, an agreed overdraft facility, which has not been fully drawn down, gives the customer a legal right against the bank and so also constitutes a chose in action.[24]

The case of *Kohn*[25] provides a useful example. D was a director of company C, which had an account with bank B. D had signing authority on the company's account. He dishonestly drew cheques on that account for personal purposes, thereby causing C's account with B to be debited. D was convicted of theft: he had stolen C's right of action, against B, for the amount by which C's account was debited.

D was not, however, convicted of theft in respect of every cheque. Most of the cheques had been drawn when C's account was in credit or within the authorised overdraft limit. In these cases D appropriated C's chose in action. One cheque, however, was drawn when the account was in overdraft beyond the authorised limit. The Court of Appeal held that in the last situation there was no theft. If an account is overdrawn beyond its agreed limit, the bank has no legal obligation to meet the cheque. Hence, C had no chose in action against B, and there was nothing for D to steal.[26]

In addition to the question of identifying what property is stolen, theft from a bank account also presents problems concerning the act of appropriation and the intention to deprive permanently. We consider these issues below, in § 13.6(vi) and § 13.7(ii)(a).

(d) Body parts

Some things, though corporeal, cannot be owned at all. At common law this included wild animals (*ferae naturae*) when at large,[27] and the human body, even when deceased;[28] so a human corpse cannot be stolen, by contrast with the corpse of a farm animal.[29] The position with regard to animals is now covered by section 4(4) (see below, § 13.3(ii)(c)). However, the question of the human body or body parts is not covered in the Theft Act, and remains somewhat uncertain. There is an interim right to possession (not ownership) of a

---

[22] Contrary to s. 11 of the Fraud Act 2006.

[23] *Foley* v. *Hill* (1848) 2 HLC 28, 9 ER 1002.

[24] *Kohn* (1979) 69 Cr App R 395.

[25] *Ibid*. Cf. *Williams (Roy)* [2001] 1 Cr App R 362, in which D, a builder, dishonestly overcharged customers for work done. D's conviction for theft was upheld on the basis that, by presenting a customer's cheque for payment, he appropriated that customer's bank account (i.e. the chose in action held by that customer against the bank).

[26] Cf. *Navvabi* [1986] 3 All ER 102. D might, however, have been guilty of stealing the proceeds of the cheque, following the decision in *Gomez* (below, § 13.6(ii)).

[27] Even a landowner does not own or possess the wild animals on his land. Cf. *Howlett and Howlett* [1968] Crim LR 222.

[28] *Williams* v. *Williams* (1880) 20 Ch D 659, 662f (extending to a corpse the logic of the proposition that a live human body cannot be subject to ownership).

[29] *Edwards* (1877) 13 Cox CC 384.

corpse which vests in those charged with its burial.[30] Apart from this, the courts have recognised a limited possessory right in a corpse or body part if being used as a medical specimen or as an exhibit in a museum, at least where the item has acquired different attributes by undergoing a lawful application of skill (e.g. dissection or embalming),[31] and the Human Tissue Act 2004 allows certain persons a right of possession to body parts in particular circumstances.

At the level of principle, there are difficult legal issues here. The fact that there may be certain limited rights to a corpse or parts thereof does not resolve the question whether that corpse or its parts can be stolen. The problem can be summarised as follows. First, although there may be possessory rights in some circumstances, it appears those rights do not amount to full ownership.[32] And if body parts are incapable of being owned, then it is arguable that they are not *property* within section 4(1), and therefore cannot be stolen.[33]

If this analysis were accepted, the courts would have to become more willing to recognise full ownership of body parts, especially where legitimate work has been done on the item (e.g. by preparation of a kidney for transplantation), although property in such things might vest only in certain eligible persons and be accompanied by stringent duties.[34] Indeed, perhaps it is time that the old rule that there can be no property in a body or its parts—a rule of dubious ancestry[35]—was itself abandoned.

The contrary position is that since possession is one of the rights of ownership, such limited rights as may be had in body parts or a corpse nonetheless amount to *property* rights, enforceable by proprietary remedies, which fall short of ownership.[36] They are rights *in rem*,[37] enforceable against third parties. And since limited property rights are available,

---

[30] *Calma* v. *Sesar* (1992) 106 FLR 446; *Dobson* v. *North Tyneside HA* [1996] 4 All ER 474, 478.

[31] *Kelly* [1998] 3 All ER 741; applying *Doodeward* v. *Spence* (1908) 6 CLR 406. In the latter case, Griffith CJ was careful not to say that a corpse could be owned, but rather that it could be in the lawful possession of someone, and that the law would protect that lawful possession. Note that preserving a brain in paraffin prior to a post-mortem examination does not turn it into an item in which others could have a right of possession or property: *Dobson* v. *North Tyneside HA* [1996] 4 All ER 474. See Maclean, "Resurrection of the Body Snatchers" (2000) 150 *NLJ* 174.

[32] *Quaere* human hair manufactured into wigs, or sperm in a sperm bank. It appears that there may be property rights in the by-products of the living body: in *Welsh* [1974] RTR 478, a man was convicted of theft of a urine sample. Cf. *Rothery* [1976] RTR 550; also *Herbert*, *The Times*, 22 December 1960, noted (1960) 25 *J Crim L* 163 (cutting off hair—though surely an offence against the person rather than property, as in *Smith* [2006] EWHC 94 (Admin)?). A.T.H Smith opines that body parts even if originally *res nullius* should, as in the case of wild animals, be able to become property by *occupatio*: "Stealing the Body and its Parts" [1976] *Crim LR* 622. This seems to be consistent with the reasoning of Griffith CJ in *Doodeward* v. *Spence* (1908) 6 CLR 406. See also Matthews, "Whose Body?" (1983) 36 *CLP* 193.

[33] Even though s. 5(1) of the Theft Act 1968 provides that for the purposes of theft, "property shall be regarded as belonging to any person having possession or control of it, or having in it any proprietary right or interest," this does not dispense with the separate requirement in ss. 1 and 4 that the thing stolen be property.

[34] Arguably, if ownership is regarded as having the largest bundle of rights available in respect of something, the extent of those available rights will naturally vary for different items—thus the fact that the bundle will be a small one in the case of body parts may still be consistent with the ascription of ownership. *Contra*, however, if the maximum bundle available lacks rights which are fundamental to any concept of ownership: cf. Honoré, "Ownership" in Guest (ed.), *Oxford Essays in Jurisprudence* (1961) 107, 108–10.

[35] Cf. Smith, "Stealing the Body and its Parts" [1976] *Crim LR* 622, 623–24. The old rule is so entrenched, however, that reform is now a matter for Parliament: *Kelly* [1998] 3 All ER 741, 749.

[36] Cf. de Stoop, "The Law in Australia Relating to the Transplantation of Organs from Cadavers" (1974) 48 *ALJ* 21, 22.

[37] I.e. a right that held *in respect of* a particular thing and which is enforceable against others generally (e.g. ownership of a car); by contrast with a right *in personam*, which is enforceable only against particular persons (e.g. a debt).

this suggests that, arguably, a corpse *is* property, albeit property that is incapable of being owned. This second analysis has now been accepted by the Court of Appeal in *Kelly*.[38] In our view, it is to be preferred: a taking in contravention of any property right suffices. Adopting such analysis has the practical advantage of allowing a conviction for theft when, say, a corpse is stolen from the executors. Even after *Kelly*, however, a second problem for the law is to identify *when* such rights can arise. For example, it remains unclear under present law whether anyone has a property right to a human embryo or to a body part designated for transplant surgery;[39] and thus whether such items can be stolen. It is certainly arguable that such items deserve the protection of the criminal law.[40]

More straightforwardly (and more generally), there is a case for statutory reform, which need not be achieved through the law of property offences. Arguably, interference with such things as body parts—in which there are no ordinary rights of ownership—is not the sort of wrongdoing for which property offences are the suitable means of control, and warrants criminalisation by means of separate, more specific legislation.

(e) Electricity, gas, and water

Section 13 of the 1968 Act enacts a separate offence of dishonestly abstracting electricity. The separate offence is needed because electricity, like other forms of energy such as heat,[41] is not property. In *Low* v. *Blease*,[42] D broke into a house and sought to warm himself by switching on the electric fire. He was held not guilty of burglary; he had not entered with intent to steal because the electricity consumed by the fire could not be stolen.

Gas, on the other hand, is property and can be stolen.[43] The same is true for water that has been placed in a container such as a pipe.[44] Water in a lake or pond is a severable part of the land on which it stands,[45] and is therefore subject to the rules governing theft of land (below).

(ii) The exceptions in section 4(2)–(4)

Notwithstanding the general rule in section 4(1) that any type of property can be stolen, section 4 itself contains special provisions applicable where the subject matter of the theft is real property, a plant growing wild, or a wild animal.

(a) Land

The ruling in section 4(1) that real property can be stolen is significantly qualified by section 4(2), which provides:

---

[38] [1998] 3 All ER 741.

[39] See, e.g., Andrews, "The Legal Status of the Embryo" (1986) 32 *Loyola LR* 257.

[40] Lavoie, "Ownership of Human Tissue: Life after *Moore* v. *Regents of the University of California*" [1989] 75 *Virginia LR* 1363.

[41] *Clinton* v. *Cahill* [1998] NI 200.

[42] [1975] Crim LR 513.

[43] *White* (1853) Dears 203, 169 ER 696; *Firth* (1869) LR 1 CCR 172.

[44] *Ferens* v. *O'Brien* (1883) 11 QBD 21.

[45] Burn, *Cheshire and Burn's Modern Law of Real Property* (15th ed., 1994) 165.

A person cannot steal land, or things forming part of land and severed from it by him or by his directions, except in the following cases, that is to say—

(a) when he is a trustee or personal representative, or is authorised by power of attorney, or as a liquidator of a company, or otherwise, to sell or dispose of land belonging to another, and he appropriates the land or anything forming part of it by dealing with it in breach of the confidence reposed in him; or

(b) when he is not in possession of the land and appropriates anything forming part of the land by severing it or causing it to be severed, or after it has been severed; or

(c) when, being in possession of the land under a tenancy, he appropriates the whole or part of any fixture or structure let to be used with the land.

Section 4(2)(a) covers trustees and the like[46] who fraudulently convert land in breach of the terms under which the land is entrusted to them. Section 4(2)(b) makes it possible for anyone to steal part of the land—including fixtures, plants, trees, and soil—by severing the item from the land, or by appropriating it after severance.[47] Under section 4(2)(c), a tenant is capable of stealing fixtures and structures which he removes from the property.[48]

(b) Things growing wild

At common law, things growing wild are part of the land on which they grow. Prima facie, therefore, under section 4(2)(b) anything growing wild on land can be stolen through being severed from the land or, once severed, through being then appropriated by D. However, section 4(3) creates a further restriction:

A person who picks mushrooms growing wild on any land, or who picks flowers, fruit or foliage from a plant growing wild on any land, does not (although not in possession of the land) steal what he picks, unless he does it for reward or for sale or other commercial purpose.

For purposes of this subsection "mushroom" includes any fungus, and "plant" includes any shrub or tree.

In essence, this means that D is exempt from liability provided:

(i)   he removes *part* of the plant (not the whole, unless it is a mushroom);

(ii) the plant is growing *wild* (not cultivated);

(iii) he *picks* it (rather than, say, chops it down); and

(iv) he does so for a non-commercial purpose.

(c) Wild creatures

At common law a wild creature is owned by no-one, and so cannot be stolen.[49] However, if such an animal is captured or killed, the person on whose land the capture or killing occurs thereupon acquires ownership of the creature.[50] Consequently, any subsequent appropriation of the animal or its carcase would prima facie be a theft. Section 4(4) abrogates this result. For the purposes of the 1968 Act:

---

[46] Cf. *Daniels* v. *Daniels* [1978] Ch 406 (company directors).

[47] Cf. *Foley* (1889) 17 Cox CC 142 (grass); *Skujins* [1956] Crim LR 266 (farm gate); *Carver* v. *Pierce* (1648) Style 66, 82 ER 534 (dung).

[48] For discussion of some of the difficulties and anomalies associated with s. 4(2) see Smith, *Property Offences* (1994) § 3.34ff.

[49] Cf. *Cresswell* v. *DPP* [2006] EWHC 3379, [2007] Env LR D8: badgers not reduced into possession are not property (either at common law or in the context of s. 10 of the Criminal Damage Act 1971).

[50] *Blades* v. *Higgs* (1865) 11 HL Cas 621, 11 ER 1474.

Wild creatures, tamed or untamed, shall be regarded as property; but a person cannot steal a wild creature not tamed nor ordinarily kept in captivity, or the carcase or any such wild creature, unless either it has been reduced into possession by or on behalf of another person and possession of it has not since been lost or abandoned, or another person is in course of reducing it into possession.

It follows that a wild creature may be stolen only if (i) it is tamed or ordinarily kept in captivity, or (ii) it has been reduced into and remains in another person's possession, or (iii) it is in the process of being reduced into possession by another person. By way of example, domestic pets or the animals in a zoo are capable of being stolen, since they are (i) tamed or ordinarily kept in captivity. Bees that return to a hive can also be stolen, not because they are tamed or kept but because (ii) they have been reduced into possession (and possession has not since been lost). A poacher, on the other hand, does not steal the rabbit he captures. But if a second person, D, takes the rabbit from the poacher when the latter is (iii) in the process of capturing it, D then steals the rabbit.[51]

§ 13.4 Belonging to another (I)

It is impossible to steal property from oneself.[52] Some other person must have an interest in the subject matter of the theft before that item can be stolen. This is not to deny that D can steal something she owns. While D may be the owner, other persons may have an immediate right to possession or control, or some proprietary interest that can be asserted against the owner: V, say, may have a lien,[53] or some other interest in the property. In such a case the property can be stolen by D (or by anyone else). But if D is the absolute owner of the property, so that no one else is joint owner or has any lesser proprietary right or a right to possession or control, she cannot steal it. It does not "belong to another" for the purposes of section 1 of the Act.

The meaning of "belonging to another" is elaborated in section 5. The key provision is section 5(1):

Property is to be regarded as belonging to any person having possession or control of it, or having in it any proprietary right or interest (not being an equitable interest arising only from an agreement to transfer or grant an interest).

In general, this means that for the purposes of theft an item "belongs" to everyone with any form of proprietary interest in the item, whatever the nature of that interest—i.e. whether it be a right of ownership or possession, or a proprietary interest existing only at equity. Generally speaking, therefore, D commits the actus reus of a theft whenever he appropriates property in which someone else has a proprietary interest.

The rule stated here gives rise to a number of special cases, which benefit by further discussion here and in § 13.5.

---

[51] This extends the common law, which formerly required that the reduction into possession be completed before the animal or carcass could be stolen. See *Roe* (1870) 11 Cox 554.

[52] Although, remarkably, one can steal property by the very act of acquiring absolute ownership of it: *Hinks* [2001] 2 AC 241. See further below, § 13.6(ii)(c).

[53] See below, § 13.4(ii).

(i) What interests are protected by section 5?

We have noted that section 5(1) protects virtually any form of proprietary interest, whether of ownership or possession, and whether at common law or equity. Although the section mentions "possession *or* control", it is not clear that the latter term adds anything much. Physical control would in any event also constitute a possessory interest, and any other right of control would presumably only qualify if it were enforceable *in rem*, i.e. if it were a proprietary interest.

On the other hand, equitable proprietary interests should be distinguished from interests that may arise when D enters into an agreement to sell goods to V on some future date. The provision in section 5(1) makes it clear that the latter sort of interest is not protected, by contrast with contracts of sale that transfer ownership immediately. Hence if, before the agreed date of the future transfer, D were to resell the goods to T, D would not commit theft from V.

The inclusion of equitable proprietary interests has opened the way for a significant expansion of the scope of theft in recent years, given the important role of the constructive trust in modern civil law. Because of the complexity of the law of constructive trusts, we will deal with this topic separately, in § 13.5(i).

The scope of theft in section 5(1) is also extended by supplementary provisions in section 5(2)–(4), which is designed to capture certain specific types of theft. These provisions are dealt with below, in § 13.5(ii)–(iv).

(ii) Theft by an owner under section 5(1)

As we have mentioned, one implication of section 5(1) is that even an owner may commit theft, provided the victim of the theft is deprived of an interest recognised under section 5. This might occur in a case where someone else has a lien[54] over the goods. In the New Zealand case of *Cox*,[55] a garage repairing a car had a lien over it. D dishonestly retrieved the car and was convicted of theft, as the lien had conferred a possessory interest. Similarly, in *Slowly*[56] V sold onions to D, for which he had not yet been paid. Until paid, V (being a seller in possession) was entitled to assert a lien over the goods.[57] Accordingly, D's dishonest taking of the goods was theft.

Another standard case in which an owner may commit theft is if there is more than one owner. If D and V are co-owners of a chattel and D dishonestly sells the chattel, D is guilty of theft. Similarly, it has been ruled that a partner may be convicted of theft of property belonging to the partnership.[58]

---

[54] That is, a right to retain possession that is enforceable even against the owner until some condition is met: *Hammonds* v. *Barclay* (1802) 2 East 227, 235, 102 ER 356, 359.

[55] [1923] NZLR 596.

[56] (1873) 12 Cox 269.

[57] Sale of Goods Act 1979, s. 39; *Dennant* v. *Skinner* [1948] 2 KB 164.

[58] *Bonner* [1970] 2 All ER 97n.

(iii) Theft by an absolute owner? When D's interest is better than V's

In principle, there should be one important exception to the general proposition that property may be stolen from anyone having a proprietary interest therein. Consider the following, fairly straightforward, case:

> Suppose that V is a thief who has stolen a television set from D. D remains absolute owner of the television, but while in possession V has a lesser proprietary (possessory) interest in the television, which he may maintain against anyone save D. V's interest is sufficient for section 5(1). Consequently, if T dishonestly removes the television from V's house, T is himself guilty of stealing from V.[59]

Now the exception. In a case of this sort, D—the owner—surely cannot steal the television by retaking it from V. This is because V has no property right in the television maintainable against D. *Vis-à-vis* D, the television belongs to no-one else. By contrast, *vis-à-vis* T, the television belongs to both D and V; hence T can steal it from V and from D.[60]

One illustration of this exception is the Crown Court decision in *Meredith*.[61] D's car had been impounded by the police and removed to a police station. Without consent, D then recovered his car from the police station. D was acquitted of theft, after the trial judge ruled that the police had no right to retain possession of the car against the owner.

Obvious as all this may seem, there is appellate authority to the contrary. In *Turner (No. 2)*,[62] D had taken his car to a garage for repair. Subsequently and dishonestly, he recovered the car without paying for the repairs. D was convicted of theft. Prima facie, this looks right: the car surely "belonged to" the garage for the purpose of section 5(1), since the garage would have been entitled to assert a lien over the car until the repairs were paid for.[63] Unfortunately, the trial judge directed the jury to disregard the issue of liens. Consequently, the Court of Appeal was obliged to consider D's appeal on the footing that there was no lien. The Court nonetheless upheld the conviction, reasoning that even as a mere bailee at will, the garage had a possessory interest in the car (maintainable against anyone except D) sufficient to qualify for section 5(1). According to the Court of Appeal, "there is no ground for qualifying the words 'possession or control' in any way," i.e. by excluding from section 5(1) any proprietary interests inferior to those of the defendant.

The decision is absurd.[64] If no lien existed, the car belonged to D and D alone. The gist of theft is interference with someone else's property rights. D did no such thing. He merely exercised proprietary rights to which he was entitled (albeit in order to evade a debt).

---

[59] *Buckley* v. *Gross* (1863) 3 B & S 566, 122 ER 213; *Daniel* v. *Rogers* [1918] 2 KB 228, 234; *Parker* v. *British Airways Board* [1982] QB 1004, 1009 (Donaldson LJ).

[60] A helpful illustration of the priority of interests is *Costello* v. *Chief Constable of Derbyshire* [2001] All ER 150 (CA). D was in possession of a stolen car that was seized by the police. The owner, however, could not be traced. In those circumstances, the Court held that D was entitled to recover the car from the police, because he had better title to the car than anyone apart from the original owner.

[61] [1973] Crim LR 253. Cf. Model Penal Code, § 223.0(7): "'property of another' includes property in which any person other than the actor has an interest *which the actor is not privileged to infringe*" (emphasis added).

[62] [1971] 2 All ER 441.

[63] Cf. *Cox* [1923] NZLR 596; above, § 13.4(ii).

[64] The same adjective is used by Smith, *Property Offences* (1994) § 4–43, and in *Arlidge and Parry on Fraud* (2nd ed., 1996) § 1.14.

(iv) Has D become an absolute owner?

Assuming that an absolute owner cannot steal her own goods, and subject to section 5(2)–(4),[65] cases will often arise when D acquires possession or control of property innocently enough but subsequently, and dishonestly, decides to keep it from the person from whom the property was acquired. For example:

> D enters into a hire-purchase contract with V Ltd. to acquire a television set. She takes the television set home, intending to honour the agreement. However, a few months later, she finds herself in financial difficulties. She stops paying V Ltd., sells the television, and pockets the proceeds.

In this case, D steals the television set when she offers it for sale.[66] In a hire-purchase agreement, possession passes but the property in the goods remains with the seller until all instalments have been paid. Thus an on-sale by the possessor is theft. Likewise, borrowing something, and then keeping it having decided not to return it, may amount to theft—on the basis of the keeping rather than the borrowing—since the borrower legitimately acquires possession but does not acquire ownership.

However, other cases may be more difficult:

> D purchases a table from V on one month's credit. When he takes delivery of the table, D intends to honour his obligation to V. Later, however, D decides not to pay. He sells the table to T, an innocent third party, and absconds with the cash.

Does D steal the table? The general rule is that if V—the person from whom the property is acquired—retains ownership or some other interest in the property, D will be guilty of theft by his later dishonest appropriation of the goods. Otherwise, if V delivers the goods and transfers property in them to D, who subsequently forms the intent not to pay for them, D does not commit theft. It is therefore crucial to determine whether, and at what point in time, D has become the owner of property that formerly belonged to V. Apart from some specific provisions in section 5(2)–(4) of the Theft Act 1968, to be considered in due course, the criminal law provides no answer to this question, which must be decided by reference to civil law rules.

The importance of this point cannot be overstated. Consistency of criminal law and civil law concepts is essential in theft, which after all is concerned with the protection of property rights.[67] It would be more than odd if D could be convicted of theft when she had not in fact interfered with V's property rights. As Williams writes, "the object of the law of theft is to attach a penal sanction to certain violations of property rights; so (it may be urged) if

---

[65] Below, § 13.5(ii)–(iv).

[66] Below, § 13.6(i).

[67] Cf. Smith, "Civil Law Concepts in the Criminal Law" [1972B] *CLJ* 197. Although see *Morris* [1984] AC 320, 334, for the dubious (and unnecessary) claim that the criminal law should not be concerned with the niceties of the civil law. The approach taken in *Walker* [1984] Crim LR 112 and in *Tillings* v. *Tillings* [1985] Crim LR 393 is to be preferred; cf. *Nabina* [2000] Crim LR 481. Compare too *Dobson* v. *General Accident Fire and Life Assurance Corp* [1989] 3 All ER 927, 937: whether property belongs to another "is a question to which the criminal law offers no answer and which can only be answered by reference to civil law principles."

there is no violation of property rights under the general (civil) law, there should be no theft."[68] It was said in this text, as far back as Chapter 1, that there ought to be no criminal-isation without harm.[69] In theft, the relevant harm is infringement of another's property rights. Protection against that harm *is the very purpose* of criminalising theft. The rights (specifically, ownership and possession) which are protected are creatures of civil law. Therefore, unless those civil law rights are in fact infringed, the harm does not occur and theft should not lie.

In deciding whether ownership has passed already to D for the purposes of section 5(1), there are two principal issues. One is to ascertain whether title has prima facie passed, or whether D merely has possession. Here one needs to look at the terms of the agreement between V and D, in particular whether V has reserved some property right in the goods.

The second issue is that, even where a prima facie transfer of title has been identified, the transfer may be vitiated. In general, there are three ways in which this may occur. First, the transaction may be induced by D's wrongful duress, fraud, false pretences, etc. In such cases, any title acquired by D will be at least voidable, if not void, and the transaction can constitute theft.[70] Secondly, even though D has not induced the transaction by any wrongdoing, V may have made a fundamental mistake. In that case, the transaction is void.[71] V retains title to the goods and they can be stolen by D. Finally, V, acting on behalf of the true owner, may not have authority to pass title. In that case, again, the transaction is void and D cannot become owner of the property.

In the following sections, we discuss aspects of these problems in more detail. (A third issue, to be discussed later, arises where D does become the legal owner of the property but is subject either to a constructive trust or to one of the extensional provisions in section 5(2)–(4), in which case theft may still be possible. These cases will be explored in § 13.5.)

(a) Has ownership passed, prima facie?

The general rule, which is subject to a number of statutory and common law provisos, is that title passes if and when the transferor so intends it to pass. It is not possible here to give a comprehensive account of the civil law regarding transfer of property. Rather, we propose briefly to mention some well-known situations, and to illustrate the relationship between the relevant civil law rules and the criminal law of theft.

Case 1: Contracts for sale of goods.

Where ascertained goods are sold, the rules on passing of title are to be found in the Sale of Goods Act 1979. The basic rule, stated in section 17, is that where there is a contract for the sale of specific or ascertained goods, property in them passes when the buyer and seller so intend. In the case of sale of unascertained goods, section 16 provides that no property in

---

[68] Glanville Williams, "Theft, Consent and Illegality" [1977] *Crim LR* 127, 138. *Per* Smith, *Property Offences* (1994) § 5–49, "if the civil law sees no reason to permit the owner to complain of an interference with his property why should the criminal law do so?"

[69] Above, § 1.2(i).

[70] The leading case is *Gomez*: below, § 13.6(ii)(a)–(b).

[71] Voidability is not an option in the case of a unilateral mistake. A transaction can be voidable, as opposed to void, only when D has acted in some way wrongfully. If P's mistake is fundamental, the transaction is void; if not, the transaction is entirely valid and unimpeachable.

them can be transferred to the buyer unless and until the goods are ascertained.[72] Section 18 provides that if there is no agreement regarding the passing of title, then property passes at the time the contract is made.[73]

One consequence of section 17 is that a seller may pass possession but reserve ownership. This is standard, for example, in hire-purchase contracts, where property remains in the seller until the buyer has paid for the goods. Although the buyer has lawful possession, a charge of theft would lie where the buyer then usurps the seller's rights of ownership over those goods, e.g. by dishonestly selling them.

Case 2: Rescission.

In *Walker,*[74] D sold V a defective video recorder which V returned for repair. After some time, V then issued a summons claiming the price of the video as the "return of money paid for defective goods." D thereafter sold the video. His conviction for theft was quashed. Arguably, the summons had the effect of rescinding the original contract of sale; revesting ownership of the machine once again in D.

Case 3: Receptacles.

The owner of a vending or similar machine, such as a coin-operated telephone, becomes the owner of any money as soon as it is inserted.[75] This is explicable on the general rule: the depositor intends to pass ownership when he inserts a coin in prepayment. Even if the machine malfunctions and he does not get what he pays for, his remedy is a refund, not a retrieval of the particular coin inserted. It is thus the actus reus of theft to retake money from such a machine, except by authorised means (e.g. pressing the refund button).

Similarly, when petrol is sold at a service station, ownership passes when the petrol is pumped into the tank of the vehicle. Thus a motorist who fills his tank intending to pay for the petrol, but then decides not to pay for it and drives off, commits no theft.[76] He already owns and has possession of the petrol before he forms the mens rea of theft, and instead commits the offence of making off without payment.[77]

Case 4: Contents.

If a person puts a valuable ring in a desk drawer, and after death her executor sells the desk, the buyer may not keep the ring on finding it since it was not included in the sale,[78] and a dishonest failure to return it would constitute theft. Ownership of the ring remains in the executor since he does not intend to pass title thereto when he sells the desk.

---

[72] See, e.g., *Re Goldcorp Exchange* [1995] 1 AC 74 (PC): buyers had no legal or equitable interest in an undifferentiated bulk of gold bullion. This rule is subject to certain exceptions for sales of undivided shares in an ascertained bulk (see, in particular, the Sale of Goods Amendment Act 1979).

[73] Provided the goods are specific and deliverable, and the contract is unconditional. Other rules in s. 18 apply where these criteria are not met.

[74] [1984] Crim LR 112.

[75] *Martin* v. *Marsh* [1955] Crim LR 781; *Hollings* (1940) 4 J Cr L 370; cf. *Jean* [1968] 2 CCC 204.

[76] *Greenberg* [1972] Crim LR 331; *Edwards* v. *Ddin* [1976] 3 All ER 705. This assumes that the controversial decision in *Hinks* [1998] Crim LR 904 (below, § 13.6(ii)(c)) applies only to circumstances where the act of appropriation is coincident with, and not subsequent to, the obtaining of ownership.

[77] Theft Act 1978, s. 3.

[78] *Thomas* v. *Greenslade* [1954] CLY 3421; *Moffatt* v. *Kazana* [1969] 2 QB 152; *Merry* v. *Green* (1841) 7 M & W 623, 151 ER 916.

(b) Is the passing of title voidable for duress, misrepresentation, etc?

It is clear that transfers, even those pursuant to a contract, are voidable at common law if they are induced by the recipient's wrongdoing, e.g. by duress or misrepresentation.[79] Similarly, transfers affected by undue influence are voidable in equity.[80] In light of the House of Lords decision in *Gomez*,[81] the dishonest receipt of goods pursuant to such a voidable transfer can now be theft. (This, strictly, puts the criminal law at odds with the civil law as a voidable title is a perfect title until the transaction conferring ownership on D is set aside.)

(c) Is the passing of title void for mistake?

O's consent to the transfer of title may be negated by a "fundamental" mistake, whether or not induced by fraud or misrepresentation. A mistake is fundamental if and only if its existence makes it reasonable to say that there is no intention on O's part to transfer *this* property to *this* person.[82] As the High Court of Australia put it, what this means is that a mistake is sufficiently fundamental if it is "as to the identity of the transferee or as to the identity of the thing delivered, or as to the quantity of the thing delivered."[83] However, applying this test is not always clear cut. Moreover, even where O's mistake is not sufficiently fundamental, it may well generate liability under section 5(4), which we will consider below (§ 13.5(iv)).

Case 1: Mistake regarding property.

Mistake as to the identity of the property will always defeat consent. In *Davies*[84] the proprietor of a nursing home induced two old ladies to endorse cheques made out to them by signing on the back, and then paid the cheques into his own account. The victims had not known that they were endorsing cheques, but merely thought that they were signing pieces of paper. For this reason property in the cheques never passed to D, who was thus rightly convicted of theft. Here the mistake was obviously fundamental: in each case V believed the property to be a valueless piece of paper, whereas in reality it was a bill of exchange—a different type of thing altogether.

Case 2: Mistake regarding quantity.

If the owner intends to deal only with a specific number of goods handed over, then there is no consent as to the excess. But if O's intention is to hand over a group of things, a mistake as to the number of items in the group does *not* negate the intention to hand them all over.

An example of the former variety is *Russell v. Smith*:[85]

---

[79] See, e.g., Furmston, *Cheshire, Fifoot and Furmston's Law of Contract* (13th ed., 1996) 292, 317; Winfield, "Quasi-Contract Arising from Compulsion" (1944) 60 *LQR* 341; *Cooper v. Joel* (1859) 1 De GF & J 240, 45 ER 350; *Wauton v. Coppard* [1899] 1 Ch 92. Indeed, in cases of grave physical duress or fundamental misrepresentation the transfer may even be void: Lanham, "Duress and Void Contracts" (1966) 29 *MLR* 615.

[80] [1993] AC 442. This should have been the approach taken by the Court of Appeal in *Hinks* [1998] Crim LR 904; below, § 13.6(ii)(c).

[81] Below, § 13.6(ii)(a).

[82] Williams, "Mistake in the Law of Theft" [1977] *CLJ* 62, 64.

[83] *Ilich* (1986) 162 CLR 110, 126.

[84] [1982] 1 All ER 513.

[85] [1958] 1 QB 27.

D was a driver for a haulage company. He was instructed to collect a one-ton load of pig meal from P. P, when loading the meal, inadvertently loaded an additional eight sacks. When D discovered the error, he appropriated the eight sacks and sold them.

P intended to give D the number of sacks corresponding to one ton of meal; there was no intention to put the additional sacks on the lorry. Thus P remained owner of the eight extra sacks, which D stole when he appropriated them. Contrast this decision with an example where P offers to sell D all the pig meal then stored at his warehouse; which P mistakenly think amounts to one ton's worth, when in fact it is eight sacks more than that weight. In the latter case, D acquires ownership of the entirety.

The distinction at work here is between a mistake which simply motivates or underlies P's intention to pass title to certain goods, and one which negates P's intention to pass title in those very goods which were in fact delivered. It is, in short, the difference between a mistake as to *what* P is passing to D, and a mistake as to *why* he is doing so.[86]

Case 3: Mistake regarding transferee.

Mistake as to the identity of the other party may vitiate consent, but only if the identity was crucial to O's decision to give consent.[87] In *Hudson*, D received and paid into his bank account a cheque which was inadvertently made out to him, but obviously intended for someone else with the same surname. He was convicted of stealing the cheque.[88]

It seems that a mistake about the transferee's identity supplies the best explanation of another well-known case, *Middleton*.[89] In that case, D went to withdraw 10 shillings from his Post Office savings account, which had at that time a balance of 11 shillings. The Post Office practice was to pay out withdrawals pursuant to a warrant obtained by D and a letter of advice from the Postmaster General sent direct to the relevant branch. Unfortunately the clerk consulted the wrong letter of advice, which related to a different account holder, and paid out £8 16s 10d. The Court of Criminal Appeal held that D was properly convicted of larceny, as the clerk's intention to pass title to the money was vitiated by his mistake. Since the clerk clearly did intend to give D £8 16s 10d, and not 10 shillings, he made no mistake about the nature or quantity of the property transferred.[90] Rather, his mistake is best seen as being about D's identity, which he had mistaken for that of the person named in the letter of advice.[91]

---

[86] Analogous to the distinction in contract law between a mistake "in the motive or reason for making the offer," and a mistake in the terms of the offer itself: *Imperial Glass* v. *Consolidated Supplies* (1960) ?? DLR (2d) 759.

[87] Thus *Cundy* v. *Lindsay* (1878) 3 App Cas 459 may be distinguished from *King's Norton Metal Co* v. *Edridge* (1897) 14 TLR 98, where the rogue's assumed name was of no particular significance.

[88] [1943] KB 458. But this is not an absolute rule, at least where the parties deal face to face. In *Ingram* v. *Little* [1961] 1 QB 31 a contract for sale of a car to a rogue under a false name (whose cheque bounced) was held void, but in *Lewis* v. *Averay* [1972] 1 QB 198 a similar sale to a rogue believing him to be a certain TV actor was held valid. Possibly the only explanation for this anomaly is that in the latter case there was no actual misrepresentation by the buyer. Even before these cases, the considerable difficulties in this area of law had been pointed out by Williams, "Mistake as to Party in the Law of Contract" (1945) 23 *Can Bar Rev* 271.

[89] (1873) 12 Cox CC 417.

[90] *Per* Bramwell B (dissenting): "No doubt the clerk did not intend to do an act of the sort described, and give to Middleton what did not belong to him. Yet he intended to do the act he did. What he did he did not do involuntarily, nor accidentally, but on purpose": (1873) 12 Cox CC 417, 428.

[91] (1873) 12 Cox CC 417, 419: the clerk "certainly meant that the prisoner should take up that money, though he only meant this because of a mistake as to the identity of the prisoner with the person really entitled to that money."

In 1972, the Court of Appeal purported to follow *Middleton* in *Gilks*.[92] G placed various bets at a betting shop, including one on "Fighting Taffy", which was unplaced in a race won by "Fighting Scot". When he went to collect his winnings on the various bets he had placed, the bookmaker mistakenly thought G had backed the winner, and calculated and paid out an amount well in excess of G's true winnings. G, realising the mistake, decided to pocket the entirety. His conviction for theft was upheld on the footing that *Middleton*[93] had established, in such cases, that property in money paid by mistake does not pass. It is submitted, however, that the Court of Appeal's reasoning was flawed. The bookmaker's error was an antecedent one of calculation[94] and not of the sort found in *Middleton*, where the clerk had paid the right amount to the wrong person. The bookmaker paid G (the right person) exactly the amount he intended. Therefore ownership of the money had passed to G,[95] and he should not have been convicted of theft.[96]

(d) Other mistakes—and the possibilities of constructive trusts or section 5(4)

The general rule is that, failing a "fundamental" mistake of the kinds identified in the foregoing paragraphs, the transaction is effective to pass title in the relevant property from O to D; thereafter, prima facie, that property cannot be stolen by D. In such cases, a charge of theft may still be available if the property is still belongs to O in equity or by virtue of section 5(1)–(4). These extensions to section 5(1) are discussed in detail below (§ 13.5); but, in the context of mistakes, it is worth drawing particular attention to the role of section 5(4) and to developments in equity. Suppose that O mistakenly imagines she owes D £100 when, in fact, she owes £70. If she then pays him £100, D normally acquires absolute title to all of the money (O makes no fundamental mistake about what she is paying him), but he becomes liable under civil law to repay the excess £30. In those circumstances, section 5(4) operates to deem that excess as belonging to O for the purposes of theft. If D dishonestly keeps the £30, he then commits theft. Section 5(4) is the subject of § 13.5(iv) below. Additionally, there is authority that, under certain conditions, O retains equitable title to the excess and D holds the excess as a constructive trustee; in which case the property still belongs to O within the core terms of section 5(1). This possibility is considered in § 13.5(i)(c).

(e) Was the transferor authorised to pass title?

Property will not pass if the transferor does not have the owner's authority to pass title. In *Bhachu*, a dishonest cashier acted in collusion with D by "selling" the goods to her at a price

---

Cf. Smith and Hogan, *Criminal Law* (1965) 354. On whether the facts really support such a finding, *contra* the dissent by Cleasby B (1873) 12 Cox CC 417, 441–2. Cf. Turner, "Two Cases of Larceny" in Turner and Radzinowicz (eds.), *The Modern Approach to Criminal Law* (1948) 356, 359.

[92] [1972] 3 All ER 280 (CA). See the criticism by J.C. Smith in [1972] *Crim LR* 586. Compare *Prince* (1868) LR 1 CCR 150.

[93] (1873) 12 Cox CC 417.

[94] Of the sort found in *Moynes* v. *Coopper* [1956] 1 QB 439; below, § 13.5(iv).

[95] There is some authority (*Chase Manhatten Bank* v. *Israel British Bank* [1981] 1 Ch 105 and *Shadrokh-Cigari* [1988] Crim LR 465) to the effect that, when making a mistake of this sort, V may retain equitable title in the money. These cases, which are controversial, are discussed in § 13.5(i)(c).

[96] Note that s. 5(4) would ordinarily apply to such overpayments, but did not do so in this case because it arose out of a wager: below, § 13.4(iv)(d), 13.5(iv).

below the authorised price.[97] In such a case, the cashier does not have the authority to pass title on O's behalf, and the goods are converted by D when she takes them out of the shop.[98] By contrast, an unintentional error on the part of an agent does not mean that the agent's conduct is unauthorised, even if the recipient is dishonest.[99]

(v) Abandonment and loss: is finding theft?

It is possible for ownership to be relinquished through abandonment. If an owner intentionally abandons goods, they become ownerless, and therefore cannot be stolen.[100] However, an item may be lost rather than abandoned. Consider the following example:

> David finds a wallet in a busy street, and picks it up. He looks in the wallet for evidence of the owner's identity and finds none, but does find some money. He puts the wallet in his pocket. Does David commit the actus reus of a theft?

Typically, in "finding" cases, it is important to resolve whether the thing found belongs to another: whether, in this scenario, there is another person with a right of property in the wallet and its contents. In turn, this is likely to depend on whether the wallet is abandoned or merely lost. If lost, then the person who originally lost the wallet remains its owner. By contrast, if abandoned, the wallet is unowned until David picks it up and puts it in his pocket.

Generally speaking, the courts are reluctant to find that goods have been "abandoned" rather than merely lost.[101] It will not suffice, for example, merely to put rubbish out for collection,[102] or to bury a dead animal.[103] Normally, as in these examples, some right in the subject matter (such as the right of exclusion of others from the subject matter) will be preserved. Abandonment of ownership requires a giving up of the owner's physical control of an item, accompanied by the cessation of any intention to possess that item and of any intention to exclude other persons from its possession—i.e. a deliberate relinquishing of all rights over the item.[104]

Let us assume, since it contains money, that in David's case the wallet was not abandoned. It is worth noting that if David had formed an honest belief that the goods were abandoned rather than lost, he would not commit theft.[105] However, this is because of the lack of mens rea (dishonesty), rather than the absence of an actus reus.

(a) When does a finder acquire ownership?

Once abandoned, ownership of items vests in the first person to take possession of them.

---

[97] (1976) 65 Cr App R 261. Cf. *Tideswell* [1905] 2 KB 273.

[98] In such circumstances, it seems that the cashier herself steals the goods when she offers to sell them at an undervalue: see *Pitham and Hehl* (1976) 65 Cr App R 45, below, § 13.6(i).

[99] *Jackson* (1826) 1 Mod 119, 168 ER 1208; *Prince* (1868) LR 1 CCR 150.

[100] Cf. *Ellerman Wilson Line* v. *Webster* [1952] 1 Lloyd's Rep 179, 180.

[101] Cf. Hudson, "Is Divesting Abandonment Possible at Common Law?" (1984) 100 *LQR* 110.

[102] *Williams* v. *Phillips* (1957) 41 Cr App R 5. As long as the rubbish remained on the owner's premises it was not abandoned; property in it passed when collected by the local authority.

[103] *Edwards* (1877) 13 Cox CC 384.

[104] Cf. Hudson, "Abandonment" in Palmer and McKendrick, *Interests in Goods* (1993); *The Crystal* [1894] AC 508.

[105] *Small* [1987] Crim LR 777; *White* (1912) 7 Cr App R 266.

Possession, in turn, is normally taken by intentionally exercising control over the items. This may be done physically (as David does with the wallet, in the example above). Where chattels are abandoned on occupied land, however, the occupier will often acquire possession even before the chattel is found. In general, there are three types of cases in which the occupier acquires a better title than the finder.[106]

First, if the thing found is embedded in,[107] under,[108] or otherwise attached[109] to the land, it belongs to the occupier or owner (as the case may be[110]) of the land regardless of who finds it.[111]

Secondly, if something is found loose by an employee on the employer's property, the employer has a superior right to possession of that thing, in priority to the employee-finder.[112]

Finally, where the item is found lying loose on the land, the occupier can acquire a prior title either by (a) restricting public access to the land upon which the items lie,[113] or (where the land is open to public access) by (b) manifesting an intention to exercise control over the land and the things thereon.[114] Obviously if the item is found by a visitor inside D's private home, D has a superior title since the public does not have general access to the home. Less straightforward illustrations of possibility (a) are the following two cases:

> In *Woodman*,[115] D took scrap metal from a factory site. E, the occupier of the site, had no knowledge of the existence of the scrap, as it had sold all the scrap on the site to B for removal. In fact, B had removed the bulk of the scrap but left some pieces behind, which B deemed too inaccessible to be worth the cost of removing. The site had been wound down and was now disused, although a barbed-wire fence had been erected around the site to exclude trespassers.

D's conviction was upheld by the Court of Appeal. Even if ownership of the remaining scrap had been abandoned by B, ownership would have reverted to D as the occupier of the land, since D had manifested an intention to exclude trespassers by fencing off the site.

> In *Hibbert* v. *McKiernan*,[116] D trespassed on a private golf course and dishonestly took eight golf balls which had been lost—and, it was found, subsequently abandoned—by their former owners.

---

[106] See Reisman, "Possession and the Law of Finders" (1939) 52 *Harv LR* 1105; Tay, "Problems in the Law of Finding" (1964) 37 *ALJ* 350; Harris, "The Concept of Possession in English Law" in Guest (ed.), *Oxford Essays in Jurisprudence* (1961) 69, 80ff.

[107] *Elwes* v. *Brigg Gas Company* (1886) 33 Ch D 562.

[108] *Rowe* (1859) Bell 93, 169 ER 1180; *South Staffordshire Water Co* v. *Sharman* [1896] 2 QB 44 (items lying under water; though in the latter case the defendant was also an employee).

[109] E.g., sealed inside a fixture: *City of London Corporation* v. *Appleyard* [1963] 2 All ER 834; *Moffatt* v. *Kazana* [1969] 2 QB 152.

[110] Itself a matter of potential controversy: see, e.g., *Elwes* v. *Brigg Gas Company* (1886) 33 Ch D 562.

[111] *Waverley* [1995] 4 All ER 756.

[112] *The Title of the Finder* (1899) 33 ILT 225; *Willey* v. *Synan* (1937) 57 CLR 200; *Grafstein* v. *Holme* [1958] 12 DLR (2d) 727.

[113] *Parker* v. *British Airways Board* [1982] QB 1004, 1013, 1019 (Donaldson LJ), 1020 (Eveleigh LJ), 1021 (Sir David Cairns).

[114] *Waverley* [1995] 4 All ER 756; cf. *Parker* v. *British Airways Board* [1982] QB 1004, 1018.

[115] [1974] QB 754.

[116] [1948] 2 KB 142.

The Divisional Court held that D was rightly convicted of theft from the golf club. Even if the balls had truly been abandoned (a doubtful conclusion, since clearly they had been lost unintentionally),[117] the golf club, as occupier of the land, had a better possessory title than D. D was a trespasser whose presence on the course was excluded.

On the other hand, where the premises are open to the public, the occupier's position is weaker, and she gains prior title only if she has (b) manifested an intention to exercise control over the things that are or might be on the premises. In *Parker v. British Airways Board*,[118] Parker found a gold bracelet in an executive lounge at Heathrow airport. He handed the bracelet in to British Airways (who, as lessees, occupied the lounge), asking that the bracelet be returned to him if unclaimed. British Airways sold the bracelet. Parker succeeded in an action for conversion of the bracelet. The Court of Appeal held that Parker's rights as finder could be displaced only if British Airways could show as occupiers an obvious intention to exercise such control over the lounge and things in it that the bracelet was in their possession before the plaintiff found it.[119] On the evidence, there was no manifestation of such an intention as would give the defendants a right superior to that of the plaintiff; the airline's instructions to staff for dealing with lost articles were not published to users of the lounge, and it did not carry out searches for lost articles.

A special exception is "treasure", as defined in section 1 of the Treasure Act 1996. Any items falling within that definition (such as articles over 300 years old when found that are comprised of at least ten per cent gold or silver) are, by virtue of the Act, the property of the Crown.

§ 13.5 Belonging to another (II): extensions in the Act and in equity

There is a variety of ways in which the reach of the criminal law has been extended to protect interests in property rights beyond those falling within section 5(1). Much of the variety is added by sections 5(2),[120] 5(3),[121] and 5(4).[122] These subsections are intended to cover specific *lacunae* in the scope of section 5(1). In at least one other area, however, liability under section 5(1) itself has been enlarged as a result of changes in the civil law, notably the expansion of the constructive trust since the passing of the 1968 Act.

---

[117] A finding made by the justices at first instance (who seem to have confused abandonment of the search with abandonment of the balls themselves) and accepted, without being approved (cf. *ibid.*, 151), by the Divisional Court for purposes of the appeal. If lost rather than abandoned, a charge of theft from the original owners of the balls would have been straightforward. A slightly different case with identical result is *Rostron* [2003] EWCA Crim 2206 where, under the rules of the club by which players were bound, lost balls were deemed to be "surrendered" to the club. Thus title passed to the club by contractual assignment rather than by the law governing possession of abandoned property; and the defendants were rightly convicted of stealing from the club.

[118] [1982] 1 All ER 834; discussed by Roberts, "More Lost Than Found" (1982) 45 *MLR* 683.

[119] It was also suggested that D's rights might be displaced had he acted dishonestly. However, unless D's dishonesty were such as to make him a trespasser *ab initio*, it is hard to see how this qualification can be justified. See Smith, *Property Offences* (1994) § 4–20, 4–21.

[120] Below, § 13.5(ii).

[121] Below, § 13.5(iii).

[122] Below, § 13.5(iv).

(i) The growth of the constructive trust

In § 13.4, we saw that section 5(1) includes almost any form of proprietary right or interest within the range of what may be stolen, including, in particular, equitable proprietary interests. Clearly, as was intended, this embraces ordinary trustees and standard cases of fiduciary relationship, e.g. between solicitor and client. However, a consequence of embracing any proprietary interest within the terms of section 5(1) is that, in recent years, developments in the law governing constructive trusts have brought a variety of new situations potentially within the net of criminal liability.

A constructive trust is a trust that arises by imposition of law, rather than pursuant to the intention of the parties. If D holds property in circumstances where, in equity and good conscience, the property ought to be owned or enjoyed by V, a constructive trust may be imposed upon D; with the consequence that, although D is the legal owner of the property, he holds that property for the benefit of V—the equitable owner. Such equitable ownership is sufficient for the purposes of section 5(1).

The law of constructive trusts is now exceedingly complicated. It is a field in its own right, and cannot be treated in any depth here. We will simply introduce and briefly discuss some of the paradigm cases. What will be said in the following paragraphs assumes—unavoidably—some familiarity with the relevant civil law concepts.

(a) Making a profit from abuse of fiduciary position

If an employee has authority to use or deal with his employer's chattel for a profit, property in the proceeds passes directly to his principal.[123] However, the position may be different where the employee uses his employer's goods outside the scope of his authority. In the nineteenth-century case of *Cullum*,[124] the captain of a barge carried cargo contrary to his instructions, and appropriated the resulting profits. It was held that he did not receive his secret profits on behalf of his employer, but on his own behalf. The employer was entitled to sue for an amount equivalent to the employee's profits, but had no proprietary claim to the proceeds themselves, which were received as the property of the employee.

On this analysis, Cullum would not be guilty of theft of the proceeds of his misconduct. But in modern law, we need also to consider whether similar facts would now give rise to a constructive trust.[125] Goff and Jones write that "a fiduciary who uses his position of trust to acquire a benefit for himself holds that benefit on constructive trust for his beneficiary."[126] This rule applies, for example, where a person in a fiduciary position derives a profit from the unauthorised use of another's property;[127] or acquires confidential information which

---

[123] *De Banks* (1884) 13 QBD 29 (D was requested to sell V's horse; he then misappropriated the proceeds. The Court held that D was a bailee of the proceeds and so guilty of larceny).

[124] (1873) LR 2 CCR 28. Cf. *A-G's Reference (No. 1 of 1985)* [1986] QB 491, discussed in the text below.

[125] Smith, "Constructive Trusts in the Law of Theft" [1977] *Crim LR* 395, 398.

[126] *The Law of Restitution* (6th ed., 2002) 713.

[127] *Ibid.*, 661. See also Goode, "The Right to Trace and Its Impact in Commercial Transactions" (1976) 92 *LQR* 360 and 528, 534–5; Youdan (ed.), *Equity, Fiduciaries and Trusts* (1989) 97, 223; Birks, *An Introduction to the Law of Restitution* (1989) 388; Goode, "Ownership and Obligation in Commercial Transactions" (1987) 103 *LQR* 433, 442–5.

he exploits for his own profit;[128] and it has also been held that a constructive trust will also arise where a fiduciary receives a secret bribe or commission.[129] As we have noted, a constructive trust would give the beneficiary an equitable proprietary right in the benefit acquired, thus bringing section 5(1) within range.

A key question, therefore, is whether D is a fiduciary. In this context, a fiduciary has been described as:[130]

> "simply, someone who undertakes to act for or on behalf of another in some particular matter or matters. That undertaking may be of a general character. It may be specified and limited. It is immaterial whether the undertaking is or is not in the form of a contract. It is immaterial that the undertaking is gratuitous. And the undertaking may be officiously assumed without request."

As a general rule, an agent[131] or a company director[132] holds a fiduciary position. Cullum himself, however, would probably not qualify, since his duties as a mere barge skipper were of a non-discretionary character. Effectively, his role was comparable to that of a modern-day lorry driver.

(b) Mere employees

Cullum was, in effect, in the position of a mere employee, one who carries out the instructions of his employer without having large measures of discretionary responsibility.[133] In *Powell* v. *MacRae*,[134] it was held in 1977 that a turnstile operator who accepted a bribe to admit someone into Wembley Stadium without a ticket was not in a fiduciary relationship with his employer, and that his retention of the money was not a theft from his employer. Authority for this proposition is *Lister & Co* v. *Stubbs*,[135] in which a foreman in a textiles firm received substantial secret commissions under an arrangement with one of the suppliers. The English Court of Appeal held that D did not hold the receipts in the capacity

---

[128] Cf. *A-G* v. *Guardian Newspapers (No. 2)* [1990] 1 AC 109 concerning use of confidential information in the book *Spycatcher; Diamond* v. *Oreamuno*, 301 NYS 2d 78 (1969): D, a director, speculated in the company's shares, using unpublished information about a potential take-over bid. See also generally Jones, "Unjust Enrichment and the Fiduciary's Duty of Loyalty" (1968) 84 *LQR* 472.

[129] *A-G for Hong Kong* v. *Reid* [1994] 1 AC 324; below, § 13.5(i)(b).

[130] Finn, *Fiduciary Obligations* (1977) 201; cf. *Bristol and West Building Society* v. *Mothew* [1996] 4 All ER 698, 71–2 (Millett LJ). See also Shepherd, "Towards a Unified Concept of Fiduciary Relationships" (1981) 97 *LQR* 51, 75.

[131] *Boston Deep Sea Fishing and Ice Co* v. *Ansell* (1888) 39 Ch D 339, 354ff.

[132] *Regal (Hastings)* v. *Gulliver* [1942] 1 All ER 378. Shares intended to be acquired by directors at par to avoid them giving a guarantee of the obligations under a lease were sold at a profit, and the directors were held to be liable to the company for the proceeds of the sale. See also *Phipps* v. *Boardman* [1967] 2 AC 46.

[133] A.T.H. Smith has suggested that arguably there should be a fiduciary relationship between employees and their employers: "Constructive Trusts in the Law of Theft" [1977] *Crim LR* 395, 398; "Theft by Persons Required to Account" [1980] 1 *Canterbury LR* 15, 21. Nonetheless, we incline to the view that since employees act under specific instructions they should not normally be regarded as fiduciaries: cf. Waters, "Banks, Fiduciary Obligations and Unconscionable Transactions" (1986) 65 *Can Bar Rev* 37, 53–4. It may be otherwise in the case of senior officers of a company who are charged by their employer "with initiatives and responsibilities far removed from the obedient role of servants": *Canadian Aero Service Ltd* v. *O'Malley* (1974) 40 CLR (3d) 371.

[134] [1977] Crim LR 571. Cf. Smith, "Embezzlement and the Disobedient Servant" (1956) 19 *MLR* 39.

[135] (1890) 45 Ch D 1. In Australia the decision has been described as anomalous and confined to its own facts: *DPC Estates* v. *Gray and Consul Development* [1974] 1 NSWLR 443 (NSW Court of Appeal). For criticism of *Lister* v. *Stubbs*, see Goff and Jones, *The Law of Restitution* (6th ed., 2002) 737–9; Oakley, *Constructive Trusts* (3rd ed., 1997) 135; contrast Birks, *An Introduction to the Law of Restitution* (1989) 378ff.

of trustee. The relationship between D and his employer was that of debtor and creditor; it was not that of trustee and beneficial owner. As Cotton LJ said:[136]

> "the moneys which under this corrupt bargain were paid by [the suppliers] to the Defendant cannot be said to be the money of the Plaintiffs before any judgment or decree in some action has been made."

However, where the employee is sufficiently senior to be regarded as a fiduciary, it appears that any bribes she takes will be subject to a constructive trust. In *A-G for Hong Kong* v. *Reid*,[137] D had accepted bribes in order to obstruct prosecutions while serving as a senior Crown prosecutor in the Colony of Hong Kong. At issue was whether the Hong Kong government held a proprietary interest in bribes received by D. It was common ground that D was a fiduciary; the question was whether he was also a constructive trustee of the money received. Ruling *Lister* v. *Stubbs* was wrongly decided on this point, the Privy Council held that:[138]

> "As soon as the bribe was received it should have been paid or transferred instanter to the person who suffered from the breach of duty. Equity considers as done that which ought to have been done. As soon as the bribe was received, whether in cash or in kind, the false fiduciary held the bribe on a constructive trust for the person injured."

What emerges from the case is that a fiduciary who receives, for himself, a bribe or commission paid for the misuse of his position will hold the money on constructive trust for his principal. That receipt falls within section 5(1) and can therefore be stolen. However, since it was conceded that Reid was a fiduciary, the question whether an employment situation will necessarily give rise to a fiduciary relationship was not considered.

The possibility that a secret profit made by an employee can be stolen was doubted by the Court of Appeal in *A-G's Reference (No. 1 of 1985)*.[139] The defendant was manager of a public house and an employee of the brewers to whom the house was tied. In contravention of the terms of his employment, he sought to sell beer purchased privately from a wholesaler to supplement his profits. The Court thought that such circumstances would not give rise to a trust and, even if it did, that it would not be such a trust as falls within the ambit of section 5(1). We will consider the policy merits of this view below, in § 13.5(i)(d). But at the level of law, the decision now seems hard to defend. On the question whether a trust arises on such facts, the Court applied *Lister* v. *Stubbs*, a Court of Appeal decision which, as we have seen, is now said to be wrongly decided by the Privy Council. More generally, on the legal question whether a constructive trust falls outside the ambit of section 5(1), the Court's interpretation is surprising. Section 5(1) expressly includes "any proprietary right or interest", and the whole point of a constructive trust is that it vests an equitable proprietary interest in someone else. If the manager is a fiduciary, his conduct amounts to theft.

---

136 (1890) 45 Ch D 1, 12–13.
137 [1994] 1 AC 324. Noted by Smith, "*Lister* v. *Stubbs* and the Criminal Law" (1994) 110 *LQR* 180.
138 [1994] 1 AC 324, 331.
139 [1986] QB 491.

(c) Property obtained by mistake

In § 13.4(iv)(c) and (d), we considered the situation where D obtains property pursuant to another's mistake. Where D has induced the mistake (e.g. by duress or deception), we saw that title to the property normally passes but is voidable, so that D may still be convicted of theft.[140] Otherwise, if the mistake is not fundamental, title passes; therefore, since D becomes absolute owner, section 5(1) does not apply and he cannot be convicted of theft unless (as will be discussed in § 13.5(iv)) the case falls exceptionally within section 5(4).

Such was the backdrop of settled law against which the Theft Act 1968 was enacted. But there is now authority that, while title passes at law, the mistaken payer can retain an equitable interest in the goods—which would be a sufficient property interest to qualify within section 5(1). In *Chase Manhattan Bank* v. *Israel British Bank*,[141] the plaintiff bank paid $2 million by mistake into another bank for the account of the defendant, which then went bankrupt. The plaintiff sought to recover the overpayment. Goulding J ruled in favour of the plaintiff, holding that a person who pays money to another under a mistake of fact retains an equitable proprietary right or interest in the money, as opposed to a purely personal right. If such an analysis is valid, section 5(1) would appear to be applicable. This was the conclusion of the court in *Shadrokh-Cigari*.[142] By error, a child's bank account was credited with £286,000. D, the child's guardian, procured the child to authorise the issue of four banker's drafts in D's favour. Applying *Chase Manhattan*, the Court of Appeal held that D stole the drafts from the bank. Since the drafts had been drawn by the bank in error, the bank retained an equitable interest in them. Hence, for the purposes of section 5(1), they belonged to the bank.

It is not clear, however, that Goulding J's analysis is a valid statement of English law.[143] The difficulty is that, traditionally, a fiduciary relationship has been a prerequisite to the availability of equitable proprietary remedies. The authority commonly cited as establishing this rule is *Re Diplock*,[144] in which the Court of Appeal interpreted an earlier decision by the House of Lords[145] as stating that an initial fiduciary relationship was necessary for equitable tracing. *Chase Manhattan* departs from the orthodox interpretation of these two cases, preferring the view that "the fund to be traced need not . . . have been the subject of fiduciary obligations before it got into wrong hands. It is enough that . . . the payment into wrong hands itself gave rise to a fiduciary relationship."[146] This reasoning has implications for the cases discussed earlier, involving employees making secret profits or taking bribes. A constructive trust might arise regardless whether the employee occupied a fiduciary position.

---

[140] Above, § 13.4(iv)(b).

[141] [1981] Ch 105, 119.

[142] [1988] Crim LR 465. Note that D's conviction was also upheld on the basis that his conduct fell within the terms of s. 5(4).

[143] The decision in *Chase Manhattan* is criticised in Goff and Jones, *The Law of Restitution* (6th ed., 2002) 203–4, but defended by Birks, *An Introduction to the Law of Restitution* (1989) 377. See also Birks, "Misdirected Funds: Restitution from the Recipient" [1980] *LMCLQ* 296, and *Agip (Africa)* v. *Jackson* [1990] Ch 265.

[144] [1948] Ch 465 (CA); *sub nom. Ministry of Health* v. *Simpson* [1951] AC 251 (HL).

[145] *Sinclair* v. *Brougham* [1914] AC 398. The reasoning in that case was said no longer to be sound by the House of Lords in *Westdeutsche Bank* v. *Islington LBC* [1996] AC 669, 709–14. At the same time, however, "[y]our Lordships should not be taken to be casting any doubt on the principles of tracing as established in *In re Diplock*" (at 714, *per* Lord Browne-Wilkinson).

[146] [1981] Ch 105, 119.

More recently, doubt has been cast on the reasoning in *Chase Manhattan* by the House of Lords in *Westdeutsche Bank* v. *Islington LBC*. According to Lord Browne-Wilkinson, Goulding J's decision was "based on a concept of retaining an equitable property in money where, prior to the payment to the recipient bank, there was no existing equitable interest."[147] Similarly, in *Halifax Building Society* v. *Thomas*[148] the Court of Appeal declined to find a constructive trust in a situation where there was no pre-existing fiduciary relationship. There are deep waters here, and it is beyond the scope of this work to chart them. Suffice it to say that the present law is unclear and that both *Shadrokh-Cigari* and *Chase Manhattan* are of doubtful authority. Moreover, although the criminal law of theft cannot decline to consider the effect of the civil law, criminal courts are not the place to develop or resolve disputed issues of civil law.[149] Accordingly, while doubt persists concerning the propriety of the ruling in *Chase Manhattan* that decision should not be employed to secure convictions for theft.

(d) The merits of criminalising theft as a constructive trustee

We noted earlier the suggestion made by the Court of Appeal in *A-G's Reference (No. 1 of 1985)*[150] that some constructive trusts might not fall within the scope of section 5(1), and that secret profits made by a publican should not be regarded as stolen from his employer. As a conclusion of law, this must be doubted. No doubt the drafters of the 1968 Act did not contemplate such cases when they framed section 5,[151] but that is not quite the point. Section 5(1) clearly applies, and was clearly intended to apply, to whatever the civil law regarded as a proprietary interest. As we have seen, the civil law has changed. Since section 5(1) is designed to protect proprietary interests, it necessarily follows that this change, which alters the scope of proprietary interests, in turn affects the reach of the criminal law.

At the level of policy, however, the reluctance of the Court of Appeal to embrace constructive trusts within section 5(1) is quite understandable, and there is a powerful case for legislative reform. The purposes for which the civil law imposes a constructive trust are characteristically irrelevant to the criminal law.[152] Very often, the main underlying consideration is whether V should have a prior claim in insolvency over a third party, T.[153] It is not obvious that the question whether D steals from V should be determined by the unrelated issue of priority between V and T.

Moreover, it is unclear that theft is the right description of D's criminality. The label "theft" does not seem accurately to capture the nature of D's wrongdoing. A charge of theft can only arise once D's receipt has been impressed with a constructive trust. But the gist of the criminal wrongdoing, if any, usually occurs *beforehand*; it is likely to be the reason the

---

[147] [1996] AC 669, 714.
[148] [1996] Ch 217.
[149] See Smith, "Judicial Lawmaking in the Criminal Law" (1984) 100 *LQR* 46.
[150] [1986] QB 491; above, § 13.5(i)(b).
[151] *Ibid.*, 505.
[152] *Per* Smith, "Constructive Trusts in the Law of Theft" [1977] *Crim LR* 395, 400: "the civil law imposes constructive trusts in situations, and for multifarious reasons, which may have nothing to do with the purposes of the criminal law."
[153] See, e.g., Paciocco, "The Remedial Constructive Trust: A Principled Basis for Priorities over Creditors" (1989) 68 *Can Bar Rev* 315; Goode, "Property and Unjust Enrichment" in Burrows (ed.), *Essays on the Law of Restitution* (1991) 215; Sherwin, "Constructive Trusts in Bankruptcy" [1989] *U Illinois LR* 297.

constructive trust is imposed. Consider the example where D accepts a bribe. The better approach would be to focus on that initial wrongdoing, not at the fact that he later keeps the money. Thus D should be prosecuted for taking a bribe,[154] and not for subsequent theft of the proceeds.

In addition to mislabelling D's wrongdoing,[155] extending theft liability to constructive trusts has the disadvantage of decreasing certainty in the law, and reducing the level of fair warning available to prospective thieves.[156] As Lord Lane pointed out in *A-G's Reference* itself, "if something is so abstruse and so far from the understanding of ordinary people as to what constitutes stealing, it should not amount to stealing."[157] When even Lord Wilberforce might say that the making of a secret profit "is no criminal offence whatever other epithet might be appropriate,"[158] one can hardly expect the man in the pub to foresee the possibility and criminal implications of a constructive trust.[159] The criminal law of theft is not the best place to resolve these issues.

(ii) Theft of an interest protected by section 5(2): trust property

As we have seen, a trustee can typically be convicted of theft of trust property under section 5(1), since any beneficiary of the trust would normally have an equitable interest in the trust property, which would qualify for protection as a proprietary interest under section 5(1). However, particularly in the case of charitable trusts, or discretionary trusts for a very large class,[160] sometimes there may be no individual beneficiary with an equitable interest in the trust. Such cases are covered by section 5(2):

> Where property is subject to a trust, the persons to whom it belongs shall be regarded as including any person having a right to enforce the trust, and an intention to defeat the trust shall be regarded accordingly as an intention to deprive of the property any person having that right.

A charitable trust is enforceable by the Attorney-General. For the purposes of theft, therefore, its property belongs to the Attorney-General, and may be stolen by the trustee.[161]

(iii) Theft of an interest protected by section 5(3): property received on account

What if a person such as stockbroker, solicitor, or estate agent, having received property from a client, fraudulently misuses it for his own benefit? One way of dealing with such persons is under section 5(3):

---

[154] Contrary to the Prevention of Corruption Act 1906, s. 1(1).

[155] Cf. the discussion of fair labelling in § 2.4.

[156] Above, § 2.3.

[157] [1986] QB 491, 507.

[158] *Tarling (No. 1)* v. *Government of the Republic of Singapore* (1979) 70 Cr App R 77, 111. Despite this statement, making secret profits has been held indictable as conspiracy to defraud: *Button* (1848) 3 Cox CC 229; *Rashid* [1977] 2 All ER 237; *Doukas* [1978] 1 All ER 1061. Even so, it is submitted that such conduct, if criminal in nature, should be regarded as a variety of fraud, rather than subsequent theft of the proceeds thereof.

[159] "There are topics of conversation more popular in public houses than the finer points of the equitable doctrine of the constructive trust": *A-G's Reference (No. 1 of 1985)* [1986] QB 491, 506.

[160] Cf. *Vestey* v. *IRC* [1980] AC 1148.

[161] The analysis was missed by the Court of Appeal in *Dyke and Munro* [2002] 1 Cr App R 404.

Where a person receives property from or on account of another, and is under an obligation to the other to retain and deal with that property or its proceeds in a particular way, the property or proceeds shall be regarded (as against him) as belonging to the other.

The section overlaps to a considerable extent with section 5(1), since persons receiving property on account will generally be fiduciaries who have legal but not equitable title to that property. In such cases, for purposes of theft the property can be stolen from the equitable owner (*per* section 5(1)) and from the person on whose account it is received (*per* section 5(3)). Section 5(3) comes into its own, however, when no-one apart from D has any legal or equitable interest in the property stolen.[162] Suppose T gives D money for a specific purpose, e.g. to pay the gas bill. There would normally be no expectation that D will pay the bill using the exact banknotes, cheque, etc., that T gives him. T intends, rather, that D should pay out either the money T gives him, its proceeds, or (if D has it) an equivalent sum; in effect, that D should maintain a sufficient fund to make the payment. In this situation D is the owner of the money, but may have a duty to account falling within section 5(3).[163]

Section 5(3) would also capture situations in which we would hold D to be under a fiduciary obligation notwithstanding that he has legal and equitable ownership of a thing. There is authority for the proposition that the residuary legatees of an estate have no proprietary interest before the estate is administered,[164] but we would think the executor guilty of theft were he dishonestly to appropriate the estate property to his own use. Another example is provided by the *Quistclose*[165] line of cases, where the transferees of money were obliged to keep it separate and to use it for specific purposes, even though there was no beneficial interest vesting in the intended recipients, nor, initially, in the transferors.

On the other hand, it is not always easy to determine when a person receives money on account. The obligation must be a *legal* obligation. A moral or social obligation is not sufficient.[166] When does this legal obligation arise?

(a) The receipt on account distinguished from mere personal liability

A duty to account does *not* exist where the relationship between D and the transferor of the property is that of debtor and creditor, such that the transferor's remedy against D is merely *in personam*. In theory, the difference between a duty to account and a liability *in personam* is clear enough. There is no duty to account when the recipient is entitled to the property both legally and beneficially, without any particular obligations attaching to her use of that property or its proceeds, so that she may deal with it as her own. In that case, the recipient's obligations operate as collateral, independent liabilities (e.g. a contractual debt). By contrast, where there is a receipt on account, D does not have untrammelled ownership of the property, and is entitled to dispose of and deal with the property or its proceeds only subject to the terms on which it was received.

---

[162] Cf. *Klineberg* [1999] 1 Cr App R 427, 432: s. 5(3) "is essentially a deeming provision by which property or its proceeds 'shall be regarded' as belonging to another, even though, on a strict civil law analysis, it does not."

[163] As the court held in *Davidge* v. *Bunnett* [1984] Crim LR 297.

[164] *Commr of Stamp Duties (Queensland)* v. *Livingstone* [1965] AC 674.

[165] *Quistclose Investments Ltd* v. *Rolls Razor Ltd* [1968] 1 All ER 613.

[166] Cf. *Huskinson* [1988] Crim LR 620; *Meech* [1974] QB 549, 554; *Hall* [1973] QB 126; Smith, "The Scope of Fraudulent Conversion" [1961] *Crim LR* 741 and 797, 799ff.

However, it is not always a simple matter to distinguish them in practice. Smith, discussing the (former) offence of fraudulent conversion, has suggested the following test where money is transferred:[167]

> "Was the transferee permitted, under the terms of the contract, to use the money as he thought fit; or was he obliged to apply it in a particular way or to retain an equivalent sum, either in his possession or in a bank? Only in the latter event can the transferee commit fraudulent conversion."

The distinction is often relevant in a civil law context, especially in an insolvency, where it may be important to decide whether the money forms part of a debtor's general assets to be distributed among creditors, or whether it may be recovered intact by the transferor.[168] In the criminal context, a simple example may be found in the travel agency business. A travel agent generally receives money from customers in return for an obligation to provide the ticket, and may use the money received from customers as he chooses. It was held in *Hall*[169] that this creates a debtor–creditor relationship. In that case, D had received deposits for air tickets and paid the money into a general trading account; he then failed to supply tickets to the clients. Although his conduct was "condemned as scandalous",[170] in the absence of special arrangements imposing on him an obligation to deal with clients' money in a particular way, he had no duty to account and therefore did not commit theft. By contrast, in *Re Kumar*[171] D, also a travel agent, had specifically agreed a trustee relationship in respect of moneys received from airline ticket sales. After deducting commission, D was required each month to remit the proceeds to IATA; which he failed to do. In these circumstances D had a duty to account and was ruled to have committed a theft.

One standard application of section 5(3) is to charity collectors.[172] In *Wain*,[173] D raised money from the public by conducting charitable discotheques and other events. Subsequently, he failed to hand the money over and instead spent it. D's conviction was upheld by the Court of Appeal on the basis that he was obliged to retain the proceeds of his fundraising for the benefit of the charity; hence, under section 5(3), the money belonged to the charity for the purposes of theft.

---

[167] "The Scope of Fraudulent Conversion" [1961] *Crim LR* 741 and 797, 800. This test was adopted in *Stephens* v. *R.* (1978) 52 ALJR 662, 669. For a useful illustration, compare *Hotine* (1904) 68 JP 143 with *Donald Smith* [1924] 2 KB 194.

[168] For example in the *Quistclose* line of cases: *Quistclose Investments Ltd* v. *Rolls Razor Ltd* [1968] 1 All ER 613.

[169] [1973] QB 126. Cf. *Robertson* [1977] Crim LR 629—but contrast *Brewster* (1979) 69 Cr App R 375 (insurance brokers).

[170] [1973] QB 126, 131.

[171] [2000] Crim LR 504.

[172] *Quaere* whether such cases in any event give rise to a constructive trust, falling within the scope of s. 5(1)-(2).

[173] [1995] 2 Cr App R 660; rightly disapproving *Lewis* v. *Lethbridge* [1987] Crim LR 59 (DC). In the latter case, D had obtained sponsorships for the benefit of a charity, but then kept the money. D's conviction was quashed because the magistrates had made no finding of fact that the charity expected D to maintain a separate fund with the money; but, as the Court in *Wain* pointed out, an obligation to account for the moneys or their proceeds need not come from the beneficiary. It can originate from the donors.

(iv) Theft of an interest protected by section 5(4): where there is an obligation to make restitution

Suppose that C is a wages clerk. When making up the pay packets one week, he accidentally puts a £50 note, which has stuck to another note, into D's packet, so that it now contains £200 instead of £150. Upon discovering the error, D resolves to say nothing and spends the money. He is guilty of stealing the £50 note. C's mistake was a fundamental one of quantity (above, § 13.4(iv)(c)), and the £50 note still belongs to the employer. Section 5(1) applies straightforwardly.

Compare, on the other hand, *Moynes* v. *Coopper*,[174] where a wages clerk miscalculated the amount due to D. Although the employee was thus overpaid, the clerk intended to pay the amount of money actually paid. Hence title in the whole amount paid passed to D, and D could not be convicted of larceny. The employer had no proprietary claim to the money in D's hands, merely a personal claim in restitution against D for money had and received.[175]

However, since the passing of the Theft Act 1968 mistakes of the latter variety are now covered by the special provisions of section 5(4):

> Where a person gets property by another's mistake, and is under an obligation to make restoration (in whole or in part) of the property or its proceeds or the value thereof, then to the extent of that obligation the property shall be regarded (as against him) as belonging to the person entitled to restoration, and an intention not to make restoration shall be regarded accordingly as an intention to deprive that person of the property or its proceeds.

Moynes would now be guilty of theft, notwithstanding that he in no way infringed his employer's property rights. The effect of section 5(4) can be seen in *A-G's Reference (No. 1 of 1983)*.[176] D, a police constable, had her salary paid by direct debit. By mistake, she was overpaid on one occasion by £74.74. On the assumption that she subsequently decided, dishonestly, not to repay the sum, the Court of Appeal ruled that she would be guilty of theft. Notwithstanding that she owned outright the content of her bank account, and was entitled to draw upon it as she wished, there was a legal obligation upon D to repay to her employer a sum equivalent to the overpayment once she discovered the mistake. By virtue of section 5(4), that sum (of £74.74) was *deemed* for the purposes of theft to belong to the employer, and so could be stolen.

The obligation must be a legal and not a moral obligation to make repayment.[177] Recall the betting case of *Gilks*,[178] discussed in § 13.4(iv)(c). While the mistake in that case was of the same type as that in *Moynes* v. *Coopper*, no legal obligation to make repayment arose in *Gilks* because the overpayment was in virtue of a wager.[179] Thus *Gilks* would not fall within the ambit of section 5(4).

---

[174] [1956] 1 QB 439. Cf. *Davis* (1988) 88 Cr App R 347 (CA).

[175] There is, however, recent controversial authority to the effect that even though title passes at law, the unilaterally mistaken payer may sometimes retain an equitable interest in the goods—which would be a sufficient property interest to qualify within s. 5(1). Because of its complexity, we consider this possibility separately, in § 13.5(i)(c).

[176] [1985] QB 182 (CA).

[177] *Gilks* [1972] 3 All ER 280, 283. Cf. the discussion of s. 5(3) above, § 13.5(iii).

[178] [1972] 3 All ER 280; above, § 13.4(iv)(c) (Case 3).

[179] Gaming Act 1845, s. 18; Gaming Act 1892, s. 1.

Although the decision in *Moynes* was much criticised at the time,[180] its undoing by section 5(4) seems something of an overreaction. The defendant in *Moynes* is a mere debtor; section 5(4) effectively makes personal liability the stuff of theft. This, surely, is a misuse of the concept of theft.

Moreover, it is debatable whether the defendant's behaviour should be criminalised under any other description either. If, through V's own error, V mistakenly gives D an unjustified windfall, prima facie his proper remedy is a civil law claim in money had and received. It is not obvious that the criminal law should wade to his rescue. This is not a case where D has done anything wrong to induce V's blunder. Like the difference between silence and active misrepresentation in contract law, taking studious advantage of another's unilateral mistake is not normally the stuff of legal intervention. Sometimes such circumstances warrant a civil law remedy; but it does not necessarily follow that the criminal law should be available here as a creditors' device.

§ 13.6 Appropriation

So far, we have considered what can be stolen: what sort of *property*, and what sort of *interest* in that property, is susceptible of theft. The third issue for the actus reus of theft is what sort of *action*, in connection with that property, is prohibited? Under section 1, D must "appropriate" the stolen property, a term elaborated upon by section 3(1):

> Any assumption by a person of the rights of an owner amounts to an appropriation, and this includes, where he has come by the property (innocently or not) without stealing it, any later assumption of a right to it by keeping or dealing with it as owner.

Although this definition is not intended to be exhaustive,[181] it appears to be at least as wide as any ordinary language concept of appropriation, and for practical purposes it is comprehensive. The history of the interpretation of section 3(1) is a sorry story of bad law and wilful misconstruction by the courts. We shall try to avoid its retelling here, save in so far as necessary. As things stand, the gist of appropriation is as follows:

> D appropriates an item when he does anything in connection with it that only an owner (or someone having rights derived from ownership) has the right to do, or that an owner has the right to exclude others from doing.

For instance, D appropriates something when he touches it, destroys it, gives it to another person, sells it, or even offers it for sale. The right to do each of these things is a right of ownership, and D assumes one of those rights when he does any of these actions. Note that D need only assume any one of the rights of ownership, not all of them, by his action.[182] Thus touching something is an appropriation even though one may do so without presuming all the facets of ownership.

Any act of appropriation is sufficient. There is no need for it to be the very act by which

---

[180] See, e.g., [1956] Crim LR 516.
[181] Cf. Report of the Criminal Law Revision Committee, *Theft and Related Offences* Cmnd. 2977 (1966) para. 34.
[182] *Morris* [1984] AC 320, where the House of Lords rejected the appellant's argument to the contrary.

D intends to deprive V of the item stolen. It is sufficient that D appropriates the item while intending that the owner should be deprived, even if that deprivation will be accomplished only by some later act of D's.[183] Suppose, for example, that D changes the labels on two products (say, product A and product B) in a supermarket, intending to buy the more expensive item, product A, at an undervalue. He steals product A as soon as he touches it, even though this act is only preliminary to the act of appropriation by which the owner will be deprived.

Before we elaborate upon this analysis in the following pages, it is worth commenting that, although this interpretation of section 3(1) must now be accepted, it seems at variance with the plain words of the statute: any assumption of "the rights of an owner" seemingly indicates an assumption of the *entirety* of the owner's rights. As we shall see, because of questionable interpretations, acts which previously would have been merely preparatory to theft—and which are not part of the gravamen of theft—are now treated as the theft itself.[184]

(i) Some examples of appropriation

It may be helpful to illustrate the variety of forms of conduct that can constitute theft. In *Pitham and Hehl*,[185] M offered to sell P and H some furniture, which all concerned knew did not belong to M. Convictions for handling by P and H were upheld on appeal, on the footing that M committed theft when he offered to sell the goods; hence P and H were guilty of handling goods that were stolen when they received them. The decision may be doubted on the facts,[186] but is clear authority that offering to sell goods assumes a right of the owner and is therefore an appropriation.

In *Chan Nai-Keung*[187] D, a director of a company which exported textiles, dishonestly sold a large quantity of the company's export quotas (a form of intangible property). D's conviction for theft was upheld by the Privy Council.

The framers of the Theft Act 1968 envisaged that the term "appropriation" would cover the same ground as the civil law concept of conversion,[188] and it seems clear that any form of conversion will also be an appropriation. This includes conversion by a person who legitimately has possession of the goods: for example, it is a theftuous conversion for a bailee to grant a chattel security over the property lent to her,[189] or to obliterate the identifying marks by painting it.[190]

---

[183] *Ibid.*

[184] In *Morris, ibid.*, Lord Roskill conceded that there was force in the view that the expression, "the rights of an owner," means all rights, not one or some. For his Lordship, however, it was decisive that s. 3(1) goes on to speak of "any later assumption of *a right.*" Remarkably, he omitted the subsequent words, "by keeping or dealing with it as an owner," which make it clear that D must keep or deal with the property by assuming the entirety of the rights to it.

[185] (1976) 65 Cr App R 45. Cf. *Rogers* v. *Arnott* [1960] 2 QB 244.

[186] Since all three knew that M had no authority to sell the furniture, M's "offer" seems to have been a mere sham rather than an appropriation. As Smith remarks, in *The Law of Theft* (8th ed., 1997) § 2–36, "D did not purport to be the owner or to be acting with his authority. It was not really an offer to sell at all but a proposal for a joint theft of the goods."

[187] *A-G of Hong Kong* v. *Chan Nai-Keung* (1987) 86 Cr App R 174.

[188] See below, § 13.6(ii)(b).

[189] Cf. *Dunbar* [1963] NZLR 253. (D had the loan of a boat, which he pledged as security for a financial transaction.)

[190] As in *Russell* [1977] 2 NZLR 20.

(ii) Restrictions on the scope of appropriation?

Prima facie, the scope of appropriation is astoundingly wide, with the consequence that the actus reus of theft is usually a simple matter for the prosecution to establish. Provided D does anything whatsoever in connection with property belonging to another person, the actus reus is made out; if he is dishonest and has an intention permanently to deprive, he steals it. Consider the following situation:

> Walter decides to steal a car. He walks down the street until he finds a Ford Mondeo with its doors unlocked. He opens the door and gets into the car. Unfortunately for him, he finds that his skeleton ignition key does not work. He gives up and goes home.

This looks like an attempted theft, subject to the question whether Walter had passed the stage of mere preparation and had in fact commenced the attempt. But it is not. It is a consummated theft, complete as soon as Walter opened the door. That was an appropriation: since all the other elements of theft were present, the offence was committed at that point.

The result is worrying as well as surprising. In Chapter 1 of this book, we discussed the proposition that criminal offences should require both harm and culpability before imposing the sanctions of conviction and punishment. Unfortunately, the modern law of theft appears virtually to have dispensed with harm. Conceptually, and at the level of ordinary language, the gist of theft is depriving another person of his property rights. Legally, theft is no such thing. Looked at objectively, D's behaviour may be ordinary and harmless, yet be the actus reus of theft. Consider the case of *Dip Kaur* v. *Chief Constable for Hampshire*:[191]

> D was in a shop where she found a pair of shoes, one of which was marked for sale at £6.99, the other at £4.99. She took the shoes to the cashier, hoping that the cashier would see the lower (incorrect) price. She was charged £4.99. Her conviction for theft was quashed, for the reason that the cashier's mistake (in thinking £4.99 was the correct price) did not negate her intention to sell the goods to D for £4.99; thus, when D left the shop, she owned the shoes and could not steal them.

As things stand, the case would now be decided differently. D stole the shoes as soon as she picked them off the sale rack—notwithstanding that the subsequent transaction was valid and she became their owner.

(a) Possible qualification 1: unauthorised or wrongful appropriations?

It might be thought that one way out of this difficulty is to read an implicit qualification into section 3(1): rather than simply "any assumption" of the rights of the owner, section 3(1) may be interpreted as requiring "any unauthorised assumption", or perhaps any "usurpation" of the owner's rights. This approach would better reflect the core idea that theft involves some form of harmful interference with another person's property rights, and that appropriation lacks a theftuous character unless it conflicts with the victim's rights.[192]

---

[191] [1981] 2 All ER 430.
[192] Cf. Model Penal Code, § 223.2 (the interference must be "unlawful").

At one point, the House of Lords appeared to favour such a qualification. In *Morris*,[193] D took goods from the shelves of a supermarket. He replaced the price labels attached to them with labels showing a lesser price than the originals. He was arrested after buying the goods at the lesser price and was subsequently convicted of theft. The House upheld the conviction, on the basis that D appropriated the goods and committed theft when he switched the price labels. The decision is clearly right, since D's act was an unauthorised appropriation of the goods. However, in the course of his judgment Lord Roskill dealt specifically with a point raised by counsel for the Crown:[194]

> "My Lords, Mr. Jeffreys sought to argue that any removal from the shelves of the supermarket, even if unaccompanied by label switching, was without more an appropriation. In one passage in his judgment in Morris's case, the learned Lord Chief Justice appears to have accepted the submission, for he said [1983] QB 587, 596 [CA]: 'it seems to us that in taking the article from the shelf the customer is indeed assuming one of the rights of the owner—the right to move the article from its position on the shelf to carry it to the check-out.' With the utmost respect, I cannot accept this statement as correct. If one postulates an honest customer taking goods from a shelf to put in his or her trolley to take to the checkpoint there to pay the proper price, I am unable to see that any of these actions involves any assumption by the shopper of the rights of the supermarket. *In the context of section 3(1), the concept of appropriation in my view involves not an act expressly or impliedly authorised by the owner but an act by way of adverse interference with or usurpation of those rights.* When the honest shopper acts as I have just described, he or she is acting with the implied authority of the owner of the supermarket to take the goods from the shelf, put them in the trolley, take them to the checkpoint and there pay the correct price, at which moment the property in the goods will pass to the shopper for the first time. . . . I do not think that section 3(1) envisages any such act as an 'appropriation,' whatever may be the meaning of that word in other fields such as contract or sale of goods law."

We have italicised the key proposition asserted by Lord Roskill, but the example he discusses is also helpful. It is this reasoning that justifies the quashing of D's conviction in *Dip Kaur* (above) where, by contrast with the defendant in *Morris*, D's handling of the shoes involved no unauthorised action. She simply picked them up and took them to the counter, something any shopper has an implied licence to do.[195]

Unfortunately, Lord Roskill's analysis was inconsistent with the earlier House of Lords decision in *Lawrence v. Metropolitan Police Commissioner*.[196] In that case D, a taxi-driver, drove a newly arrived foreign student with little English from Victoria Station to an address in London. The student had offered a £1 note for the fare, which D said was not enough before extracting a further £6 from the student's open wallet. In truth, the legally authorised fare for the journey was approximately 50 pence. Although the student had permitted D to

---

[193] [1984] AC 320; discussed by Leigh, "Some Remarks on Appropriation in the Law of Theft after *Morris*" (1985) 48 *MLR* 167. Cases exhibiting similar reasoning include *Meech* [1974] QB 549; *Hircock* (1978) 67 Cr App R 278; *Morgan* [1991] RTR 365; *Fritschy* [1985] Crim LR 745.

[194] [1984] AC 320, 332.

[195] Admittedly, it could be argued that such a licence (to carry goods within the shop) extends only to honest shoppers; a similar restriction has been allowed in the context of burglarious trespass (criticised below, § 14.3(ii)(a)). Besides being an artificial construction, however, such a move would make proof of the actus reus dependent on proving an element of mens rea, which would be to put the cart before the horse.

[196] [1972] AC 626.

take the excess money, the House upheld D's conviction for theft. The student's consent was irrelevant:[197]

> "I see no ground for concluding that the omission [from section 1(1) of the Theft Act 1968] of the words 'without the consent of the owner' was inadvertent and not deliberate, and to read the subsection as if they were included is, in my opinion, wholly unwarranted. Parliament by the omission of these words has relieved the prosecution of the burden of establishing that the taking was without the owner's consent. That is no longer an ingredient of the offence.
>
> . . . That there was appropriation in this case is clear. Section 3 (1) states that any assumption by a person of the rights of an owner amounts to an appropriation. Here there was clearly such an assumption. . . . [An appropriation] may occur even though the owner has permitted or consented to the property being taken."

The conflict in approach between *Lawrence* and *Morris* has since been resolved. In *Gomez*,[198] their Lordships affirmed *Lawrence*. D, the assistant manager of a shop, had formed a plan with R, a customer, to acquire goods in exchange for two stolen cheques. Knowing that the cheques were stolen, D deceived the shop manager into authorising the sale of the goods to R in exchange for the cheques. Instead of charging him with obtaining property by deception (as should have occurred), the prosecution charged D with theft. The Court of Appeal quashed his conviction, on the ground that ownership of the goods had passed; since the manager had consented to the transaction, possession of the goods was authorised and therefore there was no appropriation. The House of Lords restored the conviction: "The decision in *Lawrence* was a clear decision of this House upon the construction of the word 'appropriate' in section 1(1) of the Act, which had stood for 12 years when doubt was thrown upon it by obiter dicta in *Morris*. *Lawrence* must be regarded as authoritative and correct, and there is no question of it now being right to depart from it."[199]

The upshot of *Gomez* is that the scope of "appropriation" in theft is not limited to un-authorised or wrongful appropriations but includes even appropriations made with consent of the owner.[200]

(b) What's wrong with Gomez?

Quite apart from the fact that it virtually demolished any distinction between theft and the (then) offence of obtaining by deception,[201] the decision is questionable for a number of other reasons. The majority judgments by Lord Keith and Lord Browne-Wilkinson treated

---

[197] *Ibid.*, 632. Cf. *Dobson v. General Accident Fire and Life Assurance Corporation plc* [1990] 1 QB 274 (CA).

[198] [1993] AC 442.

[199] *Ibid.*, 464.

[200] See, e.g., *Williams (Roy)* [2001] 1 Cr App R 362. D dishonestly overcharged a number of clients for building work. He was convicted of stealing from his clients' bank accounts, notwithstanding that each appropriation from those accounts was with the consent of the customer who wrote the cheque.

[201] See Shute and Horder, "Thieving and Deceiving—What Is the Difference?" (1993) 56 *MLR* 548; Clarkson, "Theft and Fair Labelling" (1993) 56 *MLR* 554. A few instances of non-overlap are identified in Heaton, "Deceiving without Thieving" [2001] *Crim LR* 712. Earlier writing prior to *Gomez* includes Koffman, "The Nature of Appropriation" [1982] *Crim LR* 331; Leigh, "Some Remarks on Appropriation" (1985) 48 *MLR* 167; Gardner, "Is Theft a Rip-off?" (1990) 10 *OJLS* 441; Halpin, "The Appropriate Appropriation" [1991] *Crim LR* 426. Glazebrook, however, approves of *Lawrence* for pragmatic reasons: "Thief or Swindler: Who Cares?" [1991] *CLJ* 389. For discussion of the former offence of obtaining by deception and its successor under the Fraud Act 2006, see Chapter 15 below.

the matter largely as an issue of precedent: the analysis of appropriation in *Lawrence* was part of the *ratio decidendi* of that case, whereas it was merely *obiter dicta* in *Morris*. They barely mentioned the issues of principle at stake, and simply ignored the evidence that the legislature could not have intended such a broad interpretation of appropriation. Their Lordships' omissions are all the more surprising when one considers that the same issues are discussed at length in Lord Lowry's dissent. The majority appears to have sacrificed a restrained and coherent law of theft in favour of an *ad hoc* ruling to rescue one foolish prosecutor—who should never have charged the offence as theft.

It is submitted that if V transfers ownership of the goods to D, D as owner should be incapable of stealing those goods. As Lord Lowry shows,[202] this was certainly the view of the Criminal Law Revision Committee (CLRC), upon whose report the Theft Act 1968 was based.[203] When framing the Act, the CLRC equated appropriation with conversion[204]—a term that certainly requires unauthorised usurpation of another's property rights—and preferred the former word only because the latter was regarded as unduly technical terminology.

At the level of principle, the reasons a defendant who acquires ownership should not be convicted of theft are also compelling. The difficulty with *Gomez* is not the particular outcome, but the wider implications. The actus reus of theft has been so broadened that in practice it has no boundaries. Every transaction between two parties that pertains to property, whether corporate or private, whether consensual or involuntary, is now, apparently, the actus reus of a theft. This result has two effects. The first is to make a nonsense of the relationship between theft and the civil law of property. Bizarrely, *Gomez* means that a defendant who acquires indefeasible ownership by a transaction can also, by that very transaction, commit a crime. These two results cannot stand together. It is a long-standing rule of equity "that the Courts will not recognize a benefit accruing to a criminal from his crime":[205] no-one may benefit by his wrong.[206] If so, either there should be no crime, or the civil law must change (so that D does not get title). Given that the purpose of an offence such as theft is to protect property rights, and that the existence of property rights is a matter for the civil law, it is not for the criminal law to change the civil law of property. Unlike crimes such as assault, the rights being protected are necessarily rooted in the civil law. Remove dependence on the law of property, and property offences have no rationale. The decision in *Gomez* ignores that constraint.

The other effect of *Gomez* is to extend the offence of theft backwards in time, violating the harm principle in a second way. Earlier, we discussed the case of *Dip Kaur* v. *Chief Constable for Hampshire*,[207] and noted that this case would now be theft as soon as D picked the shoes off the sale rack—well before she approached the cashier. Previously, picking the shoes up would have been mere preparation, and not even an attempt to steal. Now (if accompanied by mens rea) it is not merely an attempt, but a full-blown theft. *This* result contravenes all the principles guiding the parsimonious criminalisation of harmless,

---

[202] *Gomez* [1993] AC 442, 470ff.

[203] Cmnd. 2977, *Theft and Related Offences* (1966).

[204] *Ibid.*, para. 34.

[205] *Beresford* v. *Royal Insurance Co Ltd* [1938] AC 586, 599 (Lord Atkin).

[206] See, e.g., *Cleaver* v. *Mutual Reserve Fund Ass.* [1892] 1 QB 147; *Re Giles, decd.* [1972] 1 Ch 546.

[207] [1981] 2 All ER 430. Above, § 13.6(ii).

preparatory activity.[208] Touching a pair of shoes inside a shop is not theftuous behaviour. It is in no way wrongful. There is no harm. Sometimes, where there is no harm and the behaviour is by itself innocent, liability for an attempt may be appropriate. But merely touching the shoes, a precursor to approaching the cashier with them, should be regarded as mere preparation for theft. Yet on the authority of *Gomez*, it constitutes the full-blown offence.

(c) Possible qualification 2: void versus voidable appropriations?

No matter how undesirable, *Gomez* is here to stay unless Parliament intervenes. At first, however, it was thought that the case was subject to one limitation. In *Gomez*, D induced the manager to part with the goods by deception. Thus, although title passed to D and his accomplice, at common law that title was voidable—like any transaction induced by deception, fraud, undue influence, or misrepresentation.[209] Arguably, therefore, *Gomez* could be distinguished from cases where D acquires full, unimpeachable ownership of the goods. *Gomez* rules that the acquisition of a voidable title is the actus reus of theft. But it does not decide that D appropriates goods when she acquires a fully valid title to them.

Unfortunately, the House of Lords rejected this distinction in the subsequent case of *Hinks*.[210] The facts were as follows:

> D had become friendly with a 53-year-old man described as naïve, gullible and of limited intelligence but with a considerable sum in his building society account. She successfully encouraged him to make a series of gifts totaling £60,000 and a TV set. The transfers were, it seems, valid gifts; as such, even after her conviction for theft, she was entitled to assert title to the money.

Nonetheless, her conviction was upheld. The money may have been hers, but she stole it. The House of Lords rejected D's argument that a finding of theft under the Act is subject to an exception where the relevant appropriation was an acquisition of title, holding that the language of the 1968 Act stipulates no such exception. Any appropriation, with or without the consent of the owner, falls within the Act. Even the *very acquisition* of indefeasible ownership, in accordance with the transferor's intentions, is an appropriation from V and the actus reus of theft. Provided D is dishonest, and intends not to return the property, she steals it.

Although, in many respects, it takes only one small step beyond *Gomez*, this is an extraordinary decision.[211] No doubt exploitation of the vulnerable warrants redress, but the law of theft is fundamentally unsuited to that task. The main problem with *Hinks* is that it turns the very rationale of property offences on its head. Theft is not a crime in thin air. It is designed to protect and reinforce property rights. That is the whole point of theft.[212] Since

---

[208] Above, § 1.2(i). Cf. Giles and Uglow, "Appropriation and Manifest Criminality in Theft" (1992) 56 *J Crim L* 179.

[209] Cf. *Wheatley and Penn* v. *The Commissioner of Police of the British Virgin Islands* [2006] UKPC 24, noted below in this section.

[210] [2001] 2 AC 241. Cf. *Hopkins and Kendrick* [1997] Crim LR 359; contra *Mazo* [1997] 2 Cr App R 518. The earlier cases are usefully discussed by Smith, *The Law of Theft* (8th ed., 1997) §§ 2–21, 2–22.

[211] A decision not, however, without defenders: see Shute, "Appropriation and the Law of Theft" [2002] *Crim LR* 445; Bogg and Stanton-Ife, "Protecting the Vulnerable: Legality, Harm and Theft" (2003) 23 *Legal Studies* 402. The law established in *Hinks* had also been advocated by Gardner, "Property and Theft" [1998] *Crim LR* 35.

[212] Cf. Simester and Sullivan, "On the Nature and Rationale of Property Offences" in Duff and Green (eds.), *Defining Crimes: Essays on the Criminal Law's Special Part* (2005) 168, § 2.

the offence has no other *raison d'être*, it is inherently dependent upon the civil law of property. If I have no property right in D's car, which is sitting on the road beside my house, I cannot complain when D drives it away. Neither am I allowed to drive it away myself without D's permission. All this is because, at civil law, the car belongs to D. Without that crucial piece of initial information, we have no way of deciding whether anything wrong has occurred, any sort of property wrong that requires the attention of the criminal law. The law of theft cannot dispense with the requirement for violation of a property right because its whole purpose is dependent upon and secondary to the allocation of rights through property law.

Hinks, alas, cuts property offences adrift from the law of property rights: the cart is now before the horse.[213] Consider the law of contract. It is standard law that if D stays silent in the face of a mistake by P which is not reflected in the terms of the transaction, P is bound to that transaction and has no remedy.[214] Adapting the facts of *Leaf* v. *International Galleries*,[215] the purchase of a painting in the mistaken belief that it was a Constable from a gallery owner, D, who knows of the mistake but says nothing is, in the law of contract, valid; and D could sue for the unpaid purchase price. But if *Hinks* is right, the price paid by the buyer is stolen by D should a jury be persuaded that D is dishonest. Such a result seems both impossible and absurd. Yet Lord Steyn contemplates just this prospect with equanimity. Perhaps surprisingly, having described this as apparently a "telling example", Lord Steyn offers no reason why it should not concern us. His Lordship simply remarks that "I am quite unpersuaded that the House [in *Gomez*] overlooked the consequences of its decision."[216] Yet *Gomez* did not decide the issue at stake in *Hinks*. The point simply did not arise in that case. What is truly telling is the subsequent case of *Wheatley and Penn* v. *The Commissioner of Police of the British Virgin Islands*,[217] in which the defendants were convicted of theft after D1 corruptly allocated government construction contracts to D2, notwithstanding that the contracts were at an appropriate price. The Privy Council, after noting that considerations of gain or loss were now irrelevant to the question of appropriation,[218] went on to emphasise that, in the present instance, "there is no dissonance between the criminal and the civil law, since the contracts made by the first appellant, contrary to his authority and with the connivance of the second appellant, were plainly voidable at the suit of the Government."[219] If *Hinks* is right, voidability is now irrelevant: that is the very point at which *Hinks* expands upon *Gomez*. Yet it is no surprise that the courts still find the point significant. *Hinks* is a very troubling decision.

Given the expansiveness of the decision, a point of limitation should be stressed. *Hinks* deals with the scenario where the act of acquiring title is charged as theft; where the acquisition of title by D is coincident with the transfer from V. From that perspective D, in the extended sense that the law allows, has appropriated property belonging to V if the

---

[213] Lord Hobhouse (dissenting) sees this when he observes that "[t]here is no law against appropriating your own property" (at 856C; see generally 854–856; also 865B).
[214] *Smith* v. *Hughes* (1871) LR 6 QB 597; *Bell* v. *Lever Brothers Ltd* [1932] AC 161.
[215] [1950] 2 KB 86.
[216] [2001] 2 AC 241, 252.
[217] [2006] UKPC 24.
[218] *Ibid.*, paras. 9–10.
[219] *Ibid.*, para. 11.

deprivation and acquisition of the property are regarded as two aspects of the one transaction. The case does not decide that once D has acquired valid title to property, any *subsequent* dishonest appropriation of that property by D, *after* absolute ownership is transferred, will amount to theft. (Such cases can only be theft if section 5(3)–(4) applies.)

One other point of qualification is made by Lord Hutton (in dissent). His Lordship observes that section 2(1)(a) of the Theft Act 1968 provides that a person's appropriation is not to be regarded as dishonest if he appropriates property in the belief that he has, in law, the right to deprive the other of it.[220] Typically, a person who acquires ownership of goods will also *believe* that she has a right to them. Where this is so, a charge of theft will fail for lack of dishonesty.[221] Hence, in the example based on *Leaf* v. *International Galleries* above, the gallery owner may say: "I know it was sharp practise, but I also knew it was permissible within the (civil) law, otherwise I would not have done it. I sought throughout to abide by the law and made all the disclosures that the law required of me in order for the transaction to be valid." In such a scenario it is arguable that, by virtue of section 2(1)(a), D may not in law be considered dishonest. Furthermore, even if D does not reason with himself in that fashion and is merely keen to make the contract at that price, he will be aware of the facts which in law make the contract valid. From the perspective of the civil law, he does not have to believe in a claim of right to the money that V pays; he simply *has* the right to the money at civil law. It is quite remarkable that persons who unreflectingly enter valid contracts may find themselves facing a charge of theft, a matter with clear implications for the fair notice protection guaranteed by Article 7 of the ECHR.

(iii) Theft by keeping or omission

The mere decision to steal is not sufficient for theft.[222] There must be conduct as well, amounting to an appropriation. We have noted, however, that this is not a very stringent restriction: picking a tin of beans off the shelves of a supermarket is theft if D does so with intent to steal. Thus, although a decision to thieve is not enough, some very preliminary conduct is.

Moreover, the conduct may be an omission, as distinct from a fresh positive act, and it is sufficient for theft that D keeps property lawfully obtained: indeed, section 3(1) expressly states that a person may steal something by "keeping . . . it as owner." In the New Zealand case of *Subritzky*,[223] failing to return a toy taken innocently by D's child was held to be theft by conversion and, it is submitted, would be theft by appropriation also. Likewise borrowing a thing, and then keeping it having decided not to return it, may amount to theft—on the basis of the keeping rather than the borrowing.

---

[220] Below, § 13.8(i).

[221] As it happens, Lord Hutton's dissent goes further: it advocates a general rule that there can never be a finding of dishonesty where the transfer of ownership is fully valid. But such a rule was implicitly rejected by the majority decision. The exploitative conduct by Karen Hinks was dishonest: everyone, and most importantly the jury, agreed on this. Nonetheless, on the particular facts of a different case, there may be room to invoke s. 2(1)(a).

[222] Cf. *Eddy* v. *Niman* (1981) 73 Cr App R 237; though the decision must now be read in light of *Gomez* [1993] AC 442 (above, § 13.6(ii)(a)).

[223] [1990] 2 NZLR 717. Similar facts occurred in the English case of *Walters* v. *Lunt* [1951] 2 All ER 645, a decision based on the old law of larceny. See also *Thomas* (1953) 37 Cr App R 169.

The possibility of theft by keeping must, however, be approached with some caution. Generally, there is no liability for omissions in the criminal law and it seems that theft by keeping may be subject to special restrictions. In *Broom* v. *Crowther*,[224] D purchased a stolen theodolite. Subsequently, he discovered that the device was stolen. D kept the theodolite for a further week until it was seized by the police. On appeal, D claimed that, after learning the truth of the matter, he had merely left the theodolite sitting in his bedroom while he pondered what to do; and that this was not an appropriation within the terms of the Theft Act 1968. The Divisional Court quashed his conviction for theft.

Usually, such a defendant may escape conviction by denying mens rea, since it will be difficult to prove dishonesty is these circumstances. It seems, however, that not all omissions to return something ("keepings") will count as appropriations. The qualifications are twofold. First, section 3(1) states that a person may steal something by "keeping . . . it *as owner.*" This suggests, as *Broom* v. *Crowther* seems to emphasise, that a mere "keeping" which does not manifest any decision to treat the property as D's own will not count as an appropriation. The keeping must amount, in effect, to a conversion: D's conduct must amount to a *usurpation* or denial of O's rights. This may depend upon the intention with which D acts: thus merely leaving the item in a drawer for safekeeping, as opposed to keeping the thing for oneself, is not a conversion[225] and, if *Broom* v. *Crowther* is right, neither is it an appropriation for the purposes of theft.

Secondly, the essence of keepings is that they are omissions. As we saw in Chapter 4, the law is rightly reluctant to impose criminal liability for mere omissions, unless the circumstances give rise to a specific duty obligating D to act. It is submitted that this general principle of the common law applies also to theft. In other words, an omission cannot be an appropriation unless it is in contravention of D's duty to return the goods to V. Suppose the following three cases:

(1) D1 has hired a car from V. The period of hire has not expired. D1 decides to keep the car, which he leaves sitting on the driveway.

(2) D2 has hired a car from V. The period of hire has not expired. D1 decides to sell the car, which he then drives to Ireland, intending to trade it in there for a new vehicle.[226]

(3) D3 has hired a car from V. The period of hire has since expired. D1 decides to keep the car, which he leaves parked on his driveway.

Case (2) is straightforwardly one of theft: D appropriates the car by his positive act of driving it to Ireland. Equally, however, it is submitted that case (1) is not theft. Since the bailment has not expired, D is under no duty to do return the car, and his omission to do so should not be regarded as an actus reus of theft.

Case (3) is more complex. D's omission to return the car is in breach of the duty he owes to V, so prima facie is a "keeping" for the purposes of section 3(1). It is necessary, therefore, also to determine whether he has kept the car "as owner", or whether the *Broom* v. *Crowther* exception is available. In our view, this is a case of theft.

---

[224] (1984) 148 JP 592. The case is also notable on a point concerning bona fide purchasers: below, § 13.6(v).
[225] Cf. *Police* v. *Moodley* [1974] 1 NZLR 644.
[226] *Morgan* [1991] RTR 365.

(iv) Multiple and continuing appropriations

Consider the following scenario, which is based on an example discussed in § 13.4(v):

> David finds a wallet in a busy street, and picks it up. He looks in the wallet for evidence of the owner's identity and finds none. The wallet contains no money. David puts the wallet in his pocket, concluding that it is lost rather than abandoned but that the true owner cannot be found. He then takes the wallet home and, on looking more carefully inside, finds the owner's name and address. Deciding to keep the wallet anyway because of its attractive appearance, he puts the wallet in a drawer. A month later, he takes the wallet out of the drawer and starts to use it.

How many times does David appropriate the wallet? When does he steal it? The key to the answer is section 3(1), which states that *any* assumption of the rights of an owner is an appropriation, "and this includes, where he has come by the property (innocently or not) *without stealing it*, any later assumption of a right to it by keeping or dealing with it as owner." The specific inclusion of later appropriations, subject to the qualification "without stealing it", means that David appropriates the wallet *every* time he does anything with it, *until* he steals it. Once there is a moment in time when all the elements of theft are present, the wallet is stolen and he does not keep restealing it thereafter.[227] Let us conclude, in the above example, that David is not dishonest and lacks the mens rea for theft until he gets home and discovers the owner's name.[228] It follows that David appropriates the wallet (*inter alia*) when he picks it up, when he looks through it, when he puts it in his pocket, when he carries it with him, and when he puts it in the drawer. But not when he starts to use it a month later: by then, it is already stolen.

Sometimes the location or timing of a theft matters. In *Atakpu and Abrahams*,[229] the defendants used false documents to hire cars in Germany and Belgium. They drove the cars to England, intending to sell them, but were arrested by customs officials on arrival at Dover. The convictions for conspiracy to steal the vehicles were quashed, on the ground that the thefts were not committed in England and therefore English courts lacked jurisdiction. On the authority of *Gomez*,[230] the cars were first appropriated in Germany and Belgium. Given that the defendants had the mens rea for theft at that time, the cars were therefore already stolen before being brought into this country.[231]

---

[227] Williams, "Appropriation: A Single or Continuous Act?" [1978] *Crim LR* 69, 69: "A man steals a watch, and two weeks later sells it. In common sense and ordinary language he is not guilty of a second theft when he sells it. Otherwise it would be possible, in theory, to convict a thief of theft of a silver teapot every time he uses it to make the tea."

[228] *Per* s. 2(1)(c): below, § 13.8(iii).

[229] [1994] QB 69. See also *Morgan* [1991] RTR 365, where D took a leased car to Ireland and traded it in for a new car; he was convicted of theft in England.

[230] Above, § 13.6(ii)(a). If *Gomez* had adopted the analysis in *Morris*, the problem would not have arisen since the first theftuous (in the sense of unauthorised) appropriation would have been when the cars were offered for sale in England.

[231] Contrast *Ashcroft* [2003] EWCA Crim 2365, where D, a haulier, was convicted of conspiring to steal goods in England which were first loaded onto his lorries in Scotland before being diverted in England. The Court of Appeal—it is submitted wrongly—dismissed D's claim that the theft occurred in Scotland, describing that analysis (paras. 43, 45) as "some way removed from reality and we do not believe that *Gomez* was ever intended to apply to

Hence, there could be no conspiracy to steal them in England.[232] As Ward J put it:[233]

> "Endeavouring to summarise it would seem that (1) theft can occur in an instant by a single appropriation but it can also involve a course of dealing with property lasting longer and involving several appropriations before the transaction is complete; (2) theft is a finite act—it has a beginning and it has an end; (3) at what point the transaction is complete is a matter for the jury to decide upon the facts of each case; (4) though there may be several appropriations in the course of a single theft or several appropriations of different goods each constituting a separate theft as in *Reg. v. Skipp* [1975] Crim LR 114, no case suggests that there can be successive thefts of the same property. . . ."

Similarly, D can be convicted of robbery only if the use or threat of force occurs immediately before or at the time of the theft.[234] Thus if D steals goods from a supermarket, and after leaving the shop threatens the driver of the taxi carrying him, D commits no robbery since the theft is already complete.

It seems that an appropriation can also be a *continuing* act,[235] as opposed to one which is always completed instantaneously. Suppose the following variation:

> D picks goods off the shelf at a supermarket and puts them inside her jacket, intending to leave without paying for them. On the authority of *Gomez*, she has already stolen the goods. While approaching the cashier, however, she is accosted by the store's security guard. D strikes the guard violently, and runs from the store with the goods.

Does D commit robbery? The common-sense answer must be yes – even though, if the goods are already stolen, it is hard to see how that answer can be justified in law. The answer is justified by holding that D's appropriation of the goods was a single continuing act, lasting (say) for the period during which she puts the goods in his jacket and carries them out of the supermarket. While such an analysis sits somewhat uneasily with *Gomez*,[236] a number of decisions appear to recognise the possibility.[237] (An alternative approach, in the specific context of robbery, might be to construe liberally the requirement in section 8(1) that the force be used "at the time of" the stealing; thereby embracing force used in the proximate aftermath of D's theftuous act.[238])

(v) Bona fide purchasers

The *nemo dat* rule means that if R steals a book from O, O retains ownership of the book even when R then sells the book to D, a purchaser who acts in good faith. Prima facie, if D

---

the sort of situation that obtains in this case. . . . In our judgment there never was in any ordinary sense of the word an 'appropriation' of the stolen goods until the conspirators removed them from the containers." But it is an ineluctable implication of *Gomez* that the goods were first appropriated in Scotland.

[232] For criticism of the jurisdictional aspects of *Atakpu* see Sullivan and Warbrick, "Territoriality, Theft and *Atakpu*" [1994] *Crim LR* 650, who argue that since the Theft Act 1968 does not have extra-territorial effect, the defendants' actions in Germany and Belgium were not appropriations within the Act. See also below, § 13.9.

[233] [1994] QB 69, 79.

[234] Theft Act 1968, s. 8(1). See below, § 14.2(iii).

[235] Cf. *Fagan* v. *Metropolitan Police Commissioner* [1969] 1 QB 438; above, § 4.1(i)(b) (Case 4).

[236] Cf. *Atakpu and Abraham* [1994] QB 69, 80; but contrast *Lockley* [1995] Crim LR 656.

were then to discover that the book was stolen, she would herself become liable to be convicted for theft. This possibility is avoided by section 3(2), which provides:

> Where property or a right or interest in property is or purports to be transferred for value to a person acting in good faith, no later assumption by him of rights which he believed himself to be acquiring shall, by reason of any defect in the transferor's title, amount to theft of the property.

In *Wheeler*,[239] a dealer purchased a variety of military antiques. He then sold one of the items, a medal. Subsequently, before delivering the medal and receiving payment, he discovered that the medal was stolen. His conviction was quashed: the application of section 3(2) meant that D committed no theft by completing the transaction. Neither was D guilty of handling.[240] (He might, however, become liable for obtaining the proceeds of the sale by deception, if the purchaser had been induced to make payment by D's representation, implied or express, that D was their owner.[241])

It appears that a purchaser will not be regarded as "in good faith" for the purposes of section 3(2) if she suspects that the goods are stolen. It is not necessary for her to be convinced of the matter. In *Broom* v. *Crowther*,[242] D purchased a theodolite from R for £5. The instrument was worth about £200. After later discovering that it was in fact stolen, D kept the theodolite for a further week until it was seized by the police. In convicting him for theft, the magistrates ruled that the defence in section 3(2) was unavailable, since D had not acted in good faith: at the time when he made the purchase, D had suspected the device was stolen and had accepted R's denial without pursuing the matter because the bargain was so advantageous.

(vi) Bank accounts

Suppose D, a company director of V Ltd., forges a cheque on V's account with bank B. Does D commit theft? The answer, it appears, is yes. V's account with B is a chose in action that can be stolen[243] and, according to the Privy Council in *Chan Man-sin*,[244] V appropriates that account when he assumes V's right, as owner, to draw cheques on the account.

It must be said that this reasoning is debatable. Prima facie, D obtained by deception; he stole nothing—at least, nothing from V.[245] In particular, although the bank account was

---

[237] e.g. *Bowden* [2002] EWCA Crim 1279; *Donaghy* v. *Marshall* [1981] Crim LR 644; *Hale* (1978) 68 Cr App R 415; *Pitham and Hehl* (1977) 65 Cr App R 45, 49 (while denying it in the instant case). See Williams, "Appropriation: A Single or Continuous Act?" [1973] *Crim LR* 69.

[238] Cf. *Hale* (1978) 68 Cr App R 415; below, 14.2(iii).

[239] (1991) 92 Cr App R 279.

[240] *Bloxham* [1983] 1 AC 109.

[241] Surprisingly, the Court also quashed D's conviction for obtaining by deception, apparently reasoning that there was no deception: because the sale was in market overt, D's implied representation that the buyer would get good title to the medal was true. But D had *expressly* stated that the medal was not stolen, which was a deception.

[242] (1984) 148 JP 592. See Spencer, "Handling, Theft and the *Mala Fide* Purchaser" [1985] *Crim LR* 92; Williams, "Handling, Theft and the Purchaser who takes a Chance" [1985] *Crim LR* 432; Spencer, "Handling and Taking Risks—A Reply to Professor Williams" [1985] *Crim LR* 440. The case is discussed earlier, in § 13.6(ii)(d), in respect of a different point taken by D in his successful appeal.

[243] Above, § 13.3(i)(c).

clearly property belonging to V, it is arguable that nothing done by D affected or was even relevant to that account. The forged cheque was a nullity, nothing more.[246] Although D *pretended* to deal with V's bank account, in law he no more dealt with V's chose in action against B than he dealt with any of the accounts held by anyone else at the bank. The real wrong was obtaining by deception the *proceeds* of the cheque[247]—but the victim of that crime was bank B, not V. No property right of V's was harmed by D. If that is right, why should V be treated as the victim of a theft?

On the other hand, and in defence of the current law, it may be argued that by pretending to deal with V's bank account, D "assumed" the right of an owner over the account and therefore appropriated it within the meaning of section 3(1).[248] Moreover, V *will* normally suffer the disadvantage of a wrongful debit against its account, which will remain in place, and cause an effective loss to V, until the forgery is discovered (if ever). So, although the law on this point is problematic, it is not without justification.

The analysis is different where the cheque is not a nullity. *Chan Man-sin* may be contrasted with the case of *Kohn*,[249] where D had authority to draw cheques.[250] He abused that authority by withdrawing money for personal gain. In that case, the cheques were valid and not mere forgeries, so that the company's bank account was rightfully debited. Thus D was properly convicted of theft, from the company, by appropriating its bank account.

Another difficult case occurs where D induces V to make a bank transfer from V's account to D's. In that case, D does not normally appropriate—assume any right over—V's account, since it is V who instructs her bank to make the transfer.[251] Moreover, unlike ordinary items of property (as will be explained in § 15.1(ii)) neither does D steal the account balance when her own account is credited; since choses in action, including bank balances, are not as such *transferred*. Rather, V's chose in action is destroyed and a new one is created. The new chose in action belongs from the outset to D and is not the same one that V held, so it is not received from V. Prior to 1997, as we shall see, such cases had to be charged as obtaining a money transfer by deception contrary to section 15A of the Theft Act 1968. They should now be charged as fraud under section 1 of the Fraud Act 2006, an offence which merely requires D to make a false pretence with intent to make an economic

---

[244] *Chan Man-sin* v. *A-G of Hong Kong* [1988] 1 All ER 1. The same analysis appears in *Burke* [2000] Crim LR 413 (CA). See also below, § 13.7(ii)(a).

[245] Unless, perhaps, he stole the paper on which the cheque was written. Given that D obtained by deception—pursuant, therefore, to a voidable transfer—the decision in *Gomez* (above, § 13.6(ii)(a)) means that he may also have stolen whatever he obtained in return for the forged cheque.

[246] *Tai Hing Cotton Mill Ltd* v. *Liu Chong Hing Bank Ltd* [1986] AC 80 (PC).

[247] This proposition is subject to further complication where the "proceeds" take the form of a money transfer (cf. *Preddy* [1996] AC 815, since remedied by s. 15A of the Theft Act 1968). See below, § 15.1(ii)(b).

[248] That was also the conclusion of the Court of Appeal in *Re Osman* [1990] 1 WLR 277, 294–5, where D, a company chairman, sent a telex instructing the company's bank to transfer money from the company's account. The Court ruled that purporting to deal with the bank account qua owner was, in itself, an appropriation regardless of the effect on the account itself and even if the account was never debited. For approving comment, see [1988] Crim LR 611.

[249] (1979) 69 Cr App R 395; discussed above, § 13.3(i)(c).

[250] To similar effect is *Hilton* [1997] 2 Cr App R 445, where D controlled a charity's bank account and had authority to instruct the bank to make transfers.

[251] *Briggs* [2004] EWCA Crim 3662; criticised in Heaton, "Cheques and Balances" [2005] *Crim LR* 747. Both Heaton and Ormerod (commenting on *Briggs* in [2004] Crim LR 495) suggest that D can still be held to appropriate

gain or to inflict an economic loss; such gains or losses are not confined to acquisitions or losses of property.

§ 13.7 Intention permanently to deprive

(i) The core definition

Dishonest borrowing is not theft, no matter how much inconvenience it causes the owner. If D, a law student, dishonestly takes a book from the law library by concealing it in his bag, he commits theft if he intends not to return the book, but not if he means to keep the book only until the end of term.[252] It is not theft even if D realises there is a chance he will be unable to return the book (e.g. because he has a habit of losing books in his possession).[253] To fulfil the requirements of theft, D must have the *intention* permanently to deprive V of her property. This requirement, stated in section 1(1), is not defined in the Theft Act 1968, although there are some complex supplementary provisions in section 6 (see § 13.7(ii)). For the most part, however, the core meaning of "intention permanently to deprive" has presented few problems. Generally, it is sufficient that D has an intention indefinitely to exclude V from exercising her right to the property.

(a) Dishonest borrowing

Some writers have questioned the rule that borrowing is not theft,[254] and its wisdom is certainly arguable. The owner may well have a civil action against D for use and enjoyment, and in many cases the very point of her ownership is to monopolise the use and enjoyment of which she is deprived by D. Suppose that O, a law student, owns a textbook on criminal law. D dishonestly takes the book, intending to keep it until the criminal law exam has been sat by both D and O. As things stand, D has not stolen the book.[255] Yet O has been frustrated in the very reason she bought the book. She is likely to have to buy another copy in the meantime. Provided D is dishonest, there is a good case for treating such behaviour as criminal.

Additionally, criminalisation of dishonest borrowing may assist in resolving an evidential difficulty. Sometimes where D claims that he intended to return the thing "borrowed" (e.g. where D takes a book from the library), it may be hard to prove that he intended to keep the thing permanently.

Against these arguments, it may be thought harsh to equate a mere borrowing with theft. Although the inconvenience to O may sometimes be comparable, as a *general* proposition the wrong of permanently taking O's property is far more substantial than the wrong of temporarily interfering with her use and enjoyment. In practice, evidential difficulties with

---

V's account because, they argue, D causes V to act. But, although D may use deception to persuade V into making the transfer, the deception is not normally (and was not in *Briggs*) directed at the transfer itself. V knows exactly what she is doing in issuing the instruction, even if she misapprehends other aspects of her agreement with D, and even if that misapprehension is relevant to her decision to issue it. Hence, so far as the instruction to make the transfer is concerned, V is an intervening agent who breaks any causal chain linking D to V's account.

[252] Cf. *Neal* v. *Gribble* [1978] RTR 409.

the present law have not been overwhelming, and are surely insufficient to justify a radical change in the substantive law. Moreover, enacting an offence of dishonest borrowing would place even greater pressure on the issue of dishonesty, itself (as we shall see) a judgement-call by the jury. To do so would leave the law of theft both extraordinarily wide and extremely vague, thereby undermining the principle of fair warning and the rule of law.

While not enacting a general offence, the 1968 Act does criminalise specific forms of borrowing. Certain cases are treated as theft by virtue of section 6, which is considered in § 13.7(ii) below. There are also some specific offences. Section 12 creates an offence of taking a motor vehicle or other conveyance without authority; section 12A enacts a related offence of aggravated vehicle-taking; while section 11 criminalises the removal (with or without an intention permanently to deprive) of items from public buildings.

(b) Deprivation

The essence of theft is deprivation, not gain. Thus, what must be intended is that the owner be deprived (permanently), not that any benefit endure to D or anyone else. Thus it is theft for D to appropriate O's goods intending to destroy them,[256] to hide them so that they are never found,[257] or to give them away. The point, which was also true under the pre-Act law of larceny,[258] is now made explicit in section 1(2) of the 1968 Act:

> It is immaterial whether the appropriation is made with a view to gain, or is made for the thief's own benefit.

(c) Change of mind

If D steals something, intending to keep it, then later changes his mind and decides to return the thing, this is theft.[259] It is too late. At the time the actus reus occurs, D has the mens rea for theft.

(d) An ulterior intention

The intent to deprive is an ulterior intention,[260] accompanying the actus reus rather than directed toward the actus reus itself. Thus the requirement is not merely that D intend the appropriation *per se*, but that the act of appropriation be done with the *further* intent that the owner be deprived permanently, either by that act or by some other act.

The importance of this point is that there is no requirement that D should intend to deprive V by *that very* act of appropriation. As was noted in § 13.6, it is sufficient that D appropriates the goods while intending that the owner should be deprived, even if the deprivation will be accomplished only by some later act of D's.[261] Suppose, for example, that D changes the labels on two products (say, product A and product B) in a supermarket,

---

[253] Cf. *Crump* (1825) 1 C & P 658, 171 ER 1357. This would be a case of recklessness whether the owner is deprived, rather than of intention: above, §§ 5.1(iii), 5.2.

[254] Williams, "Temporary Appropriation should be Theft" [1981] *Crim LR* 129; Bein, "The Theft of Use and the Element of 'Intent to Deprive Permanently' in Larceny" (1968) 3 *Israel LR* 368.

[255] Neither does s. 6(1) apply: below, § 13.7(ii)(b).

[256] *Welsh* [1974] RTR 478 (D, a motorist stopped on suspicion of drink-driving, destroyed a urine sample that he had given for analysis); cf. *Cabbage* (1815) R & R 292, 168 ER 809 (D backed a horse down a mineshaft in order to destroy evidence of the horse's theft).

intending to buy the more expensive item, product A, at the lower price of product B. He steals product A as soon as he touches it, even though this is not the act of appropriation by which the owner will be deprived.

(e) Paying for or returning similar goods

In *Velumyl*,[262] D dishonestly borrowed £1,050 from his employer's safe, without authority and in breach of company rules. D apparently intended to repay the amount borrowed. He was nonetheless convicted of theft. Although D intended to return an equivalent sum of moneys, these would not be the identical notes and coins that he had taken, merely substitute moneys to the same value. Hence, the Court concluded, D intended to deprive V permanently of the particular notes and coins that he appropriated.

Similarly, if D were to take a bag of sugar from V's kitchen, intending to buy another bag and replace it, D would still intend to deprive V permanently of the particular bag taken. *A fortiori*, a case where D intends to give V some money to pay for the sugar.[263] (Of course, an issue may arise in such cases whether D has acted dishonestly.)

(f) Conditional intention

In *Easom*,[264] D picked up a handbag in a cinema. He searched through the handbag in order to ascertain its contents, then put the handbag back having decided that none of the contents were worth stealing. D was charged with theft of "one handbag, one purse, one notebook, a quantity of tissues, a quantity of cosmetics and one pen," and at first instance was convicted. However, the Court of Appeal quashed his conviction, ruling that:[265]

> "In every case of theft the appropriation must be accompanied by the intention of permanently depriving the owner of his property. What may be loosely described as a 'conditional' appropriation will not do. If the appropriator has it in mind merely to deprive the owner of such of his property as, on examination, proves worth taking and then, finding that the booty is valueless to the appropriator, leaves it ready to hand to be repossessed by the owner, the appropriator has not stolen. If a dishonest postal sorter picks up a pile of letters, intending to steal any which are registered, but, on finding that none of them are, replaces them, he has stolen nothing."

The decision is probably right, but only in terms of the precise charge that was brought. D certainly appropriated the purse, notebook, tissues, etc., inside the handbag. However, at no time did D intend to deprive the owner of such things. He was looking for something else.

Suppose, however, that D had been charged with stealing "the contents" of the handbag. In that case, D should have been convicted.[266] Again, he certainly appropriated the contents.[267] Thus the actus reus element of theft is satisfied. This time, however, the mens

---

[257] Cf. *Wynn* (1848) 1 Den 365, 169 ER 283 (D, a postal worker, flushed letters down a lavatory in order to conceal the fact that he had sorted them incorrectly).

[258] Turner, "Larceny and Lucrum" (1941) 4 *Toronto LJ* 296.

[259] Cf. *Easom* [1971] 2 QB 315, 320.

[260] Above, § 5.1(vii).

[261] *Morris* [1984] AC 320.

[262] [1989] Crim LR 299. Cf. *McCall* (1971) 55 Cr App R 175; *Duru* [1973] 3 All ER 715; *Williams* [1953] 1 All ER 1068, 1070.

[263] Cf. Theft Act 1968, s. 2(2).

rea requirement is also satisfied—by a conditional intention.[268] Not yet knowing what they were, D intended to steal any of "the contents" of the handbag should they prove desirable. Thus, it is submitted, he appropriated the contents with intent (conditionally) to deprive the owner of them. Since conditional intention is treated in law as intention,[269] that looks like theft. The fact that he subsequently returned the bag and its contents is irrelevant. They were already stolen.[270]

At the level of policy, there seems little merit in acquitting the defendant. Pre-*Gomez*, it may have been appropriate to treat such cases either as mere preparatory action or as an attempted theft, but that possibility is now gone. D plans to steal the contents, subject only to a condition outside his control (i.e. that they are valuable); he executes the plan; he appropriates the contents. The actus reus of theft has already occurred. Certainly, D's conduct can no longer be regarded as merely preparatory. Given his moral culpability, D ought to be convicted of theft.

A different type of case is where D intends to steal valuable contents, if any, from a handbag which he has no intent to take but puts the handbag back because it is empty. That is a case of attempted theft;[271] because there is no actus reus. Although, in such a case, D has a (conditional) intent to steal the contents, he does not appropriate them since they do not exist.

There is a third type of case. Consider the following variation:

> D takes V's handbag, intending to keep the diamond ring that (he thinks) is in the bag. Later, he discovers that the handbag contains no ring, merely some credit cards (for which D has no use). He returns the bag with the credit cards inside.

D does not steal the handbag, since he has no intention to keep the bag itself. He does not steal a ring, since there is none; though he could now be charged with attempted theft of the ring.[272] Neither does he steal the credit cards *per se*, since he has no intention to deprive the owner of them. Moreover, this is not a case of conditional intention to steal anything valuable. Rather, it involves a specific, frustrated, intention to steal a diamond ring. Should D be convicted of theft of "the contents" of the handbag, or only of attempted theft of the ring?

As the law stands, it appears that D can be convicted of theft of the contents.[273] This description may seem rather vague, but it should be recalled that the Theft Act criminalises theft of any "property belonging to another". Even though it matters to D, from the point of

---

[264] [1971] 2 QB 315.

[265] *Ibid.*, 319.

[266] *Re A-G's References (Nos. 1 and 2 of 1979)* [1980] QB 180.

[267] Note that the terminology of a "conditional appropriation", coined in the quotation from *Easom* in the text, must be regarded as outmoded in the wake of *Gomez* (above, § 13.6(ii)(a)). If even an authorised touching of goods is now regarded as an appropriation, D's conduct in *Easom* is surely also an appropriation.

[268] A fine distinction exists between the case of a defendant who investigates the contents with a view to later deciding whether to steal (i.e. one who has not yet made any decision to steal) and that of one who has decided to steal the contents should they prove upon investigation to be valuable. Arguably, the close psychological relationship between decisions and intentions suggests that in the former case (and perhaps in *Easom* itself) the defendant has not yet formed an intention to steal. provided D's conduct is more than preparatory. However, such a fine distinction arguably is out of place here, since the condition upon which the decision depends is merely a matter of circumstances external to the defendant. It certainly would not operate to exculpate the postal sorter in the example cited by the Court.

view of the law the difference between a ring and credit cards is an immaterial variation.[274] D had the actus reus for theft of the cards and the mens rea for theft of a ring. Both are forms of property, which is all the Act requires.

(ii) Section 6: extensions and special cases

Often, a thief has no particular agenda regarding the fate of the property he steals. If D means to pawn stolen goods, or to use them before discarding them, he may not intend that the original owner be permanently deprived. He may be indifferent to their ultimate destiny. While many of these cases can be treated as intention on the basis that it is virtually certain the owner will be deprived permanently,[275] sometimes it may be quite likely that the owner will recover the property. In order to make it explicit that the Act extends to such cases, Parliament supplemented the work of the Criminal Law Revision Committee by enacting section 6:[276]

> (1) A person appropriating property belonging to another without meaning the other permanently to lose the thing itself is nevertheless to be regarded as having the intention of permanently depriving the other of it if his intention is to treat the thing as his own to dispose of regardless of the other's rights; and a borrowing or lending of it may amount to so treating it if, but only if, the borrowing or lending is for a period and in circumstances making it equivalent to an outright taking or disposal.
>
> (2) Without prejudice to the generality of subsection (1) above, where a person, having possession or control (lawfully or not) of property belonging to another, parts with the property under a condition as to its return which he may not be able to perform, this (if done for purposes of his own and without the other's authority) amounts to treating the property as his own to dispose of regardless of the other's rights.

Poor drafting precludes straightforward interpretation of this section. The core idea in section 6(1) is that it is sufficient for D to intend to treat the property as his own to dispose of regardless of the owner's rights. Yet what this involves remains unexplained, apart from two special cases expressly mentioned in the section.

(a) Intention to dispose

It seems that the most important aspect of "the intention to treat something as his own to dispose of regardless of the other's rights" is the element of disposal.[277] Since it is clear that merely temporary borrowing is not meant to be covered by the section, "treating something as one's own" cannot be sufficient—it is the "to dispose of" that invokes section 6. This seems apt to cover situations where D, in a bout of anti-social behaviour, takes V's property and throws it away, not caring whether the property is ever retrieved. It also applies to cases where D takes V's property and, pretending it is D's own, then sells it back to V.[278]

The courts have held that section 6(1) applies to at least two other, more controversial,

---

[269] Above, § 5.1(viii). See Campbell, "Conditional Intention" (1982) 2 *LS* 77.

[270] Cf. above, § 13.6(i)(b).

[271] Cf. *Smith and Smith* [1986] Crim LR 166.

[272] Contrast *Husseyn* (1978) 67 Cr App R 131n, a case decided before the law on impossible attempts was altered by the Criminal Attempts Act 1981 (see above, § 9.3(iii)(d), 9.4(iii)).

situations. In *DPP* v. *Lavender*,[279] D dishonestly removed two doors from a house and hung them in another house. Both houses were owned by the council. The Divisional Court ruled that D had committed theft. Although the council had not in fact been deprived of the doors, D had nonetheless "disposed" of them within the meaning of section 6(1). With respect, this result seems odd. There was no disposal of the doors—they were not thrown out, destroyed, or sold.[280] They were merely moved, and there was no suggestion by his conduct that D intended to treat them as his own, since they continued to be affixed to council property.

Another difficult case is *Chan Man-sin*,[281] discussed earlier, in which D dishonestly drew cheques on his employer's bank account. The Privy Council ruled that D had dealt with the company's property (i.e. its chose in action against the bank) as if it were his to dispose of without regard to the company's rights. But if, as we saw in § 13.6(vi), unauthorised drawings of this sort are a nullity, then arguably D did not dispose of the account at all. At law, nothing done by D in any way affected the relationship between the company and the bank. D merely tricked the bank into crediting D's own account (and purporting to debit V's account). The Privy Council appears to have equated "purporting or pretending to dispose of the thing as one's own" with "disposing of the thing as one's own." The decision is debatable. Nonetheless, as things stand, this is the law: the intent to make an apparent or pretended disposal is sufficient for section 6(1).

Arguably, section 6(1) also covers situations of the sort envisaged by J.C. Smith, where D holds a chattel for ransom, saying, for example, "I will return the picture when E (who is imprisoned) is given a free pardon."[282] However, such cases would seem to be theft independent of section 6, since D has a conditional intention to deprive permanently.[283]

(b) Borrowing or lending

When is a borrowing or lending more than temporary? Under section 6(1), when it is "equivalent to an outright taking or disposal." It may be thought that the phrase "equivalent to an outright taking or disposal" is itself opaque, for so it is. Seemingly, the test is satisfied only when the thing taken is intended to be returned either (a) in completely altered form (e.g. when D takes a horse intending to kill it and return the carcass[284]); or (b) after its "virtue", or value, has been entirely exhausted, so that it is now useless. Authority for the latter is *Lloyd*.[285] D, a film projectionist, borrowed films and passed them to E, who made and sold pirate copies of the films. The Court of Appeal ruled this was not theft:[286]

---

[273] Cf. *Re A-G's References (Nos. 1 and 2 of 1979)* [1980] QB 180.
[274] See above, § 5.7.
[275] Above, § 5.1(iv).
[276] See Spencer, "The Metamorphosis of Section 6 of the Theft Act" [1977] *Crim LR* 653.
[277] See Smith, *Property Offences* (1994) § 6–28.
[278] Cf. *Hall* (1849) 1 Den 381, 169 ER 291.
[279] [1994] Crim LR 297. Cf. *Cahill* [1993] Crim LR 141.
[280] For discussion, see Smith, *Property Offences* (1994) §§ 6–33, 6–34.
[281] [1988] 1 All ER 1; also *Burke* [2000] Crim LR 413; *Re Osman* [1990] 1 WLR 277, 294–5. See above, §§ 13.3(i)(c), 13.6(vi).
[282] *The Law of Theft* (8th ed., 1997) § 2–133.
[283] Cf. the New Zealand case of *Hare* (1910) 29 NZLR 641. D found a letter containing important business

"Borrowing is *ex hypothesi* not something which is done with intention permanently to deprive. This half of the subsection, we believe, is intended to make it clear that a mere borrowing is never enough to constitute the necessary guilty mind unless the intention is to return the 'thing' in such a changed state that it can truly be said that all its goodness or virtue is gone."

By way of example, the Court cited *Beecham*,[287] where D stole railway tickets, intending to return them only after they had been used to complete a journey; and the trial judge's example in which a battery is stolen, to be returned only when its power is exhausted. A modern illustration is *DPP v. J*,[288] in which the defendants forcibly took V's headphones, snapped them, and returned them to V. On appeal, it was held that the magistrates had been wrong to accept a submission of no case to answer: a person who took something and dealt with it for the purpose of rendering it useless demonstrated the intention of treating that article as his own to dispose of.

Contrast the example with which we began § 13.7(i)(a):

O, a law student, owns a textbook on criminal law. D dishonestly takes the book, intending to keep it until the criminal law exam has been sat by both D and O.

This is not theft, even though the case has many similarities with that of the railway ticket. So far as O is concerned, the purpose of her ownership has been frustrated entirely. However, the book itself has not been consumed in any way—it is still a book, with the same intrinsic nature that it had before being "borrowed" by D. Independent of O's particular needs, the book has retained its "goodness and virtue".

(c) Parting with property under a condition as to its return

If D dishonestly takes goods and pawns or pledges them, intending to redeem and return the goods but aware there is a risk he may be unable to do so, the operation of section 6(2) means that he commits theft. It is difficult to see why pledging goods should not count as a disposition within the scope of section 6(1),[289] in which case section 6(2) is unnecessary.

§ 13.8 Dishonesty

In addition to the other elements required for theft, D must appropriate the property *dishonestly*. Unfortunately, the 1968 Act gives no definition of dishonesty. This is not to say that the Act is silent on the matter. According to section 2:

(1) A person's appropriation of property belonging to another is not to be regarded as dishonest–
(a) if he appropriates the property in the belief that he has in law the right to deprive the other of it, on behalf of himself or of a third person; or
(b) if he appropriates the property in the belief that he would have the other's consent if the other knew of the appropriation and the circumstances of it; or

---

information. He wrote to the sender demanding money for its return, and threatening to send copies to interested persons if the money was not paid. D was convicted of theft.

[284] Cf. *Cabbage* (1815) Russ & Ry 292, 168 ER 809. For other examples, see *Morfit* (1816) Russ & Ry 307, 168 ER 817; *Richards* (1844) Car & Kir 532, 174 ER 925.

(c) (except where the property came to him as trustee or personal representative) if he appropriates the property in the belief that the person to whom the property belongs cannot be discovered by taking reasonable steps.

(2) A person's appropriation of property belonging to another may be dishonest notwithstanding that he is willing to pay for the property.

The operation of these provisions is, however, purely negative. If D falls within section 2(1), he is not dishonest. But if he falls outside the section, it does not follow that he *is* dishonest. The question whether he is dishonest must then be asked and answered independently. Similarly, section 2(2) merely excludes one defence from operating as a matter of law. If D was willing to pay for the property, he may or may not be dishonest—that question must be asked, and answered, separately—when account may be taken of the fact that she was willing to pay.

In deciding the issue of dishonesty, therefore, it is necessary to begin with section 2(1). It is only if those provisions do not apply that we must investigate the issue more generally.

(i) Belief that he has the right to deprive: section 2(1)(a)

Section 2(1)(a) codifies the old common law defence of colour of right: D's belief that he is legally entitled to act as he does forecloses any finding of dishonesty. The defence means that D does not commit theft if she honestly believes her appropriation of the thing is *legally* entitled, even where her belief is based on ignorance, mistake of fact, or even mistake of law.[290] Examples of colour of right defences abound in the common law. In *Bernhard*,[291] for example, a woman who blackmailed her former lover thought she had a right to the money claimed; she was acquitted of demanding money with menaces. Similarly, in *Skivington*,[292] D held up a wages clerk and demanded his wife's wages: though this was an assault, it was held there was no theft and therefore no robbery, since he believed he had a lawful claim.

Skivington demonstrates that since colour of right is a defence to theft, it is also a defence to other crimes in which theft or an intent to steal is an ingredient, such as robbery and burglary. In such cases, if D believes he is entitled to the money, the charge fails for lack of the theftuous element; it is irrelevant whether D believes he had a right to use force.

It may seem odd that the defence can be based on a mistake of law. But, as we have said, the moral wrong of theft is the deliberate assumption of, or interference with, another's property rights. It is D's mental state that marks out that interference as deserving the attention of the criminal law, and more than a mere tortious conversion. It follows that someone who thinks she is not violating another person's property rights lacks the guilty mind that makes her actions worth criminalising. For similar reasons, it is clear that an honest mistake is sufficient even if it be unreasonable. In *Holden*,[293] D, who worked for a

285 [1985] QB 829.
286 *Ibid.*, 836 (Lord Lane CJ). Cf. *Bagshaw* [1988] Crim LR 321.
287 (1851) 5 Cox CC 181. On tickets generally, see *Marshall* [1998] 2 Cr App R 282 and, in particular, the discussion by Smith, "Stealing Tickets" [1998] *Crim LR* 723.
288 [2002] EWHC (Admin) 291.
289 As Smith observes: *The Law of Theft* (8th ed., 1997) § 2–138.

tyre company, was charged with theft of scrap tyres from his employer. He claimed that he had seen others take tyres and had been permitted to do so by a supervisor. It was company policy that taking tyres, or permitting others to do so, was sackable conduct. D was convicted of theft after the judge directed the jury that the test of dishonesty was whether D reasonably believed he had a right to take the tyres. The Court of Appeal quashed the conviction. D's conduct was certainly a civil wrong. But, if the defendant was to be believed, he did not mean to act wrongfully. A mistake may be honest even when unreasonable, and negligent violation of another's property rights is not, and should not be, the stuff of theft.

A distinction should be drawn between the defence that D believes she has a *legal* right to the thing allegedly stolen, which operates through section 2(1)(a), and a belief that she has a *moral* justification for her act. Belief in moral justification may, but will not necessarily, include a belief that D is legally entitled to the thing taken. Where D knows she has no legal right to the thing, her belief in a moral right alone is not sufficient for the colour of right defence in section 2(1)(a).[294] It may, however, lead to her being found not dishonest on the general test (below, § 13.8(iv)).

(ii) Belief that the other would consent: section 2(1)(b)

Social life is unavoidably a co-operative enterprise. Frequently, we anticipate the generosity of our family and friends by taking and using property in their absence. When we do so, we assume that the owner will not object. For example, in a prosecution for larceny prior to the Theft Act 1968, a farmer borrowed a bale of his neighbour's hay expecting to replace it with a bale of his own.[295] Although he had an intention permanently to deprive his neighbour of the particular bale he "borrowed",[296] his behaviour was accounted not dishonest and he was acquitted of larceny. This type of case is now covered by section 2(1)(b).

(iii) Belief that the owner cannot be found: section 2(1)(c)

Section 2(1)(c) encapsulates the finder's defence.[297] Recall the example stated earlier in this chapter:[298]

> David finds a wallet in a busy street, and picks it up. He looks in the wallet for evidence of the owner's identity and finds none, but does find some money. He puts the wallet in his pocket.

Does David commit theft? Assuming the wallet is indeed lost rather than abandoned, the question turns on whether David is dishonest. If he believes the owner cannot be found by taking reasonable steps, section 2(1)(c) will operate to absolve him.

---

[290] *Bernhard* [1938] 2 KB 264.

[291] *Ibid.* V agreed to pay his mistress (D) a sum of money, which he did not; she then threatened to expose him to his wife and the public unless he paid up. D was acquitted of demanding money with menaces with intent to steal, as she—mistakenly—thought she had a valid claim to the money.

[292] [1968] 1 QB 166; cf. *Robinson* [1977] Crim LR 173.

[293] [1991] Crim LR 478.

[294] Cf. *Harris* v. *Harrison* [1963] Crim LR 497 (at common law). In *Hemmerly* (1976) 30 CCC (2d) 141, D, a drug dealer, was convicted of robbery. In his defence he argued that he was entitled to the money taken, as the victim

Three points about this defence should be emphasised. First, David need not consider whether the owner can be found if *all possible* steps are taken. Only reasonable steps need be considered. What is reasonable will depend on the circumstances. If the wallet is inexpensive and contains very little money, David will probably not be required to make any great effort (even so, were a police station close by, it may be adjudged unreasonable not to hand in the wallet). If the wallet contains hundreds of pounds, rather more may be expected.

The second point is that the question of what D *believes* is subjective. Consider the following variation:

> Joan finds a wallet in a busy street, and picks it up. She looks in the wallet for evidence of the owner's identity and finds none, but does find a few pound coins. (In fact, there is a name and address label in the wallet, but Joan's examination of the wallet is a careless one and she does not see it.) Joan puts the wallet in her pocket, concluding that it is lost rather than abandoned but that the true owner cannot be found. She then spends the money and takes the wallet home. On reaching home and looking more carefully inside the wallet, she finds the owner's name and address. Deciding to keep the wallet anyway, she puts it in a drawer.

Joan's initial mistake about the impossibility of tracing the owner need not be a reasonable one. Since she genuinely believes that that the owner cannot be found, she is entitled to be regarded as honest by virtue of section 2(1)(c). Hence, when she spends the money, she commits no theft. However, facts may change, and the defence may cease to be available—as in the example here. Joan is guilty of stealing the *wallet* when she puts it in the drawer.[299]

The foregoing points intersect at the requirement of "reasonable steps". In principle, while it is a subjective enquiry into what D's beliefs are about the circumstances, the assessment whether the steps (she believes to be) required to locate the owner are *reasonable* is an objective matter, which it is for the court to determine rather than D.[300] Suppose that D finds a wallet containing £1,000 in notes, but has little sense of obligation and genuinely believes it is unreasonable to expect her to be inconvenienced by walking some 600 yards to the nearby police station in order to notify them of her discovery (which, she recognizes, may help to locate the owner). Section 2(1)(c) would not be available.

(iv) The general test for dishonesty

Assuming the defendant cannot avail herself of the defences contained in section 2(1), dishonesty falls to be resolved under the general test. Whether the defendant was dishonest is a question of fact for the jury to decide. In *Feely* , it was said that the courts should offer them little guidance:[301]

---

owed it to him. However it was clear that D did not believe he had a legal claim to the money; although belief in a moral right might negative dishonesty, it was held not to do so in this case.

[295] Case noted [1956] Crim LR 360.

[296] Above, § 13.7(i)(e).

[297] Though its application is not restricted to finders, and would exculpate bailees where the bailor was now untraceable. See Smith, *Property Offences* (1994) § 7–42.

[298] Above, § 13.4(v).

"Jurors, when deciding whether an appropriation was dishonest can be reasonably expected to, and should, apply the current standards of ordinary decent people. In their own lives they have to decide what is and what is not dishonest. We can see no reason why, when in a jury box, they should require the help of a judge to tell them what amounts to dishonesty."

This *laissez-faire* approach has since been circumscribed, for good reason. It is unclear, under the *Feely* approach, what is to be done about the idiosyncratic defendant whose values differ from those of "ordinary decent people" (whoever they may be)—about the person who states, "others think this conduct dishonest, but in my view it is morally acceptable."

At first, the approach of the courts to such cases was to treat dishonesty essentially as a subjective test. In *Boggeln v. Williams*,[302] D's electricity had been disconnected for non-payment. He reconnected the supply himself, knowing the supplier did not consent to his doing so but notifying it of his intentions and reconnecting the electricity in such a way that his use was recorded. The Divisional Court held that the crucial question was whether D subjectively believed that what he did was honest.[303]

Where this type of situation arises, however, the leading case is now *Ghosh*,[304] in which the Court of Appeal set out a two-part test for the jury to apply:[305]

(i)   Was what was done dishonest according to the ordinary standards of reasonable and honest people?

(ii) Did the defendant realise that reasonable and honest people would regard what he did as dishonest?

If the answer to both questions is yes, the jury should conclude that the defendant was dishonest.

The *Ghosh* direction on dishonesty need not be given in every case, only when there is evidence of a divergence between the defendant's standards of honesty and those of "reasonable and honest people".[306] By contrast with the earlier, subjective approach, the defendant is no longer entitled to rely simply on her own views whether her conduct is honest. This point was made explicitly by the Court of Appeal in *Ghosh*:[307]

"For example, Robin Hood or those ardent anti-vivisectionists who remove animals from vivisection laboratories are acting dishonestly, even though they may consider themselves to be morally justified in doing what they do, because they know that ordinary people would consider those actions to be dishonest."

On the other hand, according to Lord Lane, neither is the test exclusively objective:[308]

---

[299] Cf. *Minigall v. McCammon* [1970] SASR 82.

[300] This is generally true of reasonableness requirements: cf. the justificatory defences, discussed below, § 21.2(ii), (iv). Contrast, unusually, the defence of lawful excuse under s. 5 of the Criminal Damage Act 1971: below, § 14.4(vi)(b) (a reasonable means of protection). The emphatic role of s. 5(3) in that Act finds no correspondent here.

[301] [1973] QB 530, 537–8 (CA).

[302] [1978] 2 All ER 1061.

[303] Cf. *Gilks* [1972] 3 All ER 280, 283, where the Court of Appeal approved the trial judge's direction that the jury should "try and place yourselves in [the appellant's] position at that time and answer the question whether in your view he thought he was acting honestly or dishonestly." See also *Landy* [1981] 1 All ER 491 (conspiracy to defraud); contrast *Greenstein* [1976] 1 All ER 1 (obtaining by deception).

"Take the man who comes from a country where public transport is free. On his first day here he travels on a bus. He gets off without paying. He never has any intention of paying. His mind is clearly honest; but his conduct, judged objectively by what he has done, is dishonest."

Even if the foreigner satisfies the first limb,[309] such a case is now exculpated by the second limb of the *Ghosh* test.

(a) Problems with the Ghosh test

Both *Feely* and *Ghosh* have attracted an extensive critical literature.[310] For one thing, it may be thought rather open-ended to ask the jury to apply a standard of "reasonable and honest people" (in *Ghosh*) or of "ordinary decent people" (in *Feely*). Even though, in *Ghosh* , this is done with the intention of imposing an objective standard for dishonesty, it assumes juries are heterogeneous and have consistent values. That is surely not the case. Values in this country vary widely, both across and within socio-economic and cultural divides. There is no reason to suppose such variation does not extend to judgements of dishonesty. When a batsman at cricket refuses to walk, is that dishonest? It depends who you ask. Perhaps we can agree that shoplifting is dishonest; what about making an otherwise lawful profit from information about a company that is not widely known?[311] Do we really all concur, *pace* Lord Lane, that Robin Hood was dishonest—or that openly using force to release battery hens or destroy genetically modified crops is dishonest? Obviously, if different persons can reasonably hold different views about these questions, there is a real danger of different verdicts, on the same set of facts, from different juries. In turn, this undermines the rule of law. Even an informed defendant may be unable to predict whether his behaviour will contravene the law. Arguably, such uncertainty contravenes Article 7 of the ECHR.[312]

On the other hand, the purely subjective standard envisaged in cases like *Boggeln* v. *Williams*[313] produces its own problems. To some extent, dishonesty is a matter of personal morality, but defendants cannot be permitted entirely to supplant their own values for those of the law. It is vital to the authority of a legal system that its laws set an objective touchstone. Law works by preventing people from doing what they want, through imposing a standard of acceptable behaviour and demanding that they conform to that standard. If the values that the law would have us act upon were displaced, in each case, by those of the

---

[304] [1982] QB 1053.

[305] *Ibid.*, 1064.

[306] Cf. *Roberts* (1987) 84 Cr App R 117; *Price* (1990) 90 Cr App R 409; *Brennan* [1990] Crim LR 118; *Wood* [2002] EWCA Crim 832.

[307] [1982] QB 1053.

[308] *Ibid.*, 1063.

[309] Arguably, the foreigner is not even within the first limb of the *Ghosh* test. This illustrates one of the difficulties about that test: even under limb one, D's subjective state of mind must be considered. Lord Lane's concept of "objective dishonesty" is therefore problematic.

[310] See, e.g., Elliott, "Dishonesty under the Theft Act" [1972] *Crim LR* 625; Wasik, "Mens Rea, Motive and the Problem of 'Dishonesty' in the Law of Theft" [1977] *Crim LR* 543; Campbell, "The Test of Dishonety in *R* v. *Ghosh*" [1984] *CLJ* 349; Griew, "Dishonesty: The Objections to Feely and Ghosh" [1985] *Crim LR* 341; Halpin, "The Test for Dishonesty" [1996] *Crim LR* 283; Halpin, *Definition in the Criminal Law* (2004) chap. 4.

[311] According to the Court of Appeal in *Lockwood* [1986] Crim LR 244, even in corporate frauds we apply the standards of ordinary decent people, not "current notions of fair trading among commercial men," as was suggested in *re Patrick Lyon* [1933] Ch 786, 790 and *Landy* [1981] 1 All ER 1172, 1181 ("a man of his intelligence and

particular defendant, then the law would have no standard to impose.[314] Whatever one takes to be the purposes of law, their achievement requires the co-ordination of individuals' behaviour through the external imposition of values: by ordering ("do not") rather than asking ("unless you want to"). Individuals cannot be permitted to conduct themselves above or outside the compass of the law merely because they have different moral values.

Complicating the question whether dishonesty imports a subjective or objective standard is the related issue, a standard of *what?* The case of the militant anti-vivisectionist who takes animals from a laboratory is instructive. This is theft regardless of D's undoubtedly strong moral case: because the concept of "dishonesty" in law is not merely a matter of general moral justification, but also of respect for property rights. The conscious disregard of another person's property rights must normally be regarded as dishonest in the context of a law the *raison d'être* of which is to protect property. Outside cases of emergency, the law of theft must set its face against moral arguments for systematically overriding property rights, of the kind an animal rights activist might make. Arguably, the example of the unknowing foreigner who avails herself of a bus ride without payment reveals no dishonesty not so much because she does nothing wrong, but because she has no intention to interfere with anyone else's property rights.

Yet, if this is so, how important is the general requirement of dishonesty, since the claim of *legal* right is subsumed by the defence in section 2(1)(a)? To some extent, any legal definition of dishonesty is liable to founder on these difficulties, and it is arguable that the element should be abandoned altogether in favour of specific provisions such as those contained in section 2.[315] Other cases involving defensible usurpations of others' property rights could instead be dealt with under the law's general defences of necessity and the like.

Unfortunately, with the extraordinary interpretation currently given to the element of "appropriation" in theft, the dishonesty requirement is not residual but central. It is only her honesty that prevents the ordinary shopper from being guilty of theft when she picks goods off the shelves. We are stuck with the problem, unless the House of Lords was prepared, in light of Article 7 of the ECHR and the enactment of the Human Rights Act 1998, to re-consider *Gomez* and, perhaps, to overrule the Court of Appeal's decision in *Ghosh*. At present, that possibility seems remote.

§ 13.9 Jurisdiction over Theft Act offences

Nowadays, theftuous and fraudulent conduct frequently has a transnational dimension. For example, D, from London, may obtain access by electronic means to V's New York bank account and dishonestly transfer funds from that account to an account he has opened for himself in a Swiss bank. Or D may send a deceptive telex from London to Hong Kong, causing V to transfer for D's benefit funds held in a Hong Kong bank. It may well be that the conduct just described merits trial and punishment before an English court, since there

---

experience." For discussion, see Levi, "Fraud Trials in Perspective" [1984] *Crim LR* 384; Elliott, "Directors' Thefts and Dishonesty" [1991] *Crim LR* 732.

[312] See, in particular, the discussion of this point in the Law Commission's Consultation Paper No. 155, *Fraud and*

may be damage to interests which fall properly within the purview of English criminal law.[316]

At common law, any claim to jurisdiction now requires proof that either (i) the last constituent element, or (ii) a "substantial" component, of the actus reus of the offence took place in England or Wales; and that there is no reason of comity with foreign legal systems not to try the offence here.[317] Frequently, asserting jurisdiction will be possible notwithstanding a substantial transnational element on the facts.[318] In *Re Osman*,[319] acts were done in Hong Kong (where the law of theft was the same as in England) which took effect on property situated in other countries. It was held that the property had been appropriated in Hong Kong, without prejudice to the possibility that appropriation also occurred where the property was located. Similarly, a blackmailing demand is made when a letter is posted in England, even if the addressee will receive the letter in Germany.[320]

The modern common law has fallen broadly into line with Part I of the Criminal Justice Act 1993,[321] which attempts to achieve consistency between theft and offences of fraud and dishonesty regarding jurisdiction over offences with transnational elements. If an offence is listed in Part I of the Criminal Justice Act 1993,[322] under section 2 of that Act an assumption of jurisdiction will be permitted notwithstanding that elements of the offence have taken place overseas provided a "relevant event"—i.e. any definitional element of the offence—occurs in England and Wales.[323]

It is worth mentioning that, by contrast with the predecessor deception offences contained in the Theft Acts, the new offences created by the Fraud Act 2006 (to be discussed in Chapter 15) have not been added to the list in the 1993 Act. Notably, the offences of fraud found in the Fraud Act are conduct rather than result crimes: for example, the offence of fraud by false representation merely requires the making of a dishonest false representation with intent to gain or cause loss. It is not necessary to show that any gain was made or any loss occurred. It may be concluded that English courts can assert jurisdiction over these offences even if the gains or losses intended would occur beyond the jurisdiction; provided the false pretence was made somewhere in England or Wales.

Deception (1999) § 5.33ff. A prescient early note is McKenna, "The Undefined Adverb in Criminal Statutes" [1966] *Crim LR* 548, 552–3.

[313] [1978] 2 All ER 1061; above, § 13.8(iv).

[314] "To permit one who knows but does not accede to the community valuation of interests to have an individual standard would at once destroy the law": Seavey, "Negligence—Subjective or Objective?" (1927) 41 *Harv LR* 1, 11.

[315] Cf. Elliott, "Dishonesty in Theft: A Dispensable Concept" [1982] *Crim LR* 395; Glazebrook, "Revising the Theft Acts" [1993] *CLJ* 191, 193.

[316] UK nationals, including companies, may suffer loss of property owned overseas. Moreover, the City of London and other financial centres may suffer loss of reputation and confidence if perceived as havens for international fraud: see further Law Com. No. 180, *Jurisdiction over Offences of Fraud and Dishonesty with a Foreign Element* (1989).

[317] *Smith (Wallace Duncan) (No 4)* [2004] EWCA Crim 631, [2004] QB 1418; overruling *Manning* [1999] QB 980 (CA).

[318] Save for specific statutory exceptions, English courts do not accept jurisdiction over conduct perpetrated entirely outside England and Wales, even in respect of a British subject. For common law crimes, constraints of venue and ambit ensured that "all crime is local". For statutory crimes, there is a very strong presumption that criminal statutes are concerned and only concerned with prescribing acts or omissions perpetrated in the United Kingdom: *Cox v. Army Council* [1963] AC 48.

[319] [1990] 1 WLR 277.

[320] *Treacy* [1971] AC 537.

[321] Part I came into effect in August 1999: SI 1999, No. 1189 (32); SI 1999, No. 1499 (42).

[322] The listed offences in s. 1 of the Criminal Justice Act 1993 include: theft; false accounting; false statements by

14

RELATED OFFENCES

It is impossible, in a work of this nature, to analyse all the offences besides theft which concern themselves with harms to property. In Chapter 15, fraud offences will be considered. Those are offences which, unlike theft and the offences considered in this chapter, often involve the wrongful manipulation of other persons, so that invasion of a victim's property interests is, at least prima facie, consensual: "whereas the thief makes war on a social practice from the outside, the deceiver is the traitor within."[1] Besides theft, however, there are many other property offences which are external to, and attack rather than insidiously use, the law's established processes for allocating and transferring property rights. In this chapter, we consider four such offences.

§ 14.1 Handling stolen goods

"There would not be so many thieves if there were no receivers."[2] The crime of handling is in many ways a special case of being an accessory to theft,[3] one which deserves independent criminalisation because of the important role that "fences"—and indeed end-purchasers—of stolen goods play in the economics of the offence. Recognition of the importance of handling was relatively slow in coming. As its early legal status suggests, in some respects handling *is* a secondary offence. Logically and temporally, theft is prior to handling: the latter presupposes the former. (It should be noted, however, that although receiving is normally associated with theft, the modern offence can also be committed in respect of blackmail, fraud, and by withdrawing a wrongful credit. Thus one who launders the proceeds of blackmail may be guilty of handling under the Theft Act 1968.[4]) Historically,

---

[1] Shute and Horder, "Thieving and Deceiving: What is the Difference" (1993) 56 *MLR* 548, 553.

[2] *Battams* (1979) 1 Cr App R(S) 15, 16. According to Klockars, *The Professional Fence* (1974) 165–6, "the observation itself is better understood as an hyperbolic plea for attention to the criminal receiver than as an accurate statement of his relationship to theft. . . . In brief, if there were no receivers, there would still be all sorts of thieves, and possibly more thieves of sorts we don't like than we have now."

[3] Indeed, this was how it was first criminalised, in 1692, 3 & 4 W. & M. c.13 (receivers deemed to be accessories). Earlier law disclosed an offence only if D actually received or abetted the thief himself: *Dawson's Case* (1602) 2 Bracton 337, 339, 80 ER 4. For a brief history, see Hall, *Theft, Law and Society* (2nd ed., 1952) 52–8. The old position is now reversed, and receiving the thief does not constitute receiving the goods stolen: *Wiley* (1850) 4 Cox CC 412, 169 ER 408.

[4] It is unclear why handling should be restricted to these specific crimes and not apply to the proceeds of crime more generally, as it does in some other jurisdictions. (Cf. Howarth, "Handling Stolen Goods and Handling Salmon" [1987] *Crim LR* 460.) Contrast, e.g., s. 246 of the Crimes Act 1961 (NZ), which makes it an offence to receive anything "stolen or obtained by any other crime." However, as will be noted in § 14.1(vii), the expanded scope of modern laundering legislation compasses the proceeds of any criminal conduct—effectively swallowing the traditional offence of handling.

too, theft was originally a far more significant crime than handling. Prior to the Industrial Revolution, chattels were relatively few and there was little mobility between population centres.[5] Hence, stolen property could be traced fairly easily and there were few commercial opportunities for redistribution of such property. Theft, in turn, tended to be committed to satisfy personal needs rather than for profit.

In modern society, the explosion of property offences is a simple matter of economics: in the market for stolen goods, supply has increased to meet demand. Professional fences are the brokers who make that market: handling is the channel through which commercial forces drive theft.[6] Reflecting this, the maximum penalty for handling is imprisonment for 14 years, by contrast with a maximum of seven years for theft.

In addition, those who deal in stolen goods also provide the means by which merchandise can be "laundered", so that the tangible evidence of theft effectively disappears.[7] Mass-produced items, once sold on, cannot normally be traced. By providing an outlet for the efficient disposal of such items, handlers reduce the risk that theft will be detected. Thus one, largely unrecognised, role that professional fences perform is the obstruction of justice.

Yet these considerations are somewhat abstract, and their victims not harmed so immediately as they are by the theft itself. Consequently, the wrongness of handling has never caught the popular imagination,[8] and it is arguable, even now, that the law fails to deal strongly enough with professional handling. Indeed, the Theft Act draws no distinction between the lay receiver, who may once in his lifetime buy stolen goods for his own consumption, and the criminal businessman who maintains an organisation and thus supports the theft industry.[9] No doubt, if there were no handlers, there would still be thieves. But if society were to eliminate handling, the incidence of theft surely would drop dramatically.

Section 22(1) defines handling as follows:

> A person handles stolen goods if (otherwise than in the course of the stealing) knowing or believing them to be stolen goods he dishonestly receives the goods, or dishonestly undertakes or assists in their retention, removal, disposal or realisation by or for the benefit of another person, or if he arranges to do so.

The section stipulates four main elements. The actus reus is:

(i)   that D handles goods; and
(ii)   the goods were stolen.

---

[5] Chappell and Walsh, "'No Questions Asked', A Consideration of the Crime of Criminal Receiving"(1974) 20 *Crime and Delinquency* 157, 160.

[6] Cf. Klockars, *The Professional Fence* (1974); Blakey and Goldsmith, "Criminal Redistribution of Stolen Property: The Need for Reform" (1976) 74 *Mich LR* 1512; Sutton, Schneider and Hetherington, *Tackling theft with the market reduction approach* (2001); *Shelton* (1986) 83 Cr App R 379, 385.

[7] Chappell and Walsh, "Receiving Stolen Property: The Need for a Systematic Inquiry into the Fencing Process" (1974) 11 *Criminology* 484, 494.

[8] An instructive example is *Sainthouse* [1980] Crim LR 506, where a casual (i.e. non-professional) receiver was prepared to plead guilty to handling but not to theft.

[9] "Whereas eighteenth-century English society had to learn to make distinctions between thief and receiver, our society must be prepared to distinguish among different classes of receivers and diverse patterns of fencing activity": Blakey and Goldsmith, "Criminal Redistribution of Stolen Property: The Need for Reform" (1976) 74 *Mich LR* 1512, 1544; cf. Hall, *Theft, Law and Society* (2nd ed., 1952) 155–6. The difference would, however, normally be reflected in sentencing.

The mens rea components are:

(iii)   D knows or believes the goods were stolen or dishonestly obtained; and
(iv)   dishonesty.

(i) Handling

Prior to the passing of the Theft Act 1968, the only mode of handling goods was receiving them, something that required the defendant to take possession or control over the goods. This limitation made it more difficult to convict those professional fences who facilitated dispositions of goods without themselves ever coming into physical contact with or acquiring the goods. Under section 22(1), the behavioural element of the offence can now be done in the following ways:[10]

(i)   through receiving, or arranging to receive, the goods;
(ii)   through assisting in their retention, removal, disposal, or realisation by another person, or through arranging to do so;
(iii)   through assisting in their retention, removal, disposal, or realisation for the benefit of another person, or through arranging to do so.

In each of these cases, the handling must occur otherwise than in the course of the original stealing. It must be observed, at the outset of this discussion, that the drafting of section 22(1) is rather inelegant and does not lend itself to clear elucidation. In particular, the actus reus of handling is specified in terms both wide and uncertain.[11]

(a) Receiving

The law on receiving pre-dates the Act.[12] The actus reus requirement in receiving is that H acquires (joint or sole) possession or control over the goods from another person.[13] The acquisition of possession or control is a single finite act: once possession or control is acquired, the receiving is complete and later dealing with the goods cannot be treated as a continuing or further act of receiving.

H need not take personal physical custody of the goods. Possession *or* control is sufficient. Regarding the first of these, "possession" is established by showing (i) that the goods are either in H's immediate physical custody or located at a place over which H has control (e.g. in H's house); together with (ii) a mental element, the intent by H to possess the goods.

The mental element is essential. D cannot be in possession of property that he does not know exists.[14] Suppose, for instance, that T, having stolen a wallet, disposes of it by slipping

---

[10] *Bloxham* [1983] 1 AC 109, 113–14; below, § 14.1(i)(c).

[11] Spencer, "The Mishandling of Handling" [1981] *Crim LR* 682, 683–4; Blake, "The Innocent Purchaser and Section 22 of the Theft Act" [1972] *Crim LR* 494.

[12] Cf. *Smythe* (1980) 72 Cr App R 8, 11 ("receiving, or handling as it has now become").

[13] In *Seymour* [1954] 1 All ER 1006 the Court of Criminal Appeal sought to correct a tendency to find people guilty of receiving, rather than theft, whenever they were found in possession of stolen goods. Lord Goddard CJ emphasised that to find someone guilty of receiving, the jury must be satisfied that D received from *someone else*: "[i]f he is the thief, he cannot be guilty of receiving because a man cannot receive from himself, but must receive the property from somebody else." Thus, where the evidence is as consistent with theft as it is with handling, the indictment ought to contain a count for theft and a count for handling. See below, § 14.1(vi).

[14] See also above, § 5.6 (ii).

the wallet into H's bag without H's knowledge. In such a case, for the purposes of receiving H does not take possession of the wallet, at least until she knows she has it. Similarly, if goods stolen by another are found in H's house, it must be shown either that H had arranged for them to be delivered there[15] or, alternatively, that H had realised the goods were present and intentionally exercised control over them. In *Cavendish*,[16] Lord Parker CJ put the test in the following way:

> "It is quite clear, without referring to authority, that for a man to be found to have possession, actual or constructive, of goods, something more must be proved than that the goods have been found on his premises. It must be shown either, if he was absent, that on his return he became aware of them and exercised some control over them or . . . that the goods had come, albeit in his absence, at his invitation or by arrangement."

The importance of the mental ingredient involved in acquiring possession or control can be seen in *Healey*.[17] In that case, the defendant was hired to assist in melting down some tin. The tin was stolen. The defendant's conviction for receiving was quashed by the Court of Criminal Appeal, because the trial judge had not drawn the jury's attention to the difference between a person who was merely assisting, even if dishonestly, and a person who by his assistance had become a joint possessor with the principal whom he was assisting. The Court cited a passage from *Hobson v. Impett*:[18]

> "It is not the law that, if a man knows goods are stolen and puts his hands on them, that in itself makes him guilty of receiving, because it does not follow that he is taking them into his control. The control may still be in the thief or the man whom he is assisting, and the alleged receiver may be only picking the goods up without taking them into his possession, the goods all the time remaining in the possession of the person whom he is helping."

As this passage makes clear, physical possession, e.g. in the sense of touching something, is insufficient without the accompanying intent thereby to possess or control the thing. To similar effect is the decision in *Hawes v. Edwards*.[19] A parcel containing stolen goods was delivered to D's address. After the delivery, police officers entered the premises and found the defendant together with the opened parcel. One of the officers asked D whether he had signed for the parcel, to which he responded, "No, I am examining the contents before I sign for it." D's conviction for receiving was quashed. Although he had opened the parcel, he had not yet decided whether to acquire possession from the thieves. In effect, the thieves had offered to transfer the goods to him, and D had yet to accept their offer.

Conversely, physical possession is not always *required*. If the defendant lacks actual custody of the stolen goods, she may nonetheless be found to have "control" over them. This occurs when custody is in the hands of an agent or servant acting under the defendant's direction; through whom the defendant exercises control over the goods.[20] Again, the exercise of control imports a mental element, and one cannot unknowingly exercise control over something. Hence, according to Lord Parker CJ, "a man cannot be convicted of receiving

---

[15] *Lloyd* [1992] Crim LR 361; *Cavendish* [1961] 2 All ER 856.

[16] [1961] 2 All ER 856, 858.

[17] [1965] 1 All ER 365.

[18] (1957) 41 Cr App R 138, 141 (Lord Goddard CJ). See *Healey* [1965] 1 All ER 365, 369.

[19] (1949) 113 JP 303; cf. *Freedman* (1930) 22 Cr App R 133.

[20] *Smith* (1855) Dears 494, 169 ER 818; *Miller* (1854) 6 Cox 353.

goods of which delivery has been taken by his servant unless there is evidence that he, the employer, had given the servant authority or instructions to take the goods."[21]

(b) Arranging to receive

Handling can also be committed in inchoate form. Under section 22(1) what, prior to 1968, would have been (at most) an attempt or a conspiracy to receive is now a full offence. If the prosecution can prove that H made an arrangement to receive the goods, she is guilty of handling them; there is no need to prove that she actually received the goods. However, the arrangement must be made after the goods are stolen, since it is necessary that H should know or believe the goods are stolen property at the time of making the arrangement.[22]

(c) Undertaking or assisting in the retention, removal, disposal, or realisation

Section 22(1) makes H guilty of handling if he undertakes or assists to retain, remove, dispose of, or realise the goods, by or for the benefit of another person. According to Lord Bridge:[23]

> "First, the offender may himself undertake the activity for the benefit of another person. Secondly, the activity may be undertaken by another person and the offender may assist him. Of course, if the thief or an original receiver and his friend act together in, say, removing the stolen goods, the friend may be committing the offence in both ways."

Typically, this encompasses cases where H organises the on-sale of stolen goods without herself ever taking possession of them,[24] or where H assists the thief to fence or realise the goods. The formula would also capture situations where H promises to destroy or assists in destroying (or otherwise "disposing" of) stolen property; as well as cases where H undertakes or assists to store ("retain") the stolen items.[25] Merely using the goods, however, is not sufficient. In *Sanders*,[26] D used a stolen heater in his father's garage, where D was employed. Although the father was guilty of handling, D was not.

Neither is passive acquiescence sufficient. In *Coleman*,[27] H's wife used money she had stolen to pay for legal fees which had been incurred jointly by H and his wife. H was charged with assisting his wife to dispose of the money. The Court of Appeal quashed his conviction after the trial judge misdirected the jury that it was sufficient for handling that H was dishonest and was getting the benefit of the disposal. Knowingly standing by while a benefit is conferred is not in itself assistance, though it may be circumstantial evidence supporting a wider case that H encouraged or assisted his wife in the disposal. The decision seems right, on the principle that there is generally no criminal liability for omissions. Thus, in *Brown*,[28] H's failure to tell the police that stolen goods were in his flat when instructing

---

[21] *Cavendish* [1961] 2 All ER 856, 858; a continuation of the remarks quoted earlier in this section.

[22] *Park* (1987) 87 Cr App R 164. If an agreement to handle stolen goods is made prior to the theft, the proper charge is conspiracy (*ibid.*, 173). It may also be appropriate to charge the would-be handler with abetting or inciting the contemplated theft.

[23] *Bloxham* [1983] AC 109, 113–14.

[24] Cf. the facts of *Watson* [1916] 2 KB 385.

[25] *Pitchley* (1972) 57 Cr App R 30, 37: retain means "keep possession of".

[26] (1982) 75 Cr App R 84. Cf. the law governing the taking of possession by employees who find goods: above, § 13.4(v)(a).

[27] (1985) 150 JP 175.

[28] [1970] 1 QB 105.

them to "get lost" was held not to be assisting in their retention. In the absence of a duty to disclose, H's omission was an insufficient basis for criminal liability.[29]

By contrast, in *Kanwar*,[30] H actively lied by telling the police that she had purchased articles which her husband had stolen. The effect of these lies, had they been believed by the police, would have been to assist her husband to retain the stolen articles. H's appeal against conviction for handling stolen goods was therefore dismissed by the Court of Appeal.

In *Kanwar*, the finding that positive representations by H could be assistance seems right. Nonetheless, the decision itself is problematic for a different reason: H's "assistance" was ineffective because her lies were not believed. The Court met this difficulty with the bald assertion that "[t]he requisite assistance need not be successful in its object."[31] With respect, this proposition must be qualified. It is possible to assist in a project which, ultimately, is unsuccessful. If H's lies had been temporarily believed but, later, the police had discovered the truth, it might then be reasonable to say that H provided assistance towards the retention of the stolen articles. But on the facts of the case, her lies were wholly ineffectual. She merely attempted to assist.

(d) Arranging to undertake or assist in the retention, removal, disposal, or realisation

One might think that "arranging to assist" in disposing of stolen goods has the hallmarks of an inchoate offence. But under section 22(1), it constitutes the full offence of handling. Thus if, in *Kanwar*, H had promised the thief (i.e. "undertaken") to tell lies, or had made a plan ("arrangement") with someone else to conceal stolen the stolen goods, no difficulty would have arisen: she would be guilty of handling even before the undertaking or arrangement was implemented.

Potentially, this extends the substantive law of handling far into the realm of inchoate offences. Indeed, in extreme cases it would take handling through inchoate wrongs and out the other side, into the field of mere preparation. Given that an undertaking to retain is itself inchoate in nature, making arrangements in advance of giving such an undertaking must be preparatory even to the inchoate wrong. Yet, under section 22(1), both of these constitute the full offence of handling. To some extent, the apparent width of this provision is narrowed in practice by the requirement that there be in existence, at the time, stolen goods to which H's arrangement relates. Nonetheless, it may be questioned whether the mere making of an arrangement to undertake to dispose of those goods comprises a crystallised harm sufficient to warrant criminalisation.

(e) By or for the benefit of another

The requirement that the arranging, assisting, or undertaking be "by or for the benefit of another person" is awkwardly expressed. What it seems to mean is that, apart from traditional receiving, there are two types of handling by dealing:

(i)   where H acts as a principal, by arranging or undertaking to deal with (i.e. retain, dispose of, etc.) the property *for the benefit of someone else*; and

---

[29] Above, § 4.1(i).
[30] [1982] 2 All ER 528.
[31] *Ibid.*, 529.

(ii)   where H has a secondary role, by arranging or assisting *someone else to* deal with the property (i.e. "by another person").

What this means is that if H deals with the property on his own, solely for his own benefit, he does not handle.[32] (That is, unless he receives the property.) In *Bloxham*,[33] H purchased a car in good faith. Later he realised the car was stolen, whereupon he sold it at an undervalue to T, an innocent party. H's conviction for handling was quashed by the House of Lords. Although he had disposed of the car, and T had benefited thereby, H had not dealt with the car *for the benefit* of T or anyone else. Rather, H had acted on his own behalf. Moreover, because H also acted by himself, neither could he be convicted on the alternative basis that he had arranged or assisted in the disposal *by another person.*[34]

(f) Otherwise than in the course of stealing

The original theft cannot also be a handling: the goods must be stolen before they can be handled. Section 22 re-enacts this rule, which was part of the common law of receiving,[35] by the proviso that the handling must occur "otherwise than in the course of the stealing." In so doing, it helps to preserve the functional distinctiveness of handling, which involves wrongdoing by receiving or dealing with goods *after* they are stolen.

The converse does not hold. Virtually every handling is also a theft, since both receiving and dealing with property will count as an "appropriation" for the purposes of theft.[36] This overlap is less problematic, however, since theft carries a lesser maximum penalty than handling.[37] We consider the issue of overlaps further in § 14.1(vi).

It is unclear how long a period is included within "the course of the stealing". Suppose the following example:

> D picks goods off the shelf at a supermarket and puts them inside her jacket, intending to leave without paying for them. On the authority of *Gomez*, she has already stolen the goods. As part of the plan, however, D then meets H, her accomplice, in another aisle and passes over some of the goods. H conceals them and leaves separately.

Does H handle the goods? Common sense suggests not (and that it is a joint theft), but the law has yet to answer this question unequivocally. In principle, once there is an appropriation by the thief, the offence of "theft" is complete and committed. This suggests that, in law, the theft is finished—which would make H guilty of handling.[38]

There are two possible ways round this conclusion. One is to rule that D's appropriation

---

[32] Cf. *Sloggett* [1972] 1 QB 430, 434; also the commentary on *Slater and Suddens* [1996] Crim LR 494.

[33] [1983] 1 AC 109 (HL); reversing [1981] 2 All ER 647 (CA). The decision by the Court of Appeal is strongly and rightly criticised by Spencer, "The Mishandling of Handling" [1981] *Crim LR* 682.

[34] As occurred in *Tokeley-Parry* [1999] Crim LR 578, where D arranged for T to smuggle (i.e. "remove", within the terms of s. 22(1)) stolen antiques from Egypt into England.

[35] *Seymour* [1954] 1 All ER 1006; *Thompson* [1965] Crim LR 553.

[36] Cf. *Stapylton* v. *O'Callaghan* [1973] 2 All ER 782; Smith, "Theft and/or Handling" [1977] *Crim LR* 517.

[37] Seven years' imprisonment, by contrast with 14 for handling. See ss. 7 (as amended by the Criminal Justice Act 1991, s. 26) and 22(2).

[38] Cf. *Pitham and Hehl* (1977) 65 Cr App R 45, 49, where D's offer dishonestly to "sell" V's goods to H was held to constitute theft, such that H's purporting to buy the goods and carry them away was handling. For criticism of the decision, see § 13.6(i); also the text below, § 14.2(iii).

of the goods was a single continuing act, lasting (say) until she left the supermarket. While there is no case post-*Gomez* wholeheartedly adopting such an analysis—and it is not easy to reconcile with *Gomez*[39]—the balance of the decisions appears to favour this analysis.[40]

Alternatively, and perhaps equally plausibly, it is open to the courts to rule that the phrase "the course of the stealing" covers a period extending beyond the duration of the theftuous act of appropriation.[41] As a matter of ordinary language, the term "theft" legitimately describes the whole transaction by D and H in the supermarket; moreover, it seems an appropriate word to capture the moral significance of their course of activity, when viewed as a whole. For the purposes of section 22(1), there seems no reason to restrict interpretation of "the course of the stealing" to the technical instant of appropriation required to be proved under section 1.

Even granted the analysis suggested here, however, the boundaries of theft will be vague. In the example set out above, when is the course of the theft by D (and H) completed, so that the goods can thereafter be handled? Is it after D moves past the cashier's counter, when she is outside the premises, when she is some metres down the road, or at some other moment? To some extent, the answer will involve drawing lines intuitively, depending on such factors as whether the thief is still at the scene of the crime.[42]

(ii) Stolen goods

The things handled must be "stolen", and they must be "goods", within the meaning of the Act. Both these terms require discussion.

(a) Goods

The definition of "goods" is set out in section 34(2)(b):

> "goods", except in so far as the context otherwise requires, includes money and every other description of property except land, and includes things severed from the land by stealing.

This definition is almost coextensive with the definition of "property" for the purposes of theft (above, § 13.2), with the main exception that D cannot be guilty of handling land unless severed.[43] In *A-G's Reference (No. 4 of 1979)*,[44] the Court of Appeal confirmed that things in action can be handled. Although they cannot be "received" (which requires a physical taking of possession or control over the goods), following the enactment of the 1968 Act intangible property can now be handled by retention, removal, disposal, or

---

[39] Cf. *Atakpu and Abraham* [1994] QB 69, 80. Contrast, however, *Lockley* [1995] Crim LR 656.

[40] E.g. *Hale* (1978) 68 Cr App R 415; *Donaghy v. Marshall* [1981] Crim LR 644; *Lockley* [1995] Crim LR 656; *Bowden* [2002] EWCA Crim 1279. See Williams, "Appropriation: A Single or Continuous Act?" [1973] *Crim LR* 69.

[41] Cf. *Hale* (1978) 68 Cr App R 415, regarding the requirement in robbery, per s. 8(1), that force be used "at the time of" the stealing. See below, § 14.2(iii).

[42] Contrast *Pitham and Hehl* (1976) 65 Cr App R 45 (theft of furniture complete as soon as D offered to sell it to H) with *Gregory* (1981) 77 Cr App R 41 (during a burglary, theft might continue before property is removed from the building).

[43] The possible theft of land is subject to different restrictions, set out in s. 4(2) of the Theft Act 1968. See above, § 13.3(ii).

[44] [1981] 1 All ER 1193. The decision must now be doubted on other grounds, in light of *Preddy* [1996] AC 815; below, § 15.1(ii)(b). However, there seems no reason to doubt its authority on this point.

realisation. Thus if H assists D to negotiate a cheque obtained by fraud, she becomes guilty of handling.[45]

(b) Stolen

It is not sufficient that the goods have been obtained by crime. They must have been obtained pursuant to certain particular crimes. *Per* section 24(4), the three main offences are theft contrary to section 1, blackmail contrary to section 21, and fraud contrary to section 1 of the Fraud Act 2006.[46] In light of *Gomez*,[47] cases of obtaining by blackmail or fraud generally also constitute theft, and theft is the most important principal offence lying behind convictions for handling. Goods which are obtained by offences of which theft is an element—e.g. burglary and robbery—can also be handled.[48]

It is not necessary to prove the identity of either the person who actually committed the crime or the owner of the property.[49] Provided the evidence discloses that the property was obtained by theft or another crime, even the acquittal of the particular person charged with committing that theft is irrelevant to the charge of receiving.[50] However, it *is* essential to prove that the property was stolen,[51] or obtained by blackmail or fraud that constitutes a *crime*. So, for example, where the person charged with originally stealing a thing is acquitted (or cannot be charged at all) on the ground of legal incapacity such as minority or insanity,[52] the handler cannot be convicted in the absence of other evidence showing the property was obtained by theft. An illustration of this is the pre-Act case of *Walters* v. *Lunt*,[53] in which the defendants took possession of a tricycle that their child, aged seven years, had wrongfully brought home. The Court ruled they could not be convicted of receiving since the child, being under eight years old, could not be guilty of larceny.

In cases of this sort, the defendants may still be convicted of an attempt to handle stolen goods,[54] at least where they are unaware of the circumstances exculpating the original "thief". More straightforwardly, as the Court pointed out in *Walters* v. *Lunt*, their subsequent dealing with the tricycle would itself have been larceny, and would now be theft under section 1.

---

[45] Cf. *Pitchley* (1972) 57 Cr App R 30 (money in a bank account).

[46] Section 24A(8) adds obtaining by withdrawal of a wrongful credit: thus, whereas it is now theft merely to retain a wrongful credit (s. 24A(1)); it is handling to withdraw the proceeds.

[47] Above, § 13.6(ii)(a).

[48] *Pitham and Hehl* (1976) 65 Cr App R 45; *Smythe* (1980) 72 Cr App R 8; *Gregory* (1981) 77 Cr App R 41.

[49] *Carr & Wilson* (1882) 10 QBD 76 (bonds stolen from an English ship moored in Holland, thief and circumstances of the theft unknown). In *Fuschillo* [1940] 2 All ER 489, D was charged with receiving a vast quantity of sugar, although it was not proven who had stolen it or from whom it was stolen. The Court of Criminal Appeal applied dicta in *Sbarra* (1918) 13 Cr App R 118, 120 to the effect that "the circumstances in which a defendant receives goods may of themselves prove that the goods were stolen, and further may prove that he knew it at the time when he received them. It is not a rule of law that there must be other evidence of the theft."

[50] *Close* [1977] Crim LR 107. For criticism of that decision on its particular facts, see Smith, *Property Offences* (1994) §§ 30-08, 30-09.

[51] *Cording* [1983] Crim LR 175; cf. *Creamer* [1919] 1 KB 564.

[52] Cf. *Farrell* [1975] 2 NZLR 753, in which the person from whom H received a stolen cheque was acquitted of theft on the ground of insanity. Consequently, the Court held, the evidence against H lacked an essential ingredient of the receiving charge, namely that the cheque was "stolen" within the meaning of the criminal law.

[53] [1951] 2 All ER 645.

[54] Cf. *Toye* [1984] Crim LR 555.

(c) Proceeds

The handler need not handle the whole of the thing stolen. It is sufficient, for example, that D receives parts of a car which has been stolen (e.g. the wheels or radio), or parts of a stolen stereo system, such as the tape deck or amplifier. Furthermore, the property need not be in the same state or condition as it was when stolen. A stolen car can be received even though substantially damaged in an accident before it arrives in D's hands. Similarly, section 22 would apply to the handling of mutton from a sheep that was alive when stolen.[55]

These are examples where the identity of the stolen property is unchanged in the hands of the handler, even though its character may have partially altered. What about changes of identity? At common law, the thing received had to be the actual thing that was first stolen, not its proceeds or a substitute.[56] In this form, the law was rather too generous to those involved in laundering the proceeds of theft, since it conferred an immunity from prosecution upon subsequent participants in the laundering "chain", once the original item was exchanged.[57] That immunity is now overridden by section 24(2), which extends the scope of stolen goods to include:

(a) any other goods which directly or indirectly represent or have at any time represented the stolen goods in the hands of the thief as being the proceeds of any disposal or realisation of the whole or part of the goods stolen or of goods so representing the stolen goods; and

(b) any other goods which directly or indirectly represent or have at any time represented the stolen goods in the hands of a handler of the stolen goods or any part of them as being the proceeds of any disposal or realisation of the whole or part of the stolen goods handled by him or of goods so representing them.

The upshot of this rather tortuous prose is that if a thief or handler exchanges stolen goods for other goods, the other goods are deemed also to be stolen.[58] But if an innocent person, into whose hands stolen goods fall, exchanges those stolen goods for other goods, the other goods she receives are not deemed stolen. For example:

D steals a television set. She fences it to H in exchange for a video recorder. H knows the set is stolen. In turn, H sells it at a car boot sale to T for £30. T is an innocent buyer. Later, T swaps the television with his neighbour for a lawnmower.

The television is stolen property throughout this example. The video recorder becomes stolen property when D receives it in exchange for the television. The £30 also becomes stolen when H receives it from T. The lawnmower, however, never becomes stolen property, since it was received only by T, who was innocent and neither a thief nor a handler.

---

[55] Cf. *Cowell and Green* (1796) 2 East PC 617.

[56] *Walkley* (1829) 4 C & P 133, 172 ER 640.

[57] It appears that the civil law is in the process of filling this lacuna. Common law tracing now allows P to claim the proceeds of an unauthorised exchange-transaction: see *Trustee of the Property of FC Jones and Sons v. Jones* [1997] Ch 159; *Foskett v. McKeown* [2001] AC 102. On this analysis, the victim of a theft may acquire title in the exchange proceeds, and subsequent handlers may be guilty of theft.

[58] *Forsyth* [1997] 2 Cr App R 299. See especially the commentaries at [1997] Crim LR 589 and 755.

(d) Goods which are no longer stolen

Goods are no longer stolen, and cannot be handled, once they re-enter into the possession of the legal owner or a person authorised by the owner to possess them. By section 24(3), this may occur in two ways:

> But no goods shall be regarded as having continued to be stolen goods after they have been restored to the person from whom they were stolen or to other lawful possession or custody, or after that person and any other person claiming through him have otherwise ceased as regards those goods to have any right to restitution in respect of the theft.

The first way in which goods become not stolen, then, is if they are restored to the original owner or to an authorised possessor. Suppose, for example, that the police recover stolen goods but then, with the consent of the owner, return them to the location where they were discovered in order to trap a would-be receiver. In that case, the subsequent purchaser cannot be convicted of handling.[59] However, she would remain guilty of attempting to handle the goods,[60] and would normally also commit a fresh theft.[61]

Whether goods have been reduced into possession is a question of fact, and turns on the intention of the possessor. In *A-G's Reference (No. 1 of 1974)*,[62] a policeman spotted a van containing packages of new clothing which he (rightly) suspected were stolen. He immobilised the vehicle by removing its rotor arm, and kept observation. The defendant later got into the van and attempted to start it, whereupon he was questioned by the policeman. After offering an implausible explanation for the packages, the defendant was arrested. At issue both during trial and on appeal was whether the policeman had taken possession of the clothing or whether he was merely watching it with a view to catching the handler. In the judgment of the Court of Appeal:[63]

> "it depended primarily on the intentions of the police officer. If the police officer seeing these goods in the back of the car had made up his mind that he would take them into custody, that he would reduce them into his possession or control, take charge of them so that they could not be removed and so that he would have the disposal of them, then it would be a perfectly proper conclusion to say that he had taken possession of the goods. On the other hand, if the truth of the matter is that he was of an entirely open mind at that stage as to whether the goods were to be seized or not and was of an entirely open mind as to whether he should take possession of them or not, but merely stood by so that when the driver of the car appeared he could ask certain questions of that driver as to the nature of the goods and why they were there, then there is no reason whatever to suggest that he had taken the goods into his possession or control."

The rule, then, is analogous to that governing the possession of abandoned goods:[64] a person takes possession if he intentionally exercises control over the goods. In principle, merely

---

[59] *A-G's Reference (No. 1 of 1974)* [1974] QB 744. Cf. *Dolan* (1855) Dears 436, 169 ER 794; *Schmidt* (1866) LR 1 CCR 15; *Hancock* (1878) 14 Cox CC 119. For discussion, see Blakey and Goldsmith, "Criminal Redistribution of Stolen Property: The Need for Reform" (1976) 74 *Mich LR* 1512, 1552ff.

[60] Cf. Criminal Attempts Act 1981, s. 1(2)(3); above, § 9.4(iii).

[61] *Greater Manchester Metropolitan Police Commissioner v. Streeter* (1980) 71 Cr App R 113, 119.

[62] [1974] QB 744.

[63] [1974] QB 744, 753.

[64] Above, § 13.4(v)(a).

standing by is not sufficient. However, the decision is one for the jury on the facts of each case. Consequently, the Court concluded:[65]

> "that the trial judge was wrong in withdrawing the issue from the jury. As a matter of law he was not entitled to conclude from the facts . . . that these goods were reduced into the possession of the police officer. What he should have done in our opinion would have been to have left that issue to the jury for decision, directing the jury that they should find that the prosecution case was without substance if they thought that the police officer had assumed control of the goods as such and reduced them into his possession. Whereas on the other hand, they should have found the case proved, assuming that they were satisfied about its other elements, if they were of the opinion that the police officer in removing the rotor arm and standing by and watching was doing no more than ensure that the driver should not get away without interrogation and was not at that stage seeking to assume possession of the goods as such at all."

Secondly, goods may cease to be stolen if a third party acquires indefeasible legal ownership of them, usually by purchasing them in good faith. Normally in such cases the rule *nemo dat quod non habet* will prevent other persons from acquiring ownership, since at law a person cannot transfer to another any better title to goods than she has herself.[66] However, there are some exceptions to this, enacted by statutes such as the Sale of Goods Act 1979.[67] Alternatively, where the goods are obtained by blackmail or fraud, the transaction is likely to be voidable rather than void, in which case they will cease to be stolen should the original owner elect to affirm the transaction (e.g. through ratifying the contract by which the goods were obtained), even without the intervention of a *bona fide* purchaser for value.

(iii) Knowledge or belief

At the time the actus reus occurs (i.e. the goods are received or otherwise handled), the defendant must *know or believe that the goods are stolen*. It is not necessary that the defendant should know the particular way in which the goods were obtained,[68] or their owner,[69] or even the specific nature of the goods,[70] provided she knows they were obtained by theft, fraud, or blackmail.

The meaning of "knowledge" was considered in § 5.4, where it was said that knowing means "knowing, or correctly believing."[71] In essence, this requires that the defendant must accept, or assume, and have no serious doubt, that the goods he handles were obtained by crime. In particular, it is not enough that the defendant thinks the goods are "probably" stolen.[72] Neither is it sufficient that D *suspects* the goods are stolen: " 'Knowing' is not the

---

[65] [1974] QB 744, 754.

[66] Sale of Goods Act 1979, s. 21.

[67] E.g., if the rogue has obtained a voidable title to the goods that has not been avoided at time of on-sale (Sale of Goods Act 1979, s. 23), or is a mercantile agent with authorised possession (Factors Act 1889, s. 2).

[68] Cf. *DPP* v. *Nieser* [1959] 1 QB 254.

[69] *Fuschillo* [1940] 2 All ER 489.

[70] *McCullum* (1973) 57 Cr App R 645.

[71] See also Griew, "Consistency, Communication and Codification" in Glazebrook (ed.), *Reshaping the Criminal Law* (1978) 57.

[72] *Reader* (1977) 66 Cr App R 33, 36 (CA).

equivalent of 'having a pretty good idea'. "[73] In *Griffiths*,[74] the trial judge instructed the jury that it would be sufficient if the defendant "suspects that goods are stolen and then deliberately shuts his eyes to the circumstances." The Court of Appeal held that this was a misdirection. (However, as we shall note in § 14.1(vii), suspicion may warrant a conviction for a laundering offence.)

For practical purposes, knowledge and belief are coextensive.[75] The case law has sometimes sought to draw minor distinctions between these two cognitive states. According to the 1859 case of *White*:[76]

"The knowledge charged in this indictment need not be such *knowledge* as would be acquired if the prisoner had actually seen the lead stolen; it is sufficient if you think the circumstances were such, accompanying the transaction, as to make the prisoner *believe* that it had been stolen."

Similarly, in *Hall*,[77]

"A man may be said to know that goods are stolen when he is told by someone with first-hand knowledge (someone such as the thief or the burglar) that such is the case. Belief, of course, is something short of knowledge. It may be said to be the state of mind of a person who says to himself: 'I cannot say I know for certain that these goods are stolen but there can be no other reasonable conclusion in the light of all the circumstances, in the light of all that I have heard and seen'."

But these distinctions, which merely concern the *basis* of one's knowledge or belief, are without great value. It is generally impossible to know anything with utter certainty: even the evidence of one's own eyes may occasionally be doubted. What counts is whether the defendant has a settled belief, with no serious doubt, that the goods are stolen. Consistent with this view, the better guidance is that set out by the Court of Appeal in *Moys*:[78]

"The question is a subjective one and it must be proved that the defendant was aware of the theft or that he believed the goods to be stolen. Suspicion that they were stolen, even coupled with the fact that he shut his eyes to the circumstances, is not enough, although those matters may be taken into account by a jury when deciding whether or not the necessary knowledge or belief existed. "

(a) Wilful blindness

What, however, if H suspects the goods are stolen and deliberately refrains from enquiring any further into the question? In this situation H's mental state may be described as one of *wilful blindness*. Does H's failure to make that further enquiry itself establish the requisite

---

[73] *Woods* [1969] 1 QB 447, 452. Although a pre-Act decision, this still represents the law: *Grainge* [1974] 1 All ER 928; *Reader* (1977) 66 Cr App R 33. A helpful review of the law is found in *Forsyth* [1997] 2 Cr App R 299, 317–21. More recently, the distinction between suspicion and knowledge or belief has been affirmed by the House of Lords in the context of conspiracy: *Saik* [2007] 1 AC 18, at [32] (Lord Nicholls), [78] (Lord Hope), and [120] (Lord Brown).

[74] (1974) 60 Cr App R 14, 16. Taken as a whole, however, the judge's direction was thought to be adequate, and the defendant's appeal was dismissed.

[75] Subject to the point that "knowledge" implies a *correct* belief: above, § 5.1(v).

[76] (1859) 1 F&F 665, 175 ER 898 (Bramwell B, emphasis added).

[77] (1985) 81 Cr App R 260, 264.

knowledge or belief? As was stated in § 5.4(i), generally the answer is no. That wilful blindness is not automatically deemed to be knowledge[79] for the purposes of handling was made clear by the Court of Appeal in *Griffiths*:[80]

> "To direct the jury that the offence is committed if the defendant, suspecting that the goods were stolen, deliberately shut his eyes to the circumstances as an alternative to knowing or believing the goods were stolen is a misdirection. To direct the jury that, in common sense and in law, they may find that the defendant knew or believed the goods to be stolen because he deliberately closed his eyes to the circumstances is a perfectly proper direction."

Knowledge and belief are subjective phenomena. They cannot be established by showing that the defendant *ought* to have realised the goods were stolen.[81] However, as the closing sentence of the quotation makes clear, the obviousness of the truth may be an *evidential* factor, supporting the inference that in fact H knew he was handling stolen property. A failure by H to make some enquiry may, in certain circumstances, be taken into account in considering whether the prosecution has proved beyond reasonable doubt the existence of knowledge or belief. A jury may legitimately come to the conclusion that the defendant abstained from enquiry because he knew already what the answer was going to be, and thence infer that his omission to enquire stemmed not from mere suspicion, but from his positive belief that the goods had been stolen.[82]

Nonetheless, there is still room for the wilful blindness doctrine, as the basis for deeming in law a belief that goods were stolen. It operates where H believes the goods are almost certainly stolen, and where any slight doubt on the matter could easily be resolved by his further enquiry. If H deliberately refrains from making that enquiry, especially if he does so in order later to be able to deny knowledge, he is to be attributed with knowledge. However, the scope of the doctrine is very narrow.[83] Its ambit is discussed in more detail above, in § 5.4(i).

(b) Recklessness: a case for law reform?

Apparently, the approach of the courts to wilful blindness is contrary to the intention of those who drafted the Act. According to the Criminal Law Revision Committee, commenting on the law prior to the 1968 Act:[84]

> "The man who buys the goods at a ridiculously low price from an unknown seller whom he meets in a public house may not *know* that the goods were stolen, and he may take the precaution of asking no questions. Yet it may be clear on the evidence that he *believes* that the

---

[78] (1984) 79 Cr App R 72, 76 (Lord Lane CJ); preferred in *Forsyth* (1985) 81 Cr App R 299, 321 as guidance that is "clear and more readily understandable by a jury and avoids the potential for confusion inherent in a *Hall* direction."

[79] As might be suggested by somewhat ambiguous dicta in *Atwal* v. *Massey* [1971] 3 All ER 881 (DC).

[80] (1974) 60 Cr App R 14, 18; cf. *Saik* [2007] 1 AC 18, at [62] (Lord Hope). Similarly, in *Smith* (1976) 64 Cr App R 217, 220, Lawton LJ stated: "We are satisfied that except in most unusual cases juries are capable of understanding what is meant by the word 'believing'. . . . Phrases such as 'suspecting that the goods were stolen and then wilfully shutting one's eyes to the obvious' should not be used as a definition of 'believing.' "

[81] *Atwal* v. *Massey* [1971] 3 All ER 881, 882; *Bellenie* [1980] Crim LR 437; *Havard* (1914) 11 Cr App R 2.

[82] Cf. *Crooks* [1981] 2 NZLR 53, 59 (NZCA), which contains a useful discussion of knowledge and belief.

[83] Wilful blindness is discussed further in § 5.4(i).

[84] "Theft and Related Offences" Cmnd. 2977 (1966) para. 134. But see the important gloss by Williams, "Handling, Theft and the Purchaser Who Takes a Chance" [1985] *Crim LR* 432, 433–4.

goods were stolen. In such cases the prosecution may fail (rightly, as the [pre-Act] law now stands) for want . . . of guilty knowledge."

By inserting "or believing" into the mens rea requirement for handling, the Committee seemingly sought to extend the law to capture such cases. As it turns out, they have not done so. That should not surprise, because the meaning of "believe" is too close to that of "know" to mark a meaningful extension. It certainly does *not* mean "suspect". What the Committee might have been better to do was to signal its intention more clearly by expressly widening the mens rea requirement into the realm of recklessness: e.g. by stipulating "believing the goods are probably stolen" or "believing the goods may be stolen" to be sufficient mens rea.

It is a difficult question whether the law ought to have been extended into recklessness, or whether it is right to insist on knowledge or belief. On the one hand, it is difficult to prove the mens rea of handling, hence the perceived need for a recent possession doctrine and statutory evidential aids;[85] fewer dishonest handlers would escape conviction if recklessness were sufficient. The concern about convicting for mere suspicion could be allayed by requiring, as Spencer suggests, that H believe the goods are *probably* stolen (i.e. more probably stolen than not).[86] Moreover, dishonestly buying goods which are (correctly) thought by H to be probably stolen satisfies the twin criteria of harm and culpability. It is harmful to the original owner and helpful to the thief, and it is culpable. Hence, it may be thought, there are strong reasons in favour of criminalisation.

Against this argument, it is improbable that the change would much affect the position of professional fences, who are likely to know rather than suspect the provenance of the goods. Thus its greatest value would be against the casual or occasional receiver—the purchaser at a car-boot sale, or the pawnbroker, who suspects but is uncertain whether the goods are stolen, and would not buy or accept the goods if she knew the truth. These forms of legitimate commercial activity might be stifled if the purchaser or broker were required consciously to risk criminal conviction by her activity.[87]

On balance, we incline toward the former argument. The risk of over-extending the criminal law is safeguarded against by the further mens rea requirement that the defendant must not only be reckless but also *dishonest*.[88] The pawnbroker who suspects goods are stolen but has no way of knowing the truth should not (and probably would not, by a jury) be accounted dishonest, especially if his acceptance of the goods is consistent with standard practice in the industry.[89] By insisting on knowledge or a firm belief, the law condones rather than stigmatises the "fallen off the back of a lorry" culture in our society—a culture, it must be said, that is overdue for eradication.

---

[85] Below, § 14.1(iii)(c), (d).

[86] "Handling, Theft and the *Mala Fide* Purchaser" [1985] *Crim LR* 92, 95–6. Blakey and Goldsmith, "Criminal Redistribution of Stolen Property: The Need for Reform" (1976) 74 *Mich LR* 1512, 1560 advocate a standard of awareness of "a substantial risk" that the property was stolen.

[87] See Williams, "Handling, Theft and the Purchaser Who Takes a Chance" [1985] *Crim LR* 432, 435–6.

[88] Spencer, "Handling and Taking Risks—A Reply to Professor Williams" [1985] *Crim LR* 440. See below, § 14.1(iv).

[89] On the relevance of standard practices, see Smith, *Property Offences* (1994) § 7-84.

(c) Evidence of mens rea: the doctrine of recent possession

Proof of mens rea in handling can be difficult. The prosecution may be able to establish that H had possession of stolen goods, but unless it can give some account of how those goods were acquired, or of what H intended to do with the goods, it may be very difficult to prove that H knew or believed the goods were stolen. To meet this challenge, judges have evolved a device of prima facie inference, from which proof of possession can, under certain circumstances, support an inference of criminality. This is known as the doctrine of recent possession.

The "doctrine" of recent possession, which originates in the common law, is a common-sense rule that the proof of possession by D of property recently stolen is sufficient evidence to justify a finding that D is either the thief or a dishonest receiver, in the absence of a credible explanation of how D came by the property.[90] It has been described as

> "a convenient way of referring compendiously to the inferences of fact which, in the absence of any satisfactory explanation by the accused, may be drawn as a matter of common sense from other facts, including, in particular, the fact that the accused has in his possession property which it is proved had been unlawfully obtained shortly before he was found to be in possession of it."[91]

Although in some jurisdictions it has been held that the rule is limited to theft, its application to receiving may be justified on the pragmatic ground that criminal receivers can rarely be detected in the act of receiving, so that direct evidence is rarely available.[92]

Before the inference from recent possession can be invoked, the prosecution must prove the relevant property was stolen, and that it was stolen recently. How recent is "recent"? It depends on the facts, and in particular on the nature of the property. Possession of a stolen £20 pound note would ordinarily be unlikely to support an inference of theft or handling after more than a few days; 11 months was too long for stereo equipment in *Simmons*;[93] but the doctrine was applicable after four months in the case of a corporate bond.[94]

The classic direction is found in *Aves*:[95]

> "Where the only evidence is that an accused person is in possession of property recently stolen, a jury may infer guilty knowledge (a) if he offers no explanation to account for his possession, or (b) if the jury are satisfied that the explanation he does offer is untrue. If, however, the explanation offered is one which leaves the jury in doubt whether he knew the property was stolen, they should be told that the case has not been proved, and, therefore, the verdict should be Not Guilty."

Thus stated, it is clear that recent possession is simply a matter of ordinary evidential inference from circumstances. The onus of proving both actus reus and mens rea remains

---

[90] Cf. *Smythe* (1980) 72 Cr App R 8, 11.

[91] *DPP v. Nieser* [1959] 1 QB 254, 266. See also *Raviraj* (1986) 85 Cr App R 93 (CA): the doctrine is only an extension of a general proposition that guilt may inferred from unreasonable behaviour by the accused in response to his being confronted with facts which prima facie suggest his guilt.

[92] Cf. Hall, *Theft, Law and Society* (2nd ed., 1952) 175.

[93] [1986] Crim LR 397.

[94] *Livock* (1914) 10 Cr App R 264.

[95] [1950] 2 All ER 330. See also *Ketteringham* (1926) 19 Cr App R 159; *Hepworth* [1955] 2 QB 600; *Cash* [1985] QB 801, 804 (CA).

on the prosecution. Its dependence upon the fact of possession makes the evidential inference of limited value against sophisticated professional fences, who are unlikely to take actual possession of the goods for themselves; or who, if they do take possession, are likely to take the precaution of ensuring they can offer a plausible explanation, e.g. by integrating possession of stolen goods with their other, legitimate, business activities.[96]

(d) Proof of guilty knowledge under section 27(3)

In addition to the doctrine of recent possession, the prosecutor has statutory aid. Section 27(3) provides that, in proving knowledge or belief on a charge of handling, the prosecution may give as evidence (a) the fact that other stolen property was handled by D or in D's possession at some time during the 12 months preceding the current offence charged (i.e. prior possession), or (b) the fact that D was convicted of theft or handling within the period of five years before being charged with the current offence (i.e. previous convictions).[97]

Note that paragraph (a) does not involve proof of a previous crime but only proof of two of its elements: possession, or undertaking or assistance in retention, removal, disposal, or realisation; and that the goods were stolen. Commenting on one of the predecessors to section 27(3),[98] it has been observed that "Parliament said, 'Where you find a man in possession of stolen property he may be unfortunate, and not guilty, but if you find other stolen property in his possession it may not be easy to believe that it is merely a coincidence.'"[99]

The Criminal Law Revision Committee once recommended that the section be repealed,[100] and it is easy to sympathise. The section has in practice become very complex to use and the subject of much criticism.[101] At the level of principle, moreover, section 27(3) seems undesirable. Its origins in earlier legislation trace to the days when a prisoner could not give evidence to explain away the actus reus: that constraint no longer applies, and the effect of the section now seems in danger of breaching the presumption of innocence now codified by Article 6(2) of the ECHR. This is particularly true of section 27(3)(a), whereby proof of prior possession is admissible as evidence even though the defendant was never convicted of any crime. It is submitted that the probative value of section 27(3) is outweighed by its prejudicial effect.

(iv) Dishonesty

It is an essential element of the offence that the goods have been handled dishonestly. Suppose, for instance, that H knowingly takes possession of stolen goods and passes them to someone else. H may well have done the actus reus of handling (a disposal for the benefit of another person). But if H is a police officer, recovering the goods on behalf of the owner, he is not guilty of an offence—because his actions are most unlikely to be regarded by the jury

---

[96] See Klockars, *The Professional Fence* (1974) 80–93; Hall, *Theft, Law and Society* (2nd ed., 1952) 189–90.

[97] See Munday, "Handling the Evidential Exception" [1988] *Crim LR* 345.

[98] Section 19 of the Prevention of Crimes Act 1871. See also s. 43 of the Larceny Act 1916.

[99] *Ballard* (1916) 12 Cr App R 1, 4.

[100] Eleventh Report, *Evidence (General)* Cmnd. 4991 (1971) para. 101(vii).

[101] See, e.g., *Hacker* [1995] 1 All ER 45; *Bradley* (1979) 70 Cr App R 200; Munday, "Handling the Evidential Exception" [1988] *Crim LR* 345.

as dishonest. This analysis is illustrated by the pre-Act case of *Matthews*,[102] in which the Court of Criminal Appeal held that a person who has received stolen property intending to hand it over at once to the police or the true owner could not be guilty of receiving stolen property.

The test of dishonesty in handling is the same as that in theft, and the leading case in both contexts is *Ghosh*.[103] Note, however, that the specific defences provided by section 2 of the Theft Act 1968 apply only in the context of theft and not to handling. Where such exculpatory circumstances exist on a handling charge, they operate simply as factors to be considered when determining dishonesty on general principles.[104] The issue is one of fact, and is for the jury to decide.

(v) Concurrence of actus reus and mens rea

As we saw in § 5.8, it is a fundamental principle of criminal law that the actus reus and mens rea must coincide: there must be a moment in time at which all the elements of the offence are simultaneously made out. In the context of handling, this means that knowledge acquired, or dishonesty formed, after the actus reus is insufficient.

Suppose D takes possession of goods innocently and then learns they are stolen, or receives them intending to hand the goods over to the police (so without dishonesty) and later changes her mind. At this point she cannot commit handling by receiving. Once possession is taken, it cannot be retaken; the actus reus of receiving is completed and is not a continuing act.[105] Other forms of handling, however, can be repeated or continuing.[106] Thus D would become guilty of handling if, having become dishonest, she then disposed of the goods for the benefit of another person. But if D merely retains the goods for her own benefit she does not handle. The proper charge would be theft.[107]

(vi) Handling versus theft

Even though handling must occur after the original theft is completed,[108] virtually all handlings are themselves thefts.[109] Hence, in proving handling, the prosecution generally proves two different offences constituted by the same action. In principle, there is no objection to this, since not all thefts are handlings and the two offences have different maximum penalties. Moreover, they capture quite different modes of wrongdoing to another person's property interests. Where the facts establish that D received from a thief, therefore, the prosecution should charge handling rather than theft.

However, sometimes the facts may be uncertain, so that it is unclear which of the two offences has been committed by D. This often arises when D is found in possession of stolen

---

[102] [1950] 1 All ER 137, 138.
[103] [1982] QB 1053; cf. *Brennen* [1990] Crim LR 118.
[104] See above, § 13.7.
[105] *Johnson* (1911) 6 Cr App R 218; *Matthews* [1950] 1 All ER 137, 138; *Smythe* (1980) 72 Cr App R 8, 13.
[106] Cf. *Pitchley* (1973) 57 Cr App R 30; *Smythe* (1980) 72 Cr App R 8, 13.
[107] *Matthews* [1950] 1 All ER 137, 138.
[108] Cf. s. 22(1): "otherwise than in the course of stealing."
[109] See above, § 14.1(i)(f).

goods and the prosecution cannot establish how D acquired possession of the goods (e.g. whether D stole them herself, or received them from the original thief). The doctrine of recent possession,[110] which often applies to such cases, supports a conviction for either theft or handling, without preference. Consequently, the jury may be sure beyond reasonable doubt that D is either thief or handler, without knowing which of the two.

In such cases, it is permissible for the prosecution to charge D with alternative counts of theft[111] and handling, thereby leaving the choice to the jury.[112] But this seems to bury the problem without resolving it. In principle, the prosecution must prove beyond reasonable doubt that D has committed the particular offence of which he is to be convicted—not that he is guilty of either that or another offence.[113] The difficulty is compounded by the stipulation in section 22(1) that any alleged handling must occur "otherwise than in the course of the stealing";[114] hence, prima facie, it is open to D to deny handling stolen goods by raising a reasonable doubt about whether he was, in fact, the thief. Where there is no evidence that D was actually the thief, so that D must be acquitted outright if not proved to be a handler, the Court of Appeal has ruled that there is no requirement on the prosecution (when alleging handling) to prove that D was not the original thief.[115] But that ruling, the logic of which has been questioned,[116] in any event cannot resolve the difficulty where the type of wrongdoing by D is genuinely in question.

The High Court of Australia has ruled that, in such circumstances, the jury should be directed to convict of whichever offence is the less serious[117]—presumably the offence with the lesser maximum sentence.[118] A better solution, it is submitted, is to convict D of theft since, as was noted above, virtually any act of handling will also constitute a theft (but not vice versa). So, if the jury is certain D committed theft or handling, but uncertain how possession of the stolen goods was acquired, it can be certain either way that D committed a theft[119] (which, in any event has the lesser penalty).

(vii) A whole new world: laundering

For the most part we no longer need the offence of handling, save to identify a particular form of laundering.[120] Stolen goods or their proceeds[121] are, by definition, the proceeds of a crime, and as such fall within the scope of "criminal property" within the Proceeds of Crime Act 2002.[122] By section 340(3):

---

[110] Above, § 14.1(iii)(c).

[111] Or robbery or burglary, as the case may be, depending on the circumstances of the original theft.

[112] *Shelton* (1986) 83 Cr App R 379; *Stapylton* v. *O'Callaghan* [1973] 2 All ER 782. For general discussion of the overlap, see Smith, "Theft and/or Handling" [1977] *Crim LR* 517.

[113] *A-G of Hong Kong* v. *Yip Kai-foon* [1988] AC 642 (PC); rejecting the proposal in *Langmead* (1864) Le & Ca 427, 169 ER 1459 that, having decided beyond reasonable doubt that D has committed one of the two offences, the jury should choose between them on the balance of probabilities. Cf. *Nguyen* (1992) 60 A Crim R 196, 199.

[114] See above, § 14.1(i)(f).

[115] *Cash* [1985] QB 801; *Wells* [2004] EWCA Crim 792.

[116] Hirst, "Guilty; but of what?" (2000) 4 *International J of Evidence and Proof* 31, 32-4.

[117] *Gilson* v. *R.* (1991) 172 CLR 319, not following *A-G of Hong Kong* v. *Yip Kai-foon* [1988] AC 642.

[118] Cf. *Shelton* (1986) 83 Cr App R 379, 385.

[119] *Shelton* (1986) 83 Cr App R 379, 384; *Stapylton* v. *O'Callaghan* [1973] 2 All ER 782.

[120] See generally Alldridge, *Money Laundering Law* (2003).

[121] Falling within the scope of s. 24(2); above, § 14.1(ii)(c).

[122] Cf. *Loizou* [2005] EWCA Crim 1579, [2005] Crim LR 885.

Property is criminal property if—

(a) it constitutes a person's benefit from criminal conduct or it represents such a benefit (in whole or part and whether directly or indirectly), and

(b) the alleged offender knows or suspects that it constitutes or represents such a benefit.[123]

By section 327, it is an offence to conceal disguise, convert, or transfer criminal property; section 328 makes it an offence for D to enter into or become concerned in "an arrangement which he knows or suspects facilitates (by whatever means) the acquisition, retention, use or control of criminal property by or on behalf of another person"; while section 329 creates an offence of acquiring, using, or possessing criminal property, save where the defendant pays adequate consideration for the property. Taken together, these offences are apt to cover virtually any of the activities that would fall within the ambit of handling and, like handling, they are punishable by imprisonment for up to 14 years. But, unlike handling, they do not require proof of knowledge of belief on the part of the defendant. As section 340(3) makes clear, it is sufficient that D merely *suspects* the property is stolen or a benefit from crime. Neither is there any need to prove dishonesty.[124] With this shockingly broad mens rea element, these new offences sacrifice traditional concerns for the protection and liberty of individuals in favour of the policing authority and convenience of the state. The days of the car-boot sale could be numbered.

§ 14.2 Robbery

Previously an offence at common law, robbery is now criminalised by section 8 of the Theft Act 1968:

(1) A person is guilty of robbery if he steals, and immediately before or at the time of doing so, and in order to do so, he uses force on any person or puts or seeks to put any person in fear of being then and there subjected to force.

(2) A person guilty of robbery, or of an assault with intent to rob, shall on conviction on indictment be liable to imprisonment for life.

Simply put, robbery is a species of theft which is aggravated by assault. Thus it is to some extent unusual, in that it combines a property offence with an offence of violence against the person, with penalties more severe than the punishments for those individual offences. Partly, this is because the introduction of force makes theft more likely to succeed and, conversely, the object of theft makes the assault more highly motivated, arguably exposing the victim to a greater risk of injury.[125] More importantly, however, the use of force to complete a theft changes the moral character of D's action, such that it is legitimate to criminalise D's wrong specifically by the "combined" offence of robbery. What is significant about robbery is not merely that D usurps V's property rights, but how she does so. The

---

[123] In turn, "property" includes all property, real or personal, tangible or intangible (s. 340(9)), while "criminal conduct" comprises any conduct that constitutes an offence in any part of the United Kingdom, or would do so if performed there (s. 340(2)).

[124] There is, however, a defence of making (or intending but reasonably failing to make) an authorised disclosure to the relevant authorities under s. 338.

[125] Note, "A Rationale of the Law of Aggravated Theft" (1954) 54 *Columbia LR* 84, 102.

expectations of personal and property security are preconditions of a stable, meaningful life; for both individuals and society. Robbery undermines *both* of these expectations. Unlike theft, the victim of a robbery cannot resort to any reassuring knowledge that at least her interest in personal integrity was not attacked. Thus it is perhaps misleading to suggest that robbery is a species of aggravated theft. The difference is not merely one of degree.[126]

Nonetheless, characterising robbery as a species of "theft" does reflect the law, in that the offence of robbery presupposes one of theft. The elements of robbery are as follows:

(i)   theft;

(ii)   accompanied by the use or threat of force;

(iii) which occurs immediately before or at the time of the theft; and

(iv)   where the force is used or threatened in order to commit theft.

(i) Theft

The offence of theft must be proved before there can be any question of robbery.[127] Hence, if the defendant is not dishonest, or has no intention permanently to deprive, no robbery is committed. The case of *Skivington*,[128] discussed in § 13.8(i), is instructive. D held up a wages clerk and demanded his wife's wages: though this was an assault, it was held there was no larceny (and would now be no theft) and therefore no robbery, since he believed he had a lawful claim to the wages. This amounted to a belief that he had a right to deprive the clerk of the money; therefore D was not dishonest, and would not now be dishonest within the meaning of section 2(1)(a).

Note that the claim of right asserted by D in *Skivington* will operate solely in respect of the theft element. Where theft of the property cannot be proved, it is irrelevant—for the purposes of robbery—whether D believes he has a right to use force.[129] However, the absence of justification in respect of the force used will mean that D is independently guilty of an offence against the person.[130]

The decision in *Gomez*,[131] widening the scope of appropriation in theft, consequentially also broadens the ambit of robbery. It would now be an appropriation to tug ineffectually at V's handbag, without detaching the handbag from V's grasp. Previously, where accompanied by force, that would have been only an attempt to steal or rob.

---

[126] Simester and Sullivan, "On the Nature and Rationale of Property Offences" in Duff and Green (eds.), *Defining Crimes: Essays on the Criminal Law's Special Part* (2005) 168, 194-5.

[127] *Guy* (1990) 93 Cr App R 108 (CA). The uncertainty expressed on this point by the Court of Appeal in *Forrester* [1992] Crim LR 792 was, it is submitted, unwarranted—as the note on the case observes: [1992] *Crim LR* 792, 794-5.

[128] [1968] 1 QB 166 (decided prior to the Theft Act 1968); cf. *Robinson* [1977] Crim LR 173; *Hemmings* (1864) 4 F & F 50, 176 ER 462.

[129] Cf. *Langham* (1984) 36 SASR 48. Contrast, in the United States, *People* v. *Reid* 508 NE (2d) 661 (1987); Model Penal Code, § 222.1; ruling that a claim of right that would negate a simple theft would not *ipso facto* negate robbery. Arguably, the American approach is to be preferred. In theft, the claim of right under s. 2(1)(a) implies that D did not realise he was wrongly usurping V's property rights. In *Skivington*, the claim of right was invoked by D for a more complex purpose: effectively, to justify D's forcible self-help by extra-judicial means. Arguably, where excessive force is used, a mere claim of right should not automatically exculpate D from a charge of robbery. See Note, "A Rationale of the Law of Aggravated Theft" (1954) 54 *Columbia LR* 84, 98.

[130] Cf. *Wilson* [1984] AC 242, where D was convicted of assault occasioning actual bodily harm as an alternative to burglary.

[131] [1993] AC 442; above, § 13.6(ii).

(ii) Use or threat of force

Whether or not force is used is a question of fact for the jury to decide.[132] The main difficulty that may arise is where D exerts only a slight and non-violent pressure. In *Dawson*, D1 jostled V, causing V to lose his balance and giving D2 an opportunity to relieve V of his wallet. The Court of Appeal held this was sufficient evidence of force to go to the jury.

The trial judge in *Dawson* had directed that the force used had to be "substantial". However, the Court of Appeal refused to endorse that qualification, preferring to leave the question open. There are difficult issues here, and they remain unresolved. A mere touching, involving very slight pressure that in no way interferes with V's freedom of movement, certainly should not count as force for the purposes of robbery:[133] but it is, from the perspective of physics, an application of force. What seems to be required is that the force be *significant* (rather than substantial), in that it in some way modifies V's movement or freedom of movement. A test along these lines would adequately explain *Dawson* (which was surely rightly decided). It would also explain the decision in *Hale*,[134] where D put his hand over V's mouth in order to stop V from shouting for help. The Court of Appeal affirmed D's conviction for robbery.

One upshot of this is that the crime of robbery has a very broad range, encompassing within the same label both a theft accompanied by a minor push and a theft committed using weapons and serious violence.[135] As such, the crime appears to violate principles of fair labelling, since a conviction for "robbery" does not clearly indicate the seriousness of D's wrongdoing.[136] There is a case here for law reform; in particular, for dividing the existing single crime of robbery into two or three more narrowly defined categories, according to whether the theft was accompanied merely by significant force, by the use of weapons, or by serious violence.

(a) Force against the person or against the property?

Suppose D violently snatches V's bag, without touching V herself. Is this robbery? In other words, must force be applied directly to the person, or is it sufficient that the appropriation be "by force", directed at the stolen property but impacting indirectly on V? At common law, the rule was that the force had to be directed at the person.[137] A snatching was not enough, unless the victim was thereby injured.[138]

---

[132] *Dawson and James* (1976) 64 Cr App R 170.

[133] Analogously, opening an unlocked door in the normal way does not count as a forcible entry: cf. *Ryan v. Shilcock* (1851) 7 Exch 72, 75, 155 ER 861, 862.

[134] (1978) 68 Cr App R 415.

[135] For a sense of the variety, compare O'Donnell and Morrison, "Armed and Dangerous? The Use of Firearms in Robbery" (1997) 36 *Howard J Crim Justice* 305; Gill, *Commercial Robbery: Offenders' Perspectives on Security and Crime Prevention* (2000); and Smith, *The Nature of Personal Robbery* (2003).

[136] See above, § 2.4; Ashworth, "Robbery Re-assessed" [2002] *Crim LR* 851.

[137] *Gnosil* (1824) 1 C & P 304, 1571 ER 1206: "The mere act of taking, being forcible, will not make this offence a highway robbery: to constitute the crime of highway robbery, the force must be . . . of such a nature, as to shew that it was intended to overpower the party robbed, and prevent his resisting, and not merely to get possession of the property stolen. Thus, if a man walking after a woman in the street, were by violence to pull her shawl from her shoulders, though he might use considerable violence, it would not, in my opinion, be highway robbery." See also *Baker* (1783) 1 Leach 290, 168 ER 247; *Steward* 2 East PC 702.

[138] As in *Moore* (1784) 1 Leach 335, 168 ER 270, where D snatched a diamond pin fastened to V's hair, tearing away part of her hair in the process.

It appears, however, that this distinction is not preserved in section 8(1)—contrary to the intentions of those who framed the Act.[139] In *Clouden*,[140] D tore a basket from V's grasp and ran off with it. Because D approached her from behind, V had no opportunity to resist and D offered no force directly to her person. At common law this was not robbery but, said the Court of Appeal, "the old distinctions have gone."[141] D's appeal against conviction was dismissed. Force against property, which causes force to be applied to the person, is sufficient.

It is submitted that the decision in *Clouden* is unfortunate, since it muddies the clear waters distinguishing robbery from theft. As Sir John Smith has commented, the case looks more akin to that of the pickpocket than the bank robber.[142] It contains little, if any, of the moral characteristics that justify labelling D's conduct as a "robbery", and exposing D to a maximum of life imprisonment rather than the seven years that may accompany a conviction for theft.

(b) Threats of force

The actual application of force is not required. Under section 8(1), it is sufficient if D "puts or seeks to put any person in fear of being then and there subjected to force." This is consistent with the law of assault, which includes threats to apply force as well as its actual application.[143] The victim must apprehend being subjected "there and then" to force: threatening to disclose embarrassing details about someone's past, or to apply force at a later date, unless she hands over property may be blackmail,[144] but not robbery.

(c) Third persons

The force need not be used or threatened against the victim of the theft.[145] If D points a gun at V's colleague, T, in order to obtain money from V, D commits robbery (of V). Note, however, that if force is merely threatened rather than applied, it is the person against whom force is threatened who must be "put in fear of being then and there subjected to force." Suppose, for example, that D threatens V that she will shoot V's colleague, T, unless V hands money over to D. T is out of earshot. Somewhat surprisingly, on these facts, D does not commit robbery.[146] V is not put in fear of being subjected to force, since the force is threatened against T. T is not put in fear of being subjected to force, since the threat is directed to V and T does not hear it. This could only be a case of blackmail.[147]

---

[139] Report of the Criminal Law Revision Committee, *Theft and Related Offences* Cmnd. 2977 (1966) para. 65.
[140] [1987] Crim LR 56.
[141] Citing *Dawson and James* (1976) 64 Cr App R 170.
[142] [1987] Crim LR 56, 57.
[143] Above, Chapter 11.
[144] Theft Act 1968, s. 21.
[145] See Andrews, "Robbery" [1966] *Crim LR* 524, 524–6.
[146] Section 8(1) appears in this respect to be slightly narrower than the common law. Previously, it was robbery if D took property by threatening immediately to kill the victim's child: *Donally* (1799) 2 East PC 715, 718; *Reane* (1794) 2 Leach 616, 619, 168 ER 410, 412 n. 1.
[147] Theft Act 1968, s. 21.

(iii) *Immediately before or at the time of the theft*

Suppose the following example:

> D picks V's pocket, extracting V's wallet. V realises what D has done and immediately accosts her. D violently strikes V and runs off.

Has D committed robbery, or is she guilty of separate offences of theft and battery?[148] The answer depends on whether the battery occurs "at the time of the theft". If the theft is completed and D's use of force is merely in order to escape, she is not guilty of robbery.[149] This analysis is reinforced by the requirement, to be discussed in § 14.2(iv), that the force be used or threatened in order to *commit* theft, rather than (say) to escape from it.

What time-frame does "at the time of the theft" import? This question arises elsewhere in the Theft Act, and was considered in §§ 13.6(iv) and 14.1(i)(f). Prima facie, robbery cannot be committed if the force is used or threatened after the offence of theft is completed. The difficulty with this restriction is that, under the interpretation of appropriation established in *Morris* and *Gomez*,[150] the wallet is stolen by D as soon as it is touched. Thereafter, D cannot become guilty of robbery. One example of this analysis is the decision by the Court of Appeal in *Pitham and Hehl*,[151] a handling case. M had offered to sell P and H some furniture that did not belong to him. P and H were convicted of handling and appealed on the ground that the handling occurred "in the course of" the theft by M, and so was excluded by the proviso in section 22.[152] However, the Court upheld the convictions, diagnosing that M, the thief:[153]

> "took the two appellants to 20 Parry Road, showed them the property and invited them to buy what they wanted. He was then, in the words of [s. 3(1)], 'assuming the rights of the owner.' The moment he did that he appropriated [the owner's] goods to himself. The appropriation was complete. After this appropriation had been completed there was no question of these two appellants taking part, in the words of section 22, in dealing with the goods 'in the course of stealing'. "

As a general rule, this seems too extreme.[154] It would mean that, were V to accost D—and be met with violence—while D was still extracting the wallet from V's pocket, D could not commit robbery.

The obvious solution to this difficulty is to accept that robbery cannot be committed after the theft is complete, but to describe D's appropriation of the wallet as a "continuing act", i.e. to regard the act of appropriation as continuing after D has touched the wallet. The

---

[148] Above, Chapter 11.

[149] As was intended: see the Report of the Criminal Law Revision Committee, *Theft and Related Offences* Cmnd. 2977 (1966) para. 66.

[150] Above, § 13.6, 13.6(ii).

[151] (1977) 65 Cr App R 45. Cf. *Corcoran* v. *Anderton* (1980) 71 Cr App R 104.

[152] See above, § 14.1(i)(f).

[153] (1977) 65 Cr App R 45, 49.

[154] Indeed, the Court in *Pitham and Hehl* was careful not to foreclose the possibility of an alternative conclusion in different fact situations.

balance of the case law supports this analysis. In *Hale*, for example, the Court of Appeal stated that:[155]

> "the act of appropriation does not suddenly cease. It is a continuous act and it is a matter for the jury to decide whether or not the act of appropriation has finished."

If, as seems most likely, the continuing act analysis ultimately prevails, robbery will be possible after D's act of appropriation begins but not after it ends; the determination of when the appropriation ends will depend on the facts of each case. (In the example given, it would no doubt be after D has withdrawn her hand from V's pocket, and perhaps when she begins to walk away.)

An alternative solution would be to disengage the phrase "at the time of the theft" from the technical question when the theft is committed, and interpret that phrase as referring to D's theftuous activity or escapade, viewed in its wider context. Hence, one might say "the offence of theft is established" for the purposes of section 1 as soon as D's hand touches the wallet; but that it was still "at the time of the theft" for the purposes of section 8 until D began, say, to escape.[156] One advantage of this interpretation is that it requires no manipulating of the definition of theft in order to satisfy the demands of robbery—it avoids having the cart drive the horse.

(iv) In order to commit theft

The mere coincidence of theft and force is insufficient for robbery. Force must be used, or threatened, *in order* to steal.[157] The motive counts. If D assaults V and then, while V is unconscious, decides to take V's watch, D commits assault and theft but not robbery.

Implicitly, the element of motive imports an associated requirement that D's use of force must itself be intentional. If D accidentally knocks V over while trying to pick his pocket, she cannot be guilty of robbery since she does not mean to use force in order to relieve V of his wallet.[158] Similarly, suppose that D inadvertently frightens V who, in fear, offers her money. D may commit theft should she dishonestly take advantage of V's fear and accept the money, but she does not rob.[159]

§ 14.3 Burglary

The offence of burglary is enacted by section 9 of the Theft Act 1968. As amended by the Criminal Justice Act 1991, the section provides:

---

[155] (1978) 68 Cr App R 415, 418. Note that this case was decided before *Gomez*; see also *Donaghy v. Marshall* [1981] Crim LR 644. In *Lockley* [1995] Crim LR 656, the Court of Appeal endorsed a continuing act analysis and thought that *Hale* was unaffected by *Gomez*; but *Hale* and *Gomez* were said by the same court to be difficult to reconcile in *Atakpu and Abraham* [1994] QB 69, 80. More recently, the possibility of a continuing act has been acknowledged in *Bowden* [2002] EWCA Crim 1279.
[156] Cf. the suggestion in *Atakpu and Abraham* [1994] QB 69, 80: was D still "on the job"?
[157] Cf. *Shendley* [1970] Crim LR 49; *James* [1997] Crim LR 598.
[158] Cf. *Edwards* (1843) 1 Cox CC 32.
[159] *Bruce* [1975] 3 All ER 277, 279H–J.

(1) A person is guilty of burglary if—
    (a) he enters any building or part of a building as a trespasser and with intent to commit any such offence as is mentioned in subsection (2) below; or
    (b) having entered any building or part of a building as a trespasser he steals or attempts to steal anything in the building or that part of it or inflicts or attempts to inflict on any person therein any grievous bodily harm.
(2) The offences referred to in subsection (1)(a) above are offences of stealing anything in the building or part of a building in question, of inflicting on any person therein any grievous bodily harm, and of doing unlawful damage to the building or anything therein.
(3) A person guilty of burglary shall on conviction on indictment be liable to imprisonment for a term not exceeding—
    (a) where the offence was committed in respect of a building or part of a building which is a dwelling, fourteen years;
    (b) in any other case, ten years.

In distinguishing between paragraphs (a) and (b) of section 9(1), the section creates two types of offence, one committed at the time of entry and one that is committed inside the building. The elements of the offence under section 9(1)(a) are as follows:

(a)   entry by D;
(b)   as a knowing or reckless trespasser;
(c)   into a building or part of a building;
(d1) with intent, at the time of entry, to commit one of the following ("ulterior") crimes: stealing, inflicting grievous bodily harm, or doing unlawful damage.

Under section 9(1)(b), the required elements are:

(a)   entry by D;
(b)   as a knowing or reckless trespasser;
(c)   into a building or part of a building; and
(d2) while in the building, D commits one of the following (ulterior) crimes: stealing, attempting to steal, inflicting grievous bodily harm, or attempting to inflict grievous bodily harm.

In either case, by virtue of section 9(3), for the purposes of sentence the court must also determine whether the building is a dwelling.[160] Technically, by enacting different maximum penalties for dwellings as opposed to other buildings,[161] the effect of section 9(3) is to create different offences, corresponding to the different maximum penalties.[162] There are, therefore, four types of offence in all: two for section 9(1)(a)[163] and two for section 9(1)(b).

Originally, the list of intended crimes in section 9(1)(a) included one additional crime. It was also burglary to enter as a trespasser with intent to commit rape (as will be seen when discussing the notorious case of *Collins*,[164] below). However, that version of burglary was

---

[160] At common law, a dwelling is a place that is regularly slept in: *Lyons* (1778) 1 Leach 185, 168 ER 195; *Thompson* (1796) 2 Leach 771, 168 ER 485.

[161] See too s. 111 of the Powers of Criminal Courts (Sentencing) Act 2000 (prescribing a minimum sentence of three years' imprisonment for a third domestic burglary conviction).

[162] See *Courtie* [1984] AC 463, 471 (Lord Diplock).

[163] That is, trespassory entry of a dwelling with intent to commit, etc.; and trespassory entry of a building not being a dwelling with intent to commit, etc.

[164] § 14.3(ii).

deleted by the Sexual Offences Act 2003, which introduced a separate and wider offence of trespass with intent to commit a sexual offence.[165]

(i) Entry

Entry is a physical activity rather than an instantaneous event.[166] Consequently, it can be difficult to draw the line between a completed entry, for the purposes of burglary, and an incomplete attempt. At common law, it was sufficient if any part whatsoever of the body protruded inside the building. Thus, for example, inserting a fingertip beyond the line of the window frame[167] or grasping the inner sill of a window[168] would amount to an entry. This test has the advantage of at least being reasonably straightforward to apply, even if it turns "entry" into rather a technical concept. The Theft Act 1968, which was enacted against the background of this law, makes no reference itself to what constitutes an entry, and it seems to have been assumed during the passage of the Act that the common law rules would continue to apply.[169]

Since enactment of the Act, however, modern cases have sought to qualify the common law test. In *Collins*,[170] Edmund Davies LJ stated that the entry must be "effective and substantial" to satisfy section 9. In *Brown*,[171] however, the Court of Appeal rejected "substantial" as a requirement and said that the entry need only be "effective". D had been seen standing outside, but with the top half of his body inside, a shop's display window. He was apparently rummaging inside the window for goods. While, ultimately, entry is a question of fact for the jury, the Court ruled there was no need for D's whole body to be inside the building and that, on these facts, there had clearly been an entry.

Notwithstanding *Brown*, it is unclear how important is the requirement for "effective" entry. In *Ryan*,[172] only D's head and arm entered the building before D became stuck, so that he was never in a position to steal. The Court of Appeal held that it was irrelevant whether his entry had been sufficiently effective to put D in a position to steal. This seems right, but it raises the question: can "effective" or "substantial" be given any meaningful role in qualifying the requirement for entry? If an arm and head suffice, where is the line to be drawn? How can *Ryan* be distinguished from the fingertip entry?

It is submitted that no useful line can be drawn, and that the "effective" (or "substantial") test advanced in these cases should be either disregarded or understood as a *de minimis* rule: a trivial or practically negligible entry, e.g. by the tip of a finger, is insufficient for section 9; but any significant intrusion inside the space of the building qualifies as an entry.

---

[165] Contrary to s. 63 of the Sexual Offences Act 2003.
[166] Smith, *Property Offences* (1994) § 28–27.
[167] *Davis* (1823) Russ & Ry 499, 168 ER 917. Cf. *Bailey* (1818) Russ & Ry 341, 168 ER 835, and cases cited there; *Perkes* (1824) 1 C & P 300, 171 ER 1204.
[168] *Parkin* [1950] 1 KB 155.
[169] HL Debs., vol. 290, cols. 85–86.
[170] [1973] 1 QB 100, 106. The facts of the case are set out below, in § 14.3(ii).
[171] [1985] Crim LR 212.
[172] (1995) 160 JP 610, noted [1996] Crim LR 320.

(a) Instruments

At common law, entry may be done by an instrument, unless the instrument was intruded solely to enable D to enter in person. For example, casting hooks through a window in order to drag carpets out of the building was sufficient for burglary,[173] but inserting a jemmy in order to lever open a door (and thereby enter oneself) was not.[174] Presumably, the rule that entry by instrument is sufficient will continue to apply under section 9. It is less clear, however, that the exception should be preserved for jemmies and the like which are used to secure entry. The exception arose out of the requirement at common law that there be both a "breaking" and an "entry"; it was thought that where an instrument entered the building in the activity of breaking, that could not by itself also constitute the entry.[175] Since the 1968 Act removes the element of "breaking" from burglary, this rationale no longer applies.

(ii) As a trespasser

D must be a trespasser when she enters the building. Trespass is a tort, and whether D is a trespasser is a question purely of civil law, of which only a summary can be given here. Apart from situations where entry is specifically authorised by law,[176] the main criterion is whether D has received consent to enter from someone authorised to give that consent. The most striking case on trespassory entry under the 1968 Act is *Collins*.[177] The facts of the case were as follows:

> D, naked in all material respects,[178] had climbed up to a bedroom window with intent to commit rape when he was seen by the occupier's daughter, who was in bed at the time. Mistaking D for her boyfriend, the daughter invited D to climb through the window for the purpose of having sexual intercourse. This he did, and it was only while they were in the throes of intercourse that the daughter realised her mistake; whereupon she slapped him in the face, bit him, and retired to the bathroom.

The facts disclose two possible moments at which D might have become guilty of burglary. The first possibility turned on whether D had already effected an entry through the window, onto the inner sill, when he was invited in. If so, a conviction for burglary would be straightforward and the later invitation irrelevant, since the offence under section 9(1)(a) was by then complete.

On the first question there was insufficient evidence to support D's conviction. Alternatively, therefore, assuming D entered only after he was invited in, it was necessary to

---

[173] Case determined Hilary Term, 26 Eliz; (1583) 1 Anderson 114, 123 ER 383. Cf. *Richardson and Brown* [1998] 2 Cr App R (S) 87 (using a JCB digger to ram the wall of a bank and to scoop out the cash dispenser installed there).

[174] Cf. *Hughes* (1785) 1 Leach 406, 168 ER 305.

[175] This is the best explanation of *Tucker* (1844) 1 Cox CC 73, where insertion of a knife in order to lever open a window latch was held to be an entry. D had already committed a breaking by first smashing the window pane (cf. 2 East PC, chap xv § 3).

[176] E.g. where police officers act in execution of a search warrant, or where a landlord distrains for rent.

[177] [1973] 1 QB 100. As was noted earlier, rape is no longer a qualifying offence within s. 9(1)(a).

[178] According to the Court of Appeal (*per* Edmund Davies LJ at 102–3), D had "stripped off all his clothes, with the exception of his socks, because apparently he took the view that if the girl's mother entered the bedroom it would be easier to effect a rapid escape if he had his socks on than if he was in his bare feet. That is a matter about which we are not called upon to express any view, and would in any event find ourselves unable to express one."

decide whether he was a trespasser at that later moment. The Court of Appeal ruled that D committed no burglary. Prima facie, D had received permission to enter from a person authorised to give it. As we shall see below, although the mistake vitiated that permission and D was in law a trespasser,[179] the apparent invitation prevented his entry from being a knowing or reckless trespass.[180]

(a) Authority to enter

The person who permits D's entry must be authorised to do so. Apart from the occupier of the property (usually the owner or leaseholder), any other member of the household has a general authority to invite persons on to the premises for lawful purposes,[181] although this invitation can be revoked or overridden by the occupier.[182]

D will also be a trespasser if the terms of his authority to enter are exceeded. In *Jones and Smith*,[183] D had a general licence to enter his father's house. One night, he went to the house and stole two television sets. His conviction for burglary was upheld by the Court of Appeal. D's licence did not extend so far as to permit entry for an unlawful purpose such as theft.[184]

Glanville Williams has criticised the decision in *Jones and Smith*,[185] suggesting that it forces the issue of trespass to depend on D's mental state (i.e. his criminal purpose) rather than upon any objective facts, such as the express terms of D's licence. Apart from causing burglary to look like a thoughtcrime, the possibility that D's mental state may make his entry unauthorised requires, in turn, that the courts draw lines which are not at all obvious in advance. This is contrary to the aspiration that the law should give fair warning to defendants of their potential crimes. Additionally, if it is the intent to commit theft that makes D a trespasser, the range of burglary is considerably expanded—on this view, if D enters a shop intending to shoplift, D is a burglar.[186] It is to be hoped that the rule in *Jones and Smith* will not be extended to buildings that are open generally to the public.

Notwithstanding these criticisms of *Jones and Smith*, the current law appears to be that D is a trespasser if he enters with an intention to exceed the terms of his licence while on the property.[187] Those terms may be explicit: in *Taylor* v. *Jackson*,[188] for example, V gave D permission to enter his land and hunt for rabbits. Instead, D went onto the land in order to hunt for hares. This was held to be evidence of trespass.

Alternatively, the terms of the licence may be implicit. Typically, there will be implicit restrictions which (i) exclude entry in order to commit a tort or a criminal offence.[189] They

---

[179] Below, § 14.3(ii)(b).

[180] Below, § 14.3(ii)(c).

[181] E.g. *Robson* v. *Hallett* [1967] 2 QB 939 (police officers were not trespassers when invited onto the premises by the occupier's son); *Collins* [1973] QB 100, 107.

[182] As it was in *Robson* v. *Hallett* [1967] 2 QB 939.

[183] [1976] 3 All ER 54.

[184] Arguably, the decision is better justified on the ground that D came with an accomplice, who had no authority to enter at all, and whom D abetted. For discussion, see Smith, *Property Offences* (1994) § 28–12f.

[185] *TBCL* 847ff. See Pace, "Burglarious Trespass" [1985] *Crim LR* 716.

[186] And consider the more extreme example postulated below, in n. 209.

[187] Of course, D may become a trespasser after entering, if his subsequent actions exceed the terms of his licence. But this does not help us here, since for burglary D must be a trespasser at the moment when he enters. The civil law doctrine of trespass *ab initio* has no application to the criminal law: *Collins* [1973] QB 100, 107.

[188] (1898) 78 LT 555.

[189] Cf. *Jones and Smith* [1976] 3 All ER 54.

probably (ii) also exclude other activities which are wrongful or dangerous:[190] "When you invite a person into your house to use the staircase you do not invite him to slide down the banisters."[191] Similarly, (iii) entry with an intention which is contrary to or undermines the purpose for which the licence was granted is likely also to be trespass.[192] These categories may well overlap; as in *Barker*,[193] an Australian case, where D had been asked by V, his neighbour, to keep an eye on V's house while V was away. Instead, D entered and stole some furniture. D's conviction for burglary was upheld by the High Court.

(b) Mistaken authorisation

In *Collins* (above), the daughter's invitation to enter was invalidated by a fundamental mistake regarding D's identity.[194] Hence, D did not have a genuine authorisation to enter, and did so as a trespasser. (The case turned therefore on whether D knew of the mistake, and so entered knowing he was or might be trespassing.) Where the occupier's mistake is not fundamental, authorisation to enter will nonetheless be invalid if it is obtained by deception or fraud. Presumably, by analogy with pre-Act law,[195] D's entry under these circumstances would be as a trespasser.

(c) Mental element in criminal trespass

Under civil law, an action for trespass to land lay even though the defendant had no idea that he was not entitled to enter the property. If D enters a neighbour's house, thinking by mistake it is his own, D commits a tort.[196] This rule of strict liability does not apply in the criminal law. To be guilty of burglary, D must know or be subjectively reckless about the facts that make his entry a trespass. As Edmund-Davies LJ stated in *Collins*:[197]

> "there cannot be a conviction for entering premises 'as a trespasser' within the meaning of section 9 of the Theft Act unless the person entering does so knowing that he is a trespasser and nevertheless deliberately enters, or, at the very least, is reckless as to whether or not he is entering the premises of another without the other party's consent."

This is not to require that D knows he is, *in law*, a trespasser; rather that he knows or recognises the possible existence of the *facts*, i.e. those facts which make him a trespasser. Thus in *Collins* (above), where D entered through the window at the mistaken invitation of the lady inside, D's appeal against conviction was allowed "on the basis that the jury were never invited to consider the vital question whether this young man did enter the premises as a trespasser, that is to say knowing perfectly well that he had no invitation to enter or reckless

---

[190] *Hillen and Pettigrew* v. *ICI (Alkali) Ltd* [1936] AC 65, 69.

[191] *The Calgarth, the Otarama* [1927] P 93, 110. Cited by Lord Atkin in *Hillen and Pettigrew* v. *ICI (Alkali) Ltd* [1936] AC 65, 69.

[192] "So far as he sets foot on so much as the premises as lie outside the invitation or uses them for purposes which are alien to the invitation he is not an invitee but a trespasser": *Hillen and Pettigrew* v. *ICI (Alkali) Ltd* [1936] AC 65, 69. Cf. *Savoy Hotel* v. *BBC* (1983) 133 NLJ 105, though contrast *Byrne* v. *Kinematograph Renters Society Ltd* [1958] 2 All ER 579 for a different result on analogous facts.

[193] (1983) 153 CLR 338.

[194] Cf. the discussion of mistakes, above, § 13.4(iv)(c).

[195] In *Boyle* [1954] 2 QB 292, D tricked V into permitting D to enter by pretending he was an employee of the BBC sent to investigate problems with local radio transmissions. On these facts, D was held guilty of housebreaking.

[196] *Basely* v. *Clarkson* (1682) 3 Lev 37, 83 ER 565; *Conway* v. *Wimpey & Co (No 2)* [1951] 2 KB 266, 273–4.

[197] [1973] QB 100, 105.

of whether or not his entry was with permission." Thus, had D been aware of the woman's mistake about D's identity, he would have been guilty of burglary.

(iii) A building or part of a building

What counts as a building cannot be stated with precision. According to Byles J, it is "a structure of considerable size and intended to be permanent or at least to endure for a considerable time";[198] although these words were intended to be elucidatory rather than definitive. Byles J's test would exclude a tent[199] or a Portaloo, and probably a telephone box. On the other hand, it seems the building need not be affixed to the soil. In *B and S v. Leathley*,[200] the Carlisle Crown Court, applying the statement of Byles J, ruled that a large freezer container, which was sitting on railway sleepers and could be moved by crane, was a building. The Court took into account that the container had lockable doors, was connected to an independent electricity supply, and was intended by its owner to remain *in situ* for the foreseeable future. Implicit in *B and S v. Leathley* is that detached outbuildings are also buildings for the purposes of burglary. Hence, a trespassory entry into a garage would be capable of constituting burglary.[201]

Prima facie, the definition of a building excludes vehicles.[202] However, where vehicles or vessels are inhabited, the scope of burglary is specifically extended by section 9(4), which provides:

> References in subsection (1) and (2) above to a building and the reference in subsection (3) above to a building which is also a dwelling, shall apply also to an inhabited vehicle or vessel, and shall apply to any such vehicle or vessel at times when the person having a habitation in it is not there as well as at times when he is.

Thus breaking into a caravan or houseboat would be burglary while the vehicle or boat is being used as a residence, even if the resident is away at the time. A caravan that is used only for holidays, however, would be "inhabited" only during the holiday and probably, therefore, could not be burgled at other times.[203]

(a) Part of a building

The phrase "part of a building" is included because of the possibility that D may have permission to enter a building, without being allowed access to the whole of the interior. In such cases, D can commit burglary by intruding into that part of the building where her entry is disallowed. A hotel guest, for example, commits burglary by entering another guest's room with intent to steal, even though she has permission to be in the hotel. Similarly, in *Walkington*,[204] D's general permission to enter a shop did not save her from conviction for

---

[198] (1859) 7 CBNS 99, 112, 141 ER 752, 757.
[199] Cf. Criminal Law Revision Committee, *Theft and Related Offences* Cmnd. 2977 (1966) para. 78.
[200] [1979] Crim LR 314.
[201] Cf. *Whitmore* v. *Bedford* (1843) 5 Man & G 9, 134 ER 460.
[202] E.g. an articulated lorry trailer: *Norfolk Constabulary* v. *Seekings and Gould* [1986] Crim LR 167, differing from *B and S* v. *Leathley* [1979] Crim LR 314 in that the trailer still rested on its own wheels. Compare s. 292(4) of the Canadian Criminal Code, which specifically includes railway stock, trailers, and aircraft.
[203] Cf. the common law definition of a dwelling as a place that is regularly slept in: *Lyons* (1778) 1 Leach 185, 168 ER 195; *Thompson* (1796) 2 Leach 771, 168 ER 485.
[204] [1979] 2 All ER 716.

burglary when she went behind the counter in order to plunder the till. The counter effectively bounded an area from which customers were excluded.

It is not clear whether a building can be severed into "parts" without some sort of physical division, such as the barrier that was created by the sales counter in *Walkington*. Certainly, any physical division need not be permanent, since in *Walkington* itself the counter was a movable one. In principle, it ought to be sufficient for the purposes of establishing a trespassory entry that the area is clearly demarcated, even if this is done merely by drawing lines on the floor. However, the point remains undecided.

(iv) With intent to commit, or committing, the ulterior offence

Under section 9(1)(a), the offence of burglarious entry, the prosecution must prove that *at the time he entered* D intended[205] therein to commit one of the following offences: stealing, inflicting grievous bodily harm, or doing unlawful damage. The offence is committed at point of entry; if, having entered, D then changes his mind and leaves without committing the offence, it is too late. The offence is committed and cannot be undone.

As with all future-intent offences, difficult questions sometimes arise if D's intent is conditional. Suppose that D enters a building intending to steal only if he finds something worth stealing. In principle, cases of conditional intention should be treated as ones of intention, so that D is guilty of burglary in this example.[206] Conditional intention is discussed further in the context of theft, above, in § 13.7(i)(f).[207] In the context of the difficulties there discussed, however, notice that whereas one cannot *steal* something that does not exist, one can *intend* to do so; hence D can be guilty of burglary when he enters V's house with conditional intent to steal a diamond (should it be there), even though there is no diamond.

Under section 9(1)(b), burglary is constituted by committing, or attempting, the offences either of theft or of inflicting grievous bodily harm, *after* D has entered the building as a trespasser. Thus the time at which burglary is committed is when D commits, or attempts to commit, the ulterior offence once inside the building.

Note that, under both paragraphs of section 9(1), the intended, committed or attempted offence must be within the building (or part-building) that D has entered as a trespasser. Hence if D enters V's flat without permission, solely in order to access his own adjacent flat where, for insurance purposes, he intends to stage a "theft" of electronic equipment, he does not commit burglary. His trespassory entry into V's flat was without intent to steal "therein".

(a) Stealing

For the purposes of burglary, "stealing" connotes theft, contrary to section 1, and does not refer to obtaining by fraud or blackmail.[208] Wherever "steal" carries a wider meaning than "theft", the Act makes this clear by express provision,[209] and no such provision is made for

---

[205] As the terms of s. 9(1)(a) makes clear, recklessness is insufficient: *A* v. *DPP* [2003] All ER (D) 393. For the purposes of the intoxication rules (below, § 19.3), the offence is one of specific intent: *Durante* [1972] 1 WLR 1612.

[206] *A-G's References (Nos. 1 and 2 of 1979)* [1980] QB 180.

[207] See also the general discussion above, § 5.1(viii).

[208] Cf. *Low* v. *Blease* [1975] Crim LR 513 (entry with intent dishonestly to use electricity, although contrary to s. 13, was not burglary, since using electricity was not theft within s. 1).

[209] E.g. in the case of handling: above, § 14.1(ii)(a).

burglary. Note, however, that in the wake of *Gomez*[210] any obtaining by fraud is likely anyway to be theft; thus the apparently narrow meaning of "stealing" in section 9(1) imposes few practical restrictions.[211]

(b) Inflicting grievous bodily harm

For section 9(1)(a), the relevant offence is section 18 of the OAPA 1861; for section 9(1)(b), the relevant offences are sections 18, 20, and 23 of the OAPA 1861. Those offences are discussed in Chapter 11 and will not be traversed here. One rather odd decision must, however, be mentioned. In *Wilson and Jenkins*,[212] the defendants entered a house and committed a serious assault on the occupants. They were charged with burglary under section 9(1)(b). On appeal, the Court of Appeal stated that there was no requirement in section 9(1)(b) that D's action actually be an *offence*:[213]

> "It seems unlikely that in this context Parliament intended to restrict the expression 'inflict grievous bodily harm' to the narrow area of assault. To test this proposition it may be helpful to consider a set of circumstance that could not be described as fanciful. An intruder gains access to the house without breaking in (where there is an open window, for instance). He is on the premises as a trespasser, and his intrusion is observed by someone in the house of whom he may not even be aware, and as a result that person suffers severe shock, with a resulting stroke. In such a case it is difficult to see how an assault could be alleged; but nevertheless his presence would have been a direct cause of the stroke,[214] which must amount to grievous bodily harm. Should such an event fall outside the provisions of s 9, when causing some damage to the property falls fairly within it?"

Thus, the Court concluded, whatever the proper interpretation of the words "to inflict grievous bodily harm" in the OAPA 1861, "we would be of the opinion that they have the wider meaning in section 9(1)(b) of the 1968 Act."[215]

With respect to the Court of Appeal, this conclusion—and the example given by the Court—is bizarre. While it is true that section 9(1)(a) includes, and section 9(1)(b) omits, the word "offence", in fact that omission was a mere error of drafting.[216] The Court's interpretation of section 9(1)(b) makes it possible to commit burglary by accident—turning the offence into one of strict liability.[217] There is no question but that this was not the intention of Parliament.[218] Burglary is a very serious offence which carries a substantial penalty, and it is extraordinary that it may be committed without mens rea (save to enter as

---

[210] [1993] AC 442. See above, § 13.6(ii).

[211] Bearing in mind the discussion of *Jones and Smith* [1976] 3 All ER 54 above, in § 14.3(ii)(a), this appears to suggest that someone entering a social security office intending fraudulently to claim an unemployment benefit would commit burglary. It is to be hoped that such a case would not be treated as involving a trespass.

[212] [1984] AC 242 (HL); *sub nom. Jenkins and Jenkins* [1983] 1 All ER 1000 (CA).

[213] [1983] 1 All ER 1000, 1004. No comment was made on this point by the House of Lords, which reversed the Court of Appeal's decision on other grounds.

[214] But surely not an infliction: see Gardner, "Rationality and the Rule of Law in Offences Against the Person" [1994] *CLJ* 502, 504–6.

[215] [1983] 1 All ER 1000, 1005.

[216] Smith, "Burglary under the Theft Bill" [1968] *Crim LR* 367.

[217] Strict, rather than constructive, liability, because the further element of the offence is not a mere consequence but a *novus actus* by D. See above, Chapter 6.

[218] See the commentary on *Jenkins and Jenkins* at [1983] Crim LR 386.

a trespasser, which is a wholly different type of wrongdoing). It is to be hoped that, in the future, the Court's view will come to be regarded as wrong.

(c) Unlawful damage

Damage is unlawful when it is contrary to the Criminal Damage Act 1971 (below, § 14.4–5). In particular, it is an offence under section 1 of that Act intentionally or recklessly to destroy or damage any property belonging to another. Note that unlawful damage is a relevant offence only for the purposes of burglarious *entry*, contrary to section 9(1)(a). Thus a trespasser who vandalises the interior of a building does not commit burglary unless she entered the building intending to do so.

(v) The rationale of burglary

Entry as a trespasser is not, by itself, an offence.[219] It is D's intent to commit (or commission of) the ulterior crime that radically changes the nature of her legal wrong. Given this, it might be thought odd to enact a crime of burglary when D could, on the same facts, be convicted of an attempt to commit the ulterior crime directly.[220] Recall the case of *Collins*, discussed earlier.[221] D had climbed up to a window with intent to commit rape, and was on the sill when he was invited into the house. One issue in the case was whether he had by then entered the building. But, assuming he had entered, surely the description that best captures the moral character of his conduct would have been attempted rape? Robinson asks:[222]

> "One may wonder, then, why burglary is retained as an offense in modern codes. Conviction for criminal intrusion and for attempt to commit the intended offense would seem adequately and properly to punish the conduct constituting burglary."

On this view it is all the more puzzling, one may add, that burglary carries a maximum sentence greater than theft itself. The crime is, in Robinson's view, explicable only by historical tradition; it is instructive that burglary is not an offence under the civil law codes in France and Germany.

There is much in this scepticism. It is certainly true that the gist of burglary is not trespass. However, neither is it the ulterior crime at which D aims (or ultimately commits). Burglary is not merely an aggravated form of theft, grievous bodily harm, etc. It is a wrong in its own right. The trespassory entry by D not only exposes V to risk of a serious ulterior crime; it also, in so doing, violates V's private life—an important protected interest under Article 8 of the ECHR.

---

[219] Although common law formerly knew an offence of conspiracy to trespass (*Kamara v. DPP* [1974] AC 104), this has now been abolished by s. 5 of the Criminal Law Act 1977. Some specific forms of trespass are criminalised by statute, most notably in Part II of the Criminal Law Act 1977. See also the Criminal Justice and Public Order Act 1994, especially ss. 61, 68, and 69.

[220] Or, in respect of s. 9(1)(b), of the full ulterior crime. The genesis of s. 9(1)(b) seems to be the common law rule that commission of the ulterior crime was conclusive of D's intent at the time of entry—i.e. of an offence now captured by s. 9(1)(a): 5 *English Commissioner's Reports on the Criminal Law* (1840) 4.

[221] Above, § 14.3(ii).

[222] *Criminal Law* (1997) 778.

The strongest case of this—subject under section 9(3) to distinctive sentencing provisions—is where the premises are a dwelling-house.[223] Interaction with and exposure to other members of society is integral to public life; conversely, our sense of identity and well-being as individuals depends upon our being able to reserve private space, from which other persons can be excluded. It is through controlling our private environment that we are able to have 'breathing space' from interactions with other people. Burglary compromises that space. It is hardly surprising that house burglary, in particular, causes victims great distress even if they were absent at the material time. The victim of such a burglary cannot be sure of the peaceable and secure enjoyment even of her own home. For most people, when the integrity of their private space cannot be taken for granted, one of the foundations of their well-being is destroyed.

An analogous if less powerful claim can be made for burglary of other buildings. One of the main functions of structures such as warehouses, offices, and the like is to help safeguard people and property by establishing a physical separation from the public environment. Within that secured space, people can relax at least some of the precautions they may take when in public, by putting down their handbags, remaining late to work, and the like. Conversely, if that space is not perceived to be fully secure, such practices become disrupted. Even in these non-domestic contexts, the existence and control of a realm of quasi-private space affects the manner in which we live.

The existence of secured private space also influences how we organise our property. Just as at home, goods in warehouses and offices can be arrayed or stocked without securing each individually. Thus a related harm of burglary is that it gives D unparalleled access to take (or damage) a whole range of V's goods, whether domestic or commercial, in a way that, say, pickpocketing does not. Here too, the case of a domestic burglary is an aggravated one: the goods to which D has access tend to include our highly personal things (underclothes, private letters, and the like) as well as things with high sentimental value—something that reinforces the sense of 'violation' experienced by burglary victims.

The arguments outlined here are supplemented by consequentialist considerations. Entry into a building is a significant physical step by which D commits herself to carrying out the ulterior crime. In effect, it ups the stakes, making it more likely that the ulterior offence will be committed. Moreover, because the activity occurs inside a building, it increases the probability that incidental violence will ensue should D be chanced upon by someone else:[224]

> "Frequently a person discovered in the course of committing a crime [in public] is in a position where he realizes that resistance is useless and that he must flee or surrender. Again, the person who discovers the criminal does not always have a sufficient interest to offer forcible intervention. Both of these factual situations are conducive to the non-occurrence of incidental crimes. Neither is likely to result when a trespasser is discovered while committing a crime in a dwelling;[225] rather, resistance to the criminal and consequent injury to occupants, seems probable."

---

[223] Indeed, this was originally the only variety of burglary known to the common law. See 3 Coke Inst. 63.

[224] Note, "A Rationale of the Law of Burglary" (1951) 51 *Col LR* 1009, 1026.

[225] It is submitted that this is true, to a lesser extent, of any other building.

For all these reasons, burglary deserves its status as a serious crime. Additionally, it is worth observing that while the scope of burglary may extend no further back in time than the attempted ulterior crime (so that if D is stopped by a policeman before entering a post office, he commits neither burglary nor attempted robbery),[226] its existence as a distinct offence creates the possibility of conviction for *attempted burglary*, which may lie even in circumstances that, so far as the ulterior crime is concerned, are merely preparatory.

Notice, though, that the normative core of burglary we have identified is concerned with the protection of real property rather than with the particular offence that is intended or committed therein. For this reason, it seems to us anomalous that under section 9(1) the crime is confined to only a few specified ulterior crimes. The rationale of burglary extends to penalising persons who make trespassory entries into a building and intend or commit any serious (say, indictable) crime.[227] The gravamen of the offence is both to be a trespasser and to intend or commit an indictable offence in the place wherein one has trespassed. In its aggravated domestic version, burglary is most truly a property offence in that such conduct radically undermines the enjoyment of a vital proprietary interest. In other contexts, burglary becomes more obviously associated with proscribing conduct likely to result in the commission of a serious offence; yet there too it undermines the use and purposes of the premises themselves.

§ 14.4 Criminal damage

The core offence of criminal damage is contained in section 1(1) of the Criminal Damage Act 1971:

> A person who without lawful excuse destroys or damages property belonging to another intending to destroy or damage any such property or being reckless whether any such property would be destroyed or damaged shall be guilty of an offence.

The offence, which is punishable by imprisonment for a maximum of ten years, contains six main elements. The actus reus is:

(i)   that D destroys or damages
(ii)   property; and
(iii)   the property belongs to another.

The mens rea components are:

(iv)   D intends or is reckless about destroying or damaging the property; and
(v)   D is (at least) reckless whether the property belongs to another.

Finally, the section provides for a defence:

(vi)   D's conduct is without lawful excuse.

We shall consider these elements in turn.

---

[226] *Campbell* (1990) 93 Cr App R 350. See above, § 9.3(i)(c).
[227] Compare s. 231 of the Crimes Act 1961 (NZ) (as amended).

(i) *Destroys or damages*

There must be some actual, physical damage to the property. We will focus here on the meaning of "damages" rather than "destroys", since the latter term seems to add nothing to the former, save in that it is apt to comprehend many of the more extreme or comprehensive instances of damage.

What counts as damage is a question of fact and degree for the jury, and requires evaluation of the particular circumstances of the case.[228] There is no requirement that the damage be severe. One who walks across another's lawn may damage it by flattening the grass.[229] Neither is there any requirement that the damage be permanent or irreparable. Smearing mud graffiti on the wall of a police cell, which cost £7 to clean off, has been ruled capable of being criminal damage.[230] Similarly, it has been held that erasing a computer program can be criminal damage. In *Cox* v. *Riley*,[231] D intentionally deleted the program from a printed circuit card that operated a computerised saw, rendering the saw inoperable. He was convicted of criminal damage, a conviction upheld on appeal on the ground that deletion of the program constituted damage to the circuit card, since it necessitated expending time, labour and money to reprogram the card. The Divisional Court cited a helpful discussion from the unreported case of *Henderson* v. *Battley*, in which D was charged with damaging a development land site in the Isle of Dogs. The site, which had been cleared, was flat except for one pile of crushed concrete kept for use in the laying of temporary roads during the development. Without authority, D dumped 30 lorry loads of soil and rubble and mud on the site, effectively using it as a tip. The Court of Appeal held that, even though the underlying land was not itself altered, dumping rubbish could constitute criminal damage:[232]

> "if as here there is evidence that the owner of the land reasonably found it necessary to spend about £2,000 to remove the results of the appellant's operations it is not irrelevant to the question of whether this land, as a building site, was damaged. Ultimately whether damage was done to this land was a question of fact and degree for the jury. Damage can be of various kinds. In the Concise Oxford Dictionary 'damage' is defined as 'injury impairing value or usefulness.' That is a definition which would fit in very well with doing something to a cleared building site which at any rate for the time being impairs its usefulness as such. In addition, as it necessitates work and the expenditure of a large sum of money to restore it to its former state, it reduces its present value as a building site. This land was a perfectly good building site which did not need £2,000 spending on it in order to sell or use it as such until the appellants began their operations."

The Court also relied upon early authority in *Fisher*,[233] where D inserted an object into a machine and made other alterations that temporarily rendered the machine useless. This was held capable of constituting damage, on the basis that it took two hours' labour (albeit no additional materials) to restore the machine to proper working order.

---

[228] *Roe* v. *Kingerlee* [1986] Crim LR 735 (DC); *Samuels* v. *Stubbs* [1972] 4 SASR 200, 203; *Hardman* v. *Chief Constable of Avon and Somerset* [1986] Crim LR 331 (CC).
[229] *Gayford* v. *Chouler* [1898] 1 QB 316 (DC).
[230] *Roe* v. *Kingerlee* [1986] Crim LR 735 (DC).
[231] (1986) 83 Cr App R 54 (DC).
[232] Court of Appeal, Criminal Division, 29/11/84, at 3B; quoted in *Cox* v. *Riley* (1986) 83 Cr App R 54, 57 (DC).
[233] (1865) LR 1 CCR 7.

Overall, what emerges from the cases is a two-part test: any significant alteration to property can count as damage, provided it requires more than a trivial expenditure of time, effort, or money to undo. In respect of undoing the alteration, we may contrast the smearing of mud on a wall with a scenario in which D affixes a "Post-it" note to V's door. The note can simply be lifted off, and it is submitted that D's act does not damage the door. In similar vein, spitting on a policeman's raincoat was ruled not to be damage in so far as the spittle could be removed simply by wiping it with a damp cloth.[234] Painting silhouettes on a pavement using soluble paint, on the other hand, was rightly held to be criminal damage after the local authority washed the markings away with high-pressure jets, even though they would eventually have been dissolved by rain.[235] Rainwater would not have removed the damage forthwith.

But that still leaves the question of when there is a significant alteration. Standard *indicia* are if the property is rendered either less usable[236] or less valuable.[237] To illustrate by counterexample, in *Morphitis* v. *Salmon* D removed a scaffolding bar from a barrier that was blocking an access road. The bar was subsequently found to be scratched. Even if D had caused the scratching, however, the Court ruled that this would not be criminal damage since it impaired neither the value nor the usefulness of the bar, scratching being a normal incident of scaffolding components.[238]

More difficult are the car-clamping cases. The courts have ruled that wheel clamping does not, in itself, damage the car, seemingly because it is a removable appendage that does not physically harm the vehicle. According to Laws J, in *Drake* v. *DPP*:[239]

> "But one way or another, whatever the example one chooses, there must be some intrusion into what, in the course of argument, Mann LJ described as the 'integrity of the object in question.' There was no such intrusion here. There was nothing which, as matter of ordinary language, could sensibly be regarded as damage to the car. Certainly the wheel clamp was applied to it. I do not, for my part, believe that a court could properly have held that this application amounted to 'damage.'"

It is submitted that these cases are wrongly decided. Admittedly, one may more readily think of them as involving detention rather than damage. But in light of the foregoing case law, the better view must be that clamping involves detention *by* damage. Contrast a scenario in which D erects a fence or other barrier around a car in order to prevent its departure, without affixing the barrier to the car. D does not damage the car. But if D applies a clamp directly to the car he does physically interfere so as to affect its "integrity"—no less than dumping rubbish on a land site or adding mud graffiti to a wall. Notwithstanding the assertion by Laws J, there is no necessity for any "intrusion into" the interior of the object. The requirement for a physical alteration can be satisfied either internally or externally.

---

[234] *A (A Juvenile)* v. *R* [1978] Crim LR 689 (CC).

[235] *Hardman* v. *Chief Constable of Avon and Somerset* [1986] Crim LR 331 (CC); distinguishing *A (A Juvenile)* v. *R* [1978] Crim LR 689 (CC) (above).

[236] *Roper* v. *Knott* [1898] 1 QB 868 (DC) (spoiling milk by adulterating it with water).

[237] *Foster* (1852) 6 Cox CC 25.

[238] [1990] Crim LR 48 (DC). The Court noted, *obiter*, that while D was not guilty of damaging the bar itself, he could have been convicted of criminal damage to the barrier as a whole—had he been so charged.

[239] [1994] RTR 411, 418 (DC); cf. *Lloyd* v. *DPP* [1992] 1 All ER 982 (DC).

(ii) Property

Most tangible things can be damaged. According to section 10(1) of the 1971 Act:

> In this Act "property" means property of a tangible nature, whether real or personal, including money and—
>
> (a) including wild creatures which have been tamed or are ordinarily kept in captivity, and any other wild creatures or their carcasses if, but only if, they have been reduced into possession which has not been lost or abandoned or are in the course of being reduced into possession; but
>
> (b) not including mushrooms growing wild on any land or flowers, fruit or foliage of a plant growing wild on any land.
>
> For the purposes of this subsection "mushroom" includes any fungus and "plant" includes any shrub or tree.

As with the law of theft, the scope of the offence is wide-ranging and includes most forms of tangible property known to the common law. Indeed, like the definition in section 4(1) of the Theft Act 1968, "property" is not here statutorily defined; we must begin with that concept as it is understood in the civil law,[240] and section 10(1) simply operates to modify the underlying civil law concept.

The most important difference from theft is that criminal damage requires the property to be *tangible*, something that reflects the physical nature of the concept of damage within the 1971 Act. Hence extinguishing a debt (owed to V) by appropriating V's bank account cannot be criminal damage, even though it might be said to "destroy" V's chose in action, because choses in action are intangible property and fall outwith the scope of section 10(1).

A second point of difference is that land can be damaged, without being subject to the restrictions applicable in the context of theft.[241] Additionally, things growing wild cannot be damaged, whereas they can be stolen if picked for a commercial purpose.[242]

(iii) Belonging to another

Under section 1(1), the core offence of criminal damage can be committed only when the property damaged "belongs" to someone other than V. (The aggravated offence does not require this: see below, § 14.5.) This means that, for the core offence, some other person must have an interest in the subject matter of the damage. As with theft, this does not preclude D's being the owner of the item, so long as her ownership is not absolute; as when V, say, has a lien over the property, or is a joint owner, or has some other interest in the property. In such a case the property can be criminally damaged by D (or by anyone else, including V). But if D is absolute owner of the property, she cannot commit the offence under section 1(1). It does not "belong to another" for the purposes of the Act.

The meaning of "belonging to another" is elaborated in section 10:

> (2) Property shall be treated for the purposes of this Act as belonging to any person—
> (a) having the custody or control of it;
> (b) having in it any proprietary right or interest (not being an equitable interest arising only from an agreement to transfer or grant an interest); or
> (c) having a charge on it.

(3) Where property is subject to a trust, the persons to whom it belongs shall be so treated as including any person having a right to enforce the trust.

(4) Property of a corporation sole shall be so treated as belonging to the corporation notwithstanding a vacancy in the corporation.

As with the corresponding provisions in section 5 of the Theft Act, the scope of the section is effective to protect virtually any form of proprietary interest, whether of ownership or possession, and whether at common law or equity. Although the section mentions "custody *or* control", it is not clear that the latter term adds anything much. Physical control would in any event also constitute a form of custody, and any other right of control would presumably only qualify if it were enforceable *in rem*, i.e. if it were a proprietary interest. Similarly, the inclusion of a "charge" in section 10(2)(c) is probably superfluous, since charges are normally a form of proprietary interest.

On the other hand, where there is no custody or control there *must* be a proprietary interest. Thus the section does not protect interests that may arise when D enters into an agreement to sell goods to V on some future date. Section 10(2)(b) makes it clear that the latter sort of interest is not protected, by contrast with contracts of sale that transfer ownership immediately. Hence if, before the agreed date of the future transfer, D were to destroy the goods, D would not commit criminal damage. Similarly, neither is D guilty of an offence under section 1(1) if he sets fire to his car intending to claim the insurance, because an insurer has no proprietary interest in the subject matter of the policy.[243]

(iv) Intentional or reckless damage

The *damage* (or destruction) must be done either intentionally or (subjectively) recklessly. If D throws a stone at V and misses, he does not become guilty of criminal damage when the stone misses V but goes on to break V's window, unless the risk of its doing so was foreseen by D.[244] The subjective nature of this recklessness requirement is authoritatively reasserted by the House of Lords in *G*,[245] overruling the decision in *Caldwell*[246] which was for a time authority that failing to foresee an obvious and serious risk of the actus reus could also constitute recklessness. These decisions are discussed in detail in § 5.2(i) above. In gist, the law now requires that D either intends to damage the property,[247] or actually foresees a risk that the property will be damaged by her conduct.

As with recklessness generally, in the latter case the risk she foresees must also be an unreasonable one to run.[248] No doubt, for example, by hitting a six at the village cricket ground D creates a slight risk of causing damage to a neighbouring house. Suppose that, although he does not intend such damage, he is aware of the risk. Typically, nonetheless, the

---

[240] For general discussion, see above, § 13.3.
[241] Theft Act 1968, s. 4(2); above, § 13.3(ii)(a).
[242] Theft Act 1968, s. 4(3); above, § 13.3(ii)(b).
[243] Cf. *Denton* [1981] 1 WLR 1446, 1448–9 (CA).
[244] Cf. *Pembliton* (1874) LR 2 CCC 119.
[245] [2004] AC 1034.
[246] [1982] AC 341 (HL).
[247] Above, § 5.1.
[248] This proviso is noted above, § 5.2.

risk he creates is a reasonable one and, if a window should be broken, D will not be accounted reckless.[249]

(v) Intention or recklessness whether the property belongs to another

In respect of the core offence in section 1(1), the general requirement of intention or recklessness extends to the actus reus element that the property *belongs to another*. To count as "intention" when applied to circumstances,[250] D would need either to hope, know, or believe that the property belongs to someone else.[251] But this is not especially important, since it is anyway sufficient that D is reckless about the ownership of the property. Given the meaning of the latter term in the context of circumstances,[252] D will be reckless whether the property belongs to another if she either recognises a risk that the property is not absolutely hers; or if, in the extensional case allowed for by the House of Lords in *B (a minor) v. DPP*,[253] she acts without believing that the property belongs to her (i.e. if she has no belief either way).

The importance of this mens rea element is emphasised in *Smith (David)*.[254] D, a tenant, with permission installed stereo wiring in his flat which he covered by mounting covering panels and other materials. Upon termination of the tenancy, D damaged the panels in order to remove the wiring. By operation of law, the panels had became part of the flat when installed and so belonged to the owner. Nonetheless, although D was certainly civilly liable for the damage, his conviction of criminal damage was quashed, since D honestly believed that the panels were his. In the Court's analysis:[255]

> "Construing the language of section 1(1) we have no doubt that the actus reus is 'destroying or damaging any property belonging to another.' It is not possible to exclude the words 'belonging to another' which describes the 'property'. Applying the ordinary principles of mens rea, the intention and recklessness and the absence of lawful excuse required to constitute the offence have reference to property belonging to another. It follows that in our judgment no offence is committed under this section if a person destroys or causes damage to property belonging to another if he does so in the honest though mistaken belief that the property is his own, and provided that the belief is honestly held it is irrelevant to consider whether or not it is a justifiable belief."

(vi) Without lawful excuse

As with other offences, the offence of criminal damage is only prima facie established by proof of the foregoing actus reus and mens rea elements. D may still have a defence; for example, if he acted in self-defence or in circumstances of necessity. Unusually, however, the Act offers its own supplementary definition of "lawful excuse" in section 5:

---

[249] Famously, neither is he negligent in tort law: *Miller* v. *Jackson* [1977] QB 966; *Bolton* v. *Stone* [1951] AC 850.
[250] Above, § 5.1(v).
[251] In the wider sense of belonging to another defined by s. 10; above, § 14.4(iii).
[252] Above, § 5.2(iii).
[253] [2000] 2 AC 428, 459 (Lord Mackay), 466 (Lord Nicholls).
[254] [1974] QB 354 (CA).
[255] *Ibid.*, 360.

(1) This section applies to any offence under section 1(1) above and any offence under section 2 or 3 above other than one involving a threat by the person charged to destroy or damage property in a way which he knows is likely to endanger the life of another or involving an intent by the person charged to use or cause or permit the use of something in his custody or under his control so to destroy or damage property.

(2) A person charged with an offence to which this section applies shall, whether or not he would be treated for the purposes of this Act as having a lawful excuse apart from this subsection, be treated for those purposes as having a lawful excuse —

(a) if at the time of the act or acts alleged to constitute the offence he believed that the person or persons whom he believed to be entitled to consent to the destruction of or damage to the property in question had so consented, or would have so consented to it if he or they had known of the destruction or damage and its circumstances; or

(b) if he destroyed or damaged or threatened to destroy or damage the property in question or, in the case of a charge of an offence under section 3 above, intended to use or cause or permit the use of something to destroy or damage it, in order to protect property belonging to himself or another or a right or interest in property which was or which he believed to be vested in himself or another, and at the time of the act or acts alleged to constitute the offence he believed —

(i) that the property, right or interest was in immediate need of protection; and

(ii) that the means of protection adopted or proposed to be adopted were or would be reasonable having regard to all the circumstances.

(3) For the purposes of this section it is immaterial whether a belief is justified or not if it is honestly held.

(4) For the purposes of subsection (2) above a right or interest in property includes any right or privilege in or over land, whether created by grant, licence or otherwise.

(5) This section shall not be construed as casting doubt on any defence recognised by law as a defence to criminal charges.

Section 5(2) lays down two statutory grounds of lawful excuse: consent and defence of property. For both versions, section 5(3) makes clear that the test is subjective: the availability of the defence depends on what D *believed*, rather than the actual fact of the matter or even whether D's belief was reasonable. Unusually, this is so even if D makes a mistake due to intoxication.[256] We consider the two versions in turn.

(a) Consent

Section 5(2)(a) establishes a defence of lawful excuse if D believes that the owner (or other person entitled to consent, such as the owner's representative) has consented to the damage's being inflicted, or would have done so had she known about it.[257] A striking illustration is *Denton*,[258] in which D set fire to his employer's cotton mill, causing some £40,000 worth of damage. He acted purportedly in the belief that his employer had encouraged him to do so, since the business was in difficulty and a fire would "help its financial

---

[256] *Jaggard* v. *Dickinson* [1981] QB 527 (DC). D had been given permission to treat her friend's house as her own. She broke into the wrong house one evening, drunkenly thinking it was her friend's. D's conviction was quashed on the footing that she genuinely believed she had consent to break in; and s. 5(3) stipulates a subjective rather than an objective test. See below, § 18.3(iii)(a).

[257] Compare s. 2(1)(b) of the Theft Act 1968; above, § 13.8(ii).

[258] [1981] 1 WLR 1447 (CA).

circumstances". On these facts, the Court of Appeal quashed D's conviction. The underlying fraudulent motive was irrelevant, at least to a charge of criminal damage: D's belief that he had consent, from someone he thought entitled to give such consent,[259] was sufficient to establish a lawful excuse.

(b) Defence of property

Frequently this defence will overlap with the defence of prevention of crime in section 3 of the Criminal Law Act 1967 (discussed in § 21.2). However, it is available even when the threat to property is not itself criminal.[260] In *Chamberlain* v. *Lindon*,[261] for example, following a dispute about the extent of D's right of way over part of V's land, V built a wall restricting D's vehicular access. D demolished the wall. The Divisional Court affirmed his acquittal of criminal damage, because D had acted in order to protect his right of way, which was a "right or interest in property" falling within section 5(2)(b).

In order to qualify for the defence, D must subjectively believe (i) that the property (or interest therein) belonged to himself or another; (ii) that it was in *immediate* need of protection; and (iii) that conduct was a *reasonable* means of protecting the property. D's conduct must also be undertaken (iv) *in order to* protect the property. These elements deserve separate consideration.

Belonging to himself or another.

Interestingly, there is nothing in the section to suggest that "another" cannot be the very owner of the damaged property, as when D breaks into V's house in order to put out a fire there. Section 5(2)(b) seems to require only that the property or interest being protected was thought by D to belong to *someone*, and not to be abandoned or otherwise ownerless. The point was important in *Cresswell* v. *DPP*,[262] where the defendants went onto farmland and destroyed badger traps in order to protect wild badgers. Because the badgers had not been reduced into possession they were ownerless and not property, so fell outside the scope of section 5. The defendants' convictions were upheld.

Immediate need of protection.

Whether D believes the property is in need of protection is a subjective question. But the courts have held that whether the perceived need counts as "immediate" is an *objective* question to be determined by the jury (or judge, as the case may be), in light of the facts and circumstances that D believes to exist. This point was decisive in *Hill*,[263] where D was charged with possessing articles (namely hacksaw blades) with intent to damage the perimeter fence of a naval base.[264] She claimed that her purpose was to bring about the abandonment of the base which, in the even of international hostilities breaking out, she believed would be the target of a nuclear strike with consequential damage to surrounding

---

[259] Not including God: *Blake* v. *DPP* [1993] Crim LR 586 (DC), below, § 21.2(i).

[260] But, unlike the defence of prevention of crime, there must be a threat to *property*: cf. *Cresswell* v. *DPP* [2006] EWHC 3379, [2007] Env LR D8; *Kelleher* [2003] EWCA Crim 3525, (2003) 147 SJLB 1395; *Baker* [1997] Crim LR 497.

[261] [1998] 1 WLR 1252 (QB).

[262] [2006] EWHC 3379, [2007] Env LR D8.

[263] *Hill and Hall* (1989) 89 Cr App R 74 (CA Crim Div).

[264] Contrary to s. 3 of the Criminal Damage Act 1971.

property, including hers. Even accepting her view of the facts, however, the Court of Appeal ruled that the perceived threat was not immediate. The defence requires "that she believed that immediate action had to be taken to do something which would otherwise be a crime in order to prevent the immediate risk of something worse happening."[265] On D's own account, there was no "immediate" risk at hand. It seems that this will turn, in part, on whether the perceived threat has crystallised or remains as yet conjectural. *Hill* was distinguished on this basis in *Chamberlain* v. *Lindon* (above), where D had demolished V's wall to preserve a right of way:[266]

> "The appellants in [Hill] had professed to be concerned as to the potential consequences of a possible nuclear attack in the future. Here, on the facts, as believed by the defendant, his right of way was actually being obstructed. . . . it was not a case of there being a risk of an obstruction at some future speculative date—there was a present need to remove the obstruction. The defendant was not destroying or damaging property as some sort of pre-emptive strike to prevent some future obstruction."

A reasonable means of protection.
Somewhat surprisingly, the statute makes it clear that what counts is D's own belief that her response is reasonable; the matter is not one for objective assessment by the court:[267]

> "[T]he question is not whether the means of protection adopted by the defendant were objectively reasonable having regard to all the circumstances, but whether the defendant believed them to be so. By virtue of section 5(3) it is immaterial whether his belief was justified, provided it was honestly held."

In this respect, the section 5 defence is more generous than other, more general, justificatory defences found in the criminal law, where the courts have—rightly—held that the defendant's response must be *objectively* reasonable or proportionate, regardless of D's own views on the question.[268]

In order to protect the property.
D must actually have the purpose of protecting property, although that need not be her only reason for acting.[269] Purpose is a subjective concept—it turns on *why* D acted, what she was trying to achieve. Unfortunately, the courts have occasionally got this wrong, purporting to add an objective gloss to the interpretation of "in order to protect property" in section 5(2)(b). In *Hunt*,[270] D was assisting his wife who was deputy warden in a block of old persons' flats. He discovered that the fire alarm was not working; apparently the Council had been informed but had not repaired the alarm. D subsequently set fire to some bedding in a relatively isolated part of the block of flats in order (i) to draw attention to the defective alarm and thereby (ii) to protect the block of flats from the risks posed by the defective

---

[265] (1989) 89 Cr App R 74, 79-80.
[266] [1998] 1 WLR 1252, 1260. The Court also pointed to the defendant's viewpoint that, the longer the wall remained, the more urgent the need to remove it, to avoid any suggestion of acquiescence in the obstruction.
[267] *Chamberlain* v. *Lindon* [1998] 1 WLR 1252, 1262.
[268] Below, § 21.2(ii), (iv).
[269] *Chamberlain* v. *Lindon* [1998] 1 WLR 1252, 1259.
[270] (1978) 66 Cr App R 105 (CA Crim Div).

alarm. Affirming his conviction, the Court of Appeal accepted the first purpose but rejected the second:[271]

> "The question whether or not a particular act of destruction or damage or threat of destruction or damage was done or made in order to protect property belonging to another must be, on the true construction of the statute, an objective test. Therefore we have to ask ourselves whether, whatever the state of this man's mind and assuming an honest belief, that which he admittedly did was done in order to protect this particular property, namely the old people's home in Hertfordshire?
>
> If one formulates the question in that way, in the view of each member of this Court, for the reason Slynn J gave during the argument, it admits of only one answer: this was not done in order to protect property; it was done in order to draw attention to the defective state of the fire alarm. It was not an act which *in itself* did protect or was capable of protecting property."

But purpose is a subjective, not objective concept. What this gloss amounts to is a new requirement, not found in the statute: that D's immediate action must "in itself" be capable of protecting property. But this requirement is simply not part of section 5(2), which requires that D's purpose in acting be to protect property, and that D actually believe his immediate action is a reasonable way of seeking to achieve that purpose. There is no requirement that his action should achieve the purpose *directly*.[272] Suppose that D breaks into V's house in order to telephone the fire brigade because T's house, next door, is ablaze. Breaking into the house is not "in itself" capable of protecting T's property. Yet no-one would or should deny that D has a lawful excuse under section 5(2)(b).

It is submitted that the better explanation of *Hunt* is that, notwithstanding his genuine purpose to bolster the protection mechanisms in the block of flats, the lawful excuse within section 5 was unavailable because the threat was not immediate.

(vii) Criminal damage—a distinctive wrong

Similarly to offences such as robbery and burglary, criminal damage resembles theft in that it is intrinsically bound up with the violation of another person's property rights. Indeed, to deprive the owner of a chattel by destroying it can be the actus reus of a theft.[273] Like those other offences, however, criminal damage merits separate criminalisation because of the distinctive manner in which V's rights are violated. Many typical instances of vandalism involve the infliction of damage using percussive force, fire, or explosions, conduct that may well endanger others, or cause alarm and concern even to bystanders lacking any proprietary interest in the property being damaged. (Hence, as we see in § 14.5, the enactment of aggravated criminal damage offences.) To that extent, the offence becomes part of the family of offences concerned with restraining violence and disorder—concerns generally outside the ambit of theft *simpliciter*, save for lootings in circumstances of civil tumult. And, to the extent that it is associated with these different forms of wrongful conduct, criminal damage is a proprietary wrong different in kind from theft. Vandalism frequently has an expressive dimension, communicating a contempt for society, and for the victim, which goes

---

[271] *Ibid.*, 108 (emphasis added).
[272] A similar requirement of proximity is suggested in *Hill* (1989) 89 Cr App R 74, 79.

beyond a mere appropriation of property rights; that further wrong, in turn, warrants a label distinct from theft.

Not all types of vandalism involve violence. But all cases of vandalism share a second, intrinsic feature: criminal damage is concerned with the item of property *per se*, and not just with another's rights over that item. When D steals V's book, she does not attack the item itself but, rather, pre-empts V's rights to use and exchange the book. The book itself remains usable and exchangeable; indeed, it is simply the subject of an involuntary exchange. By contrast, when E destroys V's book he attacks the use- and exchange-value of the item in anyone's hands and not merely V's. Its value is lost *tout court*, not just to V; society's store of wealth is diminished. In this respect, the harm of criminal damage differs from that of theft.

§ 14.5 Aggravated criminal damage and arson

Section 1(2) of the Criminal Damage Act 1971 creates an aggravated offence of intentionally or recklessly destroying or damaging property and thereby endangering life:

> A person who without lawful excuse destroys or damages any property, whether belonging to himself or another —
> (a) intending to destroy or damage any property or being reckless as to whether any property would be destroyed or damaged; and
> (b) intending by the destruction or damage to endanger the life of another or being reckless as to whether the life of another would be thereby endangered;
> shall be guilty of an offence.

There are three main elements to the offence, which is punishable by life imprisonment.[274] The actus reus is:

(i)   that D destroys or damages property belonging to *someone*.

The law on this is the same as for the section 1(1) offence, and is discussed above in § 14.4(i)–(iii); except that there is no requirement in section 1(2) that the property belong to someone other than D.[275] This reflects the fact that the aggravated offence is not truly a property offence at all, but rather an endangerment-based offence against the person.[276] For the same reason, the lawful excuse defence in section 5 is unavailable to a charge under section 1(2).[277] However, other general defences, such as self-defence, are available in the normal way.[278]

The mens rea components of the aggravated offence are:

---

[273] *Cabbage* (1815) Russ & Ry 292, 168 ER 809.

[274] *Per* s. 4.

[275] Cf. *A-G's Reference (No. 98 of 2001)* [2001] EWCA Crim 3068, [2002] 2 Cr App R(S) 25; *Parker* [1993] Crim LR 856 (CA).

[276] Cf. *Merrick* [1996] 1 Cr App R 130 (CA), and the critical discussion in Elliott, "Endangering life by destroying or damaging property" [1997] *Crim LR* 382, 388-9.

[277] *Per* s. 5(1), set out above in § 14.4(vi).

[278] This is made clear by the express retention of the phrase, "without lawful excuse" in the opening line of s. 1(2) notwithstanding that the supplementary definition in s. 5 is inapplicable to s. 1(2).

(ii)   D intends or is reckless about destroying or damaging the property (as above, §
        14.4(iv); and

(iii) D intends thereby to endanger the life of another, or is (at least) reckless whether the
        life of another will thereby be endangered.

Section 1(2) might be termed an ulterior mens rea offence.[279] There is no actus reus
requirement that anyone's life in fact be endangered; all that is required is that property is
damaged with the intent or in the (subjective[280]) belief that life may be endangered thereby.
This point is illustrated in *Parker*,[281] where D set fire to his semi-detached house, realising
that his neighbours' lives may be endangered. His conviction was upheld notwithstanding
that the neighbours turned out to be away.

The language of section 1(2)(b) stipulates that the endangerment must be *by* (or
"thereby") the damage or destruction. It is not enough that D's act happens to cause both
property damage and personal danger: the former must be (foreseen or intended as) a route
to the latter. In *Steer*, D fired a rifle at the windows of V's house, both intending to cause
damage and being reckless whether life would be endangered. His conviction under section
1(2) was nonetheless quashed. He was reckless whether life would be endangered *by the
bullets*, not by the damage to the house. The crucial nexus, "thereby", was missing:[282]

> "To be guilty under subsection (2) he must additionally have intended to endanger life or been
> reckless as to whether life would be endangered 'by the damage' to property which he caused.
> This is the context in which the words must be construed and it seems to me impossible to
> read the words 'by the damage' as meaning 'by the damage or by the act which caused the
> damage'."

On the other hand, D would have been guilty of the offence had he foreseen danger to life
caused by the spray of glass from the broken windows.

Relatedly, there is no requirement that the damage caused must be the same as that
which was contemplated by D. It is enough that D intends or foresees endangering life by
the property damage that he contemplates will follow from his actions; and that, by acting
as he does, D causes *some* property damage:[283]

> "Thus, if a defendant throws a brick at the windscreen of a moving vehicle, given that he
> causes some damage to the vehicle, whether he is guilty under section 1(2) does not depend
> on whether the brick hits or misses the windscreen, but whether he intended to hit it and
> intended that the damage therefrom should endanger life or whether he was reckless as to that
> outcome."

Implicitly, it is not necessary that the property damage that ultimately results from D's
actions should itself endanger life.

---

[279] Cf. Horder, "Crimes of Ulterior Intent" in Simester and Smith (eds.), *Harm and Culpability* (1996) 153.

[280] *Cooper* [2004] EWCA Crim 1382; following *G* [2003] UK HL 50, above, § 5.2(i). The Court in *Cooper* opined
at para. 12 that "[i]t is now, in the light of *G*, incumbent on a trial judge to direct a jury, in a case of this kind, that
the risk of danger to life was obvious and significant to the defendant. In other words, a subjective element is
essential before the jury can convict of this offence." *Quaere* however whether the risk now need even be obvious, as
opposed to foreseen (and, as foreseen, an unreasonable risk to run).

[281] [1993] Crim LR 856 (CA). Note that Parker was decided prior to *G* and *Cooper* (see preceding footnote) and
applied an objective standard of recklessness.

[282] [1988] AC 111, 117 (Lord Bridge). Cf. *Webster* [1995] 2 All ER 168 (CA).

[283] *Webster, ibid.*, 497; approving *Dudley* [1989] Crim LR 57.

(i) Arson

By virtue of section 1(3),[284] in cases where the criminal damage in section 1(1) or 1(2) is caused by fire, the offence is called *arson* (or arson with intent to endanger life, etc., as the case may be) and is punishable by life imprisonment.[285] The mens rea requirement is correspondingly modified: D must intend, or foresee, causing damage *by fire*. It is not enough that the contemplated damage happens unexpectedly to cause a fire, even if that fire then endangers the lives of others.[286]

---

[284] "An offence committed under this section by destroying or damaging property by fire shall be charged as arson." Section 1(3) effectively rejects the Law Commission's recommendation that there should be no separate offence of arson (although criminal damage should incur a greater maximum penalty when caused by fire): Law Com. No. 29, *Report on Offences of Damage to Property* (1970) paras. 28-33.

[285] Per s. 4.

[286] Cf. *Cooper (G) and Cooper (Y)* [1991] Crim LR 524 (CA).

15

FRAUD

Theft is not the only way of usurping another's property rights. Sometimes, the wrong-fulness of the defendant's behaviour may be more subtle. It may, for example, lie in the fact that D duped V into transferring ownership consensually[1] or into performing services for D, or in the fact that she fraudulently gained from the use of V's assets even though V suffered no loss. In common with theftuous offences, wrongdoing of this sort involves dishonest behaviour by D regarding the property of another. However, its prevention often requires the enactment of offences which differ substantially from traditional forms of theft.

The extent to which such offences are necessary has sometimes been questioned.[2] For example, although acquisition by deception may not give rise to tortious claims in trespass or conversion,[3] other civil law remedies, such as deceit, are usually available to the aggrieved party. In addition, much commercial wrongdoing is controlled by administrative regulation of the marketplace, buttressed by the civil sanctions available to professional bodies. Given such existing sanctions, and the commitment in this country to a broadly liberal economic philosophy, is it really essential to fence in the marketplace with criminal law?

The answer is yes. Our rights to private property are part of the very fabric of the modern United Kingdom.[4] Property relations are shared elements which help to structure our interpersonal relations within the community. As such, they are integral to our membership of society, and to the understanding we have of our own lives. In particular, one feature of our participation in a broadly liberal society is the autonomy we have in respect of our property—the freedom to use, control, and dispose of that property as we wish.

As was noted above, in Chapter 13, there are limitations to our autonomy as proprietors. Even the freedoms of contract and testament are substantially constrained by law. Neither may we use our assets to fund criminal activities, and we are compelled by the State to contribute through taxation to certain communal goals which may not be of direct personal benefit to us. Nonetheless, the importance of individualism to the UK polity means that personal property rights have attracted better protection from the criminal law than many more abstract social or community values, such as an unpolluted environment or a well-educated populace. By contrast with these examples, the occurrence of harms is more

---

[1] Although, following *Gomez* and *Hinks*, this case would now also be theft. See above, § 13.6(ii).

[2] See, e.g., *Jones* (1703) 2 Ld Raymond 1013, 92 ER 174; *Goodhall* (1821) Russ & Ry 461, 168 ER 898.

[3] Since possession and/or title will normally have passed, at least prima facie.

[4] Cf. Waldron, *The Right to Private Property* (1988); Ryan, *Property and Political Theory* (1986); Nozick, *Anarchy, State and Utopia* (1974); Epstein, "Property as a Fundamental Civil Right" (1992) 29 *Cal West LR* 187; Harris, *Property and Justice* (1996).

readily criminalised and prosecuted when there is an identifiable victim whose concrete individual rights have been transgressed.

This imbalance may be reason for complaint, but not on the basis that property rights deserve reduced protection. Indeed, the harms involved in property offences shade into those addressed by offences against the person, and any suggestion that offences against property are concerned solely with material loss would be misleading. The violation of our homes by a burglary, for example, may cause psychological injury and distress quite independent of the quantum of loss. Offences such as theft, fraud, and blackmail are generally categorised as property offences, and understandably so, for they involve wrongful acquisition of property. But they are also, in a very real sense, offences against the person. In each case, the conduct prohibited can be seen as an attack upon the victim's entitlement to dispose of his property by his own full and informed choice. Thus, the conduct represents an attack upon the victim's rights of free will and autonomy, and upon his freedom to exercise control over his own situation. Blackmail, for instance, involves D infringing V's legitimate control over his own affairs by imposing her free will in place of his. This subjugation of V resembles an assault as much as it does a "property" wrong. Fraud by false representation, understood in this sense, is a crime partly because it entails the manipulation or exploitation of another. Unlike the corresponding civil law remedies, property offences, in differing ways, protect the individual's entitlement to respect as an autonomous member of our society.

§ 15.1 Statutory fraud

The major measure for criminalising fraudulent conduct is the Fraud Act 2006,[5] which came into force on 15 January 2007.[6] Because, appropriately, the Act is non-retroactive, the offences it repeals will feature in trials for several years yet, as the cases come to light and are brought to court. Accordingly, later in this chapter we retain an account of the law relating to the offences of obtaining property by deception and obtaining services by deception;[7] although it must always be borne in mind that, for facts which occur after the commencement date, it is the relevant new law created by the Fraud Act 2006 that applies. As well as repealing the deception offences mentioned, the Act further abolishes separate deception offences relating variously to obtaining money transfers, pecuniary advantages, valuable securities, remission, abatement, and exemption from liabilities, and credit.[8] Whatever reservations may be made about the uncertainties and breadth of the new Act, it is a great relief to be rid of much needless prolixity and complexity.

---

[5] For helpful analysis of the key provisions, see Ormerod, "The Fraud Act 2006: Criminalising Lying?" [2007] *Crim LR* 193. See also Ormerod and Williams, *Smith on Theft* (9th ed., 2007). For background to the Act, see LCCP No. 155, *Legislating the Criminal Code: Fraud and Deception*; Law Com. No. 276, *Fraud* (on which see Sullivan, "Fraud: the Latest Law Commission Proposals" (2003) 52 *Journal of Criminal Law* 139); Home Office, *Fraud Law Reform: Consultation on Proposals for Legislation* (2004).

[6] The Fraud Act 2006 (Commencement) Order 2006 (SI 2006/3200).

[7] Below, §§ 15.4, 5.

[8] Fraud Act 2006, schedule 1.

The principal feature of the Fraud Act 2006 is a general fraud offence that can be committed in one of three ways, namely by false representation, by failing to disclose information, and by abuse of position. As there is but one offence, as a matter of substantive law it would not matter if the evidence establishes that fraud was committed in another fashion to that initially alleged by the prosecution. The prosecution may base their case on a false representation which they fail to prove, yet nonetheless establish that a fraud was perpetrated by D's failure to disclose information to V that he was under a legal duty to divulge. As a matter of practice, however, the prosecution should set out the case against D as clearly as possible,[9] and any trial must be fair within the terms of Article 6 of the ECHR.

In addition to the fraud offence, the Act creates an important new offence of obtaining services dishonestly.[10] The Act also creates offences of possession of articles for use in fraud, making or supplying articles for use in frauds and fraudulent trading using non-corporate business forms.[11] These important offences will not be considered here.[12]

Mention should be made of a provision not to be found in the Act. Despite the consistent view of the Law Commission that any new fraud act should mark the abolition of conspiracy to defraud,[13] the Government refused to abolish this "indefensible anomaly".[14] The refusal was based exclusively on pragmatism: the risk of gaps in the coverage of fraudulent conduct.[15] It seems a safe bet that any future editions of this work will continue to have a section on conspiracy to defraud.[16]

Below, we analyse the three forms of the fraud offence. Before we descend to detail the different ways of committing fraud, some features that need to be present for any conviction for fraud should be stressed at the outset. There must be proof of dishonesty, and there must be an intent to gain or to cause loss or risk of loss in money or property. We shall deal with those elements in full when examining fraud by false representation, a discussion that carries over to the other two varieties of fraud. Also common to each variety is a form of absence. Although there must be an intent to gain or to cause loss or risk of loss, neither gain nor loss need accrue or risk of loss actually arise. Each form of fraud is a conduct crime and not a result crime. In effect, fraud is an inchoate offence, although, since technically it is a substantive crime in its own right, a further layer of inchoate liability will attach.[17] Much conduct that would formerly be regarded as preliminary to fraudulent conduct—and even beyond the scope of inchoate offences—will now constitute criminal offences.

---

[9] *Maxwell* [1978] 3 All ER 1140, 1142.

[10] Section 11; replacing the offence of obtaining services by deception (below, § 15.5).

[11] Sections 6, 7, and 9 respectively. The last offence supplements corporate fraudulent trading: Companies Act 1985, s. 458.

[12] For discussion see Ormerod, "The Fraud Act 2006: Criminalising Lying?" [2007] *Crim LR* 193.

[13] Most recently Law Com. No. 276, para 1.4.

[14] *Ibid.*

[15] HL Debate, cols. 1113–16, 14 March 2006: Lord Goldsmith, Attorney General.

[16] Currently to be found at § 15.6.

[17] As is the case for the statutory offence of aiding and abetting suicide: *McCann* (1971) 56 Cr App R 359.

§ 15.2 Fraud by false representation

(i) The actus reus

This form of the fraud offence is defined by section 2 of the Fraud Act 2006. The conduct element is the making of a false representation as to fact, which will include a representation about the state of mind of D or anyone else, or as to law.[18] A representation is false "if it is untrue or misleading".[19] Whether something is true or untrue may be very difficult to resolve—is global warming (entirely) an effect of industrial activity, urban lifestyles, transportation, and agricultural activity?—but that sort of conundrum is unlikely to feature in trials for fraud. Mostly, falsity in the sense of untruth will be established by proving that D told a lie: she knew the painting was not, despite her contrary assurance to V, an unsigned old masterpiece because she was there when her partner in crime made the forgery. A lie—false representation—can be express or implied.[20] Therefore, there will be a representation when D assures V that the painting is an old master and, equally, when a price tag is put on the painting which would normally be asked only in the case of selling an old master. Less clear cut is where an expert pastiche is made, say in the style of a Vermeer, but buyers are asked merely to state their price. This leads us to the other way in which a representation may be false: it is false if it is misleading.

Clearly some representations may be literally true but are nonetheless to be regarded as false because, although true, they are misleading. When will this be? Take a hypothetical case discussed in *Hinks*:[21] a situation where D and V are negotiating the sale of D's garage. V enquires of D what the turnover of the business was, as per the latest set of accounts, and receives in response the true figures. V's subsequent offer price reflects a valuation based on the assumption that the figures were a useful guide to future profitability. D knows this, but is also aware that a bypass road to be constructed in the near future will take away practically all the passing trade. Just as the House of Lords contemplated that D's accepting V's purchase price could be theft of V's money, we must take seriously the prospect that D might now also be guilty of fraud by false representation when he gives V the accurate figures: the offence does not require the actual making of the gain or loss. Were the figures misleading? In the context of V's query it is submitted that the answer must be, yes. One problem with this answer is that it takes the criminal law beyond what constitutes a misrepresentation for the purposes of the law of contract, where the boundaries of the concept are mediated by the principle of *caveat emptor*. Extending the notion of falsity to representations that are misleading yet true will lead to further incoherence at the interface of criminal and civil law.

In this, the notion of false pretence goes beyond the legal concept of deception. But, as will be seen later in this chapter, the idea of deception has itself been extensively construed with regard to implied representations. Frequently, our conduct taken in its context will send out clear supplementary messages: as when, say, we order a meal in a restaurant. A

---

[18] Section 2(3).
[19] Section 2(2)
[20] Section 2(3).
[21] [2001] 2 AC 241, 251–2 (Lord Steyn).

straightforward implication of making the order is that the food will be paid for when the bill is presented. Thus if D orders without an intention to pay, he has deceived the serving staff,[22] and there will be a false representation by conduct for the purposes of section 2 of the Fraud Act 2006.

But the law on implied deception has been taken well beyond the sphere of such clear implications that arise from conduct. For instance, it has been held that if D uses a cheque card to guarantee a cheque drawn for an amount in excess of her credit limit, she has impliedly made a false representation to anyone who accepts the cheque that she is acting within her agreed credit limit with the bank.[23] We will not here anticipate in full the criticism below of this line of authority,[24] but note for now that these cases stretch the meaning of deception to breaking point and beyond, by asserting that V's conduct has been affected by the supposed deception when a key role of cheque cards is to relieve V of the very burden of enquiring into D's creditworthiness. It is submitted that the meaning of "false representation" for the purposes of the Fraud Act 2006 offers a fresh page, and cases on the meaning of deception considered unhelpful need not be adopted. A good reason for thinking that the credit card cases may not be followed is that, under section 2, D must intend to gain or cause loss *by making the representation*.[25] That condition is not made out if any intended gain or loss would not be caused by the false representation.

The fact that the intended gain or loss must come through the false pretence shows that, although the fraud offence is cast in an inchoate mode, causal speculation may still be necessary. If a gain has been made (or loss caused, etc.), it will provide a useful focus for determining whether the gain was made by making the representation. If no gain is actually made, the question must be along the lines of asking whether the gain that D intended would, if realised, have been made *by* making the representation. Let us say that D lands a highly paid position by a false representation that he has an Oxford degree. Assume that the truth comes out before he starts the job. Clearly any salary that would have been made would constitute a gain—but would it have been made by way of the false pretence? Changing the facts, what if the truth does not come out for ten years after his start date? Is all the salary he has earned in the meantime a gain falling within section 2? Or does a form of remoteness principle arise at some point, and, if so, when? Formerly, such speculation could be put to one side when D was charged with obtaining a pecuniary advantage by deception under the then section 16 of the Theft Act 1968, which proscribed obtaining the *opportunity* to earn remuneration by way of employment. But that is no longer an option for facts occurring after 15 January 2007, leaving the position quite unclear for this kind of case.[26]

(ii) *False representations made to systems and devices*

Under the former law of deception, only persons can be deceived.[27] However common-sensical this may seem, it left some serious gaps in the control of fraudulent conduct. For

---

[22] *Ray* [1974] AC 370.
[23] *Charles* [1977] AC 177; *Lambie* [1982] AC 449.
[24] § 15.4(iii)(a).
[25] Section 2(1)(b).
[26] For discussion in the context of the former deception offences, see below, § 15.4(iii)(b).
[27] Below, § 15.4(iii)(c).

instance; in *Re Holmes*[28] the Court of Appeal noted with regret that D would not have committed any deception offences when transferring large sums between banks by wholly automated processes. To plug this gap, section 2(5) provides:

> For the purposes of this section a representation may be regarded as made if it (or anything implying it) is submitted in any form to any system or device designed to receive, convey or respond to communications (with or without human intervention).

The language seems well adapted to its purposes and will help to ensure justice in a case such as *Re Holmes*.

But taken with the inchoate nature of the fraud offence, some very remote conduct may be criminalised. Suppose that while logged in to his email account, D types a false representation into an email that he is drafting, intending later to send it to V. It seems that the conduct element of the offence is made out.[29]

(iii) Mens rea

There are three elements to the mens rea. The false representation must be made dishonestly;[30] it must be made with intent to gain or cause loss or to expose another to the risk of loss;[31] and made with knowledge that the representation is untrue or misleading or that it might be untrue or misleading.[32]

(a) Dishonesty

The Fraud Act 2006 contains no definition of the key element of dishonesty. Of course, in run-of-the-mill cases this will cause no difficulty, as when D tells V he is collecting a debt that V owes to E, D lacking any intention to pay the money to E. If the prosecution proves these facts they will normally also have proved D's dishonesty. But suppose that E owes D money to the same value as V's debt to E, and D thinks the only way he will ever be paid is to intercept the payment that V is due to make to E? Imagine further that, after receiving the money from V by claiming he is collecting it for E, D then informs V why he did so and advises V not to make any further payment to E. If D were to be charged with *theft* of the money received from V, the issue of dishonesty would be resolved with the aid of the claim of right provision to be found in section 2(1)(a) of the Theft Act 1968.[33] As there is no similar guidance in the Fraud Act 2006, the judge presiding at D's trial for fraud by false representation can only have recourse to the test for dishonesty in disputable cases set down in *Ghosh*:[34]

---

[28] [2004] EWHC 2020.

[29] Cf. the discussion by Ormerod, "The Fraud Act 2006: Criminalising Lying?"[2007] *Crim LR* 193, 200. Professor Ormerod queries whether there is an escape route in that D could be said not to intend to gain or cause loss by *that* representation. But even if that were accepted, there is a distinct possibility of liability for attempt.

[30] Section 2(1)(a).

[31] Section 2(1)(b).

[32] Section 2(2).

[33] See the discussion above, § 13(8)(i).

[34] [1982] QB 1053, 1064. For discussion, see above, § 13(8)(iii).

(i)   Was what was done dishonest according to the ordinary standards of reasonable and honest people?

(ii) Did the defendant realise that reasonable and honest people would regard what he did as dishonest?

This failure in the 2006 Act to make special provision for recurring cases is regrettable. The case of the D–V–E debt triangle is not straightforward in terms of moral evaluation—what, for juror X, may be an example of legitimate self-help may be, for juror Y, a disreputable machination—and the law needs to set a standard for such divisive cases. The fact that the Fraud Act 2006 neglects to set any standard leaves the matter at large, with *Ghosh* the only, and uncertain, guide. We will return to this lack of clarity that the absence of even a partial definition of dishonesty engenders when examining the other mens rea elements.

(b) Intent to make a gain or cause a loss

The false representation must be made with an intent to make a gain for oneself or another, or with an intent to cause loss to another, or an intent to expose another to a risk of loss. Fraud is a property offence in that the gain or loss must be in money or property (including real property). It suffices that that the gain or loss is only intended to be temporary.[35] Gain includes keeping what one has, and loss includes not getting what one might get.[36]

Confining gains and losses to money and property at least reins in what remains a very wide offence. To make a false pretence to obtain confidential information about a forth-coming takeover bid may fall foul of insider trading legislation but it will not be fraud by false pretences, as confidential information without more is not a form of intangible property.[37] To be sure, D he may intend to make a gain by using the information to buy shares in the target company at the pre-bid price but the gain will be made by the sub-sequent sale of the shares to the bidder. Some very important gains which are not directly economic are thereby excluded from the scope of fraud, as when D gains entry to a presti-gious university by inflating his grades (and causes the loss of a vital opportunity to the better-qualified candidate he displaces); but regulation of such things as university entry procedures is best done by offences targeted on specific abuses.

In the usual case where D makes a false pretence in order to gain, the intent involved will almost invariably be the natural, core sense of the term;[38] as when D tells a deliberate lie in order dishonestly to obtain money from V. However, it is also possible to envisage circum-stances where D's intent to make a gain will be of the non-core, foresight-of-moral-certainty variety.[39] Suppose that D goes to Lord's cricket ground wearing an MCC tie. His core intent is to pass himself off as a member of the MCC among his friends and acquaintances but he knows that, as on previous occasions, he will be charged the lower admission price payable by members of the MCC. He commits fraud by false pretences.

The intent must go with the false pretence: as was noted earlier, D must intend to make the gain *by making the representation*.[40] Suppose that D enters a conversation with V and at

---

[35] Section 5(2).
[36] Section 5(3)–(4).
[37] See the discussion above, § 13.3(i)(a).
[38] Above, § 5.1(i)–(iii).
[39] Above, § 5.1(iv).
[40] Section 2(1)(b).

some point falsely claims to be an Old Etonian, merely intending to raise his status in the eyes of V. At some later point in the conversation D, having forgotten his earlier lie, success-fully asks V for a loan of £200. Even if V would not have made this loan but for his assumption about the reliability of Old Etonians, D commits no offence. At the time he made his false representation he did not intend to make money by lying. It would be different if, when asking for money, D thought his earlier lie about his schooling might favourably influence V. The false representation still has effect and now it is being deployed by D to make a gain for himself.

Where the allegation is that D intended to cause loss to another, the intent will typically be of the non-core variety, unless V is motivated by malice. So, if D borrows £50 from V, assuring her that he will pay her on Sunday but knowing that in his foreseeable financial circumstances he has no chance of doing so, he commits fraud. That still holds even if he intends to buy a lottery ticket with part of the money and fervently hopes he will be a millionaire following the draw on Saturday night. He knows it is virtually certain that V will not be paid on Sunday.

Note that it is enough to expose another to a *risk* of loss.[41] This is a considerable extension of the reach of statutory fraud, applying to each of the three ways of committing the offence. Suppose that, in a variant of the £50 loan example, D expects to be able to repay V on Sunday because he anticipates payment of a debt he is owed on Friday. However, he is aware of a risk that repayment may not happen until some time later. D knows that he has exposed V to the risk of loss which, the Act stipulates,[42] includes temporary losses. Many times each day, individuals and organisations will enter time-bounded repayment commit-ments aware that contingencies of various kinds may preclude the timely meeting of their obligation to repay. If D is aware of a non-minimal risk of time default in repaying V, he intends to expose V to the risk of loss. Making a binding commitment to pay on time will be a false pretence if D is aware of the possibility of default unless V has been made aware of and accepts the risk of untimely payment. It is submitted that much, if not most, conduct of this kind should be responded to by the renegotiation of credit terms against a backdrop of civil law enforcement of bad debts, and not remedied by the criminal law. However, whether particular incidents of this sort constitute fraud will depend now upon the vagaries of dishonesty, and the application of the *Ghosh* test.

(c) *Knowledge that the representation is or might be untrue or misleading*

This mens rea element is imported into the definition of a "false representation" by section 2(2)(b). The plainest and least problematic case will be where D knows that his represen-tation is untrue. If D says he is just about to come into a considerable inheritance when he knows that he will receive just £100 from the deceased, he is camped in the territory of fraud when he tells this lie to induce a large loan from V. Also well within the notion of fraudulent behavior is when D says to V, "I am sure this painting is a genuine Constable," when in reality he is not sure, because he is aware of the distinct possibility that it might be an expert copy.

---

[41] Section 2(1)(b)(ii). Such an intention also suffices for conspiracy to defraud: *Allsop* (1976) 64 Cr App R 29; below, § 15.6(iii)(a), (iv).
[42] Section 5(2)(b).

Yet one soon reaches territory where there is genuine doubt about the propriety of criminalising aspects of D's conduct. It is well known, for instance, that the attribution of paintings to artists long departed can be a matter of fine judgement on which experts of equal standing may disagree. Go back to the assurance that D gives to V about the attribution of a painting to Constable. After claiming that he is so convinced, D adds, "Professor Jones, perhaps our leading Constable scholar, is of that view too." All manner of nuances may be in play here. Professor Jones may well be a leading Constable scholar, but he may be notorious within his scholarly community for his willingness to make positive attributions, particularly when used as a consultant to a leading dealer with a painting of contested provenance to sell. And what if D knows that Professor Jones's positive attribution was a probabilistic, "on the balance of evidence", conclusion and he also knows that Professor Smith, regarded by his peers as *the* Constable scholar, was dismissive of the painting, convinced that it was a copy. As V dithers about spending what for him is a vast sum of money, D remarks that there has been great interest from the United States, a statement based on a tentative email from a US client. And what of V? Is it in point that he is an experienced purchaser of high-value art who will essentially make his own judgement about the value of the painting? Does the analysis change if he is a first-time buyer of high-value art, trusting of and guided by D? Does the fact that fraud by false pretences may be proved without proof that anyone was deceived, or that any gain or loss occurred, have any relevance to what constitutes a false representation? Must D's representation be misleading in some general, objective sense or is it enough that D knew it might mislead V? If the painting is subsequently shown to be a copy, bought by V at a price well in excess of its true value, a potential prosecutor of D for the offence of fraud by false pretences will have much to ponder.

§ 15.3 Fraud by failing to disclose information and fraud by abuse of position

(i) Fraud by failing to disclose information

Section 3 of the Fraud Act 2006 makes D liable for statutory fraud if he dishonestly fails to disclose information that he is under a legal duty to disclose, intending by failing to disclose the information to gain for himself or cause loss to another, or to expose another to the risk of loss. Some elements have already been discussed in the previous section: namely dishonesty; gain and loss; and the intent to make a gain or cause a loss, or expose another to the risk of loss.

The core element of this variant of fraud is the breach of a *legal* duty to disclose information. This offence will obviously be committed in circumstances such as the following:

> D is the solicitor for the estate of X and administers a probate bank account for the legatees of X. V is a distant relative of X, unaware that he is a beneficiary under the will. D deliberately omits to inform V of his legacy, intending to transfer the money to his personal account when he closes the probate account.

D's liability is clear-cut and his conduct straightforwardly deserving of criminal liability. The fact that liability is triggered by a legal duty to disclose gives a clean edge to this form of the fraud offence. One possible reservation is that liability will arise for this offence without much in the way of conduct on the part of D, which can generate temporal and other difficulties. In our probate example, D will be on the cusp of liability the moment the notice period for informing V of his legacy has elapsed. Of course, there may be all manner of reasons why a notification letter to V has not yet been sent—perhaps D is overworked or his secretary is away due to illness. But if the reason that a letter has not been sent is a dishonest intent on the part of D to acquire V's legacy, the offence is now complete notwithstanding that D soon has a change of heart and distributes the estate to the letter of X's wishes. Indeed, D arguably would be liable for attempted fraud when the expiry of the notice period was imminent provided he had formed the dishonest intent to make a gain.[43]

The ambit of this form of the fraud offence is bounded by the legal duty to disclose information. The following passage from the Law Commission's report is a useful guide:[44]

"Such a duty may derive from statute (such as provisions governing company prospectuses), from the fact that the transaction in question is one of the utmost good faith (such as a contract for insurance), from the express or implied terms of a contract, from the customs of a particular trade or market, or from the existence of a fiduciary relationship between the parties (such as agent and principal). For this purpose [the fraud offence] there is a legal duty to disclose information not only if the defendant's failure to disclose it gives the victim a cause of action for damages, but also if the law gives the victim the right to set aside any change in his or her legal position to which he or she may consent as a result of non-disclosure. For example, a person in a fiduciary position has a duty to disclose material information when entering into a contract with his or her beneficiary, in the sense that a failure to make such disclosure will entitle the beneficiary to rescind the contract and to reclaim any property transferred under it."

Undeniably, the full enforcement of this form of fraud will involve in-depth consideration of civil law issues. This is entirely appropriate in the context of a modern law of fraud. Criminal courts will have to address the civil law and the criminal law from a perspective of unity[45] and set aside their reluctance to investigate difficult civil law questions.[46]

(ii) Fraud by abuse of position

Section 4 of the Fraud Act provides that D commits fraud if he occupies a position in which he is expected to safeguard or not to act against the financial interests of another person and dishonestly abuses that position, intending by the abuse to make a gain, or to cause loss, or to expose another to the risk of loss. Abuse may take the form of act or omission.[47]

The most important threshold question is whether D occupies a qualifying position. Remarkably, this key term is undefined, deliberately so as to allow flexibility. The Law Commission not only envisaged the offence embracing persons who owe fiduciary duties,

---

[43] On whether an attempt can be committed by way of omission, see above, § 9.3(ii)(c).
[44] Law Com. No. 276, para. 7.28.
[45] Avoiding the incoherence exemplified by the decision in *Hinks* [2001] 2 AC 241; see above, § 13.6(ii)(c).
[46] As in *Morris* [1984] AC 320, 334; above, § 13.6(ii).
[47] Section 4(2).

such as trustees and company directors, but "within a family, or in the context of voluntary work, or *in any context* where the parties are not at arm's length."[48] This stance was unsurprisingly adopted by the Home Office, who advise that it may cover persons who occupy such "positions" as access to another's premises, equipment, records, or premises.[49]

To test the limits of this form of fraud, we shall take the example of a group of ten friends who decide to go to a theatre to see a play. On the theatre's booking website the tickets they want are priced at £40. D volunteers to purchase tickets for all of them, payment to be collected later, so they may sit as a group. When he orders the tickets via his computer he is pleased that there is a £5 discount for each ticket on booking ten or more tickets, and he looks forward to passing on this good news. His mood changes on finding the booking site difficult to use and two hours and two crashes later he resolves to keep the £45 discount on the nine tickets acquired for his friends as a reward for his labours. He does so with a full sense of entitlement but, as he is aware that some of his friends might not share his view of the matter, he does not tell anyone of the discount when he collects £40 from each of his friends.

It is an indication of the breadth of this form of fraud that we must give serious consideration to D's potential liability. Does D's role in purchasing the tickets entail the occupation of a position where he is expected to safeguard the financial interests of his friends or at least not act against their interests? The Law Commission intended the judge to rule on this question.[50] Certainly the parties are not at arm's length and it is not a commercial setting. So a finding that D occupies a position for the purposes of this form of fraud would be far from perverse. Did D abuse his position? He kept the discount and did not disclose that fact to his friends. The term "abuse" is not defined and seems to add nothing to the ultimate judgment of whether making a monetary gain in this manner is to be regarded as dishonest. As so often with the Fraud Act 2006, the path leads back to the two questions on dishonesty put in *Ghosh*.[51]

Where D occupies a position recognised by the law and which carries associated legal duties—positions such as trustee, solicitor, auditor, agent, and the like—there will be a complete overlap with the form of fraud created in section 3 (fraud by failing to disclose information in breach of a legal duty). Breaching a legal obligation to disclose information, an obligation which arises from one's position, in order to dishonestly make a gain or cause a loss, constitutes an abuse of position. There can be no objection whatever to an offence of fraud based on breaching legal duties in a dishonest manner to make profits or cause losses. If section 4 of the Fraud Act 2006 were confined to defendants who hold positions that carry legal duties, section 3 could be dispensed with and at least one part of the law of fraud put on a clear footing.

§ 15.4 Pre-2007 law: obtaining by deception

Prior to 15 January 2007, the day the Fraud Act 2006 came into force, the statutory deception offences were contained in the Theft Acts of 1968 and 1978. Key among these

---

[48] Law Com. No. 276, para. 7.38 (emphasis added).
[49] Home Office, *Fraud Law Reform: Consultation on Proposals for Legislation* (2004) Explanatory Notes, para. 23.
[50] Law Com. No. 276, para. 7.38.
[51] [1982] QB 1053; above, §§ 15.1(iii)(a), 13.8.

were the former offences of obtaining property by deception and obtaining services by deception. For this edition, we retain their discussion on an interim basis, since most cases in the near future are likely to involve conduct perpetrated prior to 2007 and, therefore, to fall under the old law. We begin with obtaining property by deception, enacted by section 15(1) of the Theft Act 1968:

> A person who by any deception dishonestly obtains property belonging to another, with the intention of permanently depriving the other of it, shall on conviction on indictment be liable to imprisonment for a term not exceeding 10 years.

The offence contains a variety of elements, which will be considered below:

(i)   a deliberate or reckless deception;
(ii)   an obtaining of property belonging to another;
(iii) causation or reliance;
(iv)   dishonesty and the intention permanently to deprive.

(i) Deception

There must be a deception. Surreptitiously helping oneself to another's property cannot be obtaining by deception; the proper charge would be theft. This requirement holds for all deception offences—travelling on a train without paying, or even hijacking the train, would not by itself constitute the offence of obtaining services by deception.[52] The meaning of deception is set out in section 15(4):[53]

> For purposes of this section[54] "deception" means any deception (whether deliberate or reckless) by words or conduct as to fact or as to law, including a deception as to the present intentions of the person using the deception or any other person.

Although the core term "deception" is itself left undefined, the subsection appears to require two things: (i) a representation of either fact or law, which is false; and (ii) intention or recklessness about the deceptive nature of the representation.

(a) A representation

As section 15(4) indicates, the defendant's representation must be of either law or fact. Assistance in understanding the scope of this definition may be had from the civil law. As in contract and tort, it would seem that a *mere* statement of opinion or a prediction about some future event would not normally amount to a deception. On the other hand, even a statement that is prima facie not a representation of fact or law may impliedly contain such a representation, and so may amount to a deception falling within section 15(4).

The key requirement is that the defendant's representation must be capable of being false. This means that it must contain, expressly or impliedly, a proposition of fact or law. For example, if D states to V, "the owner has authorised me to sell this car," he asserts a fact which may be true or false. That is a plain case of a representation. But other statements are

---

[52] Contrary to the former s. 1 of the Theft Act 1978. See below, § 15.2(v).
[53] See also Smith, "The Idea of Deception" [1982] *Crim LR* 721.
[54] The definition applies also to ss. 15A, 16, and 20 of the 1968 Act and to ss. 1 and 2 of the 1978 Act.

less clear-cut. Suppose that D says to V, "it is a good car for its age." This seems to express an opinion rather than state a fact. As such, the opinion itself is not capable of being false. It is similar if D's statement is about a future event: the assurance that "England will win the next World Cup" is prima facie no more than a prediction (and an unlikely one at that). Such a proposition may *become* false, but is usually not false when made.[55]

In cases such as these, it will be necessary for the prosecution to establish a further, *implied* representation by D in order to satisfy the actus reus. There are two standard implied representations in this situation. The first is *that D herself genuinely holds that opinion or believes that prediction.* This is a representation about D's existing mental state, and as such is capable of being false:[56]

> "it is very difficult to prove what the state of a man's mind at a particular time is, but if it can be ascertained it is as much a fact as anything else. A misrepresentation as to the state of a man's mind is therefore, a misstatement of fact. . . ."

In *King*,[57] for example, a second-hand car dealer stated that the mileage reading on a particular car "may not be correct". Impliedly, he also represented that he was not certain the reading was wrong. The latter representation is one of present fact, about the dealer's mental state, and capable of being a deception.

The second representation is normally inferred only if D is in a better position to express the opinion or prediction than V. In such cases, there is generally an implicit representation that D's view is a reasonable one given the information available to him. A useful statement of this rule may be found in the words of Bowen LJ in *Smith* v. *Land and House Property Corp*:[58]

> "In a case where the facts are equally well-known to both parties, what one of them says to the other is frequently nothing but an expression of opinion. . . . But if the facts are not equally known to both sides, then a statement of opinion by the one who knows the facts best involves very often a statement of a material fact, for he impliedly states that he knows facts which justify his opinion."

In recent decades the courts have become more willing to draw inferences of this sort from prima facie statements of opinion. Whereas, in 1869, a representation that the seller had a "good business" was held merely to be a matter of opinion even though the business had failed,[59] by 1966 the Court of Appeal was willing to uphold the defendants' convictions in *Jeff and Bassett*.[60] In that case, the defendants charged an old lady £35 to repair a roof, stating that the repairs were "necessary" and that £35 was "a fair and reasonable sum to charge for the work involved." In fact the repairs were not needed and the value of the work done was £5. The Court ruled that the statements involved misrepresentations of fact.

As in the civil law, an exaggeration of quality is not a deception unless carried to such an extent as to amount to a fraudulent misrepresentation of fact. The question here is whether

---

[55] See the note by White, "Trade Descriptions About the Future" (1974) 90 *LQR* 15; also Pearce, "Theft by False Promises" (1953) 101 *U Pa LR* 967.

[56] *Edgington* v. *Fitzmaurice* (1885) 29 Ch D 459, 483.

[57] [1979] Crim LR 122.

[58] (1884) 28 Ch D 7, 15. Cf. *Brown* v. *Raphael* [1958] Ch 636.

[59] *Williamson* (1869) 11 Cox CC 328.

[60] (1966) 51 Cr App R 28.

the statement goes beyond praise which does not appear to be serious or more than a mere opinion. A description of land as "fertile and improveable" has been held to be mere sales talk.[61] However, a statement that use of a carbolic smoke ball will prevent influenza is a more specific claim and may amount to a representation.[62]

(b) Implications from conduct

Implicit in the foregoing discussion is that the law does not restrict its analysis of representations merely to the literal meaning of express words used by D. Rather, the test is "what meaning was actually conveyed to the party complaining."[63] This rule is buttressed by section 15(4), which states that the representation may be "by words or conduct"[64] and thus need not be express. The best-known example of a representation by conduct is *Barnard*.[65] In that case D, by wearing a university cap and gown, was held to have falsely represented that he was a member of Oxford University in order to obtain credit from a tradesman. Whether or not he had made such a claim by words, his conduct alone constituted a false pretence.[66]

Writing a cheque implies a representation that it will be honoured when presented for payment.[67] As Robert Goff LJ said in *Gilmartin*,[68]

> "by the simple giving of a cheque, whether postdated or not, the drawer impliedly represents that the state of facts existing at the date of delivery of the cheque is such that in the ordinary course the cheque will on presentation for payment on or after the date specified in the cheque, be met."

Since this is a prediction of future events, a further representation must be implied from it that the drawer of the cheque presently intends and expects that it will be honoured when presented. Another common situation is the use of a credit card or bank card, which involves a representation that the person using it has authority to do so.[69]

Where D purports to sell goods to V, there is usually an implied representation that D has the capacity to pass ownership of the goods,[70] and that the goods are genuine.[71] Conversely,

---

[61] *Dimmock* v. *Hallett* (1866) LR 2 Ch App 21. See also *Bryan* (1857) Dears & B 265, 169 ER 1002.

[62] *Carlill* v. *Carbolic Smoke Ball Co* [1893] 1 QB 256.

[63] *Bisset* v. *Wilkinson* [1927] AC 177, 183. See *Cooper* (1877) 2 QBD 510, 513.

[64] Cf. *Giles* (1865) Le & Ca 502, 508, 169 ER 1490, 1493. For comprehensive discussion of representations implied from conduct, see Smith, *Property Offences* (1994) § 17.5.

[65] (1837) 7 C & P 784, 173 ER 342.

[66] See *Parker and Bulteel* (1916) 25 Cox CC 145: a banker who keeps his doors open and continues to trade may thereby represent that he is solvent.

[67] *DPP* v. *Turner* [1974] AC 357, 367 (Lord Reid). (Note that this representation encompasses the implied representations stated in the old case of *Hazelton* (1874) LR 2 CCR 134. It is submitted that the earlier case may now be disregarded.) See also the discussion in Smith, *Property Offences* (1994) § 17.52.

[68] [1983] QB 953, 962.

[69] *MPC* v. *Charles* [1977] AC 177; *Lambie* [1982] AC 449. These decisions, however, fail to address the causation point (below, § 15.1(iii)(a)) that the vendor accepting the card may rely only upon the minimum representation required to validate the charge transaction, i.e. that the customer is the person named on the face of the card (itself an implied representation: *Abdullah* [1982] Crim LR 122). See Smith, "The Idea of Criminal Deception" [1982] *Crim LR* 721.

[70] *Sampson* (1885) 52 LT (NS) 772. Cf. *Eichholz* v. *Bannister* (1864) 17 CB (NS) 708, 723, 144 ER 284, 290: "in almost all the transactions of sale in common life the seller by the very act of selling holds out to the buyer that he is the owner of the article he offers for sale."

[71] *Jean Jacques Williams* [1980] Crim LR 589.

where D buys or orders goods, she impliedly represents her present intention to pay for them;[72] and where payment on the spot is expected (e.g. at a restaurant or service station), she impliedly represents also that she has the ability to pay.[73] So, for instance, where D takes a taxi, she implies by her conduct that she has money for the fare.[74]

(c) Implications from silence

As in contract law, silence or non-disclosure will generally not be regarded as representation.[75] However, the general rule is qualified in some circumstances. One exception occurs in the case of half-truths, where D's silence has the effect of distorting the meaning of some positive representation that she makes. It seems clear that an incomplete representation accompanied by silence as to material facts can be a deception, if there is an implication from the circumstances that all material information has been disclosed. Thus it is a misrepresentation for a vendor to state that the properties are let, and omit the further truth that the tenants have been given notice to quit.[76]

Secondly, the failure to negate an understanding that is implied from a course of dealing may also be a deception. In *Silverman*,[77] D had been convicted of obtaining property by deception by grossly overcharging for rewiring and redecoration of a house. Although the conviction was quashed on other grounds, the Court of Appeal held that in the situation of mutual trust, which had built up over a number of years, D had impliedly represented that his firm was going to get no more than a modest profit from the work. Watkins LJ referred to dicta of Lord Reid in *DPP v. Ray* that "a man intending to deceive can build up a situation in which his silence is as eloquent as an express statement."[78] At first glance, to penalise such conduct may seem unduly severe; but this severity is tempered in practice by the need also to establish dishonesty.

In contract law, a misrepresentation may be inferred from a failure to disclose a change in circumstances which makes false a representation that originally was true.[79] It appears that the same rule applies in the criminal law.[80] In *Rai*,[81] D obtained a grant from the Birmingham City Council to install a bathroom for his aged and infirm mother. Before work was commenced, D's mother died. D refrained from notifying the council of his

---

[72] *DPP v. Ray* [1974] AC 370.

[73] *Ibid.*, 379, 382.

[74] *Waterfall* [1970] 1 QB 148, 150 (Lord Parker).

[75] Cf. *Smith v. Hughes* (1871) LR 6 QB 597; unless D is under a duty of disclosure, e.g. arising from a contract to which he is party: *Firth* (1990) 91 Cr App R 217. The relevant principles here are those governing liability for omissions: considered above, § 4.1(i)(b).

[76] *Dimmock v. Hallett* (1866) LR 2 Ch App 21. Compare *Kylsant* [1932] 1 KB 442; *Bishirgian* [1936] 1 All ER 586; also *The Siboen & the Sibotre* [1976] 1 Lloyd's Rep 293.

[77] (1988) 86 Cr App R 213; also *Stevens* (1844) 1 Cox CC 83.

[78] [1974] AC 370, 380.

[79] *With v. O'Flanagan* [1936] Ch 575.

[80] The point was discussed but not provided for by the Criminal Law Revision Committee, *Theft and Related Offences* Cmnd. 2977 (1966) para. 101(iv).

[81] [2000] 1 Cr App R 242. Contrast, in Australia, *Nelson v R.* [1987] WAR 57, 60 (Burt CJ), where it was said that the rule of equity, that a person has a duty to disclose in a pre-contractual situation where a statement inducing a contract becomes false prior to conclusion of the contract, "is not a rule which has anything to do with the criminal offence of obtaining something by a false pretence." The application of the equitable rule was also rejected by Lord Hodson in *DPP v. Ray* [1974] AC 370, 389. However, his Lordship was in the minority and the point was not taken up by the majority.

mother's death, and the council subsequently commissioned builders to install the bathroom. D's conviction for obtaining the building services by deception was upheld by the Court of Appeal, on the grounds that his silent acquiescence after the death of his mother was itself deceptive conduct.

The failure to disclose a change of circumstances or of intention may also amount to a distinct misrepresentation where the original representation is repeated, or may be regarded as continuing. An example of the latter is *DPP* v. *Ray*,[82] where D ordered food in a restaurant, ate the meal, then decided to leave without paying. The majority of the House of Lords held that by entering and ordering the meal D had represented that he intended to pay for it. This representation was analysed as an ongoing one, sustained by D's subsequent behaviour: "by continuing in the same role and behaving just as before he was representing that his previous intention continued."[83] The representation became false at the moment that D decided not to pay; thereafter, D may rightly be convicted of obtaining by deception anything that he *subsequently* ordered.[84]

(d) Deliberate or reckless

The representation must in fact be false.[85] There can be no deception where the defendant makes a statement believing it to be false, when it is in fact true.[86] (Although such cases may nowadays be prosecuted as attempts.) Additionally, the prosecution must establish that the deception is deliberate or reckless. In accordance with the ordinary definitions of intention and recklessness in respect of circumstances,[87] this means that the defendant must either know his representation is false (a deliberate deception), or recognise it might not be (recklessness). It seems that the test of D's recklessness is subjective. This follows both from the general principle that property offences cannot be committed negligently and from analogous case law.[88] Consequently a belief, however unreasonable, that the representation is true will prevent the defendant's conduct from amounting to deception.[89]

On the other hand, where D subsequently realises that her original representation was false when made, the doctrine in *Miller* may well place her under a duty to counteract the

---

[82] [1974] AC 370. Compare *Fagan* v. *Metropolitan Police Commissioner* [1969] 1 QB 439; above, § 4.1(i)(b) (Case 4); White, "Continuing Representations in Criminal Law" (1986) 37 *NILQ* 255.

[83] [1974] AC 370, 386 (Lord Morris).

[84] On the facts of the case, D changed his mind only after he had finished eating. His conviction was therefore restored by their Lordships on the basis that he had obtained *an opportunity to evade payment* (rather than food) by his continuing deception. For criticism of this analysis, see the commentary at [1974] *Crim LR* 181–3. Although the decision may be doubted on the particular facts, it is clear that D would have been guilty had he subsequently ordered more food.

[85] *Spencer* (1828) 3 C & P 420, 172 ER 483. Since this is an element of the actus reus, the onus lies on the prosecution to prove the falsity of the representation. However, proof may be either by direct evidence or by inference from the circumstances: cf. *Mandry and Wooster* [1973] 3 All ER 996.

[86] *Deller* (1952) 36 Cr App R 184. D sold a car purportedly free of encumbrances, believing that in fact he had only the use and possession of the car under a hire purchase agreement. Although made dishonestly, D's representation might indeed have been true; the purported sale and hiring back to D was arguably a sham concealing the true transaction of a loan on the security of the car, which would have been void for non-registration.

[87] Above, §§ 5.1(v), 5.2(iii).

[88] E.g. *Holden* [1991] Crim LR 478 (above, § 13.8(i)); *Large* v. *Mainprize* [1989] Crim LR 213 (furnishing false information); *Derry* v. *Peek* (1889) 14 App Cas 337 (tort of deceit).

[89] *Staines* (1974) 60 Cr App R 160; *Lewis* (1975) 62 Cr App R 206; cf. *Conrad* [1974] 2 NZLR 626. Of course, whether there were reasonable grounds for D's belief may be considered by the jury when deciding whether D in fact had that belief.

effects of that initial, innocent deception.[90] At present, this possibility remains moot: there is no case in which it has been held that the rule in *Miller* carries over into deception.

(ii) Obtaining property belonging to another

Although they are grouped together here for convenience, this element includes three distinct components: (i) an obtaining, (ii) of property, (iii) belonging to another. The requirement of an obtaining is addressed by section 15(2), which provides:

> For purposes of this section a person is to be treated as obtaining property if he obtains ownership, possession or control of it, and "obtain" includes obtaining for another or enabling another to obtain or to retain.

As section 15(2) makes clear, there is no need for D to obtain ownership *and* possession of the goods. Either will do, as will a right of control falling short of full possession. For example, it would be obtaining by deception if D were to get possession of goods by deceiving a bailee, notwithstanding that the bailee lacked the power to transfer ownership to D.

However, what must be obtained is full ownership, possession, or control. A comparison of the language in section 15(2) with that in section 5(1) of the Theft Act 1968[91] suggests that obtaining a proprietary *interest*, falling short of full ownership or possession, would be insufficient. In this respect, the scope of obtaining by deception appears to be narrower than that of theft. For example, if D were by deception to induce V to create a charge, in favour of D, over V's assets, D would not be guilty of obtaining the assets by deception.[92]

There must in fact *be* an obtaining. In *Bogdal v. Hall*,[93] D made a fraudulent application for an unemployment benefit. It was not proved that he actually received any payments. Although D had attempted to obtain property by deception, he could not be convicted of the full offence.

Under section 15(2), the person who commits the deception is guilty of an offence even though he does not obtain for himself. In *Stonehouse*,[94] the defendant fabricated his own death by drowning soon after having insured his own life for the benefit of his wife. He was convicted of attempting to obtain property by deception even though his wife was the intended beneficiary.

(a) Property

The variety of types of property that may be obtained by deception are those specified in section 4(1) of the Theft Act 1968.[95] They are discussed above, in § 13.3(i). Note, however, that the exceptions in section 4(2)–(4) are specific to theft. Consequently, so far as the

---

[90] [1983] 2 AC 161; discussed above, § 4.1(i)(b) (Case 5).

[91] Designating what interests count as "belonging to another": above, §§ 13.4–5.

[92] Neither would D obtain the charge itself by deception, because prior to its creation the charge did not exist, and therefore never belonged to anyone other than D. For discussion of this point in the context of bank transfers, see below, § 15.1(ii)(b).

[93] [1987] Crim LR 500.

[94] [1978] AC 55; discussed earlier in the context of attempts, § 9.5. See also *Duru* [1973] 3 All ER 715, 719 (overruled on other grounds by the House of Lords in *Preddy* [1996] AC 815; below, § 15.1(ii)(b)).

[95] *Per* s. 34(1).

question of property is concerned, the range of section 15 is slightly wider than that of theft. In particular, land generally cannot be stolen (except in the special cases allowed by section 4(2)). But its ownership, possession, or control may be obtained by deception.[96]

(b) Belonging to another

The definition of belonging to another in section 5(1) of the Theft Act 1968 applies to section 15 as well as to theft.[97] However, the further provisions in section 5(2)–(5) do not apply. So, for example, it would not be an obtaining by deception if D were to deceive V into allowing D's colleague to retain an overpayment that would otherwise be caught by section 5(4).[98]

A particular difficulty has arisen over the "belonging to another" requirement in the context of choses in action.[99] The problem is as follows. Where D by a false pretence induces V to make a cheque in his favour, the obtaining of the chose in action that the cheque represents (i.e. the right to sue for the amount of the cheque) will not be an offence under section 15. This is because, in order to be caught by section 15, the thing obtained must belong to another. However, the chose in action represented by the cheque has never belonged to anyone but D. In *Preddy*,[100] the defendants by deception contrived to obtain mortgage advances from building societies, which were transferred to them by debiting the lender's bank account and crediting their own accounts. The House of Lords quashed their convictions for obtaining by deception, since the thing they had obtained—a chose in action represented by the credit balance in their bank account—belonged to the defendants *ab initio*. Although there had been a transfer from the lender to the defendants, in law the effect of the "transfer"was not to pass ownership or possession of one particular asset, but to extinguish one chose in action (the lender's) and to create a different one (the defendant's).

Of course, where the chose in action is conveyed by a document such as a cheque, D may be charged with obtaining the physical document itself, *qua* piece of paper.[101] But this technique is rather artificial and gives a misleading picture of D's wrongdoing; moreover, cheques are normally returned via the drawer's bank after presentation for payment—hence there is no intention permanently to deprive. Alternatively, it has been argued that what D obtains is *a valuable security*, in the physical form of the document. If that were accepted, a charge of obtaining would lie because what is returned is no longer a valuable security but a worthless piece of paper.[102] In *Clark*,[103] however, this latter argument was reluctantly rejected by the Court of Appeal, which thought itself bound on the point by *Preddy*.[104]

---

[96] For detailed discussion, see Smith, *Property Offences* (1994) § 17-108ff; Smith, *The Law of Theft* (8th ed, 1997) § 4-50ff.

[97] *Per* s. 34(1).

[98] See above, § 13.5(iv).

[99] Smith, "Obtaining Cheques by Deception or Theft" [1997] *Crim LR* 396; Griew, "Stealing and Obtaining Bank Credits" [1986] *Crim LR* 356; Heaton, "Cheques and Balances" [2005] Crim LR 747.

[100] [1996] AC 815; confirming *Danger* (1857) 7 Cox CC 303.

[101] Cf. *O'Connell* (1992) 94 Cr App R 39; *Caresana* [1996] Crim LR 667.

[102] Cf. *Duru* [1974] 1 WLR 2, 8 (Megaw LJ); *Kohn* (1979) 69 Cr APP R 395, 409 (Lord Lane CJ). The distinction between a valuable documentary security and the paper on which it is written is also fundamental to *Davies* [1982] 1 All ER 513; above, § 13.4(iv)(c) (Case 1).

[103] [2002] 1 Cr App R 14, [2002] 1 Cr App R 141..

[104] For criticism of the view that the Court in *Clark* was bound by *Preddy*, see the commentary at [2001] *Crim LR* 572; also Heaton, "Cheques and Balances" [2005] *Crim LR* 747.

To plug the gap, Parliament inserted section 15A into the Theft Act 1968,[105] creating the new offence of obtaining a money transfer by deception. Alternatively, the defendant could have been charged under section 20(2) with procuring the execution of a valuable security. (Both of these offences are also now repealed by the Fraud Act 2006.)

(iii) Causation or reliance

Section 15(1) provides that the property must be obtained "by any deception". This implies a requirement of causation. In order for the deception to cause the obtaining, it must *both* deceive the representee *and* be an operative cause of the obtaining of the property.[106] In other words, there must be *inducement* of or *reliance* by the representee. There is therefore no offence under section 15 where the representee is aware of the falsity of the defendant's representation but hands over the property anyway, although in this situation there may be an attempt to obtain.[107]

The condition of reliance is satisfied where the deception was *one* of the reasons for which the representee acted as she did, even if not the *only* reason.[108] Conversely (subject to what will be said in the following subsection), in principle there is no reliance where she is unaffected by the representation,[109] even if she believes it, i.e. where the representation makes no difference to the representee. In *Roebuck*,[110] for example, V "confirmed" the truth of D's representation by her own enquiries, without relying on D's say-so. D was acquitted. His representation did not cause the obtaining, since it was not a reason why V handed over the property.

Note that the requirement of inducement does not mean that the false pretence must be a credible one. If V did in fact believe the representation, it does not matter that a reasonable person would not have believed it.[111]

Although the deception must cause the delivery or obtaining of the thing, it need not do so directly. For example, the offence can be committed where the deception by D causes the representee to initiate a process whereby property is obtained, even where the thing is actually obtained from someone other than the representee.[112]

(a) Cheque cards, credit cards, and but-for causation

In *Charles*,[113] D bought gaming chips at a casino, paying for them with a cheque supported by a cheque card. D's account was overdrawn and he had no authority to make further

---

[105] By the Theft (Amendment) Act 1996.

[106] Cf. *King* [1987] QB 547. Thus the deception must not be subsequent to the obtaining: *Brooks* (1859) 1 F & F 502, 175 ER 827; *Collis-Smith* [1971] Crim LR 716.

[107] *Hensler* (1870) 11 Cox CC 570. (D wrote a begging letter claiming, falsely, to be a shipwrecked and destitute widow. The recipient of the letter sent 5 shillings despite knowing the falseness of D's claims. D could not be guilty of obtaining by false pretences but was convicted of attempting to obtain.)

[108] Compare *Hamilton* (1991) 92 Cr App R 54; *English* (1872) 12 Cox CC 171; also the discussion of multiple causes, above, § 4.2(ii)(c).

[109] *Laverty* [1970] 3 All ER 432; *Dale* (1836) 7 C & P 352, 173 ER 157; *Strickland* (1850) 14 JP 784.

[110] (1856) D & B 24, 169 ER 900; cf. *Winning* (1973) 12 CCC (2d) 449.

[111] *Giles* (1865) Le & Ca 502, 169 ER 1490; *Jessop* (1858) D & B 442, 169 ER 1074.

[112] Cf. *Kovacs* [1974] 1 All ER 1236; *Charles* [1977] AC 177; *Bennitt* [1961] NZLR 452.

[113] *Commissioner of Police for the Metropolis* v. *Charles* [1977] AC 177.

drawings. D's conviction under the former section 16 of the Theft Act 1968 for obtaining pecuniary advantage (i.e. additional credit from the bank) by deception was upheld by the House of Lords.

At first glance, this may appear a sensible result. But was there any deception that induced the casino to accept the cheque? There are two possible representations to consider. First, D represented by his conduct that the cheque would be met by the bank. Clearly, this representation was relied on by the casino when accepting the cheque—but it was not a deception. The representation was true: under the terms of the cheque card, the bank was obliged to and did honour the cheque.

Secondly, D was held also to have represented by his conduct that he was authorised to use the cheque card. This was false, and so a deception. But it is at least arguable that the casino did not rely on this second representation. The manager of the casino testified that "with a cheque card, so long as the conditions on the back are met, the bank will honour that card irrespective of the state of the drawer's account or the authority, or lack of it, which he has in drawing on the account," and that "[a]ll those matters, in fact, once there is a cheque card, are totally irrelevant."[114] In other words, the casino was indifferent whether D was authorised to use the card. It relied exclusively on the first representation, that the bank would be obliged to meet D's cheque.

Nonetheless, the House of Lords thought there was sufficient evidence to support a conviction that D's deception had induced the casino manager to accept the cheque; a finding that in Sir John Smith's view, "seems, with respect, to be almost perverse."[115] It certainly dilutes the causation requirement in obtaining by deception. The rationale of the decision is that, although the deception was not directly operative on the mind of the representee, it was a "but-for" cause.[116] If the casino manager had known D was not authorised to use the card, he would not have accepted the cheque.[117] So in a hypothetical, counterfactual sense, the manager was not entirely indifferent to the truth of the deception.

It must be doubted whether counterfactual hypothesis of this sort is a proper basis for inflicting criminal convictions on people. With respect, their Lordships' analysis smacks of fiction and invention. The factual, psychological truth of the matter is that the manager decided to give credit purely because payment of the cheque was guaranteed.[118] Be that as it may, *Charles* unquestionably states the law governing the obtaining offences and was

---

[114] *Ibid.*, 193.

[115] *The Law of Theft* (8th ed, 1997) § 4-09.

[116] Above, § 4.2(i).

[117] "But in this context it has again to be borne in mind that the witness made clear that the accused's cheques were accepted only because he produced a cheque card, and he repeatedly stressed that, had he been aware that the accused was using his cheque book and cheque card 'in a way in which he was not allowed or entitled to use [them]' no cheque would have been accepted": *Charles* [1977] AC 177, 193 (Lord Edmund-Davies).

[118] An instructive contrast is the analysis in *Nabina* [2000] Crim LR 481. D obtained a number of credit cards by misrepresenting his personal circumstances. He used the cards to purchase goods and was charged with obtaining them by deception. In quashing D's conviction for misdirection, the Court of Appeal expressed doubt whether a supplier of goods would be interested in anything other than the guarantee that he would be paid. *Nabina* is, however, distinguishable from *Charles* and *Lambie* because D's misrepresentations to the card issuer merely made the issue of the card voidable, not void. Hence, unlike the other cases, D did have authority to use the card.

affirmed, on similar facts, by their Lordships in *Lambie*.[119] But-for causation, even of a hypothetical kind,[120] is sufficient.

(b) Remoteness

Sometimes, the final transaction by which something is obtained may be too remote from the original representation for causation to be established. This was said to be the case in *Clucas*, where D through a false pretence induced V, a bookmaker, to accept a bet on credit. The horse he backed won, but the money he received was held not to be obtained by the deception—the effective cause of the obtaining was not D's representation but the fact that the horse won.[121]

Although *Clucas* helpfully highlights the law's requirement of causation, the decision is doubtful on its particular facts. It seems improbable that the horse's victory was a *novus actus interveniens*, since that was precisely the subject-matter of the wager.[122] A more straightforward case is *Button*,[123] where D's representation that he had never before won a race enabled him to gain a handicap advantage and thereby win two races. Here the causal connection was clear, since the representation made it more likely that D would win the race itself.

Most situations of this type arise when the immediate cause of the obtaining is some event contemplated in a contract.[124] Where that contract is itself induced by a deception, the difficulty about causation was overcome by section 16(2)(c) (now repealed) of the Theft Act 1968, which extended the former offence of obtaining a pecuniary advantage by deception to contracts of employment and wagers.

(c) Machines

In principle, the need for deception and reliance excludes from section 15 the unauthorised obtaining of money from an automatic teller machine, or of soft drinks from a vending machine, since a machine cannot be induced to believe propositions. A useful illustration is the Australian case of *Kennison v. Daire*.[125] After D's bank account had been closed, D withdrew money from an automatic teller machine with his cashcard. The Court denied that this was an obtaining by false pretences and instead convicted D of larceny, ruling that

---

[119] [1982] AC 449. D purchased goods in a shop using a credit card. She was over her credit limit on the card and permission to use the card had been revoked. The shop assistant testified that the shop's practice, agreed with the card company, was to honour the card if the date and signature were valid and the card was not on a stop list; the shop was unconcerned whether the bearer had authority to use the card. Nonetheless, the House of Lords restored D's conviction on the basis of a deception that D was entitled to use the card.

[120] Hypothetical counterfactuals of this sort are the mark of causation by omissions (see above, § 4.2(iv)) and, effectively, *Charles* imposes liability upon D for an omission: i.e. for not informing the manager that he was exceeding his overdraft limit.

[121] [1949] 2 KB 226.

[122] Contrast *Lambassi* [1927] VLR 349, [1927] ALR 295.

[123] [1900] 2 QB 597.

[124] Compare the unreported case of *Lewis* (1922) Russell (12th ed.) Vol. II, 1186 n. 66, discussed in *King* [1987] QB 547. D obtained a teaching post by means of a forged teacher's certificate: the view was taken that her salary was obtained as a result of performing the obligations of her post, and not of the false pretence. See too the criticism of *Miller* (1992) 95 Cr App R 421 by Smith, *Property Offences* (1994) § 17.125.

[125] (1985) 38 SASR 404, 406; affirmed (1986) 160 CLR 129. Cf. dicta in *Davies v. Flackett* [1973] RTR 8, 10.

a machine cannot be deceived and does not "rely" on representations, but simply delivers money or goods in response to a certain input. According to King CJ:

> "The crime of obtaining money by false pretences requires, in my opinion, the intervention of a human being who is induced by the false pretence to part with money. A machine cannot be deceived by a false pretence or other fraud."

Although there is no binding authority applying the same rule in the United Kingdom, it has been accepted that the rule "regrettably" prevails here also.[126] Fortunately, such cases would in any event be theft.[127]

(iv) Dishonesty and the intention permanently to deprive

The principal mental elements for an offence under section 15 are (i) intention or recklessness about the deception (above, § 15.1(i)(d)); (ii) dishonesty (§ 13.8); and (iii) the intent permanently to deprive the person from whom the property is obtained (§ 13.7). These elements have each been considered earlier: dishonesty and the intention permanently to deprive bear the same meanings as they do for theft.[128]

(a) Obtaining or deprivation?

The gist of the deception offence in section 15 is the obtaining of an advantage for D, rather than the deprivation of a victim *per se*. Conversely, where a dishonest deprivation of V is intended without any benefit to D or another, it would usually have been more appropriate to charge under one of the fraud offences, such as conspiracy to defraud (below, § 15.3). Since 2007, a charge of fraud may now be apt under section 1 of the Fraud Act 2007 (above, § 15.1).

In practice, obtaining and defrauding will frequently overlap. The case of *Moses and Ansbro*[129] is a useful illustration. By false applications, the defendants managed to obtain National Insurance numbers. While rightly being convicted of conspiracy to defraud,[130] in principle they could also have been charged with obtaining property by deception, since they had obtained plastic cards bearing their National Insurance numbers. That this is so is shown by *Ashbee*,[131] in which the defendants made false applications for passports and were convicted of conspiracy[132] to obtain property (i.e. passports) by deception.

Ashbee illustrates that D may be convicted of obtaining even where the thing obtained has little or no economic value to the victim. Neither must D intend that anyone suffer a net economic loss. In *Greenstein*,[133] the defendants applied for shares in a series of public issues. In order to increase their allotments, they habitually applied for a number of shares far in excess of what they could afford. The applications were accompanied by a cheque for the full application. Contrary to an implied representation that the cheques were good, the

---

[126] *Holmes* [2004] EWHC 2020 (Admin), [2005] 1 WLR 1857, para. 11.
[127] Cf. *Hands* (1887) 16 Cox CC 188; *Cooper v. Miles* [1979] Crim LR 42; *Goodwin* [1996] Crim LR 262.
[128] Cf. *Ghosh* [1982] QB 1053 (dishonesty); s. 15(3) (intent to deprive).
[129] [1991] Crim LR 617.
[130] By deceiving a person into acting contrary to public duty: below, § 15.3(iii)(b).
[131] [1989] 1 WLR 109.
[132] That is, statutory conspiracy under s. 1 of the Criminal Law Act 1977.
[133] [1975] 1 WLR 1353.

defendants had insufficient funds to meet the cheques. However, they expected to be allocated only a small proportion of their applications; in turn, they anticipated receiving corresponding cheques refunding the portion of each application they were not allotted. Banking these would enable them to meet the cheques they had themselves written. Notwithstanding that the cheques were thus, ultimately, met—so that no-one suffered any loss—the defendants were convicted of obtaining their share allocations by deception.

There may also be an offence against section 15 even though the victim received valuable consideration, provided the transaction was induced by D's deception. In *Potger*,[134] D falsely represented that he was a student taking part in a competition to sell magazines. The fact that the magazines would have been delivered and would have been worth the purchase price did not prevent his conduct from being an offence.

§ 15.5 Pre-2007 law: obtaining services by deception

Just as private law has been reluctant to give restitution for services unless they generate an end-product,[135] the tendency to understand economic wealth in tangible terms has meant that criminal law has been slow to protect services. To deceive another person into doing work has never been an offence of obtaining property, even though intangible economic value may be involved in the transaction. Partly, this is because the performance of services does not necessarily transfer wealth, since services are not themselves a form of wealth but rather its source or product.[136] In a sense, therefore, the protection of services by criminal law is needed to protect the victim of a deception from *wasting* economically valuable activity—from loss—as much as it is to prevent the defendant's gain therefrom.

Section 1(1) of the 1978 Act addressed these needs squarely, providing that "[a] person who by any deception dishonestly obtains services from another shall be guilty of an offence."[137] Apart from its focus on services, the offence largely overlapped with that of obtaining property by deception, and the common elements of deception,[138] causation, and dishonesty will not be rehearsed here.[139] The present discussion will comment on the meaning of "services", which is further defined by section 1(2):

> It is an obtaining of services where the other is induced to confer a benefit by doing some act, or causing or permitting some act to be done, on the understanding that the benefit has been or will be paid for.

---

[134] (1970) 55 Cr App R 42.

[135] Cf. *BP Exploration Co (Libya) Ltd* v. *Hunt (No 2)* [1979] 1 WLR 783, 799 (Robert Goff J): "The identity and value of the resulting benefit to the recipient may be debatable."

[136] Marshall regards this as obvious: "services and other goods, which pass out of existence in the same instant that they come into it, are of course, not part of the stock of wealth": *Principles of Economics* (8th ed, 1947) 56. Contrast, perhaps, the *right* to a service: *per* Sachs LJ, "some have suggested that [an employee] may now be said to acquire something akin to a property in his employment": *Hill* v. *Parsons* [1972] Ch 305, 321.

[137] See Spencer, "The Theft Act 1978" [1979] *Crim LR* 24; see now the offence of obtaining services dishonestly, contrary to s. 11 of the Fraud Act 2007. Under the terms of s. 11, if D, acting for himself or another, obtains services for which payment is required in whole or in part, he will commit an offence if he fails to pay in whole or in part while knowing that payment is or might be expected, and acting with a dishonest intent to avoid payment in whole or in part. See further Ormerod, "The Fraud Act 2006: Criminalising Lying?" [2007] *Crim LR* 193, 213–16.

[138] Cf. s. 5(1) of the 1978 Act.

[139] See above, § 15.4.

Three issues arise from this definition: (i) how wide is the scope of "confer a benefit"; (ii) what restrictions are imposed by the criterion that the victim must do some act, or cause or permit some act to be done; and (iii) what is the effect of the requirement that it be understood the benefit is for payment?

(i) Confer a benefit

The phrase "confer a benefit" expands the scope of "services" well beyond its paradigm meaning, and encompasses a wider range of situations than "obtaining services" would ordinarily suggest. Most property is a benefit: hence, the offence under section 1 of the 1978 Act overlapped extensively with obtaining property by deception, under the former section 15 of the 1968 Act.[140] One advantage of this overlap, from the prosecutor's point of view, was that a dishonest hiring of property can be an offence under section 1 even though not under section 15; because there is no requirement for an intent permanently to deprive in section 1.

At first, the Court of Appeal rejected such a wide interpretation. In *Halai*,[141] D obtained a mortgage advance by deception. His conviction for obtaining services by deception was quashed *inter alia* on the ground that the advance was property, i.e. money, rather than a service, and the proper charge should have been under section 15 of the 1968 Act. Subsequently, however, the decision was effectively overruled by the Court of Appeal itself.[142] It has also been undone by legislation. A new subsection, section 1(3), was enacted to cover the difficulty:

> Without prejudice to the generality of subsection 1(2) above, it is an obtaining of services where the other is induced to make a loan, or to cause or permit a loan to be made, on the understanding that any payment (whether by way of interest or otherwise) will be or has been made in respect of the loan.

The Court of Appeal has since gone on to rule that section 1 is also apt to encompass such "services" as the opening of a bank account.[143] More straightforward scenarios falling within section 1(2) are cases where D, by falsely representing she has a driving licence, induces a rental company to lend her a car on hire; or where D, by falsely representing that she intends to pay £100 for the service, induces V to trim the trees in her garden.[144]

The boundaries of the term "benefit" have not been drawn by the courts. Presumably they would encompass—at least—anything that would qualify as consideration in a contract. In light of the point that services are not themselves a form of wealth,[145] there seems no reason to require that the defendant receive anything of marketable value. No doubt, valuable end-products are often generated by the service obtained. The end-products may not have inherent exchange value—for example, when D pretends to be an enrolled student

---

[140] Not an unwelcome consequence: Criminal Law Revision Committee, *Working Paper on Section 16 of the Theft Act 1968* (1974) para. 33.

[141] [1983] Crim LR 624.

[142] *Graham* [1997] 1 Cr App R 302, 317; *Cooke* [1997] Crim LR 436; *Naviede* [1997] Crim LR 662.

[143] *Sofroniou* [2003] EWCA Crim 3681, [2004] QB 1218, paras. 29–32.

[144] For examples, see Spencer, "The Theft Act 1978" [1979] *Crim LR* 24, 27–8.

[145] Above, § 15.2.

at a private university and has her stock of knowledge increased by receiving a tutorial on criminal law. Yet, even in this case, the criminal wrong is not that D obtains an end-product (knowledge), but the manner in which she does so: by deceiving the tutor into providing the tutorial.[146] Thus the law is justified in convicting her for obtaining services even though no realisable wealth has been transferred.

(ii) By doing some act, or causing or permitting some act to be done

A mere omission by the victim of the deception is insufficient. There must be either an act or, at least, the permitting of an act by someone else. Suppose that D, by flourishing a used stub, tricks a cinema attendant into letting her see a film without a valid ticket. This would be caught by the section, since the attendant has conferred a benefit on D by permitting D's act of entering the screening room. However, consider the following alternative. E is sitting on a train, and similarly tricks the guard into permitting him to remain on the train without a valid ticket. Here there is no act, or permitted act, that has been induced by the deception. E commits no offence of obtaining services by deception. It would be otherwise if, say, E had tricked the guard into letting him *board* the train.

(iii) On the understanding the benefit has been or will be paid for

Suppose that D, by falsely pleading poverty, induces her neighbour to cook her a meal. Although motivated by the deception, D's benefit is conferred for free. No offence is committed against section 1. The same is true even if the benefit would normally be charged for; for example where, by pretending the situation was an emergency, D procures a taxi driver to carry him to hospital without charge. In this case, the correct charge was evasion of a liability by deception, contrary to section 2(1)(c) of the 1978 Act. As the Court of Appeal put it, in *Sofraniou*:[147]

> an understanding as to payment under the section will not be satisfied unless there is an agreement or sufficient understanding that an identifiable payment or payments have been or will be made by or on behalf of the person receiving the services to the person providing them.

The understanding must be mutual, or at least putatively mutual (on the assumption that D was not dishonest).[148] Whether such an understanding exists is a question of fact: thus the opening of a bank account, for instance, may not qualify under section 1 of the 1978 Act if there are no charges attached to its operation while in credit and D does not become overdrawn.[149]

---

[146] Similarly, if D had gained the same end-product (increased knowledge) by deceiving the tutor into lending her a textbook, the charge would also focus on the intermediate means: on her obtaining services (the loan of the textbook) by deception.

[147] [2003] EWCA Crim 3681, [2004] QB 1218, para. 38.

[148] *Ibid.*, para. 37.

[149] *Ibid.*, para. 38.

The obtaining of services conferred in the expectation of non-monetary reward may also be excluded from section 1. If D tricks V into driving her somewhere by promising to cook V dinner that night, the transaction is a barter and there is arguably no understanding that the benefit will, as such, be "paid for". To the extent that section 1(2) is ambiguous on the point, the principle of strict interpretation suggests that payments in kind should be excluded from the scope of obtaining by deception. Additionally, a strict construction might help to ensure the offence is not extended too far into personal matters. Suppose that D tricks V into writing D's essay for him by implying that they will afterwards have sexual intercourse. Arguably, non-commercial transactions of this kind should lie outside the scope of criminal intervention.

Against these arguments, it may be contended that the very phrase "payment in kind" is well enough known to make reasonable the conclusion that one may "pay" for something, within the meaning of section 1(2), by non-monetary consideration. Thus, in the context of a civil action to recover rental premiums under the Landlord and Tenant (Rent Control) Act 1949, Lord Evershed once remarked:[150]

> "the word 'payment' in itself is one which, in an appropriate context, may cover many ways of discharging obligations. It may even (as is well known, although it does not arise in this case) include a discharge, not by money payment at all, but by what is called 'payment in kind'."

So far as the Theft Act 1978 is concerned, there appears to be no authority deciding this question.

§15.6 Conspiracy to defraud

Prior to the Fraud Act 2007, there was no general criminal offence of fraud. The defrauding of one individual by another did not *per se* constitute a crime.[151] For the most part, fraud was criminalised historically through more specific offences, which addressed particular forms of economic activity when done with a fraudulent intent.[152]

However, the common law does recognise an offence of *conspiracy* to defraud, operative where the fraud involves two or more persons acting together.[153] The essence of the offence is an agreement to practise a fraud on somebody.[154] In *Scott*,[155] the House of Lords thought it "clearly the law" that:

> "an agreement by two or more by dishonesty to deprive a person of something which is his or to which he is or would be or might be entitled and an agreement by two or more by dishonesty to injure some proprietary right of his, suffices to constitute the offence of conspiracy to defraud."

---

[150] *White* v. *Elmdene Estates* [1959] 2 All ER 605, 610–11.

[151] *Wheatly* (1761) 2 Burr 1125, 97 ER 746. An exception was the old offence of Cheat, which was confined to fraud "in a subject concerning the public, which, as between subject and subject, would only be actionable by a civil action": *Bembridge* (1783) 22 St Tr 1, 99 ER 679 (Lord Mansfield).

[152] See Smith, *Property Offences* (1994), especially chap. 22; *Arlidge and Parry on Fraud* (2nd ed, 1996).

[153] *Hevey* (1782) 1 Leach 232, 168 ER 218. See Hadden, "Conspiracy to Defraud" [1966] *CLJ* 248; Gillies, "The Offence of Conspiracy to Defraud" (1977) 51 *ALJ* 247.

[154] *Wai Yu-tsang* v. *R.* [1991] 4 All ER 664.

[155] *Scott* v. *Metropolitan Police Commissioner* [1975] AC 819, 840 (Viscount Dilhorne).

Although its importance has diminished with the enactment of various statutory offences, especially the Fraud Act 2007, conspiracy to defraud remains a catch-all offence covering conduct that does not fall under other substantive fraud offences. The scope of the crime is extremely wide, because of the broad definition of fraud; especially the fact that the conspiracy need not be to commit an offence, but may also be to commit a civil wrong[156] or perhaps certain kinds of moral wrongs.[157] For these reasons, the offence might be thought prima facie objectionable and one to be used sparingly. Its broad language offers little guidance to prospective offenders—by contrast, a series of offences each of which specifies an actus reus more narrowly offers better guidance to citizens, by warning clearly that proposed conduct falls within the reach of the criminal law.[158]

Even more importantly, the offence makes illegal conduct by two defendants that may not be criminal when done by only one. It is hard to see how that distinction between individual and group, and its very serious consequences, are justified. Why does the moral character of an ordinary civil or moral wrong change, *so much so that it becomes a crime*, simply because it is perpetrated by two rather than one?[159] The anomaly created by conspiracy to defraud is, moreover, difficult to reconcile with the ordinary crime of conspiracy *per se*,[160] which requires that the conduct conspired at should itself be an offence.

Aggravating these problems is the difficulty of drawing a boundary between mere sharp practice in the commercial sphere and criminal dishonesty. The two shade into each other,[161] and in practice it may be the element of conspiracy that redesignates a transaction from unscrupulous to illegal. Perhaps as a consequence of this, in the public mind fraud has tended to lack the graphic moral character of theft or receiving, and there is a continuing debate whether commercial malpractice is a proper subject for "public law", or whether it should primarily be dealt with by civil law mechanisms; particularly since such wrongdoing is often perceived to be victimless, in that there may be no identifiable individual who is directly and immediately out of pocket as a result of the defendant's activities.[162] Even where the activities are regulated by criminal law, the law's control mechanisms are different from those for street crime, in terms of the social standing of the suspects, and in terms of the comparative immunity of "white-collar crimes" from police surveillance or normal

---

[156] *Warburton* (1870) LR 1 CCR 274; *Weaver* (1931) 45 CLR 321, 334. In *Potter* [1953] 1 All ER 296, a recalcitrant debenture-holder entered into an agreement whereby he was guaranteed an additional 7 shillings in the pound on his debentures from an outside source, in return for his agreement to a scheme whereby all debenture holders were to agree to a composition of 8 shillings in the pound. D's counsel argued that the private agreement was merely unenforceable or void as a fraudulent preference, and did not constitute an indictable offence. Cassells J disagreed, holding that there was an indictable offence of conspiracy; although at trial both defendants were acquitted.

[157] *Timothy* (1858) 1 F & F 39, 175 ER 616; *Heymann* v. *R.* (1873) LR 8 QB 102, 105; cf. *Weaver* (1931) 45 CLR 321, 346–7 (but see at 349). See below, § 15.3(iii)(c).

[158] See the discussion of fair warning, above, § 2.3.

[159] For an argument that the moral character of the wrong changes when there is conspiracy, see Dennis, "The Rationale of Criminal Conspiracy" (1977) 93 *LQR* 39. But Dennis does not suggest that the moral character of the defendants' activities changes so drastically that a conspiracy to do a mere civil wrong (let alone lawful acts) should be criminalised.

[160] Contrary to s. 1(1) of the Criminal Law Act 1977. See above, § 9.2.

[161] According to the Law Commission, *Fraud* Law Com. No. 276 (2002) § 1.6, "the common law offence of conspiracy

[162] See below, § 15.3(iii)(a).

criminal prosecution.[163] Nonetheless, serious commercial fraud has increased considerably, and is extremely costly to society in economic terms. No doubt this is attributable to the evolution of commercial practices.[164] Modern credit economies enable fraudsters to manipulate wealth in large denominations, without being constrained by having to deal with its physical manifestation. The techniques of wrongdoing multiply as the variety and complexity of financial transactions increases, requiring specialist knowledge to initiate, process, and, above all, monitor. This changing nature of commercial and financial life presents at least one reason for retention of a fall-back crime such as conspiracy to defraud, since it may be impossible for specific legislation constantly to keep up with the mutating ways in which fraud may be committed, especially given modern communications and computing innovations, and the globalisation of securities and other markets.[165]

The elements of conspiracy to defraud are:

(i)   an agreement between two or more persons;
(ii)   that contemplates using fraudulent means;
(iii) to prejudice the rights of another person, or to induce another to act contrary to her public duty; and
(iv)   mens rea.

We consider these elements in turn.

(i) Agreement with another person

The law on this point is the same as for ordinary conspiracy.[166] There must be an act of agreement, constituting a joint decision to commit the fraud. Preliminary negotiations or discussions regarding the possibility of doing something fraudulent, which do not crystallise into any firm decision, are insufficient.[167] Neither is there a conspiracy where the parties each have the same thought or intention, but have not communicated this to each other: a concurrence between two people of "mere wicked thoughts not intended to be acted upon"[168] will not do. The joint decision required for conspiracy exists only if there is a genuine agreement to defraud between the parties.

In general, there are three kinds of conspiratorial agreement. The simplest variety is where each conspirator is aware of the existence of all the others and knows that they are parties to the agreement. The second, more complex, case is the "wheel" (or "cartwheel")

---

[163] Levi, *Regulating Fraud: White-collar Crime and the Criminal Process* (1987) 15. See also Hadden, "Fraud in the City: The Role of the Criminal Law" [1983] *Crim LR* 500.

[164] Cf. Hall, *Theft, Law and Society* (2nd ed., 1952) 300.

[165] See Sullivan, "Fraud and the Efficacy of the Criminal Law: A Proposal for a Wide Residual Offence" [1985] *Crim LR* 616; McBarnet and Whelan, "The Elusive Spirit of the Law: Formalism and the Struggle for Legal Control" (1991) 54 *MLR* 848; Smith, "Conspiracy to Defraud: Some Comments on the Law Commission's Report" [1995] *Crim LR* 209.

[166] See the more detailed discussion above, in § 9.2(ii); also Orchard, "'Agreement' in Criminal Conspiracy" [1974] *Crim LR* 297 and 335.

[167] This is the explanation of *Walker* [1962] Crim LR 458. D had participated in discussions about a planned payroll robbery, but later withdrew. His conviction was quashed as it was not proven that the discussions had progressed beyond the stage of negotiation before his withdrawal. See above, § 9.2(ii)(c); also *Barnard* (1980) 70 Cr App R 28.

[168] *Banks* (1873) 12 Cox CC 393, 399.

conspiracy, where A, B, and C (the spokes) are all individually in contact with D (the hub), but have never met each other.[169] The third variant is the "chain" conspiracy, where A contacts B, who contacts C, who contacts D, and so on.[170] However, it is important not to roll up a number of separate transactions in one conspiracy charge. This point is made in *Griffiths*,[171] where a lime supplier (Griffiths), his accountant, and seven farmers whom Griffiths supplied, were charged with conspiracy to defraud the government of subsidies. Their convictions were quashed on appeal, as there was no evidence of any collusion between the farmers, either directly or through the intermediation of Griffiths, but only of separate conspiracies between the supplier and individual farmers.[172]

Like statutory conspiracy, a conspiracy to defraud, once formed, does not admit of withdrawal. After an agreement is reached, and the other elements are established, the crime of conspiracy to defraud is complete and it is irrelevant that subsequently one or all of the parties decide to abandon the agreement.[173]

(ii) By fraudulent means

The conspiracy must involve the use of fraudulent or dishonest means.[174] To illustrate the importance of this requirement, suppose that a solicitor acting in her professional capacity agrees to perform certain services for her client which will cause loss to another party. These facts disclose no conspiracy to defraud unless the services go beyond her ordinary duties as a solicitor.[175] Similarly, many business decisions do—and are meant to—prejudice the economic interests of rivals, yet one is entitled to neglect those rival interests provided the decision involves a legitimate course of action. Thus in *Zemmel*,[176] the defendants' agreement to delay paying a creditor was held not to be a conspiracy to defraud.

On the other hand, the requirement of fraudulent *modus operandi* is quite easily satisfied. Obviously, the use of deceit or falsehood is sufficient (although it would now anyway fall within the scope of section 1 of the Fraud Act 2007). In *Lewis*,[177] for example, it was held

---

[169] Cf. *Ex p Coffey, Re Evans* [1971] NSWLR 434.

[170] *Ardalan* [1972] 2 All ER 257. Note, however, the cautionary words of Roskill LJ (at 262) that "words or phrases such as 'wheels', 'cartwheels', 'chain', 'sub-conspiracies' and so on are used only to illustrate and clarify the principle and for no other purpose."

[171] [1966] 1 QB 589.

[172] [1966] 1 QB 589, 599: "It is right and proper to say that the judge correctly pointed out the principle, saying that the Crown had to prove that the conspirators put their heads together to defraud the Ministry. The trouble is that it never seems to have been considered . . . whether or not in this case each farmer put his head together with Griffiths' head without any thought of a general conspiracy." Hence, although each defendant may have conspired separately with Griffiths, the convictions were unsafe since the defendants should not have been joined in a conglomerate charge.

[173] Above, § 9.2(ii)(d). Cf. *O'Brien* (1955) 2 DLR 311, 314 (Taschereau J): "If a person, with one or several others, agrees to commit an unlawful act, and later, after having had the intention to carry it through, refuses to put the plan into effect, that person is nevertheless guilty."

[174] In *Scott* [1975] AC 819, 840, this criterion is encapsulated in the phrase "by dishonesty", operating as an actus reus element; see the passage quoted above in the text at § 15.3. In order clearly to distinguish it from the mens rea component of dishonesty (below, § 15.3(iv)), we refer to this element as "by fraudulent means". Early cases express it in the requirement that a common law conspiracy be either to do an unlawful act or to do a lawful act *by unlawful means*. *Jones* (1832) 4 B & Ad 345, 349, 110 ER 485, 487.

[175] *Tighe and Maher* (1926) 26 SR (NSW) 94.

[176] (1985) 81 Cr App R 279.

[177] (1869) 11 Cox CC 404.

that an arrangement made for mock bidding at an auction could be a conspiracy to defraud, since the scheme was intended, through a deception, to induce innocent buyers to bid more than necessary. Similarly, in *A-G's Reference (No. 1 of 1982),*[178] manufacturing fake whisky was held to be a conspiracy to defraud unknowing purchasers. These are cases where the agreement involved a false representation, express or implied. But conspiracy to defraud has a much wider scope than this. In *Weaver,*[179] the High Court of Australia said that the offence embraces "every kind and description of fraudulent statement, conduct, trick, or device," including "false accounts, fabricated shares, false representations or conduct."[180] Even if there is no representation, many cases will involve deceit; as in *Hollinshead,* where the defendants agreed to manufacture and sell "black box" devices whose only purpose was to cause electricity meters to produce erroneous readings.

Moreover, there is no *requirement* that there be either a falsehood or that anyone must be deceived.[181] In *Scott,*[182] for example, the defendants bribed cinema employees to let them borrow films, which were then copied in breach of copyright. Their behaviour was certainly fraudulent, even though it involved neither falsehood nor deceit.

(iii) The object of the conspiracy

Conspiracy to defraud may be committed in either of two general forms: by conspiring to prejudice the rights of another person, or to induce another to act contrary to her public duty.

(a) To prejudice the rights of another

The paradigm case of conspiracy to defraud is where D conspires to obtain a benefit at the expense of another's assets. In many cases this can, and should, be charged under ordinary conspiracy principles; as either conspiracy to steal, or conspiracy to obtain property by deception. However, the offences of theft under section 1 and obtaining under section 15 both require that the subject matter be property belonging to another. Conspiracy to defraud is not limited in this way: thus it encompasses depriving someone of land, or exploiting another's confidential information, or even persuading a testatrix to change her will in favour of the defendants.[183] The last example would not be theft even of an equitable interest, since the (erstwhile) potential beneficiaries under a will have merely a *spes successionis,* and are not deprived of any proprietary right.

The range of interests caught by conspiracy to defraud is therefore very wide. Moreover, the core of defrauding is disadvantage to others: usually, deprivation of or prejudice to a

---

178 [1983] QB 751.
179 (1931) 45 CLR 321.
180 *Ibid.,* 334.
181 Contrast the definition by Buckley J in *Re London & Globe Finance Corp Ltd* [1903] 1 Ch 728, 732, which (wrongly) suggests that deceit is necessary for fraud: "To deceive is, I apprehend, to induce a man to believe that a thing is true which is false, and which the person practising the deceit knows or believes to be false. To defraud is to deprive by deceit: it is by deceit to induce a man to act to his injury. More tersely it may be put, that to deceive is by falsehood to induce a state of mind; to defraud is by deceit to induce a course of action."
182 [1975] AC 819. See also *Sinclair* [1968] 1 WLR 1246; *Hollinshead* [1985] AC 975.
183 *Tillings and Tillings* [1985] Crim LR 393.

victim's interests. So it is not necessary that the purpose of the conspiracy should be to benefit anyone.[184] In *Welham v. DPP*, Lord Radcliffe pointed out that:[185]

> "Although in the nature of things [defrauding] is almost invariably associated with the obtaining of an advantage for the person who commits the fraud, it is the effect upon the person who is the object of the fraud that ultimately determines its meaning."

The law thus looks at the effect of the fraud on the victim, irrespective of whether the defendants sought thereby to make a gain.

Further, if we concentrate upon the victim, we find that she may be defrauded even if she suffers no loss. It is sufficient that the conspiracy *puts at risk* the economic, or property, interests or rights of the victim.[186] In *Scott* (above, § 15.3(ii)), a conspiracy to defraud was established notwithstanding that the breach of copyright caused no direct pecuniary loss to the cinema owners, and simply had the potential to deprive them of profits. Similarly, in *Adams v. R.* it was said that there may be a conspiracy to defraud based upon an agreement dishonestly to conceal information, where the conspirator is under a duty to disclose it, or upon an agreement dishonestly to withhold information from persons entitled to require its disclosure[187]—whether or not those persons suffer financial harm as a result.

The victim need not be a particular person, and in the past the offence has been applied to conspiracies to rig markets.[188] In general, however, dishonest manipulation of a market price will now fall within insider trading regulations, and is better dealt with under that head by specialist legislation.[189] Given its potential effect on otherwise justifiable business transactions and upon the free operation of the market, it may be questionable whether criminal law is an appropriate tool at all for market regulation of this sort;[190] and it is certainly desirable to control wrongdoing with more sensitive legislation, which admits of appropriate exceptions for legitimate transactions, than with a blunt and overbroad offence such as conspiracy to defraud.

(b) To induce another to act contrary to her public duty

In addition to defrauding particular persons and unascertained persons through the marketplace, the fraud may also be on the "public" at large, where no individual's particular interests (actual or potential) are jeopardised. "Where the intended victim of a 'conspiracy

---

[184] Cf. *Cope* (1719) 1 Str 144, 93 ER 438.

[185] [1961] AC 103, 123. (D was charged with uttering forged documents with intent to defraud, contrary to s. 6 of the Forgery Act 1912.) Cf. Viscount Dilhorne in *Scott v. MPC* [1975] AC 819, 839: "'to defraud' ordinarily means, in my opinion, to deprive a person dishonestly of something which is his or of something to which he is or would or might but for the perpetration of the fraud be entitled."

[186] *Allsop* (1976) 64 Cr App R 29; *Wai Yu-tsang v. R* [1992] 1 AC 269.

[187] [1995] 1 WLR 52, 65. The Privy Council held that a conspiracy to defraud existed where company directors dishonestly agreed to conceal information relating to secret profits, so as to impede action by the company to recover those profits. However, there must still be an intention to act to the prejudice of some extant right: "A person is not prejudiced if he is hindered in inquiring into the source of moneys in which he has no interest. He can only suffer prejudice in relation to some right or interest which he possesses."

[188] Early authorities include *De Berenger* (1814) 3 M & S 67, 105 ER 536; *Burch* (1865) 4 F & F 407, 176 ER 622; *Aspinall* (1876) 1 QBD 730, affirmed 35 LT 738, 741n; *Scott v. Brown, Doering, McNab & Co* (1892) 2 QB 724.

[189] E.g. Financial Services Act 1986, s. 47 (price manipulation).

[190] For discussion, see Gillen, "Sanctions Against Insider Trading: A Proposal for Reform" (1991) 70 *Can Bar Rev* 215; Carlton and Fischel, "The Regulation of Insider Trading" (1983) 35 *Stanford LR* 857.

to defraud' is a person performing public duties as distinct from a private individual it is sufficient if the purpose is to cause him to act contrary to his duty."[191] Consequently, there may be a conspiracy fraudulently to obtain a driving licence,[192] National Insurance number,[193] confidential information,[194] or membership of a society.[195]

There is some authority that cases involving public officials are not distinctive, but rather illustrations of a more general proposition that conspiracy to defraud does not require an intention to cause loss, so that cases of "public duty" fraud might extend to victims not occupying a public office: "the expression 'intent to defraud' is not to be given a narrow meaning, involving an intention to cause economic loss to another. In broad terms, it means simply an intention to practise a fraud on another, or an intention to act to the prejudice of another man's right."[196] However, that authority should be understood as establishing no more than the proposition set out in the foregoing subsection (§ 15.3(iii)(a)), that it is ordinarily sufficient in conspiracy to defraud that the victim's rights or interests are deliberately put at risk and that there is no need for the conspirators to aim at causing loss.[197] Any wider interpretation should be doubted, since it would further extend an already vague and overbroad offence. Moreover, it would be contrary to House of Lords authority that the public duty cases are a "special line of cases",[198] a separate category,[199] perhaps a surviving variety of the now-rejected generic wrong of conspiracy to effect a public mischief.[200] Lord Kilbrandon asserts, and defends, the distinctiveness of defrauding a public official most clearly in Withers v. DPP:[201]

> "Moreover, as regards the first count, I am not prepared to accept that 'officials of banks and building societies' are public officers within the meaning of Welham v. Director of Public Prosecutions [1961] AC 103. The fact that very many people have bank accounts and some deal with

---

[191] Scott v. MPC [1975] AC 819, 841 (Lord Diplock).

[192] Potter [1958] 2 All ER 51.

[193] Moses & Ansbro [1991] Crim LR 617.

[194] DPP v. Withers [1975] AC 842.

[195] Cf. Bassey (1931) 22 Cr App R 160, where an unqualified student acting alone, who attempted to gain admission to the Inner Temple by the use of forged references and degree certificates, was held to have defrauded the Benchers of that Inn.

[196] Wai Yu-tsang v. R [1992] 1 AC 269, 276; citing Lord Denning's judgment in Welham v. DPP [1961] AC 103, 133.

[197] This analysis would explain the rejection of Lord Diplock's separate categorisation in Scott v. DPP [1975] AC 819, 841 by the Privy Council in Wai Yu-tsang v. R [1992] 1 AC 269.

[198] Welham v. DPP [1961] AC 103, 124 (Lord Radford); cf. also Withers v. DPP [1975] AC 842, 873 (Lord Simon).

[199] Scott v. MPC [1975] AC 819, 841, per Lord Diplock: "(2) Where the intended victim of a 'conspiracy to defraud' is a private individual the purpose of the conspirators must be to cause the victim economic loss by depriving him of some property or right, corporeal or incorporeal, to which he is or would or might become entitled. The intended means by which the purpose is to be achieved must be dishonest. They need not involve fraudulent misrepresentation such as is needed to constitute the civil tort of deceit. Dishonesty of any kind is enough. (3) Where the intended victim of a 'conspiracy to defraud' is a person performing public duties as distinct from a private individual it is sufficient if the purpose is to cause him to act contrary to his public duty, and the intended means of achieving this purpose are dishonest. The purpose need not involve causing economic loss to anyone." Although Lord Diplock's categorisation was disapproved by the Privy Council in Wai Yu-tsang v. R [1992] 1 AC 269, 277, the disagreement was motivated by rejection of his Lordship's analysis of category (2), in particular of the requirement that actual loss be intended.

[200] Held to disclose no offence known to law in Withers v. DPP [1975] AC 842 (HL).

[201] [1975] AC 842, 877. Unfortunately, the decision was not considered by the Privy Council in Wai Yu-tsang v. R [1992] 1 AC 269.

building societies does not change the relationship between institution and customer from a private to a public one. It would be dangerous to use analogy for the purpose of extending a meaning of fraud which has already, for the purposes of the law of conspiracy, gone beyond its common content of prejudice to proprietary rights."

Quite so.

(c) Illegality of object?

As was pointed out earlier (§ 15.3), and unlike ordinary conspiracy,[202] the object of a conspiracy to defraud need not itself constitute an offence when done. This, perhaps, is an inevitable consequence of finding a conspiracy to defraud where V's interests are merely put at risk—in the absence of a crystallised loss or gain, the contemplated activities may well be insufficiently harmful to attract the wrath of criminalisation. Nonetheless, it is submitted that the scope of conspiracy to defraud should be confined to conspiracies at least to commit a legal wrong, and that conspiracy to commit a moral wrong, *simpliciter*, should not fall within the criminal law.[203]

(d) Impossibility

What happens where the means chosen by the conspirators fail to work, e.g. because the intended victims were already aware of the facts and could not be deceived? By contrast with the modern statutory offence of conspiracy, impossibility is a defence to conspiracies at common law[204] and therefore remains a defence to the charge of conspiracy to defraud. Thus, in general, no offence is committed when the conspiracy necessarily cannot achieve its objective because of legal or physical impossibility.[205] The defence of impossibility is discussed in more detail above, in § 9.4.

(iv) Mens rea

The mens rea of conspiracy to defraud is sometimes described as an "intent to defraud". In fact, the mens rea components are more specific than this:

(i)   dishonesty; and
(ii)   intention to carry out the agreement.

The first element, dishonesty, bears the same meaning as it does for theft.[206] Although, at one time, it was suggested that the meanings were different,[207] this possibility was expressly negated by the Court of Appeal in *Ghosh*.[208] *Ghosh* is now the leading case on dishonesty for both offences.

---

[202] See above, § 9.2(i).

[203] Cf. Williams, *CLGP* §§ 222, 226.

[204] *DPP* v. *Nock* [1978] AC 979.

[205] Cf. *Bennett* (1979) 68 Cr App R 168, distinguishing cases where the means employed were physically incapable of achieving the purpose from an agreement which might have worked, but which failed because of the behaviour of some person external to the agreement.

[206] See above, § 13.8.

[207] In that the test of dishonesty was subjective for conspiracy to defraud, but objective for theft: *McIvor* [1982] 1 All ER 491, 497; *Landy* [1981] 1 All ER 1172, 1181.

[208] [1982] QB 1053, 1059–61.

Secondly, there must be an intention on the part of the alleged conspirator to carry out her part of the agreement.[209] Thus there is no conspiracy by D if he appears to agree, but secretly intends to frustrate the execution of the plan;[210] nor if D has no intention of playing his allocated role.[211] As with all crimes where motive is not part of the mens rea, a benign motive or purpose will not of itself foreclose an agreement to defraud from constituting a conspiracy. It is sufficient that the agreement exists and that D intends to carry it out.[212]

It might be thought that conspiracy to defraud requires, perhaps in addition to the above two elements, a separate intent to defraud. Not so. Proof of an intention to carry out the agreement to defraud is, of itself, sufficient to establish an intent to defraud; thus, in the context of conspiracy, the requirement of an intent to defraud adds nothing to the two elements identified here. In particular, since fraud may be committed simply by placing another's rights or interests in jeopardy, an "intent to defraud" means simply a (dishonest) intention to act to the potential prejudice of another person's rights[213]—i.e. to carry out the agreement. This includes deliberately putting V's rights at risk, whether or not actual loss is intended. As the Court of Appeal stated in *Sinclair*:[214]

> "To cheat and defraud is to act with deliberate dishonesty to the prejudice of another person's proprietary right. In the context of this case the alleged conspiracy to cheat and defraud is an agreement by a director of a company and others dishonestly to take a risk with the assets of the company by using them in a manner which was known to be not in the best interests of the company and to be prejudicial to the minority shareholders."

Similarly, in *Allsop*, the Court of Appeal remarked:[215]

> "If the deceit which is employed imperils the economic interest of the person deceived, this is sufficient to constitute fraud even though in the event no actual loss is suffered and notwithstanding that the deceiver did not desire to bring about an actual loss. . . . Interests which are imperilled are less valuable in terms of money than those same interests when they are secure and protected. Where a person intends by deceit to induce a course of conduct in another which puts that other's economic interests in jeopardy he is guilty of fraud even though he does not intend or desire that actual loss should ultimately be suffered by that other in this context."

(v) Conspiracy to defraud, statutory fraud, and clarity of law

It is perfectly reasonable to take the view that conspiracy to defraud fails to meet the standards of clarity required for a system of criminal law fit for a liberal democracy. The offence has an enormous, non-particularised scope, with its crucial reliance on the notion of dishonesty. In the *Fourteenth Report* of the Joint Parliamentary Committee on Human

---

[209] Cf. *Gemmell* [1985] 2 NZLR 740; *O'Brien* [1955] 2 DLR 311.

[210] *Anderson* [1986] AC 27, 38ff.

[211] Cf. *Thomson* (1965) 50 Cr App R 1.

[212] *Wai Yu-tsang* [1992] 1 AC 269; *Hagan* [1985] Crim LR 598. See also the discussion of *Smith* [1960] 2 QB 423, above, § 5. However, as Smith notes in his commentary on *Hagan* [1985] Crim LR 598, 599, D's motive may sometimes raise issues relevant to the question of dishonesty; e.g., when D believes he has a claim of right.

[213] *Wai Yu-tsang* [1992] 1 AC 269, 276 (Lord Goff).

[214] [1968] 1 WLR 1246, 1250. See also *Olan, Hudsson & Hartnett* (1978) 41 CCC (2d) 145.

[215] (1976) 64 Cr App R 29, 31–2.

Rights, the compatibility of conspiracy to defraud with Article 7 of the ECHR was doubted,[216] because of its over-reliance on jury findings of dishonesty.[217] It was widely anticipated that the Fraud Act 2006 would abolish conspiracy to defraud but, as we have seen, it did not. Conspiracy to defraud will operate in tandem with statutory fraud. Surprisingly, perhaps, the view was taken in the *Fourteenth Report* that the Bill which in substance became the 2006 Act was compatible with Article 7. The offence of statutory fraud proposed in the Bill was taken to have a more substantial conduct element than conspiracy to defraud, making less objectionable the recourse to dishonesty.[218] But as we have seen in our discussion of fraud by false representation[219] and, particularly, fraud by abuse of position,[220] reliance on a judgment of dishonesty is pervasive. Recall too the hollowing-out of the actus reus in theft by the decisions in *Gomez*[221] and *Hinks*,[222] which considerably increases the role of dishonesty in that offence.[223] It was once said that you could communicate the substance of property offences and offences against the person with the precept, "be honest and refrain from violence."[224] Certainly the first part of that advice is the best that can be offered by way of advance guidance about the content of large parts of the modern law of fraud and theft.

---

[216] Art. 7, which proscribes retroactive criminal law, has been interpreted as requiring minimum standards of clarity for criminal offences: above, § 2.2.

[217] Session 2004–05, para. 2.12.

[218] *Ibid.*, para. 2.14.

[219] Above, § 15.2.

[220] Above, § 15.3.

[221] [1993] AC 442.

[222] [2001] AC 241.

[223] See above, § 13.6(ii)(a)–(c).

[224] Quoted by Glanville Williams, in the preface to his *Textbook of Criminal Law* (1st ed., 1978).

16

THE MORAL LIMITS OF CRIMINALISATION

Over the past few chapters we have investigated some of the better-known common law and statutory offences. There are, of course, many other offences, both minor and serious, known to the law. Beyond that, however, there are many forms of wrongdoing that are not offences at all—and rightly so. The criminal law is not a tool to be deployed wherever someone may do wrong. As a regulatory device, it is a bluntly coercive and morally loaded tool, something to be used sparingly and with care. This is the problem of *criminalisation*: although it may frequently be appropriate, indeed necessary, to have criminal prohibitions, we should always be careful of overextending the reach of the criminal law, and of infringing too far upon citizens' rights of free choice and individual liberty. We *should* use the criminal law to prohibit conduct—but we should not over-prohibit.

The question becomes, therefore, *when* should we extend the criminal law to regulate conduct? Suppose that a responsible legislature seeks to enact an appropriate, morally justifiable, range of criminal prohibitions. What criteria should it apply when deciding whether to proscribe something? The decision whether a particular action or state of affairs is sufficiently serious to warrant criminalisation always involves difficult judgements, and will be affected by the political values, state of development, and social structure of a society. There is no sphere of industrial, commercial, or administrative activity untouched by the criminal law. As criminal lawyers, however, we may still enquire whether conduct made criminal merits that designation.

A useful starting point is that there should be parsimony in criminalisation: offences "should be created only when absolutely necessary."[1] The criminal sanction is the most drastic of the State's standard tools for regulating the conduct of individuals. It represents the most severe infringement of a person's liberty, and, as such, should be available only where there is a clear social justification.

Broadly speaking, we can identify two types of criteria that must be met if the creation of an offence is to be morally legitimate. There must, first, be a prima facie *positive* case for State regulation, in that the activity at issue must be sufficiently serious to warrant intervention. In general, as we shall argue, this requires that the conduct leads to significant levels of harm or offence being suffered by others.

Secondly, certain *negative* constraints must also be met. In particular, it must be shown that the *criminal* law offers the best method of regulation, being preferable to alternative

---

[1] *Per* Lord Williams of Mostyn, HL Deb., vol. 602, col. WA 58; June 18, 1999.

methods of legal control that are available to the State; and the practicalities must be considered of drawing up an offence in terms that are effective, enforceable, and meet rule of law and other concerns. It may be, if these negative constraints cannot be met, that the State ought not to criminalise certain types of conduct notwithstanding that initially there is a positive case for doing so.

In this chapter, we will focus mainly on the competing *positive* grounds for state intervention: the main types of reasons why the state might validly choose to intervene and criminalise some action. Later, we will briefly discuss some of the constraints that might nonetheless make the criminal law an inappropriate response.

When is behaviour, prima facie, sufficiently serious to warrant criminalisation? This question is highly controversial, because it raises squarely the issue of the limits of the state's moral authority over individuals. Joel Feinberg's classic discussion of the problem identifies four possible grounds of justifiable intervention: harm to others, offence to others, immorality, and harm to self.[2] As we shall see, liberal philosophers (including Feinberg himself) tend to endorse only the first two of those grounds, rejecting the case for criminalising conduct on purely moralistic or paternalistic grounds. Below we offer a short introduction to these four grounds of state intervention.

§ 16.1 The Harm Principle

At the core of liberalism is the proposition that the State is justified in intervening to regulate conduct only when that conduct causes *harm to others*. Conduct that merely harms oneself, or which is thought to be immoral but otherwise harmless, is on this account ineligible for prohibition. Famously, the Harm Principle was first articulated by John Stuart Mill:[3]

> "The principle is, that the sole end for which mankind are warranted, individually or collectively, in interfering with the liberty of action of any of their number is self-protection. That the only purpose for which power can rightfully be exercised over any member of a civilised community against his will is to prevent harm to others. His own good, either physical or moral, is not a sufficient warrant."

Expressed in this way, the Harm Principle is a negative constraint: in the absence of harm, the State is not morally entitled to intervene. It does not follow that, conversely, the State *is* justified in intervening whenever D's conduct causes harm to others. That conclusion can only be reached after further factors are considered, such as those to be discussed below. Perhaps more importantly, Mill offers no definition of what counts as a *harm*; without which, the application of the Harm Principle is hopelessly indeterminate.

Liberal philosophers have built on Mill's analysis in an attempt to eradicate these problems. The most detailed exposition is now offered by Feinberg, who summarises the principle as follows:[4]

---

[2] *The Moral Limits of the Criminal Law* (1984–87): vol. 1, *Harm to Others* (1984); vol. 2, *Offense to Others* (1985); vol. 3, *Harm to Self* (1986); vol. 4, *Harmless Wrongdoing* (1988).
[3] *On Liberty* chap. 1, para. 9.
[4] *Harm to Others* (1984) 26.

"It is always a good reason in support of penal legislation that it would be effective in preventing (eliminating, reducing) harm to persons other than the actor (the one prohibited from acting) and there is no other means that is equally effective at no greater cost to other values."

Notice that this is formulated as a positive claim. On Feinberg's account, if creating a criminal offence would prevent harm to others, there is a positive reason in favour of criminalisation. This leaves it possible for Feinberg, and us, to accept the legitimacy of other, supplementary, grounds for criminalisation (such as offence) where the conduct is not harmful.

In principle, one might subscribe to Feinberg's version of the Harm Principle and at the same time consistently accept that the State is also justified in criminalising some conduct on the grounds that it is immoral. That would, however, be inconsistent with the principle espoused by Mill. Especially for liberals, part of the point of the Harm Principle is that it forces an enquiry into the consequences of conduct—does it hurt anyone? According to the Harm Principle, proponents of a particular criminal offence cannot simply allege that the relevant conduct is immoral. Rather, they must identify precisely what are the particular effects of that conduct:[5] the distinct way in which it damages the lives of other persons. That claim can then be subjected to public debate. Empirical evidence of a link to the alleged harm can be demanded and scrutinised.

Consider, for example, the decision by the House of Lords in *Brown*[6] that, in the context of sadomasochistic sexual activity, it is an offence to inflict actual bodily harm on another person notwithstanding that the "victim" consents. One justification offered for this act of judicial criminalisation was that the legalisation of such activities might encourage the seduction and "corruption of young men".[7] But would it? It is a cheap claim to make when no supporting evidence is offered. Given the presumption against criminalisation, the onus is on its proponents to bring clear evidence that creating a new offence *will* prevent harm from occurring.

In the following paragraphs we consider aspects of the Harm Principle in more detail.

(i) What counts as a harm?

A harm, on Feinberg's account, is a "thwarting, setting back, or defeating of an interest."[8] When we are harmed, one or more of our interests is left in a worse state than it was beforehand. In turn, a person's *interests* comprise the things that make his life go well;[9] thus we are harmed when our lives are changed for the worse. Harm involves the impairment of

---

[5] Packer, *The Limits of the Criminal Sanction* (1968) 262.
[6] [1994] 1 AC 212. See also §§ 21.1(iv).
[7] [1994] 1 AC 212, 246 (Lord Jauncey).
[8] *Harm to Others* (1984) 33.
[9] In Feinberg's account, "One's interests . . . consist of all those things in which one has a stake. . . . These interests, or perhaps more accurately, the things these interests are *in*, are distinguishable components of a person's well-being: he flourishes or languishes as they flourish or languish. What promotes them is to his advantage or *in his interest*; what thwarts them is to his detriment or *against his interest*" (*Harm to Others* (1984) 34). See, too, his "Harm to Others: a Rejoinder" (1986) *Criminal Justice Ethics* 16, 26, where Feinberg recapitulates: "I argued that to harm a person was to set back his interest and violate his right. To have an interest, in turn, is to have a stake in some outcome, just as if one had 'invested' some of one's own good in it, thus assuming the risk of personal harm or setback."

a person's opportunities to engage in worthwhile activities and relationships, and to pursue valuable, self-chosen, goals. In this sense, harm is prospective rather than backward-looking: it involves a diminution of one's opportunities to enjoy or pursue a good life.

Characteristically, harm is brought about though the impairment of V's personal or proprietary resources. However, as Feinberg observes, what makes such impairment harmful is not the impairment *per se* but its implication for V's well-being:[10]

> "A broken arm is an impaired arm, one which has (temporarily) lost its capacity to serve a person's needs effectively, and in virtue of that impairment, its possessor's welfare interest is harmed."

Similarly, in the context of property crimes, one can say that "any harm to a person by denying him the use or the value of his property is a harm to him precisely because it diminishes his opportunities."[11]

Clearly, people have interests in their property and in their personal integrity. But we also have other interests that are capable of being harmed. Hyman Gross suggests that, before it can be said that a person has an interest in something, the thing must "be of sufficient value to [the person] that the assertion of a claim by or on behalf of [that person] based on the loss or significant impairment of X is not unreasonable."[12] He offers a four-part categorisation of the types of cases where one's interests are harmed: (i) "violations of interest in retaining or maintaining what one is entitled to have" (e.g. theft); (ii) "offences to sensibility" (e.g. obscenity); (iii) "impairment of collective welfare" (e.g. counterfeiting, which undermines the economy); and (iv) "violations of governmental interests" (e.g. contempt of court).[13]

We consider offences to sensibility in § 16.2 below, under the rubric of the Offence Principle. But categories (iii) and (iv) show that we can be harmed without directly being the victim; and, indeed, when there is no victim at all. Hence, on occasion, it may be appropriate to enact "victimless" crimes. Tax evasion is rightly a crime notwithstanding that there is no particular victim who is deprived of assets directly. Perhaps it is not the same sort of wrong as is theft. But if T illegitimately reduces his tax burden, T effectively takes from, and wrongs, his fellow taxpayers. The money must come from somewhere: if not from T, then from others. The obligation to pay tax is a collective duty, one that each person owes to his fellow citizens and not merely to the State.

Similarly, attacks on the integrity of the currency (e.g. counterfeiting) or on the operation of the judicial systems (e.g. contempt of court) matter because they undermine State-implemented regimes that exist for the benefit of us all. State intervention is warranted because the community as a whole would also suffer harm were these general

---

[10] *Harm to Others* (1984) 53. Cf. Kleinig's claim that, in the case of a temporary hurt or an abduction that has no lasting effects upon its victim, there may be interference with a welfare interest but no harm: Kleinig, "Crime and the Concept of Harm" (1978) 15 *Am Phil Q* 27, 32; Feinberg, *Harm to Others* (1984) 52–3.

[11] Raz, "Autonomy, Toleration, and the Harm Principle" in Gavison (ed.), *Issues in Contemporary Legal Philosophy* (1987) 313, 327. Cf. Perry, "Corrective v. Distributive Justice" in Horder (ed.), *Oxford Essays in Jurisprudence* (4th series, 2000) 237, 256: "The main reason that personal injury constitutes harm is that it interferes with personal autonomy. It interferes, that is to say, with the set of opportunities and options from which one is able to choose what to do in one's life."

[12] *A Theory of Criminal Justice* (1979) 116.

[13] *Ibid.*, 119–21.

regimes to be undermined. Undermining the currency, for instance, would lead to losses of value stored as currency and tend to destabilise the systems that co-ordinate a nation's economic activity;[14] which, in turn, would deprive people of many opportunities for personal and social advancement. Minimising or preventing that sort of indirect, prospective harm to our interests is rightly the business of the State.

(ii) Seriousness

Indeed, once the nature of the harm is identified, we can see why some apparently victimless crimes, such as counterfeiting, are regarded as very serious indeed. This is one of the payoffs of the Harm Principle: in forcing us to consider more precisely why we are concerned about the activity that is to be criminalised, it gives us tools with which to rank the seriousness of offences and thus decide what level of punishment, if any, is appropriate.

Von Hirsch and Jareborg have developed this point in the context of victim-oriented crimes.[15] In their seminal paper, the authors identify four generic interests that we all have directly: (i) physical integrity (health, safety, avoidance of physical pain); (ii) material support and amenity (nutrition, shelter, basic amenities); (iii) freedom from humiliation or degrading treatment; and (iv) privacy and autonomy. The justification of any existing or prospective crime can then be assessed in two steps, as follows.

First, one should identify which category of interest the crime is designed to protect. Secondly, it is necessary to assess the degree to which standard instances of that crime will adversely affect the living standard—the opportunities for V to live a good life—of a typical victim. Von Hirsch and Jareborg divide the severity of these effects into four bands: (a) subsistence (simple survival with only basic human functions); (b) minimal well-being (maintaining minimal levels of comfort and dignity); (c) adequate well-being (maintaining adequate levels of comfort and dignity); and (d) significant enhancement (above-adequate quality of life).

On this approach, we can see that homicide attacks physical integrity in such a way as to undermine even subsistence; it is, thus, more serious than a typical robbery and much more serious than petty theft or a minor assault. On the other hand, road traffic regulations become extremely important, since they too are concerned with saving lives and thus protect our fundamental interests. It may be that, because less culpable, dangerous driving should be punished less severely than murder. But, like murder, the existence of an offence of dangerous driving is justified within the Harm Principle by the desirability of saving lives.

(iii) Harms as wrongs

In Feinberg's words,[16]

> "One person wrongs another when his indefensible (unjustifiable and inexcusable) conduct violates the other's right, and in all but certain very special cases such conduct will also invade the other's interest and thus be harmful in the sense [of a setback to interests]."

---

[14] Cf. *St Margaret's Trust Ltd* [1958] All ER 289, 293.
[15] "Gauging Criminal Harm: A Living-Standard Analysis" (1991) 11 *OJLS* 1.
[16] *Harm to Others* (1984) 34.

In order to fall within the scope of the Harm Principle and be a prima facie candidate for criminalisation, the harm must also be a wrong.[17] Suppose, for example, that a judge sentences P to imprisonment for life following P's conviction of murder. One may expect that P's interests will be set back by such a sentence. He will lose his freedom and, no doubt, many opportunities to advance his life and prospects. Nonetheless, the judge does no wrong in depriving P of his freedom in this way. Her act of sentencing falls outside the Harm Principle because, although P's situation is worsened when he is deprived of his liberty, P has lost nothing to which he had a right.

The example illustrates that our interests can be set back without our being wronged. Indeed, this is something that often occurs in economic transactions. In a broadly free market, individuals are entitled to pursue their own interests. In so doing, they wrong no-one even if their self-advancing conduct has deleterious side-effects for others. Side-effects are a natural feature of competitive interaction: if D tenders successfully for a contract, D may know that in so doing she will deprive others of that contract and, in turn, weaken their commercial viability, cause employees to be laid off, and so forth. Yet D does no wrong and the case falls outside the scope of the Harm Principle.

(iv) Balancing requirements.

Even if the harm *is* wrongful, it should not necessarily be criminalised. The Harm Principle provides for a balancing of interests, one that considers the extent and likelihood of the harm involved and weighs that against the implications of criminalisation. Feinberg's account presents a number of factors to be taken into account at this stage:[18]

> "(a) the greater the gravity of a possible harm, the less probable its occurrence need be to justify prohibition of the conduct that threatens to produce it;
> (b) the greater the probability of harm, the less grave the harm need be to justify coercion;
> (c) the greater the magnitude of the risk of harm, itself compounded out of gravity and probability, the less reasonable it is to accept the risk;
> (d) the more valuable (useful) the dangerous conduct, both to the actor and to others, the more reasonable it is to take the risk of harmful consequences, and for extremely valuable conduct it is reasonable run risks up to the point of clear and present danger;
> (e) the more reasonable a risk of harm (the danger), the weaker is the case for prohibiting the conduct that creates it."

A responsible legislator should, therefore, consider the gravity and likelihood of the wrongful harm and weigh that against the social value of the conduct to be prohibited and the degree of intrusion upon citizens' lives that criminalisation would involve. The greater the gravity and likelihood of the harm, the stronger the case for criminalisation; conversely, the more valuable the conduct is, or the more the prohibition would limit liberty, the stronger the case against criminalisation. In addition, other rights that a citizen may have,

---

[17] Cf. Raz, "Autonomy, Toleration, and the Harm Principle" in Gavison (ed.), *Issues in Contemporary Legal Philosophy* (1987) 313, 328: "Since 'causing harm' by its very meaning demands that the action is prima facie wrong it is a normative concept acquiring its specific meaning from the moral theory within which it is embedded."
[18] *Harm to Others* (1984) 216.

for example to free speech or privacy, should be respected.[19] These rights may militate against creating certain types of crimes, especially (as we shall see below) in the context of offensive behaviour.

It is a calculation of this sort that justifies the setting of speed limits. In the United Kingdom, for example, it is prohibited to drive on the highway at speeds in excess of 70 miles per hour. Is this a legitimate criminal law? The answer is, yes. Driving at 75 miles per hour may not be inherently immoral or wrong. But the faster one drives, the higher the probability that if something goes wrong, serious injury and property damage will result. Hence the case falls within the scope of the Harm Principle, and is amenable to criminal regulation. On the other hand, even though setting the speed limit at (say) 20 miles per hour would save more lives, the social costs, in terms of inefficient transportation systems, would be too great. Decisions of this sort require a balancing of factors, such as the effect on public mobility of setting the limit too low, against the costs, in terms of scale and likelihood of injuries, of setting the limit too high.

Resolution of that balancing process will depend on reference to standard cases. The Harm Principle is in play here because speeding *standardly* causes or creates a risk of harm, even if not in every instance. Inevitably, the criminal law is a blunt instrument, regulating in terms of average cases and incapable of reflecting the myriad variations upon those cases that real life delivers.

To a large extent, this constraint is a matter of resources, and of their efficient use—it is simply uneconomic to frame and administer laws that take into account the particularities of every person's situation. Hence, criminal law tends to prohibit actions on the basis of their typical risks and consequences, leaving further refinement, if any, to the realm of exceptions. It is an offence, we have said, to drive faster than 70 miles per hour. This is so notwithstanding that there is no intrinsic significance to that speed. Depending on the circumstances (perhaps the road is empty) and on the particular driver (perhaps he is Lewis Hamilton), there may on occasion be no significant risk when a driver travels at a faster clip than 70. Nonetheless, specifying a precise limit is a convenient and enforceable means by which to regulate dangerous driving; and the limit itself is determined by reference to risks in standard cases.

(v) Remote harms

Andrew von Hirsch has observed that many actions are not immediately harmful but may lead to harm *remotely*.[20] My selling you a handgun, for example, does not in itself harm you but rather puts you in a position where subsequently you may harm another person. This possibility is an implicit feature of inchoate offences, such as incitement to murder; and of what are sometimes called "substantive inchoate" offences, such as the offence of "going equipped". It is a crime to be on the street at night when in possession of an article, such as a jemmy (or "crowbar"), for use in connection with a burglary.[21] The justification for this offence is not that I have the jemmy, but rather that I may use it.

---

[19] Von Hirsch characterises this as the "standard harms analysis": "Extending the Harm Principle: 'Remote' Harms and Fair Imputation" in Simester and Smith (eds.), *Harm and Culpability* (1996) 259, 261.

[20] *Ibid.*

[21] Theft Act 1968, s. 25.

Remote harms present a particular challenge for the Harm Principle. While it may sometimes be appropriate, very often there are difficulties about basing criminalisation on remote harms, especially those predicated on the eventual criminal choices of third persons. Consider the following hypothetical situation. Suppose that, as Murray has argued, there is evidence that unregulated premarital sex yields higher rates of illegitimate births, leading to more children growing up in impoverished households with weakened parental control; and that, in turn, this generates higher crime rates by these offspring.[22] If we concede the empirical links, we can conclude that unregulated premarital sex leads to harm. But, as von Hirsch argues, it does not follow that there is even a prima facie case for criminalising premarital sex. The harm is produced not by D's own conduct but by the subsequent choices of third parties (in this case, offspring) whom D does not control. That being so, it is not clear why the harm should be D's lookout: why should D be accountable, through the criminal law, for the freely chosen subsequent actions of others?[23]

> "[T]o hold him liable merely because another person chooses to follow his example, or otherwise permits herself to be influenced, infringes basic notions of the separateness of persons as choosing agents. It is that other person who has made the culpable choice of doing harm, not the original actor."

Why, in other words, should D lose an otherwise harmless option just because of the subsequent independent choices that others may make?

On occasion it is apt to prohibit an activity because of a remote harm. This may occur where D's act in some way underwrites or facilitates the later wrongdoing by others. For example, it may be appropriate to prohibit D from publishing a book detailing various ways of killing one's enemies, because the link between D's activity and murders by others influenced or helped by D's book is sufficiently close that the remote harm can fairly be imputed back to D. But in the absence of special reasons for imputing remote harms to D, the mere existence of such harms supplies no reason for criminalising D's otherwise innocent conduct.

To invoke the Harm Principle, we have noted, an action must not only be conducive to harm; it must also be a wrong. This constraint is particularly apposite to remote harm. The criminal law embodies, by its nature, an element of blame or censure. But in remote harm cases, it still needs to be shown why D should be condemned for her non-harmful action, just because that action happens to be linked, through chains of complex social interaction, to the subsequent injurious behaviour of some separate and autonomous person, E. Prima facie, it seems unjust to impose penal censure on D, at least where D has no power to control the harmful choices of E, and where D has not sought to assist or encourage those choices.

---

[22] See Murray, *The Emerging British Underclass* (London 1990); also Murray, *Underclass: The Crisis Deepens* (London 1994). Cf. von Hirsch, "Extending the Harm Principle: 'Remote' Harms and Fair Imputation" in Simester and Smith (eds.), *Harm and Culpability* (1996) 259, 266.

[23] *Ibid.*, 267.

§ 16.2 The Offence Principle

Suppose that, one day, D and E catch a bus into town. While riding on the bus, they decide to have sexual intercourse, notwithstanding the presence of the other passengers. Their conduct may not harm anyone else, and seems to fall outside the scope of the Harm Principle. Yet it will cause great offence, no doubt, to many others on the bus who are forced to witness their activity. Should conduct of that sort be criminalised?

Feinberg certainly thinks so:[24]

> "It is always a good reason in support of a proposed criminal prohibition that it would probably be an effective way of preventing serious offense (as opposed to injury or harm) to persons other than the actor, and that it is probably a necessary means to that end."

Many, probably most, liberals agree that actions may sometimes be prohibited on the grounds of their offensiveness, and there is widespread acceptance of the Offence Principle as a secondary principle of criminalisation, one that supplements the Harm Principle.

When is the Offence Principle in play? Merely showing that D's conduct is evil or unpleasant will not invoke the Offence Principle. For Feinberg, conduct is offensive when it affronts other people's sensibilities, i.e. when it causes them to undergo an unpleasant and disliked psychological experience, by way of reaction to the conduct. Causing any such affront, in his view, constitutes prima facie grounds for invoking the criminal law, provided that enough people are sufficiently affronted.

There must, however, be *serious* offence to others. Moreover, on Feinberg's account, the case for criminalisation must satisfy a sophisticated balancing test that is designed to criminalise offence more sparingly. First, a responsible legislator should consider the impact of the conduct on its audience, by examining the magnitude of the affront to see how pervasively and intensely it is felt. As part of that examination, a standard of "reasonable avoidability" is imposed: the easier it is for members of the public to avoid settings where the conduct occurs, the less serious the offence is. Pornography may cause affront to many when viewed involuntarily or unexpectedly, but V cannot reasonably complain if he has specifically visited an adult cinema to see it.

Secondly, the importance of the offending conduct should be examined from the actor's perspective. The more central the conduct is to an actor's way of life, the greater is the claim not to have the conduct prohibited. As part of this examination, a standard of "alternative opportunities" is applied: restrictions on the conduct become more acceptable if there are satisfactory alternative times and places at which the actor could perform the conduct with less offence (say by showing pornography only at home or in adult cinemas and not more generally).

The broader social impact of the conduct needs also to be considered. The more independent general usefulness the supposedly offending conduct has, the less the claim to prohibition. For this purpose, free expression of opinion is, following Mill, deemed to have its own social value, "in virtue of the great social utility of free expression and discussion generally, as well as the vital personal interest most people have in being able to speak their

---

[24] *Offense to Others* (1985) 1. See also the collection of essays in von Hirsch and Simester (eds.), *Incivilities: Regulating Offensive Behaviour* (2006).

minds fearlessly."[25] I may cause considerable and widespread offence when I advocate the legalization of, say, necrophilia; but the importance of preserving free political debate is such as to outweigh any case for criminalisation that the offence may generate.

(i) Offensive conduct as a wrong

The application of these considerations means that, on Feinberg's account, some conduct that widely offends should still be legally permissible, e.g. when committed in settings readily avoidable by others. Thus, although acts of indecent exposure may legitimately be criminalised when done on city streets, similar conduct might nonetheless be permitted at designated beaches, at which those not so inclined need not bathe.

Even so, however, Feinberg underplays a further consideration: the need for the affront to be wrongful. It is not affront *per se* to the sensibilities of others—even widespread affront—that should justify possible state intervention, but affront *plus* valid reasons for objecting to the conduct.[26] Suppose, for example, that the sight of an interracial couple holding hands causes enormous affront in a particular community. It seems to us that, regardless of the scale of the reaction, there is no case for invoking the Offence Principle here, because there is nothing wrong with that couple's behaviour.

This point is particularly important in the criminal law, which *punishes*, and censures, the offender for having done wrong. That being the case, the criminalisation of conduct should require a plausible claim of wrongdoing. With conduct that supposedly is offensive, one must therefore ask: why does the actor deserve censure? If the essence of offence is merely that the conduct displeases many people, then it is not clear that wrongdoing has occurred at all. "I don't like it" should never suffice as a basis for criminalisation, regardless of the numbers who say it. Better reasons need to be provided why there is something reprehensible about the behaviour that deserves a censuring response.

What makes offensive conduct wrong, generally speaking, is the manner in which it treats other persons. Racial insults are a paradigm of this class of case: they tend both to cause affront in the audience and to do so by communicating contempt for that audience. Another variety of offence is exhibitionism. Suppose that D is sitting peaceably in the park, but cannot concentrate on his newspaper because E and F are copulating noisily on the grass nearby. D may rightly complain. He has a legitimate claim not to have the intimate facts of E and F's relationship forced upon him. This may be singularly in point in locations like parks, which we value, *inter alia*, as places to interact with other persons who are not intimates, and where, consequently, such offensive activities are likely to cause much greater discomfort than they would in more private contexts.

(ii) A communicative and conventional wrong

In so far as offensive conduct is something that communicates to V, the person experiencing the conduct, a lack of respect and consideration, it is characteristically a form of expressive action. As such, even if one accepts the Offence Principle as a legitimate ground of

---

[25] Feinberg, *Offense to Others* (1985) 44.
[26] Simester and von Hirsch, "Rethinking the Offense Principle" (2002) 8 *Legal Theory* 269.

criminalisation, such cases should be criminalised sparingly because of the importance of allowing free expression in a society. The need to accommodate diverse and sometimes inconsistent styles of life, which may depend for their success on being publicly manifested, militates in favour of a "thick skin" approach to the regulation of expressive acts, even when those acts are offensive to others. Friction is a characteristic of social interaction, at least in a pluralistic society. Such societies require of their members a certain robustness of sensibility, so that incivility may be tolerated for the sake of personal and cultural diversity.

A second reason for caution with the Offence Principle is how close its application can resemble that of the next principle we shall discuss, Legal Moralism. Some of the most un-controversial examples of offence involve sexual activity in public places. The examples are uncontroversial because there remains a strong moral consensus disapproving of such conduct, a consensus which underpins the convention that it should not be done. What counts for the Offence Principle may be the convention, but what generates the convention is the widespread moral view.

At the same time, the convention is not *merely* the articulation of a moral view. Legal Moralism is concerned with regulating actions that are morally wrong: the Offence Principle, by contrast, is concerned with how we treat each other. Conventions such as those governing acceptable conduct in public places thus serve an important instrumental purpose, by helping to delineate the boundaries between personal and public, and setting the terms of our interaction with strangers. D's respect for V implies respect for the terms under which they (usually, by convention) interact. This holds independently of the particular terms of the convention. When D exposes himself, uninvited, to V, he both violates the applicable social convention and, further, wrongs V by failing to respect the socially agreed terms under which she interacts with others.

§ 16.3 Legal Moralism

According to the legal moralist, it is legitimate to use the criminal law to prohibit immorality *per se*. As Feinberg explains, the legal moralist holds that it "can be morally legitimate to prohibit conduct on the ground that it is inherently immoral, even though it causes neither harm nor offense to the actor or to others."[27] Legal moralism finds it justifiable to crim-inalise acts that may be termed free-floating evils, in that they neither infringe the rights of, nor harm, any other person.

Most obviously, such acts might include private immorality and the violation of religious norms.[28] A good example is *Brown*, mentioned earlier,[29] where the House of Lords held that, in the context of sadomasochistic sexual activity, the infliction of actual bodily harm upon a consenting adult "victim" was an offence. From the perspective of the Harm Principle, there is no wrong to V since the activity occurs with V's consent. But from the perspective of legal moralism, D's conduct may be regarded as inherently wrong—and therefore legitimately proscribed. (Indeed, V's consent simply makes V, too, a participant in

---

[27] *Harm to Others* (1984) 27.
[28] See, e.g., Feinberg, *Harmless Wrongdoing* (1988) 20–25.
[29] [1994] 1 AC 212; above, § 16.1; also §§ 21.1, 21.1(*v*).

the offence.) Another illustration is *Shaw* v. *DPP*,[30] in which the defendant was charged with an offence of conspiring to corrupt public morals.[31] On appeal, the count in the indictment charging this offence was upheld by the House of Lords. According to Lord Simonds, "there remains in the courts of law a residual power to enforce the supreme and fundamental purpose of the law, to conserve not only the safety and order but also the moral welfare of the state."[32]

Lord Devlin controversially argued for legal moralism on the ground that a society's moral values are an indispensable part of its structural framework.[33] In turn, if harmless immoralities were permitted, this would tend to undermine the social fabric, dissolving the moral consensus underpinning society and leading, ultimately, to social disintegration and anarchy. Strictly speaking, Devlin's argument is not an argument in favour of pure legal moralism. Rather, it rests implicitly on the Harm Principle. Social disintegration, if it occurred, would certainly be a bad thing for the lives and interests of citizens. Further, if permitting some immoral act would lead to social disintegration then, subject to the problem of remote harms noted in § 16.1(i)(e), the state has prima facie reason to criminalise the act. To do so would not violate the liberal precepts of the Harm Principle.

The main problem with Devlin's social-harm argument is the need to establish an empirical link between mere immorality and social disintegration. Adultery happens frequently and legally, but there is no sign of a causal link from it to chaos. It may be that certain, specific, immoral acts will tend to threaten the continuance of the social structure, but that possibility needs to be investigated for *each* specific act, and cannot simply be asserted as a general truth for *all* immoral acts, however minor.

More generally, pure legal moralism shares with Lord Devlin's version the characteristic of entrenching the *status quo ante*. By its nature, legal moralism is conservative, in that immorality is measured against the prevailing social mores of the time: difference in moral value is, by that standard, immoral and may therefore be suppressed. One objection to this approach, therefore, is that not all change is bad. The abolition of slavery was a good thing; so, too, it is desirable that mixed-race couples may now publicise their association, even in communities where segregation formerly was enforced. Especially in a heterogeneous society containing a wide variety of subcultures, moral stagnation enforced by the criminal law seems unattractive. Difference, even conflict, between the lives and values of citizens can be a dynamic force for the evolution of a vigorous, thriving, and valuable culture.

A related difficulty with legal moralism is the problem of identifying a stable classification of immoral acts. Is homosexuality immoral (wherefore it may be prohibited)? It depends who, when, and where one asks. Criminalisation merely on the basis of immorality leaves a great deal to the whims and fashions of the times (and, indeed, of the prevailing location or culture: adultery, not proscribed at all in many countries, is a capital offence in others). As Alldridge has pointed out, some activities that once were regarded as *malum in se* are now entirely permissible, whereas some commercial activities that formerly were permitted are now regarded as very serious wrongs.[34] Thus a private, consenting homosexual

---

[30] [1962] AC 220.

[31] Until then unknown: see above, §§ 2.2–3.

[32] [1962] AC 220, 267.

[33] Devlin, *The Enforcement of Morals* (1965) 8–14.

[34] Alldridge, "Making Criminal Law Known" in Shute and Simester (eds.), *Criminal Law Theory: Essays on the General Part* (2002) 103, 107ff.

act used to be a serious crime and now is none whatsoever[35]—yet the essential nature of the conduct has not changed in the interim. Perhaps surprisingly, this *ad hoc* view of morality is celebrated as a virtue by Lord Devlin: "*Shaw's* case settles for the purpose of the law that morality in England means what twelve men and women think it means—in other words it is to be ascertained as a question of fact."[36] Yet many areas of morality are open to honest and reasoned disagreement. Abortion and obscenity, for example, present situations where different juries may reach opposite conclusions over what is moral and what is immoral. And criminal lawyers know all too well the difficulty of applying a homogeneous standard of "dishonesty" in theft.[37] This suggests that it will not do to criminalise conduct merely on the assumption that there is for each moral dispute an "objective" resolution.[38]

Were England and Wales a uniform society comprised of citizens with identical values, Lord Devlin's approach might present few problems. But that is not the case. Ours is a multicultural environment, incorporating diverse ethnic, religious, moral and philosophical perspectives. The law regulates in order to assist in the smooth functioning of our society, yet a multicultural society also needs tolerance. The guidance provided by the Harm and Offence Principles are important aids in ensuring that tolerance, by ruling out criminal censure for mere immorality.[39] Prohibition on grounds of immorality exposes even legislators to the charge that, in truth, they are simply imposing their own moral values upon the nation.

But perhaps the most important criticism of legal moralism concerns its clash with the liberal ideal of autonomy. Criminalisation takes options away from people. It is an intrusive and condemnatory form of coercion. Accepting the general case for criminalising mere immorality will, inevitably, lead to restrictions of autonomy, especially because the criminal law is very coarse-grained, so that its prohibitions are typically framed in broad rather than narrow terms. Given the diversity of human needs and preferences, criminal prohibitions will inevitably deprive some individuals of freedoms that are valuable to them: such persons will, in effect, be harmed by the prohibitions.

The strongest cases for depriving people of opportunities in this way arise where D's activity is likely to diminish the opportunities for others to live good lives. In these cases, a condition of D's well-being (her autonomy) is weighed against a condition of V's well-being: like is compared with like. But in these very cases, D's conduct is by definition harmful. Where, by contrast, the conduct is merely immoral, the interests of persons (such as D) are being weighed only against abstract judgements of morality. There is no well-being or autonomy-based reason *for* criminalisation, only against: like is not being compared with like. In a liberal society, the interests of persons should take priority at this point. Thus it is arguable that mere immorality is, by itself, insufficient for criminalisation.

---

[35] Cf. amendment of s. 12 of the Sexual Offences Act 1956 by s. 1 of the Sexual Offences Act 1967.

[36] "Law, Democracy and Morality" (1962) 110 Pa L Rev 635, 648.

[37] Above, § 13.8(iv)(a).

[38] For this reason, it is to be welcomed that acting *contra bonos mores* has been ruled too vague to count as criminal: *Hashman and Harrup* v. *United Kingdom* (1999) 30 EHRR 241.

[39] See generally Feinberg, *Harmless Wrongdoing* (1988).

§ 16.4 Paternalism

Feinberg summarises the Paternalistic justification of criminalisation as follows:[40]

> "It is always a good reason in support of a prohibition that it is probably necessary to prevent harm (physical, psychological, or economic) to the actor himself and there is probably no other means that is equally effective at no greater cost to other values."

Like the Harm Principle, paternalism demands harm. But it goes beyond the Harm Principle in that it warrants the criminalisation of self-harm: D may be prohibited, *for her own sake*, from performing certain acts. A standard legal example of such prohibitions is the criminal law duty to wear seat belts when driving a car.[41] The duty is imposed for D's own benefit, on the grounds that persons who fail to wear a seat belt are likely to suffer much more severe injuries in an accident than are those who wear one.[42]

Prima facie, there seems little that is objectionable about a law requiring persons to wear seat belts when in a car. But this is one of the strongest cases for paternalistic intervention. The obligation is a minor one, which does not hinder the activity of driving. It is a burden easily discharged, while the harm at risk and the costs of treatment are substantial. The state's insistence that D wear a seat belt is not destructive of her style of life. Thus the case is one where the disvalue attached to the infringement of D's autonomy is minor, and arguably outweighed by the interest in D's welfare that is advanced.

Paternalistic intervention may be appropriate more generally in cases where D's choice to harm herself cannot be said to be considered or responsible. Children and the mentally defective have extensive restrictions imposed upon their ability to engage in sexual intercourse, on the grounds that their choice to do so may not be fully understood.

But even if this argument be accepted in respect of seat belts and irresponsible actors, it cannot be generalised very far. In *Harm to Self*, Feinberg considers the theory of a broadly based paternalism in detail—and rejects it:[43]

> "The cases for and against legal paternalism then can be summed up as follows. In favor of the principle is the fact that there are many laws now on the books that *seem* to have had paternalism as an essential part of their implicit rationales, and that some of these at least, seem to most of us to be sensible and legitimate restrictions. It is also a consideration in favor of paternalism that preventable personal harm (set-back interest) is universally thought to be a great evil, and that such harm is no less harmful when self-caused than when caused by others. If society can substantially diminish the net amount of harm to interests caused from *all* sources, that would be a great social gain. If that prospect provides the moral basis underlying the harm to others principle, why should it not have application as well to self-caused harm and thus support equally the principle of legal paternalism?
>
> On the other side, it is argued that a consistent application of legal paternalism would lead

---

[40] *Harm to Others* (1984) 26–7.

[41] We concentrate here on the driver on the ground that back-seat passengers who fail to wear seat belts may harm not only themselves but also those seated in front of them.

[42] It is sometimes argued that there is harm to others in such cases, since the State is likely to incur greater costs in providing healthcare to drivers who are more seriously injured after failing to wear a seat belt. This argument is not straightforward, however, since the State's intervention is voluntary; it is open to the State to refuse to treat such persons, or to require them to take out private insurance.

[43] *Harm to Self* (1986) 25.

to the creation of new crimes that would be odious and offensive to common sense, leading to the general punishment of risk-takers, the enforcement of prudence, and the interference with saints and heroes. Moreover, hard paternalistic justification of any restriction of personal liberty is especially offensive morally, because it invades the realm of personal autonomy where each competent, responsible, adult human being should reign supreme."

The obligation is on the legal paternalist to show why it is justified to coerce D and promote her welfare at the expense of her autonomy.

One way of approaching that challenge is by arguing that autonomy is only of instrumental value: having options is valuable, that is to say, only in so far as the options themselves are valuable. On this view, there is no value in permitting self-maiming, say by cutting one's arm off, because there is no value in the activity that is being permitted. However, this argument establishes only that there is no obligation on the State positively to foster or support such activities. It does not follow that the State has the right to *prohibit* valueless activities. Justified proscription through the criminal law requires something stronger: positive reasons why we should coerce, threaten, and impose sanctions upon a wrongdoer. The paternalistic legislative assertion, "We are sending you to jail for your own good," makes very little sense when addressed to responsible, autonomous, citizens in a mature liberal democracy. It amounts to saying, "we shall harm you lest you harm yourself." And punishing the choices of one autonomous agent as a deterrent to others is equally objectionable.

A moment's reflection, moreover, reveals that the potential for invasive paternalism is enormous. So many features of modern life are not especially good for us—getting drunk, playing dangerous sports, smoking, eating fatty foods, failing to take regular exercise. A consistent paternalist should seek to eliminate them all. But freedom includes the freedom to go wrong. Respect for persons as autonomous agents involves respect for individuals as deliberating agents who have the capacity independently to pursue goals and values which they have themselves adopted. If we are not allowed to choose badly then, in effect, our choices are no longer determined by our own goals and values. A paternalistic legal system which made people's choices for them may well end up alienating people from their own conduct:[44]

> "Why not interfere with someone else's shaping of his own life? . . . I conjecture that the answer is connected with that elusive and difficult notion: the meaning of life. A person's shaping his life in accordance with some overall plan is his way of giving meaning to his life; only a being with the capacity to so shape his life can have or strive for a meaningful life."

Our well-being does not just require the successful pursuit of valuable goals; it requires also that we identify and engage with those goals—that they be *our* goals. Paternalism, by contrast, imposes the state's goals and values upon us. In the criminal law, moreover, it does so coercively. When a person's choices are pre-empted by the law, she does not shape her own life.[45] And to live a meaningful life, one must shape it oneself.

---

[44] Nozick, *Anarchy, State and Utopia* (1974) 50.
[45] Raz, *The Morality of Freedom* (1986) 382.

§ 16.5 Negative grounds for intervention: regulatory alternatives

Perhaps we can establish a positive case for regulating some candidate activity through the criminal law. But we need also to consider whether, nonetheless, there are reasons *not* to criminalise. The next stage of the enquiry involves considering whether the criminal law is the most appropriate tool for regulating the activity. In particular, the advantages and disadvantages of using the criminal law should be measured against those accruing to alternative regulatory mechanisms. As a general rule, if some other form of State intervention falling short of criminalisation would be effective to regulate the conduct at issue, that alternative should be preferred. The criminal prohibition should be deployed only as a last resort.

(i) Tax

On occasions in the past, Western governments have attempted to regulate alcohol by criminal prohibition. The results were disastrous; sales and consumption simply went underground, creating a black market ripe for extortion and racketeering. Nowadays, control is exercised via licensing arrangements and tax. One of the standard modern functions of the tax system is to regulate behaviour by manipulating the cost of products in order to reduce (or sometimes, increase[46]) demand. The mechanism of tax is one means by which the State can influence, without prohibiting outright, the behaviour of citizens. Part of the overt rationale for tobacco and alcohol duties is to deter consumers from smoking and drinking and, at least in part, to ensure that the price of cigarettes and alcohol reflects the true cost to society (including healthcare costs) of these products.

Consumption taxes of this sort do, of course, affect options. If the price of his cigarettes is increased, D will have less money left for other activities. In the absence of offsetting income tax rebates, such measures tend to have a regressive effect on the poor. As such, tax measures are both an improvement on criminalisation in so far as they are less coercive and preserve more options for citizens and, at the same time, less equitable than criminalisation in so far as they are likely to affect different socio-economic classes differentially.

(ii) Tort law

A second option is for the State to regulate an activity by means of a statutory or common law tort. Intervention through the civil law involves a substantial intrusion of the legal process, but remains less coercive than the criminal justice process: there is no arrest, no imprisonment, and no record of a criminal conviction. In some situations, therefore, the creation of a statutory tort may be an excellent alternative to criminal sanctions. This is especially so when considering compliance incentives for large corporations. An industrial accident costing many lives might lead to a company being fined some tens of thousands of pounds: that same company may be far more concerned by the millions of pounds it might incur in tort damages.

---

[46] For example, in the case of children. One reason for providing benefits and/or tax credits to parents is that children are, *inter alia*, public goods; hence the State has reason to subsidise part of the cost of their upbringing.

It is not a complete alternative. Tort law effectively prices rather than prohibits; it lacks the mandatory character of the criminal law, and requires a claimant with adequate resources to bring a legal action. Moreover, in many instances tortfeasors may be able to defray the costs of liability by means of insurance.

(iii) Other mechanisms

There is a variety of other methods for addressing harmful or odious behaviour, including advertising and licensing. A classic example of the former is the campaign against drink-driving, which has been instrumental in bringing about a sea-change in public attitudes toward the wrongfulness of driving while drunk. Although not appropriate to all varieties of wrong (for example, there is normally no need to polemicise against performing acts that are already widely perceived as *mala in se*), education and advertising can in some instances raise awareness of the potential harmfulness of an activity, in circumstances where that harmfulness had previously gone unremarked.

Licensing is also a familiar form of modern regulation. The performance of many activities—e.g. running a public house, possessing a firearm, and even driving—requires a licence. All of these activities import risks of harm, either direct or remote. But each is valuable, and it may be inappropriate, because of the social costs, to criminalise the activity altogether. So the activities are permitted, but only under conditions that are regulated by means of licensing systems. The criminal law, in turn, sits in the background to prohibit persons from carrying out each activity without, or in breach of, the licence. Licensing systems represent a significant limitation of individual liberty, but fall a long way short of outright prohibition. Moreover, they offer a more flexible tool than do generalised criminal laws, since the terms of each licence can be adapted to specific cases by the magistrates or authority responsible for administering that licence.

(iv) Contra: some advantages of using the criminal law

Even though alternative methods of regulation, if practical, should normally be preferred to the criminal law, it is worth noting that there are sometimes advantages in resorting to criminalisation. Unlike any other area of law, the criminal law systematically stigmatises activities (through prohibition) and persons (though conviction and punishment). But sometimes that stigmatisation is appropriate. The symbolic significance of enacting that some activity is a criminal offence can be a reason *in favour* of criminalisation, at least where stigmatisation of the activity is desirable. If used selectively, the creation of a criminal law can be a tool for communicating to the public that the prohibited activity is a serious wrong that *must* not be done.

There are also some practical considerations. Given that the State pays the costs of investigating, prosecuting, and punishing criminal conduct, it may be better placed to regulate wrongs than are, say, private individuals through the law of tort. Suppose that my next-door neighbour throws a stone through one of the panes in my greenhouse, which it will cost some £20 to replace. It is likely to be impractical for me to pursue her through the law of tort. But a criminal prosecution will cost me only my time. In this respect, criminal regulation by the State may augment the rule of law, through increasing the consistency with which legal rights are enforced in like cases, rather than leaving the matter to irregular administration by individual claimants.

§ 16.6 negative grounds for intervention: the rule of law

If the criminal law *is* to be used, its deployment should comply with a variety of constraints, both rule of law and pragmatic. The former, which we outline here, are discussed more fully in chapter 2.

(i) Rule of law constraints on criminalization

First, it is desirable that the form of the criminal law proposed meets rule of law constraints, which were considered in §§ 2.1–4. In particular, the law should be prospective not retrospective (§ 2.2).[47] Secondly, the law should give fair warning, by defining the prohibited activity with sufficient certainty (§ 2.3). It needs to be understandable, predictable, and not vague. The more clearly defined the offence, the less potential there is for injustice with respect to those whose conduct falls close to its limits. Further, the more certainty there is in the drafting, the more confident society can be that an individual convicted under that offence is fairly labelled (§ 2.4). The law must make clear what sort of criminal each offender is—what the conviction is for. The criminal law speaks to society as well as wrongdoers when it convicts them, and it should communicate its judgment with precision, by accurately naming and describing the crime of which they are convicted.

Specificity of drafting has an additional dimension, in that more narrowly defined crimes are less likely to lead to discretionary enforcement. If an offence is too broadly drafted, so that it requires selective prosecution, the liability of defendants is, in effect, remaindered to the decisions of officials—creating the risk of unfair, inappropriate, or potentially even discriminatory prosecutions.[48] It is not unknown for defendants to be found guilty of offences even though, in the view of the court, a prosecution should not have been brought.[49] This possibility should be minimised.

---

[47] Cf. Art. 7(1) of the ECHR: "No one shall be held guilty of any criminal offence on account of any act or omission which did not constitute a criminal offence under national or international law at the time when it was committed. Nor shall a heavier penalty be imposed than the one that was applicable at the time the criminal offence was committed." This rule is also a common law principle of statutory interpretation: "in the absence of express words or a truly necessary implication, Parliament must be presumed to legislate on the assumption that the principle of legality will supplement the text." *B (a minor)* v. *DPP* [2000] AC 428, 470 (Lord Steyn).

[48] Compare the use, not intended by the legislature, of Anti-Social Behaviour Orders against prostitutes and beggars: Burney, "'No Spitting': Regulation of Offensive Behaviour in England and Wales" in von Hirsch and Simester (eds.), *Incivilities: Regulating Offensive Behaviour* (2006) 195, 206; also Simester and von Hirsch, "Regulating Offensive Conduct through Two-Step Prohibitions" in the same volume, 173, 191.

[49] E.g. *Smedleys Ltd* v. *Breed* [1974] AC 839; *Hart* v. *Bex* [1957] Crim LR 622; cf. *James & Son* v. *Smee* [1955] 1 QB 78.

(ii) The individuation of offences

How many offences do we need? Do we really need to distinguish theft from deception, rape from sexual assault, and sections 18 from 20 in the OAPA 1861? Or would it be enough just to have just a few generic crimes including, say, violation of another's property right; violation of another's person; damaging the environment; and so on? The answer to the last question is no. While the law may sometimes draw unnecessary distinctions, broad category offences would be inappropriate. Enacting only generic crimes would tend to suppress the fact that, within each field of harmful wrongdoing, each of our existing offences may involve a different wrong, a different harm, or both. It is for this reason that they are rightly separate offences.

In looking to explain and justify the existence of any offence, it is necessary to identify what harm, and what wrong, is addressed by that crime. Obtaining by deception may, for example, lead to much the same immediate harm as does theft—a straightforward diminution of V's resources—but the wrong is different. Moreover, it does not undermine the proprietary regime in the same way as does theft. As such, the two are rightly distinguished by criminal law.[50]

This claim, about the importance of drawing distinctions, is an extension of the principles of fair warning (§ 2.3) and fair labelling (§ 2.4). *Ex ante*, citizens need to know where they stand. They need advance warning concerning their actions; in particular, about whether what they are going to do is a crime and, if so, what sort of crime it is. *Ex post*, offenders ought to be labelled with an adequate degree of precision, in order that the criminal record identifies the gist of D's criminal wrongdoing. Both principles require that each offence is labelled and defined in such a way that it conveys to citizens an accurate moral picture of the prohibited conduct, one that is neither misleading nor unduly vague or overgeneralised. Offences should, so far as is practical, reflect meaningful distinctions in the public mind between different types of culpable wrongdoing. This mandates that they are drawn up in such a way that they capture, and differentiate, significant differences in the harmfulness, wrongfulness, and/or culpability of various types of action.

By way of illustration, the differences between murder, maiming, and criminal damage are significant because the harms (and indeed the wrongs) at stake are quite different. Their differences are clearly sufficient to warrant enacting separate offences, since the meaning and moral significance of each action is clearly distinguished in the public mind. Attempted murder, too, is rightly distinguished from murder because of the difference in resulting harm. Likewise, although the harms of theft and of criminal damage are similar, the manners in which they are inflicted involve two different forms of wrongdoing; forms that are sufficiently distinct in the public mind to warrant independent recognition by the criminal law.

Occasionally, too, there may be a case for distinguishing between two harmful activities on the grounds of culpability. An assault being negligent with regard to any consequential risks to life would typically lack the same culpability as an assault being reckless about those same risks—and, if ever worthy of being criminalised as form of a homicide (which we

---

[50] Cf. Simester and Sullivan, "On the Nature and Rationale of Property Offences" in Duff and Green (eds.), *Defining Crimes: Essays on the Special Part of the Criminal Law* (2005) 168, 188–90.

doubt), ought surely to be a separate offence and not lumped in with murder or reckless manslaughter.

Not every difference is worthy of capture. Even though many US states follow the old common law in drawing a rudimentary distinction between petty and grand larceny, nobody would suggest that there should be a much more refined series of theft offences, graded in minute detail (say, theft of less than £50 value; theft of less than £100 value; theft of less than £200 value; and so on). Excessively specific offences risk clogging the trial process with unmeritorious technical argument, and obfuscating the moral clarity of the law's communications. At least in the context of non-specialist activities such as property offences, people (both *ex ante* and *ex post*) need to know the law's requirements in gist and not precisely. As such, meaning is better conveyed through publicly shared moral distinctions that are broadly rather than narrowly significant, provided those broader distinctions communicate an adequately nuanced statement of the prohibited wrongdoing. The degree of specificity that the law should adopt when distinguishing various harms and wrongs is, therefore, a trade-off that depends in part on the range of moral differentiations informing the public imagination. The fragmentation of the particular must be balanced against the vagueness of the general.

§ 16.7 Negative grounds for intervention: practical constraints

Finally, in addition to rule of law constraints, a variety of other considerations must be taken into account before concluding that criminalisation through the proposed offence is the right response.

(i) What side-effects will criminalisation have?

Suppose a clearly drafted law is proposed that criminalises the failure to disclose one's HIV-positive status to a sexual partner. One thing to consider before enacting such a law is whether it will have the effect of deterring those persons who are most at risk of contracting HIV from being tested. By not knowing their status, they keep themselves outside the scope of the offence—but without advancing the underlying aim of the offence, which is to protect their partners. In these sorts of cases, the legislator should consider whether, in effect, enacting the proposed law will do more harm than good.

It has not escaped judicial notice that one of the concerns about the use of drugs is consequential criminality: the prospect that drug users will steal, deal in drugs, enter into prostitution, or commit other crimes in order to finance their habit.[51] But a responsible legislator might also think that these considerations argue for *de*criminalisation. The price of illegal drugs is high because the drugs are illegal—if not illegal, no doubt users will need less money to pay for their habits, leading (it may be thought) to a significant reduction in consequential crime. Compare, too, the eras of alcohol prohibition, which led to an upsurge in violent conflict between gangs involved in the black market that arose to replace the licit

---

[51] Cf. *R* v. *Aramah* (1982) 4 Crim App R (S) 407, 408–9 (Lord Lane CJ). See more generally Alldridge, "Dealing with Drug Dealing" in Simester and Smith (eds.), *Harm and Culpability* (1996) 239.

trade. If criminalisation of an activity is likely to produce such undesirable consequences as these, that is a powerful reason not to prohibit.

(ii) Pragmatics of the criminal justice system

A proposed offence might also be rejected for reasons of implementation. In particular, the offence needs to be capable of being administered, by enforcement authorities and prosecutors. Ideally, it will be specified in clear and unambiguous terms, so that (as well as giving fair warning to citizens) those responsible for its administration will be confident of their ability to use the new law with predictable outcomes. Further, the terms it uses will cohere with and not reinvent existing legal concepts, facilitating understanding by professionals within the criminal justice system and avoiding the need for costly retraining exercises.

Another consideration is policing. The detection of some proposed crimes may be too difficult: this is one reason not to criminalise, say, unmarried sexual intercourse in private. Alternatively, crimes may be detectable only by invasive methods of surveillance; it needs to be considered to what extent the power to use such methods is desirable. There is also the question of cost: how expensive are the means of investigation? Will enforcement agencies be able to afford to monitor the new offence? Will effective policing of the offence require additional resources and legal powers?

There are many other issues that must be resolved when a new offence is created (mode of trial, evidential requirements, sentencing options, etc.). We cannot do justice to them all here. The key point is that, even though a prima facie case can be made in favour of criminalising an activity, e.g. because it is harmful to others, it does not follow that criminal legislation is the best response. Other forms of intervention need to be considered; sometimes, it may be best not to legislate at all. The criminal law is a powerful, expensive, and invasive tool. It should not be used lightly.

§ 16.8 Anti-Social Behaviour Orders

In recent years, the UK Government has pioneered a new device to supplement standard forms of criminalisation: the Anti-Social Behaviour Order (ASBO).[52] An ASBO is an order made by a court, generally on the application of a local authority official or a chief police officer, which imposes restrictions on the future conduct of someone proved to have acted previously in an "anti-social" manner.[53] Any subsequent breach of the ASBO, which has a minimum duration of two years, then constitutes a criminal offence punishable by a maximum of five years' imprisonment. In effect, the ASBO creates a two-step route to criminal sanctions, in lieu of the more direct techniques found in the mainstream criminal law. The timeline can be summarised as follows:[54]

---

[52] Crime and Disorder Act 1998, ss. 1, 1A-1I, 2–4.

[53] Following enactment of the Police Reform Act 2002 and the Anti-Social Behaviour Act 2003, the range of eligible applicants has been extended to include the chief constable of the British Transport Police, registered social landlords, county councils, and housing action trusts.

[54] For discussion, see Simester and von Hirsch, "Regulating Offensive Conduct through Two-Step Prohibitions" in von Hirsch and Simester (eds.), *Incivilities: Regulating Offensive Behaviour* (2006) 173.

t_0:   qualifying "anti-social" behaviour by D occurs;

t_1:   ASBO issued (predicated on proof of D's behaviour at t_0, but forward-looking);

t_2:   conduct by D occurs in contravention of the ASBO, leading to criminal prosecution for violation of the order (predicated on proof of conduct at t_2).

What counts as qualifying anti-social conduct (at t_0) is defined in section 1 of the Crime and Disorder Act 1998 as behaviour by D "in a manner that caused or was likely to cause harassment, alarm or distress to one or more persons not in the same household as [D]." Perhaps needless to say, this is an extraordinarily open-ended test. There is no need to prove that anyone actually was alarmed or distressed by D's conduct, that D was aware of the risk of such consequences, or that any distress caused was justified rather than a manifestation of the "victim's" own prejudices.[55] Consequently, ASBOs have been deployed or proposed in an enormous variety of situations, including running a pirate radio station; publishing a spoof advertisement for the position of pope following the death of John Paul II; sounding a taxicab horn; feeding birds; jumping on a trampoline; even attempting suicide; and they are commonly used to repress prostitution and begging.[56] The sheer vagueness of the qualifying definition offers very little in the way of advance warning (at t_0) to those potentially subject to an ASBO, and who may suffer significant deprivations of liberty by the imposition of an Order.

The potential for deprivations of liberty arises because of the sheer range of conduct that may be enjoined by an ASBO. The content of the Order (issued at t_1) is not restricted to an injunction to "cease and desist" the complained-of behaviour by D at t_0. Rather,[57]

> The prohibitions that may be imposed by an anti-social behaviour order are those necessary for the purpose of protecting persons (whether relevant persons or persons elsewhere in England and Wales) from further anti-social acts by the defendant.

As such, the Order may make any prohibition *necessary* to prevent *any* further anti-social acts. It need not be confined to proscribing conduct that is itself anti-social, let alone the variety of conduct that D is alleged to have perpetrated at t_0. Thus the pirate broadcaster, who happened to operate from the roof of a tower block, was prohibited from *entering* any building within the borough that was more than four storeys tall—no matter what his purpose in doing so might be.[58] In practice, ASBOs standardly operate as a form of situational crime prevention, by preventing D from entering a location, such as a shopping mall or housing estate, in which anti-social behaviour might then be committed.[59]

There are certain practical advantages in using ASBOs rather than the ordinary criminal law to regulate harmful or offensive behaviour. The ASBO is, legally speaking, a civil rather

[55] This last point is mitigated somewhat by s. 1(5) of the Crime and Disorder Act 1998, which provides that, for the purpose of determining whether D's triggering conduct was anti-social, "the court shall disregard any act of the defendant which he shows was reasonable in the circumstances."

[56] See the collection in Macdonald, "A Suicidal Woman, Roaming Pigs and a Noisy Trampolinist: Refining the ASBO's Definition of 'Anti-Social Behaviour'" (2006) 69 MLR 183, 197–203.

[57] Crime and Disorder Act 1998, s. 1(6) (as substituted by the Police Reform Act 2002, s. 61(1), (7)).

[58] "Tower Blocked: The 'Anti-Social' Pirate" *The London Line* 21 April 2005; http://news.bbc.co.uk/2/hi/uk_news/magazine/4533949.stm.

[59] As in *Clingham* [2002] UKHL 39. See generally von Hirsch, Garland, and Wakefield (eds.), *Ethical and Social Perspectives on Situational Crime Prevention* (2004).

than criminal order; as such, it is subject to civil rather than criminal rules of procedure.[60] In particular, hearsay evidence is permitted. This makes it easier to obtain an ASBO in circumstances where the victims of intimidating and harassing conduct are afraid to testify directly in court. Even where the conduct complained of at t_0 itself constitutes a criminal offence, the evidential constraints upon criminal trials can mean that, in practice, it can be difficult to prosecute. As Lord Steyn observed in *Clingham*:[61]

> Often people in the neighbourhood are in fear of such young culprits. In many cases, and probably in most, people will only report matters to the police anonymously or on the strict understanding that they will not directly or indirectly be identified. . . . Unfortunately, by intimidating people the culprits, usually small in number, sometimes effectively silenced communities. Fear of the consequences of complaining to the police dominated the thoughts of people: reporting incidents to the police entailed a serious risk of reprisals.

By contrast, the admissibility of indirect evidence in civil proceedings means that a court may be able to issue an ASBO in circumstances where securing a conviction would be impossible.

A second advantage of ASBOs is that they will be available even where the initial conduct at t_0 is not itself—and perhaps should not be—a criminal offence. Sometimes, it may be inappropriate to criminalise the initial type of conduct directly. Rather, it is only repeated instances of an act (which is by itself lawful) that warrant prohibition where, in isolation, the act itself does not deserve to be criminalised. *In aggregate*, a series of minor evils may generate a significant harm to the quality of others' lives.[62] It verges on the impossible to specify, in general terms, the factors in such cases that turn merely irritating conduct into a serious wrong. As such, the ASBO offers an alternative means to regulate such conduct. It can be used to criminalise a course of conduct where single instances thereof are not suitable for prohibition, either because they are insufficiently serious wrongs in isolation, or because they are not by themselves wrongs at all, and become wrongs only when done repeatedly and for certain motives. Here, the ASBO offers a flexible—one might say, tailored—means to regulate ongoing courses of conduct without the need to prohibit every instance of that conduct, performed by anyone, *tout court*. As such, its use could even help to avoid the proliferation of minor, discrete offences.

Part of the danger of ASBOs, however, lies in that very flexibility. While not itself a conviction, the issuance of an ASBO is an *in personam* act of criminalisation. Everyone else may go to the shopping mall, but D may not. The ASBO singles D out from her fellow citizens; it creates one rule for D, and another for everyone else. As such, it undermines principles of equality between citizens. The ASBO's discriminatory prohibitions make it easier to introduce otherwise unwelcome prohibitions, by targeting them at minority or unpopular ("anti-social") elements of a community. It becomes more difficult to generate effective opposition to such measures because the majority will be unaffected. In effect, the

---

[60] *Clingham* [2002] UKHL 39. Their Lordships ruled nonetheless that the alleged anti-social conduct must be proved (in effect) to the criminal standard, i.e. beyond reasonable doubt.

[61] *Ibid.*, paras. 16–17.

[62] This possibility finds acknowledgement already in the law of harassment. The Protection from Harassment Act 1997 prohibits "a course of conduct" that is calculated to harass or annoy others. Isolated wrongs, not by themselves crimes, will not do. See above, § 11.8.

beggars, the prostitutes, the gypsies, and the downright unpopular can be suppressed without restricting the freedoms of "decent" folk. Yet by denying their access to public space, the State begins to excise such people from society. The exclusionary nature of many ASBOs tends not only to preclude the particular undesired conduct in which it originates, and the way of life to which that conduct gives expression; it may also undermine D's participation in the society itself and, ultimately, her identity as a human being.

To be sure, other court orders such as injunctions, non-molestation orders, and tree-preservation orders are also specialised forms of two-step, *ad hoc* or tailored criminalisation. But those mechanisms are narrower. The prohibitions they impose (at t_1) are limited to specific types of activity, such as chopping down trees, which are closely connected to the triggering conditions (such as owning trees of a certain age). Unlike the ASBO, they do not give administrative and judicial officials a generalised discretion to issue orders prohibiting citizens from engaging in conduct at large, and which is not already a legal wrong. In our view, no country respecting personal liberty ought to enact a scheme that gives low-level officials a generalised discretion to prohibit conduct. While guidance from appellate courts about the exercise of that discretion is welcome,[63] the legislation itself should contain far more rigorous constraints than it currently does.

---

[63] See, e.g., *Hills* v. *Chief Constable of Essex* [2006] EWHC 2633 (Admin), para. 10.

17

DEFENCES: AN OVERVIEW

In Chapters 10–15 we have outlined the elements of a number of different offences in English criminal law: murder, rape, theft, and the like. In Chapters 18–21 we will discuss a range of defences that a defendant may invoke when charged with those offences. The division made in this book relies on a basic distinction in the criminal law between offences and defences. Characteristically, if D brings about the actus reus of an offence with the requisite mens rea, then she has prima facie committed that offence. But it is recognised by most writers that these are not the only components of criminal liability. Conduct which is prima facie an offence will not lead to a conviction if the defendant has a further defence:[1]

> "[A]s a matter of analysis we can think of a crime as being made up of three ingredients, actus reus, mens rea and (a negative element) absence of a valid defence."

To illustrate this distinction, consider the following scenario:

> Imagine that you are watching a videotape showing D striking V in the face with his fist. From the film, it seems that D's conduct was deliberate. There is no indication that D was in a state of automatism[2] or that the blow was in any way accidental. You are instructed to give an account of what, if any, criminal offences D may have committed.

Taking what has been seen at face value, it appears that D has committed battery.[3] The elements of that offence, set out above in § 11.3, are satisfied. Indeed, if V has suffered any degree of injury, other more serious offences may also come into play.[4]

Before we attribute any criminal liability to D, however, certain questions must be put. Why was D striking V? D and V may have agreed to fight, so that the blow was consensual. If so, we must enquire whether they were fighting in anger or in sport and, in either case, whether and to what extent V has been injured. Alternatively, D may have hit V to pre-empt what he took to be an imminent attack. If his assumptions were correct and his response

---

[1] Lanham, "Larsonneur Revisited" [1976] *Crim LR* 276, 276; see also Smith, *Justification and Excuse in the Criminal Law* (1989) 1. On the distinction between "offence elements" and "defence elements" see generally Campbell, "Offence and Defence" in Dennis (ed.), *Criminal Law and Criminal Justice* (1987) 73; Williams, "Offences and Defences" (1982) 2 *LS* 233; above, § 1.3.

[2] Above, § 4.3.

[3] The choice of term may seem pedantry; it would be more natural to speak of D's assaulting V. But since the decision in *DPP v. Little* [1992] QB 645, we must distinguish between frightening V (assault) and hitting V (battery), save in statutory contexts where it is accepted that the term assault may be used in the sense of battery. See above, § 11.1.

[4] OAPA 1861, ss. 47, 20, 18.

proportionate to the danger posed by V, D's conduct would be justified.[5] But D may have misconstrued V's wholly peaceable intentions. Even then, D may be excused any liability provided he genuinely believed he was under attack and made a proportionate response to that perceived danger.[6] Before coming to any firm conclusion on that, we should inquire whether D acted under the influence of drink or drugs. If he did, any mistake induced by his intoxicated condition will not necessarily afford him an excuse.[7] What if D had not perceived any threat from V and struck him out of pure aggression? Even now, we should not jump to conclusions. D's aggressive behaviour may have stemmed from a psychotic condition which renders him legally insane.[8]

D's deliberate punching of V confronts us with evidence of a prima facie crime unless there is some *explanation* why, despite appearances, D has not committed that crime. Such explanations, only some of which have been canvassed above, can be described, in the broadest of terms, as defences. These explanations—defences—may take very different forms but generally fall into one of two groups. First, the explanation D offers may sustain a claim that the prosecution has failed to prove the elements of the prima facie offence charged. Alternatively, his explanation may concede that the definitional elements of the crime charged are present but contend that, nonetheless, liability should not be imposed because his conduct was justifiable or excusable.

§ 17.1 "Failure of proof" versus "substantive" defences

Strictly speaking, "defences" falling within the first group are not defences at all; they are denials of proof. For instance, the "defence" of voluntary intoxication is germane only to the question whether it can be proved that D possessed the intent required to commit a particular crime. However, it is convenient to follow conventional usage, and from now on we will eschew quotation marks and speak of these failure of proof explanations as defences. To illustrate:

> Suppose, in our example above, that D's punch broke V's jaw. D has been charged with causing grievous bodily harm with intent to cause grievous bodily harm.[9] In a case of direct attack, a finding that D intended seriously to hurt V may be inferred from the primary facts unless D can cast doubt on the reliability of the inference.[10] He may seek to do this, for example, by adducing evidence that he was intoxicated and thus did not form the intent the crime requires.[11]

If D does raise a reasonable doubt on the issue of his intent, his defence of intoxication will have succeeded. Analytically, the role of this defence is to deny mens rea.

---

[5] Below, § 21.2.
[6] Below, § 18.1(iii).
[7] Below, § 18.3.
[8] Below, § 19.1.
[9] OAPA 1861, s. 18.
[10] *Moloney* [1985] AC 905; *Beeson* [1994] Crim LR 190.
[11] *Beard* [1920] AC 479 (HL); *Sheehan* [1975] 2 All ER 960 (CA).

By contrast with such failure or proof defences, the second group comprises what may be termed substantive or true defences. Proof of the elements of the prima facie offence *is* established, but a conviction would be unjust because justificatory or excusatory circumstances were present.[12] For instance:

Assume that D struck V in order to defend himself, because V was about to attack him with a knife. D's proportionate response to the danger he was in entails that what would otherwise be unlawful is lawful. There was an intentional infliction of force on another, but a finding of battery is deflected by the justifiable nature of D's actions.

The line of demarcation between failure of proof defences and substantive defences is clear in principle but is shifting and unstable in practice. This is well illustrated by the defence of mistake. For many years, when raising a claim of mistaken belief that force was necessary in self-defence, to afford a defence, the mistake had to be based on reasonable grounds.[13] On this view of the law, if D were to raise mistaken self-defence in answer to a charge of battery, it was natural to separate what were seen as the definitional elements of battery—the intentional or reckless infliction of force—from the question whether that infliction of force was *lawful*. So if the prosecution proved that D had intentionally struck V (the prima facie offence), D would be excused only if he *reasonably* believed it was necessary to strike V in self-defence. The defence, even if it succeeded, still left in place the definitional elements of battery. Accordingly, mistake was a true or substantive defence. However, a major classificatory change ensued with the decision of the Court of Appeal in *Williams (Gladstone)*.[14] The actus reus of battery was taken to be the application of *unlawful* force, and the mens rea intentionally or recklessly inflicting unlawful force. By packing unlawfulness into the actus reus, it followed that D would lack mens rea—intent or recklessness about the actus reus of battery—if he believed, reasonably or otherwise, in the presence of circumstances which would have made his conduct lawful. Following *Williams* the defence of mistake is now, predominantly, a failure of proof defence.[15]

For many offences, whether a particular element is characterised as a constituent of the offence or as something external to it is a matter of convention, not of principle.[16] And judges will adopt different conventions. For example, in *Brown*,[17] the House of Lords had to decide, *inter alia*, whether consent by V to the force applied by D was compatible with proof of *assault* occasioning actual bodily harm.[18] For the minority,[19] lack of consent was an

---

[12] *Per* Smith, "On Actus Reus and Mens Rea" in Glazebrook (ed.), *Reshaping the Criminal Law* (1978) 95, 98: "they do not negative either traditional *mens rea* or *actus reus*, but operate in some way independently."

[13] *Rose* (1884) 15 Cox CC 540; *Chisham* (1963) 47 Cr App R 130 (CCA).

[14] [1987] 3 All ER 411.

[15] See too *Beckford* v. *R.* [1988] AC 130 (PC) and, for criticism, Simester, "Mistakes in Defence" (1992) 12 *OJLS* 295.

[16] But not always. For instance, lack of consent is integral to the conception of rape and must be part of its offence definition. A strong case can be made that the same applies to assaults and batteries that do not threaten any physical harm as when D makes what otherwise be a threatening gesture to V as part of a game. V's consent takes D's conduct outside the prohibitory norm of assault; it becomes conduct in which the criminal law has no regulatory interest.

[17] [1994] AC 212. See below, § 21.1(iv)(a).

[18] The term "assault" in s. 47 of the OAPA 1861 comprehends battery as well as "pure" assault; see above, § 11.4.

[19] Lord Mustill and Lord Slynn.

integral part of the actus reus of assault; the presence of consent precluded proof of assault. For the majority,[20] the application of force constituted the actus reus of the offence and consent was something to be raised by way of substantive defence.

In practice, this conceptual fuzziness is not a major concern because the issues to be resolved at trial remain essentially the same irrespective of whether a particular defence is conceptualised as a failure of proof defence or a substantive defence. For example, take a case where D punches V at V's request. The minority in *Brown* would say that in those circumstances there was no battery, because the absence of consent is a defining element of battery; the conduct falls beyond the prohibitory norm of the offence. The majority, by contrast, would regard the issue of consent as raising a defence to a case of battery. But, either way, the dynamics of the trial would remain the same. If the prosecution adduces convincing evidence that D deliberately struck V, a conviction for battery will ensue unless D offers some explanation to avoid conviction. Whether his explanation (V consented) is conceptualised as throwing doubt on the prosecution's prima facie case or as raising a substantive defence in response to the prima facie case, either way, an evidential onus effectively rests on D to raise the issue. If D's evidence raises the possibility of V's consent, the prosecution then assumes the probative burden of disproving the reality of V's consent.[21]

This analysis holds true for cases wherever the ultimate probative burden is on the prosecution, even though an evidential onus might have passed to the defence. There are some defences where a probative onus is placed on the defence (e.g. insanity at common law and many statutory defences).[22] These are substantive defences: they assume that the prosecution has proved its case unless D can establish the defence on the balance of probabilities.[23]

In general, success on the basis of a failure of proof defence or a substantive defence secures an acquittal. If we put aside the special case of acquittals on the ground of insanity,[24] an acquittal is an acquittal; no distinctions are drawn between acquittals afforded by different defences. Arguably, this undiscriminating approach suppresses an important distinction. D may be acquitted in circumstances where his putatively criminal conduct may be said to be wholly *justified* (e.g. proportionate response to a deadly threat). Or he may be acquitted in circumstances where he is *excused* because his conduct was insufficiently culpable for a conviction but where his actions remain an intrusion upon's V's legally protected interests (e.g. where D punches V because he unreasonably assumed that V was about to attack him). Some academics have suggested that a formal legal distinction should be drawn between justified conduct and excusable conduct, a distinction to be reflected by different forms of acquittal and in the taxonomy of criminal defences.[25] We shall not use or argue for doing so in the following chapters (save for the special case of necessity).

---

[20] Lords Templeman, Jauncey, and Lowry.

[21] Above, § 3.2. The same analysis holds for mistake even in its "failure of proof" version: "mistake is a defence . . . in the sense that it is raised as an issue by the accused. The Crown is rarely possessed of the knowledge of the subjective factors which may have caused an accused to entertain a belief in a fallacious set of facts": *Pappajohn* v. *R.* (1980) 52 CCC (2d) 481, 494 (Dickson J).

[22] See above, § 3.2(i).

[23] In *R. v. DPP, ex p Kebilene* [2000] 2 AC 326, Lord Steyn for the majority raised the possibility that the incorporation of Art. 6(2) of the ECHR (presumption of innocence) might require probative burdens of proof placed on defendants to be interpreted as imposing a mere evidential burden: see above, § 2.5(i).

[24] Criminal Procedure (Insanity) Act 1964, s. 1.

[25] Robinson, "Criminal Law Defenses: A Systematic Analysis" (1982) 82 *Columbia LR* 199.

Nonetheless, in light of the powerful arguments that have been made in favour of using the distinction to classify defences, it is necessary to explain why we have not deployed it here.

§ 17.2 Justification and excuse[26]

At one time, English law distinguished justifiable homicide from excusable homicide. A justified killer could retain his possessions whereas a person merely excused had to forfeit his possessions to the Crown. However, in 1828 forfeiture was abolished, and since then this jurisdiction has not distinguished between justification and excuse on the formal plane. Paul Robinson, for one, would reinstitute a formal distinction between cases of justification and cases of excuse. For Robinson, if D is merely excused, he should receive a verdict in the form "not guilty by reason of excuse". Although D would be acquitted, civil coercive measures may yet be allowed to further the goals of special deterrence and rehabilitation. If D's conduct is found to be justified then, according to Robinson, the verdict should be "justified" and D would be free from any form of coercive measures.[27]

Clearly, if the distinction between justification and excuse is to be as salient as Robinson proposes, a clear and usable differentiation is required between cases of justification and cases of excuse. How does Robinson mark the difference? For him, the justification of conduct does *not* require investigating the motivation and practical reasoning of the actor. Justification arises, in a utilitarian fashion, from the consequences that D's conduct brings about. If those consequences are beneficial for society, the conduct is justified. For excuses, on the other hand, the consequences of D's conduct may violate legally protected interests, but D may nonetheless be excused provided that, in all the circumstances, he is insufficiently blameworthy to merit conviction. As Robinson succinctly puts it, "an actor's *conduct* is justified; an *actor* is excused."[28]

Robinson's position is vividly illustrated by his view of the case of Motti Ashkenazi, an Israeli who, with dishonest intent, took a backpack he saw lying on a crowded beach. Unknown to Ashkenazi, the bag contained a terrorist bomb; inadvertently, he had saved many lives. Because of this, Robinson would deny that Ashkenazi committed any theft.[29] He argues that such conduct would not fall within the prohibitory norm of theft, because the criminal law is not concerned to punish beneficent outcomes. This principle, which exempts a person such as Ashkenazi, provides a derogation from the prohibitory norm of the offence in question. Following his acquittal, a law-making precedent would be established to the effect that property belonging to others may lawfully be removed if lives are thereby saved. This is a general norm about legally justified conduct, not specific to any particular actor. On Robinson's view, to be within the exemption, D need not be aware that his conduct will

---

[26] Fletcher, *Rethinking Criminal Law* (1989) chap. 10; Dressler, "New Thoughts about the Concept of Justification in the Criminal Law: A Critique of Fletcher's Thinking and Rethinking" (1984) 32 *UCLA LR* 61; Corrado (ed.), *Justification and Excuse in the Criminal Law* (1994); Horder, *Excusing Crime* (2004); Williams, "The Theory of Excuses" [1982] *Crim LR* 732; Greenawalt, "The Perplexing Borders of Justification and Excuse" (1984) 84 *Col LR* 1897; Smith, *Justification and Excuse in the Criminal Law* (1989).

[27] Robinson, "Criminal Law Defenses: A Systematic Analysis" (1982) 82 *Col LR* 199, 245–7.

[28] Robinson, *Fundamentals of Criminal Law* (1988) 664.

[29] Indeed, according to Robinson, Ashkenazi had a "right" to take the bag, in that anyone who knew the true facts would not be allowed to interfere with Ashkenazi's taking of the bag.

achieve a good outcome; indeed, as in Ashkenazi's case, his motive may be quite reprehensible.

Contrast a situation where D is merely excused; a case, say, where D misconstrues the peaceable intention of V and strikes a pre-emptive blow because he erroneously assumes that V was about to attack. D's striking V is an enchroachment on V's right to personal integrity, an event that remains a cause for concern even if we excuse D from criminal liability. In this case, when we assess D's responsibility for that harm, the focus is on his state of mind and disposition. It is because D *thought* he was under attack and therefore was not acting in an aggressive or predatory manner that we may excuse him.[30] Whether an excuse is granted requires an estimate of blameworthiness. If the mistake was an unreasonable one, arguably he should still be punished for the intrusion on V's rights; although, currently, English law merely requires that D's mistake be genuine.[31] According to Robinson, when D is excused we make a finding that in *these* circumstances it would be unjust to convict D. The judgment is personal to D; it generates no law-making precedent to guide the conduct of others in the future.[32]

Robinson's theorisation of the excuse/justification distinction has been highly influential and, if persuasive, it should be deployed as a central organising principle in any account of defences. Ultimately, however, his theorisation is unconvincing.[33] Robinson's view that questions going to D's motivation and practical reasoning should be excluded from findings of justification is not a necessary truth, merely a position that Robinson adopts. English law, for instance, does not take the view that good outcomes, *by themselves*, entail justification. In the famous case of *Dadson*,[34] D shot and wounded V, an escaping felon. The court accepted that (at that time) a person was justified in shooting to prevent the escape of fleeing felons. But D did not know V was a felon and, because of that, he was convicted of unlawful wounding with intent to do grievous bodily harm. As one would expect, Robinson has argued that *Dadson* is wrongly decided,[35] yet even he concedes that a conviction for *attempted* unlawful wounding would have been in order in the case.[36]

Moreover, once we allow, as English law does, evaluations of personal motivation and blameworthiness to enter into the question of justification, it is even possible for a bad outcome to be the result of *justified* conduct:

> Suppose, for instance, that D, an armed police officer, receives an order to kill V instantly. He has been informed by his superiors (and has no reason to doubt the information) that V is a terrorist on the point of detonating a bomb in a crowded street. D follows his orders and shoots V dead. Unfortunately, those instructing D had made a tragic error; V was going about her lawful business.

---

[30] Which is why, according to Robinson, someone apprised of the true facts would commit an offence against V if she assists D's attack.

[31] See below, § 18.1(iii).

[32] See also Fletcher, "The Individualisation of Excusing Conditions" (1974) 47 *So Cal LR* 1269.

[33] For penetrating critique of an "objectivist" view of justification, see Greenawalt, "The Perplexing Boundaries of Justification and Excuse" (1984) 84 *Col LR* 1897.

[34] (1850) 4 Cox CC 358.

[35] "Competing Theories of Justification: Deeds v. Reasons" in Simester and Smith (eds.), *Harm and Culpability* (1996) 45. But see too, from *Harm and Culpability*, Gardner, "Justifications and Reasons", 103 and Simester, "Why Distinguish Intention from Foresight?", 71, 87ff; also Sullivan, "Bad Thoughts and Bad Acts" [1990] *Crim LR* 559.

We know that according to Robinson, D should receive a verdict of "not guilty by reason of excuse" and should potentially also be subject to civil deterrent or remedial measures. But why merely excused? D's motivation was impeccable—to prevent widespread loss of life. There was no flaw in his practical reasoning—he shot the person identified as a terrorist and had no reason to think the information he was given was false. Should he receive the same order in like circumstances in the the future, he should carry out the order. He would be justified in doing so and in breach of his duty as a police officer should he decline, *irrespective of whether D was a terrorist* (provided D was unaware that V was no terrorist and had no reason to think that the order received was based on an erroneous risk assessment). Moreover, just as in the case of Ashkenazi, we can generalise the grounds of D's acquittal into a law-making precedent. The case would inform us that a person intending to use proportionate means to save lives will commit no offence, notwithstanding that he causes the death of an innocent person if he had good reason to believe that the means he employed were necessary and proportionate means.[37] Of course, from V's perspective, the structure of the situation differs radically according to his status. If he is a terrorist, any resort to force to pre-empt D's lawful use of force upon him would be an offence against D. But if V is innocent, he can lawfully defend himself even if knows that D has made a reasonable mistake. V has a right not to be killed, a right that, as an innocent person, he can enforce against D. But should D find himself on a criminal charge in respect of V's death, the reasonableness of his conduct entitles him to an unqualified acquittal.[38]

Of course, we need not employ Robinson's version of the justification/excuse divide. We could adopt a model which would consider not merely outcomes but also the nature and quality of D's motivation and practical reasoning.[39] But we will not follow that course here, for several reasons. First, there may be situations where exemption from liability is clearly warranted but where neither the head of justification nor that of excuse seems adequately to capture D's non-liability. Suppose, for example, that D is a paranoid schizophrenic who believes that V is an agent of the Devil and must be killed at all costs. It would be conventional to say that his killing V is excusable on the grounds of his insanity. (Clearly, it is not justified by his insanity.) But should we really *excuse* people such as D? When we excuse, we condescend. The excused defendant could and should have done better yet, in all the circumstances, our judgement of her conduct is not sufficiently adverse to warrant sanctions. But an insane person's conduct does not constitute a condonable lapse from the standards of self-control we might reasonably expect of him. It is not that D's action is understandable and insufficiently culpable. Rather, D is not responsible, as a deliberative agent, for her action at all. We exempt D because her mental condition places her outside

---

[36] This is a considerable concession by Robinson to the objectivist rigour of his position since, if attempt liability remains possible, the beneficent outcome does not preclude criminal liability. Robinson's theory, in allowing this concession, effectively takes a particular view on what constitutes "harm" in the context of substantive offences. The harm, in Robinson's account, is not "wounding" but "unjustified wounding"; in turn, Dadson attempted but failed to inflict an unjustified wound.

[37] Even if Robinson insists, as he would, that the bad outcome makes this a case of excuse, it is an excuse very different in structure from, say, that afforded by duress. The reasons for affording the excuse can be formulated as a guide for future conduct.

[38] If the conduct of his superiors was grossly negligent, no doubt they may be liable for manslaughter.

[39] For instance, Uniake uses the term "agent-perspectivally justified" for this approach: *Permissible Killing* (1994) 48–9.

that scheme of reference whereby moral judgements—distinctions between justification and excuse—derive their meaning.[40]

Secondly, particular defences may straddle the boundaries of justification and excuse, however those terms are defined. For instance, duress is typically characterised as an excuse. And frequently it is. In *Hudson and Taylor*,[41] we may have preferred D to be a witness of truth at a criminal trial and not to commit perjury. (Indeed in the light of *Hasan*[42] duress may now be unavailable on similar facts.[43]) We would like witnesses to pass the test of courage when threatened with death or serious bodily harm. Still, D was exempted when she failed that test. In the realm of excuse, the focus was on the fear she must have experienced and how difficult it must have been in the circumstances to do her duty as a witness. By contrast, there have been a series of cases where the defence of "duress by circumstances" has been successfully invoked in answer to motoring offences. For example, in *Willer*[44] D drove his car in a pedestrianised precinct in order to avoid a threat of death or serious bodily harm. Now, understandably, D was in very great fear and that fear, of itself, would have allowed him exemption within the terms of the defence of duress. But to focus on the fear alone is to distort D's story. If driving through the precinct was without risk to others, then it was far better that D did so rather than be killed or badly hurt. His action was justified. And even if not experiencing any of the pressures of fear—he may be icily calm—his justification is sufficient of itself.

Finally, there may be situations where there is agreement that D should not be convicted but disagreement whether, on the same facts, his conduct was justifiable or excusable. Take a case where D is charged with the battery of his son, V. D claims the defence of reasonable chastisement.[45] One strand of opinion holds that certain forms of physical punishment are fully justifiable in the case of serious misbehaviour of children. Alternatively, one may hold the view that chastisement of children is never appropriate, however serious the child's misconduct, but, given the diversity and strength of the differing views of reasonable people on this topic, think that persons of a different persuasion should not be convicted for beating their children (provided the chastisement does not exceed certain limits). Accordingly, there may be consensus among a group of individuals that a defence of reasonable chastisement should be available but a diversity of views about the nature of this defence. The spectrum may range from firm belief in the justifiable nature of corporal punishment, through persons who respect cultural diversity, to persons who think chastisement is wrong and should be punishable but consider that the time is not yet ripe for change in the law.

Because the heads of justification and excuse do not cover the entire range of defences and because there are uncertainties about the definition and application of those terms, in the following chapters we will not classify defences under these rubrics. This is subject to an exception for what may be termed non-coerced necessity. Non-coerced necessity comprises situations where D decides to contravene the letter of the law in order to achieve an outcome of greater social benefit than would accrue through compliance with law. We may

---

[40] Moore, *Law and Psychiatry* (1984) 197–8, 244–5.
[41] [1971] 2 QB 202; below, § 19.1(i)(a).
[42] [2005] 2 AC 467 (HL).
[43] For further discussion, see § 20.1(i)(b) below.
[44] (1986) 83 Cr App R 225 (CA).
[45] Below, § 21.4.

speak of such a decision as "non-coerced" if D's own person and protected interests are not under threat or danger (e.g. where D, a doctor, decides that the mentally incompetent V's best interests would be served by a sterilisation operation). A defence of necessity may be allowed in such circumstances.[46] It is a claim of justification, not of excuse. For such a defence to be afforded, D's calculation must be right; if her cost–benefit analysis is found wanting, her defence of necessity will fail.[47]

§ 17.3 The defences to be considered—an outline scheme

The present state of English law does not permit a logically derived scheme for presenting defences. In the following chapters, all that can be done is to organise our account of defences under broad and to some extent overlapping categories.

First, in Chapter 18 we will consider *failure of proof defences*, namely the defences of mistake and intoxication. In its current form, the defence of mistake of fact is mainly used to raise doubt whether D had the mens rea element of the offence charged. But here, as elsewhere, there is inconsistency and, on occasion, a claim to have made a mistake of fact will take the form of a true or substantive defence.[48] To the extent that mistake of law provides a defence, it too operates predominantly as a failure of proof defence. Intoxication, whether voluntary or involuntary, is always a failure of proof defence; its only relevance pertains to proof of the mens rea element of the crime charged.

Secondly, we will turn in Chapter 19 to *mental condition defences*. These defences concern circumstances where, in the light of some mental condition of D that arises from an internal disorder, it would be unjust to convict D either (i) for any crime, or (ii) for the crime with which she has been charged. A mental condition that exempts conviction from any crime is a condition which satisfies the criteria of insanity within the *M'Naghten* Rules. A mental condition defence that offers merely partial exemption from criminal liability is the statutory defence of diminished responsibility; murder will be reduced to manslaughter if D can demonstrate that her responsibility for a prima facie murder was substantially impaired by some internally derived mental condition that falls within section 2 of the Homicide Act 1957. Finally in Chapter 19, we will consider the defence of infancy, which can also be characterised as a form of deliberative incapacity defence.[49] Although it is a defence of status (no-one under 10 years of age can commit a crime), the status is predicated on assumptions concerning such a person's mental development and consequent moral irresponsibility for her actions. Furthermore, when determining whether children between 10 and 14 years of age are within the defence of infancy, the developmental state of the particular defendant may also be scrutinised.

---

[46] Below, § 21.3.

[47] It would be possible for D's conduct to remain within the realm of necessity (on a non-Robinsonian account) if she has made a *reasonable* mistake of fact, provided the cost–benefit analysis was appropriate to the facts she reasonably assumed.

[48] As is the case where D claims that he thought, albeit mistakenly, that he was under duress: as we shall see, such a claim must be based on reasonable grounds: *Graham* [1982] 1 All ER 801 (CA).

[49] We would be rebuked in this by Stephen: "The one is healthy immaturity, the other diseased maturity and between these there is no sort of resemblance": *A History of the Criminal Law of England* (1883) vol. II, 150–1.

Thirdly, we will turn in Chapter 20 to what we term *defences of circumstantial pressure*. These defences are available to persons who have the capacity to obey the law but are allowed exemption from liability by virtue of the pressure imposed by particular contexts. The defences of duress and marital coercion are the core members of this class of defence. We will also consider here the defences of superior orders and entrapment, although in each of these cases factors additional to the pressure placed on D are relevant to the grounds for exemption. Included too is the defence (if such a defence exists) of impossibility. A defence of impossibility, in the pure and literal sense, is a claim by D that compliance with law was physically (as opposed to morally) impossible. Strictly speaking, such a defence is *sui generis*; we include it in this section because of its focus on surrounding circumstances that affect D's non-compliance with the law.

Finally, Chapter 21 considers what will be called *defences of permissible conduct*. These are defences which permit contravention of the letter of the law provided D has acted for a qualifying reason. Unlike, say, insanity, these defences incorporate reasons in favour of acting in a particular way and, to an extent, allow a measure of planning and prediction: "I hope he will not attack but, if he does, I can defend myself." Such defences include consent, defence of self and others, prevention of crime and unlawful escapes, necessity, and reasonable chastisement. In many circumstances covered by these defences, D may find herself under considerable pressure: e.g. where she is attacked by V and fears for her life. If D then kills V in self-defence, she is permitted that defence provided her actions were a proportionate response to the danger. Unlike duress, however, any understandable fear would play no direct part in her acquittal were she to be charged with V's murder (indeed duress, controversially, is not an available defence to murder). What counts for self-defence is the reasonableness of her response: it matters not whether she defended herself in a state of terror or in a state of calm resolution.[50]

---

[50] However, some allowance is made for the frightening circumstances typical of self-defence situations when assessing the proportionality of D's response to D's attack: below, § 21.2(iv).

18

FAILURE OF PROOF: MISTAKE AND INTOXICATION

Any mistake that D makes when committing an offence will have no bearing on her criminal liability unless it causes her to lack mens rea or provides her with a legally recognised excuse. She may take valuable property thinking that it belongs to X, a wealthy person against whom she has a grudge. In fact the property belongs to V, D's best friend. But for that mistake, D would not have appropriated the property. Her mistake is quite irrelevant for her liability. All the elements of theft are present and D lacks any legally recognised excuse.

With one exception, where mistakes are legally relevant, they are relevant only to questions of exculpation. Mistakes have no inculpatory effect, even should the mistake reveal a propensity to commit criminal acts. For example, in *Taaffe*[1] D concealed a sealed packet when entering the United Kingdom. The packet was found to contain drugs. The prosecution accepted D's claim that he thought the packet contained foreign currency. He concealed the packet because he thought it was an offence to import money from overseas. That was not so; it is perfectly legal, with the abolition of exchange control, to bring in foreign money. The prosecution argued that D's belief that he was acting illegally, together with the fact that he was in possession of drugs, entailed liability for the offence of knowingly importing goods subject to import control. The House of Lords quashed his conviction. His belief that he was committing an offence did not change his lawful conduct into an offence.

There is one exception to the general principle that mistakes are relevant only to exculpation. It applies in the law of attempts. Facts may exist which render a particular crime impossible to commit. For example, suppose that X sells a cheap video recorder to D. Because the price is so low, D is sure that she is acquiring a stolen item. Were that assumption correct, she would commit the offence of handling stolen goods. If her assumption turns out to be incorrect, liability for that offence is precluded. However, since the Criminal Attempts Act 1981, she is guilty of attempting to handle stolen goods. The impossibility of committing the full offence no longer affords a defence to a charge of attempt. To that limited extent, a mistake may have an inculpatory effect.[2]

---

[1] *Taaffe* [1984] AC 539.
[2] See above, § 9.4(iii).

§ 18.1 Mistake of fact, mens rea, and the decision in Morgan

The House of Lords decision in *Morgan*[3] provides the starting point for an analysis of the defence of mistake of fact in English law. Prior to that decision, there was authority that, to afford a defence, any mistake of fact had to be a *reasonable* one.[4] This requirement gave rise to a contradiction. With the passing of section 8 of the Criminal Justice Act 1967, proof of any intention or foresight required to establish liability for an offence had to be proof of the subjective intention or foresight *possessed by the defendant.* Section 8 disallows drawing inferences of intent or foresight of a particular result solely on the basis that such a result was the natural and probable consequence of D's conduct.[5] Consequently, if D did not apprehend that his conduct would bring about a likely consequence, he could not be taken to have intended or foreseen that consequence, however foolish or indifferent his lack of awareness showed him to be. A wholly unreasonable mistake of fact may well negate intention or foresight. How then could there be an insistence, *post* section 8, that a mistake, to provide exemption, must be based on reasonable grounds if D's mistake precluded either intent or foresight with respect to a definitional element of the offence?

(i) Subjective mens rea and mistake

The matter came to a head in *Morgan*. At trial, and before the Court of Appeal,[6] it was ruled that to afford a defence to a charge of rape, a belief in the victim's consent had to be based on reasonable grounds. In the Court of Appeal, Bridge LJ finessed the contradiction between this reasonableness requirement and the terms of section 8 by asserting that unless a mistake was based on reasonable grounds there would be an insufficient basis, as a matter of evidence, on which to raise a defence of mistake.[7] The House of Lords rejected this evidential analysis. Their Lordships accepted that a reasonable mistake would typically have more credibility with a jury, yet unreasonable mistakes could be made and evidence to that effect could be adduced. Such a mistake might avoid liability for an offence because, as Lord Hailsham explained, in the context of rape:[8]

> "Once one has accepted, what seems to me abundantly clear, that the prohibited act in rape is non-consensual sexual intercourse, and that the guilty state of mind is an intention to commit it, it seems to me to follow as a matter of inexorable logic that there is no room either for a 'defence' of honest belief or mistake, or of a defence of honest and reasonable belief or mistake. Either the prosecution proves that the accused had the requisite intent, or it does not. In the former case it succeeds, and in the latter it fails."

This passage makes clear that where the issue is proof of a subjective form of mens rea it is, strictly, a misnomer to speak of a "defence" of mistake of fact. The issue is whether mens rea has been established. Thus, in rape, D must know or be reckless whether V has consented to

---

[3] [1976] AC 182 (HL).
[4] *Rose* (1884) 15 Cox CC 540; *Chisham* [1963] 47 Cr App R 130 (CA).
[5] Above, § 5.1(ix).
[6] [1975] 1 All ER 8.
[7] *Ibid.*, 14.
[8] [1976] AC 182, 214. Cf. *Smith* [1974] 1 QB 354, 360.

sexual intercourse.[9] If D is mistaken about this, he does not claim a "defence" of mistaken belief—rather, he denies mens rea.

Yet it remains a natural usage to speak in terms of a defence of mistake. If, say, the prosecution were to prove the actus reus of rape, an inference that D has mens rea would normally be straightforward from those proved facts. Accordingly, if he is to avoid the drawing of that inference, D would normally be expected to suggest some reason why it should not be drawn.[10] It is perfectly acceptable to say that D is defending himself when he attempts to raise a doubt about his mens rea. The terminology will not mislead, provided it is well understood that the burden of proving mens rea rests with the prosecution. Very often, the prosecution will discharge that task in the course of proving the actus reus, since the inference drawn from proof of the facts surrounding V's non-consent is likely to be sufficient unless D offers some explanation of his conduct.[11] If his explanation raises an evidential issue, the prosecution's probative task is joined again.

(ii) Application of Morgan to definitional elements

The approach to mistake elucidated in *Morgan* will apply straightforwardly where the mens rea required for the offence is coincident with the actus reus. One would hope that such a coincidence could be taken for granted, particularly for serious offences. Unfortunately, the "correspondence principle"[12] is of uneven application in English law. If the mens rea required for a particular offence does not correspond or embrace the entirety of the actus reus, what would otherwise be a mistake germane to liability may turn out to be immaterial. In *Ellis*,[13] for example, D was charged with knowingly evading a restriction on the importation of a Class A drug—an offence in its own right and not a mere instance of a more general offence concerned with the importation of controlled items.[14] D claimed to believe that he was bringing pornography rather than heroin into the country. The Court of Appeal ruled that the mens rea required was knowledge that the item in possession was an item subject to import control.[15] It was unnecessary that D should know the nature of the item

---

[9] Above, § 12.1.

[10] In this situation, a *tactical*—not *evidential*—burden rests on D. For explanation of the difference see above, § 3.2 n. 42.

[11] Section 35 of the Criminal Justice and Public Order Act 1994 allows the court or jury to draw such inferences as appear proper from the failure of D to give evidence or from a refusal, without good cause, to answer any question. Although s. 38(3) provides that failure to testify is not by itself to constitute a basis for conviction, in the situation under discussion, the prosecution have proved that V did not consent to intercourse with D. On the general approach to s. 35, see *Cowan* [1996] QB 373 (CA). The ECHR has declared admissible an application to review the Criminal Justice and Public Order Act 1994 provision on inferences from silence: *Condron* v. *UK* [1999] Crim LR 984.

[12] Above, § 6.5.

[13] (1986) 84 Cr Appr R 235. See too *Forbes* [2001] UKHL 40, [2002] 2 AC 512.

[14] Following the decision of the House of Lords in *Courtie* [1984] AC 463, if a statute provides that particular facts or circumstances increase the maximum penalty for an offence, a discrete offence is created incorporating those facts or circumstances as defining elements. This rule applies in the case of drugs, since greater penalties are provided for Class A drugs than for non-Class-A drugs.

[15] D was charged under s. 170(2) of the Customs and Excise Management Act 1979 which requires, *inter alia*, that D be "knowingly concerned" in the importation of a controlled drug. The requirement of knowledge relates to the item in possession. D could not have known he was in possession of pornography because he had no pornographic items in his possession. At most, he believed that he did. Whereas *true* beliefs may be accounted in law as knowledge (above, § 5.4), it strains credulity to breaking-point to classify a false belief as a form of knowledge.

in question. Accordingly, his conviction for evading the restriction of Class A drugs was confirmed. The logic of *Morgan* does not apply to the actus reus of the offence in such a case, save to this extent: D could offer a defence of mistake if he genuinely believed, however unreasonably, that he was not carrying any form of contraband.

Morgan offers welcome clarification. Yet two areas of difficulty remain. First, cognisance was taken by their Lordships of a line of authority which required that any mistake relating to a belief in a need to use defensive force had to be based on reasonable grounds if it were to have an exculpatory effect.[16] Secondly, note was also taken of the well-known and long-standing decision in *Tolson*[17] which decided, in the context of the offence of bigamy, that any belief in a capacity to enter into a valid form of marriage had to be reasonable if it was to provide an excuse. The House indicated that its decision in *Morgan* should not be read as undermining *Tolson*.[18]

We must now examine each of these reservations from the subjective approach.

(iii) Mistake of fact and defences

In *Albert* v. *Lavin*,[19] D assumed that he was under restraint by a passer-by; in fact, V was a plain-clothes police officer attempting to restrain V from queue-jumping at a bus-stop. V had intervened because he feared that D's conduct would lead to a breach of the peace in the light of the irate responses of fellow passengers.

It was argued on D's behalf that, although it may have been unreasonable for D to believe that V was not a policeman, he was entitled to a defence of mistake.[20] The Divisional Court confirmed the magistrate's ruling that such a belief, to afford a defence, had to be reasonable. *Morgan*, it was explained, concerned the *definitional* elements of offences. Here, by contrast, the definitional elements were present—D had intentionally inflicted force on V. The question for the court was not whether there had been an assault but whether the assault was an *unlawful* assault.[21] The Divisional Court approved previous authority which ruled that force based on an unreasonable belief in justificatory facts was unlawful force.[22]

The analysis applied in *Albert* v. *Lavin* was successfully challenged in *Gladstone Williams*.[23] The Court of Appeal rejected the notion that the requirement of unlawfulness was something that stood apart from the offence itself. The unlawfulness was integral to the offence and, on that view, the mens rea for assault was an intent to apply unlawful violence. Consequently, a person who believed that force was necessary to protect another from violence would lack an intent to inflict unlawful force. The approach in *Gladstone Williams*

---

[16] *Rose* (1884) 15 Cox CC 540; *Chisham* [1963] 47 Cr App R 130 (CA).

[17] (1889) 23 QBD 168 (CCR).

[18] [1976] AC 182, 201–2 (Lord Cross), 214–15 (Lord Hailsham).

[19] [1981] 1 All ER 628 (DC); affirmed on other grounds [1982] AC 546 (HL).

[20] The Divisional Court assumed that only police officers could physically restrain persons to prevent a breach of the peace. The House of Lords subsequently held that all subjects have this right. On that view, D's mistake, unreasonable or otherwise, was immaterial.

[21] [1981] 1 All ER 628, 639 (Hodgson J).

[22] *Weston* (1879) 14 Cox CC 346; *Rose* (1884) 15 Cox CC 540; *Owens* v. *HM Advocate* 1946 JC 119; *Chisham* (1963) 47 Cr App R 130.

[23] [1987] 3 All ER 411.

was endorsed by the Privy Council in *Beckford*[24] and may be regarded as authoritative for cases involving beliefs in the need for preventive or defensive force.

However, this wholly subjective approach does not apply to all mistakes. In *Graham*,[25] the Court of Appeal considered that a mistaken belief in the existence of circumstances constituting legally adequate duress must be based on reasonable grounds if it is to constitute a defence, an approach endorsed by the House of Lords in *Howe*[26] and again in *Hasan*.[27] The latter case in particular bases its refusal to endorse an subjective approach on a concern to tighten the conditions of a defence easily fabricated and abused. One cannot rule out the possibility that, at some future date, the analysis preferred in *Gladstone Williams* and *Beckford* for cases of self-defence might be reconsidered, particularly in a case where fatal force has been resorted to against a law enforcement agent on the basis of an unreasonable belief. The pragmatic concerns leading to the requirement of a reasonable belief in cases of duress could equally be pressed to require reasonable beliefs for cases of self-defence, reverting to a position that held sway for many years. It bears mentioning that there is no House of Lords authority endorsing *Gladstone Williams* and *Beckford*.

Clarkson and Keating offer a principled explanation for the current divergence of approach between cases of duress and cases of self-defence. For them, the difference may be explained on the basis that a belief in the need to use preventive force is a belief that one's conduct is justified whereas a belief that one may be subjected to duress amounts to a claim merely to be excused.[28] They rationalise this divergence on the grounds that, in the former case, a defendant believes he is acting in a lawful and justified—i.e. blameless—manner; by contrast with the latter case, where even if D were right his conduct would be neither lawful nor justified. This view implies the claim that if D1 attacks V because he unreasonably assumes that V is about to attack him, he is in better moral standing than, say, D2 who drives his car through a pedestrianised area to escape V whom he unreasonably assumed was about to kill him. D1's mistake relates to self-defence (justification) and D2's to duress of circumstances (excuse). But is far from obvious that they are in different moral case.[29]

The reason for the different approaches appears to be the happenstance that typifies our uncodified criminal law. The element of unlawfulness which must, axiomatically, be present for the commission of any offence may, as in *Gladstone Williams*, be treated as something integral to the definition of the offence. Where that analysis is employed, the wholly subjective approach taken in *Morgan* will prevail and any genuine belief in facts which would have rendered D's conduct lawful will provide an excuse. However, if the matter is not covered by authority, a court minded not to follow the subjectivism of *Morgan* may, as in *Graham*, treat the defence in question as something extraneous to the defining elements of the offence. If that analysis is employed, a court may require, as in *Graham*, that mistakes must be based on reasonable grounds to afford a defence. It has been persuasively argued that resolving such issues by reference to the categories of defining elements or defence

---

[24] [1988] AC 130. For critical commentary see Simester, "Mistakes in Defence" (1992) 12 *OJLS* 295.
[25] [1982] 1 All ER 801.
[26] [1987] AC 417.
[27] [2005] 2 AC 467.
[28] *Criminal Law: Text and Materials* (4th ed., 1998) 268–9.
[29] As argued earlier, assigning defences to the categories of either justification or excuse will run up against the difficulty that defences may operate over the two categories: § 17.2.

elements is to elevate legalism over substantive moral assessment.[30] For instance, lack of consent is clearly a defining element of rape. Yet there are good reasons why a belief in V's consent to sex should be based on reasonable grounds to afford a defence, a position now achieved under the Sexual Offences Act 2003 for rape and othe non-consensual sexual offences.[31]

Similarly, while the legislature has adopted objective standards for definitional features of serious crimes in measures such the Sexual Offences Act 2003 and the Proceeds of Crime Act 2002, at the same time the House of Lords in G[32] gave a ringing and general endorsement to the subjective approach to central elements of serious offences when abolishing *Caldwell* recklessness.[33] Ironically, in a later decision of the same name,[34] the Court of Appeal upheld the imposition of strict liability for an offence carrying a maximum penalty of life imprisonment—despite House of Lords authority[35] that (had the Court been strongly minded to do so) could have been deployed to require subjective mens rea for the element in question (the age of the victim) and hence make available a defence of mistake, even where based on unreasonable grounds.[36] English law lacks any general theory of exculpation to guide decision-making on the nature and range of the defence of mistake. A settled theory could only come by way of a criminal code, a prospect as remote as peace in the Middle East.

The need for general principle is underscored by the confusion and uncertainty engendered by a series of cases relating to mistake and defences. In *Martin (David)*,[37] the Court of Appeal ruled that it was a misdirection for the trial judge to direct that D should have had reasonable grounds to believe that his mother's life was in danger before excusing on the ground of mistaken duress. Instead, the jury should have been directed that a genuine belief, reasonable or otherwise, should suffice. While the decision has the virtue of concordance with the cases involving mistaken self-defence, confusion is shown by the cavalier treatment of the previous authority dealing with mistaken duress, where a reasonable mistake is insisted upon. In the light of the endorsement of a reasonable mistake requirement by the House of Lords in *Hasan*,[38] we can put *Martin (David)* to one side as an aberration in the case law on mistaken duress; but, nonetheless, one indicative of the instability in general terms of the approach to mistake.

In *Martin (Anthony)*,[39] a case of self-defence, the Court of Appeal confirmed that a belief in a need to defend oneself need not be based on reasonable grounds: a genuine belief sufficed. However, the Court of Appeal introduced a surprising, and untenable, distinction between (i) the facts on which D's perception that he was under attack was based and (ii)

---

[30] Tur, "Subjectivism and Objectivism: Towards Synthesis" in Shute, Gardner and Horder (eds.), *Action and Value in Criminal Law* (1993) 213.

[31] Above, §§ 12.1–4.

[32] [2003] UKHL 50; [2004] 1 AC 1034.

[33] Above § 5.2(i).

[34] G [2006] EWCA Crim 821.

[35] B (a minor) v. DPP [2000] 2 AC 428; K [2002] 1 AC 462. See further above, § 6.1(i).

[36] See above, § 12.7. In fact the defendant in G (a boy of 16) was found to have a reasonable belief that V, a 12-year-old girl, was aged 15.

[37] [2000] 2 Cr App R 42.

[38] [2005] 2 AC 467; approving the requirement therefore stated in Graham [1982] 1 All ER 801.

[39] [2002] 2 WLR 1.

the danger presented by those facts. In relation to (ii), D had claimed that his personality disorder, exacerbated by depression, induced him to perceive a greater threat to his safety arising from a burglary at his isolated farmhouse than would have been perceived by a normal person. The Court held that, whereas in relation to (i) the facts must be presumed to be as D saw them, (ii) the danger presented by those facts must be evaluated *objectively*. D's plea of mistaken self-defence therefore failed, because his response to the objectively ascertained danger (rather than his imagined danger) was excessive.

The distinction drawn by the Court of Appeal between the facts *per se* and the danger arising from the facts is spurious. Suppose that V reaches into the inside of his jacket to extract a cigarette-lighter; D assumes he is reaching for a gun. According to *Martin (Anthony)*, we are to allow D the benefit of his belief that V was reaching for a gun, however unreasonable D's belief, but must make an objective appraisal of the danger arising from these presumed facts. But what is it for a person to believe self-defence is required? It is to think that something dangerous is happening or about to happen. That is a belief about the facts: in the realm of *mistaken* beliefs, there is no division between the facts themselves and the danger to which the facts give rise.

This was perceived very clearly by the Privy Council in *Shaw* v. *R*,[40] a case decided shortly before *Martin (Anthony)* and not cited in the latter case. In *Shaw,* the appellants were appealing against a direction which invited the jury to assess the reasonableness of D's self-defence on the basis of the facts as they were rather than the facts as D believed them to be. The Privy Council expressed the proper test for self-defence as follows:[41]

> "In the opinion of the Board it was necessary for the trial judge to ask two essential questions (however expressed) for the jury's consideration. (1) Did the appellant honestly belief or may be honestly have believed that it was necessary to defend himself? (2) If so, and taking the circumstances *and the danger* as the appellant honestly believed them to be, was the amount of force which he used reasonable?"

Much the better view, then, is that D must be assessed on the basis of the danger he took to be present—a fully subjective test. As we shall see directly, D's response to that perceived danger must be reasonably proportionate: an objective test. When considering what facts D took to exist, any psychological aspect of D germane to his perceptions should be taken into account—such as D's personality disorder and depression in *Martin (Anthony)*.

(iv) The rule in Tolson

In *Tolson,*[42] the Court of Crown Cases Reserved resolved, by a majority, that there would be a defence to a charge of bigamy if D had reasonable grounds to believe that she was free to enter into marriage. Accordingly, on the facts of *Tolson*, a reasonable belief that one's husband had drowned at sea would suffice, but a belief, however strongly held, based on inadequate grounds would not. How is this approach compatible with *Morgan*?

According to Lord Cross, the explanation lies in the definition of the offence of bigamy. In

---

[40] [2001] 1 WLR 1519.
[41] [2001] 1 WLR 1519, 1527 (emphasis added).
[42] (1889) 23 QBD 168 (CCR).

so far as material, bigamy penalises, "whosoever, being married, shall marry another person during the life of the former husband or wife." It may be noted that there is no indication of what mental element, if any, is required for this offence. For Lord Cross, this was crucial:[43]

> "If the words defining an offence provide either expressly or impliedly that a man is not to be guilty of it if he believes something to be true, then he cannot be found guilty if the jury think that he may have believed it to be true, however inadequate were his reasons for doing so. But, if the definition of the offence is on the face of it 'absolute' and the defendant is seeking to escape his prima facie liability by a defence of mistaken belief, I can see no hardship to him in requiring the mistake—if it is to afford him a defence—to be based on reasonable grounds."

Lord Cross's account provides a cogent distinction between rape (the offence at issue in *Morgan*), which has an explicit mental element, and the crime of bigamy. Indeed, there are many offences which make no reference to a mental element. As a matter of judicial inter-pretation, however, the approach outlined by Lord Cross has rarely been taken. More typically, courts have either found an implication of mens rea from the statutory context or determined that the offence is one of strict liability. Strict liability tempered by a defence of reasonable mistake is an option not considered.[44] Such an approach has taken hold only in bigamy[45] and in the now-rarely prosecuted offence of taking a girl under the age of 16 from the possession of her parents or guardian.[46] As the House of Lords has now confirmed,[47] the rule in *Tolson* lacks any generality.

(v) Mistake of fact and mistake as to an applicable standard

It is customary to draw a distinction between mistakes of fact on the one hand and mistakes of law on the other, with only the former kind of mistake allowed an exculpatory effect. We shall address the fact/law divide in the next section. Before we do, it is necessary to consider another distinction which is more easily confused: the distinction between facts and standards.

Not all applicable standards are reduced to specific rules of law. For instance, section 3 of the Criminal Law Act 1967 allows force to be used in the prevention of crime provided it is "reasonable in the circumstances". What constitutes reasonable force in the particular circumstances is a question of fact. By the very nature of the reasonableness standard, it is a matter for objective appraisal. But if the matter is one of fact rather than law, arguably a person who has used unreasonable force may claim to have made a mistake of fact if she

---

[43] [1976] AC 182, 202–3.

[44] Lord Devlin has claimed, extra-judicially, that as a matter of statutory construction the choice, in practical terms, is between implying a mens rea term or reading a provision literally, thereby imposing strict liability: *Samples of Law Making* (1963) 76. Lord Devlin has in mind construction of the defining elements of the *offence*, whereas the *Tolson* approach provides a *defence* which precludes punishment of the blameless. It would have been possible for the judiciary to extend this approach beyond bigamy and kindred offences. For instance, in other Commonwealth jurisdictions, due diligence defences have been judicially created to mitigate strict liability in the regulatory sphere: see above, § 6.4.

[45] *King* [1964] 1 QB 285 (CA); *Gould* [1968] 2 QB 65 (CA).

[46] *Hibbert* (1869) LR 1 CCR 184.

[47] *B (a minor)* v. *DPP* [2000] 2 AC 428. The decision in *Tolson* was given no salience in the review of approaches to mens rea by the House of Lords in *G* [2003] UKHL 50; [2004] 1 AC 1034.

believed the force employed was appropriate to the circumstances. Such an argument was accepted by the Court of Appeal in *Scarlett*[48] where D, a pub landlord, was found guilty of constructive manslaughter at trial on the basis of having committed battery against V, a customer, whom he used excessive force to eject. On appeal, his conviction was quashed on the basis that, if D believed the circumstances called for the degree of force he used, he was entitled to a defence of mistake of fact even if his belief was unreasonable.[49]

It is submitted that *Scarlett* is wrongly decided and should not be followed. The judgment of the Court of Appeal confuses the category of fact (data concerning surrounding circumstances) with the category of standards (evaluation) which, juridically, are likened to questions of fact only because the matter is left to the jury rather than the judge to adjudicate upon. Despite their classification as matters of fact, such standards are normative, requiring an objective assessment which may well be at variance with D's own evaluation of her conduct. In *Scarlett* the court took itself to be applying the decision in *Gladstone Williams*.[50] That decision, as we have noted, merely decides that if a person mistakenly assumes that she or another is about to be attacked, her actions are to be judged as if that assumption were true. There is nothing in the case which obliges subsequent courts to accept a defendant's own view of what constitutes *a reasonable* response to the situation that she perceived herself to be in. The approach in *Scarlett* undermines section 3 of the Criminal Law Act 1967, which mandates *reasonable* force in the prevention of crime. A police officer, for instance, acting excessively but with a genuine zeal in the cause of crime prevention may, if *Scarlett* is correct, claim a defence of mistake of fact. Fortunately, in *Owino*,[51] where there was a gross disproportion between D's violent response and the threat he claimed to be facing from V, the Court of Appeal confirmed D's conviction for malicious wounding and stated that should there be any conflict between its previous decisions in *Gladstone Williams* and *Scarlett*, it was the former decision that should prevail. A similar view was expressed in *Armstrong-Braun*.[52] *Dicta* that D's response to the danger he took to exist must be reasonable and proportionate can be found in the post-*Scarlett* cases of *Armstrong-Braun*, *Shaw* v. *R.*,[53] *Martin (David)*,[54] *Leckey*,[55] and *Rashford*.[56]

Accordingly, the defence of mistake of fact is confined to facts in the sense of data about the world, misperceptions on the part of D concerning the circumstances in which she acted. Examples would be mistakes about the intentions of another, or D's taking V's umbrella mistakenly assuming that it was her own. Questions of normative standards fall outside the scope of the defence.

---

[48] [1993] 4 All ER 629 (CA).
[49] *Ibid.*, 636 (Beldam LJ).
[50] [1987] 3 All ER 411 (CA).
[51] (1996) 2 Cr App R 128 (CA).
[52] [1999] Crim LR 416.
[53] [2001] 1 WLR 1519.
[54] [2000] 2 Cr App R 42.
[55] [2005] NICA 26.
[56] [2005] EWCA Crim 3377.

§ 18.2 Ignorance and mistake of law

"Ignorance of law is no excuse" is a saying widely disseminated in our culture and, as generalisations go, it has a large core of truth.[57] In *Esop*,[58] D, a subject of the Ottoman Empire, was accused of committing buggery while aboard a ship docked in an English port. Such conduct was not an offence in his place of domicile and the court accepted that D, as a complete stranger to this country and its ways, had no reason to think that he was breaking the law. These factors were held irrelevant to the issue of liability. From *Bailey*,[59] it appears that ignorance of law will not afford an excuse even if D was in a situation where it was impossible for him to learn that the relevant law applied to him: accordingly, it did not avail D to demonstrate that the statutory provision in question had been extended to British vessels while his ship was at sea and beyond communication with England. Neither will a positive belief, based on legal advice, that one's conduct is lawful give grounds for exemption. In *Cooper* v. *Simmons*,[60] D, an apprentice, received misleading legal advice that he was no longer bound by his indentures following the death of his master. Nevertheless, he was convicted of unlawfully absenting himself from his apprenticeship.

Notwithstanding the straightforward and unyielding approach exemplified by these cases, it would be a mistake to assert that D's state of legal knowledge is invariably irrelevant to the question whether D has committed an offence. Such knowledge will, of course, be relevant where a statutory offence expressly provides that particular forms of knowledge or beliefs about legal questions are germane. Further, courts occasionally construe statutory offences as requiring, by implication, knowledge or beliefs concerning questions of law. Additionally, the expanding discretionary jurisdiction to stay criminal proceedings as an "abuse or process"[61] may well require consideration of the defendant's legal knowledge or beliefs. The importance of this jurisdiction is likely to increase with the incorporation into English law of Article 6 of the ECHR, granting to defendants a right of fair trial. Consideration must be given also to Article 7 of the ECHR, which proscribes retroactive laws. In certain circumstances, application of the maxim that ignorance of the law does not excuse will be tantamount to imposing liability on a retroactive basis.

(i) Construing offences and mistake or ignorance of law

Statutes may make explicit reference to the defendant's legal knowledge or beliefs. For instance, section 2(1)(a) of the Theft Act 1968 provides that D's appropriation of property belonging to another is not to be regarded as dishonest if she believes she has, in law, the right to deprive the other of it. Alternatively, even if the statute is not explicit, a court may conclude that the mens rea for a particular offence is negated by a mistake of law made by

---

[57] Ashworth, "Excusable Mistake of Law" [1974] *Crim LR* 652; Husak and von Hirsch, "Culpability and Mistake of Law" in Shute, Gardner, and Horder (eds.), *Action and Value in Criminal Law* (1993) 157; Smith, "Error and Mistake of Law in Anglo-American Criminal Law" (1984) 14 *Anglo-American LR* 3.

[58] (1836) 7 C & P 456, 173 ER 203.

[59] (1800) Russ & Ry 1, 168 ER 651 (CCR).

[60] (1862) 26 JP 486.

[61] Choo, *Abuse of Process and Judicial Stays of Criminal Proceedings* (1993).

[62] [1974] QB 354 (CA).

D. In *Smith*,[62] D damaged V's speakers when removing them from fixed positions. D assumed that he was removing his own speakers but, unawares, by fixing them to a wall in his rented flat he had made the items, in legal terms, fixtures and, hence, the property of the landlord V. On one view, D's conviction at trial for criminal damage is uncontroversial. He was reckless about damaging the speakers, as he anticipated that the manner of removal which he employed might damage them. He was aware of the facts that made the speakers V's property—he himself had fixed them to the wall. That D was unaware of the property-transferring effect of his conduct was regarded by the trial judge as a mistake of law, relevant to mitigation but not to liability for the offence.

The Court of Appeal quashed D's conviction. It took the gravamen of criminal damage to be the destruction or damage of property that was known or suspected by D to belong to another. The court discussed the matter in terms of mens rea, which is entirely appropriate. The point is that mens rea in the context of *Smith* required a degree of awareness on the part of D of the legal consequences of his conduct.

Another way of categorising the appellate ruling in *Smith* is to say that a mistake of civil law was in issue and questions of civil law are equivalent to questions of fact. But while it is true that courts are far readier to allow mistakes of civil law to exempt than they are to exculpate for mistakes of substantive criminal law, there is no hard and fast rule. The effect of the master's death on the legal relationship of master and apprentice is clearly a matter of civil law. Yet, as we saw in *Cooper* v. *Simmons*,[63] D's mistaken belief that the death of his master had freed him from the obligations of service did not provide a defence to a criminal charge of unlawfully absenting himself from his apprenticeship. Conversely, there are cases, albeit rare, where courts have inferred that Parliament intended that ignorance of a rule of criminal law should excuse. For instance, in *Secretary of State for Trade and Industry* v. *Hart*,[64] D acted as auditor of a company of which he was a director. In so doing, he appeared to be in breach of the terms of section 13(5) of the Companies Act 1976, which prohibits any person from acting as auditor of a company if "he knows that he is disqualified for appointment to that office." D knew all the facts (i.e. that he was a director of the company) that made for his disqualification.[65] Yet the Divisional Court held that something further was required to satisfy the requirement of knowledge: knowledge of the statutory disqualification rules was a prerequisite of liability. D's mistake was clearly a mistake of criminal law. Nonetheless, Ormrod LJ stated:[66]

> "If that means that he is entitled to rely on ignorance of the law as a defence, in contrast to the usual practice and the usual rule, the answer is that the section gives him that right."

There is no settled jurisprudence to guide us as to when the approach taken in *Hart* will be adopted. Contrast the decision in *Johnson* v. *Youden*,[67] where P built a house under the authority of a building licence that was subject to a condition limiting the price for which the house might subsequently be sold. P sold the house for a net price in excess of the limit, thereby contravening section 7 of the Building Materials and Housing Act 1945. D, P's

[63] (1862) 26 JP 486; above, § 18.2.
[64] [1982] 1 All ER 817.
[65] By virtue of s. 161(2) of the Companies Act 1948.
[66] [1982] 1 All ER 817, 822.
[67] [1950] 1 KB 544 (DC).

solicitor, was charged as an accomplice to P's offence. It was accepted that, as an accomplice, the required mens rea was knowledge of the essential elements of the offence. Despite the fact that D had read the Act and had formed the opinion that the transaction, as structured, was lawful, the Divisional Court directed the first instance justices to convict. Knowledge was satisfied on the basis of D's awareness of the terms of the licence and of the terms of the sale; the Court held it was not necessary to know that the transaction was in breach of the Act, since to require such knowledge would be to excuse D on the basis of ignorance of law.

It may seem perfectly reasonable to expect solicitors to apprise themselves of law applicable to their professional involvement. Equally, however, one would suppose that a company director should appreciate that the essence of a company audit is independent scrutiny of the financial situation of the company. All that can be said with any measure of confidence is that the line taken in *Johnson* v. *Youden* is more typical than that adopted in *Hart*. It can also be said that, generally, courts will be more receptive to claims of excuse founded on mistake or ignorance of the civil law than of the criminal law. What is signally lacking in English law is any discussion of what general principles should be invoked when determining whether, if at all, mistake or ignorance of law should provide a defence.

(ii) Mistake or ignorance of law, abuse of process, and the right to fair trial

In *Arrowsmith*,[68] D distributed leaflets to soldiers eligible to serve in Northern Ireland, urging them to desist from serving in that province. She was prosecuted under the Incitement to Disaffection Act 1934. *Inter alia*, she defended herself on the basis that a letter she received from the Director of Public Prosecutions would have led any reasonable person, including the defendant, to believe that distribution of the leaflets did not contravene the Act. Accordingly, she claimed a defence of excusable mistake of law, a claim rejected both at trial and on appeal.[69]

The case raises some difficult questions. Clearly, prosecuting authorities should not be disadvantaged by offering bona fide advice to persons seeking to stay on the right side of the law. Such advice may be optimistically interpreted or disingenuously construed and the prosecutorial task should not be stymied through such contingencies. Yet, if the nature and extent of D's proposed conduct has been clearly understood by a person in authority of appropriate standing who goes on to give an unequivocal assurance that no prosecution will ensue, there is a strong ethical case for allowing a defence of reasonable or excusable mistake of law.

An argument in favour of the unyielding stance in *Arrowsmith* is that advice, even advice reasonably relied upon, should not pre-empt the Court's right, and duty, to determine the law. Not infrequently, persons will receive legal advice to the effect, say, that premises which they own meet requirements of the Health and Safety at Work Act 1974 or that their factory

---

[68] [1975] QB 678 (CA).

[69] The facts of *Arrowsmith* were not conducive to recognition of an excusable mistake of law defence arising from official advice. D had received a letter from the Director of Public Prosecutions (whose consent was required) indicating that he would not be consenting to a prosecution in respect of earlier distributions of the pamphlet, a weak basis from which to infer that the DPP took D's conduct to be lawful. The Court of Appeal gave no indication of what the position would have been on stronger facts.

emissions comply with environmental legislation. It may well be in the public interest that such advice should be judicially scrutinised and appropriate standards imposed.

Even so, there remains room for an appropriate procedural defence. An important distinction should be drawn between advice about the law and official assurances that *particular conduct* will not be prosecuted. As Ashworth has argued, in the latter case something akin to estoppel should be seen to arise where the assurance has been given by an official of sufficient authority and has been relied upon by the person subsequently prosecuted.[70] The distinction is best observed, perhaps, not by a defence of reasonable mistake of law but by reference to notions of due process and fair trial. In *R. v. Croydon Justices, ex parte Dean*,[71] it was found to be an abuse of process to instigate criminal proceedings against a person who had agreed to give evidence in return for an assurance that he would not be prosecuted. The same reasoning would apply to a person assured that her planned conduct conforms with law, should the assurance be given by an official of appropriate standing.[72] Any trial which would constitute an abuse of process is, further, likely to contravene Article 6 of the ECHR, which secures the defendant's right to a fair trial.

(iii) Ignorance of law and Article 7 of the ECHR

In *Lim Chin Aik*,[73] D was prosecuted for being an unregistered alien present in Singapore. A registration requirement had been imposed on aliens present in Singapore by an unpublished ordinance which had not been notified to persons affected by its terms. The Privy Council construed the offence as requiring mens rea and advised that D lacked mens rea as he was unaware of any duty to register.

In its own terms, the decision is entirely satisfactory. Yet by characterising the matter as one of mens rea, the broader question of when ignorance of law may excuse is not addressed. Neither is the tension with earlier authority such as *Bailey*.[74] Broader considerations may be encouraged in future by the incorporation into English law of Article 7 of the ECHR, which proscribes retroactive penal law.[75] Of course, the mischief at work in cases such as *Lim Chin Aik* and *Bailey* is not, strictly, retroactivity: the laws under which the respective defendants were prosecuted existed at the time of their conduct. Yet from the perspective of fairness to the defendant, no distinction can be drawn between retroactive

---

[70] "Testing Fidelity to Legal Values: Official Involvement and Criminal Justice" in Shute and Simester (eds.), *Criminal Law Theory: Doctrines of the General Part* (2002) 299. Jerome Hall has objected to providing a mistake of law defence in such circumstances, on the grounds that it would give the advice greater legal potency than the view of the law taken by the court and thus contravene the principle of legality: *General Principles of Criminal Law* (2nd ed., 1960) 380–3. But such a defence would operate *in personam*. The law, in terms of its general application, would be the law as determined by the Court. The defence would merely recognise that it would be unfair to convict D *on this particular occasion* and could no more subvert the definition and interpretation of law than would, say, allowing duress to be raised in response to a charge of theft.

[71] [1993] Crim LR 758.

[72] One argument in favour of treating these cases as a matter of abuse of process is that it underscores the fact that these cases involve dimensions not merely of personal injustice but also of due process and institutional propriety. A disadvantage is the discretionary nature of the abuse of process jurisdiction.

[73] [1963] AC 160.

[74] (1800) Russ and Ry 1, 168 ER 651 (CCR).

[75] See Harris, O'Boyle, and Warbrick, *Law of the European Convention on Human Rights* (1995) chap. 7.

[76] See above, §§ 2.2–3.

law and law which cannot be known to the defendant at the time of her conduct.[76] Article 7 protection should be extended to such cases.

§ 18.3 Intoxication

The voluntary consumption of alcohol is closely associated with the subsequent commission of crimes—particularly crimes of violence and vandalism.[77] Intoxication, even involuntary intoxication,[78] will never provide a defence in its own terms. It is never enough to claim, however convincingly, that the offending behaviour in issue would not have occurred but for one's intoxicated condition. The adage, "a drunken intent is still an intent,"[79] reflects an unyielding resistance to the proposition that an intoxicated condition of itself gives rise to any form of exculpation. Indeed, for many hundreds of years, the fact of intoxication was regarded as something which aggravated rather than mitigated the commission of a crime.[80]

Intoxication may, however, form the evidential basis for claims of lack of mens rea. D may assert that because of his drunken condition he did not intend to kill or seriously hurt V when he attacked him and, accordingly, he should not be found guilty of murder. Additionally, D may argue that because of confusion induced by his condition, he thought that V was about to attack him and, on that basis, be allowed a defence of mistake of fact. The extent and frequency of such claims expand if questions relating to proof of mens rea and pleas of mistake are resolved by way of a subjective test. Section 8 of the Criminal Justice Act 1967, it will be recalled,[81] requires proof of what D intended or foresaw to be established by reference to what D *himself* intended or foresaw. The fact that a particular result was a natural and probable result of D's conduct is merely evidence that D *may* have intended or foreseen that result; it will not establish *ipso facto* that he did have intent or foresight. Recall too the decisions in *Gladstone Williams* and *Beckford*:[82] mistaken beliefs in the need for defensive or preventive force are to be judged on the basis of what D himself believed and are not subject to any limitation of reasonableness.

Consequently, if intoxicated wrongdoers were tried on the basis of the subjective principles outlined above, those principles might pave the way for many acquittals. For instance, a claim that D thought she was under attack might gain a vestige of credibility only because of D's assertion that her intoxicated state led to confusion and misperception. Likewise, a person charged with rape might claim a belief in consent made credible only by the obtuseness associated with large intakes of alcohol.

---

[77] "Alcohol is a cortical depressant. Since it is the higher and most recently evolved brain functions which are first affected by depressants, the immediate effect of a dose of alcohol is to inhibit those cerebral functions which are associated with orderly community behaviour and with finer critical judgments": Mason, *Forensic Medicine for Lawyers* (3rd ed., 1995) 351. Numerous studies have indicated that many violent offenders have taken significant amounts of drink or drugs at the time of the offence. There is, of course, no straightforward causal link: personal, gender, and cultural factors will strongly influence how intoxicated persons behave. See further Hodge, "Alcohol and Violence" in Taylor (ed.), *Violence in Society* (1993) 127; Dingwall, *Alcohol and Crime* (2005).

[78] Below, § 18.3(v).

[79] *Sheehan* [1975] 2 All ER 960, 963 (CA); *Kingston* [1995] 2 AC 355.

[80] Barlow, "Drug Intoxication and the Principle of *Capacitas Rationalis*" (1984) 100 *LQR* 639.

[81] Above, § 5.1(ix).

[82] Above, § 18.1(iii).

Unsurprisingly, the courts have proved reluctant to give full rein to a subjective approach when dealing with pleas supported evidentially by a state of voluntary intoxication. What has emerged is an uneasy compromise between the standard account of mens rea and the requirements of deterrence and social protection. Using the language that has evolved in this area of law, for offences which are designated crimes of *specific intent*, the normal principles of mens rea obtain. A state of intoxication may be adduced as evidence in order to rebut an inference of intent that otherwise would be drawn. If D may have been too drunk to intend the outcome, he will be acquitted of the offence. By contrast, for offences of *basic intent*, evidence of intoxication will not negate an inference of basic intent. Indeed, far from rebutting such an inference, on one account of the law, the state of intoxication will *constitute* the culpability required for the crime.

These matters will be addressed in more detail below. First, however, a brief discussion of what constitutes a state of "intoxication" may be helpful. No definition of intoxication exists in the case law. There is no statement concerning what level of disinhibition or confusion induced by drink or drugs is sufficient for legal purposes. For cases of specific intent, no such definition is required. The question will be whether the impact of any drink or drugs taken by D makes it reasonably possible that he did not form the intent the offence requires. The same should apply for crimes of basic intent were it the law that evidence of the voluntary consumption of drink or drugs is simply disregarded when determining whether a basic intent has been proved. However, it may be that such evidence, far from being disregarded, provides the very culpability required for the crime. If that be so, then some minimum threshold of intoxication should be required; for a crime of basic intent, the prosecution should not be relieved from its burden of proof by establishing that D had taken *some* quantity of drink or drugs prior to the conduct alleged.[83] The matter is obscure and will be revisited when analysing the leading case of *Majewski*.[84]

In deeming when an issue of intoxication arises, no distinction is drawn between alcohol and drugs such as heroin, cocaine, cannabis, and LSD.[85] Drugs such as Librium and Valium, and compounds such as insulin, when taken for therapeutic reasons, are in different case. If drugs are taken to treat the symptoms of some underlying condition of D, the normal principles of mens rea will apply and the special rules relating to voluntary intoxication will not be relevant.[86]

(i) Voluntary intoxication and crimes of specific intent

For crimes of specific intent, the position is straightforward. In *Beard*,[87] the House of Lords ruled that on a charge of murder (a crime of specific intent), evidence of D's drunkenness *was* relevant to whether D had intended to kill or seriously hurt V. Lord Birkenhead's

---

[83] There is an *obiter* remark in *Stubbs* (1989) 88 Cr App R 53, 54 that the intoxication needed to be "very extreme".
[84] [1977] AC 443 (HL).
[85] *Lipman* [1970] 1 QB 152 (CA).
[86] See below, § 18.3(iv).
[87] [1920] AC 479.
[88] *Ibid.*, 501–2 (emphasis added).
[89] [1975] 2 All ER 960.
[90] [1935] AC 462; above, § 3.2.

leading judgment caused some confusion for later courts by stating that evidence of drunkenness would be relevant in crimes of specific intent if it "showed that [D] was *incapable* of forming a specific intent."[88] In *Sheehan*,[89] however, the Court of Appeal ruled that language of Lord Birkenhead should be read in the light of the decision in *Woolmington*[90] regarding the burden of proof in criminal cases. Accordingly, the question in specific intent cases is not whether D was capable of forming the required specific intent but *whether D in fact formed the intent.* Evidence of intoxication may throw a reasonable doubt on the prosecution's case just like any other evidence germane to the issue of intent.

Accordingly, *if* a crime is a crime of specific intent, the position is clear. What is less clear is *when* a crime is one of specific rather than basic intent. The leading case on this issue is the House of Lords decision in *Majewski*.[91]

Lord Elwyn-Jones, giving the judgment of the House, considered that a crime of specific intent was a crime where the mens rea extends beyond the actus reus[92]—i.e. crimes of *ulterior* intent.[93] The idea is certainly intelligible. Burglary, for instance, must be considered a crime of specific intent because all that is required by way of an actus reus is a trespassory entry into a building. The offence is complete on entry if it can be proved that D intended to steal.[94] Moreover, according to the Court of Appeal in *Heard*,[95] a crime is a crime of specific intent even if recklessness is sufficient for an element going beyond the actus reus. The court used as an example the intentional or reckless causing of criminal damage being reckless as to whether life was endangered.[96] As the offence does not require that life actually be endangered but merely an act of criminal damage which is believed to carry that risk, on the analysis in *Heard* the crime is one of specific intent,[97] endorsing the view of Lord Edmund Davies in *Caldwell*.[98]

But despite the intelligibility of this definition, it fails to explain the case law. It is well established that murder is a crime of specific intent.[99] Yet in murder, the mens rea need not extend to the entirety of the actus reus, let alone beyond it, because an intent to cause grievous bodily harm will suffice.[100] Further, on Lord Elwyn-Jones's definition the same crime could be of either specific intent or basic intent depending on how it is committed. Section 18 of the OAPA 1861 penalises wounding with intent to cause grievous bodily harm and, additionally, causing grievous bodily harm with intent to cause grievous bodily harm. Where the actus reus of the offence takes the form of a wound insufficiently serious to constitute grievous bodily harm, the intent to be provided is a specific intent of the form indicted by Lord Elwyn-Jones. But where the actus reus has taken the form of grievous bodily harm, the intent to be proved need only correspond to the actus reus and does not go

---

[91] [1977] AC 443.
[92] *Ibid.*, 471, citing Lord Simon's speech in *Morgan* [1976] AC 182, 216.
[93] See above, § 5.1(vii).
[94] Theft Act 1968, s. 9; above, § 14.3.
[95] [2007] EWCA Crim 125; above, § 12.8.
[96] Criminal Damage Act 1971, s. 1(2)(b).
[97] [2007] EWCA Crim 125, para. 31.
[98] [1982] AC 341.
[99] *Beard* [1920] AC 479; *Gallagher* [1963] AC 349; *Sheehan* [1975] 2 All ER 960.
[100] Above, § 10.3(i)(a).
[101] *Bratty* v. *A-G for Northern Ireland* [1973] AC 386; *Pordage* [1975] Crim LR 575; *Davies* [1991] Crim LR 469.
[102] [1977] AC 443.

beyond it. It is no longer a specific intent crime in his Lordship's terms. Yet it is accepted that section 18 is a crime of specific intent whatever form its takes.[101]

Alternatively, Lord Simon, giving judgment in *Majewski*, considered that an offence of specific intent was a crime where the mens rea required proof of a "purposive element",[102] a view also endorsed in *Heard*.[103] There the court seemingly took the view that the whole territory of specific intent could be mapped by reference to ulterior intent, just discussed, and intent in the sense of purpose. But this will not do either. Murder may be committed in a fashion which fits neither category because the mental element for this offence can be established without proof of purpose: foresight of virtual certainty suffices. Furthermore, where an offence contrary to section 18 of the OAPA 1861 takes the form of causing grievous bodily harm with intent to do grievous bodily harm, foresight of the virtual certainty of causing harm of that gravity suffices.[104] But there is no doubt that an offence under section 18 is always a crime of specific intent.

In the light of this confusion, the only safe course is to follow relevant precedents. On that basis, a list of established specific intent crimes can be drawn up. Murder, wounding or causing grievous bodily harm with intent to cause grievous bodily harm, theft,[105] burglary,[106] and handling stolen goods[107] are crimes of specific intent. Most other crimes requiring proof of mens rea are crimes of basic intent. To the extent that this area of law can be explained in conceptual terms, we offer the following generalisation: crimes designated crimes of specific intent are crimes where the mens rea is exclusively (as in murder) or predominantly (as in burglary) expressed in terms of intent. Where intent is the exclusive or predominant form of culpability, on the basis of precedent we can say that the offence is a crime of specific intent even if the intent is not ulterior or purposive, despite the dicta in *Majewski* and *Heard* which would lead one to suppose that for an intent to be a specific intent it must be of the ulterior or purposive kind. The fact that one element of an offence requires intent will not of itself make for a crime of specific intent (unless the intent is an ulterior or purposive intent; in which case the offence will be a crime of specific intent at least for that element) if the predominant parts of the offence do not require proof of intent.

In *Heard*,[108] the court considered the offence of sexual assault.[109] To prove the offence, an intentional touching (*inter alia*) is required, but intention is not required for the other elements of the offence. As the Court of Appeal considered the intent for the touching need not be purposive, the offence was concluded to be a crime of basic intent. Additionally, in the light of precedent, particularly the House of Lords decision in *Majewski*,[110] we can say that where an intent other than of the purposive or ulterior kind, recklessness, or something lesser than intent or recklessness suffices as the predominant form of culpability for the offence, it is a crime of basic intent.

---

[103] [2007] EWCA Crim 125, para. 31.
[104] Above, § 11.6(ii).
[105] *Ruse* v. *Read* [1949] 1 KB 377 (DC).
[106] *Durante* [1972] 3 All ER 962 (CA).
[107] *Ibid.*
[108] [2007] EWCA Crim 125.
[109] Contrary to s. 3 of the Sexual offences Act 2003; above, § 12.3.
[110] [1977] AC 443.

Despite these complexities, the basic intent/specific intent divide has worked tolerably well in practice. In the area of violent offences where intoxication is frequently a background factor, it is well established that assault, battery, assault occasioning bodily harm, malicious wounding or inflicting grievous bodily harm, and involuntary manslaughter are crimes of basic intent, allowing convictions for these offences despite D's intoxicated condition. By contrast, murder and wounding or causing grievous bodily harm with intent are specific intent offences, where D may seek to deflect an inference of intent by reference to his intoxicated condition. Likewise, generalising from the decision in *Heard*,[111] we can say that as well as sexual assault (the offence at issue in the case), rape, assault by penetration, and causing a person to engage in sexual activety are all crimes of basic intent, since the structure of those offences sufficiently parallels sexual assault to fall within the analysis in *Heard*.[112]

That said, the structure is rickety. Crimes divide into the camps of specific intent or basic intent but the logic of the analysis in *Heard* should lead to the conclusion that one element of an offence may be a specific intent element and another element a basic intent element with the relevance of intoxication dependent upon which element is in question. Indeed, it seems that the same element may be one of basic intent or specific intent according to the facts of the case. In the crime of sexual assault whether the assault is "sexual" depends on whether it is objectively sexual or, where the act is equivocal, by refence to the purpose of the actor.[113] Where the act alleged is objectively sexual, evidence of drunkenness will not be relevant to deflect any inference that would otherwise be made that the touching was intentional. If the act is equivocal, as in *Court*,[114] in principle evidence of intoxication should be relevant to the question whether D's purpose was sexual. But whether such an approach will be taken by the courts is conjectural. It may be that a court will take a coarse-grained approach and rule that because sexual assault has been designated a crime of basic intent, evidence of intoxication is not to be used to deflect any finding of mens rea in respect of *any* element of the offence.

Equally conjectural is the position where the prosecution seeks to prove that an offence able to be committed intentionally or recklessly was, in fact, committed intentionally. Consider the offence of causing criminal damage with intent or recklessness.[115] A prosecutor may decide to charge the offence exclusively in terms of intent in order to obtain a jury finding that the damage was done intentionally. In those circumstances, is a crime (otherwise) of basic intent to be treated as a crime of specific intent? The uncertainty that exists on these issues indicates the need for legislative intervention in this area.

---

[111] [2007] EWCA Crim 125.

[112] §§ 12.1–4.

[113] Sexual Offences Act 2003, s. 78.

[114] [1989] 1 AC 28. See the discussion above, § 12.5.

[115] Criminal Damage Act 1971, s. 1.

[116] Ward, "Making Sense of Self-induced Intoxication" [1986] *CLJ* 247; Smith, "Intoxication and the Mental Element in Crime" in Wallington and Merkin (eds.), *Essays in Memory of Professor F.H. Lawson* (1986) 119; Gardner, "The Importance of Majewski" (1994) 14 *OJLS* 279.

[117] [1977] AC 443.

(ii) Voluntary intoxication and crimes of basic intent[116]

In *Majewski*,[117] D was charged with assault, an offence that can be committed recklessly or intentionally and which is therefore a crime of basic intent. D had consumed large quantities of drink and drugs. He attacked V in circumstances which, from an external perspective, indicated a deliberate assault. He claimed neither to have intended nor foreseen that he would inflict any force upon V; at the time of the incident he claimed he was "a drunken automaton", not conscious of what he was doing. It was argued for D that section 8 of the Criminal Justice Act 1967 requires that proof of D's intention or foresight must be established by reference "to all the evidence", including evidence of his intoxicated condition.

Lord Elwyn-Jones, for a unanimous House of Lords, rejected this argument. He noted that a distinction between specific intent crimes and basic intent crimes had been created long before the enactment of section 8. His Lordship observed that there was a longstanding principle of substantive law that evidence of intoxication was relevant only where the offence charged was one of specific intent. Accordingly, the statutory phrase "by reference to all the evidence" should be read as a reference to "all the *relevant* evidence".[118] The evidence of intoxication was irrelevant and, consequently, the conviction for assault could be confirmed.

That was enough to decide the case, and if matters had rested there the position for basic intent offences would have been relatively straightforward. In a case of a seemingly deliberate assault like *Majewski*,[119] a defendant would not be permitted to assert a lack of mens rea on the basis of intoxication. The prosecution would still have to establish the intention or recklessness that a conviction for assault requires but that would typically be a formality if, as on the facts of *Majewski*, the only conceivable explanation accounting for an absence of mens rea was the intoxicated condition of the defendant.

Unfortunately, the matter did not rest there. For Lord Elwyn-Jones, it was not simply a case of disregarding evidence of intoxication; rather, the condition of intoxication would *constitute* the culpability required for the offence:[120]

> "If a man of his own volition takes a substance which causes him to cast off the restraints of reason and conscience, no wrong is done to him by holding him answerable criminally for any injury he may do while in that condition. His course of conduct in reducing himself by drugs and drink to that condition in my view supplies the evidence of mens rea, of guilty mind certainly sufficient for crimes of basic intent. It is a reckless course of conduct and recklessness is enough to constitute the necessary mens rea in assault cases."

It will readily be appreciated that the recklessness involved is not the recklessness that would otherwise be required to establish assault. There is no need to prove that D foresaw any threat of force inflicted on V. The essence of this form of recklessness appears to be that D, by taking drugs or alcohol, has "cast off the restraints of reason and conscience." On one interpretation, this could mean that whenever the prosecution can establish that D would not have perpetrated the actus reus of a basic intent offence but for the taking of drink or drugs, it is relieved from any obligation to establish the mens rea that it would otherwise

---

[118] *Ibid.*, 476.
[119] D had quarrelled with V, had verbally indicated that he would hit V and, indeed, went on to hit him.
[120] [1977] AC 443, 474–5.

have to prove. The inculpatory sweep of such a principle could be very broad. To date, the outer limits of this form of "recklessness" have not been explored in the case law. The reported cases deal with defendants significantly affected by the substances taken. In such cases, the practical difference between merely excluding evidence of intoxication when determining D's mens rea and treating intoxication as a species of mens rea is small. Nonetheless, the creation of this form of drunken recklessness is an unnecessary complication. It would have been better had Lord Elwyn-Jones confined his judgment to a ruling that, in crimes of basic intent, the defendant cannot adduce evidence of his voluntary intoxication in order to cast doubt on an inference of intention or recklessness that would otherwise be drawn. As things stand, we are left with uncertainty about when the taking of drink or drugs will lead to a finding of recklessness.

It is submitted that the better view of current law is that for crimes of basic intent, evidence of intoxication cannot be adduced to rebut an inference of intent or recklessness. Such a ruling was sufficient for the House of Lords to answer the certified question in *Majewski*. But there are *obiter* passages to the effect that, for crimes of basic intent, evidence of intoxication will establish mens rea. It remains possible, therefore, that under current law the prosecution can adduce evidence of intoxication to prove basic intent.[121]

(iii) Mistake, accident, and intoxication

(a) Basic intent offences

Majewski was not a case that involved any form of mistake. D claimed that his mind was blank, not that he had formed any false view of his circumstances induced by drink and drugs. Accordingly, it would have been possible to read *Majewski* as inapplicable to mistake cases, an approach adopted by Mustill J (as he then was) in *Jaggard* v. *Dickinson*.[122] D had caused damage to a house in order to gain entry. In her intoxicated state she believed the house belonged to a friend who would have consented to her unusual method of gaining access. Section 5(2) of the Criminal Damage Act 1971 provides a defence to a charge of criminal damage if D believes the owner of the property would have consented to her actions. In allowing her appeal, Mustill J denied that quashing her conviction was to allow voluntary intoxication to preclude mens rea in crime of basic intent. Her intoxication merely lent credence to her belief. Her conviction was quashed because she *believed* she had the owner's consent and not because she was drunk.

Jaggard is in line with the standard approach to the exculpatory effect of mistakes taken in modern English criminal law. As we saw in § 18.1(iii), typically a genuine even if

---

[121] It is not known whether a prosecution has taken this course at trial. Certainly the *dicta* of Lord Elwyn-Jones suggests that it can. See also Lord Simon's judgment, at 478: "There is no juristic reason why mental incapacity (short of *M'Naghten* insanity), brought about by self-induced intoxication, to realise what one is doing or its probable consequences should not be such a state of mind stigmatised as wrongful by the criminal law; and there is every practical reason why it should be." But contrast Lord Salmon who emphasised, appositely, that the House was deciding whether intoxication could be relied upon by way of *defence*. Lord Salmon's is the better view.

[122] [1981] QB 527 (DC).

[123] In *Richardson* [1999] 1 Cr App R 392, an intoxicated belief by D that V had consented to take part in rough horseplay was allowed as a defence to a charge of maliciously inflicting grievous bodily harm—a crime of basic intent. The Court of Appeal in so ruling did not consider authority, discussed in § 18.3(iii)(b) below, which

unreasonable mistake will exempt the defendant should it negate a definitional element of the offence or generate a belief that the elements of a recognised defence are present. Drunken mistakes could be regarded as within the class of unreasonable mistakes. However, Mustill J's approach has not been generally accepted.[123] Working against it has been a concern over the propensity of intoxicated persons to make mistakes leading to violent or forceful conduct. This has led the appellate courts to treat cases of intoxicated mistakes as being within the mischief addressed by the House of Lords in *Majewski*. Doing so accords with the view, expressed by Lord Elwyn-Jones in that case, that intoxication, in the context of basic intent offences, is a form of culpability.

How far does the exclusion extend? The matter is undecided. Potentially, for basic intent offences, any mistake made by D should be disregarded if it is established that D was intoxicated at the material time. But that would go too far. Rather, the mistake should be disregarded if the prosecution can establish that but for D's intoxicated condition, his mistake would not have been made. That is the position under section 6(5) of the Public Order Act 1986 for offences under that Act. The principle should be regarded as of general application.[124]

What should be the case for accidents? What if D accidentally bumps into V when intoxicated? If the accident would have occurred in any event—V rushed round a blind corner— a battery should not be attributed to D merely because he was intoxicated. But what if the intoxication was part of the explanation as in *Brady*,[125] where D climbed a balcony above a dance floor, stood on the balcony rail, and fell onto a dancer below, causing permanent disabling injury? Neither the climb nor the fall would have occurred but for D's intoxication. Because of the way the matter was argued at trial, the Court of Appeal was limited to considering whether D's fall could be regarded as a malicious act for the purposes of maliciously inflicting grievous bodily harm within section 20 of the OAPA 1861. It was ruled that the fall did not come within the ruling in *Majewski*:[126] it was an accident, not an attack. The outcome might have been different had the court been able to consider the precursor to the fall, the non-accidental climb, which was considered, entirely reasonably, to be a cause of D's injury. Then the issue would have been whether D would have foreseen the risk of falling and injuring someone had he made the climb sober. If that would have been the case, he would be liable for maliciously inflicting grievous bodily harm.

That accidents, even if attributable to a state of intoxication, fall outside the scope of *Majewski* receives strong if *obiter* support from *Heard*,[127] where, in considered remarks, the view was taken that any accidental touching would not be treated as a deliberate touching even if D would not have made the contact with V but for his inebriated state. Even in such circumstances, "the mind must go with the body" if the touching is to be regarded as

---

disallows mistaken beliefs as to defences; nor did it consider rape cases such as *Woods* (1982) 74 Cr App R 312 (CA) and *Fotheringham* (1988) 88 Cr App R 206 (CA), which disfavour intoxicated beliefs in consent as valid defences. Consequently *Richardson*, and *Jaggard* too, must be regarded as doubtful authorities.

[124] As the Law Commission has recommended. A provision to apply this principle to non-fatal offences against the person is made in the Home Office Bill: see further below, § 18.3(viii).

[125] [2006] EWCA Crim 2413.

[126] [1977] AC 443.

[127] [2007] EWCA Crim 215.

[128] *Ibid.*, para. 17.

[129] (1969) 55 Cr App R 600.

deliberate.[128] Intriguingly, the Court of Appeal felt that the element of deliberateness would be lacking in a case such as *Lipman*[129] where D in an LSD-induced trance took himself to be grappling with a snake whereas in reality he was strangling V. But the killing in *Lipman* was not an accident; it was the product of conduct actively performed by D, albeit in a state of hallucination. There is no reason to doubt that the verdict of manslaughter reached in that case would not be repeated on similar facts.

(b) Specific intent offences

In respect of specific intent crimes, one might confidently expect that intoxication would be treated as evidence relevant to any exculpatory claim based on a mistake. So far as any mistake concerns the definitional elements of such an offence, that is certainly the position. Unfortunately, however, in two cases, *O'Grady*[130] and *O'Connor*,[131] the Court of Appeal has taken the view that mistakes which relate to defences are to be disregarded if the mistakes are induced by D's intoxicated state even where the crime is one of specific intent. In *O'Grady*, D's conviction for manslaughter was confirmed on the basis that his drunken belief that he was being attacked by V would not found a defence of mistake. As manslaughter is a crime of basic intent, the ruling is unexceptionable. However, the court, in considered *dicta*, stated that his drunken belief would be disregarded even on a charge of murder. In *O'Connor*, this view was taken to be binding even though the remarks made about murder in *O'Grady* were clearly *obiter*. *O'Connor* involved an appeal against murder: in the event, the appeal succeeded on the ground that evidence of his intoxicated state was relevant to the question whether D intended to kill or cause grievous bodily harm. So, again, remarks about the irrelevance of drunken mistakes relating to elements of defences were *obiter*.

Unfortunately these *dicta* were approved and applied in *Hatton*,[132] where D was not permitted to raise a drink-induced belief that he was under attack by way of defence to murder. Although this must now bw accepted as the state of the law, absurd distinctions arise. Take the facts of *Lipman*.[133] D, under the influence of LSD, thought he was under attack from a snake and in that deluded condition strangled V. He was acquitted of murder (although guilty of manslaughter) on the ground that he lacked an intent to kill or cause serious harm to a human being. If his delusion had taken the form of an attack by a human being, then, according to *O'Grady*, *O'Connor*, and now conclusively *Hatton*, he should have been found guilty of murder. Recall that, in *Gladstone Williams*[134] and *Beckford*,[135] the Court of Appeal and the Privy Council refused to treat mistakes going to defences any differently from mistakes going to definitional elements. That approach is equally in point for intoxicated mistakes when raised on a charge involving a specific intent offence.

[130] [1987] QB 995; see the note by Milgate at [1987] *CLJ* 381.
[131] [1991] Crim LR 135.
[132] [2005] EWCA Crim 2951. For incisive critical commentary see Spencer, "Drunken Defence" [2006] *Cambridge LJ* 267; Dingwall, "Intoxicated Mistakes about the Need for Self-defence" (2007) 70 *MLR* 127.
[133] [1970] 1 QB 152 (CA).
[134] [1987] 3 All ER 411 (CA). See above, § 18.1(iii).
[135] [1988] AC 130 (PC).
[136] [1983] 2 All ER 503 (CA).
[137] [1984] 3 All ER 848 (CA).

(iv) Intoxication arising from drugs taken for therapeutic reasons

In *Bailey*,[136] D, a diabetic, took insulin for his condition, but neglected to follow the dietary regime his doctor prescribed. In *Hardie*,[137] D, upset and agitated, took an excessive quantity of Librium belonging to someone else in an attempt to pacify himself. In the former case, D became hypoglycaemic (a condition regarded as one of automatism) and attacked V. In the latter case, D set fire to V's flat. He claimed that the drugs disorientated him, rendering him incapable of appreciating the destructive nature of his conduct.

In both cases, the Court of Appeal ruled that the trial judges had erred in directing that *Majewski* applied. Instead, the normal principles of mens rea were taken to be the applicable standard. Accordingly, the convictions were quashed.

The key to both decisions is a commendable reluctance to subject persons taking drugs for therapeutic benefit to the regime of social protection endorsed by the House of Lords in *Majewski*. *Bailey*, in particular is instructive on this point. In *Bailey*, D was not immune from criticism; his hypoglycaemic condition would have been avoided had he followed his doctor's instructions. Yet the court took appropriate and compassionate cognisance of the fact that, for a diabetic, the taking of insulin and the management of its destabilising effects is a lifetime burden. In *Hardie*, there are some distracting *dicta* to the effect that tranquilising drugs such as Librium and Valium differ in their pharmacological properties from alcohol: the former drugs are of "soporific effect" whereas the latter gives rise to "aggression and violence".[138] But this is a false distinction. The physiological properties of tranquillising drugs and alcohol are similar; their effects ensue from depressing the central nervous system. The essential point about *Hardie* is that D was taking the drug to calm his nerves, the reason why the drug is prescribed. Had the very same drugs been consumed "on the street" in order to enjoy their disinhibiting effects, then the *Majewski* regime would surely have been invoked. Of course, alcohol is often taken to "calm the nerves". But it is not a therapeutic drug. Rest assured, alcohol will incur *Majewski* for whatever reason it is consumed.

(v) Involuntary intoxication

Potentially, the largest group of persons who may claim that their intoxication is involuntary are those addicted to alcohol or other intoxicants. In *Tandy*,[139] the exculpatory potential of alcoholism was discussed in the context of the statutory defence of diminished responsibility. The view was taken that alcoholism might reduce culpability, but only if it produced involuntary drinking, a condition where D had no choice when to take her first drink of the day and was unable to refrain from drinking thereafter. A similar approach seems likely in other contexts. The conditions are so stringent that few, if any, alcoholics would satisfy them.[140]

An involuntary state of intoxication does not come within the *Majewski* regime. A firm view is taken of what constitutes "involuntary" intoxication. If D is aware that she is taking

---

[138] *Ibid.*, 853 (Parker LJ).

[139] [1989] 1 All ER 267 (CA).

[140] See further Sullivan, "Intoxicants and Diminished Responsibility" [1994] *Crim LR* 156; Mackay, *Mental Condition Defences in the Criminal Law* (1995) 196–7

[141] *Allen* [1988] Crim LR 698 (CA).

intoxicating substances any subsequent inebriation will be taken to be voluntary even if a mistake has been made about the strength of the item taken.[141]

There are, however, some settled cases of involuntary intoxication. A medically pre-scribed drug taken for therapeutic reasons may give rise to involuntary intoxication if no warning is given as to any destabilising properties of the drug. The same applies if D suffers an unpredictable, aberrant reaction to the drug[142] or if, without her knowledge, she is slip-ped a destabilising drug.[143]

(a) No discrete defence

In *Kingston*,[144] D took himself to be drinking a normal cup of coffee which in fact had been laced with destabilising drugs by a malevolent third party. D, a person with paedophile incli-nations, became disinhibited and performed non-penetrative sexual acts on an unconscious (drugged) teenage boy. The House of Lords confirmed his conviction for indecent assault. At trial, it was found that, notwithstanding the disinhibiting effects of the drugs, he intended his sexual actions. Therefore, said their Lordships, he was guilty of the offence. The only concession to the fact that he was involuntarily intoxicated took the form of not pre-suming mens rea on the basis of *Majewski*. It was irrelevant to proof of mens rea that the fault for D's condition lay with others. The term mens rea was treated as a technical expression denoting nothing more than the mental element specified for the offence in question, a mental element which was present on the facts.[145]

A more expansive view of the exculpatory effect of a state of involuntary intoxication had been taken by the Court of Appeal.[146] They were prepared to allow a defence to any crime for a person involuntarily intoxicated if it were the case that the crime committed by D would not have been perpetrated by him had he not been intoxicated. The breadth of this newly created, and short-lived, defence was alarmingly wide. Nonetheless, there is something to be said for the principle. A person who commits a crime (perhaps one less heinous than intentional killing, intentional causing of serious bodily harm, or non-consensual penetrative sex) arguably should be allowed a defence if a state of involuntary intoxication induced conduct on his part which otherwise would not have occurred and which was not characteristic of him.[147] Be that as it may, however, the House of Lords in *Kingston* took the view that any development along those or other lines was a matter for the legislature and not for the courts. The Law Commission has recommended that the current position should remain; involuntary intoxication may be adduced as evidence for all crimes of specific intent to rebut an inference of mens rea or support a claim of mistake but should not constitute any form of substantive defence.[148]

---

[142] In principle this should apply to the condition known as "pathological intoxication", where relatively small quantities of alcohol may activate a form of latent epilepsy or other conditions. However, such a phenomenon may be regarded as a form of insanity: Mackay, *Mental Condition Defences in the Criminal Law* (1995) 165–9; and see below, Chapter 19.

[143] Cf. *Kingston* [1995] 2 AC 355, 369ff (HL).

[144] *Ibid.*

[145] *Ibid.,* 366.

[146] [1994] QB 81.

[147] Sullivan, "Making Excuses" in Simester and Smith (eds.), *Harm and Culpability* (1996) 131; Sullivan, "Invol-untary Intoxication and Beyond" [1994] *Crim LR* 272; below, § 21.2(i)(b).

[148] Law Com. No. 229, *Intoxication and Criminal Liability* (1995) para. 8.36.

(vi) Intoxication and mental condition defences

Suppose that D is intoxicated. Should another mental state supervene, it need not follow that her intoxication should preclude reliance on any defence that may arise from the subsequent mental condition. In *Stripp*,[149] D, while intoxicated, fell over and sustained concussion. It was held that if the dominant cause of his automatous state was concussion rather than alcohol, he would be able to raise a plea of automatism and would not fall foul of the *Majewski* principles. A similar approach was taken in *Burns*,[150] where the cumulative effects of brain damage, alcohol, and medication rendered D an automaton. He was permitted to defend himself on the basis of automatism because his condition was primarily due to the effects of his medication. By contrast, in *Lipman*,[151] D's state of automatism was attributable to the drug he had taken; consequently the mens rea and the actus reus elements of manslaughter were attributed to him on the basis that he was voluntarily intoxicated at the material time.

Glanville Williams criticised the approach taken in *Burns*, arguing that "a verdict of insanity should be the correct one even if the outburst was triggered by taking [drink or drugs] if there is a sufficient likelihood of repetition."[152] Of course, Williams is right to point out that if the explanation of D's mental condition at the time of the offence is her disease of mind then the applicable defence is insanity. But if the predominant reason for her mental condition was some other cause, why should she not be permitted a defence related to that reason? If the dangerous propensities of such an individual give rise to concern, the appropriate response is to invoke the civil commitment procedures[153] rather than to extend the reach of the insanity defence.

(vii) Intoxication, negligence, and strict liability

As we have seen, intoxication may preclude or, in cases of basic intent, effectively provide the culpability required for an offence. Where an offence does not require any form of intent or foresight to be proved, voluntary intoxication is effectively irrelevant to any objective standard of culpability. If an offence provides for conviction on the basis of negligence, D's intoxication may explain why she did not attain the standard to be expected of a reasonable person.[154] In such cases there is no point in D drawing attention to her condition of intoxication; it will merely strengthen the case against her. The reasonable person is not voluntarily drunk.

Possibly, a different view may be taken regarding involuntary intoxication. As we have seen, "a drunken intent is still an intent" and no concession to that rule is made for

---

[149] (1978) 69 Cr App R 318 (CA).

[150] (1973) 58 Cr App R 364 (CA).

[151] [1970] 1 QB 152 (CA).

[152] (1973) 58 Cr App R 364.

[153] Mental Health Act 1983, s. 3. It may be objected that the the most dangerous class of mental disorder, "psychopathic disorder", is subject to a "treatability" criterion as a precondition of detention under s. 3. The Home Office has recently proposed measures for the civil confinement of members of that class without a treatability requirement: *Managing Dangerous People with Severe Personality Disorder* (1999). See generally below, § 19.1.

[154] Above, § 5.5(i).

involuntary intoxication.[155] However, negligence is a term of moral evaluation, a dimension absent from the word "intent". The fact that her state of intoxication was involuntary may deflect the grounds of criticism inherent in negligence. The standard applied should be the reasonable, involuntarily intoxicated person. The law, however, is uncertain. The case of *Elliott* v. *C* [156] suggests that these concessions will not necessarily be made. *Hardie,*[157] on the other hand, offers *sub silentio* support for the position argued for here.

For crimes of strict liability, there is no elbow room even for a plea of involuntary intoxication; liability is imposed on the basis of commission of the actus reus. Should involuntary intoxication lead to a condition of automatism, however, an actus reus should not be attributed to D because her conduct would not have been a voluntary act.[158]

(viii) Reform

The law relating to intoxication is complex and replete with uncertainties of conception and ambit. It need not be so. In *O'Connor,*[159] the High Court of Australia was unimpressed with the English law on this topic. In a refreshingly straightforward approach, the Court decided that intoxicated defendants could be dealt with under the ordinary principles of mens rea. Intoxication, preponderantly, is raised in the contexts of violence and vandalism. The mens rea requirements for crimes such as assault, malicious wounding, and criminal damage are hardly sophisticated mental states and are well within the capacities even of persons in advanced states of intoxication. The High Court was content to trust juries to come to appropriate decisions in cases involving intoxicated defendants.[160]

In England and Wales, the *Majewski* principle is set to remain for the indefinite future. No law reform body has recommended the abolition of the intoxication rules: the return to first principles that has occurred in Canada and Australia seems most unlikely here.

The latest proposals are contained in the Home Office Draft Bill, reforming offences against the person (excluding homicide):[161]

"For the purposes of this Act, a person who was involuntarily intoxicated at any material time must be treated—
(a) as having been aware of any risk of which he would have been aware had he not been intoxicated; and

---

[155] Above, § 18.3(v).

[156] [1983] 2 All ER 1005 (CA). The Court of Appeal disregarded D's learning disability when applying the *Caldwell* recklessness test; see above, §§ 5.2(i), 5.5(ii).

[157] [1984] 3 All ER 848. The Court of Appeal quashed D's conviction for criminal damage as the trial judge had ruled inadmissible evidence that D had not foreseen the consequences of his conduct because of medication he had taken in order to clam himself. However, the Court of Appeal's decision could alternatively be explained on the basis of an oversight that *Caldwell* recklessness was the applicable standard.

[158] Above, § 4.3(iii)(d). See also the recommendation to this effect in Law Com. No. 229, *Intoxication and Criminal Liability* (1995) para. 8.36.

[159] (1980) 146 CLR 64; Orchard, "Surviving without *Majewski* Down Under" [1993] *Crim LR* 426.

[160] Similarly, in *Daviault* (1994) 118 DLR (4th) 469, the Supreme Court of Canada ruled that to depart from ordinary principles of mens rea (as *Majewski* does) would violate the Canadian Charter of Rights and Freedoms. However it seems that dispensing with *Majewski* has not been without its difficulties in Australia and Canada: Gough, "Surviving without *Majewski*?" [2002] *Crim LR* 719.

[161] Home Office, *Violence: Reforming the Offences against the Person Act 1861* (1998) Draft Bill, cl. 19.

(b) as having known or believed in any circumstances which he would have known or believed in had he not been intoxicated."

The first part of this provision, (a), seems broadly to be satisfactory if we accept that intoxicated defendants cannot satisfactorily be treated under the normal principles of mens rea. Although it takes the form of a deeming provision, at least it does not provide that evidence of intoxication of itself establishes recklessness. It will allow a defendant to argue that, despite his intoxication, he should not be adjudged reckless because even if sober, he would not have foreseen the risk.

Part (b) seems less satisfactory. Under current law, unreasonable beliefs formed on the basis of intoxication will, largely, be discounted for the purposes of denying liability.[162] The Home Office provision goes a step further. It imposes liability—even for specific intent offences—on the basis of what D (speculatively) would have known or believed in the circumstances in which he found himself, had he not been intoxicated. The expansionary effect of this provision can best be illustrated by an example based on the facts of *Church*,[163] where D fired a gun at V mistakenly assuming that he was not endangering V (D had misunderstood the mechanism of the gun). D's mistake was found to be grossly negligent and, as V died, he was guilty of manslaughter. Had V survived, D would not have been guilty of any offence against the person. Assume now that V survives, but is badly hurt, and that D was drunk when, misunderstanding the mechanism of the gun, he fired it. On such facts, the prosecution will surely argue that a sober D would have understood the gun's mechanism and consequently would have known, as a virtual certainty, that the bullet would strike V. On that basis, D could be charged with *intentionally* causing serious injury to V.

It seems that this goes beyond anything the Home Office intended.[164] The provision should be redrafted in terms of states of mind attributable to intoxication that D *actually formed*. In line with the current law, it should provide that intoxicated mistakes or beliefs relating to definitional or defence elements should lack exculpatory effect in crimes of basic intent. For crimes of specific intent, such mistakes or beliefs should be allowed full exculpatory effect, irrespective of whether they relate to definitional or defence elements.[165]

---

[162] This is certainly true for crimes of basic intent, whether the mistake relates to definitional (§ 18.3(ii)) or defence (§ 18.3(iii)(a)) elements. It is, of course, not true for the definitional elements of specific intent offences (§ 18.3(i)). As we saw earlier (§ 18.3(iii)(b)), in crimes of specific intent the position for mistakes relating to defence elements is unclear.

[163] [1966] 1 QB 59 (CA).

[164] According to Sir John Smith: "Offences Against the Person: The Home Office Consultation Paper" [1998] *Crim LR* 317, 321.

[165] Departing from contrary dicta in *O'Grady* [1987] QB 995 and *O'Connor* [1991] Crim LR 135.

19

MENTAL CONDITION DEFENCES

§ 19.1 Insanity

A defence of insanity[1] is a long-established feature of English law, of considerable symbolic importance. It signals that the rules of the criminal law are addressed to rational persons who have the capacity to understand and comply with rules.[2] Persons lacking such capacity may need to be restrained and confined but there is a long-held sentiment that they should not be designated criminals.[3]

The defence is rarely deployed, for several reasons. First, in English law, insanity is narrowly interpreted. Many persons with medical conditions whom we would regard as insane fall outside the scope of the defence, although, paradoxically, the defence can also embrace persons who are in no sense medically insane. Secondly, an insanity plea does not result in an unqualified acquittal. The acquittal conferred as a result of a successful plea is the special verdict of "not guilty by reason of insanity",[4] which leaves the defendant under the control of the court. Prior to the Criminal Procedure (Insanity and Unfitness to Plead) Act 1991, the disposal outcome was mandatory—a period of indefinite detention in a special hospital unless and until the Home Secretary ordered release. This inflexibility has now been changed by legislation: a range of non-penal measures is available to the judge at her discretion, ranging from an absolute discharge to a hospital order without restriction of time.[5] In theory, the availability of disposal outcomes such as supervision and treatment orders should increase recourse to the insanity defence and there is some evidence of a modest increase in the number of insanity pleas raised by the defence.[6] Nonetheless, the label "insane" remains profoundly unattractive to persons afflicted with mental illness, as is any prospect of an indefinite stay in a special hospital. Accordingly, many defendants whose mental condition may undercut any culpability for the offence charged choose to plead guilty or defend themselves on other grounds.

The position is hardly satisfactory. The high incidence of mentally disordered persons in

---

[1] Mackay, *Mental Condition Defences in the Criminal Law* (1995) chap. 2; Moore, *Law and Psychiatry* (1984) chap. 6; Morris, *Madness and the Criminal Law* (1982); Morse, "Excusing the Crazy: The Insanity Defence Reconsidered" (1985) 58 *So Cal LR* 777.

[2] Bonnie, "The Moral Basis of the Insanity Defence" (1983) 69 *ABAJ* 194.

[3] The first recorded case of outright acquittal by reason of insanity in England was in 1505: Walker, *Crime and Insanity in England* (1968) 26. It seems the defendant was set free.

[4] Trial of Lunatics Act 1883, s. 2(1).

[5] Criminal Procedure (Insanity) Act 1964 as amended by the Criminal Procedure (Insanity and Unfitness to Plead) 1991 and Domestic Violence, Crimes and Victims Act 2004. For a short description of the steps by which reform proceeded, see below, § 19.1(i)(b).

[6] Mackay and Kearns, "More Facts about the Insanity Defence" [1999] *Crim LR* 714.

the prison population who should be receiving treatment for their condition[7] demonstrates that, for mentally disordered offenders, the criminal justice system is failing both in terms of justice to individual defendants and in terms of health and social policy. Yet the marginalisation of the insanity defence does not mean that it can be ignored or considered only cursorily. The minimum standard of rationality demanded by law to warrant inclusion in the class of persons who are subject to punishment is a topic of intrinsic importance for the legitimacy of state punishment. Further, even the most practically minded criminal lawyer needs to be aware of what constitutes an insanity plea. Because of the public interest in subjecting dangerous persons to restraint, not only the defendant but also the judge and even the prosecution may raise the issue of insanity if the facts of the case indicate that grounds for the defence are present. Accordingly, a defendant seeking to plead automatism or a lack of mens rea may find that her plea is treated as a plea of insanity.[8] Theoretically, the same reaction may occur if she pleads diminished responsibility to a charge of murder.[9]

(i) Mental condition of defendant prior to trial

Before considering the insanity defence, a full appreciation of the relevance of any abnormality of mind on the part of D to the criminal justice process requires consideration of two situations where an evaluation of D's mental condition may postpone or terminate the trial itself.

(a) Removal to a mental hospital by order of Home Secretary

Under the provisions of the Mental Health Act 1983, the Home Secretary, if satisfied on the basis of reports from at least two medical practitioners that D is suffering from mental illness or severe mental impairment, may order that D be detained in hospital if the minister is of the opinion that it is in the public interest to do so.[10]

On the face of it, this is an extremely wide power that, it seems, is exercised with restraint. It is, in practice, reserved for cases of profound derangement or disability, situations where it is obvious that any trial would serve no useful purpose given the current condition of D. Should D make a sufficient recovery, the practice is for D then to be brought to trial.[11]

(b) Unfitness to plead [12]

Under sections 4 and 4A of the Criminal Procedure (Insanity) Act 1964,[13] a finding may be made, on the initiative of the defence, prosecution, or judge, that D is unfit to plead. Normally the matter will be dealt with on arraignment—before the trial begins and a plea is entered. If the judge makes a finding at this stage that D is fit to stand trial, a jury is

---

[7] HO/DHSS, *Interdepartmental Working Group into Mentally Disturbed Offenders in the Prison System* (1987).

[8] *Kemp* [1957] 1 QB 399; *Sullivan* [1984] AC 156.

[9] Criminal Procedure (Insanity) Act 1964, s. 6. It seems the provision is not used.

[10] Mental Health Act 1983, ss. 47, 48.

[11] *Report of the Committee on Mentally Disordered Offenders* Cmnd. 6244 (1975) para. 3.38.

[12] Mackay, *Mental Condition Defences in the Criminal Law* (1995) chap. 5.

[13] As amended by the Criminal Procedure (Insanity and Unfairness to Plead) Act 1991 and the Domestic Violence, Crimes and Victims Act 2004.

empanelled for the trial itself. However, the judge may consider that the strength of the prosecution case should be tested before the issue of fitness is resolved: should that be the case, the judge may postpone the issue until the opening of the defence case. If, at that later stage, the judge finds that D has no case to answer, D is acquitted. Should there be a case to answer, however, the court will then determine whether D is fit to plead before hearing the defence.

Criteria of unfitness are left unspecified in the Criminal Procedure (Insanity) Act 1964, which remainders the test of unfitness to the determination of the courts. From the early 19th century, the test has been narrowly cognitive, and focused on D's capacity to "plead to the indictment" and to be "of sufficient intellect to comprehend the course of the proceedings in the trial so as to make a proper defence, to challenge a juror to whom he may wish to object and comprehend the details of the evidence."[14] What this test, still approved in the 21st century,[15] does not do is test whether D has genuine "decisional competence"—the wherewithal to reflect with a degree of insight where his best interests lie.[16] For instance, the test will not assist a defendant who, because of his affliction, irrationally refuses to allow an otherwise relevant line of defence or to testify to a particular matter. Does a person who is found fit to plead but is otherwise lacking in decisional competence receive a fair trial as guaranteed by Article 6 of the ECHR? Although much will depend on the impact of the disability at the trial itself, there is, it is suggested, one useful general principle that should be applied. If, as a result of the impact of D's disability on the course of the trial, there may be reason to think that a verdict of guilty would not have been returned had D been possessed of adequate decisional competence, the trial should be adjudged unfair. Better still would be for English law to adopt the test propounded by the US Supreme Court when determining fitness to plead: whether D has "sufficient present ability to consult his lawyer with a reasonable degree of rational understanding—and whether he has a rational as well as factual understanding of the proceedings against him."[17]

Prior to 1991, a person found unfit to plead was held at the disposal of the Home Secretary without any determination of the evidence against them. Consequently, there were cases of persons being detained for substantial periods of time despite considerable doubt over the basis of the allegations made against them. A significant and welcome reform introduced by the Criminal Procedure (Insanity and Unfitness to Plead) Act 1991 provides that, upon there being a finding of unfitness to plead, the jury shall then decide on such evidence already given (if any) and such evidence introduced by the prosecution or defence whether D did the act or made the omission charged against him as the offence. If they are not satisfied that D did the act or omission constituting the actus reus of the offence, D is to be acquitted.

Although clearly an advance on the previous position, this reform is not without its difficulties. Inevitably, a person unfit to plead may experience difficulty in effectively participating in the proceedings. As the proceedings are not a criminal trial, the full protection of

---

[14] *Pritchard* (1836) 7 C & P 303.

[15] *M* [2003] EWCA Crim 3452; *Robertson* [1968] 3 All ER 557.

[16] For very persuasive advocacy of a test of decisional competence, see Mackay, "On Being Insane in Jersey Part 3: the Case of the *Attorney General v O'Driscoll*" [2004] *Crim LR* 219.

[17] *Dusky* v. *US* 362 US 402 (1960).

Article 6 of the ECHR is not engaged and a finding that D did the act or made the omission will not be disturbed despite D's difficulties in comprehending (and refuting) the evidence called against him.[18] The focus is solely on whether D "did the act or made the omission", and this has been held in the context of murder charges to rule out evidence suggesting diminished responsibility or provocation, on the basis that this would take the hearing into questions of D's mental state whereas the legislative provision confines the enquiry into whether the actus reus of the offence can be attributed to D.[19]

Upon a finding of unfitness to plead, together with a finding that D did the act or omission alleged, D becomes subject to the disposal of the court. Following enactment of the Criminal Procedure (Insanity and Unfitness to Plead) Act 1991, the range of disposal options is now considerable, although at first this flexibility was not extended where the charge was murder. There is a range of non-punitive court orders (including involuntary confinement in a special hospital) geared to the needs of the defendant and the protection of the public.

Where the charge was murder, however, the 1991 Act permitted only one outcome: indefinite detention in a special hospital until released with the permission of the Home Secretary or by order of a Mental Health Review Tribunal.[20] Happily, this discrepancy was addressed following the case of *Grant*,[21] in which the Court of Appeal expressed doubt whether the 1991 regime for persons charged with murder would comply with Article 5 of the ECHR (protection of liberty) and associated jurisprudence, which allows the detention of the mentally ill only if necessary for treatment or protection of the patient and others. Those criteria are not addressed in the determination of whether D did the act or made the omission. As a consequence of subsequent amending legislation,[22] section 5 of the Criminal Procedure (Insanity) Act 1964 now provides the full range of disposal options for murder cases but also provides that if the grounds for a hospital order with restriction are present in such a case, then such an order must be made.

(ii) The M'Naghten Rules

In England and Wales, the insanity defence is based on the *M'Naghten* Rules.[23] These rules comprise a series of answers given by judges of the Queen's Bench in 1843 to questions put by members of the House of Lords. The occasion was prompted by the public outcry which followed the acquittal, on grounds of insanity, of Daniel M'Naghten, who had killed Sir Edmund Drummond in an attempt to murder Sir Robert Peel.[24]

---

[18] *Kerr* [2002] Crim LR 57; affirmed in *H* [2003] UKHL 1.

[19] *Antoine* [2000] 2 All ER 208 (HL). Confusingly, Lord Hutton considered that evidence of accident or mistake might be relevant to the question whether D did the act; but such matters go to mens rea and not actus reus.

[20] Pursuant to the underlying Act: Criminal Procedure (Insanity) Act 1964, s. 5(2).

[21] [2002] Crim LR 403.

[22] Domestic Violence, Crime and Violence Act 2004.

[23] (1843) 10 C & F 200, 8 ER 718.

[24] West and Walk, *Daniel McNaughton: His Trial and the Aftermath* (1977). (There is uncertainly over the correct spelling of the defendant's name: "M'Naghten" is the most common version.)

Strictly speaking, the answers given were, in formal terms, of no binding effect. However, they are regarded as an authoritative and comprehensive statement of the law, a status endorsed by the House of Lords in *Sullivan*.[25] The Rules provide that:

(i)   there is a rebuttable presumption that everyone is sane;

(ii)   proof of insanity requires proof of a defect of reason;

(iii) the defect of reason must emanate from a disease of the mind;

(iv) it must be proved that the defect of reason *either*

      (a)   caused D to be unaware of the nature and quality of his act *or*

      (b)   caused D not to know that his act was wrong.[26]

We will consider these elements in turn.

(a) Burden of proof

The presumption of sanity requires D to prove her defence of insanity.[27] Proof is discharged on a balance of probabilities and not beyond any reasonable doubt.[28] As the cases below on "disease of the mind" will illustrate, the line between a claim to have lacked mens rea and a plea of insanity may be extremely fine. It is unsatisfactory to have different standards of proof in respect of closely analogous issues. Nonetheless, that is the current law.[29] As we noted in § 2.5(i), reverse burdens of proof may be vulnerable to scrutiny under the terms of Article 6(2) of the ECHR (presumption of innocence) and may, on occasion, be "read down" to merely an evidential burden. In *Lambert*,[30] however, the Court of Appeal ruled that there was no contravention of Article 6(2) in placing the onus of proof on D to establish his diminished responsibility in response to a charge of murder. Influential upon the Court's finding was the fact that the prosecution had to prove the elements of muder before the burden was imposed on D. As we shall see below, when D claims that he did not perceive the "the nature and quality" of his act because of a disease of the mind, the applicable case law effectively requires D to prove the lack of a voluntary act and/or a lack of mens rea. In such cases, the prosecution is in effect relieved of its burden of proof on vital elements of the offence charged and in those cases it seems entirely appropriate that D's burden be reduced to an evidential one. Even if that were done, D would have to produce some medical evidence to raise the issue of insanity: section 1 of the Criminal Procedure (Insanity and Unfitness to Plead) Act 1991 provides that a verdict of not guilty by reason of insanity is not to be returned unless evidence has been given by two or more medical practitioners, including at least one medical witness duly approved as having expertise in mental health.

As things stand, no English court has addressed the tension between the burden of proof in insanity and the usual requirement for the prosecution to prove a voluntary act and mens rea attributable to D. Under section 2(1) of the Trial of Lunatics Act 1883, where insanity is

---

[25] [1984] AC 156, 171.

[26] The Rules also contain a provision relating to insane delusions. It is generally agreed that the provision adds nothing of substance to the main body of the Rules and it will not be considered here.

[27] *Bratty v. A-G for Northern Ireland* [1963] AC 386 (HL).

[28] *Carr-Briant* [1943] KB 607 (CCA).

[29] For an excellent critique of the current position, see Jones, "Insanity, Automatism and the Burden of Proof on the Accused" (1995) 111 *LQR* 475.

[30] [2001] 1 Cr App R 205 (CA).

proved, the special verdict follows provided the jury is satisfied that D "did the act or made the omission charged, but was insane." The confirms that, if D is found to be insane, the prosecution need only prove beyond reasonable doubt the actus reus of the offence; the special verdict requires no proof of any mens rea required for the crime with which D is charged.[31]

(b) Defect of reason

It is appropriate to define insanity in terms of failures of rationality. We do not regard persons whose foundational beliefs or practical reasoning are radically defective as accountable moral agents if their bizarre beliefs or deranged reasoning appear to arise from some internal pathology. If, under the influence of drink or drugs, D believes she can execute some dangerous manoeuvre, we may, other things equal, hold her morally responsible for any harm that follows her attempt to do so. Should the same belief arise from schizophrenic delusion, talk of moral responsibility would seem to miss the mark.

For the purposes of the insanity defence, the defect of reason may arise for a brief period of time and need not constitute an aspect of D's character. A temporary blackout is sufficient.[32] In *Clarke*,[33] "defect of reason" was taken to imply the cessation of a relevant deliberative faculty for however brief a period of time. The details of the case were as follows:

> D, in a depressed state, had inadvertently taken an item from a supermarket shelf and placed it in her shopping bag. In response to a charge of theft, she claimed an absence of dishonesty but was held to be raising a plea of insanity. The Court of Appeal ruled that she had not put her sanity in issue. She was not asserting a defect of reason arising from a disease of the mind. Rather, because of absent-mindedness associated with depression, she had failed to exercise a faculty she still possessed.

The reasoning is unconvincing. It would have been entirely apt to say that her mental processes were defective. Nonetheless, the disapplication of the insanity defence in *Clarke* is appropriate. It is submitted that a better way of achieving that outcome would have been to accept that D was suffering from a cognitive defect but to deny that it arose from a "disease of the mind". This would require defining the latter phrase in terms which exclude conditions such as depression. We turn now to the definition of that phrase.

(c) Disease of the mind

It needs to be stressed at the outset that what constitutes a disease of the mind within the scope of the Rules is a legal, not a medical, question. Although section 1 of the Criminal Procedure (Insanity and Unfitness to Plead) Act 1991 requires evidence to be given by two or more medical practitioners before the special verdict of acquittal on the ground of insanity may be returned, the medical witnesses will be giving evidence in response to criteria set down by law. It may be that, on a particular occasion, medical witnesses are satisfied that D is insane or not insane according to medical criteria (in so far as that term is

---

[31] *A-G's Reference (No. 3 of 1998)* [1999] 3 All ER 40 (CA).
[32] Provided, of course, that it arises from a disease of the mind: see below, § 19.1(ii)(c).
[33] [1972] 1 All ER 219 (CA).

known to medical practice). But what matters is whether the evidence demonstrates that D was within the legal conception of insanity at the time the actus reus occurred.

The well-known judgment of Devlin J in *Kemp*[34] illustrates the policy considerations which influence the legal meaning of insanity. D, by all accounts a loving husband, made a sudden and violent attack on V, his wife. He claimed to have acted in a state of automatism: evidence was given that his arteriosclerosis could produce an automatous state by cutting off the blood supply to the brain. Devlin J ruled that a plea of non-insane automatism was unavailable. A disease of the mind, for the purpose of the Rules, was any internal disorder which affected the faculties of memory, reason, or understanding. Accordingly, the evidence raised on D's behalf put his sanity in issue. It was irrelevant that such a notion of insanity might be greeted with incredulity outside a courtroom, nor did it matter that the episode of insanity was, as in the case itself, of brief duration. Devlin J's approach has been consistently followed by appellate courts and received conclusive endorsement by the House of Lords in *Sullivan*,[35] where a state of automatism arising from an epileptic fit was ruled to be a condition falling within the Rules.

The explicit policy that has driven this capacious definition of a disease of the mind is the legitimate concern that certain persons likely to be involved in repeated episodes of dangerous behaviour should be subject to restraint rather than be given an unqualified acquittal on the basis of automatism or lack of mens rea. Lord Denning forcefully expressed the view that any mental disorder which had manifested itself in violence and which was prone to recur should be classified as a disease of the mind.[36] It is submitted, however, that the legitimate concern for public safety should be resolved through civil rather than criminal procedures.[37] As things stand, persons of good character, such as the defendants in *Kemp* and *Sullivan*, may prefer to plead guilty to offences they did not commit rather than pursue an insanity plea with all its pejorative overtones.

The cardinal limiting factor on what constitutes a disease of the mind is that, to be classified as a form of insanity, the condition must arise from some psychosis, organic or functional disorder, injury, or other inherent condition; or, to use the summary expression used by the courts, from some factor "internal" to the defendant. Conversely, a state of destabilisation engendered by "external" factors is not, legally, a disease of the mind. Accordingly, in *Quick*,[38] where D became hypoglycaemic as a consequence of the insulin he had taken for his diabetic condition, the Court of Appeal ruled that the was entitled to raise a plea of non-insane automatism. By contrast, in *Hennessy*,[39] D, a diabetic, had *failed* to take his insulin. Consequently, he became *hyper*glycaemic. But he was denied a defence of non-insane automatism because his condition was a symptom of his diabetes. Each defendant

---

[34] [1957] 1 QB 399.
[35] [1984] AC 156.
[36] *Bratty v. A-G for Northern Ireland* [1963] AC 386, 410.
[37] The Mental Health Act 1983 provides for the civil commitment of persons suffering from mental disorder, severe mental impairment, mental impairment, and psychopathic disorder if such persons constitute a danger to themselves or to others. In the cases of persons suffering from mental impairment or psychopathic disorder, an additional condition of "treatability" must be satisfied. Accordingly, existing civil commitment procedures will not engage with some persons whose mental condition may create danger to others. The matter is under review by the Home Office: *Managing Dangerous People with Severe Personality Disorder* (1999).
[38] [1973] QB 910 (CA).
[39] [1989] 2 All ER 9 (CA).

had in common mismanagement of his illness and dangerousness after entering into an automatous condition. What is remarkable is their differing treatment at the hands of the law. In a case such as *Quick*, if D raises the possibility that he was an automaton at the time of the conduct alleged to constitute an offence, the burden of disproof is on the prosecution and D will receive an unqualified acquittal should that burden not be discharged. In a case like *Hennessy*, D must prove his automatism and will receive a special verdict of acquittal by reason of insanity if he does.[40]

If the court is satisfied that D's claim to have been an automaton or to have lacked mens rea stems from some form of internal disorder, he will be taken to have raised a plea of insanity even if the form of disorder afflicting D has not been identified. In *Burgess*,[41] D performed a violent act apparently while sleep. The medical evidence failed to identify any underlying cause of the incident but testimony was given that violent somnambulism was abnormal and must, in the absence of any evidence of an external cause, arise from some internal condition.[42] Accordingly, the explanation—whatever it was—constituted a disease of the mind.[43]

The approach in *Burgess* mirrors that taken by the Supreme Court of Canada in the well-known case of *Rabey*,[44] where D claimed that the shock of his girlfriend V's rejection had induced a state of disassociation at the time of his attack upon her, rendering him incapable of forming mens rea. D claimed that this condition was induced by an external factor—V's rejection of him—and should be regarded as a state of non-insane automatism. The Supreme Court held that because D's reaction was so abnormal and extreme, it must have been the product of some internal predisposing factor which was merely *triggered*, not *caused*, by V's rejection. Accordingly, insanity was the only defence available on such facts.

In *Rabey*, it was suggested, *obiter*, that if an external event is so traumatic in its impact as to cause a state of disassociation in persons of normal sensibility, a defence of non-insane automatism might be available.[45] This suggestion was followed in the trial case of *T*,[46] where D, acting in a state of disassociation induced by the effects of being raped three days earlier, was held entitled to plead non-insane automatism to a charge of robbery.

---

[40] See the remarks above, § 19.1(ii)(a).

[41] [1991] 2 All ER 769 (CA).

[42] For a very useful account of the aetiology of sleep disorders and the appropriate legal responses to sleep disordered behaviours, see Wilson *et al.*, "Violence, Sleepwalking and the Criminal Law" [2005] *Crim LR* 624.

[43] Mackay has criticised the decision on the ground that the somnambulism did not lead to the cessation of the faculties of memory, reason, and understanding; that was caused by the preceding condition of sleep, a normal condition: *Mental Condition Defences* (1995) 45–51, citing the Supreme Court of Canada's decision in *Parks* (1992) 95 DLR (4th) 27. Perhaps, in defence of *Burgess*, D's bodily movements may be said to combine with the condition of sleep, producing a discrete, disordered state, a compound of sleep and the internal disorder which leads to the ambulatory activety. Such an answer is not an argument of principle for classifying sleepwalking as a form of insanity, merely acknowledgement that it is somewhat forced to maintain a separation between somnambulism and sleep when the states are, as they must be, coincident. However, for criticism of this rationalisation of the decision in *Burgess*, see Mackay, "Sleepwalking, Automatism and Insanity" [2006] *Crim LR* 901.

[44] (1980) 114 DLR (3d) 193.

[45] *Ibid.*, 199, quoting from the decision by the Ontario Court of Appeal (1977) 79 DLR (3d) 414, 435. It is of interest that the High Court of Australia in *Falconer* (1990) 65 ALJR 20, another "psychic blow" case, has rejected the internal/external factor analysis favoured in England and Canada. A state of disassociation caused by the shock of an event is to be regarded as a form of non-insane automatism unless there is identification of some underlying disability afflicting D which is suggestive of future dangerousness.

[46] [1990] Crim LR 256; and see now *Huckerby* [2004] EWCA Crim 3251.

To summarise this section: under English law, the source of a defect of reasoning will generally be regarded as a disease of the mind if either (i) it is "internal" to the defendant (*Kemp, Sullivan, Hennessy, Burgess*); or (ii) it is an "external" trigger that would not normally produce such a result in ordinary persons (*Rabey*), so that by inference it discloses an internal cause. Where the source is external *and* the sort of event likely to cause a defect of reasoning even in normal persons (*Quick, T*), the case is not one of insanity. Finally, there may be "mixed" cases where the state of automation is a product of internal and external causes; as in *Roach*,[47] where personality disorder, prescription drugs, alcohol, and fatigue all seemingly played a part in bringing about D's automatic state. The Court of Appeal took what may be termed a "predominant cause" approach: because the predominant causes were external factors, the correct classification was therefore non-insane automatism.

(d) The nature and quality of D's act

If the defect of reason induced by the disease of the mind causes D not to perceive the nature and quality of her act, she will be entitled to an acquittal on the grounds of insanity. A person such as the defendant in *Sullivan* does not apprehend the nature and quality of his conduct if he is in a state of automatism induced by an epileptic fit. Neither, to take Stephen's example, would a person who cut off a sleeping man's head because it would be great fun to see him look for it when he woke up.[48]

The expression "nature and quality" has been construed narrowly. It has been taken to mean nothing more than the *physical* aspects of the circumstances and consequences attending D's conduct.[49] Many persons who are radically psychotic will, notwithstanding, appreciate the nature and quality of their acts in the limited sense adopted by English law. Suppose that, because of her schizophrenic delusions, D thinks she has been ordered to kill V. If she is aware that V is a person, she will fall outside this limb of the Rules. This narrow approach has been criticised and contrasts with interpretations adopted in some US jurisdictions, where the phrase "nature and quality" has been interpreted in a more liberal fashion to take into account D's full understanding of the impact and moral dimensions of her conduct.[50]

At the same time, there has been a reaction in the United States against expansive interpretations of the *M'Naghten* Rules.[51] Wider interpretation of the phrase has, in practice, led to extended testimony from expert witnesses of a speculative and impalpable character. The trial of John Hinckley for the shooting of President Reagan gave rise to a widespread sentiment, reflected in legislative initiatives in many jurisdictions,[52] that acquittals on the ground of insanity could be won by chequebook recruitment of malleable experts. Clearly, the criminal conviction of persons afflicted with grave mental illness is unjust. Yet the way forward may not be best delivered by adopting a freer interpretation of the Rules.

---

[47] [2001] EWCA 2698.
[48] *History of the Criminal Law* (1883) vol. II, 166.
[49] *Codère* (1916) 12 Cr App R 21 (CCA).
[50] Goldstein, *The Insanity Defence* (1967) 49–51.
[51] Mackay, "Post-Hinkley Insanity in the USA" [1988] *Crim LR* 88.
[52] Low, Jeffries, and Bonnie, *Criminal Law: Cases and Materials* (2nd ed., 1986) 663–4.

(e) Knowledge that D's act is wrong

Should D appreciate the nature and quality of his acts, he may still receive a verdict of insanity should it be the case that he did not know that his act was wrong. As interpreted by English courts, this is *not* a test of *moral* wrongness. D will know that his conduct is "wrong", and thereby fail this limb of the insanity test, if:

(i)   D knows that his conduct contravenes the law;[53] *or*

(ii)   D knows that his conduct transgresses "the ordinary standards adopted by reasonable men."[54]

Again, it is obviously the case that seriously deranged persons will fall outside the insanity defence because they will be aware that their conduct is "wrong" in the sense stipulated by English law.[55] In *Sutcliffe*,[56] D took it as his divinely endorsed mission to kill prostitutes. He doubtless knew his conduct was contrary to law (and that it would be disapproved of by persons of his acquaintance). He was, in fact, schizophrenic to a severe degree but still quite sane within the terms of the English law of insanity.[57]

(f) Insane delusions

There is a passage in the *M'Naghten* Rules that deals specifically with persons who are afflicted with a "partial delusion" but who are not in other respects insane. The responsibility of such a person is to be considered as if the facts with respect to which the delusion exists were real. This express provision for partial delusions does not appear to add anything to the substance of the Rules; the illustrations provided by the judges who formulated the Rules indicate that the effect of the delusion must be to prevent D knowing the nature and quality of his actions or from knowing that his actions were wrong. The superfluity of this aspect of the *M'Naghten* Rules is borne out by the lack of case law arising thereunder.

(g) The scope of the M'Naghten Rules

The Rules lay down criteria for a general defence of insanity applicable to all offences. However, that was not the view of the Divisional Court in *DPP* v. *H*,[58] which ruled that a defence of insanity had no application to an offence of strict liability. The ruling was based on an error, namely that a successful plea of insanity established a lack of mens rea. But as we have seen, this is true only of the "nature and quality" limb of the Rules: the "knowledge

---

[53]   *Windle* [1952] 2 QB 826 (CCA); *M'Naghten* (1843) 10 C & F 200, 209, 8 ER 718, 722.

[54]   *Codère* (1916) 12 Cr App R 21, 27; *M'Naghten* (1843) 10 C & F 200, 210, 8 ER 718, 723. The relevance of this second variety of "wrongness" was doubted in *Windle* [1952] 2 QB 826, 834; but the remarks on this point were *obiter* only.

[55]   In *Stapleton* v. *R*. (1952) 86 CLR 358, the High Court of Australia was of the view that the *M'Naghten* Rules were too narrowly construed in *Windle* (above, n. 46), and that a defence of insanity should be available to D if he believes that his act was right by the standards of reasonable men notwithstanding his awareness of the illegality of his conduct. For contrasting views of the decision, see Morris at (1953) 16 *MLR* 435 and Montrose at (1954) 17 *MLR* 383. There is no sign of the Australian view being adopted here.

[56]   *The Times*, 30 April 1981.

[57]   The defence of insanity is narrower in 2000 than in 1800. In *Hadfield* (1800) 27 St Tr 1281, D shot at the King in order that he, D, should hang and thereby escape the imminent destruction of the world by God. He was found insane. As Williams observes, D clearly knew his act was contrary to law, thereby establishing his sanity: *CLGP* 493–4.

[58]   [1997] 1 WLR 1406; above, § 6.2.

that the act is wrong" limb provides for a defence applicable in circumstances where D has mens rea. An important rationale of the insanity defence is to protect mentally disordered persons from punishment. This concern is engaged for all criminal offences.

(iii) The defence of insanity and the ECHR

Article 5(1) of the ECHR allows, "in accordance with a procedure prescribed by law", "the lawful detention of persons of unsound mind." Under the jurisprudence interpreting Article 5, there is a requirement that the question of unsoundness of mind must be resolved by reference to "objective medical expertise".[59] Thus the detention on grounds of insanity of anyone who, by good practice standards of the medical profession,[60] is not considered to be of unsound mind will contravene Article 5. While section 1 of the Criminal Procedure (Insanity and Unfitness to Plead) Act 1991 requires evidence from two medical practitioners before a special verdict can be returned by a jury, as Sutherland and Gearty have noted, this provision does not address the point that the category of insanity in English law allows detention of persons who are not of unsound mind in any acceptable medical sense.[61] If a medical expert witness were to testify that D's automatism stems from, say, his underlying diabetes, the common law will designate the condition as insanity.[62] Such a classification would be rejected by any reputable body of "objective medical expertise".

Decisions such as *Sullivan* and *Kemp*, where defendants who were in no sense mentally ill faced a choice between pleading guilty to crimes they did not commit or pleading insanity, therefore involve fundamental contraventions of human rights. Such persons should be allowed to contest their guilt without risk of detention under a classification of insanity.[63]

These arguments can be put directly in domestic law following implementation of the Human Rights Act 1998.[64] By virtue of section 6, a court will be obliged to apply what is required under the Convention even if that requires departing from previous decisions of the highest authority such as the House of Lords decision in *Sullivan*. In criminal law contexts, findings of insanity which are compatible with objective medical expertise would be greatly facilitated if courts would use, as a benchmark, those mental conditions which permit compulsory civil commitment.[65]

---

[59] Harris, O'Boyle and Warbrick, *Law of the European Convention on Human Rights* (1995) 121–5.

[60] *Winterwerp v. Netherlands* (1979) 2 EHRR 387. The European Court of Human Rights laid down three conditions: (i) the individual detained must be reliably shown by objective medical expertise to be of unsound mind; (ii) the individual's mental disorder must be of a kind or degree warranting compulsory confinement; and (iii) the disorder must persist throughout the period of detention.

[61] "Insanity and the European Court of Human Rights" [1992] *Crim LR* 418, 420–1; see too Baker, "Human Rights, *M'Naghten* and the 1991 Act" [1994] *Crim LR* 84; Mackay and Gearty, "On Being Insane in Jersey" [2001] *Crim LR* 560; Mackay, "On Being Insane in Jersey Part Two" [2002] *Crim LR* 728.

[62] *Hennessy* [1989] 2 All ER 9 (CA).

[63] It may be that, if a particular person can reliably be predicted to be a danger to others, a form of non-punitive civil commitment may be permissible. On the difficulty of reliable prediction see Floud and Young, *Dangerousness and Criminal Justice* (1981); Palmstierna, "One in Thirty Predictions of Assault by Discharged Psychiatric Patients will be Correct" [1999] *BMJ* 1270.

[64] See above, § 2.5.

[65] Mental Health Act 1983. The criteria in that Act are currently under review: *Reform of the Mental Health Act 1983: Proposals for Consultation* Cmnd. 4480 (1999) chap. 4.

(iv) Reform of insanity law

As interpreted in England and Wales, the *M'Naghten* Rules provide an exclusively cognitive test for determining insanity. A person who may be unequivocally "mad" in terms of diagnostic criteria may yet know the nature and quality of her act in the narrow sense of the term used in English law and know that it was contrary to law. Lord Devlin defended this emphasis on cognition on the grounds that the faculty of cognition was the main distinguishing feature between man and animals.[66] Yet in matters of criminal punishment, the key question is whether the defendant has manifested sufficient culpability to warrant being *punished* (as distinct from restrained). Questions which focus on cognition alone[67] will not capture all the dimensions of culpability. A schizophrenic under the delusion that he has divinely ordained killings to commit might find it difficult to resist the voices he hears in his head when they enjoin such killings. The clinical literature contains many examples of behaviour strongly influenced by delusions or obsessions arising from pathological states.[68] English law has not been receptive to such learning: in response to an argument that a defendant should be adjudged insane if his conduct was driven by pathological impulses, Lord Hewart described it as "a fantastical theory . . . which if it were to become part of our criminal law would be merely subversive."[69]

Conversely, when the interests of social control have appeared to judges to be best served by the insanity defence, an expansive approach has been taken to the notion of disease of the mind, leaving special verdicts the only exculpatory route for persons such as diabetics or epileptics who are sane under any non-legal meaning of that term.[70] So: a schizophrenic may not be insane, but a diabetic is. It is a conclusion only a lawyer could reach.

The narrow interpretation of the two principal limbs of the *M'Naghten* Rules is one of the main reasons why the insanity defence is not more frequently employed. For non-murder cases, the Criminal Procedure (Insanity and Unfitness to Plead Act) 1991 allows a variety of disposal outcomes after a special verdict[71] but this has not, to date, encouraged significantly more insanity pleas.[72] Arguably a more expansive mental disorder defence is required to address the needs of mentally ill persons who become defendants in criminal trials.

Such a proposal would be opposed by those who advocate the abolition of the insanity defence. Abolitionists may be sceptics such as Thomas Szasz, who in his voluminous writings time and again refers to mental illness as a convenient myth exploited by the "ill"

---

[66] "Mental Abnormality and the Criminal Law" in Macdonald (ed.), *Changing Legal Objectives* (1963) 85.

[67] This is particularly true where the matters that D must know are as narrowly conceived as they are under English law. An emphasis on questions of cognition rather than volition has been extolled as one of the virtues of the *M'Naghten* Rules in US jurisprudence, but there the interpretation of what D must know is more liberal: Livermore and Meehl, "The Virtues of M'Naghten" (1967) 51 *Minn LR* 789.

[68] Goldberg and Huxley, *Common Mental Disorders: A Biosocial Model* (1992).

[69] *Kopsch* (1925) 19 Cr App R 50, 51 (CCA).

[70] To compound the problem, while protection of the public from the recurrence of violent episodes has been the nominated policy behind this expansive approach, there is little evidence that diabetics and epileptics who have been involved in such incidents constitute an ongoing danger: Fenwick, *Automatism, Medicine and the Law* (1990) 10.

[71] Including a hospital order (with or without restriction), a guardianship order, supervision and treatment order, and an absolute discharge.

[72] Mackay and Kearns, "More Fact(s) about the Insanity Defence" [1999] *Crim LR* 714.

and their carers.[73] However, the Szasz viewpoint founders against the advances made in the reliable identification of mental disorders.[74] More telling is the abolitionist proposal made by Norval Morris.[75] He asserts that a cohort of mentally disordered persons comprising a statistically significant number and representative of the main kinds of mental disorder will contain no greater incidence of persons with offending behaviour than an equivalent sized cohort made up of randomly selected persons. Yet if we were to compare both those groups with an equivalent cohort of males, between the ages of 14 and 22, living in socially deprived circumstances in inner-city areas, we would find a much greater incidence of offenders in the last group.[76]

As Morris observes, one response to these findings is to advocate a defence of social deprivation.[77] He does not support that but instead argues that all three groups should receive the same treatment, subject to the relevance of other legally recognised defences. Personal and social circumstances should be relevant to sentencing but not to liability. Accordingly if, for a mentally disordered person, her mental condition precluded mens rea, she should receive an unqualified acquittal like anyone else. If she is considered dangerous, then civil commitment should be considered; that job should not be done through the insanity defence. If she has mens rea, she should be convicted and her disorder considered when determining what sentence or treatment she should receive.

Morris makes a powerful case. He buttresses his arguments from principle with well-founded observations of how the insanity defence operates in the US context. The majority of disordered offenders are processed through plea bargains and guilty pleas, as with other non-disordered offenders. Insanity, in practice, is confined to very serious offences, particularly capital murder. Significant advantages accrue to those offenders who can afford eminent expert witnesses—the more the better—whose evidence is frequently of a prolix and speculative character.

On the other hand, Morris's argument underplays the fact that there *are* persons so disordered or so deficient in cognitive capacities that the presence, in formal terms, of mens rea would not entail any measure of culpability.[78] For those persons, any form of conviction is wrong: an injustice is done to a person severely psychotic or profoundly learning-disabled if we record a conviction. These extreme conditions are capable of satisfactory definition; persons with such conditions should not be found guilty of crimes because they are so irrational or mentally disabled as to be beyond any moral scheme of reference.

Outside these categories, the Morris position has considerable force, since there is less diagnostic precision and more scope for debate concerning culpability. It is submitted that

---

[73] *The Manufacture of Madness* (1970); *The Myth of Mental Illness* (1961).

[74] World Health Organization, *Diagnostic and Management Guidelines for Mental Disorders* (1996).

[75] "The Criminal Responsibility of the Mentally Ill" (1982) 33 *Syracuse LR* 477.

[76] Significant research carried out after Morris's article indicates that certain diagnoses, notably schizophrenia, are predictive of violence but not strongly predictive: Bowden, "Violence and Mental Disorder" in Walker (ed.), *Dangerous People* (1996) 13. However, the point remains that age, gender, and social circumstances are more highly correlated with crime, including violent crime.

[77] Bazelon, "The Morality of the Criminal Law" (1976) 49 *So Cal LR* 385; Delgado, "Rotten Social Background: Should the Criminal Law Recognise a Defense of Severe Environmental Deprivation?" (1985) 3 *J Law and Inequality* 9.

[78] Bonnie, "The Moral Basis of the Insanity Defense" (1983) 69 *ABAJ* 194; Brady, "Abolish the Insanity Defense? No!" (1971) 8 *Houston LR* 629.

the position of mentally disordered persons whose condition falls short of severe psychosis or cognitive impairment should be the same as that of any other defendant and, importantly, they too should be allowed freedom if the elements of the offence with which they have been charged are not made out.

Accordingly, under any reformed law, a defence of mental disorder with a special verdict allowing control of the defendant should be available for any person with a serious mental disorder or severe learning disability whose conduct and state of mind satisfies the definitional elements of a crime.[79] For dangerous persons who do not fulfil these criteria, restraint should be a civil and not a criminal process.[80] For convenience and public safety it may be necessary to conjoin civil commitment with criminal proceedings in certain cases.

§ 19.2 Diminished responsibility

Diminished responsibility is a statutory defence introduced by section 2 of the Homicide Act 1957.[81] The defence is designedly broader than the insanity defence. Unlike an insanity plea, a successful defence of diminished responsibility does not secure an acquittal. The effect is to reduce the grade of offence from murder to manslaughter. For offences other than murder, there is no defence of diminished responsibility, and matters which would fall within section 2 in the context of murder become matters of mitigation and not defence. The *raison d'être* of section 2 is to avoid the fixed penalty for murder and to afford the sentencing judge the complete discretion that a verdict of manslaughter allows. A large range of culpability falls within the provision; one defendant may successfully plead the defence yet receive a life sentence, whereas another defendant may receive an absolute discharge: each outcome may be justifiable in its own terms. Section 2 of the Homicide Act 1957 provides:

(1) Where a person kills or is a party to the killing of another, he shall not be convicted of murder if he was suffering from such abnormality of mind (whether arising from a condition of arrested or retarded development of mind or any inherent causes or induced by disease or injury) as substantially impaired his mental responsibility for his acts or omissions in doing or being a party to the killing.

(2) On a charge of murder, it shall be for the defence to prove that the person charged is by virtue of this section not liable to be convicted of murder.

(3) A person who but for this section would be liable, whether as a principal or as accessory, to be convicted of murder shall be liable instead to be convicted of manslaughter.

---

[79] This is in line with the Report of the Committee on Mentally Abnormal Offenders (Cmnd. 6244, 1975), which recommends allowing a defence of mental disorder if D suffered from severe mental illness or severe subnormality. Note, however, the further constraint in the Draft Criminal Code (Law Com. No. 177, 1989), cl. 35(2), which refuses a defence to persons in that category if it is proved beyond reasonable doubt "that the offence was not attributable to the severe mental illness or severe mental handicap."

[80] Current reform proposals in England persist with a social defence model for defendants who are shown to lack the fault element for an offence because of a mental disorder: Law Com. No. 177, *A Criminal Code for England and Wales* (1989) cl. 36. It is submitted that it is wrong in principle to use coercion through the criminal justice system where the elements of guilt are not made out. Civil commitment on the basis of dangerousness is preferable, subject to reliable indicators of that condition.

[81] Mackay, *Mental Condition Defences in the Criminal Law* (1995) chap. 4; Wootton, "Diminished Responsibility: A Layman's View" (1960) 76 *LQR* 224; Sparks, "Diminished Responsibility in Theory and Practice" (1964) 27 *MLR* 9.

(i) The burden of proof

Section 2(2) places the burden of proof on the defence. On general principles, any burden placed on the defence is discharged on a balance of probabilities. The burden was placed on the defence as it was thought that it would be anomalous to arrange the matter any differently from the position prevailing for insanity. It is unfortunate that the opportunity was not taken to change the position for insanity and to provide, in either case, that the burden of disproof should ultimately fall to the prosecution should the defence discharge the evidential onus of raising insanity or diminished responsibility as a live issue. There is no reason in principle why insanity and diminished responsibility should be treated any differently from defences such as self-defence or duress in the matter of proof. The determining factor has been the presumption of sanity but that presumption could surely have been displaced on a basis of evidential onus rather than the imposition of a full probative burden.[82] Be that as it may, the Court of Appeal has held that there is no breach of Article 6(2) of the ECHR in placing the burden of proof on D, ruling it not to be disproportionate principally because the burden did not fall to D until the prosecution had proved the elements of murder.[83] Not infrequently, the same facts may raise both an issue of diminished responsibility and an issue of provocation. In the case of the latter, a burden of disproof falls to the prosecution. It cannot be easy for juries to assess the same facts raising two separate but overlapping issues under different standards of proof.[84]

(ii) Substantial impairment of responsibility

In the early cases arising under section 2, there was a judicial tendency to direct juries using the language of the section itself without any explanatory gloss. This tendency was deprecated by the Court of Criminal Appeal in *Byrne*,[85] which advised trial judges to offer guidance to the jury on the application of the section to the facts of the instant case. The court emphasised the importance of the phrase, "substantially impaired his mental responsibility for his acts." There must be something significant or salient about the mental condition of D to warrant reduction of the charge to manslaughter in cases where the prosecution had established an intent to kill or cause grievous bodily harm.

The condition of D in *Byrne* itself satisfied this requirement. D was described by expert witnesses as a dangerous sexual psychopath, responsible for a number of atrocious, sexually motivated killings of young women. The evidence was that the particular sexual drives of D were much harder for him to suppress and control than sexual urges of a normal character. Quashing his conviction for murder, the court ruled that his capacity to exercise self-control was relevant to his responsibility for his acts. It was conceded that the degree of difficulty that D experienced in controlling himself was a matter which fell beyond scientific demonstration. Juries would have to make up their collective mind in a "common sense way",

---

[82] See above, § 19.1(ii)(a).
[83] *Lambert* [2001] 1 Cr App R 205.
[84] Mackay, "Pleading Provocation and Diminished Responsibility Together" [1988] *Crim LR* 411.
[85] [1960] 2 QB 396.

taking into account not only the medical evidence but also the acts and statements of the accused, his demeanour, and any other relevant material.

The importance of *Byrne* is that, unlike the defence of insanity, volitional factors may be taken into account. D knew perfectly well what he was doing yet successfully claimed a degree of exemption on the ground that his psychopathy made it very difficult for him to refrain from such conduct. It may be noted that D received a life sentence on account of his dangerousness.

Whether the condition afflicting D is serious enough to constitute a substantial impairment of responsibility is always a question of fact for the jury. Since it is a question of fact, a judge is entitled to withdraw the issue from the jury if he considers there is insufficient evidence of the necessary degree of impairment. Thus the Court of Appeal upheld the ruling of the trial judge in *Campbell*[86] who had withdrawn the defence from D, an epileptic who was disposed to "occasional impulsive acts". That was not enough to raise an issue of substantial impairment. It is important, however, not to set the standard of exclusion too high. Several directions had referred to the diminished responsibility defence as requiring "a condition on the borderline of insanity." In *Seers*,[87] the Court of Appeal stated that this was a material misdirection. The section may accommodate persons, such as depressives, whose condition normally has no affinity with insanity.

(iii) External factors

Section 2, although broadly expressed, is limited by the need for D to identify some condition *internal* to himself attenuating responsibility for his acts. Accordingly, in *Gittens*,[88] where D argued that his psychopathy substantially reduced his powers of self-control, the Court of Appeal ruled that any disinhibiting effect on his personality arising from the alcohol he had consumed should be disregarded when considering whether his responsibility was substantially impaired.

Rightly so. It is clear from the wording of section 2 that the voluntary consumption of drink or drugs is not to be taken into account as a factor which diminishes responsibility. As a matter of policy, it would be unacceptable if self-induced conditions were to improve a defendant's prospects of a successful defence. That said, the taking of intoxicants should not *disentitle* D from successfully pleading diminished responsibility if the abnormality of mind caused by factors internal to her is sufficient, of itself, substantially to impair her responsibility. From that perspective, the Court of Appeal's subsequent decision in *Egan*[89] was open to criticism. D had brutally killed V. The majority of expert witnesses testified that D's state of "borderline subnormality" *of itself* substantially impaired D's responsibility for the killing (although, of course, the ultimate arbiter of that question is the jury). In assessing D's eligibility for a section 2 defence, the Court of Appeal stated "the vital question":[90]

> "was the appellant's abnormality of mind such that he would have been under diminished responsibility, drink or no drink?"

---

[86] (1987) 84 Cr App R 255 (CA).
[87] (1984) 79 Cr App R 261.
[88] [1984] QB 698.
[89] [1992] 4 All ER 470. See further Sullivan, "Intoxicants and Diminished Responsibility" [1994] *Crim LR* 156.
[90] *Ibid.*, 479.

Unfortunately, although it asked the right question, the Court gave the wrong answer. It interpreted *Gittens* (above) as a ruling that diminished responsibility is inapplicable unless the jury is satisfied that the killing *would* have occurred had D *not* taken drink. This is a misreading of that decision. *Gittens*, properly, rules that the disinhibiting effects of intoxicants are not to be taken into account when judging whether D's difficulties of self-control impaired his responsibility. *Egan* was a different kind of case: the question there was whether D's subnormality diminished his responsibility. Obviously, the drink taken had no part to play in constituting his subnormality. The question for the jury should, straightforwardly, have been whether his subnormality substantially impaired his responsibility for the killing. That would have been the issue put had D killed V, say, because V lost her temper with him. The question should be no different even if D would not have killed V had he not been drinking. The drink does not supervene over his underlying subnormality. That underlying condition remains, and so does the question whether that condition substantially impaired his responsibility for the killing.

The view of the law argued for here has now been endorsed by House of Lords in *Dietschmann*.[91] In that case, D killed V after drinking heavily. The fact that he might not have killed V had he not been intoxicated did not disentitle him from raising a plea of diminished responsibility based on his acute grief reaction to a recent bereavement.

If a person is addicted to intoxicants, conditions may arise therefrom which give rise to diminished responsibility. In *Tandy*[92] the Court of Appeal took the view, *obiter*, that brain damage arising from taking intoxicants would be a condition within section 2. There is support for that approach from *dicta* which regard alcoholism and delirium tremens as diseases of the mind within the *M'Naghten* Rules.[93] In *Tandy*, D was an alcoholic who argued that because she was addicted to drink, the effects on her brain of the alcohol she had taken on the day of the killing should be taken to have diminished her responsibility. There was only very limited receptiveness to this argument. She would have to demonstrate that her consumption of alcohol was involuntary and it would have that character only if she lacked any choice about when the first drink of the day was taken and if her drinking thereafter was compulsive. Most alcoholics have more self-control than that, as did D herself.

(iv) Diminished responsibility in practice

An account of the law of diminished responsibility which is based on appellate decisions may fail to convey the law as deployed at trial and in plea negotiations.[94] To an extent, this is true of textbook accounts of any part of substantive criminal law. Yet, particularly in this area, the gap between articulated judicial decisions and day-to-day practice can be a wide one and requires some comment.

Many cases involving a plea of diminished responsibility will not result in a contested

---

[91] [2003] 1 All ER 897; see too *Hendy* [2006] EWCA Crim 819.
[92] [1989] 1 All ER 267.
[93] *Davis* (1881) 14 Cox CC 563, 564; *Beard* [1920] AC 479, 501.
[94] Dell, *Murder into Manslaughter: The Diminished Responsibility Defence in Practice* (1984); Mackay, *Mental Condition Defences in the Criminal Law* (1995) 185–6; Williams, *CLGP* 551–8; Williams, *TBCL* 692–4.

trial. As a practical matter, the defence will need medical witnesses prepared to testify that the defendant was afflicted with some condition falling within the terms of section 2.[95] Not infrequently, faced with the prospect of such testimony, the prosecution will indicate that it is prepared to accept a plea of not guilty to murder but guilty of manslaughter on the ground of diminished responsibility. Very rarely will the presiding judge insist that the issue be put to trial.[96] In this manner, many killings which are more a product of the stresses of life than the result of some individual pathology will result in convictions for manslaughter rather than murder. Killings induced by abusive relationships, troublesome neighbours, familial stresses, compassion for the painfully and terminally ill, and the like may therefore be recorded as manslaughter. Diagnostic labels such as reactive depression, post-traumatic stress disorder, and morbid jealousy are sufficiently accommodating, if not interrogated too closely, to encompass essentially ordinary reactions to stressful life events. Once classified as psychiatric syndromes or disorders, conditions arising from external circumstance can be regarded as matters of D's own pathology, falling within section 2.

In view of the mandatory life sentence for murder, this pattern of practice is inevitable and, in the present context, welcome. The mandatory sentence requires matters of mitigation to be elevated into the elements of a defence if justice is to be done or mercy shown. This pattern of practice ameliorates the formal position. From first principles, however, the situation is far from ideal. This massaging of the boundaries of murder and manslaughter requires compliant expert witnesses who are prepared to put a psychiatric gloss on "normal" facets of the human condition.

This laxity would be put to an end if the 2006 Law Commission proposals for reforming diminished responsibility were to be enacted.[97] On the proposed revisions, a successful plea of diminished responsibility in this altered form would reduce first-degree murder to second-degree murder.[98] To succeed with the revised defence, D must prove[99] that he has a "recognised medical condition" or, if under 18, suffered in addition or alternatively from "developmental immaturity" that caused an abnormality of mental functioning which, in turn, substantially impaired his capacity to:

(i)   understand the nature of his or her conduct; or
(ii)   form a rational judgement; or
(iii)   control himself.

---

[95] *Dix* (1981) 74 Cr App R 306, 311 (CA). The Court spoke of medical testimony being "a practical necessity if that defence is to begin to run at all."

[96] A notorious exception to the general practice is *Sutcliffe, The Times*, 30 April 1981 (the "Yorkshire Ripper" case). Despite agreement between the defence and prosecution that D came within s. 2, the judge insisted on a trial with a consequent verdict of murder. In prison, D was diagnosed as severely schizophrenic and removed to a special hospital. The exceptional nature of the case is underscored by the earlier Court of Appeal decision in *Cox* [1968] 1 WLR 308, 310, which confirmed that where the medical evidence is clear and undisputed, the prosecution may properly accept a plea of guilty to manslaughter on the ground of diminished responsibility. For the period 1986–8, in only 9.2 per cent of cases where a plea of diminished responsibility was offered by the defence did the prosecution refuse the plea: House of Lords, *Report of the Select Committee on Murder and Life Imprisonment, Vol II—Oral Evidence, Part 1* (1988–9) 115.

[97] *Murder, Manslaughter and Infanticide* Law Com. No. 304 (2006) paras. 5.83–138; discussed in Taylor, "The Nature of 'Partial Defences' and the Coherence of Second Degree Murder" [2007] *Crim LR* 345.

[98] For discussion of the Law Commission proposals for first- and second-degree murder see above, § 10.3(ii).

[99] There is no apparent intention to change the burden of proof in Law Com. No. 304.

If one or more of these conditions is satisfied the defence will succeed, provided:

> (iv) "the abnormality, the developmental immaturity, or the combination of both *provides an explanation* for the defendant's conduct in carrying out or taking part in the killing." (Emphasis added.)

The change that this last criterion would produce can be illustrated by taking one case from a sample of cases collected as part of a study of diminished responsibility conducted for the Law Commission.[100] In Case 50, D is reported to have killed his lover V in a fit of jealousy because V had formed a romantic relationship with a third party. D had a history of schizophrenia and the prosecution accepted D's plea of guilty to manslaughter on the grounds of diminished responsibility. Essentially, the prosecution did this because of a firm diagnosis of schizophrenia. There was no finding or even a suggestion that D's schizophrenia in any way explained the killing and, of course, many killings done in jealous rage are perpetrated by persons unafflicted with any medical condition. But the admittedly awkward wording of the current defence does allow a reading whereby one's state of schizophrenia of itself diminishes one's moral responsibility, analogous to states such as infancy or learning disability. Under the Law Commission's proposals, an account would have to be given of *how* the disease explained the killing. Unless there is a connection with a symptom—for example, Peter Sutcliffe's killing of prostitutes because of his psychotic belief that God had ordered him to do so—such an explanation, if explanation there is, may lie undiscovered and the defence unavailable.

The case for this new requirement is not clear-cut. Schizophrenia supplies an instructive example. The condition raises the risk of violence by sufferers, but only to a small degree.[101] Undoubtedly, the proposed reform undoubtedly is based on a more clearly worded, more schematic provision than is section 2 of the Homicide Act 1957. But if it entails life sentences for first-degree murder for schizophrenics and others in like case, it is hardly an exercise in liberal and humane law reform.

§ 19.3 Infanticide

In strict terms, infanticide[102] is not a defence but a category of homicide. The offence of infanticide under the Infanticide Act 1938 is committed if D, the mother of V, a child under the age of 12 months, kills V when the balance of her mind is disturbed by reason of her not having fully recovered from the effect of giving birth to the child, or by reason of the effect of lactation consequent upon birth of the child. The offence provides, within its

---

[100] *Partial Defences to Murder* Law Com. No. 290 (2004) Appendix B.

[101] Walsh *et al.*, "Violence and Schizophrenia: Examining the Evidence" (2002) 180 *British Journal of Psychiatry* 490. There are significantly higher risks of violence on the part of persons diagnosed with depression, bipolar disorder, and, in particular, substance abuse disorders and personality disorders.

[102] Mackay, *Mental Condition Defences in the Criminal Law* (1995) 207–14; Maier-Katkin and Ogle, "A Rationale for Infanticide Laws" [1993] *Crim LR* 903.

limited terms of reference, a more accommodating ground of mitigation than diminished responsibility. There is no requirement that the balance of D's mind should be disturbed by a condition amounting to a clinical disorder.[103] The jury may return a verdict of infanticide as an alternative to a finding of murder,[104] or the offence may be charged in its own right. If the issue is contested, it seems that D need not prove that the balance of her mind was disturbed but must merely raise an evidential issue.[105] Most verdicts of infanticide arise from a plea of guilty to the offence. The scale of punishment is the same as manslaughter. The most frequent outcome is a probation order.

Studies of the working of the Infanticide Act 1938 indicate that a plea of guilty to infanticide will readily be accepted in cases where a mother kills her child when the child is under the age of 12 months if there is evidence of emotional disturbance at the time of the killing.[106] This liberal approach in practice contrasts with the restrictive terms of the Act. According to the statute, D's mind must be disturbed by (i) not having fully recovered from the effect of giving birth or (ii) by reason of the effect of lactation consequent upon the birth of the child. The latter condition is medically controversial[107] and we may focus attention on the first. It will be noted that, strictly, D's disturbance must be the result of the birth process and not owing to pressures, economic or emotional, arising from the introduction of a new child into D's domestic environment. In the informal world of guilty pleas, it would appear that such fine discriminations are not made.

It would be better if the law were redrafted to bring it closer to practice. The Law Commission's proposed Criminal Code would have amended infanticide with the formulation:[108]

> "A woman who, but for this section, would be guilty of murder or manslaughter of her child is not guilty of murder or manslaughter, but is guilty of infanticide, if her act is done when the child is under the age of twelve months and when the balance of her mind was disturbed by reason of the effect of giving birth or circumstances consequent upon that birth."

Even under that formulation, however, restrictions would remain which could operate with arbitrary effect. The offence would still require that the child killed be under 12 months of age and would be confined to women. It is perhaps no surprise therefore that, more recently, the Law Commission has recommended that the law should remain as it is.[109]

---

[103] From a study of 23 persons convicted of infanticide, a study found that only two could be considered mentally ill: d'Orban, "Women who Kill their Children" (1974) 134 *British Journal of Psychiatry* 560.

[104] Infanticide Act 1938, s. 1(2).

[105] The Act makes no reference to a burden of proof on D.

[106] Mackay, "The Consequences of Killing Very Young Children" [1993] *Crim LR* 21.

[107] Bluglass, "Infanticide" [1978] *Bulletin of the Royal College of Psychiatrists* 14. In Law Com. No. 304, para. 826, reference is made to a yet-unpublished study reporting a link between lactation and dopamine sensitivity which may trigger psychosis. Maier-Katkin and Ogle note that childbirth itself can give rise to mental disturbance, although social and familial pressures are more important causes of subsequent instability: "A Rationale for Infanticide Laws" [1993] *Crim LR* 903.

§ 19.4 Infancy

(i) Children below the age of 10 years

At common law, any child under the age of 7 was *doli incapax*: deemed incapable of committing a crime.[110] The qualifying age has been raised by statute to 10 years.[111] Although provision was made at one time to raise the age further to 14,[112] it was never put into effect. In fact, legislative policy has now gone into reverse, with greater emphasis on punitive responses to wrongdoing by children and young people.[113]

Whatever a child under the age of 10 does, with whatever state of mind, it cannot constitute a crime; although it may lead to the imposition of a civil care order.[114] The incapacity of the child may well affect the legal position of persons associated with the conduct perpetrated by the infant. If D, a person above the age of criminal responsibility, were to instruct C, an infant under the age of 10, to take property from V, this, all other things being equal, would constitute a theft by D through the innocent agency of C. If C were to take V's property on his own initiative and hand it on to D, D's dishonest acceptance of the property would be theft rather than handling.[115]

(ii) Children below the age of 14 years

At common law, there was a presumption that a child between the ages of 10 and 14 was *doli incapax*, a presumption rebutted if the prosecution could prove a "mischievous discretion" on the part of D—i.e. the capacity to differentiate between right and wrong.[116] The need to establish mischievous discretion was something additional to the mens rea required for the offence with which the infant was charged. This presumption of *doli incapax* came under attack predominantly on the ground that it excused those infants most in need of reformative or corrective measures.[117] It was abolished by section 34 of the Crime and Disorder Act 1998, which provides:

> The rebuttable presumption of criminal law that a child aged 10 or over is incapable of committing an offence is hereby abolished.

On the face of it, the meaning of this provision seems clear. It abolishes a presumption. Accordingly, it remains open for a child under 14 to raise the issue of *doli incapax*.[118] On general principles of proof, the child should present evidence suggestive of an incapacity to make judgements of right and wrong and then the onus will be on the prosecution to prove that the child possessed a sufficient sense of right and wrong to warrant a criminal convic-

---

[108] Law Com. No. 177, *A Criminal Code for England and Wales* (1989) cl. 64(1).
[109] Law Com No. 304, para. 8.23.
[110] Kean, "The History of the Criminal Liability of Children" (1937) 53 *LQR* 364.
[111] Children and Young Persons 1933, s. 50, as amended by the Children and Young Persons Act 1963, s. 16.
[112] Children and Young Persons Act 1969, s. 4.
[113] Criminal Justice and Public Order Act 1994; Crime and Disorder Act 1998.
[114] Children Act 1989, s. 25.
[115] *Walters* v. *Lunt* [1951] 2 All ER 645 (CCA).
[116] *Owen* (1830) 4 C & P 236, 172 ER 685; *Manley* (1844) 1 Cox CC 104; *Gorrie* (1919) 83 JP 136.

tion.[119] That was the view of the Solicitor General on the second reading of the Bill. He envisaged a child raising the defence if he has "genuine learning difficulties and . . . is genuinely at sea on the question of right and wrong."[120]

Yet, despite the seeming clarity of section 34, a view has been taken that the abolition of the presumption entails the abolition of the defence of *doli incapax* altogether for children aged 10 years and over, an interpretation endorsed in a Home Office circular on the Act.[121] This view accords with the attitude expressed by judges and politicians that the defence of *doli incapax* was an indulgence incompatible with an effective response to juvenile offending. The case law on *doli incapax* is confined to situations where the prosecution seeks to demonstrate the presence of mischievous discretion; there is no jurisprudence on raising the defence. Conditioned by that background, it is understandable, perhaps, that the abolition of the presumption has been taken to mean the abolition of the infancy defence altogether in the case of children between the ages of 10 and 14. Yet the presumption of an incapacity and the incapacity itself are clearly different things. The abolition of a long-standing defence requires language expressed in the clearest of terms. It is submitted that the defence of *doli incapax* remains for children between the ages of 10 and 14, although the issue must now be raised by the defence.

Abolition of the presumption, in itself, will bring a considerable change in the practical availability of the defence. When the presumption was operative, the prosecution could experience considerable difficulty in demonstrating sufficient moral awareness on the part of the child by reference to evidence that went beyond establishing the mens rea for the offence. The need for such evidence was confirmed in *C*,[122] where it was held that the presumption of *doli incapax* was not rebutted by evidence of intentional damage of property. To convict D of criminal damage it had to be proved that he knew it was *wrong* to damage other people's property. D would now be presumed to possess such knowledge. The evidential onus would fall on D to give some plausible reason why he did not; say, because of a learning disability or a family environment where appropriate values were not respected.

---

[117] See, especially, *C* [1996] AC 1.
[118] As is cogently argued in Walker, "The End of an Old Song" (1999) 149 *NLJ* 64.
[119] *Woolmington* [1935] AC 462 (HL).
[120] *Hansard*, Lords, 16 December 1997, col. 596.

20

DEFENCES OF CIRCUMSTANTIAL PRESSURE

§ 20.1 Duress

The common law has long conceded that if crimes (excluding murder, attempted murder, and probably treason) are committed under threat of immediate or almost immediate death or serious bodily harm, D may be exonerated. The rationale for this concession is debated. One argument has been that the deterrent force of the criminal law is ineffective when competing with countervailing threats of imminent death or serious injury. It is sound utilitarian theory to confine the imposition of sanctions to circumstances where they will secure some benefit. Why make an uncertain threat of future imprisonment or fine in the face of an unyielding and certain threat of death or serious bodily harm?[1] The point is well made in respect of individual deterrence. In terms of general deterrence, however, it may be thought particularly appropriate for the criminal law to be at its most unyielding when privately organised violence undermines the official sanctions of the criminal law, an argument not without force in a time of terrorist organisations and violent gangs.[2] Nonetheless, it is possible to subscribe to general deterrence as a justifying principle for state punishment, while insisting that the infliction of a sanction on a particular individual should satisfy the requirements of justice.[3] Those who reject utilitarianism will insist that the convictions of individuals comply with the requirements of justice. From the perspective of just deserts, it would be unacceptably Draconian to punish persons who have acted to avoid catastrophic harm to themselves, to those to whom they are attached or feel responsible.[4] For the most part, this last sentiment reflects the current state of English law.

Duress is commonly regarded as the quintessential excuse, a concession to human frailty: a conception of the defence recently endorsed by the house of Lords in *Hasan*.[5] On most occasions, it does indeed operate in the realm of excuse, which is to say that we would make D a subject of praise were he to resist the coercion and merely excuse him were he to submit to the pressure. Yet this analysis is not always appropriate. Suppose that D, a taxi-driver, is

---

[1] For this reason Bentham approved the provision of a defence of duress: *Introduction to the Principles of Morals and Legislation* (1789) chap. xiv, para. 11.

[2] "Criminal law it itself a system of compulsion on the widest scale. It is a collection of threats of injury to life, liberty, and property if people do commit crimes. Are such threats to be withdrawn as soon as they are encountered by opposing threats?": Stephen, *History of the Criminal Law of England* (1883) vol. II, 107–8.

[3] Hart, *Punishment and Responsibility* (1968) chap. vii.

[4] Some theorists, such as Schopp, believe that a conviction should be recorded against D; but not even he requires D to be punished. Schopp's views are discussed below, § 20.1(iv).

[5] [2005] UKHL 22, para. 18; [2005] AC 467, 489 (Lord Bingham).

carrying in his cab P, an armed man. P instructs him to park the vehicle outside a tobacconist's so that he may purchase cigarettes. D observes that parking is prohibited on the road adjacent to the shop; P responds he will blow D's brains out unless he does as he is told. It would be perverse to say that we *excuse* D for parking in the wrong place. He would have done the right thing, such is the disparity of the respective harms.[6] Where the balance of harms is more even, the pressure exerted on D is largely why we exonerate him. But where the discrepancy between the cost of complying with the letter of the law and the value of yielding to the threat is of the magnitude of our taxi-driver example, the focus is on the justifiability of his act. It may be that D has had a very bad day and to some degree welcomes the end of it all; still, if he decides after all to carry on living and parks his vehicle on the lines in order to do so, we should grant him the defence of duress.

Regardless whether, in particular cases, the emphasis is on excusatory pressure or on justifiable choice, duress operates in either context as a "pure" supervening defence. A valid plea of duress leaves intact the definitional elements of the offence charged. It is only when those elements have been proved against D that she need turn to duress as a way of avoiding the conviction that would otherwise follow. While, on occasion, attempts have been made to explain the defence of duress on the ground that, to be successful, it must negate actus reus or mens rea, we concur with the observation by Lord Bingham, in his wide-ranging review of the defence in *Hasan*, that "where duress is established it does not ordinarily operate to negative any legal ingredient of the crime."[7]

For centuries, duress traditionally involved situations where D committed a crime nominated by X, the person issuing the threat. Recently, the boundaries of the defence have been significantly enlarged, accommodating situations now known as "duress of circumstances".[8] These are cases where D (or another) is threatened with death or serious harm and, in order to avoid the harm, D, on his own initiative, commits what ordinarily would be a crime. The ramifications of this development are a work in progress, yet it is safe to say that duress by circumstances is now established as a discrete subdivision of the defence. In turn, this has helped prepare the way for an unequivocal recognition of a defence of necessity in English law. In this chapter we will examine the borderland between duress of circumstances and necessity, but we will defer a full consideration of the defence of necessity to Chapter 21.

(i) Duress by threat

First, we will examine duress in its traditional sense: a threat by P which will be lifted only if D commits a crime nominated by P.

---

[6] Under the rubric of duress (unlike that of necessity) we do not acquit D *for* doing the right thing: we acquit because he was under threat of death and acted in response to that threat. But where the disparity between what the duressor requires and what the duressor threatens is great, it seems right to conclude that D was justified in acting as he did unless we accord some transcendental value to compliance with the letter of the law. See further above, § 17.2.

[7] [2005] UKHL 22, para. 18. However, his Lordship took the view that duress always operates in the realm of excuse; contrasting with the view expressed here that, according to circumstances, duress may be variously excusatory or justificatory. We discuss the nature and rationale of duress further below, § 20.1(iv).

[8] Below, § 20.1(ii).

(a) The seriousness of the threat

The threat must be to inflict immediate or almost immediate *death or serious bodily harm*.[9] Nothing below that threshold is regarded, in law, as having sufficient coercive effect.[10] It is easy to envisage how other kinds of threat, e.g. to destroy a thriving business, or to expose details of a person's personal life, might be extremely effective in undermining resistance. Nonetheless, as a matter of policy, a threat of physical harm is insisted upon. Contrast the law of offences against the person, where psychological harm is regarded as bodily harm and serious psychological harm is regarded as grievous bodily harm.[11] Despite this, in *Baker*,[12] the Court of Appeal insisted that in the context of the defence of duress, a threat of physical harm was required.

There seems little immediate prospect of a more liberal approach. In *Quayle*,[13] the Court of Appeal refused to enlarge the notion of physical, bodily harm to accommodate physical *pain*, even extreme physical pain. Moreover, in *Hasan* the House of Lords took judicial notice of the increasing recourse to duress as a defence, especially in relation to drug dealing and associated offences, and of the difficulty experienced by prosecutors in rebutting this defence (particularly when raised late in the day). These considerations have prompted an overt policy to confine the defence within narrow limits.[14] In this climate, we may assume that a rigid requirement, for threats of death or serious physical harm in the most literal sense, will remain an essential condition of duress for the foreseeable future.

(b) A "present" threat: immediate or almost immediate and unavoidable

The immediacy of the threatened harm is an important requirement. At one time, the courts showed a degree of sensitivity and realism in applying this criterion. In *Hudson*,[15] D gave false testimony when she observed P, who had earlier threatened to "cut her up", staring at her intently as she was about to give evidence in a criminal trial involving defendants with a well-founded reputation for serious violence. She knew P was associated with the defendants. On appeal against D's conviction for perjury, the Court of Appeal ruled that a defence of duress should have been left to the jury. The Court took the view that a threat may be "present" or operative despite a delay in its implementation. Whereas the trial judge had been of the view that the defence must fail as D was safe in court when giving her perjured testimony, for the Court of Appeal it was enough that the threats could have been implemented later that day on the streets of Salford.[16]

In *Hussain*,[17] the Court of Appeal suggested that "imminent" was a more appropriate term than immediate and, certainly, an imminent rather than an immediate harm was at

---

[9] There are many authorities which insist that only death or serious harm will suffice; they are confirmed in an authoritative review of the defence by *Hasan* [2005] UKHL 22.

[10] In *Steane* [1947] KB 997, 1005, Goddard LCJ spoke, *obiter*, in terms of false imprisonment constituting adequate duress; but this must now be considered to be unreliable. In, *Valderrama-Vega* [1985] Crim LR 220 (CA), financial pressures and sexual blackmail were thought not to constitute legally adequate duress.

[11] *Burstow* [1998] AC 147 (HL); above, § 11.5(i)(a).

[12] [1997] Crim LR 497 (CA).

[13] [2005] EWCA Crim 1415; [2006] 1 All ER 988.

[14] [2005] UKHL 22, para. 21.

[15] [1971] 2 QB 202.

[16] By way of corollary, the Court of Appeal insisted that a realistic view should be taken of the degree of police protection available to D.

[17] [1999] Crim LR 570.

issue in *Hudson*. At the same time, "imminence" must still be understood as referring to something due to happen in the very near future. In *Cole*[18] the Court of Appeal was, it is submitted, right to reject a defence of duress to robbery when D robbed building societies in order to pay debts on a due date and thereby avoid violence on that later date. Indeed, *Hussain* itself was questionable on its facts. D and others hijacked a plane in order to travel to England from Sudan. They had good reason to fear that the Sudanese authorities might deport them to Iraq (where they were likely to be tortured and killed) at some time yet to be resolved. The Court of Appeal ruled that the trial judge was wrong to remove the issue of duress from the jury on the grounds of lack of immediately threatened harm. Arguably, a stricter view of imminence should be taken if the defence is to be kept within manageable bounds. That concern was very much to the mind of the House of Lords in *Hasan*. Although the matter did not fall for decision, Lord Bingham in his majority judgment specifically approved of the approach in *Cole* and disapproved of what he felt was a lax approach to the immediacy requirement in *Hudson* and particularly *Hussain*.[19] In the view of their Lordships, the implementation of the threat must follow "immediately or almost immediately".[20]

So it seems that "imminence" is not enough. But perhaps there is still some limited room for manoeuvre. It is possible, even in the light of Lord Bingham's stricter approach, to distinguish between *Hudson* and *Hussain*. In the latter case, the prospect of return to Iraq at the time of the hijack in Sudan was real but subject to contingencies and an uncertain time line. In *Hudson*, by contrast, P was present in court looking intently at D as she gave evidence. Furthermore, it was accepted that there was a real possibility that P and others would inflict serious violence on D later that same day. It is noteworthy that Baroness Hale, in a separate judgment, considered that the other members of the Court were overly concerned with denying the defence to criminals and their associates and insufficiently sensitive to the awful dilemmas that may confront vulnerable and innocent people caught up in the violence of others and beyond effective protection from the police and other agencies. It is submitted that it would be unfortunate if the threat in a case such as *Hudson* was considered too remote to constitute legal duress; even though Lord Bingham was clearly of the opinion that the defence should have failed in that case.

In addition to being immediate or almost immediate, the threat must also be unavoidable.[21] The exculpatory force of duress is based on the lack of viable alternatives: commit the offence or be killed (or seriously hurt). If there is a "safe avenue of escape", that should surely be taken.[22] Similarly, if effective protection is available to D, the threat is unlikely to constitute legally adequate duress.[23]

---

[18] [1994] Crim LR 582; below, § 20.1(i)(c).

[19] Baroness Hale was the only other member of the Court who gave a judgment on the duress aspect of *Hasan* and she favoured a rather less strict attitude to the defining conditions of the defence than did the other members of the bench (who concurred with Lord Bingham). The matter was *obiter* since, as will be discussed in § 20.1(i)(g), the House concurred unanimously that duress should be unavailable because D had voluntarily exposed himself to the risk of being coerced to commit offences.

[20] [2005] UKHL 22, para. 28.

[21] "No one could question that if a person can avoid the effects of duress by escaping from the threats, without damage to himself, he must do so": *Sharp* [1987] QB 853, 857 (Lord Lane CJ).

[22] *Gill* [1963] 2 All ER 688 (CA); *Hurley and Murray* [1967] VR 526.

[23] *Hudson* [1971] 2 QB 202; *Baker* [1999] 2 Cr App R 335 (CA). The need for imminence is separate from the question of protection: D may lose the defence of duress if she fails to seek effective protection even from an

In practice, immediacy will in most circumstances be strongly linked with unavoidability. But they are not inseparable: as when P points a knife at D and threatens to stab her forthwith unless she hands over the keys to the bank's safe, but D make her escape through a side door. If the threat is not of almost immediate application, then, as Lord Bingham put it, "there may be little if any room for doubt that [D] could have taken evasive action, whether by going to the police or in some other way."[24] But on particular facts, a less than completely immediate threat may nonetheless be in substance unavoidable: as the Court of Appeal recognised on the facts of *Hudson*.[25] Yet, from the negative attitude to that decision on the part of the majority in *Hasan*, it seems that a threat must be unavoidable *and* almost immediate. The fact that D acted as she did because she believed, entirely reasonably, that she would die or be very seriously hurt if she did not will not suffice. One can only hope that in deserving cases, courts will take what elbow room is needed from the qualification, *almost* immediate.

(c) Nomination of the crime

As currently interpreted, duress by threats involves an explicit or implicit requirement from X that D commits a *particular* crime. By contrast, in *Cole*,[26] D was ordered by X to make timely repayment of a debt or suffer serious harm. Consequently, he robbed a branch of a building society in order to obtain money for repayment. He was refused a defence of duress, *inter alia* because X had not *nominated*, expressly or impliedly, the crime D should commit. Robbing a building society was, rather, D's response to the predicament posed by X.

Historically, *Cole* is in line with the common law on duress by threats. Yet it is hard to discern what normative significance nomination has. Moreover, any requirement of nomination would appear now to be superseded by the evolution of the new subcategory of duress known as duress of circumstances (below, § 20.1 (ii)). Under that head, it is enough that D commits the offence (short of murder or attempted murder) as an avoiding response to an imminent threat of death or serious violence.[27] From D's perspective, the moral and legal issues at stake in duress by threats and duress of circumstances are essentially the same. "Nomination" is irrelevant. It is therefore submitted that nomination should not be a requirement for any form of duress. *Cole* is best explained on the basis of the finding that, in any event, the threat was insufficiently immediate.

(d) Resistance to the threat

In *Graham*, the Court of Appeal ruled that the threat made by X must, in all the circumstances, have been enough to overcome the resistance of a "sober person of reasonable

---

imminent threat. Conversely, if the threat (however real) is not imminent, the issue of effective protection does not arise.

[24] [2005] UKHL 22, para. 28.

[25] [1971] 2 QB 202.

[26] [1994] Crim LR 582 (CA); discussed above, § 20.1(i)(b).

[27] The Court of Appeal discussed some duress of circumstance cases but considered that the offences which fell to be excused under that head were, unlike the robberies in *Cole*, "spontaneous" reactions to the threats. The adjective is unhelpful. In every case they were *chosen* reactions, offences committed under the volition of the defendants and unnominated by anyone else.

firmness."[28] Recall that the threat must be a threat of imminent death or serious bodily harm. One might consider that most persons of reasonable firmness would succumb to pressure of that extreme kind. However, *Graham*, which was approved by the House of Lords in *Howe*,[29] makes clear that a balancing exercise must be done on each occasion between the threat and the crime that X requires D to commit. The more serious the offence and the greater its impact on innocent third parties, the more that is to be expected of D by way of resistance. As Lords Wilberforce and Edmund-Davies remarked in *Abbott*, "the more dreadful the circumstances of the [crime], . . . the stronger and more irresistible the duress needed before it could be regarded as affording any defence."[30]

Indeed, for murder or attempted murder, resistance to the threat must be unwavering. In *Howe*[31] the House of Lords ruled that duress could not be invoked as a defence to murder; further, it was immaterial whether D's involvement was as a principal or an accomplice.[32] In *Gotts*,[33] the House of Lords held that the rule in *Howe* extended to cases of attempted murder.

The exclusion of murder and attempted murder from the defence of duress is too rigid.[34] Lord Hailsham, arguing in favour of the current law, stated that to rule otherwise would be to vindicate "the coward and the poltroon."[35] Heroism is a quality to be praised, but it does not follow that its absence is reason for censure. There will be occasions where we would expect even a person of reasonable firmness to be coerced into participating in murder, for example if a taxi-driver were to find his cab commandeered by armed terrorists and himself ordered at gunpoint to be the driver for a terrorist operation. It cannot be right that the cab-driver will receive the same mandatory sentence as those who threatened him and who carried out the killings. The position is all the more anomalous given that a person who intentionally causes grievous bodily harm (which is a sufficient mens rea for murder) would be able to raise a defence of duress if his victim should survive the attack. It is noteworthy that in the context of a case where he was seeking to narrow the defence of duress, Lord Bingham stated that the argument for the extension of the defence to murder was, in logic "irresistible".[36] The Law Commission has since recommended extension of the defence to murder.[37]

(e) A sober person of reasonable firmness

What characteristics constitute the sober person of reasonable firmness, the standard of fortitude required by *Graham* and approved in *Howe*? This notional person may be attributed

---

[28] [1982] 1 All ER 801, 806.

[29] [1987] AC 417.

[30] [1976] 3 All ER 140, 152 (PC) (dissenting). The comments are made in the context of murder (and, as we shall see, are no longer applicable to that offence), but remain in point for other offences.

[31] [1987] AC 417.

[32] *Howe* overruled *Lynch* [1975] AC 653, where the House of Lords had permitted duress to be raised to *complicity* in murder, and confirmed *Abbott* [1976] 3 All ER 140, where the Privy Council had denied a defence of duress to murder as a principal.

[33] [1992] 2 AC 412.

[34] Treason may also fall outside the defence.

[35] *Howe* [1987] AC 417, 432.

[36] *Hasan* [2005] UKHL 22, para. 21.

[37] *Murder, Manslaughter and Infanticide*, Law Com. No. 304 (2006) part 6. The Law Commission's proposal places the burden of proof on D.

the age and sex of the defendant and must be assumed to be sober.[38] If the defendant is pregnant, so too is the notional person.[39] Unsurprisingly, timidity and pliancy were held in *Graham* to be non-attributable: to attribute them would have been to contradict the yardstick of reasonable firmness.[40]

In *Emery*,[41] the Court of Appeal considered *obiter* that a recognised psychiatric syndrome or mental illness could be attributed to the person of reasonable firmness. The Court envisaged that a jury could properly be asked what degree of resistance should have been shown by a woman suffering from post-traumatic stress disorder which had resulted in a condition of learned helplessness. Yet, even if D's condition is a product of psychiatric disorder, there seems to be an element of contradiction in attributing learned helplessness to "a woman of reasonable firmness". A possible way of reconciling this with an objective test is to allow such a condition to be attributed if a woman of reasonable firmness would have been afflicted with learned helplessness had she been subjected to the same experiences as D. However, this rationalisation, which is not made explicit in *Emery*, leads to singularly unattractive distinctions. Why should a state of learned helplessness generated by life's vicissitudes be treated more favourably than a similar condition which arises from a person's genetic endowment?[42]

What *is* clear, at least, is that any condition which does not amount to a mental illness or psychiatric disorder will not be attributed. The case law excludes personal characteristics such as "grossly elevated neurotic state",[43] unusual vulnerability to pressure,[44] and lack of firmness arising from sexual abuse.[45]

(f) Impact of the threat

Even if a threat of death or serious harm has been made which would have moved to action a person of reasonable firmness, it does not follow that D will be allowed a defence of duress. She *herself* must be influenced by that threat to commit the crime. If the commission of the crime is something she would have done anyway, a defence is not available. On the other hand, provided the threat was a material reason why D committed the crime, it need not have been the sole or even the dominant reason. In *Valderrama-Vega*,[46] D was confronted with threats of financial loss, exposure of his homosexuality, and physical violence. Only the last, of course, qualifies as legal duress. The Court of Appeal considered that D was entitled to raise a defence of duress if he would not have committed the crime but for

---

[38] In *Graham* [1982] 1 All ER 801, 806, Lane LCJ drew a direct (and questionable) analogy with provocation and aligned the "characteristics" applicable to pleas of provocation with characteristics allowed when applying the defence of duress.

[39] *Bowen* [1996] 4 All ER 837, 844 (CA), where there is added fear for the unborn child.

[40] Confirmed in *Bowen*, *ibid.*: "The mere fact that the accused is more pliable, vulnerable, timid, or susceptible to threats than a normal person are not characteristics [*sic*] with which it is legitimate to invest the reasonable/ordinary person for the purpose of considering the objective test."

[41] (1993) 14 Cr App R (S) 394 (CA).

[42] For a telling critique of applying an objective standard in duress, see Smith, "Duress and Steadfastness: In Pursuit of the Unintelligible" [1999] *Crim LR* 363.

[43] *Hegarty* [1994] Crim LR 353 (CA).

[44] *Horne* [1994] Crim LR 584 (CA).

[45] *Hirst* [1995] 1 Cr App R 82 (CA).

[46] [1985] Crim LR 220 (CA).

threats of violence. If so, it was immaterial that other pressures were operating at the same time.

(g) Voluntary exposure to threats

Duress may not be available as a defence if D voluntarily consorts with persons who resort to violence when committing offences or joins an organisation aware that the infliction of violence is one of its organising principles. So, if D joins a terrorist organisation or an organised criminal gang, it will not avail him that he was later faced with a choice between offending and suffering "discipline" involving serious physical harm.[47] This is a salutary principle, an important limitation on the capacity of intrinsically violent organisations to provide its membership with immunity from wrongdoing. Nonetheless, it should be open for D to show that he has left the organisation, or dissociated himself from his acquaintances, of his own volition; thereafter, he should not be precluded from raising the defence. Additionally, he should not lose the defence if he was made to join the gang by a threat of imminent violence which continued thereafter.

This exclusionary principle was considerably tightened by the decision of the House of Lords in *Hasan*.[48] D had worked as driver and minder for E, who ran an escort agency. After P, a drug dealer and a man of violence, became E's boyfriend, D was ousted from his role in working for E. Nonetheless, as the jury found, D and P had remained in contact. Subsequently, P ordered D to carry out a burglary in the company of another person, F, informing D that F would kill him unless the crime was carried out. On these facts, the House of Lords ruled that any claim of duress must fail. In the words of Lord Bingham:[49]

> "The policy of the law must be to discourage association with known criminals, and it should
> be slow to excuse the criminal conduct of those who do so. If a person voluntarily becomes or
> remains associated with others engaged in criminal activity in a situation where he knows or
> ought reasonably to know that he may be the subject of compulsion by them or their associ-
> ates, he cannot rely on the defence of duress to excuse any act which he is thereafter
> compelled to do by them."

The width of this statement should be emphasised. The fact of association is enough; D's association with P need not involve any joint criminal activity. Presumably D must know that P is a criminal although Lord Bingham does not explicitly state this. Once the fact of association is proved D will be denied access to the defence of duress if he ought reasonably to have known that P might subject him to compulsion. Note the fact that D ought to have realised that D might be violent to him is enough. It is not necessary that he should have reasonably anticipated that P might coerce him into the commission of a crime.

This is tough law, too tough for Baroness Hale. She expressed an understandable fear that women in relationships with criminal men might be denied the defence merely on the basis that they should have foreseen that P might be violent to them in the course of the relationship. She would insist that D should have foreseen that P would coerce her into

---

[47] *Sharp* [1987] QB 853 (CA). (An organised criminal gang. D was threatened with being shot when seeking to withdraw from a robbery; a defence of duress was denied.)

[48] [2005] UKHL 22; [2005] 2 AC 467.

[49] *Ibid.*, para. 38.

committing a crime, a condition which she considered would have been fulfilled on the facts of *Hasan*. The majority disavowed that limitation, confirming the decision in *Harmer*.[50] In the latter case, D was coerced by E into smuggling Class A drugs. D was a drug addict and was aware of the risk that E might be violent to him should he fail to pay on time for drugs supplied by E. D had not anticipated that E would coerce him into committing criminal acts to clear his indebtedness. Nonetheless, the Court of Appeal upheld the ruling of the trial judge in refusing D a defence of duress. The fact that D was aware of the risk of violence from E should he form an association with him precluded any reliance on E's threats as a form of duress.

(h) Threats to persons other than D

The paradigm situation in duress is where X threatens D with death or grievous bodily harm unless she commits a crime nominated by X. As we have seen, the essence of the defence is the pressure that the threat exerts on D herself, a threat sufficient to sway a person of reasonable firmness. The pressure on D may be equally or even more intense should the threat be made against E, the husband or daughter or any other person closely connected with D. There is authority that the defence of duress will accommodate such situations[51] and every reason in principle why it should. D may be able to resist a threat to herself yet be unable to allow her resistance to initiate death or serious harm to a loved one. Indeed, the defence of duress should not be constrained by any closed list of relationships. Suppose that X, a bank robber, threatens to shoot a customer unless D, a bank employee, hands over the key to the safe. It is easy to imagine how D may feel constrained to comply.[52] In *Hasan* Lord Bingham stated that the threat could be to D, his immediate family, and to any "person for whose safety the defendant would reasonably regard himself as responsible."[53]

(ii) Duress of circumstances

In a sequence of cases—*Willer*,[54] *Conway*,[55] and *Martin*[56]—the Court of Appeal has laid the foundation for a "duress of circumstances" defence. The first two cases involved driving offences; it was ruled on both occasions that a defence of duress should have been left to the jury in the light of evidence that the vehicles had been driven as they had in order to escape threats of serious violence. These rulings were confirmed in *Martin*, where the Court of Appeal ruled that D should have been allowed to raise a defence of duress in answer to a

---

[50] [2002] Crim LR 401.

[51] *Hurley and Murray* [1967] VR 526 (Victoria SC) (threats to *de facto* wife); *Ortiz* (1986) 83 Cr App R 173 (CA) (assumption that threats to wife and daughter would suffice); *Martin* [1989] 1 All ER 652 (CA) (offending to ward off a threat of suicide by wife).

[52] It is noteworthy that in *Conway* [1989] QB 290 (CA), the threat constituting duress of circumstances was to D's passenger rather than D. The Court did not investigate the nature of the relationship between D and the passenger. The Draft Criminal Code (Law Com. No. 177), cl. 42, refers to threats "to cause death or serious personal harm to himself *or another*."

[53] [2005] UKHL 22, para. 21(3).

[54] (1986) 83 Cr App R (CA).

[55] [1989] QB 290 (CA).

[56] [1989] 1 All ER 652 (CA).

charge of driving while disqualified. D's wife had threatened to kill herself unless D drove their son to his place of work.

Martin can be explained in terms of duress by threats. It is true that the threat was not directed at D, but it was (self-)directed to his wife and there is authority that a threat to one's wife will suffice.[57] Furthermore, the crime that D had to commit was implicit in the terms of the threat. *Conway* and *Willer*, however, do enter new territory. In these cases, D responded to the threat by committing a crime of his own choosing. It was certainly not a case of X's directing D to do something. X, on the account offered by D, would have preferred D to do nothing; to stay where he was so that X could inflict violence on him.

Interestingly, there is no suggestion by the Court of Appeal in either decision that any extension of the law has occurred. Prior to these cases, the predominant view was that committing a crime of one's own initiative in order to avoid harm founded, if anything, a plea of necessity rather than duress unless the circumstances fell within self-defence.[58] Further, it is thought that conduct covered by necessity must be justified conduct; conduct that is merely excused cannot be said to have been necessary. Accordingly, *Willer* and *Conway* advance the law of excuse-based defences. Properly so. A threat of death or serious bodily harm was present in each case. The crimes were committed under the pressure of such threats. It is clearly established that if X tells D to drive his car on the pavement or be shot, D would have a defence of duress were he to do as he was told. There seems little justification for treating the circumstances that arose in *Willer* differently merely because D drove on his own initiative onto the pavement to escape being shot. By analogy with duress by threats, it will be sufficient that a person of reasonable firmness would have responded to the pressure in a manner similar to D, provided D's response did not take the form of committing or attempting murder. Further, if we allow cases like *Willer* and *Conway* to fall within the law of duress, we should allow pressures arising from natural forces within the defence too. If D drives on to the pavement to avoid a herd of charging bulls he should be able to raise the defence.[59]

One important limitation on the range of threats that D can invoke by way of defence is that the threat must emanate from an external source. D cannot, for example, raise duress of circumstance in answer to a charge of prison escape by reference to the suicidal urges to which his confinement gave rise.[60]

(a) Duress of circumstances distinguished from necessity

The cases under discussion above were found relevant on the facts of *Pommell*.[61] D was arrested late at night in his bed in possession of a sub-machine gun. On his account, he came to have the gun because he had persuaded X, who was planning "to shoot some geezer with it", to hand it over to him. D, so his story went, had taken it into his custody in order to hand it to his brother who would turn it over to the police and would have done so in the

---

[57] *Hurley and Murray* [1967] VR 526 (Victoria SC); *Ortiz* (1986) 83 Cr App R 173 (CA).

[58] Elliot, "Necessity, Duress and Self-Defence" [1989] *Crim LR* 611; Horder, "Self-Defence, Necessity and Duress: Understanding the Relationship" (1998) 1 *Canadian J Law & Juris* 143.

[59] *Smith and Hogan* 314.

[60] *Rogers and Rose* (1998) 1 Cr App R 143 (CA).

[61] [1995] 2 Cr App R 607 (CA).

morning but for the inconvenience of his arrest. The trial judge had ruled that no defence issue arose on these facts, even assuming them to be true.[62] The Court of Appeal overruled him. Authorities such as *Willer* required his story, if supported by any evidence, to be put to the jury.

It should be noted that *Pommell* is a different kind of case from any of those discussed so far in this section. According to his version of events, D himself was never under any threat or pressure from X. The "geezer" whom X intended to kill was not nearby when D persuaded him to hand over the weapon. What D was doing amounted to a responsible exercise in citizenship, unconstrained by any danger or pressure. Here we are dealing with a case of necessity rather than duress. This is in some sense acknowledged by the Court, which uses the expressions "duress" and "necessity" indifferently in its judgment. D seems clearly to have been justified in what he did. Surely it is better to be in possession of a firearm without a licence than to permit X to follow his murderous path? But where D acts in such a fashion, not under coercion himself, he *must* be justified; whereas duress may be allowed to excuse. Accordingly, *Pommell* may be regarded, at least *sub silentio*, as a case of necessity, a defence to be discussed more fully below.[63]

(iii) Mistaken duress

In *Graham*,[64] the Court of Appeal considered that if D *reasonably* believed in the existence of circumstances that would have given a sober person of reasonable firmness good cause to fear death or serious injury, then he was entitled to raise the defence as if his belief were true. The Court's insistence on a reasonable mistake draws on an analogy with the defence of provocation, which is also based on a reasonable person standard. However, in provocation, the cases of *Letenock*[65] and *Wardrope*[66] go further. They allow an intoxicated belief in the existence of a provocative incident to provide a ground of excuse. This went unremarked in *Graham*. Confusingly, in *Martin (David)*,[67] the Court of Appeal endorsed a subjective approach to mistaken duress. In *Hasan*, however, the requirement for a reasonable mistake was reaffirmed by the House of Lords.[68] Although the affirmation was *obiter*, it was in the course of a wide-ranging review of the defence and should be regarded as settling the issue.

It will be recalled that beliefs relating to self-defence and the prevention of crime need only be genuine and need not be based on reasonable grounds,[69] whereas belief in the existence of duress, like consent in sexual offences, must be based on reasonable grounds.[70] It may well be that these differences are appropriate in their respective fields of application;

---

[62] Remarkably, Mr. Pommell has since come into possession of a gun for the second time and again was frustrated from handing it into police custody by premature arrest. This time he successfully raised an interesting point in the law of evidence: *Pommell* [1999] Crim LR 576 (CA).

[63] § 21.3.

[64] [1982] 1 All ER 801, 806; see too *Cairns* [1999] 2 Cr App R 137 (CA).

[65] (1917) 12 Cr App R 221 (CCA).

[66] [1960] Crim LR 770 (CCA).

[67] *Martin* [2000] 2 Cr App R 42. The favouring of an objective approach in *Graham* had been approved, *obiter*, by the House of Lords in *Howe* [1987] AC 417.

[68] [2005] UKHL 22, para. 23.

[69] Above, § 18.1(iii).

[70] See above, § 12.6.

but it merits note that the discrepancies have not been addressed in the case law, which offers no persuasive general account.

(iv) A rationale of duress

There has been considerable doctrinal uncertainty why duress should provide a defence. The claim has been made that threats as extreme as death or serious bodily harm induce conduct which is involuntary and, consequently, not fairly attributable to the person coerced.[71] On this view, duress may negate the actus reus of the offence. Yet this explanation does not convince. The involuntariness in question in cases of duress is of a less fundamental kind than the physical involuntariness of conduct occurring in a state of automatism or as a consequence of a reflex response.[72] When D commits a crime rather than be killed, she is making a choice, albeit in circumstances not of her own making.[73] Of course, a person choosing between death or committing a crime is making a choice of a different order from that involved in choosing, say, between a winter or summer holiday. Yet the decision to commit the crime is a product of deliberation. It is *her* choice, albeit a constrained choice. Even the most coercive of threats is compatible with proof of actus reus, as English law implicitly recognises when denying the defence of duress to anyone charged with murder.

Alternatively, it has been asserted that duress of sufficient potency is incompatible with a finding of mens rea.[74] Unfortunately, this is equally unconvincing, at least in English law. The term mens rea is a technical expression, a reference to the mental element required for the offence in question.[75] Sometimes the presence of duress may negate particular forms of mens rea: a manner of driving that would be accounted reckless may not deserve that description if driving as D did was the only way of escaping a threat of death or grievous bodily harm.[76] Yet there will be many occasions where the presence of duress is compatible with proof of mens rea. Indeed, this is the norm. If D commits crime X rather than be killed, she does so deliberately. D intends the wrong she commits, even if she regrets having to do so.

Thus duress is generally compatible with the definitional elements of the offence with which the defendant is charged. Schopp has argued that the presence of these elements should entail a conviction because duress does not provide any plausible ground of excuse

---

[71] *Per* Widgery LJ in *Hudson* [1971] 2 QB 202, 206, "It is clearly established that duress provides a defence . . . if the will of the accused has been overborne by threats of death or serious personal injury so that the commission of the alleged offence was no longer the voluntary act of the accused."

[72] § 4.3(i).

[73] "A criminal walking to execution is under compulsion if any man can be said to be so, but his motions are just as much voluntary as if he [were] going to leave his place of confinement and regain his liberty. He walks to his death because he prefers it to being carried": Stephen, *History of the Criminal Law of England* (1883) vol. II, 102.

[74] *Paquette* (1997) 70 DLR (3d) 129 (Supreme Court of Canada); criticised by Colvin, *Principles of Criminal Law* (2nd ed., 1991) 236–8.

[75] *Yip Chiu-cheung* [1995] AC 111 (PC); *Kingston* [1995] 2 AC 355 (HL).

[76] *Harris* [1995] 1 Cr App R 170 (CA). But see *Backshall* [1999] 1 Cr App R 35, where the Court of Appeal held, on a charge of driving without due care and attention, that the issue of necessity or duress of circumstances would be more clearly resolved by invoking those defences, rather than by assessing whether the driving was done with due care and attention.

or justification.[77] Contrasting duress with mistake-based and disability defences, Schopp observes that defendants pleading duress possess the capacities of responsible agents and possess the knowledge with which to exercise these capacities. As he puts it, defendants raising duress "act on action plans that include the acts exemplifying the objective offence elements as intended components."[78] The choice to offend is theirs. Schopp acknowledges that duress may have considerable mitigating force and concedes that in many cases no punishment whatever would be warranted. In order to allow for such cases, he proposes a special verdict to be available, "a purely vindicating conviction" from which no penal consequences would flow. For him, recording a conviction of this special kind will reflect the general community condemnation of conduct which breaches the rules of the criminal law by an agent free from disability and lacking any deficiencies in knowledge or perception.[79]

Schopp radically underestimates the stigmatic impact of a conviction for a serious offence. Allowing duress, in appropriate circumstances, to provide complete exculpation signals that the criminal law, which is a system of *blame* as well as punishment,[80] withholds its censure from conduct that merely demonstrates a failure of virtue. The criminal law does not demand perfection. The essence of duress is a pressure to conform to the will of the duressor which not even a person of reasonable firmness could have resisted. When that condition is met, it is defamatory to impose a conviction, and a form of hypocrisy that is best avoided.

The defence is based on a moral evaluation of D's conduct: can we be sure that an ordinary person of reasonable firmness would have done better than D? It is not a disability defence; as Ashworth observes, it is available to D even though she may have been "cool as a cucumber" when responding to the threat of death or serious personal injury.[81] Sometimes, the jury's task will be easy. Surely it is better that D gives a burglar the keys to V's house rather than be instantly shot? At other times, intractable decisions may arise: it must be a dreadful thing to be under threat of death at the hands of an oppressive political regime, but it is also dreadful to hijack an aeroplane, spreading insecurity and terror.[82] Either way, in resolving such questions, we can only employ the normative standard of an ordinary person of reasonable firmness with reference to the values and interests at stake in the instant case. It should not, outside the realm of defences based on disability, be enough for a defendant to claim that she, from weakness of will or timidity, could not have done better. It *should* be enough for her to answer that only persons of special virtue could have done better.

§ 20.2 Coercion

Although the terminology is not always consistent in the cases, "coercion" is the term reserved for a common law defence that used to be available to women who committed crimes in the presence of their husbands. Formerly, to what crimes the defence applied and

[77] Schopp, *Justification Defenses and Just Convictions* (1998) chap. 5.
[78] *Ibid.*, 141.
[79] *Ibid.*, 142–6.
[80] Above, § 1.1(iii).
[81] *Principles of Criminal Law* (3rd ed., 1999) 231.
[82] *Hussain* [1999] Crim LR 570.

what modes of pressure sufficed remained unclear.[83] The defence involved a presumption, rebuttable by the prosecution, that any crime committed by a wife in the presence of her husband was perpetrated under his coercion. These issues are partially resolved by section 47 of the Criminal Justice Act 1925, which abolishes the presumption:

> Any presumption of law that an offence committed by a wife in the presence of her husband is committed under the coercion of the husband is hereby abolished, but on a charge against a wife for any offence other than treason or murder, it shall be a good defence to prove that the offence was committed in the presence of, and under the coercion of, the husband.

However, what constitutes coercion is undefined in the Act and there is very little case law to offer guidance. Because a probative burden is placed on D, it seems safe to assume that the pressures which suffice to establish this defence need not be imminent threats of death or serious bodily harm; otherwise D would be better off pleading duress, where the ultimate probative burden falls to the prosecution. This view is supported by the Court of Appeal decision in *Shortland*,[84] where D's conviction was quashed because the trial judge had directed the jury in terms of threats of death or serious bodily harm. The court assumed that moral and emotional pressures would suffice, though mere loyalty to her husband would not. In the court's view the pressures must be such "that her will was overborne by the wishes of her husband," so that she was "forced unwillingly to participate" in the offence;[85] or, in an acceptable alternative phrasing, that D "was so overborne by the personality of her husband that she had no realistic alternative but to succumb to his will."[86]

The defence has significant restrictions. It is not applicable to murder or treason although, unlike duress, it would be available as a defence to attempted murder. The offence must be committed in "the presence" of the husband. One can only speculate how literally this requirement will be construed. In a different context, the complicity case of *Richards*[87] suggests that it may be necessary to be physically present at the scene of a crime before one is regarded as "present" in law. In *Richards*, D was not regarded as present despite being able to communicate with the principal offenders at the time of the offence, since she was some half a mile away from the scene of the crime. By analogy, it may be enough that the husband is able to bring pressure to bear *at the time the offence is committed*, for example where he stands outside the house in which D carries out the burglary he has coerced her to commit.

The most telling restriction is the need for a relationship of marriage. It is not enough that D believes that she is married to the person coercing her, even if that belief is based on reasonable grounds.[88] In such a case, however, although D does not fall within the terms of section 47, which clearly posits a relationship of man and wife, such a woman should be allowed a common law defence of mistake of fact by analogy with persons who reasonably

---

[83] Kenny, *Outlines of Criminal Law* (1902) 71–2.

[84] [1996] 1 Cr App R 116 (CA).

[85] *Ibid.*, 118, adopting the direction given in *Richman* [1982] Crim LR 507. "Overbear her will" should be read in a metaphorical sense. A person subject to emotional pressure is clearly capable of volitional conduct in the sense used in the criminal law.

[86] *Ibid.*

[87] [1974] QB 776 (CA).

[88] *Ditta* [1988] Crim LR 43 (CA).

believe that they are subject to duress. There is no reason of principle why the same approach should not be adopted for mistaken beliefs relating to coercion.[89]

There have also been suggestions that polygamous marriages fall outside the Act.[90] If there is to be an offence of material coercion at all, it is anomalous to exclude such marriages where coercive pressures are likely to be just as strong as in monogamous marriages. Whether there should be a defence at all is another matter. The existence of the defence cannot be accommodated to a view of marriage as a partnership of equal persons. If there is to be any relaxation of the rigour of the law of duress, this should be done in general terms and not confined to married women. Under the current law of duress, reference can be made to the gender of the person coerced.[91] There seems little value in other forms of accommodation. The Law Commission has recommended, appropriately, the abolition of the defence of marital coercion.[92]

§ 20.3 Superior orders

Criminal conduct cannot be justified or excused on the basis of the order of a superior, be that superior a public or private official. This is an important constitutional principle, founded on the lack of any dispensing power in English law.[93] A superior order may preclude liability on another ground: if D is ordered to destroy property and is instructed that it is the property of his employer, he will lack mens rea for the crime of criminal damage.[94] In general, however, in the absence of a defence of reasonable mistake of law,[95] a belief that conduct is lawful merely because of the order of a superior will not avail if the mens rea of the offence is present. Accordingly, an undercover police officer committed the offence of drug-trafficking when he took drugs from Hong Kong to Sydney because he knew the item transported to be drugs—the fact that he was part of a police operation to expose and convict drug-traffickers was held to be irrelevant.[96]

The lack of any power on the part of officials to suspend the operation of law is an admirable constitutional principle. However, in the context of criminal trials, it may produce harsh results. In *Kelly v. Minister of Defence*,[97] a civil action, a soldier shot and killed V, a person whom he took to be a terrorist. V in fact was a joy-rider. *Inter alia*, the soldier was seeking to prevent V from committing terrorist crimes in the future, a permissible justification according to the Court of Appeal of Northern Ireland. That decision is open to

---

[89] For instance, if D *mistakenly* believes that V is committing a crime, any preventive force he employs against V will fall outside the terms of s. 3 of the Criminal Law Act 1967, which requires "such force as is reasonable in the prevention of crime." Nonetheless, D will be able to raise a defence of mistake: *Williams* [1987] 3 All ER 411; above, § 18.1(iii).

[90] *Ditta* [1988] Crim LR 43.

[91] *Bowen* [1996] 4 All ER 837 (CA).

[92] Law Com. No. 83, *Defences of General Application* (1977) para. 3.9.

[93] *Entick v. Carrington* (1765) 19 St Tr 1029, 95 ER 807.

[94] *James* (1837) 8 C & P 131, 173 ER 429.

[95] Above, § 18.2.

[96] *Yip Chiu-cheung* [1995] 1 AC 111 (PC). The House of Lords in *Clegg* [1995] 1 AC 482 confirmed, *obiter*, that military orders would not afford a defence.

[97] [1989] NI 341.

serious criticism and may well be reconsidered.[98] Envisage a situation where, in circumstances such as those in *Kelly*, D received an order from E, his commanding officer, to shoot to kill V. D's options in such circumstances are unenviable: if he refused the order he might well be court-martialled for disobeying a lawful order, whereas obedience to an unlawful order may lead to a mandatory life sentence. Under the current, uncertain, state of the law if is not clear whether the order is lawful, so either outcome is possible. A junior soldier is surely in no position to decide these issues. Resolving the important and competing principles at stake in such cases is not easy, particularly as cases such as *Kelly* tend to arise in highly charged political contexts. Accommodation of the competing interests would be a great deal easier were there no mandatory penalty for murder.

§ 20.4 Entrapment

Not infrequently, police and other law enforcement officials resort to forms of incitement, pressure, or persuasion in order to obtain evidence of criminal activity.[99] For instance, E, a plain-clothes policeman, may present himself as a person anxious to acquire illegal drugs. D may be an unsuspecting drug dealer and supply drugs in response to a first request by E. Alternatively, D may not be a drug dealer but may nonetheless obtain drugs to supply E because E has offered a large sum of money for this service, or because E has frightened him into doing so by some form of threat. There may well arise situations where we can be sure that D would not have committed the offence with which he was charged but for the machinations of E. In *Sang*,[100] D was charged with dealing in counterfeit currency. He argued that he was inveigled into obtaining and supplying forged notes by the constant persuasion and insistence of E, an undercover police officer. Entrapment by an *agent provocateur*, it was claimed, should provide a complete defence to the charge in circumstances where commission of the offence was the consequence of acts of entrapment of law enforcement officials.[101] The House of Lords, however, rejected any defence of entrapment. Entrapping conduct may involve offences (as principals or accomplices) by police officers, but would not normally provide a ground of exemption for the person entrapped. Furthermore, any evidence obtained by entrapment was admissible at trial.

The rejection of an entrapment defence has been criticised. Choo, for instance argues for the recognition of a substantive defence of entrapment on the basis that entrapment:[102]

> "causes, in a broad sense, the commission of a crime. . . . The actual commission of the crime can be regarded as having been a fruit of the impropriety. . . . There is no justification for conviction of an entrapped defendant."

---

[98] Below, § 20.2(v).

[99] Heydon, "The Problems of Entrapment" [1973] *CLJ* 268.

[100] [1980] AC 402 (HL).

[101] The defence is allowed to a number of non-violent crimes in the United States, although there is division as to the rationale of the defence: contrast *Sorrells v. US* (1932) 287 US 435 (emphasising reduced culpability of offender) with *Sherman v. US* (1958) US 369 (focussing on unacceptable police methods).

[102] *Abuse of Process and Judicial Stays of Criminal Proceedings* (1993) 167.

In terms of the personal culpability of the offender, this argument is wanting. Choo is using "cause" in a very broad sense indeed; unless the mode of entrapment involves psychological coercion, a decision by D to supply drugs to E will be the act of an autonomous person, however persistent or persuasive the conduct of E. If E were simply an eager customer for drugs, any claim to exonerate D on account of E's persistence would be risible. The fact that E is an undercover policeman does not alter D's normative position. What attracts attention here is the normative position of E. To be sure, certain methods of entrapment go too far. The question then arises whether correcting certain forms of law enforcement excess is best done by providing an entrapment defence for D, notwithstanding the lack of any excuse personal to her.

To date, English law has stopped short of reversing *Sang*, while taking some steps to discourage police malpractice. There are two main mechanisms. First, section 78 of the Police and Criminal Evidence Act 1984 grants a discretion to the court to exclude evidence if, in all the circumstances, including the circumstances in which the evidence was obtained, it would have such an adverse effect on the fairness of the proceedings that the court ought not to admit it. In *Smurthwaite*,[103] the Court of Appeal considered that the phrase "fairness of the proceedings" could accommodate not only consideration of the position of the accused but also matters of "fairness to the public". In certain circumstances, evidence obtained by entrapping manœuvres could be excluded. Lord Taylor CJ laid particular emphasis on whether D would have committed the offence but for the enticement of the undercover officer, and on whether the role of the officer was active or passive.

Secondly, in *Latif*,[104] the House of Lords took the view that evidence obtained by entrapment could be excluded as an abuse of the process of the court. The House drew a comparison with exclusion under section 78 and emphasised that the judicial discretion to exclude on abuse of process grounds was focused on the public interest in the integrity of the criminal process rather than on unfairness to the individual defendant. This jurisdiction is discretionary, involving a balancing exercise between the nature and gravity of the crime and public interest in effective enforcement, on the one hand, and the nature and seriousness of the misconduct by law enforcement officers on the other.

In addition to the exclusion of evidence, the practical effect of raising the issue of entrapment may also be to obtain a reduction in sentence.[105]

Whether English law should provide a more effective protection against entrapping conduct is a question that arose following the decision of the European Court of Human Rights in *Teixeira de Castro* v. *Portugal*.[106] D, a person with no criminal record and unknown to the police, was introduced to two undercover police officers. At their request, he bought heroin on their behalf. He was convicted of drug dealing on the evidence of the officers and sentenced to six years' imprisonment. The European Court, in a strong judgment, ruled that resort to incitement on the part of the officers had deprived D of a fair trial, within the terms of Article 6 of the ECHR, "from the outset". A balancing exercise of the kind employed in the English abuse of process cases is notably absent from the Court's reasoning.

---

[103] (1994) 98 Cr App R 437 (CA).
[104] [1996] 1 All ER 353 (HL).
[105] e.g. *Springer* [1999] 1 Cr App R (S) 217 (CA).
[106] [1998] Crim LR 751.

Evidence obtained by police incitement entailed, without more, a breach of Article 6. Even in the context of drug-trafficking, the right to a fair trial could not be sacrificed in the interests of effective law enforcement.

In the conjoined appeals of *Loosely and A-G's Reference (No. 3 of 2000)*,[107] the House of Lords declined to find that the decision in *Teixeira* required provision of a substantive defence of entrapment in English law. To that extent its previous decision in *Sang* is confirmed. Yet the decision in *Teixeira* was not without impact. The House of Lords accepted that the guarantee of fair trial under Article 6 might require examination of the entirety of the prosecution process. It accepted, too, that certain forms of entrapment might generate evidence that it would be unfair to use against D. However, the House considered that issues of fairness to D could be adequately addressed by exercising the discretion to exclude evidence allowed under section 78 of the Police and Criminal Evidence Act 1984.

Notwithstanding *Teixeira*, the emphasis of the judgments in *Looseley and A-G's Reference (No. 3 of 2000)* is not on fairness to D but on the integrity of the prosecution process. The House considered that the primary check on excessive entrapment procedures should be a stay of the prosecution; on the basis that, in the light of the excess revealed, to allow the prosecution to proceed would amount to abuse of the process of the courts.

What guidance does the House of Lords provide on what might be considered excessive entrapment procedures? Unsurprisingly, nothing approaching an exact formula is provided. Much will depend on the nature of the offence, the propensities of the offender, and the difficulties of enforcement. In the broadest of terms, a distinction is drawn between providing D with an opportunity to offend—an opportunity freely taken—and conduct that unconscionably pressures or entices D into committing an offence he would not otherwise have committed.

Certainly, the police have considerable latitude under the present dispensation. In *Jones*,[108] D had left graffiti messages seeking contact with underage girls for sex. These were followed up by undercover police officers, who finally secured a rendezvous with D, after he initially failed to appear, by sending him a series of explicit text messages. The Court of Appeal held the police conduct appropriate: it did not, the Court asserted, amount to inciting D to commit underage sex offences. With respect, this reasoning must be doubted, in light of the readiness to find incitement by persons who merely respond positively to unsolicited offers to supply pornographic services.[109] The better conclusion is that it may have been incitement, but that it was not entrapment.

Given the very broad nature of the evaluations at stake, and the complex normative issues involved, further precision seems at present unobtainable. Future litigation exploring the borderland between acceptable and unacceptable entrapping procedures seems inevitable.

---

[107] [2000] 4 All ER 897; Ashworth, "Redrawing the Boundaries of Entrapment" [2002] *Crim LR* 161.
[108] [2007] EWCA Crim 1118.
[109] Above, § 9.1(i).

§ 20.5 Impossibility

As the majority of duties imposed by the criminal law are negative duties—things we must not do—the defence of impossibility[110] has a limited scope. Save for quite exceptional circumstances, which would in any event be covered by other doctrines, it is always possible to refrain from some action. It is different with offences which consist of an omission to do something or with the acquisition of some proscribed status. Circumstances may arise where the law requires an act that cannot be performed by D or where the acquisition of the proscribed status was impossible for D to avoid. If, in either case, D was not at fault in bringing about the impossibility, he should not be liable for any offence.

On rare occasions, English law has allowed an impossibility defence, though without any real consistency.[111] The courts have tended to approach questions of impossibility on the basis of interpreting the terms of a particular statute, rather than from the perspective of any general principle. It is submitted, however, that the best approach is not necessarily to recognise a defence of impossibility. Rather than being a matter of defence, impossibility raises an issue going to the very suppositions of criminal liability. If D is not responsible for the impossibility, then he may properly claim that the omission he is charged with, or the status he is blamed for acquiring, is not something which is linked to any voluntary conduct ascribable to him. That is to say: impossibility is a species of *involuntariness*. For this reason, the cases on impossibility are discussed above, in § 4.3(ii).

Criminal liability, properly understood, must always be associated with some voluntary act or omission on the part of D.[112] If, say, D is unable to discharge some legal obligation because he chose to go to bed and was asleep at the time the duty fell to be done, he may properly be convicted in respect of his failure of duty.[113] But if he cannot perform his duty because, through no fault of his own, someone has unforeseeably tied him to a bed, there is nothing on which any form of *criminal* liability can be based. It is remarkable that this simple and fundamental restraint on criminal liability is not consistently respected.[114] Constitutions which disallow "cruel and unusual punishments" proscribe liability in such circumstances.[115] A principled and consistent recognition that voluntary conduct is a prerequisite of any form of criminal liability would obviate the need for any defence of impossibility. Article 3 of the ECHR, which proscribes inhuman and degrading punishment, may assist in achieving more widespread recognition of this principle.

---

[110] Smart, "Criminal Responsibility for Failing to do the Impossible" (1987) 103 *LQR* 532; *CLGP* 746–8.

[111] See the cases discussed above, § 4.3(ii)(a)–(d).

[112] Above, § 4.1(ii); Husak, "Does Criminal Liability Require an Act" in Duff (ed.), *Philosophy and Criminal Law* (1998) 60.

[113] Antecedent fault is discussed above, § 4.3(iii).

[114] Although recognition of this principle would prevent certain forms of injustice, the principle is still compatible with the existence of very bad laws. For instance, respect for the principle would disallow, say, criminal liability for the mere fact of having curly hair; yet it would not forestall a law which required those with curly hair to shave their heads. See above, § 4.1(ii)(a).

[115] *Robinson v. California* (1962) 370 US 660; but contrast *Powell v. Texas* (1968) 392 US 514.

21

PERMISSIBLE CONDUCT

§ 21.1 Consent[1]

Normally, it would be straightforwardly harmful, wrongful, and criminal for D to hit V. Suppose, however, that V has agreed with D to enter a boxing ring to box a few rounds. As the law stands at present, neither D nor V commits an offence in hitting the other because each has consented to such contact, a consent that current law regards as effective.[2]

If English law consistently followed the precepts of classic liberalism, V's consent to conduct by D, which otherwise violates a protected interest of V (and V alone), would negate any criminal liability on the part of D. This liberal tradition[3] makes personal autonomy a key value[4] and disavows coercion through the criminal law as a means of furthering an individual's best interests.[5] The acceptable scope of the criminal law, on the classical liberal view, is to prevent harm (and some would add offence[6]) to others.[7] Of course, what constitutes harm or offence may itself be disputed. But, in principle, if the harm in question is self-regarding and freely consented to, state intervention is unjustified. Provided V has the capacity and opportunity to make a free and informed decision, the State should not interfere with V's autonomous choices. Even if, from the perspective of a reasonable bystander, what V has consented to constitutes a harm—a blow on the face, say—if V has

---

[1] Law Com. Consultation Paper No. 139, *Consent in the Criminal Law* (1995), especially Appendix C (contributed by Roberts); Roberts, "The Philosophical Foundations of Consent in the Criminal Law" (1997) 17 *OJLS* 389; Shute, "Something Old, Something New, Something Borrowed: Three Aspects of the Project" [1996] *Crim LR* 684. See also above, § 12.1(i)(b).

[2] There would be general agreement among criminal lawyers that organised boxing as sport is legal but, such is the chaotic state of English law on when effective consent may be given to the infliction of physical harm, it is impossible to give a satisfactory *legal* account of the legality of boxing; as Lord Mustill recognised in *Brown* [1994] 1 AC 212. See further Gunn and Ormerod, "The Legality of Boxing" (1995) 15 *LS* 181.

[3] Classically expounded in Mill, *On Liberty* (1859).

[4] Raz, *The Morality of Freedom* (1986).

[5] Attempts have been made to find space for a measure of paternalism within a liberal framework (Hart, *Law, Liberty and Morality* (1963)) and liberal theorists such as Raz, who allow a State interest in the worth of subjects' lives, concede, in theory, coercive interventions by the State to enhance the *worthwhile* autonomy of subjects. Classic liberalism, by contrast, protects "the right to go wrong." For a comprehensive elaboration of the classic liberal position see Feinberg, *The Moral Limits of the Criminal Law*: vol. 1, *Harm to Others* (1984); vol. 2, *Offence to Others* (1985); vol. 3, *Harm to Self* (1986); vol. 4, *Harmless Wrongdoing* (1988). For discussion of paternalism, see Dworkin, "Paternalism" (1972) 56 *Monist* 65; Dworkin, *The Theory and Practice of Autonomy* (1988) chap. 8; Glover, *Causing Death and Saving Lives* (1977) chap. 5; Kleinig, *Paternalism* (1983); above, § 1.2(i)(b).

[6] Feinberg, *Offence to Others* (1985). Feinberg allows the criminalisation of offensive conduct but only under strict conditions, the most important of which is that the offensive conduct must be something that takes place in public—such as open sexual intercourse in the view of persons who do not wish to witness the spectacle but cannot avoid doing so. See above, §1.2(i)(b).

[7] Above, § 1.2(i).

fully consented, from the liberal perspective he has not been *wronged*. If V is of the age of consent, and is of normal mental capacity, it is for her and not the state to resolve what things she may legitimately do. In theory, this sovereignty of choice for D should hold good provided her choices are self-regarding.[8] If this condition is satisfied and D has V's full consent, he would not commit an offence against V whatever it was that he did to V's person or property:[9]

> "[F]ully valid consent ought to be a defence to all the crimes that are defined in terms of individuals acting on other individuals, including battery [causing serious injury] and murder. . . . Collaborative behaviour ought never to be criminal when the collaboration is fully voluntary on both sides and no interests other than those of the collaborative parties are directly or substantially affected."

Even a cursory acquaintance with English criminal law informs that the liberal position is frequently departed from. In the sphere of harms against the person, the law allows very little scope for autonomy. Unless special considerations apply, V's consent provides D with a defence only if the harm inflicted did not amount to actual bodily harm or worse. Determining when special considerations apply is not easy. As we shall see, English law is internally inconsistent and, on occasion, irrational in determining whether consent to the risk of significant harm is effective.

The leading case is *Brown*.[10] By a three-to-two majority, the House of Lords ruled that consensual sadomasochistic activity does not fall within any recognised exception to the general legal principle that V's consent affords no defence to D should the harm inflicted be actual bodily harm or worse. That was clearly the majority decision, yet none of the judgments of the majority satisfactorily explains why consent should be irrelevant in these circumstances. In the judgments, one can discern quite clearly two different principles justifying state intervention in matters of sexual preference. First, there is a strand of legal moralism: the view that if conduct is sufficiently immoral or degrading, that *of itself* merits the punishing of persons who engage in such conduct, notwithstanding the consensual nature and self-regarding quality of the acts concerned.[11] Secondly, we may discern an attitude of paternalism: the view that the criminal law may be used to protect persons from themselves. These two principles are sometimes expressed in the same judgment.[12] While not contradictory principles, they tend to support differing conclusions, something the majority judgments do not address: if intervention in personal preferences is based on paternalism, one may well differentiate, in the context of the facts arising in *Brown*, between those who endure the pain and those who inflict it;[13] whereas legal moralism would draw no distinction.

---

[8] The boundaries of self-regard are, of course, contestable: for example, should V's choice be restricted because exposing herself to danger may impose legal duties of treatment or rescue on others?

[9] Feinberg, *Harmless Wrongdoing* (1988) 165.

[10] [1994] 1 AC 212.

[11] "Pleasure derived from the infliction of pain is an evil thing. Cruelty is uncivilised": [1994] 1 AC 212, 237 (Lord Templeman).

[12] "There were obvious dangers of serious personal injury or blood infection. . . . It is fortunate that there were no permanent injuries to a victim. . . . Such violence is injurious to the participants and unpredictably dangerous": *ibid.*, 236 (Lord Templeman).

[13] A paternalist might respond by saying that punishing those masochists who may be exploited by sadists reduces

The parameters of legally valid consent are now unstable and contestable. There are, nonetheless, clear cases where it can be said that a freely given and sufficiently informed consent by V will preclude any finding of liability against D. Conversely, there are clear cases where consent is legally irrelevant. It is in the middle ground that the lack of guiding principles is exposed.

(i) Consent: offence or defence?

The normative and legal significance of consent may operate in one of three ways, according to the nature of the particular offence.

First, consent may preclude the harm that is the subject matter of the offence. The essence of rape, for example, is intercourse without consent. There is nothing wrong or harmful about sexual intercourse: freely given consent (given by persons of the age of consent) takes sexual activity quite outside the concerns of the criminal law. The same is true of those commonplace touchings that occur in the course of ordinary life—the tap on the shoulder for attention, the playful push. Here, typically, consent may be assumed. It is only when the consent is withdrawn—"Don't tap me on the shoulder again"—that the prospect of a harm, the breach of privacy; the threat of further physical interference, constituted by the lack of consent arises.[14] In these situations, non-consent is an integral part of the actus reus of the offence. If there is consent to such things, there is no datum for the criminal law to process.

Secondly, there are situations where a harm does occur but consent precludes any liability from following. Take a situation where D and V have agreed to fight. D punches V in the face without causing him any physical injury. There is a form of harm here; ordinarily, being punched in the face is unwelcome and unsettling. However, no offence of battery has been committed, because D consented. Although D inflicts the sort of harm that is normally a battery, his conduct is effectively privileged and outside the criminal law. On liberal principles even if there is harm there is no wrong. It is unclear whether, in legal terms, consent operates here as an element of the offence (i.e. is part of the actus reus) or as a defence. According to the minority in *Brown*, the actus reus of battery is the infliction of force on V *without the consent of V*. Although the majority treated consent as something external to the offence of battery, a defence that might justify it, that analysis was in the context of cases where the battery occasions actual bodily harm.

The position certainly changes if D's punch causes V actual bodily harm or worse. Under English law, that degree of injury cannot be consented to unless special circumstances apply. Establishing special circumstances that render V's consent effective in law involves raising a *defence* of consent. However, as we shall see in § 21.1(v), the scope of this defence is uncertain. In our fighting example, D will not incur liability if he inflicts actual bodily harm or worse, provided he is fighting V in an organised boxing tournament or sparring in a

---

the number of people who submit to sadists, thereby advancing welfare overall. But even in its own terms, the response is problematic. It would be very difficult to measure what further increments of deterrence are achieved by punishing masochists in addition to sadists. Further, the punishment of a member of the protected class is a disvalue to be set against any advance in welfare achieved for that individual and in the quantum of welfare generally.

[14] Above, § 11.2(i)(a).

gym, but he will be liable for criminal offences if fighting with his bare fists in a public or private place.[15] There are many other situations where the legality of consensual fighting which may cause injury—free-fighting; Thai boxing; full contact karate—is entirely unclear.[16] Conceptually, we can, as indicated, distinguish between lack of consent as a constituent of the offence or as raising an issue of consent by way of defence. The distinction may impinge on matters of proof. When lack of consent is a constituent of the actus reus, the prosecution must prove a lack of consent of its own motion. When the presence of consent operates as a defence, an evidential onus will lie on the defence to raise the issue. If it can do that, a probative onus to disprove the presence of consent will fall to the prosecution.[17] On occasion, this difference may affect the dynamics and shape of a trial. Suppose that D throws what appears to be a friendly arm over D's shoulder. If it was indeed a friendly arm, no offence, no actus reus, has occurred. To make a battery of it the prosecution would have to show that, for example, D was a stranger to V and his action was sudden and threatening. Contrast the case where D walks up to V and punches him hard on the nose. Prove that and the prosecution has proved its case unless the defence can plausibly suggest some exonerating explanation (perhaps it was a film stunt that miscarried). Only if the defence can come up with something plausible must the prosecution then rebut it.

(ii) The definition of consent

There is no general, analytical definition of consent in English law. Conceptual tidiness and predictability of outcome would be furthered if such a definition could be successfully formulated, a definition that would descend from the realm of concepts to marshal the messier world of facts and value. But it is hard to fashion an analytical/conceptual definition that would be serviceable in all the contexts where consent may arise as an issue. The truth of the matter is that whether a valid consent has been given frequently involves normative as well as analytical questions, and the normative issues may change according to context.[18] The closest thing that we have to a general definition is section 74 of the Sexual Offences Act 2003 which, for sexual offences based on the absence of consent, provides that a person "consents if he agrees by choice and has the freedom and capacity to make that choice." As we saw in the context of sexual offences, however, section 74 does not help in the difficult case.[19] In cases where the presence or absence of consent is contestable it merely poses questions for the debate.

There are many straightforward cases of non-consent, where D simply overrides V's decision-making capacities. If D forces himself sexually upon V by using violence, we can say categorically that V does not consent to sex with D. The same applies where D overcomes V's resistence to sexual contact by threats of violence.[20] She cannot be said to be

---

[15] A-G's Reference (No. 6 of 1980) [1981] QB 715 (CA).

[16] See Law Com. Consultation Paper No. 139, Consent in the Criminal Law (1995) Appendix D.

[17] Woolmington [1935] AC 462 (HL); above, § 3.2.

[18] Wertheimer, Coercion (1987); Dripps, "For a Negative, Normative Model of Consent, with a Comment on Preference Skepticism" (1996) 2 Legal Theory 113.

[19] § 12.6.

[20] Surprisingly, s. 75(2) of the Sexual Offences Act 2003 merely creates a rebuttable presumption of lack of

exercising her autonomy; she is merely mitigating some of the features of her appalling situation. In law, submission is not consent.

More room for argument arises where V does not encounter a prospect of physical violence but is confronted with a choice of unwelcome options presented by D. For example, D may threaten to inform her employer of her past criminal record or refuse her access to her children unless she agrees to sexual intercourse. In *Olugboja*,[21] the Court of Appeal drew a distinction between consent, albeit reluctant consent, on the one hand and mere submission on the other. The Court provided no criteria with which to draw this distinction, indicating that it would be for the jury to use their common sense. This approach has been criticised for vacuity and, indeed, it merely states the problem without providing any resources with which to solve it.[22] Yet, in fairness, the constituents of consent are elusive and cannot be reduced to any simple test, particularly when we move beyond violence and the threat of violence.

(iii) Factors that may vitiate consent

(a) Force and fear of force

That force or the fear of force vitiates consent is uncontroversial and is mentioned here merely for completeness. The force or threat of force need not involve serious bodily harm. D rapes V if he obtains sex by threatening to punch her in the face; it need not be the case that the blow, if struck, would cause V serious hurt. In principle, force should also comprehend any extreme fears or phobias with which V is afflicted. If D threatens to lock V in a cupboard, knowing her to be claustrophobic, that should constitute force sufficient to vitiate consent.[23]

(b) Non-physical coercion

There is authority that pressure falling short of physical harm or the threat of such harm is insufficiently coercive to render a hard choice a case of submission rather than consent. In *Latter* v. *Braddell*,[24] a civil case, V, a maid, was ordered to submit to an intimate medical examination to check for pregnancy as a condition of further employment. V underwent the test under tearful protest. It was held that V had consented to this procedure and could not succeed in her action for assault. In an unreported decision,[25] Winn J ruled that a policeman charged with rape on the basis of obtaining sexual intercourse with V by threatening to make false reports against her had no case to answer. Glanville Williams has supported the line taken in these two cases. His view, taken with particular reference to the appropriate

---

consent to sexual conduct where D uses or threatens force immediately beforehand. Perhaps, in a sexual context, the participants' preferences may accommodate some violence in the course of the activity but, where violence or the threat of violence is used to overcome resistance, we can surely speak in categoric terms about a lack of consent.

[21] [1982] QB 320.

[22] For further discussion of *Olugboja* see above, § 12.1(i)(b) and Gardner, "Appreciating *Olugboja*" (1996) 16 *LS* 275.

[23] Cf. s. 75(2) of the Sexual Offences Act 2003; above, § 12.6.

[24] (1881) 50 LJQB 166.

[25] The decision is referred to in *Olugboja* [1982] QB 320 (see above, § 12.1(i)(b)) and Gardner, "Appreciating *Olugboja*" (1996) 16 *LS* 275.

scope of the offence of rape, is that once beyond violence or the threat of violence, the line between reluctant consent and mere submission is unacceptably vague and should not be used to determine liability for serious offences. He is not averse to penalising the policeman's conduct in the case above, but advises creating offences which do not employ consent as a constituent element.[26]

Arguably, the restrictive approach advocated by Williams is no longer tenable following the decision in *Olugboja*.[27] V had been driven to a house and raped there by X. D then informed her that he was going to have sex with her and ordered her to remove her trousers. V complied with his wishes and did not physically resist D. Confirming D's conviction for rape, the Court of Appeal held, as we noted in § 21.1(ii), that it is for the jury to distinguish on the facts before it between consent and mere submission. Importantly, the Court did not require a direction to the effect that consent would be absent only if V complied under threat of violence from D. It should be noted, however, that in the factual circumstances of *Olugboja*, V was in an inherently threatening situation; indeed, she had already been raped by someone still present in the house. If the direction to the jury is read against these facts, arguably no extension of the law beyond the point advocated by Williams was involved.

In the Rhodesian case of *McCoy*,[28] a more expansive approach was adopted unequivocally. V, an airline hostess, had broken company rules and was anticipating a period of "grounding" with consequent loss of pay. D, her manager, offered to cancel her grounding order if she would submit to a caning on her bottom. He was convicted of indecent assault, affirmed on appeal, on the basis that V's compliance with his wishes was a coerced submission and not a product of her consent. Similarly, in *Wellard*,[29] when discussing D's appeal against sentence, the Court of Appeal made no adverse comment on the propriety of his previous conviction for rape, a conviction sustained on the basis of obtaining sexual intercourse by threatening, in his capacity as a security guard, to report aspects of V's sexual conduct.

The better view, it is submitted, is that there is no categorical rule that only violence or the threat of violence has sufficient coercive effect to negate consent. As a matter of principle, threats of a non-physical kind are surely capable of inducing submission rather than consent. Whether the threat at issue in the instant case has the necessary weight should, ultimately, be a question of fact for the jury. Such an approach is open on the state of the authorities and, arguably, is endorsed by *Olugboja*. In the context of non-consensual sexual offences, the test is now framed in terms of whether V had the "freedom and capacity to choose".[30] This is in effect another way of asking a jury to choose between submission and consent, a normative as much as an analytical question.

(c) Threats and opportunities

In the case of non-physical threats, a helpful distinction should be borne in mind, namely the distinction between threats and opportunities. The latter may involve agonising choices

---

[26] *TBCL* 551–8.
[27] [1982] QB 320.
[28] 1953 (2) SA 4 (Rhodesian CA).
[29] (1978) 67 Cr App R 364, 368 (CA).
[30] Section 75(2) Sexual Offences Act 2003.

for the agent but it is typically only the former that constrain and vitiate consent. The distinction may be elaborated by contrasting the facts of *Wellard*[31] with *McCoy*.[32]

In *Wellard*, D, by threatening to report his observations of V unless she submitted to intercourse with him, confronted V with two awful alternatives. She was faced with two entirely negative choices because of D's actions and can truly be said to have submitted rather than consented to one fate rather than the other; or, in the language of section 75(2) of the Sexual Offences Act, she lacked freedom and capacity to choose in respect of each alternative, merely submitting as to one unchosen outcome rather than the other.

In *McCoy*, V broke her rules of employment and faced a sanction. D, in making his proposal, however unsavoury, was increasing V's options from the starting-point of V's self-created baseline. *Pace* the Court of Appeal of Rhodesia, it is hard to understand how V was constrained by D's proposal.[33] She appears to have accepted it because it offered, all things considered, a new and better way forward from her current situation.

In distinguishing between threats and opportunities, it is important to keep in mind V's existing rights and legitimate expectations. V, an actor, is entitled to be considered for the part on her thespian merits. If the casting-couch is an obligatory way-station for auditioning for the part it constitutes a threat; if it is a way of stealing a march on her competitors, it is an opportunity. The threat/opportunity divide should only be used for guidance; it is not a "bright-line" rule. There may arise situations where V's baseline situation is so unenviable and the stakes so high that the price for an opportunity may be paid without true consent.[34]

(d) Mistake or ignorance on the part of V regarding D's conduct or its consequences

In the famous case of *Clarence*,[35] D had sexual intercourse with V, his wife, neglecting to inform her that he was infected with gonorrhoea. Consequently, V contracted this disease and D was charged with a number of offences against the person. A central issue in the case was whether V, given her ignorance of D's dangerous condition, had given an effective consent to intercourse. The Court for Crown Cases Reserved held that his failure to disclose his infection did not vitiate V's consent. According to the court, she understood the *nature* of the act she consented to. Her ignorance related to a mere *attribute* of D's conduct, its propensity to pass on infection.

Essentially, the analysis in *Clarence* was confirmed by the Court of Appeal in *EB*,[36] with its ruling that D's failure to disclose his HIV-positive status did not entail that he had raped V when he had intercourse with her without disclosing his condition. That rape had not occurred might at first seem surprising, because V would not have agreed to sex had she

---

[31] *Ibid.*

[32] 1953 (2) SA 4.

[33] Perhaps, as Lamond argues, the threat/opportunity distinction depends also on D's reasons for implementing the unwelcome alternative: "Coercion, Threats, and the Puzzle of Blackmail" in Simester and Smith (eds.), *Harm and Culpability* (1996) 215.

[34] The facts of *Latter v. Bradell* (above, § 21.1(iii)(b)) illustrate this limitation of the threat/opportunity distinction. V had no legal right to further employment; accordingly, D's offer of further employment on condition of an intimate examination to check for pregnancy was, strictly, an opportunity. Yet the available options for a Victorian domestic servant were likely to be exceedingly limited, arguably rendering D's proposal a coercive act (despite the finding of the Court in that case).

[35] (1888) 22 QBD 23 (CCR).

[36] [2006] EWCA Crim 2945

known of his infected condition. Yet the same opinion was also expressed, *obiter,* in *Dica*[37] and in *Konzani.*[38] We now seem to have a well-established rule that failure to disclose a sexually transmitted disease (STD), however serious the condition is, does not vitiate the consent to the sex act *in the dimension of sexual activity.* However, in *Konzani* it was ruled that, in passing on HIV to V without fully informing her of his positive status, D had maliciously inflicted grievous bodily harm contrary to section 20 of the OAPA 1861, a conclusion anticipated in *Dica.*[39] So now we have a situation where, in law, it may be possible for V to consent to D's act in one dimension but not consent to other facets of the act that, for the purposes of the criminal law, belong in a different dimension. This is the case even if V would have refused D's act *tout court* had she known the true position.

A further level of complexity is introduced by the insistence in *Konzani* that any valid consent by V to D's act in the dimension of risk of infection had to be a "fully informed" consent, a condition only satisfied if, prior to sexual intercourse, V was aware of his HIV-positive status. This is a more demanding test of consent than is required for the act of intercourse *qua* sex. It is simply not the case that valid consent is given to sexual conduct in the dimension of sexual activity only if the nature of the conduct is understood in all its aspects by V before it occurs. But it now seems to be the case that different tests for consent may be in play with respect to different aspects of the same act.[40]

It would be possible to regulate cases of mistake and ignorance much more straight-forwardly than this. Jonathan Herring proposes a beguilingly simple test for sexual offences:[41]

"If at the time of the sexual activity a person:
(i)   is mistaken as to a fact; and
(ii) had s/he known the truth about that fact would not have consented to it
then s/he did not consent to the sexual activity."

This is a much more sweeping principle of vitiation than currently applies. Adopting such a principle would entail a conviction for rape on facts such as *Konzani,* in addition to liability under section 20 of the OAPA 1861. While on balance we do not favour liability for rape in those circumstances, a finding of rape is in no sense outlandish where the matter undisclosed is of such vital importance and so tightly bound to the act of sexual intercourse.[42] But a conviction for rape would also follow if D, say, has sexual intercourse with his partner after deceitfully agreeing to her proposal to visit relatives at the weekend,

---

[37] [2004] QB 1257 (CA).

[38] [2005] 2 Cr App R 13 (CA).

[39] In *Clarence* the wording of s. 20 was taken to preclude any liability unless the harm was inflicted by way of battery, a view now superseded; above, § 11.5(i). That caveat aside, several members of the court in *Clarence* took STDs to be a form of grievous bodily harm, a position confirmed in *Konzani* and *Dica.*

[40] For strong criticism of this aspect of *Konzani* see Weait, "Knowledge, Autonomy and Consent" [2005] *Crim LR* 673. In our view, contra Weait, that the approach in *Konzani* employing different standards of consent for different aspects of conduct is defensible. Whereas consent to sexual conduct may be dynamic and evolving during an episode of conduct, and be expressed solely in deeds, consent as to latent physical dangers must have a firm knowledge base. It is not unreasonable to set the knowledge standard at actual awareness of the danger rather than an appreciation of a risk of the danger if the focus is exclusively on the harm done to V. In the broader picture of public health, it is far from obvious that vigorous enforcement of the law against the reckless spread of infection will encourage disclosure of sexual contacts and the seeking out of treatment.

[41] Herring, "Mistaken Sex" [2005] *Crim LR* 511, 517.

[42] The Supreme Court of Canada has upheld a conviction for rape on such facts: *Curriet* [1998] SCR 371.

without disclosing his plans instead to be travelling in the opposite direction to watch a rugby match. He may have told his lie not with sex in mind but to postpone the inevitable row they will have when he reveals that his plans for the weekend are different from hers. Yet later that evening, when they have fully mutual and enjoyable sex, under a Herring dispensation, he will be in the process of raping V if, according to Herring, he knew or ought to have known that she would not have agreed to sex on that occasion had she known the truth about his plans for the weekend.[43]

A finding that D had raped V in those circumstances is preposterous.[44] Besides, a law of rape constructed on those lines would require police-state methods to be fully enforced. And yet, from the perspective of findings of full consent, with its focus on the state of knowledge and disposition of V, there is considerable force in Herring's position. There is a literal truth to the proposition that consent to some activity is vitiated if an agent would not have permitted the activity but for a mistake or ignorance of a fact that, if disclosed, would have resulted in the agent's not consenting. The difficulty is that if we allow full sway to that truth, we will in some cases, even in cases where lack of consent is placed at the heart of the offence, find D liable for wrongs that he did not commit.

To avoid such outcomes, we must set aside the cut-and-dried method of Herring and try a more nuanced approach. In *Clarence*,[45] an attempt to do this was made in terms of a distinction between the core nature of an act and the mere attributes of an act. For the Court in *Clarence*, if V understood the nature of the act notwithstanding any ignorance or mistake about some of its aspects, she would give a valid consent. The risk of serious infection was seen as merely a concomitant, not part of the defining core of sexual intercourse with an infected person. On this analysis, only when a sexually motivated act is passed off as something non-sexual is there non-consent to sex.[46] But one difficulty with this approach is that a purportedly analytical distinction between the core nature and the mere attributes of an act may have little bearing on the facts that matter to V, the things that count for her in deciding to consent to an act. For V1 the fact that the act is sexual may outweigh any other consideration; even being the unwitting victim of a plausible subterfuge which inveigles her into sexual activity may entail a devastating loss of status in her cultural community. For V2, sex not fully chosen may constitute a matter for anger and regret but on a different and lesser plane to the harm of a life-threatening infection. We can see how a preoccupation with the consent of V in circumstances where she is mistaken or ignorant of facts relevant to her decision-making may deflect attention from the more salient issue of what *wrong* D does to V when he exploits her mistake or ignorance to induce a consent that would not have been obtained had V been apprised of the full picture.

A focus on the wrong D has done to V underlies some recent decisions involving ignorance or mistake on the part of V as to facts relevant to consent. In *Dica*[47] and *Konzani*,[48] the Court of Appeal entertained no doubt that V may give a valid consent to sexual activity

---

[43] [2005] *Crim LR* 511, 517.

[44] See Gross, "Rape, Moralism and Human Rights" [2007] *Crim LR* 220; Herring, "Human Rights and Rape: A Reply to Hyman Gross" [2007] *Crim LR* 228.

[45] (1888) 22 QBD 23.

[46] As in *Rosinski* (1824) 1 Lew CC 11.

[47] [2004] QB 1257.

[48] [2005] 2 Cr App R 13.

with D despite a failure by D to disclose his HIV-positive status. The gravamen of D's wrong in such circumstances was taken to be the infection of V. On balance this seems correct, although from V's perspective the harm might not have been confined to infection, serious though that was. If a relationship was involved, the breach of trust may well put a retrospective blight on the sexual aspects of the relationship. Accordingly, conviction for an offence against the person may not capture all aspects of Ds wrongdoing against V. But attempting to bring V fully to book by conjoining charges of rape to charges based on causing physical harm arguably takes us too far beyond current legal and cultural understandings of rape. Less uncertainty may be had about the decision in *Linekar*,[49] where D had sex with V, a prostitute, and then ran off without paying. The Court of Appeal rightly held that D had not raped V. The wrong that is rape had not occurred. If V regularly made herself available for sex for payment and, all other things equal, her decisions about providing sexual services were based purely on economics, she was not sexually violated. She was conned into providing sexual services and, at the time, D could have been better charged with obtaining sexual intercourse by false pretences.[50] That offence was abolished by the Sexual Offences Act 2003. Even in the absence of a suitable charge,[51] courts should resist stretching the boundaries of offences based on sexual violation to reach such conduct.

We may now understand better the role of consent in cases where V is mistaken or ignorant as to aspects or the consequences of D's conduct. The focus is exclusively on V only when we ask the threshold question of whether the mistake or ignorance at issue was material in terms of her decision to consent to what D proposed to do. So, if on facts similar to *Linekar* it should turn out that V was only hoping to be paid by D, that she would have had sex with him with or without payment, consent is present and there is no offence of any kind by D. But if, as in the case itself, payment was the condition of consent, then it is logical to conclude that there was no full consent to sexual intercourse. Staying in the realm of logic, it would then be possible to conclude that V had been raped by D. Deflecting that logic entails going beyond questions that are exclusively concerned with V's psychological state and turning to an evaluation of the wrong that D did to V when he exploited V's mistake, or ignorance, as to some aspect of the conduct or its consequences. When evaluating the wrong D did to V, we may have to return to V's understanding of D's act. She may, despite any mistake or ignorance affecting her decision-making, have sufficient understanding of D's act in one of its dimensions to rule out any wrongdoing by D *in that regard*; but may still be wronged by D in respect of other matters of which she was insufficiently aware.

(e) Mistake or ignorance on the part of V regarding D's identity or status

Whether a mistake by V about D's identity vitiates her consent very much depends on the nature of the conduct at issue. In the case of non-commercial sexual activity, one might suppose that the identity of one's partner is crucial and any mistake on that matter destructive of consent. Surprisingly, in *Barrow*,[52] it was held not to be a case of rape where

---

[49] [1995] QB 250.

[50] Sexual Offences Act 1956, s. 3.

[51] Such conduct should fall within the offence of dishonestly obtaining services by deception, contrary to s. 11 of the Fraud Act 2006.

[52] (1868) LR 1 CCR 81.

D impersonated V's husband. Subsequently, however, it was enacted that a man commits rape if he obtains a woman's consent by representing himself as her husband. The narrow terms of this legislative reversal allowed the view that if the impersonation was of someone other than a husband, the general principle in *Barrow* still stood—that mistake as to personal identity of a sexual partner does not vitiate one's essential understanding of the act consented to. That argument, thankfully, did not impress the Court of Appeal in *Elbekkay*,[53] which ruled that the question of personality went to the heart of consent in sexual matters. Consequently, D was guilty of raping V when obtaining sexual intercourse with her by passing himself off as her boyfriend. For non-consensual sexual offences the matter is now placed on a secure statutory footing by section 76(2) of the Sexual Offences Act 2003, which applies an irrebutable presumption of non-consent where D impersonates "a person known personally to the complainant".

Matters relating to the status or qualifications of D may also be germane to consent. In *Richardson*,[54] at trial it was held that V had made the equivalent to a mistake of indentity when she submitted to dental treatment by D, assuming him to be a qualified dentist, whereas he was suspended from practice. The conviction was quashed on the ground that the finding below unduly distorted the natural meaning of "identity". *Richardson* must be contrasted with *Tabassum*,[55] where the conviction of D for indecent assault was confirmed following D's intimate examination of women in what may (or may not)[56] have been genuine research into the incidence of breast cancer. D had been aware that the subjects of the examinations wrongly assumed him to be medically qualified (although he did have academic qualifications useful for the research he claimed to be conducting). The reconciliation of *Tabassum* with *Richardson* is not obvious. To the extent that the decisions can be squared, the answer does not lie in any claim that a mistake of identity was made in *Tabassum*. The answer, if there is one, is that in the case of intimate examinations, the procedure when carried out by a doctor is something fundamentally different from the procedure when carried out by a lay-person.

For less intimate forms of contact, the importance of D's identity will very much depend on the circumstances. In the case of forcible contact in the sphere of sport, for example, identity should only be an issue if V has made it clear that her participation is dependent on D's identity.

(f) The age of understanding for effective consent

In order to give an effective consent, V must possess a sufficiently mature capacity to understand the nature of the interaction that D proposes. For certain acts, legislation designates an age under which consent will be ineffective, such as 16 for sexual activity. For medical treatment, consent given at the age of 16 is taken to be effective, other things being equal.[57] It does not follow that the consent of a younger person will be ineffective. As the House of Lords explained in *Gillick*,[58] a person under that age may nonetheless give consent

---

[53] [1995] Crim LR 163.
[54] [1999] QB 444.
[55] [2000] 2 Cr App R 328.
[56] Bearing in mind the burden of proof on the prosecution, D should be given the benefit of any doubt as to his true purpose.
[57] Family Law Reform Act 1969, s. 8.
[58] [1986] AC 112.

to treatment which is in her best interests if she has sufficient maturity and understanding to assess her interests.

It was widely assumed that a "*Gillick*-competent" young person could refuse as well as consent to treatment. Donaldson MR thought differently in *Re R*,[59] when he ordered treatment for a 15-year-old girl with an eating disorder, even though he accepted that her refusal of treatment was a refusal on the part of a *Gillick*-competent person. He introduced the notion of "joint key-holders"; she could unlock the door, making her treatment lawful by virtue of her consent, but so too could other competent persons, such as the court exercising its wardship jurisdiction, on her behalf.

This asymmetry between refusal of treatment and consent to treatment has been widely attacked and, indeed, it would be hard to follow if the sole value informing *Gillick*-competence were personal autonomy.[60] But it is not. *Gillick* was, *inter alia*, a case concerned to ensure that treatment in the best interests of a patient is delivered. The leading consideration in *Gillick* was ensuring that sexually active girls under the age of 16 received contraception even in circumstances where parents or guardians would not be involved in the decision-making. In *Re R*, again the underlying concern was that a patient with volatile mood swings would receive therapy which would (and did) save her life. The cases reflect the fact that the consequences of accepting treatment are typically beneficent, whereas the outcomes ensuing from the refusal of treatment may be catastrophic. In that sense, the decisions in *Gillick* and *Re R* have a greater affinity than may at first appear.[61]

If, on policy or moral grounds, the court disapproves of the interaction between D and V, it may be astute to find a lack of competence on the ground of age. That appears to have been the case in *Burrell* v. *Harmer*,[62] where D tattooed V, a 13-year-old boy, for payment. According to the Divisional Court, this constituted an assault on V, based on the questionable finding that he did not understand the nature of the act that D had performed upon him.[63]

(iv) The limits of consent

(a) The general rule

As we have seen, V's consent will generally be ineffective if D's conduct causes actual bodily harm or worse. Actual bodily harm need not involve any injury of any significance; it consists of harm which "need not be permanent, but must, no doubt, be more than transient or trifling."[64] Cuts, bruises, and bloody noses fall within the category. In *A-G's Reference (No. 6 of 1980)*, a case where D and V fought by agreement in a public street, Lord Lane CJ put the position as follows:[65]

---

[59] [1991] 3 WLR 592 (CA).
[60] Grubb, "Treatment Decisions" in Grubb (ed.), *Choices and Decisions in Health Care* (1993) 54–68.
[61] See further Teff, *Reasonable Care* (1994) 146–52.
[62] [1967] Crim LR 169.
[63] D's conduct would now be more straightforwardly dealt with under the Tattooing of Minors Act 1969.
[64] *Donovan* [1934] 2 KB 498, 509.
[65] [1981] QB 715, 719 (emphasis added).

"it is not in the public interest that people should try to cause, or should cause, each other actual bodily harm for no good reason . . . it is an assault if actual bodily harm is *intended and/or caused*."

These remarks were approved by the House of Lords in *Brown*.[66] The most obvious feature of the current law is the extremely limited scope for effective consent. It will be noted that consent is taken to be ineffective not merely when D *intends* to cause V actual bodily harm but also when he *in fact* causes actual bodily harm. In *Boyea*,[67] D, with V's consent, indulged in "vigorous sex"; so vigorous that it was considered likely to cause actual bodily harm. It was accepted that it was not D's intention to cause V harm, neither did he foresee that he would. If harm had *not* been caused, the sexual interchange between D and V would have been entirely lawful. The Court of Appeal ruled that the fact that harm was caused rendered V's consent ineffectual, applying the *dictum* of Lord Lane (above) in *A-G's Reference (No. 6 of 1980)*.

Boyea may be contrasted with *Kimber*,[68] where the Court of Appeal ruled that lack of consent was a definitional requirement of assault and that, consequently, D would lack the mens rea for assault if he mistakenly believed that he had V's consent. *Kimber* supports the view that the essence of assault (as with rape) is the lack of consent. Where significant bodily harm occurs, other forms of criminal liability may ensue but it would remain the case that, if V consented to D's act, V would not have been *assaulted. Boyea* holds otherwise. A consensual act may yet be an assault if D intends actual bodily harm (or worse) or inadvertently causes actual bodily harm.

In summary: under current law, the general rule is that what would otherwise be an offence against the person such as assault and battery can be consented to, provided actual bodily harm (or worse) is neither intended nor in fact caused. More serious offences, such as assault occasioning actual bodily harm, cannot be consented to.

(b) Exceptions to the general rule

Exception 1: Organised sports.

It was accepted in *Brown*, confirming earlier authority, that in the course of "properly organised sports" V could lawfully take the risk of being *seriously* hurt by D. The extent of this exception is far from clear. Obviously well-established sports with rule-making bodies such as association football, rugby football, hockey, and cricket fall within this exception. In a very useful review of the sports exception,[69] Lord Woolf emphasised the importance of open public performance, rules of the game, and disciplinary and governing bodies. The better regulated the "zone of toleration", the more secure the participants from interference under the general law. Yet, as the Law Commission observed, the position of minority sports such as Thai boxing and full contact karate is less secure.[70]

The case law on sports injuries and criminal liability also draws a distinction between injuries, including foreseen injuries, which are a by-product of play and intentionally

---

[66] [1994] 1 AC 212.
[67] [1992] Crim LR 574.
[68] [1983] 3 All ER 316. See also the trial case of *Slingsby* [1995] Crim LR 570.
[69] *Barnes* [2005] 1 WLR 910.
[70] Law Com. Consultation Paper No. 139, *Consent in the Criminal Law* (1995) Part XII.

inflicted injury. In *Bradshaw*,[71] it was said that an act intended to cause serious injury would be unlawful even if it complied with the rules of the game. But provided there is no intent to cause injury, there may be effective consent to injuries inflicted outside the rules of the game. In *Barnes*,[72] the Court of Appeal confirmed the category of what may be called the conventional foul, the kind of thing that players should expect and thereby consent to when they participate in a particular kind of game.

Intent seems to be the key. If the move by D is intended to cause V injury, it may well constitute an offence against the person irrespective of whether D's play is within or outside the rules of the game. If what D did is within the rules of the game, it is submitted that the intent in question should be direct or core intent.[73] This is because it is possible that forms of well accepted conduct—well-timed, full-impact tackles in rugby—might, on a particular occasion, satisfy a *Woollin*-based[74] test of intentionally causing injury. It is not appropriate that participants in well-recognised sports should be liable for serious offences for conduct which is consistent with the rules of the sport. In this context, a parallel may be drawn with the constriction of intent to core intent in medical contexts.[75]

Notoriously, the sport of boxing does not fit the picture just sketched. The causing of serious injury with a direct intent to cause such injury seems to be at the heart of the sport, notwithstanding pious references to the "noble art of self-defence". Lord Mustill, a dissentient in *Brown*, was at a loss to understand how intentionally causing serious injury for financial gain could be considered lawful, whereas inflicting painful but non-serious injury for sexual gratification, as in *Brown*, was illegal.[76] The legality of boxing, if such it is, does not rest on any statute or well-regarded appellate case. In favour of the legality of boxing is its openness, its rule book, its governing bodies—factors given salience for sport generally in *Barnes*—and, above all, the generally held assumption of legality that has stood for many years. Were boxing suddenly to be regarded as illegal in the course of criminal litigation, there would be a real question of retroactive law and grounds for challenge under Article 7 of the ECHR. But just as with the former immunity granted to husbands who raped their wives,[77] the legality of boxing could crumble without the need for legislation should public and judicial opinion turn decisively against the sport as an acceptable form of activity within the moral framework of current society. There is no indication that that stage has been reached.

We tentatively offer the following summary:

(i)   In games which do not involve fighting as the defining activity: where the injury is intentionally inflicted, criminal liability may arise even if the incident falls within the rules of the particular game. If the incident does fall within the rules of a

---

[71] (1878) Cox CC 83.

[72] [2005] 1 WLR 910.

[73] See above, § 5.1.

[74] [1999] 1 AC 82. For a wide-ranging discussion of the legality of boxing see Gunn and Ormerod, "The Legality of Boxing"(1995) 15 *LS* 181.

[75] Ashworth, "Criminal Liability in a Medical Context; The Treatment of Good Intentions" in Simester and Smith, *Harm and Culpability* (1996) 173.

[76] [1994] 1 AC 212.

[77] *R v. R.* [1992] 1AC 599; above, § 2.2.

long-accepted, publicly open and properly organised game, the intention to cause injury should be a direct intention before criminal liability may ensue.

(ii) In games which do not involve fighting as the defining activity: where the injury is non-intentional and a foreseeable consequence of playing the game, the rules of the game may be considered very strong evidence of what risks are consented to by the players. Further, incidents falling beyond the rules of the game but within its bounds of tolerance—e.g. marginally late tackles in rugby or football—will also fall within the boundaries of effective consent.

(iii) In the anomalous case of sports that involve rule-governed fighting, all manner of injury, up to and including death, would seem to be within the purview of effective consent, provided the injury is inflicted within the rules of the sport. (This rule is offered with confidence only for fighting sports long tolerated and openly presented and organised, such as boxing and wrestling, when conducted under the auspices of the relevant controlling bodies. New fighting sports or fighting sports new to this jurisdicion, e.g. free- or cage-fighting and Thai boxing, are of doubtful legality notwithstanding their public performance and extensive media coverage.)

(iv) Intentionally inflicted injuries falling outside the rules of any game should lead straightforwardly to criminal liability. The intention may be either direct or oblique (i.e. virtually certain).

Exception 2: Horseplay.
In addition to organised sport, "rough, undisciplined play" allows scope for consent even to the risk of serious harm of the kind that occurred in *Aitken*,[78] where airforce officers in an after-dinner mess game amused themselves, *inter alia*, by dousing each other with fuel and setting it alight. The idea, apparently, was to test the fire-resistance properties of their flying-suits. As all concerned had consented to this exceedingly dangerous activity, it was held that no offence had been committed against V, a participant, who suffered horrendous burns. The activity must constitute "play": if injury is intentionally inflicted, the conduct will lose its character as play.

Other exceptions.
Beyond the categories of sport and play, the exceptions from the general rule are eclectic and of uncertain scope. Therapeutic surgery is clearly lawful. So too, it seems, are non-therapeutic plastic surgery, contraceptive surgery, and sex-change operations.[79] Body piercing and tattooing of non-minors are now prevalent and apparently lawful,[80] including the fearsome "do-it-yourself" branding by hot knife that occurred in *Wilson*.[81] Female circumcision is clearly unlawful because of legislative intervention[82] though we must still assume that religiously ordained male circumcision is lawful.[83] The legality of customary and tribal scarifications and markings is debatable, particularly in the case of minors. We

---

[78] [1992] 4 All ER 541 (CA). See too *Jones* (1986) 83 Cr App R 375.
[79] Discussed in Law Com. Consultation Paper No. 139, *Consent in the Criminal Law* (1995) Part VIII.
[80] *Ibid.*, Part IX.
[81] [1997] QB 47 (CA); below, § 21.1(v).
[82] The Prohibition of Female Circumcision Act 1985.
[83] Law Com. Consultation Paper No. 139, *Consent in the Criminal Law* (1995) para. 9.2.

may bring this confusing and miscellaneous list to a close by mentioning "dangerous exhibitions": there is high authority that such displays, whatever precisely they are, are lawful.[84]

(v) The limits of consent—critique

Any account of consent which seeks an acceptable degree of consistent principle and policy is confounded by the *ad hoc* nature of the legal materials to hand.[85] The confusing nature of the current situation can best be exemplified by contrasting the decision of the House of Lords in *Brown*[86] with the subsequent Court of Appeal decision in *Wilson*.[87] In the former case, an organised group of homosexual men had devised elaborate and ritualised methods of inflicting pain on consenting group members. Although bodily harm was inflicted, no member of the group required medical assistance as a consequence of these bizarre activities. In the latter case, a wife requested that her husband brand his initials on her buttocks. She required medical treatment to salve the burns that he inflicted with her consent. In *Brown*, there were convictions for occasioning actual bodily harm and malicious wounding: in *Wilson*, the defendant was acquitted. Why the difference?

The decision in *Brown*, though controversial in policy terms, at least can be expressed straightforwardly. The House of Lords confirmed the general rule that effective consent could not be given if the harm amounted to actual bodily harm or worse. The value of free sexual expression between consenting adults did not weigh sufficiently to displace the general rule. The rule was characterised as a rule about the control of violence and the infliction of harm to that degree was considered a token of violence. The sexual motivation of the defendants did not supervene on the violence and change its nature to private sexual conduct; an opinion confirmed by the European Court of Human Rights in finding that the conviction of the defendants did not infringe the right to privacy under Article 8 of the ECHR.[88] The Court of Appeal in *Wilson* found three grounds of differentiation with *Brown*.[89] First, in *Wilson*, there was no "aggressive intent", as had been present in *Brown*. The distinction is spurious. If a person were to be branded without consent, it would be a violent act. In both *Brown* and *Wilson* there was no aggressive intent because of consent. Secondly, the Court of Appeal described *Brown* as a "truly extreme" case, involving "physical torture". Yet only in *Wilson* was medical attention needed. Finally, the branding procedure was characterised as a form of tattooing and not, like the various acts in *Brown*, as acts of violence. At this point, we must abandon any attempt at classification and analysis. Why violence perpetrated for sport, horseplay, or ornamentation has an acceptability denied to sexual fulfilment lies beyond reason.[90] All that can be done is to note and docket the

---

[84] *A-G's Reference (No 6 of 1980)* [1981] QB 715 (CA).

[85] Kell, "Social Disutility and the Law of Consent"(1994) 14 *OJLS* 121.

[86] [1994] 1 AC 212.

[87] [1997] QB 47.

[88] *Laskey et al* v. *United Kingdom* (1997) 24 EHRR 39.

[89] *Ibid.*, 50.

[90] "The position is unprincipled and incoherent. . . . [R]ecognition of individual autonomy [concerns] the right of individuals of sufficient understanding to make their own decisions about what is good for them. In principle, this should apply to people's sexual preferences. Indeed, it is hard to see how the interest (whether public or private) in allowing people to express their sexuality, which forms a fundamental part of people's personality, could be less important than the interest in allowing people to play sports": Feldman, *Civil Liberties and Human Rights* (1993) 517.

decisions of the courts as and when they arise. In *Emmett*,[91] D and V, a couple soon to be married,[92] indulged in two episodes of consensual sexual risk-taking which miscarried, causing actual bodily harm on each occasion. The harm, unlike the harm in *Brown*, was not intended, though the risk of harm was clearly present. The Court of Appeal confirmed D's conviction for assault occasioning actual bodily harm. *Wilson* was distinguished as a tattooing case. In the light of the ruling in *Dica*[93] and the considered dicta in *Konzani*[94] which allow that, if fully informed, V may give a valid consent to the risk of contracting an STD (again, *Brown* was distinguished as a case concerned with violence) we can now say that consent may be given in sexual contexts even to a risk of death, if the risk arises from a potential infection; but there will be zero tolerance for all other forms of risk that arise in the course of sexual activity.

A law which employs such distinctions is a law ripe for change. The Law Commission's Second Consultation Paper on the role of consent in the criminal law provides a useful agenda for reform. The core suggestion of the Commission's Report is that consent to harm on the part of competent persons should be effective in all spheres of activity provided the harm consented-to falls short of serious injury.[95] This strikes a balance between the values of paternalism and autonomy, allowing greater weight to the latter but denying validity to choices that favour the infliction of serious injury on the basis that an agent opting for harm of that gravity can be assumed not to be acting in her own best interests.

The Law Commission's recommendation has been attacked as a muddled and unstable compromise. Paul Roberts, for instance, has argued that the only principled stance for a modern, heterogeneous democracy is thorough-going liberalism, a liberalism that would enjoin respect and freedom for *any* self-regarding choice made by a competent agent.[96] Certainly the liberal position in its pure form is cut and dried. In terms of individual choice, the freedom to choose is maximised and the shadow of the criminal law removed. The self-regarding choice of a competent agent precludes any finding of a wrong done to the agent and, in the absence of any wrong, with it any ground of intervention for the consistent liberal. Yet if persons are to be allowed complete freedom to choose, inevitably some very dark choices will be made; such as the choices of Bernd Brandes and Armin Miewes, that the latter should make a meal of parts of the former's body, some parts to be mutually consumed while Brandes was being hacked by Miewes to his inevitable death, the rest for Miewes later.[97] Given that neither Miewes nor Brandes were incompetent decision-makers in terms of their mental capacities,[98] the sentence of life imprisonment for man-slaughter handed down by a German court was a great injustice to Miewes from the classic

---

[91] *Emmett (Stephen Roy), The Times*, 15 October 1999 (CA).

[92] They were married at the time of D's trial.

[93] [2004] QB 1257.

[94] [2005] 2 Cr App R 13.

[95] Law Com. Consultation Paper No. 139, *Consent in the Criminal Law* (1995) paras. 4.46–53.

[96] Roberts, "The Philosophical Foundations of Consent in the Criminal Law" (1997) 17 *OJLS* 389.

[97] This macabre case is discussed by Bergelson, "The Right To be Hurt; Testing the Boundaries of Consent" (2007) 75 *George Washington LR* 165, 167.

[98] Consistent liberalism is constantly threatened by reading back from bizarre choices an inference that the chooser in making such a choice has demonstrated his mental incapacity and hence his ineligibility for autonomous agency. If that temptation is avoided in the cases of Brandes and Miewes, there was nothing to cast doubt on their mental capacities.

liberal perspective. From that vantage, the consent of Brandes entailed that no wrong had been done to him and that should have entailed that Miews had committed no crime.

Yet even many liberals, on learning of Miewes's sentence, will not experience the sense of indignation that is the typical reaction on encountering an injustice. Indeed the real and imagined horrors that may flow from unrestrained choice led Joel Feinberg, the leading philosopher on the application of liberal principles to the criminal law, to concede that the criminal law could intervene to suppress what he terms"free floating evils".[99] One token of such an evil acknowledged by Feinberg was a commercially sponsored gladiatorial contest to the death. If such a contest is to be regarded as evil, then for Feinberg it is of the free floating kind, as the consent of the contestants entails that no-one has been wronged. But he allows that a society that permits such public events debases itself, loses civic virtue, and that it may be permissible to depart from the liberal framework to suppress such evils in the general societal interest. Other commentators have striven to bring proscription of extreme choices within the liberal paradigm by challenging the claim that a freely chosen harm by an autonomous agent can never constitute a wrong to the agent.

Duff maintains that the gladiatorial contestants have been wronged, their interests as human subjects have been set back, as even chosen participation degrades and dehumanises those involved. For a state not to intervene to prevent the degradation of the participants would be a wrong by that state. Preventing such contests advances the interests of those who would otherwise have participated.[100] In similar vein, Dan-Cohen maintains that to allow participation in such spectacles is to disrespect the participants, to regard them as lacking moral worth.[101] Whether the liberal framework is left intact after such adjustments is doubtful. When read in full, it is clear that Duff and Dan-Cohen would deploy their arguments for interventions overriding consent sparingly, yet differences emerge between them; with Dan-Cohen, for instance, more receptive to respecting the choices of sado-masochists than is Duff. If we turn from differences between liberally minded philosophers to the state of public opinion, there will be a signal lack of consensus over what freely chosen activities dehumanise, degrade, or disrespect the moral worth of the participants. If we opt for liberalism all the way down, we have a clear-cut basis for intervention but are likely to end up with more "free floating evils" than public opinion is prepared to tolerate. If we allow intervention on the back of such culturally contestable criteria as degradation and disrespect, we may give too much elbow room to pressures for conformity and intolerance.

The radically different cultural, social, and religious groups present within the juris-diction of England and Wales renders impossible any large and stable consensus on the limits of consent. Indeed, because of the lack of any consensus emerging from its consultation exercise and the absence of any political enthusiasm to liberalise the current law to any degree, the Law Commission has dropped the consent project.[102] However realistic, this is a matter for regret for anyone wishing to move on from the chaotic and overly punitive condition of the current law. Allowing effective consent to any harm falling short of serious harm would have significantly advanced tolerance and freedom. Considerable scope would

---

[99] *Harmless Wrongdoing* (1988) 3-33.
[100] Duff, "Harms and Wrongs" (2001) 5 *Buffalo Crim LR* 13, 39.
[101] "Basic Values and the Victim's State of Mind" (2000) 88 *California LR* 759.
[102] Law Commission, *Eighth Programme (2001-02)* HC 227, at 44.

still have been left for paternalism or, if you will, authoritarian communitarianism, a political necessity it seems. If scope is to be allowed to paternalism, it is important that the ground of intervention should be a genuine concern for the interests of the harmed agent and not mere moralism. For that to be the case, only the person inflicting the harm should be subject to penal sanctions. The person harmed should not also be liable as a joint principal or accomplice. Currently, outside the narrow scope of the *Tyrrell*[103] principle, no distinction is drawn in terms of exposure to criminal liability between the person harmed and the person causing the harm. This is difficult to square with a paternalistic concern for the interests of the harmed agent. Apologists for the current dispensation, under which those who harm and those who submit to harm are eligible for punishment, will invoke deterrence to defend the status quo in terms of paternalism. But what increments of deterrence are added by punishing both camps is entirely conjectural and to be set against conjectured gains is the palpable damage that convictions and punishments do to those who endure them. The present dispensation sits best with legal moralism. And legal moralism is not a proper basis for the deployment of criminal law in a modern, plural democracy.

§ 21.2 Self-defence and the prevention of crime[104]

Section 3 of the Criminal Law Act 1967 provides:

(1) A person may use such force as is reasonable in the circumstances in the prevention of crime, or in effecting or assisting in the lawful arrest of offenders or suspected offenders or of persons unlawfully at large.

(2) Subsection (1) above shall replace the rules of the common law on the question when force used for a purpose mentioned in the subsection is justified by that purpose.

If force is employed in circumstances which are within subsection (1), then, as indicated by subsection (2), the old common law no longer applies: the lawfulness or otherwise of the force will be determined by reference to the very broad standard of reasonableness prescribed in subsection (1). No reference is made to the common law defence of self-defence. There is no reason to think that this defence was abolished by section 3.

Historically, the defence of self-defence had a more restrictive application than the criteria set out in section 3.[105] However, the idea of *reasonable* response to violence or the imminent threat of violence is at the heart of both defences. Moreover, where the conduct of V is violent or threatens violence it will, almost invariably, constitute a criminal act on the part of V. Should D defend himself against V, his reaction is aptly characterised as an act of self-defence but it is, at one and the same time, something done to prevent V from committing or continuing a crime even though D's primary purpose is to protect himself. It would be most unsatisfactory if the criteria against which D's defensive conduct is judged were to differ according to whether we describe it as self-defence or crime prevention. Indeed, it would be pointless to conceive of the common law of self-defence as more narrow

---

[103] [1894] 1 QB 710; above, § 7.6(ii)(a).

[104] Smith, *Justification and Excuse in the Criminal Law* (1989) chap. 4; Leverick, *Killing in Self-Defence* (2006).

[105] Cf. the rule that D must take any safe avenue of retreat before responding violently to the threat posed by V: below, § 21.2(iii).

than section 3, should both defences be applicable on the facts. Accordingly, where V's violent or threatening conduct constitutes an offence, it is submitted that the legality of D's defensive response should be assessed solely in terms of the reasonableness standard set by the Criminal Law Act 1967.[106]

There will, however, be some exceptional situations where D may act in justifiable self-defence against V even though V's conduct does not constitute a crime. D may fend off an attack launched by an insane person, or by an infant, or by a person who has mistakenly assumed that D was about to attack him. In these cases, section 3 of the Criminal Law Act 1967 will not apply and it is possible to argue that the traditional, more restrictive, law of self-defence still governs. This is no authority directly in point. It would be anomalous, however, if the legality of D's conduct were to be judged by different standards in these kinds of cases, for instance by imposing a strict duty of safe retreat. Whether English law should resolve all issues that may arise when evaluating the legitimacy of defensive force merely by reference to a standard of reasonableness is debatable.[107] Yet this approach prevails at the present time and all defendants raising an issue of defensive force should be treated alike unless there is good reason to do otherwise. It will be assumed here that a plain reasonableness standard obtains for all cases of self-defence, whether or not the assailant is committing a criminal act.[108]

In one obvious way, force used in the prevention of crime is wider than self-defence in that crimes may prevented by recourse to reasonable force even where no threat to life or limb is present. D may be about to break into an empty building to commit theft and can lawfully be prevented from doing so by forcible means if necessary. However, it seems that the crime to be prevented must at least be a crime triable in England or Wales. In Jones,[109] the defendants claimed that various forms of damage inflicted on RAF property were instances of reasonable force used to prevent crimes of aggression to be committed by Her Majesty's Government in Iraq. It was ruled that section 3 was not engaged because its application is restricted to crimes justiciable in England and Wales, whereas crimes of aggression are crimes contrary to international law and not crimes contrary to English law. The Court noted that there is nothing in the legislative history of section 3 suggestive of an extra-territorial reach.

(i) Force

A claim to have used force in self-defence or prevention of crime is a claim to have used legitimate force. The term "force" is used in section 3 and is employed at common law. Clearly, "force" comprehends any violence that D has resorted to and, additionally, covers such conduct as the breaking of a window or the battering down of a door. The term, as a matter of ordinary language, will not cover any acts that lack a violent or percussive

---

[106] For further discussion of the interplay between s. 3 and the common law see Harlow, "Self-Defence: Public Right or Private Privilege" [1974] *Crim LR* 528.

[107] Ashworth, "Self-Defence and the Right to Life" [1975] *CLJ* 272.

[108] The assumption appears warranted by *McInnes* [1971] 3 All ER 295 and *Devlin v. Armstrong* [1971] NI 13: it was assumed in each of these decisions that, with the passing of s. 3 of the Criminal Law Act 1967, failure to retreat before resorting to violence was merely a factor to be considered when assessing the reasonableness of D's conduct.

[109] [2005] QB 259; but note the reservation in the text below, § 21.3(iv).

character. Accordingly, in *Blake*,[110] it was held that D could not raise a defence within the terms of section 3 where his conduct took the form of writing on V's property with a felt-tip pen. Likewise, in *Hutchinson* v. *Newbury Magistrate's Court*,[111] it was held that wire-cutting a perimeter fence did not constitute "force".

The decision is unexceptionable in terms of the literal meaning of the word force, but it may have unfortunate consequences. Suppose that D's only way of warning X that X's life is in danger is to write a message on V's whitewashed wall. D could not raise a section 3 defence to a charge of criminal damage if he painted his message on V's wall—but he could raise the issue if he brought a hammer and chisel to the task. On the principle that the "greater includes the lesser", if D can justify an act of force as a response to particular circumstances, *a fortiori* justification should be accorded to a lesser, non-forceful response to the same situation.[112] Yet the decision in *Blake* indicates the contrary, and it is notable that in the cases of *Conway*[113] and *Willer*,[114] where, in each case, D escaped unlawful serious violence by committing a driving offence, a defence was allowed by way of duress of circumstances rather than self-defence or the prevention of crime. It will be recalled that a defence of duress is available only if the harm threatened is death or serious bodily harm and cannot be raised to a charge of murder. Further, mistaken duress must, if it is to afford a defence, be based on reasonable grounds.[115] These restrictions do not apply to the use of defensive force or to mistaken belief in the need for such force.[116] To have a stricter regime for non-violent responses seems insupportable. In *Bayer*,[117] the Divisional Court expressed sympathy for the view that all forms of conduct directed at preventing crime should be appraised within the terms of section 3 of the Criminal Law Act 1967 and that conduct otherwise criminal but not involving force should not lead to liability if it was a reasonable measure to prevent the commission of a crime.

(ii) Reasonable force—a question of fact

Force used in self-defence or the prevention of crime must be "such force as is reasonable in the circumstances" if it is to be lawful. Difficult issues may arise when appraising a particular incident involving force. Broadly, they will involve questions concerning the *necessity* to use force at all and whether the amount of force used was a *proportionate* response to the circumstances. Whether the force used by D was reasonable in the circumstances is a question of fact to be determined by the jury. As with any question of fact, guidance, including strong guidance, may be given by the presiding judge. The jury should be advised that the judgment of reasonableness should be on broad and liberal grounds—jewellers' scales are not required.[118] That said, if a judge should come to the view

---

[110] [1993] Crim LR 586 (DC). See also the discussion of force in the context of robbery: above, § 14.2(ii).
[111] *The Independent*, 20 November 2000 (QBD).
[112] Perhaps such a case could now be defended on the basis of necessity: below, § 21.3.
[113] [1989] QB 290 (CA).
[114] (1987) 83 Cr App R 225 (CA).
[115] Above, § 20.1(iii).
[116] Above, § 18.1(iii).
[117] [2004] Crim LR 663.
[118] *Reed* v. *Wastie* [1972] Crim LR 221 (DC).

that, even on the most favourable view of the evidence, no reasonable jury could find that the force D employed was either necessary or proportionate, the correct course is to withdraw the issue from the jury.

This conclusion is at odds with the decision in *Scarlett*,[119] where D caused the death of V, a trespasser, by using excessive force when ejecting him from the premises. On appeal, D's conviction for manslaughter was quashed on the basis that if D thought the force he employed was reasonable (even though it was in fact excessive), he was entitled to a defence of mistake. The decision in *Scarlett* is based on a misreading of *Gladstone Williams*,[120] where it was decided that if D makes a mistake of fact, his conduct is to be evaluated as if his mistaken assumption were a true assumption. *Williams*, however, does not require D to be given the benefit of his mistaken view about what constitutes reasonable force. *Williams* involved a mistake of circumstantial fact, a mistaken assumption that V was an aggressor whereas in truth he was a police officer making an arrest; *Scarlett* involves a mistake of normative evaluation.[121] This was clearly perceived in two subsequent decisions of the Court of Appeal, namely *Owino*[122] and *Armstrong-Braun*.[123] In neither case was *Scarlett* said to be wrong but the "correct" reading of *Gladstone Williams* was emphasised. It seems safe to conclude that *Scarlett* will not be followed.

(iii) Force as a necessary means

Force cannot be justified to prevent a crime or to defend against an attack unless it was a necessary means of doing so. If D is aware that a safe alternative to the use of force is available, ordinarily he should take it. So, if D can prevent the entry of V, a burglar, by locking a door, she should do that rather than allow V to enter and then subject him to force.

The common law of self-defence required D to take any safe avenue of retreat.[124] On one view, this is a sensible rule entailed by the necessity principle. A deliberate failure to retreat rendered the subsequent use of force something that was avoidable. However, the Court of Appeal in *Julien*[125] held that, with the passing of section 3 of the Criminal Law Act 1967, the question is now simply whether D's use of force was reasonable: a failure to retreat is merely a factor to be taken into account when determining the reasonableness of D's conduct.

The approach in *Julien* is welcome in that it allows due weight to be given to D's right to autonomy. If D is behaving in a non-threatening, law-abiding manner in a place where she has a right to be, she should be under no duty to exert herself at the unlawful behest of V. The question of necessity to use force should take, as its baseline, D's right to autonomy.

---

[119] [1993] 4 All ER 629 (CA).

[120] [1987] 3 All ER 411 (CA).

[121] Although the reasonableness of D's force is a question of "fact" in the sense that it is for the jury rather than the judge to resolve, it is not the same type of fact as the circumstantial facts mistaken by the defendant in *Williams*. For further discussion of the distinction see above, § 18.1(v).

[122] (1996) 2 Cr App R 128 (CA).

[123] [1999] Crim LR 416.

[124] Turner, *Kenny's Outlines of Criminal Law* (16th ed., 1952) 113–14.

[125] [1969] 1 WLR 839 (CA). See too the discussion above, § 21.2.

This is reflected in the important case of *Field*,[126] which rules that D may remain at a place of lawful resort notwithstanding his knowledge that V may attack him should he stay there. By electing to visit a place of known danger, he does not forfeit his right to defend himself once there.

This conclusion is supported by *Redmond-Bate*,[127] where the Divisional Court had to decide whether D and others had legitimately been arrested for breach of the peace. D had been preaching, quite lawfully, on cathedral steps. A crowd of about 100 gathered, some of whom showed hostility to D. D was arrested when she refused to desist from preaching. In finding the arrest unlawful, the Court held that citizens could not be called upon to desist from lawful conduct. Only when lawful conduct gives rise to a reasonable apprehension that it will, *by interfering with the rights or liberties of others*, provoke violence, is a police officer empowered to take steps to prevent it.

Accordingly, it may be concluded that D will not lose the right to defend himself by maintaining a lawful voluntary presence.[128] Note, however, that we are dealing with *defensive* force. If D deliberately provokes V in order that he, D, may "defend" himself against V's attack, D will not ordinarily be afforded a right of self-defence.[129] In other cases, however, it does not follow that D will lose the right to defend himself whenever he is the first to initiate violence. D may launch an attack on V with his fists. If V were to produce a knife in order to kill D to terminate the attack, then D could defend himself against V's knife attack if that attack were a disproportionate response to the danger V was in.[130]

(iv) Force and proportionality

Force which is disproportionate to the needs of the occasion is unreasonable force. As remarked already, questions of proportionality need to be resolved in a broad and liberal manner, eschewing the benefits of hindsight. Only in the plainest case should a judge, after finding that some force was necessary, remove a defence from the jury on the grounds of disproportionality:[131]

> "If there has been an attack so that defence is reasonably necessary it will be recognised that a person defending himself cannot weigh to a nicety the exact measure of his necessary defensive action. If a jury thought that in a moment of unexpected anguish a person attacked had only done what he honestly and instinctively thought was necessary, that would be the most potent evidence that only reasonable defensive action had been taken."

If a jury should find that the force was excessive, the defence of self-defence will fail *in toto*.

---

[126] [1972] Crim LR 435 (CA).

[127] [1999] Crim LR 998.

[128] The conclusion might be contested by Ashworth, "Self-Defence and the Right to Life" [1975] *CLJ* 272. For Ashworth, D's right to maintain a lawful presence wherever he chooses must be balanced against V's "right to life". The drawing of the appropriate baseline is very important here. V's right to life is unalloyed while he goes about his lawful business. But that right has to be accommodated to D's right to defend himself when attacked by V. It is only at the point of attack, and no sooner, that V's right to life becomes qualified by D's right to defend himself. See further Fletcher, *Rethinking Criminal Law* (1978) 864–70.

[129] *Mason* (1756) 1 East PC 239; *Browne* [1973] NI 96, 107.

[130] *Rashford* [2005] EWCA Crim 3377.

[131] *Palmer* [1971] 1 AC 814 (PC) (Lord Morris).

If there was an entitlement to use *some* force, this may be thought to attenuate culpability to an extent. Where the sentence is subject to the discretion of the judge, any diminution of culpability can be reflected in the sentence passed. That is, of course, not possible where the sentence is fixed by law, as it is for the crime of murder. In certain states of Australia, a form of manslaughter was judicially created to allow for such a verdict where D had killed with the mens rea for murder but in circumstances where he was entitled to use a degree of force, albeit a lesser degree than the force he resorted to.[132] A similar judicial initiative has been consistently refused here, most recently by the House of Lords in *Clegg*.[133] Indeed, the idea has been dropped in the land of its origin, on the ground that directions to juries required an excessive degree of complexity.[134] This seems unfortunate. As a matter of principle, a right to use a degree of violence towards the victim must surely, on occasion, diminish the moral turpitude of D. A suitable direction to juries would appear no more intractable than for the cognate issues of provocation and diminished responsibility.[135]

Questions of proportionality may require difficult judgments by juries. The only guidance they have is their own sense of what is reasonable. A particular jury may find that it was permissible to kill to avoid serious bodily harm, for example, whereas another jury in a similar case may find such means excessive when compared to the threat. There is something to be said for more explicit guidance on commonly recurring situations, as is done, for example, in the Model Penal Code.[136] Judgments may be particularly difficult to make when incommensurable values are in play. It is often said that it can never be justified to kill in order to protect property.[137] Yet it is not obviously a categoric truth that any individual's life is of more intrinsic worth than any item of property. Is it necessarily unreasonable to kill a terrorist if such is the only means of preventing the destruction of priceless historic artefacts? The answer depends, in part, on one's core values. The lack of consensus on such issues suggests that the law should provide specific rules rather than leave such matters to *ad hoc* evaluations.

(v) Pre-emptive force

The effective prevention of a crime or an attack may require pre-emptive force. There is no requirement that D must wait until V actually attacks him before making a defensive response. It suffices that V's attack was imminent; thenceforth, D may defend himself.

---

[132] *McKay* [1957] ALR 648; *Howe* (1958) 100 CLR 448.

[133] [1995] 1 AC 482; see *Palmer* [1971] 1 All ER 1077 (PC).

[134] *Zecevic* (1987) 61 ALJR 375.

[135] The Law Commission has recently recommended that a proposed offence of first-degree murder should be reduced to second-degree murder if D killed V because he was in fear of serious violence and a person of ordinary stability might have done the same or something similar in the circumstances: *Murder, Manslaughter and Infanticide* Law Com. No. 304 (2006).

[136] The Code has a number of provisions (3.04–08) which occupy several pages of close print dealing separately with self-protection; protection of other persons; protection of property; law enforcement; and persons with special responsibilities for care and safety of others. And see too Law Com. No. 177, *A Criminal Code for England and Wales* (1989) cl. 44.

[137] Killing to protect property is not one of the circumstances where life may be legitimately taken without contravening Article 2 of the ECHR. Were an English court to hold that it was lawful to use deadly force to protect any item of property, there would arguably be a breach of Article 2 however priceless in terms of culture and heritage the item that otherwise would have been destroyed.

Focusing on the prevention of crime rather than self-defence, there is authority that the time-frame for preventive responses is more generous. If D, a police officer, is sure that V will commit a serious offence in the future, arguably it is reasonable to use force to prevent that crime even though its commission is not yet imminent. Such a view was endorsed by the Court of Appeal of Northern Ireland in *Kelly*,[138] where D, a soldier, shot and killed V, the driver of a car. There was reason to think that V and his fellow passengers were terrorists and that, if allowed to escape, they would commit terrorist offences in the future. It was held that this (false[139]) belief justified the use of force, even though D was not firing to prevent V from committing some imminent, identified, offence; he was preventing non-specific crimes at some future time.

It is submitted that *Kelly* is unsustainable.[140] The criminal law contains significant restrictions on the use of force and restraint which are at odds with this decision. If we turn to the law of arrest, a pre-emptive arrest is not possible until V is "about to" commit a crime.[141] The law of criminal attempt requires an act which is sufficiently proximate to the commission of the crime.[142] It is somewhat paradoxical that on facts such as *Kelly* D could not have used the slightest degree of restraint to make an arrest to prevent a crime yet to be committed but, nonetheless, was entitled to use fatal force for that end. This inconsistency cannot be tolerated. The laws of arrest and criminal attempt set parameters for the deployment of preventative force under section 3 of the Criminal Law Act 1967, parameters which were overlooked in *Kelly*.

Although the use of force should be subjected to strict time restraints, more latitude may be allowed for pre-emptive measures which fall short of actual violence. In *Cousins*,[143] D presented a shotgun to V and threatened that he would use it at some future time unless X, a close relative of V, withdrew his threat to kill D. On appeal D's conviction for making threats to kill was quashed because, contrary to the ruling of the trial judge, D was entitled to raise a section 3 defence despite the fact that his life was not in imminent danger. The Court of Appeal emphasised that the case involved the threat of violence and not the use of force. In *A-G's Reference (No. 2 of 1983)*,[144] the Court of Appeal ruled that D's possession of petrol bombs was possession for a lawful purpose, the purpose being to defend his shop premises from ransack at a time of urban riots. The Court assumed that D would have been entitled to use petrol bombs to defend his premises should they come under attack. It followed that he was entitled to put himself in a position to use such means.

In both *Cousins* and *A-G's Reference*, the Court of Appeal considered that offences other than the offences charged *had* been committed: in the former case, unlawful possession of a firearm because of a lack of licence, and, in the latter, the unlawful manufacture and storing

---

[138] [1989] NI 341.

[139] In fact, V and his passengers were joyriders and not terrorists.

[140] Surprisingly, the decision was upheld by the European Commission of Human Rights (*Kelly* v. *UK* (1993) 74 DR 139), who found no contravention of Art. 2 of the ECHR on the basis that the force was used to effect a lawful arrest within the terms of Art. 2. As Professor Sir John Smith observes, how can a shooting carried out with an intent to kill be spoken of as an "arrest"? See Smith, "The Right to Life and the Right to Kill in Law Enforcement" (1994) 144 *NLJ* 354.

[141] Police and Criminal Evidence Act 1984, s. 24(7)(a).

[142] Above, § 9.3(i).

[143] [1982] QB 26 (CA).

[144] [1984] QB 456 (CA).

of explosives.[145] These *obiter dicta* need to be treated with some caution. If the firearm and explosives, respectively, were obtained prior to the existence of the relevant threats, then liability for those offences ensues. Yet if the items were obtained by way of response to the threats, liability should not arise. If the use of a firearm as a threat is lawful in particular circumstances, it would be inconsistent to hold that acquiring a firearm to use lawfully in particular *identified* circumstances is unlawful. *Smith and Hogan* gives an example of V's threatening D with a gun, whereupon D wrests the gun from V and uses it to defend himself. If D's use of the weapon is lawful, the learned authors convincingly assert that to convict D of the unlawful possession of the weapon because he lacked a licence to possess a weapon would be absurd.[146] As we are dealing with conduct preliminary to the threat or use of force, prima facie it should not matter how items such as guns or explosives are acquired, provided they are acquired in order to respond to identified circumstances where the use or threatened use of such items would be lawful. (Contrast a scenario where D acquires a gun "just in case".) Of course, the longer D has possessed the gun, explosives, etc., the more difficult it will be to associate the acquisition of the item with a particular identifiable threat.

The imminence requirement may work harshly for D when she is subjected to episodes of violence by V, a more powerful person than D; D's only defensive option may be to take advantage of some moment of calm where D is unawares and vulnerable. The difficult is that providing a full defence, particularly for fatal violence inflicted pre-emptively, would be very difficult to confine to deserving circumstances. For instance, one would not want to legitimate anticipatory gangland killings, however real the "kill or be killed" dilemma that prompted them. A useful compromise is the Law Commission's proposal to reduce first-degree murder to second-degree murder if D killed V in fear of serious violence from V in circumstances where a person of ordinary stability or temperament may have done the same or something similar.[147]

(vi) Force and non-criminal threats

If D defends himself against conduct of V's which is not criminal, section 3 of the Criminal Law Act 1967 will not be in play since any defensive force by D will not prevent a crime on the part of V. Nonetheless, as we noted earlier,[148] it is probable that the legitimacy of his defensive response will be assessed according to the same standard of reasonableness. Although it could be argued that the common law of self-defence remains unmodified for these kinds of cases, it would be distinctly anomalous if this were so.

It is generally accepted that D may defend himself against unjustified force even if she knows that the force in question does not constitute a criminal act. Suppose that D, a nurse in a mental health hospital, is attacked by V, a patient she knows to be insane. It is submitted that she can take all reasonable steps to defend herself including, should it be

---

[145] See too *Fegan* [1972] NI 80 (CA), where it was held that possession of a firearm to protect oneself against violence would be possession for a lawful object even though the possession was in itself unlawful for being unlicenced.

[146] *Smith and Hogan* 267.

[147] *Murder, Manslaughter and Infanticide* Law Com. No. 304 (2006).

[148] Above, § 21.2, 21.2(iii).

necessary, the use of fatal force. Were this incident assessed from the perspective of the right to life, it could be argued that V, if sufficiently deranged to be within the defence of insanity, has not forfeited any of his rights by making this attack. From a right-to-life perspective, there is no obvious reason why it should be V rather than D who dies. Yet, though D and V have rights to life of equal standing, it is V, albeit blamelessly, who has violated D's right to autonomy. D is under no obligation to surrender her life for the benefit of V's life. Her right to autonomy allows self-preference, the sustaining of her own life with its responsibilities to those close to her, provided she does not actively violate the right to autonomy of others.[149]

The logic of this analysis flows to any situation where V's conduct constitutes an encroachment of D's autonomy and a threat to her security of person. It is not necessary that V's conduct should take the form of an attack on D. Take a situation that arose in the course of the Zeebrugge ferry disaster.[150] D and others were seeking to climb a rope ladder in order to leave the hold of a ship that was filling with seawater. The way was barred by V who, immobilised by fear, clung to the ladder despite urgent requests to climb it. D, in order to save himself and others from drowning, tore V from the ladder. Consequently, V died from drowning; D and others climbed to safety. It may be objected that D's act was not done in self-defence or in defence of others because V was not attacking anyone. Yet V's behaviour constituted an immediate threat of death to others and encroached on their autonomy by restricting, without justification, their freedom of movement. There seems no difference of principle between this situation and being attacked by a mad person. It may be said that the ferry disaster situation is a case of duress by circumstances and, possibly, of necessity. Conceptually, such a classification is possible (though not exhaustive). The drawback of rejecting the equally plausible characterisation of D's conduct as self-defence is that duress and (generally) necessity are not available defences to a charge of murder.[151] It is important to repeat that the right to self-defence will arise only if V's conduct is a threat to D's security of person *and* an encroachment on her autonomy. To take a famous example, suppose that in open seas V is first to a wooden plank, sufficient to support her but nobody else. D will drown unless he is able to take sole occupancy of it.[152] In a sense, V's possession of the plank is an immediate threat to D's life. Yet D should not be permitted to remove her from it. By taking possession of the plank, V exercised her own autonomy without violating D's.

In *Re A (Children)*,[153] Ward LJ justified a separation operation that entailed the survival of one conjoined twin J and the certain death of the other twin M. M's own heart and lungs were inadequate to sustain M's life. While joined to J, M survived only by relying on J's heart to pump the blood oxygenated by J. It was estimated that J's heart would fail under the strain within three to six months, with the inevitable consequence that both J and M would die. If a successful separation operation were to be carried out, J's prospects for a healthy life were good.

Ward LJ equated M's life-sapping dependence on J's heart and lungs as tantamount to an

---

[149] See further Uniacke, *Permissible Killing—The Self-defence Justification of Homicide* (1994) 158–93.
[150] Discussed in Smith, *Justification and Excuse in the Criminal Law* (1989) 73–4.
[151] See §§ 20.1(ii)(b), 21.3(ii)(e).
[152] Cicero, *De Officiis* iii, 23.
[153] [2001] Fam 147.

attack upon J, an attack from which J was entitled to be defended. In resolving that the killing of M would be lawful self-defence, he stressed J's prospects for a normal life, by contrast with M who was "self-designated" for death. On first impression this reference to "self-designation" sits oddly with a right of self-defence.[154] If V launches an unlawful attack on D that, of itself, gives D an entitlement to defend himself, even if D is an old man with a terminal illness and V a young, healthy man. Yet in the context of *Re A* the drawing of a contrast between the life prospects of M, on the one hand, and J, on the other, is understandable. It was the fact that M's dependence radically cut down J's life expectancy that made their coexistence a threat to J; it would have been quite otherwise had J's outlook have been as dire as M's.

It would be unwise to hazard any generalisation concerning the scope of self-defence from facts so specific as those in *Re A (Children)*, particularly as only Ward LJ based his judgment on this ground. Moreover, there is a considerable technical difficulty in subsuming the facts of the case under self-defence, namely the imminence requirement. J, at the time of the operation, was estimated to have three to six months to live, yet it would have been grotesque to delay the intervention until she was at death's door. Nonetheless, the case gives support for the view that facts such as those dismissed above arising in the course of Zeebrugge tragedy would fall within the purview of self-defence.

(vii) The defence of others

Clearly, under section 3 of the Criminal Law Act 1967, if D intervenes to defend E from the commission of a crime against E, intervention will be justified provided reasonable force is used. There is every reason to adopt the same rule for circumstances where D intervenes to prevent V from inflicting non-criminal but unjustified force on E (D, a nurse, intervenes to prevent V, a patient afflicted with insanity, from attacking another patient). A right to intervene on behalf of others is recognised at common law[155] and, presumably, still applies to situations where intervention is warranted to protect another from unjustified force.

(viii) Fatal force and Article 2 of the ECHR

Article 2 of the ECHR provides that everyone's right to life shall be protected by law. Deprivation of life will not contravene Article 2 if, *inter alia*, it results from the use of force which is no more than *absolutely necessary*:

    (a) in defence of any person from unlawful violence; or
    (b) in order to effect a lawful arrest or to prevent the escape of a person lawfully detained.

Should the action of a State official, such as a police officer or soldier, contravene Convention standards, that conduct will directly implicate the United Kingdom. Through its official, the State itself has breached the Convention. Accordingly, post-incorporation, when concerned with acts by state officials the English courts should construe the broad terms of

---

[154] Quite apart from the difficulty of characterising M as an innocent attacker, since she was not *acting* at all: cf. Chan and Simester, "Duress, Necessity: How Many Defences?" (2005) 16 *King's College LJ* 121, 128-9.
[155] Smith and Hogan, *Criminal Law* (1965) 235.

section 3 of the Criminal Law Act 1967 to conform with Article 2.[156] Although the Convention standard of "absolute necessity" contrasts with the reasonableness standard prescribed by section 3, the Convention jurisprudence does not take the phrase literally—a *reasonable* belief in the need for force will comply with Article 2.[157] As we have seen, an unreasonable belief in the need for force will ground a defence of mistake in English law.[158] Under the Convention, however, for law enforcement officials a reasonable belief may now be required.

Where a private individual uses force against another individual, the State is not directly implicated in any wrong that may have arisen. The State may be in breach of Article 2, however, if the current law provides inadequate protection for the lives of its citizens.[159] The question then arises whether allowing private individuals a defence of unreasonable mistake, in cases involving death, insufficiently protects the right to life of persons overall. Here an issue of balance arises: the protection of the public may need to be reconciled with the degree of culpability required for just punishment. Empirical questions surface too: how much more dangerous is a society that allows a defence of unreasonable mistake in homicide contexts? One would need also to note that not all unreasonable mistakes excuse. A grossly negligent mistake will allow a conviction for manslaughter. A belief that force was proportionate will not avail if the force is found to be excessive.[160] On balance, it is submitted that allowing some latitude to unreasonable mistakes for homicides perpetrated by private individuals does not bring the United Kingdom into breach of Article 2.[161]

Article 2 permits the use of fatal force to prevent unlawful violence. There is no reference to the defence of property and, because Article 2 is regarded as a fundamental provision to be construed strictly,[162] use of fatal force to protect property surely contravenes the Convention. It seems very likely that any law of self-defence which allowed private citizens to take life in order to protect property will therefore be found wanting. Earlier in this chapter (§ 21.2(iv)), we questioned whether it would always be unreasonable to take life to defend property but, under the Convention, that appears to be the position.

§ 21.3 Necessity[163]

English case law contains some vigorous rejections of any notion that necessity may be invoked as an excuse or justification for a crime. In *Kitson*, D,[164] who was asleep on the back

---

[156] This includes taking into account any settled jurisprudence of the ECHR relating to Art. 2: Human Rights Act 1998, s. 2.

[157] *McCann and others* v. *UK* (1996) 21 EHRR 97; *Andronicou* v. *Cyprus* (1998) 25 EHRR 491.

[158] Above, § 18.1(iii).

[159] As was found in respect of the defence of "reasonable chastisement" that English law affords to parents of children: *A* v. *UK* [1998] Crim LR 892; below, § 21.4.

[160] *Clegg* [1995] 1 AC 482.

[161] For differing view of this question see Leverick, "Is English Self-defence Law Incompatible with Art 2 of the ECHR?" [2002] *Crim LR* 347; Smith, "The Use of Force in Public or Private Defence and Article 2" [2002] *Crim LR* 958; Leverick, "The Use of Force in Public and Private Defence and Article 2: A Reply to Professor Smith" [2002] *Crim LR* 963.

[162] Harris, O'Boyle and Warbrick, *Law of the European Convention on Human Rights* (1995) 37.

[163] Fletcher, *Rethinking Criminal Law* (1978) 759–97, 818–35, 855–75; Smith, *Justification and Excuse in the Criminal Law* (1989) chap. 3; Schopp, *Justification Defences and Just Convictions* (1998) chap. 6; Brudner, "A Theory of Necessity" (1987) 7 *OJLS* 338; Gardner, "Necessity's Newest Inventions" (1991) 11 *OJLS* 125.

[164] (1955) 39 Cr App R 66 (CCA).

seat of a car, awoke to find the car was moving down the hill on which it was parked. To avert catastrophe, he assumed control of the vehicle and steered it safely to a stationary position on the side of the road. The fact that he was responding to an emergency and refrained from driving any further once the situation was resolved did not exempt him from liability for driving a car when unfit due to drink. In *Buckoke* v. *GLC*,[165] the Court of Appeal had to decide whether a driver of a fire-engine on an emergency call could elect to go past a red traffic light. The answer was a resounding no, an answer to be given even if the road was clear and a person some 50 yards from the now stationary vehicles required immediate life-saving rescue from the fire service. A final example is afforded by *Southwark LBC* v. *Williams*,[166] where the Court of Appeal rejected an argument that homeless people could take temporary refuge in vacant council premises without committing acts of trespass.

The intransigent approach in these cases is no longer so easy to take. Case law since then has made it impossible to deny the existence of a general defence of necessity in English law. But before we move on to this new development, it is important to recognise the concern underlying the earlier decisions since, as we shall see, it may help to illuminate current difficulties raised by the recognition of a general plea of necessity. Earlier rejection of the defence was driven by an understandable reluctance to allow individuals to be the judge of when to dispense with the letter of the law:[167]

> "The law regards with the deepest suspicion any remedies of self-help, and permits these remedies to be resorted to only in very special circumstances. The reason for such circumspection is clear—necessity can very easily become simply a mask for anarchy."

This is a Rule of Law argument. The legal system will simply not work if its authority is optional. Derogation from its rules is not permitted save in specific, confined circumstances. It is clearly in the public interest that traffic signals be rigidly obeyed: general security would be much diminished if overriding discretions were allowed. The use of vacant council properties is best resolved by the local political decision-making processes, implemented by consistent administration rather than *ad hoc* self-help. And so on. The drawback produced by this unyielding stance is that it exposes to criminal liability persons whose conduct may have brought about significant benefit and whose motivation may have been impeccable. This is a powerful consideration and warrants the admissibility of a necessity plea. Yet it is a plea that imports considerable difficulties of definition and ambit.

(i) Recognition of a necessity defence in modern case law

The recent re-emergence of a defence of necessity did not arise from any considered reflection; effectively, it has arrived inadvertently by way of the defence of duress by circumstances and, in a more considered way, in cases of protective interventions for incompetent persons. Recall the cases of *Conway*[168] and *Willer*,[169] where defences of duress were afforded to defendants who had elected to commit motoring offences rather than remain in the

---

[165] [1971] 1 Ch 655 (CA).
[166] [1971] 1 Ch 734 (CA).
[167] *Southwark London Borough* v. *Williams* [1971] Ch 734, 740 (Edmund Davies LJ). Cf. Brudner, "A Theory of Necessity" (1987) 7 *OJLS* 338, 342–4.
[168] [1989] QB 290 (CA).
[169] (1987) 83 Cr App R 225 (CA).

presence of a threat of serious bodily harm or worse. As we noted in § 20.1(ii), these decisions involved a considerable enlargement of the defence of duress. Nonetheless, they remain close to the informing idea of duress, namely that the defendant's act was coerced by a fear of immediate death or serious bodily harm. Essentially, the content of the legal norm violated is not being challenged by claiming the priority of a competing value;[170] rather, the argument is that compliance with law cannot reasonably be expected from a person under such pressure.

Duress of circumstances was extended to a very different situation in the case of *Pommel*.[171] Recall that D took possession of a sub-machine gun from a person who had it in mind "to kill some geezer". D himself was not that "geezer" and was under no threat. Essentially, his reasoning was that it was better to take possession of the gun, despite the lack of a licence, rather than to allow it to remain in the hands of a person intending to use it to kill. D was asserting the value of saving life over the letter of the gun-control laws while at the same time furthering the ultimate goals of gun laws, namely keeping weapons out of the wrong hands. This is a defence of necessity; as seems implicitly to have been recognised by the Court of Appeal, which used the terms necessity and duress interchangeably.[172]

More explicit recognition of a defence of necessity has been effected by the House of Lords in two cases involving incompetent patients. In the first, *F v. West Berkshire Health Authority*,[173] the legality of a sterilisation operation on a sexually active but learning-disabled patient was in issue. Pregnancy was judged to be something which it was in the interests of the patient to avoid at all costs; measures short of sterilisation were assessed as ineffective or impracticable. Lords Brandon and Goff premised the legality of the operation on ground of necessity. In *R v. Bournewood Community and Mental Health NHS Trust*,[174] the legality of the detention and treatment of an informally admitted mentally incompetent patient whose detention fell outside the regime provided by the Mental Health Act 1983 was held, unanimously, to be justified by necessity. The latter case unequivocally declares that a defence of necessity is known to English law.[175] What the decision (and previous decisions) lacks, however, is any considered discussion of the rationale and ambit of the defence.[176]

(ii) The rationale and ambit of necessity

Discussion of necessity inevitably contains a large measure of conjecture. The idea behind

---

[170] Because such claims are so troubling to the coherence of the legal order, the Supreme Court of Canada was of the opinion in *Perka* (1984) 13 DLR (4th) 1 that necessity claims must operate in the realm of excuse. But as we shall see, necessity pleas will be raised in circumstances where D herself is unpressurised; as, for example, where D, a surgeon, decides that V's best interests as a severely learning disabled person who is sexually active will be served by a sterilisation operation. It should not be enough to excuse D for carrying out such a radical intervention without V's consent: the operation must be, all things considered, the right thing to do.

[171] [1995] 2 Cr App R 607 (CA); above, § 20.1(ii)(a).

[172] In *Quayle* [2005] EWCA Crim 1415, paras. 41 and 42, there is recognition that *Pommel* is in different case from the other duress by circumstances authorities.

[173] [1990] 2 AC 1.

[174] [1998] 3 All ER 289 (HL).

[175] In *Hasan* [2005] 2 AC 467 and *Quayle* [2005] EWCA Crim 1415, one can find *dicta* sceptical about whether talk of a general defence of necessity is grounded in legal reality but at the same time a recognition that cases such as *Re F* and *Bournewood* cannot really be placed under the rubric of duress of circumstances.

[176] [1998] 3 All ER 673 (CA).

the defence is simple and beguiling: achieve the greater good rather than slavishly follow the letter of the law. There will be occasions where following this injunction will produce incontrovertible gains in welfare and an absence of countervailing harms. Yet an absence of countervailing harms is not a necessary condition for establishing the defence. A balance of harms test may be allowed in some circumstances; whereas in other situations vested legal rights will be given priority, thereby precluding on those occasions a necessity defence based on a balance of harms test. The devil is in the detail. The leading cases are short on guidance about these issues. On the following pages, we will do what we can to delineate the ambit of this defence.

There is no unitary rationale of the necessity defence.[177] Rather, within the general rubric of "necessity", the defence cloaks a number of intertwined justificatory reasons. What they have in common is at least a degree of urgency, which may fall short of immediate emergency. Sometimes it may be possible to seek the assistance of the courts *ex ante* to determine the legality of a proposed course of action. In medical cases, the courts have shown a commendable degree of procedural flexibility in advising on the legality of proposed surgery, surgery that would constitute a criminal (and tortious) act unless warranted by necessity. Where prior guidance of the courts is feasible, the Rule of Law concerns discussed above are less pressing. Yet there will be occasions where immediate action is called for—unless D takes V's car she will not be able to save E. Nowadays, a court may rule, *ex post facto*, that D was entitled to drive V's car, without prior permission from V, to save the life of E. But what must be present in every case is a harm which can only be avoided if, in the near future, the letter of the law is breached. If the harm is more remote than that (particularly where the harm has a degree of conjecture and imprecision), D cannot take the law into her own hands and must address her concerns in some other fashion. In *Shayler*,[178] D, a civil servant employed in MI5, was concerned that the kind of covert actions supported by the service threatened rather than enhanced public security. He was held to be in breach of the Official Secrets Act 1989, consequent on sharing secret information with a newspaper. Even on the assumption that his concerns were warranted, he was not attempting to avert some imminent catastrophe by the only possible and proportionate means. There was no forthcoming incident his actions were intended to avert, merely a fear that the covert operations of MI5 threatened public security generally.

Since necessity has an uncertain scope and is not tightly confined in the way that other defences generally are, its recognition could potentially undermine the authority of law. If defendants were permitted to break laws *whenever* there was, say, a lesser-evils justification (below), the generality of those laws would be undermined and their application would have to be reassessed on a case-by-case basis. It is for the legal system to determine when its prima facie laws may be broken. Ideally, in a democracy, the freedom of action that a perceived necessity requires should be afforded by legislative change. Yet constraints of time may preclude resort to legislation. In those circumstances, wherever possible, guidance from a court should be sought before the putatively illegal action is taken; as was done, for instance, in the conjoined twins separation case of *Re A (Children)*.[179] Where that is impossible and the only recourse is direct action by D, D may be found to have been justified by necessity.

---

[177] Cf. Chan and Simester, "Duress, Necessity: How Many Defences?" (2005) 16 *King's College LJ* 121.
[178] [2001] 1 WLR 2206.
[179] [2001] Fam 147.

(a) A lesser-evils justification

The most obvious rationale for allowing necessity is a recognition that, on occasion, more welfare may ensue from breaking than from keeping the law. The defence looks to the consequences of particular episodes of conduct rather than to the desert of the actor. To be sure, on many occasions where a necessity defence may be invoked, the defendant is meritorious or blameless. Yet if, say, a driver of a fire-engine decides to pass a red light with complete safety on a clear road in order to effect a life-saving rescue, it misses the point to say that a conviction for a road traffic offence is not merited on retributivist grounds. The gain in welfare arising from saving a life rather than opting for pedantic compliance with regulatory law is so salient that it eclipses any issues of culpability and blame typically associated with law-breaking. The conduct in question is incontrovertibly worthwhile, like giving to charity or researching cures for deadly diseases. It is not that D acted wrongly and is insufficiently culpable: it is that D did the right thing.

The fire-engine case is an easy example because the offence in question was a victimless offence; no-one's rights or interests were overridden when making the rescue. Contrast the following case:

> D takes money from V to give to X so that X may have a life-saving operation only available to those who can travel abroad and pay for it. V is an elderly billionaire who lives alone in a large mansion full of cardboard boxes stuffed with money. He has no relatives, has made no will, and possesses no plans whatever for his money. Yet he resolutely refuses to give any of it away.

To take any of V's money should surely be theft, even if D is able to take the money in circumstances causing V no distress whatever (e.g. D takes one box from hundreds and V remains wholly unaware that it has gone). Where breaching the law involves violating a prima-facie right, the lesser-evils justification is insufficient, by itself, to support a necessity defence.

(b) Intervention in V's own interests where V is incompetent

Are we to say, then, that a defence of necessity will be stopped short whenever it comes into conflict with an innocent person's legal rights? As we saw in § 21.2(i), that is clearly not the position taken by English law. In *West Berkshire*,[180] a compulsory operation was lawfully carried out. In *Bournewood*,[181] a learning-disabled person was detained for compulsory treatment even though his adoptive family were anxious to bring him home. The rights overridden were of the most fundamental nature. Was it to the point that the persons whose rights were overridden were deemed incompetent to know their best interests and the procedures were carried out for the presumed benefit of these subjects? Probably; particularly in light of the Court of Appeal's decision in *St George's Healthcare NHS Trust* v. *S*,[182] which vindicated the right of a pregnant woman to refuse a caesarian operation, notwithstanding that the operation was required to preserve the life of the mother and of the

---

[180] [1990] 2 AC 1.
[181] [1998] 3 All ER 289.
[182] [1998] 3 All ER 673 (CA).

unborn child. The judgement of best interests in these cases is a sensitive and troubling matter, something recognised particularly by Lord Steyn in *Bournewood*.[183]

(c) Violating rights of an autonomous innocent victim

The most important constraint on the necessity plea is that it cannot be invoked in circumstances where D overrides a legal right of a non-consenting person whose conduct constitutes no threat to the person or property of others. That is why D cannot take any money from V, the misanthropic billionaire, in the example discussed in § 21.2(a). It is why a person in a rare blood group cannot be forced to donate blood, however urgent the need for blood from this group. This fundamental limitation is not expressly stated in any English case. Yet its existence can be assumed with some assurance, particularly in the light to the decision in *St George's Healthcare NHS Trust* v. *S*[184] which, as we noted above, unequivocally upholds the right of a competent person to refuse any form of medical or surgical intervention however, pressing the need for assistance. Furthermore, the case decides that a life-saving procedure cannot be forced upon an unwilling person even if, at one and the same time, another significant interest—here the safe delivery of a late-term foetus—would be secured. If a person's legal rights cannot be overridden in order to treat her own medical needs, they cannot be violated in order to further the treatment of someone else.

(d) Violating property rights

This important limitation is subject to some *de minimis* exceptions. On occasion, the infringement of a right may be transitory and inflict no lasting setback to the interests of the right holder by comparison with the value being protected, e.g. where the infringement is required to preserve life. As Devlin J remarked in *Esso Petroleum Co Ltd* v. *Southport Corporation*, a tort case:[185]

> "The safety of human lives belongs to a different scale of values from the safety of property. The two are beyond comparison and the necessity for saving life has at all times been considered a proper ground for inflicting such damage as may be necessary upon another's property."

For example: it may be necessary to trespass across land to effect the rescue of X. Or it may be necessary to break into the absent V's house in order to telephone an ambulance required to take D to hospital for vital emergency treatment. In each of these cases, provided the situation is an emergency, such minor infringements of rights are compatible with allowing a necessity plea. Sufficient regard of V's interests will be offered if he is entitled to full compensation for any loss sustained.[186] If this analysis is correct, D may, say, pick up V's mobile phone from the table to alert emergency services even should V have declined D's request to use the phone. It may well be that D is entitled to use a reasonable degree of force should V attempt to take back the phone until the emergency call is made. But could D use

---

[183] [1998] 3 All ER 289, 307–9.
[184] [1998] 3 All ER 673.
[185] [1956] AC 218, 228 (first instance judgment).
[186] Cf. the famous tort case of *Vincent* v. *Lake Erie Transportation Co.* 124 NW 221 (1910).

a degree of force on V to access the phone in the first place? When, if ever, can V's right to personal integrity be violated in order to secure a greater good?

(e) Violating rights of personal integrity

Given the paramount importance of personal autonomy in a liberal democracy, it is difficult to imagine circumstances where the *de minimis* exception would ever permit the violation of an innocent (and competent) victim's *person*, in however minor a form. The view that the personal integrity of competent persons may never be violated is supported by the strong body of judicial opinion, most recently expressed by Lord McKay in *Howe*[187] (a duress case), that the famous case of *Dudley and Stephens*[188] precludes the raising of necessity as a defence to murder. In *Dudley*, D and others, survivors of a shipwreck, were adrift in an open boat in the South Atlantic. They killed and consumed without his consent the youngest and weakest member of their party. But for this act, D and his companions would probably have died prior to rescue.[189] The case clearly decides that there is no defence to murder in such circumstances. Why the defence was unavailable does not emerge clearly from the judgment. In so far as D was arguing that the threat of imminent death excused his act, the denial of a defence can be understood; he was raising what we now would call a defence of duress of circumstances and, for better or worse, it is well established that a defence of duress is not available for murder.[190] Alternatively, we can read D's defence as a claim that he did the right thing: had this drastic step not been taken, all would have died including the victim of the killing. An emphasis on the value of the act raises the defence of necessity, giving weight to an interpretation of *Dudley* to the effect that necessity is not available as a defence to murder. Either way, it appears that current law refuses to countenance a defence to murder unless the circumstances can be brought within the rubrics of self-defence or the prevention of crime (above, § 21.2).

There *may* be one exception to this rule: where V is the source of the danger faced by D. It is important to notice that *Dudley* was not concerned with that possibility. Coleridge LCJ referred to the victim as "a weak and unoffending boy." He was an autonomous individual and constituted no threat to anyone else. Because of this, he had a right to be left alone. It does not follow from *Dudley* that D may never cause personal injury to V. Consider the following case:

> D and others have survived a shipwreck. They are in a lifeboat on the open seas, which is filled to capacity. V, who is in the water, is holding on to the side of the boat. D realises that the weight of all the passengers, combined with V's actions, is

---

[187] [1987] AC 417.

[188] (1884) 14 QBD 273 (CCR).

[189] A fascinating historical and socio-legal account of the case is given by Simpson, *Cannibalism and the Common Law* (1984). The jury, by special verdict, found that D and others would probably have died had they not killed and consumed V. The killing took place on the eighth day adrift and rescue came on the twentieth day. Legally speaking, therefore, D's act was necessary for survival, particularly in the light of the prosecution's burden of proof. Despite this, Coleridge LCJ queried the necessity of the act as an act of survival by noting that D might have been picked up next day or not picked up at all and, in either case, the killing would have been profitless. But D must be tried on the facts as they occurred and not on the basis of what might have been. To judge necessity on the basis of speculating on the range of possible worlds from a given baseline would be, effectively, to eliminate the defence.

[190] *Howe* [1987] AC 417.

causing the lifeboat to ship water. If V is allowed to continue holding on, the boat will ultimately sink entailing the death of everyone.

On these facts, D is presumably entitled to fend V off, even if that means V will drown more quickly. The case is similar to that which occurred during the Zeebrugge ferry disaster, described above in § 21.2(vi). Arguably, such situations should be accommodated within the defence of self-defence, which permits violence to the person extending even to murder. But if not self-defence,[191] then a defence of necessity should in principle be available. The prospects for the availability of such a defence are enhanced to a degree by the judgment of Brooke LJ in *Re A (Children)*.[192] As already discussed, the Court of Appeal permitted a separation operation to be carried out to preserve a normal life for J even though the surgery inevitably entailed the death of her conjoined twin M. Alone of the three appellate judges, Brooke LJ squarely based his decision on the grounds of necessity (although it should be noted that Ward LJ expressed his agreement with Brooke LJ's decision). Brooke LJ found the operation to be justified on a straightforward application of the following three criteria, endorsed originally by Stephen:

(i) the act is needed to avoid inevitable and irreparable evil;
(ii) no more should be done than is reasonably necessary for the purpose to be acheived; and
(iii) the evil inflicted must not be disproportionate to the evil avoided.

Taken at face value, these criteria are overinclusive. They would allow extreme invasions of the personal integrity of autonomous, non-threatening persons whenever, on a consequentialist weighing of advantage, welfare overall would be increased. The facts of *Re A* should be stressed. Innocent though she indubitably was, M's demands on J's bodily resources were characterised as a direct threat to the life of J, a threat that would terminate an otherwise viable life within three to six months. From that perspective, the affinity with the emergency that arose in the context of the Zeebrugge ferry is reasonably close, M being the source of the threat. One factor informing these situations is that V's position is not significantly worsened by D's intervention. Either way, V will die. Even in *Re A*, the operation aside, M was "self-designated for a very early death." This consideration may well be crucial if personal injury is ever to be permitted under the guise of necessity. Suppose the following example:

> D, V, and others are speleologists. They are exploring a series of caves underground. Unfortunately, and through no-one's fault, V becomes trapped in the mouth of one of the caves. The waters in the cave are rapidly rising, and the cave will soon be flooded. The trapped man is immovable. He is preventing the escape and survival not only of himself but also of his fellow speleologists. The only way of unblocking

---

[191] If self-defence is confined to repulsing attacks, then fending off V may not fall with its purview.
[192] [2001] Fam 147. For discussion see Uniacke, "Was Mary's Death Murder?" (2001) 9 *Medical LR* 9; Huxtable, "Separation of the Conjoined Twins: where next for English Law?" [2002] *Crim LR* 549; Michalowski, "Sanctity of Life: Are Some Lives More Sacred Than Others?" [2002] *LS* 377; Chan and Simester, "Duress, Necessity: How Many Defences?" (2005) 16 *King's College LJ* 121.

the exit is by cutting off his arm. Even though V objects, D does so and everyone survives.

Necessity would surely be available here as a defence to a charge of inflicting grievous bodily harm. Unlike the shipwreck example, this is not a case in which D is protecting his life against a threat posed by V's actions, so this is unlikely to be a case of self-defence. Rather, the speleologists face a common danger. It matters here not only (i) that like cases of self-defence, D's response is addressed to the source of the peril (and not to a third party), but also (ii) that V's interests are served as well as D's—D has not simply preferred his own interests to those of V. The latter condition is not a requirement of the defence of self-defence.

Condition (i) is also significant. Suppose that T, a terrorist, threatens to shoot D unless D, in turn, participates in a mission to murder V. If D does so, the case is neither self-defence nor necessity. It can only be argued as one of duress (and, as we saw, in § 20.1(i)(d), it would fail under the current law of duress). It would have been otherwise if D had responded by shooting T. Justification requires addressing the source of the danger, not deflecting it upon someone else.

To summarise: the defence of necessity generally does not permit the infliction of personal harm. In principle, however, it may do so under certain very stringent conditions, outlined here. At the level of principle, where these conditions are met necessity should be available as a defence to all crimes, including murder. Under current law, *Dudley* is regarded as authority that necessity is unavailable to murder. But, on the facts, *Dudley* need not have decided any specific rule for murder. In principle, a defence of necessity should have been unavailable in *Dudley* anyway—because the cabin boy was an autonomous individual who posed no threat to D.

(iii) Conclusion

Recent cases, particularly *Bournewood*,[193] have unequivocally recognised a defence of necessity. This defence must be carefully distinguished from the newly emerged defence of duress of circumstances. Under the latter head, the primary focus is on the pressure that D was under, an excusatory claim premised on a threat of death or serious bodily harm. In the case of a necessity plea, attention is paid foremost to the value of D's act, the claim that by breaking the letter of the law more benefit was obtained than would have been the case with compliance. In principle, necessity should be available as a defence for all offences, including (sometimes) murder. Affording a necessity defence should not be at the expense of legal rights held by competent non-consenting persons. This principle is subject to a *de minimis* exception which will allow some infringements of rights by reason of necessity but subject to full compensation to the right holder. Rarely, if ever, will this exception permit the violation of V's body. The bodies of non-competent persons may be violated on the ground of necessity but only where the necessitous intervention is for the benefit of the person violated.

---

[193] [1998] 3 All ER 289 (HL).

(iv) Necessity and parliamentary sovereignty

Necessity is a common law principle. Accordingly, it should yield wherever statutory provision has been made for the emergency, crisis, or interest invoked to justify D's act. If, for example, as a consequence of the decision in *West Berkshire Health Authority*,[194] Parliament had enacted that sterilisation operations could not be carried out without the consent of the patient, necessity could never again be invoked in the circumstances of the *Berkshire* case. In *Bournewood*, the Court of Appeal took the view that the Mental Health Act 1983 provided a comprehensive regime for the detention and treatment of mentally incompetent patients.[195] V fell outside this scheme and, appropriately, on its view of the Act, the Court of Appeal ruled that necessity could not be invoked to allow V's continuing detention. By contrast, the House of Lords held (convincingly, in the light of the legislative history) that the scheme of the 1983 Act was not comprehensive and had designedly made no provision for patients such as V who were compliant and did not object to detention but who essentially lacked any means of volition to accept or reject detention and treatment. Accordingly, the immediate best interests of that class of patient could be addressed under the head of common law necessity.

Contrast the decision of the Court of Appeal in *Quayle*:[196] one aspect of the case concerned persons who had involved themselves in providing cannabis and various cannabis derivatives for other persons who, it appeared, could only find palliative relief for very painful symptoms by using these substances. Both possession and supply of these substances contravened provisions of the Misuse of Drugs Act 1971. That Act, as well as proscribing in general terms the possession, supply, etc., of controlled drugs, sets up an elaborate scheme for their lawful possession. The Court of Appeal took this scheme to be comprehensive and complete. It did not make general provision for doctors, let alone non-medically qualified persons, to supply cannabis for pain relief. Express provision was made for the medical use of opiates but no express provision was made for cannabis. Consequently, there was no space for a judicial ruling allowing the palliative use of cannabis on the ground of common law necessity. The area of concern was regulated by a statutory scheme.

As well as bowing out where the area of concern is already regulated, courts will be reluctant to intervene under the head of necessity where a claim of necessitous intervention is used to legitimate forms of direct action by way of protest or opposition to government actions or policies which involve criminal acts on the part of the protestors. In *Jones*,[197] D and others perpetrated acts of criminal damage at RAF airbases and claimed vindication on the ground that their otherwise criminal acts were reasonable force in the prevention of crime within the terms of section 3 of the Criminal Law Act 1967, the crime in question being the international law crime of aggression, committed, it was alleged, by the United Kingdom against Iraq. Entanglement in this issue was avoided by ruling that section 3 was only concerned with crimes justiciable within England and Wales. (One may wonder whether such a ruling would have been forthcoming against a person who used reasonable

---

[194] [1996] 2 AC 1.
[195] [1998] 1 All ER 634.
[196] [2005] EWCA Crim 3377.
[197] [2005] QB 259.

force in England against V, a French citizen, to prevent him from leaving England to carry out a murder in France.) An analogous upshot occurred in *Shayler*,[198] where D claimed it had been essential to breach official secrecy legislation to alert the public to the dangers they were in due to secret service incompetence. The Court of Appeal dismissed the necessity claim on the merits, as previously discussed: the House of Lords thought any discussion of necessity to be an irrelevancy.

Simon Gardner has argued that necessity claims cannot be avoided, however politically embarrassing a particular claim may be, if they raise a matter of legality and principle against Her Majesty's Government and not a mere difference of policy.[199] He turns to the ECHR as the major constraint on what the government may legitimately do and advocates the legal protection of forms of direct action which attempt to secure government compliance with the Convention. For instance, he envisages the courts protecting persons who have forcibly released prisoners whose detention is found to have been in breach of Article 5 of the ECHR. We anticipate that courts will rule, contra Gardner, that the only avenue of redress for unlawful detention is by way of legal challenge and not through the *ex post* vindication of forms of criminal conduct.

Necessity is a doctrine to be used sparingly to cover crises and gaps in provision which lead to an urgent need for remedial action; it is not a major organising principle of a modern legal system. Where a social problem is structural and continuous, it must be addressed through the legislative and political process.[200] A homeless person cannot occupy an empty property as a home.[201] But anyone may take temporary shelter in such a property to avoid an immediate catastrophe.

§ 21.4 Chastisement[202]

At common law, disciplinary chastisement of an apprentice, servant, or child was permitted provided it was done by a person with the authority to do so and was of a "moderate, reasonable nature".[203] Nowadays, it may be asserted confidently that the age of legal corporal punishment for apprentices and junior employees has long gone. The social and legal substrata permitting force against persons in these categories have completely disappeared, and with them any colour of justification for disciplinary force.

Parents and persons *in loco parentis* are still allowed a common law power of reasonable and moderate chastisement.[204] Recently, a stepfather who frequently and severely beat his stepson with a garden cane was acquitted of battery by a jury on the ground of reasonable

---

[198] [2001] 1 WLR 2206; above, § 21.3(ii).

[199] "Direct Action and the Defence of Necessity" [2005] *Crim LR* 371.

[200] This was a matter which weighed heavily with the Court of Appeal in *Quayle*. The problem of pain relief was persistent and ongoing. See further, Lenckner, "The Principle of Interest Balancing as a General Basis of Justification" in Eser and Fletcher (eds.), *Justification and Excuse: Comparative Perspectives* (1987) vol. 1, 493. Arguably, the decision in *Bournewood* [1998] 3 All ER 289 is at odds with this limitation since, although the Court was faced with an emergency, the problem was systemic.

[201] *Southwark London Borough Council* v. *Williams* [1971] 1 Ch 734 (CA).

[202] Rogers, "Chastisement" [2002] *Crim LR* 98.

[203] Kenny, *Outlines of Criminal Law* (1st ed., 1902) 108–9.

[204] *Hopley* (1860) 2 F & F 202, 175 ER 1024; *Clearly* v. *Booth* [1893] 1 QB 465.

chastisement. An application on behalf of the boy was made to Strasbourg where the ECHR ruled that the common law provided insufficient protection for children, since it had exculpated (in that case) a degree of chastisement that constituted "inhuman and degrading treatment" within the terms of Article 3 of the Convention.[205] Under the Human Rights Act 1998, English courts are obliged to limit permissible chastisement to force not proscribed by Article 3. What degree of force falls outside Article 3 is unclear. Using a cane to sharp effect is clearly outlawed. Physical punishment *per* se is not banished.[206] But what physical punishment remains allowable under the Convention is a matter of conjecture. Neither does the Children Act 2004 proscribe physical chastisement, provided no bodily harm is caused.[207]

Schoolteachers are the largest class of persons who are regularly *in loco parentis* to children. Under pressure of earlier ECHR rulings, there has been legislation relating to the use of corporal punishment by teachers.[208] Briefly summarised, the right of teachers to use corporal punishment as a form of discipline is effectively now revoked.

---

[205] *A* v. *UK* [1998] Crim LR 892. The breach of Art. 3 by the United Kingdom was on the basis of allowing too broad a defence of chastisement which might allow the inhuman and degrading treatment of children. Exception was taken to the fact that it was for the prosecution to prove that the chastisement was not reasonable and moderate.

[206] *H* [2002] 1 Cr App R 59; Rogers, "A Criminal Lawyer's Response to Chastisement in the European Court of Human Rights" [2002] *Crim LR* 98.

[207] See s. 58.

[208] Children and Young Persons Act 1933, s. 1; Education Act 1996, ss. 548, 549.

22

DEFENCES AND BLAME: SOME OBSERVATIONS

In §§ 1.3 and 17, we discussed the structure of an offence. There, we noted that many questions of criminal liability can be resolved by deploying a threefold analysis along the following lines:

(i)   Is there an actus reus?
(ii) Is there mens rea?
(iii) Is there any supervening defence?

Employing this procedure will frequently be straightforward and useful. A negative answer to (i) or (ii) will preclude liability and it is appropriate to ascertain whether the definitional elements of a crime are present before turning, if necessary, to such matters as justification and excuse. If English law were more precise and consistent in its terminology, we might expect the term "defence" to be confined to issues arising under (iii), whereas matters contested within the terms of (i) or (ii) should go to questions of "definition" rather than defence. As we have seen, however, English law does not follow this pattern of usage. What are termed defences in the case law may arise under any of these headings. An ascription of an actus reus may be contested by raising a "defence" of automatism. Mens rea may be denied by claiming a "defence" of mistake. If what otherwise would be a crime is committed in response to an immediate threat of death, a defence of duress may be raised. Only this last case is a case of defence, within the terms of the threefold analysis.

It would be a mistake, however, to become preoccupied with correct usage. After all, it is perfectly natural to say that D is defending herself when she contests an issue on which her liability depends. So D may argue that to take V's new car without his permission and return it after driving 10,000 miles is not theft, because she lacked an intent to deprive V of his car permanently. Conceptually, whether she has an intent to deprive permanently is a question about the defining elements of theft but there is no vice in describing D's arguments as her defence to the charge of theft. What matters, substantively, is that the issues in dispute are clearly defined and the burden of proof is appropriately allocated. Provided these conditions are met, it is pedantry rather than rigour to insist on terminological exactitude.

Moreover, there is often an overlap between defences and elements of the offence. If D takes £10 from V's wallet in an emergency (e.g. to pay for a taxi ride to hospital), she may not need to plead a defence of necessity, since she can plausibly deny that she was dishonest—which is part of the mens rea requirement for theft. Many mens rea terms, such as dishonesty, recklessness, and negligence, import an evaluative as well as a cognitive element. It would be odd, for instance, to characterise the driver who justifiably mounts a pavement in order to avoid an out-of-control vehicle as driving "recklessly".[1]

Nonetheless, it is important to understand the nature and role of what we may term "true" or "supervening"[2] defences. These are defences which go to (iii), relating to pressures, exemptions, and permissions, rather than denials of actus reus or mens rea. When defining or interpreting the ambit of offences, legislatures and courts seek to identify particular types of wrongs. Delineation of these wrongs requires specification of the defining elements— actus reus and mens rea. To collide with someone accidentally is not to assault that person: an assault is something done intentionally or recklessly. The wrong that is murder has intentionality at its core. When identifying and individuating wrongs, we should seek as much clarity and precision as is feasible. In so far as possible, we must capture the essence of the wrong *ex ante*, in order to afford fair warning[3] and to avoid false labelling.[4] Inevitably, however, circumstances will arise when the defining elements of a particular offence are made out but where blame and punishment are unwarranted because of the presence of culpability-reducing factors unspecified in the offence. Here we see what may be termed the default role of supervening defences. They serve to ensure justice is done to defendants who would otherwise be convicted because their conduct satisfies the definition of an offence. Typically, when that definition is met, blame and punishment are merited. But not always: it is for those times when the move from liability to punishment should be blocked that we provide supervening defences.

§ 22.1 Some things defences cannot do

Broadly speaking, defences are provided to ensure that a person whose conduct does not exhibit sufficient culpability for conviction of an offence will not be convicted of that offence. A conviction, especially for a stigmatic criminal offence, is harmful *per se*: D suffers a significant setback to her interests if she is convicted of a serious offence, even if she receives an absolute discharge. A conviction is a public act of blame and it must be warranted. Defences help to safeguard against unwarranted convictions. Unfortunately, the defences currently allowed under English law provide inadequate protection. As things stand, persons may be convicted of offences despite the lack of sufficient—or indeed any— culpability.

This is for two sorts of reason. First, there are systemic limitations to the varieties of exoneration that any criminal law system can recognise. Under the conventions of our criminal law, only a limited range of conditions may be taken into account when assessing whether, despite the presence of the definitional elements of an offence, D may nonetheless be exempted from liability. These limitations are intrinsic to a system reliant on the application of rules. They entail the conviction of certain defendants who may be morally

---

[1] *Harris* [1995] 1 Cr App R 170; but see *Backshall* [1999] 1 Cr App R 35.
[2] A term coined in Simester, "Mistakes in Defence" (1992) 12 *OJLS* 295.
[3] Above, § 2.3.
[4] Above, § 2.4.

blameless. At least at the formal level of adjudication, even the fairest systems of criminal law will convict some people who do not deserve to be blamed.

That melancholy fact provides no excuse for the second type of case. There are many situations where defences *could* be, but are not, made available to blameless persons despite the lack of any systemic need to deny them. We shall discuss some of these situations below, in § 22.2. Before that, however, we begin by considering some of the systemic constraints on defences.

(i) Justifications and divergent values

Inevitably, any judgement of blamelessness in the context of legal adjudication is constrained by the substantive values to be found in the norms of the criminal law. Imagine a society where there is a large majority view that homosexuals should be allowed the same degree of sexual freedom as heterosexuals. However, a ruling elite has been able to retain political power and the law of the state continues to proscribe same-gender sexuality. If D transgresses the law by having homosexual sex he is blameworthy within the conventions of that legal system. Any assessment of criminal culpability must accept as a *datum* the substantive morality contained in the norms of the criminal law.

This constraint is bound up with the authority of a legal system. Law works, *inter alia*, by coercing people, by imposing a standard of legally acceptable behaviour and demanding that they conform to that standard. If the norms that the law would have us observe were displaced, in each case, by those of the particular defendant, then the law would have no standard to impose.[5] Whatever one takes to be the purposes of law, their achievement requires the co-ordination of individuals' behaviour by ordering ("do not") rather than asking ("unless you want to"). Individuals cannot be legally justified in conducting themselves above or outside the compass of the law merely because they have different moral values—even if they are right. Any criminal legal system which aims to prevent wrongs must be able to determine wrongful behaviour by a standard independent of the defendant.

The claim to authority that legal norms exert has significant implications for the availability of particular defences. Consider the rule *ignorantia juris non excusat*: ignorance of the law does not excuse.[6] Suppose D is unaware of a prima facie offence that mandates behaviour she would not otherwise choose. The most difficult cases of this type arise in offences *mala prohibita*—when the defendant's action is to be avoided only because proscribed. For example, the main wrong about driving only slightly in excess of the speed limit is that one does so in defiance of law, rather than of the reasons for which that law was made. From D's perspective, even if she desires to comply with the law, no reason to modify

---

[5] "To permit one who knows but does not accede to the community valuation of interests to have an individual standard would at once destroy the law": Seavey, "Negligence—Subjective or Objective?" (1927) 41 *Harv LR* 1, 11. It is, of course, a further question whether the law's claim to authority is itself justified. In an unjust society, persons who receive few material advantages may have little attachment or regard for the prevailing social order, particularly if unequal outcomes track systemic divisions of race and gender. In such societies, defiance of aspects of the criminal law may be a warranted moral and political stance. Yet even then the reasons that ground morally legitimate defiance do not form any basis for exculpation *within* the terms of the criminal law itself. Intrinsically, the criminal law protects the status quo and criminal law defences must fall within that framework.

[6] Above, § 18.2.

her behaviour is generated by such offences unless D is aware of the potential violation. As such, D's ignorance is analogous to mistakes of fact and blameless when reasonable. Yet the law may have institutional reasons to disallow her defence. Sometimes, as in the driving example, D can be regarded as culpable for failing to ascertain relevant law before embarking on a course of conduct. But the main arguments are instrumental; based, especially, upon the difficulty of proving the defendant ought to have known the law, and upon the need to provide incentives for citizens to become acquainted with law.[7] The literature on ignorance of law is vast[8] and we cannot conclude the debate here. The point is that these instrumental arguments depend on the need for the legal system to be effective rather than morally accurate. Thus they point toward a rule governing mistakes of law that is, at least partly, disconnected from judgments of culpability.

In § 21.3, we noted that similar concerns about the authoritative status of law have, traditionally, hampered recognition of a defence of necessity. People are not permitted to choose for themselves whether some legal prohibition should be obeyed in particular circumstances; that, the courts have said, would be a recipe for anarchy.[9] This is a consideration that informs all justificatory defences. In general, individuals are not free to choose to break the law unless the situation is urgent, so that it cannot be resolved by recourse to the legal system. D cannot raze V's field to create a firebreak, thereby protecting the villagers against the realistic *prospect* of a forest fire, unless authorised by law. But she may do so if the fire is real and upon them.

(ii) Limiting excuses

Implicit in the claim to authority are further limitations. It is important that the practical scope of excusatory defences does not undermine the capacity of criminal law to sustain a system of order through rules.[10] Consequently, many episodes of blameless conduct which fall within the defining elements of offences must nonetheless be regarded as crimes, where they are the products of the normal and countless vicissitudes of life. Consider, for example, D, a man devastated by the recent departure of his partner. He drinks alcohol by way of solace and, being unaccustomed to alcohol, he rapidly becomes intoxicated. While in that condition, he is taunted by V and, in his disinhibited state, D lashes out at V with his fists. Even if D's life was exemplary up to that point, he must still be held liable for his assault. Were we to allow an excuse based on his current life situation, we would then be committed to entertaining many other narratives of how "normal" life had dealt harshly with an

---

[7] "The principle that ignorance of the law should not be a defence in criminal matters is not justified because it is fair, it is justified because it is necessary, even though it will sometimes produce an anomalous result": *Campbell* (1972) 21 CRNS 273, 280 (Kerans DCJ). Compare *People* v. *O'Brien* 31 Pac 45, 47 (1892). For an instrumental counter-argument, see *State* v. *O'Neil* (1910) 126 NW 454, 456.

[8] In the criminal context see, e.g., Ashworth, "Excusable Mistake of Law" [1974] *Crim LR* 652; Brett, "Mistake of Law as a Criminal Defence" (1966) 5 *Melbourne ULR* 179; Hall and Seligman, "Mistake of Law and *Mens Rea*" (1940–41) 8 *U Chicago LR* 641; Keedy, "Ignorance and Mistake in the Criminal Law" (1908) 22 *Harv LR* 75; Williams, *Textbook of Criminal Law* (2nd ed, 1983) 451–63; Fletcher, *Rethinking Criminal Law* (1978) 736–58; Hall, *General Principles of Criminal Law* (2nd ed., 1947) 376–92.

[9] *Southwark London Borough* v. *Williams* [1971] Ch 734, 740 (Edmund Davies LJ).

[10] For a thorough and nuanced discussion of the nature and limits of excusatory claims see Horder, *Excusing Crime* (2004).

accused. Yet, if we change our example to a situation where D did not know he was drinking alcohol because his soft drinks were surreptitiously laced, arguably he should have now a supervening defence. An excuse based on the fact of involuntary intoxication is exceptional, bounded, and forensically manageable. Were it to choose to do so, English law could, within certain limits, afford a defence of involuntary intoxication without undermining a system of ordering by rule.[11]

No doubt this conclusion would be attacked by critical theorists, who may regard a distinction between agents who drink while in thrall to strong emotions and agents who drink unwittingly as yet another of the arbitrary distinctions that undermine any claim of the criminal law to be based on defensible principles.[12] Norrie, for instance, has made much of the fact that we allow a defence of duress based on violence but disallow, as any excuse, the impact of poverty deprivation on conduct.[13] In some situations,[14] his critique has considerable force. Assessed in terms of culpability, there may be little difference if D shoplifts because she has been threatened with violence by her husband or shoplifts because she cannot face the disappointment of her children at Christmas. The short explanation for the variance is that we can sustain a law of theft even if we allow an excuse on the basis of violent coercion but not if we excuse on the grounds of economic deprivation. Maintenance of a law of theft in an unequal society may well entail the conviction of persons who must be held blameworthy within the terms of the criminal law but whose conduct does not merit punishment when judged by a wider frame of reference.

The fact that the criminal law must employ a conception of blame that will, on occasion, include persons of good character suggests that the criminal law has little concern with the quality of a defendant's character. Its concern is with particular episodes of conduct and whether a finding of blame, in the sense under discussion, can be made in respect of them.[15] The character of D is relevant to liability (as opposed to mitigation) only if it can be presented as afflicted by some form of pathology germane to a mental condition defence. D may be a firm believer in euthanasia, and, moved by compassion for V, she may bring about his death in a calm and resolute manner. The fact that D has led an impeccable life of selfless public service will have no bearing on her liability for murder. If, however, her concern for V has caused her to become extremely depressed, she may be able to raise a plea of diminished responsibility to a murder charge.

The disassociation of background character from questions of liability is particularly poignant in cases where, for reasons beyond her control, D has undergone a radical change of character. Such was the claim of Patty Hearst, who was abducted and indoctrinated, as she claimed, by a cell of urban terrorists before participating in bank robberies and other

---

[11] Sullivan, "Making Excuses" in Simester and Smith (eds.), *Harm and Culpability* (1996) 131.

[12] Kelman, "Interpretive Construction in the Substantive Criminal Law" (1981) 33 *Stanford LR* 591.

[13] *Crime, Reason and History* (2nd ed., 2001). See too Norrie, *Punishment, Resposibility and Justice* (2000), discussed in Sullivan, "Is Criminal Law Possible"(2001) 22 *OJLS* 424.

[14] But not all. It is true that many criminal convictions are imposed on persons who lead lives of great social and economic deprivation. The association of such disadvantages with criminal behaviour is, statistically, irrefutable. That fact, as Norrie notes, has no bearing on whether a particular defendant from such a background is eligible for a criminal conviction. But it may also have little, if any, bearing on whether that defendant is eligible for moral blame. That D is poor does not entitle her to kill V.

[15] Moore, "Choice, Character and Excuse" in Paul, Miller and Paul (eds.), *Crime, Culpability and Remedy* (1990) 29; but see also Arenella, "Character, Choice and Moral Agency" in *ibid.*, 59.

criminal acts.[16] Yet, within the set of values that she had been induced to adopt, her acts were the product of her volition and comported with her practical reasoning. To allow Ms Hearst a defence on the basis that her criminogenic character was something unchosen by her would merely underscore the fact that, to a large extent, everyone's character is something beyond volitonal control.[17] If, in our present circumstances, we are capable of practical reasoning and are physically and psychologically unconstrained, we are judged accountable for what we do. The test is always whether, as we are now and regardless of how we came to be what we are, we are capable of moral agency. If we satisfy that test, we are responsible and cannot evade *conviction*. It does not follow, however, that someone in the position of Patty Hearst should be *punished*. If she has been restored to her former law-abiding character at the time of her trial, no obvious retributivist or consequentialist purpose seems served by imposing punishment. Punishment can be withheld in such an exceptional case without threat to the foundations and practice of criminal liability.

(iii) Responsibility for one's character: free will and incapacity

The case of Patty Hearst raises questions about the extent to which not only our actions, but also the motives that lie behind those actions, are free. As we saw in § 4.3, the criminal law exculpates conduct that is physically involuntary. Otherwise, however, the law assumes that all adult citizens are capable of understanding and complying with its rules, an assumption displaced only if D's transgression is attributable to a condition falling within the *M'Naghten* Rules. It does not, for instance, excuse to demonstrate that D was *psychologically* incapable of obeying the law on a particular occasion. D, a chronic alcoholic, is guilty of theft if he takes a bottle of spirits belonging to V, notwithstanding his craving for alcohol and lack of funds.[18]

In light of these doctrinal strictures, it is frequently claimed that the criminal law assumes free will. In fact, it need make no commitment to free will, nor to determinism, nor to any compatibilist theory which mediates between these two positions.[19] Rather, the criminal law simply makes a categoric assumption that, save for special cases, D is responsible for her conduct. If particular conduct is in breach of the letter of the law, then, prima facie, D is taken to be at fault and a candidate for blame and sanction. It must then be resolved whether there is any reason not to make a finding of guilt. Criminal law legislation and adjudication cannot, on any long-term basis, stray too far from strong community sentiments concerning the immorality of particular forms of conduct.[20] If D stabs and kills V while in thrall to a schizophrenic belief that V was about to kill him, there may be a general acceptance that D should be confined in a place of safety but not be punished. Contrast the feelings likely to be generated by the conduct of D, who has had penetrative sexual relations with young children. Even in the face of evidence that he has a

---

[16] See Alldridge, "Brainwashing as a Criminal Law Defence" [1984] *Crim LR* 726.

[17] Vuoso, "Background Responsibility and Excuse" (1987) 96 *Yale LJ* 1661.

[18] *Powell* v. *Texas* 392 US 514 (1968).

[19] For an excellent account of the relevance of the free will–determinism debate to the form and practice of criminal liability, see Westen, "Getting the Fly out of the Bottle: The False Problem of Free Will and Determinism"(2005) 8 *Buffalo Crim LR* 101.

[20] Robinson and Darley, *Justice, Liability and Blame: Community Views and the Criminal Law* (1995).

form of psychological disorder which makes sexual control difficult, nonetheless there will be a strong demand for blame and punishment.

The difference in likely popular reaction to these two cases is explained by what Strawson has famously called "reactive attitudes".[21] It may well be that the propensity to act upon schizophrenic delusions is of the same order of force as the propensity to surrender to the urgings of a pathological libido. It is the "otherness" of a person afflicted with schizophrenia that attenuates the urge to blame and punish. Yet if a particular pathological condition does not impair a person's cognitive and reasoning capacities that person remains firmly within the community of blame. Consequently, even if a strong version of determinism were to be accepted as the best working hypothesis to explain and predict all forms of human behaviour, the institutions of state punishment are unlikely to wither away and be replaced by forms of preventive detention. Atrocious conduct would continue to elicit strong negative reactions. Those reactions will in part be expressed in a system of formal blame and sanction. The conventions of blame can withstand an acceptance that human beings are located in the natural order, an order constituted by causal regularities.

These are issues that arise prior to law. They affect our conceptions of humanity and morality. In particular, there are unanswerable questions about when a person's character is "normal" and, as Bernard Williams noted, disputes about the degree to which that should count.[22] Law, morality, and society each works with a concept of the "voluntary" that informs judgements of wrongdoing. But that concept is not profound. Even if D's action is done with mens rea and in a normal state of mind, there are deeper questions about why D is someone who wants to act as she does; whether it is within her choice or control to be such a person; whether her character is itself "voluntarily" chosen. One might then ask: is it fair that D should be subject to state punishment because she is the sort of person she is (when, one might say, that is not something D is responsible for)?

The concept of voluntariness offers no assistance with such questions. It shapes our analysis of physical conduct and casts no deeper light. Voluntariness may discern whether, given who and how she is, D deserves criminal sanctions, but cannot reveal whether D deserves to be that person she is.

(iv) Summary

Judgements about whether particular conduct is blameworthy must operate within the framework of substantive values contained in the norms of whatever criminal jurisdiction is in issue. Exemptions from blame cannot delve too deeply into the particularities of defendants' lives because the provision of defences must remain a matter of rule rather than discretion. Such constraints entail, from time to time, the blaming and punishment of persons who have not forfeited a claim to be of good character.

These constraints on findings of blamelessness are considerable and can lead some theorists to reject the criminal law as a system of principle rather than a system of coercion.

---

[21] "Freedom and Resentment" in *Freedom and Resentment* (1974) 1. See too Horder, "Criminal Law: Between Determinism, Liberalism, and Criminal Justice" (1996) 49 *Current Legal Problems* 159.

[22] "Moral Responsibility and Political Freedom" [1997] *CLJ* 96, 101–2. A reply by Duff and von Hirsch follows: "Responsibility, Retribution and the 'Voluntary': A Response to Williams" [1997] *CLJ* 103.

But one must continue to strive for principle in a hostile social climate. Criminal law and criminal justice are nowadays highly politicised subjects in England and Wales; to gain electoral support the main political parties frequently resort to proposals to extend criminal liability and increase punishments.[23] In such times as these, it is particularly appropriate for advocates and judges to create and develop defence doctrine, albeit within the ineluctable constraints of the criminal law.[24]

§ 22.2 Some things the defences fail to do

Within its institutional limitations, one might reasonably anticipate that the defences afforded by the criminal law of England and Wales will, largely, ensure acquittals for the blameless. Broadly, supervening defences fall within two major categories. First, there are defences which focus on some aspect of D himself, an aspect which renders him morally irresponsible for the conduct forming the substance of the offence charged. Within that group are infancy, insanity, non-insane automatism, and, to an extent, diminished responsibility. Secondly, rather than picking out a particular quality of D's that pre-empts her moral responsibility for the offence,[25] there are defences which arise on the basis that any person, placed in the same set of circumstances or making the same factual assumptions as was D, could not fairly have been expected to comply with the letter of the law. This second category includes excuses[26] and justifications: indeed, falling within this latter group may be situations where, from a societal perspective, committing a prima facie offence is the preferred option.

Unfortunately, even where the constraints of institutional possibility do not apply, English law does not always exculpate the blameless.

(i) Irresponsibility defences

(a) Exemptions for infancy and insanity

Certain mental conditions may be incompatible with justified blame. Young children afford an obvious example. From an early age, children are capable of aggressive and predatory conduct. Such conduct may need to be restrained but a degree of maturity, a capacity for self-criticism, is required before formal pronouncements of blame and punishment are apt. English law takes the age of 10 as the threshold for criminal guilt. There must be considerable doubt whether pre-teenage children have, as a class, sufficient insight and maturity to be full candidates for blame and punishment. Particular concern arises where young

---

[23] For an instructive if depressing evaluation of the politicisation of criminal law and justice see Ashworth, "Is Criminal Law a Lost Cause?" (2000) 116 *LQR* 225..

[24] The Law Commission's Draft Code would allow judges the capacity to develop common-law defences: Law Com. No. 177, *A Criminal Code for England and Wales* (1989) cl. 4(4).

[25] This generalisation is subject to any allowances made, within the "reasonable man" standards that operate in excuses such as duress and provocation, for weaknesses peculiar to the defendant: above, §§ 10.5(iii)(c), 20.1(i)(e). Thus the division we have made here is not clear-cut.

[26] Thus, as Gardner points out, excuses do not deny responsibility: "The Gist of Excuses" (1998) 1 *Buffalo Crim LR* 575, 588ff.

children receive long terms of incarceration for a serious offence. In *R. v. Secretary of State for the Home Department, ex p Venables*, two 10-year-old boys were detained at Her Majesty's pleasure for murder.[27] Even if we assume a culpability commensurate with that gravest of crimes, the 15-year "tariff" the pair received raises a major issue of principle. All other things being equal, at the age of 18 they were to be transferred to young offender institutions and thereafter to prison. To what extent is a person of, say, 22 years the "same" person as he was at 10? Even if he is not in any perceptible sense a better person at 22, is there a sufficient link between his present self and his earlier conduct to justify a continuing expiation of it? The trial and punishment of young children raises questions concerning not only a sufficiency of culpability at the time of the crime but also the connection between past conduct and present guilt during a period of growth and change.

In addition to infancy, insanity has long been accepted in many cultures as incompatible with moral agency. The idea has not gone unchallenged. Szasz,[28] among others, has rejected the acceptance of insanity as an exculpating condition. For him, insanity is just another form of survival strategy, a chosen mode of existence. It is no disrespect to Szasz to say that his is, nowadays, almost a lone voice. The reality of insanity is a matter of vivid report in case histories and there are increasing prospects of identifying major mental pathologies with underlying physiological conditions. The "otherness" of persons afflicted with psychotic disorders—their profoundly disturbed sense of reality—places such persons beyond any community of blame constituted by a sufficient core of shared assumptions guiding practical reason.

Alas, the *M'Naghten* Rules exclude many profoundly disturbed people. The class of psychotic persons outside the Rules may be said to constitute a body who should properly be ineligible for blame and are victims of injustice when convicted and punished. To some extent this situation is remedied by the partial statutory defence of diminished responsibility, albeit the remedy is confined to the offence of murder and diminishes but does not exclude blame and punishment. This defence also embraces persons whose cognitive and reasoning capacities are unimpaired but who may, because of a personality disorder, experience considerable difficulty in restraining criminogenic impulses. Peter Arenella[29] has argued forcefully argued that persons with profoundly disordered personalities, who are incapable of any degree of identification or sympathy with the interests of others, should be dealt with outside the framework of the criminal law. However, the concept of personality disorder or psychopathy is controversial medically and has gained no purchase in the realm of public sympathy or understanding. While there are now proposals to confine, without the need of a criminal conviction, persons with personality disorder on account of the danger they may present,[30] there are no proposals to exempt from conviction personality-disordered defendants who do perpetrate crimes.

---

[27] [1998] AC 407. Ultimately, the boys were released on parole after spending eight years in custody.

[28] *The Manufacture of Madness* (1970); *The Myth of Mental Illness* (1961).

[29] "Convicting the Morally Blameless: Reassessing the Relationship Between Legal and Moral Accountability" (1992) 39 *UCLA LR* 1511.

[30] Home Office, *Managing Dangerous People with Severe Personality Disorder: Proposals for Policy Development* (1999). The Mental Health Bill 2007 contains provisions for the detention of persons assessed to be dangerous on account of personality disorder even though effective treatment for the condition of the person detained may not be to hand.

(b) Destabilisation?

Persons who are not insane or personality-disordered may nonetheless find themselves in a destabilised condition and, in such a state, may perpetrate the actus reus of a crime. Where the condition is not self-induced and is incompatible with proof of mens rea, no conviction for the crime is possible. If, however, the definitional elements of a crime are present, liability will ensue. Recall *Kingston*,[31] where it is ruled that a "drunken intent is a criminal intent" even in circumstances where the drunken condition was involuntarily induced through the machinations of a third party. The House of Lords reversed the decision of the Court of Appeal,[32] which had allowed involuntary intoxication to serve as a defence to any crime provided the actus reus would not have been perpetrated but for the effects of the drink.

In correcting the generosity of the Court of Appeal, the House of Lords took an unduly formal view of the nature of criminal guilt. Guilt, for their Lordships, consisted merely of the presence of the definitional elements of the crime and the absence of any legally recognised justification or excuse. Even if the defendant were blameless, he would still be guilty of the offence. This approach completely disregards the reputational consequences of a conviction for a stigmatic offence: the public judgement of blame that inheres in the fact of conviction alone. It is submitted that if a court accepts D is blameless, the conditions that explain his blamelessness should provide, wherever systemically possible, the basis of a defence.

There are a number of personal conditions compatible with mens rea that preclude a sufficient moral culpability for conviction of that crime. Non-exhaustively, these include involuntary intoxication, confused states of consciousness induced by medication, the destabilising effects of post-traumatic stress disorder, premenstrual tension, epilepsy, arteriosclerosis, cerebral tumours, and diabetes. Such conditions may trigger outbursts of motiveless violence from persons who are otherwise morally well-disposed. The way that English law deals with these conditions at the present time is manifestly unsatisfactory.[33] Sometimes sympathy for a defendant may influence a court to find that the mental element for a crime is not made out—even though this may seem at variance with the facts of the case. If the mental element is held to be absent, either a straightforward acquittal or a qualified verdict of insanity will follow, depending on whether the court characterises the condition as arising from internal or external factors. If the mental element is found to be present then an acquittal cannot follow. Arguably, a general defence *should* be available for those afflicted with any of these conditions, notwithstanding the presence of mens rea. Of course, the availability of such a defence should be subject to a number of restrictive conditions.[34] But, where those conditions are met, it is submitted that this class of blameless persons could be excluded from liability without undermining the structure and cohesion of the criminal law.

---

[31] [1995] 2 AC 355; above, § 18.3(v)(a).

[32] [1993] 4 All ER 373.

[33] Sullivan, "Making Excuses" in Simester and Smith (eds.), *Harm and Culpability* (1996) 131, 145–50.

[34] In particular, provided (i) D would not have committed the offence but for being in a state of disequilibrium occasioned by his diabetes, post-traumatic stress, etc.; (ii) the offence at issue is not amongst the most serious of crimes, such as murder, rape, etc.; and (iii) D has not previously been convicted for a similar offence.

In our discussion of murder,[35] we noted the Law Commission proposals which reformulated the provocation defence.[36] These proposals will allow the culpability-reducing factors of gross provocation and the fear of serious violence to be taken into account at the trial stage. The introduction of such a partial defence is particularly in point for murder because of the mandatory penalty.[37] There is nothing, in principle, however, against the introduction of forms of legal mitigation (as opposed to sentencing discretion) for other offences. Jeremy Horder, for instance, has advocated the extension of diminished responsibility to offences other than murder.[38] If diminished responsibility were to be established in a non-homicide context, perhaps one could "cap" the maximum penalty that could be imposed to, say, half the maximum sentence provided for the offence. This form of mitigation would thus become a matter of *entitlement*, to be won in argument at trial or by concession on the part of the prosecution. There is merit in acknowledging the diminution of guilt in the realm of law rather than judicial discretion. Accordingly, forms of legal mitigation such as provocation and diminished responsibility which are currently confined to murder arguably should be available for offences generally.

(ii) When conformity with law cannot reasonably be expected

For defences in this second category, D's claim is, loosely, that in the circumstances any ethically well-disposed person could not reasonably have been expected to comply with the letter of the law. It is not that there is anything peculiar to himself which precludes liability. *Anyone*—or at least, anyone like D[39]—placed in similar circumstances could not reasonably have been expected to do differently. The emphasis is on the reasons or explanations why D acted as he did or found himself in the situation that he was, reasons or explanations potentially applicable to any actor.

Expectations of conformity with law may be pitched at unattainable levels. The most glaring situation of this kind is where, for reasons beyond the control of D and in circumstances that do not reveal any fault on her part, criminal liability is attached by way of an involuntarily acquired status, as in the notorious case of *Larsonneur*.[40] In principle, questions of involuntariness and control should be accommodated within the concept of actus reus.[41] Failing that, the blamelessness of defendants should be accommodated by way of a defence of impossibility.[42] But at present, English law tends to disregard principle in favour of *ad hoc* decisions, frequently tailored to the language of the particular offence.

Almost as fundamental in their unfairness are cases where liability will be incurred as an inevitable concomitant of carrying on a lawful trade or business. If peas are to be canned on an industrial scale, it is inevitable that some cans will contain foreign bodies, whatever

---

[35] Above, § 10.5(vii).
[36] *Murder, Manslaughter and Infanticide* Law Com. No. 304 (2006) part 5.
[37] Under the Law Commission's scheme, first degree murder would be reduced to second degree murder, displacing the mandatory penalty.
[38] "Pleading Involuntary Lack of Capacity" [1993] *CLJ* 298, 316. See also Wasik, "Partial Excuses in the Criminal Law" (1982) 45 *MLR* 516, 522.
[39] Above, n. 23.
[40] (1933) 149 LT 542; above, 4.1(ii)(a).
[41] Above, § 4.3.
[42] Above, § 20.5.

reasonable checks and controls are put in place.[43] If videos, tobacco, or lottery tickets are allowed as items of commerce, then even careful shopkeepers and their assistants will sell or hire such items to persons who look older than they are, whatever precautions are taken.[44] To date, there seems no judicial inclination to mitigate the inherent unfairness of strict liability by way of a due diligence offence. Such a defence would also be relevant to a plea of excusable ignorance or mistake of law.

Less frequently encountered, but potentially productive of grave injustice when it arises, is the failure of English law to recognise any defence of superior orders. Consider a situation where D, an armed soldier, is ordered by his commanding officer, E, to shoot V. The reason for the order is, let us suppose, the belief that if V were allowed to escape, he will commit terrorist offences at some future time. It is probably the case that the order is unlawful; force used in the prevention of crime is likely to be found lawful only when the crime is imminent, although *Kelly*[45] favours a more expansive approach. The position of D is invidious. If he disobeys the order, adverse career and disciplinary consequences may well follow. Besides, D may believe, quite reasonably, that the order given by E is an order to do something which is lawful. Were he to be tried for murder consequent upon following the order, the prospect of a conviction on such facts would appear to be strong. Equally strong, it is submitted, is a plea for excuse on the part of D.

Currently, a defence of superior orders is uncountenanced even in circumstances where D's conduct is morally *justifiable*. In *Yip Chiu-cheung*,[46] D and E were charged with conspiring to traffic in controlled drugs. Their conviction depended on proof that F, who was not a defendant, was guilty of drug trafficking, in taking drugs from Hong Kong to Sydney. F was found to have committed the offence, notwithstanding that he was an undercover police officer whose only motivation was to bring D and E to justice, an endeavour for which the Privy Council had only praise. The matter is put as one of high constitutional principle—the unconstitutionality of any dispensing power entailed that F was guilty. But this is a situation where F acted not to undermine but to reinforce the law's authority. It is legitimate to speculate whether that line of analysis would have held if F had actually been prosecuted for the offence.

In respect of the other defences recognised by English law, claims that blameless people are insufficiently accommodated are more controversial. The scope of the defence of duress has been criticised on the grounds that it is unavailable to a charge of murder.[47] Yet it is not *obviously* wrong to deny impunity for killing an innocent person in order to escape death or serious harm to oneself, and the counterarguments should be acknowledged even if one favours extending the defence to murder.[48] Similarly, whether the defences of mistaken self-defence or prevention of crime are under-inclusive of the blameless is a matter of controversy.[49] On the other hand, the law shows a meaner spirit when disallowing a defence

---

[43] *Smedleys Ltd* v. *Breed* [1974] AC 839 (HL). See above, Chapter 6.

[44] *Harrow LBC* v. *Shah* [1999] 3 All ER 302 (DC).

[45] [1989] NI 341. See above, § 20.3.

[46] [1995] 1 AC 111.

[47] Smith, *Justification and Excuse in the Criminal Law* (1989) 92–5; above, §201(i)(d). The Law Commission has recently proposed the exrension of duress to murder: Law Com. No. 304 (2006) part 6.

[48] For some thoughtful points, see Horder, "Occupying the Moral High Ground? The Law Commission on Duress" [1994] *Crim LR* 334, 335–6, 339–40.

[49] Simester, "Mistakes in Defence" (1992) 12 *OJLS* 295; above, § 18.1(iii).

where D kills an innocent person in order to avoid harm to innocent persons other than herself, particularly where she enjoys a close relationship with those whose welfare she prioritises. Arguably, too, English law is unduly restrictive in denying any form of mitigation to a person who was entitled to use some degree of force but who used force excessive for the occasion.[50] Certainly in the context of murder, the availability of a manslaughter verdict in such circumstances would be a welcome departure from the rigidity of the mandatory life sentence.

§ 22.3 Defence doctrine and judicial creativity

In principle, therefore, more could be done to exculpate blameless defendants. What chance is there of judicial innovation to meet these needs? In *Lynch*,[51] the House of Lords decided, by a majority, to extend the defence of duress to the crime of murder (a decision later reversed in *Howe*[52]). In the judgments two very different attitudes to enlarging the coverage of defences were expressed. For the majority, Lord Wilberforce said:[53]

> "I have no doubt that it is open to us, on normal judicial principles, to hold the defence admissible. We are here in the domain of the common law: our task is to fit what we can see as principle and authority to the facts before us, and it is no obstacle that these facts are new. The judges have always assumed responsibility for deciding questions of principle relating to criminal liability and guilt, and particularly for setting the standards by which the law expects normal men to act."

For the majority of the House, extending the defence of duress to acts of complicity in murder was an appropriate task for the highest appellate court, notwithstanding long-standing institutional authority that the defence was not available in such circumstances. For the minority, this amounted to a usurpation of legislative authority. Lord Simon castigated the majority's approach:[54]

> "I can hardly conceive of circumstances less suitable than the instant for five members of an appellate committee of your Lordships' House to arrogate to ourselves so momentous a law-making initiative."

In the context of *defence* doctrine, the more expansive approach of Lord Wilberforce is to be preferred. The judicial role is well suited to expanding defence doctrine and even, when circumstances require so, the creation of a novel defence. In terms of the propriety of judicial law-making, one may distinguish between grounds of inculpation, on the one hand, and grounds of exculpation on the other.[55] In the former case, clarity and generality of application are important virtues when defining the prima facie offence. Further, any significant enlargement of a class of conduct which may be punished is a task for the legislature and not for an unelected judiciary. For exculpatory questions, however, it is possible

---

[50] Above, § 21.2(iv).
[51] [1975] AC 653.
[52] [1987] AC 417.
[53] [1975] AC 653, 684.
[54] *Ibid.*, 696.
[55] See, e.g., Smith, "Judicial Law Making in the Criminal Law" (1984) 100 *LQR* 46, esp. 63–7.

to craft principled responses to the quiddity of a particular case without undermining the normative framework of the criminal law. The recent development of the defence of duress of circumstances and the overdue recognition of a defence of necessity indicate the willingness of some contemporary judges to give practical effect to findings of blamelessness.

But there are other judicial voices too. The House of Lords and Privy Council have each held that there may be a conviction for a serious stigmatic offence in circumstances where the defendant is blameless. Further, in *Clegg*,[56] the House of Lords expressed a reserved attitude to the judicial creation and extension of defences. In *C v. DPP*,[57] the House of Lords, in reinstating the presumption of *doli incapax* for 10- to 14-year-olds, spoke in general terms of the propriety of judicial lawmaking in criminal law. Speaking for the appellate committee, Lord Lowry laid down what he termed "aids of navigation". They are:[58]

> "(1) If the solution is doubtful, the judges should beware of imposing their own remedy. (2) Caution should prevail if Parliament has rejected opportunities of clearing up a known difficulty or has legislated, while leaving the difficulty untouched. (3) Disputed matters of social policy are less suitable areas for judicial intervention than purely legal problems. (4) Fundamental legal doctrines should not be lightly set aside. (5) Judges should not make a change unless they can achieve finality and certainty."

These navigational aids are intended for general guidance. But, it is submitted, they are too restrictive when applied to the development of defence doctrine, by contrast with enlarging the scope of offences. At risk of repetition, what should drive the development of defence doctrine is a refusal to countenance the conviction of a blameless person for a serious criminal offence. We must accept that full expression of that principle is limited by the nature of the criminal law itself. But subject to that important proviso, what *can* be done by way of exempting of blameless persons, should be done. This may require a disregard for some of Lord Lowry's navigational aids, particularly the matter of finality and certainty. For example, consider the decision in *Bournewood*[59] which at long last recognised a defence of necessity. Beyond the facts of *Bournewood*, the limits of the defence are impossible to state with any assurance. That brings a degree of disvalue; but the disvalue is outweighed by the value of providing the defence. The primary norms of the criminal law remain intact as a guide to action and are not unduly undermined by allowing departures from the letter of law in cases of obvious necessity.

On the matter of sensitivity to the condition of blamelessness, it may be that we are set to enter a new judicial era. In an important extra-judicial lecture, Mrs Justice Arden (then Chairman of the Law Commission) gave her views on the centrality of the Human Rights Act 1998 to the substantive criminal law and, in particular, her view of the likely impact of Article 3 of the ECHR which proscribes torture and "inhuman and degrading treatment or punishment." The hypothetical case that she poses is so resonant of future possibilities that it may be quoted in full:[60]

---

[56] [1995] 1 AC 482.

[57] [1996] AC 1.

[58] *Ibid.*, 28.

[59] [1998] 3 All ER 289; above, § 21.3(i).

[60] "Criminal Law at the Crossroads: The Impact on Human Rights from the Law Commission's Perspective and the Need for a Code" [1999] *Crim LR* 439, 450; above, § 2.5(i).

"Suppose as a result of an accident, which was not the result of any negligence or intention, a factory owner pollutes the environment around his factory. He admits that the damage was caused by his factory and he pays a large sum of money to clear up the mess with a view to limiting the damage to his reputation. Suppose that he is then prosecuted for an environmental offence involving strict liability which carries an unlimited fine and he resists conviction on the ground that the accident had occurred accidentally and without fault. He contends that a conviction would cause him great loss of reputation. Can he successfully contend that for the law to impose strict liability, so that a person can show that the damage was not due to any negligence on his part, and that he has taken all the steps required to rectify the damage caused, has no defence, infringes his rights under Article 3?"

Mrs Justice Arden considers the likely answer to this question is affirmative and envisages a court creating a "due diligence and all reasonable steps to rectify" defence under the wide powers of construction provided by section 3 of the Human Rights Act 1998. She also adverts to Article 6(2), which provides that "everyone charged with a criminal offence shall be presumed innocent until proved guilty according to law," and queries the legitimacy of strict liability offences in the light of this presumption.

Strict liability has been judicially tolerated for a long time and has been confirmed at the appellate level.[61] Yet if other judges, in addition to Mrs Justice Arden, were to read the ECHR and the interpretative possibilities of the Human Rights Act 1998 as boldly as she does, the lot of blameless defendants may significantly improve.

---

[61] The Court of Appeal has recently confirmed the ECHR-compatibility of strict liability even in serious offences: G [2006] EWCA Crim 821.

BIBLIOGRAPHY

Adams, F., "Homicide and the Supposed Corpse" (1968) 1 *Otago LR* 278.

Advisory Council on the Penal System, *Sentences of Imprisonment: A Review of Maximum Penalties* (London: HMSO, 1978).

Advisory Group on the Law of Rape (Heilbron Committee), *Report of the Advisory Group on the Law of Rape* Cmnd. 6352 (London: HMSO, 1975).

Alexander, L., "Criminal Liability for Omissions: An Inventory of Issues" in S. Shute and A.P. Simester (eds.), *Criminal Law Theory: Doctrines of the General Part* (Oxford: Oxford University Press, 2000) 121.

——, "The Moral Magic of Consent (II)" (1996) 2 *Legal Theory* 165.

Alldridge, P., "Common Sense, Innocent Agency, and Causation" (1992) 3 *Criminal Law Forum* 299.

——, "Dealing with Drug Dealing" in A.P. Simester and A.T.H. Smith (eds.), *Harm and Culpability* (Oxford: Oxford University Press, 1996) 239.

——, "The Doctrine of Innocent Agency" (1990) 2 *Criminal Law Forum* 45.

——, "Making Criminal Law Known" in S. Shute and A.P. Simester (eds.), *Criminal Law Theory: Doctrines of the General Part* (Oxford: Oxford University Press, 2002) 103.

——, *Money Laundering Law* (Oxford: Hart Publishing, 2003).

Allen, C., *Legal Duties and Other Essays in Jurisprudence* (Oxford: Oxford University Press, 1931).

André, J., "Nagel, Williams and Moral Luck" (1983) 43 *Analysis* 202.

Andrews, L.B., "The Legal Status of the Embryo" (1986) 32 *Loyola LR* 257.

Andrews, J.A., "Robbery" [1966] *Criminal LR* 524.

——, "Wilfulness: a Lesson in Ambiguity" (1981) 1 *Legal Studies* 303.

Annas, J., "How Basic are Basic Actions?" (1977–78) 78 *Proceedings of the Aristotelian Society* 195.

Archibald, B.P., "The Constitutionalisation of the General Part of the Criminal Law" (1988) 67 *Canadian Bar Review* 403.

Arden, M., "Criminal Law at the Crossroads: The Impact on Human Rights from the Law Commission's Perspective and the Need for a Code" [1999] *Criminal LR* 439.

Arenella, P., "Character, Choice, and Moral Agency" in E.F. Paul, F.D. Miller, and J. Paul (eds.), *Crime, Culpability and Remedy* (Oxford: Blackwell, 1990) 59.

——, "Convicting the Morally Blameless: Reassessing the Relationship Between Legal and Moral Accountability" (1992) 39 *UCLA LR* 1511.

Arlidge, A., "The Trial of Dr David Moor" [2000] *Criminal LR* 31.

Arlidge, A., Parry, J., and Gatt, I., *Arlidge and Parry on Fraud* (London: Sweet and Maxwell, 2nd ed., 1996).

Ashworth, A., "Belief, Intent, and Criminal Liability" in J. Eekelaar and J. Bell (eds.) *Oxford Essays in Jurisprudence* (Oxford: Oxford University Press, 3rd Series, 1987) 1.

——, "Criminal Attempts and the Role of Resulting Harm under the Code and in the Common Law" (1988) 19 *Rutgers LJ* 725.

——, "Criminal Liability in a Medical Context: the Treatment of Good Intentions" in A.P. Simester and A.T.H. Smith (eds.), *Harm and Culpability* (Oxford: Oxford University Press, 1996) 173.

——, "Defining Criminal Offences without Harm" in P. Smith (ed.), *Criminal Law: Essays in Honour of J.C. Smith* (London: Butterworths, 1987) 7.

——, "Excusable Mistake of Law" [1974] *Criminal LR* 652.

——, "Interpreting Criminal Statutes: a Crisis of Legality?" (1991) 107 *Law Quarterly Review* 419.

——, "Is the Criminal Law a Lost Cause?" (2000) 116 *Law Quarterly Review* 225.

——, "Principles, Pragmatism and the Law Commission's Recommendations on Homicide Law Reform" [2007] *Criminal LR* 345.

——, "Reason, Logic and Criminal Liability" (1975) 91 *Law Quarterly Review* 102.

——, "Redrawing the Boundaries of Entrapment" [2002] *Criminal LR* 161.

——, "Robbery Re-assessed" [2002] *Criminal LR* 851.

——, "Self-Defence and the Right to Life" [1975] *Cambridge LJ* 272.

——, "Taking the Consequences" in S. Shute, J. Gardner and J. Horder (eds.), *Action and Value in Criminal Law* (Oxford: Oxford University Press, 1993) 107.

——, "Testing Fidelity to Legal Values: Official Involvement and Criminal Justice" in S. Shute and A.P. Simester (eds.), *Criminal Law: Doctrines of the General Part* (Oxford: Oxford University Press, 2002) 299.

——, "The Doctrine of Provocation" [1976] *Cambridge LJ* 292.

——, "The Elasticity of Mens Rea" in C. Tapper (ed.), *Crime, Proof and Punishment* (London: Butterworths, 1981) 45.

——, "The European Convention and Criminal Law" in Cambridge Centre for Public Law, *The Human Rights Act and the Criminal and Regulatory Process* (Oxford: Hart Publications, 1999) 37.

——, "The Human Rights Act and the Substantive Criminal Law: A non-minimalist view" [2000] *Criminal LR* 564.

——, "The Scope of Criminal Liability for Omissions" (1989) 105 *Law Quarterly Review* 424.

——, "Transferred Malice and Punishment for Unforeseen Consequences" in P. Glazebrook (ed.), *Reshaping the Criminal Law* (London: Sweet and Maxwell, 1978) 77.

——, *Principles of Criminal Law* (Oxford: Oxford University Press, 2nd ed., 1995; 3rd ed., 1999).

Ashworth, A. and Blake, M., "The Presumption of Innocence in English Criminal Law" [1996] *Criminal LR* 306.

Ashworth, A. and Emmerson, B., *Human Rights and Criminal Justice* (London: Sweet and Maxwell, 2001).

Atiyah, P.S., "Common Law and Statute Law" (1985) 48 *Modern Law Review* 1.

——, *Vicarious Liability in the Law of Torts* (London: Butterworths, 1969).

Baker, B.M., "Mens Rea, Negligence and Criminal Law Reform" (1987) 6 *Law and Philosophy* 53.

Baker, E., "Human Rights, McNaghten and the 1991 Act" [1994] *Criminal LR* 84.

Baldwin, R., "Why Rules Don't Work" (1990) 53 *Modern Law Review* 321.

Bamforth, N., "The Application of the Human Rights Act 1998 to Public Authorities and Private Bodies" [1999] *Cambridge LJ* 159.

Barlow, N.L.A., "Drug Intoxication and the Principle of *Capacitas Rationalis*" (1984) 100 *Law Quarterly Review* 639.

Bayles, M., "Character, Purpose and Criminal Responsibility" (1982) 1 *Law and Philosophy* 5

Bazelon, D., "The Morality of the Criminal Law" (1976) 49 *Southern California LR* 385.

Becker, B.C., "Human Being: The Boundaries of the Concept" (1974) 4 *Philosophy and Public Affairs* 334.

Bein, D., "The Theft of Use and the Element of 'Intent to Deprive Permanently' in Larceny" (1968) 3 *Israel LR* 368.

Bell, J. and Engle, G., *Cross on Statutory Interpretation* (London: Butterworths, 3rd ed., 1995).

Bennett, J., "Morality and Consequences" in S. McMurrin (ed.), *The Tanner Lectures in Human Values* (Cambridge: Cambridge University Press, 1981) 47.

——, *The Act Itself* (Oxford: Oxford University Press, 1995).

Bentham, J., *An Introduction to the Principles of Morals and Legislation* (1789).

Bergelson, V., "The Right To be Hurt; Testing The Boundaries of Consent" (2007) 75 *George Washington LR* 165.

Beynon, H., "Causation, Omissions and Complicity" [1987] *Criminal LR* 539.

——, "Doctors as Murderers" [1982] *Criminal LR* 17.

Birks, P., "Misdirected Funds: Restitution from the Recipient" (1980) *Lloyds Maritime and Commercial Law Quarterly* 296.

——, *An Introduction to the Law of Restitution* (Oxford: Oxford University Press, 1989).

Blake, L.W., "The Innocent Purchaser and Section 22 of the Theft Act" [1972] *Criminal LR* 494.

Blake, M., "Physician-assisted Suicide: A Criminal Offence or a Patient's Right?" (1997) 5 *Medical LR* 294.

Blakey, G.R. and Goldsmith, M., "Criminal Redistribution of Stolen Property: The Need for Reform" (1976) 74 *Mich LR* 1512.

Blom-Cooper, L. and Morris, T., *With Malice Aforethought* (Oxford: Hart Publishing, 2004).

Bluglass, R., "Infanticide" [1978] *Bulletin of the Royal College of Psychiatrists* 14.

Bogart, J.H., "Commodification and Phenomenology: Evading Consent in Theory Regarding Rape" (1996) 2 *Legal Theory* 253.

Bogg, A. and Stanton-Ife, J., "Protecting the Vulnerable: Legality, Harm and Theft" (2003) 23 *Legal Studies* 402.

Bohlander, M., "The Sexual Offences Act 2003 and the *Tyrell* Principle – Criminalising the Victims" [2005] *Criminal LR* 701.

Bonnie, R.J., "The Moral Basis of the Insanity Defense" (1983) 69 *American Bar Assoc J* 194.

Bowden, P., "Violence and Mental Disorder" in N. Walker (ed.), *Dangerous People* (London: Blackstone Press, 1996) 13.

Bowley, M., "Talking about Sex" (1999) 149 *New LJ* 1739.

Brady, J.B., "Abolish the Insanity Defense? No!" (1971) 8 *Houston LR* 629.

Brett, P., "Mistake of Law as a Criminal Defence" (1966) 5 *Melbourne ULR* 179.

——, "Strict Responsibility: Possible Solutions" (1974) 37 *Modern Law Review* 417.

——, "The Physiology of Provocation" [1970] *Criminal LR* 640.

——, *Inquiry into Criminal Guilt* (London: Sweet and Maxwell, 1960).

Broderick, P.A., "Conditional Objectives of Conspiracies" (1985) 94 *Yale LJ* 895.

Bronitt, S., "Defending *Giorgianni*" (1993) 17 *Criminal LJ* 242 and 305.

——, "Spreading Disease and the Criminal Law" [1994] *Criminal LR* 21.

Brudner, A., "A Theory of Necessity" (1987) 7 *Oxford Journal of Legal Studies* 338.

——, "Guilt under the Charter: The Lure of Parliamentary Supremacy" (1998) 40 *Criminal Law Quarterly* 287.

Buard, J., "'Intent'" [1978] *Criminal LR* 5.

Burn, E.H., *Cheshire and Burn's Modern Law of Real Property* (London: Butterworths, 15th ed., 1994) 165.

Buxton, R., "By any Unlawful Act" (1966) 82 *Law Quarterly Review* 174.

——, "Complicity in the Criminal Code" (1969) 85 *Law Quarterly Review* 252.

——, "Some Simple Thoughts on Intention" [1988] *Criminal LR* 484.

——, "The Human Rights Act and the Substantive Criminal Law" [2000] *Criminal LR* 331.

Cambridge Centre for Public Law, *Constitutional Reform in the United Kingdom. Practice and Principles.* (Oxford: Hart Publishing, 1998).

——, *The Human Rights Act and the Criminal Justice and Regulatory Process* (Oxford: Hart Publishing, 1999).

Camp, P., "Section 69 of the Army Act 1955" [1999] *New LJ* 1736.

Campbell, K., "Conditional Intention" (1982) 2 *Legal Studies* 77.

——, "Offence and Defence" in I. Dennis (ed.), *Criminal Law and Criminal Justice* (London: Sweet and Maxwell, 1987) 73.

——, "The Test of Dishonesty in *R* v. *Ghosh*" [1984] *Cambridge LJ* 349.

Card, R., *Card, Cross and Jones: Criminal Law* (London: Butterworths, 14th ed., 1998).

Carlton, D.W. and Fischel, D.R., "The Regulation of Insider Trading" (1983) 35 *Stanford LR* 857.

Carson, W.G., "Symbolic and Instrumental Dimensions of Early Factory Legislation" in R. Hood (ed.), *Crime, Criminology and Public Policy: Essays in Honour of Sir Leon Radzinowicz* (London: Heinemann Educational, 1974).

——, "The Conventionalisation of Early Factory Crime" (1979) 7 *Int J Soc Law* 37.

Chan, W. and Simester, A.P., "Duress, Necessity: How Many Defences?" (2005) 16 *King's College LJ* 121.

Chappell, D. and Walsh, M., "'No Questions Asked,' A Consideration of the Crime of Criminal Receiving"(1974) 20 *Crime and Delinquency* 157.

——, "Receiving Stolen Property: The Need for a Systematic Inquiry into the Fencing Process" (1974) 11 *Criminology* 484.

Choo, A.L-T., *Abuse of Process and Judicial Stays of Criminal Proceedings* (Oxford: Oxford University Press, 1993).

Clarkson, C.M.V., "Complicity, *Powell* and Manslaughter" [1998] *Criminal LR* 556.
——, "Corporate Manslaughter: Yet More Government Proposals" [2005] *Criminal LR* 677.
——, "Kicking Corporate Bodies and Damning Their Souls" (1996) 59 *Modern Law Review* 557.
——, "Theft and Fair Labelling" (1993) 56 *Modern Law Review* 554.
Clarkson, C.M.V., Cretney, S., Davis, G., and Shepherd, J., "Assaults: the Relationship between Seriousness, Criminalisation and Punishment" [1994] *Criminal LR* 4.
Clarkson, C.M.V. and Keating, H., *Criminal Law: Text and Materials* (4th ed., 1998).
Coffee, J., "Does 'Unlawful' Mean 'Criminal'?: Reflections on the Disappearing Tort/Crime Distinction in American Law" (1991) 71 *Boston ULR* 193.
——, "No Soul to Damn: No Body to Kick: An Unscandalized Inquiry into the Problem of Corporate Punishment" (1981) 79 *Michigan LR* 386.
Cohen, M.D., "The 'Actus Reus' and Offences of 'Situation'" (1972) 7 *Israel LR* 186.
Coke, E., *Third Institute* (1641).
Colvin, E., "Criminal Law and the Rule of Law" in P. Fitzgerald (ed.), *Crime, Justice and Codification: Essays in Commemoration of Jacques Fortin* (Toronto: Carswell, 1986) 125.
Committee on Mentally Abnormal Offenders, *Report of the Committee on Mentally Abnormal Offenders* Cmnd. 6244 (London: HMSO, 1975).
Committee on the Penalties for Homicide, *Report on the Penalties for Homicide* Cmnd. 5137 (Edinburgh: HMSO, 1972).
Cooke, R., *Turning Points of the Common Law* (London: Sweet & Maxwell, 1997).
Corrado, M. (ed.), *Justification and Excuse in the Criminal Law: An Anthology* (New York: Garland Publishing, 1994).
Criminal Law Revision Committee, Eleventh Report, *Evidence (General)* Cmnd. 4991 (1971).
——, Fourteenth Report, *Offences Against the Person* Cmnd. 7844 (1980).
——, Fifteenth Report, *Sexual Offences* Cmnd. 9213 (1984).
——, Eighth Report, *Theft and Related Offences* Cmnd. 2977 (1966).
——, *Working Paper on Section 16 of the Theft Act 1968* (1974).
Cripps, Y., "The Public Interest Defence to the Action for Breach of Confidence and the Law Commission's Proposals on Disclosure in the Public Interest" (1984) 4 *Oxford Journal of Legal Studies* 361.
Cross, J.T., "Protecting Confidential Information under the Criminal Law of Theft and Fraud" (1991) 11 *Oxford Journal of Legal Studies* 264.
Cross, R., "Duress and Aiding and Abetting (A Reply)" (1953) 69 *Law Quarterly Review* 354.
Cross, R. and Jones, P.A., *An Introduction to Criminal Law* (London: Butterworths, 3rd ed., 1953).
Crown Prosecution Service, *Offences Against the Person Charging Standards* (2nd ed., 1996).
d'Orban, P.T., "Women who Kill their Children" (1979) 134 *British Journal of Psychiatry* 560.
Dan-Cohen, M., "Basic Values and the Victim's State of Mind" (2000) 88 *California LR* 759.
——, *Rights, Persons and Organisations: A Legal Theory for Bureaucratic Society* (Berkeley: University of California Press, 1986).
Davidson, D., "Agency" in *Essays on Actions and Events* (Oxford: Oxford University Press, 1980) 43.
Davies, C.R., "Protection of Intellectual Property – a Myth?" [2004] *Journal of Criminal Law* 398.
Delgado, R., "Rotten Social Background: Should the Criminal Law Recognize a Defence of Severe Environmental Deprivation?" (1985) 3 *J Law and Inequality* 9.
Dell, S., *Murder into Manslaughter: The Diminished Responsibility Defence in Practice* (London: Institute of Psychiatry, 1984).
Denning, A.T., *Responsibility Before the Law: A Lecture* (Jerusalem: Magnes Press, 1961).
Dennis, I., "Intention and Complicity: A Reply" [1988] *Criminal LR* 649.
——, "Reverse Onuses and the Presumption of Innocence: In Search of Principle" [2005] *Criminal LR* 901.
——, "The Criminal Justice and Public Order Act 1994: The Evidence Provisions" [1995] *Criminal LR* 4.
——, "The Rationale of Criminal Conspiracy" (1977) 93 *Law Quarterly Review* 39.
——, "The Mental Element for Accessories" in P. Smith (ed.), *Criminal Law: Essays in Honour of J.C. Smith* (London: Butterworths, 1987) 40.

Department of Health, *Protecting Children, Supporting Parents: A Consultation Document on the Physical Punishment of Children* (London: Department of Health, 2000).

Devlin, P., "Law, Democracy and Morality" (1962) 110 *Pennsylvania LR* 635, 648.

——, "Mental Abnormality and the Criminal Law" in R.St.J. Macdonald (ed.), *Changing Legal Objectives* (Toronto: Toronto University Press, 1963) 85.

——, *Samples of Lawmaking* (London: Oxford University Press, 1962).

——, *The Enforcement of Morals* (Oxford: Oxford University Press, 1965).

Dickens, B., "Death" in I. Kennedy and A. Grubb (eds.), *Principles of Medical Law* (Oxford: Oxford University Press, 1998) 868.

Dillof, A.M., "Transferred Intent: an Enquiry into the Nature of Criminal Culpability" [1998] *Buffalo Criminal LR* 501.

Dingwall, G., *Alcohol and Crime* (London: Cavendish Publishing, 2005).

Dressler, J., "Battered Women Who Kill Their Sleeping Tormenters: Reflections on Maintaining Respect for Human Life while Killing Moral Monsters" in S. Shute and A.P. Simester (eds.), *Criminal Law Theory: Doctrines of the General Part* (Oxford: Oxford University Press, 2002) 259.

——, "New Thoughts about the Concept of Justification in the Criminal Law: A Critique of Fletcher's Thinking and Rethinking" (1984) 32 *UCLA LR* 61.

——, "Provocation: Partial Justification or Partial Excuse" (1988) 51 *Modern Law Review* 467.

——, "Reassessing the Theoretical Underpinnings of Accomplice Liability: New Solutions to an Old Problem" (1985) 37 *Hastings LJ* 91.

——, "Rethinking Heat of Passion: A Defence in Search of a Rationale" (1982) 73 *J Criminal Law and Criminology*

Dripps, D., "For a Negative, Normative Model of Consent, with a Comment on Preference-Skepticism" (1996) 2 *Legal Theory* 113.

Duff, R.A., "Attempted Homicide" (1995) 1 *Legal Theory* 149.

——, "'Can I help you?' Accessorial Liability and the Intention to Assist" (1990) 10 *Legal Studies* 165.

——, "Choice, Character and Criminal Liability" (1993) 12 *Law and Philosophy* 345.

——, "Fitness to Plead and Fair Trials" [1994] *Criminal LR* 419.

——, "Harms and Wrongs" (2001) 5 *Buffalo Criminal LR* 13.

——, "Intentionally Killing the Innocent" (1973) 34 *Analysis* 16.

——, "Intentions Legal and Philosophical" (1989) 9 *Oxford Journal of Legal Studies* 76.

——, "Professor Williams and Conditional Subjectivism" [1982] *Cambridge LJ* 273.

——, "The Circumstances of an Attempt" [1991] *Cambridge LJ* 100.

——, "The Obscure Intentions of the House of Lords" [1986] *Criminal LR* 771.

——, *Criminal Attempts* (Oxford: Oxford University Press, 1996).

——, *Intention, Agency and Criminal Liability* (Oxford: Blackwell, 1990).

Duff, R.A. and Garland, D. (eds.), *A Reader on Punishment* (Oxford: Oxford University Press, 1994).

Duff, R.A. and von Hirsch, A., "Responsibility, Retribution and the 'Voluntary': A Response to Williams" [1997] *Cambridge LJ* 103.

Dworkin, G., "Paternalism" (1972) 56 *Monist* 65.

——, *The Theory and Practice of Autonomy* (Cambridge: Cambridge University Press, 1988).

Dworkin, R., "Hard Cases" in *Taking Rights Seriously* (London: Duckworth, 1977) 81.

——, *Life's Dominion: An Argument About Abortion and Euthanasia* (London: HarperCollins, 1993).

Edwards, J., "Duress and Aiding and Abetting" (1953) 69 *Law Quarterly Review* 226.

Elliott, D.W., "Directors' Thefts and Dishonesty" [1991] *Criminal LR* 732.

——, "Dishonesty in Theft: A Dispensable Concept" [1982] *Criminal LR* 395.

——, "Dishonesty under the Theft Act" [1972] *Criminal LR* 625.

——, "Endangering life by destroying or damaging property" [1997] *Criminal LR* 382.

——, "Frightening a Person into Injuring Himself" [1974] *Criminal LR* 15.

——, "Mens Rea in Statutory Conspiracy" [1978] *Criminal LR* 202.

——, "Necessity, Duress and Self-Defence" [1989] *Criminal LR* 611.

Elliott, I.D., "Responsibility for Involuntary Acts: *Ryan* v. *The Queen*" (1968) 41 *Australian LJ* 497.

Emmerson, B. and Ashworth, A., *Human Rights and Criminal Justice* (London: Sweet and Maxwell, 2001).

Engelhardt, H.T., "The Ontology of Abortion" (1973) 84 *Ethics* 217.

English, P., "What Did Section Three do to the Law of Provocation?" [1970] *Criminal LR* 249.

Epstein, R., "Property as a Fundamental Civil Right" (1992) 29 *Cal West LR* 187.

Evans, J., *Statutory Interpretation* (Auckland: Oxford University Press, 1988).

Farrier, M.D., "The Distinction between Murder and Manslaughter in its Procedural Context" (1976) 39 *Modern Law Review* 415

Fauconnet, P., *La Responsabilité: Étude de Sociologie* (Paris: F. Alcan, 1920).

Feinberg, J., "Action and Responsibility" in M. Black (ed.), *Philosophy in America* (Ithaca: Cornell University Press, 1965) 134.

——, "Harm to Others: A Rejoinder" (1986) *Criminal Justice Ethics* 16.

——, *Harm to Others* (New York: Oxford University Press, 1984).

——, *Harm to Self* (New York: Oxford University Press, 1986).

——, *Harmless Wrongdoing* (New York: Oxford University Press, 1988).

——, *Offense to Others* (New York: Oxford University Press, 1985).

Feldman, D., *Civil Liberties and Human Rights* (Oxford: Oxford University Press, 1993).

Fenwick, H., *Automatism, Medicine and the Law* (Cambridge: Cambridge University Press, Psychological Medicine Monograph 17: 1990).

Finch, E., "The Perfect Stalking Law: An Evaluation of the Efficacy of the Protection from Harrasment Act 1997" [2002] *Criminal LR* 702.

——, *The Criminalisation of Stalking: Constructing the Problem and Evaluating the Solution* (London: Cavendish Publishing, 2001).

Finkel, N. *et al.*, "Lay Perspectives on Legal Conundrums: Impossible and Mistaken Act Cases" (1995) 19 *Law and Human Behaviour* 593.

Finn, J., "Culpable Non-Intervention: Reconsidering the Basis for Party Liability by Omission" (1994) 18 *Criminal LJ* 90.

Finn, P., *Fiduciary Obligations* (Sydney: Law Book Company, 1977).

Finnis, J., "*Bland*: Crossing the Rubicon?" (1993) 109 *Law Quarterly Review* 329.

——, "Intention and Side-effects" in R.G. Frey and C.W. Morris (eds.), *Liability and Responsibility* (Cambridge: Cambridge University Press, 1991) 32.

——, "The Rights and Wrongs of Abortion: a Reply to Judith Jarvis Thomson" (1973) 2 *Philosophy and Public Affairs* 117.

Fisse, B. and Braithwaite, J., "The Allocation of Responsibility for Corporate Crime: Individualism, Collectivism and Accountability" (1988) 11 *Sydney LR* 468.

——, *Corporations, Crime, and Accountability* (Cambridge: Cambridge University Press, 1993).

Fitzgerald, P.G. and Williams, G., "Carelessness, Indifference and Recklessness: Two Replies" (1962) 25 *Modern Law Review* 49.

Fleming, J., *The Law of Torts* (Sydney: Law Book Company, 7th ed., 1987; 8th ed., 1992).

Fletcher, G., "On the Moral Irrelevance of Bodily Movements" (1994) *U Pennsylvania LR* 1443.

——, "The Individualisation of Excusing Conditions" (1974) 47 *Southern California LR* 1269.

——, *Rethinking Criminal Law* (Boston: Little Brown, 1978).

Floud, J. and Young, W., *Dangerousness and Criminal Justice* (London: Heinemann, 1981).

Freckelton, I., "When Plight Makes Right: The Forensic Abuse Syndrome" (1994) 18 *Criminal LJ* 29.

Freedman, D., "Restoring Order to the Reasonable Person Test in the Reference of Provocation" [1998] *King's College LJ* 26.

French, P., "Fishing the Red Herrings out of a Sea of Moral Responsibility" in E. LePore and B.P. McLaughlin (eds.), *Actions and Events: Perspectives on the Philosophy of Donald Davidson* (Oxford: Blackwell, 1985) 73.

——, *Collective and Corporate Responsibility* (New York: Columbia University Press, 1984).

Furmston, M., *Cheshire, Fifoot and Furmston's Law of Contract* (London: Butterworths, 13th ed., 1996).

Galligan, D.J., "The Return to Retribution in Penal Theory" in C. Tapper (ed.), *Crime, Proof and Punishment* (London: Butterworths, 1981) 144.

——, "The Right to Silence Reconsidered" [1988] *Current Legal Problems* 69.

Gardner J., "Justifications and Reasons" in A.P. Simester and A.T.H. Smith (eds.), *Harm and Culpability* (Oxford: Oxford University Press, 1996) 103.

——, "Rationality and the Rule of Law in Offences Against the Person" [1994] *Cambridge LJ* 502.

——, "The Gist of Excuses" (1998) 1 *Buffalo Criminal LR* 575.

Gardner, J. and Macklem T., "Compassion without Respect? Nine Fallacies of *R v Smith*" [2001] *Criminal LR* 623.

——, "Provocation and Pluralism" (2001) 64 *Modern LR* 815.

Gardner, J. and Shute, S., "The Wrongness of Rape" in J. Horder (ed.), *Oxford Essays in Jurisprudence* (4th Series, Oxford: Oxford University Press, 2000) 193.

Gardner, S., "Appreciating *Olugboja*" (1996) 16 *Legal Studies* 275.

——, "Direct Action and the Defence of Necessity" [2005] *Criminal LR* 371.

——, "Is Theft a Rip-Off?" (1990) 10 *Oxford Journal of Legal Studies* 441.

——, "Necessity's Newest Inventions" (1991) 11 *Oxford Journal of Legal Studies* 125.

——, "Property and Theft" [1998] *Criminal LR* 35.

——, "Reckless and Inconsiderate Rape" [1991] *Criminal LR* 172.

——, "Stalking" (1998) 114 *Law Quarterly Review* 33.

——, "The Importance of Majewski" (1994) 14 *Oxford Journal of Legal Studies* 279.

Gearty, C.A., "Reconciling Parliamentary Democracy and Human Rights" (2002) 118 *Law Quarterly Review* 248.

Geddes, L., "On the Intrinsic Wrongness of Killing Innocent People" (1973) 33 *Analysis* 93.

Giesen, D., *International Medical Malpractice Law* (London: Nijhoff, 1988).

Gill, M., *Commercial Robbery: Offenders' Perspectives on Security and Crime Prevention* (London: Blackstone Press, 2000).

Gillen, M., "Sanctions Against Insider Trading: A Proposal for Reform" (1991) 70 *Canadian Bar Review* 215.

Giles, M. and Uglow, S., "Appropriation and Manifest Criminality in Theft" (1992) 56 *J Criminal Law* 179.

Gillies, P., "The Offence of Conspiracy to Defraud" (1977) 51 *Australian LJ* 247.

Glaze, C.L., "Combatting Prenatal Substance Abuse: Court Ordered Protective Custody of the Fetus" (1997) 80 *Marquette LR* 793.

Glazebrook, P.R., "A Better Way of Convicting Business of Avoidable Deaths and Injuries" [2002] *Cambridge LJ* 405.

——, "Criminal Omissions: The Duty Requirement in Offences Against the Person" (1960) 76 *Law Quarterly Review* 386.

——, "Revising the Theft Acts" [1993] *Cambridge LJ* 191.

——, "Situational Liability" in Glazebrook (ed.), *Reshaping the Criminal Law* (London: Sweet and Maxwell, 1978) 108.

——, "Structuring the Criminal Code: Functional Approaches to Complicity, Incomplete Offences and General Defences" in A.P. Simester and A.T.H. Smith (eds.), *Harm and Culpability* (Oxford: Oxford University Press, 1996) 195.

——, "Thief or Swindler: Who Cares?" [1991] *Cambridge LJ* 389.

——, (ed.), *Blackstone's Statutes on Criminal Law* (London: Blackstone Press, 9th ed., 1999)

Glover, J., *Causing Death and Saving Lives* (Harmondsworth: Penguin, 1977).

Gobert, J., "Corporate Criminality. New Crimes for the Times" [1994] *Criminal LR* 722.

Gobert, J. and Punch, M., *Rethinking Corporate Crime* (London: Butterworths, 2003).

Goff, R., "The Mental Element in the Crime of Murder" (1988) 104 *Law Quarterly Review* 30.

Goff, R. and Jones, G., *The Law of Restitution* (London: Sweet and Maxwell, 4th ed., 1993).

Goldberg, D. and Huxley, P., *Common Mental Disorders: A Biosocial Model* (London: Tavistock/Routledge, 1992).

Goldstein, A.S., *The Insanity Defence* (New Haven: Yale University Press, 1967).

Goode, R., "Ownership and Obligation in Commercial Transactions" (1987) 103 *Law Quarterly Review* 433.

——, "Property and Unjust Enrichment" in A. Burrows (ed.), *Essays on the Law of Restitution* (Oxford: Oxford University Press, 1991) 215.

——, "The Right to Trace and Its Impact in Commercial Transactions" (1976) 92 *Law Quarterly Review* 360 and 528.

Goodhart, A.L., "The *Shaw* Case: The Law and Public Morals" (1961) 77 *Law Quarterly Review* 560.

Gordon, G.H., *The Criminal Law of Scotland* (Edinburgh: Green, 2nd ed., 1978).

Gough, S., "Surviving without *Majewski*?" [2002] *Criminal LR* 719.

Gray, K., "Property in Thin Air" [1991] 50 *Cambridge LJ* 252.

Gray, O., "The Standard of Care for Children Revisited" (1980) 45 *Missouri LR* 597.

Greaves, C.S., *the Criminal Law Consolidation and Amendment Acts of the 24 & 25 Vict. With Notes, Observations, and Forms for Summary Proceedings* (London: V. & R. Stevens, 2nd ed., 1862).

Greenawalt, K., "The Perplexing Borders of Justification and Excuse" (1984) 84 *Columbia LR* 1897.

Grey, "The Disintegration of Property" in *NOMOS xxii: Property* (1980) 69.

Griew, E., "Consistency, Communication and Codification—Reflections on Two Mens Rea Words" in P.R. Glazebrook (ed.), *Reshaping the Criminal Law* (London: Sweet and Maxwell, 1978) 57.

——,"Dishonesty: The Objections to Feely and Ghosh" [1985] *Criminal LR* 341.

——, "Reckless Damage and Reckless Driving: Living with *Caldwell* and *Lawrence*" [1981] *Criminal LR* 743.

——, "Stealing and Obtaining Bank Credits" [1986] *Criminal LR* 356.

Gross, H., "Rape, Moralism and Human Rights" [2007] *Criminal LR* 220.

——, *A Theory of Criminal Justice* (New York: Oxford University Press, 1979).

Grubb, A., "Treatment Decisions: Keeping it in the Family" in A. Grubb (ed.), *Choices and Decisions in Health Care* (Chichester: Wiley, 1993) 37.

Grubin, D., "What Constitutes Fitness to Plead" [1998] *Criminal LR* 748.

Gunn, M.J. and Ormerod, D., "The Legality of Boxing" (1995) 15 *Legal Studies* 181.

Hadden, T.B., "Conspiracy to Defraud" [1966] *Cambridge LJ* 248.

——, "Fraud in the City: The Role of the Criminal Law" [1983] *Criminal LR* 500.

Hall, J., "Negligent Behaviour Should be Excluded from Penal Liability" (1963) 63 *Columbia LR* 632.

——, *General Principles of Criminal Law* (Indianapolis: Bobbs-Merrill, 2nd ed, 1960).

——, *Theft, Law and Society* (Indianapolis: Bobbs-Merrill, 2nd ed., 1952).

Hall, L., "Strict or Liberal Construction of Penal Statutes" (1935) 48 *Harvard LR* 748.

Hall, L. and Seligman, S.J., "Mistake of Law and *Mens Rea*" (1940–41) 8 *U Chicago LR* 641.

Halpin, A., "The Appropriate Appropriation" [1991] *Criminal LR* 426.

——, "The Test for Dishonesty" [1996] *Criminal LR* 283.

——, *Definition in the Criminal Law* (Oxford: Hart Publishing, 2004).

Hampton, J., "Mens Rea" in E.F. Paul, F.D. Miller, and J. Paul (eds.), *Crime, Culpability and Remedy* (Oxford: Blackwell, 1990) 1

Hanink, J.G., "Some Light on Double Effect" (1975) 35 *Analysis* 147.

Harlow, C., "Self-Defence: Public Right or Private Privilege" [1974] *Criminal LR* 528.

Harris, D.J., O'Boyle, M., and Warbrick, C., *The Law of the European Convention on Human Rights* (London: Sweet and Maxwell, 1995).

Harris, D.R., "The Concept of Possession in English Law" in A. Guest (ed.), *Oxford Essays in Jurisprudence* (Oxford: Oxford University Press, 1961) 69.

Harris, J., *Property and Justice* (Oxford: Oxford University Press, 1996).

Harris, J. and Grace, S., *A Question of Evidence? Investigating and Prosecuting Rape in the 1990's* Home Office Research Study No. 196 (London: Home Office, 1999).

Hart, H.L.A., "Definition and Theory in Jurisprudence" (1954) 70 *Law Quarterly Review* 37.

——, *Law, Liberty and Morality* (Oxford: Oxford University Press, 1963).

——, *Punishment and Responsibility* (Oxford: Oxford University Press, 1968)

Hart, H.L.A. and Honoré, A.M., *Causation in the Law* (Oxford: Oxford University Press, 2nd ed., 1985)

Hawkins, K., *Environment and Enforcement: Regulation and the Social Definition of Pollution* (Oxford: Oxford University Press, 1984).

——, *Law as Last Resort* (Oxford: Oxford University Press, 2003).

Heaton, R., "Cheques and Balances" [2005] *Criminal LR* 747.

——, "Deceiving without Thieving" [2001] *Criminal LR* 712.

Herring, J., "Human Rights and Rape: A reply to Hyman Gross" [2007] *Criminal LR* 228.

——, "Mistaken Sex"[2005] *Criminal LR* 511.

——, "The Duty of Care in Gross Negligence Manslaughter" [2007] *Criminal LR* 24.

Heuston, R.F.V. and Buckley, R.A., *Salmond and Heuston on the Law of Torts* (London: Sweet and Maxwell, 20th ed., 1992).

Heydon, J.D., "The Corroboration of Accomplices" [1973] *Criminal LR* 264.

——, "The Problems of Entrapment" [1973] *Cambridge LJ* 268.

Hirsch, A. von, "Extending the Harm Principle: 'Remote' Harms and Fair Imputation" in A.P. Simester and A.T.H. Smith (eds.), *Harm and Culpability* (Oxford: Oxford University Press, 1996) 259.

——, "The Offence Principle in Criminal Law: Affront to Sensibility or Wrongdoing?" (2000) 11 *King's College LJ* 78.

——, *Censure and Sanctions* (Oxford: Oxford University Press, 1993).

——, *Doing Justice: the Choice of Punishments* (New York: Hill and Wang, 1976).

Hirsch, A. von and Ashworth, A. (eds.), *Principles of Sentencing: Readings on Theory and Policy* (Oxford: Hart Publishing, 2nd ed., 1998).

Hirsch, A. von, Garland, D. and Wakefield, A. (eds.), *Ethical and Social Perspectives on Situational Crime Prevention* (Oxford: Hart Publishing, 2004).

Hirsch, A. von and Jareborg, N., "Gauging Criminal Harm: A Living-Standard Analysis" (1991) 11 *Oxford Journal of Legal Studies*, 1.

Hirsch, A. von and Simester, A.P. (eds.), *Incivilities: Regulating Offensive Behaviour* (Oxford: Hart Publishing, 2006).

Hirsch, A. von *et al.*, *Criminal Deterrence and Sentencing Severity: an analysis of recent research* (Oxford: Hart Publishing, 1999).

Hirst, M., "Assault, Battery and Indirect Violence" [1999] *Criminal LR* 577.

——, "Guilty; but of what?" (2000) 4 *International Journal of Evidence and Proof* 31.

Hodge, J., "Alcohol and Violence" in P. Taylor (ed.), *Violence in Society* (London: Royal College of Physicians of London, 1993) 127.

Hogan, B., "The Criminal Attempts Act and Attempting the Impossible" [1984] *Criminal LR* 584.

——, "The *Dadson* Principle" [1989] *Criminal LR* 679.

——, "Victims as Parties to Crime" [1962] *Criminal LR* 683.

Hogg, P.W., *Constitutional Law of Canada* (Scarborough, Ontario: Carswell, 4th ed., 1997).

Hohfeld, W.N., *Fundamental Legal Conceptions as Applied in Judicial Reasoning* (New Haven: Yale University Press, 1919).

Home Office, *Corporate manslaughter: the Government's draft bill for reform* Cm. 6497 (London: The Stationery Office, 2005).

——, *Criminal Statistics, England and Wales 1996* Cmnd. 3764 (London: Stationery Office, 1997).

——, *Fraud Law Reform: Consultation on Proposals for Legislation* (London: Home Office, 2004).

——, *Managing Dangerous People with Severe Personality Disorder: Proposals for Policy Development* (London: Home Office, 1999).

——, *Racial Violence and Harassment: A Consultation Document* (London: Home Office, 1997).

——, *Reforming the Law on Involuntary Manslaughter: The Government's Proposals* (London: Home Office, 2000).

——, *Setting the Boundaries – Reforming the Law on Sex Offenders* (London: Home Office, 2000).

——, *Stalking the Solutions: A Consultation Paper* (London: Home Office, 1996).

——, *Violence: Reforming the Offences against the Person Act 1861* (London: Home Office, 1998).

Home Office and Department of Health and Social Security, *Interdepartmental Working Group into Mentally Disturbed Offenders in the Prison System* (London: Home Office, 1987).

Honoré, A.M., "Necessary and Sufficient Conditions in Tort Law" in D. Owen (ed.), *Philosophical Foundations of Tort Law* (Oxford: Oxford University Press, 1995) 363.

——, "Ownership" in A. Guest (ed.), *Oxford Essays in Jurisprudence* (Oxford: Oxford University Press, 1961) 107.

——, "Responsibility and Luck: The Moral Basis of Strict Liability" (1988) 104 *Law Quarterly Review* 530.

Hooper, M., "The Impact of the Human Rights Act on Judicial Decision-Making" [1998] *European Human Rights Law Review* 676.

Horder, J., "A Critique of the Correspondence Principle in Criminal Law" [1995] *Criminal LR* 759.

——, "Cognition, Emotion and Criminal Culpability" (1990) 106 *Law Quarterly Review* 469.

——, "Crimes of Ulterior Intent" in A.P. Simester and A.T.H. Smith (eds.), *Harm and Culpability* (Oxford: Oxford University Press, 1996) 153.

——, "Criminal Law: Between Determinism, Liberalism, and Criminal Justice" (1996) 49 *CLP* 159.

——, "Gross Negligence and Criminal Culpability" (1997) 47 *U Toronto LJ* 495.

——, "How Culpability Can, and Cannot, be Denied in Under-age Sex Crimes" [2001] *Criminal LR* 15.

——, "Occupying the moral high ground? The Law Commission on Duress" [1994] *Criminal LR* 343.

——, "Pleading Involuntary Lack of Capacity" [1993] *Cambridge LJ* 298.

——, "Questioning the Correspondence Principle—A Reply" [1999] *Criminal LR* 206.

——, "Reconsidering Psychic Assault" [1998] *Criminal LR* 392.

——, "Re-Shaping the Subjective Element in the Provocation Defence" (2005) 25 *Oxford Journal of Legal Studies* 123.

——, "Rethinking Non-Fatal Offences against the Person (1994) 14 *Oxford Journal of Legal Studies* 335.

——, "Strict Liability, Statutory Construction, and the Spirit of Liberty" (2002) 118 *Law Quarterly Review* 458.

——, "Transferred Malice and the Remoteness of Unexpected Outcomes from Intentions" [2006] *Criminal LR* 383.

——, "Whose Values Should Determine When Liability is Strict?" in A.P. Simester, (ed.), *Appraising Strict Liability* (Oxford: Oxford University Press, 2005) 105.

——, *Excusing Crime* (Oxford: Oxford University Press, 2004).

——, *Provocation and Responsibility* (Oxford: Oxford University Press, 1992).

Horder, J. and McGowan, L., "Manslaughter by Causing Another's Suicide" [2006] *Criminal LR* 1035.

House of Lords, *Report of the Select Committee on Murder and Life Imprisonment* (Session 1988–89) HL Paper 78 (London: HMSO).

Howard, C., "Strict Responsibility in the High Court of Australia" (1960) 76 *Law Quarterly Review* 547.

——, *Strict Responsibility* (London: Sweet and Maxwell, 1963).

Howarth, W., "Handling Stolen Goods and Handling Salmon" [1987] *Criminal LR* 460.

Hudson, A.H., "Abandonment" in N. Palmer and E. McKendrick (eds.), *Interests in Goods* (London: LLP, 1993) 423.

——, "Is Divesting Abandonment Possible at Common Law?" (1984) 100 *Law Quarterly Review* 110.

Hughes, G., "Criminal Omissions" (1958) 67 *Yale LJ* 590.

Hume, D., *A Treatise of Human Nature* (Oxford: Oxford University Press, Selby-Bigge and Nidditch, eds., 2nd ed., 1978).

Hurd, H., "The Moral Magic of Consent" (1996) 2 *Legal Theory* 121, 165.

Husak, D.N., "Does Criminal Liability Require an Act" in R.A. Duff (ed.), *Philosophy and Criminal Law* (Cambridge: Cambridge University Press, 1998) 60.

——, "Recreational Drugs and Paternalism" (1989) 8 *Law and Philosophy* 353

——, "The Nature and Justifiability of Nonconsumate Offences" (1995) 37 *Arizona LR* 151.

——, "Transferred Intent" (1996) 10 *Notre Dame Journal of Legal Ethics and Public Policy* 65.

——, *Philosophy of the Criminal Law* (New Jersey: Rowman and Littlefield, 1987).

Husak, D. and von Hirsch, A., "Culpability and Mistake of Law" in S. Shute, J. Gardner and J. Horder (eds.), *Action and Value in Criminal Law* (Oxford: Oxford University Press, 1993) 157.

Hutchinson, A.C., "Sault Ste. Marie, Mens Rea and the Halfway House: Public Welfare Offences Get a Home of Their Own" (1979) 17 *Osgoode Hall LJ* 415.

Hutter, B., *The Reasonable Arm of the Law* (Oxford: Oxford University Press, 1988).

Huxtable, R., "Separation of the Conjoined Twin: Where Next for English Law?" [2002] *Criminal LR* 549.

Jackson, B.S., "*Storkwain*: A Case Study in Strict liability and Self-Regulation" [1991] *Criminal LR* 892.

Jackson, J., "Curtailing the Right to Silence: Lessons from Northern Ireland" [1991] *Criminal LR* 404.

Jareborg, N., "What Kind of Criminal Law do we Want" in A. Snare (ed.), *Scandinavian Studies in Criminology* vol. 14 (Oslo: Pax Forlag A/S, 1995) 17

Jeffries, J.C., "Legality, Vagueness, and the Construction of Penal Statutes" (1985) 71 *Virginia LR* 189.

Jeffries, J.C. and Stephan, P.B., "Defences, Presumptions, and Burden of Proof in the Criminal Law" (1979) 88 *Yale LJ* 1325.

Johnson, R., "The Unnecessary Crime of Conspiracy" (1973) 61 *California LR* 1137.

Jones, G., "Unjust Enrichment and the Fiduciary's Duty of Loyalty" (1968) 84 *Law Quarterly Review* 472.

Jones, T.H., "Causation, Homicide and the Supply of Drugs" (2006) 26 *Legal Studies* 139.

——, "Insanity, Automatism and the Burden of Proof on the Accused" (1995) 111 *Law Quarterly Review* 475.

Jos, P.H., Marshall, M.F., and Perlmutter, M., "The Charleston Policy on Cocaine use during Pregnancy: A Cautionary Tale" (1995) 23 *J Law, Medicine and Ethics* 120.

JUSTICE, *Breaking the Rules: the Problem of Crimes and Contraventions* (London: JUSTICE, 1980).

Kadish, S., "Some Observations on the Use of Criminal Sanctions in Enforcing Economic Regulations" (1963) 30 *U Chicago LR* 423.

——, *Blame and Punishment* (New York: MacMillan, 1987).

Kant, *Foundations of the Metaphysics of Morals* (1785).

Kaufman, R.M., "Legal Recognition of Independent Fetal Rights: The Trend Towards Criminalizing Prenatal Maternal Conduct" (1997) 17 *Children's Legal Rights J* 20.

Kean, A.W.G., "The History of the Criminal Liability of Children" (1937) 53 *Law Quarterly Review* 364.

Keedy, E.R., "Ignorance and Mistake in the Criminal Law" (1908) 22 *Harvard LR* 75.

Kell, D., "Social Disutility and the Law of Consent" (1994) 14 *Oxford Journal of Legal Studies* 121.

Kelman, M., "Interpretative Contraction in the Substantive Criminal Law" (1981) 33 *Stanford LR* 591.

Kennedy, I.M., "Switching Off Life Support Machines: The Legal Implications" [1977] *Criminal LR* 443.

Kenny, A., "Intention and Purpose in Law" in R.S. Summers (ed.), *Essays in Legal Philosophy* (London: Blackwells, 1968) 146.

Kenny, C.S., *Outlines of the Criminal Law* (Cambridge: Cambridge University Press, 1902; 2nd ed., 1904).

Kentridge, S., "The Incorporation of the European Convention on Human Rights" in Cambridge Centre for Public Law, *Constitutional Reform in the United Kingdom: Practice and Principles* (Oxford: Hart Publishing, 1998) 69.

Keown, J., "Restoring Moral and Intellectual Shape to the Law after *Bland*" (1997) 113 *Law Quarterly Review* 481.

Kleinig, J., "Crime and the Concept of Harm" (1978) *American Philosophical Quarterly* 27.

——, *Paternalism* (Manchester: Manchester University Press, 1983).

Klockars, C.B., *The Professional Fence* (New York: Free Press, 1974).

Koffman, L., "The Nature of Appropriation" [1982] *Criminal LR* 331.

——, "The Rise and Fall of Proportionality: The failure of the Criminal Justice Act 1991" [2006] *Criminal LR* 281.

Kremnitzer, M., "Interpretation in Criminal Law" [1986] 21 *Israel LR* 358.

Kugler, I., *Direct and Oblique Intention in the Criminal Law: an inquiry into degrees of blameworthiness* (Aldershot: Ashgate, 2002).

Lacey, N., "Beset by Boundaries: The Home Office Review of Sex Offenders" [2001] *Criminal LR* 3.

Lamond, G., "Coercion, Threats, and the Puzzle of Blackmail" in A.P. Simester and A.T.H. Smith (eds.), *Harm and Culpability* (Oxford: Oxford University Press, 1996) 215.

Lanham, D.J., "Accomplices and Withdrawal" (1981) 97 *Law Quarterly Review* 575.

——, "Complicity, Concert and Conspiracy" (1980) 4 *Criminal LJ* 276.

——, "Drivers, Control, and Accomplices" [1982] *Criminal LR* 419.

——, "Duress and Void Contracts" (1966) 29 *Modern Law Review* 615.

——, "Larsonneur Revisited" [1976] *Criminal LR* 276.

——, "Primary and Derivative Criminal Liability: An Australian Perspective" [2000] *Criminal LR* 707.

——, "Wilful Blindness and the Criminal Law" (1985) 9 *Criminal LJ* 261.

Lavoie, J., "Ownership of Human Tissue: Life after *Moore v. Regents of the University of California*" [1989] 75 *Virginia LR* 1363.

Law Commission, No. 177, *A Criminal Code for England and Wales* (London: HMSO, 1989).

——, Consultation Paper No. 177, *A New Homicide Act for England and Wales?* (London: HMSO, 2006).

——, Consultation Paper No. 131, *Assisting and Encouraging Crime* (London: HMSO, 1993).

——, No. 102, *Attempt and Impossibility in Relation to Attempt, Conspiracy and Incitement* (London: HMSO, 1980).

——, No. 143, *Codification of the Criminal Law* (London: HMSO, 1985).

——, Consultation Paper No. 139, *Consent in the Criminal Law* (London: HMSO, 1995).

——, No. 76, *Conspiracy and Criminal Law Reform* (London: HMSO, 1976).

——, No. 83, *Defences of General Application* (London: HMSO, 1977).

——, No. 89, *Draft Criminal Liability (Mental Element) Bill* (London: HMSO, 1978).

——, No. 276, *Fraud* (London: HMSO, 2002)

——, Consultation Paper No. 155, *Fraud and Deception* (London: HMSO, 1999).

——, No. 10, *Imported Criminal Intent (Director of Public Prosecutions v. Smith)* (London: HMSO, 1967).

——, No. 300, *Inchoate Liability for Assisting and Encouraging Crime* (London: HMSO, 2006).

——, No. 229, *Intoxication and Criminal Liability* (London: HMSO, 1995).

——, No. 180, *Jurisdiction over Offences of Fraud and Dishonesty with a Foreign Element* (London: HMSO, 1989).

——, Consultation Paper No. 155, *Legislating the Criminal Code: Fraud and Deception* (London: HMSO, 1999).

——, No. 237, *Legislating the Criminal Code: Involuntary Manslaughter* (London: HMSO, 1996).

——, Consultation Paper No. 122, *Legislating the Criminal Code: Offences against the Person and General Principles* (London: HMSO, 1992).

——, No. 218, *Legislating the Criminal Code: Offences against the Person and General Principles* (London: HMSO, 1993).

——, Working Paper No. 23, "Malicious Damage" (London: HMSO, 1969).

——, No. 304, *Murder, Manslaughter and Infanticide* (London: HMSO, 2006).

——, No. 290, *Partial Defences to Murder* (London: HMSO, 2004).

——, No. 305, *Participation in Crime* (London: HMSO, 2007).

——, No. 29, *Report on Offences of Damage to Property* (London: HMSO, 1970).

Leavens, A., "A Causative Approach to Omissions" (1988) 76 *California LR* 547.

Lederman, E., "Models for Imposing Corporate Criminal Liability: From Adaptation and Imitation Toward Aggregation and the Search for Self-identity" (2001) *Buffalo Criminal LR* 642.

Leigh, L.H., "Some Remarks on Appropriation in the Law of Theft after *Morris*" (1985) 48 *Modern Law Review* 167.

——, *Strict and Vicarious Liability* (London: Sweet and Maxwell, 1982).

Lenckner, T., "The Principle of Interest Balancing as a General Basis of Justification" in A. Eser and G. Fletcher (eds.), *Justification and Excuse: Comparative Perspectives* (Freiburg: Max Planck Institut, 1987) vol. 1, 493.

Leverick, F., "Is English Self-defence Law Incompatible with Article 2 of the ECHR?" [2002] *Criminal LR* 347.

——, "The Use of Force in Public and Private Defence and Article 2: A Reply to Professor Smith" [2002] *Criminal LR* 963.

——, *Killing in Self-Defence* (Oxford: Oxford University Press, 2006).

Levi, M., "Fraud Trials in Perspective" [1984] *Criminal LR* 384.

——, *Regulating Fraud: White-collar Crime and the Criminal Process* (London: Tavistock, 1987) 15.

Lewis, D., "The Punishment that Leaves Something to Chance" (1989) 18 *Philosophy and Public Affairs* 53.

Livermore, J.M. and Meehl, P.E., "The Virtues of M'Naghten" (1967) 51 *Minnesota LR* 789.

Locke, J., *Two Treatises of Civil Government* (New York: Dutton, 1924).

Low, P., Jeffries, J., and Bonnie, R., *Criminal Law: Cases and Materials* (New York: Foundation Press, 2nd ed., 1986).

Lowry, D.R., "The Blind and the Law of Tort" (1972) 20 *Chittys LJ* 253.

Lucas, J.R., "The Philosophy of the Reasonable Man" (1963) 13 *Philosophical Quarterly* 97.

Lynch, A.C.E., "The Mental Element in the Actus Reus" (1982) 98 *Law Quarterly Review* 109.

MacCormick, D.N. and Summers, R.S. (eds.), *Interpreting Statutes: a Comparative Study* (Aldershot: Dartmouth, 1991).

Macdonald, S., "A Suicidal Woman, Roaming Pigs and a Noisy Trampolinist: Refining the ASBO's Definition of 'Anti-Social Behaviour'" (2006) 69 *Modern LR* 183.

MacKay, R.D., "Intoxication as a Factor in Automatism" [1982] *Criminal LR* 146.

——, "On Being Insane in Jersey Part Two: the appeal in *Jason Prior v Attorney General*" [2002] *Criminal LR* 728.

——, "On Being Insane in Jersey Part Three: the case of the *Attorney General v O'Driscoll*" [2004] *Criminal LR* 219.

——, "Pleading Provocation and Diminished Responsibility Together" [1988] *Criminal LR* 411.

——, "Post-Hinkley Insanity in the USA" [1988] *Criminal LR* 88.

——, "Sleepwalking, Automatism and Insanity" [2006] *Criminal LR* 901.

——, "The Abnormality of Mind Factor in Diminished Responsibility" [1999] *Criminal LR* 117.

——, "The Consequences of Killing Very Young Children" [1993] *Criminal LR* 21.

——, "The Trial of the Facts and Unfitness to Plead" [1997] *Criminal LR* 644.

——, *Mental Condition Defences in the Criminal Law* (Oxford: Oxford University Press, 1995).

Mackay, R.D. and Gearty, C., "On Being Insane in Jersey: the case of *Attorney General v Jason Prior*" [2001] *Criminal LR* 560.

Mackay, R.D. and Kearns, G., "More Fact(s) about the Insanity Defence" [1999] *Criminal LR* 714.

——, "The Continued Underuse of Unfitness to Plead and the Insanity Defence" [1994] *Criminal LR* 576.

Mackay, R.D. and Mitchell, B.J., "But is this Provocation? Some thoughts on the Law Commission's Report on Partial Defences to Murder" [2005] *Criminal LR* 44.

Mackie, J.L., "Causes and Conditions" in E. Sosa (ed.), *Causation and Conditionals* (London: Oxford University Press, 1975) 15.

Maclean, A.R., "Resurrection of the Body Snatchers" (2000) 150 *NLJ* 174.

Macklem, T. and Gardner J., "Provocation and Pluralism" (2001) 64 *Modern LR* 815.

Maier-Katkin, D. and Ogle, R., "A Rationale for Infanticide Laws" [1993] *Criminal LR* 903.

Manchester, C., "Knowledge, Due Diligence and Strict Liability in Regulatory Offences" [2006] *Criminal LR* 213 .

Mandil, D.M., "Chance, Freedom and Criminal Liability" (1987) 87 *California LR* 125.

Mann, K., "Punitive Civil Sanctions: The Middle Ground Between Criminal and Civil Law" (1992) 101 *Yale LJ* 1795.

Mannheim, H., "Mens Rea in German and English Criminal Law" (1935) 17 *J Comparative Legislation* 82, 236, and (1936) 18 *J Comparative Legislation* 78.

Marcus, P., "Criminal Conspiracy Law: Time to Turn Back from an Ever Expanding, Ever More Troubling Area" (1992) 1 *William and Mary Bill of Rights J* 1.

——, "The Criminal Agreement in Theory and in Practice (1977) 65 *Georgetown LJ* 925.

Marshall, A., *Principles of Economics* (New York: Macmillan, 8th ed., 1947).

Marshall, B., Webb, B., and Tilley, N., *Rationalisation of Current Research on Guns, Gangs and other Weapons: Phase 1* (London: University College, 2005).

Marston, G., "Contemporaneity of Act and Intention in Crimes" [1970] 86 *Law Quarterly Review* 208.

Mason, J.K., *Forensic Medicine for Lawyers* (London: Butterworths, 3rd ed., 1995).

Mason, J.K. and McCall Smith, R.A., *Law and Medical Ethics* (London: Butterworths, 5th ed., 1999).

Matthews, P., "Whose Body? People and Property" (1983) 36 *Current Legal Problems* 193.

McAuley, F., "Anticipating the Past: The Defence of Provocation in Irish Law" (1987) 50 *Modern Law Review* 133.

McBarnet, D. and Whelan, C., "The Elusive Spirit of the Law: Formalism and the Struggle for Legal Control" (1991) 54 *Modern Law Review* 848.

McColgan, A., "Common Law and the Relevance of Sexual History Evidence" (1996) 15 *Oxford Journal of Legal Studies* 275.

——, "In Defence of Battered Women who Kill" (1993) 130 *J Law and Soc* 508.

McEwan, J. and Robilliard, St.J., "Recklessness: the House of Lords and the Criminal Law" (1981) 1 *Legal Studies* 267.

McHarg, A., "Reconciling Rights and the Public Interest: Conceptual Problems and Doctrinal Uncertainty in the Jurisprudence of the European Court of Human Rights" (1999) 62 *Modern Law Review* 671.

McKenna, B., "The Undefined Adverb in Criminal Statutes" [1966] *Criminal LR* 548.

Merry, A. and McCall-Smith, A., *Errors, Medicine and the Law* (Cambridge: Cambridge University Press, 2001).

Michalowski, S., "Sanctity of Life: Are Some Lives More Sacred Than Others?" (2002) 22 *Legal Studies* 377.

Mill, J.S., *On Liberty* (1859).

Milsom, S.F.C., *Historical Foundations of the Common Law* (London: Butterworths, 1969; 2nd ed., 1981).

Mitchell, B., "In Defence of a Principle of Correspondence" [1999] *Criminal LR* 195.

——, "Multiple Wrongdoing and Offence Structure: A Plea for Consistency and Fair Labelling" (2001) 64 *Modern LR* 395.

Moore, M.S., "Choice, Character, and Excuse" in E.F. Paul, F.D. Miller, and J. Paul (eds.), *Crime, Culpability and Remedy* (Oxford: Blackwell, 1990) 29

——, *Act and Crime* (Oxford: Oxford University Press, 1993)

——, *Law and Psychiatry: Rethinking the Relationship* (Cambridge: Cambridge University Press, 1984).

Morris, N., "The Criminal Responsibility of the Mentally Ill" (1982) 33 *Syracuse LR* 477.

——, *Madness and the Criminal Law* (Chicago: University of Chicago Press, 1982).

Morse, S., "Excusing the Crazy: The Insanity Defence Reconsidered" (1985) 58 *Southern California LR* 777.

Moxon, D., *Sentencing Practice in the Crown Court*, Home Office Research Study No. 103 (London, HMSO: 1988).

Munday, R.J., "Handling the Evidential Exception" [1988] *Criminal LR* 345.

Murphy, J.G. and Hampton, J., *Forgiveness and Mercy* (Cambridge: Cambridge University Press, 1998).

Murray, C., *The Emerging British Underclass* (London: IEA Health and Welfare Unit, 1990).

——, *Underclass: The Crisis Deepens* (London: IEA Health and Welfare Unit, 1994).

Nagel, T., "Moral Luck" in *Mortal Questions* (Cambridge: Cambridge University Press, 1979) 24.

Nicholas, S., Povey, D., Walker, A., and Kershaw, C., *Crime in England and Wales 2004-05* Home Office Statistical Bulletin 11/05 (London: Home Office, 2005).

Nicholson, D., "Telling Tales: Gender Discrimination Gender Construction and Battered Women who Kill" (1995) 3 *Feminist Leg Stud* 185.

——, "The Citizen's Duty to Assist the Police" [1992] *Criminal LR* 611.

Nicholson, D. and Sanghvi, R., "Battered Women and Provocation: The Implications of *R v. Ahluwalia*" [1993] *Criminal LR* 728.

Norrie, A., "A Critique of Criminal Causation" (1991) 54 *Modern Law Review* 685.

——, "After *Woollin*" [1999] *Criminal LR* 532.

——, "Between Orthodox Subjectivism and Moral Contextualism: Intention and the Consultation Paper" [2006] *Criminal LR* 486.

——, "From Criminal Law to Legal Theory: The Mysterious Case of the Reasonable Glue Sniffer" (2002) 65 *Modern LR* 38.

——, "'Simulacra of Morality?' Beyond the Ideal/Actual Antinomies of Criminal Justice" in Duff (ed.), *Philosophy and the Criminal Law* (Cambridge: Cambridge University Press, 1998) 101.

——, *Crime, Reason and History* (London: Weidenfeld and Nicholson, 2nd ed., 2001).

——, *Punishment, Responsibility and Justice* (Oxford: Oxford University Press, 2000).

Note, "A Rationale of the Law of Aggravated Theft" (1954) 54 *Columbia LR* 84.

Note, "A Rationale of the Law of Burglary" (1951) 51 *Columbia LR* 1009.

Nourse, V., "Passion's Progress; Modern Law Reform and the Provocation Defence" (1997) 106 *Yale LJ* 1331.

Nozick, R., *Anarchy, State and Utopia* (Oxford: Oxford University Press, 1974).

O'Connor, D. and Fairall, P.A., *Criminal Defences* (Sydney: Butterworths, 2nd ed., 1988).

O'Donnell, I. and Morrison, S., "Armed and Dangerous? The Use of Firearms in Robbery" (1997) 36 *Howard J Criminal Justice* 305.

O'Donovan, K., "Defences for Battered Women who Kill" (1991) 18 *J Law and Society* 219.

Oakley, A., *Constructive Trusts* (London: Sweet and Maxwell, 3rd ed., 1997).

Office for National Statistics, *Mortality Statistics: Injury and Poisoning* (London: HMSO, 1994).

Orchard, G., "The Defence of Absence of Fault in Australasia and Canada" in P.F. Smith (ed.), *Criminal Law: Essays in Honour of J.C. Smith* (London: Butterworths, 1987) 114.

Orchard, G., "'Agreement' in Criminal Conspiracy" [1974] *Criminal LR* 297 and 335.

——, "Provocation—Recharacterisation of 'Characteristics'" (1996) 6 *Canterbury LR* 202.

——, "Surviving without Majewski—A View from Down Under" [1993] *Criminal LR* 426.

——, "The Golden Thread—Somewhat Frayed" (1988) 6 *Otago LR* 615.

——, "The Judicial Categorisation of Offences" (1983) 2 *Canterbury LR* 81.

Ormerod, D., "Cheating the Public Revenue" [1998] *Criminal LR* 627.

Ormerod, D. and Fortson, R., "Drug Suppliers as Manslaughterers (Again)" [2005] *Criminal LR* 819.

Ormerod, D. and Williams, D., *Smith: The Law of Theft* (Oxford: Oxford University Press, 9th ed., 2007).

Oryang, G. and Shiner, R.A., "Organisations and Agency" (1995) 1 *Legal Theory* 283.

Pace, P.J., "Burglarious Trespass" [1985] *Criminal LR* 716.

——, "Delegation: A Doctrine in Search of a Definition" [1982] *Criminal LR* 627.

Paciocco, D.W., "The Remedial Constructive Trust: A Principled Basis for Priorities over Creditors" (1989) 68 *Canadian Bar Review* 315.

Packer, H.L., *The Limits of the Criminal Sanction* (Stanford: Stanford University Press, 1968).

Padfield, N., "The high price of participation in criminal activities" [1993] *Cambridge LJ* 373.

Palmstierna, T., "One in Thirty Predictions of Assault by Discharged Psychiatric Patients will be Correct" [1999] *British Medical J* 1270.

Patient, I., "Some Remarks about the Element of Voluntariness in Offences of Absolute Liability" [1968] *Criminal LR* 23.

Pearce, A.R., "Theft by False Promises" (1953) 101 *U Pennsylvania LR* 967.

Pedain, A., "Intention and the Terrorist Example" [2004] *Criminal LR* 284.

Perkins, R.M., "Parties to Crime" (1941) 89 *U Pennsylvania LR* 581.

——, "The Law of Homicide" (1946) 36 *J Criminal Law and Criminology* 391.

Perkins, R.M. and Boyle, R.N., *Criminal Law* (Mineola, N.Y.: Foundation Press, 3rd ed., 1982).

Perry, S., "Corrective Justice v. Distributive Justice" in J. Horder (ed.), *Oxford Essays in Jurisprudence* (4th Series, Oxford: Oxford University Press, 2000) 237.

Phillipson, G., "The Human Rights Act, 'Horizontal Effect' and the Common Law: a Bang or a Whimper" (1999) 62 *Modern Law Review* 824.

——, "(Mis)-Reading Section 3 of the Human Rights Act" (2003) 119 *Law Quarterly Review* 183.

Pickard, T., "Culpable Mistakes and Rape: Relating Mens Rea to the Crime" (1980) 30 *U Toronto LJ* 75.

Pollock, F. and Maitland, F.W. *The History of English Law Before the Time of Edward I* (Cambridge: Cambridge University Press, 2nd ed., 1911).

Popper, K., *The Poverty of Historicism* (London: Routledge and Kegan Paul, 1957).

Posner, R., *An Economic Theory of the Criminal Law* (1985) 85 *Columbia LR* 1193.

Pound, R., "Common Law and Legislation" (1907) 21 *Harvard LR* 383.

Power, H., "Provocation and Culture" [2006] *Criminal LR* 871.

Price, D.P.T., "Assisted Suicide and Refusing Medical Treatment: Linguistics, Morals and Legal Contentions" (1996) 4 *Medical LR* 270.

Quick, O. and Wells, C. "Getting Tough with Defences" [2006] *Criminal LR* 514.

Rawls, J., *A Theory of Justice* (Cambridge, Mass.: Harvard University Press, 1971).

Raz, J., "Autonomy, Toleration, and the Harm Principle" in R. Gavison (ed.), *Issues in Contemporary Legal Philosophy* (Oxford: Clarendon Press, 1987) 313.

——, *The Authority of Law* (Oxford: Oxford University Press, 1979).

——, *The Morality of Freedom* (Oxford: Oxford University Press, 1986).

Reiman, J. and van den Haag, E., "On the Common Saying that it is Better that Ten Guilty Persons

Escape than that One Innocent Suffer: *Pro* and *Con*" in E.F. Paul, F.D. Miller, and J. Paul (eds.), *Crime, Culpability and Remedy* (Oxford: Blackwell, 1990) 226.

Reisman, D., "Possession and the Law of Finders" (1939) 52 *Harvard LR* 1105.

Reiss, A., "Selecting Strategies of Social Control over Organizational Life" in K. Hawkins and J.M. Thomas (eds.), *Enforcing Regulation* (Boston: Kluwer-Nijhoff, 1984) 25.

Richardson, G., "Strict Liability for Regulatory Crime: The Empirical Research" [1987] *Criminal LR* 295.

Richardson, G., Ogus, A., and Burrows, P., *Policing Prosecution* (Oxford: Oxford University Press, 1982).

Robbins, I.P., "Double Inchoate Crimes" (1989) 26 *Harv J Legislation* 1.

Roberts, P., "Strict Liability and the Presumption of Innocence" in A.P. Simester (ed.), *Appraising Strict Liability* (Oxford: Oxford University Press, 2005) 151.

——, "Taking the Burden of Proof Seriously" [1995] *Criminal LR* 783.

——, "The Philosophical Foundations of Consent in the Criminal Law" (1997) 17 *Oxford Journal of Legal Studies* 389.

——, "The Presumption of Innocence Brought Home" (2002) 118 *Law Quarterly Review* 41.

Roberts, S., "More Lost Than Found" (1982) 45 *Modern Law Review* 683.

Robinson, P.H., "Causing the Conditions of One's Own Defence: A Study in the Limits of Theory in Criminal Law Doctrine" (1985) 71 *Virginia LR* 1.

——, "Competing Theories of Justification: Deeds v. Reasons" in A.P. Simester and A.T.H. Smith (eds.), *Harm and Culpability* (Oxford: Oxford University Press, 1996) 45.

——, "Criminal Law Defenses: A Systematic Analysis" (1982) 82 *Columbia LR* 199.

——, "The Criminal-Civil Distinction and the Utility of Desert" (1996) 76 *Boston ULR* 201.

——, *Criminal Law* (New York: Aspen Law and Business, 1997).

——, *Fundamentals of Criminal Law* (Boston: Little Brown, 1988).

Robinson, P.H. and Darley, J.M., "Objectivist Versus Subjectivist View of Criminality: A Study in the Role of Social Science in Criminal Law Theory" (1998) 18 *Oxford Journal of Legal Studies* 409.

——, *Justice, Liability and Blame: Community Views and the Criminal Law* (1995).

Rock, P., *After Homicide: practical and political responses to bereavement* (Oxford: Clarendon Press, 1998).

Rogers, J., " A Criminal Lawyer's Response to Chastisement in the European Court of Human Rights" [2002] *Criminal LR* 98.

——, "Chastisement" [2002] *Criminal LR* 98.

Royal College of Physicians Working Group, "Criteria for the Diagnosis of Brain Stem Death" (1995) 29 *J Royal College of Physicians* 381.

Royal Commission on Capital Punishment, *Report of the Royal Commission on Capital Punishment, 1949–1953* Cmnd. 8932 (London: HMSO, 1953).

Rumney, P., "Review of Sex Offenders and Rape and Law Reform: Another False Dawn?" [2001] 64 *Modern LR* 801.

Ryan, A., *Property and Political Theory* (Oxford: Blackwell, 1984).

Ryan, S., "Reckless Transmission of HIV: Knowledge and Culpability" [2006] *Criminal LR* 981.

Saunders, J.B., *Mozley & Whiteley's Law Dictionary* (London: Butterworths, 9th ed., 1977).

Sayre, F.B., "Criminal Responsibility for the Acts of Another" (1930) 43 *Harvard LR* 678.

——, "Mens Rea" (1932) 45 *Harvard LR* 974.

——, "Public Welfare Offences" (1933) 33 *Columbia LR* 55.

——, "The Present Significance of *Mens Rea* in the Criminal Law" in R. Pound (ed.), *Harvard Legal Essays* (Harvard: Harvard University Press, 1934) 399.

Schopp, R.F., *Justification Defences and Just Convictions* (Cambridge: Cambridge University Press, 1998).

Schott, L., "Fetal Protection—An Overview of Recent State Legislative Responses" (1991) 22 *Memphis State University LR* 119.

Schulhofer, S.J., "Harm and Punishment: A Critique of Emphasis on the Results of Conduct in the Criminal Law" (1974) 122 *U Pennsylvania LR* 1497.

Searle, J.R., *The Construction of Social Reality* (London: Allen Lane, 1995).

Seavey, W., "Negligence—Subjective or Objective?" (1927) 41 *Harvard LR* 1.

Shepherd, J.C., "Towards a Unified Concept of Fiduciary Relationships" (1981) 97 *Law Quarterly Review* 51.

Sherwin, E., "Constructive Trusts in Bankruptcy" (1989) *U Illinois LR* 297.

Shulman, H., "The Standard of Care Required of Children" (1928) 37 *Yale LJ* 618.

Shute, S., "Appropriation and the Law of Theft" [2002] *Criminal LR* 445.

——, "Knowledge and Belief in the Criminal Law" in S. Shute and A.P. Simester (eds.), *Criminal Law Theory: Doctrines of the General Part* (2002) 184.

——, "Something Old, Something New, Something Borrowed: Three Aspects of the Project" [1996] *Criminal LR* 684.

Shute, S. and Horder, J., "Thieving and Deceiving—What is the Difference?" (1993) 56 *Modern Law Review* 548;

Shyllon, F.O., "The Corruption of 'Corruptly'" [1969] *Criminal LR* 250.

Simester, A.P., "Can negligence be culpable?" in J. Horder (ed.), *Oxford Essays in Jurisprudence* (4th Series, Oxford: Oxford University Press, 2000) 85.

——, "Mistakes in Defence" (1992) 12 *Oxford Journal of Legal Studies* 295.

——, "Moral Certainty and the Boundaries of Intention" (1996) 16 *Oxford Journal of Legal Studies* 445.

——, "Murder, Mens Rea and the House of Lords—Again" (1999) 115 *Law Quarterly Review* 17.

——, "Why Distinguish Intention from Foresight?" in A.P. Simester and A.T.H. Smith (eds.), *Harm and Culpability* (Oxford: Oxford University Press, 1996) 71.

——, "Why Omissions are Special" (1995) 1 *Legal Theory* 311.

—— (ed.), *Appraising Strict Liability* (Oxford: Oxford University Press, 2005).

Simester, A.P. and Chan, W., "Intention Thus Far" [1997] *Criminal LR* 704.

Simester, A.P. and Hirsch, A. von, "Regulating Offensive Conduct through Two-Step Prohibitions" in A. von Hirsch and A.P. Simester (eds.), *Incivilities: Regulating Offensive Behaviour* (Oxford: Hart Publishing, 2006) 173.

——, "Rethinking the Offense Principle" (2002) 8 *Legal Theory* 269.

Simester, A.P. and Roberts, P., "Strict Liability in UK Regulation" in R. Macrory, *Regulatory Justice: Sanctioning in a post-Hampton World* Consultation Document (London: Cabinet Office, 2006) Annex E.

Simester, A.P. and Smith, A.T.H., (eds.) *Harm and Culpability* (Oxford: Oxford University Press, 1996).

Simester, A.P. and Sullivan, G.R., "On the Nature and Rationale of Property Offences" in R.A. Duff and S.P. Green (eds.), *Defining Crimes: Essays on the Criminal Law's Special Part* (Oxford: Oxford University Press, 2005) 168.

Simmonds, N., "The Possibility of Private Law" in J. Tasioulas (ed.), *Law, Values and Social Practices* (Aldershot: Dartmouth, 1997) 129.

Simpson, A.W.B., *Cannibalism and the Common Law* (Chicago: University of Chicago Press, 1984).

Singer, P., *Rethinking Life and Death: the Collapse of Our Traditional Ethics* (Oxford: Oxford University Press, 1994).

Skegg, P., *Law, Ethics and Medicine: Studies in Medical Law* (Oxford: Oxford University Press, 1984).

Smart, A., "Criminal Responsibility for Failing to Do the Impossible" (1987) 103 *Law Quarterly Review* 532.

Smith, A.T.H., "Constructive Trusts in the Law of Theft" [1977] *Criminal LR* 395.

——, "Error and Mistake of Law in Anglo-American Criminal Law" (1984) 14 *Anglo-American LR* 3.

——, "Judicial Law Making in the Criminal Law" (1984) 100 *Law Quarterly Review* 46.

——, "On Actus Reus and Mens Rea" in P. Glazebrook (ed.), *Reshaping the Criminal Law* (London: Sweet and Maxwell, 1978) 95.

——, "Stealing the Body and its Parts" [1976] *Criminal LR* 622.

——, "The Human Rights Act and the Criminal Lawyer: The Constitutional Context" [1999] *Criminal LR* 251.

——, "The Idea of Deception" [1982] *Criminal LR* 721.

——, "The Use of Force in Public or Private Defence and Article 2" [2002] *Criminal LR* 958.

——, "Theft by Persons Required to Account" [1980] 1 *Canterbury LR* 15.

——, *Property Offences* (London: Sweet and Maxwell, 1994).

Smith, H., "Culpable Ignorance" (1983) 92 *The Philosophical Review* 543.

Smith, J., *The Nature of Personal Robbery* Home Office Research Study 254 (London: Home Office, 2003).

Smith, J.C., "A Note on 'Intention'" [1990] *Criminal LR* 85.

——, "Aid, Abet, Counsel, or Procure" in P. Glazebrook (ed.), *Reshaping the Criminal Law* (London: Sweet and Maxwell, 1978) 120

——, "Burglary under the Theft Bill" [1968] *Criminal LR* 367.

——, "Civil Law Concepts in the Criminal Law" [1972B] *Cambridge LJ* 197.

——, "Codification of the Criminal Law" [1987] *Denning LJ* 134.

——, "Conspiracy to Defraud: Some Comments on the Law Commission's Report" [1995] *Criminal LR* 209.

——, "Conspiracy under the Criminal Law Act 1977" [1977] *Criminal LR* 598 and 638

——, "Criminal Liability of Accessories: Law and Law Reform" (1997) 113 *Law Quarterly Review* 453.

——, "Embezzlement and the Disobedient Servant" (1956) 19 *Modern Law Review* 39.

——, "'Intent': A Reply" [1978] *Criminal LR* 14.

——, "Intention in Criminal Law" (1974) 27 *Current Legal Problems* 93.

——, "Intoxication and the Mental Element in Crime" in P. Wallington and R. Merkin (eds.), *Essays in Memory of Professor F.H. Lawson* (London: Butterworths, 1986) 119.

——, "*Lister* v. *Stubbs* and the Criminal Law" (1994) 110 *Law Quarterly Review* 180.

——, "Mens Rea in Statutory Conspiracy: (3) Some Answers" [1978] *Criminal LR* 210.

——, "Obtaining Cheques by Deception or Theft" [1997] *Criminal LR* 396.

——, "Offences against the Person : the Home Office Consultation Paper" [1998] *Criminal LR* 317.

——, "Secondary Participation and Inchoate Offences" in C. Tapper (ed.), *Crime, Proof and Punishment* (London: Butterworths, 1981) 21.

——, "Secondary Participation in Crime—can we do without it?" (1994) 144 *New LJ* 679.

——, "Stealing Tickets" [1998] *Criminal LR* 723.

——, "The Element of Chance in Criminal Liability" [1971] *Criminal LR* 63.

——, "The Presumption of Innocence" (1987) 38 *Northern Ireland Law Quarterly* 223.

——, "The Right to Life and the Right to Kill in Law Enforcement" (1994) 144 *New LJ* 354.

——, "The Scope of Fraudulent Conversion" [1961] *Criminal LR* 741 and 797.

——, "The Use of Force in Public or Private Defence and Article 2" [2002] *Criminal LR* 958.

——, "Theft and/or Handling" [1977] *Criminal LR* 517.

——, *Justification and Excuse in the Criminal Law* (London: Sweet and Maxwell, 1989).

Smith, J.C. and Hogan, B., *Criminal Law* (London: Butterworths, 1st ed., 1965; 5th ed., 1983; 7th ed., 1992; 8th ed., 1996, 10th ed., 2002).

Smith, K.J.M., "Duress and Steadfastness: In Pursuit of the Unintelligible" [1999] *Criminal LR* 363.

——, "Proximity in Attempt : Lord Lane's Midway Course" [1991] *Criminal LR* 576.

——, "Withdrawal in Complicity: A Restatement of Principles" [2001] *Criminal LR* 769.

——, *A Modern Treatise on the Law of Criminal Complicity* (Oxford: Oxford University Press, 1991).

Snelling, H.A., "The Alternative Verdict of Manslaughter" (1958) 32 *Australian LJ* 137.

Sparks, R.F., "Diminished Responsibility in Theory and Practice" (1964) 27 *Modern LR* 9.

Spencer, J.N., "Handling and Taking Risks—a Reply to Professor Williams" [1985] *Criminal LR* 440.

——, "Handling, Theft and the *Mala Fide* Purchaser" [1985] *Criminal LR* 92.

——, "The Metamorphosis of Section 6 of the Theft Act" [1977] *Criminal LR* 653.

——, "The Mishandling of Handling" [1981] *Criminal LR* 682.

——, "The Theft Act 1978" [1979] *Criminal LR* 24.

——, "Trying to help another person commit a crime" in P. Smith (ed.), *Criminal Law: Essays in Honour of J.C. Smith* (London: Butterworths, 1987) 148.

Spencer, S., "Assault with Intent to Rape—Dead or Alive?" [1986] *Criminal LR* 110.

Stannard, J.E., "Making up for the Missing Element: A Sideways Look at Attempts" (1987) 7 *Legal Studies* 194.

Stephen, J.F., *A History of the Criminal Law of England* (1883).

Stephen, *Digest of the Criminal Law* (4th ed., 1887).

Stoop, D.F. de, "The Law in Australia Relating to the Transplantation of Organs from Cadavers" (1974) 48 *Australian LJ* 21.

Strawson, P., "Freedom and Resentment" in *Freedom and Resentment* (London: Methuen, 1974) 1.

Stuart, D., "The *Actus Reus* in Attempts" [1970] *Criminal LR* 505.

Stuckey, J.E., "The Equitable Action for Breach of Confidence: Is Information Ever Property?" (1981) 9 *Sydney LR* 402.

Sullivan, G.R., "Anger and Excuse: Reassessing Provocation" (1992) 12 *Oxford Journal of Legal Studies* 380.

——, "Bad Thoughts and Bad Acts" [1990] *Criminal LR* 559.

——, "Cause and the Contemporaneity of *Actus Reus* and *Mens Rea*" [1993] *Cambridge LJ* 487.

——, "Contemporaneity of Actus Reus and Mens Rea" [1993] *Cambridge LJ* 487.

——, "Corporate Killing – Some Government Proposals" [2001] *Cambridge LJ* 31.

——, "Crossing the Rubicon in Miami" (1978) 41 *Modern Law Review* 215.

——, "Expressing Corporate Guilt" (1995) 15 *Oxford Journal of Legal Studies* 551.

——, "Fault Elements and Joint Enterprise" [1994] *Criminal LR* 252.

——, "Fraud and the Efficacy of the Criminal Law: a Proposal for a Wide Residual Offence" [1985] *Criminal LR* 616.

——, "Fraud: the Latest Law Commission Proposals" (2003) 52 *Journal of Criminal Law* 139.

——, "Inchoate Liability for Assisting and Encouraging Crime – The Law Commission Report" [2006] *Criminal LR* 1047.

——, "Intent, Purpose and Complicity" [1988] *Criminal LR* 641.

——, "Intent, Subjective Recklessness and Culpability" (1992) 12 *Oxford Journal of Legal Studies* 380

——, "Intoxicants and Diminished Responsibility" [1994] *Criminal LR* 156.

——, "Involuntary Intoxication and Beyond" [1994] *Criminal LR* 272.

——, "Is Criminal Law Possible?" (2001) 22 *Oxford Journal of Legal Studies* 424.

——, "Knowledge, Belief and Culpability" in S. Shute and A.P. Simester (eds.), *Criminal Law Theory: Doctrines of the General Part* (Oxford: Oxford University Press, 2002) 207

——, "Making Excuses" in A.P. Simester and A.T.H. Smith (eds.), *Harm and Culpability* (Oxford: Oxford University Press, 1996) 131.

——, "Strict Liability for Criminal Offences in England and Wales Following Incorporation into English Law of the ECHR" in A.P. Simester (ed.), *Appraising Strict Liability* (Oxford: Oxford University Press, 2005) 195.

——, "The Attribution of Culpability to Limited Companies" [1996] *Cambridge LJ* 515.

——, "The Law Commission Consultation Paper on Complicity: Fault Elements and Joint Enterprise" [1994] *Criminal LR* 252.

——, "The Need for a Crime of Sexual Assault" [1989] *Criminal LR* 331.

——, "The Particularity of Serious Fraud" in P. Birks (ed.), *Pressing Problems in the Law* vol. 1 (Oxford: Oxford University Press, 1995) 99.

——, "Violent Self-help" (1983) 46 *Modern Law Review* 78.

Sullivan, G.R. and Warbrick, C., "Ship Routeing Schemes and the Criminal Liability of the Master" [1983] *Lloyds Maritime and Commercial Law Quarterly* 23.

——, "Territoriality, Theft and *Atakpu*" (1994) *Criminal LR* 650.

Sutherland, P. and Gearty, C., "Insanity and the European Court of Human Rights" [1992] *Criminal LR* 418.

Sutton, M., Schneider, J., and Hetherington, S., *Tackling theft with the market reduction approach* Home Office Crime Reduction Research Series Paper 8 (London: Home Office, 2001).

Syrota, G., "A Radical Change in the Law of Recklessness?" [1982] *Criminal LR* 97.

Szasz, T., *The Manufacture of Madness: A Comparative Study of the Inquisition and the Mental Health Movement* (New York: Harper & Row, 1970).

——, *The Myth of Mental Illness* (New York: Harper & Row, 1961; 2nd ed., 1976).

Tadros, V., *Criminal Responsibility* (Oxford: Oxford University Press, 2005).

Tadros, V. and Tierney, S., "The Presumption of Innocence and the Human Rights Act" (2004) 67 *Modern Law Review* 402.

Tay, A., "Problems in the Law of Finding" (1964) 37 *Australian LJ* 350.

Taylor, R.D., "Complicity and Excuses" [1983] *Criminal LR* 656.

Taylor, R., "The Nature of 'Partial Defences' and the Coherence of Second Degree Murder" [2007] *Criminal LR* 345.

Teff, H., *Reasonable Care: Legal Perspectives on the Doctor-Patient Relationship* (Oxford: Oxford University Press, 1994).

Temkin, J., "Pre-Natal Injury, Homicide and the Draft Criminal Code" [1986] *Cambridge LJ* 414.

——, "Sexual History Evidence—the Ravishment of Section 2" [1993] *Criminal LR* 3.

Temkin, J. and Ashworth, A., "Rape, Sexual Assaults and the Problems of Consent" [2004] *Criminal LR* 328.

Tigar, M., "The Right of Property and the Law of Theft" (1984) 62 *Texas LR* 1443.

Tur, R., "Legislative Technique and Human Rights: The Sad Case of Assisted Suicide" [2003] *Criminal LR* 3.

——, "Subjectivism and Objectivism: Towards Synthesis" in S. Shute, J. Gardner and J. Horder (eds.), *Action and Value in Criminal Law* (Oxford: Oxford University Press, 1993) 213.

Turner, J.W.C., "Larceny and Lucrum" (1941) 4 *Toronto LJ* 296.

——, "The Mental Element in Crimes at Common Law" in L. Radzinowicz and J.W.C. Turner (eds.), *The Modern Approach to Criminal Law* (London: Macmillan, 1948) 195.

——, "Two Cases of Larceny" in L. Radzinowicz and J.W.C. Turner (eds.), *The Modern Approach to Criminal Law* (London: Macmillan, 1948) 356.

——, *Kenny's Outlines of Criminal Law* (Cambridge: Cambridge University Press, 16th ed., 1952; 17th ed., 1958; 19th ed., 1965).

——, *Russell on Crime* (London: Stevens, 12th ed., 1964).

Uniacke, S., "Was Mary's Death Murder?" (2001) 9 *Medical LR* 9.

——, *Permissible Killing—the Self-defence Justification of Homicide* (Cambridge: Cambridge University Press, 1994).

Vuoso, G., "Background Responsibility and Excuse" (1987) 96 *Yale LJ* 1661.

Wade, H.W.R., "The United Kingdom's Bill of Rights" in Cambridge Centre for Public Law, *Constitutional Reform in the United Kingdom: Practice and Principles* (Oxford: Hart Publishing, 1998) 59.

Waldron, J., *The Right to Private Property* (Oxford: Oxford University Press, 1988).

Walker, N., "The End of an Old Song" (1999) 149 *New LJ* 64.

——, *Crime and Insanity in England* (Edinburgh: Edinburgh University Press, 1968).

Walker, N. and Padfield, N., *Sentencing: Theory, Practice and Law* (London: Butterworths, 2nd ed., 1996).

Walsh, E., *et al.*, "Violence and Schizophrenia: examining the evidence" (2002) 180 *British Journal of Psychiatry* 490.

Ward, A.R., "Making Sense of Self-induced Intoxication" [1986] *Cambridge LJ* 247.

Ward, T., "Magistrates, Insanity and the Common Law" [1997] *Criminal LR* 796.

Warren, E.H., "Qualifying as Plaintiff in an Action for Conversion" (1936) 49 *Harvard LR* 1084.

Wasik, M., "A Learner's Careless Driving" [1982] *Criminal LR* 411.

——, "Abandoning Criminal Intent" [1980] *Criminal LR* 785.

——, "Mens Rea, Motive and the Problem of 'Dishonesty' in the Law of Theft" [1977] *Criminal LR* 543.

——, "Partial Excuses in the Criminal Law" (1982) 45 *Modern LR* 516.

Wasik, M. and Thompson, M.P., "Turning a Blind Eye as Constituting Mens Rea" (1981) 32 *Northern Ireland Law Quarterly* 328.

Waters, D., "Banks, Fiduciary Obligations and Unconscionable Transactions" (1986) 65 *Canadian Bar Review* 37.

Watkins, J.W.N., "Historical Explanation in the Social Sciences" (1957–58) 8 *British Journal for the Philosophy of Science* 104.

Weait, M., "Knowledge, Autonomy and Consent: *R v Konzani*" [2005] *Criminal LR* 763.

——, "Taking the Blame: Criminal Law, Social Responsibility and the Sexual Transmission of HIV" (2001) 23 *Journal of Social Welfare and Family Law* 441.

Weisiger, G.B., "Negligence of the Physically Infirm" (1946) 24 *North Carolina LR* 187.

Wells, C., "Battered Women Syndrome and Defences to Homicide: Where Now?" (1994) 14 *Legal Studies* 266.

——, "Stalking: the Criminal Law Response" [1997] *Criminal LR* 463.

——, *Corporations and Criminal Responsibility* (Oxford: Oxford University Press, 1993; 2nd ed 2001).

Wertheimer, A., *Coercion* (Princeton: Princeton University Press, 1987).

West, D.J. and Walk, A. (eds.), *Daniel McNaughton: His Trial and the Aftermath* (Ashford, Kent: Headley, 1977).

West, R., "A Comment on Consent, Sex, and Rape" (1996) 2 *Legal Theory* 233.

Westen, P., "Getting the Fly out of the Bottle: the False Problem of Free Will and Determinism" (2005) 8 *Buffalo Criminal LR* 101.

Wheat, K., "The Law's Treatment of the Suicidal" [2000] *Medical LR* 182.

White, A.R., "Intention, Purpose, Foresight and Desire" (1976) 92 *Law Quarterly Review* 569.

——, "The Identity and Time of the Actus Reus" [1977] *Criminal LR* 148.

——, "Trade Descriptions About the Future" (1974) 90 *Law Quarterly Review* 15.

White, S., "Continuing Representations in Criminal Law" (1986) 37 *Northern Ireland Law Quarterly* 255.

Williams, B., "Moral Luck" in *Moral Luck* (Cambridge: Cambridge University Press, 1981) 20.

——, "Moral Responsibility and Political Freedom" [1997] *Cambridge LJ* 96.

——, "The Actus Reus of Dr Caligari" (1994) 142 *U Pennsylvania LR* 1661.

——, *Ethics and the Limits of Philosophy* (London: Fontana, 1985).

Williams, G., "Absolute Liability in Traffic Offences" [1967] *Criminal LR* 142 and 194.

——, "Appropriation: A Single or Continuous Act?" [1978] *Criminal LR* 69.

——, "Causation in Homicide" [1957] *Criminal LR* 429.

——, "Complicity, Purpose and the Draft Code" [1990] *Criminal LR* 4.

——, "Convictions and Fair Labelling" [1983] *Cambridge LJ* 85.

——, "Criminal Omissions—The Conventional View" (1991) 107 *Law Quarterly Review* 86.

——, "*Finis* for *Novus Actus?*" (1989) 48 *Cambridge LJ* 391.

——, "Handling, Theft and the Purchaser who takes a Chance" [1985] *Criminal LR* 432.

——, "Homicide and the Supernatural" (1949) 65 *Law Quarterly Review* 491.

——, "Innocent Agency and Causation" (1992) 3 *Criminal Law Forum* 289.

——, "Mistake as to Party in the Law of Contract" (1945) 23 *Canadian Bar Review* 271.

——, "Mistake in the Law of Theft" [1977] *Cambridge LJ* 62.

——, "Obedience to Law as a Crime" (1990) 53 *Modern Law Review* 445.

——, "Oblique Intention" (1987) 46 *Cambridge LJ* 417.

——, "Offences and Defences" (1982) 2 *Legal Studies* 233.

——, "Recklessness Redefined" [1981] *Cambridge LJ* 252.

——, "Temporary Appropriation should be Theft" [1981] *Criminal LR* 129.

——, "The Definition of Crime" (1955) *Current Legal Problems* 107.

——, "The Mens Rea for Murder: Leave it Alone" (1989) 105 *Law Quarterly Review* 387.

——, "The Theory of Excuses [1982] *Criminal LR* 732.

——, "The Unresolved Problem of Recklessness" (1988) 8 *Legal Studies* 74.

——, "Theft, Consent and Illegality" [1977] *Criminal LR* 127

——, "Three Rogues' Charters" [1980] *Criminal LR* 263.

——, "Venue and Ambit in the Criminal Law" (1961) 77 *Law Quarterly Review* 81: 276, 395, 518.

——, "Victims and Other Exempt Parties in Crime" (1990) 10 *Legal Studies* 245.

——, "Victims as Parties to Crimes—A Further Comment" [1964] *Criminal LR* 686.

——, "What should the Code do about Omissions?" (1987) 7 *Legal Studies* 92.

——, *Criminal Law: The General Part* (London: Stevens, 2nd ed., 1961)

——, *Textbook of Criminal Law* (London: Stevens, 2nd ed., 1983).

——, *The Mental Element in Crime* (Jerusalem: Magnes Press, 1965).

——, *The Proof of Guilt: A Study of the English Criminal Trial* (London: Stevens, 2nd ed., 1958).

Wilson, W., "A Plea for Rationality in the Law of Murder" (1990) 10 *Legal Studies* 307.

——, "The Structure of Criminal Homicide" [2006] *Criminal LR* 471.

Wilson, W. *et al.*, "Violence, Sleepwalking and the Criminal Law" [2005] *Criminal LR* 624.

Winfield, P.H., "Death as Affecting Liability in Tort" (1929) 29 *Columbia LR* 239.
——, "Quasi-Contract Arising from Compulsion" (1944) 60 *Law Quarterly Review* 341.
Winslade, W.J., "Brady on Recklessness" (1972) 33 *Analysis* 31.
Wolf, S., "The Legal and Moral Responsibility of Organisations" in J.R. Pennock and J.W. Chapman (eds.), *Criminal Justice* (New York: New York University Press, 1985).
Wootton, B., "Diminished Responsibility: A Layman's View" (1960) 76 *Law Quarterly Review* 224.
——, *Crime and the Criminal Law* (London: Sweet and Maxwell, 2nd ed., 1981).
World Health Organisation, *Diagnostic and Management Guidelines for Mental Disorders* (Geneva: World Health Organisation, 1996).
Wright, R.S., *Law of Criminal Conspiracies and Agreements* (London: Butterworths, 1873).
Yale, D.E.C., "A Year and a Day in Homicide" [1989] *Cambridge LJ* 202.
Yeo, S., "Sex, Ethnicity, Power of Self-Control and Provocation Revisited" (1996) 18 *Sydney LR* 304.
Youdan, T.G. (ed.), *Equity, Fiduciaries and Trusts* (Toronto: Carswell, 1989).

INDEX